Lecture Notes in Computer Science 4741

Christian Bessiere (Ed.)

Principles and Practice of Constraint Programming – CP 2007

13th International Conference, CP 2007
Providence, RI, USA, September 23-27, 2007
Proceedings

Volume Editor

Christian Bessiere
LIRMM
CNRS/University of Montpellier
France
E-mail: bessiere@lirmm.fr

Library of Congress Control Number: 2007934641

CR Subject Classification (1998): D.1, D.3.2-3, I.2.3-4, F.3.2, I.2.8, F.4.1, J.1

LNCS Sublibrary: SL 2 – Programming and Software Engineering

ISSN 0302-9743
ISBN-10 3-540-74969-1 Springer Berlin Heidelberg New York
ISBN-13 978-3-540-74969-1 Springer Berlin Heidelberg New York

Springer is a part of Springer Science+Business Media

springer.com

Printed in Germany

Typesetting: Camera-ready by author, data conversion by Scientific Publishing Services, Chennai, India
Printed on acid-free paper SPIN: 12124312 06/3180 5 4 3 2 1 0

Preface

The 13th International Conference on Principles and Practice of Constraint Programming (CP 2007) was held in Providence, RI, USA, September 23–27, 2007, in conjunction with the International Conference on Automated Planning and Scheduling (ICAPS). Held annually, the CP conference series is the premier international conference on constraint programming. The conference focuses on all aspects of computing with constraints. The CP conference series is organized by the Association for Constraint Programming (ACP). Information about the conferences in the series can be found on the Web at `http://www.cs.ualberta.ca/~ai/cp/`. Information about ACP can be found at `http://www.a4cp.org/`.

CP 2007 launched two calls for contributions: a call for research papers, describing novel contributions in the field, and a call for application papers, describing applications of constraint technology in the industrial world. The research track received 143 submissions and the application track received 22 submissions. Research papers were reviewed under a double-blind scheme. They received three reviews that the authors had the opportunity to see and to react to before the papers and their reviews were discussed extensively by the members of the Program Committee. Application papers were reviewed by a separate Application Committee. The Program Committee and the Application Committee then selected 43 research papers and 9 application papers to be published in full in the proceedings, and an additional 14 research papers to be published as short papers. The full papers were presented at the conference in two parallel tracks and the short papers were presented in a poster session. The paper "Solution Counting Algorithms for Constraint-Centered Search Heuristics," by Alessandro Zanarini and Gilles Pesant, was selected by a subcommittee—consisting of Javier Larrosa, Christophe Lecoutre, Christian Schulte and myself—to receive the best paper award. This subcommittee also selected the paper "Propagation = Lazy Clause Generation," by Olga Ohrimenko, Peter J. Stuckey and Michael Codish, to receive ACP's best student paper award.

The Program Committee invited two prominent researchers, Fahiem Bacchus and Matt Ginsberg, to give guest lectures. Their summary is included in the proceedings. The program also contained a talk by Rina Dechter, recipient of the "Award for Research Excellence in Constraint Programming." This award was given by the ACP during the conference. The tutorial chair selected four tutorials to be part of the program: "Ants and Constraint Programming," by Christine Solnon, "SAT solving," by Inês Lynce, "ECLIPSE by example," by Joachim Schimpf, and a final tutorial in which recent CP solvers were presented. The conference hosted a panel, organized by Barry O'Sullivan, where people from the industry discussed their use of CP technology and gave feedback on the strengths and weaknesses of current solvers. Lastly, I would like to emphasize the fact that all the sessions of the conference were held in parallel to ICAPS sessions and that CP and ICAPS participants could freely attend any session they wanted. In addition, there were joint CP-ICAPS sessions.

CP 2007 continued the tradition of the CP doctoral program, in which PhD students presented their work, listened to tutorials on career issues, and discussed their work with senior researchers via a mentoring scheme. This year, the doctoral program received 37 submissions and selected 30 of them for financial support.

The first day of the conference was devoted to satellite workshops tackling some of the important directions of research in constraint programming. This year, seven workshops were held, one of which was joined with ICAPS. The complete list of workshops is provided below. Each workshop printed its own proceedings.

In conclusion, I would like to thank all the people who, by their hard work, made this conference a great success. Thank you to Laurent Michel and Meinolf Sellmann, the Conference Chairs, who had the huge task of organizing, budgeting and planning the whole event. Thank you to Brahim Hnich and Kostas Stergiou, the Doctoral Program Chairs, for having set up a fantastic program for the students. Thank you to Pedro Meseguer, the Workshop and Tutorial Chair, for the energy he put into creating an excellent workshop and tutorial program. Thank you to Carmen Gervet, the Publicity Chair, who worked hard designing a logo and who was always mindful of the aesthetic quality of the conference Web site. Thank you to Guillaume Verger, who helped me in the final rush of collecting all the material for the proceedings. Thank you to Javier Larrosa, Christophe Lecoutre and Christian Schulte, the members of the Best Paper Committee, who accepted the intensive task of reading all candidate papers in a few days, in addition to their work as Program Committee members. Thank you to all the members of the Program Committee and Application Committee. Not only did they review all their assigned papers on time, but they participated intensively in online discussions for selecting the papers. The quality of the technical program is largely due to their terrific work. Thank you to Barry O'Sullivan and Helmut Simonis for their many ideas on the kind of event we could run to fill the gap between industrial applications and academic research. We implemented only a few of their great ideas. Thank you to Barry O'Sullivan, the Sponsor Chair and Conference Coordinator, who worked hard in close collaboration with the Conference Chairs to produce a balanced budget (thanks to the numerous sponsors they attracted). Thank you to all the institutions (listed below) that supported the conference. Thank you to Frdric Benhamou, Francesca Rossi and Peter van Beek for their helpful advice on how to deal with the stressful job of being Program Chair, and thank you to the Executive Committee of the ACP for having chosen me to carry out this exciting job!

September 2007 Christian Bessiere

Organization

Conference Organization

Conference Chairs	Laurent Michel, University of Connecticut, USA
	Meinolf Sellmann, Brown University, USA
Program Chair	Christian Bessiere, LIRMM-CNRS, France
Workshop/Tutorial Chair	Pedro Meseguer, IIIA-CSIC, Spain
Doctoral Program Chairs	Brahim Hnich, Izmir University of Economics, Turkey
	Kostas Stergiou, University of the Aegean, Greece
Publicity Chair	Carmen Gervet, Boston University and Brown University, USA
Sponsor Chair	Barry O'Sullivan, 4C, University College Cork, Ireland

Program Committee

Fahiem Bacchus, Canada
Roman Bartak, Czech Republic
Christopher Beck, Canada
Frdric Benhamou, France
Alexander Brodsky, USA
Mats Carlsson, Sweden
Hubie Chen, Spain
Rina Dechter, USA
Boi Faltings, Switzerland
Pierre Flener, Sweden
Thom Frühwirth, Germany
Maria Garcia de la Banda, Australia
Carla Gomes, USA
Narendra Jussien, France
Brahim Hnich, Turkey
Javier Larrosa, Spain
Christophe Lecoutre, France
Jimmy Lee, Hong Kong
Olivier Lhomme, France
Felip Manya, Spain
Joao Marques-Silva, UK
Amnon Meisels, Israel
Laurent Michel, USA
Ian Miguel, UK
Bertrand Neveu, France
Barry O'Sullivan, Ireland
Gilles Pesant, Canada
Francesca Rossi, Italy
Thomas Schiex, France
Christian Schulte, Sweden
Meinolf Sellmann, USA
Kostas Stergiou, Greece
Peter van Beek, Canada
Willem-Jan van Hoeve, USA
Gérard Verfaillie, France
Toby Walsh, Australia
Roland Yap, Singapore

Application Track Committee

Barry O'Sullivan, Ireland
Jean-Franois Puget, France
Helmut Simonis, UK
Pascal Van Hentenryck, USA
Mark Wallace, Australia

Additional Referees

Slim Abdennadher
Magnus Ågren
Raffaetà Alessandra
Carlos Ansótegui
Albert Atserias
Jorge Baier
Nicolas Beldiceanu
Hariolf Betz
Ateet Bhalla
Stefano Bistarelli
Manuel Bodirsky
Simon Boivin
Eric Bourreau
Sebastian Brand
Hadrien Cambazard
Tom Carchrae
Martine Ceberio
Ondrej Cepek
Gilles Chabert
Kenil C.K. Cheng
Marc Christie
Víctor Dalmau
Jessica Davies
Romuald Debruyne
Simon de Givry
Yves Deville
Bistra Dilkina
Marek J. Druzdzel
Lei Duan
Esra Erdem
Franois Fages
Hlne Fargier
Alan M. Frisch
Michel Gagnon
Jonathan Gaudreault
Hector Geffner
Ian Gent
Alfonso Gerevini
Amir Gershman
Omer Giménez
Vibhav Gogate
Alexandre Goldsztejn
Frdric Goualard
Laurent Granvilliers
Tal Grinshpon
Emmanuel Hebrard
Federico Heras
Yannet Interian
Chris Jefferson
Christophe Jermann
George Katsirelos
Tom Kelsey
Philip Kilby
Matthew Kitching
Zeynep Kiziltan
Andras Kovacs
Lukas Kroc
Oliver Kullmann
Mikael Z. Lagerkvist
Arnaud Lallouet
Yat-Chiu Law
Yahia Lebbah
Daniel Le Berre
C. Likitvivatanavong
Jiming Liu
Xavier Lorca
Inês Lynce
Santiago Macho
Vasco Manquinho
Radu Marinescu
Chris Mears
Marc Meister
Pedro Meseguer
Bernd Meyer
Jean-Nol Monette
Eric Monfroy
António Morgado
Nicholas Nethercote
Albert Oliveras
Lars Otten
Justin Pearson
Karen Petrie
Jakob Pichinger
Jordi Planes
Cdric Pralet
Nicolas Prcovic
Steven Prestwich
Riccardo Pucella
Jakob Puchinger
Luis Quesada
Claude-Guy Quimper
Frank Raiser
Philippe Refalo
Guillaume Richaud
Louis-Martin Rousseau
Ashish Sabharwal
Rida Sadek
Horst Samulowitz
Marti Sanchez Fibla
Frdric Saubion
Pierre Schauss
Tom Schrijvers
Andrew See
Uri Shapen
Eyal Shimony
Charles Siu
John Slaney
Barbara Smith
Peter Stuckey
Thomas Stutzle
Pavel Surynek

Radoslaw Szymanek
Sebastien Tabary
Guido Tack
Gilles Trombettoni
Charlotte Truchet
Marc R.C. van Dongen
Andrew Verden
Xuan-Ha Vu
Mark Wallace
Jean-Paul Watson
Ryan Williams
Armin Wolf
May Woo
Hui Wu
Neil Yorke-Smith
Changhe Yuan
Alessandro Zanarini
Yuanlin Zhang
Roie Zivan
Matthias Zytnicki

Administrative Council of the ACP

President	Francesca Rossi, Italy
Vice-president	Peter van Beek, Canada
Secretary	Pedro Meseguer, Spain
Treasurer	Christian Bessiere, France
Conference Coordinator	Barry O'Sullivan, Ireland
Executive Committee	Frédéric Benhamou, Narendra Jussien, Javier Larrosa, Jimmy H.M. Lee, Pedro Meseguer, Michela Milano, Barry O'Sullivan, Jean-Charles Régin, Francesca Rossi, Christian Schulte, Michael Trick, Peter van Beek

Workshops

Autonomous Search
Distributed Constraint Reasoning
Constraint Modelling and Reformulation
Local Search Techniques in Constraint Satisfaction
Constraint Programming for Graphical Applications
Constraint Satisfaction Techniques for Planning and Scheduling Problems
Symmetry and Constraint Satisfaction Problems

Sponsoring Institutions

Association for Constraint Programming
Brown University
Cork Constraint Computation Centre
Fidelity Investments
Google
IBM
ILOG
Intelligent Information Systems Institute, Cornell University
National ICT Australia
Nokia
Springer
University of Connecticut

Table of Contents

Invited Lectures

Application Papers

Full Research Papers

Short Research Papers

Caching in Backtracking Search

Fahiem Bacchus

University of Toronto
Canada
fbacchus@cs.toronto.edu

As backtracking search explores paths in its search tree it makes various inferences about the problem. The inferences search computes can be very computationally expensive to compute statically. However, in most backtracking CSP solvers this information is discarded when the search backtracks along the current path.

In this talk we will investigate the alternative—caching these inferences and using them to improve the efficiency of the rest of the search. Caching provides radical improvements to the theoretical power of backtracking, and can also yield significant improvements in practice. Sometimes, however, obtaining improvements in practice might not be so straightforward. We will examine CSP caching techniques for the problem of finding a single solution, counting the number of solutions, and finding an optimal solution. Time permitting we will also look at caching techniques that would be useful for QCSPs.

C. Bessiere (Ed.): CP 2007, LNCS 4741, p. 1, 2007.

Of Mousetraps and Men: A Cautionary Tale

Matt Ginsberg

On Time Systems, Inc.
and
Computational Intelligence Research Laboratory
University of Oregon
mginsberg@otsys.com

This talk consists of two interwoven stories. The Happy Story presents a technical solution to the problem of optimizing for cost instead of the more normal metric of duration. We describe a mechanism whereby the optimization problem is split into an evaluation component, where the projected cost of a schedule is evaluated using dynamic programming techniques, and a search component, where search is conducted in "window space" to find a cost-efficient schedule.

The Sad Story explains what happens when you build a better mousetrap. The people beating a path to your door are the fat cats, who are reimbursed for their mouse catching on a cost-plus basis.

C. Bessiere (Ed.): CP 2007, LNCS 4741, p. 2, 2007.

Estimation of the Minimal Duration of an Attitude Change for an Autonomous Agile Earth-Observing Satellite

Grégory Beaumet[1], Gérard Verfaillie[1], and Marie-Claire Charmeau[2]

[1] ONERA
2 avenue Édouard Belin, BP 74025, 31055 Toulouse Cedex 4, France
{Gregory.Beaumet,Gerard.Verfaillie}@onera.fr
[2] CNES
18 avenue Édouard Belin, 31401 Toulouse Cedex 9, France
Marie-Claire.Charmeau@cnes.fr

Abstract. Most of the currently active Earth-observing satellites are entirely controlled from the ground: observation plans are regularly computed on the ground (typically each day for the next day), uploaded to the satellite using visibility windows, and then executed onboard as they stand. Because the possible presence of clouds is the main obstacle to optical observation, meteorological forecasts are taken into account when building these observation plans. However, this does not prevent most of the performed observations to be fruitless because of the unforeseen presence of clouds. To fix this problem, the possibility of equipping Earth-observing satellites with an extra instrument dedicated to the detection of the clouds in front of it, just before observation, is currently considered. But, in such conditions, decision upon the observations to be performed can be no longer made offline on the ground. It must be performed online onboard, because it must be performed at the last minute when detection information is available and because visibility windows between Earth-observing satellites and their control centers are short and rare. With agile Earth-observing satellites which are the next generation ones, decision-making upon observation requires the computing of an as short as possible attitude trajectory allowing the satellite to point to the right ground area within its visibility window. In this paper, we show the results of an experiment consisting in using a continuous constraint satisfaction problem solver (RealPaver) to compute such optimal trajectories online onboard.

1 The Problem

1.1 Applicative Context

Earth-observing satellites are placed on heliosynchronous low altitude circular orbits around the Earth. Most of them are equipped with optical observation instruments, with a mass memory able to record observation data, and with a high-rate antenna able to download it towards ground mission centers. When

C. Bessiere (Ed.): CP 2007, LNCS 4741, pp. 3–17, 2007.

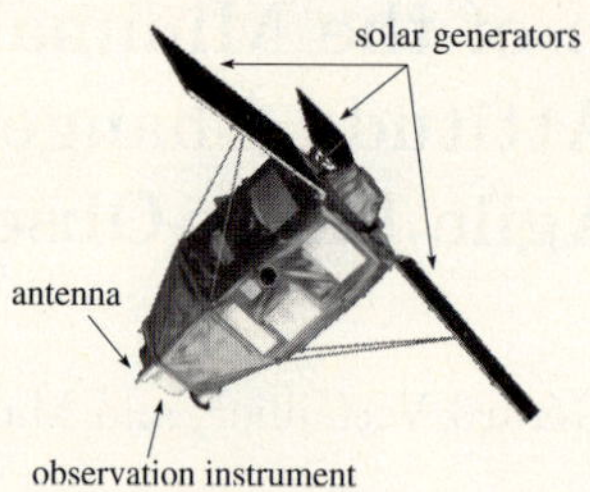

Fig. 1. A PLEIADES satellite

they are not agile, that is keeping pointing to the Earth center, as the current French SPOT satellites do, they can observe specific ground areas thanks to mirrors placed in front of their instruments and orientable along the roll axis. When they are agile, that is keeping controlling their attitude movement along the roll, pitch, and yaw axes thanks to reaction wheels or to gyroscopic actuators, as the future French PLEIADES satellites will do, this is the whole satellite which orientates itself to observe specific ground areas (see Figure 1; for more details, see http://smsc.cnes.fr/PLEIADES/).

The main advantage of *agility* is to offer more freedom in terms of observation. With non agile satellites, the realization window of an observation is fixed, because observation is only possible when the satellite flies over the target ground area. With agile ones, this realization window can be freely chosen within a wide visibility window, because observation is now possible before, when, or after the satellite flies over the target ground area. This freedom may allow more observations to be performed because observations which conflict with each other in the context of non agile satellites may no longer conflict in the context of agile ones. This is illustrated by Figure 2 which represents five candidate observations, from 1 to 5. With a non agile satellite (see Figure 2(a)), observations 1 and 2 conflict with each other, because their realization windows overlap. This is also the case with observations 3 and 4. As a result, it is only possible to perform three observations, for example observations 1, 3, and 5. With an agile satellite (see Figure 2(b)), all these conflicts can be resolved and the five observations can be performed.

Agile or not, these satellites are assumed to perform observations following observation requests emitted by users. With each request, are usually associated a ground area, a priority, and some observation conditions. For each candidate observation, it is then necessary to decide on whether, when, and how it will be performed. For almost all the currently active Earth-observing satellites, these decisions are made *on the ground* under the supervision of human operators in centralized mission centers. Typically, an observation *plan* is built each day for the next day, taking into account the current set of candidate observations (see [1] for a description of the problem in the context of a non agile satellite and [2] for a similar description in the context of an agile one). The resulting optimization problem may be huge and hard to be solved, even when using powerful computers and sophisticated algorithms running for tens of minutes.

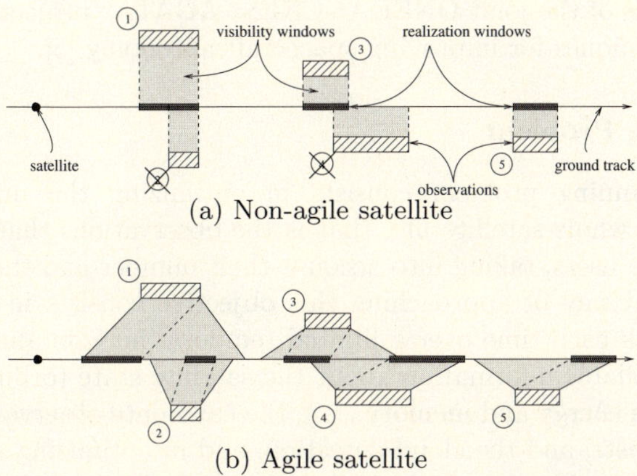

(a) Non-agile satellite

(b) Agile satellite

Fig. 2. Agile *vs* non-agile satellite

When a plan has been produced, it is uploaded to the satellite using a visibility window and executed as it stands without any execution freedom. The only notable exception to this organizational scheme is the US EO-1 satellite which is equipped with onboard planning and replanning capabilities [3].

Unfortunately, optical observation is sensitive to clouds and it is very difficult to foresee the actual presence of clouds the next day over a given ground area. Despite the use of meteorological forecasts by the planning algorithms, many observations (until 80%) remain fruitless due to the presence of clouds. To fix this problem, engineers are currently considering the possibility of equipping Earth-observing satellites with an extra instrument dedicated to the detection of the clouds in front of it, just before observation becomes possible. But, if one wants to exploit information coming from the detection instrument, it is no longer possible to decide upon observations offline each day for the next day. Decisions must be made *online* at the last minute, when detection information is available. Moreover, because Earth-observing satellites are not often within the visibility of their control centers, decisions can no longer be made on the ground. They must be made *onboard* the satellite. The previously offline long-term optimization problem, using unreliable information about cloud presence, becomes an online short-term decision problem, using far more reliable information about cloud presence. One may hope that information reliability will compensate for a quick decision performed over a limited temporal horizon and that globally more fruitful observations will be performed.

This is such a scenario we are currently working on: an agile PLEIADES-like satellite equipped with a cloud detection instrument and with autonomous decision capabilities. This work can be seen as an extension to the case of agile satellites of a similar work performed in the context of non agile ones [4]. It is one of the pieces of the joint ONERA[1]-CNES[2] AGATA[3] project, which aims at developing techniques for improving spacecraft autonomy [5].

1.2 Planning Problem

The global planning problem consists in optimizing the mission feedback throughout the whole satellite life, that is the observations that are performed and delivered to users, taking into account their number and their priorities.

One practical way of approaching this objective consists in optimizing the mission feedback each time over a limited temporal horizon ahead, taking into account the available information about the satellite state (orbital position, attitude, available energy and memory . . .), the candidate observations, the meteorological forecasts, and the cloud detection, and in optimizing again each time the current temporal horizon ends or changes occur. In the particular case of an agile Earth-observing satellite, possible actions are:

- the *observation* of any ground area;
- the *downloading* of any observation data by pointing the satellite and thus its antenna to any ground station;
- the *detection* of clouds in front of the satellite by pointing the satellite 30 degrees ahead;
- the *recharge* of its batteries by orienting its solar generators towards the Sun;
- a *geocentric pointing* when it "has nothing to do" or must remain in a safety mode;
- an *orbital manoeuvre* when the drift of its orbital trajectory from the reference orbit becomes too important.

All these actions impose strong constraints on the satellite attitude and on its attitude speed. They are thus systematically in conflict with each other and must be executed *sequentially*, with a necessary *attitude movement* between two successive ones.

The basic decision problem is thus to decide before the current action ends which action to perform next. To make such a decision, one must be able to assess the feasibility and the effects of each candidate action, including the attitude movement necessary to start it.

In planning problems, assessing the feasibility and the effects of a candidate action is usually easy and what is difficult is to make the right choice among all the feasible candidates. In our problem, this assessment is itself difficult, because it requires reasoning on the attitude movement necessary to start the candidate action and then to perform it.

Considering only the attitude movement necessary to start a candidate action a and only temporal constraints enforcing that a must start within a given temporal

[1] ONERA: the French Aerospace Lab, http://www.onera.fr

[2] CNES: the French Space Agency, http://www.cnes.fr

[3] AGATA: Autonomy Generic Architecture, Tests and Applications, http://www.agata.fr

window w, one must be able to check whether or not a can start within w. If this is possible, it may be moreover useful to compute the minimal time t at which a can start within w. This is the planning subproblem we focused on.

1.3 Attitude Change Subproblem

This attitude change subproblem can be formulated as follows. Let be:

- an *initial state* specified by the attitude and the attitude speed at the end of the current action;
- a *goal state* specified by constraints on the time, the attitude, and the attitude speed at the beginning of the next action;
- *constraints on the attitude movement* such as maximal moments and torques in terms of attitude.

The decision problem consists in checking if a goal state is reachable. If the answer is positive, the associated optimization problem consists in computing the minimal time at which this is possible.

Constraints on the goal depend on the nature of the next action to be performed. For example, if the next action is a Sun pointing, the goal must be reached before the satellite be in eclipse, the goal attitude is fixed, and the associated speed is consequently null (see Section 3.2). If the next action is a data downloading towards any ground station, the goal must be reached before the end of the visibility window between the satellite and the station, and the goal attitude and attitude speed are functions of the time at which the goal is reached because the satellite is moving on its orbit and the Earth is rotating on itself. In fact, the problem can be seen as the problem of tracking a mobile target from a mobile engine. Things are similar if the next action is an observation of any ground area a, with only extra constraints on the goal attitude and attitude speed to allow the line of sensors of the observation instrument to scan a in the right direction at the right speed (see Section 3.3).

To simplify the problem, we decompose the attitude movement into *three parallel movements*, each one performed along one axis (roll, pitch, or yaw) using one actuator. Moreover, we enforce that each of these movements be decomposed into *three successive phases* (see Figure 3):

- a first phase with a *constant torque* T_1;
- a second phase with a *constant moment* L_2;
- a third phase with a *constant torque* T_3.

Such a strategy can be justified as follows. To get a given goal attitude as soon as possible, it is necessary to start with an acceleration until a maximum speed (first two phases). But, to get at the same time a given goal attitude speed, it may be necessary to end with a deceleration phase (third phase). Each of these phases may be empty. To get an intuition of the problem at hand, think that you are driving a car at a given speed on a highway and that you want to go as soon as possible behind the car of a friend who is driving at another speed.

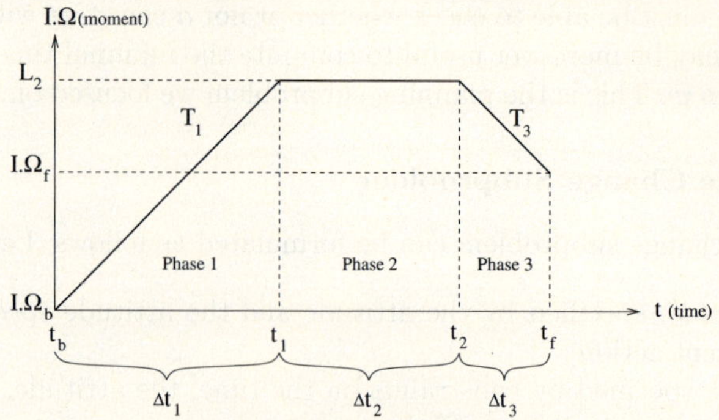

Fig. 3. The three successive attitude movement phases along one axis

The start time t_b of the first phase and the end time t_f of the last one must be obviously equal along the three axes. But in addition, in order to limit the disturbances due to the instantaneous acceleration/deceleration changes, we enforce that the phase commutation times t_1 and t_2 be equal along the three axes too.

The problem consists now in determining the three common *phase end times* t_1, t_2, and t_f, and, along each axis, the *torques* T_1 and T_3 in the first and third phases and the *moment* L_2 in the second one. This is this problem we tried to model as a continuous CSP problem and to solve using a continuous CSP solver.

2 Why Constraint Programming ?

2.1 Existing Methods

Numerical methods exist to solve this kind of problem. In particular, CNES has developed a library called MANIAC [6] which includes an algorithm dedicated to the computing of attitude changes for families of satellites whose attitude is controlled thanks to reaction wheels (MYRIADE, PROTEUS, ...). This algorithm allows the feasibility of an attitude change of a given duration between an initial attitude and a observation goal attitude to be checked. The minimal duration of such an attitude change is obtained thanks to an iterative call to this algorithm. In the context of the future PLEIADES satellites whose attitude is controlled thanks to gyroscopic actuators, CNES has developed a similar library called GOTlib. However, these methods have several drawbacks:

- they have been developed to be used *on the ground* in the context of the regular production of activity plans; they are time consuming and cannot be used in an online context as they stand;
- they consist in searching the values for which a function gets null thanks to *gradient-based* mechanisms such as Newton and Lagrange algorithms; they offer consequently no optimality guarantee in terms of attitude change duration;

– they use *no explicit model* of the problem to solve: initial and goal states, constraints on the attitude movement; this model is hidden in the algorithms.

2.2 Why Considering Constraint Programming ?

Interval analysis has been already used in robotics [7]. In the same direction, we explored the use of constraint programming to remedy the drawbacks of the existing methods. The main *a priori* advantages of such an approach are:

– the use of an *explicit model* of the problem, what is consistent with the model-based approach followed by the AGATA project at all the levels of the autonomous control of a spacecraft, for both situation tracking and decision;
– the ability to use the same model to answer *various requests*, by changing only the optimization criterion (see Section 3.5);
– the ability to get the *global optimum* and not only a local one, or at least a *bound on this optimum*, for example a lower bound on the minimal duration of an attitude change, allowing the decision algorithm to remove infeasible candidate actions.

3 How Constraint Programming ?

3.1 Kinematic Models

The first task is to build a simplified kinematic model of the various bodies which come into play (Sun, Earth, and satellite): movement of the Earth around the Sun and on itself, of the satellite orbit around the Earth, and of the satellite on its orbit and on itself.

Reference Frames. Let $R_\phi(\alpha)$, $R_\theta(\alpha)$, and $R_\psi(\alpha)$ be the rotation matrix of any angle α around respectively the first, the second, and the third base vector. Let $\boldsymbol{u}^{\boldsymbol{R_i}}$ be the vector $\boldsymbol{u}$ expressed in any reference frame R_i. When no reference frame is specified, the vector is assumed to be expressed in the inertial reference frame R_c: $\boldsymbol{u} = \boldsymbol{u}^{\boldsymbol{R_c}}$.

The chosen inertial reference frame is the geocentric equatorial reference frame $R_c = \{\boldsymbol{x_c}; \boldsymbol{y_c}; \boldsymbol{z_c}\}$, with $\boldsymbol{z_c}$ in the direction of the Earth inertial rotation vector and $\boldsymbol{x_c}$ pointing to the vernal equinox point[4] γ.

For any ground area to observe starting in point M, we define the reference frame $R_a = \{\boldsymbol{x_a}; \boldsymbol{y_a}; \boldsymbol{z_a}\}$ with $\boldsymbol{z_a}$ pointing to the zenith and $\boldsymbol{x_a}$ in the direction of the observation.

We define the satellite local orbital reference frame $R_{lo} = \{\boldsymbol{x_{lo}}; \boldsymbol{y_{lo}}; \boldsymbol{z_{lo}}\}$ with $\boldsymbol{z_{lo}}$ pointing to the zenith and $\boldsymbol{y_{lo}}$ in the direction of the kinetic moment of the satellite moving around the Earth.

[4] The vernal equinox point is one of the two points on the celestial sphere where the celestial equator intersects the ecliptic. It is defined as the position of the Sun on the celestial sphere at the vernal equinox time.

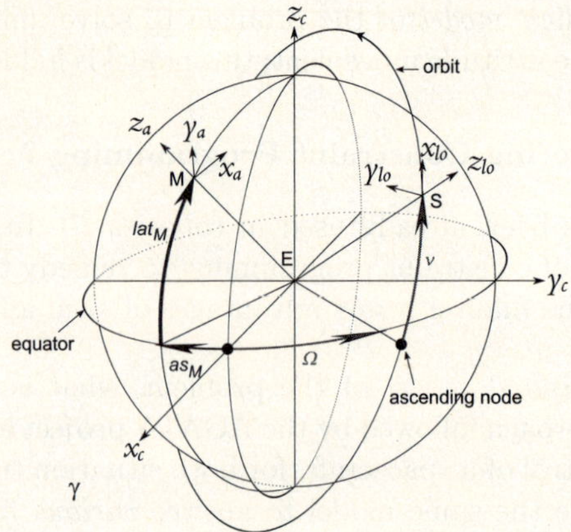

Fig. 4. Used reference frames

Finally, we define the satellite reference frame $R_s = \{\boldsymbol{x_s}; \boldsymbol{y_s}; \boldsymbol{z_s}\}$ with $\boldsymbol{z_s}$ in the opposite direction to the observation instrument direction and $\boldsymbol{y_s}$ in the direction of the line of sensors of the observation instrument. When the satellite points to the Earth center, R_s and R_{lo} are the same (see Figure 4 and see [8] for more details).

Movement of a Point at the Earth Surface. An ground area to observe is defined by a point M on the Earth surface and a course (the observation direction). The latitude lat_M of M is constant and the right ascension[5] $as_M(t)$ of M at any time t is defined by the following equation:

$$as_M(t) = as_{M_b} + \Omega_E(t - t_b)$$

where as_{M_b} is its right ascension at time t_b and $\Omega_E = \frac{2\pi}{86400}$ rd.s^{-1} is the Earth inertial rotation speed. The orientation of the ground area reference frame R_a is given by the transformation matrix from the inertial reference frame R_c to R_a:

$$M_{ca}(t) = R_\theta(-\frac{\pi}{2})R_\phi(\pi)R_\phi(as_M(t))R_\theta(lat_M)R_\psi(course)$$

Consequently, the location $\boldsymbol{EM}(t)$ of M in R_c at any time t is given by:

$$\boldsymbol{EM}(t) = M_{ca}(t) \begin{bmatrix} 0 \\ 0 \\ R_E \end{bmatrix}^{R_a} = \begin{bmatrix} R_E \cos(lat_M)\cos(as_M(t)) \\ R_E \cos(lat_M)\sin(as_M(t)) \\ R_E \sin(lat_M) \end{bmatrix}^{R_c}$$

where $R_E = 6378.13$ km is the Earth radius. Its velocity $\boldsymbol{V_M}(t)$ is given by:

$$\boldsymbol{V_M}(t) = \Omega_E \boldsymbol{z_c} \wedge \boldsymbol{EM}(t)$$

[5] The right ascension is the angular distance of a celestial body or point on the celestial sphere, measured eastward from the vernal equinox.

Movement of the Satellite Orbit around the Earth. The satellite circular orbit is characterized by its radius R_o and its inclination i. The right ascension $\Omega(t)$ of its ascending node[6] at any time t is defined by the following equation:

$$\Omega(t) = \Omega_b + \dot{\Omega}(t - t_b)$$

where Ω_b is the right ascension of its ascending node at time t_b and $\dot{\Omega}$ its constant rotation speed around $\boldsymbol{z_c}$.

Movement of the Satellite on its Orbit. The satellite location on its orbit at any time t is defined by its true anomaly[7] $\nu(t)$ defined by the following equation:

$$\nu(t) = \nu_b + \dot{\nu}(t - t_b)$$

where ν_b is its true anomaly at time t_b and $\dot{\nu}$ its mean motion. The orientation of the local orbital reference frame R_{lo} is given by the transformation matrix from the inertial reference frame R_c to R_{lo}:

$$M_{clo}(t) = R_\psi(\Omega(t))R_\phi(i)R_\psi(\frac{\pi}{2})R_\phi(\frac{\pi}{2})R_\theta(\nu(t))$$

Consequently, the location $\boldsymbol{ES}(t)$ of the satellite in R_c at any time t is given by the vector:

$$\boldsymbol{ES}(t) = M_{clo}(t) \begin{bmatrix} 0 \\ 0 \\ R_o \end{bmatrix}^{R_{lo}}$$

Its velocity $\boldsymbol{V_S}(t)$ is given by:

$$\boldsymbol{V_S}(t) = \boldsymbol{\Omega_{clo}} \wedge \boldsymbol{ES}(t) = (\dot{\Omega}\boldsymbol{z_c} + \dot{\nu}\boldsymbol{y_{lo}}) \wedge \boldsymbol{ES}(t)$$

Movement of the Satellite on itself. The attitude movement of the satellite is constrained by its inertial matrix I and the maximum moment and torque vectors L_{max} and T_{max}:

$$I = \begin{pmatrix} I_x & 0 & 0 \\ 0 & I_y & 0 \\ 0 & 0 & I_z \end{pmatrix} = \begin{pmatrix} 850 & 0 & 0 \\ 0 & 850 & 0 \\ 0 & 0 & 750 \end{pmatrix} \text{ m}^2.\text{kg}$$

$$\begin{bmatrix} L_{x_{max}} \\ L_{y_{max}} \\ L_{z_{max}} \end{bmatrix} = \begin{bmatrix} 45 \\ 45 \\ 20 \end{bmatrix} \text{ N.m} \qquad \begin{bmatrix} T_{x_{max}} \\ T_{y_{max}} \\ T_{z_{max}} \end{bmatrix} = \begin{bmatrix} 7 \\ 7 \\ 6 \end{bmatrix} \text{ N.m}$$

---

6 The orbit ascending node is the orbit point where the satellite crosses the equatorial plane headed from south to north.

7 The satellite true anomaly is the angular distance, viewed from the Earth center and measured in the orbital plane from the perigee to the current location of the satellite.

3.2 Attitude Change with a Fixed Goal Attitude

We start by considering the simplest case, where the goal attitude is fixed. This happens when the candidate next action is a battery recharge with the solar generators oriented towards the Sun. Because of the huge distance between the Earth and the Sun and the relatively slow movement of the Earth around the Sun, we can indeed consider that the attitude A_{Sun} required by battery recharge remains constant during a non-eclipse period (more than half a revolution of the satellite around the Earth, which lasts about 100 minutes; see Figure 5).

As the satellite attitude movement has been decomposed into three parallel movements, each one along one axis, each other constrained by only the three common phase end times (see Section 1.3), we can consider the attitude movement along one axis.

Let α_b (resp. α_f) be the initial (resp. goal) attitude, with $\Delta\alpha = \alpha_f - \alpha_b$. Let Ω_b (resp. Ω_f) be the initial (resp. goal) attitude speed. Let t_b be the initial time and t_1 (resp. t_2 and t_f) be the end time of phase 1 (resp. 2 and 3) with $\Delta t_1 = t_1 - t_b$, $\Delta t_2 = t_2 - t_1$, and $\Delta t_3 = t_f - t_2$. Let T_1 (resp. T_3) be the constant torque during phase 1 (resp. 3) and L_2 be the constant moment during phase 2 (see Figure 3). The moment $I \cdot \Omega(t)$ at any time t is given by the following equations:

- during phase 1: $I \cdot \Omega(t) = I \cdot \Omega_b + T_1(t - t_b)$;
- during phase 2: $I \cdot \Omega(t) = L_2$
- during phase 3: $I \cdot \Omega(t) = I \cdot \Omega_f + T_3(t - t_f)$;

Moment continuity at times t_1 and t_2 enforces that $I \cdot \Omega_b + T_1(t_1 - t_b) = I \cdot \Omega_f + T_3(t_2 - t_f) = L_2$. This results in Equations 1 and 2:

$$T_1 = \frac{L_2 - I \cdot \Omega_b}{\Delta t_1} \tag{1}$$

$$T_3 = \frac{I \cdot \Omega_f - L_2}{\Delta t_3} \tag{2}$$

If we consider the attitude change $\Delta\alpha$ between t_b and t_f, we get:

$$I \cdot \Delta\alpha = \int_{t_b}^{t_f} I \cdot \Omega(t)\, dt = I \cdot \Omega_b \cdot \Delta t_1 + T_1 \cdot \frac{{\Delta t_1}^2}{2} + L_2 \cdot \Delta t_2 + I \cdot \Omega_f \cdot \Delta t_3 + T_3 \cdot \frac{{\Delta t_3}^2}{2}$$

Combined with equations 1 and 2, this results in Equation 3.

$$I \cdot \Delta\alpha = \frac{L_2 + I \cdot \Omega_b}{2} \Delta t_1 + L_2 \cdot \Delta t_2 + \frac{L_2 + I \cdot \Omega_f}{2} \Delta t_3 \tag{3}$$

The problem consists now in minimizing t_f with constraints given by Equations 1, 2, and 3, at which must be added the following inequalities:

$$t_b \le t_1 \le t_2 \le t_f$$

$$-L_{max} \le L_2 \le L_{max}$$

$$-T_{max} \le T_1, T_3 \le T_{max}$$

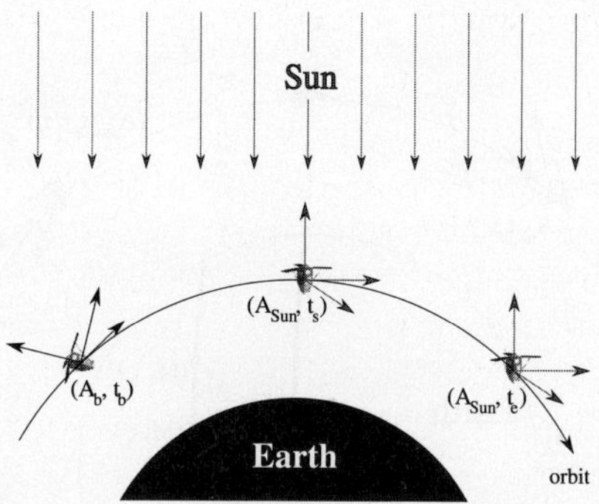

Fig. 5. Reaching a Sun pointing attitude

It is worth emphasizing that, because the decision variables are t_1, t_2, t_f, L_2, T_1, and T_3, the resulting problem is not linear.

3.3 Attitude Change with a Variable Goal Attitude

Except when the next candidate action is a battery recharge, the goal attitude and attitude speed are not fixed. They are variable and depend on the time t_f at which the attitude movement ends. This is the case when the candidate next action is an observation, a data downloading, a detection, a geocentric pointing, or an orbital manoeuvre.

We consider here the most constrained case when the candidate next action is the observation of any ground area a (see Figure 6 which shows how the goal attitude depends on the time at which observation starts, anywhere in the visibility window $[t_s; t_e]$ of a). All the constraints described in the previous section for the case of an attitude change with a fixed goal attitude remain valid, except that α_f and Ω_f are no longer constant. They are variable, but constrained due to the following requirements:

- the observation instrument must point to the starting point M of a:

$$\boldsymbol{z_s} = \frac{\boldsymbol{ES}(t_f) - \boldsymbol{EM}(t_f)}{||\boldsymbol{ES}(t_f) - \boldsymbol{EM}(t_f)||}$$

- the sensor line of the observation instrument must be orthogonal to the observation direction of a:

$$\boldsymbol{x_s} = \boldsymbol{y_a}(t_f) \wedge \boldsymbol{z_s}$$

So, the orientation of the satellite reference frame R_s at time t_f is given by the transformation matrix from the inertial reference frame R_c to R_s:

$$M_{cs} = \left(\boldsymbol{x_s} \; \boldsymbol{z_s} \wedge \boldsymbol{x_s} \; \boldsymbol{z_s} \right)$$

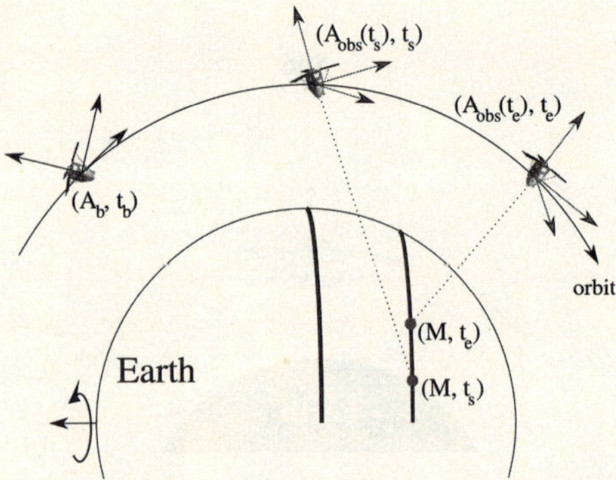

Fig. 6. Reaching an observation attitude

– the speed of the projection on the ground of the sensor line of the of the observation instrument must be equal to the sum of the ground area speed and of the required scanning observation speed v_{scan}:

$$\boldsymbol{V_S}(t_f) + \boldsymbol{\Omega_{cs}}(t_f) \wedge (\boldsymbol{EM}(t_f) - \boldsymbol{ES}(t_f)) = \boldsymbol{V_M}(t_f) + v_{scan}\boldsymbol{x_a}(t_f)$$

where $\boldsymbol{\Omega_{cs}}(t)$ is the rotation speed of the satellite reference frame R_s in the inertial reference frame R_c at any time t.

3.4 CSP Model

The problem can be cast into the following continuous CSP [9].

Variables representing the attitude movement:

$t_f \in [t_s; t_e]$	$T_{1x}, T_{3x} \in [-T_{maxx}; T_{maxx}]$	$L_{2x} \in [-L_{maxx}; L_{maxx}]$
$t_1, t_2 \in [t_b; t_e]$	$T_{1y}, T_{3y} \in [-T_{maxy}; T_{maxy}]$	$L_{2y} \in [-L_{maxy}; L_{maxy}]$
	$T_{1z}, T_{3z} \in [-T_{maxz}; T_{maxz}]$	$L_{2z} \in [-L_{maxz}; L_{maxz}]$

Variables representing the goal state at time t_f:

$M_{ca} \in \mathcal{M}_3(\mathbb{R})$	$\boldsymbol{x_a} \in [-1, 1]^3$	$\boldsymbol{y_a} \in [-1, 1]^3$
$M_{clo} \in \mathcal{M}_3(\mathbb{R})$	$\boldsymbol{\Omega_{cs}} \in]-\infty; +\infty[^3$	$\boldsymbol{\Omega_{cs}^{R_s}} \in]-\infty; +\infty[^3$
$M_{cs} \in \mathcal{M}_3(\mathbb{R})$	$\boldsymbol{x_s} \in [-1, 1]^3$	$\boldsymbol{z_s} \in [-1, 1]^3$
$\Delta\phi \in [-\pi; \pi]$	$\Delta\theta \in [-\pi; \pi]$	$\Delta\psi \in [-\pi; \pi]$

Constraints:

$t_b \leq t_1 \leq t_2 \leq t_f$ and Equations 1, 2, and 3 along the three axes

$$M_{ca} = M_{ca}(t_f) = R_\theta(-\tfrac{\pi}{2})R_\phi(\pi)R_\phi(as_M(t_f))R_\theta(lat_M)R_\psi(course)$$

$\boldsymbol{x_a} = M_{ca}\boldsymbol{x_c}$ $\qquad$ $\boldsymbol{y_a} = M_{ca}\boldsymbol{y_c}$

$$M_{clo} = M_{clo}(t_f) = R_\psi(\Omega(t_f))R_\phi(i)R_\psi(\tfrac{\pi}{2})R_\phi(\tfrac{\pi}{2})R_\theta(\nu(t_f))$$

$$\boldsymbol{z_s} = \frac{\boldsymbol{ES}(t_f)-\boldsymbol{EM}(t_f)}{||\boldsymbol{ES}(t_f)-\boldsymbol{EM}(t_f)||} \qquad \boldsymbol{x_s} = \boldsymbol{y_a} \wedge \boldsymbol{z_s}$$

$$M_{cs} = (\boldsymbol{x_s}\ \boldsymbol{z_s} \wedge \boldsymbol{x_s}\ \boldsymbol{z_s}) \qquad \boldsymbol{\Omega_{cs}} = M_{cs}\boldsymbol{\Omega_{cs}^{R_s}}$$

$$\boldsymbol{V_S}(t_f) + \boldsymbol{\Omega_{cs}} \wedge (\boldsymbol{EM}(t_f) - \boldsymbol{ES}(t_f)) = \boldsymbol{V_M}(t_f) + v_{scan}\boldsymbol{x_a}$$

$$\Delta\phi = \arctan(\frac{(M_{cs})_{32}}{(M_{cs})_{33}}) \qquad \Delta\theta = -\arcsin((M_{cs})_{31}) \qquad \Delta\psi = \arctan(\frac{(M_{cs})_{21}}{(M_{cs})_{11}})$$

3.5 Resolution with RealPaver

We used the RealPaver continuous CSP solver [10] to compute the minimal duration of an attitude change. We present an example of computation where the satellite attitude is A_b at time $t_b = 0$ and the candidate action consists in observing point M ($lat_M = 40.1\,^\circ$, $as_{M_b} = 1.0$ rd, and $course = 0.5$ rd) with a null scanning speed ($v_{scan} = 0$ m.s^{-1}) within the visibility window $[t_s; t_e] = [0; 100]$ s.

The considered satellite orbit is characterized by its radius $R_o = 7204.8$ km, its inclination $i = 98.72\,^\circ$, its ascending node rotation speed $\dot{\Omega} = 1.99e^{-7}$ rd.s^{-1}, and its ascending node right ascension $\Omega_b = -2.23$ rd at time t_b. The satellite mean motion is $\dot{\nu} = 1.03e^{-3}$ rd.s^{-1} and its true anomaly at time t_b is $\nu_b = 2.3$ rd.

$$A_b = \{\begin{bmatrix}\psi_b\\ \theta_b\\ \phi_b\end{bmatrix}, \begin{bmatrix}\dot{\psi}_b\\ \dot{\theta}_b\\ \dot{\phi}_b\end{bmatrix}\} = \{\begin{bmatrix}1.34\\ -0.0682\\ -0.254\end{bmatrix} \text{rd}, \begin{bmatrix}0.0495\\ 0.0133\\ 0.0494\end{bmatrix} \text{rd.s}^{-1}\}$$

Figure 7 shows the result of the computation of a *lower bound* on the attitude change minimal duration ($\Delta T = t_f - t_b \approx 16.75$ s) obtained in 240 ms. From that, we just know that there is no attitude change whose duration is shorter than 16.75 seconds, but know neither the minimal duration, nor the associated attitude movement.

Figure 8 shows the result of the computation of an *upper bound* on the attitude change minimal duration ($\Delta T \approx 49.02$ s) obtained in 600 ms. This upper bound has been obtained by fixing the remaining degrees of freedom on the trajectory, more precisely by setting the torques T_1 and T_3 to the maximal acceleration and deceleration along the axis for which the angular movement to perform is the greatest, in this case the x axis, with $T_{1x} = -T_{x_{max}}$ and $T_{3x} = T_{x_{max}}$. From that, we get an attitude movement whose duration is an upper bound on the attitude change minimal duration.

But attempts to get the minimal duration and the associated attitude movement within a reasonable CPU time were unsuccessful. So, it remains to explore other ways, possibly more sensible, of fixing the remaining degrees of freedom on the trajectory.

Interestingly, it is possible to use the same model to optimize another criterion. If there are many observations to perform, minimizing the attitude change duration may be sensible. But, if there are only few observations, it may be more sensible to try and optimize their quality. One way of doing that consists in

```
OUTER BOX: HULL of 1 boxes
  tf             in [16.75 , 16.77]
  delta_psi      in [-1.5 , -1.499]
  delta_theta    in [-0.1763 , -0.1761]
  delta_phi      in [1.144 , 1.146]
  T1x            in [-7 , -0.1952]
  T3x            in [-7 , +7]
  T1y            in [-7 , +7]
  T3y            in [-7 , +7]
  T1z            in [-6 , -1.016]
  T3z            in [-6 , +6]
  L2x            in [-45 , +41.59]
  L2y            in [-45 , +45]
  L2z            in [-20 , +20]
  t1             in [2.84 , 16.77]
  t2             in [2.84 , 16.77]
  [...]

  precision: 90, elapsed time: 240 ms
```

Fig. 7. Lower bound computation

```
OUTER BOX: HULL of 1 boxes
  tf             in [49.02 , 49.04]
  delta_psi      in [-1.552 , -1.551]
  delta_theta    in [-0.3708 , -0.3704]
  delta_phi      in [1.207 , 1.209]
  T1x            = -7 **point**
  T3x            = 7 **point**
  T1y            in [-1.697 , -1.688]
  T3y            in [0.5936 , 0.6169]
  T1z            in [-1.398 , -1.382]
  T3z            in [-3.478 , -3.413]
  L2x            in [-45 , -44.91]
  L2y            in [-9.745 , -9.662]
  L2z            in [19.68 , 19.84]
  t1             in [12.43 , 12.45]
  t2             in [43.27 , 43.31]
  [...]

  precision: 59.6, elapsed time: 600 ms
```

Fig. 8. Upper bound computation

```
OUTER BOX: HULL of 1 boxes
  cos_a-1        in [1.036 , 1.038]
  tf             in [107.4 , 107.5]
  delta_psi      in [1.363 , 1.365]
  delta_theta    in [-0.7951 , -0.7948]
  delta_phi      in [1.349 , 1.351]
  T1x            in [-7 , +1.02]
  T3x            in [-7 , +7]
  T1y            in [-7 , +7]
  T3y            in [-7 , +7]
  T1z            in [-6 , -0.1586]
  T3z            in [-6 , +6]
  t1             in [2.84 , 107.5]
  t2             in [2.84 , 107.5]
  [...]

  precision: 105, elapsed time: 4,760 ms
```

Fig. 9. Observation angle optimization

minimizing the observation angle[8]. Figure 9 shows the result of the computation of a *lower bound* on the new criterion `cos_a-1` $= \frac{1}{<z_s, z_{lo}>}$ obtained in 4,760 ms, with $\Delta T \approx 107.4$ s. However, we can observe that the CPU time is significantly greater than with the previous optimization criterion.

4 Added Value of Constraint Programming

The main lessons we draw from this work are the following ones:

- maybe, the main advantage of using constraint programming tools is to compel oneself to write an *explicit model* of the problem, which can be used as a reference for any algorithmic development; moreover, the same model can be used with different *optimization criteria*;

[8] The observation angle is defined as the angle between the base vectors z_s and z_{lo}.

- unlike gradient-based methods, interval analysis allows *bounds* to be computed; in our case, the lower bound on the minimal duration of an attitude change may allow infeasible candidate actions to be removed;
- unfortunately, the recursive domain splitting used by constraint programming tools does not allow *optimal solutions* to be produced within a reasonable CPU time; in practice, some heuristic choices are necessary to get solutions of reasonable quality.

References

1. Bensana, E., Lemaître, M., Verfaillie, G.: Benchmark Problems: Earth Observation Satellite Management. Constraints 4(3), 293–299 (1999)
2. Verfaillie, G., Lemaître, M.: Selecting and Scheduling Observations for Agile Satellites: Some Lessons from the Constraint Reasoning Community Point of View. In: Walsh, T. (ed.) CP 2001. LNCS, vol. 2239, pp. 670–684. Springer, Heidelberg (2001)
3. Chien, S., et al.: The EO-1 Autonomous Science Agent. In: Kudenko, D., Kazakov, D., Alonso, E. (eds.) Adaptive Agents and Multi-Agent Systems II. LNCS (LNAI), vol. 3394. Springer, Heidelberg (2005)
4. Damiani, S., Verfaillie, G., Charmeau, M.C.: Cooperating On-board and On the ground Decision Modules for the Management of an Earth Watching Constellation. In: Proc. of i-SAIRAS-05 (2005)
5. Charmeau, M.C., Bensana, E.: AGATA: A Lab Bench Project for Spacecraft Autonomy. In: Proc. of i-SAIRAS-05 (2005)
6. Parraud, P., Flipo, A., Jaubert, J., Lassalle-Balier, G.: Computing Smooth Attitude Guidance Laws for Homing Maneuvers. In: Proc. of the International Symposium on Space Technology and Science (2006)
7. Merlet, J.P.: Interval Analysis and Robotics (Invited Presentation). In: Benhamou, F. (ed.) CP 2006. LNCS, vol. 4204, p. 15. Springer, Heidelberg (2006)
8. Hoots, F.: Theory of the Motion of an Artificial Earth Satellite. Celestial Mechanics and Dynamical Astronomy (1979)
9. Granvilliers, L., Benhamou, F.: Continuous and Interval Constraints. In: Rossi, F., Beek, P.V., Walsh, T. (eds.) Handbook of Constraint Programming, pp. 571–603. Elsevier, Amsterdam (2006)
10. Granvilliers, L., Benhamou, F.: RealPaver: an Interval Solver using Constraint Satisfaction Techniques. ACM Trans. Math. Softw. 32(1), 138–156 (2006)

Solving an Air Conditioning System Problem in an Embodiment Design Context Using Constraint Satisfaction Techniques

Raphaël Chenouard[1], Patrick Sébastian[1], and Laurent Granvilliers[2]

[1] ENSAM Bordeaux, TRansferts Ecoulements FLuides Energétique, CNRS, F-33405, Talence Cedex

[2] University of Nantes, Laboratoire d'Informatique de Nantes Atlantique, CNRS, BP 92208, F-44322 Nantes Cedex 3

Abstract. In this paper, the embodiment design of an air conditioning system (ACS) in an aircraft is investigated using interval constraint satisfaction techniques. The detailed ACS model is quite complex to solve, since it contains many coupled variables and many constraints corresponding to complex physics phenomena. Some new heuristics and notions based on embodiment design knowledge, are briefly introduced to undertake some embodiment design concepts and to obtain a more relevant and more efficient solving process than classical algorithms.

The benefits of using constraint programming in embodiment design are discussed and some difficulties for designers using CP tools are shortly detailed.

1 An Air Conditioning System Problem

1.1 Context

The design process is a sequence of phases ranging from the definition of needs and requirements to preliminary design and detailed design (Pahl & Beitz 1996). Preliminary design includes conceptual design leading to product schemes, and embodiment design, where feasibility studies are investigated according to geometric constraints, physics behaviors and interactions between the product, its components, and its environments.

Nowadays, no real software exist to solve complex embodiment design problems. In this context, a constraint solver, namely *Constraint Explorer*, was developed within a partnership between Dassault Aviation and several research laboratories. This partnership was created through the french RNTL project *CO2*. Our work starts from this project and aims to express some other difficulties using constraint programming in embodiment design, where problems are highly coupled according to a design point of view. We use Elisa [1], an open C++ library for constraint programming and constraint solving techniques based on interval arithmetic (Moore 1966), where we develop some new concepts and algorithms.

[1] http://sourceforge.net/projects/elisa/

C. Bessiere (Ed.): CP 2007, LNCS 4741, pp. 18–32, 2007.

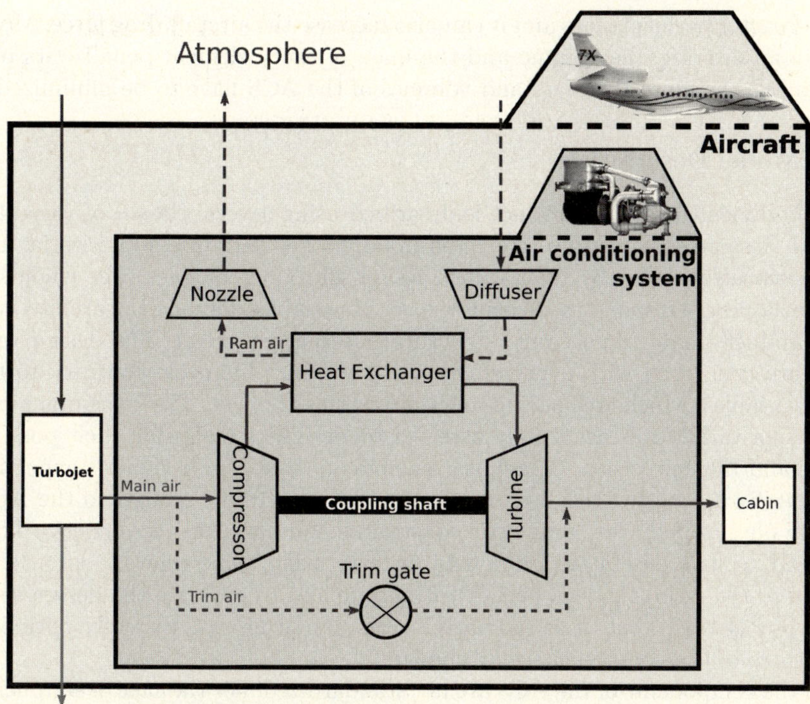

Fig. 1. Bloc functional diagram for an aircraft air conditioning system

In this paper, the embodiment of an air conditioning system (ACS) for an aircraft (see Figure 1) is investigated. Figure 1 describes the main components of an ACS and functional fluxes circulation. The ACS may be viewed as a bootstrap, composed of: a turbo-machine (a compressor, a turbine and a coupling shaft), an exchanger, a trim gate, a diffuser and a nozzle. This bootstrap corresponds to a reverse Joule-Brayton cycle. A trim gate is used to regulate the air cooling system and guarantee a suitable air pressure and temperature in most of the aircraft life situations. The main air is taken from the turbo-reactor and flows through the compressor. The pressure and temperature of the main air increase a lot; this improves the heat tranfers inside of the heat exchanger. Indeed, the heat exchanger uses the dynamic cold air from atmosphere to cool down the main air flow, which is very hot. Then, the main air is released through the turbine and its pressure and temperature significantly drop. The coupling shaft transmits the energy given by the turbine rotation to the compressor. If the main air temperature is not suitable for humans (i.e.: too cold), then the trim gate can mix hot air from the turbo-reactor with the main air flow.

In an aircraft, several essential criteria must be taken into account. Indeed, the air pressure and temperature of the cabin must be guaranteed for the well-being of the passengers, but the air flows taken from the turbo-reactor and from the atmosphere have to be carefully managed. Indeed, it can decrease the turbo-reactor performances and it can also increase the aircraft drag force. Moreover in an aircraft, the volume and the mass of every element penalize its performances, therefore the mass and volumes of the ACS have to be minimized.

1.2 Model Description

In embodiment design, a product is described using several classes of variables. Indeed, designers are mainly interested in only a few variables and criteria. The *design variables* define by their values design solution principles. The whole design variables correspond to the smallest set of variables defining the architecture of a product (main dimensions, structural alternatives, etc.). The design variables are concerned with every stage of the product life cycle contrary to the other variables, which are specific to the investigated phase. Thus, the domain of the design variables is accurately assessed by designers regarding their possible values and their precision. These assessments are based on designer's expertise. The *auxiliary variables* are used to express the constraints related to the ACS, namely physics behavior, geometric constraints and performances criteria. They are used to link design variables and criteria using some relevant knowledge related to the ACS. Criteria permit to validate and to evaluate the design solutions, but at this point, it is too early in the design process to really optimize, since some of the components may change.

All the components of the ACS are not standardized. For the sake of simplicity, only the exchanger and the trim gate are embodied, since the ACS performances seem to be mainly depending on the characteristics of the exchanger. In this way, other components are mainly expressed with efficiency coefficients (provided by manufacturers) and energy balances. Although these simplifications are used, the model of the exchanger is really complex and several coupled physics phenomena interfere.

Our model is composed of 156 variables. There are 5 design variables (1 for the trim gate and 4 describing the exchanger). The 151 other variables are some auxiliary variables. Most of them (85 variables) may be considered as explicit variables. Indeed, these variables are explicitly defined by a constraint, since they correspond to intermediary computations. Their mathematical definition could act as a substitute for them, but they are maintained within the model, because they express well-known physical variables (for instance Reynolds or Nusselt dimensionless numbers) or criteria used by designers. These variables preserve the model expressivity and intelligibility. The 66 other auxiliary variables are mainly related to the exchanger (fin characteristics, pressures, temperatures, efficiency, etc.). Explicit variables' values are often used to estimate the validity of the model and to check that no error occurs in the expressed knowledge. Many variables can be considered as explicit variables, if their significance in the model is minor regarding the designer expertise and if they are alone on the left part of one equation.

Constraints may also be classified. For instance, there are 2880 basic unary constraints describing a catalogue of 48 exchange surfaces (Kays & London 1984). Indeed, 2 exchange surfaces (hot and cold sides) are detailed using 30 characteristics (fins thickness and spacing, interpolation coefficients, etc.). 9 constraints describe the energy balances of the 8 components used in the model. 94 other constraints express the ACS characteristics and behavior (geometry, temperature, pressure losses, etc.), most of them defining the explicit variables.

1.3 Embodiment Design Solutions

A design solution corresponds to a product architecture, which satisfy all constaints and criteria. As a consequence, a design solution is represented by design variable values. The multiple auxiliary variables values must not be taken into account when considering design solutions, since their domain exploration may induce duplicated design variable solutions. However the auxiliary variables exploration is mandatory to check the product behavior and the physics reality.

2 Why CP?

In Embodiment design, designers have to determine sets of design solutions to support decision making. They need tools to globally explore the solutions search space.

Stochastic methods are mainly used. They are developed in engineering departments using simulation tools coupled with optimization tools. This method requires the development of simulation codes, specific to the investigated problems. For instance, a tool using an optimization approach based on an evolutionary method was developed to investigate the ACS presented in this paper (Sébastian et al. 2007). These simulation codes are often powerful, but they are not easily maintainable and reusable. The solving algorithm must be redefined for each application, even though it is often time consuming to develop. In the context of a preliminary design phase, many decisions are not taken at that point and the model may evolve several times. Moreover the evolutionary approaches do not compute the entire set of solutions. In particular if some parameters of the genetic algorithm are not finely tuned, some areas of the search space may not be explored. The embodiment design phase is used to detect feasibility areas in the search space and leaving out some may be detrimental to take the appropriate decisions.

The CP approach allows to write the design models without developing their solving methods, thus the cost is lesser when a parameter or a component changes. It is already used in configuration and in conceptual design (O'Sullivan 2001, Gelle & Faltings 2003, Yannou et al. 2003) and it seems promising for embodiment design (Zimmer & Zablit 2001, Fischer et al. 2004). The search space is explored entirely and it is easier to determine the shapes of the solution set. This entire set of solutions allows designers to take more robust decisions, since they can investigate more easily the model response to some characteristics changes (for instance components, dimensions or criteria) and thus preserve one design architecture and some of its performances validity from future changes.

3 How CP?

In our air conditioning system application, we use a general CP framework based on a branch-and-prune algorithm (Van-Hentenryck et al. 1997).

3.1 Model Formulation

We consider the classical triplet representation of CSP problems: $\langle V, D, C \rangle$. Variables are defined using discrete or continuous domains. During computations, discrete domains are converted into an interval hull and it is later refined using the discrete values it holds. The constraints are based on arithmetic expressions, using the classical equality and weak inequality operators.

However, some physics laws were established through experiments, and they are expressed as piecewise nonlinear functions. We focus on piecewise phenomena which are defined by one variable. Indeed, most physics phenomena are estimated using some representative and well-known variables (for instance in fluid mechanics: Nusselt, Reynolds, Prandtl numbers, etc.). We define a global piecewise constraint to efficiently compute theses piecewise nonlinear functions, quite similarly to Refalo's approach on linear piecewise functions (Refalo 1999). Moreover this global constraint allows to define easily the range of choices using a unique reference for a component, corresponding to a disjunction between all the components to choose.

3.2 Solving Algorithms

The robust classical round-robin strategy on the variables choices for exploration often gives slow solving times for embodiment design problems and generates many duplicated design solutions. The main explanation is the useless computation steps made on auxiliary variables. Indeed, they may have a very large domain, whereas splitting on their domain may result on only few reductions of the overall search space. That's why we develop a heuristic custom search based on variable classes linked to the embodiment design point of view. Indeed, design variables are relating to the main structuring characteristics and models are often established around them and around criteria. Auxiliary variables are only introduced to express performance criteria, physics behavior, etc. (see figure 2). Thus, this choice strategy promotes design variables to compute the design architectures (or design principles of solution) as soon as possible. Auxiliary variables' domain often appear to be more quickly reduced than using the round-robin strategy.

In addition, some of the auxiliary variables are explicitly defined according to other variables. They correspond to intermediary computation steps, but they are maintained in the model to ensure its intelligibility. To avoid some useless exploration steps according to these variables, their precision are defined to the infinite value, so that their precisions are always achieved. Their values are computed by the consistency pruning process based on 2B (Lhomme 1993) and box consistency (Benhamou et al. 1999). It is important to highlight, that

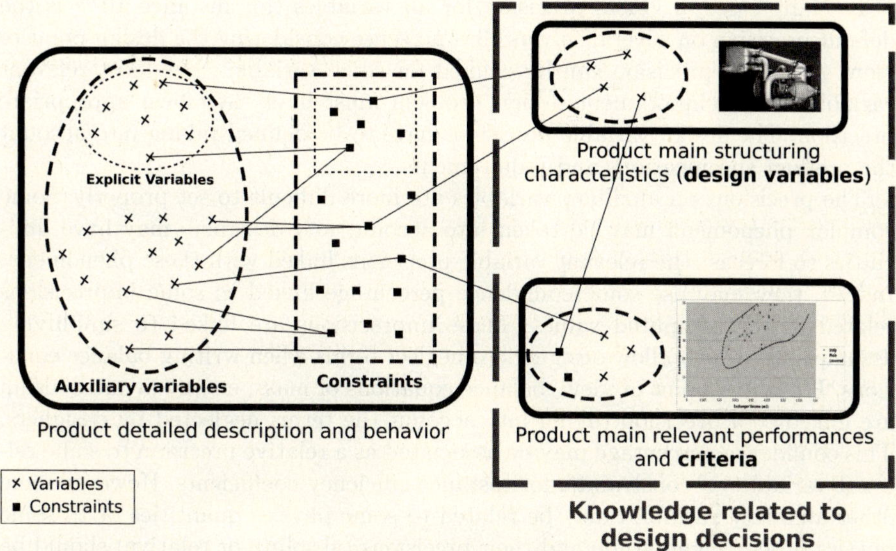

Fig. 2. Knowledge classification in an embodiment design model

explicit variables may be defined using other explicit variables. In this case, no dependency cycle has to stand between them. Some small design problems are presented using such variables or not in Vu's work (Vu 2005).

These algorithms and the use of explicit variables allow us to compute more efficiently the entire solution set of embodiment design problems in a few hours, whereas other algorithms do not compute the first solution after several hours (the solving process was stopped after about 5 hours without any results).

In some other works, models are decomposed in small blocks organized in a directed acyclic graph (Reddy et al. 1996, Bliek et al. 1998, Neveu et al. 2006). It may be interpreted to a variables solving order, where blocks are fully solved before starting the next one in the graph. It is an efficient approach for problems, where coupled variables are not too numerous. Indeed, when there are several sets of coupled variables, the model is decomposed in big blocks and the hardness of the problem remains. Moreover, preliminary design problems are often under-constrained, and many start variables have to be chosen to compute a decomposition of the constraint network. In this case, these variable domains are explored almost exhaustively and it may induce useless computation steps on irrelevant variables.

3.3 Precision Management

The management of the precisions variables appears to be fundamental to ensure a relevant solution set for designers. Indeed, each design variable has a precision representing the interval width, which defines solutions according to the design point of view. These precisions are linked with tolerances and real-world feasibility.

In many cases, a global precision for all variables (for instance 10^{-8} is the default precision on several solvers) has no sense considering the design point of view. A default precision can be defined for some variables, but most relevant variables of an embodiment design problem must have their own appropriate precision. The design variable precisions have to be defined taking into account the product specifications and requirements.

The precisions on auxiliary variables are more difficult to set properly. Some complex phenomena may be taken into account and designers may have difficulties to forecast the relevant variable precisions linked with these phenomena. Indeed, they may use some confidence percentage linked to some imprecisions related to the computed values. These imprecisions are linked to simplifying assumptions, which allow designers to neglect terms when writing balance equations. From this point of view, balance equations of mass, energy or momentum are linked to a precision taking into account the terms neglected by designers. This confidence percentage may be associated as a relative precision to some relevant variables of constraints, for instance efficiency coefficients. However some other auxiliary variables may be related to some physics quantities or to some physics order of magnitude and their precisions (absolute or relative) should be defined taking this knowledge into account.

The precision management is really fundamental to obtain efficient solving time (not completely useless search space explorations) and relevant solutions (not too many duplicated design solutions).

3.4 Model Implementation

All the constants, variables, domains and constraints of the ACS problem are detailed in the following tables. The c or h indexes related to some variables identify the cold or hot side of the exchanger. We do not define the domain of the variables from the Kays & London database and explicit variables, since it is useless. For a variable x, $p(x)$ denotes the precision of x.

Constants	
Air properties	$Cp = 1000$ J/kg.K, $r = 287$ J/kg/K, $\gamma = 1.4$
Flight conditions	$Z = 10500$ m, $M = 0.8$
Turbo-reactor characteristics	$TC_{TR} = 8$, $\eta_{TRd} = 0.9$, $\eta_{TRc} = 0.8$
Components efficiency	$\eta_c = 0.75$, $\eta_{AT} = 0.95$, $\eta_t = 0.8$, $\eta_{NO} = 0.9$, $\eta_{DI} = 0.9$
Air sent into the cabin	$T_5 = 278.15$ K, $p_5 = 85000$ Pa, $q = 0.7$ kg/s
Plates characteristics	$kp = 20$ W/m/K, $tp = 0.001$ m

Design variables	
Width of the exchanger (m)	Lx $\in [0.1, 1]$, p(Lx)$= 0.01$
Mass capacity ratio (-)	$\tau \in [1, 8]$, p(τ)$= 0.5$
Hot-side exchange surface reference (-)	$ExSurf_h \in [1, 48]$: int
Cold-side exchange surface reference (-)	$ExSurf_c \in [1, 48]$: int
Trim gate radius (m)	Rv $\in \{0.01, 0.02, ..., 0.2\}$

Auxiliary variables	
Exchanger material characteristics	$roex \in [0, 10000]$, $kw \in [0, 500]$
Exchanger pressures (Pa)	$p_2 \in [0, 1000000] \wedge p(p_2) = 5\%$, $p_3 \in [0, 1000000] \wedge p(p_3) = 5\%$ $pe_{ic} \in [0, 1000000] \wedge p(pe_{oc}) = 5\%$, $pe_{oc} \in [0, 1000000] \wedge p(pe_{oc}) = 5\%$
Exchanger temperatures (K)	$T_2 \in [0, 1000] \wedge p(T_2) = 5\%$, $T_3 \in [0, 1000] \wedge p(T_3) = 5\%$ $Te_{ic} \in [0, 1000] \wedge p(Te_{ic}) = 5\%$, $Te_{oc} \in [0, 1000] \wedge p(Te_{oc}) = 5\%$
Exchanger pressure losses (Pa)	$\Delta Pe_h \in [-\infty, +\infty] \wedge p(\Delta Pe_h) = 10\%$ $\Delta Pe_c \in [-\infty, +\infty] \wedge p(\Delta Pe_c) = 10\%$
Exchanger efficiency coefficient (-)	$\epsilon \in [0, 1] \wedge p(\epsilon) = 5\%$
Air flows in the exchanger (kg/s)	$q_{ra} \in [0, +\infty] \wedge p(q_{ra}) = 0.001$ $q_{ma} \in [0, +\infty] \wedge p(q_{ma}) = 0.001$
Pressure after the turbine (Pa)	$p_4 \in [0, 1000000] \wedge p(p_4) = 5\%$
Temperature after the turbine (K)	$T_4 \in [0, 1000] \wedge p(T_4) = 5\%$

Auxiliary variables relating to the K&L database	
Fins characteristics	b_h, rh_h, δ_h, β_h, b_c, rh_c, δ_c, β_c
Colburn interpolation coefficients	JS_{h1}, JS_{h2}, JS_{h3}, JS_{c1}, JS_{c2}, JS_{c3}
Fanning interpolation coefficients	fS_{h1}, fS_{h2}, fS_{h3}, fS_{c1}, fS_{c2}, fS_{c3}
Kc interpolation coefficients	KcS_{h1}, KcS_{h2}, KcS_{h3}, KcS_{h4}, KcS_{h5}, KcS_{h6} KcS_{h7}, KcS_{h8}, KcS_{h9} KcS_{c1}, KcS_{c2}, KcS_{c3}, KcS_{c4}, KcS_{c5}, KcS_{c6}] KcS_{c7}, KcS_{c8}, KcS_{c9}
Ke interpolation coefficients	KeS_{h1}, KeS_{h2}, KeS_{h3}, KeS_{h4}, KeS_{h5}, KeS_{h6} KeS_{h7}, KeS_{h8}, KeS_{h9} KeS_{c1}, KeS_{c2}, KeS_{c3}, KeS_{c4}, KeS_{c5} , KeS_{c6} KeS_{c7}, KeS_{c8}, KeS_{c9}

Auxiliary variables defined as explicit variables	
Exchanger dimensions (m)	$Ly = Lx$, $Lz = 0.25 * Lx$
Fins characteristics	$\alpha_h = \frac{(b_h * \beta_h)}{(b_h + b_c + 2 * \delta_h)}$, $\alpha_c = \frac{(b_c * \beta_c)}{(b_h + b_c + 2 * \delta_c)}$, $\sigma_h = \alpha_h * rh_h$, $\sigma_c = \alpha_c * rh_c$
Fins efficiency	$\eta f_h = \frac{\tanh ml_h}{ml_h}$, $\eta f_c = \frac{\tanh ml_c}{ml_c}$
Exchange surface dimensions	$A_h = \alpha_h * (Lx * Ly * Lz)$, $A_c = \alpha_c * (Lx * Ly * Lz)$, $Aw = Lx * Ly * n$, $Ac_h = \sigma_h * Af_h$, $Ac_c = \sigma_c * Af_c$, $Af_h = Lx * Lz$, $Af_c = Ly * Lz$
Exchange surface efficiency	$\eta 0_h = 1 - \frac{Af_h}{A_h} * (1 - \eta f_h)$, $\eta 0_c = 1 - \frac{Af_c}{A_c} * (1 - \eta f_c)$

Exchanger inner wall thickness (m)	$tw = \frac{(\delta_h+\delta_c)}{2}$
Number of plates (-)	$n = \frac{Lz}{b_h+b_c+2*\delta_h}$
Air characteristics in the exchanger	$G_h = \frac{q_{ma}}{Ac_h}, G_c = \frac{q_{ra}}{Ac_c},$ $\mu_h = \frac{-1.075e^{-5}-2.225e^{-9}*T_3+1.725e^{-6}*\sqrt{T_3}}{2} + \frac{-1.075e^{-5}-2.225e^{-9}*T_2+1.725e^{-6}*\sqrt{T_2}}{2},$ $\mu_c = \frac{-1.075e^{-5}-2.225e^{-9}*Te_{oc}+1.725e^{-6}*\sqrt{Te_{oc}}}{2} + \frac{-1.075e^{-5}-2.225e^{-9}*Te_{ic}+1.725e^{-6}*\sqrt{Te_{ic}}}{2},$ $\rho_2 = \frac{p_2}{r*T_2}, \rho_3 = \frac{p_3}{r*T_3},$ $\rho_{ic} = \frac{pe_{ic}}{r*Te_{ic}}, \rho_{oc} = \frac{pe_{oc}}{r*Te_{oc}},$ $Cp_{oh} = 1003.7 + 6.8e^{-2} * (T_3 - 273.15) + 2.22e^{-4} * (T_3 - 273.15)^2,$ $Cp_{ih} = 1003.7 + 6.8e^{-2} * (T_2 - 273.15) + 2.22e^{-4} * (T_2 - 273.15)^2,$ $Cp_h = \frac{Cp_{oh}+Cp_{ih}}{2},$ $Cp_{oc} = 1003.7 + 6.8e^{-2} * (Te_{oc} - 273.15) + 2.22e^{-4} * (Te_{oc} - 273.15)^2,$ $Cp_{ic} = 1003.7 + 6.8e^{-2} * (Te_{ic} - 273.15) + 2.22e^{-4} * (Te_{ic} - 273.15)^2$ $Cpc = \frac{Cp_{oc}+Cp_{ic}}{2}$
Exchanger mass (kg)	$m_{ex} = \rho_{ex} * Lx * Ly * ((\frac{\sigma_h*\delta_h}{rh_h} + \frac{\sigma_c*\delta_c}{rh_c}) * Lz + n * tw)$
Exchanger volume (m3)	$V = Lx * Ly * Lz$
Air speed in the exchanger (m/s)	$C_h = \frac{q_{ma}}{Ac_h*\rho_2}, Cc = \frac{q_{ra}}{Ac_c*\rho_{ic}}$
Heat transfer characteristics	$\lambda = \frac{q_{ra}*Cp_{ic}}{q_{ma}*Cp_{ih}},$ $Nut = \frac{q_{ma}*Cp_{ih}}{\frac{1}{\eta 0_h*h_h*A_h}+\frac{tw}{kw*Aw}+\frac{1}{\eta 0_c*h_c*A_c}},$ $h_h = J_h * G_h * Cp_h * Pr_h^{-2/3},$ $hc = J_c * G_c * Cp_c * Pr_c^{-2/3}$
Colburn Coefficients (-)	$J_h = e^{JS_{h1}*log^2(Re_h)+JS_{h2}*log(Re_h)+JS_{h3}},$ $J_c = e^{JS_{c1}*log^2(Re_c)+JS_{h2}*log(Re_c)+JS_{h3}}$
Fanning friction factor (-)	$f_h = e^{fS_{h1}*log^2(Re_h)+fS_{h2}*log(Re_h)+fS_{h3}},$ $f_c = e^{fS_{c1}*log^2(Re_c)+fS_{h2}*log(Re_c)+fS_{h3}}$
Prandtl number (-)	$Pr_h = \frac{(0.825-0.00054*T_3+5.0e-7*T_3^2)}{2} + \frac{(0.825-0.00054*T_2+5.0e^{-7}*T_2^2)}{2},$ $Pr_c = \frac{0.825-0.00054*Te_{oc}+5.0e^{-7}*Te_{oc}^2}{2} + \frac{0.825-0.00054*Te_{ic}+5.0e^{-7}*Te_{ic}^2}{2}$
Reynolds number (-)	$Re_h = \frac{4*rh_h*G_h}{\mu_h}, Re_c = \frac{4*rh_c*G_c}{\mu_c}$
Inlet pressure losses coefficient	$Kc_h = KcS_{h1} * \sigma_h^2 + KcS_{h2} * \sigma_h + KcS_{h3} * log^2(Re_h) + KcS_{h4} * \sigma_h^2 + KcS_{h5} * \sigma_h + KcS_{h6} * log(Re_h) + KcS_{h7} * \sigma_h^2 + KcS_{h8} * \sigma_h + KcS_{h9},$ $Kc_c = KcS_{c1} * \sigma_c^2 + KcS_{c2} * \sigma_c + KcS_{c3} * log^2(Re_c) + KcS_{c4} * \sigma_c^2 + KcS_{c5} * \sigma_c + KcS_{c6} * log(Re_c) + KcS_{c7} * \sigma_c^2 + KcS_{c8} * \sigma_c + KcS_{c9}$

Outlet pressure losses coefficient	$Ke_h = KeS_{h1} * \sigma_h^2 + KeS_{h2} * \sigma_h + KeS_{h3} * log^2(Re_h)+$ $KeS_{h4} * \sigma_h^2 + KeS_{h5} * \sigma_h + KeS_{h6} * log(Re_h)+$ $KeS_{h7} * \sigma_h^2 + KeS_{h8} * \sigma_h + KeS_{h9},$ $Ke_c = KeS_{c1} * \sigma_c^2 + KeS_{c2} * \sigma_c + KeS_{c3} * log^2(Re_c)+$ $KeS_{c4} * \sigma_c^2 + KeS_{c5} * \sigma_c + KeS_{c6} * log(Re_c)+$ $KeS_{c7} * \sigma_c^2 + KeS_{c8} * \sigma_c + KeS_{c9}$
Atmosphere characteristics	$T_a = 288.2 - 0.00649 * Z,\ p_a = 101290 * (\frac{T_a}{288.08})^{5.256}$
Turbo-reactor temperatures (K) Turbo-reactor pressures (Pa)	$T_0 = T_a * (1 + \frac{M^2*(\gamma-1)}{2})$ $T_1 = T_0 * (1 + \frac{1}{\eta_{TRc}} * ((\frac{p1}{p0})^{\frac{\gamma-1}{\gamma}} - 1))$ $p_0 = p_a * (\eta_{TRd} * \frac{M^2*(\gamma-1)}{2} + 1)^{\frac{\gamma}{\gamma-1}},$ $p_1 = TC_{TR} * p_0$
Diffuser pressures (Pa) and temperatures (K)	$po_{Dc} = pi_{Dc} * (\eta_{DI} * M^2 * \frac{\gamma-1}{2} + 1)^{\frac{\gamma}{\gamma-1}}$ $To_{Dc} = Ti_{Dc} * (1 + M^2 * \frac{\gamma-1}{2})$ $pi_{Dc} = p_a,\ Ti_{Dc} = T_a$
Nozzle pressure (Pa) and temperatures (K)	$pi_{Bc} = pe_{oc},\ po_{Bc} = p_a,\ Ti_{Bc} = Te_{oc}$ $To_{Bc} = Ti_{Bc} * (1 + \eta_{NO} * (-1 + (\frac{po_{Bc}}{pi_{Bc}})^{\frac{\gamma-1}{\gamma}}))$
Trim gate descripion	$\nu = \frac{r*T_1}{p_1},\ p_4 = p_5,\ q_{mav} = q - q_{ma}$ $ksi_\alpha = e^{(4.03108e^{-4}*\alpha^2+8.50089e^{-2}*\alpha-1.59295}$
Various explicit variables	$m_h = \sqrt{\frac{2*h_h}{kw*\delta_h}},\ m_c = \sqrt{\frac{2*h_c}{kw*\delta_c}},$ $ml_h = \frac{m_h*b_h}{2},\ ml_c = \frac{m_c*b_c}{2},$ $CPam_h = Kc_h + 1 - (\sigma_h^2),\ CPd_h = 2 * (\frac{\rho_2}{\rho_3} - 1),$ $CPr_h = f_h * \frac{A_h}{Ac_h} * (2 * \frac{\rho_2}{\rho_2+\rho_3}),$ $CPav_h = (Ke_h + \sigma_h^2 - 1) * \frac{rho2}{rho3},$ $CPam_c = Kc_c + 1 - \sigma_c^2,\ CPd_c = 2 * (\frac{\rho_{ic}}{\rho_{oc}} - 1),$ $CPr_c = f_c * \frac{A_c}{Ac_c} * (2 * \frac{\rho_{ic}}{\rho_{ic}+\rho_{oc}}),$ $CPav_c = (Ke_c + \sigma_c^2 - 1) * \frac{\rho_{ic}}{\rho_{oc}}$

Constraints	
Catalogue of exchange surfaces	$exchSurf_h = 1 \rightarrow JS_{h1} = 0.0314 \wedge \cdots \wedge KcS_{h9} = 1.717231$ $\vdots$ $exchSurf_h = 48 \rightarrow JS_{h1} = 0.0369 \wedge \cdots \wedge KcS_{h9} = 1.551097$ $exchSurf_c = 1 \rightarrow JS_{c1} = 0.0314 \wedge \cdots \wedge KcS_{c9} = 1.717231$ $\vdots$ $exchSurf_c = 48 \rightarrow JS_{c1} = 0.0369 \wedge \cdots \wedge KcS_{c9} = 1.551097$
Materials choice for the exchanger	$T_2 \leq 473 \rightarrow roex = 8440 \wedge kw = 30$ $T_2 \geq 473 \rightarrow roex = 8440 \wedge kw = 30$
Exchanger description: Air flow ratio Heat efficiency for the hot-side	$\tau = \frac{q_{ra}}{q_{ma}}$ $\epsilon = 1 - e^{\lambda*Nut^{0.22}*(e^{\frac{-Nut^{0.78}}{\lambda}}-1)}$ $\epsilon = \frac{T_2-T_3}{T_2-T_0}$

Hot-side energy balance	$T_3 = T_2 - \epsilon * (T_2 - Te_{ic})$
Hot-side pressure losses	$\Delta Pe_h = p_2 - p_3$
	$\Delta Pe_h = \frac{G_h^2}{2*\rho_2} * (CPam_h + CPd_h + CPr_h + CPav_h)$
Cold-side energy balance	$Te_{oc} = \frac{q_{ma}*Cp_{ih}}{q_{ra}*Cp_{ic}} * (T_2 - T_3) + Te_{ic}$
Cold-side pressure losses	$\Delta Pe_c = pe_{ic} - pe_{oc}$
	$\Delta Pe_c = \frac{G_c^2}{2*\rho_{ic}} * (CPam_c + CPd_c + CPr_c + CPav_c)$
Components energy balances:	
Compressor	$\eta_c * (\frac{T_2}{T_1} - 1) = (\frac{p_2}{p_1})^{\frac{\gamma}{\gamma-1}} - 1$
Coupling shaft	$(T_2 - T_1) = \eta_{AT} * (T_3 - T_4)$
Turbine	1-T4/T3 $= \eta_t * (1 - (\frac{p_4}{p_3})^{\frac{\gamma-1}{gamma}})$
Trim gate	$q * Cp * T_5 = q_{ma} * Cp * T_4 + q_{mav} * Cp * T_1$
	$p_1 - p_4 = ksi_\alpha * \nu * \frac{q_{mav}^2}{2*(\pi*Rv^2)^2}$
	$To_{Dc} = Te_{ic}$
	$po_{Dc} = pe_{ic}$

3.5 ACS Solutions

Using all this knowledge about the ACS model during the solving process permit us to compute a finite set of 322 design solution principles in a few hours on a personal computer at 2 GHz (see figure 3 and 4). Using a classical Round-Robin strategy with relevant precisions, but without taking into account design variable classes, give a set of 388608 solutions in several hours.

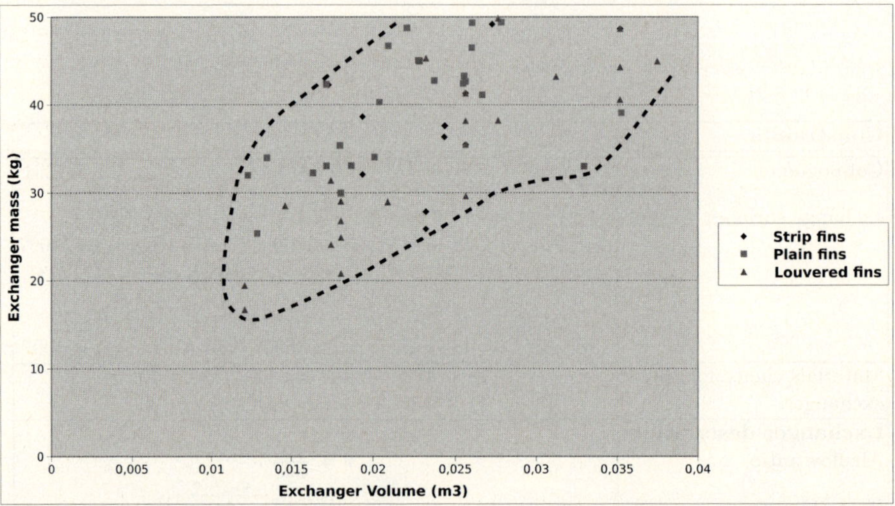

Fig. 3. ACS solutions considering the main system performance criteria: volume and mass of the exchanger

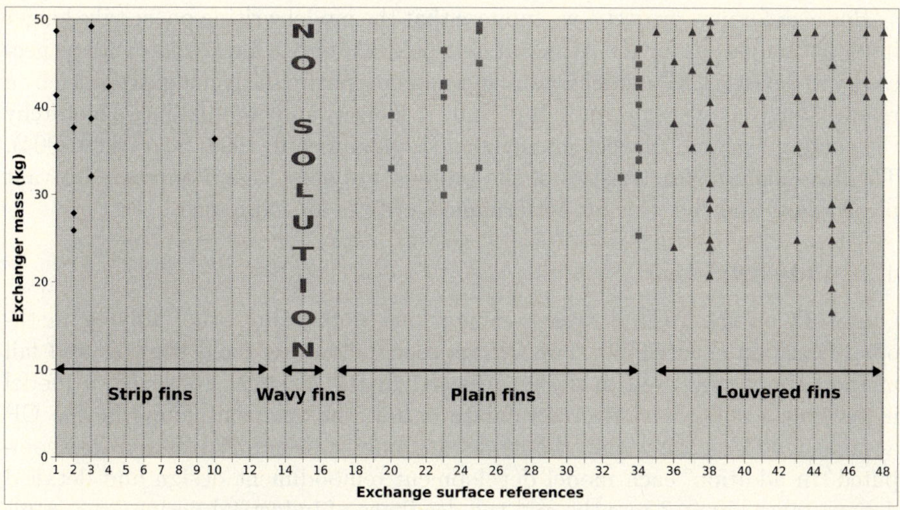

Fig. 4. ACS solutions considering the exchanger mass sorted by hot-side exchange surface references

Figure 3 illustrates the distribution of the solution set considering 2 major criteria: the volume of the exchanger and its mass. The three symbols used to plot solutions represent the exchange surface types used for the hot-side in the exchanger. The dashed line was made by hand and permits to perceive the overall shape of the solution space. Figure 4 shows the solutions sorted by the exchange surface references from the catalogue for the hot side of the exchanger. It is important to highlight that there are no solutions with the wavy exchange surfaces from the catalogue and the best ones are from the louvered exchange surface family.

Considering all this results, designers may have a better understanding of the solution set of the ACS. These results allow us to validate some factual knowledge about the design of air conditioning systems in an aircraft. Some exchange surfaces families appear to participate in more powerful ACS and it could save time in the upstream phases of ACS design.

4 Added Value of CP?

4.1 Development Cost

This application was developed in several steps, because of the complexity of the model. A first model without fins between the exchanger plates was developed. It took a few days to get a preliminary model, since we used the data from an evolutionary approach and previous work on this system. However several days were needed to get a model with valid physics behaviors. Finally the entire model with fins data was built after several weeks. We do not count the development time of the heuristics search in the solver.

However for new projects, we suppose that the model writing phase take longer if it is as complex as for the ACS, but we think that only a few weeks could be necessary to devise a CSP model for design problems, particularly if it is preceded by a relevant analysis of the product. It permits to identify and organize into a hierarchy the components and physics phenomena (Szykman et al. 1999, Scaravetti 2004). Then the main characteristics of the product are defined and only the relevant physics laws and the relevant performances criteria are expressed.

4.2 Industrial Use

Our work on the ACS is based on previous work using other solving methods (Sébastian et al. 2007). The CP approach allows to avoid the test and fail method commonly used in design process. In the classical approach, a model is developed and then criteria validate or not the solutions found.In the CP approach, criteria are within the model and only satisfactory solutions are computed. In addition, each model development (embodiment design and detailed design) takes about 3 months and the deadlines of industrial design are incompatible with several model developments.

Our ACS model is quite complete considering an embodiment stage, since it takes into account more detailed knowledge related to components and their performances than previously used models, namely the exchanger and its exchange surfaces. The results from an equivalent model were taken into account for the design of the ACS in a vehicle subjected to confidentiality constraints developed by Dassault Aviation.

4.3 Feedback and User Experience

The use of constraint satisfaction techniques in embodiment design appears promising, although the solving process is not always efficient. Indeed, solving some models may be time consuming compared to the evolutionary approach and the solution set is not always relevant, since there are many duplicated solutions realted to the design point of view.

We think that most CP tools or constraints solvers are not enough designed for beginners in constraints and particularly designers, although the constraints languages are often intuitive. Solvers are mainly concerned with mathematical results, leaving aside other needs. Most solvers do not take into account fundamental notions of design, as for instance the design and auxiliary variables, explicit variables, piecewise constraints, matrix calculus, models and data from catalogues or databases, etc. More to the point, the results obtained with a constraint solver are not reusable for the next phases of the design process, where CAD tools are mainly used.

Moreover, the development of real applications with many constraints and large amounts of data is difficult. Indeed, the inconsistencies are often complex to explain, since only little information is available about the solving failures and only how familiar the user is with the problem may really help. In our application, this lack of information about the solving process and the inconsistencies have drastically increased the development time of the ACS model.

Finally, we think that solvers must not be some black box tools. They have to be flexible and tuneable to fit every problem type. The definition of heuristics at several levels should make it possible to undertake all model specificities, like, for instance, considering the relevance of variable classes according to a design point of view, or more specific strategies related to the investigated problem.

5 Conclusion

In this paper, the model of an air conditioning system in an aircraft is investigated according to the embodiment design context. Indeed, some simplifications are made on several components, whereas others are more detailed, adding the reality of complex physics phenomena at several scales. Some new concepts and new heuristics are defined according to variable classes and relevant precisions in order to support decision making. Indeed, many duplicated design solutions are eliminated when compared to a classical CP solving approach and the entire set of design solutions is computed. These new notions increase the efficiency of the solving process, but we believe that some improvements can still be made to undertake additional design model specificities.

Solving embodiment design models with constraint programming seems promising, although some difficulties may appear for beginners in constraints. Indeed, most solvers are mathematical tools, where design concepts are missing. The difficulty for CP is to keep within a general approach to solve problems in order to keep its easy-to-use feature, and at the same time to solve efficiently all types of problems.

However, several fundamental notions may be integrated in solvers to help designers with their task, as for instance the variable types in design, piecewise constraints, etc. The constraints solvers should also be linked with other tools commonly used in design (CAD tools), and perhaps use an object or component oriented approach to express constraints and to facilitate the writing of knowledge and to reuse it in other tools.

On the other hand, the CP approach allows designers to avoid backtracks in the design process, since criteria are used in the solving process to compute only satisfactory architectures. Thus, designers can choose among several architectures and have a better overview of product possibilities.

References

[Benhamou et al. 1999]Benhamou, F., Goualard, F., Granvilliers, L., Puget, J.-F.: Revising Hull and Box Consistency. In: International Conference on Logic Programming, pp. 230–244. MIT Press, Cambridge (1999)

[Bliek et al. 1998]Bliek, C., Neveu, B., Trombettoni, G.: Using Graph Decomposition for Solving Continuous CSPs. In: Maher, M.J., Puget, J.-F. (eds.) Principles and Practice of Constraint Programming - CP98. LNCS, vol. 1520. Springer, Heidelberg (1998)

[Fischer et al. 2004]Fischer, X., Sebastian, P., Nadeau, J.-P., Zimmer, L.: Constraint based Approach Combined with Metamodeling Techniques to Support Embodiment Design. In: SCI'04, Orlando, USA.

[Gelle & Faltings 2003]Gelle, E., Faltings, B.: Solving Mixed and Conditional Constraint Satisfaction Problems. Constraints 8, 107–141 (2003)

[Kays & London 1984]Kays, W.M., London, A.L.: Compact Heat Exchangers. Mc Graw-Hill, New York (1984)

[Lhomme 1993]Lhomme, O.: Consistency Techniques for Numeric CSPs. In: IJCAI'93, Chambéry, France (1993)

[Moore 1966]Moore, R.: Interval Analysis. Prentice-Hall, Englewood Cliffs (1966)

[Neveu et al. 2006]Neveu, B., Chabert, G., Trombettoni, G.: When Interval Analysis Helps Interblock Backtracking. In: Benhamou, F. (ed.) CP 2006. LNCS, vol. 4204. Springer, Heidelberg (2006)

[O'Sullivan 2001]O'Sullivan, B.: Constraint-Aided Conceptual Design. Professional Engineering Publishing (2001)

[Pahl & Beitz 1996]Pahl, G., Beitz, W.: Engineering Design: A Systematic Approach. Springer, Heidelberg (1996)

[Reddy et al. 1996]Reddy, S.Y., Fertig, K.W., Smith, D.E.: Constraint Management Methodology for Conceptual Design Tradeoff Studies. In: Design Theory and Methodology Conference, Irvine, CA (1996)

[Refalo 1999]Refalo, P.: Tight Cooperation and Its Application in Piecewise Linear Optimization. In: Jaffar, J. (ed.) Principles and Practice of Constraint Programming – CP'99. LNCS, vol. 1713, pp. 375–389. Springer, Heidelberg (1999)

[Scaravetti 2004]Scaravetti, D., Nadeau, J.P., Sébastian, P., Pailhès, J.: Aided Decision-Making for an Embodiment Design Problem. In: International IDMME, Bath, UK (2004)

[Sébastian et al. 2007]Sébastian, P., Chenouard, R., Nadeau, J.P., Fischer, X.: The Embodiment Design Constraint Satisfaction Problem of the BOOTSTRAP facing interval analysis and Genetic Algorithm based decision support tools. International Journal on Interactive Design and Manufacturing (2007) ISSN: 1955-2513.

[Szykman et al. 1999]Szykman, S., Racz, J.W., Sriram, R.D.: The Representation of Function in Computer-based Design. In: Proceedings of the 1999 ASME Design Engineering Technical Conferences (11th International Conference on Design Theory and Methodology) (1999) DETC99/DTM-8742.

[Van-Hentenryck et al. 1997]Van-Hentenryck, P., Mc Allester, D., Kapur, D.: Solving Polynomial Systems Using Branch and Prune Approach. SIAM Journal on Numerical Analysis 34(2), 797–827 (1997)

[Vu 2005]Vu, X.-H.: Rigorous Solution Techniques for Numerical Constraint Satisfaction Problems. PhD thesis, Swiss Federal Institute of Technology in Lausanne (EPFL) (2005)

[Yannou et al. 2003]Yannou, B., Simpson, T.W., Barton, R.R.: Towards a Conceptual Design Explorer using Metamodeling Approaches and Constraint Programming. In: ASME DETC'03, Chicago, USA (2003)

[Zimmer & Zablit 2001]Zimmer, L., Zablit, P.: Global Aircraft Predesign based on Constraint Propagation and Interval Analysis. In: CEAS-MADO'01, Koln, Germany (2001)

Solving the Salinity Control Problem in a Potable Water System*

Chiu Wo Choi and Jimmy H.M. Lee

Department of Computer Science and Engineering
The Chinese University of Hong Kong
Shatin, N.T., Hong Kong
{cwchoi,jlee}@cse.cuhk.edu.hk

Abstract. Salinity is the relative concentration of salts in water. In a city of southern China, the local water supply company pumps water from a nearby river for potable use. During the winter dry season, the intrusion of sea water raises the salinity of the river to a high level and affects approximately the daily life of 450,000 residents of the city. This paper reports the application of constraint programming (CP) to optimize the logistical operations of the raw water system so as to satisfy the daily water consumption requirement of the city and to keep the potable salinity below a desirable level for as many days as possible. CP is the key to the success of the project for its separation of concerns and powerful constraint language that allows for rapid construction of a functional prototype and production system. Flexibility and adaptiveness allow us to deal with our clients' many changes in the requirements. Deriving good variable and value ordering heuristics, and generating useful implied constraints, we demonstrate that branch-and-bound search with constraint propagation can cope with an optimization problem of large size and great difficulty.

1 Introduction

Salinity is the relative concentration of salts in water measured in parts per million (ppm). All types of water, except distilled water, contain different concentration of salts. The salinity of very clean water is about 50 ppm, while sea-water is about 35,000 ppm.

In a city of southern China, the local water supply company pumps water into a raw water system from a nearby river for supplying water to the city. The pumped water is to be stored and mixed with water in a number of reservoirs in the raw water system. The water is also treated before supplying to the general public for daily consumption.

The geographic location of the pumping station is close to the river estuary. During the winter dry season, the water level of the river is low due to lack of rainfall. Tidal flows and other weather conditions lead to the intrusion of sea-water into the river. As a result, the salinity of the water pumped from the river could drastically rise to such levels as 2,500 ppm while the desirable salinity level of potable water is below 250 ppm. During the *salinity period*, the daily life of some 450,000 residents is affected.

* We thank the anonymous referees for their insightful comments. The work described in this paper was substantially supported by a grant (Project no. CUHK4219/04E) from the Research Grants Council of the Hong Kong SAR.

C. Bessiere (Ed.): CP 2007, LNCS 4741, pp. 33–48, 2007.

There are a number of ways to better prepare for the crisis. On the engineering side, the water company can improve the monitoring of the salinity levels and the pumping system. Reservoirs can be topped up with fresh water before the dry season begins. Better leak detection at the water pipes and the reservoirs can reduce water loss.

Before attempting on larger scale engineering work, such as seawater desalination, the water company decided to tackle the salinity issue as an optimization problem. The idea is to carefully plan when and how much water to pump from the river using supplied prediction information of the salinity profile at the water source, and how much water should be transferred among the reservoirs in the raw water system. The aim is to satisfy the daily water consumption while optimizing the number of days in which the salinity of the potable water is below a given desirable level.

In the beginning of this project, the water supply company required us to handle at most 90 days for the duration of the salinity period. Later, upon receiving satisfactory preliminary results, the water supply company requested us to extend the duration to at most 180 days, the problem model of which consists of about 4,500 variables and 9,000 constraints. The search space of such model is about $(3,612,000)^{180}$. In addition to the shear size, the problem consists of physical conditions expressible as a mixture of linear and non-linear constraints, as well as ad hoc conditions which can only be modeled as a table constraint. In view of the stringent requirements and tight production schedule, we adopt constraint programming (CP) as the key technology of the project, following the success of the CLOCWiSe project [1].

The rest of this paper is organized as follows. Section 2 discusses the current practice and why constraint programming (CP) is used in this project. Section 3 details the application domain. Operations of the raw water system, as well as the objective of the problem, are described in length. Section 4 describes how CP is applied to model the problem. Section 5 describes the improvements to increase search efficiency, followed by a discussion of some testing results in Section 6. In Section 7, we discuss the added values of CP and other possible approaches that have been tried to solve the problem. We conclude the paper in Section 8.

2 Current Practice Versus Constraint Programming

The water supply company has developed a spreadsheet to optimize the operations of water pumping and transfer during the salinity period. The spreadsheet approach is primitive and uses manual trial-and-error method to perform optimization. The spreadsheet consists of macros that encode equations on the law of conservation of matters. Users of the spreadsheet have to input the given data and guess some values for the number of pumping hours and amount of water to be transferred between reservoirs. The macro will then compute automatically the potable salinity using the given inputs. Users have to check whether the resulting potable salinity is satisfactory; if not, the guessed values must be manually tuned repeatedly until a satisfactory result is obtained.

The major weakness of such manual method is that it is tedious and time consuming. The problem on hand is usually too large and too complex for humans to perform such manual optimization process. Users of the spreadsheet often obtain solutions that violate some constraints of the problem, since some constraints stated above cannot be enforced automatically using a spreadsheet. Field workers in the pumping stations and reservoirs often lack the knowledge of operating a spreadsheet.

The water supply company would like to have an automated system with a more realistic model and a simple interface so as to generate solutions which satisfy all the constraints of the problem. Moreover, the system should be flexible enough to cater for changes in the topology of the water system and additional constraints.

We propose the application of CP to develop an automated optimization engine for solving the salinity problem. A key advantage of CP is the separation of modeling and solving. By modeling, we mean the process of determining the variables, the associated domains of the variable, the constraints and the objective function. The availability of a rich constraint language allows for a constraint model relatively close to the original problem statement, making the model easy to verify and adaptable to changes. Indeed, during the development of the system, our client changed the constraints and requirements a good many times. CP allowed us to change the model quickly and meet the tight development schedule.

Although efficient commercial constraint solvers are available, out-of-the-box execution strategies usually fail to handle even small testing instances of the problem. We make two improvements to speed up solution search and quality of solutions. First, by studying the problem structure and insights of human experts in depth, we devise good search heuristics for both variables and values that allow us to find solutions faster. We also program an opportunistic iterative improvement strategy. Second, we give a general theorem that allows us to derive useful implied constraints from a set of linear equalities. Adding these implied constraints into the model can increase the amount of constraint propagation, which in turns reduces the search space substantially.

Our application exemplifies the advantage of separation of concerns offered by CP. After the problem model was constructed, we never had to touch the model again except when users requested changes in the requirements. The focus of the development is thus on improving search and looking for better heuristics.

3 Application Domain Description

The entire water supply system consists of the raw water system, water treatment plant and potable water distribution network. In the raw water system, water is pumped from the river and carried to the treatment plant. Surplus water are stored in reservoirs for emergency and salinity control during dry season. In order to ensure that the water supplied to the city is safe for drinking, raw water is treated in the treatment plant before being carried by the distribution network to general households and commercial establishments. It is important to note that the water treatment plant is incapable of removing salt from the raw water since salt is highly soluble and tends to stay dissolved. In this project, we focus on optimizing the logistical operations of the raw water system to control the salinity of potable water.

3.1 The Raw Water System

Figure 1 shows the topology of the water supply system. The raw water system consists of 3 pumping stations (X, Y and Z) denoted by black dots, 4 reservoirs (A, B, C and

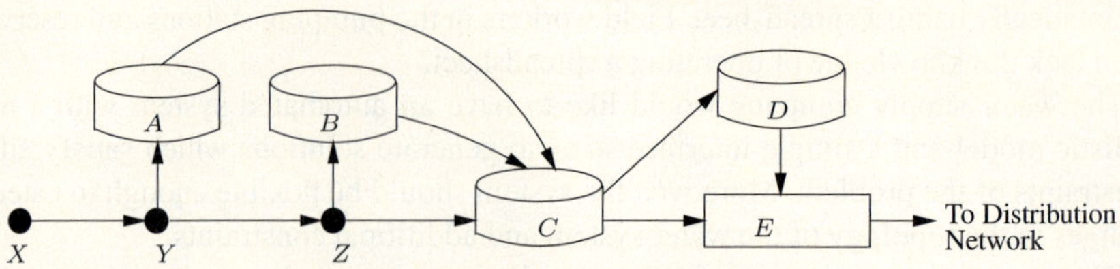

Fig. 1. The Raw Water System Model

D) denoted by cylinders and a water treatment plant (E) denoted by a rectangle. Arrows denote connecting pipes and the direction of water flow. Raw water (from the river) is pumped at pumping station X and carried all the way to reservoir C for storage. Surplus water is delivered, via pumping stations Y and Z, to and stored in reservoirs A and B respectively for future use. Water in reservoirs A and B can be transferred and mixed with water in reservoir C for regulation of salinity of water during the dry seasons. Water is carried from reservoir C to reservoir D for storage and to the water treatment plant E which is connected directly to the distribution network. In the water treatment plant E, water from reservoir C can be mixed with water from reservoir D. Water is treated in the water treatment plant E before being supplied to the general public for consumption.

There are several (reasonable) assumptions made by the water supply company for the raw water system to simplify the computational model. The unit of measurement for volume is cubic meter (m^3) and the unit of measurement for operation of pumps is in hours. Salinity concentration in each reservoir is homogeneous and instantaneous mixing occurs when water is poured in each reservoir. There is little rainfall during the dry seasons and the river is the only source of raw water. The computational model operates on a day-by-day basis, so that the predicted salinity data represent daily averages. Since salinity of the raw water varies during a single day, operators at the pumping station would use their experience to decide the best time during the day to pump water with lower salinity.

3.2 Physical and Human Constraints

There are three types of constraints concerning the raw water system. The first type of constraints is about the law of conservation of matters (i.e. water and salts). The general form for the law of conservation of water of a reservoir is

$$\text{volume today} = \text{volume yesterday} - \text{volume flow-out} + \text{volume flow-in}. \quad (1)$$

Analogously, the general form for the law of conservation of salts of a reservoir is

$$(\text{salinity today} \times \text{volume today}) = (\text{salinity yesterday} \times \text{volume yesterday}) - (\text{salinity flow-out} \times \text{volume flow-out}) + (\text{salinity flow-in} \times \text{volume flow-in}) \quad (2)$$

The second type of constraints is about physical limitation on the capacity of pumps, reservoirs and pipes. Each pumping station has a maximum number of usable pumps and each pump has a given capacity measured in cubic meters per hour. Each reservoir has a

Table 1. Constraint on Water Flowing Out of Reservoir C

Volume of Reservoir C (m^3)	Maximum Flow-out Capacity of Reservoir C (m^3/day)
2,345,650 – 2,454,590	211,395
⋮	⋮
1,200,000 – 1,256,250	160,445

minimum and maximum capacity. It is impossible to pump water out of a reservoir when it is at the minimum capacity, and overflowing a reservoir at its maximum capacity for dilution is forbidden. Each reservoir also has a volume threshold which reserves certain amount of water above the minimum capacity for emergency use. The volume threshold for each reservoir is different from one day to another, and the volume threshold overrides the minimum capacity. The pipes, which connect reservoirs A and B to reservoir C and the pipe which connects reservoir D to the treatment plant E, have a maximum capacity measured in cubic meters per day.

Flowing from reservoir C located at a high topographical level, water is carried by gravity to reservoir D and the water treatment plant E. Therefore, the maximum amount of water that can flow out of reservoir C depends on the water pressure which decreases as the water level of reservoir C goes down. Due to the complex nature of the physics behind the water transfer mechanism, the constraint is given in the form of a table constructed empirically using measurement and experimentation. The water supply company provides a table (see Table 1) to specify such constraint.

The third type of constraints is about the requirements of the general public on water consumption. It is mandatory to have enough water supply to the general public everyday. There is a maximum level of potable salinity to ensure that water is safe for drinking. Between any two consecutive days, the salinity level of potable water should not increase too drastically; otherwise, the general public will feel a sudden increase in saltiness of drinking water and that will raise public discontent. There are *no corresponding constraints to restrict sudden decreases*, since drop in salinity is generally welcome by the public.

3.3 Problem Statement

To control the salinity of potable water, the water supply company needs to control carefully when and how much water is pumped from the river and how much water is transferred among the reservoirs. The aim is to satisfy all the constraints stated in Section 3.2 and to keep the salinity of potable water below a desirable level for as many days as possible during the salinity period. The given data include the initial volume and salinity level of reservoirs and the prediction[1] of salinity level of the river during the salinity period.

---

[1] The prediction of salinity level of the river is supplied to us by the water supply company. The prediction model is beyond the scope of this project.

4 Problem Modeling

Let n denote the duration of the given salinity period, (i.e. $n \leq 180$ days). Since values in our model are defined on a day-by-day basis, we have a set of variables for each day $i \in \{1, \ldots, n\}$, and each set contains seven variables. The first three variables are P_i^X, P_i^Y and P_i^Z which denote the number of pumping hours to operate at pumping stations X, Y and Z respectively. The other four variables are O_i^A, O_i^B, O_i^C and O_i^D which denote the amount of water flowing out of reservoirs A, B, C and D respectively.

4.1 Domains Discretization

The associated domains of the above variables are all continuous in nature, i.e. time for pumping hours and volume for water transfers. After consulting the water supply company, we learn that it does not make sense to operate the pumps for a very short time (e.g. 3 minutes) or to transfer a very small amount of water (e.g. 10 m^3). Therefore, we discretize the domains to reflect this reality and to reduce the search space. Assuming the pumps are operated in unit of ϕ pumping hours (e.g. $\phi = 6$ hours), the domains D of the 3 pump variables are

$$D(P_i^X) = \{0, \ldots, \lfloor N^X \cdot 24/\phi \rfloor\} \qquad D(P_i^Y) = \{0, \ldots, \lfloor N^Y \cdot 24/\phi \rfloor\}$$
$$D(P_i^Z) = \{0, \ldots, \lfloor N^Z \cdot 24/\phi \rfloor\}$$

where N^X, N^Y and N^Z denote the maximum number of usable pumps in pumping stations X, Y and Z respectively. Assuming water is transferred in unit of τ m^3 (e.g. $\tau = 5,000$m^3), the domains D of the 4 flow-out variables are

$$D(O_i^A) = \{0, \ldots, \lfloor F^A/\tau \rfloor\} \quad D(O_i^B) = \{0, \ldots, \lfloor F^B/\tau \rfloor\}$$
$$D(O_i^C) = \{0, \ldots, \lfloor F^C/\tau \rfloor\} \quad D(O_i^D) = \{0, \ldots, \lfloor F^D/\tau \rfloor\}$$

where F^A, F^B, F^C, and F^D denote the maximum amount of water that can flow out of reservoirs A, B, C, and D respectively. We also have a number of other variables but they are auxiliary in the sense that the values of the auxiliary variables are fixed once the values of the decision variables are known.

4.2 Constraints and Objective Function

To express the constraints on the law of conservation of water for the reservoirs, we derive the following constraints from Equation 1,

$$V_i^A = V_{i-1}^A - (O_i^A \cdot \tau) + I_i^A \tag{3}$$
$$V_i^B = V_{i-1}^B - (O_i^B \cdot \tau) + I_i^B \tag{4}$$
$$V_i^C = V_{i-1}^C - (O_i^C \cdot \tau) + (O_i^A \cdot \tau) + (O_i^B \cdot \tau) + I_i^X - I_i^A - I_i^B \tag{5}$$
$$V_i^D = V_{i-1}^D - (O_i^D \cdot \tau) + I_i^D \tag{6}$$

where V_i^A, V_i^B, V_i^C and V_i^D are auxiliary variables denoting the volume of the four reservoirs on day $i \in \{1, \ldots, n\}$; I_i^A, I_i^B, I_i^X and I_i^D are auxiliary variables denoting the amount of water to flow into the four reservoirs on day $i \in \{1, \ldots, n\}$. We express the amount of water pumps from the pumping stations using the constraints

$$I_i^A = P_i^Y \cdot \phi \cdot K^Y \quad I_i^B = P_i^Z \cdot \phi \cdot K^Z \quad I_i^X = P_i^X \cdot \phi \cdot K^X$$

where K^Y, K^Z and K^X denote the capacity of the pumps in pumping stations Y, Z and X respectively. We use the following constraints to express that there is only a single source of water flowing into reservoir D,

$$I_i^D = (O_i^C \cdot \tau) - U_i \qquad\qquad V_i^E = U_i + (O_i^D \cdot \tau)$$

where V_i^E denotes the amount of water consumption on day $i \in \{1, \ldots, n\}$, and U_i denotes the surplus water flowing out of reservoir C after some water is supplied for consumption .

To express the constraints on the law of conservation of salts for reservoirs A, B, C, D, we derive the following constraints from Equation 2,

$$\begin{aligned}
(S_i^A \cdot V_i^A) &= (S_{i-1}^A \cdot V_{i-1}^A) - (S_{i-1}^A \cdot O_i^A \cdot \tau) + (S_i^X \cdot I_i^A)\\
(S_i^B \cdot V_i^B) &= (S_{i-1}^B \cdot V_{i-1}^B) - (S_{i-1}^B \cdot O_i^B \cdot \tau) + (S_i^X \cdot I_i^B)\\
(S_i^C \cdot V_i^C) &= (S_{i-1}^C \cdot V_{i-1}^C) - (S_{i-1}^C \cdot O_i^C \cdot \tau) + (S_{i-1}^A \cdot O_i^A \cdot \tau) +\\
&\quad (S_{i-1}^B \cdot O_i^B \cdot \tau) + (S_i^X \cdot I_i^X) - (S_i^X \cdot I_i^A) - (S_i^X \cdot I_i^B)\\
(S_i^D \cdot V_i^D) &= (S_{i-1}^D \cdot V_{i-1}^D) - (S_{i-1}^D \cdot O_i^D \cdot \tau) + (S_{i-1}^C \cdot I_i^D)
\end{aligned}$$

where S_i^A, S_i^B, S_i^C, S_i^D are auxiliary variables denoting the salinity level of the four reservoirs on day $i \in \{1, \ldots, n\}$, and S_i^X is the (given) predicted value of salinity level of the river. We also need a constraint to specify the law of conservation of salts for potable water

$$(S_i^E \cdot V_i^E) = (S_{i-1}^C \cdot U_i) + (S_{i-1}^D \cdot O_i^D \cdot \tau)$$

where V_i^E and S_i^E denote the amount of water consumption and the potable salinity on day $i \in \{1, \ldots, n\}$. Note that the variables denoting salinity level are continuous, and the constraints associated to these variables involve both finite domain and continuous variables.

We can express the physical limitation on the volume of the reservoirs using the following constraints,

$$\begin{aligned}
V_{\min}^A + H_i^A \le V_i^A \le V_{\max}^A \qquad V_{\min}^B + H_i^B \le V_i^B \le V_{\max}^B\\
V_{\min}^C + H_i^C \le V_i^C \le V_{\max}^C \qquad V_{\min}^D + H_i^D \le V_i^D \le V_{\max}^D
\end{aligned}$$

where $V_{\min}^A$, $V_{\min}^B$, $V_{\min}^C$ and $V_{\min}^D$ denote the minimum capacity of the four reservoirs, $V_{\max}^A$, $V_{\max}^B$, $V_{\max}^C$ and $V_{\max}^D$ denote the maximum capacity of the four reservoirs, and H_i^A, H_i^B, H_i^C and H_i^D denote the volume threshold of the four reservoirs on day $i \in \{1, \ldots, n\}$.

The following set of constraints expresses the requirements given in Table 1,

$$O_i^C \le \begin{cases} 211,395 \textit{ if } 2,345,650 < V_i^C \le 2,454,590 \\ \vdots \qquad\qquad \vdots \\ 160,445 \textit{ if } 1,200,000 < V_i^C \le 1,256,250 \end{cases}$$

We have intentionally used $<$ and $\leq$ to specify the bounds on each level to avoid potential conflict with domain discretization.

Last but not least, we have the following constraints to express the requirements of the general public on potable salinity,

$$S_i^E \leq S_{\max}^E \qquad\qquad S_i^E \leq S_{i-1}^E + \delta$$

where $S_{\max}^E$ denotes the maximum level of potable salinity and δ denotes the maximum allowable daily increase in potable salinity. Clearly, the objective of the problem is to *maximize* the sum

$$\sum_{i=1}^{n} (S_i^E \leq S_{\text{desire}}^E)$$

which represents the total number of days that potable salinity is below the desirable level S_{desire}^E.

5 Improving Search

We implement the above model using ILOG Solver 6.0 [5]. Out-of-the-box execution strategies used in our initial implementation fails to handle even small testing instances of the problem. There are two important issues in applying CP to solve problems. The first issue is to use an appropriate search strategy so that (good) solutions appear earlier in the search. There is no definite rule for discovering what is a good search strategy. By studying the problem structure and insights of human experts in depth, we are able to come up with a good search strategy. The second issue is that the model should also have *strong* propagation: that is, it should be able to quickly reduce the domains of the variables of the problem. We give a theorem for deriving useful implied constraints from a set of linear equalities to increase the amount of constraint propagation.

5.1 Variable and Value Ordering Heuristics

Since values in our model are defined on a day-by-day basis, it does make sense to label the variables chronologically by the days. We propose to pick first the seven decision variables for day 1, then day 2, and so on until day n. Such variable ordering has the advantages of turning many of the non-linear constraints into linear constraints, since constraint propagation on linear constraints is usually stronger than that on non-linear constraints.

Within day $i \in \{1, \ldots, n\}$, we propose to pick the variables based on the following order: $(P_i^X, P_i^Y, P_i^Z, O_i^C, O_i^D, O_i^A, O_i^B)$. This ordering is the best we have so far after extensive experiments. The rationale is that the river is the only source of water, the pumps dictate the amount of salts to take into the reservoirs and are very important in controlling the salinity of potable water. In the raw water system, reservoirs A and B serve only as storage for surplus water which can be used to dilute the water pumps from the river, and hence are less important than reservoirs C and D.

Different variables represent different control parameters of the raw water system. Rather than using a single value ordering heuristic for all variables, we have different heuristics for different variables depending on their strategic roles in the raw water system.

- For variable P_i^X, the value ordering heuristic depends on the salinity of river S_i^X on day $i \in \{1, \ldots, n\}$. In order to control the salinity, it is common sense to pick lower value for P_i^X (i.e. pump less water) if S_i^X is high (i.e. salty river water); and pick higher value for P_i^X otherwise. We make use of a user-supplied salinity level *avoidPump* to indicate when the salinity should be considered high. If S_i^X is less than *avoidPump*, then larger values in the domain of S_i^X can be tried first; and vice versa, otherwise. In comparing S_i^X and *avoidPump*, the magnitude of their difference is taken into account too.
- For variables P_i^Y and P_i^Z, the value ordering heuristic picks the middle value first. Pumping stations Y and Z pump the water coming from pumping station X, and we prefer to pump more water from the river when it is less salty. We lean on pumping more water into Reservoirs A and B for dilution, but at the same time do not want to overdo it (since it is dangerous when the salinity of the water from pumping station X is high).
- For variable O_i^C, rather than choosing the values one-by-one from the domains, we use bisection to perform domain splitting. Bisection divides the values in a variable domain into two equal halves, and this process is repeated recursively forming a binary tree with leave nodes containing only a single value. The water supply company prefers to use more water in reservoir C for consumption. Therefore, our heuristic prefers to visit the branch with larger domain values first each time the domains are bisected.
- For variable O_i^D, the water supply company wants to avoid using too much water from reservoir D. If $S_{i-1}^C \leq S_{\text{desire}}^E$, we use bisection and visit first the branch with smaller domain values. Otherwise, our heuristic picks the value which gives the minimum amount of water required to satisfy $S_i^E \leq S_{\text{desire}}^E$.
- For variable O_i^A and O_i^B, we use bisection and visit first the branch with smaller values. The rationale is to keep more fresh water in reservoirs A and B for dilution.

For most of the test cases given by the water supply company, the above search strategy performs well. We called this strategy the NORMAL strategy. However, there are some stringent (unrealistic) test cases where the amount of daily water consumption is usually higher than the maximum amount of water that can flow out of reservoir C. If we are too frugal in supplying water from reservoirs A and B to C, reservoirs C and D alone would not be able to handle the high daily water consumption. To deal with such situation, we propose another set of value ordering heuristic, called the HIGH strategy, especially for test cases with such stringent daily water consumption pattern. The only modification is to visit first the branch with larger domain values when bisecting domains of variables O_i^A and O_i^B. The rationale is to keep reservoir C as full as possible.

5.2 Greedy Search Strategy

The basic solution search technology is branch-and-bound with constraint propagation. The *avoidPump* user input parameter turns out to have great impact on the quality of the solutions generated. Since our value ordering heuristics are designed to generate good quality solutions earlier in the search, prolonging the search effort could be fruitless. We adopt an opportunistic iterative improvement approach.

Our search strategy encompasses trying different *avoidPump* values in succession with a *timeout* (300 seconds) period for each value. After consultation with human operators and extensive experimentations, we adopt to try the following *avoidPump* values in sequence: $600, 700, \ldots, 1500$. A smaller (larger) *avoidPump* value implies a more conservative (aggressive) approach to pumping water. In other words, we progress from a more conservative to a more aggressive approach.

For every *avoidPump* value, we start execution with the best solution from the last execution as guidance. After a *timeout* period expires, the system examines if a better solution is found. If yes, execution continues for another *timeout* period; otherwise, the next *avoidPump* value is tried. The rationale is that if a better solution is found within the *timeout* period for a particular *avoidPump* value, the value is good and should be given more chance to search for even better solution. On the other hand, a *avoidPump* value failing to find any good solutions within the *timeout* period is probably no good and there is probably no point to search further.

5.3 Adding Implied Constraints

Most of the constraints in our model are linear equalities denoting the law of conservation of water and salts. Given a set of linear equalities sharing common terms, we can introduce a new variable to denote the common terms and reformulate the linear equalities in terms of the new variables. The resulting set of linear equalities can be added as implied constraints to increase the amount of constraint propagation. Modern constraint solvers use bounds propagation [6] for linear arithmetic constraints. We state without proof the following theorem based on the work of Harvey and Stuckey [4] and Choi *et al.* [2,3].

Theorem 1. *Let* $c_1 \equiv \sum_i(a_i)(x_i) + \sum_j(b_j)(y_j) = d_1$ *and* $c_2 \equiv \sum_j(b_j)(y_j) + \sum_k(c_k)(z_k) = d_2$*, we can reformulate* c_1 *and* c_2 *as* $c_3 \equiv \sum_j(b_j)(y_j) - v = 0$*,* $c_4 \equiv \sum_i(a_i)(x_i) + v = d_1$*, and* $c_5 \equiv v + \sum_k(c_k)(z_k) = d_2$*. Bounds propagation on* $\{c_1, c_2, c_3, c_4, c_5\}$ *is stronger than bounds propagation on* $\{c_1, c_2\}$*.*

For instance, observe that there is a common term $-(O_i^A \cdot \tau) + I_i^A$ between Equations 3 and 5, similarly a common term $-(O_i^B \cdot \tau) + I_i^B$ between Equations 4 and 5. We can reformulate Equations 3, 4 and 5 as follow

$$W_i^A = -(O_i^A \cdot \tau) + I_i^A \qquad W_i^B = -(O_i^B \cdot \tau) + I_i^B$$
$$V_i^A = V_{i-1}^A + W_i^A \qquad V_i^B = V_{i-1}^B + W_i^B$$
$$V_i^C = V_{i-1}^C - (O_i^C \cdot \tau) + I_i^X - W_i^A - W_i^B$$

where W_i^A and W_i^B are auxiliary variables representing the common term. We can add the above equalities as implied constraints to our model. Suppose $\tau = 5000$ and the domain D is such that: $D(V_0^A) = \{1300000\}$, $D(V_0^B) = \{1237350\}$, $D(V_0^C) = \{2450000\}$, $D(V_1^A) = \{320000, \ldots, 1500000\}$, $D(V_1^B) = \{100000, \ldots, 1260000\}$, $D(V_1^C) = \{1200000, \ldots, 2450000\}$, $D(O_1^A) = \{0, \ldots, 15\}$, $D(O_1^B) = \{0, \ldots, 15\}$, $D(O_1^C) = \{27, \ldots, 42\}$, $D(I_1^A) = \{0, \ldots, 36000\}$, $D(I_1^B) = \{0, \ldots, 36000\}$, and

$D(I_1^X) = \{0, \ldots, 432000\}$. Constraint propagation with the original set of constraints returns the domains D' such that $D'(I_1^X) = \{0, \ldots, 282000\}$, while constraint propagation with the new and enlarged set of constraints returns the domains D'' such that $D''(I_1^X) = \{0, \ldots, 268650\}$. The latter is stronger in propagation.

6 Experiments

We have tested the system using both real-life and handcrafted data provided by the water supply company. We have chosen three representative sets of data to illustrate the performance of our system. Each set of data has a different characteristic, aiming to test the versatility and robustness of our engine. The three sets of data differ in terms of:

- the duration of the salinity period (n),
- the predicted salinity level of river (S_i^X),
- the daily water consumption of the city (V_i^E),
- the volume thresholds for the reservoirs (H_i^A, H_i^B,H_i^C and H_i^D), and
- the initial volumes and salinity values of the reservoirs (V_0^A, S_0^A, V_0^B, S_0^B, V_0^C, S_0^C, V_0^D, S_0^D).

Figure 2 gives the salinity curves of the prediction data.

The following experiments are executed using a Linux Workstation (Intel Pentium-III 1GHz with 1GB memory) running Fedora Core release 3. We choose ILOG Solver 6.0 [5] as our implementation platform. The time limit for the system to run is set to one hour. Execution is aborted when the time limit is reached, and the best solution located so far is reported.

For this project, there is no way to do comparison with the existing manual method based on spreadsheet. We cannot make any meaningful comparison in terms of the quality of solution since the manual method often fails to obtain a solution satisfying all constraints. We also cannot make any fair comparison in terms of time since one is a manual method and the other is an automated method. Therefore, we present only the results obtained from our system.

Table 2 shows the result of Set 1. The first two columns with heading "salinity" indicate the different combination of desirable and maximum salinity level. The next

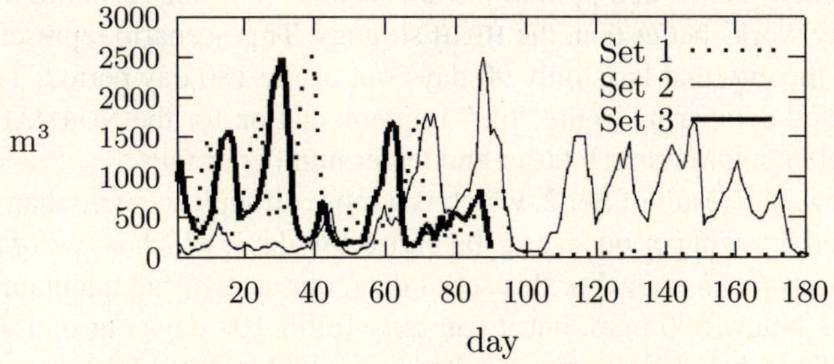

Fig. 2. Salinity Prediction Curves for Data Sets 1 to 3

Table 2. Result of Set 1, Duration = 180 days

salinity		normal			high			old		
desire	max	days	secs	fails	days	secs	fails	days	secs	fails
200	300	157	21	3	126	619	134,520,603	104	44	2,367
250	350	180	21	3	168	621	134,520,602	162	330	30,005
250	400	180	23	3	168	623	1,807	162	333	30,013
250	500	180	29	3	168	627	134,520,602	162	337	30,013
250	600	180	34	3	168	631	1,807	162	342	30,013
250	1,000	180	58	3	168	649	134,520,602	162	364	30,013
300	600	180	35	3	180	32	4	180	215	20,678
300	1,000	180	62	3	180	50	4	180	238	20,678

Table 3. Result of Set 2, Duration = 180 days

salinity		normal			high			old		
desire	max	days	secs	fails	days	secs	fails	days	secs	fails
200	300	–	–	–	–	–	–	–	–	–
250	350	–	–	–	–	–	–	–	–	–
250	400	–	–	–	–	–	–	–	–	–
250	500	107	1,222	269,201,686	107	1,222	134,725,593	–	–	–
250	600	117	926	269,080,063	117	925	134,604,570	–	–	–
250	1,000	117	943	269,063,234	117	943	134,582,923	73	53	520
300	600	137	952	269,096,832	129	1,225	269,196,833	–	–	–
300	1,000	146	647	269,041,205	146	646	78,408	114	52	605

three columns with heading "normal" indicate the results using the NORMAL strategy. We measure the number of days for which the potable salinity is below the desirable level (column "days"), the runtime in seconds (column "secs") and the total number of fails (column "fails"). The next three columns with heading "high" indicate the results using the HIGH strategy. The last three columns with heading "old" indicate the results of an earlier implementation without the custom heuristics and implied constraints listed in Section 5. Our system performs very well for Set 1 and is able to fulfill all 180 days with the potable salinity below 250 ppm in just 21 seconds. For this scenario, the NORMAL strategy clearly works better than the HIGH strategy. This scenario represents a typical dry season of the city that lasts only 90 days out of the 180 day period. The search is clearly improved comparing to the "old" implementation for the NORMAL strategy is able to find better solution much faster and lesser number of fails.

Table 3 shows the result of Set 2, which is a more difficult scenario than Set 1. Set 2 has a prolonged drought period lasting the entire 180 days, which is *one of the worst in the last 150 years for the city*. For this set of data, our system can maintain the potable salinity always below 500 ppm, but it can only fulfill 107 days out of 180 days with the potable salinity below 250 ppm. It takes around 20 minutes for our system to find this solution. If we can relax the desirable salinity level to 300 ppm and the maximum salinity level to 1000 ppm, our system can return a better solution fulfilling 146 days

Table 4. Result of Set 3, Duration = 90 days

salinity		normal			high			old		
desire	max	days	secs	fails	days	secs	fails	days	secs	fails
200	300	–	–	–	–	–	–	–	–	–
250	350	–	–	–	–	–	–	–	–	–
250	400	–	–	–	21	2,403	404,174,730	–	–	–
250	500	–	–	–	28	1,803	269,394,622	12	4	9
250	600	–	–	–	28	1,803	269,480,570	12	4	9
250	1,000	–	–	–	28	1,805	639,731	12	6	9
300	600	–	–	–	45	1,803	269,441,669	24	4	5
300	1,000	–	–	–	45	1,805	135,072,897	24	6	5

out of 180 days with the potable salinity below 300 ppm. The system is now able to find the solution in 10 minutes. This example illustrates the flexibility of our system. If we allow the desirable salinity level to raise slightly higher, our system would be able to distribute the salinity level of potable water more evenly among the days to improve the quality of solution.

Table 4 shows the result of Set 3, which is an artificially handcrafted scenario. The salinity level of the river for Set 3 is similar to the first 90 days of Set 1. The difficulty of Set 3 lies in the unrealistically high daily water consumption[2] comparing to Set 1 and Set 2 as shown in Figure 3. Set 1 (the bold dotted line) has constant daily water

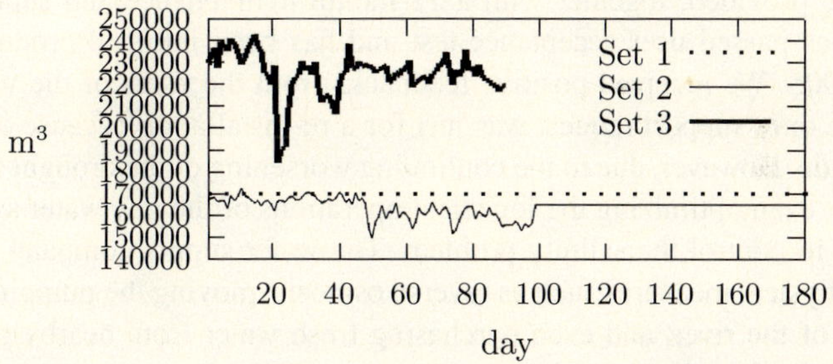

Fig. 3. Daily Water Consumption (V_i^E)

consumption. Set 2 (the thin line) has a fluctuating daily water consumption. Set 3 (the bold line) has a more fluctuating daily water consumption that is usually higher than the maximum amount of water that can flow out of reservoir C (i.e. 211,395 m^3/day). Set 3 suffers from the problem discussed at the end of Section 5.1, which makes the NORMAL strategy fail. The HIGH strategy is able to find a solution fulfilling 28 days out of 90 days with the potable salinity below 250 ppm and maintaining the potable salinity always below 500 ppm. It takes about 30 minutes to find this solution.

[2] The capacities of the reservoirs are: $A = 1,500,000$ m^3, $B = 1,260,000$ m^3, $C = 2,450,000$ m^3, and $D = 2,060,000$ m^3 for comparison with the daily consumption.

7 Discussions

In this project, we collaborate with the International Institute for Software Technology, United Nations University (UNU/IIST). We are responsible for the design and implementation of the core optimization engine, while UNU/IIST is responsible for constructing a web user interface to invoke our optimization engine. We discuss in the following issues regarding system development and deployment.

7.1 Added Values of CP

Our client gave us the problem in late September, 2004, only a couple of months before the beginning of the winter dry season. During that time, the city was suffering from one of the most serious drought in the last 150 years. Due to the urgency of the problem, we were given only 2 weeks to come up with a functional prototype, and to release a fully functional production system in early December, 2004, just before the winter dry season began. This version replicates and automates the functionalities and model of the client's spreadsheet model described in Section 2. We came up with a version to model the table constraint (water flow limit from Reservoir C to D) plus a large number of change requests in another month's time. The project involves the authors coming up with the model and techniques for improving search, and two undergraduate students for the implementation effort. The use of CP allowed us to meet the deadline and come up with the first fully functional production system in just 2 months of development. We spent another 5 months to study and experiment with various search improvements.

We have delivered the system to the water supply company. Installation and user trainings were provided, together with a 12-month maintenance and support period. The system has passed user acceptance test and has been into full production mode since June, 2005. We received positive feedbacks from the users of the water supply company. The only support request was just for a re-installation because of the ILOG product upgrade. However, due to the continuing worsening of the drought condition in the past years, even optimizing the logistical operations of the raw water system alone is insufficient to control the salinity problem. The water supply company is seriously considering physical measures such as reverse osmosis, moving the pumping station to upper stream of the river, and even purchasing fresh water from nearby provinces to effectively handle the salinity crisis.

The optimization engine is abstracted from the web interface, the end-users do not need to understand CP at all. Indeed, our client does not care about the optimization methodology we use, and wanted only a practical solution for the salinity problem that could be developed in 2 months, although our method has no guarantee for optimality.

7.2 Reasons for Choosing Finite Domain

Although the domain of the salinity problem is continuous (real numbers), a more natural choice seems to be modeling the problem using interval constraints instead of finite domain constraints. However, we still decided to use finite domain constraints for the following practical considerations. First, as discussed in Section 4.1, it does not make sense to operate the pumps for a very short time (e.g. 3 minutes) or to transfer a very small amount of water (e.g. 10 m^3). Therefore, we decided to discretize the domains. Second, finite domain constraints have had many successful industrial applications including scheduling, time-tabling, resource allocation, etc. Third, the development schedule was extremely tight and opportunity cost was high. At the time we were given the problem, we simply could not afford a lot of experimentation but had to adopt a proven technology.

7.3 Other Optimization Methodologies

Besides CP, we have investigated with UNU/IIST in applying Evolver [7], which is a genetic algorithm based optimization engine for Microsoft® Excel, to the project. Experimental results show that this approach is less efficient both in terms of execution time and quality of solution. Moreover, Evolver is only semi-automatic, requiring expert human guidance during the search for solutions. This approach is also unstable and unpredictable with regard to convergence. Nevertheless, such an approach is good for fast prototyping.

We also works with the operations research (OR) colleagues in our university to investigate the use of linear programming (LP) [8] for solving the salinity problem. The advantage of using LP is that the domain of the salinity problem is continuous in nature (i.e. real numbers); hence, there is no need to discretize the domains. However, the major obstacle to the LP approach is the *nonlinear* constraints in the problem, i.e. constraints on the law of conservation of salts and the table constraints on the water flowing out of reservoir C. The idea is to construct an *approximate* model of the problem with only linear constraints and objectives. Preliminary results are encouraging, outperforming our engines in selected test cases. The possibility of combining the LP model and the CP model is a promising research direction.

8 Conclusion

By applying CP, we have developed a fully automated optimization engine incorporating a more realistic model for solving the salinity problem. Experimental results demonstrate that the engine is more efficient and can produce higher quality solutions than the human counterpart. Now, even a non-domain expert can make use of our engine to plan for water management operations and experiment with different salinity scenarios in advance.

In summary, the choice of CP has immense impact on the successful delivery of the project. First, the rich constraint language available in commercial constraint solvers allows efficient modeling of the problem. Separation of concerns of CP allows us to focus on programming search heuristics. We were thus able to complete a working prototype and a functional production system within a tight development schedule. Second, CP is flexible and adaptive to changes. During the course of development, our client requested for numerous, often unreasonable, changes to the requirement specification. Without CP as the core technology, we were not sure if we could deal with all the requests in a timely and mostly effortless manner. Third, we were also able to adopt and generalize latest research result in propagation redundancy [4,2,3] to come up with useful implied constraints for our implementation, thus enhancing the constraint propagation in the salinity control engine. And this work on the model is orthogonal to the search strategies we employ. This is again a triumph of separate of concerns.

References

1. Brdys, M., Creemers, T., Riera, J., Goossens, H., Heinsbroek, A.: Clockwise: Constraint logic for operational control of water systems. In: The 26th Annual Water Resources Planning and Management Conference, pp. 1–13 (1999)
2. Choi, C.W., Harvey, W., Lee, J.H.M., Stuckey, P.J.: Finite domain bounds consistency revisited. In: Australian Conference on Artificial Intelligence, pp. 49–58 (2006)
3. Choi, C.W., Lee, J.H.M., Stuckey, P.J.: Removing propagation redundant constraints in redundant modeling. ACM Transactions on Computational Logic (to appear 2007)
4. Harvey, W., Stuckey, P.J.: Improving linear constraint propagation by changing constraint representation. Constraints 8(2), 173–207 (2003)
5. ILOG, S.A.: ILOG Solver 6.0: User's Manual (2003)
6. Marriott, K., Stuckey, P.J.: Programming with Constraints: an Introduction. MIT Press, Cambridge (1998)
7. Palisade Corporation: Evolver 4.0 (2005), Available from `http://www.palisade.com`
8. Vanderbei, R.J.: Linear Programming—Foundations and Extensions, 2nd edn. Springer, Heidelberg (2001)

Exploring Different Constraint-Based Modelings for Program Verification

Hélène Collavizza and Michel Rueher

Université de Nice–Sophia-Antipolis – I3S/CNRS
930, route des Colles - B.P. 145, 06903 Sophia-Antipolis, France
{helen,rueher}@polytech.unice.fr

Abstract. Recently, constraint-programming techniques have been used to generate test data and to verify the conformity of a program with its specification. Constraint generated for these tasks may involve integer ranging on all machine-integers, thus, the constraint-based modeling of the program and its specification is a critical issue. In this paper we investigate different models. We show that a straightforward translation of a program and its specification in a system of guarded constraints is ineffective. We outline the key role of Boolean abstractions and explore different search strategies on standard benchmarks.

1 Introduction

Constraint programming techniques have been used to generate test data (e.g., [6,13]) and to develop efficient model checking tools (e.g. [10,4]). SAT based model checking platforms have been able to scale and perform well due to many advances in SAT solvers [11]. Recently, constraint-programming techniques have also been used to verify the conformity of a program with its specification [3,8].

To establish the conformity between a program and its specification we have to demonstrate that the union of the constraints derived from the program and the negation of the constraints derived from its specification is inconsistent. Roughly speaking, pruning techniques -that reduce the domain of the variables- are combined with search and enumeration heuristics to demonstrate that this constraint system has no solutions.

Experimentations reported in [8] demonstrate that constraint techniques can be used to handle non-trivial academic examples. However, we are far from the state where this techniques can be used automatically on real applications. Modeling is a critical issue, even on quite small programs. That's why we investigate different models in this paper.

The framework we explore in this paper can be considered as a very specific instance of SMT solvers[1]

[1] For short, a Satisfiability Modulo Theories (SMT) problem consists in deciding the satisfiability of ground first-order formulas with respect to background theories such as the theory of equality, of the integer or real numbers, of arrays, and so on [5,12,1].

C. Bessiere (Ed.): CP 2007, LNCS 4741, pp. 49–63, 2007.

The different models and search strategies we did experiment with, showed that a straightforward translation of a program and its specification in a system of guarded constraints is ineffective[2]. These experimentations also clearly outlined the key role of appropriate Boolean abstractions.

The verification of the conformity between a program and its specification is highly dependant on the programming language and the specification language. In this paper, we restrict ourseleves to *Java programs* and *JML specifications* (for "Java Modeling Language" see www.cs.iastate.edu/˜leavens/JML).

To illustrate the advantages and limits of the models and search strategies we introduce, we will use the following examples:

- `S1` (see figure 1) : This is a very simple example of a Java program and its JML specification : it returns 1 if $i < j$ and 10 otherwise. `S1` will help us to understand how to introduce boolean abstractions. For each model, we will give the complete constraint system for `S1`.
- `S2` : This is also a very simple example derived from `S1`. The only difference with `S1` is that it returns the result of a calculus on input variables instead of constant values, i.e., it returns $i + j$ when S1 returns 1 (line 5 in figure 1) and $2 * i$ when S1 returns 10 (line 6 in figure 1). The main idea is to evaluate the impact of arithmetic during the resolution process.
- `Tritype` : This is a famous example in test case generation and program verification. This program takes three numbers that must be positive. These numbers represent the lengths of three sides of a triangle. It returns 4 if the input is not a triangle, 3 if it is an equilateral triangle, 2 if it is isosceles and 1 if it is a scalene triangle.
- `Tri-perimeter` : This program has the same control part than the *tritype* program. It returns -1 if the three inputs are not the lengths of triangle sides, else it returns the perimeter of the triangle. The specification returns $i+j+k$ while the program returns either $3*i$, $2*i+j$, $2*i+k$, $2*j+i$ or $i+j+k$.

The program and the specification of *tritype* and *tri-perimeter* can be found at www.polytech.unice.fr/˜rueher/annex_tritype_triperimeter.pdf.

All the java programs of the examples in this paper conform to their JML specifications. This corresponds to the much difficult problem, since the search must be complete. Indeed, detection of non-conformity is much easier in practice (it stops when the first solution is found) even if the difficulty from a theoretical point of view is the same.

The rest of this paper is organised as follows. Section 2 recalls some basics on the translation process we have implemented to generate the constraint systems. Section 3 details the different models we propose whereas section 4 introduces different solving strategies. Section 5 describes the experimental results and section 6 discusses some critical issues.

[2] A full translation in Boolean constraints is also ineffective as soon as numeric expression occurs in the program or in the specification. Indeed, in this case we need to translate each integer operation into bit-vector calculus. Thus, even SMT solvers like SMT-CBMC [2] which use specialized solver for bit-vector calculus fail to solve some trivial problems.

```
/* @ public normal_behavior
   @ ensures ((i<j)=>\result=1) && ((i>=j)=>\result=10)
 */
int simple(int i, int j) {
  int result;
  int k=0;
  if (i <= j) k=k+1;
  if (k==1 && i!=j) result=1;
     else result =10;
  return result;
}
```

Fig. 1. S1 example : JML specification and Java program

2 Translation of a Program and its Specification into Constraints

This section recalls basic techniques for translating a Java program and its JML specification into a set of constraints.

For the sake of simplicity, we only consider here a very restricted form of Java and JML programs. For the JML specification, we restrict ourselves to normal behaviour, i.e., we do not consider exceptions such as overflows. We also assume that the JML specification contains an `\ensures` statement, a logical expression defining the post-condition. It may also contain a `\requires` statement defining the pre-condition. Likewise, we only consider Java program where all variables are integers and we assume that functions have only one return statement. Finally, we do not detail here the process for handling loops. Interested readers can find details on the way we handle loops and several JML statements such as `\forall` statement in [8].

2.1 Translation Process

We only recall here the basics which are required to understand this paper. More details on SSA form can be found in [9].

Translating the Program into a Set of Constraints. We first transform the program into its SSA "Single State Assignment" form [9]: for each new definition of a program variable, we introduce a fresh variable. In order to manage control instructions, we use ϕ–functions for `if then else` statements.

Basic statements. Each assignment $var = value$ is translated as a constraint $var_i = value$ where i is the current number of definition of variable var. For example, the following piece of code $x = x + 1; y = x * y; x = x + y;$ is translated as the set of constraints : $\{x_1 = x_0 + 1, y_1 = x_1 * y_0, x_2 = x_1 * y_1\}$.

Conditional execution flow. Conditional execution flows are translated into *guarded constraints*. Guarded constraints are conditional constraints whose evaluation depends upon other constraints. $C_0 \to C_1$ denotes a guarded constraint where C_0 and C_1 are conjunctions of basic constraints. Relation $C_0 \rightarrow C_1$ states that constraints C_1 have to be added to the current constraint store when the solver can prove that constraints C_0 hold. More precisely, let C_0 be a boolean expression and C_1 a set of constraints, the guarded constraint $C_0 \rightarrow C_1$ behaves as follows:

- When the solver can prove that C_0 is true, then constraints C_1 are added to the store of constraints;
- When the solver can prove that C_0 is false, then the guarded constraint is just discarded;
- When the solver can neither prove that C_0 is true, nor prove that C_0 is false, that is when not enough variables of C_0 are instantiated, then the guarded constraint is suspended.

The solver tries to prove that the guard C_0 of a suspended constraint holds whenever the domain of some variable occurring in C_0 has been reduced.

One major difficulty with guarded constraints is that nothing can be done before the solver can demonstrate that the condition is either *true* or *false*. Let us consider a very simple piece of code:

```
//@ ensures \result ≥ 0
public int absolute(int i, int j) {
   if (i<j) return j - i;
       else return i - j;
}
```

This code is translated into the following set of constraints:
$\{i < j \rightarrow r = j - i, !(i < j) \rightarrow r = i - j, r < 0\}$
A standard CSP solver cannot achieve any pruning on this system since nothing is known about i and j. So a very costly enumeration process is started: the inconsistency is only detected when the domain of i and j are reduced to one value.

That's why we introduce Boolean variables and handled in a better way guarded constraints (see part 3.2).

The `If then` statement. For the sake of clarity, we only focus on the assignment of a single variable. Trivially, the same process could be applied individually for each variable appearing in a block with many variable assignments.

Let us consider the statement `S : if (cond) {var=val}`. Assume that *var* has already been defined p times before this statement. S is translated into the following set of guarded constraints where $SSA(s)$ denotes the constraint corresponding to the SSA form of the basic statement s.

if part :	SSA(cond)	$\rightarrow$	$var_{p+1} = \text{SSA}(val)$
else part :	SSA(!cond)	$\rightarrow$	$var_{p+1} = var_p$

The else part just ensures that the var_{p+1} fresh variable will not remain uninstantiated in the corresponding CSP.

The `If then else` statement. Let us consider the statement `S : if (cond) {v=`x_1`;v=`x_2`; ...;v=`x_q`;} else {v=`y_1`;v=`y_2`;...; v=`y_r`;}`. Assume that v has already been defined p times before this statement and assume that $q < r$. Since v has not the same number of definitions in the `if` part and the `else` part, we need to introduce a guarded constraint to take the place of the ϕ function. So, S is translated into the following set of guarded constraints :

// if part
SSA(cond) $\rightarrow$ $(v_{p+1}$=SSA$(x_1))$&$(v_{p+2}$=SSA$(x_2))$&...&$(v_{p+q}$=SSA$(x_q))$
// else part
SSA(!cond) $\rightarrow$ $(v_{p+1}$=SSA$(y_1))$&$(v_{p+2}$=SSA$(y_2))$&...&$(v_{p+r}$=SSA$(y_r))$
// ϕ function
SSA(cond) $\rightarrow$ $(v_{p+q+1}=v_{p+q})$&$(v_{p+q+2}=v_{p+q})$&...&$(v_{p+r}=v_{p+q})$

Remark: if $q > r$ the same principle is applied and the guarded constraints of the ϕ function are guarded by $SSA(\neg\ cond)$. If q=r then no ϕ function is required. Figure 2 gives an example of translation of an overlapped `if then else`.

```
1   if  (i < j) x = 0;            (i<j) --> x1=0
    else {
2     if (i < 30)                 (!(i<j)&(i<30))-->(x1=x0+1&x2=x1+y0)
         { x = x+1;
           x = x+y;}
      else {
3       if (j > 43) x=2;          (!(i<j)&!(i<30)&(j>43))--> x1=2
            else x=3;             (!(i<j)& !(i<30)& !(j>43))--> x1=3
      }                           // phi-function for #2 if
    }                             (!(i<j)&!(i<30)) --> x2=x1
                                  // phi-function for #1 if
                                  (i<j) --> x2=x1
```

Fig. 2. example of if then else translation

Translating the Specification. The JML specification we handle is decomposed into two parts : the `\requires` statement and the `\ensures` statement. The `\requires` statement is a logical expression on input variables and the `\ensures` statement is a logical expression both on input variables and `\result`, which denotes in JML the value returned by the method. We translate the JML specification in the following way :

- each logical expression is translated into the corresponding constraint,
- the `\result` JML variable is associated to a new variable of the CSP named *result* which establishes the link between the program and the specification,
- we add the constraints issued from the `\requires` statement,
- we add the negation of constraints issued from the `\ensures` statement.

2.2 Characteristics of a CSP for Software Validation

We define a CSP for software validation as a tuple formed with a set of *integer variables*, a set of *boolean variables* (possibly empty) used to improve performance of guarded constraints propagation, a set of *guarded constraints* issued from the program and the specification and an *abstraction table* which gives the correspondence between the boolean abstract variables and the integer expressions. This is detailed in figure 3.

1. *Variables*
   - INT_VAR : set of finite variables with domain [min,max]
   - BOOL_VAR : set of boolean variables with domain [0,1]
   - result ∈ INT_VAR : the variable which makes the link between the program (Java return statement) and the specification (`\result` JML statement)
2. *Constraints*
   - PROG_CONST : set of guarded constraints from the program
   - REQUIRE_CONST : set of guarded constraints from the JML `\requires` statement
   - ENSURE_CONST : set of guarded constraints from the negation of the JML `\ensures` statement
3. *Abstraction table*
   - SEMANTICS(b_i) provides the finite domain constraint that is modelled by the boolean abstract variable b_i.

Fig. 3. CSP for software validation

3 Modeling Issues

We present here different models –from the less abstract one to the most abstract one– that we studied during our experiments. All the models are illustrated on example *S1* of figure 1. To help the reading, in the successive figures for example *S1* , we start by '*' the lines which have changed from one model to the next one. When solving the CSPs, all the models are also evaluated on the two more significant benchmarks *tritype* and *tri-perimeter.*

3.1 `INT_CSP`: A Model Without Boolean Abstraction

In this model, we do not introduce any boolean variable : the guarded constraints are couples (g,c) where g and c are expressions on integer variables. Figure 4 illustrates this model on example *S1.*

3.2 `HYBRID_CSP_1`: Using Boolean Abstraction for the Program Guards

In this model, we introduce a boolean variable for each guard involved in the constraints of the program. The advantage is that the enumeration process begins with boolean variables and so guards are evaluated first. In this way, a

```
1. Variables
   INT_VAR = {i,j,r_0,r_1,k_0,k_1} in [min,max]
   BOOL_VAR = empty
   result in [min,max]
2. Constraints
   PROG_CONST :
     1   r_0=0
     2   k_0=0
     3   i<=j --> k_1=k_0+1
     4   !(i<=j) --> k_1=k_0
     5   k_1=1 & i!=j --> r_1=1
     6   !(k_1=1 & i!=j) --> r_1=10
     7   result=r_1
   REQUIRE_CONST : empty
   ENSURE_CONST :
     8   !(((i<j) --> result=1) & ((i>=j) --> result=10))
3. Abstraction table : empty
```

Fig. 4. Example S1: INT_CSP

constraint c can be posted even if the integer variables involved in its guard are not instantiated. The introduction of boolean entails a *non standard* processing of guarded constraints. For instance, consider the guarded constraint $i < j \rightarrow k_1 = k_0 + 1$ and assume that the boolean variable b_0 is associated to the guard $i < j$. When b_0 is set to true, both constraints $i < j$ and $k_1 = k_0 + 1$ are added to the constraint store.

Figure 5 shows this model on example *S1*. With respect to figure 4 we have introduced two boolean variables, g_0 for the guard of constraints 3 and 4 and g_1 for the guard of constraints 5 and 6.

3.3 HYBRID_CSP_2: Using Boolean Abstraction for Expressions Appearing in Several Guards

One drawback of the previous model is that it looses too much semantics; for instance, it doesn't take into account that the same logical expressions may be involved in distinct guards. That's why we introduce in the model HYBRID_CSP_2 a boolean variable for each sub-expression which appears several times in the guards of the program constraints or in the specification constraints.

In the previous modeling of *example S1* (see figure 5), the sub-expression $i < j$ appears both in guard g_0 and in the specification constraints. So we introduced a new boolean variable to abstract this expression (see figure 6).

3.4 HYBRID_CSP_3: Adding Boolean Abstraction for Expressions Involving the Variable *result*

In order to have a better link between the program and the specification, we extend the HYBRID_CSP_2 model by introducing a boolean abstraction for each

```
1. Variables
   INT_VAR = {i,j,r_0,r_1,k_0,k_1} in [min,max]
*  BOOL_VAR = {g_0,g_1} in [0,1]
   result in [min,max]
2. Constraints
   PROG_CONST :
      1   r_0=0
      2   k_0=0
*     3   g_0 --> k_1=k_0+1
*     4   !g_0 --> k_1=k_0
*     5   g_1 --> r_1=1
*     6   !g_1 --> r_1=10
      7   result=r_1
    REQUIRE_CONST : empty
    ENSURE_CONST :
      8   !(((i<j) --> result=1) & ((i>=j) --> result=10))
3. Abstraction table
*  SEMANTICS(g_0) = i<=j
*  SEMANTICS(g_1) = k_1=1 & i!=j
```

Fig. 5. Example S1 : HYBRID_CSP_1

expression on the *result* variable. This variable is part both of the program and the specification and so it can be helpful to cut some branches during the resolution process. Since we can only assign variable *result* once, we add a constraint which states that only one abstract variable can be true at the same time.

For example *S1*, we introduced two boolean variables in the model of figure 6 : one for the expression *result=1* and the other for the expression *result=10*; the link between the possible values of variable *result* is done by constraint 7 in figure 7.

3.5 BOOL_CSP: Boolean Model

In this model, we introduce a boolean variable for each expression in the program and the specification. This is the model which is used by SAT solvers when the expressions do not contain any arithmetic expression. If they do, basic arithmetic operations must also be modelled with boolean constraints.

4 Solving the CSP

We have explored various strategies for solving hybrid CSP with boolean and integer variables. These strategies are closely related to the models we presented in the previous section. We operated with JSolver4Verif[7]: it is a Java version of Ilog solver[3] with specific propagation rules based on congruence techniques. However, on all the examples contained in this paper the performances of JSolver are very similar to the one of Solver.

[3] See http://www.ilog.com/products/cp/.

```
1. Variables
    INT_VAR = {i,j,r_0,r_1,k_0,k_1} in [min,max]
*   BOOL_VAR = {g_0,g_1,g_2} in [0,1]
    result in [min,max]
2. Constraints
   PROG_CONST
      1  r_0=0
      2  k_0=0
*     3  (g_0||g_1) --> k_1=k_0+1
*     4  !(g_0||g_1) --> k_1=k_0
*     5  g_2 --> r_1=1
*     6  !g_2 --> r_1=10
      7  result=r_1
   REQUIRE_CONST : empty
   ENSURE_CONST
      8  !((g_0 --> result=1) & (!g_0 --> result=10)))
3. Abstraction table
*  SEMANTICS(g_0) = i<j
*  SEMANTICS(g_1) = i=j
*  SEMANTICS(g_2) = k_1=1 & !g_1
```

Fig. 6. S1 example : HYBRID_CSP_2

4.1 Solving an Integer CSP

In order to solve INT_CSP we only have to perform a search on the CSP. If a solution is found, then it is an error test case (a data that satisfies the constraints of the program and of the negation of its specification); otherwise the program is conform to its specification.

4.2 Solving a Hybrid CSP Using a CSP Solver

We show here two strategies for solving hybrid CSP for models HYBRID_CSP_1, HYBRID_CSP_2 and HYBRID_CSP_3:

– Strategy 1 : searching for all solutions.
  Roughly speaking, this strategy consists into searching a solution to the hybrid CSP and then to construct an integer CSP which has the semantics of the current solution of the hybrid CSP. This process is detailed in figure 9. The goal of this strategy is to take advantage of of the forward and backward propagation process on guarded constraints.
– Strategy 2 : enumerating on boolean variables only
  This is the same algorithm as *Strategy 1* except that in line 1 of figure 9 we start the search by enumerating on boolean variables only (i.e. on B_VAR variables only).

  This strategy is mandatory when we use models HYBRID_CSP_2 or HYBRID_CSP_3. In these models, some boolean variables depend from other boolean variables and do not appear directly in the constraints of the program and the specification. So they may remain uninstantiated during the search on the HYBRID_CSP.

```
1. Variables
     INT_VAR = {i,j,r_0,r_1,k_0,k_1\} in [min,max]
*    BOOL_VAR = {g_0,g_1,g_2,b_0,b_1} in [0,1]
     result in [min,max]
2. Constraints
     PROG_CONST :
         1  r_0=0
         2  k_0=0
         3  (g_0||g_1) --> k_1=k_0+1
         4  !(g_0||g_1) --> k_1=k_0
*        5  g_2 --> b_0
*        6  !g_2 --> b_1
*        7  b_0 + b_1 = 1
     REQUIRE_CONST : empty
     ENSURE_CONST :
*        8  !((g_0 --> b_0) & (!g_0 --> b_1))
3. Abstraction table
*   SEMANTICS[g_0] = i<j
*   SEMANTICS[g_1] = i=j
*   SEMANTICS[g_2] = k_1=1 & !g_1
*   SEMANTICS[b_0] = result=1
*   SEMANTICS[b_1] = result=10
```

Fig. 7. S1 example : HYBRID_CSP_3

5 Experimental Results

5.1 Experimental Results

In this section we evaluate the various models and strategies on the *S1* and *S2* programs and also validate our conclusions on the two more realistic examples *tritype* and *tri-perimeter*.

In each table, we consider signed integers and we give the time performance according to the number of bits they are coded with. Since our purpose is to compare different modeling issues, we use a time out limit of ten minuts (denoted '–' in the tables). Nevertheless, we give the solving time required for the largest size of integers we could handle in some cases (in italic). *bool* denotes the number of boolean solutions, that's to say the number of finite domain CSPs which are generated, and which have to be disproved to demonstrate the conformity between the program and its specification.

The constraint systems for these different programs have been generated automatically. Primary boolean expressions are stored on the fly in a hash map and each expression is replaced with a boolean variable if it is used more than once, depending on the model. All experiments were performed on a Processor Intel Core 2 Duo E6400 (2,13 GHz, 1G memory).

```
  1. Variables
       INT_VAR = {i,j,r_0,r_1,k_0,k_1} in [min,max]
  *    BOOL_VAR = {g_0,g_1,g_2,b_0,b_1,b_2,...,b_11} in [0,1]
       result in [min,max]
  2. Constraints
       PROG_CONST :
  *       1  b_0
  *       2  b_1
  *       3  (g_0||g_1) --> b_2
  *       4  !(g_0||g_1) --> b_3
  *       5  g_2 --> b_4
  *       6  ! g_2 --> b_5
  *       7  b_2 + b_3 = 1
  *       8  b_4 + b_5 = 1
       REQUIRE_CONST : empty
       ENSURE_CONST :
  *       9  !((g_0 --> b_4) & (!g_0 --> b_5))
  3. Abstraction table
       SEMANTICS(g_0) = i<j               SEMANTICS(g_1) = i=j
       SEMANTICS(g_2) = k_1=1 & !g_1
  *    SEMANTICS(b_0) = r_0=0             SEMANTICS(b_1) = k_0=0
  *    SEMANTICS(b_2) = k_1=k_0+1         SEMANTICS(b_3) = k_1=k_0
  *    SEMANTICS(b_4) = result=1          SEMANTICS(b_5) = result=10
```

Fig. 8. Example S1 : BOOL_CSP

Let HYBRID_CSP={I_VAR, B_VAR, CONST, SEMANTICS} where I_VAR is the set of integer variables including result*, B_VAR the set of boolean variables, CONST is the union of constraints from program and specification and SEMANTICS is the abstraction table*

boolean conform(HYBRID_CSP)

1 start a search on HYBRID_CSP

2 if HYBRID_CSP has no solution print **program conform with its specification**; **return true**

3 else

4 while HYBRID_CSP has a solution

5 - search next **solution S** of HYBRID_CSP

6 - build integer CSP **S_INT** :

- . for each variable I in I_VAR add a variable S_I in S_INT with initial domain equals to the domain of I in solution S
- . add the constraints of CONST where each variable I has been renamed as S_I
- . for each variable B_i in B_VAR,
  if B_i is true in solution S add the constraint SEMANTICS(b_i)
  else if b_i is not an abstraction of an assignement of variable *result*,
  then add the constraint (!SEMANTICS(b_i))

7 - start a search on **S_INT** : if there is a solution it is an **error test-case**; **return false**

8 print **program conform with its specification; return true**.

Fig. 9. Strategy 1: solving an hybrid CSP

5.2 INT_CSP Model

As mentioned in subsection 3.2, the INT_CSP model cannot achieve any filtering as long as the integer variables involved in the guards are not instantiated. So, the search process is very slow: table 1 shows that even for the very simple examples, the INT_CSP model cannot be solved for integers coded on 32 bits.

Table 1. CSP_INT solving

# bit	*S1*	S2	tritype	tri-perimeter
8	0.577 s	0.766 s	66.582 s	406.27 s
10	5.422 s	9.255s	-	-
16	*21663.778 s (6 hours)*	-	-	-
32	-	-	-	-

5.3 Hybrid CSP Models

Table 2 provides the results for *S1* and *tritype* programs.

In these programs, the returned value is a constant so the `HYBRID_CSP_3` is not relevant. Indeed, in this case there is little interest to introduce a boolean abstraction for each expression on the *result* variable.

Searching all solutions (strategy 1) is rather inefficient with the `HYBRID_CSP_1` model. Strategy 2 (searching only boolean solutions) is clearly better both with `HYBRID_CSP_1` and `HYBRID_CSP_2`.

An essential observation is that strategy 1 searches for all the solutions, that is to say, even for solutions which differ on integer variables but are equals for boolean variables. As said before, we evaluated this strategy because the inverse propagation of guarded constraints may eliminate values for boolean variables on some problems. Indeed, for a guarded constraint (g, c), if c is proved false due to other constraints, then the negation of g is added to the constraint store; this information may cut some branches for other guarded constraints which share guard g.

The difference between the results for the various models highlights that introducing boolean variables is a key issue when these variables are shared by many constraints.

Table 3 compares the performances of models HYBRID_CSP_2, HYBRID_CSP_3 and BOOL_CSP on the *S2* and *tri-perimeter* examples using strategy 2.

First, let us note that the performances are weaker on these two examples. This is due to the arithmetic operations, which occur in these two examples. Indeed, *S2* (resp. *tri-perimeter*) differs from *S1* (resp. *tritype*) only on the operative part (calculus on inputs instead of constant value).

Another essential observation is that in model `BOOL_CSP`, we provide a constraint which states that the boolean variables which correspond to several assignements of a single variable cannot be true at the same time. This is a critical point: if we remove this constraint for *tri-perimeter* with integers coded on 8 bits there are 778240 boolean solutions and it takes 319.028s to solve the problem.

Table 2. HYBRID_CSP_1 and HYBRID_CSP_2 solving

S1 and tritype						
# bit	HYBRID_CSP_1 strategy 1		HYBRID_CSP_1 strategy 2		HYBRID_CSP_2 strategy 2	
	S1	*tritype*	*S1*	*tritype*	*S1*	*tritype*
8	57.116 s 131072 bool	-	0.194 s 4 bool	0.999 s 565 bool	0.182 s 4 bool	1.768 s 4520 bool
10	-	-	0.221 s 4 bool	4.157 s 565 bool	0.186 s 4 bool	1.926 s 4520 bool
16	-	-	0.568 s 4 bool	-	0.221 s 4 bool	8.522 s 4520 bool
32	-	-	-	-	*1520.82 s* 4 bool	-

Table 3. HYBRID_CSP_2, HYBRID_CSP_3 and BOOL_CSP solving

S2 and tri-perimeter						
# bit	HYBRID_CSP_2		HYBRID_CSP_3		BOOL_CSP	
	S2	*tri-perimeter*	*S2*	*tri-perimeter*	*S2*	*tri-perimeter*
8	0.477 s 8 bool	15.056 s 5056	0.185 s 4 bool	6.57 s 22464 bool	0.2 s 4 bool	3.42 s 6080 bool
10	2.946 s 8 bool	-	0.2 s 4 bool	10.489 s 22464 bool	0.286 s 4 bool	3.654 s 6080 bool
16	-	-	0.274 s 4 bool	-	0.292 s 4 bool	4.809 s 6080 bool
32	-	-	*2516.156 s* 4 bool	-	-	-

6 Discussion

Verification and validation are two of the most critical issues in the software engineering process. Numerous techniques, ranging from formal proofs to testing methods have been used during the last years to verify the conformity of a program with its specification. However, such a verification remains a difficult task, even for small programs. Our experimentations [8] showed that constraint techniques can be very efficient on some non trivial problems. Performance of CSP techniques behave clearly better than state of art SMT solvers [8,2]

In this paper, we did investigate different CSP models on a few simple but non-trivial academic examples. As expected, a straightforward translation of a program and its specification in a system of guarded constraints is ineffective, even on very simple examples. Boolean abstraction is clearly a critical issue for efficiency. An appropriate Boolean abstraction is an essential support for the search process.

Of course, additional work is required before these techniques can be used on real applications. Further work to try is on the cooperation of CSP and SAT solvers as well as new filtering techniques.

When the set of Boolean constraints becomes larger, a collaboration between a SAT solver and CSP solver is probably more appropriate to handle such problems. We have performed some very preliminary experimentation with SAT4J(see www.sat4j.org) and Jsolver4Verif. A technical difficulty concerns the enumeration of all solutions by a SAT solvesr. Indeed, the most efficient SAT solver are not designated to enumerate all solutions. Moreover, the transfer to the SAT solver of failure information from CSP solver –which is a key issue– is far from being obvious.

Specific filtering techniques[4] may also drastically improve the refutation of the generated CSP over finite domains. Likewise, linear solvers or difference constraint solvers may be used to check the consistency of constraint defining the semantics of guards.

References

1. Aït-Kaci, H., Berstel, B., Junker, U., Leconte, M., Podelski, A.: Satisfiability Modulo Structures as Constraint Satisfaction: An Introduction. In: Procs. of JFLA, 8 pages (2007)
2. Armando, A., Mantovani, J., Platania, L.: Bounded Model Checking of C Programs using a SMT solver instead of a SAT solver Technical Report, AI-Lab, DIST, University of Genova, 16 pages (December 19, 2005)
3. Bouquet, F., Dadeau, F., Legeard, B., Utting, M.: JML-Testing-Tools: a Symbolic Animator for JML Specifications using CLP. In: Halbwachs, N., Zuck, L.D. (eds.) TACAS 2005. LNCS, vol. 3440, pp. 551–556. Springer, Heidelberg (2005)
4. Clarke, E., Kroening, D., Sharygina, N., Yorav, K.: SATABS: SAT-Based Predicate Abstraction for ANSI-C. In: Halbwachs, N., Zuck, L.D. (eds.) TACAS 2005. LNCS, vol. 3440, pp. 570–574. Springer, Heidelberg (2005)
5. Ganzinger, H., Hagen, G., Nieuwenhuis, R., Oliveras, A., Tinelli, C.: DPLL(T): Fast Decision Procedures. In: Alur, R., Peled, D.A. (eds.) CAV 2004. LNCS, vol. 3114, pp. 175–188. Springer, Heidelberg (2004)
6. Gotlieb, A., Botella, B., Rueher, M.: Automatic Test Data Generation using Constraint Solving Techniques. In: Proc. ISSTA 98, ACM SIGSOFT, vol. 2, pp. 53–62 (1998)
7. Leconte, M., Berstel, B.: Extending a CP Solver with Congruences as Domains for Program Verification. In: Procs. of CSTVA06, 1st Workshop on Constraints in Software Testing, Verification and Analysis, Nantes (2006)
8. Collavizza, H., Rueher, M.: Software Verification using Constraint Programming Techniques. In: Hermanns, H., Palsberg, J. (eds.) TACAS 2006 and ETAPS 2006. LNCS, vol. 3920, pp. 182–196. Springer, Heidelberg (2006)
9. Cytron, R., Ferrante, J., Rosen, B., Wegman, M., Zadeck, K.: Efficently Computing Static Single Assignment Form and the Control Dependence Graph. Transactions on Programming Languages and Systems 13(4), 451–490 (1991)

[4] See for instance [7] where congruence domains are introduced.

10. Ganai, M., Gupta, A., Ashar, P.: DiVer: SAT-Based Model Checking Platform for Verifying Large Scale Systems. In: Halbwachs, N., Zuck, L.D. (eds.) TACAS 2005. LNCS, vol. 3440, pp. 575–580. Springer, Heidelberg (2005)
11. Moskewicz, M., Madigan, C., Zhao, Y., Zhang, L., Malik, S.: Chaff: Engineering an Efficient SAT Solver. In: Proc. of DAC, pp. 530–535 (2001)
12. Nieuwenhuis, R., Oliveras, A., Tinelli, C.: Solving SAT an SAT Modulo Theories: from an Abstract Davis-Putnam-Logemann-Loveland Procedure to DPLL(T). Journal of the ACM (to appear)
13. Sy, N.T., Deville, Y.: Automatic test data generation for programs with integer and float variables. In: Proc of. 16th IEEE International Conference on Automated Software Engineering(ASE01). IEEE Computer Society Press, Los Alamitos (2001)

An Application of Constraint Programming to Generating Detailed Operations Schedules for Steel Manufacturing

Andrew Davenport[1], Jayant Kalagnanam[1], Chandra Reddy[1], Stuart Siegel[1], and John Hou[2]

[1] IBM T.J.Watson Research Center, 1101 Kitchawan Road, Yorktown Heights, NY 10598, USA

[2] IBM Taiwan Business Consulting Services, Shong-Ren Rd, Taipei, Taiwan, Republic of China

davenport@us.ibm.com, jayant@us.ibm.com, creddy@us.ibm.com, ssiegel@us.ibm.com, kwhou@tw.ibm.com

Abstract. We present an overview of a system developed by IBM for generating short-term operations schedules for a large steel manufacturer. The problem addressed by the system was challenging due to the combination of detailed resource allocation and scheduling constraints and preferences, sequence dependent setup times, tight minimum and maximum inventory level constraints between processes, and constraints on the minimum and maximum levels of production by shift for each product group. We have developed a domain-specific decomposition based approach that uses mixed-integer programming to generate a high-level plan for production, and constraint programming to generate a schedule at fine level of time granularity taking into account detailed scheduling constraints and preferences. In this paper we give an overview of the problem domain and solution approach, and present a detailed description of the constraint programming part of the system. We also discuss the impact the system is having with the customer on their manufacturing operations.

1 Introduction

In this paper we present an overview of a system developed by IBM for generating short-term detailed operations schedules for a large steel manufacturer. The problem addressed by the system involves generating schedules subject to detailed constraints and preferences at a fine level of time granularity (30 seconds or less). Scheduling problems with such low-level constraints and preferences are typically handled well by constraint programming techniques [1,3]. However the problem also contains constraints and objectives that are stated at a coarser level of time granularity, and might be considered to be more at the "planning level". Examples of such constraints and objectives are deciding which orders to produce over the next few days from an order pool, subject to capacity constraints on the number of orders of each product type that can be produced within each shift, and maximizing the number of orders scheduled on their preferred start date. This aspect of the problem is often handled well using mixed

C. Bessiere (Ed.): CP 2007, LNCS 4741, pp. 64 – 76, 2007.

integer programming techniques. In order to combine the advantages of both constraint programming and integer programming, we developed a hybrid solution approach that decomposes the full problem into a high level integer programming based planning problem to determine what orders to produce and roughly when on the available process stages, and a low-level constraint programming based scheduling problem to determine a detailed second-by-second schedule on specific machines at each process. However the complex global nature of some of the detailed scheduling constraints, combined with the requirement to achieve a high level of resource utilization, resulted in this decomposition-based approach producing poor solutions that were not acceptable to the customer. In order to overcome this drawback, we developed a simple integration mechanism between the planning and detailed scheduling stages that was found to significantly improve solution quality. A detailed description of the mixed integer programming formulations used in this decomposition-based approach is presented in [6]. In this paper we present an overview of the application domain and the integrated problem solving approach, and discuss in detail the constraint programming aspects of solving this problem.

2 The Problem

The scope of the problem addressed by the system is to produce a multi-day operations schedule for the manufacture of steel products from raw material inputs. The main processes involved in the manufacturing of steel are illustrated in Figure 1. The four main process areas addressed by the system are:

1. The *Blast Furnace* (far left in Figure 1) where iron is heated to a very high temperature to become molten. There is a continuous flow of molten iron from the blast furnace to the downstream processes. This flow is given as input to the scheduling problem formulation specified on an hourly basis.
2. The *Basic Oxygen Furnace* is the first process that all production must pass through after leaving the blast furnace. At this process, molten iron starts to become differentiated with respect to grade and chemical composition.
3. The *Refining Processes* consist of a number of steps such as reheating, ladle furnace and stirring. Not all production will pass through all of these steps, and these steps are not ordered (the steps that are used depend on the chemical composition of the final products.)
4. The *Continuous Casters* (far right in Figure 1): All production passes from the refining stage to the final continuous casting process. In this process, molten steel is poured into a long, adjustable copper mold. As the steel passes through the mold, it is cooled by water jets and solidifies into slabs of a specific dimension.

Steel is usually produced on a make to order basis. Customer orders are batched into units of production called "charges". All distinct operations (activities in the scheduling model) from the basic oxygen furnace and the refining process stages take place on a single charge of steel. At the continuous casting stage, operations take place on a sequence of (2-12) contiguous charges, which is called a "cast". The batching of orders into charges and the sequencing of charges into casts is provided as input to the scheduling system. These batching and sequencing steps form the basis of a complex, multi-criteria sequencing problem, the descriptions of which are outside of the scope of this paper, but which were part of the overall system developed by IBM for the customer.

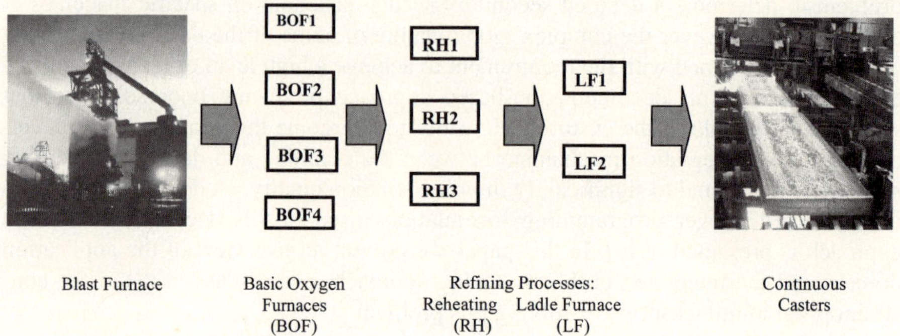

Fig. 1. An illustration of the basic process flow for the manufacture of steel

We divide the full problem into two problem stages: the downstream cast scheduling problem, which corresponds to the high-level planning problem, and the upstream processes detailed scheduling problem. We describe each of these problems stages in the sections which follow.

2.1 Detailed Scheduling Problem Model

Figure 2 presents a Gantt chart view illustrating how the concept of charges and casts are reflected in the formulation of the scheduling model. The Figure shows the schedule for the activities involved in the production of a single cast of steel. The interesting aspects of this formulation to note are that:

1. Each set of activities, for example A_1, A_2, A_3 and A_4 represent the set of operations required to produce a single charge of steel. This corresponds to a single job in the scheduling model. All activities are non-preemptible.
2. In the final casting process a cast is produced consisting of a sequence of contiguous charges. This sequence is given as input to the problem. The processing of consecutive charges in a single cast on the casting processes must be without interruption. In Figure 2, the activities A_4, B_3 and C_2 are scheduled as a cast on the casting process. Hence the start time of activity B_3 must occur at the end time of activity A_4, and the start time of activity C_2 must occur at the end time of activity B_3.
3. There are tight minimum and maximum time lag constraints between consecutive activities in the same job[1], for instance the maximum time lag between the end of activity A_1 and start of activity A_2 might be 20 minutes.

[1] Maximum time lags arise as a result of the movement of the molten steel between processes. If the steel cools down, it is necessary to reheat it, which is expensive in terms of energy consumption. Minimum time lags arise from the transfer time of materials between processes.

4. At each process stage there are a number of resources (machines) that can be used to process an activity (between 2 and 5). The scheduling system needs to determine which resource at each process stage each activity is assigned to[2]. Each resource has different operating characteristics and a different physical location. As a result, the processing time of an activity at a process stage, as well as the transfer time between processes, will depend on the specific resources at each process the activity is assigned to.
5. For each charge we are given a preferred recipe specifying the sequence of process steps that the charge must pass through. We are also given between 0 and 3 alternate recipes that can be used, should there not be sufficient capacity on the preferred recipe process stages. In practice, most (85-95%) of charges will be assigned to their preferred recipes.

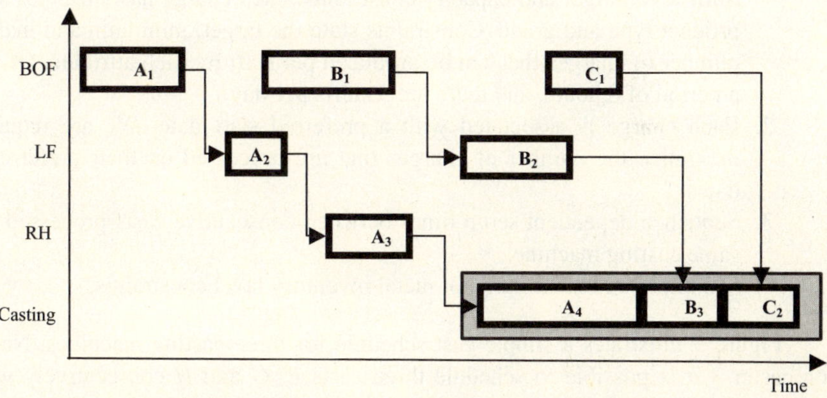

Fig. 2. A Gantt chart illustration of the activities involved in manufacturing a single cast in a steel plant, from the basic oxygen furnace (BOF) to the refining processes (reheating (RH), and ladle furnace (LF)) to the casting process

All the scheduling resources in the problem model have unary capacity (at most one activity at any time point can be executing on a specific resource.) However some resources are state resources, whose state is represented by the number of activities it has processed since the last "setup" activity on the resource. Once the resource has processed a maximum number of activities, it is required to perform another setup activity. Charges on a state resource have a range specifying the minimum and maximum values with respect to the resource state, within which they can be processed on the resource.

2.2 Cast Scheduling Problem Model

We are required to schedule between 60 and 100 casts each composed of 2-12 charges on one of a number (3-9) of distinct casting machines and upstream processes over a

[2] There is an exception for the casting process, where every charge in a cast executes on the same casting machine that is given as input to the scheduler.

1-2 day horizon. The system selects which casts to schedule within the horizon from a pool of around 200 available casts given as input.

As mentioned earlier, there is a continuous flow of molten iron from the blast furnace. The amount of this flow over time is specified as a problem input in terms of number of tons per hour. We consider some quantity of molten iron to be consumed by the first activity of each job when it starts processing at the basic oxygen furnace process. Between the blast furnace and the basic oxygen furnace there is finite capacity buffer, where the molten iron is stored until some activity is scheduled to consume it. There are tight constraints on the minimum and maximum quantity of molten iron that can be allowed to accumulate in this buffer.

The cast schedule specifies which casts are to be processed at what time on the available casting machines, subject to the following constraints:

1. Shift level target and capacity constraints: each charge has attributes such as product type and grade. Constraints state the target, minimum and maximum number of charges that can be produced per shift by each attribute. (A shift is a period of 8 hours, and there are 3 shifts per day.)
2. Each charge is associated with a preferred start date. We are required to maximize the number of charges that are processed on their preferred start dates.
3. Sequence dependent setup times between consecutive casts processed on the same casting machine.
4. Minimum and maximum hot metal inventory level constraints.

Figure 3 illustrates a simple cast schedule for three casting machines. Note that on caster-3 it is possible to schedule three casts *F*, *G* and *H* consecutively with no setup time between them. Although there is no explicit objective to minimize setup time used in the schedule, in practice the maximum hot metal inventory constraint and constraints on the minimum number of charges to schedule per shift require us to use as little setup time as possible.

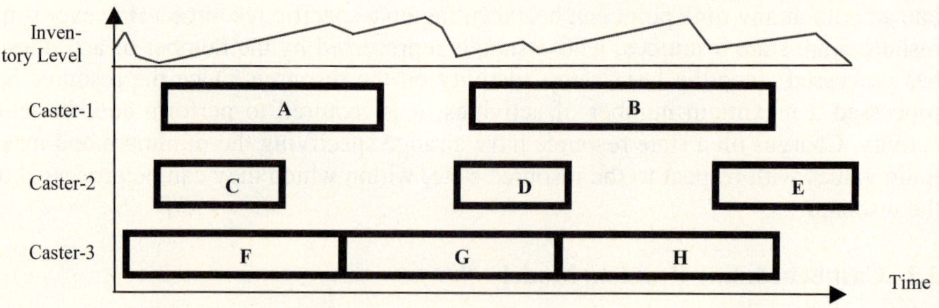

Fig. 3. An illustration of a Gantt chart that specifies a cast schedule

3 Why CP?

The system developed by IBM was designed to be used as a decision support tool for the scheduling department at a steel manufacturing plant. Prior to our involvement, all scheduling was performed manually by a group of scheduling experts. The nature of steel manufacturing is such that production planning, design and operations scheduling are generally more complex than is found in other industries. In particular, optimization problems in the steel industry often involve many constraints expressed at a very low level of detail, yet the tightness of these constraints can have a major impact on the solution at a global level. Furthermore, most steel industry problems that we have encountered contain multiple, often competing objectives. As a result, off-the-shelf supply chain tools, even with some customization, are usually not able to cope with the complexity of optimization problems found in the steel industry.

The complexity of the problem model we encountered for this problem is such that constraint programming seemed a natural choice for the detailed scheduling part of the system. Some of the detailed constraints in the problem, such as those involving state resources, would be quite difficult to model and maintain using an integer programming formulation. Even so, this problem was still quite challenging to solve using constraint programming, since some aspects of the problem have received little attention in the research literature. Examples of such aspects include scheduling with non-substitutable resource alternatives and alternative recipes [7,9] and taking into account detailed preferences on resource and recipe assignments for each activity or set of activities. (One example of the source of such preferences was that if something goes wrong during execution, the schedule should be designed in such a way that it was easy for the human experts to take out "chunks" of the schedule to reschedule elsewhere as quickly as possible.) As such, we were required to experiment and develop solution approaches for dealing with these aspects of the problem during the project. One advantage of using constraint programming, compared with integer programming approaches, is the relative ease with which the constraint programming model and solution approach could quickly and flexibly accommodate change requests over the lifespan of the project.

Although constraint programming seemed like a good choice of technology for the detailed scheduling aspect of the problem, the cast scheduling problem contains constraints and objectives that are more amenable to an integer programming approach. As such, the solution approach we developed decomposes the full problem into two sub-problems that are solved in sequence:

1. ***Downstream cast scheduling***: Cast scheduling determines which casts we are going to schedule and when; satisfying hot metal inventory constraints, shift level capacity constraints, sequence-dependent setup times between casts and preferred start times of casts. We do not consider the scheduling of any upstream processes of casting at this stage. We model this problem using a time-indexed integer programming formulation with a time granularity of 15-30 minutes and solve it using ILOG CPLEX[3].

[3] For the purposes of cast scheduling, we assume all charges will be scheduled on their preferred route. The upstream detailed scheduling stage may reassign routes.

2. ***Upstream process detailed scheduling***: From the solution of the cast-scheduling problem we create a constraint-programming model for scheduling the processes upstream of casting, taking into account detailed scheduling constraints and preferences (such as minimum and maximum time lags between activities, resource exclusion constraints, state resource constraints, preferences on recipe and resource assignments.) This model is formulated at a fine level of time granularity (30 seconds.) Since the cast schedule has already been determined, we do not need to take into account any of the cast scheduling constraints in this model[4].

This solution approach exploits the fact that we have fairly tight maximum time lag constraints between all consecutive pairs of activities in a single job for a charge (this may be as little as 20-40 minutes.) As a result, the schedule for a single cast over all processes will necessarily be localized in time both on the casting process and the upstream processes.

4 How CP?

We solve the cast scheduling problem using mixed-integer programming, formulating the problem using a time-indexed formulation and modeling the shift level capacity constraints, the sequence dependent setup times and the hot metal inventory constraints as side constraints. The scheduling horizon in the time-indexed model is divided into a set of contiguous time periods of equal size (between 15 and 30 minutes.) We present the full mixed integer programming model in [6]. In the sections that follow, we discuss in detail the use of constraint programming in the overall system and give an overview of the integration between the integer programming model and the constraint programming model.

4.1 Constraint-Programming Detailed Scheduling Solver

Given a cast schedule that specifies which casts are to be scheduled in the horizon and an approximate starting time for each selected cast, the goal of the detailed scheduler is to schedule all processes upstream of casting, subject to the following:

1. Select a recipe from a number of available alternate recipes for each charge in each cast to follow in the schedule;
2. Select a resource (machine) from a number of available non-substitutable resources for each job at each process stage;
3. Assign start times to activities on each resource at each process stage, subject to unary resource capacity constraints and precedence constraints with minimal and maximal time lags;
4. Take into account preferences on alternate recipe and resource assignments.

[4] The detailed scheduler is based on a C++ constraint-programming library for manufacturing scheduling developed by IBM (currently known as the "Watson Scheduling Library").

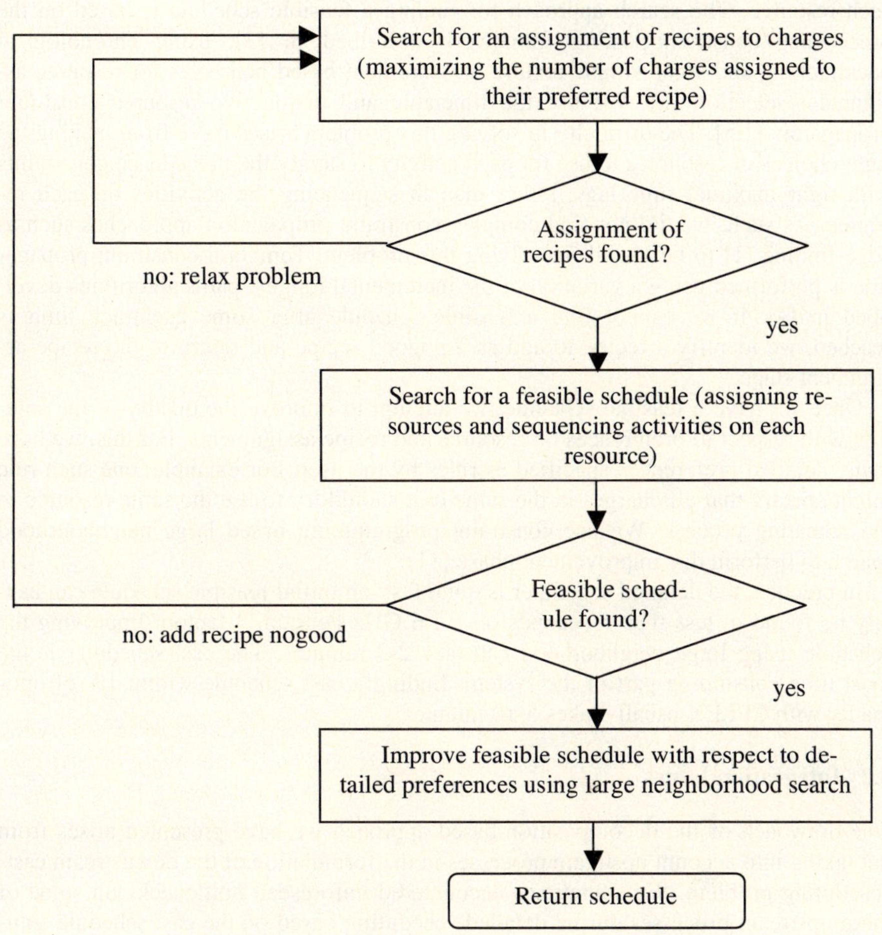

Fig. 4. Problem solving flow for detailed scheduling

We use constraint programming to perform detailed scheduling [1]. An outline of the constraint programming approach we use to perform detailed scheduling is presented in Figure 4.

The problem solving process takes place in several stages. Firstly, we search for a complete feasible assignment of recipes to charges. We perform depth-first search with chronological backtracking. We use a chronological variable ordering heuristic, following the initial start time for each cast specified by the cast scheduling solution. Alternate recipes for each charge are tried in order of preference. Usually we can find an assignment of recipes that uses the most preferred recipe for each charge. In rare cases that a feasible assignment of recipes cannot be found, we relax the problem by selecting a cast to remove from the schedule.

The next stage is to find a feasible schedule that for each recipe, assigns a resource to each activity at each process stage in the recipe, and sequences all activities on each resource. The search approach for finding a feasible schedule is based on the precedence constraint-posting framework described in [3], using chronological backtracking and some simple texture-measurement based heuristics for resource assignment selection [2]. We use the timetable and disjunctive resource constraint propagators [1,5]. The difficulty in solving this problem arises more from making the right choices of resources to use for each activity to satisfy the precedence constraints with tight maximal time lags, rather than in sequencing the activities on each resource. As such, we did not find complex constraint propagation approaches such as edge-finding [1] to be useful for solving this problem. Temporal constraint propagation is performed using a variation of the incremental longest-paths algorithms developed in [4]. If we cannot find a feasible schedule after some backtrack limit is reached, we identify a recipe to add as a nogood recipe and return to the recipe assignment stage.

Once we have a feasible schedule, we attempt to improve the quality of the solution with respect to preferences on resource and recipe assignments. For this, we have many detailed preferences specified as rules by the user. For example, one such rule might specify that all charges in the same cast should try to use the same resource in the reheating process. We use constraint programming based large neighbourhood search to perform this improvement phase [11].

In practice, the detailed scheduler is quite fast: an initial feasible schedule can usually be found in less than 5 seconds on a 1.6 GHz Pentium 4 laptop. Improving the schedule using large neighborhood can take 2-3 minutes. The cast scheduler is the most time consuming part of the system: finding a cast schedule within 1% of optimality with CPLEX usually takes 5-10 minutes.

4.2 Integration Issues

One drawback of the decomposition-based approach we have presented arises from not taking into account upstream processes in the formulation of the downstream cast-scheduling problem. We sometimes encountered unforeseen bottlenecks on some of these upstream processes during detailed scheduling based on the cast schedule solution. Sometimes this results in the solution to the cast scheduling problem found by the integer programming solver being infeasible on the processes upstream of casting.

One solution to this problem is to extend the cast-scheduling model to perform some scheduling of the upstream bottleneck processes. However, the time-indexed formulation of the cast-scheduling problem is at a relatively coarse level of time granularity (15-30 minutes), relative to the time granularity of the detailed scheduling constraints (at the 30 second level.) Using a finer time granularity in the cast-scheduling model in order to accommodate such constraints significantly increases the size and complexity of the model and the time taken to find a solution.

We developed an alternative approach to avoiding upstream bottlenecks by adding capacity constraints on the upstream bottleneck processes as side constraints to the cast-scheduling integer programming model. In order to formulate such capacity constraints, we need to be able to estimate for each cast how much capacity of the upstream processes they are expected to utilize, and when. This is illustrated in Figure 5, where we represent part of the time-indexed cast-scheduling formulation involving a single cast of 3 charges, *A*, *B* and *C*, starting in time period 5 on the Caster and using 3 time periods (5-7) of Caster capacity. In this example if charge *A* in the cast starts in period 5 on the Caster, we might estimate that it will use 1 time period of upstream BOF capacity in period 2. Note that later detailed scheduling of the upstream processes may determine that the actual BOF capacity used by these charges is somewhere else in the schedule. However, since we have tight maximum wait time constraints between consecutive activities in a job for each charge, our working assumption is that we can estimate upstream capacity utilization for each cast that is fairly accurate with respect to the final upstream schedule.

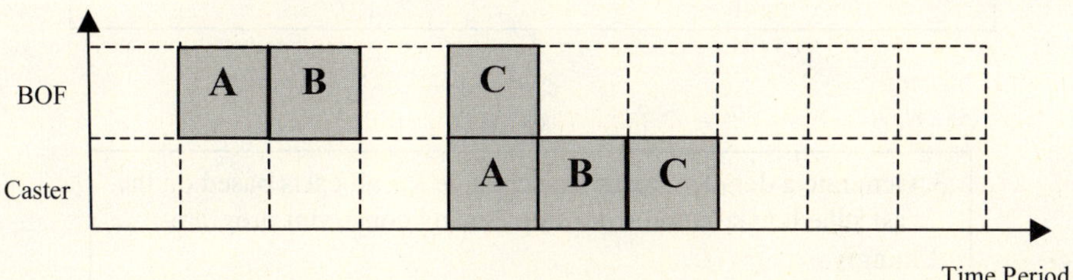

Fig. 5. An illustration of the estimated capacity utilization profile on the upstream process BOF for a cast startin g on the Caster process in time period 5

More specifically, for each cast and each time period *t* in the time-indexed integer programming model and for each upstream bottleneck process, we estimate the capacity used by the cast on the process if it starts processing in time period *t* on the casting process. (In practice it is not necessary to estimate this for every time period: it is sufficient to generate a single estimation for all time periods where the capacity constraints do not change.) We use this estimation as a basis to formulate the upstream process capacity constraints to add to the time-indexed integer programming model. For such an estimation to be useful, it should take into account the detailed scheduling constraints on the upstream processes. We do this by generating a detailed schedule for each cast on all upstream processes, independently of all other casts, using the constraint programming scheduling solver. We use the solution generated by this solver as the basis to estimate upstream capacity utilization for each cast.

Experiments on customer problem data show that by using capacity constraints generated from a constraint programming solution for a single cast can improve both the quality of the final schedule with respect to number of orders scheduled, and well as speed up execution time of the solver. We present the exact formulation of these capacity constraints, as well as experimental results comparing the performance of constraint-programming generated capacity constraints to those generated using simple heuristics, in [6].

We summarize the full high-level problem solving flow used by the system for a generating a steel-making schedule in Figure 6.

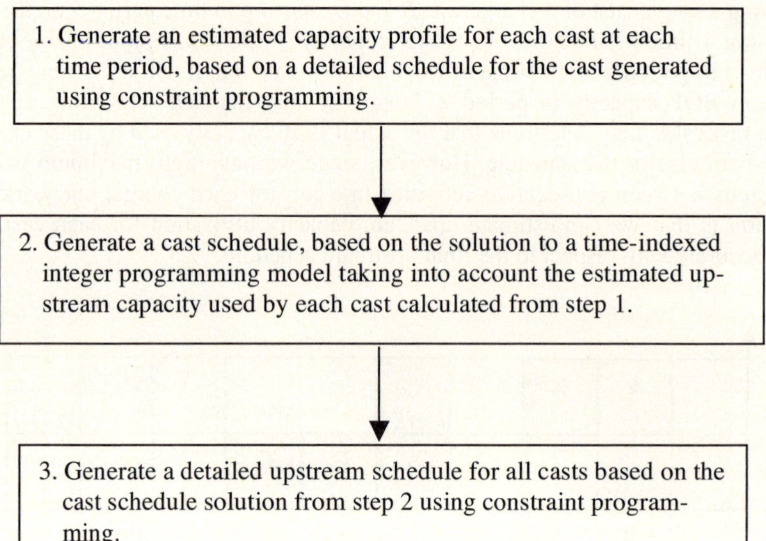

Fig. 6. High-level solution approach process flow using constraint programming and mixed integer programming

5 Added Value of CP?

The scheduling system described in this paper was just one part of a large, multi-million dollar development project that interacted with an upstream optimization module to design the casts that are input to the system, and a downstream module to perform hot strip mill sequencing of the production scheduled by the system. The scheduling system module was developed by two researchers at IBM over a period of 18 months.

The users acknowledge that this scheduling problem is extremely complex, in part due to the complexity of the manufacturing processes and the wide diversity of product types produced. The impetus for the user to improve their scheduling processes arose from the growing pressure from their customers to improve on-time delivery and provide shorter ordering promising time. There were several attempts in the past by the user to develop a scheduling system in-house. This included developing a rule-based system and experimenting with heuristic scheduling approaches, but the results unsatisfactory.

As of writing, the system has just started to go into use by the end user, in parallel with their current system. Initial feedback has been very favourable. The users interact with the system through a graphical user interface, allowing them to influence aspects of the solution such as stating that some casts must be included in the schedule within some specified time range. The users are very impressed that the IBM system is able to generate schedules that achieve higher resource utilization, by scheduling up to 10% more charges, than that of hand-generated schedules prepared by the expert human schedulers. Furthermore, the system can generate full 2-day schedules within 5-10 minutes on a 3GHz Opteron Linux machine, as opposed to many hours needed for the human experts to generate a schedule. This is important, since in practice the users may use the system to perform some kind of "what-if" analysis, experimenting with problem parameters and upstream optimization modules to generate and select from multiple possible schedules. Since the shop floor is very dynamic, some real-time adjustment of the schedules generated by the system is performed by the users during execution.

6 Related Work

Due to the nature of the manufacturing processes, the complexity of production planning and operations scheduling is usually higher in the steel industry than in many other industries. As a result, many commercial "off-the-shelf" tools cannot adequately address the full scope and complexity of production planning and scheduling in the steel industry. We believe that constraint programming can be an important component of decision-support solutions in this area. Some other applications of constraint programming in the steel industry include the system presented in [12] to perform bloom sequencing at what was formerly British Steel. The bloom-sequencing problem is an "upstream" optimization problem to the system presented in this paper: it is used to design the casts whose production is then scheduled by the steelmaking scheduling system. (A system to perform bloom sequencing (as well as plate and coil sequencing) was designed and implemented by IBM as part of the overall project, but is not described in this paper. This system uses a decomposition-based approach utilizing integer programming and specialized bin-packing heuristics [10].) Constraint programming is also used in the COORDIAL system developed using CHIP for real-time scheduling of the production of steel for the Sollac Group in France [13].

7 Conclusions

We have presented an overview of a system for generating detailed schedules for steel production that has developed by IBM for a large steel manufacturer. The full scheduling problem addressed by the system involves solving two related problems for the upstream and downstream processes of steel manufacturing. The downstream, cast-scheduling problem requires the selection and sequencing of groups of contiguous jobs (casts) on a number of machines, subject to shift-level capacity constraints, inter-process inventory constraints and sequence-dependent setup times. The upstream scheduling problem involves determining a detailed schedule for processes upstream of the casting processes, taking into account preferences on how resources are allocated (such as alternate recipes and resources used by each job), precedence constraints with tight minimum and maximum time lags and complex state resources. We have presented an integrated, decomposition-based approach that uses mixed-integer programming to generate a production plan for downstream cast scheduling at a coarse level of time granularity, and constraint programming to schedule upstream processes subject to detailed scheduling constraints at a fine level of time granularity. Initial end-user feedback has been very favourable.

References

[1] Baptiste, P., LePape, C., Nuijten, W.: Constraint-Based Scheduling: Applying Constraint Programming to Scheduling Problems. In: International Series in Operations Research and Management Science, vol. 39. Kluwer, Dordrecht (2001)

[2] Beck, J.C., Davenport, A.J., Sitarski, E.M., Fox, M.S.: Texture-Based Heuristics for Scheduling Revisited. In: Proceedings of the 14th National Conference on Artificial Intelligence (AAAI-97), pp. 241–248. AAAI Press / MIT Press (1997)

[3] Cheng, C.C., Smith, S.F.: Applying constraint satisfaction techniques to job shop scheduling. Annals of Operations Research, Special Volume on Scheduling: Theory and Practice 1 (1996)

[4] Katriel, I., Van Hentenryck, P.: Maintaining Longest Paths in Cyclic Graphs. In: Proc. 11th International Conference on Principles and Practice of Constraint Programming. Springer, Heidelberg (2005)

[5] Laborie, P.: Algorithms for propagating resource constraints in AI planning and scheduling: existing approaches and new results. Artificial Intelligence Journal 143(2), 151–188 (2003)

[6] Davenport, A., Kalagnanam, J.: Scheduling steel production using mixed-integer programming and constraint programming. In: Proceedings of the 3rd Multidisciplinary International Scheduling Conference: Theory and Applications (2007)

[7] Beck, J.C., Fox, M.S.: Scheduling Alternative Activities. In: Proceedings of the Sixteenth National Conference on Artificial Intelligence (AAAI-99) (1999)

[8] Kramer, L.A., Smith, S.F.: Maximizing Flexibility: A Retraction Heuristic for Oversubscribed Scheduling Problems. In: Proceedings of the 18th International Joint Conference on Artificial Intelligence (IJCAI-03) (2003)

[9] Focacci, F., Laborie, P., Nuijten, W.: Solving Scheduling Problems with Setup Times and Alternative Resources. In: Proceedings of the 5th International Conference on Artificial Intelligence Planning and Scheduling Systems (AIPS 2000), pp. 92–111 (2000)

[10] Lee, H.S., Trumbo, M.: An Approximate 0-1 Edge-Labeling Algorithm for Constrained Bin-Packing Problem. In: Proceedings of the 15th International Joint Conference on Artificial Intelligence (IJCAI-97), pp. 1402–1411 (1997)

[11] Shaw, P.: Using Constraint Programming and Local Search Methods to Solve Vehicle Routing Problems. In: Maher, M.J., Puget, J.-F. (eds.) Principles and Practice of Constraint Programming - CP98. LNCS, vol. 1520. Springer, Heidelberg (1998)

[12] Smith, A.W., Smith, B.: Constraint Programming Approaches to a Scheduling Problem in Steelmaking. School of Computing Research Report 97.43, University of Leeds (September 1997)

[13] http://www.cosytec.com/constraint_programming/cases_studies/steel_industry.htm

An Efficient Model and Strategy for the Steel Mill Slab Design Problem

Antoine Gargani[1] and Philippe Refalo[2]

[1] ILOG, 9, rue de Verdun, BP85,
94253 Gentilly Cedex, France
agargani@ilog.fr

[2] ILOG, Les Taissounières, 1681, route des Dolines,
06560 Sophia-Antipolis, France
refalo@ilog.fr

Abstract. The steel mill slab design problem from the CSPLIB is real-life problem from the steel industry. Finding optimal solutions to this problem is difficult. Existing constraint programming approaches can solve problems up to 30 orders. We propose a strong constraint programming model based on logical and global constraints. By designing a specific strategy for variable and value selection, we are able to solve instances having more than 70 orders to optimality using depth-first search. Injecting this strategy into a large neighborhood search, we are able to solve the real-life instance of the CSPLIB having 111 orders in just 3 seconds.

1 Introduction

The steel mill slab design problem (referenced in the CSP library[1] as problem 38) is difficult to solve to optimality. This problem arises from operations planning in the process industry. The problem consists of packing a set of orders onto slabs so as to minimize the total capacity of the slabs needed to fulfill the order book. In practice, two constraints must be satisfied. First, the total weight of the orders assigned to a slab cannot exceed the slab weight. Second, there is a route specification associated with each order represented by the *color* of the order. Packing different colors on a slab involves cutting the slab in different pieces. The cutting machine being the bottleneck of production line, the number of allowed cuttings must not exceed one, and thus the number of different colors on a slab must not exceed two.

The slab design problem is the second step of a more general problem that optimizes the process of orders in a steel mill (see [6]). Before designing and producing slabs, the orders are matched with a slab surplus inventory. Some orders may be assigned to existing slabs, and thus only the orders that were not matched are used in the slab design problem. This inventory matching problem has some similarities with the slab design problem, but the number of available

[1] CSPLIB problems are available at http://www.csplib.org.

C. Bessiere (Ed.): CP 2007, LNCS 4741, pp. 77–89, 2007.

slabs is limited, and a cost for non-packed orders must be handled. This inventory matching problem was addressed with integer programming techniques and in particular by developing approximation algorithms [1] More recently, better results were found using a column generation approach [2].

In the slab design problem, there is no limit on the number of available slabs, and all orders must be packed. This problem, described in the CSP library, has been addressed with constraint programming techniques. In the CSPLIB, an instance with 111 orders is available that so far could not be solved to optimality by constraint programming approaches. A study of different models has been presented in [3], and the role of symmetries has been discussed and experienced in [4]. A hybrid approach combining constraint programming and linear relaxations described in [5] gave the best results and could solve an instance with 30 orders (a subinstance of the 111 orders instance) in about 1000s. Local search techniques were also used in [7]. In this report, the local search solver for pseudo booleans WSAT(OIP) [12] is applied to the decision problem where the cost function is forced to the lower bound of the problem (the sum of order weights). A solution to the 111 instance could be found in about 2000s.

The models used for constraint programming approaches to this problem were basically linear models over binary variables. While such models are suited for integer programming solvers that can tighten the formulation by cutting-plane generation, these models are notoriously not well suited to a constraint programming approach because of the limited domain reductions they produce.

We introduce in this article a strong constraint programming model based on logical and global constraints that achieves more domain reduction. This new model is simple and elegant; it does not contain binary variables but exploits the structure of the problem. By designing a specific strategy for variable and value selection, we are able to use depth-first search to solve instances having more than 70 orders to optimality in less than 200s. We have used this strategy in a large neighborhood search, and we are able to solve the largest instance with 111 orders in just 3s.

2 Problem Description

The problem consists in producing n orders from a set of slabs. Several orders can be made from the same slab but there is no limitation on the number of slabs that can be requested. Each order o has a color c_o and requires an amount of capacity (weight) w_o of the slab to which it is assigned. Each slab has a weight that must be chosen from the increasing set of weights $\{u_1, u_2, \ldots, u_k\}$. The constraints of the problem are

1. an order must be produced from a single slab, and
2. the sum of order weights on a slab must not exceed the slab weight, and
3. a slab can be used to produce orders of at most two different colors.

The first two constraint describe a bin-packing problem. The third one is called the color constraint. Therefore this problem is also called a *variable sized bin-packing problem with color constraints* in the literature [1]. In the steel mill slab design problem, the objective is to produce a few slabs as possible to satisfy the demande. More precisely, the objective is to minimize the cumulative sum of the weights of the slabs used. An obvious lower bound to this problem is the sum of order weights.

Example 1. *Here is a small, illustrative example of an instance and of a solution. Assume that we have 10 orders whose weights and colors are*

Order	*1*	*2*	*3*	*4*	*5*	*6*	*7*	*8*	*9*	*10*
Weight	*1*	*3*	*2*	*9*	*9*	*11*	*3*	*3*	*5*	*2*
Color	*Red*	*Black*	*Black*	*Red*	*Red*	*White*	*Red*	*White*	*Black*	*Red*

and let the set of possible slab weight be $\{5, 7, 9, 11, 15, 18\}$. *A solution to this problem is to use 4 slabs and assign the orders in the following way:*

Slab	*Orders*	*Weight sum*	*Slab weight*
1	*1, 2, 3*	*6*	*7*
2	*4, 5*	*9*	*9*
3	*6, 7, 8*	*17*	*18*
4	*9, 10*	*7*	*7*

Note that in this solution

- *there are no more than two different colors on the same slab;*
- *the maximum slab weight is not exceeded;*
- *the slab weight is just large enough for producing the orders;*
- *the cost of this solution (the sum of the slab weights) is 41;*
- *a lower bound is the sum of order weights that is 39.*

3 A Basic Model

The basic model described here is very similar to the model used for a constraint programming solver in [4]. The model uses primarily binary variables.

Assume that O is the set of orders and S is the set of slabs. Since there is no limitation on slab weight, we artificialy create as many slabs as orders and $|S| = |O|$. Let C bet the set of colors of orders in O and let Q be the set of slab weights $Q = \{u_0 = 0, u_1, u_2, \ldots, u_k\}$. The value 0 introduced in the set is the weight of unused slabs.

The variables of the problem are binary variables. The first matrix of variables determines the positions of the orders:

$$x_{os} \in \{0, 1\} \text{ for } o \in O, s \in M$$

We have $x_{os} = 1$ when order o is packed onto the slab s. The second matrix of variables determines the weight of a slab:

$$y_{sq} \in \{0, 1\} \text{ for } s \in O, q \in Q$$

We have $y_{sq} = 1$ when the slab s has weight q. The third matrix of variables is related to colors:

$$z_{cs} \in \{0, 1\} \text{ for } c \in C, s \in S$$

We have $z_{cs} = 1$ when at least one order of color c is assigned to slab s.

The first constraint of the problem states that an order must be on a single slab:

$$\sum_{o \in O} x_{os} = 1 \text{ for every slab } s \in S$$

The second one states that a slab must have a single weight:

$$\sum_{q \in Q} y_{sq} = 1 \text{ for every slab } s \in S$$

The third constraint states that the orders must fit within the slab weight:

$$\sum_{o \in O} w_o x_{os} \leq \sum_{q \in Q} q \times y_{qm} \text{ for every slab } s \in S$$

When an order is on a slab, then its color is on a slab

$$x_{os} \leq z_{c_o s} \text{ for } o \in O, s \in M$$

There are orders of at most two different colors on the same slab:

$$\sum_{c \in C} z_{cs} \leq 2 \text{ for every slab } s \in S$$

Finally, the objective function is to minimize the sum of the slab weights:

$$\min \sum_{s \in S, q \in S} q \times y_{sq} \text{ for } s \in S$$

In addition, the authors introduced in [5] a variable for each order whose value is the slab it uses ($Order[o] \in S$). These variables are linked to the binary variables via channeling constraints like ($Order[o] = s) \leftrightarrow (x_{os} = 1)$. The purpose of these variables is to state symmetry-breaking constraints and to define the search strategy. The strategy used is to choose first the order variable $Order[o]$ with minimum domain size and assign it to the slab with the smallest index. Pure constraint programming could solve problems having up to about 20 orders. By hybridizing constraint programming and integer programming, instances with 30 orders could be solved in about 1000s [5].

The basic model defined above is basically a linear model over binary variables. Such a model is well-suited to an integer programming solver. Integer programming solvers can tighten the formulation by adding cutting planes and use the relaxed optimal solution to guide the search. However for constraint programming solvers, this model involves few domain reductions and can be seen as a typical worst case. Moreover, this model involves different groups of binary variables, and it is not easy to determine how to branch on them. Should we start branching with order variables, or with slab weight variables ? Should we merge the groups ? A comparison has been made in [5] but there is no clear winner.

4 A Stronger Constraint Programming Model

The constraint programming model we propose is rather different from the basic one. For clarity, we will consider the minimization of the unused capacity of the selected slab, also called the *loss*. This is equivalent to the objective function of the basic model up to a constant. An obvious lower bound is 0. It is reached when the orders assigned to slabs fit exactly the slab weights. Consequently, it gives a clearer view of solution cost and of the distance to optimality that no longer depends on the order weights.

Example 2. *The solution in Example 1 above induces an total loss of* 2 *because slabs 1 and 3 are not fully filled*

Slab	*Orders*	*Weight sum*	*Slab weight*	*Loss*
1	*1, 2, 3*	*6*	*7*	*1*
2	*4, 5*	*9*	*9*	*0*
3	*6, 7, 8*	*17*	*18*	*1*
4	*9, 10*	*7*	*7*	*0*

To design a stronger constraint programming model we had to *unlinearize* the basic model in order to replace linear constraints by global and logical constraints which achieve more propagation more efficiently.

The first model change is in regards to the variables. Since an order uses a single slab, we can avoid creating a binary variable for each couple (order, slab) and instead introduce a single variable for each order that specifies the slab it uses. That is for each order $o \in O$ a variable x_o whose domain is S is created. The constraint stating that an order uses a single slab becomes implicit.

The variables x_o are the decision variables of the problem; the instantiation of these variables suffices to define completely a solution to the problem and the value of the objective function. Therefore, a good approach is to state all constraints only on those variables or, at most, to introduce auxiliary variables that are all fixed to a value when the decision variables are fixed. This permits the search strategy to be applied to the decision variables only and avoids the need to determine priorities between groups of variables. These priorities are often quite difficult to determine, and this is one of the drawbacks of the basic model.

Packing orders onto slabs can be expressed directly over the variables x_o. A straightforward approach is to constrain, for each slab s, the sum of weights of orders using the slab:

$$\sum_{o \in O} (x_o = s) \times w_o \leq u_k$$

where u_k is the maximum capacity of a slab. However, to compute the loss we need to know the load of each slab. An auxiliary load variable $l_s \in \{0, \dots, u_k\}$ can be introduced for each slab s and an equivalent constraint is stated instead:

$$l_s = \sum_{o \in O} (x_o = s) \times w_o$$

The upper bound on the l_s variables enforces constraint on the maximum slab weight. Note that variables l_s are all fixed when the variables x_o are all fixed. This formulation could be strengthened by replacing each linear constraint by a knapsack constraint. An arc-consistency algorithm has been given in [10]. Knapsack global constraints are also used in the `Comet` system [11]. An alternative stronger formulation is to replace the whole set of inequalities by the global packing constraint introduced in [9]. It constrains a set of items, given with their sizes, to be packed into a set of bins. The load of each bin is given as a variable. Upper bounds on load variables can be used to model the bin capacity. The packing constraint can be used to strengthen formulations not ony for bin-packing problem, but more generaly on assignment problems where capacity is involved such as warehouse location or resource allocation. The packing constraint achieves more domain reductions than the set of linear constraints above. We have used it to pack orders on slabs. It is stated over variables x_o and l_s and uses order weights w_o as item sizes:

$$\text{pack}([l_1, \ldots, l_n], [x_1, \ldots, x_n], [w_1, \ldots, w_n])$$

A straightforward way to express the loss on each slab is to introduce a variable $y_i \in \{0, u_1, u_2, \ldots, u_k\}$ representing the weight of the slab i. We can then state that the loss on slab s is $\text{loss}_s = (y_s - l_s)$. To achieve more propagation we can observe that the loss on a slab is simply a function of its load. For instance in the Example 1 above for a load of 12, the loss is 5, that is the difference between the load and the smallest slab weight that can contain the orders on that slab. The loss of a slab can thus be defined by

$$\text{loss}(\text{load}) = \min\{u_j \mid j \in \{1, \ldots, k\} \wedge u_j \geq \text{load}\} - \text{load}$$

Therefore the loss of a slab s can be expressed by a constraint in extension (that lists the set of solutions) where the number of solutions is equal to the largest slab weight. Most of the constraint solvers achieve arc-consistency on this constraint. In the Example 1 above the set of solutions is:

load	0	1	2	3	4	**5**	6	**7**	8	**9**	10	**11**	12	13	14	**15**	16	17	**18**
loss	0	4	3	2	1	0	1	0	1	0	1	0	3	2	1	0	2	1	0

A simpler way to express this constraint with the same perfect domain reduction is to use the good old element constraint that indexes the array of precomputed loss with the load variable l_s. This expression is $\text{element}(l_s, \text{loss})$. The objective function is thus

$$\min \sum_{s \in S} \text{element}(l_s,\ \text{loss})$$

Note that when the objective function is to minimize the sum of the slab weights, the loss array is replaced by the array of slab weights indexed by the load.

Now we can express the color constraints without introducing extra variables. First we need an expression that is equal to one when a color k is used on a

```
1.  using CP;

2.  int nbSlabs   = 10;
3.  int nbOrders  = 10;
4.  int nbColors  = 3;
5.  int nbCap     = 7;
6.  int capacities[1..nbCap] = [0, 5, 7, 9, 11, 15, 18];
7.  int weight[1..nbOrders] = [1, 3, 2, 9, 9, 11, 3, 3, 5, 2];
8.  // White = 0, Black = 1, Red = 2
9.  int colors[1..nbOrders] = [2, 1, 1, 2, 2, 0, 2, 0, 1, 2];

10. int maxCap  = max(i in 1..nbCap) capacities[i];
11. int loss[c in 0..maxCap]
12.       = min(i in 1..nbCap : capacities[i] >= c) capacities[i] - c;

13. dvar int x[1..nbOrders] in 1..nbSlabs;
14. dvar int l[1..nbSlabs] in 0..maxCap;

15. minimize sum(s in 1..nbSlabs) loss[l[s]];
16. subject to {
17.   pack(l, x, weight);
18.   forall(s in 1..nbSlabs)
19.     sum (c in 1..nbColors)
20.         (or(o in 1..nbOrders : colors[o] == c) (x[o] == s)) <= 2;
21. }
```

Fig. 1. An OPL 5.2 model for the steel mill slab design problem

slab s. Such an expression is simply modeled by a disjunction over order position variables x_o whose color c_o is equal to k:

$$\bigvee_{\{o \in O,\ c_o = \ k\}} (x_o = s)$$

The color constraint on a slab is then

$$\sum_{k \in C} \left(\bigvee_{\{o \in O,\ c_o = \ k\}} (x_o = s) \right) \leq 2$$

Figure 1 shows a complete OPL 5.2 model whose objective is to minimize the total loss. ILOG OPL 5.2 includes ILOG CP Optimizer 1.0, which is the ILOG constraint programming C++ library. From lines 2 to 9, the constants and arrays of the instance used in Example 1 are initialized. The `maxCap` constant is set to the maximum capacity of a slab at line 10. The array `loss` initialized at lines 11 and 12 contains the loss induced by each slab load. This is to be used in the objective function. At lines 13 and 14, the variables x (that represent order positions) and l (the slab load) are created. The cost function is defined at line 15. An element constraint in OPL is created by indexing a constant array with a variable. The pack constraint is stated at line 17. And for each slab, a color constraint is stated at lines 18 to 20.

5 A Search Strategy

The steel mill slab design can be seen as a bin-packing problem with color constraints. The orders must be packed onto slabs. Therefore we have implemented a typical search strategy for solving bin-packing problems. The strategy consists of

- choosing the order with the largest weight first and
- placing that order in the first available slab.

The choice of the variable follows the first-fail principle strategy: largest orders are the most difficult to assign and placing them first reduces the search space. The choice of a value involves grouping orders on a small set of slabs. Avoiding the orders being spread on too many slabs reduces the chances of creating a loss on several slabs and thus avoids producing solutions with a large loss. This strategy has been implemented within a depth-first search.

5.1 Test Instances

The instance provided with the problem definition in the CSPLIB is one with 111 orders. Previous studies of this problem have considered subinstances of this instance by keeping only the k first orders with k varying from 12 to 30. In order to have a precise evaluation of the effectiveness of our choices, we have considered all subinstances from $k = 12$ to $k = 110$ and, of course, the original instance. Every instance has a solution where the total loss is zero.

Our comparisons measure the computation time needed to reach an optimal solution. The experiments were made with ILOG CP Optimizer 1.0, a constraint programming library in C++ and we have run the test with a time limit of 1000 seconds on a PC with a Pentium-4 processor at 2.6 Mhz. The results given by our strategy are presented in Figure 2. The instances index the x-axis while the computation time (in seconds) to reach an optimal solution is on the y-axis. We were able to solve all the instances ranging from 12 to 74 orders in less than 200 seconds. This is much better than all previous constraint programming approaches to this problem.

5.2 Symmetry Breaking

Previous studies on the solution of the steel mill slab design problem insist on the importance of breaking symmetries by adding extra constraints. In [4], two main classes of symmetries are identified:

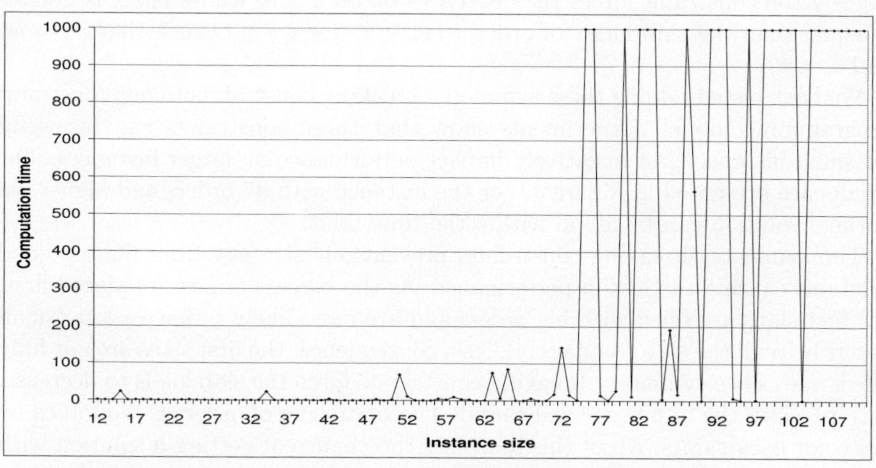

Fig. 2. Depth-first search

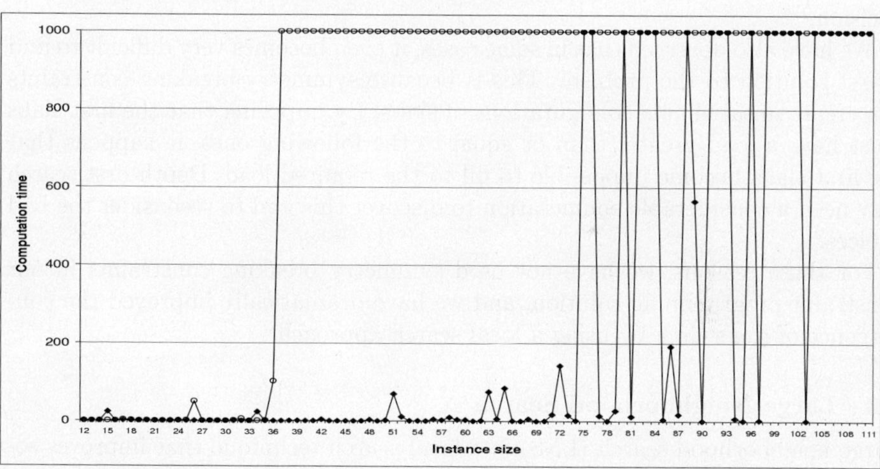

Fig. 3. Symmetry-breaking constraints (circles) versus no symmetry-breaking constraints (diamond-shaped)

1. Slab weight symmetries: slabs weights can be permuted without changing the objective value of the solution.
2. Identical order symmetries: two identical orders (w.r.t. weight and color) on different slabs can be swapped.

To avoid the search strategy producing symmetrical solutions, some additional constraints can be added. The first symmetry can be broken by forcing the slab s to be of greater or equal weight than $s+1$ ($l_s \geq l_{s+1}$). The second symmetry can be broken by adding a constraint for each pair or identical orders i and j.

If $i > j$ the constraint forces the order i to be on a slab whose index is greater or equal than the slab index of order j ($x_i \geq x_j$ for $i, j \in O$ such that $w_i = w_j$ and $c_i = c_j$) .

We have tested adding these symmetry breaking constraints to our constraint programming model. Experiments show that these constraints can be useful for small instances but negatively impact performance on larger instances. The results are presented in Figure 3. For the instance with 37 orders and higher, no optimal solution can be found within the time limit.

The symmetry-breaking constraints prevent our strategy from finding good solutions causing the loss in performance. As the biggest orders are placed first, the first slabs are filled with big orders and are more likely to have a loss (small orders help fill the slab completely). As a consequence, the first slabs are not fully filled, and, since symmetry breaking constraints force the slab loads to decrease, this increases the number of slabs used. The scattering of orders is reinforced by the color constraints. All of this increases the chance of getting a solution with a high loss. Depth-first search makes this even worse as a bad decision made at the beginning of the search to satisfy the symmetry-breaking constraints will be reconsidered only when search has exhausted the whole tree below that bad decision.

We have also observed that in some cases, it even becomes very difficult to find a first solution to the problem. This is because symmetry breaking constraints can create unsatisfiable configurations of slabs. By imposing that the first slabs must have a load greater than or equal to the following ones, it happens that the first slabs become impossible to fill to the required load. Depth-first search may need a considerable enumeration to discover this and to reconsider the bad choices.

For these reasons, we have not used symmetry breaking constraints in our constraint programming solution, and we have dramatically improved the convergence of the search by using a local search approach.

5.3 Large Neighborhood Search

Large neighborhood search (LNS) is a local search technique that improves solutions by solving small decision problems [8].

Assume we want to solve the optimization model

$$\min f(x) \text{ s.t. } M$$

where x are the decision variables, f is the objective function and M is the set of constraints. The LNS method starts from a solution x^* of M whose objective value is f^*. It first chooses a fragment F that is a set of equations $x_i = x_i^*$ and injects it in the model M. That is, it fixes the variables of the fragment to their value in the current solution but keeps the other variables unfixed. Additionally, a constraint is stated on the objective function to force it to be improved. This new model is called a *submodel* since its solution set is included in the solution set of M. A search method is then applied to the submodel

$$R = M \cup F \cup \{f(x) \leq f^* - \epsilon\}$$

Where ϵ is the (positive) optimality tolerance. Consequently when a solution is found in the submodel, it has a necessarily better objective function than the previous one, and it shares with the current solution the values of variables that are in the fragment F. The new solution found becomes the current solution, and the process is repeated.

This method is well suited to optimization in constraint programming because constraint programming is good at finding solutions in small constrained problems.

Example 3. *If we reconsider the data and solution in Example 1, the current solution is* $x_1^* = 1, x_2^* = 1, x_3^* = 1, x_4^* = 2, x_5^* = 2, x_6^* = 3, x_7^* = 3, x_8^* = 3, x_9^* = 4, x_{10}^* = 4$ *and the objective value of this solution is* 2. *Let* M *be the strong constraint programming model of Section 4. A possible fragment for LNS is* $F = \{x_2 = 1, x_3 = 1, x_4 = 2, x_5 = 2, x_6 = 3, x_9 = 4, x_{10} = 4\}$ *where only* x_1 *and* x_8 *are unfixed. The subproblem solved by LNS in this case is*

$$R = M \cup F \cup \{f(x) \leq 1\}$$

The subproblem is solved with a standard constraint programming search that is comprised of depth-first search and constraint propagation. If a good strategy is known for the solving the problem with depth-first search, it is in general also good for solving the subproblem as both have basically the same structure.

Example 4. *The submodel of the previous example contains an optimal solution. Instantiating the variable* x_1 *to* 3 *permits the reduction of the weight of slab* 1 *from* 7 *to* 5, *and its loss becomes 0. The slab 3 now has an order of weight one more, and it fills slab completely. The loss is thus 0. The new solution is*

Slab	*Orders*	*Weight sum*	*Slab weight*	*Loss*
1	*2, 3*	*5*	*5*	*0*
2	*4, 5*	*9*	*9*	*0*
3	*6, 7, 8, 1*	*18*	*18*	*0*
4	*9, 10*	*7*	*7*	*0*

This solution would have been harder to find than the previous one with the full search space. Having a small search space to explore (and of course, the right fragment) makes it easier to find.

In order for the LNS method to explore several neighborhoods and thus several fragments, the submodel is not solved completely. It is crucial to set a limit on the solution method. It can be a limit in time or on the size of the search tree. For instance, when the strategy has encountered a certain number of failures without finding a solution, one can consider that the fragment is not likely to lead to a solution and the search can be stopped. This limit on failures is often used in constraint programming based LNS methods, and the failure limit used is often quite small.

Large neighborhood search has improved dramatically the convergence of our search strategy. For the steel mill slab design problem, we have used the following configuration:

- the fragment size is chosen randomly (between 50% and 95% of the variables are fixed in the fragment);
- variables appearing in the fragment are chosen randomly until the required size is reached;
- load variables l_s are never included in the fragment, the load must not be fixed in order to allow the uninstantiated orders to be assigned to any slab to improve the solution;
- the search strategy for solving the subproblems is the one used for depth-first search (largest orders first, smallest index slab first);
- the failure limit is set to 60.

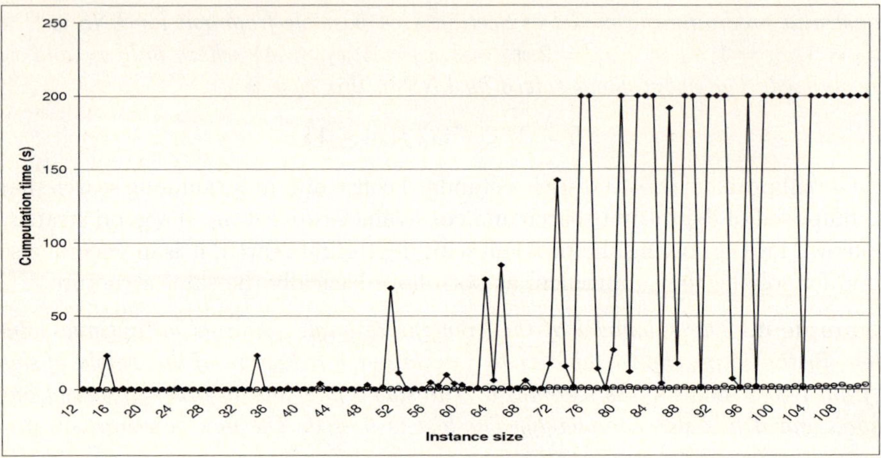

Fig. 4. Large neighborhood search (circles) versus depth-first search (diamond-shaped)

The results are shown in Figure 4. The largest instance with 111 orders is solved in 2.98 seconds and only 27 fragments are explored. All other smaller instances are solved in less than 3 seconds. Interestingly, even with different random seeds, the computation time does not vary much. This demonstrates the robustness of this approach.

6 Conclusion

The constraint programming model we have presented is based on logical and global constraints and is more effective than a linear model over binary variables. A dedicated search strategy used in conjunction with large neighborhood search was able to solve the CSPLIB instance in a few seconds. This demonstrates that a combination of a strong model, a dedicated strategy and randomization can make large neighborhood search effective.

The solutions developed for solving the steel mill slab design can be applied to solving the first-step problem (inventory matching) where orders are not necessarily all packed. Minimizing the weight of unpacked orders is also part of the objective function. The pack global constraint cannot be used any longer, and the strategy would need to be adapted. This is the topic of our current research.

References

1. Dawande, M., Kalagnanam, J., Sethuraman, J.: Variable-sized bin packing with color constraints. Electronic Notes in Discrete Mathematics 7 (2001)
2. Forrest, J., Ladanyi, L., Kalagnanam, J.: A column-generation approach to the multiple knapsack problem with color constraints. INFORMS Journal on Computing 18(1), 129–134 (2006)
3. Frisch, A., Miguel, I., Walsh, T.: Modelling a steel mill slab design problem. In: Proceedings of the IJCAI-01 Workshop on Modelling and Solving Problems with Constraints (2001)
4. Frisch, A., Miguel, I., Walsh, T.: Symmetry and implied constraints in the steel mill slab design problem. In: Walsh, T. (ed.) CP 2001. LNCS, vol. 2239. Springer, Heidelberg (2001)
5. Hnich, B., Kiziltan, Z., Miguel, I., Walsh, T.: Hybrid modelling for robust solving. Annals of Operations Research 130(1-4), 19–39 (2004)
6. Kalagnanam, J., Dawande, M., Trumbo, M., Lee, H.S.: Inventory matching problems in the steel industry. Technical Report RC 21171, IBM Research Report, T.J. Watson Research Center (1988)
7. Prestwich, S.: Search and modelling issues in steel mill slab design. Technical Report 4/148, Cork Constraint Computation Center (2002)
8. Shaw, P.: Using constraint programming and local search methods to solve vehicle routing problems. In: Maher, M.J., Puget, J.-F. (eds.) Principles and Practice of Constraint Programming - CP98. LNCS, vol. 1520, pp. 417–431. Springer, Heidelberg (1998)
9. Shaw, P.: A constraint for bin-packing. In: Wallace, M. (ed.) CP 2004. LNCS, vol. 3258, pp. 648–662. Springer, Heidelberg (2004)
10. Trick, M.: A dynamic programming approach for consistency and propagation for knapsack constraints. In: Proceedings of the Third International Workshop on Integration of AI and OR Techniques in Constraint Programming for Combinatorial Optimization Problems (CPAIOR-01), Lille, France, pp. 113–124 (2001)
11. van Hentenryck, P., Michel, L.: Constraint-Based Local Search. MIT Press, Cambridge, Mass. (2005)
12. Walser, J.P.: Solving linear pseudo-boolean constraints with local search. In: Proceedings of the Eleventh Conference on Artificial Intelligence, pp. 269–274 (1997)

Constraint-Based Temporal Reasoning for E-Learning with LODE

Rosella Gennari and Ornella Mich

KRDB, CS Faculty, Free University of Bozen-Bolzano
Piazza Domenicani 3, 39100 Bolzano, Italy
gennari@inf.unibz.it, mich@itc.it

Abstract. LODE is a logic-based web tool for Italian deaf children. It aims at stimulating global reasoning on e-stories written in a verbal language. Presently, we are focusing on temporal reasoning, that is, LODE stimulates children to reason with global temporal relations between events possibly distant in a story. This is done through apt exercises and with the support of a constraint programming system. Children can also reinvent the e-story by rearranging its events along a new temporal order; it is the task of the constraint system to determine the consistency of the temporally reorganised story and provide children with feedback. To the best of our knowledge, LODE is the first e-learning tool for Italian deaf children that aims at stimulating global reasoning on whole e-stories.

Keywords: constraint programming, automated temporal reasoning, e-learning, assistive technology.

1 Introduction

In the last years, much research in deaf studies and computer science has been devoted to applications for sign languages; roughly speaking, a *sign language* is a gestural-visual language with signs as lexical units, whereas a *verbal language* is an oral-auditive language with words as lexical units. Less attention seems to be paid to e-learning tools for improving the literacy of deaf children in verbal languages. Our LOgic-based e-tool for DEaf children (LODE) belongs in this latter class. In the following, we motivate the need of an e-learning tool such as LODE and then briefly outline our LODE tool.

1.1 The Problem

Learning to read and write effectively can be a difficult task for deaf people. Due to a limited exposition to the language in its spoken form in their first years of life, they lack the primary, natural means of acquiring literacy skills: "deaf children have unique communication needs: unable to hear the continuous, repeated flow of language interchange around them, they are not automatically exposed to the enormous amounts of language stimulation experienced by hearing children" [24].

C. Bessiere (Ed.): CP 2007, LNCS 4741, pp. 90–104, 2007.

Research on deaf subjects points out that deaf people hardly achieve verbal language literacy; they tend to reason on single episodes and show difficulties in formulating coherent global relations, such as temporal relations, between episodes of narratives in a verbal language [5], to the effect that their ability of reading does not often go beyond that of a eight-year old child [20]. As reported in [5], this attitude can also depend on the kind of "literacy interventions addressed to deaf children" which tend to "focus on single sentences and the grammatical aspects of text production". A novel literacy e-tool for them should thus focus on global deductive reasoning.

1.2 Our Proposal

Given that limited literacy skills constitute an obstacle to the integration of deaf people into our society, our purpose is to develop an e-learning tool for deaf children which stimulates the global reasoning on texts written in verbal Italian. To this end, LODE presents children with e-stories and invites children to globally reason on each of them; that is, children are elicited to analyse and produce relations between events, even distant in the story, so that the relations are consistent with the story and possibly implicit in it.

In its current version, LODE focuses on a specific type of relations, namely, temporal relations; it narrates temporally rich stories and then stimulates children to create a coherent network of temporal relations out of each LODE's story. In order to do so, LODE heavily employs an automated reasoner, namely, a constraint programming system.

Section 2 provides the essential background on reasoning with temporal relations by using constraint programming. Then the paper delves into LODE. Section 3 outlines the educational exercises of LODE and how they aim at stimulating global reasoning with temporal relations. The architecture of LODE is discussed in Sect. 4; there, we explain the pivotal role of constraint programming and how it allows us to implement the educational exercises of LODE. We relate LODE to other e-tools for deaf children in Sect. 5, highlighting its novelty in the e-learning landscape of e-tools for deaf children, and conclude with an assessment of our work in Sect. 7.

2 Background on Temporal Reasoning with Constraints

Temporal Reasoning is a branch of Artificial Intelligence (AI) and involves the *formal representation of time* and a computational *reasoning system* for it. An instance of a temporal reasoning problem is given by the following exercise of LODE; the excerpt is taken from a simplified version of *The Ugly Duckling* by H.C. Andersen.

> Mammy duck is brooding: she has five eggs, four are small, and one is big. All of a sudden, while she is still brooding, the small eggshells crack and four little yellow ducklings peep out. Mammy duck watches the big

egg but sees no signs of cracking... So she decides to keep on brooding. After some days, while she is brooding, also the big eggshell cracks and an ugly grey duckling peeps out...

Exercise: *do the small eggshells crack* before *the big eggshell cracks?*

We use it in the remainder to explain the time representation, in Subs. 2.1, and the computational reasoning system, in Subs. 2.2, that LODE adopts.

2.1 Time Representation à la Allen

Here we adopt intervals as the primitive entities for representing time; each interval is uniquely associated with a time event. Between any two pairs of events, there is an *atomic Allen* relation, namely, a relation of the form

before, meets, overlaps, starts, during, finishes, equals

or rel^{-1}, where rel is one of the above relations and rel^{-1} is the inverse of rel. See Fig. 1 for an intuitive graphical representation of the atomic Allen relations between two events, $e1$ and $e2$. The Allen relations are employed whenever

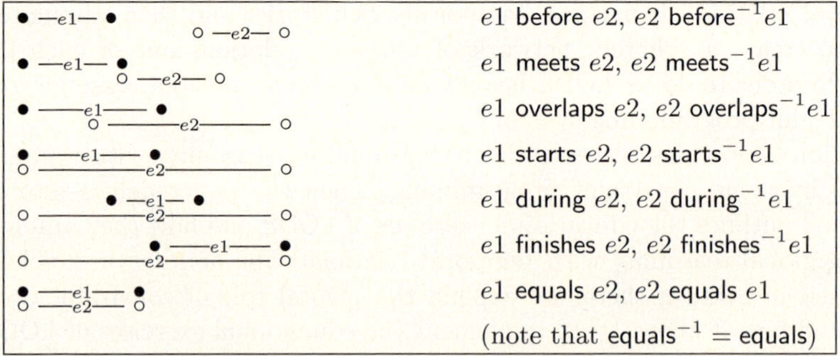

Fig. 1. The atomic Allen relations

temporal information boils down to qualitative relations between events, e.g.,

"the small eggshells crack *while* Mammy duck broods"; (1)

in terms of the Allen relations, the sentence (1) states that the relation during can hold between the event "the small eggshells crack" and the event "Mammy duck broods". By way of contrast, "the small eggshells crack *after 2 days*" is a quantitative temporal information.

As Allen arguments [1], "uncertain information" can be represented by means of unions of the atomic Allen relations. Formally, let A denote the class of the atomic Allen relations. Then the class 2^A forms a relational algebra with the operations of union $\cup$, composition $\odot$, and inverse $^{-1}$. In particular, the composition operation is used in deductions with the Allen relations. For instance, the result of the composition before ⊙ before is before; this means that

`if` $e1$ before $e2$ and $e2$ before $e3$
`then` $e1$ before $e3$.

2.2 Constraint Programming for Automated Temporal Reasoning

Constraint programming is a flourishing programming paradigm implemented in several constraint programming systems, e.g., ECL^{i}PS^e, a Constraint Logic Programming (CLP) system. Performing automated temporal reasoning with constraint programming means first modelling a temporal problem in a suitable formalism and then solving it in an automated manner with a constraint programming system. In the following, we introduce the basics on constraint modelling and solving, taking them from [4].

Constraint modelling. Given the temporal reasoning problem above, the constraint programmer *models* it as a *constraint satisfaction problem.* In essence, this is given by

- finitely many variables, $x_1, \ldots, x_n$,
- each ranging on a domain D_i of values,
- and a set of constraints, namely, relations of the form $C \subseteq D_{i_1} \times \cdots \times D_{i_m}$.

A tuple of domain values $a_1, \ldots, a_n$ for the variables $x_1, \ldots, x_n$ is a *solution* to the problem if it belongs to all the constraints of the problem. When a value a_i for x_i participates in a solution to the problem, we will say that a_i is *consistent* with the problem.

A temporal reasoning problem can be modelled as a constraint problem as done in [3]. We expound this modelling in the context of LODE in Sect. 4. As an example, take the temporal reasoning problem in p. 91. The ordered pair of events "the small eggshells crack" and "the big eggshell cracks" gives a variable; its domain is the set of the atomic Allen relations; the temporal reasoning problem restricts the domain of the variable to before, and this is a unary constraint. The relation before is consistent with the considered problem.

Constraint solving. Once a temporal reasoning problem is modelled as a constraint problem in a suitable programming language (e.g., CLP), a constraint programming system (e.g., ECL^{i}PS^e) can be invoked to *solve* it. In this setting, to solve a problem means

- to decide on the consistency of a relation with the problem, e.g., before between "the big eggshells crack" and "the small eggshell cracks",
- or to deduce an/all the Allen relation/relations between two events, e.g., "the big eggshell cracks" and "the small eggshells crack", which are consistent with the problem and implicit in it.

The LODE's exercises rely on both these solving capabilities of a constraint programming system, namely, that of deciding on and that of deducing new Allen relations, consistent with a LODE's story. First we need to present such exercises, then we can return to constraint programming by explaining its role in the LODE's architecture and in solving the exercises.

3 LODE: Educational Exercises

LODE presents a list of e-stories the child can choose among. They are simplified versions of traditional children tales, such as *The Ugly Duckling*, so that the language is more suitable to a 8-year old deaf child; they are also enriched with explicit temporal relations so as to focus the attention of the child on temporal reasoning. The child has to choose a story from the list in order to begin his/her work session.

3.1 Dictionary of Difficult Words

The first exercises build a sort of dictionary of the most unusual words for deaf children. Single words are proposed on the screen together with an image explaining their meaning and a short textual explanation; example sentences are also available. This preliminary phase simplifies the comprehension of the story and the association grapheme-meaning in beginning readers, a step which may be necessary with young deaf users. Children can also consult back the dictionary during the other work sessions of LODE.

Future versions of LODE will also feature a translation of the dictionary words into Italian Sign Language (*Lingua Italiana dei Segni*, LIS) to facilitate their comprehension to LIS speakers.

3.2 Global Reasoning Exercises

Then the chosen story is presented, split across different pages. There are two or three sentences with an explanatory image on each page. The text is visually predominant so that the child must concentrate on it and not on the image. Every few pages, the child starts a new exercise session for *reasoning* on the tale. In LODE, we have two main types of reasoning exercises: comprehension exercises and production exercises.

Comprehension. In comprehension exercises, the child is presented with temporal relations connecting events of the story; the relations may be implicit in it. More precisely, the child is proposed four temporal relations. The child is asked to judge which relations are inconsistent with the text he/she has already read, playing the role of the teacher who eliminates the incoherent ones. The four cases are constructed with the assistance of the constraint programming system to determine which temporal relations are (in)consistent with the story.

Production. The child is asked to tackle three main kinds of production exercises, explained in the following.

P1. The child is shown an unordered sequence of temporal events extracted from the story; his/her task is to drag the events into the right temporal sequence, namely, one which is consistent with the story. The consistency is decided by the constraint programming system.

P2. The child is shown scattered sentence units extracted from the given story; then he/she should compose a grammatically correct sentence with them, forming a temporal relation consistent with the story and which may be implicit in the story. For instance, suppose that the available sentence units are: `before`, `while`, `after`, `the big eggshell`, `cracks`, `the small eggshells`, `crack`. Two are the possible correct sentences the child can compose, consistent with the tale. One is: `the small eggshells crack before the big eggshell cracks`. The other sentence is: `the big eggshell cracks after the small eggshells crack`. If the child composes a wrong sentence, because it is ungrammatical or inconsistent with the story, LODE will suggest how to correct the sentence with the help of the constraint programming system and a natural language processor for Italian.

P3. The child can also reinvent the chosen e-story by using selected events of the e-story. More precisely, first LODE proposes a set of events extracted from the chosen e-story. Then the child re-creates his/her own story by reordering the events along the timeline, to the child's liking. Anytime, the child can check whether the temporal relations are consistent in his/her story, e.g., it is not the case that an event is simultaneously before and during another; he/she can also ask for the assistance of LODE, or better, of the constraint programming system of LODE in setting new temporal relations between events, consistent with his/her story.

3.3 Final Remarks

LODE assists children in all the exercises, e.g., they are shown the events they may reason on. The difficulty of the exercises for reasoning increases with the portion of the story the child has to reason on. Thus, first LODE proposes the simpler exercises: these relate two temporal events which occur in the portion of the tale, temporally rich, that the child has just read. If the score reached so far by the child is reasonably good, then LODE proposes the more challenging exercises, namely, those that require a deep global understanding of the story and the creation of global temporal relations: these exercises relate two temporal events, one of the current session and the other of a previous session—the farther is this session the more difficult is the exercise.

Moreover, note that the comprehension exercises aim at stimulating the deduction of global relations between events of the story; the production exercises demand this and something else, that is, to compose parts of the story. Therefore, the production exercises also aim at teaching children Italian grammar. To stimulate children to write, web users of LODE will also be invited to collaborate and exchange their productions via a blog.

Through all its exercises, LODE stimulates children to learn and reason on e-stories in an inductive and implicit manner.

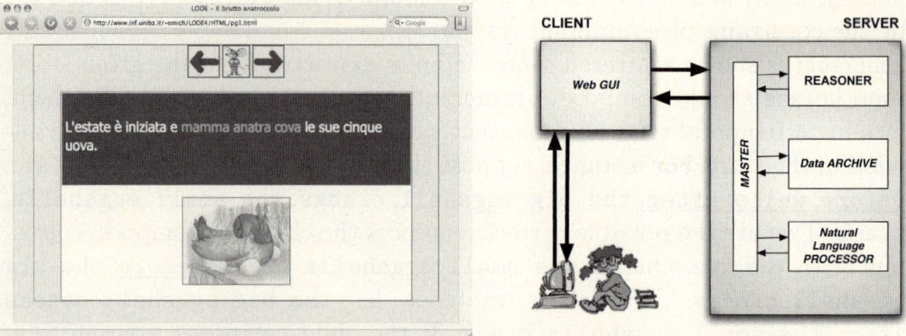

Fig. 2. LODE: a screen-shot of a client session on the left and the client-server architecture on the right

4 LODE: The Architecture and the Constraint-based Module

LODE has a web-based client-server architecture; see Fig. 2. We opt for this for several reasons. First, it makes LODE independent of the Operating System (OS). Therefore, users are free to run LODE on the preferred OS with their web browser. Second, it makes easier the updating of LODE; new features can be implemented without affecting the users, e.g., no need of installing new versions of LODE. Third, a web-based architecture promotes collaborative study: when they are on-line, the LODE users can work together and exchange their own stories or comments.

4.1 The Modular Architecture

The client is a graphical user interface (GUI); see the left side of Fig. 2. This is an AJAX application compatible with most web browsers, e.g., Firefox-Mozilla, Internet Explorer, Safari, Opera. It works as the interface between the LODE user and the real system, the server, which runs on a remote machine.

The server has a modular structure. The main modules are: 1) the *stories' database*, 2) the *Constraint-based Automated Reasoner* and 3) the *Natural Language Processor*; see the right side Fig. 2.

1) The current stories' database is a simple repository structured as a file system. It contains temporally enriched versions of famous children stories, in XHTML format. Events and relations are tagged in XHTML à la TimeML [23], the main difference being that the used Allen relations can be non-atomic; see Fig. 3 for an example.
2) The *Constraint-based Automated Reasoner* is composed of three main parts: a) ECL^{i}PS^e, the constraint (logic) programming system; b) the *knowledge base*, namely, an ECL^{i}PS^e program with the inverse and composition operations for the Allen relations; c) the *domain knowledge*, consisting of constraint problems modelling the temporal information of the e-stories in the

database. The Constraint-based Automated Reasoner is employed in the composition and production exercises to assist children in their deductions.

3) The *Natural Language Processor* will check if the user's sentences are grammatically correct in the production exercises.

The most important module of the architecture is the Constraint-based Automated Reasoner.

4.2 The Constraint-Based Automated Reasoner

Each e-story in the database is modelled as a constraint problem in a semi-automated manner; the problem is included in the domain knowledge and then solved by the chosen constraint programming system. Let us make precise what we mean by modelling and solving in the context of LODE; for their more general presentation, refer back to Subsect. 2.2.

Constraint modelling in LODE. First we illustrate the main steps of the modelling with an example and then we generalise it.

Example. Hereby is part of the excerpt of the LODE's story introduced in Sect. 2:

> The small eggshells crack. Mammy duck watches the big egg... After some days, [...] the big eggshell cracks. (2)

The excerpt has 3 temporal events, tagged in the XHTML code as illustrated in Fig. 3:

– "the small eggshells crack", classified as E1;
– "Mammy duck watches the big egg", classified as E2;
– "the big eggshell cracks", classified as E3;

The corresponding constraint problem, stored in the domain knowledge of $\mathsf{ECL}^i\mathsf{PS}^e$, has variables

```
<EVENT class="E1">
  The small eggshells crack
</EVENT>
<EVENT class="E2">
  Mammy duck watches the big egg
</EVENT>
<TLINK event="E1" relatedToEvent="E2" relType="before OR meets"/>
<EVENT class="E3">
  The big eggshell cracks
</EVENT>
<TLINK event="E2" relatedToEvent="E3" relType="before"/>
```

Fig. 3. A sample of a tagged story in LODE

- E1E2 with domain the set of the atomic Allen relations between E1 and E2,
- E2E3 with domain the set of the atomic Allen relations between E2 and E3,
- E1E3 with domain the set of the atomic Allen relations between E1 and E3,

and constraints of two main types:

C1. unary constraints formalising the temporal relations of the excerpt (which are tagged with `TLINK` in the XHTML code in Fig. 3), that is: a constraint stating that E1E2 is before or meets; a constraint stating that E2E3 is before;
C2. a ternary constraint on E1, E2 and E3 formalising the Allen composition operation; the ternary constraint on E1, E2 and E3 yields that before can hold between E1 and E3 since before can hold between E1 and E2, and between E2 and E3.

See Fig. 4 for the straightforward translation of the above constraints in the language of ECL^{i}PS^e.

```
E1E2 &:: [before,meets],
E2E3 &:: [before],
allen_composition(E1E2, E2E3, E1E3)
```

Fig. 4. The constraint model in ECL^{i}PS^e corresponding to the sample in Fig. 3

Model. As illustrated in the above example, here we adopt the same constraint model for qualitative temporal reasoning as in [3]. More precisely, the knowledge base contains

- the set A of atomic Allen relations providing the domain of the variables,
- a ternary relation, namely, allen_composition, for the composition of the Allen relations, e.g., allen_composition(before, before, before).

Let $E := \{\text{E1}, \ldots, \text{En}\}$ be the set of events tagged in a story of LODE. Then the domain knowledge of the constraint-based module contains the following:

- variables EiEj of ordered pairs of events Ei and Ej of E; the domain of the EiEj is the set A of the atomic Allen relations;
- for each variable EiEj, a unary constraint C(EiEj) on EiEj which restricts the relations from A to those that are declared in the story (e.g., see item C1 above);
- for each triple Ei, Ej and Ek of events from E, a ternary constraint C(EiEj, EjEk, EiEk) stating that each relation in EiEk comes from the composition of EiEj and EjEk (e.g., see item C2 above).

Constraint solving in LODE. In LODE, we employ both the following solving capabilities of a constraint programming system such as ECL^{i}PS^e:

- that of deciding on the consistency of a temporal constraint problem in the domain knowledge,

– that of deducing a/all the consistent Allen relation/relations between two events of a temporal constraint problem in the domain knowledge.

These constraint solving capabilities are employed in LODE in two main manners:

– to assist the LODE developers in the creation of the exercises; the constraint programming system allows us to automatically *deduce* the relations between events which are consistent with the e-story, such as before between E1 and E3 of (2);
– to assist children in the resolution of exercises. In the comprehension exercises and in some production exercises (see Sect. 3), the constraint programming system can be used to *decide* on the consistency of the relations proposed by children. Moreover, in specific production exercises, a child can recreate his/her own story, setting a different order among events of the story along the timeline; then he/she can (transparently) query the constraint system to *decide* on the consistency of the recreated story or to *deduce* a/the consistent relation/relations between the considered events.

Final remarks: Why Constraint Programming in LODE. Constraint programming is thus a backbone of LODE; in the following, we try to sum up the main reasons for using constraint programming in LODE; we split our summary in two parts, one for constraint modelling, the other for constraint solving.

Constraint modelling

– First of all, the constraint modelling is human readable as it is closer to the structure of the temporal reasoning problem; by way of contrast, a SAT encoding would be less manageable and readable for the modeller.
– The modelling can also be semi-automated: events and explicit relations of an e-story are first tagged in XHTML; then a script automatically reads the XHTML tags and translates them into variables and constraints of the corresponding constraint problem.
– Last but not least, the constraint model for temporal reasoning that we adopted here allows us to employ a generic constraint programming system, such as $\mathsf{ECL}^i\mathsf{PS}^e$, as is. In other words, this constraint model does not demand to implement dedicated algorithms for temporal reasoning with Allen relations; for instance, with this model, we can exploit constraint propagation in the form of hyper-arc consistency which is already available in the propia library of $\mathsf{ECL}^i\mathsf{PS}^e$; instead, with the constraint model described in [12], we should use and implement path consistency.

Constraint solving

– Thanks to the solving capabilities of the constraint programming system, users of LODE can create new temporally consistent e-stories out of the available ones: a user of LODE can query the constraint programming system to decide on the consistency of the relations in his/her story, or to deduce new temporal relations that can be consistently added to his/her story.

- Using constraint programming spares the LODE developers manual work in the creation of the exercises, a task which is tedious and prone to human errors: instead of creating, manually, a series of exercises, e-stories are first modelled as constraint problems; then the relations of the reasoning exercises, introduced in Sect. 3, are deduced using the constraint programming system.
- Moreover, the exercises created in this manner can be easily updated, new exercises can be introduced and solved on the fly using the constraint programming system.
- Although the efficiency in solving temporal problems is not a critical feature of LODE at present, it may become a critical issue in future and more ambitious versions of the tool; in this respect, the model and the different constraint propagation and search procedures already available in the chosen constraint programming system will be of pivotal importance.

5 Related Work

Currently, research in deaf studies and computer science seems to mostly revolve around applications for sign languages, such as LIS, e.g., see [7,16]. Considerable less attention seems to be devoted to the development of e-learning tools for the literacy of deaf children in verbal languages. This impression is confirmed by our overview of this type of e-learning tools. We present the main ones related to LODE in the remainder.

5.1 Italian Tools

In Italy, three systems were developed in the '90s to tackle different aspects of verbal Italian lexicon or grammar: *Articoli* [6] aims at teaching Italian articles (e.g., gender agreement); *Carotino* [8] is an interactive tool for teaching simple Italian phrases; *Pro-Peanuts* [21] deals with the correct use of pronouns. Please, note that none of these tools were developed exclusively for deaf children. This is clear in a tool such as Carotino, where instructions for children presume a certain knowledge of written verbal Italian and do not focus on issues with verbal Italian which are specific to deaf children.

There are several tools that aim at teaching stories to deaf or hearing-impaired children. In order to facilitate the integration of a deaf girl into an Italian primary school, teachers and students of the school created *Fabulis* [11], a collection of famous stories for children narrated using text and images, based on gestures and LIS signs. Another application born at school is *Nuvolina* [19], the result of a project realised in a fourth class of an Italian primary school. Also this project aimed at integrating a deaf girl into the class. *Nuvolina* is a multimedia tale with contents in Italian, English and French, written and spoken. The version in verbal Italian is also presented in LIS by means of short videos.

In the area of bilingual tools, employing LIS and verbal Italian, we found *Gli Animali della Savana* [2]. This is a multimedia software based on text, images and videos, featuring an actor who translates the written text in LIS; assisted by a cartoon (a lion), the user navigates through a series of pages presenting the life of 10 wild animals. A more recent and ambitious project is *Tell me a Dictionary* [15,22], the purpose of which is to offer both deaf and hearing children an interactive instrument to discover and compare the lexicon of LIS and Italian. *Tell me a Dictionary* is a multimedia series of six DVDs plus book volumes [15].

We also found references to a tool developed in 1994, *Corso di Lettura* [10], which aims at improving the reading capabilities of hearing-impaired children. Alas, we could not find further information on the tool besides this.

5.2 English Tools

The primary goal of the ICICLE [14,17] researchers was to employ natural language processing and generation to tutor deaf students on their written English. ICICLE's interaction with the user takes the form of a cycle of user input and system response. The cycle begins when a user submits a piece of writing to be reviewed by the system. The system then performs a syntactic analysis on this writing, determines its errors, and constructs a response in the form of tutorial feedback. This feedback is aimed towards making the student aware of the nature of the errors found in the writing and giving him or her the information needed to correct them.

CornerStones [18] is a technology-infused approach to literacy development for early primary children who are deaf or hard of hearing. Academic experts in literacy and deafness, along with teachers of deaf students participated in its development. An essential element of Cornerstones is a story taken from the PBS's literacy series *Between the Lions*, complemented by versions of the story in American Sign Language and other visual-spatial systems for communicating with deaf children. Cornerstones developers evaluated their system with children and teachers and results of their evaluation demonstrated an increase in students' knowledge of selected words from pre-test to post-test.

FtL [9] has not been developed for deaf or hard of hearing children, but this type of users has also been considered. FtL is a comprehensive computer-based reading program that has been designed to teach beginning and early readers to read with good comprehension. FtL consists of three integrated components: a Managed Learning Environment (MLE) that tracks and displays student progress and manages an individual study plan for each student; Foundational Skills Reading Exercises, which teach and practice basic reading skills, such as alphabet knowledge and word decoding, providing the foundation for fluent reading; Interactive Books, which represent the state of the art in integration of human language and animation technologies to enable conversational interaction with a Virtual Tutor that teaches fluent reading and comprehension of text. The final evaluation of FtL produced significant learning gains for letter and word recognition for kindergarten students.

5.3 Final Remarks

According to our overview of Italian and non-Italian projects for deaf children, and to the best of our knowledge, LODE is the first web e-learning tool that tackles literacy issues of deaf children which go beyond the lexicon and grammar of a verbal language, that is: LODE addresses *global deductive reasoning* on stories, and LODE does it with the support of a constraint-based automated reasoner. Table 1 gives a summative analysis of LODE, comparing it with the principal and assessed tools for the literacy improvement of deaf children.

Table 1. Tools for literacy improvement: a comparative analysis

	ICICLE	Cornerstones	FtL	LODE
Content type	user's input	famous stories	interactive books	famous stories
Use of sign language	yes	yes	no	planned
Dialogue interface	yes	no	yes	yes
Reading comprehension	no	no	yes	yes
Active feedback	yes	no	no	yes
Syntax/grammar analysis	yes	no	no	planned
Speech recognition	no	no	yes	no
Global deductive reasoning	no	no	no	yes

6 Future Work

LODE is being evaluated into three main phases. The first evaluation phase is almost over; LIS interpreters and teachers for deaf children from the Talking Hands Association and the Italian National Institute for the Assistance and Protection of the Deaf (ENS), logopaedists and a cognitive psychologist have tested a preliminary version of LODE and provided us with positive informative feedback on its learning goals and strategies.

The second and third evaluation phases will directly involve deaf children; the second phase will be done in class with the assistance of a teacher from ENS and a cognitive psychologist; the third phase will involve children at home. The second evaluation phase will test the usability of LODE and, in particular, which is the most effective way of visually representing the exercises of LODE. The third evaluation phase will test the effectiveness of LODE and will involve circa 15 deaf children. As confirmed by our own experience, the assistance of children and their teachers is fundamental for developing a tool interesting and useful for children.

Last but not least, the application of constraint programming in LODE goes beyond temporal reasoning: after the evaluation phase, we are going to extend LODE to other kinds of global deductive reasoning, critical for deaf children and for which constraint programming can be beneficial.

7 Conclusions

In this paper, we presented our e-learning web-based tool for deaf children: LODE. The tool tackles problematic issues encountered in their written productions in a verbal language, related to deductive global reasoning; see Subsect. 1.1.

Presently, we are focusing on global temporal reasoning. In Sect. 2, we introduced temporal reasoning with Allen relations and motivated their use in the context of LODE; note that the relations are visually represented as explained in [13] because LODE is for deaf children. In Sect. 3, we summed up the educational exercises of LODE; we showed how the so-called reasoning exercises aim at stimulating global reasoning on stories, and not on isolated sentences of the stories.

In particular, these exercises of LODE demand the use of the automated reasoner embedded in LODE, namely, a constraint programming system. In Sect. 4, explaining the web-based architecture of LODE, we presented in details and motivated such a use of constraint programming in LODE, both in terms of the adopted constraint model for temporal reasoning problems and in terms of the constraint solving capabilities of a system such as $\mathsf{ECL}^i\mathsf{PS}^e$.

In Sect. 5, we overviewed and compared with LODE several e-learning tools that address literacy issues of deaf or hearing-impaired people. According to our overview and to the best of our knowledge, LODE is the first web-based e-learning tool which aims at stimulating global deductive reasoning on whole e-stories in a verbal language, such as Italian, by employing a constraint-based automated reasoner.

Acknowledgement. Among the others, we wish to thank B. Arfé, S. Brand, the ENS of Trento (in particular, N. Hy Thien), Talking Hands (in particular, F. De Carli), M. Valente and the anonymous referees for their assistance.

References

1. Allen, J.F.: Mantaining Knowledge about Temporal Intervals. Comm. of ACM 26, 832–843 (1983)
2. Animali della Savana, G.: Retrieved (October 24, 2006) from `http://www.areato.org/noquadri/ausiliDinamici/AusDnm_00_Titolo.Asp?IDAUSILIO=106&FORMATO=G`
3. Apt, K.R., Brand, S.: Constraint-based Qualitative Simulation. In: Proc. of the 12th International Symposium on Temporal Representation and Reasoning (TIME'05), pp. 26–34 (2005)
4. Apt, K.R., Wallace, M.G.: Constraint Logic Programming using ECLiPSe. Cambridge University Press, Cambridge (2006)
5. Arfé, B., Boscolo, P.: Causal Coherence in Deaf and Hearing Students' Written Narratives. Discourse Processes 42(3), 271–300 (2006)
6. Articoli: Retrieved (October 24, 2006) from `http://www.anastasis.it/AMBIENTI/NodoCMS/CaricaPagina.asp?ID=36`
7. Bartolini, S., Bennati, P., Giorgi, R.: Sistema per la Traduzione in Lingua Italiana dei Segni: Blue Sign Translator / Wireless Sign System. In: Proc. of the 50th AIES National Conference (2004)
8. Carotino: Retrieved (October 24, 2006) from `http://www.anastasis.it/AMBIENTI/NodoCMS/CaricaPagina.asp?ID=40`
9. Cole, R., Massaro, D., Rundle, B., Shobaki, K., Wouters, J., Cohen, M., Beskow, J., Stone, P., Connors, P., Tarachow, A., Solcher, D.: New Tools for Interactive Speech and Language Training: Using Animated Conversational Agents in the Classrooms of Profoundly Deaf Children

10. di Lettura, C.: Retrieved (October 24, 2006) from http://www.anastasis.it/AMBIENTI/NodoCMS/CaricaPagina.asp?ID=35
11. Fabulis: Retrieved (October 24, 2006) from http://www.bonavitacola.net/fabulis/
12. Gennari, R.: Temporal Reasoning and Constraint Programming: a Survey. CWI Quarterly 11(2–3) (1998)
13. Gennari, R., Mich, O.: LODE: Global Reasoning on e-Stories for Deaf Children. In: Proc. of the Engineered Applications of Semantic Web (SWEA 2007), invited session of the 11th KES conference, to be published in the LNAI/LNCS series (2007)
14. ICICLE: Retrieved (January 24, 2007) from http://www.eecis.udel.edu/research/icicle/
15. Insolera, E., Militano, G., Radutzky, E., Rossini, A.: Pilot Learning Strategies in Step with New Technologies: LIS and Italian in a Bilingual Multimedia Context 'Tell me a Dictionary'. In: Vettori, C. (ed.) Proc. of the 2nd Workshop on the Representation and Processing of Sign Languages, LREC 2006 (2006)
16. Mertzani, M., Denmark, C., Day, L.: Forming Sign Language Learning Environments in Cyberspace. In: Vettori, C. (ed.) Proc. of the 2nd Workshop on the Representation and Processing of Sign Languages, LREC 2006 (2006)
17. Michaud, L.N., McCoy, K.F., Pennington, C.: An Intelligent Tutoring System for Deaf Learners of Written English. In: Proc. of ASSETS'00 (2000)
18. NCAM-CornerStones: Retrieved (January 24, 2007) from http://ncam.wgbh.org/cornerstones/overview.html
19. Nuvolina: Retrieved (October 24, 2006) (1998) from http://www.areato.org/noquadri/ausiliDinamici/AusDnm_01_Dettaglio.Asp?IDAUSILIO=229 IDSEZIONE=5&FORMATO=G&VETRINA=N
20. Paul, P.V.: Literacy and Deafness: the Development of Reading, Writing, and Literate Thought. Allyn & Bacon (1998)
21. Pro-peanuts: Retrieved (October 24, 2006) (1998) from http://www.ciscl.unisi.it/persone/chesi/laurea/str.htm
22. Tell me a Dictionary: Retrieved (October 24, 2006) (2005) from http://www.lismediait/demo01/home.html
23. TimeML: Retrieved (March 10, 2007) from http://www.cs.brandeis.edu/~jamesp/arda/time/
24. UNESCO: Education of Deaf Children and Young People. Guides for Special Needs Education. Paris (1987)

Scheduling for Cellular Manufacturing

Roman van der Krogt[1], James Little[1], Kenneth Pulliam[2], Sue Hanhilammi[2], and Yue Jin[3]

[1] Cork Constraint Computation Centre
Department of Computer Science
University College Cork, Cork, Ireland
{roman,jlittle}@4c.ucc.ie
[2] Alcatel-Lucent System Integration Center, Columbus, Ohio
[3] Bell Labs Research Center Ireland

Abstract. Alcatel-Lucent is a major player in the field of telecommunications. One of the products it offers to network operators is wireless infrastructure such as base stations. Such equipment is delivered in cabinets. These cabinets are packed with various pieces of electronics: filters, amplifiers, circuit packs, etc. The exact configuration of a cabinet is dependent upon the circumstances it is being placed in, and some 20 product groups can be distinguished. However, the variation in cabinets is large, even within one product group. For this reason, they are built to order.

In order to improve cost, yield and delivery performance, lean manufacturing concepts were applied to change the layout of the factory to one based on *cells*. These cells focus on improving manufacturing through standardised work, limited changeovers between product groups and better utilisation of test equipment. A key component in the implementation of these improvements is a system which schedules the cells to satisfy customer request dates in an efficient sequence.

This paper describes the transformation and the tool that was built to support the new method of operations. The implementation has achieved significant improvements in manufacturing interval, work in process inventory, first test yield, headcount, quality (i.e. fewer defects are found during the testing stage) and delivery performance. Although these benefits are mainly achieved because of the change to a cell layout, the scheduling tool is crucial in realising the full potential of it.

1 Introduction

Alcatel-Lucent is a major player in the field of telecommunications. One of the products they deliver to network operators is wireless infrastructure. A key component of wireless infrastructure is the base station. Such equipment is delivered in *cabinets*, an example of which is pictured in Figure 1.[1] Located between the

[1] Although the cabinet is only the outer casing of the equipment, this is the term the company uses to refer to the equipment. In this paper, we will therefore also use the term 'cabinet' to refer to the whole item.

C. Bessiere (Ed.): CP 2007, LNCS 4741, pp. 105–117, 2007.

antennae and the ground network, their function is to handle the signals the antennae receive and send. Depending on the model, their size is roughly that of a standard kitchen refrigerator and they are packed with various pieces of electronics: filters, amplifiers, circuit packs, etc. The exact configuration of a cabinet is dependent upon the circumstances it is being placed in: the type of network (e.g. CDMA or UMTS), the frequency (the GSM standard defines eight frequency bands, for example), physical location (inside or outside), network density (is it expected to handle a high or low volume of calls, what is the area the cabinet covers), etc. Some 20 product groups can initially be distinguished. However, as one can understand from the many aspects that are taken into consideration, the variation in cabinets is large, even within one product group. For this reason, they are built to order.

Fig. 1. A cabinet

The site that we worked with, the Systems Integration Center in Columbus, Ohio, produces several hundred cabinets per week on average. The production takes place in three stages: assembly, wiring and testing. The durations of each the stages depends on the particular product group of the cabinet.

Assembly. The first series of steps takes as input a partially pre-populated cabinet. This has certain basic features such as power supplies, cooling and the back plane. To this, they add the required amplifiers, filters, circuit packs and other hardware according to a predetermined schema. The cabinet passes through a number of stations. Each station is dedicated to one or more types of modules that are fitted into the cabinet.

Wiring. The second step involves physically interconnecting the hardware that was added during assembly. Each component has a number of input and output ports that have to be connected with a wire to the outputs and inputs of other modules, again according to a predefined schema.

Testing. The final step involves the validation of the completed system. For this, each cabinet is connected to a test station that subjects it to a specially designed set of test signals. If the output of the cabinet is not according to specifications (e.g. due to a cable that is not firmly fixed in place), the test engineer diagnoses the system and corrects the fault.

Of the three stages, assembly is a relatively low skill operation and requires the least amount of training. The wiring step is more complicated, because a great number of connections has to be made between a great number of connectors that all look identical. Moreover, there is a high degree of freedom in the way the connections can be made. Not in terms of the inputs and outputs that have to be connected (these are fixed), but in terms of the order in which the connections are made (i.e. which cables run in front of other cables), the position of the cables (e.g. along the left or the right side of the cabinet) and which cables are tied together. The final step of testing is also complicated, as it involves making diagnoses for the detected anomalies and repairing them. Notice that the high variability in orders exacerbates the complexity in wiring and testing. To address these issues, the management decided to introduce a new setup that allows wirers and test engineers to specialise on product groups. However, this means that production has to be matched to available operator capabilities. The CP-based scheduling system we describe in this paper does exactly that.

The remainder of this paper is organised as follows. In the next section, we describe this change in operations in more detail and show why the use of a scheduling tool is necessary in the new situation. Section 3, then, describes the system that we built in detail. The paper finishes with an evaluation on the system itself and the use of CP in general.

2 Introducing CP

As indicated in the introduction, the wirers and test engineers face a great difficulty because of the huge variety in cabinets. Part of the problem in the original situation, as depicted in Figure 2.a, is that all wirers and all test engineers are considered to be a pool. Assembly puts populated cabinets into a buffer, from which the wirers take their cabinets. In their turn, wirers put finished cabinets into a buffer for testing. In this situation, only a very crude scheduling is employed. Based on the due dates of the orders, it is decided which orders are to be produced on a given day. The assembly stage then starts populating the required cabinets and places them in a buffer for wiring. When a wirer finishes a cabinet, he chooses one of the cabinets from the buffer to work on. Similarly, testers pull a cabinet out of the buffer for testing. In this way, cabinets trickle down the three stages on their way to completion. Aside from the selection of which orders to produce on a given day, no scheduling is performed. This may lead to several issues. For example, when a particular wirer has finished there is a few specific cabinets available in the buffer. Perhaps, the only product groups available are ones that he has no great familiarity with, which may lead to errors. As a second example, consider that a wirer consistently makes the same mistake over a particular period of time. These may be spread over several testers, all of whom will have to diagnose the fault and may not notice the repeated nature of it. Moreover, cabinets from product groups that are hard to wire, may have to wait in the wiring buffer for a long time, since other, easier, cabinets are preferred by the wirers.

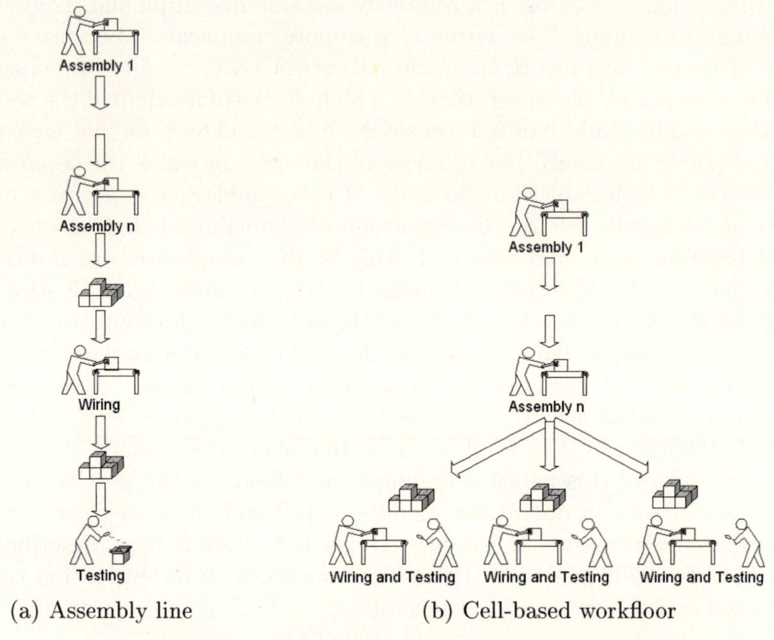

(a) Assembly line (b) Cell-based workfloor

Fig. 2. From assembly line to cell-based work floor

To prevent these and similar issues, management had decided to move from what was essentially an assembly line to a (partially) cell-based work floor [6]. In particular, the company wanted to integrate the wiring and testing activities into a *cell*, as depicted in Figure 2.b. Such a cell is made up of a dedicated team consisting of wirers and testers that focuses on a limited number of product groups. One of the key benefits that the company hopes to achieve by this change in setup is an improved quality of wiring and hence lower testing times. However, since the cells are dedicated to certain product groups, the order in which cabinets are assembled becomes much more important. An incorrect sequence may starve certain cells, or lead to building a stock of cabinets waiting to be processed on an already overloaded cell (or indeed both). For this reason, a scheduling tool was required.

The choice of technology was influenced by several factors. Firstly, the problem is a scheduling one in which time needed to be represented at the minute level. Therefore, a CP or IP based approach would be considered. There was uncertainty about what a good schedule would look like and so we would be required to iterate through a number of search strategies and objective functions to achieve the type of schedule they needed. This required an environment to try different options quickly, one of the reasons to work with Ilog OPL Studio. Once we analysed the problem more we could see that here was a variety of complex scheduling constraints which would have been too onerous to model in IP; the high level scheduling concepts of CP-based scheduling provided the ideal medium.

2.1 Related Work

Constraint-based scheduling is a modelling and solving technique successfully used to solve real-world manufacturing problems in, for example, aircraft manufacturing [4], production scheduling [8] and the semiconductor industry [1]. In the area of telecommunications, Little *et al.* [5] have already applied CP to the complex thermal part of the testing of circuit packs. This type of testing is not present in the plant we are concerned with; however, the work was influential in convincing the company of the suitability of the CP technology.

The area of cellular manufacturing is traditionally more about layout and design; where the actual design of the cells, what they are to do, their location and possible performance is of concern. Love [6] gives a clear overview on this type of problem. In particular, Golany *et al.* [2] are concerned with identifying the optimal level of work in progress (WIP) and the best strategy to deal with backlogs, rather than producing a day to day schedule. Also in our case, the cells location, number and they types of operations that they do, has been decided in advance. Ponnabalam *et al.* [9] consider simulation of manufacturing through a cell in light of uncertainty. They propose new heuristics to decide on the allocation of jobs to machines. They are working on theoretical problems here, but also simulating scheduling rather than creating an optimal (or near optimal) schedule.

3 The Program

The basis of the model was developed over the course of a one week site visit. As indicated above, the tool that we used for this was Ilog OPL Studio 3.7.1 with the Ilog Scheduler [7]. Perhaps the most significant reason to use OPL Studio was that we had effectively a time window of one week in which to develop a model which would convince the company of the potential benefits. A rapid prototyping system such as Ilog's OPL 3.7.1 with its variety of solvers seemed a good choice. Additionally, it offers the ability to try a variety of options quickly, while investigating different strategies and objective functions. After the initial model was built and verified, we returned home and finished the details of the model and built a user interface around it. (More on our procedure is outlined in the next section.)

The scheduling system produces a weekly schedule given the list of orders for that week. It does so by iteratively considering each day, extending the schedule built for the previous day(s). For each day, it first produces a schedule for each of the cells, assuring that assembly is possible in principle. Then, in a second phase, it optimises the assembly process. It then fixes this schedule and continues with the next day. Satisfactory results are obtained with optimising each day for 60 CPU-seconds.[2] The user runs the tool twice daily, computing a schedule from scratch each time (but taking into account work in progress). This way, changes to e.g. due dates and availability of material, and disruptions (e.g. machine break-downs) are taken into account. If necessary, the tool can be run when a disruption occurs to immediately take it into account.

Each order o is characterised by a product group *group*[o], an earliest start time *releaseTime*[o], a due date *dueDate*[o], a measure for the availability of components needed for the cabinet *matAvailability*[o], a priority *priority*[o] and a partial preference ordering over the shifts *preference*[o].

3.1 The Model

From Figure 2.b one can see that there are essentially two processes in the new configuration: that of assembly, and the work being carried out on the cells. As the operations within each those processes are a sequence of steps, we opted not to model each of the substeps, but regard each of the cells and the assembly line as a single resource. A number of cabinets is assembled or processed at the same time, however, so we used a *discrete resource* to model these.[3] Unfortunately, the semantics of a discrete resource imply that if we allow n cabinets simultaneously on the assembly line, these might all start at the same time. Clearly this is not the intended behaviour: although a number of cabinets can be assembled simultaneously, these would have to be at different stations (i.e. stages in the process). Therefore, for each discrete resource, we also create a corresponding *unary resource* to regulate the flow.[4] For each cabinet we now create two sets of two of activities: one group to represent the usage of the assembly line, and another to represent the usage of the cell. Both groups consist of an activity for the discrete resource (with a duration equal to the complete process time), and one activity for the unary resource (with a duration chosen according to the desired flow through the resource). Constraints are put in place to ensure that the activities in one group start at the same time. Figure 3 illustrates this behaviour.Here, *cellFlowAct*[i] is the unary activity on a cell for cabinet i, and *wireAndTestAct*[i] is the corresponding discrete activity. The duration of the former activity regulates the inflow (it equals the duration of the first wiring step); the duration of the latter equals the amount of time it takes for a cabinet to be wired and tested. Notice that the variability in process times in all but one of the stages is limited for all of the product groups; only the test stage has an uncertain duration. However, the user recognised that this uncertain behaviour

[2] The 60 seconds per day are required to get good results in weeks with a heavy load, where orders have to be shifted to earlier days to achieve the requested due dates. If this is not the case, 20 seconds per day suffice.

[3] Discrete resources "are used to model resources that are available in multiple units, all units being considered equivalent and interchangeable as far as the application is concerned." [3]

[4] A unary resource "is a resource that cannot be shared by two activities." [3]

affects the efficiency of the cell as a whole. Therefore, they implemented a policy to move cabinets that take more than a standard time to test to a special cell. Hence, we are dealing with deterministic processing times, and can use fixed durations in the schedule. In order to implement an efficient search, we make

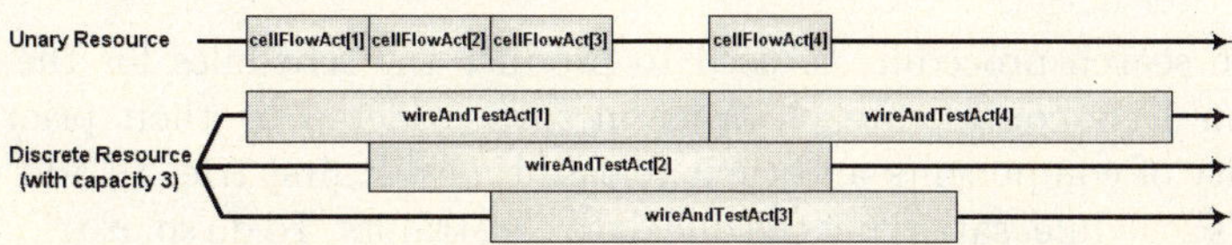

Fig. 3. Example of using both a discrete resource and a unary resource to represent a single entity (in this case: the cell)

use of a boolean matrix *orderOnCellShift*$[o, c, s]$. An entry in this matrix is true iff order o is scheduled on cell c during shift s. Let O be the set of all orders, C the set of all cells, and S the set of all shifts, then the following constraint holds:

$$\forall_{o \in O} \sum_{s \in S} \sum_{c \in C} \mathit{orderOnCellShift}[o, c, s] = 1$$

Orders that are assigned a certain shift are started during that shift (but may only be finished in a later shift):

$$\forall_{o \in O} \sum_{s \in S} \sum_{c \in C} \mathit{orderOnCellShift}[o, c, s] \times \mathit{shift}[s].\mathit{start} \leq \mathit{wireAndTestAct}[o].\mathit{start}$$

$$\forall_{o \in O}\ \mathit{wireAndTestAct}[o].\mathit{start} \leq \sum_{s \in S} \sum_{c \in C} \mathit{orderOnCellShift}[o, c, s] \times \mathit{shift}[s].\mathit{finish}$$

Cells have an associated *availability* matrix which indicates during which shifts they are active, as well as a *capability* matrix that specifies the product groups that these cells can run.

$$\forall_{o \in O} \forall_{c \in C} \sum_{s \in S} \mathit{orderOnCellShift}[o, c, s] \leq \mathit{capability}[c, \mathit{group}[o]]$$

$$\forall_{o \in O} \forall_{c \in C} \forall_{s \in S}\ \mathit{orderOnCellShift}[o, c, s] \leq \mathit{availability}[c, s]$$

Some days, not all orders can be scheduled, and some will have to be postponed to a later date. A boolean variable *delayed*$[o]$ is used to indicate that the due date may be missed (but the order is still included in today's schedule). Another variable *postponed*$[o]$ (which implies *delayed*$[o]$) indicates that the order will be left for the next scheduling iteration.

$$\forall_{o \in O}\ (1 - \mathit{delayed}[o]) \times \mathit{wireAndTestAct}[o].\mathit{end} \leq \mathit{dueDate}[o]$$

In addition to the above constraints, there are constraints linking the activities to their corresponding resources, precedence constraints as well as special constraints that keep track of the assignments that have been made so far, in order to make decisions during search. The criterion is a minimisation of the makespan, combined with the number of orders that have to be postponed. However, as we shall see next, the search is geared towards clustering of product groups to ensure few changeovers during a shift.

3.2 Search

A custom search procedure is used to produce the schedules for the cells, see Algorithm 1. It considers each order in turn, ordered by their priorities, the availability of components and their release times. It first tries to add the order to today's schedule, satisfying the due date constraints. To do so, it tries to assign the order to each valid shift / cell combination. It does so following an order. In this case, it first tries shifts with the highest preferences, and cells that have already one or more cabinets of the same product group assigned. The latter is to direct towards solutions that have a low number of different product groups (and hence changeovers) that are assigned to a cell. If a shift / cell combination is chosen, the order is assigned the earliest possible start time on that cell during the shift.

If all these options fail, the search procedure next considers running late with the order. This means that the order is started *before* it's due time, but is only finished *after*. Notice that we only have to consider the last possible shift of the current time window in this case. Starting the processing of a cabinet during one of the earlier shifts will result in the cabinet being finished in time, and the previous step of the search procedure has shown that this cannot lead to a valid solution. Finally, if neither of the previous steps result in a valid assignment for the order, it is left for the next day's schedule.

Once the cells have been assigned, a second search procedure is started that optimises the assembly operations. The first stage finds ensures the existence of a valid schedule for the assembly operations (to ensure that the schedule for the cells is valid), but it does not try to optimise it, as the focus is on optimising the usage of the cells. In this second phase, the schedule for the cells is kept fixed, while the maximum time between the completion of assembly of a cabinet and the start of the cell operations on that cabinet is minimised. The search procedure for this stage is shown in Algorithm 2. This greedy algorithm iteratively selects the order for which the minimum possible time that is spent in the buffer between assembly and wiring is currently the largest.[5] For this order, it tries to assign the best possible time left, or removes it from the domain. It does so for all orders, until all orders have been assigned a time to start the assembly.

[5] The **dmax**(v) function returns the maximum value in the domain of the variable v. The function **unbound**(v) returns *true* if the variable v is unbound (i.e. has not been assigned a value yet), and *false* otherwise.

Algorithm 1. Search procedure for the first stage

```
begin
  forall orders o ∈ O ordered by increasing ⟨priority[o], matAvailability[o],
  releaseTime[o]⟩
    try
      // first try to schedule it for today
      delayed[o] = 0
      postponed[o] = 0
      forall shifts s ∈ S ordered by increasing ⟨preference[o], s⟩
        forall cells c ∈ C ordered by increasing ⟨usage, s⟩
          try
            orderOnCellShift[o, c, s] = 1
            assign minimum time
          or
            orderOnCellShift[o, c, s] = 0
    or
      // consider finishing too late
      delayed[o] = 1
      postponed[o] = 0
      select s ∈ S : s is the last shift in the current window
      forall cells c ∈ C ordered by increasing ⟨usage, s⟩
        try
          orderOnCellShift[o, c, s] = 1
          assign minimum time
        or
          orderOnCellShift[o, c, s] = 0
    or
      // wait for tomorrow's schedule
      delayed[o] = 1
      postponed[o] = 1
end
```

Algorithm 2. Search procedure for the second stage

```
begin
  while ∃o ∈ O : unbound(assemblyStart[o]) do
    select o ∈ O : unbound(assemblyStart[o]) ordered by decreasing
    ⟨cellStart[o] − dmax(assemblyStart[o]) ⟩
    try
      assemblyStart[o] = dmax(assemblyStart[o])
    or
      assemblyStart[o] < dmax(assemblyStart[o])
end
```

3.3 The GUI

The user interface is built in Microsoft Excel using Visual Basic. The reason for this is twofold. On the one hand, the users are comfortable using the Microsoft Office suite, which means that no extra training is required. On the other hand, it allowed for easy integration with the existing Work floor Management System that tracks all activities and can generate reports in the Excel file format.

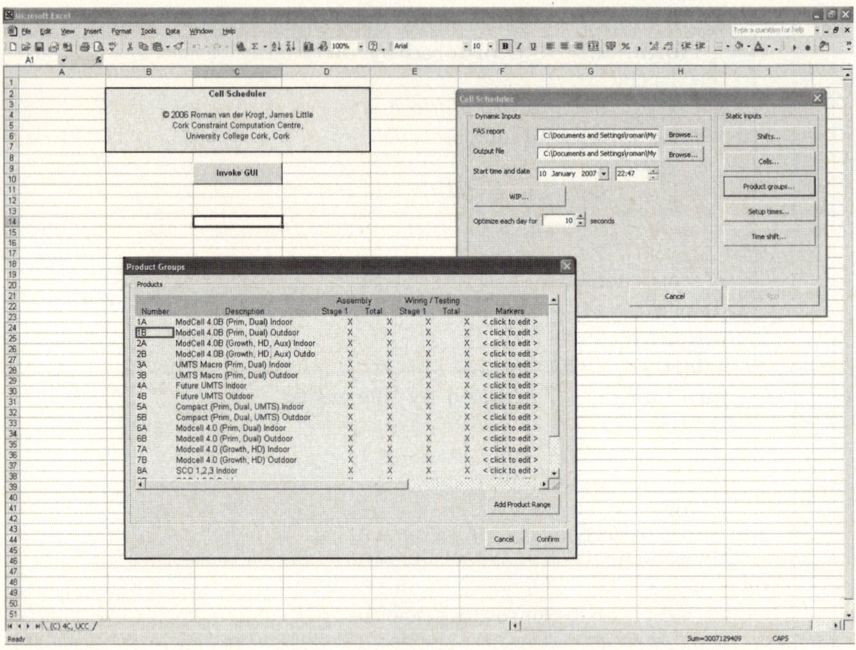

Fig. 4. Screenshot of the GUI

Figure 4 shows the user interface. The window in the top right (labeled "Cell Scheduler") forms the heart of the interface. On the left-hand side, it allows the input of some general data (the input file for orders and the output file for the resulting schedule, for example) and on the right-hand side there is a number of buttons that allow the user to specify the more static input to the scheduler. This includes things like the number of cells, their capabilities and availabilities, changeover times between product groups, and the product groups themselves. (This last window is shown in the foreground.)

The output of the scheduling tool is presented as an Excel file, see Figure 5. This file consists of two sheets: one for assembly and one for the cells. On each tab, it shows per shift which work is to be done and when and where each activity is to take place. The rows in bold face correspond to work that was in progress when the scheduling tool was run. Each row lists the order number, the start en finish times of assembly (if applicable), the start and finish times of wiring and testing(i.e. the

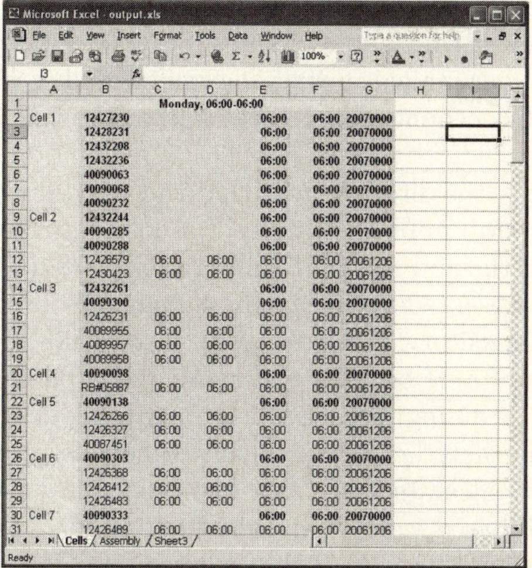

Microsoft Excel - output.xls

	A	B	C	D	E	F	G
1			Monday, 06:00-06:00				
2	Cell 1	12427230			06:00	06:00	20070000
3		12428231			06:00	06:00	20070000
4		12432208			06:00	06:00	20070000
5		12432236			06:00	06:00	20070000
6		40090063			06:00	06:00	20070000
7		40090068			06:00	06:00	20070000
8		40090232			06:00	06:00	20070000
9	Cell 2	12432244			06:00	06:00	20070000
10		40090285			06:00	06:00	20070000
11		40090288			06:00	06:00	20070000
12		12426579	06:00	06:00	06:00	06:00	20061206
13		12430423	06:00	06:00	06:00	06:00	20061206
14	Cell 3	12432261			06:00	06:00	20070000
15		40090300			06:00	06:00	20070000
16		12426231	06:00	06:00	06:00	06:00	20061206
17		40089955	06:00	06:00	06:00	06:00	20061206
18		40089957	06:00	06:00	06:00	06:00	20061206
19		40089958	06:00	06:00	06:00	06:00	20061206
20	Cell 4	40090098			06:00	06:00	20070000
21		RB#05887	06:00	06:00	06:00	06:00	20061206
22	Cell 5	40090138			06:00	06:00	20070000
23		12426266	06:00	06:00	06:00	06:00	20061206
24		12426327	06:00	06:00	06:00	06:00	20061206
25		40087451	06:00	06:00	06:00	06:00	20061206
26	Cell 6	40090303			06:00	06:00	20070000
27		12426368	06:00	06:00	06:00	06:00	20061206
28		12426412	06:00	06:00	06:00	06:00	20061206
29		12426483	06:00	06:00	06:00	06:00	20061206
30	Cell 7	40090333			06:00	06:00	20070000
31		12426489	06:00	06:00	06:00	06:00	20061206

Cells / Assembly / Sheet3

Fig. 5. Screenshot of the resulting output (censored)

activity on the cell) and the original due date. The cell sheet (which is shown in Figure 5) groups the orders by cell, whereas the assembly sheet merely shows the orders over time.

4 Evaluation

4.1 From Prototype to Production

The scheduling system is currently in the final stages of testing. As said before, the project started with the authors visiting the site for a week in October 2006. During the first two days of the week, we had meetings with the key figures in the factory and were painted a detailed picture of the processes going on. We then worked on a prototype model, confirming our decisions and asking for clarifications as we needed them. Although very intense (for both sides), this proved to be a very fruitful setup: by the end of the week we could present an initial version of our system. After presenting our first results, the company was confident that the CP-based scheduling approach that we proposed could deliver the tool they needed. So confident, in fact, that they decided to buy the necessary licenses, a considerable investment, during the course of our presentation. (The option of re-engineering the model in another language was also considered, but rejected because of time constraints.) We took the model home, further refined it, and added the GUI as discussed in Section 3.3. Early January, we produced the first schedules in parallel to the schedules the company made themselves. Eventually, when enough confidence in the schedules was gained, the system's schedules were used as the basis for the company's own schedules. From the second half of March, the company is using the schedules as is. As all recent issues are of a cosmetic nature, we expect to move into full production mode shortly. This would mean that the project has taken roughly eight months from the start. Note, however, that due to issues obtaining a license to OPL for the company the project was stalled during December, and it was worked on part-time. Taking this into account, the project has taken three to four months of full-time work.

It is hard to quantify the direct benefit that the scheduling tool has delivered, as it is part of the overall implementation of a different way of working. Moreover, the transition to the new setup has only recently been completed. However, already, the user has observed significant improvements in manufacturing interval, work in process inventory, first test yield, head count, quality and delivery performance. Although these benefits are mainly achieved because of the change to a cell layout, the scheduling tool is crucial in realising the full potential of this layout. The feeling is that the return on investment is considerable, although no figures have been calculated yet. Due to its success, the company considers extending the cell-based work floor concept to other areas of the factory. A CP-based scheduler would be part of that extension.

4.2 Lessons Learned

The week that we spent on-site developing the first model was intensive (for all parties), but great to kick start the project. By the end of the week, the outline of the complete system could be seen, which acted as a motivator to keep things going. However, to achieve this required commitment from the people in the factory, who had to spend a lot of time interacting with us. The engineers at the site had experience with the Theory of Constraints. As such, they had intuitive notions of what a constraint is and how to identify them. This helped us greatly in the initial modelling and getting the feedback on that model. Both these factors were required for the success of our visit. If these requirements are met, however, we can recommend this approach as it helps the developers to get to grips with the problem quickly, and builds a strong relationship between the developer and the user.

From our point of view, the main lesson learned is that it is harder than it seems to successfully deploy a system. This may seem obvious to some, but the amount of work it takes to go from prototype to a system robust enough to withstand user interaction is considerable. Moreover, the variety of situations that is encountered in practice means that the model itself has to be robust enough to allow for very different input profiles. This either calls for a large data set during development, or a period of building this robustness during the testing process. As there was no data available on the new layout when we started, we opted for the latter. In this case it is important to make the user realise that the initial phase of testing will be slow and not not very smooth at times, as the tool is adjusted to match the reality on the shop floor.

4.3 Final Remarks

This project shows the strength of the combination of lean manufacturing techniques and (CP-based) scheduling. The former techniques allow a business to take a critical look at its operations to identify areas for improvement, whereas the latter technique can be used to realise the potential of the improvements. This becomes more and more an issue as businesses move to more advanced methods of operation. As the user puts it: "*The amount of constraints the program has to handle points out the need for it. Scheduling manually would not allow us to service our customers as well.*"

Acknowledgements

Roman van der Krogt is supported by an Irish Research Council for Science, Engineering and Technology (IRCSET) Postdoctoral Fellowship. James Little is supported by Science Foundation Ireland under Grant- 03/CE3/I405 as part of the Centre for Telecommunications Value-Chain-Driven Research and Grant-05/IN/I886.

The authors would like to thank everybody at the Systems Integration Center in Columbus, Ohio for their warm welcome and support.

References

1. Bixby, R., Burda, R., Miller, D.: Short-interval detailed production scheduling in 300mm semiconductor manufacturing using mixed integer and constraint programming. In: The 17th Annual SEMI/IEEE Advanced Semiconductor Manufacturing Conference (ASMC-2006), pp. 148–154. IEEE Computer Society Press, Los Alamitos (2006)
2. Golany, B., Dar-El, E.M., Zeev, N.: Controlling shop floor operations in a multi-family, multi-cell manufacturing environment through constant work-in-process. IIE Transactions 31, 771–781 (1999)
3. Ilog: Ilog OPL Studio 3.7.1 help files (2005)
4. Bellone, J., Chamard, A., Fischler, A.: Constraint logic programming decision support systems for planning and scheduling aircraft manufacturing at dassault aviation. In: Proceedings of the Third International Conference on the Practical Applications of Prolog, pp. 111–113 (1995)
5. Creed, P., Berry, S., Little, J., Goyal, S., Cokely, D.: Thermal test scheduling using constraint programming. In: Proceedings of the 12th IFAC Symposium on Information Control Problems in Manufacturing (2006)
6. Love, D.: International Encyclopedia of Business and Management. In: The Design of Manufacturing Systems, vol. 4, pp. 3154–3174. Thompson Business Press (1996)
7. Nuijten, W., Le Pape, C.: Constraint-based job shop scheduling with IILOG SCHEDULER. Journal of Heuristics 3, 271–286 (1998)
8. Le Pape, C.: An application of constraint programming to a specific production scheduling problem. Belgian Journal of Operations Research, Statistics and Computer Science (1995)
9. Ponnambalam, S.G., Aravindan, P., Reddy, K.R.R.: Analysis of group scheduling heuristics in a manufacturing cell. The International Journal of Advanced Manufacturing Technology 15, 914–932 (1999)

A Constraint Store Based on Multivalued Decision Diagrams

H.R. Andersen[1], T.Hadzic[1], J.N. Hooker[2], and P. Tiedemann[1]

[1] IT University of Copenhagen
{hra,tarik,petert}@itu.dk
[2] Carnegie Mellon University
john@hooker.tepper.cmu.edu

Abstract. The typical constraint store transmits a limited amount of information because it consists only of variable domains. We propose a richer constraint store in the form of a limited-width multivalued decision diagram (MDD). It reduces to a traditional domain store when the maximum width is one but allows greater pruning of the search tree for larger widths. MDD propagation algorithms can be developed to exploit the structure of particular constraints, much as is done for domain filtering algorithms. We propose specialized propagation algorithms for alldiff and inequality constraints. Preliminary experiments show that MDD propagation solves multiple alldiff problems an order of magnitude more rapidly than traditional domain propagation. It also significantly reduces the search tree for inequality problems, but additional research is needed to reduce the computation time.

1 Introduction

Propagation through a constraint store is a central idea in constraint programming, because it addresses a fundamental issue in the field. Namely, how can a solver that processes individual constraints recognize the global structure of a problem? Global constraints provide part of the answer, because they allow the solver to exploit the global structure of groups of constraints. But the primary mechanism is to propagate the results of processing one constraint to the other constraints. This is accomplished by maintaining a constraint store, which pools the results of individual constraint processing. When the next constraint is processed, the constraint store is in effect processed along with it. This partially achieves the effect of processing all of the original constraints simultaneously.

In current practice the constraint store is normally a domain store. Constraints are processed by filtering algorithms that remove values from variable domains. The reduced domains become the starting point from which the next constraint is processed. An advantage of a domain store is that domains provide a natural input to filtering algorithms, which in effect process constraints and the domain store simultaneously. A domain store also guides branching in a natural way. When branching on a variable, one can simply split the domain in the current domain store. As domains are reduced, less branching is required.

A serious drawback of a domain store, however, is that it transmits relatively little information from one constraint to another, and as a result it has a limited

C. Bessiere (Ed.): CP 2007, LNCS 4741, pp. 118–132, 2007.

effect on branching. A constraint store can in general be regarded as a relaxation of the original problem, because any set of variable assignments that satisfies the original constraint set also satisfies the constraint store. A domain store is a very weak relaxation, since it ignores all interactions between variables. Its feasible set is simply the Cartesian product of the variable domains, which can be much larger than the solution space.

This raises the question as to whether there is a natural way to design a constraint store that is more effective than a domain store. Such a constraint store should have several characteristics:

1. It should provide a significantly stronger relaxation than a domain store. In particular, it should allow one to adjust the strength of the relaxation it provides, perhaps ranging from a traditional domain store at one extreme to the original problem at the other extreme.
2. It should guide branching in a natural and efficient way.
3. In optimization problems, it should readily provide a bound on the optimal value (to enable a branch-and-bound search).
4. It should provide a natural input to the "filtering" algorithms that process each constraint.

In this context, a "filtering" algorithm would not simply filter domains but would tighten the constraint store in some more general way.

We propose a *multivalued decision diagram* (MDD) [1] as a general constraint store for constraint programming, on the ground that it clearly satisfies at least the first three criteria, and perhaps after some algorithmic development, the fourth as well. MDDs are a generalization of binary decision diagrams (BDDs) [2,3], which have been used for some time for circuit design/verification [4,5] and very recently for optimization [6,7,8]. The MDD for a constraint set is essentially a compact representation of a branching tree for the constraints, although it can grow exponentially, depending on the structure of the problem and the branching order. We therefore propose to use a *relaxed* MDD that has limited width and therefore bounded size. The MDD is relaxed in the sense that it represents a relaxation of the original constraint set.

An MDD-based constraint store satisfies the first three criteria as follows:

1. By setting the maximum width, one can obtain an MDD relaxation of arbitrary strength, ranging from a traditional domain store (when the maximum width is fixed to 1) to an exact representation of the original problem (when the width is unlimited).
2. One can easily infer a reduced variable domain on which to branch at any node of a branching tree.
3. A relaxed MDD provides a natural bounding mechanism for any separable objective function. The cost of a particular shortest path in the MDD is a lower bound on the optimal value.

The primary research issue is whether fast and effective "filtering" algorithms can be designed for limited-width MDDs. Rather than reduce domains, these algorithms would modify the current MDD without increasing its maximum width. The feasibility of this project can be demonstrated only gradually by examining a number of constraints and devising MDD filters for each, much as was done for conventional domain filtering. As a first step in this direction we present an MDD filter for the all-different (alldiff) constraint and for inequality constraints (i.e., constraints that bound the value of a separable function).

2 Related Work

The limitations of the domain store's ability to make inferences across constraints are well known, but few attempts have been made to generalize it. In [9] meta-programming is proposed for overcoming the limitations. The idea is to allow *symbolic propagation* by giving the programmer detailed access to information about constraints at runtime and thereby allow for early detection of failures by symbolic combination of constraints.

Decision diagrams have been used previously for Constraint Satisfaction as a compact way of representing ad-hoc global constraints [10] as well as for no-good learning both in CSP and SAT solving [11]. This is however quite different from the goal of this paper, which is to utilize an MDD as a relaxation of the solution space.

3 MDDs and Solution Spaces

We are given a constraint set $\mathcal{C}$ defined over variables $X = \{x_1, \ldots, x_n\}$ with finite domains $D_1, \ldots, D_n$ giving rise to the declared domain of solutions $D = D_1 \times \cdots \times D_n$. Each constraint $C \in \mathcal{C}$ is defined over a subset of variables $\text{scope}(C) \subseteq X$. An MDD for $\mathcal{C}$ can be viewed as a compact representation of a branching tree for the constraint set.

For example, an MDD for the two constraints

$$\begin{aligned} &x_1 + x_3 = 4 \ \vee \ (x_1, x_2, x_3) = (1, 1, 2), \\ &3 \le x_1 + x_2 \le 5 \end{aligned} \tag{1}$$

with $x_1, x_2, x_3 \in \{1, 2, 3\}$ appears in Fig. 1(a). The edges leaving node u_1 represent possible values of x_1, those leaving u_2 and u_3 represent values of x_2, and so forth. Only paths to 1 are shown.

Formally, an MDD M is a tuple (V, r, E, var, D), where V is a set of vertices containing the special terminal vertex 1 and a root $r \in V$, $E \subseteq V \times V$ is a set of edges such that (V, E) forms a directed acyclic graph with r as the source and 1 as the sink for all maximal paths in the graph. Further, $var : V \to \{1, \ldots, n+1\}$ is a labeling of all nodes with a variable index such that $var(1) = n + 1$ and D is a labeling $D_{u,v}$ on all edges (u, v) called the *edge domain* of the edge. We require that $\emptyset \neq D_{u,v} \subseteq D_{var(u)}$ for all edges in E and for convenience we take $D_{u,v} = \emptyset$ if $(u, v) \notin E$.

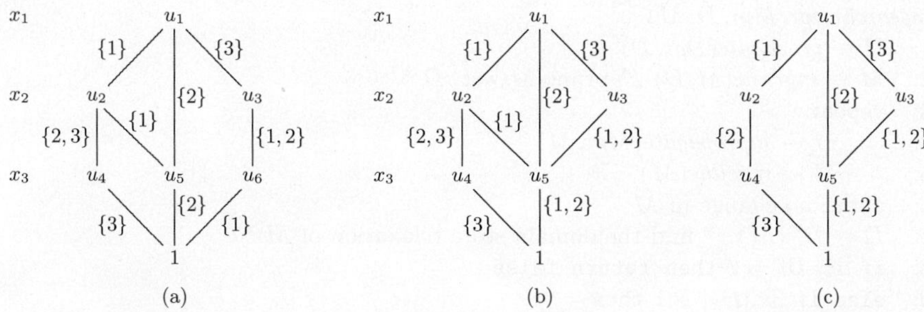

Fig. 1. (a) MDD for problem (1). (b) Same MDD relaxed to width 2. (c) Result of propagating alldiff in (b).

We work only with *ordered* MDDs. A total ordering $<$ of the variables is assumed and all edges (u, v) respect the ordering, i.e. $var(u) < var(v)$. For convenience we assume that the variables in X are ordered according to their indices. Ordered MDDs can be considered as being arranged in n *layers* of vertices, each layer being labeled with the same variable index. If $i = var(u)$ and $j = var(v)$, we say that (u, v) is a *long edge* if its skips variables $(i+1 < j)$. We use $N_{u,v}$ for the set of indices $\{i+1, i+2, \ldots, j-1\}$ skipped by the long edge, with $N_{u,v} = \emptyset$ if (u, v) is not a long edge.

Each path from the root to 1 in an MDD represents a set of feasible solutions in the form of a Cartesian product of edge labels. Thus the path $(u_1, u_2, u_4, 1)$ in Fig. 1(a) represents the two solutions (x_1, x_2, x_3) in the Cartesian product $\{1\} \times \{2, 3\} \times \{3\}$. Note that the path $(u_1, u_5, 1)$ does not define the value of x_2, which can therefore take any value in its domain. This path represents the three solutions in $\{2\} \times \{1, 2, 3\} \times \{2\}$. Formally, a path $p = (u_0, \ldots, u_m)$, $u_0 = r$, $u_m = 1$ defines the set of solutions $Sol(p) = \prod_{i=0}^{m-1}(D_{u_i,u_{i+1}} \times \prod_{k \in N_{u_i,u_{i+1}}} D_k)$. Every path can in this way be seen as a traditional domain store. The solutions represented by an MDD are a union of the solutions represented by each path. One of the key features of an MDD is that due to sharing of subpaths in the graph, it can represent exponentially more paths than it has vertices. This means that we can potentially represent exponentially many domain stores as an approximation of the solution set.

An MDD M induces a Cartesian product *domain relaxation* $D^{\times}(M)$ whose k'th component is defined by

$$D_k^{\times}(M) = \begin{cases} D_k & \text{if there exists } (u, v) \text{ with } k \in N_{u,v}, \\ \bigcup\{D_{u,v} \mid var(u) = k\} & \text{otherwise.} \end{cases}$$

This relaxation shows that an MDD is a refined representation of the associated domain store. For a given set of solutions $S \subseteq D = D_1 \times \cdots \times D_n$, it is convenient to let $S_{x_i=\alpha}$ be the subset of solutions in which x_i is fixed to α, so that $S_{x_i=\alpha} = \{(\alpha_1, \ldots, \alpha_n) \mid \alpha_i = \alpha\}$. If MDD M represents solution set S, we let $M_{x_i=\alpha}$ be the MDD that represents $S_{x_i=\alpha}$ obtained by replacing the labels with $\{\alpha\}$

msearch(*Dpr*, *Mpr*, D, M)
1: $D \leftarrow$ *propagate*(*Dpr*, D)
2: $M \leftarrow$ *mprune*(M, D) /* prune M wrt. D */
3: `repeat`
4: $M \leftarrow$ *mpropagate*(*Mpr*, M)
5: $M \leftarrow$ *mrefine*(M)
6: `until` no change in M
7: $D \leftarrow D^{\times}(M)$ /* find the domain store relaxation of M */
8: `if` $\exists k.\ D_k = \emptyset$ `then return false`
9: `else if` $\exists k. |D_k| > 1$ `then`
10: pick some k with $|D_k| > 1$
11: `forall` $\alpha \in D_k$: `if` *msearch*(*Dpr*, *Mpr*, $D_{x_k=\alpha}$, $M_{x_k=\alpha}$) `then return true`
12: `return false`
13: `else return true` /* $\forall k.\ |D_k| = 1$, i.e., D is a single solution */

Fig. 2. The MDD-based search algorithm. The algorithms uses a set of domain propagators *Dpr* and a set of MDD-propagators *Mpr*. It works on a domain store relaxation D and an MDD constraint store M. In line 1 *propagate* is the standard domain propagation on D and in line 2 M is pruned with respect to the result of the domain propagation. Lines 3-6 mix MDD propagation and refinement until no further change is possible. This is followed by a new computation of the domain store relaxation, which is then used in guiding the branching in lines 10-11. An important operation is that of restricting the MDD store when a branch is made in line 11: $M_{x_k=\alpha}$. There are several options when implementing this operation as discussed in the main text.

on every edge leaving a vertex u with $var(u) = i$. Also for a given D we let $mprune(M, D)$ be the MDD that results from replacing each edge domain $D_{u,v}$ with $D_{u,v} \cap D_{var(u)}$.

We use an MDD of limited width as a constraint store (i.e., as a relaxation of the given constraint set). The *width* of an MDD is the maximum number of nodes on any level of the MDD. For example, Fig. 1(b) is a relaxed MDD for (1) that has width 2. It represents 14 solutions, compared with 8 solutions for the original MDD in Fig. 1(a). The relaxation is considerably tighter than the conventional domain store, which admits all 27 solutions in the Cartesian product $\{1, 2, 3\} \times \{1, 2, 3\} \times \{1, 2, 3\}$.

4 MDD-Based Constraint Solving

The MDD-based constraint solver is based on *propagation* and *search* just as traditional solvers. During search, branches are selected based on the domains represented in the MDD store. Propagation involves the use of a new set of MDD propagators and a *refinement* step. The overall algorithm is shown in Fig. 2.

The algorithm is a generalization of the normal constraint solving algorithm [12]. If lines 3–7 are omitted we get the domain store algorithm. The steps in line 1–2 are included for efficiency. If more powerful and efficient MDD propagators are developed, they might not be necessary. Further, the branching used in lines

10–11 could be replaced by more general branching strategies [12]. The operation $M_{x_k=\alpha}$ can be implemented in several ways. The effect is that the constraint store is reduced to reflect the choice of $x_k = \alpha$. If the branching follows the MDD variable ordering, this is very simple as the new MDD store can be represented by moving the root to the node reached by following the edge corresponding to $x_k = \alpha$. If another order is used, the operation will have to be implemented through a marking scheme keeping track of the "live" parts of the MDD store, or by explicitly reducing the MDD store. The major logical inferences are made by the MDD (and domain) propagators.

Propagators work by pruning edge domains, and if a domain $D_{u,v}$ is pruned down to the empty set, the edge (u, v) is removed. This can lead to further reduction of the MDD, if after the removal of the edge some other edges do no longer have a path to 1 or can be reached by a path from r. MDD propagators are described in section 5.

The purpose of refinement is to refine the relaxation represented by the MDD so that further propagation can take place. Refinement is achieved through *node splitting* which refines the MDD by adding nodes while ensuring the maximal width is not exceeded (see section 6).

MDD-Based Constraint Optimization. The MDD-based solver can be readily used for optimization. A separable objective function $\sum_i f_i(x_i)$ can be minimized over an MDD through efficient shortest path computations. Suppose for example we wish to minimize the function

$$20x_1^2 - 10x_2^2 + 15x_3^2 \tag{2}$$

subject to (1). The MDD is shown in Fig. 3(a). The corresponding edge weights appear in Fig. 3(b). Thus the weight of the edge (u_2, u_4) is $\min_{x_2 \in \{2,3\}}\{-10x_2^2\} = -90$, and the weight of the edge (u_1, u_5) is

$$\min_{x_1 \in \{2\}} \{20x_1^2\} + \min_{x_2 \in \{1,2,3\}} \{-10x_2^2\} = -10\,.$$

Formally, given a separable objective function $\sum_i f_i(x_i)$ each edge (u, v) with $i = var(u)$ is associated with the weight $w_f(u, v)$:

$$\min_{x_i \in D_{u,v}} \{f_i(x_i)\} + \sum_{k \in N_{u,v}} \min_{x_k \in D_k} f_k(x_k)\,. \tag{3}$$

A branch-and-bound mechanism computes a lower bound on the optimal value as the cost of the shortest path in the current MDD relaxation wrt. weights $w_f(u, v)$. The more relaxed the MDD representation, the weaker the bound. For example, the shortest path for the MDD in Fig. 3(b) is $(u_1, u_5, 1)$ and has cost 50. The lower bound wrt. the relaxed MDD of Fig. 1(b) (edge weights indicated in Fig. 3(c)) is 5. Finally, the lower bound based only on the domain store is -55.

If the bound is greater than the cost of the current incumbent solution b, the search is cut of. This is achieved by adding a new inequality constraint $\sum_i f_i(x_i) \leq b$ to the set of constraints and propagating it in future using a standard inequality propagator (discussed in section 5).

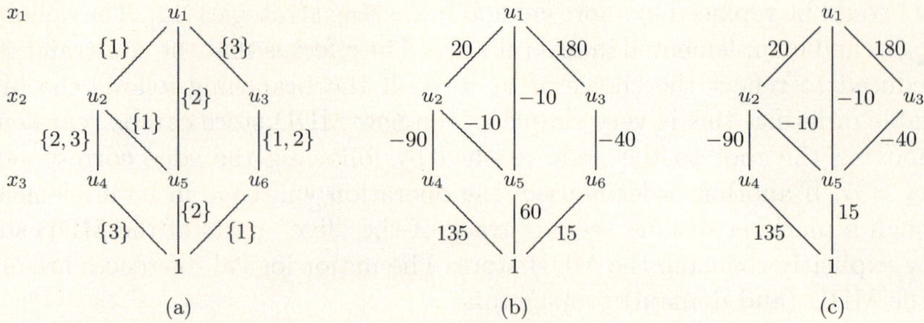

Fig. 3. (a) MDD for problem (1) copied from Fig. 1. (b) The same with edge weights for objective function (2). (c) Weights when the MDD is relaxed to width two.

5 Propagation

To characterize the strength of MDD propagators we define the notion of *MDD consistency* for a constraint C and an MDD M as the following condition: for every edge $(u, v) \in E$ and every value $\alpha \in D_{u,v}$, if α is removed from $D_{u,v}$ then there is at least one solution in M satisfying C that is lost. When the MDD is a single path, MDD consistency is equivalent to generalized arc consistency (GAC).

A key observation is that even if a constraint C has a polynomial-time algorithm that enforces GAC, it can be NP-hard to enforce MDD consistency for C on a polynomial sized MDD. This is because the Hamiltonian path problem, which is NP-hard, can be reduced to enforcing MDD consistency on an MDD of polynomial size. Consider the n-walk constraint on a graph G. Variable x_i is the ith vertex of G visited in the walk, and the only restriction is that x_{i+1} be vertex adjacent to x_i. Then $x_1, \ldots, x_n$ is a Hamiltonian path in G if and only if $x_1, \ldots, x_n$ is an n-walk on G and alldiff$(x_1, \ldots, x_n)$ is satisfied.

The MDD for the n-walk constraint has polynomial size because there are at most n nodes at each level in the MDD: From the root node there is an edge with domain $\{i\}$ to a node corresponding to each vertex i of G. From any node on level $k < n$ corresponding to vertex i there is an edge with domain $\{j\}$ to a node corresponding to each vertex j that is adjacent to i in G. Thus there may be no poly-time algorithm for MDD consistency even when there is a poly-time algorithm for domain consistency (unless P=NP).

Re-using domain propagators. An intermediate step towards implementing customized MDD-based propagators is to reuse existing domain propagators. Though the above result on MDD consistency means that we should not expect a general polynomial time algorithm that can enforce MDD consistency, we can still reuse domain propagators to achieve tighter consistency than GAC.

Let *Dpr* be the set of domain propagators we wish to reuse. In order to apply such propagators to the MDD store, we must supply them with a domain in such a way that any domain reductions made by the propagators can be utilized for edge domain reductions. To this end consider an edge (u, v) and let $M_{u,v}$ be the MDD obtained by removing all paths in M not containing the edge. Note that the domain relaxation $D^\times(M_{u,v})$ might be significantly stronger than $D^\times(M)$. We can now compute the simultaneous fixpoint D^{dom} of the propagators in Dpr over $D^\times(M_{u,v})$. For each assignment $x_k = \alpha$ consistent with $D^\times(M_{u,v})$ but not with D^{dom} we place a no-good $x_k \neq \alpha$ on the edge (u, v). We can use such a no-good to prune as follows. If (u, v) corresponds to the variable x_k we prune α from $D_{u,v}$ and remove the no-good. Otherwise, if (u, v) corresponds to a variable x_j,where $j < k$, we move the no-good to all incoming edges of u if the same no-good occurs on all other edges leaving u. In the case $j > k$, the no-good is moved to all edges leaving v if all incoming edges to v have the no-good. Intuitively, no-goods move towards the layer in the MDD which corresponds to the variable they restrict, and are only allowed to move past a node if all paths through that node agree on the no-good. This ensures that no valid solutions will be removed.

As an example, consider propagating an alldiff over Fig. 1(b). Examining (u_2, u_4) yields a no-good $x_2 \neq 3$ which can be immediately used for pruning D_{u_2,u_4}. Examining (u_1, u_2), yields the nogood $x_2 \neq 1$, which can be moved to (u_2, u_5) and (u_2, u_4), resulting in the former edge being removed. The result is shown in Fig. 1(c).

This type of filtering will reach a fixpoint after a polynomial number of passes through the MDD, and will hence only apply each domain propagator polynomially many times. However, since many domain store propagators can be quite costly to invoke even once it is important to develop specialized propagators that not only take direct advantage of the MDD store but also obtain stronger consistency.

Inequality Propagator. Consider a constraint which is an inequality over a separable function:

$$\sum_i f_i(x_i) \leq b\,.$$

We can propagate such a constraint on an MDD by considering shortest paths in the MDD wrt. edge weights $w_f(u, v)$ (equation (3) in section 4). For each node u we calculate $L_{up}(u)$ and $L_{down}(u)$ as the shortest path from the root to u and from u to 1 respectively. L_{up} and L_{down} can be computed for all nodes simultaneously by performing a single bottom-up and top-down pass of the MDD. A value α can now be deleted from an edge domain $D_{u,v}$ iff every path through the edge (u, v) has weight greater than b under the assumption that $x_{var(u)} = \alpha$, that is if

$$L_{up}(u) + w_f(u, v) + L_{down}(v) > b\,.$$

Further details (for propagation in BDDs) can be found in [8]. We observe that this inequality propagator achieves MDD consistency as a value α in an edge domain $D_{u,v}$ is always removed unless there exists a solution to the inequality in the MDD going through the edge (u, v).

Alldiff Propagator. As implied by the hardness proof of MDD consistency, a polynomial time MDD consistent propagator for the alldiff constraint would imply that P=NP. In this section we therefore suggest a simple labeling scheme that provides efficient heuristic propagation of an alldiff constraint over the MDD store.

To each node u we attach four labels for each alldiff constraint C: ImpliedUp, ImpliedDown, AvailUp and AvailDown. The label $\text{ImpliedUp}_C(u)$ is the set of all values α such that on all paths from the root to u there is an edge (v, w) where $x_{var(v)} \in \text{scope}(C)$ and $D_{v,w} = \{\alpha\}$. The label $\text{ImpliedDown}_C(u)$ is defined similarly for paths from u to the 1-terminal. Given these labels for a node u we can remove the value α from the domain of an edge (v, w) if $\alpha \in \text{ImpliedUp}(v)$ or $\alpha \in \text{ImpliedDown}(w)$.

In addition we use the label $\text{AvailUp}_C(u)$, which contains values α such that there exists at least one path from the root to u containing some edge (v, w) where $x_{var(v)} \in \text{scope}(C)$ and $\alpha \in D_{v,w}$.

Given some node u, consider the set of variables $X_a = \text{scope}(C) \cap \{x_k \mid k < var(u)\}$. If $|X_a| = |\text{AvailUp}_C(u)|$ (i.e., X_a forms a Hall Set [13]) the values in $\text{AvailUp}_C(u)$ cannot be assigned to any variables not in X_a. This allows us to prune these values from the domain of any outgoing edge of u. AvailDown_C is defined and used analogously.

When the labels of the parents of a node u are known, it is easy to update the labels ImpliedUp and AvailUp of u as follows. Let $\{(u_1, \alpha_1), \ldots, (u_k, \alpha_k)\}$ be pairs of parents and values, corresponding to incoming edges to u (nodes are repeated if the edge domain label on an edge contains more than one value). We then have

$$\text{ImpliedUp}_C(u) = \bigcap_{1 \le j \le k} (\text{ImpliedUp}_C(u_j) \cup \{\alpha_j\})$$

$$\text{AvailUp}_C(u) = \bigcup_{1 \le j \le k} (\text{AvailUp}_C(u_j) \cup \{\alpha_j\})$$

Using this formulation it is easy to see that computing ImpliedUp and AvailUp as well as pruning values based on these can be trivially accomplished in a single top-down pass of the MDD store. Similarly ImpliedDown and AvailDown can be computed in a single bottom-up pass.

6 Refining

Refining is achieved by *node splitting* in an MDD M. A node $u \in V$ is selected for splitting. We then add a new node u' to V and add edges as follows. Let $In_u = \{s \in V \mid (s, u) \in E\}$ be the set of vertices with an edge to u and let $Out_u = \{t \in V \mid (u, t) \in E\}$ be the set of vertices with an edge from u. The new edges are then $E' = \{(s, u') \mid s \in In_u\} \cup \{(u', t) \mid t \in Out_u\}$. The domains for the outgoing edges of u' are the same as for u: $D_{u',t} = D_{u,t}$ for all $t \in Out_u$. For the ingoing edges we select some domains $D_{s,u'} \subseteq D_{s,u}$ and remove these values from the domains in $D_{s,u}$, i.e., we update $D_{s,u}$ to $D_{s,u} \setminus D_{s,u'}$. A good selection

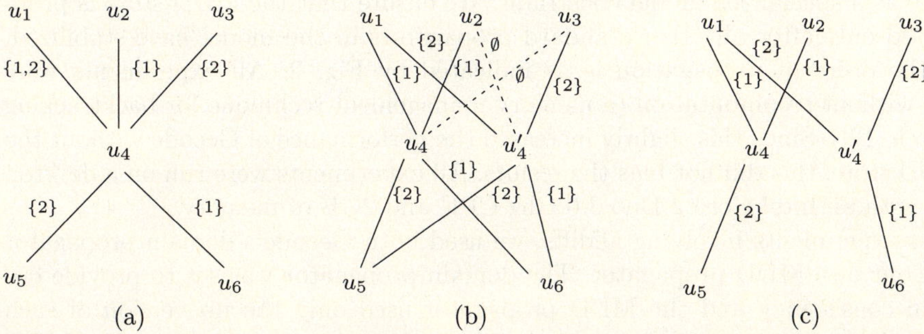

Fig. 4. (a) Part of an MDD store representing a relaxation of a global alldiff, just before splitting on the node u_4. Note that while there are obvious inconsistencies between the edge domains (such as label 1 in domains of (u_1, u_4) and (u_4, u_6)), we cannot remove any value. (b) A new node u_4' has been created and some of the edge domain values to u_4 have been transferred to u_4'. There are no labels on (u_2, u_4') and (u_3, u_4), so the edges need not be created. (c) After the split we can prune inconsistent values and as a result remove edges (u_4, u_6) and (u_4', u_5).

of the node u and the new ingoing edge domains will help the future MDD propagators in removing infeasible solutions from the MDD store. A good split should yield an MDD relaxation that is fine-grained enough to help propagators detect inconsistencies, but that is also coarse enough so that each removal of a value from an edge domain corresponds to eliminating a significant part of the solution space of the MDD. Fig. 4 shows an example of a node split and subsequent propagation.

The selection of the splitting node u and the ingoing edge domain splits is performed by a *node splitting heuristic.* We will use a heuristic that tries to select nodes that 1) are involved in large subsets of the solution space, and 2) have the potential of removing infeasible solutions during subsequent propagation steps. These criteria – estimating the strength of a split – must be balanced against the limit on the width of the MDD store and the increase in memory usage resulting from adding the new node and edges. For alldiffs C, the heuristic can utilize the labels ImpliedUp_C computed by the alldiff propagators. If $var(u) \in \text{scope}(C)$ then the larger the size of the ImpliedUp-set the more pruning could happen after splitting the node u. Also, the ability to prune significantly increases with the number of different constraints involving $var(u)$. Therefore, an estimate of strength for u could be the product of the sizes of the ImpliedUp_C-sets for each alldiff C s.t. $var(u) \in \text{scope}(C)$.

7 Computational Results

To obtain experimental results we integrated the MDD store into Gecode [14,15,16], a standard domain-store based solver. We implemented the MDD store as a specialized global constraint. We ensure that the MDD store is propagated only after all other standard propagators in the model have stabilized, so the order of propagation is as indicated by Fig. 2. All experiments were run without recomputation (a memory management technique for backtracking search [12]). Since this slightly increased the performance of Gecode without the MDD store, this did not bias the results. All experiments were run on a desktop PC with an Intel Core 2 Duo 3.0 Ghz CPU and 2GB of memory.

In experiments involving alldiffs, we used both Gecode's domain propagator and our own MDD propagator. The domain propagator was set to provide domain consistency and the MDD propagator used only the up version of each label. Experiments involving optimization or linear inequalities over the MDD store used only the MDD-versions of inequality propagators. All instances were randomly generated.

We first compared the *size of the search tree* of domain-based search ST_D and MDD-based search ST_M. This gives an idea of how the extra processing at each node influences the search tree. We then took into account this extra processing, by counting the *total number of node-splits* NS_M and comparing ST_D against $ST_M + NS_M$. Finally, we compared the total running times T_D and T_M for domain-based and MDD-based search respectively.

The first set of experiments was carried out for several different MDD widths. The problems consisted of three overlapping alldiff constraints. Each instance was parameterized by the triple (n, r, d), where n is the number of variables, r the size of the scope of each alldiff, and d the size of a domain. We ordered variables in decreasing order of the number of alldiffs covering them. This variable ordering was then used both as the ordering in the MDD store and for the search.

Remarkably, the MDD-based search never backtracked. The MDD-based refinement was strong enough to either detect infeasibility immediately, or to guide branching so that no backtracking was necessary. Hence, the size of the MDD-search tree is incomparably small – at most n. We therefore report only the comparison of ST_D against the $ST_M + NS_M$. This is shown in Fig. 5(a), for different widths. Fig. 5(b) compares the total running time for different widths. We can see, that when the total search effort is taken into account, the MDD-store still outperforms domain-based search by several orders of magnitude. We also see that the actual time closely corresponds to the number of node splits.

Width clearly has a dramatic effect both on the total computational effort $ST_M + NS_M$, as well as the running time T_M. The smallest width tested with the MDD store is 5 for the $(10, 9, 9)$ instances and 10 for the $(12, 10, 10)$ instances. The runtime is worse with the MDD store for small widths but becomes more than an order of magnitude better for larger widths. In the $(10, 9, 9)$ instances a width of 10 suffices to outperform the domain store, while 25 is required in the $(12, 10, 10)$ instances.

The second set of experiments minimized $\sum_i c_i x_i$ subject to $\sum_i a_i x_i \leq \alpha L$ and a single alldiff, where L is the maximum value of the left-hand side of the inequality constraint and $\alpha \in [0, 1]$ is a tightness parameter. The instances were parameterized by (n, k), where n is the total number of variables, and k

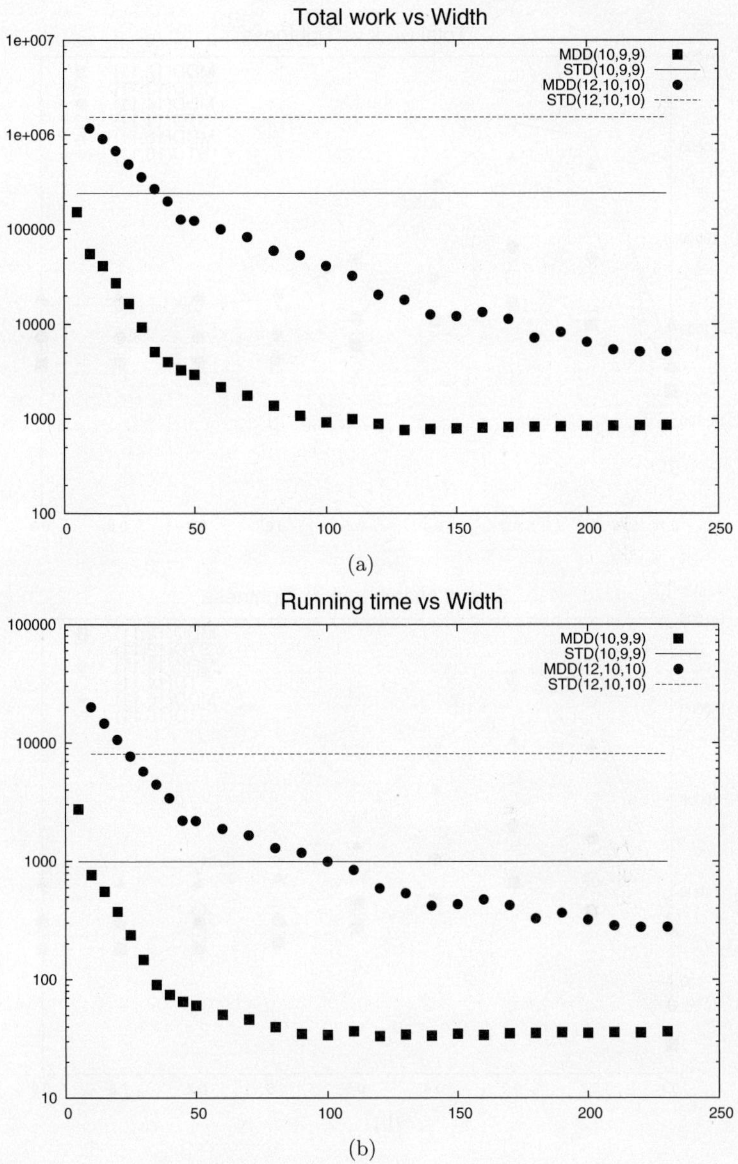

Fig. 5. (a) The two curves labeled MDD(n, r, d) show the total computational effort $ST_M + NS_M$ that resulted from an MDD constraint store on instances with parameters (n, r, d); every problem was solved without backtracking. The two lines labeled STD show the search tree size that resulted from a standard domain store. Each instance set consists of 60 randomly generated instances. Twenty instances were feasible for the $(10, 9, 9)$ set, 16 for the $(12, 10, 10)$ instances. (b) The same as before, but showing the actual running time in milliseconds. Note the close relation between $ST_M + NS_M$ and the time used.

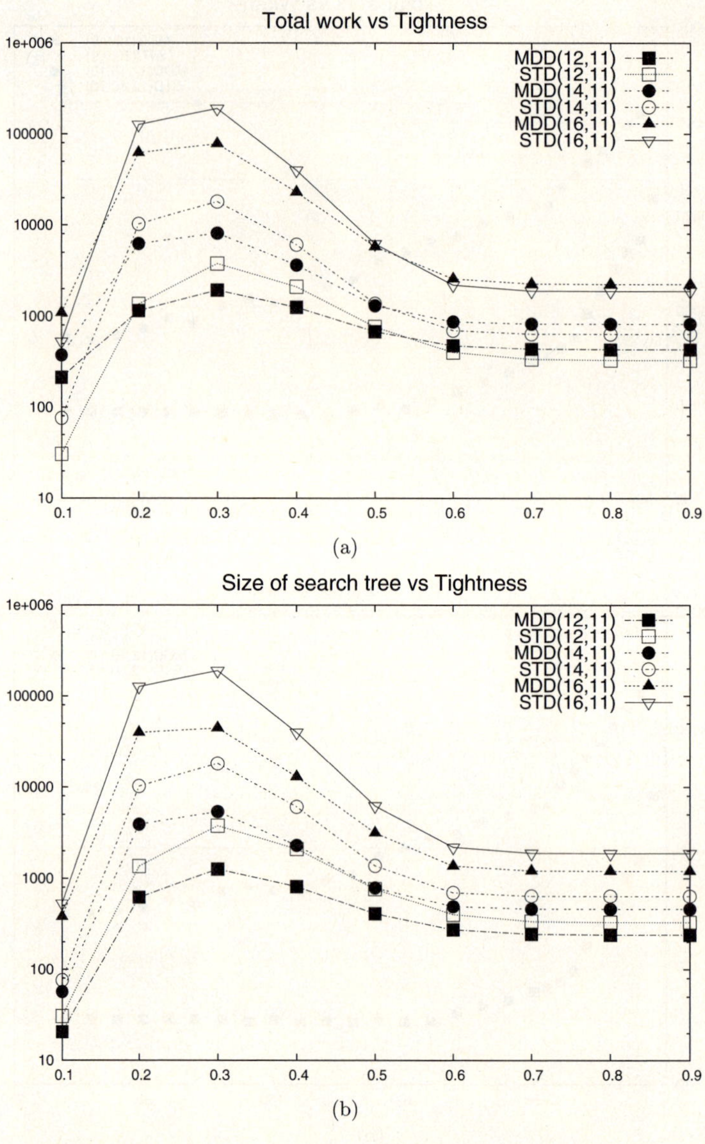

Fig. 6. (a) Total computation effort vs. the tightness α when minimizing $\sum_i c_i x_i$ subject to $\sum_i a_i x_i \leq \alpha L$ and a single alldiff, where L is the maximum size of the left-hand side of the inequality. MDD(n,k) denotes the MDD-based results for instances parameterized by (n,k), and STD denotes results based on standard domain filtering. For MDD-based results, computational effort is the sum $ST_M + SN_M$ of the number search tree nodes and the number of splits, and for domain filtering it is the number ST_D of search tree nodes. (b) Number of search tree nodes vs. the tightness α when minimizing $\sum_i c_i x_i$ subject to $\sum_i a_i x_i \leq \alpha L$ and a single alldiff.

the number of variables in the alldiff. The coefficients a_i and c_i were drawn randomly from the interval $[1, 100]$. We made the same comparisons as in the previous experiment.

The MDD store resulted in a consistently smaller search tree (Fig. 6(b)). The size of the search tree explored using the mdd store (ST_M) was as little as one-fifth the number explored by Gecode (ST_D). The total number of splits NS_M was also significantly smaller than ST_D in most cases (Fig. 6(a)). However, the computation time T_M was an order of magnitude greater than T_D. Similar results were obtained when minimizing the same objective functions subject to a single alldiff.

8 Conclusions and Future Work

Preliminary experiments indicate that an MDD-based constraint store can substantially accelerate solution of multiple-alldiff problems. Even a rather narrow MDD allows the problems to be solved without backtracking, while the traditional domain store generates about a million search tree nodes. As the MDD width increases, the MDD-based solution becomes more than an order of magnitude faster than a solver based on traditional domain filtering.

Conventional wisdom tells us that in constraint satisfaction problems, reducing the search tree through enhanced processing at each node often does not justify the additional overhead—perhaps because the added information is not transmitted in a conventional domain store. Our results suggest that intensive processing can be well worth the cost when one uses a richer constraint store.

We obtained less encouraging results for the optimization problems involving inequalities, where more intensive processing at each node is generally worthwhile. The MDD store required less branching than a traditional domain store, but the computation time was greater. An important factor affecting performance is that we cannot identify a feasible solution until we have branched deeply enough in the search tree to fix every variable to a definite value. This is time consuming because MDDs are processed at each node along the way.

This problem is avoided in branch-and-cut methods for integer programming by solving the relaxation at each node and checking whether the solution happens to be integral. Very often it is, which allows one to find feasible solutions high in the search tree. This raises the possibility that we might "solve" the MDD relaxation (by heuristically selecting solutions that it represents) and check whether the solution is feasible in the original problem. This is an important project for future research and could substantially improve performance.

Overall, the results suggest that an MDD-based constraint store can be an attractive alternative for at least some types of constraints. Naturally, if an MDD is not useful for a certain constraint, the solver can propagate the constraint with traditional domain filtering.

A number of issues remain for future research, other than the one just mentioned. MDD-based propagators should be built for other global constraints, additional methods of refining the MDD developed, and MDD-based constraint stores tested on a wide variety of problem types.

Acknowledgments. We would like to thank the anonymous reviewers for their valuable suggestions which helped us improve the presentation significantly.

References

1. Kam, T., Villa, T., Brayton, R.K., Sangiovanni-Vincentelli, A.L.: Multi-valued decision diagrams: Theory and applications. International Journal on Multiple-Valued Logic 4, 9–62 (1998)
2. Andersen, H.R.: An introduction to binary decision diagrams. Lecture notes, available online, IT University of Copenhagen (1997)
3. Akers, S.B.: Binary decision diagrams. IEEE Transactions on Computers C-27, 509–516 (1978)
4. Bryant, R.E.: Graph-based algorithms for boolean function manipulation. IEEE Transactions on Computers C-35, 677–691 (1986)
5. Lee, C.Y.: Representation of switching circuits by binary-decision programs. Bell Systems Technical Journal 38, 985–999 (1959)
6. Becker, Behle, Eisenbrand, Wimmer: BDDs in a branch and cut framework. In: Nikoletseas, S.E. (ed.) WEA 2005. LNCS, vol. 3503. Springer, Heidelberg (2005)
7. Hadzic, T., Hooker, J.: Postoptimality analysis for integer programming using binary decision diagrams. Technical report, Carnegie Mellon University. In: Presented at GICOLAG workshop (Global Optimization: Integrating Convexity, Optimization, Logic Programming, and Computational Algebraic Geometry), Vienna (2006)
8. Hadzic, T., Hooker, J.N.: Cost-bounded binary decision diagrams for 0-1 programming. Technical report, Carnegie Mellon University (to appear)
9. Muller, T.: Promoting constraints to first-class status. In: Proceedings of the First International Conference on Computational Logic, London (2000)
10. Cheng, K.C., Yap, R.H.: Maintaining generalized arc consistency on ad-hoc n-ary boolean constraints. In: Proceeedings of The European Conference on Artificial Intelligence (2006)
11. Hawkins, P., Stuckey, P.J.: A hybrid BDD and SAT finite domain constraint solver. In: Van Hentenryck, P. (ed.) PADL 2006. LNCS, vol. 3819, pp. 103–117. Springer, Heidelberg (2005)
12. Schulte, C., Carlsson, M.: Finite domain constraint programming systems. In: Rossi, F., van Beek, P., Walsh, T. (eds.) Handbook of Constraint Programming. Foundations of Artificial Intelligence, pp. 495–526. Elsevier Science, Amsterdam, The Netherlands (2006)
13. van Hoeve, W.J.: The alldifferent constraint: A survey. In: Sixth Annual Workshop of the ERCIM Working Group on Constraints (2001)
14. Schulte, C. (ed.): Programming Constraint Services. LNCS (LNAI), vol. 2302. Springer, Heidelberg (2002)
15. Schulte, C., Stuckey, P.J.: Speeding up constraint propagation. In: Wallace, M. (ed.) CP 2004. LNCS, vol. 3258, pp. 619–633. Springer, Heidelberg (2004)
16. Schulte, C., Szokoli, G., Tack, G., Lagerkvist, M., Pekczynski, P.: Gecode. Software download and online material at the website: `http://www.gecode.org`

GAC Via Unit Propagation

Fahiem Bacchus

Department of Computer Science,University of Toronto, Canada
fbacchus@cs.toronto.edu

Abstract. In this paper we argue that an attractive and potentially very general way of achieving generalized arc consistency (GAC) on a constraint is by using unit propagation (UP) over a CNF encoding of the constraint. This approach to GAC offers a number of advantages over traditional constraint specific algorithms (propagators): it is easier to implement, it automatically provides incrementality and decrementality in a backtracking context, and it can provide clausal reasons to support learning and non-chronological backtracking. Although UP on standard CNF encodings of a constraint fails to achieve GAC, we show here that alternate CNF encodings can be used on which UP does achieve GAC. We provide a generic encoding applicable to any constraint. We also give structure specific encodings for the **regular**, **among**, and **gen-sequence** constraints on which UP can achieve GAC with the same run time bounds as previously presented propagators. Finally, we explain how a UP engine can be added to a CSP solver to achieve a seamless integration of constraints encoded in CNF and propagated via UP and those propagated via traditional constraint specific propagators.

1 Introduction

Unit propagation (UP) is a local propagation mechanism for propositional formulas expressed in conjunctive normal form (CNF). Any constraint over finite domain variables can be converted to CNF using the direct encoding of [17]. However, UP on that encoding (or on the other encodings presented in [17]) does not achieve GAC—it has only the power of forward checking. In this paper we demonstrate that alternate CNF encodings can be constructed that allow UP to efficiently achieve GAC.

Using UP on a CNF encoding to achieve GAC has a number of advantages over the specialized constraint specific algorithms (propagators) that are typically used. Intuitively, these advantages arise from the fact that propagators are procedural where as the CNF encoding utilized by UP is declarative. In particular, the sequencing of operations defining a propagator is typically quite rigid. Altering these operations so as to support features like interleaving with the propagators for other constraints or incrementality and decrementality in a backtracking context often requires non-trivial modifications.

In contrast UP can be run on a CNF encoding in flexible ways. In particular, UP can easily interleave the propagation of multiple constraints; it is always incremental; decrementality can be achieved almost without cost; and it readily supports the derivation of new clauses (generalized nogoods [12]) that can be used to improve search performance via learning and non-chronological backtracking. First, once encoded in CNF a constraint's clauses need not be distinguished from the clauses encoding other constraints.

C. Bessiere (Ed.): CP 2007, LNCS 4741, pp. 133–147, 2007.

Thus, UP can interleave its GAC propagation across different constraints in arbitrary ways. For example, if the constraints C_1 and C_2 are both encoded in CNF then UP can detect that a value for a variable has become inconsistent for constraint C_1 while it is in the middle of propagating the clauses for computing GAC on C_2. Furthermore, this pruned value will then automatically be taken into account during the rest of UP's computation of GAC on C_2. Second, UP works by forcing the truth value of propositions; the order in which these truth values are set is irrelevant to the final result. Hence, it is irrelevant to UP if some of these propositions already have their truth value set: i.e., UP is always incremental. Third, the modern technique for implementing UP employs a lazy data structure called watch literals. One of the salient features of watch literals is that they need not be updated on backtrack. Thus, with UP decrementality can be achieved essentially without cost: only the forced truth assignments need to be undone. Fourth, if UP detects a contradiction, existent techniques can be used to learn powerful nogoods that can improve search performance. These techniques learn generalized nogoods (clauses) which are more powerful than standard nogoods [12].

Previous work has investigated the connections between SAT propagation mechanisms (including UP) and various CSP propagation mechanisms (e.g., [6,3,9,17]). Most of this work, however, has been confined to binary constraints and thus has addressed AC rather than GAC. However, Hebrard et al. [11] building on the work of [9] present an CNF encoding for an arbitrary constraint that allows UP to achieve relational k-arc-consistency. Although that paper did not directly address achieving GAC via UP, their encoding can easily be adapted accomplish this. Furthermore, UP on this encoding achieves GAC in the same time complexity as a generic GAC algorithm like GAC-Schema [4] (GAC-Schema can however have a lower space complexity). Here one of our contributions is to elaborate the connection between GAC and UP on generic constraints, showing how Hebrard et al.'s encoding idea can be adapted to achieve GAC and how a more direct CNF encoding of the constraint can also allow UP to achieve GAC.

The main benefit of GAC in Constraint Programming, however, lies not so much with generic constraints, but rather in the fact that for a number of constraints specialized algorithms exist, called propagators, that can compute GAC in time that is typically polynomial in the arity of the constraint. This is a significant speed up over generic GAC algorithms which require time exponential in the arity of the constraint.

The main contribution of this paper is to demonstrate that just as some constraints admit specialized algorithms for computing GAC, some constraints also admit specialized CNF encodings on which UP can compute GAC much more efficiently. In this paper, we demonstrate such encodings for three different constraints: **regular**, **among** and **gen-sequence**. However, UP on our encoding for **gen-sequence** is not quite sufficient to achieve GAC. Nevertheless, a simple extension of UP called the **failed literal test** is able to achieve GAC on this encoding. The failed literal test retains the advantages of UP mentioned above.

An additional contribution of the paper is to explain how a CSP solver can easily be modified to integrate a state of the art UP engine that can then be used to achieve GAC for some constraints while the other constraints are propagated using traditional mechanisms. It is worth noting that a UP engine does not need to be implemented from scratch. Rather, *very* efficient state of the art UP engines are publically available. For example, the open source MiniSat SAT solver [7] (a consistent winner of recent SAT solver competitions) contains a clearly coded UP engine that can be extracted and utilized for this purpose—the code can be freely used even for commercial purposes.

In the sequel we first present the background properties of GAC and UP needed for the rest of the paper, and explain what is already known about the connection between GAC and UP. We then give a new result that elaborates on this connection. These results illustrate how generic GAC can be accomplished by UP. We then illustrate how a UP engine can be seamlessly integrated into a CSP solver. Turning to global constraints, we then present encodings for the afore mentioned constraints that allow UP to achieve GAC in polynomial time. We close with some final conclusions and ideas for future work.

2 Background

Let $\mathcal{V} = \{V_1, \ldots, V_n\}$ be a sequence of variables each of which has a finite domain of possible values $dom[V_i]$. Corresponding to the variable sequence $\mathcal{V}$ is the Cartesian product of the variable domains. We extend *dom* to apply to sequences of variables: $dom[\mathcal{V}] = dom[V_1] \times \cdots \times dom[V_n]$. A constraint C is a function over a sequence of variables $scope(C)$. The size of $scope(C)$ is called the **arity** of C. C maps tuples from $dom[scope(C)]$ to **true**/**false**. That is, if $scope(C) = \langle X_1, \ldots, X_k \rangle$ and $\tau \in dom[X_1] \times \cdots \times dom[X_k]$, then $C(\tau) =$ **true**/**false**. If $C(\tau) =$ **true** we say that τ **satisfies** C, else it **falsifies** it. We also view τ as being a set of assignments and say that $V = d \in \tau$ if τ's V'th dimension is equal to d.

A constraint C is said to be GAC if for every variable $X \in scope(C)$ and every value $d \in dom[X]$ there exists a $\tau \in dom[scope(C)]$ with $X = d \in \tau$ and $C(\tau) =$ **true**. A satisfying tuple τ containing $X = d$ is called a **support** for $X = d$. A constraint can be made GAC by simply removing every unsupported value from the domains of its variables. If the value $d \in dom[V]$ is unsupported by C we say that the assignment $V = d$ is **GAC-inconsistent** for C.

GAC propagation is the process of making some or all of the constraints of the problem GAC. If more than one constraint is to be made GAC, then GAC propagation will be an iterative process as making one constraint GAC might cause another constraint to no longer be GAC. However, since enforcing GAC (making a constraint GAC) is a monotonic process of removing unsupported values from the domains of variables, propagation must converge in at most a polynomial number of steps.

Unit propagation (UP) works on propositional formulas expressed in conjunctive normal form (CNF). A CNF formula is a conjunction of clauses, each of which is a disjunction of literals, each of which is a variable of the formula valued either positively or negatively. Given a CNF formula F and a literal ℓ we denote the reduction of F by ℓ as $F\big|_\ell$. The reduction $F\big|_\ell$ is a new CNF formula obtained from F by removing all clauses of F containing ℓ and then removing $\neg\ell$ (the negation of ℓ) from all remaining clauses. UP works by iteratively identifying all unit clauses of F (i.e., clauses containing only a single literal). Each unit clause $(\ell) \in F$ entails that ℓ must be true. Hence if (ℓ) is a unit clause of F then F is equivalent to $F\big|_\ell$. UP forces ℓ and transforms F to $F\big|_\ell$ whenever it finds a unit clause (ℓ). Furthermore, since $F\big|_\ell$ might contain additional unit clauses UP iteratively identifies unit clauses and continues to reduce the formula until no more units exist.

It is not hard to demonstrate that the final formula produced by UP does not depend on the order in which UP removes the unit clauses. Similarly, if GAC is being achieved for a collection of constraints, the order in which these constraints are processed (and reprocessed) has no effect on the final set of reduced variable domains. It can also be seen that UP runs in time linear in the total size of the input formula F (the sum of the lengths of the clauses of F): each clause of length k need only be visited at most k times to remove literals or force the last literal during UP. GAC also runs in time linear in the size of a tabular representation of the constraint: by processing each satisfying tuple of the constraint GAC can identify all supported variable values.[1] However, the tabular representation of a constraint has size exponential in the constraint's arity. It can be shown that when taking the arity of the constraint as the complexity parameter achieving GAC is NP-Hard. Both UP and GAC are sound rules of inference. That is, if d is removed from the domain of V by GAC, then no tuple of assignments satisfying C can contain $V = d$. Similarly, if UP forces the literal ℓ then ℓ must be true in all truth assignments satisfying F. Finally, Both GAC and UP can detect contradictions. If UP produces an empty clause during its propagation, the initial formula is UNSAT, and if GAC produces an empty variable domain the constraint cannot be satisfied.

UP can also be utilized for look-ahead. In particular the **failed literal rule** [8] involves adding the unit clause (ℓ) and then doing UP. If this yields a contradiction we can conclude that $\neg\ell$ is implied by the original formula.

2.1 Achieving Generic GAC with UP

In [11] a CNF encoding for a constraint was given on which UP is able to achieve relational k-arc consistency. Although GAC was not mentioned in that paper, their idea can be easily be adapted to allow UP to compute GAC on an arbitrary constraint.

The required encoding contains clauses for representing the variables and their domains of possible values. We call these clauses the **Variable Domain Encoding** (**VDom**). **VDom** consists of the following propositional variables and clauses. For every multi-valued variable V with $dom[V] = \{d_1, \ldots, d_m\}$:

1. m **assignment variables** $A_{V=d_j}$ one for each value $d_j \in dom[V]$. This variable is true when $V = d_j$, it is false when V cannot be assigned the value d_j, i.e., V has been assigned another value, or d_j has been pruned from V's domain.
2. The $O(m^2)$ binary clauses $(\neg A_{V=d}, \neg A_{V=d'})$ for every $d, d' \in dom[V]$ such that $d \neq d'$, capturing the condition that V cannot be assigned two different values.
3. The single clause $(A_{V=d_1}, \ldots, A_{V=d_m})$ which captures the condition that V must be assigned some value.

One important point about the **VDom** clauses is that although there are $O(km^2)$ clauses, UP can be performed on these clauses in time $O(km)$. In particular, it is easy to modify a UP engine so that the information contained in the **VDom** clauses is given a more compact $O(km)$ representation and propagated in $O(km)$ time (e.g., the e-clauses described in [5]). In the sequel we will assume that this optimization to the UP engine is used, so as to avoid an unnecessary m^2 factor in our complexity results.

[1] Practical GAC algorithms employ support data structures that make re-establishing GAC more efficient and that save space when the constraint is intensionally represented.

In addition to the **VDom** clauses, the encoding contains additional clauses used to capture the constraint C. These constraint clauses utilize additional propositional variables $t_1, \ldots, t_m$, each one representing one of the m different tuples over $dom[scope(C)]$ that satisfies C. Let τ_i be the satisfying tuple represented by the propositional variable t_i. Using the t_i variables the clauses capturing C are as follows:

1. For the variable $V \in scope(C)$ and value $d \in dom[V]$, let $\{s_1, \ldots, s_i\}$ be the subset of $\{t_1, \ldots, t_m\}$ such that the satisfying tuples represented by the s_i are precisely the set of tuples containing $V = d$. That is, the s_i represent all of the supports for $V = d$ in the constraint C. Then for each variable and value $V = d$ we have the clause $(s_1, \ldots, s_i, \neg A_{V=d})$, which captures the condition that $V = d$ cannot be true if it has no support.
2. For each satisfying tuple of C, τ_i, and assignment $V = d \in \tau_i$ we have the clause $(A_{V=d}, \neg t_i)$, which captures the condition that the tuple of assignments τ_i cannot hold if $V = d$ cannot be true.

When building this encoding, any value $d \in dom[V]$ that is unsupported in C will yield a unit clause $\neg A_{V=d}$ in item 1. Thus for every value $d \in dom[V]$ pruned by GAC, UP will force $\neg A_{V=d}$. More interestingly, in a dynamic context if d is pruned (say by GAC on another constraint), then the clauses of item 2 will allow UP to negate all tuple variables t_i such that $V = d \in \tau_i$. Then the clauses of item 1 will allow UP to delete any newly unsupported domain values. This propagation will continue until all unsupported domain values have been removed and GAC has been re-established.

It can also be observed that the size of this encoding (i.e., the sum of the lengths of the clauses) is linear in the size of the constraint's tabular representation: $O(mk)$ where m is the number of satisfying tuples, and k is the constraint's arity. In particular, t_i appears in only k clauses from item 1 (which bounds to total length of these clauses), and k clauses from item 2 (which are all of length 2). Hence UP on this encoding will operate in time linear in the size of the constraint's tabular representation, i.e., the same time complexity as a generic GAC algorithm.

3 UP for Generic GAC Revisited

We now present an new method for achieving GAC on a generic constraint via UP. Our method does not introduce any new propositional variables (only assignment variables are used).

In the new encoding we have the **VDom** clauses encoding the multi-valued variables in $scope(C)$, as before. Then for each **falsifying** tuple of assignments $\tau = \langle V_1 = d_1, V_2 = d_2, \ldots, V_k = d_k \rangle$ to the variables in $scope(C)$ we add the clause $(\neg A_{V_1=d_1}, \ldots, \neg A_{V_k=d_k})$ which blocks this tuple of assignments. Call this set of clauses $direct(C)$ [17]. Let the total set of clauses encoding C be $T =$ **VDom** $\cup\, direct(C)$. Now we replace T with its set of prime-implicates.

Definition 1. *If F is a CNF formula then the clause c is a* ***prime implicate*** *of F if $F \models c$ and for any c' that is a sub-clause of c ($c' \subsetneq c$), then $F \not\models c'$.*

Letting $PI(T)$ be the set of prime implicates of T we have the following result.

Theorem 1. *If the constraint C is satisfied by some tuple of assignments, UP on the CNF theory $PI(T)$ achieves GAC on C. That is, the assignment $V = d$ is GAC-inconsistent for C iff UP on $PI(T)$ forces $\neg A_{V=d}$. If C has no satisfying tuple, UP on $PI(T)$ will generate the empty clause (and GAC will generate an empty domain).*

Proof: First we observe that the set of satisfying tuples of C and the set of models of T are in 1-1 correspondence. From any model of T we must have one and only one assignment variable $A_{V=d}$ being true for each variable $V \in scope(C)$. Furthermore, this set of true assignments do not correspond to any falsifying tuple, else they would falsify one of the clauses encoding C. Similarly, from a satisfying tuple for C we can make the corresponding assignment variables of T true, this will falsify all other assignment variables and thus satisfy all the clauses encoding C.

Hence, if GAC prunes $V = d$, $A_{V=d}$ cannot be true in any model of T, thus $T \models (\neg A_{V=d})$ and this unit clause must be part of $PI(T)$. On the other hand if UP on $PI(T)$ forces $\neg A_{V=d}$ then $A_{V=d}$ must be false in every model of $PI(T)$, hence false in every model of T (since $PI(T)$ is logically equivalent to T), hence $V = d$ cannot be part of any satisfying tuple, and hence it will be pruned by GAC. Finally, if C is unsatisfiable, T will be UNSAT, and $PI(T)$ will contain only the empty clause. ■

Corollary 1. *If after establishing GAC by running UP on $PI(T)$ we additionally prune the assignment $V = d$ (say by GAC on another constraint), then UP on $PI(T) \cup (\neg A_{V=d})$ will re-establish GAC.*

This corollary can be seen to be true by observing that UP on $PT(T) \cup (\neg A_{V=d})$ is the same as UP on $PT(T)\big|_{\neg A_{V=d}}$ and that this is the set of prime implicates of $T\big|_{\neg A_{V=d}}$.

Computing the set of prime implicates of a theory can be expensive; in the worst case it is exponential in the sum of the domain sizes of the variables in $scope(C)$. Nevertheless, we can make the following observations. First, the prime implicate encoding can be computed prior to search. Furthermore, once a constraint has been converted to its prime implicate encoding that encoding can be reused in any CSP containing the constraint. Second, some constraints might have a special structure that permit a more efficient computation of their prime implicates. And third even partial computation of some of the implicates of T could allow UP to derive more consequences even if it fails to achieve GAC.

4 Using a UP Engine in a CSP Solver

The two encodings presented above facilitate achieving GAC on an arbitrary constraint, but the complexity remains exponential in the constraint's arity. In the next section we investigate encodings that exploit constraint specific structure to move from exponential to polynomial complexity. But before presenting those results we first discuss how an UP engine could be utilized in a CSP solver.

The architecture would be as illustrated in the figure to the right. The UP engine operates on a set of clauses encoding some of the constraints $C_1, \ldots, C_k$. These clauses would also include the **VDom** clauses encoding variable domains. The other constraints of the problem, $D_1, \ldots, D_i$ are handled by a standard CSP propagator (e.g., a GAC propagator). Both UP and GAC communicate with each other and with an underlying solver. The communication required is simple. Whenever GAC (the solver) prunes a value d from $dom[V]$ (assigns $V = d$) it informs the UP engine that the associated literal $\neg A_{V=d}$ ($A_{V=d}$) has become true. UP can then propagate this literal which might result in other variables $A_{X=a}$ being forced true or false. If $A_{X=a}$ becomes true, then the assignment $X = a$ is forced and all of X's other values have been pruned. The GAC engine can then propagate the fact that $X \neq d$ for all $d \neq a$. If $A_{X=a}$ becomes false, then the GAC engine can propagate the pruned value $X \neq a$. Either engine might be able derive a contradiction, at which point the search engine can backtrack. On backtrack the search engine will inform the GAC and UP engines to backtrack their state. For UP this is the simple process of unassigning all literals set to be true since the backtrack point.

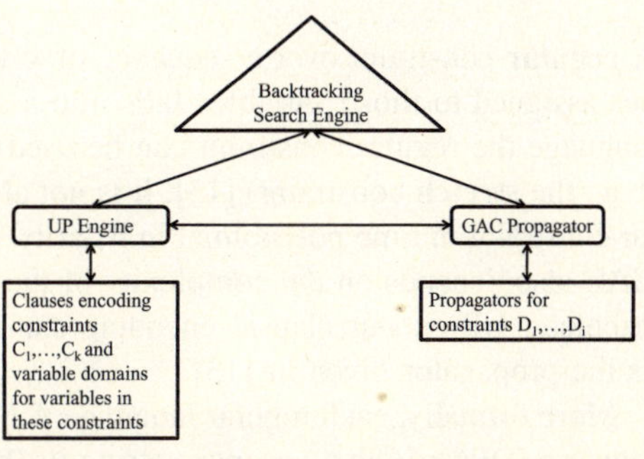

Note that UP can also return a clausal reason for every assignment variable it forces. These clausal reasons can then be utilized by the search engine to perform non-chronological backtracking and clause learning. Since these clauses can contain both positive and negative instances of the assignment variables they are more general than standard nogoods (which contain only positive instances of assignment variables). As shown in [12] this added generality can yield a super-polynomial speedup in search. With the GAC engine, however, we have to modify each specialized propagator to allow it to produce an appropriate clausal reason for its pruned values. [12] gives some examples of how this can be accomplished.

5 Constraint Specific UP Encodings

GAC propagators are one of the fundamental enablers of GAC in CSP solvers. Propagators are constraint specific algorithms that exploit the special structure of a constraint so as to compute GAC in time polynomial in the constraint's arity.

Our main contribution is to demonstrate that constraint specific structure can also be exploited by a UP engine for a range of constraints. In particular, we present specialized clausal encodings for three different constraints, **regular**, **among**, and **gen-sequence**, such that UP on these encodings achieve GAC as efficiently as currently known propagators.

There has been some previous work on exploiting structure via specialized CNF encodings of constraints, e.g., [2,15,10,1]. These works however are mostly aimed at obtaining better performing CNF encodings for use in a SAT solver. In particular, either UP on these encodings does not achieve GAC or when it does it is not as efficient as standard GAC propagators.

5.1 Regular

A **regular** constraint over a sequence of k variables asserts that the sequence of values assigned to those variables falls into a specific regular language. By varying the language the regular constraint can be used to capture a number of other constraints (e.g., the **stretch** constraint) [13]. It is not always possible to achieve GAC on a regular constraint in time polynomial in its arity. In particular, the complexity of achieving GAC also depends on the complexity of the regular language being recognized. Nevertheless, UP on our clausal encoding can achieve the same complexity guarantees as the propagator given in [13].

More formally, each regular language $\mathcal{L}$ has an associated Deterministic Finite Automaton (DFA) M that accepts a string iff that string is a member of $\mathcal{L}$. M is defined by the tuple $\langle Q, \Sigma, \delta, q_0, F\rangle$, where Q is a finite set of automaton states, Σ is an input alphabet of symbols, δ is a transition function mapping state-input symbol pairs to new states $Q \times \Sigma \mapsto Q$, q_0 is the initial state, and F is a set of accepting states. A DFA takes as input a string of characters. Each character $c \in \Sigma$ causes it to transition from its current state q to the new state $\delta(q, c)$. The DFA starts off in the state q_0 and a string S over the alphabet Σ is said to be accepted by the DFA M if S causes M to transition from q_0 to some accepting state in F.

Let $\mathcal{L}$ be a regular language over the alphabet of symbols $\bigcup_{i=1}^{k} dom[V_i]$, and M be a DFA that accepts $\mathcal{L}$. The regular constraint over the sequence of variables $\langle V_1, \ldots, V_k\rangle$ and the language $\mathcal{L}$, $\textbf{regular}_{\mathcal{L}}(\langle V_1, \ldots, V_k\rangle)$ is satisfied by a sequence of assignments $\langle V_1 = d_1, \ldots V_k = d_k\rangle$ iff the sequence of values $\langle d_1, \ldots, d_k\rangle$ is accepted by the DFA associated with $\mathcal{L}$.

Our clausal encoding of regular utilizes the insight of [13] that GAC can be achieved by looking for paths in a layered directed graph. The graph has k layers each of which represents the possible states the DFA can be in after s inputs ($0 \le s \le k$). Any input string generates a path in this graph, and an accepted string must generate a path starting at q_0 and ending in some state of F. Our encoding captures the structure of this graph in such a way that UP can determine whether or not any particular value $d \in dom[V_i]$ lies on an accepting path (is part of a satisfying tuple). The encoding contains the assignment variables $A_{V_i=d}$ ($d \in dom[V_i]$) along with the **VDom** clauses encoding the variable domains. In addition it also contains the following variables and clauses:

1. For each step s of M's processing, $0 \le s \le k$, and each state $q_i \in Q$, the state variable q_i^s. This variable is true if M is in state q_i after having processed s input symbols.
2. For each transition $(q_i, d) \mapsto q_j \in \delta$ and each step s, $1 \le s \le k$ such that $d \in dom[V_s]$, the transition variable $t^s_{q_i\langle d\rangle q_j}$. This variable is true if M's s-th input symbol is d and on processing this symbol it transitions from state q_i to q_j.
3. For each transition variable the clauses $(\neg t^s_{q_i\langle d\rangle q_j}, q_i^{s-1})$, $(\neg t^s_{q_i\langle d\rangle q_j}, q_j^s)$, and $(\neg t^s_{q_i\langle d\rangle q_j}, A_{V_s=d})$. These clauses capture the condition that if the transition $t^s_{q_i\langle d\rangle q_j}$ is true, M must be in state q_i at step $s{-}1$, q_j at step s, and V_s must be assigned the value d.
4. For each state variable q_i^s let $\{t^{s+1}_{q_i\langle *\rangle *}\}$ be the set of transition variables representing transitions out of q_i at step $s{+}1$ and $\{t^s_{*\langle *\rangle q_i}\}$ be the set of transition

variables representing transitions into q_i at step s. For each q_i^s the encoding contains the clauses $(\{t^{s+1}_{q_i\langle *\rangle *}\}, \neg q_i^s)$ and $(\{t^s_{*\langle *\rangle q_i}\}, \neg q_i^s)$, capturing the condition that at least one incoming and one outgoing transition must be true for state q_i to hold at step s. For step 0 we omit the clauses for incoming transitions, and for step k we omit the clauses for outgoing transitions.

5. For each assignment variable $A_{V_s=d}$ let $\{t^s_{*\langle d\rangle *}\}$ be the set of transition variables representing transitions enabled by the assignment $V_s = d$ at step s. Then for each assignment variable the encoding contains the clause $(\{t^s_{*\langle d\rangle *}\}, \neg A_{V_s=d})$ capturing the condition that at least one supporting transition must be true for this assignment to be possible.
6. For each state variable q_i^0 such that $i \neq 0$, the encoding contains the clause $(\neg q_i^0)$, capturing the condition that M must start in step 0 in the initial state q_0. For each state variable q_i^k such that q_i is not an accepting state of M, the encoding contains the clause $(\neg q_i^k)$, capturing the condition that M must finish in some accepting state.

Theorem 2. *If the constraint* **regular**$_{\mathcal{L}}(\langle V_1, \ldots, V_k\rangle)$ *is satisfied by some tuple of assignments, UP on the above encoding achieves GAC on the constraint in time* $O(km|Q|)$, *where* k *is the arity of the constraint,* m *is the maximum sized domain, and* $|Q|$ *is the number of states of the DFA accepting* $\mathcal{L}$. *That is, the assignment* $V_i = d$ *is GAC-inconsistent for* **regular**$_{\mathcal{L}}(\langle V_1, \ldots, V_k\rangle)$ *iff UP on this encoding forces* $\neg A_{V_i=d}$. *If* **regular**$_{\mathcal{L}}(\langle V_1, \ldots, V_k\rangle)$ *has no satisfying assignment UP will generate the empty clause (GAC will generate an empty domain).*

Proof: First we address the size of the encoding. There are $|Q|k$ state variables (where k is the arity of the constraint and $|Q|$ is the number of states of M), and if m is the maximal sized domain of any of the variables V_i, at most $km|Q|$ transition variables. In particular, M is deterministic, hence for each transition variable $t^s_{q_i\langle d\rangle q_j}$ if any two of the three parameters q_i, d, or q_j are fixed the last parameter can only have a single value (s ranges from 1 to k).

Associated with each transition variable are 3 clauses from item 3 for a total size of $O(km|Q|)$. Associated with each of the $k|Q|$ state variables is a clause of length $|\{t^{s+1}_{q_i\langle *\rangle *}\}| + 1$ and a clause of length $|\{t^s_{*\langle *\rangle q_i}\}| + 1$, from item 4. These clauses are at most $m + 1$ in length (given the input symbol the other (input or output) state is determined): again a total size of $O(km|Q|)$. Finally, associated with each of the $O(km)$ assignment variables is a single clause of length $|\{t^s_{*\langle d\rangle *}\}| + 1$. These clauses can be most length $|Q| + 1$ (fixing the input or output state determines the other state): once again a total size of $O(km|Q|)$. Hence the total size of the clausal encoding is $O(km|Q|)$ which gives the space as well as the time complexity of UP (UP runs in time linear in the total size of the encoding).[2] This is the same time and space complexity of the propagator given in [13].

Now we prove that UP achieves GAC assuming that the constraint is satisfied by some tuple of assignments. First, if $V_i = d_i$ is not pruned by GAC then UP cannot

[2] As discussed Section 2.1 we are exploiting the fact that the km^2 **VDom** clauses can be represented and propagated in $O(km)$ space and time.

force $\neg A_{V_i=d_i}$. If $V_i = d_i$ is not pruned by GAC it must have a supporting tuple, $\langle V_1 = d_1, \ldots, V_i = d_i, \ldots, V_k = d_k\rangle$. This sequence of inputs to M will cause M to transition through a sequence of states $\langle q_{\pi(0)}, q_{\pi(1)}, \ldots, q_{\pi(k)}\rangle$ starting at the initial state $q_{\pi(0)} = q_0$ and ending at an accepting state $q_{\pi(k)} \in F$. Setting all of the corresponding assignment variables $A_{V_i=d_i}$, state variables $q^s_{\pi(s)}$, and transition variables $t^s_{q_{\pi(s-1)}\langle d_s\rangle q_{\pi(s)}}$ to be true, and and all other variables to be false, we observe that all clauses become satisfied. Hence $A_{V_i=d_i}$ is part of a satisfying truth assignment and since UP is sound it cannot force $\neg A_{V_i=d_i}$. We conclude by contraposition that if UP forces $\neg A_{V_i=d_i}$ then GAC must prune $V_i = d_i$

Second, if UP does not force $\neg A_{V_i=d_i}$ then GAC will not prune $V_i = d_i$, and by contraposition we have that if GAC prunes $V_i = d_i$ then UP must force $\neg A_{V_i=d_i}$. Given that UP has been run to completion and $\neg A_{V_i=d_i}$ has not been forced, then by the clauses of item 5 there must exist some transition variable $t^i_{q_h\langle d_i\rangle q_j}$ that also has not be falsified by UP. By the clauses of item 2, it must also be the case that the state variables q^{i-1}_h and q^i_j have not been falsified. By the clauses of item 4 there must be corresponding transition variables $t^{i-1}_{q_g\langle d_{i-1}\rangle q_h}$ incoming to q^{i-1}_h and $t^{i+1}_{q_j\langle d_{i+1}\rangle q_k}$ outcoming from q^i_j, neither of which have been falsified. By the clauses of item 2 the assignment variables $A_{V_{i-1}=d_{i-1}}$ and $A_{V_{i+1}=d_{i+1}}$ cannot be falsified. Continuing this way we arrive at a input sequence that includes $V_i = d_i$ and that causes M to transition from q_0 to an accepting state. That is, $V_i = d_i$ has a supporting tuple, and GAC will not prune it.

Finally, if $\textbf{regular}_{\mathcal{L}}(\langle V_1, \ldots, V_k\rangle)$ has no satisfying assignment then no value $d \in dom[V_i]$ is supported (for any variable V_i). By the above UP will force $\neg A_{V_i=d}$ for every $d \in dom[V_i]$ thus making the **VDom** clause $(A_{V_i=d_1}, \ldots, A_{V_i=d_m})$ empty. ■

Corollary 2. *If after initial GAC we additionally prune the assignment $V_i = d_i$, then adding the unit clause $\neg A_{V_i=d_i}$ and again performing UP re-establishes GAC.*

That is, we can incrementally maintain GAC on $\textbf{regular}_{\mathcal{L}}(\langle V_1, \ldots, V_k\rangle)$ by simply falsifying the assignment variables for every pruned assignment and then redoing UP. As noted in the introduction UP is inherently incremental, so no changes need to be made to achieve an incremental propagator. This corollary can be proved by observing that the proof of the theorem continues to apply even if some of the assignment variables have initially been set to be false.

In [14] a CNF encoding for the **grammar** constraint has been developed. That encoding is based on the grammar rules view of languages, and uses CNF to encode a dynamic programming parsing algorithm. UP on the encoding is able to achieve GAC for context free grammar constraints. Since regular languages are a subset of context free languages, this encoding supplies an alternate way of using UP to achieve GAC on **regular**. However, as demonstrated below our encoding for **regular** can be extended to provide an encoding for **gen-sequence** whereas the encoding of [14] does not provide an immediate solution for **gen-sequence**. Furthermore, the argument that UP might be a useful general way of achieving GAC is not put forward in that paper.

5.2 Among

An **among** constraint over a sequence of k variables, $\langle V_1, \ldots, V_k\rangle$ asserts that at least $\min$ and at most $\max$ of these variables can take on a value from a specific set S. More formally, **among**$(\langle V_1, \ldots, V_k\rangle, S, \min, \max)$ is satisfied by a tuple of assignments $\langle d_1, \ldots, d_k\rangle$ iff $\min \leq |\langle d_1, \ldots, d_k\rangle \cap S| \leq \max$.

To simplify our notation we can consider **among**$(\langle V_1, \ldots, V_k\rangle, \{1\}, \min, \max)$ in which all of the variables in $\langle V_1, \ldots, V_k\rangle$ have domain $\{0, 1\}$ and S is $\{1\}$. Any **among** constraint **among**$(\langle X_1, \ldots, X_k\rangle, S', \min, \max)$ can be reduced to this case by introducing the $\langle V_1, \ldots, V_k\rangle$ as new variables and imposing a constraint between X_i and V_i $(1 \leq i \leq k)$ such that $V_i = 1$ iff X_i has a value in S'. In fact, although we omit the details here, the constraint between the original X_i variables and the V_i variables can be captured with a CNF encoding and enforced with the same UP engine used to enforce **among**.

We can specify a CNF encoding for **among** by constructing a DFA that has $\max$ states, $q_0, \ldots, q_{\max}$. The states $q_{\min}, \ldots q_{\max}$ are all accepting states. The input alphabet is the two conditions V_i and $\neg V_i$ (the V_i are binary values thus they can be treated as propositions with $V_i \equiv V_i = 1$ and $\neg V_i \equiv V_i = 0$). The transition function is simply defined by the condition that an V_i input causes a transition from q_j to q_{j+1}, while a $\neg V_i$ input causes a transition from q_j back to q_j. In other words, the states of the DFA simply keep track of the number of variables taking values in S and accepts iff the total number over all k variables lies in the range $[\min, \max]$. Thus the **among** constraint can be encoded as a CNF on which UP achieves GAC by using the previously specified encoding for this DFA.

Encoding **among** as a CNF is not particularly practical, as **among** has a very simple propagator that is more efficient than UP on this CNF encoding. The real use of the CNF encoding of **among** comes from applying it to conjunctions of **among** constraints. It can also be noted that [1,15] both provide CNF encodings for the Boolean Cardinality Constraint which is equivalent to the above **among** constraint. Their encodings allow UP to achieve GAC, but as with the above encoding, their encodings are not as efficient as the standard propagator.

5.3 Generalized Sequence Constraint

A **gen-sequence** constraint over a sequence of variables $\langle V_1, \ldots, V_k\rangle$ is a conjunction of **among** constraints. However, it is not an arbitrary collection of **among** constraints. In particular, all of the **among** constraints are over sub-sequences of the same global sequence $\langle V_1, \ldots, V_k\rangle$. Furthermore, the **among** constraint all count membership in a fixed subset of domain values S.[3] More formally,

$$\textbf{gen-sequence}(\langle V_1, \ldots, V_k\rangle, S, \langle \sigma_1, \ldots, \sigma_m\rangle, \langle \min_1, \ldots, \min_m\rangle, \langle \max_1, \ldots, \max_m\rangle) \equiv \textstyle\bigwedge_{j=1}^{m} \textbf{among}_j(\sigma_j, S, \min_j, \max_j),$$

where each σ_j is a sub-sequence of $\langle V_1, \ldots, V_k\rangle$.

[3] The algorithm provided in [16] also requires that the set S be fixed over all **among** constraints.

We present an encoding on which the failed literal test achieves GAC. That is, with this encoding, each value of each variable can be tested to determined if it is supported by doing a single run of UP. It is particularly important that modern implementations of UP are decremental almost without cost. Thus all that needs to be done between testing successive variable values is to undo the truth assignments forced by the previous run of UP. Using the failed literal test to achieve GAC on this constraint achieves the same time complexity guarantee as the propagator given in [16].

Since the set S is fixed across all of the **among** constraints, we can apply the same transformation used in the previous section to convert them to **among** constraints over variables with domain $\{0, 1\}$ and $S = \{1\}$. With this simplifying transformation our CNF encoding for **gen-sequence** consists of the encoding generated by a simple DFA along with some additional clauses. In particular, to obtain a CNF encoding for **gen-sequence**($\langle V_1, \ldots, V_k\rangle$, $\{1\}$, $\langle \sigma_1, \ldots, \sigma_m\rangle$, $\langle \min_1, \ldots, \min_m\rangle$, $\langle \max_1, \ldots, \max_m\rangle$) (abbreviated as **gen-sequence**($\langle V_1, \ldots, V_k\rangle$)) where $S = \{1\}$ and the variables are all have domain $\{0, 1\}$, we first generate the CNF encoding for **among**($\langle V_1, \ldots, V_k\rangle, S, 0, k$).

This encoding captures a DFA that simply keeps track of the number of variables in $\langle V_1, \ldots, V_k\rangle$ that lie in S: all states are accepting. In the CNF encoding each step s ($0 < s \leq k$) contains s state variables q_i^s ($0 \leq i \leq s$) indicating that i of the first s variables $V_1, \ldots, V_s$ took a value in S. The transition variables $t^s_{q_i \langle V_s \rangle q_{i+1}}$ and $t^s_{q_i \langle \neg V_s \rangle q_i}$ capture the transitions $q_i \rightarrow q_{i+1}$ made when V_s takes a value in S and $q_i \rightarrow q_i$ made when V_s takes a value not in S.

In addition to the clauses encoding this "base" DFA, for every constraint **among**$_j$ (σ_j, S, $\min_j$, $\max_j$) in the **gen-sequence** we have the following clauses.

1. Let σ_j be the subsequence of variables $\langle V_g, \ldots, V_h\rangle$, for every state variable at step $g-1$, q_i^{g-1} ($0 \leq i \leq k$) we have the clause ($q^h_{i+\min_j}, \ldots, q^h_{i+\max_j}, \neg q_i^{g-1}$) encoding the condition that if the count by time we have reached step h does not lie in the range $[i + \min_j, i + \max_j]$ then we cannot have started with the count at i at step $g-1$.
2. The clause ($q^{g-1}_{i-\max_j}, \ldots, q^{g-1}_{i-\min_j}, \neg q_i^h$) encoding the condition that if the count by time we reach step h is i then we must have started off in the range $[i - \max_j, i - \min_j]$ at step $g-1$.

Theorem 3. *If the constraint **gen-sequence**($\langle V_1, \ldots, V_k\rangle$) is satisfied by some tuple of assignments, the failed literal test on the above encoding achieves GAC on the constraint in time $O(mk^3)$, where k is the arity of the constraint, and m is the number of **among** constraints in the **gen-sequence** constraint. That is, the assignment V_i (i.e., $V_i = 1$) is GAC-inconsistent iff the failed literal test on V_i yields a contradiction. Similarly for the assignment $\neg V_i$ (i.e., $V_i = 0$). If **gen-sequence**($\langle V_1, \ldots, V_k\rangle$) has no satisfying assignment then UP (without use of the failed literal test) will generate the empty clause (GAC would generate an empty domain).*[4]

[4] Note that in [16] the claim is made that their propagator runs in time $O(k^3)$. However, a close look at their algorithm demonstrates that it in fact requires $O(mk^3)$. In particular, each time a PUSHUP operation (at most $O(k^2)$) in their CHECKCONSISTENCY

Proof: We show that V_i is GAC inconsistent iff the failed literal test on $\neg V_i$ yields a contradiction. The argument for $\neg V_i$ is similar.

Consider the relevant parts of the CNF encoding of **gen-sequence**. These are the clauses encoding the base DFA that counts the number of variables taking values in S, along with the clauses of item 1 and 2 above capturing the relationship between the initial and final counts for each **among** constraint.

If GAC does not prune V_i then there must be some supporting tuple of values containing it $\langle V_1, \ldots, V_k \rangle$. We can then generate a path through the base DFA from this input sequence of V_j values. As with the proof of Theorem 2 this sequence can be used to assign **true** to the state, and transition lying along this accepting path, with all other variables assigned **false**. It can then be observed that all clauses of the DFA will be satisfied, and further since the sequence also satisfies all m **among** constraints so will all clauses for the m **among** constraints (items 1 and 2 above). Thus UP cannot not force $\neg V_i$ since V_i is part of a satisfying assignment. Furthermore, the failed literal test on V_i cannot yield a contradiction. By contraposition we conclude that if the failed literal test yields a contradiction then GAC will prune the value.

To prove the other direction consider what happens after UP (but not failed literal) has been run. There will be some **set** of unfalsified state variables Q_s at each step s. If any of these sets, say Q_i is empty, UP must have produced an empty clause. In particular, the clauses of item 3 of the DFA encoding (specifying that a transition cannot be true if its final state is false) will allow UP to falsify all incoming transitions variables into states of step s, and this in turn will allow UP to falsify both "alphabet symbols" V_i and $\neg V_i$ using the clauses of item 5 of the DFA. This will give rise to a contradiction and an empty clause. By the previous paragraph this means that the constraint has no satisfying tuple, as each satisfying tuple yields a model of the clauses.

Say that none of these sets Q_s is empty, let $\langle q_0, q_{\pi(1)}, \ldots, q_{\pi(k)} \rangle$ be the sequence of states such that $\pi(i)$ is the minimal indexed state variable of Q_i. This sequence of states corresponds to the minimal unfalsified counts in the DFA after UP. We claim that this sequence of states corresponds to a satisfying tuple for **gen-sequence**. First, we have that either $\pi(i{+}1) = \pi(i)$ or $\pi(i{+}1) = \pi(i) + 1$, that is these counts can increase by zero or one at each step. If $\pi(i{+}1) < \pi(i)$, then the only transitions into $q^{i+1}_{\pi(i+1)}$ are from q^i_j with $j < \pi(i)$. However, all such state variables have been falsified as $q^i_{\pi(i)}$ is the minimal indexed state variable at step i, hence the clauses of item 3 of the DFA would have falsified all transitions variables coming into $q^{i+1}_{\pi(i-1)}$, and the clauses of item 4 of the DFA would falsify $q^{i+1}_{\pi(i+1)}$: a contradiction. Similarly, if $\pi(i{+}1) > \pi(i) + 1$ then all outgoing transitions from $q^i_{\pi(i)}$ would be falsified and so would $q^i_{\pi(i)}$. Second, if $\pi(i{+}1) = \pi(i)$ the variable $\neg V_i$ cannot be false and if $\pi(i{+}1) = \pi(i) + 1$ the variable V_i cannot be false: if these variables were false then one or both of $q^i_{\pi(i)}$ and $q^{i+1}_{\pi(i+1)}$ would fail to have any incoming or outgoing transitions and would thus be falsified by UP. Finally, this sequence must satisfy each

algorithm is performed it could require first checking all m **among** constraints to see if any are violated. This yields an $O(mk^2)$ complexity for CHECKCONSISTENCY and an overall $O(mk^3)$ complexity for achieving GAC.

among constraint because of the clauses from each of these constraints. Consider the clauses $(q^h_{\pi(g+\min_j)}, \ldots, q^h_{\pi(g+\max_j)}, \neg q^{g-1}_{\pi(g-1)})$ and $(q^{g-1}_{\pi(h-\max_j)}, \ldots, q^{g-1}_{\pi(h-\min_j)}, \neg q^h_{\pi(h)})$ from **among** constraint j. Since $q^{g-1}_{\pi(g-1)}$ is the minimal indexed state variable at step g and $q^h_{\pi(h)}$ is the minimal indexed state variable at step h, we can see that if $\pi(g) - \pi(h)$ lies outside of the range $[\min_j, \max_j]$ then one of $q^{g-1}_{\pi(g-1)}$ or $q^h_{\pi(h)}$ will be falsified by UP from these clauses. For example, if $\pi(g) - \pi(h) > \max_j$ then all of the step h state literals in $(q^h_{\pi(g+\min_j)}, \ldots, q^h_{\pi(g+\max_j)}, \neg q^{g-1}_{\pi(g-1)})$ would be falsified and thus $q^{g-1}_{\pi(g-1)}$ would also be falsified by UP. Hence, these minimal states and the corresponding transitions and V_j variables between them define a satisfying tuple for **gen-sequence**. We also see that if the constraint has no satisfying tuple, at least one of the sets Q_s must be empty and by the previous paragraph UP yields the empty clause. This proves the last claim of the theorem.

If we apply the failed literal test to V_i, this will force V_i and thus if there is no contradiction the minimal path after UP must contain V_i in the satisfying tuple it defines. Thus V_i is supported, and so GAC will not prune this assignment. By contraposition, if GAC prunes V_i then the failed literal test must generate a contradiction.

Turning now to the complexity, note that the encoding for the base DFA is of size (total length of clauses) $O(k^2)$; in particular $|Q| = k$ and $m = 2$ since the base DFA only has to symbols V_j and $\neg V_j$ in its alphabet. The clauses encoding the **among** constraints total m (the number of **among** constrains) times $O(k^2)$; each **among** constraint generates k clauses from item 1 and k clauses of item 2, each of these clauses is of length $O(k)$. So in total we have a CNF theory of total size $O(mk^2)$. At most we have to do $O(k)$ failed literal tests each of which runs in time $O(k^2)$. This gives us a total complexity for achieving GAC of $O(mk^3)$ in the worst case. ■

Some additional comments can be made about the practicality of this approach to GAC on **gen-sequence**. First, the failed literal test can be quite efficient. In particular, no work needs to be done to reset the "data structures" (i.e., the clauses) between successive failed literal tests. Second, UP on this encoding achieves incremental GAC, it is not difficult to see that if we prune values from the domains of the variables V_i so as to force the value of V_i, UP can incrementally re-establish GAC. Third, the initial UP and each successive failed literal test yields a supporting tuple. If V_i or $\neg V_i$ appears in any of these tuples, we need not do a failed literal test on it: it is already supported. Furthermore, by analogous reasoning it is not hard to see that the sequence of **maximum** indexed state variables in the sets Q_s also forms a satisfying tuple. Thus the initial UP and each subsequent failed literal test can yield up to two satisfying tuples, each of which can be used to avoid testing some as yet untested V_i literals.

6 Conclusions

In this paper we have shown that GAC can be efficiently achieved by using the approach of converting a constraint to a CNF and then employing a UP engine to do propagation in that CNF. As discussed in the introduction this approach has a number of advantages, including the fact that it is immediately incremental and decremental. We have also shown that special structure in a constraint can in some cases be exploited so that UP can achieve GAC with the same complexity as a constraint specific propagation algorithm.

A number of questions remain open. First, there is the empirical question of how this approach performs in practice. On that front we are quite optimistic given the highly tuned nature of publically available UP engines. Second, there is the question of just how general is this approach; can it be applied to other well known constraints? One thing to note with respect to this question is that **regular** is already quite a general constraint. Nevertheless, further research along this line is definitely required. It should be noted that the CNF encodings presented here exploits structure that had already been uncovered and exploited in previous propagators. So it is feasible that other propagation algorithms could similarly exploited.

References

1. Bailleux, O., Boufkhad, Y.: Efficient cnf encoding of boolean cardinality constraints. In: Rossi, F. (ed.) CP 2003. LNCS, vol. 2833, pp. 108–122. Springer, Heidelberg (2003)
2. Bailleux, O., Boufkhad, Y.: Full cnf encoding: The counting constraints case. In: Hoos, H.H., Mitchell, D.G. (eds.) SAT 2004. LNCS, vol. 3542, Springer, Heidelberg (2005)
3. Bennaceur, H.: A comparison between sat and csp techniques. Constraints 9, 123–138 (2004)
4. Bessière, C., Régin, J.C.: Arc consistency for general constraint networks: Preliminary results. In: Proc. IJCAI, pp. 398–404 (1997)
5. Chavira, M., Darwiche, A.: Compiling bayesian networks with local structure. In: Proc. IJCAI-2005, pp. 1306–1312 (2005)
6. Dimopoulos, Y., Stergiou, K.: Propagation in csp and sat. In: Benhamou, F. (ed.) CP 2006. LNCS, vol. 4204, pp. 137–151. Springer, Heidelberg (2006)
7. Eén, N., Sörensson, N.: Minisat solver, `http://www.cs.chalmers.se/Cs/Research/FormalMethods/MiniSat/MiniSat.html`
8. Freeman, J.W.: Improvements to Propositional Satisfiability Search Algorithms. PhD thesis, University of Pennsylvania (1995)
9. Gent, I.: Arc consistency in sat. In: ECAI, pp. 121–125 (2002)
10. Gent, I., Nightingale, P.: A new encoding of all-different into SAT. In: Proc. 3rd International Workshop on Modelling and Reformulating Constraint Satisfaction Problems, pp. 95–110 (2004)
11. Hebrard, E., Bessière, C., Walsh, T.: Local consistencies in sat. In: Giunchiglia, E., Tacchella, A. (eds.) SAT 2003. LNCS, vol. 2919, pp. 400–407. Springer, Heidelberg (2004)
12. Katsirelos, G., Bacchus, F.: Generalized nogoods in csps. In: Proc. of AAAI, pp. 390–396 (2005)
13. Pesant, G.: A regular language membership constraint for finite sequences of variables. In: Wallace, M. (ed.) CP 2004. LNCS, vol. 3258. Springer, Heidelberg (2004)
14. Quimper, C.-G., Walsh, T.: Decomposing global grammar constraints. In: Proc. of CP2007 (2007)
15. Sinz, C.: Towards an optimal cnf encoding of boolean cardinality constraints. In: van Beek, P. (ed.) CP 2005. LNCS, vol. 3709, pp. 827–831. Springer, Heidelberg (2005)
16. van Hoeve, W.J., Pesant, G., Rousseau, L.M., Sabharwal, A.: Revisiting the Sequence Constraint. In: Benhamou, F. (ed.) CP 2006. LNCS, vol. 4204. Springer, Heidelberg (2006)
17. Walsh, T.: Sat v csp. In: Dechter, R. (ed.) CP 2000. LNCS, vol. 1894, pp. 441–456. Springer, Heidelberg (2000)

Solution Directed Backjumping for QCSP

Fahiem Bacchus[1] and Kostas Stergiou[2]

[1] Department of Computer Science, University of Toronto, Canada
fbacchus@cs.toronto.edu
[2] Department of Information and Communication Systems Engineering,
University of the Aegean, Greece
konsterg@aegean.gr

Abstract. In this paper we present new techniques for improving backtracking based Quantified Constraint Satisfaction Problem (QCSP) solvers. QCSP is a generalization of CSP in which variables are either universally or existentially quantified and these quantifiers can be alternated in arbitrary ways. Our main new technique is solution directed backjumping (SBJ). In analogue to conflict directed backjumping, SBJ allows the solver to backtrack out of solved sub-trees without having to find all of the distinct solutions normally required to validate the universal variables. Experiments with the solver QCSP-Solve demonstrate that SBJ can improve its performance on random instances by orders of magnitude. In addition to this contribution, we demonstrate that performing varying levels of propagation for universal vs. existential variables can also be useful for enhancing performance. Finally, we discuss some techniques that are technically interesting but do not yet yield empirical improvements.

1 Introduction

In this paper we present new techniques for improving the performance of solvers for Quantified Constraint Satisfaction Problems (QCSPs). QCSPs are an extension of standard constraint satisfaction problems (CSPs) that can compactly represent a wider range of problems than the standard CSP formalism. Whereas all of the variables of a CSP are implicitly existentially quantified, QCSPs also allow variables to be universally quantified. Furthermore, universal and existential variables can be alternated in arbitrary ways in a QCSP. From a theoretical point of view, these added features make QCSPs PSPACE complete; any problem in PSPACE can be encoded as a polynomially sized (poly-sized) QCSP. CSPs, on the other hand, are NP complete; any problem in NP can be encoded as a poly-sized CSP. It is known that both NP $\subseteq$ PSPACE and co-NP $\subseteq$ PSPACE, and it is widely believed that these containments are proper, i.e., that there are problems outside of NP and co-NP that still lie in PSPACE. Such problems will not have a poly-sized CSP representation, but will have a poly-sized QCSP representation.

From a practical point of view, this difference means that if effective QCSP solvers can be developed they would enable a wide range of practical applications that lie beyond the reach of CSP solvers. Even though CSP and QCSP solvers both have the same exponential worst case complexity, experience has shown that solvers can often achieve reasonable run times in practice. The real issue separating CSP and QCSP solvers lies

C. Bessiere (Ed.): CP 2007, LNCS 4741, pp. 148–163, 2007.

in size of the problem representation, i.e., the size of the input. If NP $\neq$ PSPACE, then there will exist problems for which a CSP formalization will always be exponentially larger than the equivalent QCSP representation. Thus a CSP solver could not even get started on the problem—the problem would contain too many variables and constraints. The QCSP representation, on the other hand, would still be polynomial in size and thus potentially solvable by a QCSP solver if that solver was able to achieve reasonable run times in practice.

A good illustration of this point comes from the area of circuit diagnosis. In [1] an innovative application of quantified boolean formulas (QBF is a restricted form of QCSP), for diagnosing hardware circuits is given. The key feature of the approach is that the QBF encoding is many times smaller than the equivalent SAT encoding (SAT is a restricted form of CSP). In fact, in experiments the SAT encoding grew so large that it could no longer be solved by existent SAT solvers, whereas the QBF encoding remained compact and was solvable by existent QBF solvers. Other applications of QCSP come from areas like conditional planning and planning under incomplete knowledge [14], non-monotonic reasoning [9], and hardware verification and design [7,1].

In this paper we present new techniques for improving backtracking based QCSP solvers. Our main contribution is to demonstrate how the technique of cubes, utilized in QBF solvers [16,12], can be extended to QCSPs in a technique we call solution directed backjumping (SBJ). SBJ allows the solver to backtrack intelligently after having encountered a solution. SBJ subsumes and improves on the technique of solution directed pruning (SDP) [11], in an manner analogous to how conflict directed backjumping (CBJ) extends ordinary backjumping. In particular, SBJ computes information that can be used at internal nodes of the tree rather than just at the leaf nodes. Experiments demonstrate that SBJ can improve performance by orders of magnitude.

In addition to SBJ, we demonstrate that performing varying levels of propagation for universal vs. existential variables can enhance performance. In particular, we show that enforcing very high levels of consistency on universal variables can pay off, as detecting a locally inconsistent value of a universal variable immediately forces a backtrack. We also discuss validity pruning, a technique that can be used to prune the domains of universally quantified variables. Our current empirical investigations with random problems indicate that validity pruning does not yield significant improvements. Nevertheless, it has the potential to be useful in other types of problems.

This paper is structured as follows. Section 2 gives the necessary definitions and background on QCSPs. Section 3 describes methods to enhance propagation in QCSPs, while in Section 4 we present SBJ, a method to enhance intelligent backtracking in QCSPs. Section 5 gives experiments results demonstrating the efficiency of the proposed methods. Finally, in Section 6 we conclude.

2 Background

We are concerned here with QCSPs defined over finite valued variables. Let $V = \{v_1, \ldots, v_n\}$ be a set of variables. Each variable v_i has an associated finite domain of values $dom[v_i]$. We write $v = d$ if the variable v has been assigned the value d always requiring that $d \in dom[v]$, i.e., a variable can only be assigned a value from its domain. A constraint c is a function from a subset of the variables in V to $\{\mathbf{true}, \mathbf{false}\}$ (1/0). This subset of variables is called the **scope** of c, $scope(c)$, and the cardinality of this set is the **arity** of the constraint. Any tuple τ of values for the variables in $scope(c)$ will be mapped by c to **true** or **false**. If $c(\tau) = \mathbf{true}$, τ is said to be a **satisfying** tuple of c, else $c(\tau) = \mathbf{false}$ and τ is a falsifying tuple of c. We will consider τ to be a set, and write $v = d \in \tau$ if v has the value d in τ.

A conjunction of constraints $C = c_1 \wedge \cdots \wedge c_m$, their associated variables $V = \bigcup_{j=1}^{m} scope(c_j)$, and domains for these variables $D = \{dom[v] : v \in V\}$ define a standard CSP, $C[D]$, which forms the **body** of a QCSP. Let τ be a tuple of values for all of the variables in V, and for each constraint $c_i \in C$ let τ_i be the subset of τ containing the values assigned to variables in $scope(c_i)$. τ is a **solution** of the body $C[D]$ if each τ_i is a satisfying tuple of c_i.

Definition 1 (QCSP). *Given a body $C[D]$ a Quantified Constraint Satisfaction Problem (**QCSP**) is a formula of the form $Q.C[D]$ where Q is a quantifier prefix consisting of the variables of $\bigcup_{c_j \in C} scope(c_j)$ arranged in some sequence and each proceeded by either an existential ($\exists$) or universal quantifier ($\forall$).*

For example

$$\forall v_1, \exists v_2, \forall v_3, \exists v_4 . c_1(v_1, v_2) \wedge c_2(v_1, v_3, v_4) \wedge c_3(v_2, v_3, v_4)$$
$$[\{dom[v_1] = \{a, b\}, dom[v_2] = \{a, b, c\}, dom[v_3] = \{a\}]$$

is a QCSP with the quantifier prefix $\forall v_1, \exists v_2, \forall v_3, \exists v_4$. This QCSP asserts that for all values of v_1 there exists a value of v_2 (perhaps dependent on the particular value of v_1) such that for all values of v_3 there exists a value of v_4 (perhaps dependent on the particular values of v_1, v_2 and v_3) such that all the constraints c_1, c_2 and c_3 are satisfied.

A **quantifier block** qb of Q is a maximal contiguous subsequence of Q such that every variable in qb has the same quantifier type. For two quantifier blocks qb_1 and qb_2 we say that $qb_1 \leq qb_2$ iff qb_1 is equal to or appears before qb_2 in Q. Each variable v in Q appears in some quantifier block $qb(v)$ and we say that $v_1 \leq_q v_2$ if $qb(v_1) \leq qb(v_2)$ and $v_1 <_q v_2$ if $qb(v_1) < qb(v_2)$. We also say that v is **universal (existential)** if its quantifier in Q is $\forall$ ($\exists$).

A QCSP makes an assertion that is either true or false. The assertion made by $Q.C[D]$ is true iff $Q.C[D]$ has a Q-Model. A Q-Model for a $Q.C[D]$ is a tree in which each node except for the root is labeled by a variable assignment and that is subject to the following conditions. Let n and m be any two nodes in the tree such that n's label is $x = a$ while m's label is $y = b$.

1. If n is an ancestor of m, then it must be the case that $x \leq_q y$. That is, the sequence of assignments along any path from the root to a leaf must respect the ordering of the quantifier blocks.
2. If x is universally quantified, then n must have $k - 1$ siblings where k is the size of $dom[x]$. For each value $d \in dom[x]$, n or one of its $k - 1$ siblings must be labeled by $x = d$. On the other hand if x is existentially quantified, then n has no siblings.
3. The tuple of assignments along any path from the root to a leaf node must be a solution to $C[D]$.

Hence in a Q-Model there is a path for every possible setting of the universal variables in Q each of which is a CSP solution to the body of the QCSP. Thus a Q-Model of a QCSP containing k universal variables will contain $2^{O(k)}$ solutions to the body. From this definition it can be seen that any CSP can be viewed as a QCSP with all its variable existentially quantified. The Q-Models of such existential only QCSPs contain only a single path, and determining the truth of such QCSPs (the existence of a Q-Model) is equivalent to determining if the CSP has a solution.

The **reduction** of $C[D]$ by an assignment $v = d$, $C[D]\big|_{v=d}$ is the new body obtained by removing from the domain of v all values not equal to d (i.e., reducing $dom[v]$ set to the singleton set $\{d\}$). We can also reduce the body by pruning a value from the domain of a variable: $C[D]\big|_{v\neq d} = C[(D(dom[v])/(dom[v]-d))]$. The reduction by a set of assignments or value prunings is defined as the sequential application of these reductions. Note that if any variable domain is reduced to the empty set, then the QCSP is false. It cannot have a Q-Model as every Q-Model must assign every variable a value from its domain along each path.

Proposition 1. *Let v be a variable and d be some value in its domain. If v is universal then $Q.C[D] \Rightarrow Q.C[D]\big|_{v\neq d}$. If v is existential then $Q.C[D]\big|_{v\neq d} \Rightarrow Q.C[D]$.*

Proof: If v is universal and $Q.C[D]$ has a Q-Model then so does $Q.C[D]\big|_{v\neq d}$: we simply remove all subtree rooted by nodes labeled $v = d$ from $Q.C[D]$'s Q-Model. If v is existential then any Q-Model of $Q.C[D]\big|_{v\neq d}$ is a Q-Model of $Q.C[D]$.

A common way of solving a QCSP is via backtracking search. In its most basic form such a search works much like CSP backtracking search except for two additional conditions: (1) the variable ordering along any branch must respect the ordering of the quantifier blocks (although it is free to dynamically reorder the variables within each block), and (2) for every universal variable v the search needs to solve for every value in $dom[v]$.

The search tries to find a Q-Model: a successful run verifies that a Q-Model exists by traversing a Q-Model during its search while a failed run has tried to traverse all possible Q-Models thus verifying that one does not exist. In particular, at any node n the search tree that has been reached by making the sequence of assignments $\pi_k = \langle v_1 = d_1, \dots, v_k = d_k \rangle$, the search in the subtree below n attempts to find a Q-Model for $Q.C[D]\big|_{\pi_k}$. Thus at the root the search attempts to find a Q-Model for the original problem $Q.C[D]$.

The key to making backtracking search for QCSPs effective is by developing techniques that allow unsuccessful subtrees to be refuted more efficiently, and successful subtrees to be verified more efficiently. Efficient refutation of unsuccessful subtrees is also the goal in backtracking CSP solvers, but here we aim to exploit the additional structure of QCSPs to develop better methods for achieving this goal. Efficient verification of successful subtrees, on the other hand, has no analogue in CSP solvers which typically can stop as soon as a single solution is found. With a QCSP however, a successful subtree has an exponential number of solutions and finding each of these would be very slow. Here again our aim is to exploit the additional structure of QCSPs to develop methods for verifying that all of these solutions exist without having to actually find each one.

In the sequel we report on some new methods for achieving these two goals as well as on our empirical evaluation of their effectiveness. From here on we will confine our attention to QCSPs with constraints of arity at most two. It can be noted that any QCSP with non-binary constraints can be converted to an equivalent QCSP containing only binary constraints by applying the hidden variable transformation (see e.g., [2]) to convert the body to a binary CSP and then adding all of the newly introduced hidden variables as new existential variables to the end of the quantifier prefix. Whether or not this is a effective way of dealing with non-binary constraints is a topic for future work. The alternative of dealing directly with non-binary constraints poses some considerable additional formal and practical challenges and is also a topic for future work.

3 Propagation

Our first techniques arise from the standard idea of constraint propagation. These techniques use the constraints of the QCSP body to provide additional information that can simplify the task of searching the subtree below the current node.

3.1 Detecting Inconsistent Values

An assignment $v = d$ is **inconsistent** for $Q.C[D]$ if it does not appear in *any* Q-Model of $Q.C[D]$. If $v = d$ is inconsistent and v is existential then $Q.C[D] \equiv Q.C[D]\big|_{v \neq d}$: any Q-model for $Q.C[D]$ must also be a Q-Model for $Q.C[D]\big|_{v \neq d}$ since it cannot contain $v = d$, while Prop. 1 supplies the opposite direction. On the other hand if v is universal then $Q.C[D]$ is **false**: any Q-Model must contain $v = d$.

Of course it is in general hard to detect inconsistent values, but as with CSPs various local checks can be performed that detect some but not all inconsistent values. Such checks can be done at every node n of the search (including prior to search at the root). In particular, if an inconsistent existential value is detected it can be pruned before searching the subtree below n, and if an inconsistent universal value is detected the search can immediately backtrack from n.

Since every path in a Q-Model is a standard CSP solution to the body, any standard CSP technique for detecting inconsistent values can be used: any value inconsistent for the body cannot appear in any Q-Model. Additionally, we can do better than this by exploiting the additional structure of QCSPs. In particular, as shown in [6,13], arc consistency (AC) can be extended to QCSPs to support the detection of values that are inconsistent for the QCSP even though they are not inconsistent for the CSP body. AC for binary QCSPs has been implemented in the QCSP-Solve system that we employ in our empirical evaluations. QCSP-Solve uses AC only as a preprocessing step (i.e., at the root), as FC (forward checking) seems to be more cost effective during search [11].

The key feature of AC for QCSPs is that it allows many of the constraints of the body to be removed at the root. In particular, the only constraints $c(x, y)$ that remain in the problem after AC preprocessing are those where both x and y are existential, and those where x is universal, y is existential, and $x <_q y$ (see [11] for more details).

Pruning inconsistent values improves the efficiency of search in the subtree below, but local consistency checking has its greatest impact when it allows us to avoid that search altogether. This happens when either all values of an existential are pruned or a single value of a universal is pruned. It is more likely that local propagation can prune a single universal value than all values for some existential. Hence, it can be worth while to expend more effort checking for inconsistency universal values. This intuition already appears to some extent in the QCSP-Solve system via its FC1 and MAC1 propagation. In these propagation methods, whenever a universal variable x is to be branched on, before descending deeper in the search tree all of its possible values are tried and FC or AC performed after each trial assignment. If any of these assignments yield a contradiction the algorithm can immediately backtrack. This extra work on universals was shown to be cost effective in the experiments of [11].

Our first new technique is to further investigate the technique of doing more work on the consistency checking of universals. In particular, we investigate applying a different and stronger level of consistency checking on universals and a weaker, and thus cheaper, level of consistency on existentials, in addition to the technique of checking all universal values prior to descending deeper, used in [11].

3.2 Strong Levels of Consistency on Universals

Like QCSP-Solve after any existential is assigned we perform FC. But further to QCSP-Solve we also check all future universal variables to ensure that they are arc consistent in all of the constraints they participate in. Like QCSP-Solve if a universal is about to be assigned we check each of its values first. But further to QCSP-Solve we check each value with a much higher level of local consistency than FC. The particular form of local consistency we found to be effective is a mixture of path consistency (PC) and max restricted path consistency (maxRPC). If any value of the universal fails this local consistency test we backtrack. If they all pass this test, we then assign the universal a value and then perform FC followed by enforcing AC on all constraints involving a future universal. Hence, we have two changes from QCSP-Solve: (1) after each instantiation we check that the future universals are AC in their constraints, and (2) checking a higher level of consistency on all values of a universal prior to assigning it a specific value.

Now we specify more precisely the local consistency test we employ on the values of an about to be assigned universal. A pair of values (d_i, d_j), $d_i \in dom[v_i]$ and $d_j \in dom[v_j]$, is *path consistent* (PC) iff the two values are compatible and for any third variable v_k there exists a value $d_k \in dom[v_k]$ that is compatible with both d_i and d_j. A value $d_i \in dom[v_i]$ is *max Restricted Path Consistent* (maxRPC) [8] iff for any variable v_j constrained with v_i there exists a value $d_j \in dom[v_j]$ that is compatible with d_i and has the following property: for any third variable v_k, there exists a value $d_k \in dom[v_k]$ that is compatible with both d_i and d_j. In this case we say that d_j is a maxRPC-support of d_i. In other words d_i is maxRPC if it is a member of *some* path consistent pair in every constraint it participates in while path consistency ensures that every pair d_i of is path consistent. When during search we are about the assign the universal v_i, after having some set of assignments π, the local consistency test we employ is specified in Figure 1.

In Figure 1 when a universal v_i is reached during search we check that each of its values d_i has a maxRPC support in the domain of each existential it is constrained with, and that d_i is path consistent with all future universals. AC preprocessing ensures there

function maxRPC+PC_Propagation $(Q.C[D], \pi, v_i)$
1: **for** each value $d_i \in dom[v_i]$
2: **for** each unassigned existential variable v_j constrained with v_i
3: **if** d_i has no maxRPC-support in $dom[v_j]$
4: **then return** FAIL
5: **for** each unassigned universal variable v_j
6: **for** each value $d_j \in dom[v_j]$
7: **if** (d_i, d_j) is not path consistent
8: **then return** FAIL

Fig. 1. Strong propagation on universal variables

are no constraints over two universals, thus to check the consistency of pairs of universal values we must consider the existentials they are jointly constrained with; hence our use of path consistency.

The following example demonstrates how the application of PC and maxRPC prunes the search space upon reaching a universal variable.

Example 1. *Consider the QCSP*

$$\exists v_1, \forall v_2, \exists v_3, \forall v_4, \exists v_5.(v_1 \neq v_5 - 2 \wedge v_2 = v_3 \wedge v_2 \neq v_5 \wedge v_3 \neq v_5 - 1 \wedge v_4 = v_5)$$
$$[dom[v_1] = dom[v_2] = dom[v_3] = dom[v_4] = \{0, 1\}, dom[v_5] = \{0, 1, 2\}]$$

A chronological backtracking algorithm that applies PC and maxRPC upon reaching a universal will solve the problem as follows. Variable v_1 is assigned value 0. Forward checking removes 2 from $dom[v_5]$. The next variable v_2 is a universal. We will now call the function of Figure 1 to apply PC and maxRPC on v_2's values. v_3 is existential and is constrained with v_2. Therefore, we check if value 0 of v_2 has a maxRPC-support in $dom[v_3]$ (line 3). The only value compatible with 0 in $dom[v_3]$ is 0 and there is no value in $dom[v_5]$ that is compatible with both $0 \in dom[v_2]$ and $0 \in dom[v_3]$. Therefore, value 0 of v_2 is not maxRPC and the algorithm immediately backtracks and assigns 1 to v_1. Again the function of Figure 1 is called. Value 0 of v_2 now has a maxRPC-support in $dom[v_3]$ (value 0), because 2 has been restored to $dom[v_5]$ and it is compatible with both $0 \in dom[v_2]$ and $0 \in dom[v_3]$. v_4 is a universal so we now apply PC on its values. That is, we check if the values of v_4 have a support in v_5 that is also a support for value 0 of v_2 (lines 6-8). This is not the case for value 0 of v_4 and therefore the algorithm backtracks and determines that the problem is false.

3.3 Detecting Valid Values

In QCSPs a duality exists between universal and existential variables that manifests itself in various aspects of the processing that can be done when solving a QCSP. With respect to detecting inconsistent values the dual notion is detecting valid values.

An assignment $v = d$ is **valid** for a constraint c if for every tuple τ of assignments to the variables in $scope(d)$ with $v = d \in \tau$ we have $c(\tau) =$ **true**. In other words the assignment $v = d$ renders c vacuous. We say that an assignment $v = d$ is valid for a conjunction of constraints C if it is valid for every constraint in C that has v in its scope.

This notion of validity corresponds both to that defined in [3] and to the notion of **purity** defined in [11]. It is also related to notions described in [5]. A useful fact from

[3] is that validity is the dual of inconsistency with respect to GAC. That is, $v = d$ is valid for a constraint c if and only if $v = d$ is GAC inconsistent for $\neg c$, where $\neg c$ is the negation of c. That is, $scope(\neg c) = scope(c)$ and for any tuple of assignments τ, $\neg c(\tau) =$ **true** iff $c(\tau) =$ **false**.

If $v = d$ is valid for C in the QCSP $Q.C[D]$ and v is existential then $Q.C[D] \equiv Q.C[D]\big|_{v=d}$: we can assign v the value d. In particular, if $Q.C[D]$ has a Q-Model, then we can replace every assignment to v in that Q-Model by $v = d$. Since $v = d$ is valid this change cannot cause any constraint to be violated, hence the modified Q-Model is still a Q-Model for $Q.C[D]\big|_{v=d}$. Prop.1 provides the opposite direction. On the other hand if v is universal then $Q.C[D] \equiv Q.C[D]\big|_{v\neq d}$: we can prune d from $dom[v]$. In this case if $Q.C[D]\big|_{v\neq d}$ has a Q-Model we can add the node $v = d$ as a new sibling to all sets of siblings labeled by the other assignments to v and then simply copy the subtree below one of these other assignments to create subtree below $v = d$. Since $v = d$ is valid the other assignment's subtree will continue to be a tree of solutions under $v = d$. This modified Q-Model is a Q-Model of $Q.C[D]$. Prop.1 provides the opposite direction.

Validity was previously utilized in QCSP-Solve by waiting until a variable was about to be assigned. At that point the values of the variable would be checked to see if any of them were valid (pure). For an existential the valid value would immediately be assigned, and for a universal the valid values would be pruned, in accord with the above observations.

An alternative to the approach of QCSP-Solve is to do validity propagation. In particular, instead of waiting until a variable is about to be assigned one could detect valid values of future variables and prune or assign them dependent on their type. Validity propagation can be achieved by exploiting the relationship cited above between GAC (AC) on the negation of a constraint and validity. That is, it is fairly easy to alter AC lookahead to detect valid values of future variables by running AC on the negations of the constraints.

It should be noted that validity propagation does not affect the size of the search tree: a valid value of a future variable will still be exploited even if it is only detected at the time the variable is about to be assigned. Potentially, it can be more efficient to determine that a value is valid once near the top of the search tree, rather than each time the variable is to be assigned. On the other hand, one could waste time detecting valid values for variables that are never reached because an inconsistency is found before they are instantiated. The main potential benefit of validity propagation over future variables lies in the fact that it dynamically alters the size of the variable domains; potentially differently along different branches of the search tree. As noted above, although the order in which variables are instantiated is restricted by the ordering of the quantifier blocks, within a quantifier block the variable ordering can be selected heuristically. Hence, validity propagation could potentially provide "within a block" dynamic ordering with useful information about varying domains sizes.

We implemented validity propagation and used it in conjunction with dynamic variable ordering within quantifier blocks. Our experimental results were disappointing, but we only tested random problems. Potentially this technique could be useful on other QCSPs.

4 Intelligent Backtracking

Our second set of techniques arises from the idea of keeping track of the reasons a path failed or succeeded so that irrelevant variables can be backtracked over. QCSP-Solve already utilizes conflict directed backjumping (CBJ), as described in [11]. Hence, when backtracking from a failure node irrelevant variables can be skipped over. However, CBJ does not support intelligent backtracking from successful nodes. Extending intelligent backtracking so that it can be applied after success is achieved by our new technique of solution directed backjumping (SBJ).

4.1 Solution Directed Backjumping (SBJ)

In QBF solvers cube learning is an technique used to backtrack from successful nodes [16,12]. Cubes are computed at solution leaves of the search tree by identifying a subset of the assigned literals sufficient to satisfy all clauses of the QBF. The aim is to identify universal variables whose setting was irrelevant to the discovered solution. Potentially those variables can be backtracked over without having to test if their other value is solvable.

In a QBF solver the leaf cubes (cubes computed as solution leaf nodes) support backtrack to the deepest universal they contain, and at internal nodes cubes computed for each setting of a universal can be combined to support further non-chronological backtracking. Since a successful subtree in QBF (or QCSP) can contain an exponential number of solutions, backtracking out of such subtrees by using cubes can provide a considerable performance improvement. For example, if at a any node a cube consisting entirely of existential literals is computed, then the search can immediately terminate.

In QCSPs however a straight forward application of this idea is not effective. In particular it is hardly ever the case that a universal variable is completely irrelevant to the solution found. Rather, the solution found at a leaf node might continue to be a solution under some other settings of the universal variable, but not under other settings. Hence the idea behind SBJ is to keep track of the values of the universals that are verified by the current solution so that on backtrack these values need not be verified again. It is however slightly easier to formalize SBJ as keeping track of the complement of the verified values.

Definition 2 (QCSP Cube). *Let qbe be a set containing (a) a set of existential assignments* $(v = a)$ *and (b) for each universal variable* v *a set of values* $uncovered[v] \subset dom[v]$. *Let* $C[D]\big|_{qbe}$ *be the reduction of* $C[D]$ *by* $v = a$ *for each existential assignment* $(v = a) \in qbe$ *and by* $v \neq d$ *for each* $d \in uncovered[v]$ *for each universal variable* v. *The set qbe is a* ***cube*** *iff* $Q.C[D]\big|_{qbe}$ *is* ***true*** *(i.e., has a Q-Model).*

We use the convention of omitting mention of the set $uncovered[v]$ from a cube if it is empty, and we say that the universal variable v_u **is in a cube**, qbe, if $uncovered[v_u] \in qbe$ (i.e., $uncovered[v_u] \neq \emptyset$). An existential assignment $v_e = a \in qbe$ is called **tailing** if for all universal variables $v_u \in qbe$ we have $v_u <_q v_e$.

Observation 1. *If* $v_e = a$ *is a tailing existential in a cube* qbe *then* $qbe - \{v_e = a\}$ *is also a cube. That is, tailing existential assignments can be removed from a cube.*

```
function ComputeLeafCube (Q.C[D], π)
1: qbe = the assignments to the existential variables in π
2: for each universal variable v_i
3:   uncovered[v_i] = {}
4:   for each d ∈ dom[v_i]
5:     if π(v_i=d) does not satisfy C
6:       uncovered[v_i] = uncovered[v_i] ∪ {d}
7:   qbe = qbe ∪ {uncovered[v_i]}
8: qbe = remove tailing existentials from qbe
```

Fig. 2. Computing a QCSP cube at a solution leaf node

Proof: $Q.C[D]\big|_{qbe}$ is **true** (by definition) and $Q.C[D]\big|_{qbe} \Rightarrow Q.C[D]\big|_{qbe-\{v_e=a\}}$ (Prop 1). Hence $Q.C[D]\big|_{qbe-\{v_e=a\}}$ is also **true** and $qbe - \{v_e = a\}$ is a cube.

Figure 2 gives the algorithm for computing a QCSP cube at a solution leaf. Let π be the sequence of assignments made on the path to this leaf node. (π satisfies all of the constraints of the body). In this algorithm $\pi(v_i{=}d)$ denotes the set of assignments π modified so that v_i is now assigned the value d. The algorithm computes $uncovered[v_i]$ for each universal variable v_i; this is the set of values of v_i that are incompatible with the current solution. Note that $uncovered[v_i]$ can never contain v_i's current value (the condition on line 5 cannot be satisfied since π satisfies all constraints).

Proposition 2. *The set qbe returned by* `ComputeLeafCube` *is a cube.*

Proof: Consider *qbe* before tailing existentials are removed (line 8). At this point *qbe* contains an assignment for every existential variable. We must show that $Q.C[D]\big|_{qbe}$ has a Q-Model. Such a Q-Model will be a tree with paths for every combination of assignments to the universal variables not in the *uncovered* sets. Construct such a tree by assigning the existential variables along every path its value in *qbe*. Due to our restriction to binary constraints and preprocessing of the problem $C[D]$ only contains constraints $c(v_u, v_e)$ between a universal and an existential and constraints $c(v_{e_1}, v_{e_2})$ between two existentials. Since the existential assignments in *qbe* came from a solution π all constraints between two existentials are satisfied. Furthermore, line 5 ensures that all constraints between a universal and an existential are satisfied by any universal value not in the *uncovered* sets. Hence each path in this tree is a solution to $C[D]$, and $Q.C[D]\big|_{qbe}$ has a Q-model (is **true**). By the previous observation *qbe* remains a cube after its tailing existentials have been removed.

Let v be the deepest universal in *qbe*, i.e., the universal assigned at the deepest level along the path to the current solution leaf with $uncovered[v] \neq \emptyset$. Let n be the node assigning v its current value. The fact that *qbe* is a cube tells us that the subtree under n has been solved: this subtree is attempting to solve $Q.C[D]\big|_{\pi_v}$ where π_v is set of assignments in the path to n. π_v agrees with *qbe* on the assignment to its existential variables but further restricts its universal variables to assignments that lie in the domains of $C[D]\big|_{qbe}$. By Prop. 1 $Q.C[D]\big|_{qbe} \Rightarrow Q.C[D]\big|_{\pi_v}$, and thus $Q.C[D]\big|_{\pi_v}$ must be **true** since *qbe* is a cube. Furthermore, *qbe* also verifies that the subtrees of the other assignments to v not in $uncovered[v]$ are also solved: by the same reasoning all of these

```
function ComputeInternalCube (Q.C[D], v, π_v, qbe_1, ..., qbe_k)
1: qbe = the assignments to the existential variables in π_v
2:   for each universal variable v_i ≠ v
3:     uncovered[v_i] = ⋃_{j=1}^{k} uncovered[v_i] ∈ qbe_j
4:     qbe = qbe ∪ {uncovered[v_i]}
5:   qbe = remove tailing existentials from qbe
```

Fig. 3. Computing a QCSP cube at an internal node where the universal variable v was assigned

subproblems are also **true**. Hence, the search can backtrack to the node that assigned v, and from that point only attempt to solve the values for v in $uncovered[v]$ that have not been previously verified.

Each time the search backtracks to a universal variable v a new cube is returned, and at least one more value from v's domain has been verified (v's current assignment must be verified by the cube). Say that the search backtracks to v a total of k times before all of v's domain has been verified, in the process returning k cubes $qbe_1, \ldots, qbe_k$. At that point, the function in Figure 3 is invoked to compute a new cube (where π_v is the sequence of assignments made before v was selected to be assigned).

In ComputeInternalCube each universal's uncovered values is the union of its uncovered values in the k cubes $qbe_1, \ldots, qbe_k$. Note also that $uncovered[v]$ is omitted from the new cube (i.e., $uncovered[v]$ is implicitly empty). Since v was the deepest universal in each of the cubes qbe_i, we see that the newly computed cube also contains no universals deeper that v. Nor does it contain any existential assignments deeper than v due to line 5 and the fact that each $cube_i$ also previously had their tailing existentials removed.

Once qbe is has been computed the search can once again backtrack to the node assigning the deepest universal v' in qbe, and at that point continue by solving all values of v' in $uncovered[v'] \in qbe$ that have not be previously verified. If all of these values were previously verified ComputeInternalCube will be invoked again on the set of cubes that were returned to v' (i.e., qbe and any other cubes returned by earlier backtracks to v'). The new cube it returns will then generate yet another backtrack.

Proposition 3. *Assume that $qbe_1, \ldots, qbe_k$ are all cubes, have been existentially reduced, agree on all existential assignments, have v as their deepest universal, and together verify all of the values in $dom[v]$ (i.e., for each $a \in dom[v]$ there exists j such that $a \notin uncovered[v] \in qbe_j$). Then the set qbe returned by* ComputeInternal Cube *is a cube.*

This proposition can be proved by constructing a Q-Model for $Q.C[D]\big|_{qbe}$ using parts of the k Q-Models known to exist for $Q.C[D]\big|_{qbe_i}$. Subject to the assumed conditions these Q-Models are sufficiently compatible that these parts can be put together to cover all values for the universal variable v and all values in the universal domains of $C[D]\big|_{qbe}$.

The above propositions demonstrate that SBJ computes correct cubes and that these cubes verify that the backtracking described above is sound. In particular, SBJ will backtrack to the root of the search tree if and only if it has verified that the empty set is a cube. That is, $Q.C[D]\big|_{\emptyset} = Q.C[D]$ is **true**. Finally, two more observations about SBJ can be made. First, SBJ's space requirements are bounded by $O(dn^2)$, where d is the maximal sized variable domain and n is the number of variables. In particular, at each node along the current path (max n nodes) we need only store the union of the cubes that have been returned to that node so far. Furthermore, this set can be deleted when we backtrack from the node. Second, at each node the cubes contain all of the previously assigned existentials, so we need not explicitly store these in cube. These existentials would be needed however if we wanted to store the cubes to use along future paths of the search tree (i.e., if we were to perform cube learning).

5 Empirical Study

The random QCSP instances used in our empirical study were generated following the generation model introduced in [11]. As in [15] we added an extra parameter that denotes the number of universal blocks. The generator takes 8 parameters: $\langle n$, $n_\exists$, $n_\forall$, d, p, $q_{\forall\exists}$, $q_{\exists\exists}$, $b_\forall\rangle >$ where n is the number of variables, $n_\exists$ is the number of existentials in each block, $n_\forall$ is the number of universals in each block, d is the uniform domain size, p is the number of binary constraints as a fraction of all possible constraints, and $b_\forall$ is the number of universal blocks. $q_{\exists\exists}$ is the fraction of satisfying tuples in constraints between existentials. The satisfying tuples in a constraint between a universal and an existential later in the variable sequence are specified as follows. A random total bijection is generated from the domain of the universal to the domain of the existential. All 2-tuples not in the bijection satisfy the constraint. Parameter $q_{\forall\exists}$ is the fraction of satisfying tuples from the d tuples in the bijection.

Constraints between universals or an existential and a universal later in the variable sequence are not generated as these can be removed by preprocessing [11]. With certain parameter settings the randomly generated instances are free from the flaw described in [10]. Variables are quantified in blocks with alternating quantification starting with a block of $n_\exists$ existentials.

5.1 SBJ and Strong Consistency on Universals

To evaluate the effects of SBJ and the constraint propagation methods for universals, we have compared QCSP-Solve against three solvers obtained by extending QCSP-Solve with these features. The first solver (QCSP-Solve prop) augments QCSP-Solve with strong propagation on universals. The second one (QCSP-Solve+) augments QCSP-Solve with SBJ. The third one (QCSP-Solve++) applies both SBJ and strong propagation on universals. We used random problems with a variety of parameter settings. The results presented hereafter are averages over 100 instances generated at each data point. In each figure the value of $q_{\exists\exists}$ is varied in steps of 0.05. For the experiments of this section variables were instantiated according to the quantifier sequence. Values were always ordered lexicographically.

Figure 4 shows cpu times and node visits from problems where $n = 24$, $n_\exists = n_\forall = 8$, $b_\forall = 1$, $d = 9$, $p = 0.15$, $q_{\forall\exists} = 0.44$. Under these parameter settings all instances are guaranteed to be flaw-free.

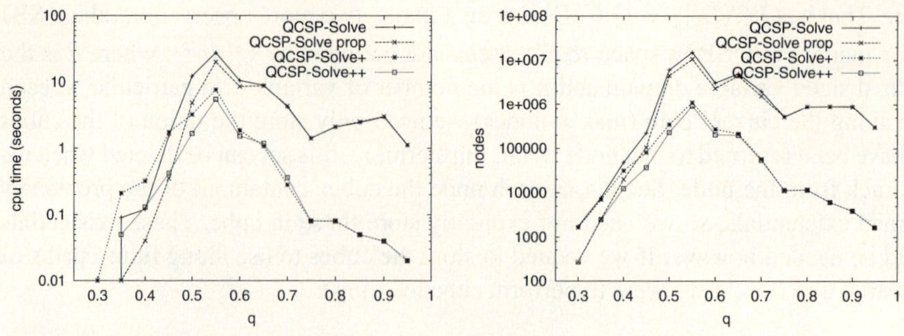

Fig. 4. Cpu times (left) and node visits (right)

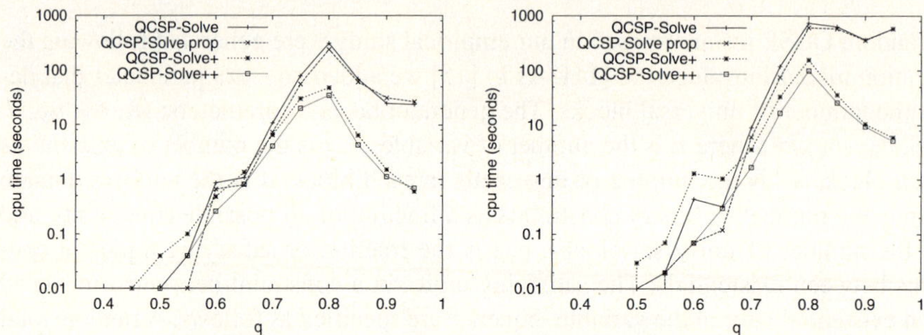

Fig. 5. Cpu times on problems with 25 variables (left) and 28 variables (right)

The results given in Figure 5 are from problems generated using similar parameter settings as in [15]. The left plot in Figure 5 shows cpu times from problems where $n = 25$, $n_\exists = n_\forall = 5$, $b_\forall = 2$, $d = 8$, $p = 0.20$, $q_{\forall\exists} = 0.50$. The right plot in Figure 5 shows cpu times from problems where $n = 28$, $n_\exists = n_\forall = 4$, $b_\forall = 3$, $d = 8$, $p = 0.20$, $q_{\forall\exists} = 0.50$. Note that neither of these parameter settings guarantees flaw-free instances.

In all sets of problems QCSP-Solve++ is considerably faster than QCSP-Solve. For high values of $q_{\exists\exists}$, where most instances are soluble, the speed-up obtained can be up to two orders of magnitude. This is because, through the use of SBJ, the solver avoids repeatedly searching for solutions involving all sequences of assignments to universals. For low values of $q_{\exists\exists}$, where most problems are insoluble, SBJ has little effect and the computation/maintainance of solution cubes is an overhead that slows down search. However, the early failure detection offered by the strong consistencies applied on universals outweighs this and speed-ups compared to QCSP-Solve are obtained. Comparing QCSP-Solve to QCSP-Solve prop and QCSP-Solve+ to QCSP-Solve++ shows that the effects of SBJ and strong propagation on universals are more or less orthogonal.

As is evident from the results shown in the figures, a small increase in the number of variables and quantifier alternations can have a significant impact on the difficulty of the problem.

Other Approaches to QCSP Solving. Apart from QCSP-Solve, two direct solvers for QCSPs have been developed and a number of encodings of QCSP into QBF have been proposed. The two solvers are BlockSolve [15] and QeCode [4]. BlockSolve is a bottom-up solver that displays very good performance on soluble instances, but as a downside requires exponential space. QeCode is built on top of Gecode and hence is equipped with many advanced CSP techniques. However, it lacks specialized features for QCSPs, such as pure value handling.

Although we have not directly compared our work to these solvers, we can make some conjectures by observing the performance of the solvers on instances generated with similar parameters. SBJ makes QCSP-Solve far more competitive with BlockSolve than before on soluble instances. However, BlockSolve still holds an advantage, as it can achieve a speed-up of up to four orders of magnitude over QCSP-Solve; albeit with an exponential memory cost. At the phase transition and to its left, where problems are insoluble, BlockSolve is outperformed by our techniques. This conjecture is based on the observation that BlockSolve displays roughly the same performance as QCSP-Solve at the phase transition while it is slower in the insoluble region [15]. Experiments with QeCode showed that it displays roughly similar performance as QCSP-Solve [4]. Therefore, we conjecture that SBJ makes QCSP-Solve considerably more efficient than QeCode on soluble instances. QBF solvers that run on the efficient adapted and enhanced log encodings are typically slower than QCSP-Solve on insoluble instances and faster on soluble ones [10,11]. We conjecture that SBJ makes QCSP-Solve at least competitive with the encodings on soluble instances.

5.2 Validity Pruning and Dynamic Variable Ordering

We now study the effect of validity pruning and dynamic variable ordering (DVO) within blocks. In Figure 6 we compare three variations of QCSP-Solve++ augmented with validity pruning. The first one (QCSP-Solve++.1) applies validity pruning to achieve early detection of valid values and uses a static variable ordering. Its performance is very close to that of QCSP-Solve++ (it is negligibly slower). The second variation (QCSP-Solve++.2) dynamically reorders variables within both existential and universal blocks. The third variation (QCSP-Solve++.3) applies DVO only within existential blocks and orders the universals statically. The heuristic used is dom/deg. The left plot in Figure 6 gives results from the problems of Figure 4 while the right plot gives results from the problems of Figure 5 (the ones with 25 variables).

Not surprisingly, DVO is effective on insoluble problems with large existential blocks. However, is has little effect on soluble problems, and even slows down search

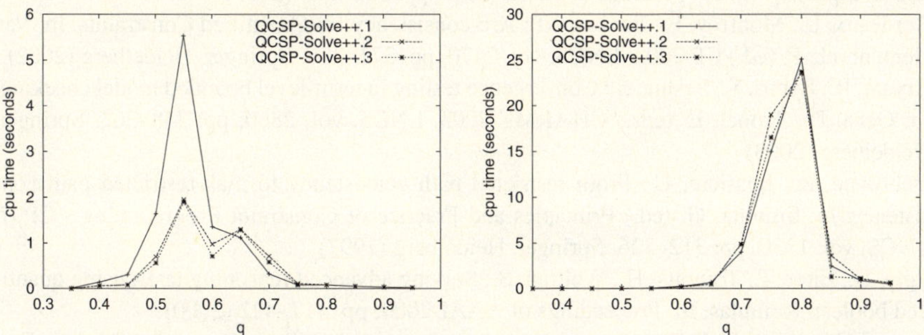

Fig. 6. Cpu times on problems with 25 variables (left) and 28 variables (right)

in some cases. Again unsurprisingly, problems with blocks of small size do not benefit from DVO. Finally, since QCSP-Solve++.2 and QCSP-Solve++.3 yield similar results, it seems that the reordering of universals does not improve the performance of the solver. However, fail-first heuristics like dom/deg may not be ideal for universal variables, so it is possible that better heuristics, which exploit the information offered by validity pruning, will be designed in the future.

6 Conclusions

We have presented new techniques for improving the performance of backtracking based QCSP solvers. Our main contribution is the development of solution directed backjumping for QCSPs. In analogue to conflict directed backjumping, SBJ allows the solver to backtrack out of solved sub-trees without having to find all of the distinct solutions normally required to validate that all sequences of assignments to the universal variables lead to solutions. We also demonstrated that performing varying levels of propagation for universal vs. existential variables can be useful for enhancing performance. Experiments with the solver QCSP-Solve demonstrate that both these techniques, and especially SBJ, can significantly improve the performance of backtracking solvers. Finally, we discussed validity pruning, a potentially useful technique that can be used to prune the domains of universally quantified variables during search.

References

1. Ali, M.F., Safarpour, S., Veneris, A., Abadir, M.S., Drechsler, R.: Post-verification debugging of hierarchical designs. In: International Conf. on Computer Aided Design (ICCAD), pp. 871–876 (2005)
2. Bacchus, F., van Beek, P.: On the conversion between non-binary and binary constraint satisfaction problems. In: Proceedings of AAAI-98, pp. 311–318 (1998)
3. Bacchus, F., Walsh, T.: Propagating logical combinations of constraints. In: Proc. of 19th IJCAI, pp. 35–40 (2005)
4. Benedetti, M., Lallouet, A., Vautard, J.: Reusing CSP propagators for QCSPs. In: Hnich, B., Carlsson, M., Fages, F., Rossi, F. (eds.) CSCLP 2005. LNCS (LNAI), vol. 3978. Springer, Heidelberg (2006)
5. Bordeaux, L., Cadoli, M., Mancini, T.: CSP Properties for Quantified Constraints: Definitions and Complexity. In: Proceedings of AAAI-2005, pp. 360–365 (2005)
6. Bordeaux, L., Monfroy, E.: Beyond NP: Arc-consistency for Quantified Constraints. In: Van Hentenryck, P. (ed.) CP 2002. LNCS, vol. 2470, pp. 371–386. Springer, Heidelberg (2002)
7. Bryant, R., Lahiri, S., Seshia, S.: Convergence testing in term-level bounded model checking. In: Geist, D., Tronci, E. (eds.) CHARME 2003. LNCS, vol. 2860, pp. 348–362. Springer, Heidelberg (2003)
8. Debruyne, R., Bessière, C.: From restricted path consistency to max-restricted path consistency. In: Smolka, G. (ed.) Principles and Practice of Constraint Programming - CP97. LNCS, vol. 1330, pp. 312–326. Springer, Heidelberg (1997)
9. Egly, U., Eiter, T., Tompits, H., Woltran, S.: Solving advanced reasoning tasks using quantified boolean formulas. In: Proceedings of AAAI-2000, pp. 417–422 (2000)
10. Gent, I., Nightingale, P., Rowley, A.: Encoding Quantified CSPs as Quantified Boolean Formulae. In: Proceedings of ECAI-2004, pp. 176–180 (2004)

11. Gent, I., Nightingale, P., Stergiou, K.: QCSP-Solve: A Solver for Quantified Constraint Satisfaction Problems. In: Proceedings of IJCAI-2005 (2005)
12. Giunchiglia, E., Narizzano, M., Tacchella, A.: Learning for quantified boolean logic satisfiability. In: Eighteenth national conference on Artificial intelligence, pp. 649–654 (2002)
13. Mamoulis, N., Stergiou, K.: Algorithms for Quantified Constraint Satisfaction Problems. In: Wallace, M. (ed.) CP 2004. LNCS, vol. 3258, pp. 752–756. Springer, Heidelberg (2004)
14. Rintanen, J.: Constructing conditional plans by a theorem-prover. Journal of Artificial Intelligence Research 10, 323–352 (1999)
15. Verger, G., Bessière, C.: Blocksolve: a Bottom-Up Approach for Solving Quantified CSPs. In: Benhamou, F. (ed.) CP 2006. LNCS, vol. 4204, pp. 635–649. Springer, Heidelberg (2006)
16. Zhang, L., Malik, S.: Towards symmetric treatment of conflicts and satisfaction in quantified boolean satisfiability solver. In: Van Hentenryck, P. (ed.) CP 2002. LNCS, vol. 2470, pp. 185–199. Springer, Heidelberg (2002)

Reformulating CSPs for Scalability with Application to Geospatial Reasoning

Kenneth M. Bayer[1], Martin Michalowski[2], Berthe Y. Choueiry[1,2], and Craig A. Knoblock[2]

[1] Constraint Systems Laboratory, University of Nebraska-Lincoln
{kbayer,choueiry}@cse.unl.edu
[2] University of Southern California, Information Sciences Institute
{martinm,knoblock}@isi.edu

Abstract. While many real-world combinatorial problems can be advantageously modeled and solved using Constraint Programming, scalability remains a major issue in practice. Constraint models that accurately reflect the inherent structure of a problem, solvers that exploit the properties of this structure, and reformulation techniques that modify the problem encoding to reduce the cost of problem solving are typically used to overcome the complexity barrier. In this paper, we investigate such approaches in a geospatial reasoning task, the building-identification problem (BID), introduced and modeled as a Constraint Satisfaction Problem by Michalowski and Knoblock [1]. We introduce an improved constraint model, a custom solver for this problem, and a number of reformulation techniques that modify various aspects of the problem encoding to improve scalability. We show how interleaving these reformulations with the various stages of the solver allows us to solve much larger BID problems than was previously possible. Importantly, we describe the usefulness of our reformulations techniques for general Constraint Satisfaction Problems, beyond the BID application.

1 Introduction

Geospatial data integration aims at combining geospatial information from traditional and non-traditional data sources to infer information that is not available in any one source. The inadvertent bombing of the Chinese Embassy in Belgrade [2] illustrates the importance of geospatial data integration. That event could have been avoided by reasoning about the information that was available at the time (i.e., telephone books and maps) to identify the buildings shown in a satellite image. More generally, the information gained by data integration can be used to verify and augment geospatial databases (e.g., gazetteers), and extend the capabilities of geospatial systems (e.g., Google Maps, Google Earth, and Microsoft VirtualEarth).

Michalowski and Knoblock [1] identified and studied the Building Identification (BID) problem as an application of significant intelligence and civilian impact. The task is to assign a potentially incomplete list of postal addresses, collected from various 'phone-book' sources, to buildings appearing in a satellite image. A map provides the names of the streets and the positions of the buildings, but we do not know the addresses of the buildings or, for a building located on a street corner, on which street the building's address lies. They modeled the problem as a Constraint Satisfaction Problem (CSP) and

C. Bessiere (Ed.): CP 2007, LNCS 4741, pp. 164–179, 2007.

used an existing solver (CPlan [3]) to find *all possible* matchings of addresses to buildings that are consistent with the phone book and with the geographical layout in the image. Their work established the feasibility of the approach and *identified an important new area where CP techniques are useful for solving real-world problems*. However, their approach resisted scaling because their model included high-arity constraints and their generic solver failed to take advantage of the structural information in the application domain. While we show in this paper that the particular BID problem studied in [1] is tractable, it is clear that only a careful theoretical study can determine whether or not a given set of constraints in the BID problem yields a tractable problem. The value of a CP approach is its flexibility in solving new problems with arbitrary constraints even when the problem's tractability is unknown. This paper addresses the scalability of the CP approach to the BID problem with the use of reformulation techniques, and discusses the use of the proposed reformulations to general CSPs.

First, we propose an improved constraint model that reflects the topology of the streets layout, and accommodates the addition of new constraints locally to express variations of street-numbering schemas around the world. *Second*, we introduce a custom solver, based on backtrack search, that exploits structural properties of a problem instance, such as identifying backdoor variables [4] and exploiting them to decompose the problem into tractable components. *Third*, we introduce four reformulation techniques to reduce the cost of problem solving. These techniques are (1) reformulating the BID problem from a counting problem to a satisfiability one, (2) reducing the domains size of variables in the scope of a global constraint that we identify and characterize, (3) relaxing the satisfiability problem into a matching problem, (4) using symmetry to generate efficiently all possible solutions of the relaxed version of the original BID counting problem. *Fourth*, as we introduce each reformulation technique, we also discuss its application to general CSPs. *Fifth*, we evaluate the benefits of 3 of our reformulations on the BID problem, showing that we can now solve instances involving 206 buildings while the problem solved by Michalowski and Knoblock included only 34 buildings.

This paper is structured as follows. Section 2 positions our adopted perspective on reformulation. Section 3 describes the new CSP model and custom solver for the BID problem. Sections 4, 5, 6, and 7 describe our reformulations of the BID problem and their utility for general CSPs. Section 8 evaluates our techniques on real-world BID instances. Finally, Section 9 describes related work and concludes the paper.

2 Background

Choueiry et al. [5] characterized a reformulation as a transformation of a problem $\mathcal{P}$ from one encoding to another, where a problem is given by a *formulation* and a *query*, $\mathcal{P} = \langle \mathcal{F}, \mathcal{Q} \rangle$. The transformation may change the query and/or any of the components of the formulation. The goal of the reformulation is to 'simplify' problem solving, where the benefit of the 'simplification' and other effects of the reformulation are clearly articulated in the particular problem-solving context. The reformulation techniques discussed in this paper operate on various aspects of a Constraint Satisfaction Problem (CSP) in order to improve the performance of problem solving. The problem formulation of a CSP is given by $\mathcal{F} = (\mathcal{V}, \mathcal{D}, \mathcal{C})$ where $\mathcal{V}= \{V_i\}$ is a set of variables,

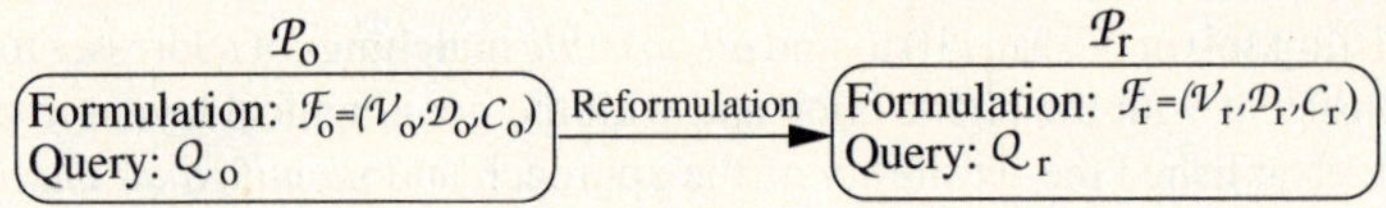

Fig. 1. The general pattern of a CSP transformation

$\mathcal{D}= \{D_{V_i}\}$ the set of their respective domains, and $\mathcal{C}$ a set of constraints. A constraint is a relation over a subset of the variables specifying the allowable combinations of values for the variables in its scope. A solution is an assignment to the variables such that all constraints are satisfied. The query is usually to find one consistent solution or all possible solutions. In this paper, we describe a reformulation of a CSP as a transformation of the original problem $\mathcal{P}_o = \langle \mathcal{F}_o, \mathcal{Q}_o \rangle$ into the reformulated problem $\mathcal{P}_r = \langle \mathcal{F}_r, \mathcal{Q}_r \rangle$, where $\mathcal{F}_i$ indicates a formulation and $\mathcal{Q}_i$ indicates a query, as illustrated in Figure 1.

3 Modeling and Solving the BID Problem as a CSP

The task is to assign possible addresses to the buildings that appear in a satellite image. Each address consists of the combination of a street name and a number. The names of the streets are provided by a map and the positions of the buildings are extracted from a satellite image. Thus, we know the street names and the positions of the buildings, but we do not know the addresses of the buildings or, for buildings located on corners, on which street the buildings are located. The addresses can be partially retrieved from a variety of data sources such as a phone books, gazetteers, or property records. We generically refer to the addresses given as input as phone-book addresses regardless of their actual source. Figure 2 shows a BID instance with 10 buildings. The set of phone-book addresses may be *incomplete*, that is, there could be fewer addresses than there are buildings in an image. However, we assume that the reverse does not hold, that is, every phone-book address must be assigned to a building on the image. A solver must infer addresses for buildings that do not have an address in the phone book. In addition to the phone-book addresses, we may have information about street-numbering schemas used in a given region in the world, such as the 100-block increment in the addresses across street intersections used in the US or the red-black numbering used in Italy. Also, we may know the exact address of one or more *landmarks*, such as the residence of the Prime Minister in London.

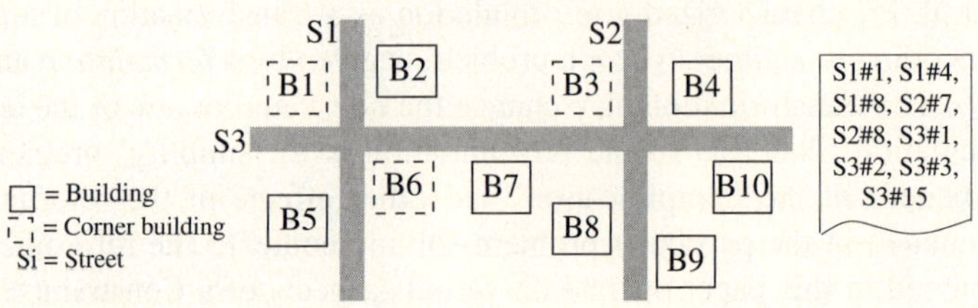

Fig. 2. An example of the building-identification problem

3.1 A New Constraint Model

Below we describe the variables and constraints in our CSP model of the BID problem. Our model uses three types of variables: *orientation*, *corner*, and *building*. In general, there are four *orientation variables*. These Boolean variables determine the global orientation properties of the map. The first two are *ordering* variables and indicate whether or not addresses increase in value when moving toward the north and to the east. The remaining two are *parity* variables and indicate on which side of the street odd addresses occur. The *corner variables* represent the possible *streets* on which a corner building might be. We generate one corner variable for each corner building, whose domain is the list of streets on which the building could lie. *The corner buildings are natural 'backdoors' [4] in the constraint network*: once the solver assigns values to all corner buildings, the network degenerates into a set of chains (corresponding to buildings along street segments) that can be solved in a backtrack-free manner. Thus our solver instantiates corner variables as soon as possible. The *building* variables represent the addresses (i.e., numbers) of the buildings. We generate a building variable for every building on the map. The domain of a variable is every possible address on the building's streets.

Our model has five types of constraints: *parity*, *ordering*, *corner*, *phone book*, and *grid*. *Parity constraints* are binary constraints and ensure that the numbers assigned to buildings respect the values assigned to the parity (orientation) variables. *Ordering constraints* are ternary constraints, and link an ordering variable to two building variables along the same street. These constraints ensure that the addresses assigned to the building variables respect the ordering specified by the ordering variable. *Corner constraints* are binary constraints that apply to the pair of variables of each corner building, namely, the corner variable (which determines the street), and the building variable (which determines the address on the street). It reinforces that the address assigned to the building is consistent with the street chosen for the building. *Phone-book constraints* exist for each street on the map. These constraints ensure that the solver assigns every address in the phone book to some building along that street. These constraints usually have a high arity, because their scope is the set of buildings along the street. *Grid constraints* exist between buildings across certain artificial grid-lines, depending on the region we are modeling. These constraints ensure that the addresses of adjacent buildings across the grid-lines are in separate numeric increments. For example, in many cities in the United States, addresses increase to the next increment of 100 across intersections.

Our new model improves the original one proposed in [1] as follows. The number of variables for non-corner buildings is reduced by half, reducing number of variables between 37% and 43% in our test cases. Domains of the building variables in [1] were enumerated and upper bounds chosen arbitrary. They are represented as intervals with potentially infinite bounds in the new model. We reduced constraint arity from four to two for parity constraints, and from six to three for ordering constraints. Corner constraints are new and allow early decomposition of the problem. Grid constraints are also new and allow a more precise modeling of the real world. Interestingly, we show, in Section 6, that in the absence of grid constraints, the BID problem is tractable. The tractability of the BID problem in the presence of grid constraints remains an open question. Thus, modeling the BID problem as a CSP remains a pertinent approach because it gives us the flexibility to represent arbitrary constraints such as grid constraints and other street-addressing schemas used around the world.

3.2 A Custom Backtrack-Search Solver

Our custom solver, written in Java, is a backtrack-search procedure. We adapted the conflict-directed backjumping mechanism MAC-CBJ of [6] to handle constraints of any arity with nFC3, a look-ahead strategy for non-binary CSPs [7], yielding nFC3-CBJ. Key to the solver's success are the domain representation and the variable ordering. Domains of building variables are represented as a list of intervals, where an interval is a sequence of values. This representation allows us to restrict propagation to the boundaries of the intervals, as in bound consistency, whenever possible, and iterate over the individual values only when necessary. Using intervals with arbitrary large bounds is crucial when the phone book is incomplete and the smallest or largest address number on a given street is not known. Variables are ordered as follows: building and corner variables corresponding to landmark buildings, orientation variables, corner variables, then building variables. Because corner variables are backdoor variables, *satisfiability can be determined without instantiating the building variables*, which are instantiated only when full solutions are sought. Further, instantiating the backdoor variables (corner variables) decomposes the problem into chains, one for each entire street.

4 Query Reformulation

Michalowski and Knoblock [1] searched for all solutions in order to retrieve for each building on the map the set of acceptable addresses. *When the phone book is complete*, the problem has few solutions. Our solver, but not the one in [1], can easily find all solutions for *all* real-world examples we tested. *When the phone book is not complete*, the number of solutions quickly increases. The sheer number of solutions to be enumerated forced us to reconsider the task and reformulate the original query as explained below.

4.1 Per-Variable Solutions

Finding all solutions of a CSP is $O(d^n)$ where n is the number of variables and d is the maximum domain size. In practice, this process is prohibitively expensive. We consider the situation where we do not need to find all solutions, but only the values that each variable takes in any solution. We call this problem *finding the per-variable solutions*[1]. Thus, we reformulate the query from $\mathcal{Q}_\text{o}$= enumerating all solutions, to $\mathcal{Q}_\text{r}$= finding the per-variable solutions, where $\mathcal{Q}_\text{r}$ is "$\forall V_i,\ x \in D_{V_i}$, find if $\mathcal{P}_\text{o} \wedge (V_i \leftarrow x)$ is satisfiable" as illustrated in Figure 3. This query changes the complexity class of the problem from a counting problem to a satisfiability one.

[1] Formally, this query corresponds to finding the minimal CSP. It is also equivalent to the inverse consistency property introduced in [8], and to relational $(1,|\mathcal{C}|)$-consistency defined in [9].

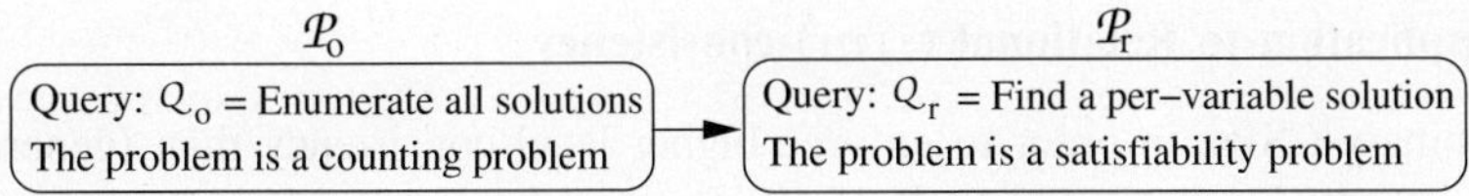

Fig. 3. Reformulation for the per-variable solution query

Algorithm 1 tests for every variable-value pair (V_i, x) if the CSP with $V_i \leftarrow x$ is solvable. When it is, x is added to the data structure returned by the algorithm. Algorithm 1 returns the set of variables along with all their values that appear in a solution.

```
Input: P =(V, D, C)
Output: S, a per-variable solution
1  foreach Vi ∈ V do
2  |  S[Vi] ← ∅
3  end
4  foreach Vi ∈ V do
5  |  foreach x ∈ D_Vi do
6  |  |  if P with Vi←x has a solution then
7  |  |  |  S[Vi] ← S[Vi] ∪ {x}
8  |  |  end
9  |  end
10 |  if |S[v]| = 0 then
11 |  |  return P has no solutions
12 |  end
13 end
14 return S
```

Algorithm 1. Finding the per-variable solutions

The inner loop of the algorithm runs $O(nd)$ times. Each iteration requires determining the satisfiability of a CSP. This operation appears costly, but in cases where the original CSP has significantly more than nd solutions, Algorithm 1 can perform significantly better than enumerating all solutions to the CSP.

When the test in Line 6 is executed by finding a solution to the CSP, the values for the variables in the solution found can be collected, and excluded from future calls in the loops on Lines 1 and 5 thus reducing the number of loops[2]. In the BID problem, we are not able to exploit this improvement for the following reason. A variable-value pair in Algorithm 1 for the BID problem is a combination of a building and a street name and number. However, the satisfiability of the BID instance is determined, and search is terminated, after the assignment of the backdoor variables and without instantiating the building variables (see Section 3.2). The benefit of continuing search and generating solutions after the instantiation of the backdoor variables in order to exploit the above improvement remains to be assessed.

[2] This improvement was suggested by an anonymous reviewer.

4.2 Application to Relational (i, m)-consistency

In non-binary CSPs, in order to enforce higher level consistency than (generalized) arc-consistency, Dechter and van Beek [9]introduced *relational* (i, m)*-consistency* as the consistency of m non-binary constraints over every subset of i variables in the CSP. Dechter [10] proposed the algorithm $RC_{(i,m)}$ for computing relational (i, m)-consistency. $RC_{(i,m)}$ works as follows. For every set C_m of m constraints in a constraint network, join the m constraints and project the result on each subset of i variables. The algorithm is not practical for large values of m, because the memory requirements for computing and storing a join of m constraints rises exponentially with the number of variables in the scopes of these constraints.

Algorithm 1 computes a minimal network, and the resulting network is the same as if we had executed $RC_{(1,m)}$. The difference between the two algorithms is that Algorithm 1 is polynomial space, whereas $RC_{(1,m)}$ is exponential space. We can easily generalize Algorithm 1 to consider sets of i variables (and all tuples in the Cartesian product of their domain) rather than a single variable (and a single variable-value pair). This extension would allow Algorithm 1 to produce the same results as $RC_{i,m}$. The memory requirement rises exponentially with i, which quickly becomes impractical, but remains more efficient than $RC_{(i,m)}$ whose space complexity is exponential in the size of the union of the m constraints scopes.

5 Domain Reformulation Using Symbolic Values

If the phone book is incomplete, we must infer the missing numbers to add to the variables' domains. Michalowski and Knoblock [1] proposed to enumerate all numbers between 1 and the largest address that appears on the street. Their approach has two problems. First, the choice of the upper limit is arbitrary. When the largest address is not in the phone book, this approach may yield incorrect solutions. The second problem with this approach is that the size of the domains becomes prohibitively large on real-world data. We propose a reformulation of the variables domains that reduces their size using symbolic variables, thus solving both problems.

5.1 Symbolic Values in the BID Problem

Assume we have, on the even side of a street S, the set of buildings B_S=$\{B_1, B_2, \ldots, B_5\}$, the set of phone-book addresses of even parity P_S=$\{$S#12, S#18$\}$, and the range of address numbers [2,624]. Any assignment cannot use more than 3 numbers in each of [2,12), (12,18), and (18,624]. Using symbolic values to represent an address in a solution, we replace the domain [1,624] of each variable B_S with the significantly smaller set $\{s_1, s_2, s_3, 12, s_4, s_5, 18, s_6, s_7, s_8\}$ where $s_1, s_2, s_3 \in$ [2,12), $s_4, s_5 \in$ (12,18), and $s_6, s_7, s_8 \in$ (18,624] and s_i<s_j for i<j. This process allows us to choose arbitrarily large bounds on a given street. Figure 4 illustrates this transformation. More generally, when [min,max] is the range of address numbers on the considered side of S, the address numbers in P_S partition [min,max] into consecutive convex intervals. In any such interval (i_1, i_2), we cannot use more than minimum($|B_S|$-$|P_S|$, $\lfloor\frac{(i_2-i_1)-1}{2}\rfloor$) addresses. Below we introduce ALLDIFF-ATMOST as a global constraint useful in such situations and

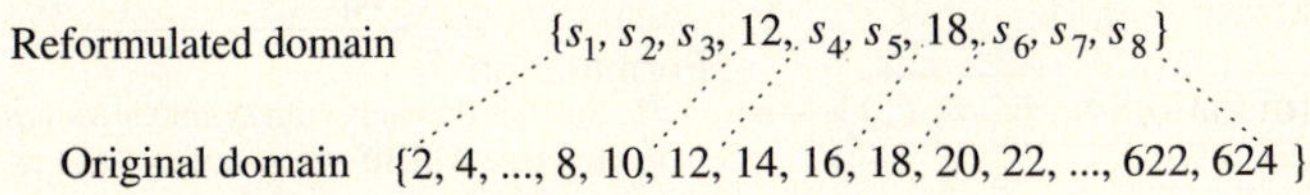

Reformulated domain $\{s_1, s_2, s_3, 12, s_4, s_5, 18, s_6, s_7, s_8\}$

Original domain $\{2, 4, ..., 8, 10, 12, 14, 16, 18, 20, 22, ..., 622, 624\}$

Fig. 4. Domain reformulation for the building-identification problem

discuss how to reformulate the domains of the variables in the scope of this constraint in order to reduce their size both for general and totally ordered domains.

5.2 The ALLDIFF-ATMOST Global Constraint

Example 1. An emerging country received an aid to build 7 hospitals on its territory, but does not want to put more than 2 hospitals in areas with high volcanic activity.

We propose the constraint ALLDIFF-ATMOST to model this situation. Given a set of variables $\mathcal{A} = \{V_1, V_2, ..., V_n\}$ with domains D_{V_i}, ALLDIFF-ATMOST$(\mathcal{A}, k, d)$, where $d \subseteq D_{V_i}$ for $i \in [1, n]$, $k \in \mathbb{N}$, and $k \leq |d|$, requires that (1) all variables take different values and (2) at most k variables in $\mathcal{A}$ have values from d. Note that while the domains D_{V_i} may be different, d must be a subset of each one of them and D_{V_i}, and d and D_{V_i} may be finite or infinite[3].

Example 2. Consider with the variables $\mathcal{A}$=$\{V_1, V_2, V_3, V_4\}$ of a CSP, with D_i=$\{1, 2, \ldots, 8\}$ and the constraint ALLDIFF-ATMOST*($\mathcal{A}$, 2, $\{1, 3, 4, 5, 8\}$). The assignment $V_1 \leftarrow 5$, $V_2 \leftarrow 2$, $V_3 \leftarrow 7$ and $V_4 \leftarrow 4$ satisfies the constraint.*

We can express the above described situation for the BID problem as ALLDIFF-ATMOST(B_S, k_a, (i_1, i_2)) with k_a=minimum($|B_S|$-$|P_S|$, $\lfloor \frac{(i_2-i_1)-1}{2} \rfloor$).

5.3 ALLDIFF-ATMOST Reformulation

Our reformulation of the domains of the variables in a ALLDIFF-ATMOST constraint is theorem constant, in the sense that solutions to the reformulated problem map to solutions to the original problem [12]. The benefit of this reformulation is the reduction of the domain sizes. Because the complexity of many CP techniques depends on the sizes of the domains, the reformulation improves the solver performance.

We reformulate the domains of the variables in the scope of the constraint ALLDIFF-ATMOST$(\mathcal{A}, k, d)$ by introducing k values s_l that we call *symbolic values* as follows:

$$\forall V_i \in \mathcal{A} \; D_{V_{i_r}} = \{s_1, s_2, \ldots, s_k\} \cup (D_{V_i} \setminus d) \tag{1}$$

where the symbolic values s_j $(1 \leq j \leq k)$ can take any distinct values in d. Applying this reformulation on Example 2 yields the following domains for all four variables: D_{V_i}=$\{s_1, s_2, 2, 6, 7\}$, where s_1, s_2 can take any different values in $\{1, 3, 4, 5, 8\}$.

[3] Many definitions of the ATMOST constraint exist (e.g., ECLiPse and on page 148 of [11]). Our definition of ALLDIFF-ATMOST allows us to express a situation of interest to resource allocation problems where our reformulation can be used to reduce the domain size.

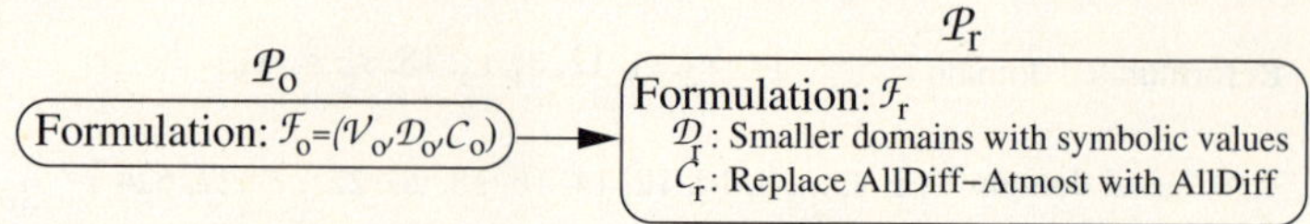

Fig. 5. The reformulation of ALLDIFF-ATMOST

In Example 1, the domains become $\{s_1, s_2\} \cup \{\text{sites in non-volcanic areas}\}$ where s_1, s_2 are different and range over sites with volcanic activities.

This reformulation operates on the problem formulation and affects, strictly speaking, both the ALLDIFF-ATMOST constraint and the domains of the variables in its scope, see Figure 5. However the most significant modification is the domain reformulation. We transform $\mathcal{D}_o$ to $\mathcal{D}_r$, where in $\mathcal{D}_r$ the domains of variables in $\mathcal{A}$ have been reformulated according to Equation (1). Replacing d with k symbolic values reduces the domains sizes by $|d| - k$, which is useful when d is large or infinite.

This operation is particularly useful during backtrack search where the domain values are enumerated. If we want to assign 'ground' values to each symbolic value, we can do so as a post-processing step while ensuring that two symbolic values are always mapped back to distinct ground values. While a solution to the reformulated problem does not map to a unique solution to the original problem, we can generate any solution to the original problem from some solution to the reformulated problem. Of particular concern is the interaction between this reformulation and the other constraints in the problem. When all the constraints in a problem can be checked on the symbolic values, as in the case of the BID problem, the reformulation is sound. When one or more constraints in a problem must be checked on the 'ground' values, then propagation must run on the appropriate representation for each constraint and, as soon as domain filtering causes $|d| \leq k$, then reformulated domains should be dropped and ALLDIFF-ATMOST replaced with a ALLDIFF constraint, as is the case in a BID instance with a complete phonebook. While this double representation works for constraint propagation, using it during backtrack search requires further investigation.

5.4 Symbolic Intervals

When the values in the variables domains follow a total order, as in numeric domains, the domains are commonly represented as intervals and constraint propagation is typically restricted to the endpoints of these intervals, as in box-consistency algorithms. The reformulation of an ALLDIFF-ATMOST in the presence of totally ordered domains obviously remains valid. However, in order to *restrict propagation to the endpoints of the intervals* representing the domains, the following is needed:

1. We require the values in d to form a convex interval.
2. We must add total ordering constraints between the symbolic values: $s_1 < s_2 < \ldots < s_k$.
3. We must add total ordering constraints between the two extreme symbolic values, s_1 and s_k, and their closest neighbors in the reformulated domains. Let $D^{\mathrm{l}}_{V_{ir}}$ and $D^{\mathrm{r}}_{V_{ir}}$ be respectively the intervals of $D_{V_i} \backslash d$ to the left and right of, and adjacent to, d. The right endpoint of $D^{\mathrm{l}}_{V_{ir}}$ must be less than s_1, and the left endpoint of $D^{\mathrm{r}}_{V_{ir}}$ must be greater than s_k. Figure 6 illustrates this transformation.

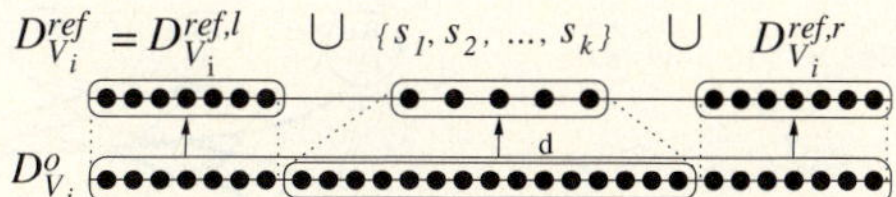

Fig. 6. ALLDIFF-ATMOST reformulation for totally ordered domains

4. When mapping the symbolic values back to ground values, the ground values must respect the total ordering imposed on the symbolic values.

In the BID problem, we use this particular form of the reformulation of the ALLDIFF-ATMOST on the building variables, which have totally ordered domains.

6 Problem Relaxation by Constraint Removal

Removing (or adding) a constraint in a problem formulation to yield a necessary (or sufficient) tractable approximation of the problem is a typical reformulation strategy. Examples abound and include: In AI, admissible heuristics generation for A* (page 107 in [11]) and theory approximation [13]; in mathematical programming, linear relaxation of integer programs, Lagrangian relaxation [14], and the cutting-plane method. Below, we show that removing the grid constraint from the BID problem yields a tractable problem that is a tractable necessary approximation of the BID problem.

6.1 A Tractable Necessary Approximation of the BID Problem

We describe a construction to efficiently solve the BID problem in the absence of grid constraints by finding a maximum matching in a bipartite graph. We first recall some terminology. Let $G = (X \cup Y, E)$ be a bipartite graph with edge set E, vertex set $V = X \cup Y$, and partitions X and Y, which are independent sets of vertices. We define a *match count* for each vertex in $v \in V$, which we denote $m(v)$, to be a positive (non-null) integer. A *matching* in G is a set of edges $M \subseteq E$ such that for all $v \in V$ there exists at most one edge $e \in M$ incident to v. In this paper we consider a matching in G to be a set of edges $M \subseteq E$ such that for all $v \in V$ there exists at most $m(v)$ edges $e \in M$ incident to v. Further, we say that a matching M saturates vertex v iff M has exactly $m(v)$ edges incident to v; and a matching M saturates a set S iff M saturates all vertices in S. A matching that saturates S can be computed in polynomial time [15].

Given an instance of the BID problem without grid constraints, we construct a bipartite graph $G = (B \cup S, E)$ as follows. First, assume an assignment to the orientation variables (there are 2^4 such assignments). For each building β in the problem, add a vertex b to B and set its match count to 1. For each street σ in the problem, add two vertices s_{odd} and s_{even} to S, one for each side of the street. Set the match count of each s_i to the number of phone-book addresses on street s with parity i. For each building β, add an edge between vertex b and the street vertex corresponding to the street side on which β may be. (Note that corner buildings are on two streets.) Figure 7 shows the construction of G for the map in Figure 2 where we assume that odd numbers appear on the North and West sides of the street. We can show that a

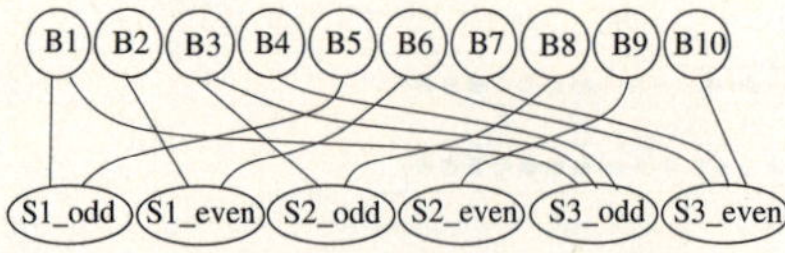

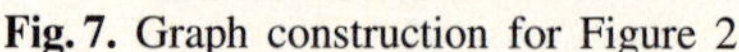

Fig. 7. Graph construction for Figure 2

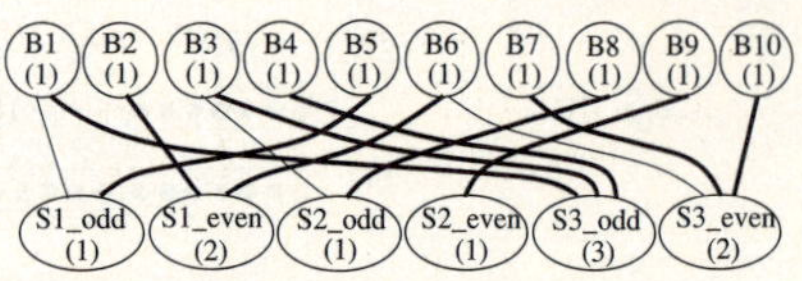

Fig. 8. A saturating matching for Figure 7

matching in this graph that saturates S corresponds to a satisfactory assignment of streets to corner buildings[4]. We find a maximum matching using an $O(n^{5/2})$ algorithm by Hopcroft and Karp [16] after replacing each vertex in the bipartite graph by as many vertices as its match count.

Figure 8 shows a saturating matching for the graph of Figure 7, where the edges of the matching are darkened and the numbers in parentheses indicate the match count. This matching determines the satisfiability of the relaxed BID problem, and yields assignments to all corner variables in the corresponding CSP. For a complete solution, we still need to instantiate the building variables, which can be done in linear time because the constraint network becomes a set of chains after the instantiation of the backdoor (corner) variables. While the matching approach is powerful, it does not model the grid constraint. The tractability of the problem with grid constraints remains an open question.

6.2 Relaxing Resource Allocation Problems

At the core of many resource allocation problems lies the problem of matching between the elements of two sets: the tasks and the resources. In general, the resource allocation problem may be complex (and likely intractable). However, we may sometimes be able to identify those constraints that, when removed, reduce the original problem into the problem of finding a matching in a bipartite graph that saturates one of the two partitions as described above. Figure 9 illustrates this relaxation.

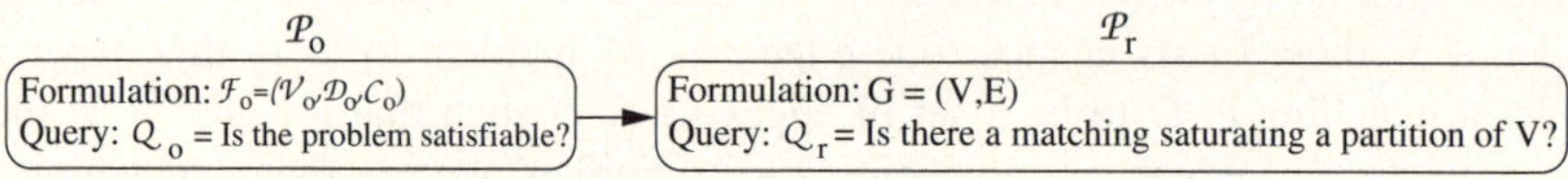

Fig. 9. Relaxing a CSP as a matching problem

6.3 Using the Relaxation in Problem Solving

We can use the above relaxation in four ways for the BID problem and for other applications that can be relaxed as a matching problem:

1. To solve problem instances that do not have the grid constraints, e.g. [1].
2. As a first preprocessing step to quickly rule out unsatisfiable instances, i.e. before Line 1 in Algorithm 1. Our experiments on the BID problem (not included here

[4] The matching must saturate S because the BID problem assumes that all addresses in the phone book, whether complete or incomplete, must be assigned to a building.

for lack of space) showed that this early preprocessing is effective only on tight problems.

3. As a second preprocessing between Line 5 and Line 6 in Algorithm 1, see Section 8.
4. As a lookahead mechanism when using search at Line 6 in Algorithm 1. We use the construction of [17] to filter out, from the domains of the future variables, those values that cannot yield a solution. As such, the relaxed problem appears as a (special version of the) all-diff constraints of [17], added to the problem as a *new* but redundant constraint to enhance propagation, see Section 8.

7 Generating Solutions by Symmetry

The set of solutions to the relaxed problem of Section 6 can be obtained by enumerating all maximum matchings using an algorithm such as the one proposed by Uno [18]. In this section, we characterize all maximum matchings in a bipartite graph as symmetric to a single base matching, and proposed to use this symmetry to enumerate all solutions.

Our symmetry detection relies on two graph constructions described by Berge [19]: *alternating cycles* (AltCyc) and *even alternating paths starting at a free vertex* (EvAltP). An AltCyc or EvAltP in a graph G relative to a matching M alternate between edges in M and edges not in M. If we take a maximum matching M and a AltCyc or EvAltP P, we can produce another maximum matching M' by computing the symmetric difference of M and P, denoted $M \Delta P$. We use that mechanism to identify all maximum matchings in a bipartite graph G as symmetric of a single maximum matching M. Let $\mathcal{S}$ be the set of all AltCyc's and EvAltP's relative to M. We construct another maximum matching M_i by choosing a disjoint subset $\mathcal{S}_i \subseteq \mathcal{S}$ and computing $M \Delta \mathcal{S}_i$. M_i is symmetrical to M in that it is identical to M in all edges except those in $\mathcal{S}_i$. In fact, for any maximum matching M_j of G, we prove[5] that there exists an $\mathcal{S}_j$ such that $M_j = M \Delta \mathcal{S}_j$. We generate $\mathcal{S}$ by first orienting G using the construction described by Hopcroft and Karp [16]. From the oriented graph, we enumerate the alternating paths by finding all EvAltP's, as defined by Berge [19]. We enumerate the AltCyc's from the strongly connected components in the oriented graph as described by Régin [17]. Thus, to store the information necessary to enumerate all alternating paths and cycles, and therefore all maximum matchings, we only need to store a single base matching, the set of free vertices, and the set of strongly connected components[6].

Consider the bipartite graph $G = (X \cup Y, E)$, where $X = \{x_1, x_2, x_3, x_4\}$, $Y = \{y_1, y_2, y_3\}$, and E=$\{(x_1, y_1), (x_2, y_1), (x_2, y_2), (x_3, y_2), (x_3, y_3), (x_4, y_2), (x_4, y_3)\}$. Figure 10 (a) shows a maximum matching M in G. $P = x_1y_1x_2$ is an alternating path and $C = x_3y_2x_4y_3x_3$ is an alternating cycle. We find other maximum matchings using the symmetric difference operator. Figure 10 (b) show $M \Delta P$, Figure 10 (c) shows $M \Delta C$, and Figure 10 (d) shows $M \Delta (C \cup P)$.

Figure 11 illustrates the two reformulations of $\mathcal{P}_o$, the problem of enumerating all maximum matchings. We can reformulate $\mathcal{P}_o$ as $\mathcal{P}_{r1}$, the set of all maximum matchings, using Uno's algorithm. Alternatively, we can reformulate the problem as $\mathcal{P}_{r2}$,

[5] The proof is omitted for lack of space.

[6] An improvement suggested by an anonymous reviewer.

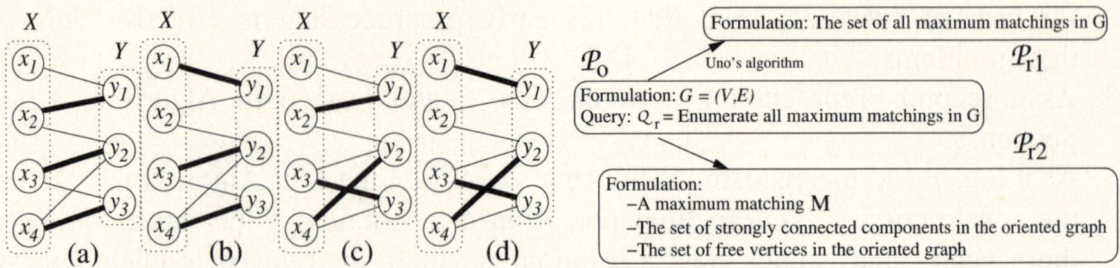

Fig. 10. Multiple matchings saturating Y

Fig. 11. Finding all maximum matchings

a base matching and its corresponding sets of strongly connected components and free vertices. All matchings can be enumerated from $\mathcal{P}_{r2}$ as needed. Our construction has the same time complexity as Uno's, which is linear in the number of maximum matching. However, our characterization of the solutions as symmetries has valuable properties which we do not fully exploit:

1. It provides a more compact representation of the set of solutions. Rather than storing all matchings, we store a single matching, a set of strongly connected components, and a set of free vertices.
2. In case one is indeed seeking *all*, or a given number of, the solutions to BID problem (similarly, to a resource allocation problem that has a maximum matching relaxation), we can generate every symmetric matching to that known single matching and test if it satisfies the additional constraints of the non-relaxed problem, when it does not, the matching is a solution to the non-relaxed problem found without search. Naturally, the number of maximum matchings can be large.

8 Experiments

We integrate our techniques in the flowchart shown in Figure 12, which implements the instruction in Line 6 of Algorithm 1. Table 1 describes the properties of the regions of the the city of El Segundo (CA), on which we ran our experiments. The number of calls refers to the total number of calls to Line 6 of Algorithm 1. Each call to Line 6 was timed out after one hour. We report the number of timed out executions. The completeness of the phone book indicates what percent of the buildings on the map have a corresponding address in the phone book. We created the complete phone books using property-tax data, and the incomplete phone books using the real-world phone-book.

Effect of domain reformulation. Table 2 shows the effect of domain reformulation by comparing the domain sizes and the cost of BT before and after reformulation. When the phone book is complete, the reformulation is not used as no ALLDIFF-ATMOST constraints exist. The advantage of the reformulation increases with the incompleteness of the phone book.

Effect of query reformulation. As stated in Section 4, the sheer number of solutions made it impossible to solve problem instances with incomplete phone-books using the query of enumerating all solutions. Thus, without the query reformulation, we would not have been able to solve the incomplete phone-book instances.

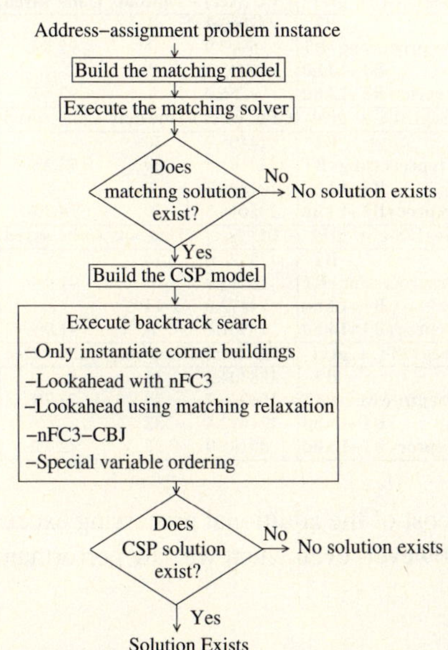

Fig. 12. Implementing Line 6 of Algorithm 1

Table 1. Case studies used in experiments

Case study	Phone book completeness	Number of bldgs	crnr bldgs	blks	calls
NSeg125-c	100.0%	125	17	4	4160
NSeg125-i	45.6%				1857
NSeg206-c	100.0%	206	28	7	4879
NSeg206-i	50.5%				10009
SSeg131-c	100.0%	131	36	8	3833
SSeg131-i	60.3%				2375
SSeg178-c	100.0%	178	46	12	4852
SSeg178-i	65.6%				2477

Table 2. Domain reformulation

Case study	Avg. domain size Orig.	Ref.	Runtime [sec] Orig.	Ref.	Timeouts Orig.	Ref.
NSeg125-i	1103.1	236.1	2943.7	744.7	0	0
NSeg206-i	1102.0	438.8	14818.9	5533.8	0	0
SSeg131-i	792.9	192.9	67910.1	66901.1	18	17
SSeg178-i	785.5	186.3	119002.4	117826.7	32	29

Table 3. Solvers' performance (no grid)

Case study	Runtime [sec] BT	Matching	Matching + Symmetry
NSeg125-c	139.2	4.8	0.03
NSeg125-i	744.7	2.5	*
NSeg206-c	4971.2	16.3	0.06
NSeg206-i	5533.8	8.5	*
SSeg131-c	38618.3	7.3	0.26
SSeg131-i	66901.1	3.1	*
SSeg178-c	117279.1	22.5	0.41
SSeg178-i	117826.7	4.9	*

* Did not finish in 1 hour.

Effect of finding symmetrical maximum matchings. In the absence of grid constraints, the building-identification problem can be solved in polynomial time by the matching solver. Here we compare backtrack search, a solver that uses Algorithm 1 with a matching solver, and a solver that uses the reformulation of symmetric matchings from Section 7. Finding all symmetric matchings requires enumerating all matchings, which isn't feasible for the under-constrained incomplete phone-book problems. Thus, those problem instances timed out and are indicated by asterisks. However, when the number of solutions was small, such as when the phone-book is complete, the symmetry solver had significantly better performance than the per-variable matching solver. The benefit in terms of runtime reduction is shown in Table 3.

Effect of relaxing a CSP into a matching problem. To test the use of the matching relaxation as a preprocessing step and lookahead mechanism, we added grid constraints to each region. Table 8 shows the results of these experiments, comparing the performance of: (1) the backtrack search (BT), (2) BT with matching for preprocessing (Preproc+BT), (3) BT with matching for lookahead (Lkhd+BT), and (4) BT with matching for both purposes (Preproc+BT+Lkhd). We report runtime, number of timeouts, and number of calls to the CSP solver saved by the preprocessing. In all cases, the same solutions were found. Our results indicate that, in general, the integration of the matching and BT improves

Table 4. Improvements due to preprocessing and lookahead

NSeg125-c + grid	CPU [sec]	#Timeouts	Calls saved
BT	100.8	0	-
Preprocessing+BT	33.2	0	97.0%
BT+Lkhd	140.2	0	-
Preproc+BT+Lkhd	39.6	0	97.0%
NSeg125-i + grid	**CPU [sec]**	**#Timeouts**	**Calls saved**
BT	1232.5	0	-
Preprocessing+BT	1159.1	0	62.6%
BT+Lkhd	726.6	0	-
Preproc+BT+Lkhd	701.1	0	62.6%
NSeg206-c + grid	**CPU [sec]**	**#Timeouts**	**Calls saved**
BT	2277.5	0	-
Preprocessing+BT	614.2	0	98.9%
BT+Lkhd	1559.2	0	-
Preproc+BT+Lkhd	443.8	0	98.9%
NSeg206-i + grid	**CPU [sec]**	**#Timeouts**	**Calls saved**
BT	4052.8	0	-
Preprocessing+BT	3806.7	0	87.8%
BT+Lkhd	3499.5	0	-
Preproc+BT+Lkhd	3510.0	0	87.8%

SSeg131-c + grid	CPU [sec]	#Timeouts	Calls saved
BT	17063.3	0	-
Preprocessing+BT	5997.9	0	92.5%
BT+Lkhd	9745.8	0	-
Preproc+BT+Lkhd	4256.0	0	92.5%
SSeg131-i + grid	**CPU [sec]**	**#Timeouts**	**Calls saved**
BT	114405.9	30	-
Preprocessing+BT	114141.3	29	74.2%
BT+Lkhd	107896.3	30	-
Preproc+BT+Lkhd	108646.5	30	74.2%
SSeg178-c + grid	**CPU [sec]**	**#Timeouts**	**Calls saved**
BT	78528.6	14	-
Preprocessing+BT	15717.9	1	91.9%
BT+Lkhd	74172.0	14	-
Preproc+BT+Lkhd	13961.1	1	91.9%
SSeg178-i + grid	**CPU [sec]**	**#Timeouts**	**Calls saved**
BT	138404.2	35	-
Preprocessing+BT	103244.7	25	72.7%
BT+Lkhd	121492.4	32	-
Preproc+BT+Lkhd	85185.9	22	72.7%

performance. There are exceptions, when the cost of the additional processing exceeds the gains in terms of reduced search space. However, even when we saw performance degradation, the degradation was minimal.

9 Related Work and Conclusions

Reformulation has been applied to a wide range of CSP problems with much success. The literature also encompasses approaches to modeling, abstraction, approximation, and symmetry detection[7]. Nadel studied 8 different models of the n-Queens problem, some of which much easier to solve than others [20]. Glaisher proposed avoiding symmetry in the Eight Queens as far back as 1874 [21]. Holte and Choueiry provide a general discussion on abstraction and reformulation in AI including CSPs [22]. Razgon et al. [23] studied a class of problems that is similar to the one we investigate, and which they call Two Families of Sets constraints (TFOS). They introduced a technique for reformulating TFOS problems into network flow problems. Conceptually, the relaxed problem we study in Section 6 constitutes a special case of the TFOS problem.

An interesting feature of our work is the design of several techniques and their integration in a comprehensive framework for solving the BID problem while highlighting their usefulness for general CSPs. Also, our query reformulation facilitates a much wider use of relational consistency algorithms than was possible before. In the future, we intend to evaluate these techniques in other application settings. For example, we believe that many resource allocation problems have matching relaxations like we described.

Acknowledgments. Experiments were conducted on the Research Computing Facility at UNL. This research is supported by NSF CAREER Award #0133568 and the Air Force Office of Scientific Research under grant numbers FA9550-04-1-0105 and FA9550-07-1-0416.

[7] Some successful dedicated meetings are: Symposium on Abstraction, Reformulation and Approximation, Workshop on Modeling and Reformulation, Workshop on Symmetry in CSPs.

References

1. Michalowski, M., Knoblock, C.: A Constraint Satisfaction Approach to Geospatial Reasoning. In: AAAI 2005, pp. 423–429 (2005)
2. Pickering, T.: Speech by Under Secretary of State T. Pickering on 06/17/1999 to the Chinese Government Regarding the Accidental Bombing of the PRC Embassy in Belgrade (1999)
3. van Beek, P., Chen, X.: CPlan: A Constraint Programming Approach to Planning. In: AAAI 1999, pp. 585–590 (1999)
4. Kilby, P., Slaney, J., Thiébaux, S., Walsh, T.: Backbones and Backdoors in Satisfiability. In: AAAI 2005, pp. 1373–1468 (2005)
5. Choueiry, B.Y., Iwasaki, Y., McIlraith, S.: Towards a Practical Theory of Reformulation for Reasoning About Physical Systems. Artificial Intelligence 162 (1–2), 145–204 (2005)
6. Prosser, P.: MAC-CBJ: Maintaining Arc Consistency with Conflict-Directed Backjumping. Technical Report 95/177, Univ. of Strathclyde (1995)
7. Bessière, C., Meseguer, P., Freuder, E., Larrosa, J.: On Forward Checking for Non-binary Constraint Satisfaction. In: Jaffar, J. (ed.) Principles and Practice of Constraint Programming – CP'99. LNCS, vol. 1713, pp. 88–102. Springer, Heidelberg (1999)
8. Freuder, E., Elfe, C.: Neighborhood Inverse Consistency Preprocessing. In: AAAI 1996, pp. 202–208 (1996)
9. Dechter, R., van Beek, P.: Local and Global Relational Consistency. Journal of Theoretical Computer Science (1996)
10. Dechter, R.: Constraint Processing. Morgan Kaufmann, San Francisco (2003)
11. Russell, S., Norvig, P.: Artificial Intelligence: A Modern Approach. Prentice-Hall, Englewood Cliffs (2003)
12. Giunchiglia, F., Walsh, T.: A Theory of Abstraction. Artificial Intelligence 57(2-3), 323–389 (1992)
13. Selman, B., Kautz, H.: Knowledge Compilation and Theory Approximation. Journal of the ACM 43(2), 193–224 (1996)
14. Milano, M. (ed.): Constraint and Integer Programming: Toward a Unified Methodology. Kluwer Academic Publishers, Dordrecht (2004)
15. Gallai, T.: Über extreme Punkt- und Kantenmengen. Ann. Univ. Sci. Budapest, Eotvos Sect. Math. 2, 133–139 (1959)
16. Hopcroft, J., Karp, R.: An $n^{5/2}$ Algorithm for Maximum Matchings in Bipartite Graphs. SIAM 2, 225–231 (1973)
17. Régin, J.: A Filtering Algorithm for Constraints of Difference in CSPs. In: AAAI 1994, pp. 362–367 (1994)
18. Uno, T.: Algorithms for Enumerating All Perfect, Maximum and Maximal Matchings in Bipartite Graphs. In: Leong, H.-V., Jain, S., Imai, H. (eds.) ISAAC 1997. LNCS, vol. 1350, pp. 92–101. Springer, Heidelberg (1997)
19. Berge, C.: Graphs and Hypergraphs. American Elsevier, New York (1973)
20. Nadel, B.: Representation Selection for Constraint Satisfaction: A Case Study Using n-Queens. IEEE Expert 5(3), 16–24 (1990)
21. Glaisher, J.: On the Problem of the Eight Queens. Philosophical Magazine 4(48), 457–467 (1874)
22. Holte, R.C., Choueiry, B.Y.: Abstraction and Reformulation in Artificial Intelligence. Philosophical Trans. of the Royal Society Sect. Biological Sciences 358(1435), 1197–1204 (2003)
23. Razgon, I., O'Sullivan, B., Provan, G.: Generalizing Global Constraints Based on Network Flows. In: Workshop on Constraint Modelling and Reformulation, pp. 74–87 (2006)

A Generic Geometrical Constraint Kernel in Space and Time for Handling Polymorphic k-Dimensional Objects

N. Beldiceanu[1], M. Carlsson[2], E. Poder[1], R. Sadek[1], and C. Truchet[3]

[1] École des Mines de Nantes, LINA FRE CNRS 2729, FR-44307 Nantes, France
{Nicolas.Beldiceanu,Emmanuel.Poder,Rida.Sadek}@emn.fr
[2] SICS, P.O. Box 1263, SE-164 29 Kista, Sweden
Mats.Carlsson@sics.se
[3] Université de Nantes, LINA FRE CNRS 2729, FR-44322 Nantes, France
Charlotte.Truchet@univ-nantes.fr

Abstract. This paper introduces a geometrical constraint kernel for handling the location in space and time of polymorphic k-dimensional objects subject to various geometrical and time constraints. The constraint kernel is generic in the sense that one of its parameters is a set of constraints on subsets of the objects. These constraints are handled globally by the kernel.

We first illustrate how to model several placement problems with the constraint kernel. We then explain how new constraints can be introduced and plugged into the kernel. Based on these interfaces, we develop a generic k-dimensional lexicographic sweep algorithm for filtering the attributes of an object (i.e., its shape and the coordinates of its origin as well as its start, duration and end in time) according to all constraints where the object occurs. Experiments involving up to hundreds of thousands of objects and 1 million integer variables are provided in 2, 3 and 4 dimensions, both for simple shapes (i.e., rectangles, parallelepipeds) and for more complex shapes.

1 Introduction and Presentation of the Kernel

This paper introduces a constraint kernel $geost(k, \mathcal{O}, \mathcal{S}, \mathcal{C})$ for handling in a generic way a variety of geometrical constraints $\mathcal{C}$ in space and time between polymorphic k-dimensional objects $\mathcal{O}$ ($k \in \mathbb{N}^+$), where each object takes a shape among a set of shapes described by $\mathcal{S}$ during a given time interval and at a given position in space. This line of research can be seen as a continuation and generalisation of previous work on non-overlapping parallelepipeds [1,2,3,4].

Each shape is defined as a finite set of shifted boxes, where each shifted box is described by a box in a k-dimensional space at a given offset (from the origin of the shape) with given sizes. More precisely, a *shifted box* $s = \text{sbox}(sid, t[], l[]) \in \mathcal{S}$ is an entity defined by its shape id $s.sid$, shift offset $s.t[d]$, $0 \leq d < k$, and sizes $s.l[d]$ ($s.l[d] > 0, 0 \leq d < k$). All attributes of a shifted box are integer values. Then, a *shape* is defined as the union of shifted boxes sharing the same shape id. Each *object* $o = \text{object}(id, sid, x[], start, duration, end) \in \mathcal{O}$ is an entity defined by its unique object id $o.id$, shape id $o.sid$, origin $o.x[d]$, $0 \leq d < k$, start in time $o.start$, duration in time

C. Bessiere (Ed.): CP 2007, LNCS 4741, pp. 180–194, 2007.

$o.duration$ ($o.duration \geq 0$) and end in time $o.end$.[1] All these attributes correspond to domain variables.[2] Typical constraints from the list of constraints $\mathcal{C}$ can express, for instance, the fact that a given subset of objects from $\mathcal{O}$ do not pairwise overlap or that they are all included within a given bounding box. Constraints always have two first arguments $\mathcal{A}_i$ and $\mathcal{O}_i$ (followed by possibly some additional arguments) which resp. specify:

- A list of distinct dimensions (integers in $[0, k-1]$) that the constraint considers.
- A list of identifiers of the objects to which the constraint applies.

Example 1. Assume we have a 3D placement problem (i.e., $k = 3$) involving a set of parallelepipeds $\mathcal{P}$ and one subset $\mathcal{P}'$ of $\mathcal{P}$, where we want to express the fact that (1) no parallelepipeds of $\mathcal{P}$ should overlap, and (2) no parallelepipeds of $\mathcal{P}'$ should be piled. Constraints (1) and (2) resp. correspond to *non-overlapping*$([0,1,2], \mathcal{P})$ and to *non-overlapping*$([0,1], \mathcal{P}')$. Within the first *non-overlapping* constraint, the argument $[0,1,2]$ expresses the fact that we consider a non-overlapping constraint according to dimensions 0, 1 and 2 (i.e., given any pair of parallelepipeds p' and p'' of $\mathcal{P}$ there should exist at least one dimension d ($d \in \{0,1,2\}$) where the projections of p' and p'' on d do not overlap). Similarly, the argument $[0,1]$ of the second non-overlapping constraint expresses the fact that, given any pair of parallelepipeds p' and p'' of $\mathcal{P}'$, there should exist at least one dimension d ($d \in \{0,1\}$) where p' and p'' do not overlap).

$geost(k, \mathcal{O}, \mathcal{S}, \mathcal{C})$ is defined in the following way: given a constraint $ctr_i(\mathcal{A}_i, \mathcal{O}_i)$ from the list of constraints $\mathcal{C}$ between a subset of objects $\mathcal{O}_i \subseteq \mathcal{O}$ according to the attributes $\mathcal{A}_i$, let $\mathcal{MC}_i$ denote the sets of cliques stemming from the objects of $\mathcal{O}_i$ that all overlap in time.[3] The constraints of $geost(k, \mathcal{O}, \mathcal{S}, \mathcal{C})$ hold if and only if $\forall ctr_i \in \mathcal{C}, \forall \mathcal{O}_{\mathcal{MC}_i} \in \mathcal{MC}_i : ctr_i(\mathcal{A}_i, \mathcal{O}_{\mathcal{MC}_i})$ holds.

Example 2. Fig. 1 presents a typical example of a dynamic 2D placement problem where one has to place four objects, in time and within a given box, so that objects that overlap in time do not overlap in space. Parts (A), (B), (C) and (D) resp. represent the potential shapes associated with the four objects to place, where the origin of each object is represented by a black square ■. Part (E) shows the position of the four objects of the example as the time varies, where the first, second, third and fourth objects were resp. assigned shapes S_1, S_5, S_8 and S_9:

- During the first time interval $[2, 9]$ we have only object O_1 at position $(1, 2)$.
- Then, at instant 10 objects O_2 and O_3 both appear. Their origins are resp. placed at positions $(2, 1)$ and $(4, 1)$.
- At instant 14 object O_1 disappears and is replaced by object O_4. The origin of O_4 is fixed at position $(1, 1)$. Finally, at instant 22 all three objects O_2, O_3 and O_4 disappear.

The corresponding arguments are:

---

[1] The time dimension is treated specially since the $duration$ attribute may not be fixed, which is not the case for the sizes of a shifted box. Also, the geometrical constraints only apply on objects that intersect in time.

[2] A *domain variable* v is a variable ranging over a finite set of integers denoted by $\mathrm{dom}(v)$; let $\underline{v}$ and $\overline{v}$ resp. denote the minimum and maximum possible values for v.

[3] In fact, these cliques (of an interval graph) are only used for defining the declarative semantics of $geost$'s constraints.

```
01 geost(2,
02       [object(1,1,[1,2], 2,12,14), object(2,5,[2,1],10,12,22),
03        object(3,8,[4,1],10,12,22), object(4,9,[1,1],14, 8,22)],
04       [sbox(1,[0,0],[2,1]), sbox(1,[0,1],[1,2]), sbox(1,[1,2],[3,1]),
05        sbox(2,[0,0],[3,1]), sbox(2,[0,1],[1,3]), sbox(2,[2,1],[1,1]),
06        sbox(3,[0,0],[2,1]), sbox(3,[1,1],[1,2]), sbox(3,[2,2],[3,1]),
07        sbox(4,[0,0],[3,1]), sbox(4,[0,1],[1,1]), sbox(4,[2,1],[1,3]),
08        sbox(5,[0,0],[2,1]), sbox(5,[1,1],[1,1]), sbox(5,[0,2],[2,1]),
09        sbox(6,[0,0],[3,1]), sbox(6,[0,1],[1,1]), sbox(6,[2,1],[1,1]),
10        sbox(7,[0,0],[3,2]), sbox(8,[0,0],[2,3]), sbox(9,[0,0],[1,4])],
11       [non-overlapping([0,1],[1,2,3,4]),included([0,1],[1,2,3,4],[1,1],[5,4])])
```

Its first argument 2 is the number of dimensions of the placement space we consider. Its second and third arguments resp. describe the four objects and the shifted boxes of the nine shapes we have. For instance, the 3 boxes of shape S_1 (depicted by 3 thick rectangles in Part (A) of Fig. 1) respectively correspond to the 3 boxes declared at line 04 of the example. Finally, its last argument gives the list of geometrical constraints imposed by *geost*: the first constraint expresses a non-overlapping constraint between the four objects, while the second constraint imposes the four objects to be located within the box containing all points (x, y) such that $1 \leq x \leq 1+5-1$ and $1 \leq y \leq 1+4-1$. The constraints of *geost* hold since the four objects do not simultaneously overlap in time and in space and since they are completely included within the previous box (i.e., see Part (E) of Fig. 1).

Within the scope of $geost(k, \mathcal{O}, \mathcal{S}, \mathcal{C})$, this paper presents a filtering algorithm that prunes the domain of each attribute of every object o = object$(id, sid, x[], start,$

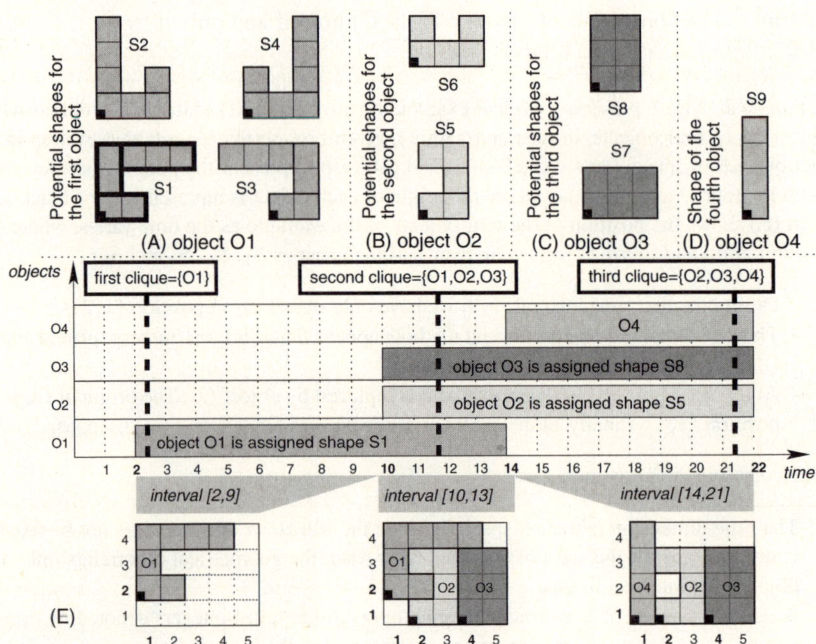

Fig. 1. Example with 4 objects, 9 shapes, one *non-overlapping* and one *included* constraints

duration, *end*) $\in \mathcal{O}$. All values found infeasible are deleted from the shape attribute *sid*; for the other attributes (i.e., the origin $x[]$, the start, the duration and the end), the minimum and maximum are adjusted.

The paper is organised as follows. Section 2 provides an overview of placement problems that can be modelled with the constraints currently available in *geost*. Section 3 presents the overall architecture of the geometrical kernel. It explains how to define geometrical constraints in terms of a programming interface by the geometrical kernel. Section 4 focusses on the main contribution of this paper: a multi-dimensional lexicographic sweep algorithm used for filtering the attributes of an object of *geost*. Section 5 evaluates the scalability of the *geost* kernel as well as its ability to deal with a variety of specific placement problems. Before we conclude, Section 6 compares *geost* with related work and suggests future directions.

2 Modelling Problems with *geost*

As illustrated by Fig. 2 in the context of *non-overlapping*, *geost* allows to model directly a large number of placement problems:

- Case (A) corresponds to a non-overlapping constraint among three segments.
- The second and third cases (B,C) correspond to a non-overlapping constraint between rectangles where (B) is a special case where the sizes of all rectangles in the second dimension are equal to 1; this can be interpreted as a *machine assignment problem*.
- Case (D) corresponds to a non-overlapping constraint between rectangles where each rectangle can have two orientations. This is achieved by associating with each rectangle two shapes of respective sizes $l \times h$ and $h \times l$. Since their orientation is not initially fixed, the *included* constraint enforces the three rectangles to be included within the bounding box defined by the origin's coordinates $1, 1$ and sizes $8, 3$.
- Case (E) corresponds to a non-overlapping constraint between more complex objects where each object is described by a given set of rectangles.
- Case (F) describes a placement problem where one has to first assign each rectangle to a strip so that all rectangles that are assigned to the same strip do not overlap.
- Case (G) corresponds to a non-overlapping constraint between parallelepipeds.
- Case (H) can be interpreted as a non-overlapping constraint between parallelepipeds that are assigned to the same container. The first dimension corresponds to the identifier of the container, while the next three dimensions are associated with the position of a parallelepiped inside a container.
- Case (I) describes a rectangle placement problem over three consecutive time-slots: rectangles assigned to the same time-slot should not overlap in time. We initially start with the three rectangles 1, 2 and 3. Rectangle 3 is no longer present at instant 2 (the triangle ▼ within rectangle 3 at time 1 indicates that rectangle 3 will disappear at the next time-point), while rectangle 4 appears at instant 2 (the triangle ▲ within rectangle 4 at time 2 denotes the fact that the rectangle 4 appears at instant 2). Finally, rectangle 2 disappears at instant 3 and is replaced by rectangle 5.

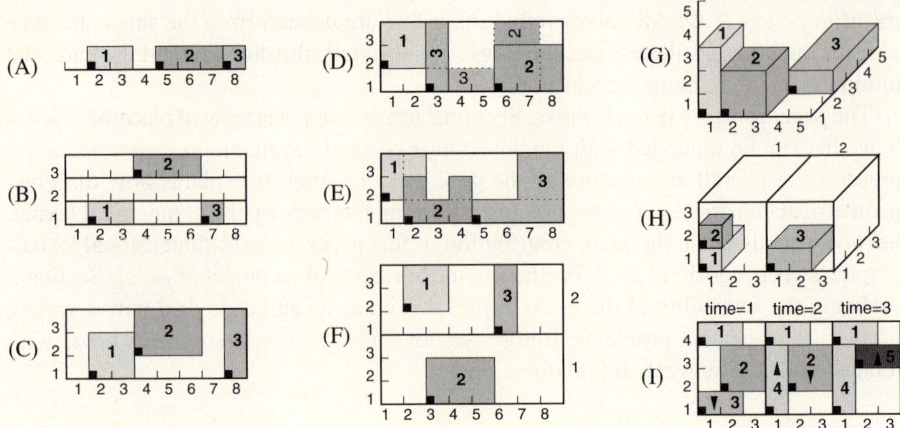

Fig. 2. Nine typical examples of use of *geost*

3 Standard Representation of Geometrical Constraints

The key idea for handling multiple geometrical constraints in a common kernel is the following. For each type of geometrical constraint found in $\mathcal{C}$ (also called *external* constraints), one has to provide a service that computes necessary conditions (also called *internal* constraints) for a given object and shape. Given an external geometrical constraint $ectr_i(\mathcal{A}_i, \mathcal{O}_i)$ ($\mathcal{A}_i \subseteq \{0, 1, \ldots, k-1\}, \mathcal{O}_i \subseteq \mathcal{O}$), one of its object $o \in \mathcal{O}_i$ and one potential shape s of o, such a necessary condition generated by $ectr_i$, o and s is a unary[4] constraint $ictr(o.x)$ such that: $o.sid = s \wedge ectr_i(\mathcal{A}_i, \mathcal{O}_i) \Rightarrow ictr(o.x)$. Now, the key to being able to globally treat such necessary conditions in the kernel is to give them a uniform representation. We have chosen the following one:

– A constraint $\text{outbox}(t, l)$ on $o.x$ holds iff $o.x$ is located outside the shifted box defined by its origins point $t[d]$, $0 \leq d < k$, and sizes $l[d]$, $0 \leq d < k$ (i.e., $\exists d \in [0, k-1] \mid o.x[d] < t[d] \vee o.x[d] > t[d] + l[d] - 1$).

Thus, an outbox corresponds to a box-shaped set of points that are infeasible for $o.x$. The purpose of the introduction of outboxes is to have a common representation for the kernel, suitable for the k-dimensional lexicographic sweep algorithm presented in the next section, which considers all the outboxes, for a selected object and shape, in one run.

Consequently, for each type of external geometrical constraint, found in $\mathcal{C}$ a service $\text{GenOutboxes}(ectr_i, o, s) : (ictrs)$, responsible for generating outboxes, must be provided. This service is assumed to generate outboxes that intersect the domains of the origin coordinates of o. Also, if all attributes mentioned by $ectr_i$ belonging to objects other than o are fixed, those outboxes are assumed to be necessary and sufficient conditions, lest the kernel accept false solutions.

[4] Unary, since it involves the k coordinates of a *single* object.

Example of External Geometrical Constraints. We now illustrate some external geometrical constraints that are currently available within the constraint kernel. As we saw in the introduction, an external constraint always has at least two arguments that resp. correspond to a list of distinct dimensions and to a list of object identifiers to which the constraint applies.

The *included* **and** *non-overlapping* **external constraints.** The $included(\mathcal{A}_i, \mathcal{O}_i, t, l)$ and the *non-overlapping*$(\mathcal{A}_i, \mathcal{O}_i)$ external constraints take as input a list of distinct dimensions $\mathcal{A}_i$ in $\{0, 1, \ldots, k-1\}$ and a list $\mathcal{O}_i$ of distinct object identifiers of $geost$. In addition, the $included$ constraint considers a shifted box defined by its origin point $t[d], 0 \le d < k$, and size $l[d], 0 \le d < k$.

The $included$ constraint enforces for each object o (with $o.id \in \mathcal{O}_i$) and for any corresponding shifted box s (with $o.sid = s.sid$) the condition $\forall d \in \mathcal{A}_i \mid t[d] \le o.x[d] + s.t[d] \wedge o.x[d] + s.t[d] + s.l[d] - 1 \le t[d] + l[d] - 1$ (i.e., s is included within the shifted box attribute defined by the parameters t and l of the $included$ constraint). Depending on which shape of an object we actually consider, the $included$ constraint can be translated to $2k$ outbox constraints.

The *non-overlapping* constraint enforces the following condition: given two distinct objects o and o' (with $o.id, o'.id \in \mathcal{O}_i$) that overlap in time, no shifted box s (with $o.sid = s.sid$) should overlap any shifted box s' (with $o'.sid = s'.sid$); i.e. it should hold that $\exists d \in \mathcal{A}_i \mid o.x[d] + s.t[d] + s.l[d] \le o'.x[d] + s'.t[d] \vee o'.x[d] + s'.t[d] + s'.l[d] \le o.x[d] + s.t[d]$ (i.e., there exists a dimension where they do not intersect). While focussing on an object o we can easily generate an outbox constraint for each object o' that should not overlap o by reusing the results of [2].

4 The Geometrical Kernel: A Generic k-Dimensional Lexicographic Sweep Algorithm

In this section, we first present the sweep algorithm used for filtering the coordinates of the origin of an object o of $geost$ when each object has one single shape. We initially assume that time is treated exactly like the space dimensions, i.e. that the $o.x$ array is extended by one element. Toward the end of this section, we explain in detail how to treat the time attributes of an object. We also assume for now that the shape attribute is fixed, and explain later how to handle multiple potential shapes for an object (i.e., polymorphism). We now introduce some notation used throughout this section.

Notation. Assume v and w are vectors of scalars of k components. Then $v \leftarrow w$ denotes the element-wise assignment of w to v, $w + d$ (resp. $w - d$) denotes the element-wise addition of d (resp. $-d$) to w. Given a scalar d, $0 \le d \le k-1$, $\text{rot}(v, d, k)$ denotes the vector $(v[d], v[(d+1) \mod k], \ldots, v[(d-1) \mod k])$. That is, in the rotated vector, $v[d]$ is the most significant element, which is what we need when running the sweep algorithm on dimension d.

The Sweep Algorithm. This algorithm first considers all outboxes $\mathcal{IC}_o$ derived from $\mathcal{C}$ where object o actually appears, and then performs a recursive traversal of the placement space for each coordinate and direction (i.e., min or max). Without loss of generality, assume we want to adjust the minimum value of the dth coordinate $o.x[d]$,

$0 \le d < k$, of the origin of o. The algorithm starts its recursive traversal of the placement space at point $c = \mathrm{rot}(\underline{o.x}, d, k)$ and could in principle explore all points of the domains of $o.x$, one by one, in increasing lexicographic order, until a point is found that is not inside any outbox, in which case $c[0]$ is the computed new minimum value. To make the search efficient, instead of moving each time to the successor point, we arrange the search so that it skips points that are known to be inside some outbox.[5]

Thus, we compute the lexicographically smallest point c' such that:

1. c' is lexicographically greater than or equal to c,
2. every element of c' is in the domain of the corresponding element of $o.x$,
3. c' is not inside any outbox of $\mathcal{IC}_o$.

If no such c' exists, the constraint fails. Otherwise, the minimum value of $o.x[d]$ is adjusted to $c'[0]$. As we saw, the sweep algorithm moves in increasing lexicographic order a point c from its lexicographically smallest potential feasible position to its lexicographically largest potential feasible position through all potential points. The algorithm uses the following data structures:

- The current position c of the sweep.
- A vector $n[0..k-1]$ that records knowledge about already encountered sets of infeasible points while moving c from its first potential feasible position. The vector n is always element-wise greater than c and maintained as follows. Let inf, sup denote the vectors $\mathrm{inf} = \mathrm{rot}(\underline{o.x}, d, k)$ and $\mathrm{sup} = \mathrm{rot}(\overline{o.x} + 1, d, k)$:
  - Initially, $n = \mathrm{sup}$.
  - Whenever an outbox f containing c is found, n is updated by taking the element-wise minimal value of n and the upper boundary of $\mathrm{rot}(f, d, k)$, indicating the fact that new candidate points can be found beyond that value.
  - Whenever we skip to the next candidate point, we reset the elements of n that were used to the corresponding values of sup.

  The following invariant holds for the vector n, and is used when advancing c to the next candidate point. Let i be the smallest j such that $n[j+1] = \mathrm{sup}[j+1] \wedge \cdots \wedge n[k-1] = \mathrm{sup}[k-1]$ and suppose c is known to be in some outbox. Then, the next point, lexicographically greater than c and not yet known to be in any outbox, is $(c[0], \ldots, c[i-1], n[i], \mathrm{inf}[i+1], \ldots, \mathrm{inf}[k-1])$.

Algorithm 1 implement this idea. The algorithm prunes the bounds of each coordinate of every object wrt. its relevant outboxes, iterating to fix-point.

Efficiency. The main inefficiency in this sweep algorithm lies in searching the set of outboxes (line 4 of PruneMin). In order to make this search more efficient, we can make the sweep algorithm more sophisticated by the following modifications to PruneMin:

- We extend the state of the algorithm by an *event point series*, ordered in lexicographically increasing order. These events correspond to the lexicographically smallest (insert events) and largest (delete events) relevant infeasible point associated with each outbox $ictr_o \in \mathcal{IC}_o$. They are sorted in lexicographically increasing order, and we maintain a pointer into the series in sync with point c.

[5] Potential holes in the domains are reflected in outboxes.

```
PROCEDURE FilterCtrs(k, O, S, C) : bool
nonfix ← true                                              // fixpoint not yet reached
while nonfix do
   nonfix ← false                                          // assumes no filtering will be done
   for all o ∈ O do
      I ← ⋃_{e∈C} GenOutboxes(e, o, o.sid)                 // build the set of outboxes on o
      I ← I ∪ ⋃_{0≤d<k} possible outboxes corresponding to holes in o.x[d]
      for d ← 0 to k − 1 do
         if ¬PruneMin(o, d, k, I) ∨ ¬PruneMax(o, d, k, I) then
            return false                                   // no feasible origin
         else if o.x was pruned then
            nonfix ← true                                  // fixpoint not yet reached
         end if
      end for
   end for
end while
return true                                                // feasible origin
PROCEDURE PruneMin(o, d, k, I) : bool
b ← true                                                   // b =true while we have not failed
c ← o.x (lower)                                            // initial position of the point
n ← o.x (upper) + 1                                        // upper limits+1 in the different dimensions
while b ∧ ∃f ∈ I | c ∈ f do
   n ← min(n, f.t + f.l)                                   // update vector naccording to an outbox f containing c
   b ← false                                               // no new point to jump to yet
   for j ← k − 1 downto 0 do
      j' ← (j + d)  mod k                                  // rotation wrt. d, k
      c[j'] ← n[j']                                        // use vector n to jump
      n[j'] ← o.x (upper)[j'] + 1                          // reset component of n to maximum value
      if c[j'] ≤ o.x (upper)[j'] then
         b ← true                                          // jump target found
         j ← 0                                             // exit for loop
      else
         c[j'] ← o.x (lower)[j']                           // reset component of cfor exhausted a dimension
      end if
   end for
end while
if b then
   o.x (lower)[d] ← max(o.x (lower)[d], c[d])
end if
return b
```

Algorithm 1: FilterCtrs is the main filtering algorithm associated with $geost(k, \mathcal{O}, \mathcal{S}, \mathcal{C})$, where k, $\mathcal{O}$, $\mathcal{S}$ and $\mathcal{C}$ resp. correspond to the number of dimensions, to the objects, to the shapes and to the external geometrical constraints. PruneMin adjusts the lower bound of the dth coordinate of the origin of object o where I is the set of outboxes associated with object o (since PruneMax is similar to PruneMin it is omitted). The given fixpoint loop is an over-simplification. The implementation maintains a set of objects that need filtering. Whenever an object o is pruned, all non-fixed objects connected to o by an external constraint are added to this set. When the set becomes empty, the fixpoint is reached.

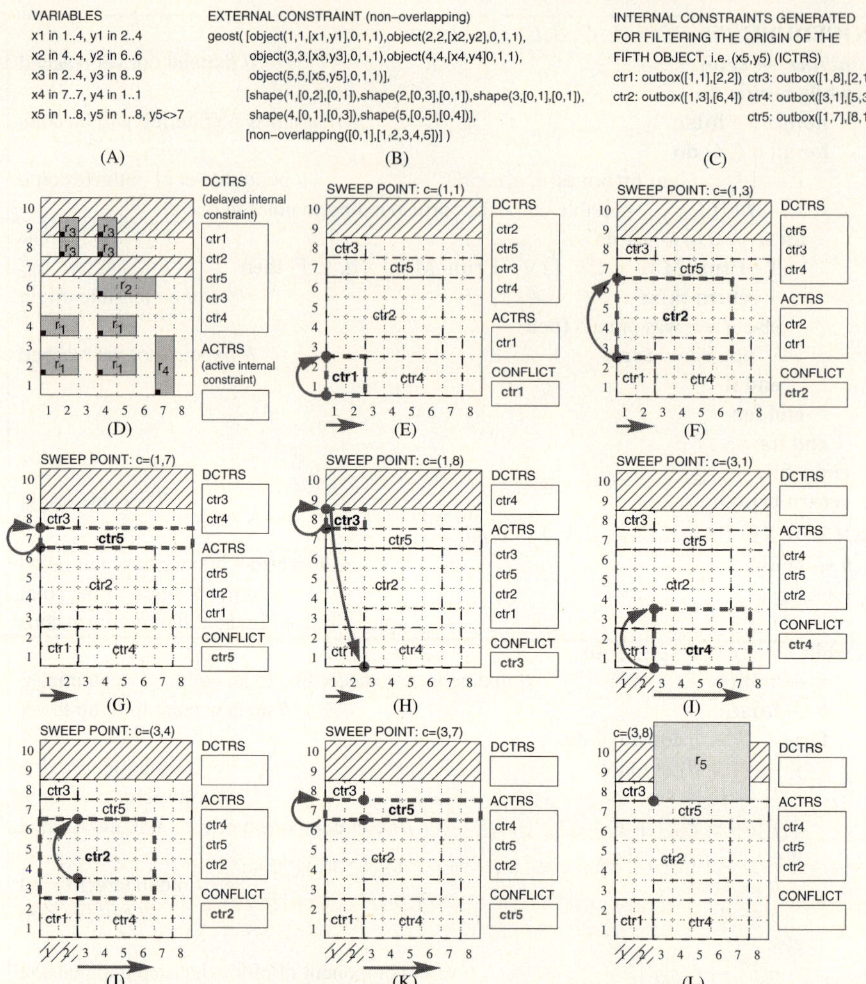

Fig. 3. Illustration of the lexicographic sweep algorithm for adjusting the minimum value of the abscissa of rectangle r_5

- We maintain the set of *active outboxes*, corresponding to all outboxes $ictr_o \in \mathcal{IC}_o$ such that c is between its lexicographically smallest and largest infeasible points. This set is initially empty.
- When c is initialized in line 2 as well as when c is incremented in lines 7-17, the relevant events up to point c from the event point series are processed, and the corresponding outboxes are added to or deleted from the set of active outboxes.
- In line 4, only the active outboxes are considered.

Example 3. Fig. 3 illustrates the k-dimensional lexicographic sweep algorithm in the context of $k = 2$. Parts (A) and (B) provide the variables of the problem (i.e., the abscissa and ordinate of each rectangle r_1, r_2, r_3, r_4 and r_5) as well as the non-overlapping constraint between the five previous rectangles. On Part (D) we have represented the extreme possible feasible positions of each rectangle (i.e., rectangles r_1 to r_4): for instance the leftmost lower corner of rectangle r_1 can only be fixed at positions $(1,2)$, $(1,3)$, $(1,4)$, $(2,2)$, $(2,3)$, $(2,4)$, $(3,2)$, $(3,3)$, $(3,4)$, $(4,2)$, $(4,3)$ and $(4,4)$. Parts (C) to (L) of Fig. 3 detail the different steps of the algorithm for adjusting the minimum value of the abscissa of rectangle r_5. Part (C) provides the outboxes associated with the fact that we want to prune the coordinates of r_5: constraints ctr_1, ctr_2, ctr_3 and ctr_4 resp. correspond to the fact that rectangle r_5 should not overlap rectangles r_1, r_2, r_3 and r_4, while constraint ctr_5 represents the fact that the ordinate of r_5 should be different from 7. Part (D) represents the initialisation phase of the algorithm where we have all five outboxes with their respective lexicographically smallest infeasible point (i.e., $(1,1)$ for ctr_1, $(1,3)$ for ctr_2, $(1,7)$ for ctr_5, $(1,8)$ for ctr_3 and $(3,1)$ for ctr_4). Part (E) represents the first step of the sweep algorithm where we start the traversal of the placement space at point $c = (1,1)$. We first transfer to the list of active outboxes all outboxes for which the first lexicographically smallest infeasible point is lexicographically greater than or equal to the current position of the sweep $c = (1,1)$ (i.e., constraint $ctr_1 = \text{outbox}([1,1],[2,2])$). We then search through the list of active constraints (represented on the figure by a box with the legend ACTRS on top of it) the first constraint for which $c = (1,1)$ is infeasible. In fact, since ctr_1 is infeasible (represented on the figure by a box with the legend CONFLICT on top of it) we compute the vector $f = (3,3)$ that tells how to get the next potentially feasible point in the different dimensions. Consequently the sweep moves to the next position $(1,3)$ (see Part (F)) and the process is repeated until we finally find a feasible point for all outboxes (i.e., point $(3,8)$ in Part (L)). Note that, when the lexicographically largest infeasible point associated with an active outbox is lexicographically less than the current position of the sweep, we remove that constraint from the list of active outboxes. This is for instance the case in Part (I), where we remove constraint ctr_3 from the list of active outboxes (since its lexicographically largest infeasible point $(2,8)$ is lexicographically less than the position of the sweep $c = (3,1)$).

Complexity. Rather than analysing the complexity of the *geost* kernel for a fixed k, which depends both on the type of each external constraint (i.e., the complexity of a given external constraint for generating all its corresponding outboxes as well as their number), we rather focus on PruneMin for adjusting the minimum value of the dth coordinate of the origin of an object. Assuming that the maximum number of outboxes is equal to n we give an upper bound on the maximum number of jumps of PruneMin (i.e., the maximum number of times the sweep is moved).

First note that we always jump to an upper border (+1) of an outbox (i.e., see line 5 of PruneMin) or that we reset some coordinates of the sweep to its minimum value (i.e., see line 15 of PruneMin). Consequently, all coordinates of the sweep are always equal to an upper border (+1) of some outboxes or to a minimum possible value. Since we want to evaluate the maximum number of jumps, let us assume that for every dimension d $(0 \leq d < k)$ the upper limits of all the n outboxes are distinct. Having this in mind we can construct a maximum of $(n+1)^k$ points. Even if we found a systematic construction where this number of jumps is reached, the performance evaluation of Section 5 indicates that we can handle a reasonable number of objects for $k = 2, 3, 4$.

From a memory consumption point of view, the algorithm only records the coordinates of the sweep from one invocation to the next, in order not to restart the search from scratch (i.e., $2k$ points for each object).

Handling Time. Given an object $o \in \mathcal{O}$ of *geost*, the sweep algorithm that we have introduced in the previous section can be easily adapted to handle the start in time

$o.start$, duration in time $o.duration$ and end in time $o.end$. Beside maintaining bound consistency for the constraint $o.end = o.start + o.duration$, we add an extra *time* dimension to the geometric coordinates of object o. Roughly, this new time coordinate corresponds to $o.start$ resp. $o.end$ depending on whether we are adjusting the minimum or maximum.

Handling Polymorphism. In order to handle the fact that objects can have several potential shapes we modify the previous algorithm in the following way. For adjusting the minimum value of the coordinate of the origin of an object that has more than one shape we call the sweep algorithm for each potential shape of the object (i.e., for each value of its shape variable). Then we take the smallest minimum value obtained (i.e., we use constructive disjunction) and prune the shape variable of an object if we did not find any feasible point for a given potential shape of that object.

Other Internal Constraints. The standard representation of geometrical constraints given in Section 3 is an over-simplification. For some constraints, e.g. distance constraints, outboxes are not a suitable representation, as the set of forbidden coordinates cannot be covered by a small number of boxes. Therefore, the constraint kernel internally handles other representations of necessary conditions, with an appropriate internal API. For details, see the technical report [5].

5 Performance Evaluation

We evaluate the implementation[6] of the *geost* kernel from three perspectives:

Wanting to measure the speed and the scalability of the sweep algorithm for finding a first solution on loosely constrained placement problems (i.e., 20% spare space), we generated one set of random problem instances of m k-dimensional boxes for $k \in \{2, 3, 4\}$ involving $t \in \{1, 16, 256, 1024\}$ distinct types of boxes, and for $m \in \{1024, 2048, \ldots, 262144\}$. The results for $k = 2$ are shown in Fig. 4 (top left) and indicates that the approach is sensible to the number of distinct types of boxes. It can typically pack 1024 2D, 3D and 4D distinct boxes in at most 200 msec. The longest time, 13694 seconds (close to 4 hours), was obtained for packing 262144 4D parallelepipeds (over 1 million domain variables) with a memory consumption of 351MB.

Wanting to get an idea of the performance of the *geost* kernel on very tight placement problems (i.e., 0% spare space), we considered the *perfect squared squares problem* [1,6] as well as the *3D pentominoes problem* [7]:

- A *perfect squared square of order* n is a square that can be tiled with n smaller squares where each of the smaller squares has a different integer size. We used the data available (i.e., the size of the small squares to pack) from the catalogue [8] and tested the corresponding 207 instances. The labelling strategy is roughly to repeat the following, first for the x dimension, then for the y dimension:
  1. Find the smallest position where some square can be placed.
  2. Find a square to place in that position.

[6] The experiments were run in SICStus Prolog 4 compiled with gcc -02 version 4.0.2 on a 3GHz Pentium IV with 1MB of cache.

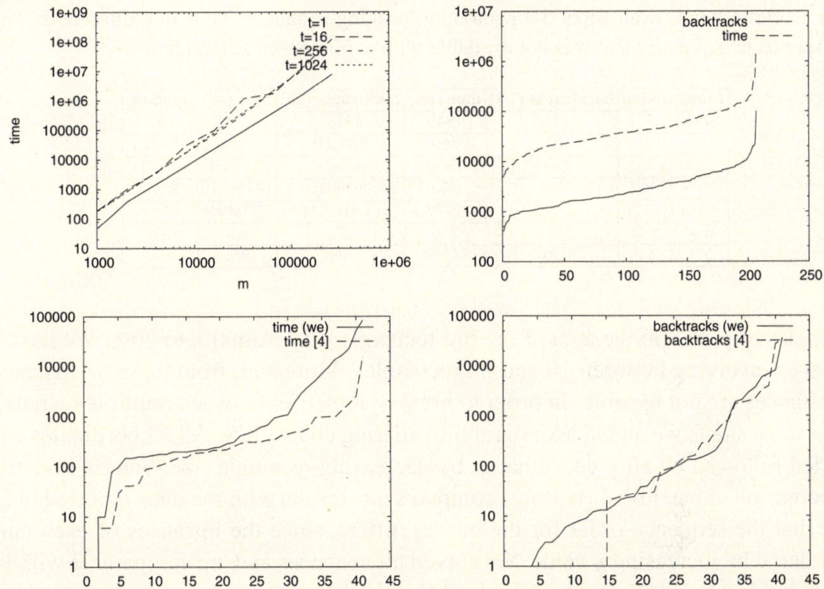

Fig. 4. Performance evaluation. Top left: scalability, $t \in \{1, 16, 256, 1024\}$. Top right: Perfect Squared Squares, runtime and backtracks. Bottom: 2D Orthogonal Packing, runtime (left) and backtracks (right). Time in milliseconds. In each curve, the instances are ordered by increasing y value.

- *Pentominoes* are pieces made of 5 connected unit cubes laid on a plane surface. Their shapes look like the 12 letters $F, I, L, P, N, T, U, V, W, X, Y$ and Z. We considered the problem of finding the different ways of putting 12 distinct shapes that can be reflected and rotated in a box having a volume of 60 unit cubes. Our labelling strategy is roughly to repeat the following:
  1. Find a slot in the space that has not yet been filled by some piece.
  2. Find a piece that can fill that slot.

Fig. 4 (top right) and Table 1 respectively report, for the squared squares and the pentominoes problems, the time and number of backtracks for exploring all the search space[7] without breaking any symmetry. For the squared squares problems the maximum time of 1585 seconds was spent on problem 48; on the other hand, 148 problems were completely solved within 60 seconds. For the 3D pentomino packing instances, performance results for comparison can be found in [7]. However, they stop the search when the first 100 solutions have been found, so the results are only partly comparable.

Finally, wanting to compare the *geost* kernel with a recent exact state of the art method for the 2D orthogonal packing problem [4], we reused the benchmarks proposed by Clautiaux et al. [9]. This is a feasibility problem which consists in determining whether a set of rectangles that cannot be rotated, can be packed or not into a rectangle of fixed size. In these instances the discrepancy between the sum of the areas of the

[7] Finding all solutions and proving that there is no other solution.

Table 1. Performance evaluation. 3D pentomino packing instances. Time in milliseconds. "n/a" corresponds to a quantity that was not available with a time-out of several hours.

configuration	backtracks (1st)	time (1st)	backtracks (all)	time (all)	solutions
$20 \times 3 \times 1$	1434	1840	47381	49740	8
$15 \times 4 \times 1$	290	560	888060	939060	1472
$12 \times 5 \times 1$	1594	1850	3994455	4112870	4040
$10 \times 6 \times 1$	111	260	9688985	10726810	9356
$10 \times 3 \times 2$	1267	2370	1203511	1778980	96
$6 \times 5 \times 2$	157	730	n/a	n/a	n/a
$5 \times 4 \times 3$	3567	14930	n/a	n/a	n/a

rectangles to pack and the area of the big rectangle vary from 0% to 20%. We have 41 instances involving between 10 and 23 rectangles. Moreover, from these 41 instances, 26 instances are not feasible. In order to break symmetries between multiple rectangles of the same shape we added lexicographic ordering constraints. All x coordinates were labelled followed by all y coordinates, by decreasing rectangle size. Values were tried by increasing value. Fig. 4 (bottom) compares our results with the ones reported in [4]. Note that the sequence order for the curves differs, since the instances of each curve are ordered by increasing y value. We solved all instances and are comparable with [4], although 8 instances are much easier for [4] and 10 instances are much easier for us.

Note that for the last three problems (i.e., Squared Squares, Pentominoes and 2D orthogonal packing) extra filtering algorithms mostly based on cumulative relaxation were integrated within our kernel. Since this paper focusses on the constraint kernel and because of space limitations these methods were not detailed.

6 Related Work and Future Directions

The rectangles packing problem has been studied by Clautiaux et al. [9,4] where scheduling-based reasoning is used [1]. The use of sweep algorithms in constraint filtering algorithms was introduced in [3] and applied to the non-overlapping 2D rectangles constraints. This paper generalizes and extends that work in several ways.

- The 2D sweep is generalized to a lexicographic sweep, independent of the number of dimensions.
- The notion of forbidden regions for non-overlapping rectangles is generalized to necessary conditions for general geometric constraints.

The idea of generating necessary conditions is reminiscent of indexicals [10], a.k.a. projection constraints [11]. An indexical for a constraint $c(x_1, \ldots, x_n)$ computes a unary constraint on a single variable x_i, i.e. a set S of values such that $c \Rightarrow x_i \in S$, in reaction to domain changes in $x_1, \ldots, x_n$. The constraint kernel then immediately enforces $x_i \in S$. Our kernel generalizes this in two ways:

- We compute necessary conditions in the form of k-dimensional forbidden regions.
- We treat all such forbidden regions, for a selected object and shape, in one run of the sweep algorithm. Projecting a single forbidden region on one coordinate often does not yield any pruning, whereas considering the union of forbidden regions is much more effective.

Dal Palù et al. in [12] proposed a constraint solver specialized for 3D discrete domains. Their solver was targeted to the study of problems in molecular, chemical and crystal structures. Our work, however, remains in the setting of mainstream finite domain constraint systems, whereas our kernel internally handles k-dimensional objects.

Even though the *geost* kernel has been designed over discrete domains, it could rather easily be extended to continuous domains with the coordinates of the objects approximated by the floating-point numbers $\mathbb{F}$. Since switching from $\mathbb{N}$ to $\mathbb{F}$ may cause rounding errors at this level, the sweep algorithm needs to handle these rounding errors when moving the sweep out of an outbox constraint. If the projections of the forbidden regions on all dimensions are intervals of real bounds we can proceed as follows. On continuous domains, an outbox will have an very thin strip at the border where the feasibility of the corresponding internal constraint is unknown. The region inside this strip is strictly forbidden, and outside, the constraints is certainly satisfied. The outbox must be computed including this strip, by taking lower and upper approximations of the region's coordinates. In that case, the solutions are guaranteed to be valid, but the solver may not be complete, because it may (rarely) happen that the real forbidden region allows positions that are forbidden by its approximation.

This research was conducted under the European Union project "Net-WMS", a major task of which is to study packing problems in warehouse management. In this context, our constraint kernel is a step towards being able to capture a large set of packing rules in a constraint programming setting. Future work involves extending our set of external geometric constraints to include such packing rules.

7 Conclusion

The main contribution of this paper is a geometrical constraint kernel for handling the location in space and time of polymorphic k-dimensional objects subject to various geometrical and time constraints. The constraint kernel is generic in the sense that one of its parameters is a set of constraints on subsets of the objects. These constraints are handled globally by the kernel.

We have presented a sweep algorithm for filtering the attributes of the objects. Thanks to its architecture, new geometric constraints can be plugged into this sweep algorithm without modifying it. The strong point of this sweep algorithm is that it considers all the geometrical constraints for a selected object and shape in one run. As a first result, more deduction can be performed by combining sets of forbidden points coming from multiple geometrical constraints. Secondly, it can handle within one single constraint problems involving up several tens of thousands of objects without memory consumption problems, which is often a weak point for constraint programming environments. We have also shown that we could handle tight 2D or 3D placement problems, which were traditionally solved by specific approaches.

Acknowledgements

This research was conducted under European Union Sixth Framework Programme Contract FP6-034691 "Net-WMS".

References

1. Aggoun, A., Beldiceanu, N.: Extending CHIP in order to solve complex scheduling and placement problems. Mathl. Comput. Modelling 17(7), 57–73 (1993)
2. Beldiceanu, N., Guo, Q., Thiel, S.: Non-overlapping constraints between convex polytopes. In: Walsh, T. (ed.) CP 2001. LNCS, vol. 2239, pp. 392–407. Springer, Heidelberg (2001)
3. Beldiceanu, N., Carlsson, M.: Sweep as a generic pruning technique applied to the non-overlapping rectangles constraints. In: Walsh, T. (ed.) CP 2001. LNCS, vol. 2239, pp. 377–391. Springer, Heidelberg (2001)
4. Clautiaux, F., Jouglet, A., Carlier, J., Moukrim, A.: A new constraint programming approach for the orthogonal packing problem. Computers and Operation Research (to appear)
5. Beldiceanu, N., Carlsson, M., Poder, E., Sadek, R., Truchet, C.: A generic geometrical constraint kernel in space and time for handling polymorphic k-dimensional objects. SICS Technical Report T2007:08, Swedish Institute of Computer Science (2007)
6. Van Hentenryck, P.: Scheduling and packing in the constraint language cc(FD). In: Zweben, M., Fox, M. (eds.) Intelligent Scheduling, Morgan Kaufmann, San Francisco (1994)
7. Colmerauer, A., Gilleta, B.: Solving the three-dimensional pentamino puzzle. Technical report, Laboratoire d'Informatique de Marseille (1999), `http://www.lim.univ-mrs.fr/~colmer/ArchivesPublications/Giletta/misc99.pdf`
8. Bouwkamp, C.J., Duijvestijn, A.J.W.: Catalogue of simple perfect squared squares of orders 21 through 25. Technical Report EUT Report 92-WSK-03, Eindhoven University of Technology, The Netherlands (November 1992)
9. Clautiaux, F., Carlier, J., Moukrim, A.: A new exact method for the two-dimensional orthogonal packing problem. European Journal of Operational Research (to appear)
10. Van Hentenryck, P., Saraswat, V., Deville, Y.: Constraint processing in cc(FD). Manuscript (1991)
11. Sidebottom, G.: A Language for Optimizing Constraint Propagation. PhD thesis, Simon Fraser University (1993)
12. Palù, A.D., Dovier, A., Pontelli, E.: A new constraint solver for 3D lattices and its application to the protein folding problem. In: Sutcliffe, G., Voronkov, A. (eds.) LPAR 2005. LNCS (LNAI), vol. 3835, pp. 48–63. Springer, Heidelberg (2005)

Local Symmetry Breaking During Search in CSPs

Belaïd Benhamou and Mohamed Réda Saïdi

Laboratoire des Sciences de l'Information et des Systèmes (LSIS)
Centre de Mathématiques et d'Informatique
39, rue Joliot Curie - 13453 Marseille cedex 13, France
Belaid.Benhamou@cmi.univ-mrs.fr, saidi@cmi.univ-mrs.fr

Abstract. Many research works on symmetry in CSPs appeared recently. But, most of them deal only with the global symmetry[1] of the studied problem and give no strategy that can be used to detect and eliminate local symmetry[2]. Eliminating global symmetry is shown to be useful, but exploiting only these symmetries could not be sufficient to solve some hard locally symmetrical problems. That is, a problem can have few or no initial symmetries and become very symmetrical at some nodes during the search. In this paper we study a general principle of semantic symmetry and define a syntactic symmetry which is a sufficient condition for semantic symmetry. We define a weakened form of this syntactic symmetry, and show how to detect and how to eliminate it locally to increase CSP tree search methods efficiency. Experiments confirm that local symmetry breaking is profitable for CSP solving.

1 Introduction

As far as we know, the principle of symmetry is first introduced by Krishnamurty [1] to improve resolution in propositional logic. Symmetries for Boolean constraints are studied in depth in [2,3,4], the authors showed how to detect them and proved that their exploitation is a real improvement for several automated deduction algorithms. The notion of interchangeability in CSPs is introduced in [5] and symmetry for CSPs are studied in [6,7].

Since that, many research works on symmetry have appeared. For instance, the static approach used by James Crawford et al. in [8] for propositional logic theories consists in adding constraints to break the global symmetries of the problem. This technique has been improved in [9] and extended to 0-1 Integer Logic Programming in [10].

Since a great number of constraints could be added, some researchers proposed to add the constraints during the search. In [11,12,13], authors post some conditional constraints which remove the symmetric of the partial interpretation

[1] The symmetry of the initial problem appearing at the root of the search tree.
[2] The symmetry of the resulting CSP at a node of the search tree corresponding to a partial instantiation.

C. Bessiere (Ed.): CP 2007, LNCS 4741, pp. 195–209, 2007.

in case of backtracking. In [14,15,16,17], authors proposed to use each subtree as a no-good to avoid exploration of some symmetric interpretations and the group equivalence tree conceptual for value symmetry elimination is introduced in [18]. These techniques are called respectively SBDS, SBDD and GE-Tree.

Recently, a method which breaks symmetries between the variables of an Alldiff constraint is studied in [19], a nice method which eliminates all value symmetries in surjection problems is given in [20], and a work gathering all the known different symmetry definitions to *solution symmetry* or to *constraint symmetry* is done in [21]. More recently, in [22], Puget studied a new lex constraints symmetry breaking method in the term of dynamic lex leader solutions, and in [23] Walsh studied various new propagators to break various symmetries among them the one acting simultaneously on both variables and values.

One drawback of all these approaches is that only the symmetry of the initial problem is considered (the global symmetry) and no method that allows dynamic detection and exploitation of local symmetry is given. Recently, researchers called this, conditional symmetry [24,25].

In this paper we developed the general concept of semantic symmetry for CSPs that Benhamou first initiated in [7]. We also study and extend the principle of syntactic symmetry that we prove to be a sufficient condition for semantic symmetry. We show how local symmetry is detected and eliminated during search, and show how its removal simplifies the search space of tree search algorithms.

This paper is organized as following: CSP background is given in Section 2. *Semantic symmetry* is defined in Section 3. Section 4 discusses the notion of *syntactical symmetry* which is a sufficient condition for *semantic symmetry*. Section 5 shows how symmetry is detected and eliminated locally during search and how a tree search method (here Forward Checking) takes advantage of symmetrical values to reduce its search space. In section 6 we evaluate the proposed techniques by experimental results and Section 7 concludes the work.

2 Background

A CSP is a quadruple $\mathcal{P} = (V, D, C, R)$ where: $V = \{v_1, ..., v_n\}$ is a set of n variables; $D = \{D_1, \ldots, D_n\}$ is the set of finite discrete domains associated to the CSP variables, D_i includes the set of possible values of the CSP variable v_i, d_i denotes the fact that the value d belongs to the domain D_i, $C = \{C_1, ..., C_m\}$ is a set of m constraints each involving a subset of the CSP variables. A binary constraint is a constraint which involves at most two variables v_i, v_j, and is denoted by C_{ij}; $R = \{r_1, ..., r_m\}$ is a set of relations corresponding to the constraints of C. r_i represents the list of value tuples permitted by the constraint $C_i \in C$. A binary CSP $\mathcal{P}$ (a CSP involving only binary constraints) can be represented by a constraint graph $G(V, E)$ where the set of vertices V is the set of the CSP variables and each edge $(v_i, v_j) \in E$ connects the variables v_i and v_j involved in the constraint $C_{ij} \in C$. The microstructure [5,26,21] of the CSP $\mathcal{P}$ is a graph $\mathcal{M}_{\mathcal{P}}(V \times \cup_{i \in [1,n]} D_i, \acute{E})$, where each edge of $\acute{E}$ corresponds either to a tuple allowed by a specific constraint or to an allowed tuple because there is no constraints between the associated variables. An instantiation $\mathcal{I} = (\langle v_1, a_1 \rangle, \langle v_2, a_2 \rangle, \ldots, \langle v_n, a_n \rangle)$ is the variable assignment $\{v_1 = a_1, v_2 = a_2, \ldots, v_n = a_n\}$ where a value a_i of the domain D_i is assigned to the variable v_i . A constraint $C_i \in C$ is satisfied by $\mathcal{I}$ if the projection of $\mathcal{I}$ on the variables involved in C_i is a tuple of r_i. The instantiation $\mathcal{I}$ is consistent if it satisfies all the constraints of C, thus $\mathcal{I}$ is a solution of the CSP. An instantiation of a subset of the CSP variables V is called a partial instantiation, it defines a nogood when it is inconsistent. Each partial instantiation $\mathcal{I}$ defines a node $n_{\mathcal{I}}$ in the search tree which corresponds to the local CSP $\mathcal{P}_{\mathcal{I}}$ resulting from $\mathcal{P}$ by considering $\mathcal{I}$ and its induced propagations. An instantiation is total if it is defined on all the CSP variables. Given a CSP, the main question is to decide its consistency or to find its set of solutions. We assume that the reader knows a minimal background on permutations and groups. For the sake of simplicity we restricted the study to binary CSPs, however, the notion of symmetry remains valuable for non-binary CSPs as well.

3 Semantic Symmetry

Because we are interested in two problems in CSPs: the problem of finding a solution and the problem of finding all the solutions of the CSP, we define two levels of semantic symmetry.

Definition 1 (Semantic symmetry for consistency). *Two variable-value pairs $\langle v_i, b_i \rangle \in V \times D_i$ and $\langle v_j, c_j \rangle \in V \times D_j$ are symmetrical for consistency iff the following assertions are equivalent:*

1. *There is a solution of the CSP which assigns the value b_i to the variable v_i;*
2. *There is a solution of the CSP which assigns the value c_j to the variable v_j.*

Variable-value pairs can be not only symmetrical for consistency, but symmetrical for the set of all solutions as well. Thus, if $sol(\mathcal{P})$ denotes the set of solutions of the CSP $\mathcal{P}$, then we define a second level of semantic symmetry as follows:

Definition 2 (Semantic symmetry for all solutions). *Two variable-value pairs $\langle v_i, b_i \rangle \in V \times D_i$ and $\langle v_j, c_j \rangle \in V \times D_j$ are symmetrical for $sol(\mathcal{P})$ if and only if each solution of the CSP assigning the value b_i to v_i can be mapped into a solution assigning the value c_j to v_j and vice-versa.*

This means that the set of solutions in which the assignment $v_i = b_i$ participates is isomorphic to the one in which $v_j = c_j$ participates. These are symmetrical solutions.

Remark 1. 1. If the variables v_i and v_j designate a same variable, then both previous definitions concern symmetry of values of a same domain.
2. Symmetry for all solutions implies symmetry for consistency.

Identifying semantic symmetry is clearly time consuming, since this requires solving the problem. We study in the next section the syntactical symmetry notion which is more tractable computationally and which is a sufficient condition to handle semantic symmetry.

4 Syntactic Symmetry

In [7], the author studied syntactical symmetry of values of a same CSP domain variable, here syntactic symmetry is extended to the possible variable-value pairs of the CSP. This leads to a similar definition as the one of constraint symmetry given in [21]

Definition 3. *A syntactical symmetry of a CSP $\mathcal{P} = (V, D, C, R)$ having the microstructure $\mathcal{M}_{\mathcal{P}}$, is a mapping $\sigma : V \times \cup_{i\in[1,n]} D_i \longrightarrow V \times \cup_{i\in[1,n]} D_i$, that preserves the edges and the non-edges of $\mathcal{M}_{\mathcal{P}}$.*

Remark 2. A syntactical symmetry of a CSP $\mathcal{P}$ is an automorphism of its microstructure $\mathcal{M}_{\mathcal{P}}$. The set of syntactic symmetries of a CSP $\mathcal{P}$ is identical to the set of its *constraint symmetries* [21] which is equivalent to the automorphism group $Aut(\mathcal{M}_{\mathcal{P}})$ of its microstructure. Syntactical symmetries preserve the solutions of the CSP.

Definition 4. *Two variable-value pairs $\langle v_i, b_i\rangle \in V \times D_i$ and $(v_j, c_j) \in V \times D_j$ are syntactically symmetrical iff there exists a syntactical symmetry σ of $\mathcal{P}$, such that $\sigma(\langle v_i, b_i\rangle)=\langle v_j, c_j\rangle$.*

Theorem 1. *If two variable-value pairs $\langle v_i, b_i\rangle \in V \times D_i$ and $\langle v_j, c_j\rangle \in V \times D_j$ are syntactically symmetrical, then they are semantically symmetrical for all solutions of the CSP.*

Proof. It is based on the fact that syntactical symmetry preserves solutions.

4.1 The Weakened Syntactic Symmetry Conditions

A weakened symmetry condition has been defined in [27,28] for the restricted framework of Not-equals CSPs and had been shown to be useful in practice. Here, we show how to extend this weakened condition to General CSPs. Before doing that, we define the notion of assignment trees and failure trees corresponding to the enumerative search method used to prove the consistency of a considered CSP.

Definition 5. *We call an assignment tree of a CSP $\mathcal{P}$ corresponding to a given search method and a fixed variable ordering, a tree which gathers the history of all the variable assignments made during search, where the nodes represent the variables of the CSP and where the edges outgoing from a node v_i are labeled by the different values used to instantiate the corresponding CSP variable v_i.*

The root of the tree is the first variable in the ordering. In this work, the considered search method is Forward Checking [29].

In an assignment tree of a CSP, a path connecting the root of the tree to a node defines a partial instantiation $\mathcal{I}$ of the CSP. The variables of the partial instantiation $\mathcal{I}$ are the nodes of the considered path. The last node $n_{\mathcal{I}}$ of the path corresponds to the last affected variable in the instantiation or to a variable having an empty domain.

We associate to each inconsistent partial instantiation, corresponding to a given path in the assignment tree, a failure tree defined as follows:

Definition 6. *Let T be an assignment tree of the CSP $\mathcal{P}$, $\mathcal{I} = (\langle v_1, a_1\rangle, \langle v_2, a_2\rangle, \ldots, \langle v_i, a_i\rangle)$ an inconsistent partial instantiation of the variables v_1,v_2,...,v_i corresponding to the path $\{v_1, v_2, ..., v_i\}$ in T. We call a failure tree of the instantiation $\mathcal{I}$, the sub-tree of T denoted by $T_\mathcal{I}$ such that:*

1. *The root of the tree T and the root of the sub-tree $T_\mathcal{I}$ are joined by the path corresponding to the instantiation $\mathcal{I}$;*
2. *All the CSP variables corresponding to the leaf nodes of $T_\mathcal{I}$ have empty domains.*

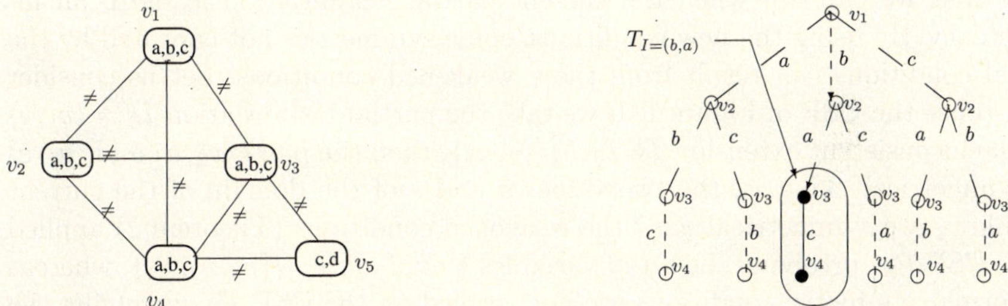

Fig. 1. The constraint graph of a graph coloring instance, its assignment tree and the failure tree of $\mathcal{I}$=$(\langle v_1, b\rangle, \langle v_2, a\rangle)$

Example 1. Take the CSP on the left part of Figure 1 and apply a Forward Checking process on it w.r.t the variable ordering $\{v_1, v_2, v_3, v_4, v_5\}$. The right part of Figure 1 illustrates the assignment tree of the considered CSP. If we take the partial instantiation $\mathcal{I} = (\langle v_1, b\rangle, \langle v_2, a\rangle)$, then the failure tree $T_\mathcal{I}$ of the instantiation $\mathcal{I}$ is the part of the assignment tree shown in a box.

We can now give the weakened conditions of syntactic symmetry. The main idea is to weaken the syntactic symmetry conditions when an inconsistent partial instantiation is generated during the search. That is, for a local CSP $\mathcal{P}_\mathcal{I}$ where the partial instantiation $\mathcal{I}$ is inconsistent, the conditions of syntactic symmetry (Definition 3) are restricted to only the variables involved in the failure tree $T_\mathcal{I}$, rather than to all the un-instantiated variables.

Theorem 2. *Let $\mathcal{P}(V, C, D, R)$ be a CSP, $\mathcal{I}_0 = (\langle v_1, a_1\rangle, \ldots, \langle v_{i-1}, a_{i-1}\rangle)$ a partial instantiation of $i-1$ variables instantiated before the current variable v_i such that the extension $\mathcal{I} = \mathcal{I}_0 \bigcup \{\langle v_i, a_i\rangle\}$ is inconsistent, $T_\mathcal{I}$ is the failure tree of $\mathcal{I}$ and $Var(T_\mathcal{I})$ the set of the variables corresponding to the nodes of $T_\mathcal{I}$. If $\langle v_i, a_i\rangle$ is syntactically symmetrical to $\langle v_j, b_j\rangle$ in the CSP $\acute{\mathcal{P}}_{\mathcal{I}_0}$ derived from $\mathcal{P}_{\mathcal{I}_0}$ by restricting its set of variables to $Var(T_\mathcal{I}) \cup \{v_i\}$, then the extension $\mathcal{J} = \mathcal{I}_0 \bigcup \{\langle v_j, b_j\rangle\}$ is inconsistent.*

Proof. The CSP $\acute{\mathcal{P}}_{\mathcal{I}_0}$ is $\mathcal{P}_{\mathcal{I}_0}$ where the set of variables is restricted to $Var(T_{\mathcal{I}}) \cup \{v_i\}$. By the hypothesis, $T_{\mathcal{I}}$ is a failure tree of $\mathcal{I}$ in $\mathcal{P}$. This implies that the assignment of the value a_i to v_i leads to a failure in $\acute{\mathcal{P}}_{\mathcal{I}_0}$. In other words, $\langle v_i, a_i \rangle$ does not participate in any solution of $\acute{\mathcal{P}}_{\mathcal{I}_0}$. By the hypothesis, the pair $\langle v_i, a_i \rangle$ is symmetrical to $\langle v_j, b_j \rangle$ in $\acute{\mathcal{P}}_{\mathcal{I}_0}$. This implies that $\langle v_j, b_j \rangle$ does not participate in any solution of $\acute{\mathcal{P}}_{\mathcal{I}_0}$. Thus $\langle v_j, b_j \rangle$ does not participate in any solution of $\mathcal{P}_{\mathcal{I}_0}$ as well. This implies that the partial instantiation $\mathcal{J} = \mathcal{I}_0 \bigcup \{\langle v_j, b_j \rangle\}$ is inconsistent in $\mathcal{P}$. (QED)

Remark 3. In the case of a failure during search, the symmetry conditions are restricted to only the variables participating in the failure.

Theorem 2 gives an interesting weakening of the conditions of syntactic symmetry that we can use when the current partial instantiation leads to an inconsistency. By using the new conditions, some symmetries not captured by the normal conditions can result from these weakened conditions. Let us consider for instance the CSP of Figure 1. If we take the partial instantiation $\mathcal{I}_0 = \langle v_1, b \rangle$ and the inconsistent extension $\mathcal{I}{=}\mathcal{I}_0 \cup \{\langle v_2, a \rangle\}$, then the pairs $\langle v_2, a \rangle$ and $\langle v_2, c \rangle$ are symmetrical. That is, the two values a and c of the domain of the current variable v_2 are symmetrical *w.r.t* the weakened conditions (Theorem 2) applied on the CSP $\acute{\mathcal{P}}_{\mathcal{I}_0}$ involving the set of variables $Var(T_{\mathcal{I}}) \cup v_2 {=} \{v_2, v_3, v_4\}$, whereas the normal symmetry conditions are not verified on the CSP $\mathcal{P}_{\mathcal{I}_0}$ involving the set of all un-instantiated variables $\{v_2, v_3, v_4, v_5\}$. The branch corresponding to the assignment of c to v_2 is not explored during search thanks to Theorem 2. This defines a more powerfull symmetry cut that we use to shorten CSP search trees.

Besides, this weakening property can be used in other known symmetry breaking methods [2,3,4]. That is, symmetry conditions have to be checked only on the variables involved in the failure when a partial instantiation is shown to be inconsistent.

Below we show how local symmetry is detected and eliminated, and how a tree search method (Forward Checking) can take advantage of symmetry.

5 Local Symmetry Detection and Exploitation

5.1 Symmetry Detection and Breaking

Local symmetries have to be detected dynamically at each node of the search tree. Dynamic symmetry detection had been studied in CSPs, a local syntactic domain symmetry search method had been given in [7].

As an alternative to this symmetry search method, we adapted Saucy [9] to detect local syntactic symmetries and show how to break such symmetries during search. Saucy is a tool for computing the automorphism group of a graph. Other tools like Nauty [30] or the most recent methods AUTOM [31] or the one described in [32] can be adapted to search local symmetry. It is shown in [31] that AUTOM is the best method. Because the source code of AUTOM is not free, we chose Saucy. Since the syntactic symmetry group of a CSP $\mathcal{P}$ is identical to the automorphism group of its microstructure $\mathcal{M}_{\mathcal{P}}$, we can use Saucy on $\mathcal{M}_{\mathcal{P}}$ to detect the syntactic symmetry group of $\mathcal{P}$. Saucy returns a set of generators *Gen* of the symmetry group from which we can deduce each symmetry. Saucy offers the possibility to color the microstructure such that, a node is allowed to be permuted with another node if they have the same color. This restricts the permutations to the nodes having the same color. We use this coloration possibility to guide the symmetry search and detect local value symmetries. The source code of Saucy can be found at (http://vlsicad.eecs.umich.edu/BK/SAUCY/).

Symmetry detection: Consider a CSP $\mathcal{P}$, and a partial instantiation $\mathcal{I}$ of $\mathcal{P}$, defining a state in the search corresponding to the current node $n_{\mathcal{I}}$. The main idea is to maintain dynamically the microstructure $\mathcal{M}_{\mathcal{P}_{\mathcal{I}}}$ of the CSP $\mathcal{P}_{\mathcal{I}}$ corresponding to the local sub-problem defined at each current node $n_{\mathcal{I}}$, then color the microstructure $\mathcal{M}_{\mathcal{P}_{\mathcal{I}}}$ and compute its automorphism group $Aut(\mathcal{M}_{\mathcal{P}_{\mathcal{I}}})$. The CSP $\mathcal{P}_{\mathcal{I}}$ can be viewed as a new problem corresponding to the unsolved part. Computing all the automorphisms of the dynamic microstructure at each node of the search tree may be expensive. To remedy this, two coloration strategies of the microstructure are considered:

1. **The multi-colors-strategy:** A first compromise is to limit permutations to only values of the same domains. To do that, a color is associated to each variable. Every node of the microstructure belonging to a variable is colored with the same color. Now by applying Saucy on this colored microstructure we can get the generator set *Gen* of the symmetry sub-group existing between values of the same domains of the CSP.
2. **The two-colors-strategy:** A second compromise is to associate to the current variable v_i (under instantiation) one color and all the other variables another color. That is, we color the dynamic microstructure $\mathcal{M}_{\mathcal{P}_{\mathcal{I}}}$ with two colors. All the nodes of the microstructure belonging to the current variable v_i have the first color and all the other nodes the second one. Finally apply Saucy to compute the generators of the automorphism sub-group corresponding to this coloration. This returns the generators *Gen* of the symmetry group allowing variable-value permutations on the other variables different from v_i, but the values of v_i are permuted together.

Remark 4. The total local symmetry group is reached when using only one color on the microstructure $\mathcal{M}_{\mathcal{P}_{\mathcal{I}}}$.

Symmetry elimination: We use Theorem 2 to prune search spaces of tree search methods. Indeed, if the assignment $\langle v_i, b_i \rangle$ of the current variable v_i at a given node $n_{\mathcal{I}}$ of the search tree is shown to participate in no solution of the CSP $\mathcal{P}$, then all the pairs $\langle v_j, c_j \rangle$ which are symmetrical to $\langle v_i, b_i \rangle$ in $\mathcal{P}_{\mathcal{I}}$ do not (i.e. these pairs are the ones corresponding to the orbit of the conflicted pair $\langle v_i, b_i \rangle$ that can be computed by using only the symmetry group generators). Then we remove the value c_j from the domain of the un-instantiated variable v_j, and prune the sub-space which corresponds to its assignment to v_j in the search tree.

If the variable v_i and v_j are the same (as in our implementation), then the previous reasoning handles symmetries between values of the domain D_i. The domain D_i of the current variable v_i is partitioned into sub-sets of symmetrical values *w.r.t* the detected local symmetries at the corresponding node of the search tree. To avoid generating local symmetrical solutions, we consider one value from each sub-set of symmetrical values in D_i. If we need to check CSP consistency only, we stop the search when a first solution is found.

5.2 Symmetry Advantage in Tree Search Algorithms

Now we are in the position to show how these symmetrical values can be used to increase the efficiency of CSP tree search algorithms. We choose in our implementation the Forward Checking method to be the baseline method that we want to improve by local symmetry elimination. The resulting procedure called FC-sym is given in Figure 2.

If $\mathcal{I}$ is an inconsistent partial instantiation in which the assignment $\langle v_i, d_i \rangle$ of the current variable v_i is shown to participate in no solutions of the CSP $\mathcal{P}$, then according to Theorem 2, all the pairs $\langle v_j, d_j \rangle$ which are symmetrical to $\langle v_i, d_i \rangle$ in $\mathcal{P}_\mathcal{I}$ do not. Thus we remove d_j from the domain of v_j, and prune the sub-space which corresponds to its assignment to v_j.

The function $orbit(\langle v_{k+1}, d_{k+1} \rangle, Gen)$ is elementary, it computes the orbit of the pair $\langle v_{k+1}, d_{k+1} \rangle$ from the set of generators *Gen* returned by Saucy.

6 Experiments

Now, we shall investigate the performances of our search techniques by experimental analysis. We choose for our study some classical problems to show the local symmetry behavior in CSP resolution. We expect that symmetry breaking will be more profitable in real-life applications. Here, we tested and compared four methods:

1. **No-sym:** search without symmetry breaking;
2. **Global-sym:** search with global symmetry breaking restricted to values of a same domain. The same symmetries as the ones considered in the GE-tree method, with a slight difference that we break only global symmetries between values of a same domain;
3. **Local-sym1:** search with local value symmetry breaking (the weakened symmetry). This method implements the multi-colors strategy (see Section 5.1).
4. **Local-sym2:** search with restricted local variable-value symmetry breaking (the weakened symmetry). This method implements the two-colors strategy (see Section 5.1).

on different problems: random graph coloring problems, Dimacs graph coloring instances and n-Queens problems. An implementation of the $Local-sym1$ strategy in GECODE system is successfully used in [33] to break local symmetry in the subgraph pattern matching problem. The common baseline search method

```
Procedure FC-sym(D, I, k);{I = [⟨v1, d1⟩, ⟨v2, d2⟩, ..., ⟨vk, dk⟩]}
begin
  if k = n then I is a solution, return(I)
  else
  begin
   for each vi ∈ V, such that Cik ∈ C, vi ∈future(vk) do
     for each value di ∈ Di do
       if (di, dk) ∉ rik then
         delete di from Di;
   if ∀vi ∈ future(vk), Di ≠ ∅ then
   begin
     vk+1=next-variable(vk)
     repeat
       take dk+1 ∈ Dk+1
       Dk+1 = Dk+1 − {dk+1}
       I=I ∪ {⟨vk+1, dk+1⟩};
       J=FC-sym(D, I, k + 1);
       I=I-{⟨vk+1, dk+1⟩};
       if J ∈ Sol(P) then Gen=Saucy(P_I);
       else Gen=Saucy(P_{Var(T_I)∪vk+1});
       SymClass(⟨vk+1, dk+1⟩)=orbit(⟨vk+1, dk+1⟩,Gen);
       Dk+1=Dk+1-SymClass(⟨vk+1, dk+1⟩)
     until Dk+1 = ∅
   end
  end
end;
```

Fig. 2. Forward Checking method with symmetry

for the four previous methods is Forward Checking. The complexity indicators are the number of nodes of the search tree and the CPU time. The time needed for computing symmetries is added to the total CPU time. The source codes are written in C and compiled on a Pentium 4, 2.8 GHZ and 1 Go of RAM.

6.1 Random Graph Coloring Problems

Random graph coloring problems are generated with respect to the following parameters: (1) n : the number of vertices (variables), (2) *Colors*: the number of colors (domain values) and (3) d: the density which is a number between 0 and 1 expressed by the ratio : the number of constraints (the number of edges in the constraint graph) to the number of all possible constraints. For each test corresponding to some fixed values of the parameters n, *Colors* and d, a sample of 100 instances are randomly generated and the measures (CPU time, nodes) are taken on the average.

Figure 3, shows the performances of the four methods in number of nodes of the search tree, respectively, in CPU time (in seconds) on random graph coloring problems, whose number of variables is fixed to $n = 15$ and the density to $d = 0.9$. We reported here experiments on instances having hight density, because they

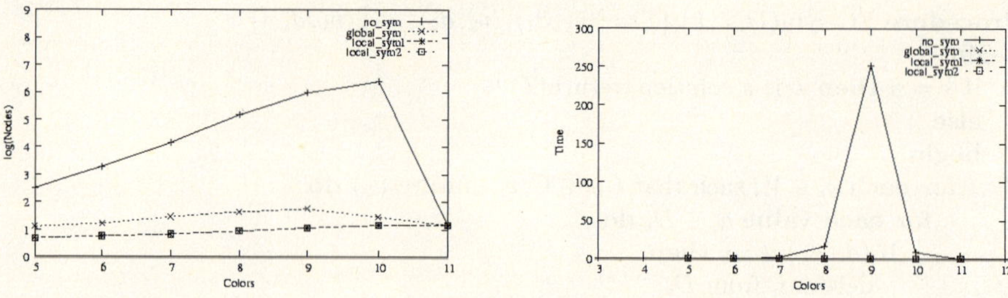

Fig. 3. Node and Time curves where $n = 15$ and $d = 0.9$

are the hardest instances, and symmetry presents a similar behavior for average and weak density instances. The curves on the left are plotted in a logarithmic scale, they represent the performances in number of nodes *w.r.t* the number of colors. The ones on the right are plotted in the usual scale and express the performances in CPU time *w.r.t* the number of colors. As expected, we can see that all the methods exploiting symmetry outperform dramatically the search without symmetry (No-sym) in both the number of nodes and the CPU time. We can also see on the node curves that local symmetry elimination (Local-sym1 and Local-sym2) reduces more the search tree than global symmetry elimination (Global-sym). That is, local symmetries are more frequent during the search than the global symmetries stabilizing the partial instantiation. Both Local-sym1 and Local-sym2 have the same behavior in number of nodes; their node curves are almost identical. We can distinguish on the CPU time curve of No-sym a critical region where the instances are harder. All the methods using symmetry solved these instances in less than 0.1 seconds, then their CPU time curves are confused with x-axis and do not appear.

Since Figure 3 does not allow a CPU time comparison of the methods exploiting symmetry, we reported in Figure 4 the practical results of the methods: Global-sym, Local-sym1 and Local-sym2, on the random graph coloring problem where the number of variables is increased to $n = 35$ and where we keep the same density ($d = 0.9$) as in Figure 3.

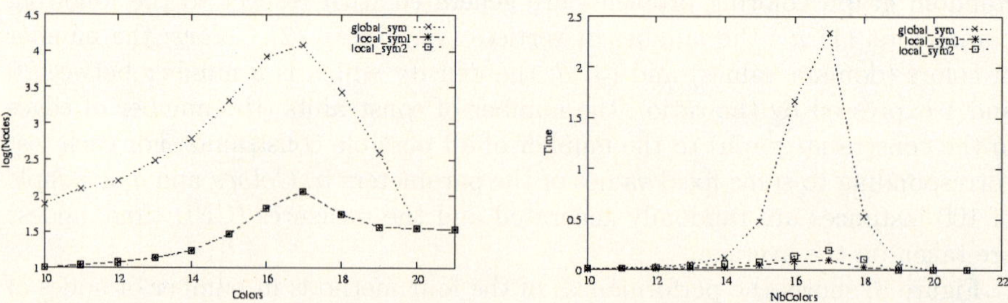

Fig. 4. Node and Time curves of the three symmetry methods on random graph coloring where $n = 35$ and $d = 0.9$

We can see on the node curves (the curves on the left plotted in a logarithmic scale) that both Local-sym1 and Local-sym2 detect and eliminate more symmetries than the Global-sym method. The reason is that the local symmetry detected at a node during the search by both Local-sym1 and Local-sym2 includes the global symmetry stabilizing the partial instantiation at that node exploited by Global-sym. The node curves of both Local-sym1 and Local-sym2 compare well. From the CPU time curves (the curves on the right), we can see that both Local-sym1 and Local-sym2 are faster than Global-sym. Near the peak of difficulty, Local-sym2 seems to be 12 times faster than Global-sym and Local-sym1 about 24 times faster than Global-sym. Therefore, Local symmetry elimination is profitable for solving random graph coloring instances in the hard region and outperforms dramatically global symmetry breaking on these problems. We can also see on the CPU time that Local-sym1 improves Local-sym2, thus the good compromise looks to be the multi-color strategy corresponding to domain value symmetry. These remarks will be confirmed by the experiments on Dimacs benchmarks in the next section.

6.2 Dimacs Graph Coloring Benchmarks

Here, we tested and compared the four methods on some graph coloring benchmarks taken from the Dimacs challenge (http://mat.gsia.cmu.edu/COLOR04/).

Table 1 shows the results of the methods on some of the benchmarks. It gives the instance, the chromatic number found (k), the number of nodes of the search tree and the CPU time for each method. We seek for each instance the minimal number k of colors needed to color the vertices of the corresponding graph (called the chromatic number). The search of the chromatic number consists in proving the consistency of the problem with k colors (the existence of a k-coloration of the graph); and in proving its inconsistency when using $k-1$ colors (not colorable). The symbol "-" means that the corresponding method does not solve the instance in one hour.

Table 1. Results on some Dimacs graph coloring benchmarks

		No-sym		Global-sym		Local-sym1		Local-sym2	
Instance	*k*	*Nodes*	*Time*	*Nodes*	*Times*	*Nodes*	*Time*	*Nodes*	*Time*
myciel4	5	30,976	0.16	2,764	0.03	1,260	0.01	1,260	0.04
myciel5	6	-	-	8,040,259	59.84	2,413,556	22.21	2,406,945	25.36
anna	11	-	-	3,403	0.59	168	0.05	168	0.08
david	11	-	-	3,896	0.23	124	0.03	124	0.03
queen7_7	7	2,452	0.01	513	0.02	502	0.01	502	0.0
queen8_8	9	-	-	10,629,131	262.54	1,399,436	29.7	1,396,774	30.16
school1	14	-	-	-	-	76,192	17.28	75,985	17.85
school1_nsh	14	-	-	-	-	1,487,287	257.57	1,486,523	270.4
2-Insertion_3	4	832,150	1.02	277,408	0.73	135,953	0.48	115,737	0.52
2-FullIns_3	5	2,294,396	7.63	193,347	1.14	49,202	0.59	48,076	0.65
mugg88_1	4	-	-	-	-	2,882,284	53.91	2,882,284	93.55
mugg88_25	4	-	-	-	-	881,784	6.74	881,784	9.4
mugg100_1	4	-	-	-	-	3,325,453	24.85	3,325,453	40.15
mugg100_25	4	-	-	-	-	2,727,178	17.3	2,727,178	30.92
zeroin.i.1	49	-	-	-	-	268	7.0	268	35.49
zeroin.i.2	30	-	-	-	-	262	0.75	262	3,675
zeroin.i.3	30	-	-	-	-	262	0.76	262	3,675
mulsol.i.2	31	-	-	-	-	237	0.85	237	10.14
mulsol.i.3	31	-	-	-	-	237	0.9	237	10.14
le450_5a	5	178,753	13.88	170,123	13.75	167,787	32.0	167,703	32.23
le450_5b	5	1,349	0.11	1,110	0.09	927	0.11	927	0.19
le450_5c	5	1,984	0.15	1,984	0.17	1,983	0.31	1,975	0.34
le450_5d	5	5,795	0.54	4,563	0.34	3,452	0.62	3,452	0.68
DSJC125.1	5	55,358	0.85	43,773	1.34	40,809	1.44	40,809	1.48

Table 1 shows that both No-sym and Global-sym are not able to solve several instances under the time limit, but Global-sym is better than No-sym in both numbers of nodes and CPU time on these problems. We can see that both Local-sym1 and Local-sym2 are in general better than Global-sym in both the number of nodes and the CPU time. That is, local symmetry is more profitable than global symmetry on these problems. We can also see that Local-sym1 eliminates the same symmetries as the ones eliminated by Local-sym2, but Local-sym1 is faster than Local-sym2. This confirms that eliminating local domain value symmetries by using the multi-color strategy implemented in Local-sym1 is the best compromise on these problems.

6.3 The n-Queens Problems

Finding *all* solutions of the n-queens problem is still a challenge. We compared the four methods on some instances of this problem.

Table 2 summarizes the results obtained. For each method we give the number of computed solutions (*Sols*), the number of nodes, and the CPU time in seconds. Note that for the methods exploiting symmetry, the number of solutions (*Sols*) is the number of non-symmetrical solutions found *w.r.t* the applied symmetry breaking strategy. The number of solutions of No-sym is the total set of solutions of the problem. We can see that both Local-sym1 and Local-sym2 represent the set of solutions slightly in a more compact way than Global-sym. This means that Local-sym1 and Local-sym2 compact some local symmetrical solutions in addition to the global symmetrical ones compacted by Global-sym. We can also see that Local-sym2 detects some local symmetrical solutions which are not considered by Local-sym1. This is due to some variable-value symmetries considered in Local-sym2 that detect some local symmetrical solutions which are not detected in Local-sym1. Now, if we compare globally the methods in number of solutions, in the number of nodes and in CPU time, the method Global-sym seems to be the best on the average. Indeed, global symmetry is sufficient to solve efficiently the n-queens problems and local value symmetry does not abound like

Table 2. Results on the n-queens problem

	No-sym			Global-sym		
n	*Sols*	*Nodes*	*Time*	*Sols*	*Nodes*	*Times*
8	92	1,360	0.0	46	680	0.01
9	352	5,399	0.0	179	2,800	0.0
10	724	19,744	0.03	362	9,872	0.03
11	2,680	85,939	0.1	1,382	43,958	0.07
12	14,200	416,828	0.28	7,100	208,414	0.25
13	73,712	2,154,845	2.69	37,361	1,093,606	1.99
14	365,596	11,799,746	46.95	51,726	5,899,873	20.65

	Local-sym1			Local-sym2		
n	*Sols*	*Nodes*	*Time*	*Sols*	*Nodes*	*Times*
8	45	664	0.01	45	662	0.01
9	172	2,645	0.02	168	2,625	0.05
10	355	9,656	0.07	353	9,640	0.08
11	1,309	42,154	0.25	1,305	42,078	0.31
12	6,883	204,901	2.05	6,839	203,611	2.19
13	35,525	1,055,366	11.44	35,312	1,053,053	11.58
14	44,334	5,777,244	69.6	43,257	5,765,594	75.6

in the graph coloring. We believe that local variable symmetry will be more profitable for n-queens.

7 Discussion and Conclusions

Here, we extended symmetry detection and elimination to local symmetry. That is, the symmetries of each sub-CSP defined at a given node of the search tree and which is derived from the initial CSP by considering the partial instantiation corresponding to that node. We adapted Saucy to compute this local symmetry by maintaining dynamically the microstructure of the sub-CSP defined at each node of the search tree. Unlike the methods using GAP tools, here local symmetry detection is fully automated. Saucy is called with the microstructure of the local sub-CSP as the input graph, and then return the set of generators of the automorphism group of the microstructure which is shown to be equivalent to the local symmetry group of the considered sub-CSP. Detecting and exploiting all the local symmetry groups of the different nodes generated during the search may be time consuming. To remedy this, we proposed two coloration strategies in order to guide and restrict the symmetry search to domain value permutations (the multi-color strategy) and to some restricted variable-value permutations (the two color strategy). Both local symmetry strategies are implemented and exploited in the tree search method FC to prove either CSP consistency or to compute the not-local symmetrical solutions of the CSP. Experimental results confirmed that local symmetry breaking is profitable for CSP solving and improves global symmetry breaking in most of the considered problems.

As a future work, we are looking to implement a one-color symmetry detection strategy, then experiment it and compare it with the two strategies studied in this work.

An other interesting point, is to extend our approach to variable local symmetry breaking. One can try to detect local variable symmetries and post dynamic constraints to break them, it will be important to consider the possibilities of combining local variable and local value symmetries.

Finally, we are interested to adapt our symmetry results for other look-ahead CSP methods like MAC, and export local symmetry breaking to other research domains like biology or operational research to tackle real life applications.

References

1. Krishnamurty, B.: Short proofs for tricky formulas. Acta informatica 22, 253–275 (1985)
2. Benhamou, B., Sais, L.: Theoretical study of symmetries in propositional calculus and application. In: Eleventh International Conference on Automated Deduction, Saratoga Springs, NY, USA (1992)
3. Benhamou, B., Sais, L.: Tractability through symmetries in propositional calculus. Journal of Automated Reasoning (JAR) 12, 89–102 (1994)

4. Benhamou, B., Sais, L., Siegel, P.: Two proof procedures for a cardinality based language. In: Enjalbert, P., Mayr, E.W., Wagner, K.W. (eds.) STACS 94. LNCS, vol. 775, pp. 71–82. Springer, Heidelberg (1994)
5. Freuder, E.: Eliminating interchangeable values in constraints satisfaction problems. In: Proc AAAI-91, pp. 227–233 (1991)
6. Puget, J.F.: On the satisfiability of symmetrical constrained satisfaction problems. In: Komorowski, J., Raś, Z.W. (eds.) ISMIS 1993. LNCS, vol. 689. Springer, Heidelberg (1993)
7. Benhamou, B.: Study of symmetry in constraint satisfaction problems. In: Borning, A. (ed.) PPCP 1994. LNCS, vol. 874. Springer, Heidelberg (1994)
8. Crawford, J., Ginsberg, M.L., Luck, E., Roy, A.: Symmetry-breaking predicates for search problems. In: KR'96. Principles of Knowledge Representation and Reasoning, pp. 148–159. Morgan Kaufmann, San Francisco, California (1996)
9. Aloul, F.A., Ramani, A., Markov, I.L., Sakallak, K.A.: Solving difficult sat instances in the presence of symmetry. IEEE Transaction on CAD 22(9), 1117–1137 (2003)
10. Aloul, F.A., Ramani, A., Markov, I.L., Sakallak, K.A.: Symmetry breaking for pseudo-boolean satisfiabilty. In: ASPDAC'04, pp. 884–887 (2004)
11. Backofen, R., Will, S.: Excluding symmetries in constraint-based search. In: Jaffar, J. (ed.) Principles and Practice of Constraint Programming – CP'99. LNCS, vol. 1713. Springer, Heidelberg (1999)
12. Gent, I.P., Smith, B.M.: Symmetry breaking during search in constraint programming. In: Proceedings ECAI'2000 (2000)
13. Gent, I., Harvey, W., Kelsey, T.: Groups and constraints: Symmetry breaking during search. In: Van Hentenryck, P. (ed.) CP 2002. LNCS, vol. 2470, pp. 415–430. Springer, Heidelberg (2002)
14. Focacci, F., Milano, M.: Global cut framework for removing symmetries. In: Walsh, T. (ed.) CP 2001. LNCS, vol. 2239, pp. 77–82. Springer, Heidelberg (2001)
15. Fahle, T., Schamberger, S., Sellmann, M.: Symmetry breaking. In: Walsh, T. (ed.) CP 2001. LNCS, vol. 2239, pp. 93–108. Springer, Heidelberg (2001)
16. Puget, J.: Symmetry breaking revisited. In: Van Hentenryck, P. (ed.) CP 2002. LNCS, vol. 2470, pp. 446–461. Springer, Heidelberg (2002)
17. Gent, I.P., Hervey, W., Kesley, T., Linton, S.: Generic sbdd using computational group theory. In: Rossi, F. (ed.) CP 2003. LNCS, vol. 2833. Springer, Heidelberg (2003)
18. Roney-Dougal, C.M., Gent, I.P., Kelsey, T., Linton, S.A.: Tractable symmetry breaking using restricted search trees. In: Proceedings of ECAI'04, pp. 211–215 (2004)
19. Puget, J.: Breaking symmetries in all diffrent problems. In: Proceedings of IJCAI, pp. 272–277 (2005)
20. Puget, J.: Breaking all value symmetries in surjection problems. In: van Beek, P. (ed.) CP 2005. LNCS, vol. 3709, pp. 490–504. Springer, Heidelberg (2005)
21. Cohen, D., Jeavons, P., Jefferson, C., Petrie, K., Smith, B.: Symmetry definitions for constraint satisfaction problems. In: van Beek, P. (ed.) CP 2005. LNCS, vol. 3709, pp. 17–31. Springer, Heidelberg (2005)
22. Puget, J.: Dynamic lex constraints. In: Benhamou, F. (ed.) CP 2006. LNCS, vol. 4204, pp. 453–467. Springer, Heidelberg (2006)
23. Walsh, T.: General symmetry breaking constraints. In: Benhamou, F. (ed.) CP 2006. LNCS, vol. 4204, pp. 650–664. Springer, Heidelberg (2006)
24. Gent, I.P., Kelsey, T., Linton, S.A., McDonald, I., Migeul, I., Smith, B.: Conditional symmetry breaking. In: van Beek, P. (ed.) CP 2005. LNCS, vol. 3709, pp. 256–270. Springer, Heidelberg (2005)

25. Zampelli, S., Deville, Y., Dupont, P.: Symmetry breaking in subgraph pattern matching. In: SymCon'06, pp. 35–42 (2006)
26. Jegou, P.: Decomposition of domains based on the micro-structure of finite constraint satisfaction problems. In: Proceedings AAAI'93 (1993)
27. Benhamou, B., Saïdi, M.R.: Reasoning by dominance in not-equals binary constraint networks. In: Benhamou, F. (ed.) CP 2006. LNCS, vol. 4204, pp. 670–674. Springer, Heidelberg (2006)
28. Benhamou, B., Saïdi, M.R.: Some improvements in symmetry elimination in not-equals binary constraint networks. In: van Beek, P. (ed.) CP 2005. LNCS, vol. 3709, pp. 1–7. Springer, Heidelberg (2005)
29. Haralik, R.M., Elliot, G.L.: Increasing tree search efficiency for constraint satisfaction problems. Artificial Intelligence 14, 263–313 (1980)
30. McKay, B.: Practical graph isomorphism. Congr. Numer. 30, 45–87 (1981)
31. Puget, J.F.: Automatic detection of variable and value symmetries. In: van Beek, P. (ed.) CP 2005. LNCS, vol. 3709, pp. 474–488. Springer, Heidelberg (2005)
32. Mears, C., de la Banda, M.G., Wallace, M.: On implementing symmetry detection. In: Benhamou, F. (ed.) CP 2006. LNCS, vol. 4204, pp. 1–8. Springer, Heidelberg (2006)
33. Zampelli, S., Deville, Y., Saïdi, M.R., Benhamou, B., Dupont, P.: Breaking local symmetries in subgraph pattern matching. In: The International Symmetry Conference (ISC 2007), Edinburgh, SCOTLAND (2007)

Encodings of the SEQUENCE Constraint

Sebastian Brand[1], Nina Narodytska[2], Claude-Guy Quimper[3], Peter Stuckey[1], and Toby Walsh[2]

[1] NICTA and University of Melbourne
[2] NICTA and University of NSW
[3] Omega Optimisation

Abstract. The SEQUENCE constraint is useful in modelling car sequencing, rostering, scheduling and related problems. We introduce half a dozen new encodings of the SEQUENCE constraint, some of which do not hinder propagation. We prove that, down a branch of a search tree, domain consistency can be enforced on the SEQUENCE constraint in just $O(n^2 \log n)$ time. This improves upon the previous bound of $O(n^3)$ for each call down the tree. We also consider a generalization of the SEQUENCE constraint – the Multiple SEQUENCE constraint. Our experiments suggest that, on very large and tight problems, domain consistency algorithms are best. However, on smaller or looser problems, much simpler encodings are better, even though these encodings hinder propagation. When there are multiple SEQUENCE constraints, a more expensive propagator shows promise.

1 Introduction

Global constraints are an important factor contributing to the success of constraint programming. They capture common modelling patterns and provide efficient propagators for these patterns. Research has started to show that some global constraints can be efficiently and effectively encoded and propagated using a small number of building blocks. For instance, a wide range of useful global constraints like AMONG, ATMOST, LEX, and STRETCH can be efficiently and effectively encoded using Pesant's REGULAR constraint [1]. Such REGULAR constraints can themselves be efficiently and effectively encoded into ternary transition constraints [2].

Encoding global constraints in this way offers several advantages. First, it is easy to incorporate such encodings into existing solvers. Second, encodings can provide efficient *incremental* propagators. For example, with the ternary encoding of the REGULAR constraints, only those ternary constraints involving variables whose domains have changed need wake up. Third, encodings can make it easier to construct nogoods for learning and backjumping. Fourth, the encoding gives heuristics an ability to "look inside" the global constraint when making branching decisions.

In this paper we propose and compare half a dozen different encodings of the SEQUENCE constraint. The SEQUENCE constraint was introduced by Beldiceanu and Contejean [3]. It constrains the number of values taken from a given set in any sequence of k variables. It is useful in staff rostering to specify, for example, that every employee has at least 2 days off in any 7 day period. Another application is car sequencing problems (prob001 in CSPLib). The SEQUENCE constraint can be used to specify,

C. Bessiere (Ed.): CP 2007, LNCS 4741, pp. 210–224, 2007.

for example, that at most 1 in 3 cars along the production line can have a sun-roof fitted. Several propagators for the SEQUENCE constraint have previously been proposed against which we will compare these new encodings.

2 Background

A constraint satisfaction problem (CSP) consists of a set of variables, each with a finite domain of values, and a set of constraints specifying allowed combinations of values for subsets of variables. We use capital letters for variables (e.g. X, Y and S), and lower case for values (e.g. d and d_i). A solution is an assignment of values to the variables satisfying the constraints. Constraint solvers typically explore partial assignments enforcing a local consistency property using either specialized or general purpose propagation algorithms. A *support* for a constraint C is a tuple that assigns a value to each variable from its domain which satisfies C. A *bounds support* is a tuple that assigns a value to each variable which is between the maximum and minimum in its domain which satisfies C. A constraint is *domain consistent* (*DC*) iff for each variable X_i, every value in the domain of X_i belongs to a support. A constraint is *bounds consistent* (*BC*) iff for each variable X_i, there is a bounds support for the maximum and minimum value in its domain. A CSP is DC/BC iff each constraint is DC/BC. A CSP is *singleton domain consistent* (*SDC*) iff for each variable X_i, we can assign any value in the domain of X_i and make the resulting subproblem domain consistent. Consider, for example, a problem with two constraints: $X_1 \neq X_2$, $X_1 + X_2 = X_3$, where $D(X_1) = \{0, 1, 2\}$, $D(X_2) = \{1, 3\}$ and $D(X_3) = \{1, 2, 3\}$. All constraints are domain consistent, but enforcing SDC on these constraints removes the value 1 from the domain of X_1 and the value 2 from the domain of X_3. A CSP is *singleton bounds consistent* (*SBC*) iff for each variable X_i, we can assign the maximum (minimum) value of X_i and make the resulting subproblem bounds consistent. In the previous example enforcing SBC does not prune any values. A constraint is *monotone* iff there exists a total ordering $\prec$ of the domain values such that for any two values v, w if $v \prec w$ then v can be replaced by w in any support for C.

We will compare local consistency properties applied to sets of constraints, c_1 and c_2, that are logically equivalent. As in [4], a local consistency property Φ on c_1 is as strong as Ψ on c_2 iff, given any domains, if Φ holds on c_1 then Ψ holds on c_2; Φ on c_1 is stronger than Ψ on c_2 iff Φ on c_1 is as strong as Ψ on c_2 but not vice versa; Φ on c_1 is equivalent to Ψ on c_2 iff Φ on c_1 is as strong as Ψ on c_2 and vice versa; they are incomparable otherwise. For the complexity results, we assume the propagation engine wakes each propagator whose variables are changed in constant time per propagator, and that the propagation cost for a linear constraint on n variables is $O(n)$. Modern propagation engines respect this.

3 The SEQUENCE Constraint

The AMONG constraint restricts the number of occurrences of some given values in a sequence of k variables. More precisely, AMONG$(l, u, [X_1, X_2, \ldots, X_k], v)$ holds iff $l \leq |\{i \mid X_i \in v\}| \leq u$. That is, between l and u of the variables take values in v.

The AMONG constraint can be encoded by channelling into 0/1 variables using $Y_i \leftrightarrow X_i \in v$ and $l \leq \sum_{i=1}^{k} Y_i \leq u$. Since the constraint graph of this encoding is Berge-acyclic, this does not hinder propagation. Consequently, except in Section 5 we will simplify notation and consider AMONG (and SEQUENCE) on Boolean variables Y with $v = \{1\}$. If $l = 0$, AMONG becomes an ATMOST constraint. If $u = k$, AMONG becomes an ATLEAST constraint. ATMOST (and ATLEAST) is monotone since given a support, we also have support for any larger (smaller) value [5].

The SEQUENCE constraint is a conjunction of overlapping AMONG constraints. More precisely, SEQUENCE$(l, u, k, [X_1, X_2, \ldots, X_n], v)$ holds iff for $1 \leq i \leq n-k+1$, AMONG$(l, u, [X_i, X_{i+1}, \ldots, X_{i+k-1}], v)$ holds. We shall refer to the decomposition of the SEQUENCE constraint into a sequence of AMONG constraints as the AMONG decomposition (*AD*). Clearly, this decomposition hinders propagation. However, if the AMONG constraint is monotone then enforcing DC on the decomposition is equivalent to enforcing DC on the SEQUENCE constraint [5]. An extension proposed in [6] is that each AMONG constraint can have different parameters (l, u and k). All the encodings proposed here can easily be extended to deal with this generalization.

Several filtering algorithms exist for SEQUENCE constraints. Régin and Puget propose a filtering algorithm for the Global Sequencing constraint (GSC) that combines a SEQUENCE and a Global Cardinality constraint (GCC) [7]. GSC$([X_1, \ldots, X_n], l, u, v, k, [l_1, \ldots, l_m], [u_1, \ldots, u_m])$ is satisfied iff for each $i \in \{1, \ldots, m\}$, $l_i \leq |\{j \mid X_j = i\}| \leq u_i$ and for each $p \in \{1, \ldots, n-k\}$, $l \leq |\{j \mid X_j \in v \,\&\, p \leq j \leq p+k-1\}| \leq u$. They encode the GSC constraint into a set of GCC constraints. This encoding hinders propagation as domain consistency on the encoding may not achieve domain consistency on the original SEQUENCE constraint. Beldiceanu and Carlsson propose a greedy filtering algorithm for the CARDPATH constraint that can be used to propagate the SEQUENCE constraint, but this again may not achieve domain consistency [8]. Régin proposes decomposing GSC into a set of variable disjoint AMONG and GCC constraints [9]. Again, this decomposition hinders propagation. Bessière *et al.* [5] encode SEQUENCE using a SLIDE constraint, and give a domain consistency propagator that runs in $O(nd^{k-1})$ time (d is the maximal domain size). Finally, van Hoeve *et al.* [6] propose two filtering algorithms that establish domain consistency. The first algorithm is based on an encoding into a REGULAR constraint and runs in $O(n2^k)$ time, whilst the second is based on computing cumulative sums and runs in $O(n^3)$ time (we call this *HPRS* after the initials of the authors). One of our contributions here is to improve on this bound.

3.1 Domain Consistency Filtering Algorithms Based on REGULAR (*LO*)

As mentioned above, van Hoeve *et al.* give an encoding using the REGULAR constraint [6]. The states of the automata used in this encoding record which of the last k values encountered are from the set v. We can improve upon this encoding very slightly by having states record just the last $k-1$ values encountered. A transition is then permitted iff the last $k-1$ values encountered plus the current variable have the correct frequency of values from the given set.

We now give an alternative encoding using the REGULAR constraint. The REGULAR $([X_1, \ldots, X_n], \mathcal{A})$ constraint ensures that the string defined by the sequence of variables $X_1, \ldots, X_n$ is accepted by the deterministic finite automaton (DFA) $\mathcal{A}$. The encoding exploits two features of many car sequencing and staff rostering problems. First, such problems typically only place upper bounds on occurrences (e.g. at most 1 in 3 cars can have the sun-roof). Second, in many problems the lower and upper bounds are typically small (e.g. in all data files in Prob001 in CSPLib, $u \leq 2$ and $k \leq 5$).

Suppose we wish to ensure that at most 1 in k Boolean variables Y_i take the value 1. Consider an automaton whose states record the minimum of k and the distance back to the last occurrence of 1. If 1 has not yet occurred, the distance is taken to be k. The transition function from the state q on seeing Y_i is $t(q, Y_i) = \min(k, q + 1)$ if $Y_i = 0$ and $t(q, Y_i) = 1$ if $q = k$ and $Y_i = 1$. The initial state of the automaton is k and any state is accepting (Figure 1(a)). A similar automaton can be constructed for $u > 1$, but we need states to record the distances back to the last u occurrences of value 1. Now, suppose we wish to ensure at least 1 in k variables take the value 1. The states of the automaton record the distance back to the last occurrence of 1. If 1 has not yet occurred, the distance is taken to be the number of variables seen so far. The transition function from the state q on seeing Y_i is $t(q, Y_i) = q + 1$ if $Y_i = 0$ and $q < k$, and $t(q, Y_i) = 1$ if $q \leq k$ and $Y_i = 1$. The initial state of the automaton is 1 and any state is accepting (Figure 1(b)).

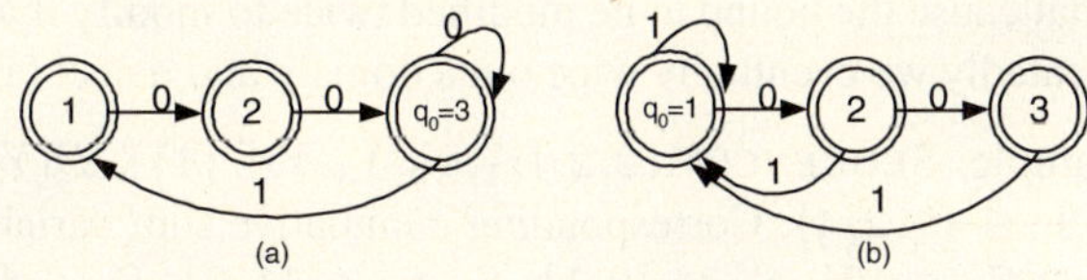

Fig. 1. (a) An automaton for the ATMOSTSEQ constraint with $u = 1$ and $k = 3$. (b) An automaton for the ATLEASTSEQ constraint with $l = 1$ and $k = 3$.

Thus, to encode a SEQUENCE constraint, we convert it into a sequence of ATLEAST and ATMOST constraints. We can convert the sequence of ATLEAST constraints into a sequence of ATMOST constraints (or vice versa depending on which representation gives smaller complexity) by inverting the value being counted. For example,the constraint that at least 3 in any 5 days must be work days is equivalent to at most 2 in 5 days are rest days. Finally, we construct the product of the automata for the two sequences of ATMOST or ATLEAST constraints. The complexity of enforcing domain consistency on SEQUENCE using this encoding is $O(nk^{\min(l,k-l)+\min(u,k-u)})$. We will refer to this encoding as *LO* as the automaton records the last occurrence(s).

3.2 Domain Consistency Filtering Algorithm Based on Cumulative Sums (*CS*)

Our next encoding is based on computing cumulative sums. We introduce a sequence of *cumulative sum* integer variables S_j where $S_j = \sum_{i=1}^{j} Y_i$, each with domain $[0, j]$. We encode this linearly as $S_0 = 0$ and $S_i = Y_i + S_{i-1}$ for $1 \leq i \leq n$. We then post $S_j \leq S_{j+k} - l$ and $S_{j+k} \leq S_j + u$ for $1 \leq j \leq n - k + 1$. We call this the *CS* encoding. Not surprisingly, this encoding hinders propagation. However, if we enforce a slightly stronger level of local consistency on the encoding, propagation is unhindered.

Theorem 1. *Singleton bounds consistency on CS enforces domain consistency on* SEQUENCE *and takes $O(n^3)$ time to enforce down a branch of a search tree.*

Proof. It is easy to show that if *CS* is BC then setting each S_i variable to its upper bound u_i, and setting each $Y_i = u_i - u_{i-1}$ gives a solution of *CS* and the SEQUENCE constraint. Hence SBC on *CS* clearly enforces DC of SEQUENCE.

For the complexity argument, first note that propagation for *CS* is $O(n^2)$ having $O(n)$ constraints which can wake at most $O(n)$ times each. A priori it would appear that enforcing SBC at each node down the search tree is $O(n^3)$ since we must check $O(n)$ assignments. But we can show for each assignment, either incremental propagation is $O(n)$ or it is $O(n^2)$ and the assignment causes failure. Since each failure fixes an Y_i variable in any forward computation this can occur at most $O(n)$ times. Hence the total complexity down the tree is $O(n^3)$. Using shadow variables for the Y_i we can disconnect the SBC propagation of the *CS* encoding from the rest of the problem. Since copying from the Y_i to their shadows and back is $O(n)$ the implementation of SBC is $O(n^3)$.

Incremental BC of *CS* after fixing a single Y_i variable proceeds to modify upper and lower bounds of S_j variables. Either every bound is modified at most once, in which case the propagation is $O(n)$, or some bound is modified twice. We can use the sequence of propagations that cause the bound to be modified twice to modify it again. Applying this sequence repeatedly we eventually wipe out a domain and detect failure. □

Consider, for example, SEQUENCE$(1, 2, 2, [Y_1, Y_2, Y_3, Y_4], \{1\})$, $D(Y_3) = \{0\}$ and $D(Y_i) = \{0, 1\}, i \in \{1, 2, 4\}$. Corresponding cumulative sum variables S have the following domains: $S_0 \in \{0\}$, $S_1 \in \{0, 1\}$, $S_2, S_3 \in \{1, 2\}$, $S_4 \in \{2, 3\}$. All constraints in *CS* are bounds consistent. However, enforcing singleton bounds consistency on *CS* prunes the value 0 from the domains of Y_2 and Y_4. We can see SBC applied to *CS* as a reworking of the original *HPRS* algorithm in different terms, with a tighter complexity argument.

3.3 Domain Consistency Filtering Algorithm Based on Difference Constraints (*CD*)

The key constraints in the *CS* encoding are difference constraints of the form $S \leq S' + d$, a well studied class with connections to shortest path algorithms [10]. We can modify the encoding to use only reified difference constraints, and then use efficient methods for handling these constraints. We replace each constraint $S_i = Y_i + S_{i-1}$ by the equivalent $S_i \leq S_{i-1} + 1$, $S_{i-1} \leq S_i$, $Y_i \Leftrightarrow S_{i-1} \leq S_i - 1$. We denote this the *CD* encoding.

We can convert a conjunction of difference constraints C into a weighted directed graph $G_C = (N_C, E_C)$ defined as $N_C = vars(C)$ and $E_C = \{S \xrightarrow{c} S' \mid S \leq S' + c \in C\}$, where $S \xrightarrow{c} S'$ is a directed edge from S to S' with weight c.

The connection with shortest path algorithms is well known:

Proposition 1. *(Theorem 1 from [10]) C is satisfiable iff G_C contains no negative length cycles. Assuming C is satisfiable then C implies $S \leq S' + c$ iff the shortest path from S to S' in G_C is length $c' \leq c$.* □

We construct a *DC* propagator by using the current Y assignment to construct a conjunction of difference constraints C. After checking the satisfiability of C, we then check whether C implies $S_{i-1} \leq S_i - 1$ in which case we set $Y_i = 1$, or if it implies $S_i \leq S_{i-1}$ (the negation of $S_{i-1} \leq S_i - 1$) in which case we set $Y_i = 0$.

Theorem 2. *The difference constraints propagator on the CD encoding enforces domain consistency of* SEQUENCE *in* $O(n^2 \log n)$ *time down a branch of a search tree.*

Proof. Suppose that $Y_i = 1$ has no support given the current domains. Since each solution of the SEQUENCE constraint can be extended to a solution of *CD*, there can be no solution to *CD* with $Y_i = 1$. Hence the difference constraints will imply $S_i \leq S_{i-1}$ and the algorithm will set $Y_i = 0$. The reasoning is analogous for $Y_i = 0$.

Cotton and Maler [10] define incremental algorithms for (a) detecting negative cycles in a weighted directed graph after addition of a new edge in $O(|E| + |N| \log |N|)$, and (b) checking whether the shortest path has changed after addition of a new edge for a set P of pairs of nodes in $O(|E| + |N| \log |N| + |P|)$. For the *CD* encoding $P = \{(S_i, S_{i-1}), (S_{i-1}, S_i) \mid 1 \leq i \leq n\}$ and $|N_C|$, $|E_C|$, and $|P|$ are all $O(n)$; hence the complexity of incremental propagation after adding a single edge (e.g. when Y_i is fixed) is $O(n \log n)$. Since we only add $O(n)$ edges overall, the total complexity over a branch of the search tree is $O(n^2 \log n)$. □

Our current implementation of *CD* uses incremental all-pairs shortest path algorithms, rather than the single-source shortest path algorithms of [10]. Let s_{ij} be the shortest path from S_i to S_j for $1 \leq i, j \leq n$. Adding a single new arc $S_k \xrightarrow{c} S_l$ then there exists a negative cycle iff $s_{lk} + c < 0$. If no negative cycle exists then we can update all shortest paths variables s_{ij} by $s_{ij} = \min\{s_{ij}, s_{ik} + c + s_{lj}\}$. The cost for adding a single arc is then $O(n^2)$ and hence $O(n^3)$ down a branch of the search tree.

Consider, for example, $\text{SEQUENCE}(1, 2, 2, [Y_1, Y_2, Y_3, Y_4], \{1\})$, $D(Y_i) = \{0, 1\}$, $i \in \{1, \ldots, 4\}$. The initial constraint graph and the corresponding transitive closure of its adjacency matrix are presented in Figure 2(a). Assigning Y_3 to 0 causes addition of the edge from S_3 to S_2 with cost 0. After updating all shortest path variables s, we get that $s_{1,2}$ and $s_{3,4}$ are equal to -1. Consequently, value 0 can be pruned from domains of Y_2 and Y_4 (Figure 2(b)).

3.4 Domain Consistency Filtering Algorithm Based on Partial Sums (*PS*)

The fourth encoding is arguably the simplest encoding which gives domain consistency. The *PS* encoding simply decomposes the constraint into a set of equations based on partial sums: $P_{i,j} = \sum_{l=i}^{j} Y_l$ each with domain $[0, \min(u, j-i+1)]$. The *PS* encoding of the SEQUENCE constraint is $P_{i,i+k-1} \leq u$ and $P_{i,i+k-1} \geq l$ for $1 \leq i \leq n-k+1$ as well as $P_{i,i} = Y_i$ for $1 \leq i \leq n$ and most importantly, all possible ways of adding two of these variables to create another: $P_{i,j} = P_{i,m} + P_{m+1,j}$ for $1 \leq i \leq m < j \leq n, j \leq i + k - 1$. Note there are $O(nk^2)$ constraints of the last form.

Lemma 1. *Bounds consistency on the PS encoding enforces domain consistency of the* SEQUENCE *constraint in* $O(nk^2 u)$ *down a branch of a search tree.*

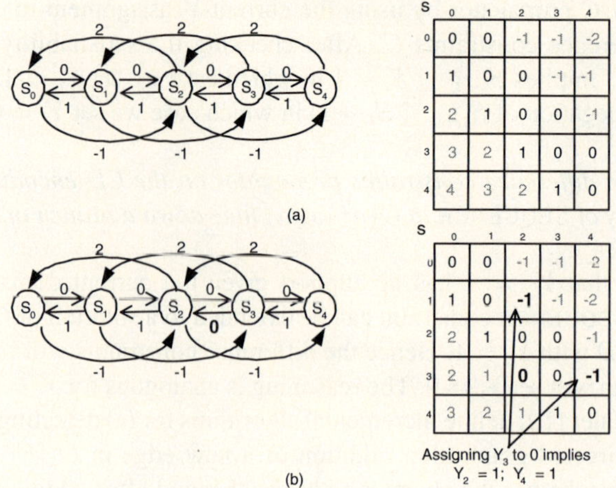

Fig. 2. The *CD* encoding for SEQUENCE$(1, 2, 2, [Y_1, Y_2, Y_3, Y_4], \{1\})$, $D(Y_i) = \{0, 1\}$, $i \in \{1, \ldots, 4\}$. (a) The initial constraint graph and the transitive closure of its adjacency matrix. (b) The constraint graph and the transitive closure of its adjacency matrix after assigning Y_3 to 0.

Proof. Define domain D to bounds capture C if for each $Y_i + \cdots + Y_j \leq c \in C$, $\max D(P_{i,j}) \leq c$ and for each $Y_i + \cdots + Y_j \geq c \in C$, $\min D(P_{i,j}) \geq c$. Clearly the domain resulting from BC applied to *PS* bounds captures the *AD* encoding.

We show that if D is BC with *PS* and bounds captures C then it also bounds captures C' which results from eliminating the least (or greatest) indexed variable Y_i.

We consider the least variable Y_i, the greatest is similar. Consider Fourier elimination of Y_i. For each pair of constraints in C of the form $Y_i + \cdots + Y_{j_1} \leq c_1$ and $Y_i + \cdots + Y_{j_2} \geq c_2$, Fourier elimination creates the constraint (a) if $j_1 > j_2$ then $Y_{j_2+1} + \cdots + Y_{j_1} \leq c_1 - c_2$, (b) if $j_1 < j_2$ then $Y_{j_1+1} + \cdots + Y_{j_2} \geq c_2 - c_1$, or (c) if $j_1 = j_2$ then $0 \leq c_1 - c_2$. Now since D bounds captures C we have $\max D(P_{i,j_1}) \leq c_1$ and $\min D(P_{i,j_2}) \geq c_2$. For case (a) by BC on the constraint $P_{i,j_1} = P_{i,j_2} + P_{j_2+1,j_1}$ we have $\max D(P_{j_2+1,j_1}) \leq c_1 - c_2$, for (b) BC on $P_{i,j_2} = P_{i,j_1} + P_{j_1+1,j_2}$ gives $\min D(P_{j_1+1,j_2}) \geq c_2 - c_1$, and for (c) the new constraint is $true$ since otherwise $D(P_{i,j_1}) = \emptyset$. Hence the new constraint is bounds captured by D.

To prove DC of SEQUENCE, let C be the *AD* encoding plus inequalities fixing Y variables in the current domain D (which we assume is BC with *PS*). Clearly D bounds captures C. Consider any variable Y_i, and eliminate from C in order $Y_1, \ldots, Y_{i-1}, Y_n, Y_{n-1}, \ldots, Y_{i+1}$ to obtain C'. Now C' only involves the variable Y_i. By the correctness of Fourier elimination[1] there are solutions of C extending any solution of C'. Since D bounds captures C' by repeated use of the above argument we have that there are solutions to C for each $d \in D(Y_i)$.

For the complexity argument, we note that the domains of the variables in each constraint $P_{i,j} = P_{i,m} + P_{m+1,j}$ can change at most $3u$ times in a forward computation. Each propagation is $O(1)$ hence the overall complexity down a branch is $O(nk^2u)$. □

[1] While Fourier is for real variable elimination, it coincides with integer elimination on C.

3.5 A Log Based Encoding of SEQUENCE (*LG*)

Our final encoding, called *LG*, is based on a simple dynamic program that builds up partial sums on counts. We introduce variables $L_{i,j}$ with domain $[0, \min(u, 2^{i-1})]$ for the partial sums $\sum_{k=j}^{j+2^i-1} Y_k$ where $0 \leq i \leq \lfloor \log k \rfloor$ and $1 \leq j \leq n - 2^i + 1$. Note that $L_{i,j} = P_{j,j+2^i-1}$. This requires the constraints $L_{0,j} = Y_j, 1 \leq j \leq n$ and $L_{i,j} = L_{i-1,j} + L_{i-1,j+2^{i-1}}, 1 \leq j \leq n, i > 0$. Suppose $k = \sum_{i=1}^{m} 2^{a_i}$ where $a_1 < \ldots < a_m$ (in other words, a_i is the ith bit set in the binary representation of k). We also need the vector Z_1 to Z_{n-k+1}, each with domain $[l, u]$, and the constraint

$$Z_j = \sum_{i=1}^{m} L[a_i, j + \sum_{k=1}^{i-1} 2^{a_k}].$$

Figure 3 shows the intra-variable dependencies for an example.

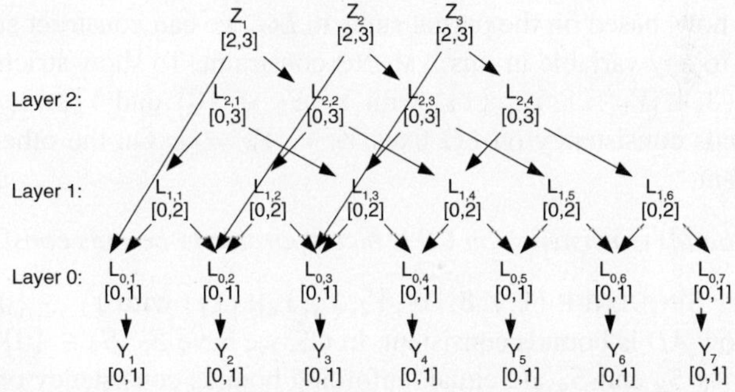

Fig. 3. Dependencies between partial sum variables L and Y and their initial domains for the SEQUENCE$(2, 3, 5, [Y_1, \ldots, Y_7])$ constraint

We have $O(n \log k)$ variables L that are subject to $O(n \log k)$ ternary constraints and $O(n)$ variables Z that are subject to $O(n)$ linear constraints of arity $O(\log k)$. The constraint propagation cost equals the number of invocations of the filtering algorithm for this constraint times the cost of one invocation. The number of invocations is bounded by the number of values in the domains of the variables. Hence, the propagation cost of a ternary constraint is $O(u)$. For all ternary constraints we have a cost of $O(u)O(n \log k) = O(nu \log k)$. Also, we have $O(n)$ variables Z that are subject to $O(n)$ linear constraints. We split linear constraints of the form $a = b_1 + b_2 +, \ldots, +b_{p-2} + b_{p-1} + b_p$ into ternary constraints as follows: $a = b_1 + (b_2 + (, \ldots, (b_{p-2} + (b_{p-1} + b_p))))$. Each parenthesised expression creates an additional variable. Instead of having $O(n)$ linear constraints of arity $O(\log k)$, we have $O(n \log k)$ ternary constraints. The cardinality of each variable domain in these constraints is $O(u)$. Consequently, the propagation cost for the original linear constraints is $O(u)O(n \log k) = O(nu \log k)$. Therefore we can enforce bounds consistency on this encoding in $O(nu \log k) + O(nu \log k) = O(nu \log k)$ time down a branch of a search tree. However, this may not achieve domain consistency on the SEQUENCE constraint.

There are a number of redundant constraints we can add to improve propagation. In fact, we can add any permutation of partial sums that add up to k. It is not hard to show that such additional redundant constraints can help propagation.

4 Theoretical Comparison

We compare theoretically those encodings on which we may not achieve domain consistency on the SEQUENCE constraint. We will show that we get more propagation with *LG* than *AD*, but that *AD*, *CS* and *LG* are otherwise incomparable. During propagation, all auxiliary variables in *CS*, *LG*, *AD* and *PS* encodings will always have ranges as their domains; consequently, bounds consistency is equivalent to domain consistency for them.

Theorem 3. *Bounds consistency on LG is strictly stronger than bounds consistency on AD.*

Proof. Suppose *LG* is bounds consistent. Consider any AMONG constraint in *AD*. It is not hard to see how, based on the partial sums in *LG*, we can construct support for any value assigned to any variable in this AMONG constraint. To show strictness, consider SEQUENCE $(3, 3, 4, [Y_1, \ldots, Y_6], \{1\})$ with $Y_1, Y_2 \in \{0\}$ and $Y_3, \ldots, Y_6 \in \{0, 1\}$. Enforcing bounds consistency on *LG* fixes $Y_5 = Y_6 = 1$. On the other hand, *AD* is bounds consistent. □

Theorem 4. *Bounds consistency on CS is incomparable to bounds consistency on AD.*

Proof. Consider SEQUENCE $(1, 1, 3, [Y_1, Y_2, Y_3, Y_4], \{1\})$ with $Y_1 \in \{0\}$ and Y_2, Y_3, $Y_4 \in \{0, 1\}$. Now *AD* is bounds consistent. In *CS*, we have $S_0, S_1 \in \{0\}$, $S_2 \in \{0, 1\}$, $S_3, S_4 \in \{1\}$. As S_3 and S_4 are equal, enforcing bounds consistency on *CS* prunes 1 from the domain of Y_4.

Consider SEQUENCE $(1, 2, 2, [Y_1, Y_2, Y_3, Y_4], \{1\})$ with $Y_3 \in \{0\}$ and Y_1, Y_2, $Y_4 \in \{0, 1\}$. In *CS*, we have $S_0 \in \{0\}$, $S_1 \in \{0, 1\}$, $S_2, S_3 \in \{1, 2\}$, $S_4 \in \{2, 3\}$. All constraints in *CS* are bounds consistent. Enforcing bounds consistency on *AD* prunes 0 from the domains of Y_2 and Y_4. □

From the proof of Theorem 4 it follows that bounds consistency on *CS* does not enforce domain consistency on SEQUENCE when SEQUENCE is monotone.

Theorem 5. *Bounds consistency on CS is incomparable with bounds consistency on LG.*

Proof. Consider SEQUENCE $(2, 2, 4, [Y_1, Y_2, Y_3, Y_4, Y_5], \{1\})$ with $Y_1 \in \{1\}$ and Y_2, Y_3, Y_4, $Y_5 \in \{0, 1\}$. All constraints in *LG* are bounds consistent. In *CS*, we have $S_0 \in \{0\}$, $S_1 \in \{1\}$, $S_2, S_3 \in \{1, 2\}$, $S_4 \in \{2\}$, $S_5 \in \{3\}$. As S_4 and S_5 are ground and $S_5 = S_4 + 1$, Enforcing bounds consistency on *CS* fixes $Y_5 = 1$.

Consider SEQUENCE $(2, 3, 3, [Y_1, Y_2, Y_3, Y_4], \{1\})$ with $Y_1 = 1$ and Y_2, Y_3, $Y_4 \in \{0, 1\}$. Now *CS* is bounds consistent. However, enforcing bounds consistency on *LG* prunes 0 from Y_4. □

Recall that singleton bounds consistency on *CS* is equivalent to domain consistency on SEQUENCE. We therefore also consider the effect of singleton consistency on the other encodings where propagation is hindered. Unlike *CS*, singleton bounds consistency on *AD* or *LG* may not prune all possible values.

Theorem 6. *Domain consistency on* SEQUENCE *is strictly stronger than singleton bounds consistency on LG.*

Proof. Consider SEQUENCE $(2, 2, 4, [Y_1, Y_2, Y_3, Y_4, Y_5], \{1\})$ with $Y_1 \in \{1\}$ and Y_2, Y_3, Y_4, $Y_5 \in \{0, 1\}$. Consider $Y_5 = 0$ and the *LG* decomposition. We have $P_{0,1} \in \{1\}$, $P_{0,2}, P_{0,3}, P_{0,4} \in \{0, 1\}$, $P_{0,5} \in \{0\}$, $P_{1,1}, P_{1,2} \in \{1, 2\}$, $P_{1,3}, P_{1,4} \in \{0, 1\}$, $P_{2,1}, P_{2,2} \in \{2\}$. All constraints in *LG* are bounds consistent. Consequently, we do not detect that $Y_5 = 0$ does not have support. □

Theorem 7. *Domain consistency on* SEQUENCE *is strictly stronger than singleton bounds consistency on AD.*

Proof. By transitivity from Theorems 6 and 3. □

We summarise relations among the decompositions in Figure 4.

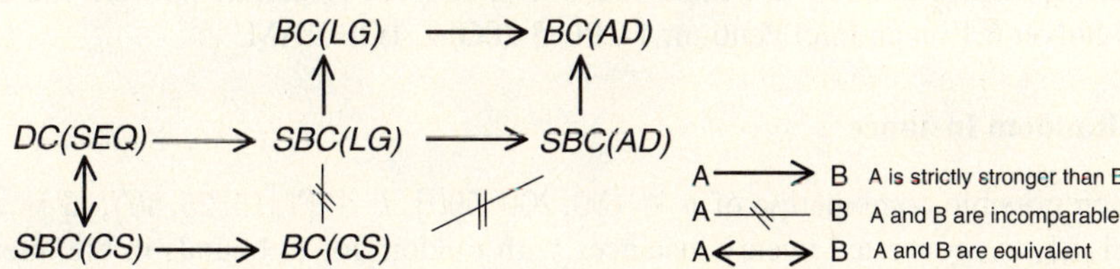

Fig. 4. Relations among decompositions of the SEQUENCE constraint

5 The Multiple SEQUENCE Constraint (*MR*)

We often have multiple SEQUENCE constraints applied to the same sequence of variables. For instance, we might insist that at most 1 in 3 cars have the sun roof option and

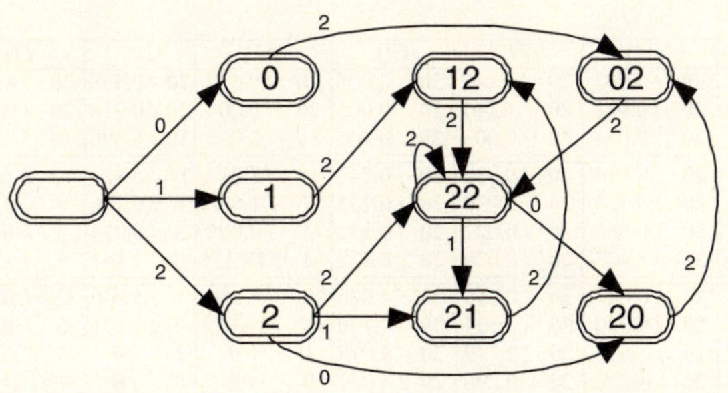

Fig. 5. The automaton for the Multiple SEQUENCE constraint with two SEQUENCEs: SEQUENCE$(0, 1, 2, [X_1, \ldots, X_n], \{1\})$ and SEQUENCE$(2, 3, 3, [X_1, \ldots, X_n], \{2\})$ with $D(X_i) = \{0, 1, 2\}$, for $i \in \{1, \ldots, n\}$

simultaneously that at most 2 in 5 of those cars have electric windows. We propose an encoding for enforcing domain consistency on the conjunction of m such SEQUENCE constraints (we shall refer to this as *MR*). Suppose that the jth such constraint, $j \geq 1$, is SEQUENCE$(l_j, u_j, k_j, [X_1, \ldots, X_n], v_j)$. We suppose that the values being counted are disjoint. We channel into a new sequence of variables Y_i where $Y_i = j$ if $X_i \in v_j$ else $Y_i = 0$. We now construct an automaton whose states record the last $k' - 1$ values used where k' is the largest k_j. Transitions of the automaton ensure that all SEQUENCE constraints are satisfied. Domain consistency can therefore be enforced using the REGULAR constraint in $O(nm^{k'-1})$ time. The automaton for the Multiple SEQUENCE with 2 SEQUENCEs is presented in Figure 5.

6 Experimental Results

To compare performance of the different encodings, we carried out a series of experiments. The first series used randomly generated instances so we could control the parameters precisely. The second series used some nurse rostering benchmarks and car sequencing benchmarks to test more realistic situations. Experiments were run with ILOG Solver 6.1 on an Intel Pentium 4 CPU 3.20Ghz, 1GB RAM.

6.1 Random Instance

For each possible combination of $n \in \{50, 200, 500\}$, $k \in \{7, 15, 25, 50\}$, $\Delta = u - l \in \{1, 5\}$, we generated twenty instances with random lower bounds in the interval $[0, k - \Delta)$. We used a random value and variable ordering and a time-out of 100 sec. Results are given in Tables 1–2.

Instances can be partitioned into two groups. In the first group, $n > 50$ and $\Delta < 3$. On these instances, assignment of one variable has a strong impact on other variables. In the extreme case when $\Delta = 0$ instantiation of one variable assigns on average another n/k variables. So, we expect DC propagators to significantly shrink variable domains

Table 1. Randomly generated instances with a single SEQUENCE constraint and $\Delta = 1$. Number of instances solved in 100 sec / average time to solve.

n	k	*PS*	*HPRS*	*CD*	*AD*	GSC	*LG*	*CS*
50	7	**20** / 0.003	**20** / **0.002**	**20** / 0.005	**20** / 0.133	**20** / 0.538	**20** / 0.044	**20** / **0.002**
	15	**20** / 0.023	**20** / **0.001**	**20** / 0.005	**20** / 0.004	**20** / 0.018	**20** / 0.003	**20** / **0.001**
	25	**20** / 0.094	**20** / 0.003	**20** / 0.005	19 / 0.066	19 / 0.396	19 / 0.034	**20** / **0.001**
200	7	**20** / 0.016	**20** / 0.030	**20** / 0.242	15 / 2.517	14 / 5.423	17 / **0.003**	**20** / 0.020
	15	**20** / 0.120	**20** / 0.030	**20** / 0.235	7 / 1.850	6 / 0.106	9 / 0.083	**20** / **0.016**
	25	**20** / 0.661	**20** / 0.027	**20** / 0.235	3 / 0.005	3 / 0.039	3 / **0.004**	**20** / 0.016
	50	**20** / 5.423	**20** / 0.028	**20** / 0.232	4 / 18.255	3 / 1.361	6 / 5.926	**20** / **0.014**
500	7	**20** / 0.043	**20** / 0.336	**20** / 4.086	9 / 6.756	8 / 1.046	13 / **0.009**	**20** / 0.150
	15	**20** / 0.320	**20** / 0.334	**20** / 4.130	4 / 13.442	3 / 0.121	6 / **0.012**	**20** / 0.100
	25	**20** / 1.816	**20** / 0.279	**20** / 4.017	1 / **0**	1 / **0**	3 / 0.013	**20** / 0.085
	50	**20** / 16.762	**20** / 0.290	**20** / 4.032	0 / **0**	0 / **0**	2 / 11.847	**20** / 0.086
	TOTALS							
	solved/total	**220** /220	**220** /220	**220** /220	102 /220	97 /220	118 /220	**220** /220
	avg time for solved	2.298	0.124	1.566	2.376	1.115	0.524	**0.045**
	avg bt for solved	**0**	**0**	**0**	42830	4319	3239	33

Table 2. Randomly generated instances with a single SEQUENCE constraint and $\Delta = 5$. Number of instances solved in 100 sec / average time to solve.

n	k	*PS*	*HPRS*	*CD*	*AD*	GSC	*LG*	*CS*
50	7	**20** / 0.004	**20** / **0.001**	**20** / 0.005	**20** / **0.001**	**20** / 0.003	**20** / 0.002	**20** / 0.002
	15	**20** / 0.025	**20** / **0.001**	**20** / 0.006	**20** / **0.001**	**20** / 0.005	**20** / **0.001**	**20** / 0.002
	25	**20** / 0.100	**20** / **0.001**	**20** / 0.006	**20** / **0.001**	**20** / 0.008	**20** / 0.002	**20** / 0.002
200	7	**20** / 0.016	**20** / 0.020	**20** / 0.262	**20** / **0.003**	**20** / 0.017	**20** / 0.005	**20** / 0.024
	15	**20** / 0.133	**20** / 0.031	**20** / 0.251	**20** / **0.005**	**20** / 0.026	**20** / 0.005	**20** / 0.028
	25	**20** / 0.665	**20** / 0.030	**20** / 0.242	**20** / 0.007	**20** / 0.038	**20** / **0.006**	**20** / 0.020
	50	**20** / 5.538	**20** / 0.039	**20** / 0.242	**20** / 0.012	**20** / 0.073	**20** / **0.010**	**20** / 0.019
500	7	**20** / 0.047	**20** / 0.195	**20** / 4.362	**20** / **0.012**	**20** / 0.085	**20** / 0.012	**20** / 0.154
	15	**20** / 0.358	**20** / 0.383	**20** / 4.183	**20** / **0.015**	**20** / 0.119	**20** / 0.017	**20** / 0.235
	25	**20** / 1.786	**20** / 0.411	**20** / 4.127	**20** / **0.019**	**20** / 0.146	**20** / 0.021	**20** / 0.201
	50	**20** / 17.016	**20** / 0.342	**20** / 4.077	11 / 0.034	11 / 0.298	12 / **0.033**	**20** / 0.120
	TOTALS							
	solved/total	**220** /220	**220** /220	**220** /220	211 /220	211 /220	212 /220	**220** /220
	avg time for solved	2.335	0.132	1.615	**0.009**	0.065	**0.009**	0.073
	avg bt for solved	**0**	**0**	**0**	2	2	1	19

and reduce the search tree. As can be seen from Table 1, DC propagators outperform non-DC propagators. Surprisingly, *CS* has the best time of all combinations and solved all instances. Whilst it takes more backtracks compared to the DC propagators which solve problems without search, it is much faster. The *CD* algorithm is an order of magnitude slower compared to the *HPRS* propagator but in the current implementation we use incremental all-pairs shortest path algorithms, rather than the single-source shortest path algorithms of [10]. The *PS* algorithm is much slower compared to other DC algorithms and its relative performance decays for larger k.

In the second group, $n \leq 50$ or $\Delta \geq 3$. On these instances, assignment of a variable does not have a big influence on other variables. The overhead of using DC propagators to achieve better pruning outweighs the reduction in the search space. The clear winner in this case are those propagators that do not achieve DC. When $k < 25$ *AD* is best. When k gets larger, *LG* solves more instances and is faster.

6.2 Nurse Rostering Problems

Instances come from `www.projectmanagement.ugent.be/nsp.php`. For each day in the scheduling period, a nurse is assigned to a day, evening, or night shift or takes a day off. The original benchmarks specify minimal required staff allocation for each shift and individual preferences for each nurse. We ignore these preference and replace them with a set of constraints that model common workload restrictions for all nurses. The basic model includes the following three constraints: each shift has a minimum required number of nurses, each nurse should have at least 12 hours of break between 2 shifts, each nurse should have at least two consecutive days on any shift. Each model was run on 50 instances. The scheduling period is 14 days. The number of nurses in each instance was set to the maximal number of nurses required for any day over the period of 14 days. The time limit for all instances was 100 sec. For variable ordering, we branched on the smallest domain. Table 3 gives results for those instances that were solved by each propagator. In these experiments $n < 50$. As expected from the random experiments, the *AD* decomposition outperforms all other decompositions.

Table 3. Models of the nurse rostering problem using the SEQUENCE constraint. Number of instances solved in 100 sec / average time to solve.

SEQUENCE	*PS*	*LO*	*HPRS*	*CD*	*AD*	GSC	*LG*	*CS*
$(1,3,3,\{O\})$	**43** / 0.47	**43** / 0.64	**43** / 0.54	**43** / 0.63	**43** / **0.45**	**43** / 0.60	**43** / **0.45**	39 / 2.49
$(3,5,5,\{O\})$	**44** / 2.43	**44** / 2.11	**44** / 2.28	**44** / 2.61	**44** / **1.84**	**44** / 2.84	**44** / 1.87	40 / 3.53
$(2,2,5,\{O\})$	39 / 5.41	39 / **4.76**	**40** / 7.41	38 / 4.97	36 / 7.50	35 / 7.73	36 / 8.56	36 / 5.36
$(2,2,7,\{O\})$	**23** / 9.09	**23** / 7.92	**23** / 5.64	**23** / 7.50	22 / 11.16	22 / 18.21	22 / 11.66	**23** / **4.53**
$(2,3,5,\{O\})$	26 / 4.65	26 / 4.92	**27** / 6.77	26 / **3.91**	**27** / 5.47	26 / 4.27	**27** / 5.81	26 / 5.77
$(2,5,7,\{O\})$	22 / 3.45	**23** / 6.90	22 / 2.22	22 / 2.43	**23** / 6.06	22 / 3.28	22 / **2.10**	22 / 2.28
$(1,3,4,\{O\})$	**27** / 7.02	26 / 5.25	**27** / 6.75	26 / **4.35**	**27** / 5.80	26 / 4.69	**27** / 6.05	25 / 6.18
TOTALS								
solved/total	224 /350	224 /350	**226** /350	222 /350	222 /350	218 /350	221 /350	211 /350
avg time for solved	4.169	4.068	4.263	**3.475**	4.776	5.170	4.676	4.218
avg bt for solved	11045	9905	13804	**8017**	20063	12939	18715	17747

The only exception are instances with $\Delta = 0$ and non-DC propagators lose to DC algorithms and the *CS* decomposition.

6.3 Car Sequencing Problems

In this series of experiments we used car sequencing problems benchmarks. All instances are taken from CSPLib (the first set of benchmarks). We used the car sequencing model from the Ilog distribution as the basic model and added each encoding as a redundant constraint to this model. The time limit for all instances was 100 sec. All SEQUENCE constraints in these benchmarks are monotone. Hence, GSC enforces DC on the SEQUENCE part of it, and an introduction of redundant constraints does not give extra pruning. As Table 4 shows, the basic model gives the best performance.

Table 4. The Car Sequencing Problem. Number of instances solved in 100 sec / average time to solve.

	The basic model from the Ilog distribution +							
	PS	*LO*	*HPRS*	*CD*	*AD*		*LG*	*CS*
CarSequencing	**36** / 8.21	**36** / 8.26	35 / 7.59	34 / 7.85	**36** / 8.15	**36** / 7.95	**36** / 8.10	35 / **5.91**
TOTALS								
solved/total	**36** /78	**36** /78	35 /78	34 /78	**36** /78	**36** /78	**36** /78	35 /78
avg time for solved	8.21	8.26	7.59	7.85	8.15	7.95	8.10	**5.91**
avg bt for solved	518	518	265	**211**	518	518	518	265

6.4 Multiple SEQUENCE Constraints

We also evaluated performance of the different propagators on problems with multiple SEQUENCE constraints. We again used randomly generated instances and nurse rostering problems. For each possible combination of $n \in \{50, 100\}$, $k \in \{5, 7\}$, $\Delta = 1$, we generated twenty random instances with four SEQUENCE constraints. All variables had domains of size 5. An instance was obtained by selecting random lower bounds in the interval $[0, k - \Delta]$. We excluded instances where $\sum_{i=1}^{m} l_i \geq k$ to avoid unsatisfiable instances. We used a random variable and value ordering and a time-out of 100 sec. All SEQUENCE constraints were enforced on disjoint sets of cardinality one.

Experimental results are given in Table 5. The Multiple SEQUENCE propagator significantly outperforms other propagators in both the time to find a valid sequence and

Table 5. Randomly generated instances with 4 SEQUENCE constraints and $\Delta = 1$. Number of instances solved in 100 sec / average time to solve.

n	k	*MR*	*PS*	*LO*	*HPRS*	*CD*	*AD*	GSC	*LG*	*CS*
50	5	**20** / 0.05	6 / 12.58	6 / 17.03	5 / 0.81	5 / 4.76	6 / 13.75	5 / 10.59	7 / 15.05	0 / **0**
	7	**20** / 0.86	6 / 20.85	6 / 16.89	7 / 23.99	4 / **0.15**	6 / 14.02	5 / 15.90	8 / 26.81	2 / 5.80
100	5	**20** / 0.11	0 / **0**	0 / **0**	0 / **0**	0 / **0**	0 / **0**	0 / **0**	0 / **0**	0 / **0**
	7	**20** / 1.83	2 / 8.98	2 / 7.52	2 / 10.48	1 / **0**	1 / **0**	1 / **0**	1 / **0**	0 / **0**
TOTALS										
solved/total		**80** /80	14 /80	14 /80	14 /80	10 /80	13 /80	11 /80	16 /80	2 /80
avg time for solved		**0.71**	15.61	15.61	13.78	2.44	12.81	12.04	19.99	5.80
avg bt for solved		**0**	72078	72078	64579	2214	185747	51413	257831	106008

Table 6. Models of the nurse rostering problem using the SEQUENCE constraint. Number of instances solved in 100 sec / average time to solve.

	MR	*PS*	*LO*	*HPRS*	*CD*	*AD*	GSC	*LG*	*CS*
Model 1	**9** / 10.62	4 / 12.61	4 / 14.78	4 / 7.38	4 / 19.00	4 / 6.41	4 / 16.87	4 / **5.58**	4 / 5.64
Model 2	**8** / 1.40	4 / 0.08	4 / 0.11	4 / **0.04**	4 / 0.06	4 / **0.04**	4 / 0.08	4 / **0.04**	4 / **0.04**
TOTALS									
solved/total	**17** /100	8 /100	8 /100	8 /100	8 /100	8 /100	8 /100	8 /100	8 /100
avg time for solved	6.28	6.35	7.45	3.71	9.53	3.22	8.47	**2.81**	2.84
avg bt for solved	**3470**	30696	30696	30696	30696	30232	30232	30430	30749

the number of solved instances. For bigger values of n, the Multiple SEQUENCE propagator is the only one able to solve all instances. However, due to its space complexity, to use this propagator, k and m need to be relatively small and $n < 100$.

In the second series of experiments we used nurse scheduling benchmarks. We removed the last constraint from the basic model described in the previous section and added two sets of non-monotone SEQUENCE constraints to give two different models. In the first model, each nurse has to work 1 or 2 night shifts in 7 consecutive days, 1 or 2 evening shifts, 1 to 5 day shifts and 2 to 5 days-off. In the second model, each nurse has to work 1 or 2 night shifts in 7 consecutive days, and has 1 or 2 days off in 5 days. In order to test the performance of the Multiple SEQUENCE constraint on large problems, we built a schedule over a 28 days period. The number of nurses was equal to the maximum number of nurses required for any day over the period multiplied by 1.5. The total number of variables in an instance is about 500. Table 6 shows the number of instances solved by each propagator. The Multiple SEQUENCE propagator again solved the most instances.

7 Conclusion

The SEQUENCE constraint is useful in modelling a range of rostering, scheduling and car sequencing problems. We proved that down a branch of a search tree domain consistency can be enforced on the SEQUENCE constraint in just $O(n^2 \log n)$ time. This improves upon the previous bound of $O(n^3)$ for each call down the branch [6]. To propagate the SEQUENCE constraint, we introduced half a dozen new encodings, some of which do not hinder propagation. We also considered a generalization of SEQUENCE constraint – the Multiple SEQUENCE constraint. Our experiments suggest that, on very large and tight problems, the existing domain consistency algorithm is best. However, on smaller or looser problems, much simpler encodings are better, even though these encodings hinder propagation. When there are multiple SEQUENCE constraints, especially when we are forcing values to occur, a more expensive propagator shows promise.

This study raises a number of questions. For example, what other global constraints can be efficiently and effectively propagated using simple encodings? As a second example, can we design heuristics to choose an effective encoding automatically?

Acknowledgements

We would like to thank Willem-Jan van Hoeve for providing us with the implementation of the *HPRS* algorithm, as well as the reviewers for useful feedback.

References

1. Pesant, G.: A regular language membership constraint for finite sequences of variables. In: Wallace, M. (ed.) CP 2004. LNCS, vol. 3258, pp. 482–495. Springer, Heidelberg (2004)
2. Quimper, C.G., Walsh, T.: Global grammar constraints. [11], pp. 751–755
3. Beldiceanu, N., Contejean, E.: Introducing global constraints in CHIP. Mathematical and Computer Modelling 12, 97–123 (1994)
4. Debruyne, R., Bessière, C.: Some practicable filtering techniques for the constraint satisfaction problem. In: 15th Int. Joint Conf. on Artificial Intelligence (IJCAI'97), pp. 412–417. Morgan Kaufmann, San Francisco (1997)
5. Bessière, C., Hebrard, E., Hnich, B., Kiziltan, Z., Walsh, T.: The SLIDE-meta constraint. Technical report (2007)
6. van Hoeve, W.J., Pesant, G., Rousseau, L.M., Sabharwal, A.: Revisiting the Sequence constraint. [11], pp. 620–634
7. Régin, J.C., Puget, J.F.: A filtering algorithm for global sequencing constraints. In: Smolka, G. (ed.) Principles and Practice of Constraint Programming - CP97. LNCS, vol. 1330, pp. 32–46. Springer, Heidelberg (1997)
8. Beldiceanu, N., Carlsson, M.: Revisiting the cardinality operator and introducing the cardinality-path constraint family. In: Codognet, P. (ed.) ICLP 2001. LNCS, vol. 2237, pp. 59–73. Springer, Heidelberg (2001)
9. Régin, J.C.: Combination of Among and Cardinality constraints. In: Barták, R., Milano, M. (eds.) CPAIOR 2005. LNCS, vol. 3524, pp. 288–303. Springer, Heidelberg (2005)
10. Cotton, S., Maler, O.: Fast and flexible difference constraint propagation for DPLL(T). In: Biere, A., Gomes, C.P. (eds.) SAT 2006. LNCS, vol. 4121, pp. 170–183. Springer, Heidelberg (2006)
11. Benhamou, F. (ed.): CP 2006. LNCS, vol. 4204. Springer, Heidelberg (2006)

On Inconsistent Clause-Subsets for Max-SAT Solving*

Sylvain Darras, Gilles Dequen, Laure Devendeville, and Chu-Min Li

LaRIA, FRE 2733 – Université de Picardie Jules Verne
33, Rue St-Leu, 80039 Amiens Cedex 01, France
{sylvain.darras,gilles.dequen,laure.devendeville,
chu-min.li}@u-picardie.fr

Abstract. Recent research has focused on using the power of look-ahead to speed up the resolution of the Max-SAT problem. Indeed, look-ahead techniques such as Unit Propagation (UP) allow to find conflicts and to quickly reach the upper bound in a Branch-and-Bound algorithm, reducing the search-space of the resolution. In previous works, the Max-SAT solvers $maxsatz9$ and $maxsatz14$ use unit propagation to compute, at each node of the branch and bound search-tree, disjoint inconsistent subsets of clauses in the current subformula to estimate the minimum number of clauses that cannot be satisfied by any assignment extended from the current node. The same subsets may still be present in the sub-trees, that is why we present in this paper a new method to memorize them and then spare their recomputation time. Furthermore, we propose a heuristic so that the memorized subsets of clauses induce an ordering among unit clauses to detect more inconsistent subsets of clauses. We show that this new approach improves $maxsatz9$ and $maxsatz14$ and suggest that the approach can also be used to improve other state-of-the-art Max-SAT solvers.

Keywords: Max-SAT, Unit Propagation, Inconsistent Subset.

1 Introduction

The Max-SAT (short for Maximum Satisfiability) problem is to find an assignment of logical values to the variables of a propositional formula expressed in terms of a conjunction of clauses (i.e. disjunction of literals) that satisfies the maximum number of clauses. This optimization problem is a generalization of the Satisfiability Decision problem. During the last decade, the interest in studying Max-SAT has grown significantly. These works highlight Max-SAT implications in real problems, as diverse as scheduling [1], routing [2], bioinformatics [3], ..., motivating considerable progresses concerning efficient Max-SAT solving based on the Branch-and-Bound (BnB) scheme.

The almost common characteristic of the successive progresses for the BnB scheme is to propose new ways of computing the Lower Bound (LB). Given a Max-SAT instance Σ, the BnB algorithm implicitly enumerates the search-space of all possible assignments using a binary search-tree. At every node, BnB compares the Upper Bound (UB), which is the minimum number of conflict clauses in Σ obtained so far for a complete assignment, with LB which is an underestimation of the minimum number of conflict clauses of Σ by any complete assignment obtained by extending the partial assignment at the current node. If $LB \geq UB$, the algorithm prunes the subtree below

* This work was partially supported by Région Champagne-Ardennes.

C. Bessiere (Ed.): CP 2007, LNCS 4741, pp. 225–240, 2007.

the current node, since a better solution cannot be obtained from the current node. In previous works, the quality of LB was improved of several manners. Thus, [4,5,6] define new inference rules based on special cases of resolution that are able to outperform state-of-the-art solvers [7,8]. In addition, another way to improve LB is to make an intensive use of unit propagation with look-ahead techniques at each node of the BnB algorithm in order to find disjoint inconsistent clause-subsets (named ICS in the following) [9,10]. These inconsistent cores of clauses allow LB to quickly equal or exceed UB and to decrease the mean-size of the BnB search-tree. However, some characteristics as the mean number of clauses belonging to these cores influence on the quality of LB and consequently on the efficiency of the BnB algorithm. Moreover, the detection of these disjoint inconsistent clause-subsets is not incremental in [9,10]. In other words, a number of inconsistent clause-subsets detected at a node are detected over and again in the two subtrees of the node.

In this paper, we focus on the study of the characteristics of the inconsistent clause-subsets and their influence on the lower bound quality. After presenting some preliminaries, we study structures and characteristics of inconsistent clause-subsets and propose a heuristic to estimate the usefulness of a given inconsistent subset of clauses in LB calculus. We then describe our heuristic-based approach to improve LB and to make the LB calculus more incremental. This approach is applied to the Max-SAT solvers $maxsatz9$ [10] and $maxsatz14$ [4], and experimental results on random and Max-Cut instances where some are from the 2007 Max-SAT evaluation[1] show that our approach significantly improves $maxsatz9$ and $maxsatz14$.

2 Preliminaries

A *CNF-formula* (Conjunctive Normal Form formula) Σ is a conjunction of clauses where each clause is a disjunction of literals. A literal is the (positively or negatively) signed form of a boolean variable. An *interpretation* of Σ is an assignment over the truth values space $\{True, False\}$ to its variables. It is a partial interpretation if only a subset of the variables of Σ are assigned. A positive (resp. negative) literal is satisfied if the corresponding variable has the value $True$ (resp. $False$). A clause is satisfied if at least one of its literals is satisfied. Σ is satisfied according to an interpretation if all its clauses are satisfied. The Max-SAT problem is to find an assignment which minimizes the number of falsified clauses of Σ. This optimization problem is a generalization of the Satisfiability decision problem which is to determine whether a satisfying assignment of all clauses of Σ exists or not.

In this paper, each further reference of *formula* means *CNF-formula*. Moreover, a conjunction of clauses $c_1 \wedge c_2 \wedge ... \wedge c_m$ is simply represented by a set of clauses $\{c_1, c_2, \ldots, c_m\}$. We denote k-*cl* a clause which contains exactly k literals. The 1-*cl* and 2-*cl* clause may be respectively named *unit* and *binary* clause. A k-SAT formula is a formula which exclusively consists of k-*cl*. An empty clause contains no literal; it represents a conflict since it cannot be satisfied. When one literal l is assigned to $True$, applying

one-literal rule consists in satisfying all clauses containing l (i.e. removing them from the formula) and removing all $\neg l$ from all remaining clauses. The *Unit Propagation* (denoted UP) is the iterative process which consists in applying one-literal rule to each

[1] `http://www.maxsat07.udl.es/`

literal appearing in at least one unit clause. This process continues until all unit clauses disappear from Σ or an empty clause is derived.

We focus our work on complete Max-SAT solvers which are based on a BnB algorithm. This class of solvers actually provides the best performances on Max-SAT solving[2]. Given Σ, these solvers implicitly enumerate the whole search-space of the formula by constructing a depth-first search-tree. At every node, they use two important values: UB, the minimum number of conflict clauses in Σ obtained so far for a complete assignment, and LB, an underestimation of the minimum number of conflict clauses of Σ by any complete assignment extending the partial assignment at the current node. If $LB < UB$, the current partial assignment is extended by choosing a decision variable x, which is successively set to $True$ and $False$ in order to split the current sub-formula into two new simplified ones using the one-literal rule, the process being recursively continued from each of the two new formulas. If $LB \geq UB$ the solvers prune the subtree under the current node, since all complete assignments extending the current partial assignment are worse than the best one found so far. The solution of a BnB solver is the assignment with the minimum UB after enumerating all assignments.

As it allows to prune subtrees, LB is essential in efficient Max-SAT solving. In [11], LB is defined as follows:

$$LB(\Sigma_A) = \#Empty(\Sigma_A) + \sum_{x \in \Sigma_A} \min(\#Unit(x, \Sigma_A), \#Unit(\neg x, \Sigma_A)) \quad (1)$$

where $\#S$ is the number of elements of the set S, Σ_A is the current state of a formula Σ according to a partial assignment A, $Empty(\Sigma_A)$ is the set of empty clauses of Σ_A, and $Unit(lit, \Sigma_A)$ is the set of unit clauses containing the literal lit. Many works have extended this estimation. The equation 1 can be generalized to:

$$LB(\Sigma_A) = \#Empty(\Sigma_A) + \#ICS(\Sigma_A) \quad (2)$$

where $ICS(\Sigma_A)$ is a set of disjoint inconsistent clause-subsets from the formula Σ_A. Subsets of the form $\{x, \neg x\}$, $x \in \Sigma_A$ are included in $ICS(\Sigma_A)$. Thanks to binary clauses using the Directional Arc Consistency notion (DAC) defined in [12] for Max-CSP, [13,14] have improved the LB computation.

More recently, the equation 2 has led to new rules:

1. The Star rule ([15,16]) consists in searching inconsistent cores of clauses of the form $\{l_1, ..., l_k, \neg l_1 \vee ... \vee \neg l_k\}$.
2. The UP-rule [9] detects inconsistent clause-subsets in Σ_A using unit propagation. The detection can be described as follows. Let Σ_{A1} be a copy of Σ_A. Unit propagation repeatedly applies one-literal rule to simplify Σ_{A1} until there is no more unit clause or an empty clause is derived. If an empty clause is derived, let S be the set of clauses used to derive the empty clause. Then S is an inconsistent subset of clauses, i.e., all clauses in S cannot simultaneously be satisfied by any assignment. For example, let us consider the following set of clauses of a formula Σ_1:

$$\Sigma_1 = \left\{ \begin{array}{lll} c_1 : x_1 & c_4 : \neg x_2 \vee \neg x_4 & c_7 : \neg x_4 \vee x_6 \\ c_2 : \neg x_1 \vee x_2 & c_5 : \neg x_1 \vee \neg x_3 \vee x_4 & \\ c_3 : \neg x_1 \vee \neg x_2 \vee x_3 & c_6 : \neg x_1 \vee x_5 & \end{array} \right\}$$

[2] see http://www.iiia.csic.es/~maxsat06/

Following the UP process, x_1 has to be $True$, c_2 and c_6 become unit clauses, and so on. Finally, c_5 is empty and the set $S = \{c_1, c_2, c_3, c_4, c_5\}$ is an inconsistent subset of clauses.

The detection of other disjoint inconsistent subformula continues, after excluding the clauses of S, until no more empty clause can be derived. LB is then the number of empty clauses in Σ_A plus the total number of disjoint inconsistent subsets of clauses detected.

3. The failed literals technique [10] (denoted UP^*_{FL}) is an extension of UP-rule. After applying UP-rule to Σ_A to detect disjoint subsets of clauses, it detects additional disjoint inconsistent subsets of clauses by finding failed literals after excluding the inconsistent subsets of clauses already found from Σ_A. This detection can be illustrated as follows. If unit propagation in $\Sigma_A \cup \{x\}$ and unit propagation in $\Sigma_A \cup \{\neg x\}$ both lead to a conflict then clauses in Σ_A implying the two contradictions constitute an inconsistent subset.

The UP^*_{FL} heuristic has been proved much more effective in $maxsatz9$ [10] and $maxsatz14$ [4] than previous state-of-the-art lower bounds. However, the LB calculus based on UP^*_{FL} in $maxsatz9$ and $maxsatz14$ is not incremental (in $maxsatz14$, an incremental part of the LB is computed by $inference\ rules$; we mention them in section 5.2) . When LB is still less than UB, the solver should extend the current partial assignment i.e., the solver should branch. Before branching to a new node, all the inconsistent clauses-subset are erased. The new node does not inherit neither the inconsistent clause-subsets detection of its parent, nor the information of these inconsistent clause-subsets such as their size. The UP^*_{FL} function is entirely re-executed at the new node.

The aim of our work is to enable a search-tree node to inherit some inconsistent clause-subsets of its parent, which avoids the entire re-execution of the UP^*_{FL} function and could improve the quality of LB.

3 Improving UP^*_{FL}

The purpose of UP^*_{FL} is to detect as many inconsistent clause-subsets as possible in a formula. Since an inconsistent subset of clauses has to be excluded before detecting other inconsistent subsets of clauses, UP^*_{FL} should detect small enough inconsistent subsets of clauses, leaving more clauses in the formula to facilitate the detection of other inconsistent subsets of clauses. UP^*_{FL} uses a heuristic on the ordering of unit clauses during unit propagation to detect small inconsistent clause-subsets, but when there are several unit clauses in the formula, it selects one in an undetermined ordering to start an unit propagation. However, we believe that the number of inconsistent subsets detected by UP^*_{FL} is strongly correlated to the ordering of initial unit clauses. Moreover, as we noticed above, UP^*_{FL} recomputes the whole inconsistent subset detection in every node of a search-tree, which is time-consuming.

For example, let Σ_2 be the following set of clauses

$$\Sigma_2 = \left\{ \begin{array}{llll} c_1 : x_1 & c_5 : \neg x_3 \vee x_5 & c_9 : \neg x_6 \vee x_4 & c_{13} : \neg x_8 \vee x_9 \\ c_2 : \neg x_1 \vee x_2 & c_6 : \neg x_4 \vee \neg x_5 & c_{10} : \neg x_6 \vee x_5 & c_{14} : \neg x_8 \vee x_{10} \\ c_3 : \neg x_2 \vee x_3 & c_7 : \neg x_9 \vee \neg x_{10} & c_{11} : \neg x_3 \vee x_7 & \\ c_4 : \neg x_3 \vee x_4 & c_8 : x_6 & c_{12} : \neg x_7 \vee x_8 & \end{array} \right\}$$

1. *unit clause ordering in UP^*_{FL} detection.*
   - UP^*_{FL} first calls *UP-rule* detection. Following the empirical UP^*_{FL} techniques of the $maxsatz$ solver, c_1 is propagated first, then new unit clauses produced during the unit propagation are stored in a queue and propagated in a first in first out ordering. Thus, the UP-rule first assigns $x_1 = True$ through the clause c_1. The variables $x_2 = True$, $x_3 = True$, $x_4 = True$, $x_5 = True$, and $x_7 = True$, through c_1, c_2, c_3, c_4, c_5, c_{11} respectively. We then get an empty clause c_6 and the inconsistent subset of clauses S is equal to $\{c_1, c_2, c_3, c_4, c_5, c_6\}$. Only clauses $\{c_7, c_8, c_9, c_{10}, c_{11}, c_{12}, c_{13}, c_{14}\}$ can participate in finding other inconsistent clause-subsets. However, while propagating c_8, the UP-rule assigns $x_6 = True$, $x_4 = True$, $x_5 = True$ through c_8, c_9, c_{10}, respectively, no more conflict is found.
   - Consider now another ordering of the unit clauses in Σ_2 that propagates first c_8. The following assignments are then performed: $x_6 = True$, $x_4 = True$, and $x_5 = True$ through c_8, c_9, and c_{10}, respectively. We encounter an empty clause c_6. The associated inconsistent subset of clauses is $S' = \{c_6, c_8, c_9, c_{10}\}$. The candidates clauses belonging to other inconsistent clause-subsets are then $\{c_1, c_2, c_3, c_4, c_5, c_7, c_{11}, c_{12}, c_{13}, c_{14}\}$. We then propagate c_1, $x_1 = True$, $x_2 = True$, $x_3 = True$, $x_4 = True$, $x_5 = True$, $x_7 = True$, $x_8 = True$, $x_9 = True$, and $x_{10} = True$ through c_1, c_2, c_3, c_4, c_5, c_{11}, c_{12}, c_{13}, and c_{14}, respectively. As c_7 is now empty, a second and disjoint inconsistent clause-subset $S'' = \{c_1, c_2, c_3, c_7, c_{11}, c_{12}, c_{13}, c_{14}\}$ is obtained.
2. *Re-computation of inconsistent clause-subsets.*
   Let us consider now the same subformula Σ_2 and assuming that the next decision variable chosen by the solver does not belong to $\{x_1, x_2, x_3, x_4, x_5, x_6, x_7, x_8, x_9, x_{10}\}$. Σ_2 is unchanged. UP^*_{FL} probably finds the same conflicts, so the re-computation could be avoided if the inconsistent clause-subsets of the parent node were memorized.

Within a practical framework, we propose a method to solve totally or partially the UP^*_{FL} weaknesses mentioned above. The idea is to memorize the small inconsistent subsets of clauses computed at a given node and maintain them for all the corresponding subtrees. This allows to avoid costly re-detection of inconsistent subsets and induce a natural ordering UP^*_{FL} detection. Indeed, storing (small) inconsistent subsets of clauses is equivalent to grant a privilege to the variables which minimize the number of clauses to detect a conflict. We could just store a sorted list of variables, which would give us the same "good" conflictual clause subsets at each node than if we had memorized these sets: it draws a variable ordering. Thus, the goal of our approach is double:

- Inconsistent subsets of clauses stored at a node of the search-tree will not be re-computed at the child-nodes. These subsets are directly added to LB. Once a small inconsistent subset is found, the solver does not spend time to detect it again.
- Since we will empirically determine "interesting" inconsistent clause-subsets, UP^*_{FL} begins its computation in the child-nodes with the stored interesting subsets. In addition to the advantage that these interesting inconsistent clause-subsets are given without specific detection, they induce a natural ordering of unit clauses for detecting small inconsistent subsets of clauses so as to improve LB.

For example, let Σ_3 be the following set of clauses

$$\Sigma_3 = \left\{ \begin{array}{llll} c_1 : x_1 & c_5 : \neg x_3 \vee x_5 & c_9 : \neg x_6 \vee x_4 & c_{13} : \neg x_8 \vee x_9 \\ c_2 : \neg x_1 \vee x_2 & c_6 : \neg x_4 \vee \neg x_5 & c_{10} : \neg x_6 \vee x_5 & c_{14} : \neg x_8 \vee x_{10} \\ c_3 : \neg x_2 \vee x_3 \vee x_{11} & c_7 : \neg x_9 \vee \neg x_{10} & c_{11} : \neg x_3 \vee x_7 & \\ c_4 : \neg x_3 \vee x_4 & c_8 : x_6 & c_{12} : \neg x_7 \vee x_8 & \end{array} \right\}$$

Propagating c_1, UP^*_{FL} does not find any empty clause. Propagating c_8, UP^*_{FL} finds an inconsistent subset $S' = \{c_6, c_8, c_9, c_{10}\}$ as for Σ_2 in the previous example, which we store. After branching next on x_{11} and assigning $False$ to x_{11}, Σ_3 becomes Σ_2. Without the storage of S', UP^*_{FL} propagates c_1 and finds an unique inconsistent clause-subsets S=$\{c_1, c_2, c_3, c_4, c_5, c_6\}$ as in the previous example, since after the clauses in S are removed from Σ_2, no more conflict is found using unit propagation.

However, with the storage of the inconsistent subset $S' = \{c_6, c_8, c_9, c_{10}\}$, after branching next on x_{11} and assigning $False$ to x_{11}, S' is first counted in LB and its clauses are excluded in the conflict detection. UP^*_{FL} naturally detects the second inconsistent subset $S'' = \{c_1, c_2, c_3, c_7, c_{11}, c_{12}, c_{13}, c_{14}\}$.

The above example shows that by memorizing small inconsistent subsets of clauses and "forget" large ones, we are able to detect more inconsistent subsets of clauses.

4 Clause Sets Storage

We have seen in the previous section that the storage of inconsistent subsets of clauses and their reuse are helpful. We should now answer two questions: (i) should we memorize all inconsistent subsets of clauses for child-nodes? (ii) if not, what are inconsistent subsets of clauses that should be stored? For this purpose, we should analyze the impact of branching on a variable.

Let us consider an inconsistent subset $S_k = \{c_{k_1}, c_{k_2}, ..., c_{k_n}\}$ found at a node of the search-tree by UP^*_{FL}. Note that S_k is a minimal inconsistent subset of clauses in the sense that it becomes consistent if any clause is removed from it, meaning that any literal in S_k should also have its negated literal in S_k. Let x be the next branching variable. We can distinguish three cases:

1. *Variable x appears in clauses of S_k.*
   In this case, the literals x and $\neg x$ belong to S_k. S_k has no meaning anymore after branching because it contains satisfied clauses, and S_k remains inconsistent but is not probably minimal anymore. We should then find the minimal inconsistent subset of S_k and allow other clauses of S_k to be used in the detection of other conflicts.

   To illustrate this case, let us consider the following inconsistent clause subset:

$$S_k = \left\{ \begin{array}{lll} c_1 : \neg x \vee y & c_3 : \neg y \vee \neg z & c_5 : \neg z \vee t \\ c_2 : \neg y \vee z & c_4 : x \vee z & c_6 : \neg z \vee \neg t \end{array} \right\}$$

   On the one hand, when x is set to $True$, the clause c_4 is then satisfied. The subset of clauses $\{y, \neg y \vee z, \neg y \vee \neg z\}$ from c_1, c_2 and c_3 is inconsistent. This allows the set of clauses $\mathcal{R} = \{\neg z \vee t, \neg z \vee \neg t\}$ from c_5 and c_6 to take part of other conflictual sets. On the other hand, when x is set to $False$, the subset of clauses $\{z, \neg z \vee t, \neg z \vee \neg t\}$ from c_4, c_5 and c_6 is inconsistent and $\mathcal{R} = \{\neg y \vee z, \neg y \vee \neg z\}$ from c_2 and c_3 can be used to detect other conflicts.

2. *Variable x does not appear in clauses of the S_k, but some of the clauses shortened by the assignment of x form a smaller inconsistent subset S'_k using some clauses of S_k.*

   S'_k and S_k are inconsistent but not disjoint. Only one of S'_k and S_k can contribute to increase LB. It would be more useful to keep S'_k instead of S_k.
   For example, consider the inconsistent clause-subset S_k such as:

$$S_k = \begin{Bmatrix} c_1 : \neg w \vee y & c_3 : \neg y \vee \neg z & c_5 : \neg z \vee t \\ c_2 : \neg y \vee z & c_4 : w \vee z & c_6 : \neg z \vee \neg t \end{Bmatrix}$$

   and the two clauses $c_7 : \neg x \vee z \vee t$ and $c_8 : \neg x \vee z \vee \neg t$. After branching to x and x=$True$, c_7 and c_8 are reduced to $z \vee t$ and $z \vee \neg t$, respectively. Thus, one can exhibit S'_k which consists of:

$$S'_k = \begin{Bmatrix} c_5 : \neg z \vee t & c_7 : z \vee t \\ c_6 : \neg z \vee \neg t & c_8 : z \vee \neg t \end{Bmatrix}$$

   In order to maximize the possibility of finding other inconsistent clause-subsets, a solver should forget S_k in order to detect S'_k, allowing clauses in $S_k \setminus S'_k$ to participate in further conflict detection.
3. *Variable x does not appear in clauses of S_k and there is no new smaller inconsistent subset using clauses of S_k.*

   In this third case, it is generally useful to memorize S_k, since otherwise UP^*_{FL} would probably re-detect it at the child-nodes. Memorizing it avoids this re-detection.

Given a formula Σ, the first aim of our work is to induce a natural ordering for unit clauses of Σ so that as many inconsistent subsets of clauses as possible are detected. The second aim is to avoid the repeated detections of the same inconsistent subsets of clauses at different nodes of a search-tree to make the LB computation more incremental. For these two aims, we should keep all inconsistent subsets of clauses in case 3 and avoid keeping any inconsistent subset of clauses in case 1 and case 2 when branching.

Figure 1 shows the branch and bound algorithm for Max-SAT with storage of inconsistent subsets of clauses. The first call to the function is max-sat($\Sigma, \#clauses, \emptyset$). Given a formula Σ, the algorithm begins by removing all clauses in each inconsistent subset stored in $ICSS$ (lines 4-6). Then it computes the set C of further inconsistent subsets of clauses using UP^*_{FL} (line 7). If LB reaches UB the solver backtracks, otherwise all removed clauses are reinserted (lines 13-15). The heuristic $decideStorage(S)$ decides if the new inconsistent subset of clauses S should be stored (lines 17-19). This heuristic is essentially based on the probability that S is in case 2. Finally, in lines 21-25, all inconsistent subsets containing the next branching variable x are removed from $ICSS$ before branching so that any inconsistent subset of clauses in case 1 is not stored anymore.

Since all inconsistent subsets of clauses containing the next branching variable x (case 1) are excluded, the heuristic $decideStorage(S)$ only decides if S would probably lead to the case 2. If the heuristic performs well, most inconsistent subsets of clauses

max-sat$(\Sigma, UB, ICSS)$

Require: A CNF formula Σ, an upper bound UB, and a set of inconsistent subsets of clauses $ICSS$

Ensure: The minimal number of unsatisfied clauses of Σ

```
if Σ = ∅ or Σ only contains empty clauses then
    return #Empty(Σ);
end if
for all inconsistent subset S in ICSS do
    remove clauses of S from Σ
end for
C ← UP*_FL(Σ);
LB ← #Empty(Σ) + #ICSS + #C
if LB ≥ UB then
    return ∞;
end if
x ← selectVariable(Σ)
for all inconsistent subset S in ICSS do
    reinsert clauses of S into Σ
end for
for all inconsistent subset S in C do
    if decideStorage(S)=True then
        ICSS ← ICSS ∪ {S}
    end if
end for
for all inconsistent subset S in ICSS do
    if S contains x (case 1) then
        remove S from ICSS
    end if
end for
UB ← min(UB, max-sat(Σ_x̄, UB, ICSS))
return min(UB, max-sat(Σ_x, UB, ICSS))
```

Fig. 1. A branch and bound algorithm for Max-SAT with storage of inconsistent subsets of clauses

stored in $ICSS$ should be in case 3 and consequently an effective lower bound LB can be obtained. So the heuristic $decideStorage(S)$ is essential in our approach.

It is obviously not conceivable to build a function that could definitely decide if a clause subset would never hide a smaller set since it would need to consider every node of the subtrees rooted at the current node. So we rather use a heuristic to define $decideStorage(S)$.

We conjecture that the more clauses an inconsistent clause-subset S contains, the higher is the probability that some of its clauses are involved in a smaller new inconsistent subset of clauses after branching. In other words, a larger inconsistent clause-subset S has higher probability to be in case 2 and a smaller inconsistent clause-subset S has higher probability to be in case 3. This conjecture suggests that the size of S is an effective characteristic to be used in $decideStorage(S)$ to decide if S is in case 3 and should be stored. Our empirical results in the next section seem to confirm this conjecture.

5 Experimental Results

As indicated in Algorithm 1, our approach can be implemented in all branch-and-bound methods dedicated to complete Max-SAT solving of which the LB computation is based on the detection of disjoint inconsistent subsets of clauses. We have chosen to graft it into the $maxsatz$ solver [10] which is the best performing Max-SAT solver in the Max-SAT evaluation 2006[3]. Nevertheless, in order to validate the strength of our approach, we have tested it on the two last versions of $maxsatz$: version 9 with "Failed Literals" [10] (denoted $maxsatz9$) and version 14 with "Failed Literals" and "Inference Rules" [4] (denoted $maxsatz14$). These two solvers extended by our approach are respectively named $maxsatz9_{icss}$ and $maxsatz14_{icss}$ in the following, where $icss$ denotes Inconsistent Clause Subset Storage. Moreover, we compare $maxsatz9_{icss}$ and $maxsatz14_{icss}$ with $Toolbar_{v3}$ [17,18] and $MaxSolver$ [19], two other state-of-the-art Max-SAT solvers. The experimentations have been done on a 2.6 GHz Bi-Opteron with 2 GB of RAM under Linux OS (kernel 2.6).

5.1 Size of the Inconsistent Clause-Subsets

We use a heuristic based on the size of an inconsistent subset S of clauses to indicate whether S is in case 3 or not. We empirically determine that S should probably be in case 3 if it contains at most five clauses of which at most two unit clauses. Figure 2 shows the influence of the storage of inconsistent clause-subsets according to their size. It compares the mean run-time of the $maxsatz14$ solver on sets of 2-SAT and 3-SAT formulae with 80 variables when the $\frac{\#clauses}{\#vars}$ ratio increases, where the $decideStorage$ predicate in algorithm 1 chooses to store inconsistent subsets with at most five clauses ($maxsatz9/14_{icss}(5)$), of which at most two unit clauses, and with all inconsistent subsets ($maxsatz9/14_{icss}(yes)$), with at most two unit clauses, respectively. The reason of limiting the number of unit clauses in a stored inconsistent subset is that an unit

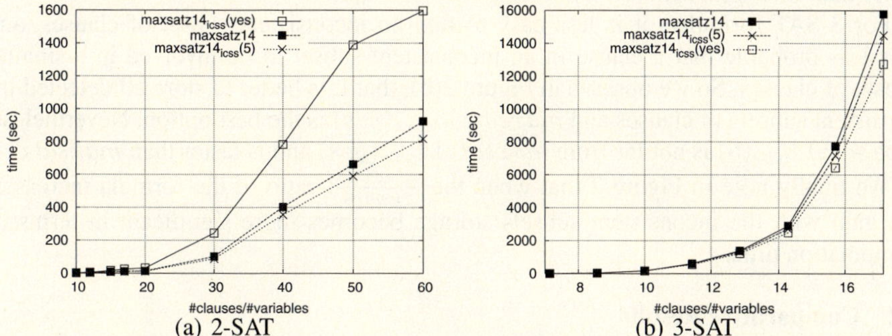

(a) 2-SAT (b) 3-SAT

Fig. 2. Mean computation time of the $maxsatz14$ solver with or without inconsistent subsets storage for randomly generated 2-SAT formulae and 3-SAT formulae with 80 variables with the ratio $\frac{\#clauses}{\#vars}$ from 10 to 80 (2-SAT) and from 7 to 17 (3-SAT). The $decideStorage$ heuristic chooses to store all inconsistent subsets ($maxsatz14_{icss}(yes)$) or the inconsistent subsets of at most five clauses ($maxsatz_{icss}(5)$) with at most two unit clauses, respectively.

[3] see `http://www.iiia.csic.es/~maxsat06/`

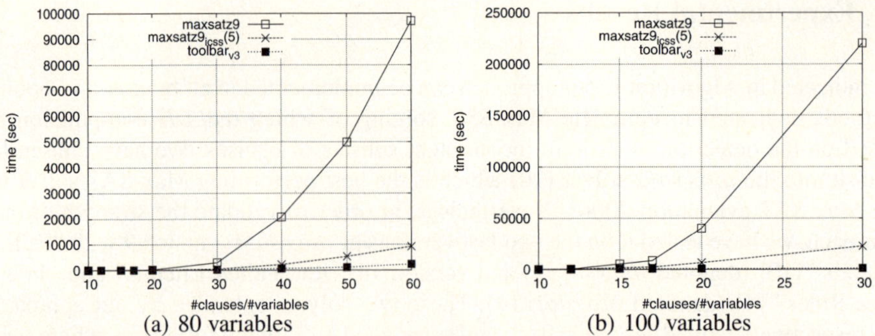

(a) 80 variables (b) 100 variables

Fig. 3. mean computation time of $maxsatz9$ and $maxsatz9_{icss}(5)$ on sets of randomly generated 2-SAT formulae of 80 and 100 variables according to the ratio $\frac{\#clauses}{\#vars}$ from 10 to 60/30

clause is likelier to be involved in other inconsistent subsets detected by unit propagation, so that inconsistent subsets containing more than two unit clauses should not be stored, since these unit clauses can be used to possibly detect more inconsistent subsets after branching. We have developed a $maxsatz9/14_{icss}(yes)$ without limit on the number of unit clauses which gives the worst results on each instance. Note that both $maxsatz14_{icss}(5)$ and $maxsatz14_{icss}(yes)$ are based on $maxsatz14$, the currently fastest solver for Max-2-SAT and Max-3-SAT in our knowledge.

Considering the 2-SAT curve with high $\frac{\#clauses}{\#vars}$ ratios in Figure 2(a), the mean time is more than twice faster when the $decideStorage$ predicate chooses to store subsets with a low number of clauses (see $maxsatz14_{icss}(5)$ curve) than for an unlimited storage (see $maxsatz14_{icss}(yes)$ curve). Moreover, at this point of the curve, the search-tree size of $maxsatz14_{icss}(yes)$ is almost three times bigger than the search-tree size of $maxsatz14_{icss}(5)$ (see table 4). Note that $maxsatz14_{icss}(yes)$ is slower than $maxsatz14$ in which no inconsistent subset is stored, but $maxsatz14_{icss}(5)$ is faster than $maxsatz14$.

For 3-SAT formulae, it is less easy to find an inconsistent subset of clauses, and it is less probable that a clause in an inconsistent subset to be involved in a smaller subset of clauses. So we observe in Figure 2(b), that it is better to store all detected inconsistent subsets of clauses and $maxsatz14_{icss}(yes)$ is the best option. Nevertheless, $maxsatz14_{icss}(5)$ is not far from $maxsatz14_{icss}(yes)$ and is faster than $maxsatz14$.

We finally note in Figure 2 that when the $\frac{\#clauses}{\#vars}$ ratio of the formula increases, the gain with the inconsistent subsets storage becomes more significant in terms of computation time.

5.2 Comparative Results

Figure 3 and Figure 4 compare $maxsatz9_{icss}(5)$, $maxsatz9$, and $Toolbar_{v3}$ on Max-2-SAT and Max-3-SAT problems. It is clear that with the inconsistent clause-subsets storage, $maxsatz9_{icss}(5)$ is significantly faster than $maxsatz9$. Using powerful inference rules, $Toolbar_{v3}$ is faster than $maxsatz9_{icss}(5)$ and $maxsatz9$ for Max-2-SAT, but both $maxsatz9_{icss}(5)$ and $maxsatz9$ are faster than $Toolbar_{v3}$ for Max-3-SAT.

Figure 5 and Figure 6 compare $maxsatz14$, $maxsatz14_{icss}(5)$ and $Toolbar_{v3}$ on Max-2-SAT and Max-3-SAT problems. Both $maxsatz14$, $maxsatz14_{icss}(5)$ are sub-

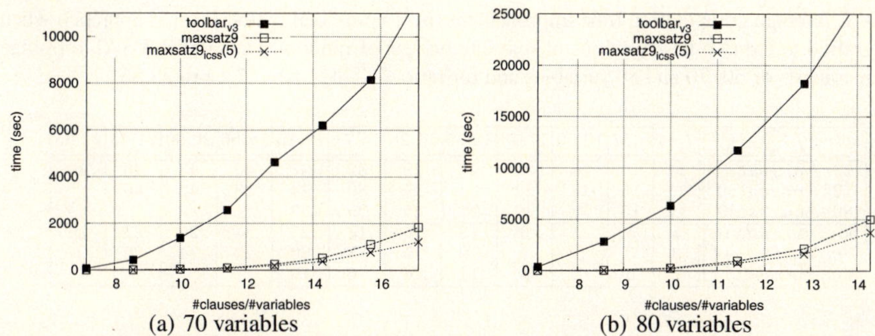

(a) 70 variables (b) 80 variables

Fig. 4. Mean computation time of $maxsatz9$, $maxsatz9_{icss}(5)$ and $Toolbar_{v3}$ on sets of randomly generated 3-SAT formulae which consists of 70 and 80 variables according to the ratio $\frac{\#clauses}{\#vars}$ from 7 to 17/15

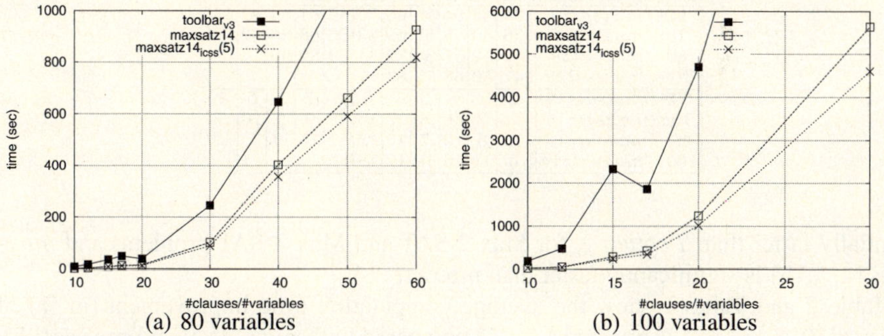

(a) 80 variables (b) 100 variables

Fig. 5. Mean computation time $maxsatz14$, $maxsatz14_{icss}(5)$ and $Toolbar_{v3}$ on sets of randomly generated 2-SAT formulae of 80 and 100 variables according to the ratio $\frac{\#clauses}{\#vars}$ from 10 to 60/30

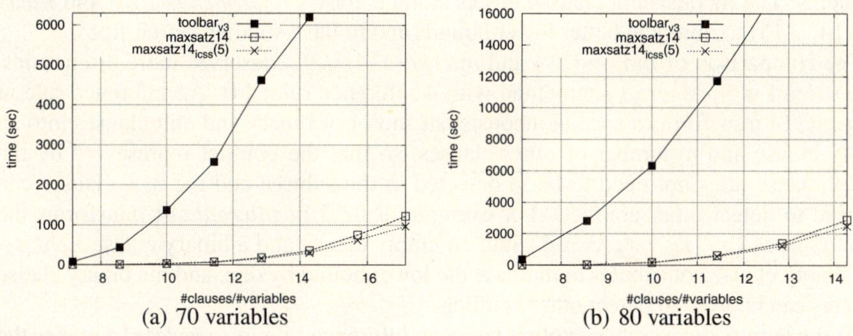

(a) 70 variables (b) 80 variables

Fig. 6. Mean computation time of $maxsatz14$, $maxsatz14_{icss}(5)$ and $Toolbarv3$ on sets of randomly generated 3-SAT formulae which consists of 70 and 80 variables according to the ratio $\frac{\#clauses}{\#vars}$ from 7 to 17/15

Table 1. Average computation time improvement (in %) provided by the $icss(5)$ approach when it is grafted to the two best versions of maxsatz on sets of randomly generated 3-SAT formulae which consists of 60, 70 and 80 variables and for ratio $\frac{\#clauses}{\#vars}$ from 7.14 to 22.85

$solver/\frac{\#clauses}{\#vars}$	7.14	8.57	10.00	11.43	12.85	14.28	15.71	17.15	18.56	20.00	21.43	22.85
$60v/maxsatz9$	11	14	18	22	25	29	32	37	40	43	46	49
$70v/maxsatz9$	11	15	18	20	24	27	30	34	38	42	46	
$80v/maxsatz9$	12	15	18	20	24	25	29	33				
$60v/maxsatz14$	5	5	9	9	13	16	18	21	24	25	27	29
$70v/maxsatz14$	3	5	6	9	12	15	17	20	22	24	26	
$80v/maxsatz14$	3	5	7	8	11	14	16	19				

Table 2. Average computation time improvement (in %) provided by the $icss(5)$ approach when it is grafted to the two best versions of maxsatz on sets of randomly generated 2-SAT formulae which consists of 60 to 100 variables and for ratio $\frac{\#clauses}{\#vars}$ from 10 to 80

$solver/\frac{\#clauses}{\#vars}$	10	12	15	17	20	30	40	50	60	70	80
$60v/maxsatz9$	34	39	54	59	65	76	80	81	84	82	83
$70v/maxsatz9$	36	50	55	57	69	83	86	88	88	87	
$80v/maxsatz9$	42	52	57	64	72	84	89	89	90		
$100v/maxsatz9$	47	50	68	72	83						
$60v/maxsatz14$	2	1	5	3	7	5	6	7	7	6	8
$70v/maxsatz14$	−6	2	9	8	6	10	9	9	9	10	
$80v/maxsatz14$	13	8	10	7	12	13	11	10	11		
$100v/maxsatz14$	0	11	16	19	17	18					

stantially faster than $Toolbar_{v3}$ for Max-2-SAT and Max-3-SAT problems and $maxsatz14_{icss}(5)$ is significantly faster than $maxsatz14$.

Table 2 and Table 1 show the average computation time improvement (in %) of $maxsatz9_{icss}(5)$ and $maxsatz14_{icss}(5)$ compared with $maxsatz9$ and $maxsatz14$, respectively, for Max-2-SAT and Max-3-SAT problems. It is clear that the improvement becomes more important when the $\frac{\#clauses}{\#vars}$ increases.

Table 4 and Table 3 compare the size of search-trees of $maxsatz9$, $maxsatz14$, $maxsatz9_{icss}(5)$, $maxsatz14_{icss}(5)$, and $Toolbar_{v3}$ for Max-2-SAT and Max-3-SAT problems. The inconsistent clause subsets storage allows $maxsatz9_{icss}(5)$ and $maxsatz14_{icss}(5)$ to compute better lower bounds and to have smaller search-trees.

The comparison of $maxsatz14$ and $maxsatz14_{icss}(5)$ deserves more discussions. $maxsatz14$ is $maxsatz9$ augmented with 4 inference rules [4]. An inference rule in $maxsatz14$ transforms a special inconsistent subset of binary and unit clauses into an empty clause and a number of other clauses, so that the conflict represented by the empty clause does not need to be re-detected in the subtree and the new clauses can be used to detect other conflicts. For example, Rule 3 in $maxsatz14$ transforms the set of clauses $\{x_1, x_2, \neg x_1 \vee \neg x_2\}$ into an empty clause and a binary clause $x_1 \vee x_2$. The empty clause contributes to increase the lower bound by one, and the binary clause $x_1 \vee x_2$ can be used to detect other conflicts.

So the empty clause made explicit using an inference rule in $maxsatz14$ makes the lower bound computation in different search-tree nodes more incremental, since the conflict does not need to be re-detected in the subtree. The new added clauses using the inference rule allows to improve the lower bound.

The inference rules implemented in $Toolbar_{v3}$ are independently designed for weighted Max-SAT, and are similar to those implemented in $maxsatz14$ when applied

Table 3. Average search-tree size (in 10^4 nodes) of $Toolbar_{v3}$, $maxsatz9$, $maxsatz9_{icss}(5)$, $maxsatz14$ and $maxsatz14_{icss}(5)$ on sets of randomly generated 3-SAT formulae of 60, 70 and 80 variables with ratio $\frac{\#clauses}{\#vars}$ from 8.57 to 22.85

$Algorithms/\frac{\#clauses}{\#vars}$	8.57	10.00	12.85	14.28	17.15	20.00	21.43	22.85
$60v/maxsatz9$	1.21	3.22	14.61	27.44	59.65	130.18	180.79	262.86
$60v/maxsatz9_{icss}(5)$	1.18	3.13	14.13	26.12	53.80	109.98	148.24	209.32
$60v/Toolbar_{v3}$	115.06	258.54	878.23	1,279.87	2,465.58	4,034.10	4,065.77	4,439.90
$60v/maxsatz14$	1.20	2.54	9.88	17.32	33.03	64.01	84.47	114.44
$60v/maxsatz14_{icss}(5)$	1.19	2.52	9.83	17.19	32.70	63.27	82.96	112.02
$70v/maxsatz9$	4.93	19.61	94.64	166.50	471.22	1,397.55	2,188.83	
$70V/maxsatz9_{icss}(5)$	4.75	19.01	92.35	161.23	436.11	1,199.83	1,796.31	
$70v/Toolbar_{v3}$	987.95	2,615.78	4,228.95	5,229.80	3,941.12	3,941.12	3,941.12	
$70v/maxsatz14$	4.80	14.84	63.75	104.27	268.73	694.23	1,012.11	
$70v/maxsatz14_{icss}(5)$	4.78	14.83	63.31	103.21	264.87	681.41	994.00	
$80v/maxsatz9$	22.57	113.01	644.61	1,303.28	5,388.91			
$80v/maxsatz9_{icss}(5)$	21.64	109.11	632.50	1,278.88	5,095.61			
$60v/Toolbar_{v3}$	5,629.36	7,927.10	4,530.50	4,530.50				
$80v/maxsatz14$	19.67	81.28	409.06	716.40	2,965.09			
$80v/maxsatz14_{icss}(5)$	19.53	80.80	406.62	710.32	2,921.41			

Table 4. Average search-tree size (in 10^4 nodes) of $Toolbar_{v3}$, $maxsatz9$, $maxsatz9_{icss}(5)$, $maxsatz14$ and $maxsatz14_{icss}(5)$ on sets of randomly generated 2-SAT formulae of 60 to 100 variables with ratio $\frac{\#clauses}{\#vars}$ from 10 to 60

$Algorithms/\frac{\#clauses}{\#vars}$	10	12	15	17	20	30	40	50	60
$60v/maxsatz9$	0.1	0.2	0.6	1.1	1.3	4.7	8.3	13.8	19.0
$60v/maxsatz9_{icss}(5)$	0.1	0.1	0.4	0.7	0.8	2.2	3.6	5.5	7.0
$60v/Toolbar_{v3}$	0.8	1.1	1.8	3.2	3.0	5.6	8.1	12.9	11.8
$60v/maxsatz14$	0.03	0.04	0.09	0.15	0.14	0.27	0.44	0.66	0.71
$60v/maxsatz14_{icss}(5)$	0.03	0.04	0.09	0.1	0.1	0.3	0.4	0.6	0.7
$70v/maxsatz9$	0.3	0.5	2.4	4.1	10.6	54.1	131.3	282.6	434.3
$70v/maxsatz9_{icss}(5)$	0.2	0.4	0.1	0.3	5.6	18.3	41.7	75.1	121.2
$70v/Toolbar_{v3}$	2.1	2.6	6.3	12.4	15.6	48.3	46.3	88.3	109.1
$70v/maxsatz14$	0.07	0.09	0.3	0.4	0.7	1.9	2.7	4.9	7.1
$70v/maxsatz14_{icss}(5)$	0.08	0.1	0.3	0.4	0.8	1.8	2.6	4.7	6.8
$80v/maxsatz9$	1.3	5.1	12.3	21.2	25.6	238.9	1,238.2	2,161.4	3,317.6
$80v/maxsatz9_{icss}(5)$	1.1	4.0	7.9	11.4	11.2	71.5	283.4	523.1	734,6
$80v/Toolbar_{v3}$	14.3	25.7	43.5	51.31	35.19	166.39	345.93	578.73	322.58
$80v/maxsatz14$	0.3	0.5	1.2	1.5	1.5	6.3	19.2	24.9	27.8
$80v/maxsatz14_{icss}(5)$	0.2	0.5	1.2	1.5	1.4	6.1	18.4	23.7	25.7
$100v/maxsatz9$	33.6	69.4	768.4	1,078.4	4,364.8	12,348.8			
$100v/maxsatz9_{icss}(5)$	26.0	48.2	324.9	404.6	1,040.2	2,349.1			
$100v/Toolbar_{v3}$	236.8	528.8	2,235.3	1,489.5	3,307.4	8,513.2			
$100v/maxsatz14$	3.8	7.2	32.1	40.8	95.6	258.3			
$100v/maxsatz14_{icss}(5)$	4.1	7.0	29.7	36.9	88.8	233.8			

to (unweighted) Max-SAT. Note that all these inference rules are limited to unit and binary clauses.

Unfortunately, the inference rules implemented in $maxsatz14$ and $Toolbar_{v3}$ are for special subsets of clauses and cannot be applied to transform all inconsistent subsets of clauses. For example, no inference rule is applied in $maxsatz14$ and $Toolbar_{v3}$ to the inconsistent clause set $\{x_1, x_2, x_3, \neg x_1 \vee \neg x_2 \vee \neg x_3\}$, which has to be re-detected in every node of a search-tree. This set is indeed equivalent to the set $\{\emptyset, x_1 \vee x_2, x_1 \vee x_3, \neg x_1 \vee x_2 \vee x_3\}$, which is time-consuming to detect and to treat. $maxsatz14$ is limited to detect some special patterns which are shown practically efficient as inference rules.

Table 5. Mean computation time (in sec.) of $maxsatz9$, $maxsatz9_{icss}(5)$, $maxsatz14$, $maxsatz14_{icss}(5)$, $Toolbar_{v3}$ and $MaxSolver$ on some families of Max-Cut and Max-SAT evaluation benchmarks

$Benchmarks$	$maxsatz9$	$maxsatz9_{icss}(5)$	$Toolbar_{v3}$	$maxsolver$	$maxsatz14$	$maxsatz14_{icss}(5)$
$brock200$	98.43	38.40	40.33	18,902	7.58	6.58
$brock400$	350.22	141.00	118.88	> 25,200	27.22	24.49
$brock800$	53.47	19.37	16.74	18,917	3.21	2.90
$c-fat200$	1.09	0.48	0.33	2.46	0.07	0.08
$c-fat500$	10,743.42	10,658.90	12,737	12,615.07	7,313.89	7,353.20
$hamming6$	12,605	12,601	12,600	> 25,200	12,600.27	12,600.22
$hamming8$	12,603.77	12,601.53	12,600	12,609.13	12,600.22	12,600.20
$hamming10$	15,013.98	14,009.33	13,337.14	> 25,200	12,858.69	12,803.17
$johnson16$	7.40	3.40	1.00	> 25,200	0.39	0.30
$johnson32$	2,535.20	1,066.03	311.27	> 25,200	127.13	111.03
$keller$	116.13	45.21	13.02	> 25,200	4.47	3.39
$max_{c}ut_{6}0_{4}20$	11.68	2.99	5.88	122.90	0.90	0.88
$max_{c}ut_{6}0_{5}00$	68.76	15.86	27.01	523.37	3.00	2.94
$max_{c}ut_{6}0_{5}60$	210.64	47.47	67.27	> 25,200	6.40	6.03
$max_{c}ut_{6}0_{6}00$	365.98	81.89	96.24	> 25,200	9.20	8.58
$p_{h}at300$	164.27	63.14	81.92	8,400.58	10.82	8.60
$p_{h}at500$	356.30	142.48	165.31	8,404.01	33.06	31.07
$p_{h}at700$	123.76	49.01	54.66	8,400.79	14.60	12.13
$p_{h}at1000$	51.28	20.09	21.80	8,401.15	3.56	2.89
$san200_{0}$	4,033.84	1,878.20	1,345.57	> 25,200	451.01	404.92
$san400_{0}$	1,250.98	561.10	434.97	20,161.99	127.99	113.26
$san1000$	4.03	1.62	1.25	15.28	0.23	0.22
$sanr200$	1,354.37	617.36	516.93	> 25,200	134.10	116.50
$sanr400$	42.63	15.28	13.17	12,606,03	2.49	1.80
$t4pm3-6666.spn$	0.80	0.03	10.18	0.45	0.05	0.04
$t5pm3-7777.spn$	209.82	51.96	> 25,200	15,336.68	116.72	65.70
$ram_{k}3_{n}10.ra0$	262.230	261.850	594.46	> 25,200	293.430	294.530
$ram_{k}3_{n}9.ra0$	0.120	0.120	0.27	> 25,200	0.140	0.140
$spinglass4_{2}.pm3$	0.160	0.070	17.81	> 25,200	0.160	0.120
$spinglass5_{10}.pm3$	190.310	54.200	> 25,200	> 25,200	101.290	60.910
$spinglass5_{1}.pm3$	394.140	108.020	> 25,200	> 25,200	229.330	137.820
$spinglass5_{3}.pm3$	309.470	87.590	> 25,200	> 25,200	160.510	105.610
$spinglass5_{5}.pm3$	105.100	25.300	> 25,200	> 25,200	45.310	25.530
$spinglass5_{6}.pm3$	578.410	154.120	> 25,200	> 25,200	343.910	206.920
$spinglass5_{7}.pm3$	272.320	61.110	> 25,200	> 25,200	117.880	65.090
$spinglass5_{9}.pm3$	162.930	47.600	> 25,200	> 25,200	102.170	62.310

Our inconsistent clause subsets storage approach allows to complete the inference rules. In other words, when no inference rule is applicable, the inconsistent clause subset can be stored to make the lower bound computation incremental and to improve the lower bound. The experimental results show the effectiveness of our approach.

We have also tested $MaxSolver$ [19], which is too slow to be showed in Figures 3, 4, 5 and 6, and in Tables 2, 1, 4, and 3.

Table 5 compares $MaxSolver$, $maxsatz9$, $maxsatz14$, $maxsatz9_{icss}(5)$, $maxsatz14_{icss}(5)$, and $Toolbar_{v3}$ on max-cut instances submitted to the Max-SAT evaluation 2006. Observe that $maxsatz9_{icss}(5)$ is significantly faster than $maxsatz9$ and $maxsatz14_{icss}(5)$ is also generally faster than $Toolbar_{v3}$ and $maxsatz14$ as the inconsistent clause-subsets storage complete inference rules in $maxsatz14$.

6 Conclusion

We study the detection of disjoint inconsistent subsets of clauses in $maxsatz9$ and $maxsatz14$ and find that the detection could be more incremental and that the ordering of initial unit clauses in a CNF formula is important for the lower bound computation. We then propose an approach to store some inconsistent clause subsets at a node for its subtrees. The selection of a clause subset S to be stored is determined by a heuristic based on the size of the clause subset, estimating the probability that the clauses of S are used to detect smaller inconsistent subsets than S in the subtrees. The experimental results show that our approach improves $maxsatz9$ and $maxsatz14$ in terms of run-time and search-tree size, by making the lower bound more incremental and by inducing a natural ordering of initial unit clauses in a CNF formula. Our approach completes the inference rules in $maxsatz14$ and could be also used in any Max-SAT solver which computes the lower bound by detecting disjoint inconsistent subsets of clauses.

As future work we also plan to apply the incremental lower bound to Max-SAT solvers that deal with the many-valued clausal formalism defined in [20,21,22] and to partial Max-SAT solvers [23].

References

1. Watson, J., Beck, J., Howe, A., Whitley, L.: Toward an understanding of local search cost in job-shop scheduling (2001)
2. Iwama, K., Kambayashi, Y., Miyano, E.: New bounds for oblivious mesh routing. In: European Symposium on Algorithms, pp. 295–306 (1998)
3. Zhang, Y., Zha, H., Chao-Hsien, C., Ji, X., Chen, X.: Towards inferring protein interactions: Challenges and solutions. EURASIP Journal on Applied Signal Processing (2005)
4. Li, C.M., Manyà, F., Planes, J.: New inference rules for max-sat. Journal of Artificial Intelligence Research (to appear, 2007)
5. Heras, F., Larrosa, J.: New inference rules for efficient max-sat solving. In: AAAI (2006)
6. Lin, H., Su, K.: Exploiting inference rules to compute lower bounds for max-sat solving. In: ijcai07 (2007)
7. Xing, Z., Zhang, W.: Maxsolver: an efficient exact algorithm for (weighted) maximum satisfiability. Artificial Intelligence 164(1-2), 47–80 (2005)
8. Larrosa, J., Schiex, T.: In the quest of the best form of local consistency for weighted csp. In: IJCAI, pp. 239–244 (2003)
9. Li, C.M., Manyà, F., Planes, J.: Exploiting unit propagation to compute lower bounds in branch and bound Max-SAT solvers. In: van Beek, P. (ed.) CP 2005. LNCS, vol. 3709, pp. 403–414. Springer, Heidelberg (2005)
10. Li, C.M., Manyà, F., Planes, J.: Detecting disjoint inconsistent subformulas for computing lower bounds for max-sat. In: AAAI, pp. 86–91 (2006)
11. Wallace, R., Freuder, E.: Comparative studies of constraint satisfaction and davis-putnam algorithms for maximum satisfiability problems. In: Cliques, Colouring and Satisfiability, pp. 587–615 (1996)
12. Wallace, R.J.: Directed arc consistency preprocessing. In: Constraint Processing, Selected Papers, pp. 121–137. Springer, London, UK (1995)
13. Larrosa, J., Meseguer, P., Schiex, T.: Maintaining reversible dac for max-csp. Artif. Intell. 107(1), 149–163 (1999)
14. de Givry, S., Larrosa, J., Meseguer, P., Schiex, T.: Solving max-sat as weighted CSP. In: Rossi, F. (ed.) CP 2003. LNCS, vol. 2833, pp. 363–376. Springer, Heidelberg (2003)
15. Shen, H., Zhang, H.: Study of lower bounds functions for max-2-sat. In: AAAI 2004, pp. 185–190 (2004)
16. Alsinet, T., Manyà, F., Planes, J.: Improved exact solver for weighted Max-SAT. In: Bacchus, F., Walsh, T. (eds.) SAT 2005. LNCS, vol. 3569, pp. 371–377. Springer, Heidelberg (2005)
17. de Givry, S.: Singleton consistency and dominance for weighted csp. In: Wallace, M. (ed.) CP 2004. LNCS, vol. 3258. Springer, Heidelberg (2004)

18. Larrosa, J., Schiex, T.: In the quest of the best form of local consistency for weighted csp. In: IJCAI 2003 (2003)
19. Xing, Z., Zhang, W.: Maxsolver: an efficient exact algorithm for (weighted) maximum satisfiability. Artif. Intell. 164(1-2), 47–80 (2005)
20. Béjar, R., Manyà, F.: Solving combinatorial problems with regular local search algorithms. In: Ganzinger, H., McAllester, D., Voronkov, A. (eds.) LPAR 1999. LNCS, vol. 1705, pp. 33–43. Springer, Heidelberg (1999)
21. Béjar, R., Hähnle, R., Manyà, F.: A modular reduction of regular logic to classical logic. In: ISMVL'01, pp. 221–226 (2001)
22. Ansótegui, C., Manyà, F.: Mapping problems with finite-domain variables into problems with boolean variables. In: Hoos, H.H., Mitchell, D.G. (eds.) SAT 2004. LNCS, vol. 3542, pp. 1–15. Springer, Heidelberg (2005)
23. Argelich, J., Manyà, F.: Exact Max-SAT solvers for over-constrained problems. Journal of Heuristics 12(4–5), 375–392 (2006)

An Abstract Interpretation Based Combinator for Modelling While Loops in Constraint Programming

Tristan Denmat[1], Arnaud Gotlieb[2], and Mireille Ducassé[1]

[1] IRISA/INSA
[2] IRISA/INRIA
Campus universitaire de Beaulieu 35042 Rennes Cedex, France
{denmat,gotlieb,ducasse}@irisa.fr

Abstract. We present the w constraint combinator that models while loops in Constraint Programming. Embedded in a finite domain constraint solver, it allows programmers to develop non-trivial arithmetical relations using loops, exactly as in an imperative language style. The deduction capabilities of this combinator come from abstract interpretation over the polyhedra abstract domain. This combinator has already demonstrated its utility in constraint-based verification and we argue that it also facilitates the rapid prototyping of arithmetic constraints (e.g. power, gcd or sum).

1 Introduction

A strength of Constraint Programming is to allow users to implement their own constraints. CP offers many tools to develop new constraints. Examples include the global constraint programming interface of SICStus Prolog *clp(fd)* [5], the ILOG concert technology, iterators of the GECODE system [17] or the Constraint Handling Rules [8]. In many cases, the programmer must provide propagators or filtering algorithms for its new constraints, which is often a tedious task. Recently, Beldiceanu et al. have proposed to base the design of filtering algorithms on automaton [4] or graph description [3], which are convenient ways of describing global constraints. It has been pointed out that the natural extension of these works would be to get closer to imperative programming languages [4].

In this paper, we suggest to use the generic w constraint combinator to model arithmetical relations between integer variables. This combinator provides a mechanism for prototyping new constraints without having to worry about any filtering algorithm. Its originality is to model iterative computations: it brings while loops into constraint programming following what was done for logic programming [16]. Originally, the w combinator has been introduced in [9] in the context of program testing but it was not deductive enough to be used in a more general context. In this paper, we base the generic filtering algorithm associated to this combinator on case-based reasoning and Abstract Interpretation over the polyhedra abstract domain. Thanks to these two mechanisms, w performs non-trivial deductions during constraint propagation. In many cases, this combinator

C. Bessiere (Ed.): CP 2007, LNCS 4741, pp. 241–255, 2007.

can be useful for prototyping new constraints without much effort. Note that we do not expect the propagation algorithms generated for these new constraints to always be competitive with hand-written propagators.

We illustrate the w combinator on a relation that models $y = x^n$. Note that writing a program that computes x^n is trivial whereas building finite domain propagators for $y = x^n$ is not an easy task for a non-expert user of CP. Figure 1 shows an imperative program (in C syntax) that implements the computation of x^n, along with the corresponding constraint model that exploits the w combinator (in CLP(FD) syntax). In these programs, we suppose that N is positive although this is not a requirement of our approach.

```
power(X, N){               power(X, N, Y) :-
  Y = 1;                      w([X, 1, N], [Xin, Yin, Nin], [Xin, Yout, Nout], [_, Y, _],
  while(N ≥ 1){                 Nin #>= 1,
    Y = Y * X;                  [Yout #= Yin * Xin,
    N = N - 1};                  Nout #= Nin - 1]).
  return Y;}
```

Fig. 1. An imperative program for $y = x^n$ and a constraint model

It is worth noticing that the w combinator is implemented as a global constraint. As any other constraint, it will be awoken as soon as X, N or Y have their domain pruned. Moreover, thanks to its filtering algorithm, it can prune the domains of these variables. The following request shows an example where w performs remarkably well on pruning the domains of X, Y and N.

```
| ?- X in 8..12, Y in 900..1100, N in 0..10, power(X,N,Y).

N = 3, X = 10, Y = 1000
```

The w combinator has been implemented with the *clp(fd)* and *clpq* libraries of SICStus prolog. The above computation requires 20ms of CPU time on an Intel Pentium M 2GHz with 1 Gb of RAM.

Contributions. In this paper, we detail the pruning capabilities of the w combinator. We describe its filtering algorithm based on case-based reasoning and fixpoint computations over polyhedra. The keypoint of our approach is to reinterpret every constraint in the polyhedra abstract domain by using Linear Relaxation techniques. We provide a general widening algorithm to guarantee termination of the algorithm. The benefit of the w combinator is illustrated on several examples that model non-trivial arithmetical relations.

Organization. Section 2 describes the syntax and semantics of the w operator. Examples using the w operator are presented. Section 3 details the filtering algorithm associated to the combinator. It points out that approximation is crucial to obtain interesting deductions. Section 4 gives some background on abstract interpretation and linear relaxation. Section 5 shows how we integrate abstract interpretation over polyhedra into the filtering algorithm. Section 6 discusses some related work. Section 7 concludes.

2 Presentation of the *w* Constraint Combinator

This section describes the syntax and the semantics of the w combinator. Some examples enlight how the operator can be used to define simple arithmetical constraints.

2.1 Syntax

Figure 2 gives the syntax of the finite domain constraint language where the w operator is embedded.

W	$::=$ $\mathbf{w}(Lvar, Lvar, Lvar, Lvar, Arith\_Constr, LConstr)$
If	$::=$ $\mathbf{if}(Lvar, Arith\_Constr, LConstr, LConstr)$
$Lvar$	$::=$ var $Lvar \mid \varepsilon$
$LConstr$	$::=$ $Constr\ LConstr \mid \varepsilon$
$Constr$	$::=$ var **in** int..int $\mid Arith\_Constr \mid W \mid If$
$Arith\_Constr$	$::=$ var $Op\ Expr$
Op	$::= < \mid \leq \mid > \mid \geq \mid \neq \mid =$
$Expr$	$::= Expr + Expr \mid Expr - Expr \mid Expr * Expr \mid$ var $\mid$ int

Fig. 2. syntax of the w operator

As shown on the figure, a w operator takes as parameters four lists of variables, an arithmetic constraint and a list of constraints. Let us call these parameters $Init, In, Out, End, Cond$ and Do. The $Init$ list contains logical variables representing the initial value of the variables involved in the loop. In variables are the values at iteration n. Out variables are the values at iteration $n + 1$. End variables are the values when the loop is exited. Note that $Init$ and End variables are logical variables that can be constrained by other constraints. On the contrary, In and Out are local to the w combinator and do not concretely exist in the constraint store. $Cond$ is the constraint corresponding to the loop condition whereas Do is the list of constraints corresponding to the loop body. These constraints are such that $vars(Cond) \in In$ and $vars(Do) \in In \cup Out$.

Line 2 of Figure 2 presents an *if* combinator. The parameter of type $Arith\_Constr$ is the condition of the conditional structure. The two parameters of type $LConstr$ are the "then" and "else" parts of the structure. $Lvar$ is the list of variables that appear in the condition or in one of the two branches. We do not further describe this operator to focus on the w operator.

The rest of the language is a simple finite domain constraint programming language with only integer variables and arithmetic constraints.

2.2 Semantics

The solutions of a w constraint is a pair of variable lists $(Init, End)$ such that the corresponding imperative loop with input values $Init$ terminates in a state where final values are equal to End. When the loop embedded in the w combinator never terminates, the combinator has no solution and should fail. This point is discussed in the next section.

2.3 First Example: Sum

Constraint sum(S,I), presented on Figure 3, constrains S to be equal to the sum of the integers between 1 and I: $S = \sum_{i=1}^{n} i$

```
sum(I){
   S = 0;
   while(I > 0){
        S = S + I;
        I = I - 1;
   }
   return S;
```

```
sum(S,I) :-
   I > 0,
   w([0,I],[In,Nin],[Out,Nout],[S,_],
        Nin > 0,
        [Out = In + Nin,
         Nout = Nin - 1]).
```

Fig. 3. The sum constraint derived from the imperative code

The factorial constraint can be obtained by substituting the line Out = In + Nin by Out = In * Nin and replacing the initial value 0 by 1. Thanks to the w combinator, sum and factorial are easy to program as far as one is familiar with imperative programming. Note that translating an imperative function into a w operator can be done automatically.

2.4 Second Example: Greatest Common Divisor (gcd)

The second example is more complicated as it uses a conditional statement in the body of the loop. The constraint gcd(X,Y,Z) presented on Figure 4 is derived form the Euclidian algorithm. gcd(X,Y,Z) is true iff Z is the greatest common divisor of X and Y.

```
gcd(X,Y){
   while(X > 0){
        if(X < Y){
             At = Y;
             Bt = X;
        }else{
             At = X;
             Bt = Y;
        }
        X = At - Bt;
        Y = Bt;
   }
   return Y;
```

```
gcd(X,Y,Z) :-
     w([X,Y],[Xin,Yin],[Xout,Yout],[_,Z],
           Xin > 0,
           [if([At,Bt,Xin,Yin],
                Xin < Yin,
                [At = Yin, Bt = Xin],
                [At = Xin, Bt = Yin]),
           Xout = At - Bt,
           Yout = Bt]).
```

Fig. 4. The gcd constraint

3 The Filtering Algorithm

In this section we present the filtering algorithm associated to the w operator introduced in the previous section. The first idea of this algorithm is derived from the following remark. After n iterations in the loop, either the condition is false and the loop is over, or the condition is true and the statements of the body are executed. Consequently, the filtering algorithm detailed on Figure 5 is basically a constructive disjunction algorithm. The second idea of the algorithm is to use abstract interpretation over polyhedra to over-approximate the behaviour of the loop. Function w^∞ is in charge of the computation of the over-approximation. It will be fully detailed in Section 5.3.

The filtering algorithm takes as input a constraint store $((X, C, B)$ where X is a set of variables, C a set of constraints and B a set of variable domains), the constraint to be inspected $(w(Init, In, Out, End, Cond, Do))$ and returns a new constraint store where information has been deduced from the w constraint. $\tilde{X}$ is the set of variables X extended with the lists of variables In and Out. $\tilde{B}$ is the set of variable domains B extended in the same way.

Input:
A constraint, $w(Init, In, Out, End, Cond, Do)$
A constraint store, (X, C, B)
Output:
An updated constraint store

w_filtering
1 $(X_{exit}, C_{exit}, B_{exit}) := propagate(\tilde{X},\ C \wedge Init = In = Out = End \wedge \neg Cond,\ \tilde{B})$
2 **if** $\emptyset \in B_{exit}$
3   **return** $(\tilde{X}, C \wedge Init = In \wedge Cond \wedge Do \wedge$
4         $w(Out, FreshIn, FreshOut, End, Cond', Do'), \tilde{B})$
5 $(X_1, C_1, B_1) := propagate(\tilde{X}, C \wedge Init = In \wedge Cond \wedge Do, \tilde{B})$
6 $(X_{loop}, C_{loop}, B_{loop}) := w^\infty(Out, FreshIn, FreshOut, End, Cond', Do', (X_1, C_1, B_1))$
7 **if** $\emptyset \in B_{loop}$
8   **return** $(\tilde{X}, C \wedge Init = In = Out = End \wedge \neg Cond, \tilde{B})$
9 $(X', C', B') := join((X_{exit}, C_{exit}, B_{exit}), (X_{loop}, C_{loop}, B_{loop}))_{Init,End}$
10 **return** $(X', C' \wedge w(Init, In, Out, End, Cond, Do), B')$

Fig. 5. The filtering algorithm of w

Line 1 posts constraints corresponding to the immediate termination of the loop and launches a propagation step on the new constraint store. As the loop terminates, the variable lists $Init, In, Out$ and End are all equal and the condition is false ($\neg Cond$). If the propagation results in a store where one variable has an empty domain (line 2), then the loop must be entered. Thus, the condition of the loop must be true and the body of the loop is executed: constraints $Cond$ and Do are posted (line 3). A new w constraint is posted (line 4), where the initial variables are the variables Out computed at this iteration, In and Out are replaced by new fresh variables ($FreshIn$ and $FreshOut$) and End variables remain the same. *Cond′* and *Do′* are the constraints *Cond* and *Do* where variable names *In* and *Out* have been substituted by *FreshIn* and *FreshOut*. The initial w constraint is solved.

Line 5 posts constraints corresponding to the fact that the loop iterates one more time (*Cond* and *Do*) and line 6 computes an over approximation of the rest of the iterations via the w^{∞} function. If the resulting store is inconsistent (line 7), then the loop must terminate immediately (line 8). Once again, the w constraint is solved.

When none of the two propagation steps has led to empty domains, the stores computed in each case are joined (line 9). The *Init* and *End* indices mean that the join is only done for the variables from these two lists. After the join, the w constraint is suspended and put into the constraint store (line 10).

We illustrate the filtering algorithm on the `power` example presented on Figure 1 and the following request:
`X in 8..12, N in 0..10, Y in 10..14, power(X,N,Y).`

At line 1, posted constraints are:
`Xin = X, Nin = N, Yin = 1, Y = Yin, Nin < 1.` This constraint store is inconsistent with the domain of `Y`. Thus, we deduce that the loop must be entered at least once. The condition constraint and loop body constraints are posted (we omit the constraints $Init = In$):
`N >= 1, Yout = 1*X, Xout = X, Nout = N-1` and another w combinator is posted:

```
w([Xout,Yout,Nout],[Xin',Yin',Nin'],[Xout',Yout',Nout'],[_,Y,_],
  Nin'>= 1,[Yout' = Yin'*Xin', Xout' = Xin', Nout' = Nin'-1]).
```

Again, line 1 of the algorithm posts the constraints `Y = Yout, Nout < 1`. This time, the store is not inconsistent. Line 5 posts the constraints
`Nout >= 1, Yout' = Yout*X, Xout' = X, Nout' = Nout - 1`, which reduces domains to `Nout in 1..9, Yout' in 64..144, Xout' in 8..12`. On line 6,
w^{∞}`([Xout',Yout',Nout'],FreshIn,FreshOut,[_,Y,_],Cond,Do,Store)`
is used to infer `Y >= 64`. `Store` denotes the current constraint store. This is a very important deduction as it makes the constraint store inconsistent with `Y in 10..14`. So `Nout < 1,Y = X` is posted and the final domains are
`N in 1..1, X in 10..12, Y in 10..12`. This example points out that approximating the behaviour of the loop with function w^{∞} is crucial to deduce information.

On the examples of sections 2.3 and 2.4 some interesting deductions are done. For the *sum* example, when S is instantiated the value of I is computed. If no value exist, the filtering algorithm fails. Deductions are done even with partial information: `sum(S,I), S in 50..60` leads to $S = 55, I = 10$.

On the request `gcd(X,Y,Z), X in 1..10, Y in 10..20, Z in 1..1000`, the filtering algorithm reduces the bounds of Z to 1..10. Again, this deduction is done thanks to the w^{∞} function, which infers the relations $Z \leq X$ and $Z \leq Y$. If we add other constraints, which would be the case in a problem that would use the *gcd* constraint, we obtain more interesting deductions. For example, if we add the constraint $X = 2 * Y$, then the filtering algorithm deduces that Z is equal to

Y. On each of the above examples, the required computation time is not greater than 30 ms.

Another important point is that approximating loops also allows the filtering algorithm to fail instead of non terminating in some cases. Consider this very simple example that infinitely loops if X is lower than 10.

```
loop(X,Xn) :-
   w([X],[Xin],[Xout],[Xn],
        X < 10,
        [Xout = Xin])
```

Suppose that we post the following request, `X < 0, loop(X,Xn)`, and apply the case reasoning. As we can always prove that the loop must be unfolded, the algorithm does not terminate. However, the filtering algorithm can be extended to address this problem. The idea is to compute an approximation of the loop after a given number of iterations instead of unfolding more and more the loop. On the `loop` example, this extension performs well. Indeed the approximation infers `Xn < 0`, which suffices to show that the condition will never be satisfied and thus the filtering algorithm fails. If the approximation cannot be used to prove non-termination, then the algorithm returns the approximation or continue iterating, depending on what is most valuable for the user: having a sound approximation of the loop or iterating hoping that it will stop.

4 Background

This Section gives some background on abstract interpretation. It first presents the general framework. Then, polyhedra abstract domain is presented. Finally, the notion of linear relaxation is detailed.

4.1 Abstract Interpretation

Abstract Interpretation is a framework introduced in [6] for inferring program properties. Intuitively, this technique consists in executing a program with abstract values instead of concrete values. The abstractions used are such that the abstract result is a sound approximation of the concrete result. Abstract interpretation is based upon the following theory.

A lattice $\langle L, \sqsubseteq, \sqcap, \sqcup \rangle$ is complete iff each subset of L has a greatest lower bound and a least upper bound. Every complete lattice has a least element $\bot$ and a greatest element $\top$. An ascending chain $p_1 \sqsubseteq p_2 \sqsubseteq \ldots$ is a potentially infinite sequence of ordered elements of L. A chain eventually stabilizes iff there is an i such that $p_j = p_i$ for all $j \geq i$. A lattice satisfies the ascending chain condition if every infinite ascending chain eventually stabilizes. A function $f : L \rightarrow L$ is monotone if $p_1 \sqsubseteq p_2$ implies $f(p_1) \sqsubseteq f(p_2)$. A fixed point of f is an element p such that $f(p) = p$. In a lattice satisfying ascending chain condition, the least fixed point $lfp(f)$ can be computed iteratively: $lfp(f) = \bigsqcup_{i \geq 0} f^i(\bot)$.

The idea of abstract interpretation is to consider program properties at each program point as elements of a lattice. The relations between the program properties at different locations are expressed by functions on the lattice. Finally, computing the program properties consists in finding the least fixed point of a set of functions.

Generally, interesting program properties at a given program point would be expressed as elements of the lattice $\langle \mathcal{P}(\mathbb{N}), \subseteq, \cap, \cup \rangle$ (if variables have their values in $\mathbb{N}$). However, computing on this lattice is not decidable in the general case and the lattice does not satisfy the ascending chain condition. This problem often appears as soon as program properties to be inferred are not trivial. This means that the fixed points must be approximated. There are two ways for approximating fixed points. A static approach consists in constructing a so-called abstract lattice $\langle M, \sqsubseteq_M, \sqcap_M, \sqcup_M \rangle$ with a Galois connection $\langle \alpha, \gamma \rangle$ from L to M. $\alpha : L \to M$ and $\gamma : M \to L$ are respectively an abstraction and concretization function such that $\forall l \in L, l \sqsubseteq \gamma(\alpha(l))$ and $\forall m \in M, m \sqsubseteq_M \alpha(\gamma(m))$. A Galois connection ensures that fixed points in L can be soundly approximated by computing in M. A dynamic approximation consists in designing a so-called widening operator (noted ∇) to extrapolate the limits of chains that do not stabilize.

4.2 Polyhedra Abstract Domain

One of the most used instanciation of abstract interpretation is the interpretation over the polyhedra abstract domain, introduced in [7]. On this domain, the set of possible values of some variables is abstracted by a set of linear constraints. The solutions of the set of linear constraints define a polyhedron. Each element of the concrete set of values is a point in the polyhedron. In this abstract domain, the join operator of two polyhedra is the convex hull. Indeed, the smallest polyhedron enclosing two polyhedra is the convex hull of these two polyhedra. However, computing the convex hull of two polyhedra defined by a set of linear constraints requires an exponential time in the general case.

Recent work suggest to use a join operator that over-approximates the convex hull [15]. Figure 6 shows two polyhedra with their convex hull and weak join.

Intuitively, the weak join of two polyhedra is computed in three steps. Enlarge the first polyhedron without changing the slope of the lines until it encloses the second polyhedron. Enlarge the second polyhedron in the same way. Do the intersection of these two new polyhedra.

In many works using abstract interpretation on polyhedra, the standard widening is used. The standard widening operator over polyhedra is computed as follows: if P and Q are two polyhedra such that $P \sqsubseteq Q$. Then, the widening $P \nabla Q$

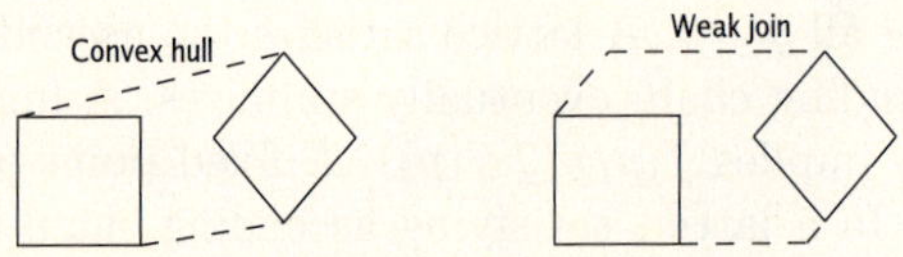

Fig. 6. Convex Hull vs Weak Join

is obtained by removing from P all constraints that are not entailed in Q. This widening is efficient but not very accurate. More accurate widening operators are given in [1].

4.3 Linear Relaxation of Constraints

Using polyhedra abstract interpretation requires us to interpret non linear constraints on the domain of polyhedra. Existing techniques aim at approximating non linear constraints with linear constraints. In our context, the only sources of non linearity are multiplications, strict inequalities and disequalities. These constraints can be linearized as follows:

Multiplications. Let $\underline{X}$ and $\overline{X}$ be the lower and upper bounds of variable X. A multiplication $Z = X * Y$ can be approximated by the conjunction of inequalities [12]:

$$(X - \underline{X})(Y - \underline{Y}) \geq 0 \wedge (X - \underline{X})(\overline{Y} - Y) \geq 0 \\ \wedge (\overline{X} - X)(Y - \underline{Y}) \geq 0 \wedge (\overline{X} - X)(\overline{Y} - Y) \geq 0$$

This constraint is linear as the product $X * Y$ can be replaced by Z. Fig.7 shows a slice of the relaxation where $Z = 1$. The rectangle corresponds to the bounding box of variables X, Y, the dashed curve represents exactly $X * Y = 1$, while the four solid lines correspond to the four parts of the inequality.

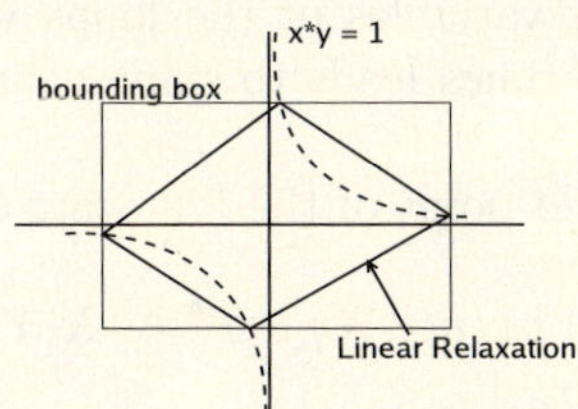

Fig. 7. Relaxation of the multiplication constraint

Strict inequalities and disequalities. Strict inequalities $X < Var$ (resp. $X > Var$) can be rewritten without approximation into $X \leq Var - 1$ (resp. $X \geq Var + 1$), as variables are integers. Disequalities are considered as disjunctions of inequalities. For example, $X \neq Y$ is rewritten into $X =< Y - 1 \vee X >= Y + 1$. Adding the bounds constraints on X and Y and computing the convex hull of the two disjuncts leads to an interesting set of constraints. For example, if X and Y are both in 0..10, the relaxation of $X \neq Y$ is $X + Y \geq 1 \wedge X + Y \leq 19$.

5 Using Abstraction in the Filtering Algorithm of w

In this section, we detail how abstract interpretation is integrated in the w filtering algorithm. Firstly, we show that solutions of w can be computed with a fixed point computation. Secondly, we explain how abstract interpretation over polyhedra allows us to compute an abstraction of these solutions. Finally, the implementation of the w^∞ function is presented.

5.1 Solutions of w as the Result of a Fixed Point Computation

Our problem is to compute the set of solutions of a w constraint:

$$Z = \{((x_1, \ldots, x_n), (x_1^f, \ldots, x_n^f)) \mid w((x_1, \ldots, x_n), In, Out, (x_1^f, \ldots, x_n^f), Cond, Do)\}$$

Let us call S_i the possible values of the loop variables after i iterations in a loop. When $i = 0$ possible variables values are the values that satisfy the domain constraint of *Init* variables. We call S_{init} this set of values. Thus $S_0 = S_{init}$. Let us call T the following set:

$$T = \{((x_1, \ldots, x_n), (x'_1, \ldots, x'_n)) \mid (x_1, \ldots, x_n) \in S_{init} \wedge \exists i (x'_1, \ldots, x'_n) \in S_i\}$$

T is a set of pairs of lists of values (l, m) such that initializing variables of the loops with values l and iterating the loop a finite number of times produce the values m. The following relation holds

$$Z = \{(Init, End) \mid (Init, End) \in T \wedge End \in sol(\neg Cond)\}$$

where $sol(C)$ denotes the set of solutions of a constraint C. The previous formula expresses that the solutions of the w constraint are the pairs of lists of values (l, m) such that initializing variables of the loops with values l and iterating the loop a finite number of times leads to some values m that violate the loop condition.

In fact, T is the least fixed point of the following equation:

$$T^{k+1} = T^k \cup \{(Init, Y) \mid (Init, X) \in T^k \wedge (X, Y) \in sol(Cond \wedge Do\})\} \quad (1)$$

$$T^0 = \{(Init, Init) \mid Init \in S_{init}\} \quad (2)$$

Cond and *Do* are supposed to involve only *In* and *Out* variables. Thus, composing T^k and $sol(Cond \wedge Do)$ is possible as they both are relations between two lists of variables of length n.

Following the principles of abstract interpretation this fixed point can be computed by iterating Equation 1 starting from the set T^0 of Equation 2.

For the simple constraint: `w([X],[In],[Out],[Y],In < 2,[Out = In+1])` and with the initial domain `X in 0..3`, the fixed point computation proceeds as follows.

$$\begin{aligned}
T^0 &= \{(0,0), (1,1), (2,2), (3,3)\} \\
T^1 &= \{(0,1), (1,2)\} \cup T^0 \\
&= \{(0,0), (0,1), (1,1), (1,2), (2,2), (3,3)\} \\
T^2 &= \{(0,1), (0,2), (1,2)\} \cup T^1 \\
&= \{(0,0), (0,1), (0,2), (1,1), (1,2), (2,2), (3,3)\} \\
T^3 &= T^2
\end{aligned}$$

Consequently, the solutions of the w constraint are given by

$$\begin{aligned} Z &= \{(X,Y) \mid (X,Y) \in T^3 \wedge Y \in sol(In \geq 2)\} \\ &= \{(0,2),(1,2),(2,2),(3,3)\} \end{aligned}$$

Although easy to do on the example, iterating the fixed point equation is undecidable because Do can contain others w constraints. Thus, Z is not computable in the general case.

5.2 Abstracting the Fixed Point Equations

We compute an approximation of T using the polyhedra abstract domain. Let P be a polyhedron that over-approximates T, which means that all elements of T are points of the polyhedron P. Each list of values in the pairs defining T has a length n thus P involves $2n$ variables. We represent P by the conjunction of linear equations that define the polyhedron.

The fixed point equations become:

$$P^{k+1}(Init, Out) = P^k \sqcup (P^k(Init, In) \wedge Relax(Cond \wedge Do))_{Init,Out} \quad (3)$$
$$P^0(Init, Out) = \alpha(S_{init}) \wedge Init = Out \quad (4)$$

Compared to equations 1 and 2, the computation of the set of solutions of constraint C is replaced by the computation of a relaxation of the constraint C. $Relax$ is a function that computes linear relaxations of a set of constraints using the relaxations presented in Section 4.3. P_{L_1,L_2} denotes the projection of the linear constraints P over the set of variables in L_1 and L_2. Projecting linear constraints on a set of variables S consists in eliminating all variables not belonging to S. Lists equality $L = M$ is a shortcut for $\forall i \in [1,n] L[i] = M[i]$, where n is the length of the lists and $L[i]$ is the ith element of L. $P_1 \sqcup P_2$ denotes the weak join of polyhedron P_1 and P_2 presented in Section 4.2.

In Equation 4, S_{init} is abstracted with the α function. This function computes a relaxation of the whole constraint store and projects the result on $Init$ variables.

An approximation of the set of solutions of a constraint w is given by

$$Q(Init, In) = P(Init, In) \wedge Relax(\neg Cond) \quad (5)$$

We detail the abstract fixed point computation on the same example as in the previous section. As the constraints $Cond$ and Do are almost linear their relaxation is trivial: $Relax(Cond \wedge Do) = X_{in} \leq 1, X_{out} = X_{in} + 1$. X_{in} is only constrained by its domain, thus $\alpha(S_{init}) = X_{in} \geq 0 \wedge X_{in} \leq 3$. The fixed point is computed as follows

$$\begin{aligned} P^0(X_{in}, X_{out}) &= X_{in} \geq 0 \wedge X_{in} \leq 3 \wedge X_{in} = X_{out} \\ P^1(X_{in}, X_{out}) &= (P^0(X_{in}, X_0) \wedge X_0 \leq 1 \wedge X_{out} = X_0 + 1)_{X_{in},X_{out}} \\ &\quad \sqcup P^0(X_{in}, X_{out}) \\ &= (X_{in} \geq 0 \wedge X_{in} \leq 1 \wedge X_{out} = X_{in} + 1) \sqcup P^0(X_{in}, X_{out}) \\ &= X_{in} \geq 0 \wedge X_{in} \leq 3 \wedge X_{out} \leq X_{in} + 1 \wedge X_{out} \geq X_{in} \end{aligned}$$

$$\begin{aligned}
P^2(X_{in}, X_{out}) &= (P^1(X_{in}, X_1) \wedge X_1 \leq 1 \wedge X_{out} = X_1 + 1)_{X_{in},X_{out}} \\
&\quad \sqcup P^1(X_{in}, X_{out}) \\
&= (X_{in} \geq 0 \wedge X_{in} \leq 3 \wedge X_{in} \leq X_{out} - 1) \sqcup P^1(X_{in}, X_{out}) \\
&= X_{in} \geq 0 \wedge X_{in} \leq 3 \wedge X_{out} \leq X_{in} + 2 \wedge X_{out} \geq X_{in} \wedge X_{out} \leq 4 \\
P^3(X_{in}, X_{out}) &= (P_2(X_{in}, X_2) \wedge X_2 \leq 1 \wedge X_{out} = X_2 + 1)_{X_{in},X_{out}} \\
&\quad \sqcup P^2(X_{in}, X_{out}) \\
&= (X_{in} \geq 0 \wedge X_{in} \leq 3 \wedge X_{in} \leq X_{out} - 1) \sqcup P^2(X_{in}, X_{out}) \\
&= P^2(X_{in}, X_{out})
\end{aligned}$$

Figure 8 shows the difference between the exact fixed point computed with the exact equations and the approximate fixed point. The points correspond to elements of T^3 whereas the grey zone is the polyhedron defined by P^3.

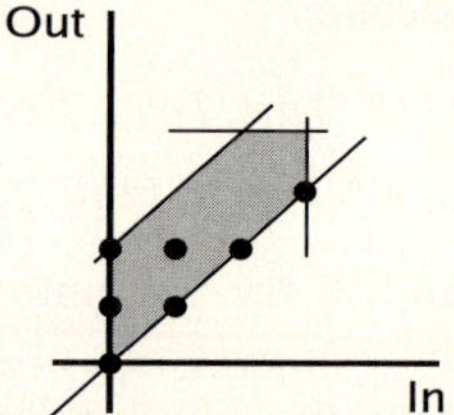

Fig. 8. Exact vs approximated fixed point

An approximation of the solutions of the w constraint is

$$\begin{aligned}
Q &= P^3(X_{init}, X_{end}) \wedge X_{end} \geq 2 \\
&= X_{end} \geq 2 \wedge X_{end} \leq 4 \wedge X_{in} \leq X_{end} \wedge X_{in} \leq 3 \wedge X_{in} \geq X_{end} - 2
\end{aligned}$$

On the previous example, the fixed point computation converges but it is not always the case. Widening can address this problem. The fixed point equation becomes:

$$\begin{aligned}
P^{k+1}(Init, Out) = P^k(Init, Out) \nabla \\
(P^k \sqcup (P^k(Init, In) \wedge Relax(Cond, Do))_{Init,Out})
\end{aligned}$$

In this equation ∇ is the standard widening operator presented in Section 4.2.

5.3 w^∞: Implementing the Approximation

In Section 3, we have presented the filtering algorithm of the w operator. Here, we detail more concretely the integration of the abstract interpretation over polyhedra into the constraint combinator w via the w^∞ function.

w^∞ is an operator that performs the fixed point computation and communicates the result to the constraint store. Figure 9 describes the algorithm. All the operations on linear constraints are done with the *clpq* library [10].

Input:
$Init, In, Out, End$ vectors of variables
$Cond$ and Do the constraints defining the loop
A constraint store (X, C, B)
Output:
An updated constraint store

w^∞ :
1 $P^{i+1} := project(relax(C, B), [Init]) \wedge Init = Out$
2 **repeat**
3 $\quad P^i := P^{i+1}$
4 $\quad P^j := project(P^i \wedge relax(Cond \wedge Do, B), [Init, Out])$
5 $\quad P^k := weak\_join(P^i, P^j)$
6 $\quad P^{i+1} := widening(P^i, P^k)$
7 **until** $includes(P^i, P^{i+1})$
8 $Y := P^{i+1} \wedge relax(\neg Cond, B)$
9 $(C', B') := concretize(Y)$
10 **return** $(X, C' \wedge w(Init, In, Out, End, Cond, Do), B')$

Fig. 9. The algorithm of w^∞ operator

This algorithm summerizes all the notions previously described. Line 1 computes the initial value of P. It implements the α function introduced in Equation 4. The *relax* function computes the linear relaxation of a constraint C given the current variables domains, B. When C contains another w combinator, the corresponding w^∞ function is called to compute an approximation of the second w. The $project(C, L)$ function is a call to the Fourier variable elimination algorithm. It eliminates all the variables of C but variables from the list of lists L. Lines 2 to 7 do the fixed point computation following Equation 3. Line 6 performs the standard widening after a given number of iterations in the repeat loop. This number is a parameter of the algorithm. At Line 7, the inclusion of P^{i+1} in P^i is tested. $includes(P^i, P^{i+1})$ is true iff each constraint of P^i is entailed by the constraints P^{i+1}.

At line 8, the approximation of the solution of w is computed following Equation 5. Line 9 concretizes the result in two ways. Firstly, the linear constraints are turned into finite domain constraints. Secondly, domains of *End* variables are reduced by computing the minimum and maximum values of each variable in the linear constraints Y. These bounds are obtained with the simplex algorithm.

6 Discussion

The polyhedra abstract domain is generally used differently from what we presented. Usually, a polyhedron denotes the set of linear relations that hold between variables at a given program point. As we want to approximate the solutions of a w constraint, our polyhedra describe relations between input and output values of variables and, thus, they involve twice as many variables. In abstract interpretation, the analysis is done only once whereas we do it each time a w operator is awoken. Consequently, we cannot afford to use standard libraries to handle polyhedra, such as [2], because they use the dual representation, which is a source of exponential time computations. Our representation implies, nevertheless, doing many variables elimination with the Fourier elimination algorithm. This remains costly when the number of variables grows. However, the abstraction on polyhedra is only one among others. For example, abstraction on intervals is efficient but leads to less accurate deductions. The octagon abstract domain [13] could be an interesting alternative to polyhedra as it is considered to be a good trade-off between accuracy and efficiency.

Generalized Propagation [14] infers an over-approximation of all the answers of a CLP program. This is done by explicitely computing each answer and joining these answers on an abstract domain. Generalized Propagation may not terminate because of recursion in CLP programs. Indeed, no widening techniques are used. In the same idea, the 3r's are three principles that can be applied to speed up CLP programs execution [11]. One of these 3r's stands for *refinement*, which consists in generating redundant constraints that approximate the set of answers. Refinement uses abstract interpretation, and more specifically widenings, to compute on abstract domains that have infinite increasing chains. Hence, the analysis is guaranteed to terminate. Our approach is an instantiation of this theoretical scheme to the domain of polyhedra.

7 Conclusion

We have presented a constraint combinator, w, that allows users to make a constraint from an imperative loop. We have shown examples where this combinator is used to implement non trivial arithmetic constraints. The filtering algorithm associated to this combinator is based on case reasoning and fixed point computation. Abstract interpretation on polyhedra provides a method for approximating the result of this fixed point computation. The results of the approximation are crucial for pruning variable domains. On many examples, the deductions made by the filtering algorithm are considerable, especially as this algorithm comes for free in terms of development time.

Acknowledgements

We are indebted to Bernard Botella for his significant contributions to the achievements presented in this paper.

References

1. Bagnara, R., Hill, P.M., Ricci, E., Zaffanella, E.: Precise widening operators for convex polyhedra. In: Cousot, R. (ed.) SAS 2003. LNCS, vol. 2694, pp. 337–354. Springer, Heidelberg (2003)
2. Bagnara, R., Ricci, E., Zaffanella, E., Hill, P.M.: Possibly not closed convex polyhedra and the parma polyhedra library. In: Hermenegildo, M.V., Puebla, G. (eds.) SAS 2002. LNCS, vol. 2477, pp. 213–229. Springer, Heidelberg (2002)

3. Beldiceanu, N., Carlsson, M., Demassey, S., Petit, T.: Graph properties based filtering. In: Benhamou, F. (ed.) CP 2006. LNCS, vol. 4204, pp. 59–74. Springer, Heidelberg (2006)
4. Beldiceanu, N., Carlsson, M., Petit, T.: Deriving filtering algorithms from constraint checkers. In: Wallace, M. (ed.) CP 2004. LNCS, vol. 3258, pp. 107–122. Springer, Heidelberg (2004)
5. Carlsson, M., Ottosson, G., Carlson, B.: An open-ended finite domain constraint solver. In: Hartel, P.H., Kuchen, H. (eds.) PLILP 1997. LNCS, vol. 1292, pp. 191–206. Springer, Heidelberg (1997)
6. Cousot, P., Cousot, R.: Abstract interpretation: A unified lattice model for static analysis of programs by construction or approximation of fixpoints. In: POPL'77. Proc. of Symp. on Principles of Progr. Lang., pp. 238–252. ACM Press, New York (1977)
7. Cousot, P., Halbwachs, N.: Automatic discovery of linear restraints among variables of a program. In: POPL'78. Proc. of Symp. on Principles of Progr. Lang., pp. 84–96. ACM Press, New York (1978)
8. Fruhwirth, T.: Theory and practice of constraint handling rules. Special Issue on Constraint Logic Progr., Journal of Logic Progr. 37(1-3) (1998)
9. Gotlieb, A., Botella, B., Rueher, M.: A CLP framework for computing structural test data. In: Palamidessi, C., Moniz Pereira, L., Lloyd, J.W., Dahl, V., Furbach, U., Kerber, M., Lau, K.-K., Sagiv, Y., Stuckey, P.J. (eds.) CL 2000. LNCS (LNAI), vol. 1861, pp. 399–413. Springer, Heidelberg (2000)
10. Holzbaur, C.: OFAI clp(q,r) Manual. Austrian Research Institute for Artificial Intelligence, Vienna, 1.3.3 edn.
11. Marriott, K., Stuckey, P.J.: The 3 r's of optimizing constraint logic programs: Refinement, removal and reordering. In: POPL'93. Proc. of Symp. on Principles of Progr. Lang., pp. 334–344. ACM Press, New York (1993)
12. McCormick, G.P.: Computability of global solutions to factorable nonconvex programs: Part 1 - convex underestimating problems. Math. Progr. 10, 147–175 (1976)
13. Miné, A.: The octagon abstract domain. Higher-Order and Symbolic Computation Journal 19, 31–100 (2006)
14. Le Provost, T., Wallace, M.: Domain independent propagation. In: FGCS'92. Proc. of the Int. Conf. on Fifth Generation Computer Systems, pp. 1004–1011 (1992)
15. Sankaranarayanan, S., Colòn, M.A., Sipma, H., Manna, Z.: Efficient strongly relational polyhedral analysis. In: Emerson, E.A., Namjoshi, K.S. (eds.) VMCAI 2006. LNCS, vol. 3855, pp. 115–125. Springer, Heidelberg (2005)
16. Schimpf, J.: Logical loops. In: Stuckey, P.J. (ed.) ICLP 2002. LNCS, vol. 2401, pp. 224–238. Springer, Heidelberg (2002)
17. Schulte, C., Tack, G.: Views and iterators for generic constraint implementations. In: Hnich, B., Carlsson, M., Fages, F., Rossi, F. (eds.) CSCLP 2005. LNCS (LNAI), vol. 3978, pp. 118–132. Springer, Heidelberg (2006)

Tradeoffs in the Complexity of Backdoor Detection

Bistra Dilkina, Carla P. Gomes, and Ashish Sabharwal

Cornell University, Department of Computer Science, Ithaca, NY 14850, USA
{bistra,gomes,sabhar}@cs.cornell.edu

Abstract. There has been considerable interest in the identification of structural properties of combinatorial problems that lead to efficient algorithms for solving them. Some of these properties are "easily" identifiable, while others are of interest because they capture key aspects of state-of-the-art constraint solvers. In particular, it was recently shown that the problem of identifying a strong Horn- or 2CNF-backdoor can be solved by exploiting equivalence with deletion backdoors, and is NP-complete. We prove that strong backdoor identification becomes harder than NP (unless NP=coNP) as soon as the inconsequential sounding feature of empty clause detection (present in all modern SAT solvers) is added. More interestingly, in practice such a feature as well as polynomial time constraint propagation mechanisms often lead to much smaller backdoor sets. In fact, despite the worst-case complexity results for strong backdoor detection, we show that Satz-Rand is remarkably good at finding small strong backdoors on a range of experimental domains. Our results suggest that structural notions explored for designing efficient algorithms for combinatorial problems should capture both statically and dynamically identifiable properties.

1 Introduction

Capturing and exploiting problem structure is key to solving large real-world combinatorial problems. For example, several interesting tractable classes of combinatorial problems have been identified by restricting the constraint language used to characterize such problem instances. Well-known cases include 2CNF, Horn, Linear Programming (LP), and Minimum Cost Flow problems (MCF). In general, however, such restricted languages are not rich enough to characterize complex combinatorial problems. A very fruitful and prolific line of research that has been pursued in the study of combinatorial problems is the identification of various structural properties of instances that lead to efficient algorithms. Ideally, one prefers structural properties that are "easily" identifiable, such as from the topology of the underlying constraint graph. As an example, the degree of acyclicity of a constraint graph, measured using various graph width parameters, plays an important role with respect to the identification of tractable instances — it is known that an instance is solvable in polynomial time if the treewidth of its constraint graph is bounded by a constant [8, 9, 6, 10, 5, 21]. Interestingly, even though the notion of bounded treewidth is defined with respect

C. Bessiere (Ed.): CP 2007, LNCS 4741, pp. 256–270, 2007.

to tree decompositions, it is also possible to design algorithms for constraint satisfaction problems of bounded (generalized) hypertree width that do not perform any form of tree decomposition (see e.g., [3]). Other useful structural properties consider the nature of the constraints, such as their so-called functionality, monotonicity, and row convexity [7, 24].

Another approach for studying combinatorial problems focuses on the role of *hidden structure* as a way of analyzing and understanding the efficient performance of state-of-the-art constraint solvers on many real-world problem instances. One example of such hidden structure is a backdoor set, i.e., a set of variables such that once they are instantiated, the remaining problem *simplifies* to a tractable class [25, 26, 12, 4, 15, 23, 20]. Note that the notion of tractability in the definition of backdoor sets is not necessarily syntactically defined: it may often be defined only by means of a polynomial time algorithm, such as unit propagation. In fact, the notion of backdoor sets came about as a way of explaining the high variance in performance of state-of-the-art SAT solvers, in particular heavy-tailed behavior, and as a tool for analyzing and understanding the efficient performance of these solvers on many real-world instances, in which the propagation mechanisms of fast "sub-solvers" play a key role. In this work the emphasis was not so much on efficiently identifying backdoor sets, but rather on the fact that many real-world instances have surprisingly small sets of backdoor variables and that once a SAT solver instantiates these variables, the rest of the problem is solved easily. In this context, randomization and restarts play an important role in searching for backdoor sets [25, 26].

Even though variable selection heuristics, randomization, and learning in current SAT/CSP solvers are quite effective at finding relatively small backdoors in practice, finding a *smallest backdoor* is in general intractable in the worst case. This intractability result assumes that the size of the smallest backdoor is unknown and can grow arbitrarily with n. However, if the size of the backdoor is small and fixed to k, one can search for the backdoor by considering all $\binom{n}{k}$ subsets of k variables and all 2^k truth assignments to these candidate variables. This is technically a polynomial time process for fixed k, although for moderate values of k the run time becomes infeasible in practice. Can one do better? This is a question considered in the area of fixed-parameter complexity theory. A problem with input size n and a parameter k is called *fixed-parameter tractable* w.r.t. k if it can be solved in time $O(f(k)n^c)$ where f is any computable function and c is a constant. Note that c does not depend on k, meaning that one can in principle search fairly efficiently for potentially large backdoors if backdoor detection for some class is shown to be fixed parameter tractable. Indeed, Nishimura, Ragde, and Szeider [19] showed that detecting strong backdoors (cf. Section 2 for a formal definition) w.r.t. the classes 2CNF and Horn is NP-complete but, interestingly, fixed-parameter tractable. This result for 2CNF and Horn formulas exploits the equivalence between (standard) strong backdoors and "deletion" backdoors, i.e., a set of variables that once deleted from a given formula (without simplification) make the remaining formula tractable. Note, however, that this result is only w.r.t. the tractable classes of *pure* 2CNF/Horn.

In particular, certain kinds of obvious inconsistencies are not detected in these classes, such as having an empty clause in an *arbitrary* formula — clearly, any basic solver detects such inconsistencies. We show that such a seemingly small feature increases the worst-case complexity of backdoor identification, but, perhaps more importantly, can dramatically reduce the size of the backdoor sets.

More specifically, we prove that strong Horn- and 2CNF-backdoor identification becomes both NP- and coNP-hard, and therefore strictly harder than NP assuming NP $\neq$ coNP, as soon as empty clause detection is added to these classes. This increase in formal complexity has however also a clear positive aspect in that adding empty clause detection often considerably reduces the backdoor size. For example, in certain graph coloring instances with planted cliques of size 4, while strong Horn-backdoors involve $\approx 67\%$ of the variables, the fraction of variables in the smallest strong backdoors w.r.t. mere empty clause detection converges to 0 as the size of the graph grows.

Encouraged by the positive effect of slightly extending our notion of Horn-backdoor, we also consider backdoors w.r.t. RHorn (renamable Horn), UP (unit propagation), PL (pure literal rule), UP+PL, and SATZ. For each of these notions, we show on a variety of domains that the corresponding backdoors are significantly smaller than pure, strong Horn-backdoors. For example, we consider the smallest deletion RHorn-backdoors. We provide a 0-1 integer programming formulation for finding such optimal backdoors, and show experimentally that they are in general smaller than strong Horn-backdoors. In particular, in the graph coloring domain, while strong Horn-backdoors correspond to $\approx 67\%$ of the variables, deletion RHorn-backdoors correspond to only $\approx 17\%$ of the variables. More interestingly, when considering real-world instances of a car configuration problem, while strong Horn-backdoor sets vary in size between 10-25% of the variables, deletion RHorn-backdoor sets vary only between 3-8%.

At a higher level, our results show that the size of backdoors can vary dramatically depending on the effectiveness of the underlying simplification and propagation mechanism. For example, as mentioned earlier, empty clause detection can have a major impact on backdoor size. Similarly, Horn versus RHorn has an impact. We also show that there can be a substantial difference between deletion backdoors, where one simply removes variables from the formula, versus strong backdoors, where one factors in the variable settings and considers the propagation effect of these settings. Specifically, we contrast deletion RHorn-backdoors with strong RHorn-backdoors. We prove by construction that there are formulas for which deletion RHorn-backdoors are exponentially larger than the smallest strong RHorn-backdoors.

Finally, despite the worst-case complexity results for strong backdoor detection, we show that *Satz-Rand* [16, 11] is remarkably good at finding small strong backdoors on a range of experimental domains. For example, in the case of our graph coloring instances, the fraction of variables in a small strong SATZ-backdoor converges to zero as the size of the graph grows. For the car configuration problem, strong SATZ-backdoor sets involve 0-0.7% of the variables. We next consider synthetic logistics planning instances over n variables that are known to have strong UP-backdoors of size $\log n$ [13]. For all these instances, the size of the strong SATZ-backdoor sets is either zero or one. In contrast, the size of deletion RHorn-backdoors corresponds to over 48% of the variables, increasing with n. We also consider instances from game theory for which one is interested in determining whether there is a pure Nash equilibrium. For these instances, while strong Horn-backdoors and deletion RHorn-backdoors involve $\approx$ 68% and $\approx$ 67% of the variables, respectively, strong SATZ-backdoors are surprising small at less than 0.05% of the variables.

These results show that real-world SAT solvers such as *Satz* are indeed remarkably good at finding small backdoors sets. At a broader level, this work suggests that the study of structural notions that lead to efficient algorithms for combinatorial problems should consider not only "easily" identifiable properties, such as being Horn, but also properties that capture key aspects of state-of-the-art constraint solvers, such as unit propagation and pure literal rule.

2 Preliminaries and Related Work

A *CNF formula* F is a conjunction of a finite set of clauses, a *clause* is a disjunction of a finite set of literals, and a *literal* is a Boolean variable or its negation. The literals associated with a variable x are denoted by x^ϵ, $\epsilon \in \{0,1\}$. $var(F)$ denotes the variables occurring in F. A (partial) *truth assignment* (or assignment, for short) is a map $\tau : X_\tau \to \{0,1\}$ defined on some subset of variables $X_\tau \subseteq var(F)$. A *solution* to a CNF formula F is a complete variable assignment τ (i.e., with $X_\tau = var(F)$) that satisfies all clauses of F. $F[\epsilon/x]$ denotes the simplified formula obtained from F by removing all clauses that contain the literal x^ϵ and removing, if present, the literal $x^{1-\epsilon}$ from the remaining clauses. For a partial truth assignment τ, $F[\tau]$ denotes the simplified formula obtained by setting the variables according to τ.

A *unit clause* is a clause that contains only one literal. A *pure literal* in F is a literal x^ϵ such that $x \in var(F)$ and $x^{1-\epsilon}$ does not occur in F. A *Horn clause* is a clause that contains at most one positive literal. A *binary clause* is a clause that contains exactly two literals. A formula is called *Horn* (resp., *2CNF*) if all its clauses are Horn (binary). We also use Horn and 2CNF to denote the two corresponding classes of formulas. *Renaming* or flipping a variable x in F means replacing every occurrence of x^ϵ in F with $x^{1-\epsilon}$. F is *Renamable Horn*, also called RHorn, if all clauses of F can be made Horn by flipping a subset of the variables. Following Nishimura et al. [19], we define the *deletion* of a variable x from a formula F as syntactically removing the literals of x from F: $F - x = \{c \setminus \{x^0, x^1\} \mid c \in F\}$. For $X \subseteq var(F)$, $F - X$ is defined similarly.

The concept of backdoors and their theoretical foundations were introduced by Williams, Gomes, and Selman [25, 26]. Informally, a strong backdoor set is a set of variables such that for each possible truth assignment to these variables, the simplified formula is tractable. The notion of tractability is quite general, and it even includes tractable classes for which there is not a clean syntactic characterization. It is formalized in terms of a polynomial time sub-solver:

Definition 1 (sub-solver [25]). *A* sub-solver *S is an algorithm that given as input a formula F satisfies the following conditions:*

1. Trichotomy: *S either rejects F or correctly determines it (as unsatisfiable or satisfiable, returning a solution if satisfiable),*
2. Efficiency: *S runs in polynomial time,*
3. Trivial solvability: *S can determine if F is trivially true (has no clauses) or trivially false (has an empty clause, $\{\}$), and*
4. Self-reducibility: *If S determines F, then for any variable x and value $\epsilon \in \{0,1\}$, S determines $F[\epsilon/x]$.*

Definition 2 (strong S-backdoor [25]). *A set B of variables is a* strong backdoor set *for a formula F w.r.t a sub-solver S if $B \subseteq var(F)$ and for every truth assignment $\tau : B \to \{0,1\}$, S returns a satisfying assignment for $F[\tau]$ or concludes that $F[\tau]$ is unsatisfiable.*

Clearly, if B is a strong S-backdoor for F, then so is any B' such that $B \subseteq B' \subseteq var(F)$. For any sub-solver S, given $\langle F, k\rangle$ as input, the problem of deciding whether F has a strong S-backdoor of size k is in the complexity class Σ_2^{P}: we can formulate it as, "does *there exist* a $B \subseteq var(F), |B| = k$, such that *for every* truth assignment $\tau : B \to \{0,1\}$, S correctly determines $F[\tau/B]$?" We are interested in the complexity of this problem for specific sub-solvers.

The most *trivial sub-solver* that fulfills the conditions in Definition 1 is the one that only checks for the empty formula and for the empty clause. Lynce and Marques-Silva [17] show that the search effort required by the SAT solver *zChaff* [18] to prove a random 3-SAT formula unsatisfiable is correlated with the size of the strong backdoors w.r.t. this trivial sub-solver.

More relevant sub-solvers employed by most state-of-the-art SAT solvers are Unit Propagation and Pure Literal Elimination, and their combination. Given a formula F, the Unit Propagation sub-solver (UP) checks whether the formula is empty or contains the empty clause, in which case it is trivially solvable, otherwise it checks whether the formula contains a unit clause. If yes, it assigns the variable in the unit clause the corresponding satisfying value, and recurses on the simplified formula. If the formula does not contain any more unit clauses, it is rejected. The Pure Literal Elimination sub-solver (PL) checks for variables that appear as pure literals, assigning them the corresponding value and simplifying, until the formula is trivially solvable or is rejected (when no more pure literals are found). The sub-solver that uses both of these rules is referred to as UP+PL.

We note that unit propagation by itself is known to be sufficient for computing a satisfying assignment for any satisfiable Horn formula: set variables following unit propagation until there are no more unit clauses, and set the remaining variables to 0. A similar result is known for RHorn formulas. Interestingly, this does not mean that the smallest UP-backdoors are never larger than Horn- and RHorn-backdoors. For example, any (satisfiable) Horn formula with $k \geq 2$ literals per clause has a strong Horn-backdoor of size zero but no strong UP-backdoor of size $k - 2$.

Szeider [23] studied the complexity of finding strong backdoors w.r.t. the above sub-solvers. For $S \in \{\text{UP, PL, UP+PL}\}$ and with k as the parameter of interest, he proved that the problem of deciding whether there exists a strong C-backdoor of size k is complete for the parameterized complexity class W[P]. Interestingly, the naïve brute-force procedure for this problem is already in W[P]; it has complexity $O(n^k 2^k n^\alpha)$ and works by enumerating all subsets of size $\leq k$, trying all assignments for each such subset, and running the $O(n^\alpha)$ time sub-solver. Hence, the in the worst case we cannot hope to find a smallest strong backdoor w.r.t. UP, PL, or UP+PL more efficiently than with brute-force search.

Satz [16] is a DPLL-based SAT solver that incorporates a strong variable selection heuristic and an efficient simplification strategy based on UP and PL. Its simplification process and lookahead techniques can be thought of as a very powerful sub-solver. Kilby et al. [15] study strong SATZ-backdoors: sets of variables such that for every assignment to these variables, *Satz* solves the simplified formula without any branching decisions (i.e., with a "branch-free" search). They measure problem hardness, defined as the logarithm of the number of search nodes required by *Satz*, and find that it is correlated with the size of the smallest strong SATZ-backdoors.

A sub-solver S correctly determines a subclass of CNF formulas and rejects others, and hence implicitly defines the class C_S of formulas that it can determine. A natural variation of the definition of the backdoor does not explicitly appeal to a sub-solver, but rather requires the remaining formula, after setting variables in the backdoor, to fall within a known tractable sub-class, such as 2CNF, Horn, or RHorn. We will refer to such backdoors as Horn-backdoor, RHorn-backdoor, etc. Note that this way of defining the backdoor de facto corresponds to relaxing the assumption of the sub-solver's trivial solvability and therefore trivially satisfiable or unsatisfiable formulas need not lie within the tractable class. For example, an arbitrary formula with an empty clause may not be Horn. Such formulas — with an empty clause in them — are important for our discussion and we use the following notation:

Definition 3. *$C_{\{\}}$ is the class of all formulas that contain the empty clause, $\{\}$. For any class C of formulas, $C^{\{\}}$ denotes the class $C \cup C_{\{\}}$.*

We will show that strong backdoors w.r.t. $2\text{CNF}^{\{\}}$ and $\text{Horn}^{\{\}}$ behave very differently, both in terms of the complexity of finding backdoors as well as backdoor size, compared to 2CNF and Horn. In our arguments, we will use two properties of formula classes defined next.

Definition 4. *A class C of formulas is* closed under removal of clauses *if removing arbitrary clauses from any formula in C keeps the formula in C.*

Definition 5. *A class C of formulas is said to* support large strong backdoors *if there exists a polynomial (in k) time constructible family $\{G_k\}_{k\geq 0}$ of formulas such that the smallest strong C-backdoors of G_k have size larger than k.*

Note that (pure) 2CNF, Horn, and RHorn are closed under removal of clauses, while $C^{\{\}}$ is in general not: removing the empty clause may put a formula outside

$C^{\{\}}$. Further, 2CNF and Horn support large strong backdoors as witnessed by the following simple single-clause family of formulas: $G_k = (x_1 \vee x_2 \vee \ldots \vee x_{k+3})$. It can be easily verified that the all-0's assignment to any set of k variables of G_k leaves a clause with three positive literals, which is neither 2CNF nor Horn.

A different notion of backdoors, motivated by the work of Nishimura et al. [19], involves a set of variables such that once these variables are "deleted" from the formula, the remaining formula falls into a given tractable class (without considering any simplification due to truth assignments). Formally,

Definition 6 (deletion C-backdoor). *A set B of variables is a deletion backdoor set of a formula F w.r.t. a class C if $B \subseteq var(F)$ and $F - B \in C$.*

When membership in C can be checked in polynomial time, the problem of deciding whether F has a deletion C-backdoor of size k is trivially in NP. This problem is in fact NP-complete when C is 2CNF [19], Horn [19], or RHorn [2].

In general, a deletion C-backdoor may not be a strong C-backdoor. E.g., when C includes $C_{\{\}}$, any 3CNF formula F has a trivial deletion C-backdoor of size 3: select any clause and use its variables as the deletion backdoor. Unfortunately, such a "backdoor" set is of limited practical use for efficiently solving F. When the class C is closed under removal of clauses, every deletion C-backdoor is indeed also a strong C-backdoor. Conversely, strong C-backdoors often are not deletion C-backdoors, because assigning values to variables usually leads to further simplification of the formula. Nonetheless, for $C \in \{\text{2CNF, Horn}\}$, deletion and strong backdoors are equivalent, a key fact underlying the fixed parameter algorithm of Nishimura et al. [19]. We will show that this equivalence between deletion backdoors and strong backdoors does not hold for RHorn.

Paris et al. [20] studied deletion RHorn-backdoors. They proposed a two step approach: find a renaming that maximizes the number of Horn clauses using a local search method and then greedily delete variables from the remaining non-Horn clauses until the renamed formula becomes Horn. The variables deleted in the second step form a deletion RHorn-backdoor. They find that branching on these variables can significantly speed up DPLL solvers.

3 Theoretical Results

In this section, we first prove that the two problems of deciding whether a formula has a strong backdoor w.r.t. 2CNF$^{\{\}}$ and Horn$^{\{\}}$, respectively, are NP-hard as well as coNP-hard. This shows that unless NP=coNP, this problem is much harder than detecting strong backdoors w.r.t. 2CNF and Horn, which are both known to be in NP [19]. Recall that adding $C_{\{\}}$ to 2CNF and Horn corresponds to adding empty clause detection to the two classes. We then consider the class RHorn and prove that strong RHorn-backdoors can be exponentially smaller than deletion RHorn-backdoors, and are therefore more likely to succinctly capture structural properties of interest in formulas.

Lemma 1. *Let $C \in \{\text{Horn, 2CNF}\}$. Given a formula F and $k \geq 0$, the problem of deciding whether F has a strong $C^{\{\}}$-backdoor of size k is NP-hard.*

Proof. We extend the argument originally used by Nishimura et al. [19] for (pure) 2CNF/Horn. The polynomial time reduction is from the NP-complete Vertex Cover problem: given an undirected graph $G = (V, E)$ and a number $k \geq 0$, does G have a vertex cover of size k? Recall that a vertex cover U is a subset of V such that every edge in E has at least one end point in U. Given an instance $\langle G, k \rangle$ of this problem, we will construct a formula F_{Horn} with all positive literals such that F_{Horn} has a strong Horn$^{\{\}}$-backdoor of size k iff G has a vertex cover of size k. Similarly, we will construct F_{2CNF}.

F_{Horn} has $|V|$ variables and $|E|$ clauses. The variables are x_v for each $v \in V$. For each edge $e = \{u, v\} \in E, u < v$, F_{Horn} contains the binary clause $(x_u \vee x_v)$. It is easy to see that if G has a vertex cover U, then the corresponding variable set $X_U = \{x_u \mid u \in U\}$ is a strong Horn$^{\{\}}$-backdoor: for any assignment τ to X_U, $F[\tau/X_U]$ only contains unit clauses or the empty clause, and is thus in Horn$^{\{\}}$. For the other direction, suppose X_U is a strong Horn$^{\{\}}$-backdoor. We claim that variables of X_U must touch every clause of F_{Horn} so that the corresponding vertices U touch every edge of G and thus form a vertex cover. To see this, consider the all-1's assignment τ_1 to X_U. Since X_U is a strong Horn$^{\{\}}$-backdoor and assigning variables according to τ_1 cannot result in creating the empty clause, $F_{\text{Horn}}[\tau_1/X_U]$ must be Horn. If X_U did not touch a clause c of F_{Horn}, then c would appear in $F_{\text{Horn}}[\tau_1/X_U]$ as a binary clause with two positive literals, violating the Horn property. Hence, the claim holds.

F_{2CNF} has $|V| + |E|$ variables and $|E|$ clauses. The variables are x_v for each $v \in V$ and $y_{u,v}$ for each $\{u, v\} \in E, u < v$. For each such $\{u, v\}$, F_{2CNF} contains the ternary clause $(x_u \vee x_v \vee y_{u,v})$. The argument for the correctness of the reduction is very similar to above, relying on the all-1's assignment. The only difference is that if we have a strong backdoor X_U, it may contain some of the y variables, so that there is no direct way to obtain a vertex cover out of X_U. However, this is easy to fix. If X_U contains $y_{u,v}$ and also at least one of x_u and x_v, we can simply disregard $y_{u,v}$ when constructing a vertex cover. If X_U contains $y_{u,v}$ but neither x_u nor x_v, we can replace $y_{u,v}$ with either of these two variables and obtain a backdoor set with fewer (and eventually no) such y variables. □

We now prove coNP-hardness of backdoor detection w.r.t. Horn$^{\{\}}$ and 2CNF$^{\{\}}$, exploiting the notions introduced in Definitions 4 and 5.

Lemma 2. *Let C be a class of formulas such that (1) C is closed under removal of clauses and (2) C supports large strong backdoors. Then, given a formula F and $k \geq 0$, the problem of deciding whether F has a strong $C^{\{\}}$-backdoor of size k is coNP-hard.*

Proof. Let UNSAT denote the coNP-complete problem of deciding whether a given CNF formula is unsatisfiable. We prove the lemma by reducing UNSAT to $C^{\{\}}$-backdoor detection. Let H be a CNF formula over variables V_H, $|V_H| = k$. We create a formula F such that F has a strong $C^{\{\}}$-backdoor of size k iff H is unsatisfiable. The idea is to start with H and append to it a formula on a disjoint set of variables such that for any assignment to k backdoor variables, the combined formula does not reduce to a formula in C and must therefore contain the empty clause in order to belong to $C^{\{\}}$.

F is constructed as follows. Using the fact that C supports large strong backdoors, construct in polynomial time a formula G over a disjoint set of variables (i.e., variables not appearing in H) such that G does not have a strong C-backdoor of size k. Now let $F = H \wedge G$. We prove that $H \in$ UNSAT iff F has a strong $C^{\{\}}$-backdoor of size k.

($\Rightarrow$) Suppose H is unsatisfiable. This implies that every truth assignment τ to V_H, the variables of H, violates some clause of H. It follows that for each such τ, $F[\tau/V_H] = H[\tau/V_H] \wedge G[\tau/V_H]$ contains the empty clause and is therefore in $C^{\{\}}$. Hence V_H gives us the desired backdoor of size k.

($\Leftarrow$) Suppose F has a strong $C^{\{\}}$-backdoor B of size k. Partition B into $B_H \cup B_G$, where B_H has the variables of H and B_G has the variables of G. By the construction of G and because $|B_G| \leq k$, B_G cannot be a strong C-backdoor for G. In other words, there exists an assignment τ_G to B_G such that $G[\tau_G/B_G] \notin C$. Because of the closure of C under removal of clauses and and the variable disjointness of H and G, it follows that $F[\tau/B] \notin C$ for every extension $\tau = (\tau_H, \tau_G)$ of τ_G to all of B. However, since B is a strong $C^{\{\}}$-backdoor for F, it must be that $F[\tau/B] \in C^{\{\}}$, and the only possibility left is that $F[\tau/B] \in C_{\{\}}$. Since $G[\tau_G/B_G] \notin C_{\{\}}$, it must be that $H[\tau_H/B_H] \in C_{\{\}}$ for all such extensions τ of τ_G. In words, this says that $H[\tau_H/B_H]$ contains a violated clause for every truth assignment to B_H. Therefore, H is unsatisfiable as desired. □

Lemmas 1 and 2 together give us our main theorem:

Theorem 1. *Let $C \in$ {Horn, 2CNF}. Given a formula F and $k \geq 0$, the problem of deciding whether F has a strong $C^{\{\}}$-backdoor of size k is both NP-hard and coNP-hard, and thus harder than both NP and coNP, assuming NP $\neq$ coNP.*

We now turn our attention to the relationship between strong and deletion backdoors. While these two kinds of backdoors are known to be equivalent for the classes 2CNF and Horn, we prove an exponential separation for the class RHorn. The main idea is the following. Suppose B is a strong RHorn-backdoor for F. Then for each assignment τ to the variables in B, there exists a renaming r_τ such that $F[\tau/B]$ under the renaming r_τ yields a Horn formula. If F is such that for different τ, the various renamings r_τ are different and mutually incompatible, then there is no single renaming r under which $F - B$, the formula obtained by deleting the variables in B, becomes Horn.

The following example illustrates this point, which we will generalize to an exponential separation in the proof of Theorem 2. Let $F = (x_1 \vee x_2) \wedge (\neg y_1 \vee \neg y_2) \wedge (\neg x_1 \vee y_1 \vee z) \wedge (\neg x_1 \vee y_2 \vee \neg z) \wedge (\neg x_2 \vee y_1 \vee z) \wedge (\neg x_2 \vee y_2 \vee \neg z)$. First we observe that $B = \{z\}$ is a strong RHorn-backdoor for F because for $z = 0$ we can rename x_1 and y_1, and for $z = 1$ we can rename x_1 and y_2 to get a Horn formula. On the other hand, $\{z\}$ certainly does not work as a deletion backdoor because we must rename at least one of x_1 and x_2, which forces both y_1 and y_2 to be renamed and violates the Horn property. In fact, it can be easily verified both $\{x_1\}$ and $\{y_1\}$ are also not deletion RHorn-backdoors. From the symmetry between x_1 and x_2 and between y_1 and y_2, it follows that F does not have a deletion RHorn-backdoor of size 1.

Theorem 2. *There are formulas for which the smallest strong RHorn-backdoors are exponentially smaller than any deletion RHorn-backdoors.*

Proof. Let s be a power of 2, $t = s+\log_2 s$, and $n = s+\log_2 s+t = 2\cdot(s+\log_2 s)$. We will prove the theorem by explicitly constructing a family of formulas $\{F_n\}$ such that F_n is defined over n variables, F_n has a strong RHorn-backdoor of size $\log_2 s = \Theta(\log n)$, and every deletion RHorn-backdoor for F_n is of size at least $s + \log_2 s - 1 = \Theta(n)$.

F_n is constructed on three kinds of variables: $\{x_i \mid 1 \leq i \leq t\}$, $\{y_j \mid 1 \leq j \leq s\}$, and $\{z_k \mid 1 \leq k \leq \log_2 s\}$. Variables z_k are used to encode all s 0-1 sequences of length $\log_2 s$. Specifically, for $1 \leq j \leq s$, let D_z^j be the unique clause involving all z variables where each z_k appears negated in D_z^j iff the kth bit of j, written in the binary representation, is a 1. For example, for $j = 01101$, $D_z^j = (z_1 \vee \neg z_2 \vee \neg z_3 \vee z_4 \vee \neg z_5)$. Note that D_z^j is falsified precisely by the unique assignment that corresponds to the binary representation of j.

F_n has exactly $st+2$ clauses: $C_x = (x_1 \vee x_2 \vee \ldots \vee x_t)$, $C_y = (\neg y_1 \vee \neg y_2 \vee \ldots \vee \neg y_s)$, and for each $i \in \{1, \ldots, t\}, j \in \{1, \ldots, s\}$, the clause $C_z^{i,j} = (\neg x_i \vee y_j \vee D_z^j)$.

We now analyze RHorn-backdoors for F_n. First, we show that $\{z_k \mid 1 \leq k \leq \log_2 s\}$ is a strong RHorn-backdoor for F_n. To see this, fix any assignment $\tau \in \{0,1\}^{\log_2 s}$ to the z variables. By the discussion above, τ satisfies all but one clause D_z^j. Let us denote this falsified clause by D_z^τ. It follows that the reduced formula, $F_n[\tau/z]$, consists of C_x, C_y, and for each $i \in \{1, \ldots, t\}$, the binary clause $(\neg x_i \vee y_\tau)$. We can convert this formula to Horn by renaming or flipping the signs of all x_i, and of y_τ. This renaming makes C_x Horn. Further, it preserves the Horn property of C_y as well as of each of the t residual binary clauses. Hence the z variables form a strong RHorn-backdoor of size $\log_2 s$.

To derive a lower bound on the size of every deletion RHorn-backdoor B, notice that if B includes at least $t-1$ of the x variables, then $|B| \geq t - 1 = s + \log_2 s - 1$, as claimed. Otherwise, B does not contain at least two of the x variables, and we must therefore rename at least one of these two variables, say x_1, to make C_x Horn. This implies that we must flip all variables $y_j \notin B$ because of the clauses $C_z^{1,j}$ which now already have a positive literal, x_1. However, because of the clause C_y, we can flip at most one y variable, and it follows that at least $s-1$ of the y variables are in B. Moreover, we also have that all $\log_2 s$ of the z variables are in B, because otherwise, irrespective of how the z variables are renamed, in at least one $C_z^{1,j}$ clause a z variable will appear positively, violating the Horn property. Hence, $|B| \geq s - 1 + \log_2 s$, as claimed. This finishes the proof. □

4 Computing the Smallest Backdoors

Smallest Strong Horn-Backdoors: The problem of finding a smallest strong Horn-backdoor can be formulated as a 0-1 integer programming problem using the equivalence to deletion backdoors [19]. Given a formula F, associate with each Boolean variable x_i a 0-1 variable y_i, where $y_i = 0$ denotes that the corresponding variable x_i is deleted from F (and added to the backdoor). For a clause $c \in F$, let $c^+ = \{i \mid x_i^1 \in c\}$ and $c^- = \{i \mid x_i^0 \in c\}$. The smallest (deletion) Horn-backdoor problem is formulated as follows:

$$\begin{array}{lll} \text{minimize} & \sum_{i \in var(F)} (1 - y_i) & \\ \text{subject to} & \sum_{i \in c^+} y_i \leq 1, & \forall c \in F \\ & y_i \in \{0,1\}, & \forall x_i \in var(F) \end{array}$$

The constraints ensure that each clause is Horn (in each clause, the total number of not-deleted positive literals is at most one). The objective function minimizes the size of the backdoor.

Smallest Deletion RHorn-Backdoors: The problem of finding a smallest deletion RHorn-backdoor can be formulated similarly. Given a formula F, associate with each Boolean variable x_i three 0-1 variables y_{1i}, y_{2i}, y_{3i}, where $y_{1i} = 1$ denotes that x_i is not renamed in F, $y_{2i} = 1$ denotes that x_i is renamed in F, and $y_{3i} = 1$ denotes that x_i is deleted from F (and added to the deletion backdoor). The smallest deletion RHorn-backdoor problem is formulated as follows:

$$\begin{array}{lcl} \text{minimize} & \sum_{i \in var(F)} y_{3i} & \\ \text{subject to} & y_{1i} + y_{2i} + y_{3i} = 1, & \forall x_i \in var(F) \\ & \sum_{i \in c^+} y_{1i} + \sum_{i \in c^-} y_{2i} \leq 1, & \forall c \in F \\ & y_{1i}, y_{2i}, y_{3i} \in \{0,1\}, & \forall x_i \in var(F) \end{array}$$

The first set of constraints ensures that each Boolean variable x_i is either not-renamed, renamed, or deleted. The second set of constraints ensures that each clause is Horn (in each clause, the total number of not-renamed positive literals and renamed negative literals is at most one). The objective function minimizes the size of the backdoor.

We use the above encodings and the ILOG CPLEX libraries [14] for experimenting with Horn- and RHorn-backdoors.

Smallest Strong SATZ-, UP-, and (UP+PL)-Backdoors: Following previous work [25, 15], we consider strong backdoors w.r.t. branch-free search by *Satz-Rand* [11], a randomized version of *Satz* [16]. These are referred to as SATZ-backdoors. We obtain an upper bound on the size of the smallest strong SATZ-backdoors by running *Satz-Rand* without restarts multiple times with different seeds and recording the set of variables on which the solver branches when proving unsatisfiability. We also record the set of variables not set by UP and PL. This gives us an upper bound on the strong (UP+PL)-backdoor size. Similarly we record all variables set in *Satz-Rand* by anything but the UP procedure to obtain an upper bound on the smallest strong UP-backdoor size.

Table 1. Strong backdoor sizes for various ensembles of instances: Graph Coloring (gcp), MAP planning (map), Pure Nash Equilibrium (pne), and Automotive Configuration (Cxxx). Each row reports the average over several instances. Backdoor sizes are shown as the average % of the number of problem variables. The RHorn numbers are for deletion backdoors. Horn- and RHorn-backdoor sizes are for the smallest corresponding backdoors, while the rest are upper bounds.

instance set	num vars	num clauses	Horn %	RHorn (del) %	SATZ %	UP+PL %	UP %	$C_{\{\}}$ %
gcp_100	300	7557.7	66.67	17.00	0.30	1.20	1.23	4.00
gcp_200	600	30122.0	66.67	16.83	0.17	0.60	0.60	2.00
gcp_300	900	67724.4	66.67	16.78	0.11	0.51	0.60	1.33
gcp_400	1200	119997.4	66.67	16.75	0.08	0.38	0.55	1.00
gcp_500	1500	187556.0	66.67	16.73	0.07	0.28	0.80	0.80
map_5_7	249	720	38.96	37.75	0	2.01	2.01	
map_10_17	1284	5000	44.55	44.31	0	1.17	1.17	
map_20_37	5754	33360	47.31	47.25	0	0.61	0.61	
map_30_57	13424	103120	48.21	48.19	0	0.41	3.23	
map_40_77	24294	232280	48.66	48.65	0	0.31	3.20	
map_50_97	38364	438840	48.93	48.92	0	0.25	3.19	
pne	2000	40958.9	67.88	66.86	0.05	0.38	0.42	
pne	3000	60039.7	67.66	66.55	0.00	0.17	0.20	
pne	4000	79666.4	67.96	66.92	0.00	0.14	0.16	
pne	5000	98930.8	67.80	66.80	0.00	0.13	0.15	
C168_FW_SZ	1698	5646.8	14.32	2.83	0.16	0.77	5.70	
C168_FW_UT	1909	7489.3	23.62	5.50	0.00	0.36	1.03	
C170_FR_SZ	1659	4989.8	9.98	3.57	0.13	0.57	15.19	
C202_FS_SZ	1750	6227.8	12.31	4.55	0.13	0.61	9.42	
C202_FW_SZ	1799	8906.9	14.48	6.12	0.22	0.89	10.86	
C202_FW_UT	2038	11352.0	21.25	7.61	0.00	0.20	1.86	
C208_FA_SZ	1608	5286.2	10.52	4.51	0.06	0.40	6.50	
C208_FA_UT	1876	7335.5	23.13	7.46	0.00	0.05	0.05	
C208_FC_RZ	1654	5567.0	10.28	4.59	0.36	1.12	12.91	
C208_FC_SZ	1654	5571.8	10.47	4.68	0.16	0.63	10.41	
C210_FS_RZ	1755	5764.3	11.64	4.22	0.55	1.25	12.12	
C210_FS_SZ	1755	5796.8	11.77	4.35	0.30	0.91	15.56	
C210_FW_RZ	1789	7408.3	12.54	4.81	0.65	1.42	12.97	
C210_FW_SZ	1789	7511.8	13.74	5.37	0.23	0.78	11.15	
C210_FW_UT	2024	9720.0	20.73	7.31	0.00	0.64	4.42	
C220_FV_SZ	1728	4758.2	9.14	2.92	0.19	0.46	8.88	

5 Experimental Evaluation

For our experimental evaluation, we considered four problem domains: graph coloring, logistics planning, equilibrium problems from game theory, and car configuration. The results are shown in Table 1.

We generated graph coloring instances using the clique hiding graph generator of Brockington and Culberson [1]. All instances were generated with the probability of adding an edge equal to 0.5 and with a hidden clique of size 4. All SAT-encoded instances are unsatisfiable when the number of colors is 3. The twelve variables representing color assignments to the four vertices in the hidden 4-clique constitute a strong $C_{\{\}}$-backdoor, since any assignment of colors to these four vertices will fail at least one coloring constraint. This domain illustrates how the strong Horn-backdoors and deletion RHorn-backdoors can be significantly larger than backdoors w.r.t. empty clause detection; it also shows that deletion RHorn-backdoors (involving $\approx 17\%$ of the variables) are considerably smaller than strong Horn-backdoors ($\approx 67\%$). We note that *Satz* is very efficient at finding the small backdoors corresponding to the planted cliques.

The MAP problem domain is a synthetic logistics planning domain for which the size of the strong UP-backdoors is well understood [13]. In this domain, n is the number of nodes in the map graph and k is the number of locations to visit. All MAP instances considered are unsatisfiable, encoding one planning step less than the length of the optimal plan. Hoffmann et al. [13] identify that MAP instances with $k = 2n-3$ (called asymmetric) have logarithmic size DPLL refutations (and backdoors). We evaluate the size of the backdoors in asymmetric MAP instances of various sizes ($n = 5..50$). In this domain, strong Horn-backdoors and deletion RHorn-backdoors are of comparable size and relatively large (37-48%); as expected strong UP-backdoors are quite small. Interestingly, *Satz* solves these instances without any search at all, implying that the smallest strong SATZ-backdoor is of size 0.

The game theory instances encode the problem of computing an equilibrium strategy. In a game, interactions between players can be represented by an undirected graph where nodes represent players and edges represent mutual dependencies between players. Each player has a finite set of actions and a payoff function that assigns a real number to every selection of actions by him and his neighbors. Here we consider binary games, where each player has exactly two action choices. Our focus will be on random graphical games where each payoff value is chosen uniformly and independently at random from the interval $[0,1]$ and the interaction graphs are drawn from the Erdös-Rényi random graph model $\mathbb{G}(n,p)$. In a pure Nash equilibrium (PNE), each player chooses an action and has no incentive to unilaterally deviate and change his action, given the actions chosen by the other players (i.e. each player has chosen a best response action to the choices of his neighbors). We encode the problem of deciding whether a graphical game has a PNE as a CNF formula that is satisfiable iff the given game has a PNE. For every player p, there is a Boolean variable x_p encoding the action chosen by p. For each possible action assignment for the neighbors of p, we add a clause ruling out the non-best response action of p. For this domain, while strong Horn-backdoor sets and deletion RHorn-backdoor involve $\approx 68\%$ and $\approx 67\%$ of the variables, respectively, strong SATZ-backdoors are surprisingly small, close to 0% of the variables.

Finally, we also consider a real-world SAT benchmark from product configuration. The instances encode problems from the validation and verification of automotive product configuration data for the Daimler Chrysler's Mercedes car lines [22]. We consider a set of unsatisfiable instances available at http://www-sr.informatik.uni-tuebingen.de/~sinz/DC/. Here, while strong Horn-backdoors vary between 10-25% of the variables, RHorn-backdoor sets are considerably smaller at 3-8%. Strong SATZ-backdoors involve only 0-0.7% of the variables.

6 Conclusions

The complexity of finding backdoors is influenced significantly by the features of the underlying sub-solver or tractable problem class. In particular, while the problem of identifying a strong Horn- or 2CNF-backdoor is known to be in NP and fixed parameter tractable, strong backdoor identification w.r.t. to Horn and 2CNF becomes harder than NP (unless NP=coNP) as soon as the seemingly small feature of empty clause detection (present in all modern SAT solvers) is incorporated. While such a feature increases the worst-case complexity of finding backdoors, our experiments show that in practice it also has a clear positive impact: it reduces the size of the backdoors dramatically. For the class RHorn, we prove that deletion backdoors can be exponentially larger than strong backdoors, in contrast with the known results for 2CNF- and Horn-backdoors. Nonetheless, we show experimentally that deletion RHorn-backdoors can be substantially smaller than strong Horn-backdoors. We also demonstrate that strong backdoors w.r.t. UP, PL, and UP+PL can be substantially smaller than strong Horn-backdoors and deletion RHorn-backdoors. Finally, despite the worst-case complexity results for strong backdoor detection, we show that *Satz-Rand* is remarkably good at finding small strong backdoors on a range of problem domains.

Acknowledgments

The authors would like to thank Joerg Hoffmann for providing the generator for the MAP domain, and the reviewers for their thoughtful comments. This research was supported by IISI, Cornell University, AFOSR Grant FA9550-04-1-0151.

References

[1] Brockington, M., Culberson, J.C.: Camouflaging independent sets in quasi-random graphs. In: Johnson, D.S., Trick, M.A. (eds.) Cliques, Coloring, and Satisfiability: Second DIMACS Implementation Challenge, American Mathematical Society, vol. 26, pp. 75–88 (1996)

[2] Chandru, V., Hooker, J.N.: Detecting embedded Horn structure in propositional logic. Information Processing Letters 42(2), 109–111 (1992)

[3] Chen, H., Dalmau, V.: Beyond hypertree width: Decomposition methods without decompositions. In: van Beek, P. (ed.) CP 2005. LNCS, vol. 3709, pp. 167–181. Springer, Heidelberg (2005)

[4] Chen, H., Gomes, C., Selman, B.: Formal models of heavy-tailed behavior in combinatorial search. In: Walsh, T. (ed.) CP 2001. LNCS, vol. 2239, Springer, Heidelberg (2001)

[5] Dechter, R.: Constraint Processing. Morgan Kaufmann Publishers Inc., San Francisco (2003)

[6] Dechter, R., Pearl, J.: Network-based heuristics for constraint-satisfaction problems. Artif. Intell. 34(1), 1–38 (1987)

[7] Deville, Y., Van Hentenryck, P.: An efficient arc consistency algorithm for a class of csp problems. In: IJCAI'91, pp. 325–330 (1991)

[8] Freuder, E.C.: A sufficient condition for backtrack-free search. J. ACM 29(1), 24–32 (1982)

[9] Freuder, E.C.: A sufficient condition for backtrack-bounded search. J. ACM 32(4), 755–761 (1985)

[10] Freuder, E.C.: Complexity of k-tree structured constraint satisfaction problems. In: AAAI'90, Boston, MA, pp. 4–9 (1990)

[11] Gomes, C., Selman, B., Kautz, H.: Boosting Combinatorial Search Through Randomization. In: AAAI'98, New Providence, RI, pp. 431–438 (1998)

[12] Gomes, C.P., Selman, B., Crato, N., Kautz, H.: Heavy-tailed phenomena in satisfiability and constraint satisfaction problems. J. Autom. Reason. 24(1-2), 67–100 (2000)

[13] Hoffmann, J., Gomes, C., Selman, B.: Structure and problem hardness: Goal asymmetry and DPLL proofs in SAT-based planning. Logical Methods in Computer Science 3(1:6) (2007)

[14] ILOG, SA.: CPLEX 10.1 Reference Manual (2006)

[15] Kilby, P., Slaney, J.K., Thiébaux, S., Walsh, T.: Backbones and backdoors in satisfiability. In: AAAI'05, pp. 1368–1373 (2005)

[16] Li, C.M., Anbulagan: Heuristics based on unit propagation for satisfiability problems. In: IJCAI'97, pp. 366–371 (1997)

[17] Lynce, I., Marques-Silva, J.: Hidden structure in unsatisfiable random 3-SAT: An empirical study. In: ICTAI'04 (2004)

[18] Moskewicz, M.W., Madigan, C.F., Zhao, Y., Zhang, L., Malik, S.: Chaff: engineering an efficient SAT solver. In: DAC'01, pp. 530–535 (2001) ISBN 1-58113-297-2.

[19] Nishimura, N., Ragde, P., Szeider, S.: Detecting backdoor sets with respect to Horn and binary clauses. In: Hoos, H.H., Mitchell, D.G. (eds.) SAT 2004. LNCS, vol. 3542. Springer, Heidelberg (2005)

[20] Paris, L., Ostrowski, R., Siegel, P., Sais, L.: Computing Horn strong backdoor sets thanks to local search. In: ICTAI'06, pp. 139–143 (2006), http://.ieeecomputersociety.org/10.1109/ICTAI.2006.43 ISSN 1082-3409

[21] Samer, M., Szeider, S.: Constraint satisfaction with bounded treewidth revisited. In: Benhamou, F. (ed.) CP 2006. LNCS, vol. 4204, pp. 499–513. Springer, Heidelberg (2006)

[22] Sinz, C., Kaiser, A., Küchlin, W.: Formal methods for the validation of automotive product configuration data. Artificial Intelligence for Engr. Design, Analysis and Manufacturing 17(1), 75–97 (2003)

[23] Szeider, S.: Backdoor sets for DLL subsolvers. J. of Automated Reasoning (2005)

[24] van Beek, P., Dechter, R.: On the minimality and global consistency of row-convex constraint networks. J. ACM 42(3), 543–561 (1995)

[25] Williams, R., Gomes, C., Selman, B.: Backdoors to typical case complexity. In: IJCAI'03, pp. 1173–1178 (2003)

[26] Williams, R., Gomes, C., Selman, B.: On the connections between heavy-tails, backdoors, and restarts in combinatorial search. In: Giunchiglia, E., Tacchella, A. (eds.) SAT 2003. LNCS, vol. 2919, pp. 222–230. Springer, Heidelberg (2004)

Model-Driven Visualizations of Constraint-Based Local Search*

Grégoire Dooms[1], Pascal Van Hentenryck[1], and Laurent Michel[2]

[1] Brown University, Box 1910, Providence, RI 02912
[2] University of Connecticut, Storrs, CT 06269-2155

Abstract. Visualization is often invaluable to understand the behavior of optimization algorithms, identify their bottlenecks or pathological behaviors, and suggest remedies. Yet developing visualizations is a tedious activity requiring significant time and expertise. This paper presents a framework for the visualization of constraint-based local search (CBLS). Given a high-level model and a declarative visualization specification, the CBLS visualizer systematically produces animations to visualize constraints and objectives, violations, and conflicts, as well as the temporal behavior of these measures. The visualization specification is composed of a triple (*what,where,how*) indicating what to display, where, and how. The visualizer architecture is compositional and extensible, and focuses almost exclusively on static aspects, the dynamic aspects being automated by invariants. The paper highlights various functionalities of the visualizer and describes a blueprint for its implementation.

1 Introduction

The visualizations of optimization algorithms have been an integral part of constraint programming (CP) since its inception. Systems such as CHIP [5] already featured graphical interfaces to understand and explain the behavior of constraint programs. Visualization and debugging of constraint programs became a major research topic in the 1990s. It led to the DISCiPl project [4] and some exciting developments such as the visualization of search trees (e.g., [3,9,10,16]), global constraints (e.g., [2,6,11]), and the effect of propagation on the variable domains (e.g., [10,16]). High-level visualization tools are desirable for at least two reasons. On the one hand, building visualizations typically requires significant time, care, and expertise because of the large gap between what users would like to see and the abstractions provided by traditional graphical packages. On the other hand, visualizations are often invaluable in analyzing the behaviour of optimization algorithms, exhibiting their pathological behaviors, identifying their bottlenecks, and suggesting avenues for improvements.

This research proposes a visualization framework for constraint-based local search (CBLS) [15]. Inspired by earlier research, it is also motivated by the fact

* Partially supported by NSF awards DMI-0600384 & IIS-0642906 and ONR Award N000140610607.

C. Bessiere (Ed.): CP 2007, LNCS 4741, pp. 271–285, 2007.

that, although CP and CBLS models are often quite close, the information to visualize is fundamentally different in the two paradigms. Indeed, in CP, it is often important to visualize the effect of constraint propagation and branching heuristics on the search space and the search tree. In CBLS however, the search algorithm typically works with a complete assignment of the decision variables and it becomes critical to visualize such concepts as violations, variable gradients, and conflicts, as well as their evolution over time. Our visualization framework thus aims at providing a high-level visualization tool for CBLS algorithms, leveraging and amplifying the contributions from CP visualizers.

Our CBLS visualizer recognizes the inherent difficulty in implementing visualizations and strives to automate the visualization process, systematically exploiting the substructures within CBLS models. It is based on the slogan

CBLS Animation = Model + Visualization Specification

capturing that a CBLS animation is obtained automatically from a model and a visualization specification. The specification is declarative and expressed in a small, compositional language, describing *what* must be visualized (e.g., variable conflicts), *how* to represent it visually (e.g., using arcs to link variables in conflict), and *where* to display the visualization (e.g., on a variable/value view). Modelers can thus focus on what to visualize, not on how to build animations.

Moreover, our CBLS visualizer features an extensible and compositional architecture, focusing almost exclusively on the static aspects of visualization. Its implementation proceeds by successive refinements, transforming the model and the visualization specification into increasingly specific abstractions. In particular, the CBLS visualizer first extracts the relevant *model concepts* (e.g., conflict sets), transforms them into *visual concepts* (set of arcs), before producing *graphical concepts* (set of arcs with constrained logical coordinates). All these steps are concerned with *static* descriptions of what must be visualized; they do not deal with the dynamic aspects of the visualizations which are often most challenging and require low-level concepts such as callbacks. Instead, the animation is obtained by the use of *invariants* to maintain the model, visual, and graphical concepts incrementally. The incremental variables associated with each concept type are thus the interface between the various abstraction layers, while the declarative graphical layer automates the dynamic aspects of the visualization.

Our two main contributions can thus be summarized as follows:

1. We show how to systematically derive CBLS animations from high-level models and declarative visualization specifications, exploiting the structure of constraints and objectives.
2. We present a compositional and extensible architecture for the CBLS visualizer, focusing almost exclusively on the static parts of the visualization.

The goal of this paper (best viewed in color) is to convey these two contributions. The paper first illustrates interesting animations for a variety of models, illustrating the functionalities of the tool and its relationship with prior work. It then presents the visualizer architecture with two goals in mind: To explain how the animations are systematically derived and to highlight its compositionality, extensibility, and its "declarative" nature. The CBLS visualizer is entirely written on top of the COMET system and consists of about 5,000 lines of code.

2 The CBLS Visualizer at Work

Visualizing Constraints: Figure 1 depicts how to visualize the car-sequencing model in COMET [14]. Lines 1–6 depict the COMET model, while lines 7–8 specify the visualization by declaring a CBLS visualizer and requesting that all (soft) constraints be visualized. The resulting animation is sketched in Figure 2. Each row in the display corresponds to a sequence constraint (one for each option), each red rectangle highlights a slot in the assembly line for which the sequence constraint is violated, and each yellow rectangle shows a slot requiring the option. This animation provides the counterpart for CBLS of the constraint-based visualizations in CP (e.g., [11]), exploiting the structure and semantics of the high-level model to provide a meaningful animation of CBLS concepts. *But it goes one step beyond by cleanly separating the model from the visualization specification.* Indeed, the visualization only receives the model as input and cleanly separates the model and the visualization. It is the responsibility of the visualizer to collect the constraints from the model.

```
1 model m {
2  var{int} line[Cars](Configs);
3  hard: atmost(demand,line);
4  forall(o in Options)
5    soft: sequence(line,options[o],n[o],len[o]);
6 }
7 CBLSVisualizer visu();
8 visu.displayConstraints(m);
```

Fig. 1. Animating The Car Sequencing Problem

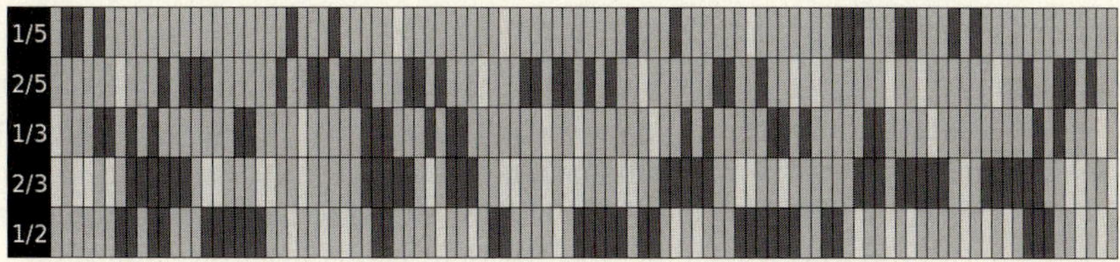

Fig. 2. The Car-Sequencing Animation

```
model m {
 var{int} boat[Periods,Groups](Hosts);
 forall(g in Groups)
   soft(2): alldifferent(all(p in Periods) boat[p,g]);
 forall(p in Periods)
   soft(2): knapsack(all(g in Groups) boat[p,g],crew,cap);
 forall(i in Groups, j in Groups : j > i)
   soft(1): atmost(1,all(p in Periods) boat[p,i] == boat[p,j]);
}
```

(a) The Progressive Party Problem.

```
model m {
   var{bool} open[w in Warehouses]();
   minimize: sum(w in Warehouses) fcost[w] * open[w] +
             sumMinCost(open,tcost);
}
```

(b) The Warehouse Location Problem.

Fig. 3. Models for The Running Applications

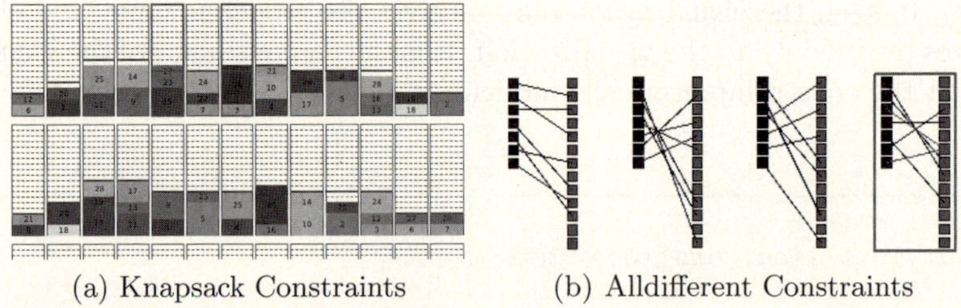

(a) Knapsack Constraints (b) Alldifferent Constraints

Fig. 4. Visualizing Knapsack and Alldifferent Constraints in the Progressive Party

Figure 3 depicts the models for the progressive party and warehouse location problems used to illustrate visualizations (we also use standard n-queens and sudoku models). On the progressive party problem, the instructions

```
CBLSVisualizer visu();
visu.displayKnapsacks(m);
visu.displayAlldiffs(m);
```

produce two new windows animating all the knapsack and alldifferent constraints separately. A snapshot of these visualizations is shown in Figure 4. The knapsack visualization shows the item allocation to the knapsacks and the constraint violations. This display is inspired from the bin packing display for `cumulative` in [11], with the difference that we also display the constraint violations. The alldifferent constraints are visualized as bipartite variable/value graphs, highlighting their violations. Such visualizations are often critical in identifying bottlenecks in local search algorithms. In particular, the knapsack visualizations were instrumental in suggesting new moves for the progressive party problem,

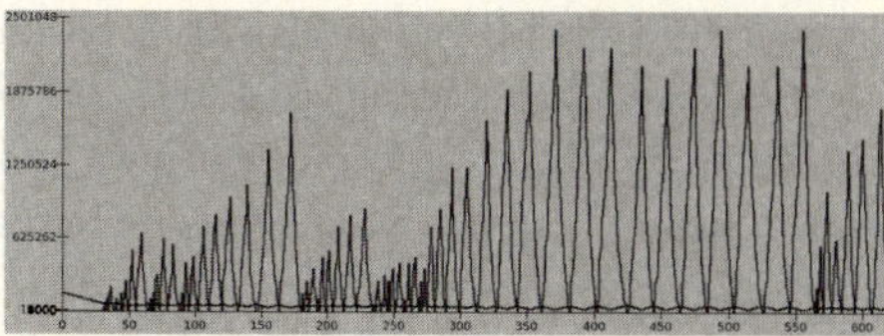

Fig. 5. The Objective Function in Warehouse Location on the GAP Instance

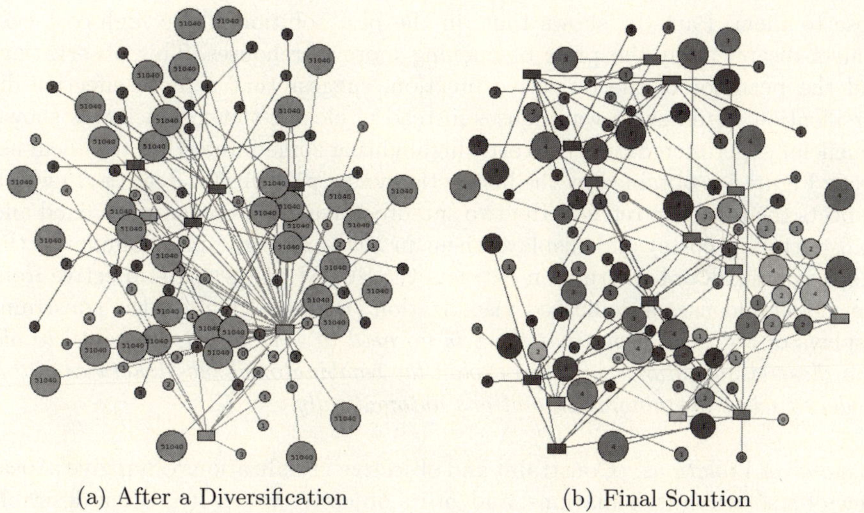

(a) After a Diversification (b) Final Solution

Fig. 6. Visualizing the SUMMINCOST Objective in Warehouse Location

producing some significant improvements in performance [13]. The visualization highlighted that assignments would rarely reduce the knapsack violations and suggested the use of specific swaps for this problem.

Visualizing Objectives: Dedicated visualizations are also available for objective functions. In this context, the visual information includes, not only the assignment, but the value of the objective (instead of the violations). Consider the warehouse location model applied to one of the challenging GAP instances. On these instances, using variable neighborhood search, the objective function exhibited a surprising, highly chaotic behavior with high peaks followed by deep valleys. This is depicted in Figure 5 which displays the fixed and transportation costs over time. The visualization of the SUMMINCOST objective function

```
visu.displaySumMinCost(m,WithBipartite());
```

provided a clear explanation of this behavior, as shown in Figure 6. Part (a) of the figure is a snapshot of the visualization after a diversification of the variable neighborhood search. Part (b) depicts the best solution found. In the visualization, warehouses are shown by rectangles, while the customers are shown by circles. Obviously, the constraint visualization has no knowledge about the application and simply visualizes the min-cost assignment and the costs (the *what*). The visualisation must view `tcost` as a bipartite cost matrix (the *how*) and the positioning of the customers and warehouses is automatically obtained by a planar embedding algorithm balancing spacing between nodes and the (often non-metric) distances in the cost matrix. The visualization reflects not only the assignment, but also the cost of each assignment (bigger circles mean more expensive customers). Part (a) of the figure shows that, after a solution, many of the customers entail a significant penalty because there is no open warehouse close to them. Part (b) shows that, in the best solution, these high-cost customers disappear at the price of opening more warehouses. This observation, and the behavior of the objective function, suggest that a more effective diversification would swap warehouses instead of closing them, which was shown beneficial experimentally. It is worth highlighting some interesting technical aspects. Figure 5 is obtained by the instruction `visu.plotObjToLevel(m,1)` which inspects the model to retrieve the two sub-objectives (representing the fixed and transportation costs) and displays them in the same time plot. Similarly, the `displaySumMinCost` instruction extracts the SumMinCost sub-objective from the model and uses a dedicated visualization (Figure 6) like for the constraint displays of Figure 4. *Note that there is no need to instrument the model to obtain these visualizations, yet they exploit the combinatorial sub-structures of this model to select meaningful animations automatically.*

Visualizing Violations: Constraint and objective visualizations often give a local view of a solution, its violations, and/or its objective value. It is often desirable to look at these concepts more globally in order to identify potential bottlenecks. Consider the progressive party problem again and the visualization specification:

```
1  CBLSVisualizer visu();
2  VariableDisplay vd = visu.getMatrixIntDisplay(m).labelValues();
3  plot(ConstraintViolations(m),vd,withDefault("red"));
4  plot(VariableViolations(m),vd,withDefault("red"));
5  plot(ViolationNature(m),vd, withColors());
```

This specification first creates a variable view in line 2 to display the variables as a matrix. It then requests to visualize the constraint violations on such a view (line 3). It also requests to visualize the variable violations. Finally, it asks for visualizing the nature of the violations, also on a variable view. Note that the `plot` instruction specifies *what*, *where*, and *how* to visualize. Only the *what* and the *how* vary in this specification, but we will illustrate various *where* subsequently. Figure 7 shows a snapshot of this visualization.

Part (a) shows the knapsack constraints horizontally, the alldifferent constraints vertically, and the atmost constraints with arcs below the variable view. Their violation degrees are given in various intensities of red. *This visualization nicely illustrates the expressivity of model-based visualizations.* The constraint violations (the *what*) are transformed in the visual concept of highlighting a set of variables. The variable view (the *where*) automatically identifies the constraints

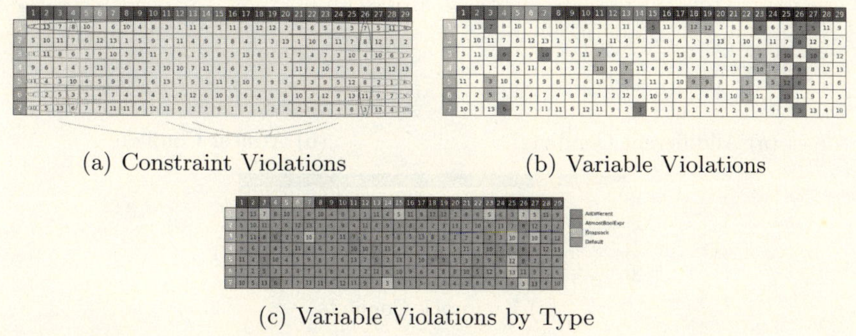

(a) Constraint Violations

(b) Variable Violations

(c) Variable Violations by Type

Fig. 7. Constraint and Variable Violations for Progressive Party

with rows (knapsacks), columns (alldifferent), and pairs of columns (atmost). Part (b) shows the variable violations, the intensity reflecting the violation degree again. Part (c) depicts the nature of the violations, using different colors for each violation type. In particular, the knapsack violations are shown in light blue, the atmost violations in green, and the alldifferent violations in light green. The visualization in Part (c) is obtained by creating constraint subsystems for each type of constraint and retrieving the variable violations of each subsystem. Such constraint subsystems are reminiscent of the S-boxes in [6].

These three snapshots are for the same configuration and the overall visualizations were valuable in understanding the new neighborhood for the progressive party problem. Indeed, allowing swaps for knapsack constraints has essentially shifted the bottleneck from knapsack to atmost constraints, confirming our intuition about the benefits of knapsack swaps.

Visualizing Conflicts: The violations are sometimes a bit too coarse to expose some underlying structure in CBLS algorithms: Discovering chains of dependencies or subsets of highly interdependent variables may require a finer grained visualization. The CBLS visualizer supports the concept of conflict: Informally speaking, a conflict for a constraint C is a set of variables whose current assignment violates C, independently of the values of the remaining variables in C. The visualization specification

```
1  CBLSVisualizer visu();
2  VariableDisplay vd = visu.getMatrixIntDisplay(m).labelValues();
3  plot(AllDiffConflicts(m),vd, withArcs("red"));
4  plot(AtmostConflicts(m),vd, withArcs("red"));
5  plot(KnapsackConflicts(m),vd, withRectColor());
```

requests the visualization of the alldifferent and atmost conflicts (the *what*) with red arcs (the *how*) (lines 3–4) and the knapsack conflicts with colored rectangles (another *how*) (line 5). The snapshots, at the same point in time as the earlier violation visualizations, are shown in Figure 8. Observe how the alldifferent conflicts are visualized with a clique of arcs, how the atmost conflicts clearly identify the pairs in conflict, and how the knapsack conflicts isolate the variables

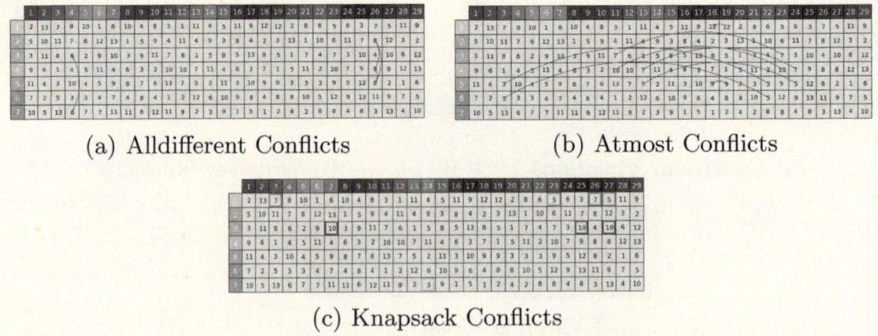

(a) Alldifferent Conflicts

(b) Atmost Conflicts

(c) Knapsack Conflicts

Fig. 8. Conflict for the Progressive Party Problem

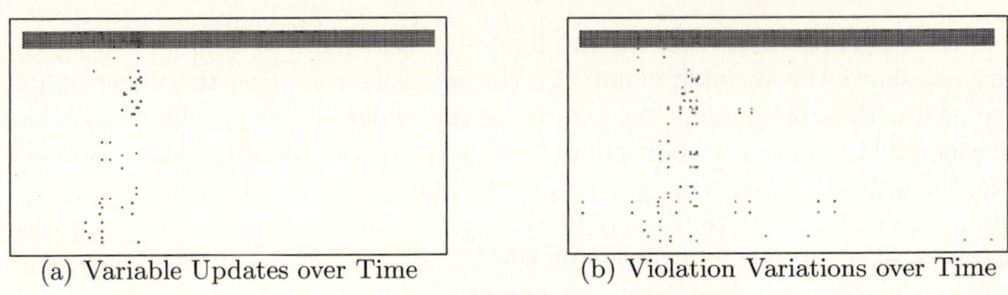

(a) Variable Updates over Time

(b) Violation Variations over Time

Fig. 9. Visualizing Temporal Behavior

in conflict with rectangles. Note that the atmost constraint is a meta-constraint posted on equations, which the visualizer inspects to collect the conflicting variables. These snapshots reveal some interesting structure about the applications. First, the alldifferent constraint is violated by the largest group (variable 26 on the horizontal axis), which also violates another knapsack constraint (see Figure 4(a)). Second, the atmost constraints tend to be localized at some specific region. Understanding this structure better and finding ways to avoid these behaviors may suggest new algorithmic improvements.

Visualizing Temporal Behavior: The visualizations presented so far require humans to infer the temporal behavior of the search from successive snapshots. As shown by search tree visualizations in CP, it is often desirable to assist humans in that activity by displaying the behavior of the algorithms over time. In CBLS, the algorithm typically performs one or multiple random walks and it is important to visualize its behavior along these walks. This information may help to identify cyclic behavior due to short tabu list, dependencies between variables, or neighborhoods that are too small to reach different parts of the search space.

Figure 9(a) visualizes how variables change over time. It is obtained by the instruction `displayTemporal(Changes(Variables(m)),MoveClock))`, which specifies to visualize the variable changes using move events. The lower and largest part of the figure depicts which variables have changed in the last 200 iterations. In this example, some variables tend to change much more often than the others, a consequence of a (too) short tabu list. The upper part of the figure presents 5 arrays of colored squares. The top array represents the total number of changes over the complete execution of the algorithm and the four arrays below depict changes over the last 100, 50, 20, and 10 moves.

The CBLS visualizer is compositional: it can display the temporal behavior of any scalar function and supports high-order functions to generate interesting functions. For instance, Figure 9(b) depicts the amount of change in variable violations over time: Green squares indicate decreases in violations, while red squares show violation increases. The figure is obtained by instruction `displayTemporal(Derivative(VariableViolation(m)))`, using a high-order function for differentiation.

These temporal displays are inspired by update views in [10] and stacked variable views in the VIFID tool [2]. Our visualizer adds the possibility to plot user-defined functions and presents the last N values of this function. Moreover, the time points are either automatically derived from the model (e.g., when a variable violation changes in the second example) or specified by users (e.g., when the search procedure makes a move as in the first example). This last functionality is similar in spirit to the spy-points in [2]. However, events in Comet avoid to clutter the code with spy points, cleanly separating the visualization, the model, and the search.

Variable Views: Visualizations are often specified with a triplet *(what,where,how)*. We have shown many examples of *what*, some of *how*, but the *where* component was almost always a two-dimensional variable view. Like some earlier tools [16,10], the CBLS visualizer offers alternative variable views. A popular variable view for one-dimensional arrays adds a dimension for values. Figure 10(a) visualizes the queens conflicts on such a view and is obtained by the instructions

```
CBLSVisualizer visu();
VariableDisplay vd = visu.displayArray2D(m);
plot(AllDiffConflicts(m),vd, withArcs("red"));
```

The same variable/value view is also available for matrices and is illustrated for the Sudoku conflicts in Figure 10(c). It shows the same information as Figure 10(b) but is much more readable. Those displays are obtained by the instructions

```
CBLSVisualizer visu();
VariableDisplay v2D = visu.getMatrixIntDisplay(m).colorLabelValues();
plot(AllDiffConflicts(m),v2D, withArcs("red"));
VariableDisplay v3D = visu.getMatrix3DDisplayByVal(m);
plot(AllDiffConflicts(m),v3D, withLines("red"));
```

In Figure 10(c), each value is associated with a table, which shows the variables assigned to the value and their conflicts.

3 The Visualizer Architecture and Its Implementation

This section considers the visualizer architecture and presents a blueprint for its implementation. It has a dual role: (1) To show how the CBLS visualizer is

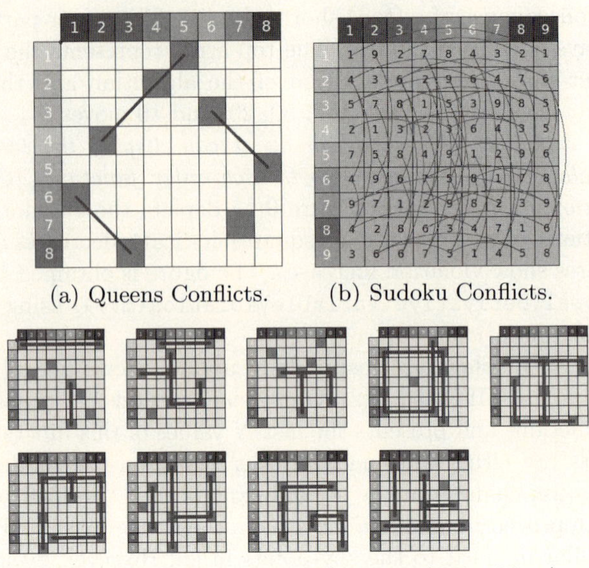

(a) Queens Conflicts. (b) Sudoku Conflicts.

(c) Sudoku Conflicts Again (Variable/Value View).

Fig. 10. Conflics and Variable Views for the Queens and Sudoku Problems

capable of deriving the visualizations from the model and the visualization specification; (2) to highlight the compositional, extensible, and declarative nature of the visualizer itself. The high-level architecture is shown in the top part of Figure 11. Starting from the model and the visualization specification, the visual interpreter creates declarative graphical objects, which are then transmitted to the graphics engine to produce an animated display. This process is executed once at the beginning of the animation. The declarative graphical objects are expressed in terms of incremental variables and invariants, which are maintained automatically by COMET. The declarative graphics engine uses these incremental variables and events to produce the animation.

3.1 The Visual Interpreter

The visual interpreter provides a number of functionalities depicted in the middle part of Figure 11, each of which focuses on some elements of the visualization language. Space does not allow us to describe all of them in detail. Instead this section focuses on a vertical slice of the visual interpreter: the transformation of model concepts into graphical concepts occurring in many of the `plot` instructions described earlier.

Recall that the plot instruction is composed of three components: the *what* (e.g., visualizing alldifferent conflicts), the *where* (e.g., on a variable/value view), and the *how* (e.g., with arcs). The visual interpeter receives these components and proceeds in stepwise refinements as depicted in the bottom part of

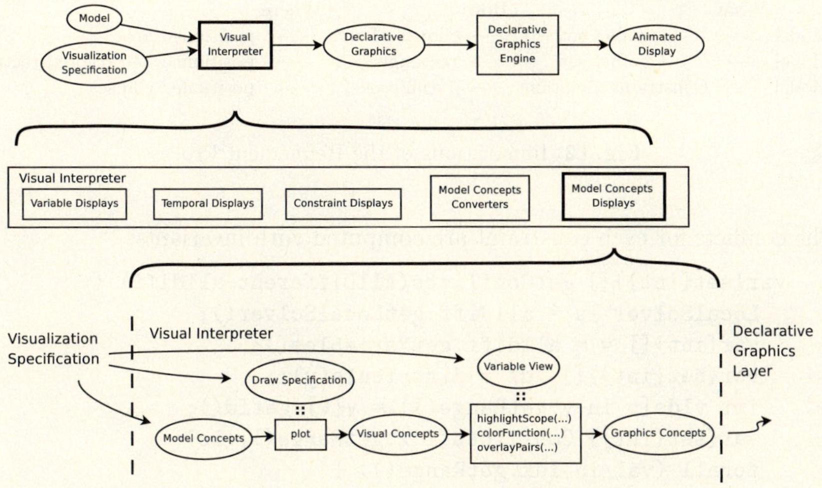

Fig. 11. The Architecture of the CBLS Visualizer

Figure 11. In particular, the model concepts (e.g., the *what*) are transformed into visual concepts (the *what* + *how*), which are then extended into graphical concepts by adding logical coordinates, colors, and other attributes. Figure 12 illustrates this process on several examples from the previous sections. The first line specifies the transformation for alldifferent or atmost conflicts in Figures 8(a) and 8(b). The second line illustrates the knapsack conflicts in Figure 8(c). The last line illustrates the refinements for the constraint violations in Figure 7(a).

We now dive into the actual implementation for a specific example. This slice of the visual interpreter illustrates its genericity, the significant role of invariants which enables the interpreter to focus solely on static aspects, and the clean separation of many visualization aspects (e.g., coordinates) until they are finally combined at the lowest level. The running example considers the instruction

```
plot(AllDiffConflicts(m),vd,withArcs("red"));
```

i.e., how to visualize conflicts in the alldifferent constraints using red arcs on a matrix→scalar variable view.

The What: The first step for the visual interpreter is to compute the conflicts for the alldifferent constraints and to create a model concept to encapsulate them.

```
ModelConcept collectAllDiffConflicts(LocalModel m) {
   ModelConcept x();
   forall (c in getAllDifferentInstances(m))
      x.add(getConflicts(c),c.getVariables());
   return x;
}
```

	What		How		Where
Model	⟶	Conflict set	⟶ cliques of arcs	⟶	positioned arcs
Model	⟶	Conflict set	⟶ rectangle sets	⟶	positioned and colored rectangles
Model	⟶	Constraint violations	⟶ ellipses	⟶	positioned ellipses

Fig. 12. Illustrations of the Refinement Process

The conflicts for each constraint are computed with invariants:

```
1  var{set{int}}[] getConflicts(AllDifferent alldiff) {
2    LocalSolver ls = alldiff.getLocalSolver();
3    var{int}[] y = alldiff.getVariables();
4    var{set{int}}[] Idx = distribute(y);
5    int vIds[v in y.getRange()] = y[v].getId();
6    var{set{int}} Conflicts[Idx.getRange()](ls);
7    forall (val in Idx.getRange()) {
8       var{set{int}} Ids(ls) <- collect(i in Idx[val]) (vIds[i]);
9       Conflicts[val] <- (card(Ids) > 1 ? Ids : {} );
10   }
11   return Conflicts;
12 }
```

Line 4 uses the `distribute` invariant to compute the indices of variables assigned to each value, i.e., for each value `v`, `Idx[v]` stores the sets of variable indices which are assigned value `v`. Since the visualization is concerned with all variables, each of these sets of indices is converted to a set `Ids` of variable identifiers using the `collect` invariant on line 8. Finally, on line 9, if the resulting set has cardinality 2 or more, it is a conflict set and must be preserved. Otherwise, the conflict set corresponding to that value is empty. *Observe that this computation takes place once: By stating these invariants, the implementation guarantees that the array* `Conflicts` *will incrementally maintain all the conflict sets over time, allowing the visual interpreter to focus on static aspects of the visualization.*

The How: The `withArcs` function returns a drawing specification (the *how*) whose method `plot` is called with the model concept (the *what*) and a variable view (the *where*). Its implementation is given by the snippet:

```
1 void DrawArc::plot(ModelConcept w, VariableView h) {
2   forall(i in w.getSetRange()) {
3      var{set{pair}} Conf(ls) <- w.getSet(i) cross w.getSet(i);
4      h.overlayPairs(ArcPairOverlay(Conf,_color));
5   }
```

Since it must highlight a set of variables with arcs, the visual interpreter generates the clique of all pairs of variables, which is again maintained by an invariant (line 3). The interpreter then calls method `overlayPairs` on the variable view (line 4) to visualize pairs with arcs (a visual concept).

The Where: The last step of the refinements, the `overlayPairs` method of the variable display,

```
1  void VDisp2DS::overlayPairs(VisualPairConcept vc) {
2     GraphicalArcPairs gc(vc,_Xcoords, _Ycoords);
3     animate(gc,_board,_table);
4  }
```

adds the logical coordinates to the identifiers pairs and the pair visualization (line 2) to create a graphical concept. This graphical concept is then transmitted to the graphics engine with the drawing board and the coordinate transformer `_table` capable of transforming logical coordinates into physical coordinates for a table. The coordinate variables `_Xcoords` and `_Ycoords` are instance variables of the class `VariableView` which `VDisp2DS` subclasses. In this example, these logical coordinates do not vary during the animation. They do in variable/value views (such as in the queens problem in Figure 10(a)), in which case, these incremental variables automatically maintain the variable coordinates.

3.2 The Declarative Graphics Layer

It is also instructive to dive into a slice of the declarative graphics engine to illustrate how the dynamic aspects of the visualization are handled at this lowest level of abstraction. The snippet

```
1  void GraphicalPairsAnimator::animate() {
2    var{set{pair}} edges = _vc.getPairs();
3    forall (e in edges)
4       overlayOnePair(e);
5    whenever edges@insert(pair e)
6       overlayOnePair(e);
7    whenever edges@remove(pair e)
8       unOverlayOnePair(e);
9  }
```

shows the core of the pair animator. It first displays the current pairs (lines 2–3) and then uses events to update the display when new pairs (e.g., new conflicts) are added or removed (lines 4–7). COMET events make it natural to deal with this data-driven aspect of the visualization. The snippet

```
void GraphicalPairAnimator::overlayOnePair(pair p) {
   PairOverlay ph = _vc.getGraphics(_board,_x[e.f],_y[e.f],
                                    _x[e.s],_y[e.s]);
   _board.add(p,ph);
}
```

shows how to highlight a pair. It creates a pair overlay from the visual concept using the physical coordinates and adds it to the board with the pair identifier. The `PairOverlay` encapsulates a declarative graphical line or arc whose attributes are specified by incremental variables. The physical coordinates are obtained from the logical coordinates with invariants of the form

```
px <- offsetx + lx*xs + xs/2;
py <- offsety + ly*ys + ys/2;
```

where px, py (resp. lx, ly) are the physical (resp. logical) coordinates, liberating the engine from some of the dynamic aspects of the visualization. To un-highlight one pair, it suffices to remove the pair (and its associated object) from the board, i.e.,

```
void GraphicalPairAnimator::unOverlayOnePair(pair p){
   _board.rem(p);
}
```

This declarative layer supports graphical objects similar to those in other graphics frameworks (e.g. [1,7,12]). *However, one of the contributions of the architecture is to show that this declarative graphics layer can be lifted into a declarative visualization layer thanks to the expressivity of invariants in* COMET.

4 Conclusion

This paper presented a visualization framework for Constraint-Based Local Search based on the slogan

CBLS Animation = Model + Visualization Specification.

Starting from a model and a specification stating *what*, *where*, and *how* to visualize, the visualizer systematically produces animations to visualize constraints and objectives, violations, and conflicts, as well as the temporal behavior of these measures. The visualization exploits the high-level structure of the models to highlight the behavior of CBLS algorithms in an informative and structured way, relieving modelers and programmers from the tedious and time-consuming task. The paper introduced new concepts and methods for visualizing CBLS programs, and adapted existing ones from constraint programming to this new setting. The paper also presented a blueprint for the visualizer architecture, whose main contribution is to lift a declarative graphics layer into a declarative visualization language. Thanks to invariants, the implementation focuses almost exclusively on static aspects, pushing the dynamic updating to the declarative graphics engine, the lowest abstraction level. The architecture is also compositional and extensible, proceeding in stepwise refinements to produce successively model, visual, and graphical concepts. Finally, the paper indicated that the resulting visualizations have already been useful in identifying suprising behaviors, suggesting new algorithms, and isolating bottlenecks. Research avenues are numerous and range from identifying new interesting visualization concepts, to aggregating results (e.g., for multi-start algorithms), visualizing algorithm-specific concepts, and developing an interactive visual tool. A particularly intriguing avenue is to use COMET itself to produce a layout of many animation components that satisfy user constraints, using ideas from document layout [8].

References

1. Borning, A.: The Programming Language Aspects of ThingLab, a Constraint-Oriented Simulation Laboratory. ACM Transaction on Programming Languages and Systems 3(4), 353–387 (1981)
2. Carro, M., Hermenegildo, M.: Tools for Constraint Visualisation: The VI-FID/TRIFID Tool. In: Analysis and Visualization Tools for Constraint Programming (2000)
3. Carro, M., Hermenegildo, M.: Tools for Search-Tree Visualisation: The APT Tool.. In: Analysis and Visualization Tools for Constraint Programming (2000)
4. Deransart, P., Hermenegildo, M., Maluszynski, J. (eds.): Analysis and Visualization Tools for Constraint Programming, Constrain Debugging (DiSCiPl project). Springer, London, UK (2000)
5. Dincbas, M., Van Hentenryck, P., Simonis, H., Aggoun, A., Graf, T., Berthier, F.: The Constraint Logic Programming Language CHIP. In: Proceedings of the International Conference on Fifth-Generation Computer Systems (1988)
6. Goualard, F., Benhamou, F.: Debugging Constraint Programs by Store Inspection. In: Analysis and Visualization Tools for Constraint Programming (2000)
7. Helm, R., Marriott, K.: Declarative Graphics. In: Shapiro, E. (ed.) Third International Conference on Logic Programming. LNCS, vol. 225, pp. 513–527. Springer, Heidelberg (1986)
8. Hosobe, H.: A Scalable Linear Constraint Solver for User Interface Construction.. In: Dechter, R. (ed.) CP 2000. LNCS, vol. 1894, pp. 218–232. Springer, Heidelberg (2000)
9. Schulte, C.: Oz Explorer: A visual constraint programming tool. In: ICLP'97, Leuven, Belgium, pp. 286–300 (July 1997)
10. Simonis, H., Aggoun, A.: Search-Tree Visualisation. In: Analysis and Visualization Tools for Constraint Programming (2000)
11. Simonis, H., Aggoun, A., Beldiceanu, N., Bourreau, E.: Complex Constraint Abstraction: Global Constraint Visualisation. In: Analysis and Visualization Tools for Constraint Programming (2000)
12. Sutherland, I.E.: Sketchpad, A Man-Machine Graphical Communication System. In: Outstanding Dissertations in the Computer Sciences. Garland Publishing (1963)
13. Van Hentenryck, P.: Constraint Programming as Declarative Algorithmics. In: Benhamou, F., Jussien, N., O'Sullivan, B. (eds.) Trends in Constraint Programming, Hermes (2007)
14. Van Hentenryck, P., Michel, L.: Synthesis of Constraint-Based Local Search Algorithms from High-Level Models. In: AAAI'07 (July 2007)
15. Van Hentenryck, P., Michel, L.: Constraint-Based Local Search. MIT Press, Cambridge (2005)
16. Van Hentenryck, P., Michel, L., Paulin, P., Puget, J.F.: The OPL Studio Modeling System. In: Kallrath, J. (ed.) Modeling Languages in Mathematical Optimization, pp. 43–76. Kluwer Academic Publishers, Dordrecht (2004)

Dealing with Incomplete Preferences in Soft Constraint Problems

Mirco Gelain, Maria Silvia Pini, Francesca Rossi, and K. Brent Venable

Dipartimento di Matematica Pura ed Applicata, Università di Padova, Italy
{mgelain,mpini,frossi,kvenable}@math.unipd.it

Abstract. We consider soft constraint problems where some of the preferences may be unspecified. This models, for example, situations with several agents providing the data, or with possible privacy issues. In this context, we study how to find an optimal solution without having to wait for all the preferences. In particular, we define an algorithm to find a solution which is necessarily optimal, that is, optimal no matter what the missing data will be, with the aim to ask the user to reveal as few preferences as possible. Experimental results show that in many cases a necessarily optimal solution can be found without eliciting too many preferences.

1 Introduction

Traditionally, tasks such as scheduling, planning, and resource allocation have been tackled using several techniques, among which constraint reasoning is one of the winning ones: the task is represented by a set of variables, their domains, and a set of constraints, and a solution of the problem is an assignment to all the variables in their domains such that all constraints are satisfied. Preferences or objective functions have been used to extend such scenario and allow for the modelling of constraint optimization, rather than satisfaction, problems. However, what is common to all these approaches is that the data (variables, domains, constraints) are completely known before the solving process starts.

On the contrary, the increasing use of web services and in general of multi-agent applications demands for the formalization and handling of data that is only partially known when the solving process works, and that can be added later, for example via elicitation. In many web applications, data may come from different sources, which may provide their piece of information at different times. Also, in multi-agent settings, data provided by some agents may be voluntarily hidden due to privacy reasons, and only released if needed to find a solution to the problem.

Recently, some lines of work have addressed these issues by allowing for open settings in CSPs: both open CSPs [5,7] and interactive CSPs [11] work with domains that can be partially specified, and in dynamic CSPs [4] variables, domains, and constraints may change over time. It has been shown that these approaches are closely related. In fact, interactive CSPs can be seen as a special case of both dynamic and open CSPs [10].

Here we consider the same issues but we focus on constraint optimization problems rather than CSPs, thus looking for an optimal solution rather than any solution. In particular, we consider problems where constraints are replaced by soft constraints, in which

C. Bessiere (Ed.): CP 2007, LNCS 4741, pp. 286–300, 2007.

each assignment to the variables of the constraint has an associated preference coming from a preference set [1]. In this setting, for the purpose of this paper we assume that variables, domains, and constraint topology are given at the beginning, while the preferences can be partially specified and possibly added during the solving process.

Constraint optimization has also been considered in the context of open CSPs, in a cost-minimization setting in [6] and in a fuzzy setting in [7]. However, the incompleteness considered in [7,6] is on domain values as well as on their preferences or costs. We assume instead that all values are given at the beginning, and that some preferences are missing. Because of the setting of [7], the assumption that new values and costs are provided monotonically is needed, while it is not necessary here. Working under this assumption means that the agent that provides new values/costs for a variable knows all possible costs, since it is capable of providing the best value first. If the cost computation is expensive or time consuming, then computing all such costs (in order to give the most preferred value) is not desirable. This is not needed in our setting, where single preferences are elicited.

There are several application domains where such setting is useful. One regards the fact that quantitative preferences, and needed in soft constraints, may be difficult and tedius to provide for a user. Another one concerns multi-agent settings, where agents agree on the structures of the problem but they may provide their preferences on different parts of the problem at different times. Finally, some preferences can be initially hidden because of privacy reasons.

Formally, we take the soft constraint formalism when preferences are totally ordered and we allow for some preferences to be left unspecified. Although some of the preferences can be missing, it could still be feasible to find an optimal solution. If not, then we ask the user and we start again from the new problem with some added preferences.

More precisely, we consider two notions of optimal solution: *possibly optimal* solutions are assignments to all the variables that are optimal in *at least one way* in which currently unspecified preferences can be revealed, while *necessarily optimal* solutions are assignments to all the variables that are optimal in *all ways* in which currently unspecified preferences can be revealed. This notation comes from multi-agent preference aggregation [12], where, in the context of voting theory, some preferences are missing but still one would like to declare a winner.

Given an incomplete soft constraint problem (ISCSP), its set of possibly optimal solutions is never empty, while the set of necessarily optimal solutions can be empty. Of course what we would like to find is a necessarily optimal solution, to be on the safe side: such solutions are optimal regardless of how the missing preferences would be specified. However, since such a set may be empty, in this case there are two choices: either to be satisfied with a possibly optimal solution, or to ask users to provide some of the missing preferences and try to find, if any, a necessarily optimal solution of the new ISCSP. In this paper we follow this second approach, and we repeat the process until the current ISCSP has at least one necessarily optimal solution.

To achieve this, we employ an approach based on branch and bound which first checks whether the given problem has a necessarily optimal solution (by just solving the completion of the problem where all unspecified preferences are replaced by the worst preference). If not, then finds the most promising among the possibly optimal solutions (where the promise is measured by its preference level), and asks the user to reveal the missing preferences related to such a solution. This second step is then repeated until the current problem has a necessarily optimal solution.

We implemented our algorithm and we tested it against classes of randomly generated binary fuzzy ISCSPs, where, beside the usual parameters (number of variables, domain size, density, and tightness), we added a new parameter measuring the percentage of unspecified preferences in each constraint and domain. The experimental results show that in many cases a necessarily optimal solution can be found by eliciting a small amount of preferences.

2 Soft Constraints

A soft constraint [1] is just a classical constraint [3] where each instantiation of its variables has an associated value from a (totally or partially ordered) set. This set has two operations, which makes it similar to a semiring, and is called a c-semiring. More precisely, a c-semiring is a tuple $\langle A, +, \times, \mathbf{0}, \mathbf{1}\rangle$ such that: A is a set, called the carrier of the c-semiring, and $\mathbf{0}, \mathbf{1} \in A$; $+$ is commutative, associative, idempotent, $\mathbf{0}$ is its unit element, and $\mathbf{1}$ is its absorbing element; $\times$ is associative, commutative, distributes over $+$, $\mathbf{1}$ is its unit element and $\mathbf{0}$ is its absorbing element.

Consider the relation $\leq_S$ over A such that $a \leq_S b$ iff $a+b = b$. Then: $\leq_S$ is a partial order; $+$ and $\times$ are monotone on $\leq_S$; $\mathbf{0}$ is its minimum and $\mathbf{1}$ its maximum; $\langle A, \leq_S\rangle$ is a lattice and, for all $a, b \in A$, $a + b = lub(a, b)$. Moreover, if $\times$ is idempotent, then $\langle A, \leq_S\rangle$ is a distributive lattice and $\times$ is its glb.

Informally, the relation $\leq_S$ gives us a way to compare (some of the) tuples of values and constraints. In fact, when we have $a \leq_S b$, we will say that *b is better than a*. Thus, $\mathbf{0}$ is the worst value and $\mathbf{1}$ is the best one.

Given a c-semiring $S = \langle A, +, \times, \mathbf{0}, \mathbf{1}\rangle$, a finite set D (the domain of the variables), and an ordered set of variables V, a constraint is a pair $\langle def, con\rangle$ where $con \subseteq V$ and $def : D^{|con|} \to A$. Therefore, a constraint specifies a set of variables (the ones in con), and assigns to each tuple of values of D of these variables an element of the semiring set A. A soft constraint satisfaction problem (SCSP) is just a set of soft constraints over a set of variables.

Many known classes of satisfaction or optimization problem can be cast in this formalism. A classical CSP is just an SCSP where the chosen c-semiring is: $S_{CSP} = \langle\{false, true\}, \vee, \wedge, false, true\rangle$. On the other hand, fuzzy CSPs [13,9] can be modeled in the SCSP framework by choosing the c-semiring: $S_{FCSP} = \langle[0, 1], max, min, 0, 1\rangle$. For weighted CSPs, the semiring is $S_{WCSP} = \langle\Re^+, min, +, +\infty, 0\rangle$. Here preferences are interpreted as costs from 0 to $+\infty$, which are combined with the sum and compared with min. Thus the optimization criterion is to minimize the sum of costs. For probabilistic CSPs [8], the semiring is $S_{PCSP} = \langle[0, 1], max, \times, 0, 1\rangle$. Here preferences are interpreted as probabilities ranging from 0 to 1, which are combined using the product and compared using max. Thus the aim is to maximize the joint probability.

Given an assignment t to all the variables of an SCSP, we can compute its preference value $pref(t)$ by combining the preferences associated by each constraint to the subtuples of the assignments referring to the variables of the constraint. More precisely, $pref(P,s) = \Pi_{\langle idef,con\rangle \in C} def(s_{\downarrow con})$, where Π refers to the $\times$ operation of the semiring and $s_{\downarrow con}$ is the projection of tuple s on the variables in con.

For example, in fuzzy CSPs, the preference of a complete assignment is the minimum preference given by the constraints. In weighted constraints, it is instead the sum of the costs given by the constraints.

An optimal solution of an SCSP is then a complete assignment t such that there is no other complete assignment t'' with $pref(t) <_S pref(t'')$. The set of optimal solutions of an SCSP P will be written as $Opt(P)$.

3 Incomplete Soft Constraint Problems (ISCSPs)

Informally, an incomplete SCSP, written ISCSP, is an SCSP where the preferences of some tuples in the constraints, and/or of some values in the domains, are not specified. In detail, given a set of variables V with finite domain D, and c-semiring $S = \langle A, +, \times, 0, 1\rangle$ with a totally ordered carrier, we extend the SCSP framework to incompleteness by the following definitions.

Definition 1 (incomplete soft constraint). *Given a set of variables V with finite domain D, and a c-semiring $\langle A, +, \times, 0, 1\rangle$, an incomplete soft constraint is a pair $\langle idef, con\rangle$ where $con \subseteq V$ is the scope of the constraint and $idef : D^{|con|} \longrightarrow A \cup \{?\}$ is the preference function of the constraint. All tuples mapped into ? by $idef$ are called incomplete tuples.*

In an incomplete soft constraint, the preference function can either specify the preference value of a tuple by assigning a specific element from the carrier of the c-semiring, or leave such preference unspecified. Formally, in the latter case the associated value is ?. A soft constraint is a special case of an incomplete soft constraint where all the tuples have a specified preference.

Definition 2 (incomplete soft constraint problem (ISCSP)). *An incomplete soft constraint problem is a pair $\langle C, V, D\rangle$ where C is a set of incomplete soft constraints over the variables in V with domain D. Given an ISCSP P, we will denote with $IT(P)$ the set of all incomplete tuples in P.*

Definition 3 (completion). *Given an ISCSP P, a completion of P is an SCSP P' obtained from P by associating to each incomplete tuple in every constraint an element of the carrier of the c-semiring. A completion is partial if some preference remains unspecified. We will denote with $C(P)$ the set of all possible completions of P and with $PC(P)$ the set of all its partial completions.*

Example 1. A travel agency is planning Alice and Bob's honeymoon. The candidate destinations are the Maldive islands and the Caribbean, and they can decide to go by ship or by plane. To go to Maldives, they have a high preference to go by plane and a low preference to go by ship. For the Caribbean, they have a high preference to go by ship, and they don't give any preference on going there by plane.

Assume we use the fuzzy c-semiring $\langle [0,1], max, min, 0, 1\rangle$. Then we can model this problem by using two variables T (standing for $Transport$) and D (standing for

Destination) with domains $D(T) = \{p, sh\}$ (p stands for $plane$ and sh for $ship$) and $D(D) = \{m, c\}$ (m stands for $Maldives$, c for $Caribbean$), and an incomplete soft constraint $\langle idef, con\rangle$ with $con = \{T, D\}$ and with preference function as shown in Figure 1. The only incomplete tuple in this soft constraint is (p, c).

Also, assume that for the considered season the Maldives are slightly preferrable to the Caribbean. Moreover, Alice and Bob have a high preference to plane as a way of transport, while they don't give any preference to ship. Moreover, as far as accommodations, which can be in a standard room, a suite, or a bungalow, assume that a suite in the Maldives is too expensive while a standard room in the Caribbean is not special enough for a honeymoon. To model this new information we use a variable A (standing for *Accommodation*) with domain $D(A) = \{r, su, b\}$ (r stands for $room$, su for $suite$ and b for $bungalow$), and three constraints: two unary incomplete soft constraints, $\langle idef1, \{T\}\rangle$, $\langle idef2, \{D\}\rangle$ and a binary incomplete soft constraint $\langle idef3, \{A, D\}\rangle$. The definition of such constraints is shown in Figure 1. The set of incomplete tuples of the entire problem is $IT(P) = \{(sh), (p, c), (su, c), (su, m), (r, m), (b, c)\}$.

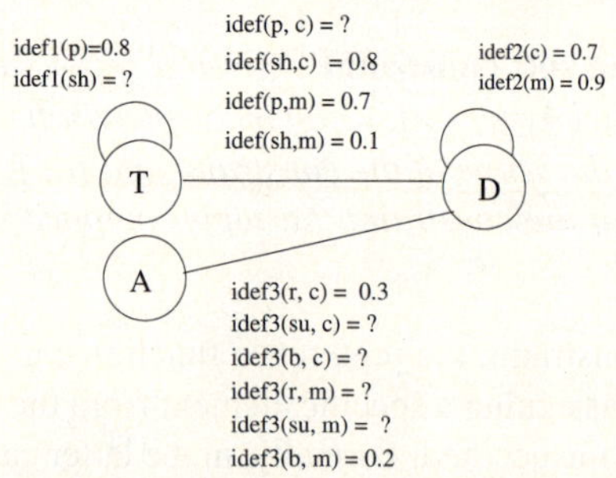

Fig. 1. An ISCSP

Definition 4 (preference of an assignment, and incomplete tuples). *Given an ISCSP $P = \langle C, V, D\rangle$ and an assignment s to all its variables we denote with $pref(P, s)$ the preference of s in P. In detail, $pref(P, s) = \Pi_{<idef,con>\in C | idef(s_{\downarrow con}) \neq ?} idef(s_{\downarrow con})$. Moreover, we denote by $it(s)$ the set of all the projections of s over constraints of P which have an unspecified preference.*

The preference of an assignment s in an incomplete problem is thus obtained by combining the known preferences associated to the projections of the assignment, that is, of the appropriated subtuples in the constraints. The projections which have unspecified preferences, that is, those in $it(s)$, are simply ignored.

Example 2. Consider the two assignments $s_1 = (p, m, b)$ and $s_2 = (p, m, su)$, we have that $pref(P, s_1) = min(0.8, 0.7, 0.9, 0.2) = 0.2$, while $pref(P, s_2) = min(0.8, 0.7, 0.9) = 0.7$. However, while the preference of s_1 is fixed, since none of its projections is incomplete, the preference of s_2 may become lower that 0.7 depending on the preference of the incomplete tuple (su, m).

As shown by the example, the presence of incompleteness generates a partition of the set of assignments into two sets: those which have a certain preference which is independent of how incompleteness is resolved, and those whose preference is only an upperbound, in the sense that it can be lowered in some completions.

Given an ISCSP P, we will denote the first set of assignments as $Fixed(P)$ and the second with $Unfixed(P)$. In Example 2, $Fixed(P) = \{s_1\}$, while all other assignments belong to $Unfixed(P)$.

In SCSPs we have that an assignment is an optimal solution if its global preference is undominated. This notion can be generalized to the incomplete setting. In particular, when some preferences are unknown, we will speak of necessarily and possibly optimal solutions, that is, assignments which are undominated in all (resp., some) completions.

Definition 5 (necessarily and possibly optimal solution). *Given an ISCSP $P = \langle C, V, D \rangle$, an assignment $s \in D^{|V|}$ is a necessarily (resp, possibly) optimal solution iff $\forall Q \in C(P)$ (resp., $\exists Q \in C(P)$ such that) $\forall s' \in D^{|V|}$, $pref(Q, s') \not> pref(Q, s)$.*

Given an ISCSP P, we will denote with $NOS(P)$ (resp., $POS(P)$) the set of necessarily (resp., possibly) optimal solutions of P. Notice that, while $POS(P)$ is never empty, in general $NOS(P)$ may be empty. In particular, $NOS(P)$ is empty whenever the available preferences do not allow to determine the relation between an assignment and all the others.

Example 3. In the ISCSP P of Figure 1, we can easily see that $NOS(P) = \emptyset$ since, given any assignment, it is possible to construct a completion of P in which it is not an optimal solution. On the other hand, $POS(P)$ contains all assignments not including tuple (sh, m).

4 Characterizing POS(P) and NOS(P)

In this section we characterize the set of necessarily and possibly optimal solutions of an ISCSP given the preferences of the optimal solutions of two of the completions of P. In particular, given an ISCSP P defined on a totally ordered c-semiring $\langle A, +, \times, \mathbf{0}, \mathbf{1} \rangle$, we consider:

- the SCSP $P_0 \in C(P)$, called the $\mathbf{0}$-completion of P, obtained from P by associating preference $\mathbf{0}$ to each tuple of $IT(P)$.
- the SCSP $P_1 \in C(P)$, called the $\mathbf{1}$-completion of P, obtained from P by associating preference $\mathbf{1}$ to each tuple of $IT(P)$.

Let us indicate respectively with $pref_0$ and $pref_1$ the preference of an optimal solution of P_0 and P_1. Due to the monotonicity of $\times$, and since $\mathbf{0} \leq \mathbf{1}$, we have that $pref_0 \leq pref_1$.

In the following theorem we will show that, if $pref_0 > \mathbf{0}$, there is a necessarily optimal solution of P iff $pref_0 = pref_1$, and in this case $NOS(P)$ coincides with the set of optimal solutions of P_0.

Theorem 1. *Given an ISCSP P and the two completions $P_0, P_1 \in C(P)$ as defined above, if $pref_0 > \mathbf{0}$ we have that $NOS(P) \neq \emptyset$ iff $pref_1 = pref_0$. Moreover, if $NOS(P) \neq \emptyset$, then $NOS(P) = Opt(P_0)$.*

Proof. Since we know that $pref_0 \leq pref_1$, if $pref_0 \neq pref_1$ then $pref_1 > pref_0$. We prove that, if $pref_1 > pref_0$, then $NOS(P) = \emptyset$. Let us consider any assignment s of P. Due to the monotonicity of $\times$, for all $P' \in C(P)$, we have $pref(P', s) \leq pref(P_1, s) \leq pref_1$.

- If $pref(P_1, s) < pref_1$, then s is not in $NOS(P)$ since P_1 is a completion of P where s is not optimal.
- If instead $pref(P_1, s) = pref_1$, then, since $pref_1 > pref_0$, we have $s \in Unfixed(P)$. Thus we can consider completion P'_1 obtained from P_1 by associating preference $\mathbf{0}$ to the incomplete tuples of s. In P'_1 the preference of s is $\mathbf{0}$ and the preference of an optimal solution of P'_1 is, due to the monotonicity of $\times$, at least that of s in P_0, that is $pref_0 > \mathbf{0}$. Thus $s \notin NOS(P)$.

Next we consider when $pref_0 = pref_1$. Clearly $NOS(P) \subseteq Opt(P_0)$, since any assignment which is not optimal in P_0 is not in $NOS(P)$. We will show that $NOS(P) \neq \emptyset$ by showing that any $s \in Opt(P_0)$ is in $NOS(P)$. Let us assume, on the contrary, that there is $s \in Opt(P_0)$ such that $s \notin NOS(P)$. Thus there is a completion P' of P with an assignment s' with $pref(P', s') > pref(P', s)$. By construction of P_0, any assignment $s \in Opt(P_0)$ must be in $Fixed(P)$. In fact, if it had some incomplete tuple, its preference in P_0 would be $\mathbf{0}$, since $\mathbf{0}$ is the absorbing element of $\times$. Since $s \in Fixed(P)$, $pref(P', s) = pref(P_0, s) = pref_0$. By construction of P_1 and monotonicity of $\times$, we have $pref(P_1, s') \geq pref(P', s')$. Thus the contradiction $pref_1 \geq pref(P_1, s') \geq pref(P', s') > pref(P', s) = pref_0$. This allows us to conclude that $s \in NOS(P) = Opt(P_0)$. □

In the theorem above we have assumed that $pref_0 > \mathbf{0}$. The case in which $pref_0 = \mathbf{0}$ needs to be treated separately. We consider it in the following theorem.

Theorem 2. *Given ISCSP $P = \langle C, V, D \rangle$ and the two completions $P_0, P_1 \in C(P)$ as defined above, assume $pref_0 = \mathbf{0}$. Then, if $pref_1 = \mathbf{0}$, $NOS(P) = D^{|V|}$. Also, if $pref_1 > \mathbf{0}$, $NOS(P) = \{s \in Opt(P_1) | \forall s' \in D^{|V|}$ with $pref(P_1, s') > \mathbf{0}$ we have $it(s) \subseteq it(s')\}$.*

The formal proof is omitted for lack of space. Intuitively, if some assignment s' has an incomplete tuple which is not part of another assignment s, then we can make s' dominate s in a completion by setting all the incomplete tuples of s' to $\mathbf{1}$ and all the remaining incomplete tuples of s to $\mathbf{0}$. In such a completion s is not optimal. Thus s is not a necessarily optimal solution. However, if the tuples of s are a subset of the incomplete tuples of all other assignments then it is not possible to lower s without lowering all other tuples even further. This means that s is a necessarily optimal solution.

We now turn our attention to possible optimal solutions. Given a c-semiring $\langle A, +, \times, \mathbf{0}, \mathbf{1} \rangle$, it has been shown in [2] that idempotency and strict monotonicity of the $\times$ operator are incompatible, that is, at most one of these two properties can hold. In the following two theorems we show that the presence of one or the other of such two properties plays a key role in the characterization of $POS(P)$ where P is an ISCSP.

In particular, if $\times$ is idempotent, then the possibly optimal solutions are the assignments with preference in P between $pref_0$ and $pref_1$. If, instead, $\times$ is strictly monotonic, then the possibly optimal solutions have preference in P between $pref_0$ and

$pref_1$ and dominate all the assignments which have as set of incomplete tuples a subset of their incomplete tuples.

Theorem 3. *Given an ISCSP P defined on a c-semiring with idempotent $\times$ and the two completions $P_0, P_1 \in C(P)$ as defined above, if $pref_0 > \mathbf{0}$ we have that: $POS(P) = \{s \in D^{|V|} | pref_0 \leq pref(P,s) \leq pref_1\}$.*

The formal proof is omitted for lack of space. Informally, given a solution s such that $pref_0 \leq pref(P,s) \leq pref_1$, it can be shown that it is an optimal solution of the completion of P obtained by associating preference $pref(P,s)$ to all the incomplete tuples of s, and $\mathbf{0}$ to all other incomplete tuples of P. On the other hand, by construction of P_0 and due to the monotonicity of $\times$, any assignment which is not optimal in P_0 cannot be optimal in any other completion. Also, by construction of P_1, there is no assignment s with $pref(P,s) > pref_1$.

Theorem 4. *Given an ISCSP P defined on a c-semiring with a strictly monotonic $\times$ and the two completions $P_0, P_1 \in C(P)$ as defined above, if $pref_0 > \mathbf{0}$ we have that: an assignment $s \in POS(P)$ iff $pref_0 \leq pref(P,s) \leq pref_1$ and $pref(P,s) = max\{ pref(P,s') | \, it(s') \subseteq it(s)\}$.*

The intuition behind the statement of this theorem is that, if assignment s is such that $pref_0 \leq pref(P,s) \leq pref_1$ and $pref(P,s) = max\{pref(P,s')|it(s') \subseteq it(s)\}$, then it is optimal in the completion obtained associating preference $\mathbf{1}$ to all the tuples in $it(s)$ and $\mathbf{0}$ to all the tuples in $IT(P) \setminus it(s)$. On the contrary, if $pref(P,s) < max\{pref(P,s')|it(s') \subseteq it(s)\}$, there must be another assignment s'' such that $pref(P,s'') = max\{pref(P,s')|it(s') \subseteq it(s)\}$. It can then be shown that, in all completions of P, s is dominated by s''.

In constrast to $NOS(P)$, when $pref_0 = \mathbf{0}$ we can immediately conclude that $POS(P) = D^{|V|}$, independently of the nature of $\times$, since all assignments are optimal in P_0.

Corollary 1. *Given an ISCSP $P = \langle C, V, D \rangle$, if $pref_0 = \mathbf{0}$, then $POS(P) = D^{|V|}$.*

The results given in this section can be summarized as follows:

- when $pref_0 = \mathbf{0}$
  - not enough information to compute $NOS(P)$ (by Theorem 2);
  - $POS(P) = D^{|V|}$ (by Corollary 1);
- when $pref_0 = pref_1 = \mathbf{0}$
  - $NOS(P) = D^{|V|}$ (by Theorem 2);
  - $POS(P) = D^{|V|}$ (by Corollary 1) ;
- when $\mathbf{0} = pref_0 < pref_1$
  - $NOS(P) = \{s \in Opt(P_1) | \forall s' \in D^{|V|}$ with $pref(P_1, s') > \mathbf{0}$ we have $it(s) \subseteq it(s')\}$ (by Theorem 2);
  - $POS(P) = D^{|V|}$ (by Corollary 1);
- when $\mathbf{0} < pref_0 = pref_1$
  - $NOS(P) = Opt(P_0)$ (by Theorem 1);
  - if $\times$ is idempotent: $POS(P) = \{s \in D^{|V|} | pref_0 \leq pref(P,s) \leq pref_1\}$ (by Theorem 3);

  - if $\times$ is strictly monotonic: $POS(P) = \{s \in D^{|V|} | pref_0 \leq pref(P,s) \leq pref_1, pref(P,s) = max\{ pref(P,s') | it(s') \subseteq it(s)\}\}$ (by Theorem 4);
- when $\mathbf{0} < pref_0 < pref_1$
  - $NOS(P) = \emptyset$ (by Theorem 1);
  - $POS(P)$ as for the case when $\mathbf{0} < pref_0 = pref_1$.

5 A Solver for ISCSPs

We want to find a necessarily optimal solution of the given problem, if it exists. In most cases, however, the available information will only allow to determine the set of possibly optimal solutions. In such cases, preference elicitation is needed to discriminate among such assignments in order to determine a necessarily optimal one of the new problem with the elicited preferences. In this section we describe an algorithm, called *Find-NOS*, to achieve this task.

Algorithm 1. Find-NOS

```
Input: an ISCSP P
Output: an ISCSP Q, an assignment s, a preference p
P0 ← P[?/0]
s0, pref0 ← BB(P0, −)
s1 ← s0
pref1 ← pref0
smax ← s0
prefmax ← pref0
repeat
    P1 ← P[?/1]
    if pref1 > prefmax then
        smax ← s1
        prefmax ← pref1
    s1, pref1 ← BB(P1, prefmax)
    if s1 ≠ nil then
        S ← it(s1)
        P ← Elicit(P, S)
        pref1 ← pref(P, s1)
until s1 = nil ;
return P, smax, prefmax
```

Algorithm *Find-NOS* takes in input an ISCSP P over a totally ordered c-semiring and returns an ISCSP Q which is a partial completion of P, and an assignment $s \in NOS(Q)$ together with its preference p. Given an ISCSP P, *Find-NOS* first checks if $NOS(P)$ is not empty, and, if so, it returns P, $s \in NOS(P)$, and its preference. If instead $NOS(P) = \emptyset$, it starts eliciting the preferences of some incomplete tuples.

In detail, *Find-NOS* first computes the $\mathbf{0}$-completion of P, written as $P[?/0]$, called P_0, and applies Branch and Bound (BB) to it. This allows to find an optimal solution of P_0, say s_0, and its preference $pref_0$.

In our notation, the application of the BB procedure has two parameters: the problem to which it is applied, and the starting bound. When BB is applied without a starting bound, we will write $BB(P, -)$. When the BB has finished, it returns a solution and its preference. If no solution is found, we assume that the returned items are both nil.

Variables s_1 and $pref_1$ (resp., s_{max} and $pref_{max}$) represent the optimal solution and the corresponding preference of the **1**-completion of the current problem (written $P[?/1]$) (resp., the best solution and the corresponding preference found so far). At the beginning, such variables are initialized to s_0 and $pref_0$.

The main loop of the algorithm, achieved through the **repeat** command, computes the **1**-completion, denoted by P_1, of the current problem. In the first iteration the condition of the first **if** is not satisfied since $pref_1 = pref_{max} = pref_0$. The execution thus proceeds by applying BB to P_1 with bound $pref_{max} = pref_0 \geq \mathbf{0}$. This allows us to find an optimal solution of P_1 and its corresponding preference, assigned to s_1 and $pref_1$. If BB fails to find a solution, s_1 is nil. Thus the second **if** is not executed and the algorithm exits the loop and returns P, $s_{max} = s_0$, and $pref_{max} = pref_0$.

If instead BB applied to P_1 with bound $pref_{max}$ does not fail, then we have that $pref_0 < pref_1$. Now the algorithm elicits the preference of some incomplete tuples, via procedure $Elicit$.

This procedure takes an ISCSP and a set of tuples of variable assignments, and asks the user to provide the preference for such tuples, returning the updated ISCSP. The algorithm calls procedure $Elicit$ over the current problem P and the set of incomplete tuples of s_1 in P. After elicitation, the new preference of s_1 is computed and assigned to $pref_1$.

Since $s_1 \neq nil$, a new iteration begins, and BB is applied with initial bound given by the best preference between $pref_1$ and $pref_{max}$. Moreover, if $pref_1 > pref_{max}$, then s_{max} and $pref_{max}$ are updated to always contain the best solution and its preference. Iteration continues until the elicited preferences are enough to make BB fail to find a solution with a better preference w.r.t. the previous application of BB. At that point, the algorithm returns the current problem and the best solution found so far, together with its preference.

Theorem 5. *Given an ISCSP P in input, algorithm* Find-NOS *always terminates and returns an ISCSP Q such that $Q \in PC(P)$, an assignment $s \in NOS(Q)$, and its preference in Q.*

Proof. At each iteration, either $pref_{max}$ increases or, if it stays the same, a new solution will be found since after elicitation the preference of s_1 has not increased. Thus, either $pref_{max}$ is so high that BB doesn't find any solution, or all the optimal solutions have been considered. In both cases the algorithm exits the loop.

At the end of its execution, the algorithm returns the current partial completion of given problem and a solution s_{max} with the best preference seen so far $pref_{max}$. The **repeat** command is exited when $s_1 = nil$, that is, when $BB(P[?/1], pref_{max})$ fails. In this situation, $pref_{max}$ is the preference of an optimal solution of the **0**-completion of the current problem P. Since BB fails on $P[?/1]$ with such a bound, by monotonicity of the $\times$ operator, $pref_{max}$ is also the preference of an optimal solution of $P[?/1]$. By Theorems 1 and 2, we can conclude that $NOS(P)$ is not empty. If $pref_{max} = \mathbf{0}$, then $NOS(P)$ contains all the assignments and thus also s_0. The algorithm correctly returns the same ISCSP given in input, assignment s_0 and its preference $pref_0 = \mathbf{0}$. If instead $0 < pref_{max}$, again the algorithm is correct, since by Theorem 1 we know that $NOS(P) = Opt(P[?/0])$, and since $s_{max} \in Opt(P[?/0])$. □

Notice also that the algorithm performs preference elicitation only on solutions which are possibly optimal in the current partial completion of the given problem (and thus also in the given problem). In fact, by Theorems 3 and 4, any optimal solution of the **1**-completion of the current partial completion Q is a possibly optimal solution of Q. Thus no useless work is done to elicit preferences related to solutions which cannot be necessarily optimal for any partial completion of the given problem. This also means that our algorithm works independently of the properties of the $\times$ operator.

6 Experimental Setting and Results

We have implemented Algorithm *Find-NOS* in Java and we have tested it on randomly generated ISCSPs with binary constraints and based on the Fuzzy c-semiring. To generate such problems, we use the following parameters:

- n: number of variables;
- m: cardinality of the domain of each variable;
- d: density of the constraints, that is, the percentage of binary constraints present in the problem w.r.t. the total number of possible binary constraints that can be defined on n variables;
- t: tightness, that is, the percentage of tuples with preference 0 in each constraint w.r.t. the total number of tuples (m^2 since we have only binary constraints), and in each domain;
- i: incompleteness, that is, the percentage of incomplete tuples (formally, tuples with preference ?) in each constraint and in each domain.

For example, if the generator is given in input $n = 10$, $m = 5$, $d = 50$, $t = 10$, and $i = 30$, it will generate a binary ISCSP with 10 variables, each with 5 elements in the domain, 22 constraints on a total of $45 = n(n-1)/2$, 2 tuples with preference 0 and 7 incomplete tuples over a total of 25 in each constraint, and 1 missing preference in each domain.

Notice that we use a model B generator: density and tightness are interpreted as percentages, and not as probabilities. Also, when we simulate the Elicit procedure, we randomly generate values in $(0, 1]$.

We have generated classes of ISCSPs by varying one parameter at a time, and fixing the other ones. The varying parameters are the number of variables, the density, and the incompleteness. When the number of variables varies (from $n = 5$ to $n = 20$, with step 3), we set $m = 5$, $d = 50$, $t = 10$, and $i = 30$. When we vary the density (from $d = 10$ to $d = 80$ with step 5), we set $n = 10$, $m = 5$, $t = 10$, and $i = 30$. Finally, when we vary the incompleteness (from $i = 10$ to $i = 80$ with step 5), we set $n = 10$, $m = 5$, $d = 50$, and $t = 10$.

In all the experiments, we have measured the number of tuples elicited by Algorithm *Find-NOS*. We also show the percentage of elicited tuples over the total number of incomplete tuples of the problem in input. For each fixed value of all the parameters, we show the average of the results obtained for 50 different problem instances, each

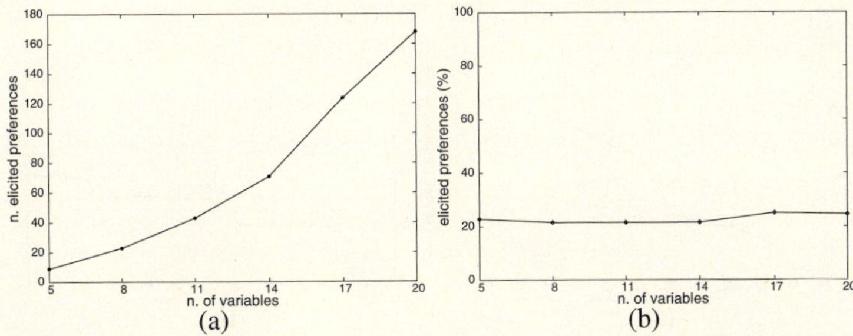

Fig. 2. Number and percentage of elicited preferences, as a function of the number of variables. Fixed parameters: $m = 5$, $d = 50$, $t = 10$, $i = 30$.

given in input to *Find-NOS* 10 times. This setting is necessary since we have two kinds of randomness: the usual one in the generation phase and a specific one when eliciting preferences.

Figure 2 shows the absolute number and the percentage of elicited preferences when the number of variables varies. As expected, when the number of variables increases, the absolute number of elicited preferences increases as well, since there is a growth of the total number of incomplete tuples. However, if we consider the percentage of elicited tuples, we see that it is not affected by the increase in the number of variables. In particular, the percentage of elicited preferences remains stable around 22%, meaning that, regardless of the number of variables, the agent is asked to reveal only 22 preferences over 100 incomplete tuples. A necessarily optimal solution can be thus found leaving 88% of the missing preferences unrevealed.

Similar results are obtained when density varies (see Figure 3). We can see that the absolute number of elicited preferences grows when density increases. The maximum number of elicited preferences reached is however lower that the maximum reached when varying the variables (see Figure 2(a)). The reason for this is that the largest problems considered when varying the number of variables have more incomplete tuples than the largest obtained when varying the density. In fact, a problem with $n = 20$, given the fixed parameters, has around 685 incomplete tuples, 165 of which (about 22%) are elicited. On the other hand, a problem with $d = 80$, given the fixed parameters, has around 262 incomplete tuples, 55 (about 22%) of which are elicited. This is

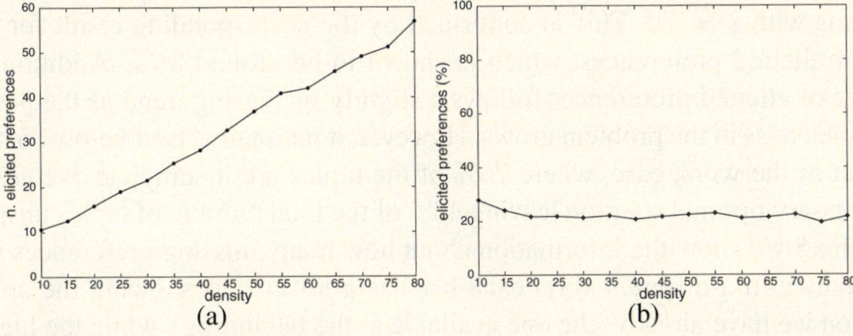

Fig. 3. Number and percentage of elicited preferences, as a function of the density. Fixed parameters: $n = 10$, $m = 5$, $t = 10$, $i = 30$.

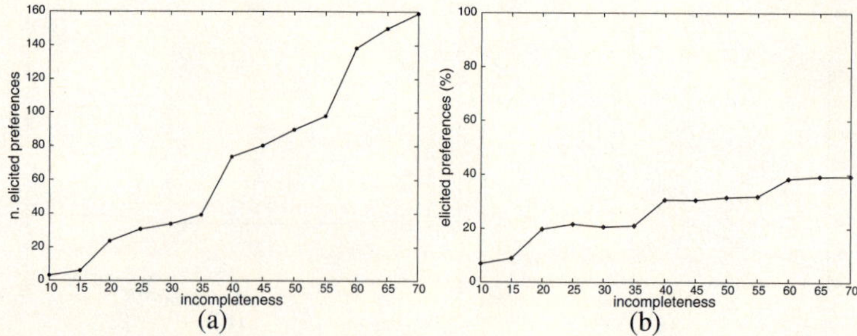

Fig. 4. Number and percentage of elicited preferences, as a function of the incompleteness. Fixed parameters: $n = 10$, $m = 5$, $t = 10$, $d = 50$.

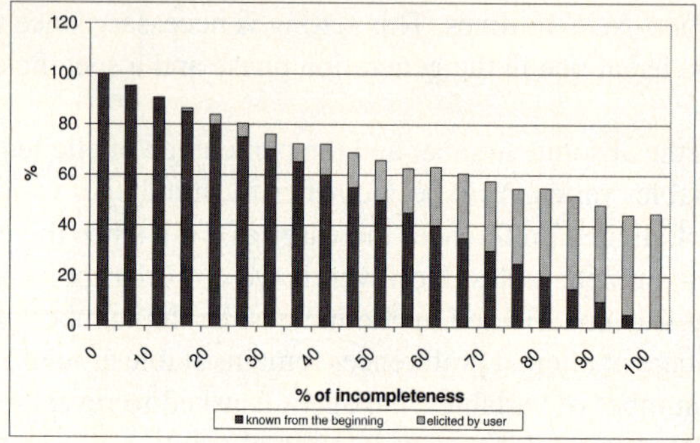

Fig. 5. Amount of preferences initially available and elicited as a function of the incompleteness. Fixed parameters: $n = 10$, $m = 5$, $t = 10$, $i = 30$.

coherent with the fact that the results on the percentage of elicited preferences when varying the density and the number of variables are very similar.

The last set of experiments vary the percentage of incompleteness (see Figure 4). As for density and number of variables, the absolute number of elicited preferences grows when the percentage of incompleteness increases. The maximum number of elicited preferences reached is close to that reached when varying the variables. However, the number of incomplete tuples of the problems with $i = 70$ is around 460 and thus smaller than that of problems with $n = 20$. Thus the percentage of elicited preferences is larger in problems with $i = 70$. This is confirmed by the corresponding result for the percentage of elicited preferences, which is shown to be around 35%. Additionally, the percentage of elicited preferences follows a slightly increasing trend as the percentage of incompleteness in the problem grows. However, it maintains itself below 35%, which means that in the worst case, where 70% of the tuples are incomplete, we are able to find a necessary optimal solution leaving 46% of the total number of tuples unspecified.

In Figure 5 we show the information about how many missing preferences we need to ask the user in a different way: each bar has a lower part showing the amount of information we have already (the one available at the beginning), while the higher part shows how much more information we need to ask the user for in order to find a necessarily optimal solution. It is possible to see that, when we have already some initial

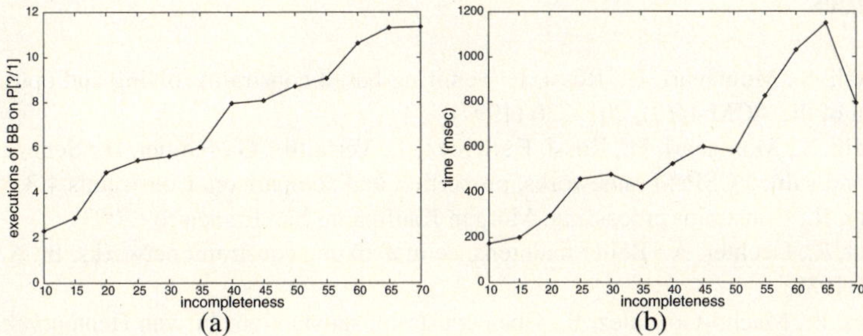

Fig. 6. CPU time and BB runs as a function of the incompleteness. Fixed parameters: $n = 10$, $m = 5$, $t = 10$, $i = 30$.

information, usually we need to ask the user for more even if the initial information amount is large. This is because some of the preferences available initially may be not useful for the computation of an optimal solution. On the other hand, if we start with no initial preferences (rightmost bar), we need to ask the user only for about 40% of the preferences.

The focus of this work is on how many elicitation steps need to be done before finding a necessarily optimal solution. In fact, our Branch and Bound procedure could certainly be improved in terms of efficiency. However, we show in Figure 6 the CPU time needed to solve some incomplete problems (when incompleteness varies) and also the number of runs of the Branch and Bound on the 1-completion.

7 Ongoing and Future Work

We are currently working on several variants of the algorithm described in this paper, where elicitation occurs not at the end of an entire BB search tree, but at the end of every complete branch or at every node. In this case, the algorithm runs BB only once before finding a necessarily optimal solution. Moreover, we are also considering variants of the Elicit function that asks for just one of the missing preferences: for example, in the context of fuzzy constraints, it just asks for the worst one, since it is the most useful one due to the drowning effect.

Future work will consider partially ordered preferences and also other ways to express preferences, such as qualitative ones a la CP nets, as well as other kinds of missing data, such as those considered in dynamic, interactive, and open CSPs. Moreover, other solving approaches can be considered, such as those based on local search and variable elimination.

We also would like to consider the specification of intervals, rather than a fixed preference or nothing. This would not change much our setting. We consider the [0,1] interval where no preference is specified, and thus the 0-completion and the 1-completion. With generic intervals, we can consider the "lower bound completion" and the "upper bound completion".

References

1. Bistarelli, S., Montanari, U., Rossi, F.: Semiring-based constraint solving and optimization. Journal of the ACM 44(2), 201–236 (1997)
2. Bistarelli, S., Montanari, U., Rossi, F., Schiex, T., Verfaillie, G., Fargier, H.: Semiring-based CSPs and valued CSPs: Frameworks, properties, and comparison. Constraints 4(3) (1999)
3. Dechter, R.: Constraint processing. Morgan Kaufmann, San Francisco (2003)
4. Dechter, R., Dechter, A.: Belief maintenance in dynamic constraint networks. In: AAAI, pp. 37–42 (1988)
5. Faltings, B., Macho-Gonzalez, S.: Open constraint satisfaction. In: Van Hentenryck, P. (ed.) CP 2002. LNCS, vol. 2470, pp. 356–370. Springer, Heidelberg (2002)
6. Faltings, B., Macho-Gonzalez, S.: Open constraint optimization. In: Rossi, F. (ed.) CP 2003. LNCS, vol. 2833, pp. 303–317. Springer, Heidelberg (2003)
7. Faltings, B., Macho-Gonzalez, S.: Open constraint programming. Artif. Intell. 161(1-2), 181–208 (2005)
8. Fargier, H., Lang, J.: Uncertainty in constraint satisfaction problems: a probalistic approach. In: Moral, S., Kruse, R., Clarke, E. (eds.) ECSQARU 1993. LNCS, vol. 747, pp. 97–104. Springer, Heidelberg (1993)
9. Fargier, H., Schiex, T., Verfaille, G.: Valued Constraint Satisfaction Problems: Hard and Easy Problems. In: IJCAI-95, pp. 631–637. Morgan Kaufmann, San Francisco (1995)
10. González, S.M., Ansótegui, C., Meseguer, P.: On the relation among open, interactive and dynamic CSP. In: The Fifth Workshop on Modelling and Solving Problems with Constraints (IJCAI'05) (2005)
11. Lamma, E., Mello, P., Milano, M., Cucchiara, R., Gavanelli, M., Piccardi, M.: Constraint propagation and value acquisition: Why we should do it interactively. In: IJCAI, pp. 468–477 (1999)
12. Lang, J., Pini, M.S., Rossi, F., Venable, K.B., Walsh, T.: Winner determination in sequential majority voting. In: IJCAI, pp. 1372–1377 (2007)
13. Ruttkay, Z.: Fuzzy constraint satisfaction. In: Proceedings 1st IEEE Conference on Evolutionary Computing, Orlando, pp. 542–547 (1994)

Efficient Computation of Minimal Point Algebra Constraints by Metagraph Closure

Alfonso Gerevini and Alessandro Saetti

Dipartimento di Elettronica per l'Automazione
Università degli Studi di Brescia, via Branze 38, 25123 Brescia, Italy
{gerevini,saetti}@ing.unibs.it

Abstract. Computing the minimal network (or minimal CSP) representation of a given set of constraints over the Point Algebra (PA) is a fundamental reasoning problem. In this paper we propose a new approach to solving this task which exploits the timegraph representation of a CSP over PA. A timegraph is a graph partitioned into a set of chains on which the search is supported by a metagraph data structure. We introduce a new algorithm that, by making a particular closure of the metagraph, extends the timegraph with information that supports the derivation of the strongest implied constraint between any pair of point variables in constant time. The extended timegraph can be used as a representation of the minimal CSP. We also compare our method and known techniques for computing minimal CSPs over PA. For CSPs that are sparse or exhibit chain structure, our approach has a better worst-case time complexity. Moreover, an experimental analysis indicates that the performance improvements of our approach are practically very significant. This is the case especially for CSPs with a chain structure, but also for randomly generated (both sparse and dense) CSPs.

1 Introduction

Constraint-based qualitative temporal reasoning is a widely studied area with application to various fields of AI (for a recent survey see [2]). The Point Algebra [9,10] is one of the first and most prominent frameworks for representing qualitative temporal constraints and reasoning about them. PA consists of three basic relations between time point variables that are jointly exhaustive and pairwise disjoint ($<$, $>$, $=$), all possible unions of them ($\leq$, $\geq$, $\neq$, and $\top$, where $\top$ is the universal relation), and of the empty relation. The *convex* Point Algebra contains all the relations of PA except $\neq$.

Given a set C of temporal constraints over PA (or a temporal CSP), a fundamental reasoning problem is computing the minimal CSP representation of C.[1] A temporal CSP is *minimal* if, for every pair of variables i, j, the relation R between i and j is the strongest relation (or minimal constraint) between i and j that is entailed by the CSP. In other words, every basic relation $r \in R$ is feasible, i.e., there exists a solution of the temporal CSP where the values assigned to i and j satisfy r.

[1] This problem is also called *deductive closure* problem in [9], *minimal labeling* problem in [5,7] and computing the *feasible relations* in [6].

C. Bessiere (Ed.): CP 2007, LNCS 4741, pp. 301–316, 2007.

Computing the minimal CSP of a temporal CSP involving n variables can be accomplished in $O(n^3)$ time by using a path-consistency algorithm, if the CSP is over the convex PA [9,10], and in $O(n^3 + n^2 \cdot c_{\neq})$, if the CSP is over the full PA [6,4], where $c_{\neq}$ is the number of input $\neq$-constraints.

An alternative approach to qualitative temporal reasoning in the context of PA is the "graph-based approach" [1,3]. Instead of computing the minimal CSP, we build a particular graph-based representation of the input CSP that supports efficient computation of the minimal constraints at query time. This method has been proposed with the aim of addressing scalability especially for large data sets forming sparse CSPs (in which the number of constraints is less than quadratic) and exhibiting particular structure (e.g., a collection of time chains [3] or series-parallel graphs [1]).

The minimal CSP representation supports the derivation of the strongest entailed relation between any pair of variables in constant time. On the contrary, in the graph-based representation this has a computational cost that depends on the structure and sparseness of the input temporal CSP; in the best case it can be constant time, while in the worst case it can be quadratic time with respect to the number of the CSP point variables. On the other hand, in practice computing the minimal CSP representation using known techniques is significantly slower than computing the graph-based representation of a sparse CSP [1,3].

In this paper, we investigate a combined approach. We propose a new method for computing the minimal CSP representation by exploiting the *timegraph* representation [3]. A timegraph is a graph partitioned into a set of time chains on which the search is supported by a *metagraph* data structure. We introduce a new algorithm that, by making a particular closure of the metagraph, extends the timegraph with information that supports the derivation of the strongest entailed relation between any pair of point variables in constant time. The extended timegraph can be seen as a representation of the minimal CSP. By using our approach the (explicit) minimal CSP can be computed in $O(\hat{n} \cdot \hat{e} + n^2)$ time (convex PA) and $O(\hat{e} \cdot \hat{n} + \hat{e}_{\neq} \cdot (\hat{e} + \hat{n}) + n^2)$ time (full PA), where $\hat{n}$, $\hat{e}$ and $\hat{e}_{\neq}$ are the metanodes, metaedges and $\neq$-metaedges, respectively, in the timegraph.

We compare our method and the known techniques for computing minimal CSPs over PA. For CSPs that are sparse or exhibit chain structure, our approach has a better worst-case time complexity. Moreover, an experimental analysis indicates that in practice our approach is significantly faster. This is the case not only for CSPs with a chain structure, but also for general randomly generated (both sparse and dense) CSPs.

The paper is organized as follows. Section 2 gives the necessary background. Section 3 presents our new method for computing the minimal CSP. Section 4 concerns the experimental analysis. Finally, Section 5 gives the conclusions.

2 Background: TL-Graphs, Timegraphs and Metagraphs

A **temporally labeled graph** (*TL-graph*) [3] is a graph with at least one vertex and a set of labeled edges, where each edge (v, l, w) connects a pair of distinct

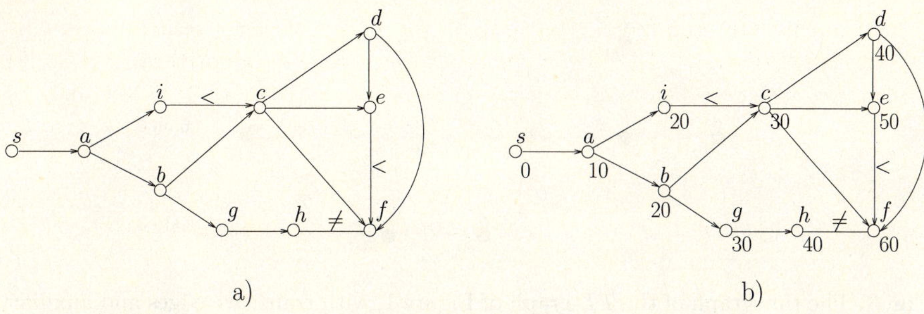

Fig. 1. Examples of TL-graph and ranked TL-graph. Edges with no label are assumed to be labeled "≤".

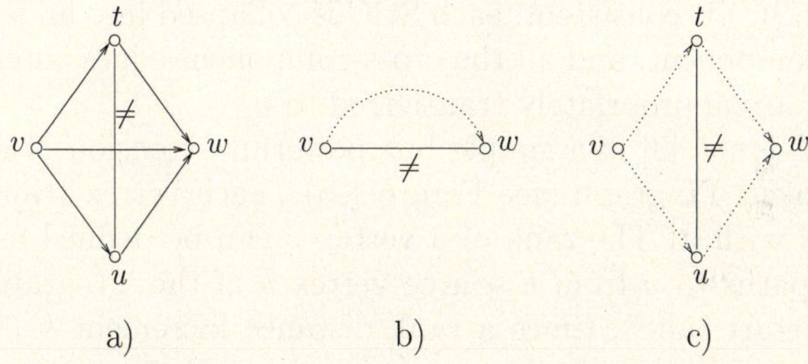

Fig. 2. a) van Beek's forbidden graph; b) and c) the two kinds of implicit < relation in a TL-graph. Edges with no labels are assumed to be labeled "≤". Dotted arrows indicate paths, solid lines ≠-edges. In each graph there is an implicit < between v and w.

vertices v, w representing point variables. Each edge represents a PA-constraint and is either directed and labeled $\leq$ or $<$, or undirected and labeled $\neq$. Figure 1.a) shows an example of TL-graph. A path in a TL-graph is called a $\leq$-path if each edge on the path has label $<$ or $\leq$. A $\leq$-path is called a $<$-path if at least one of the edges has label $<$.

A TL-graph $\mathcal{G}$ contains an *implicit* $<$ relation between two vertices v_1, v_2 when the strongest relation entailed by the temporal CSP from which $\mathcal{G}$ has been built is $v_1 < v_2$ and there is no $<$-path from v_1 to v_2 in $\mathcal{G}$. Figures 2.b) and 2.c) show the two possible TL-graphs which give rise to an implicit $<$ relation. All TL-graphs with an implicit $<$ relation contain one of these subgraphs [4,6].

An acyclic TL-graph without implicit $<$ relations is an *explicit* TL-graph. In order to make explicit a TL-graph containing implicit $<$ relations, we can add new edges with label $<$ [3]. For example, in Figure 2 we add the edge $(v, <, w)$ to the graph. An important property of an explicit TL-graph is that it entails $v \leq w$ if and only if there is a $\leq$-path from v to w; it entails $v < w$ if and only if there is a $<$-path from v to w, and it entails $v \neq w$ if and only if there is a $<$-path from v to w or from w to v, or there is an edge $(v, \neq, w)$.

Given a CSP C over PA with c constraints, we can construct a TL-graph $\mathcal{G}$ representing C in $O(c)$ time; In order to check consistency of C and transform $\mathcal{G}$ into an equivalent acyclic TL-graph, we can use van Beek's method for PA [6].

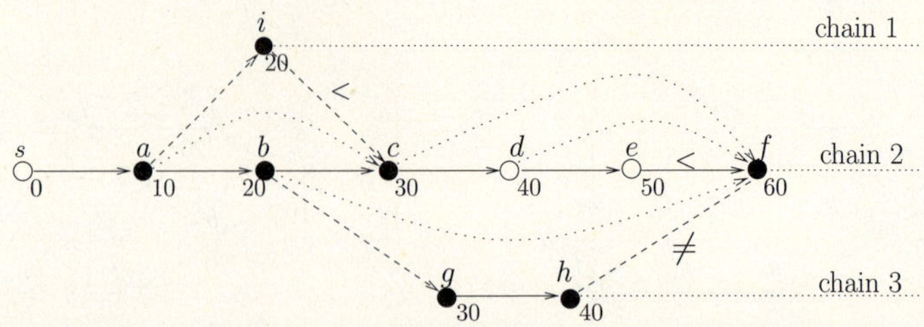

Fig. 3. The timegraph of the TL-graph of Figure 1, with transitive edges and auxiliary edges omitted. Dotted links between nodes on the same chain are nextgreater links. Edges with no label are assumed to be labeled "≤".

If the TL-graph (C) is consistent, each SCC is collapsed into an arbitrary vertex v within that component, and all the cross-component edges entering or leaving the component are appropriately transferred to v.

A *ranked TL-graph* [3] is a simple but powerful extension of an acyclic TL-graph. In a ranked TL-graph (see Figure 1.b) , each vertex (time point) has a *rank* associated with it. The rank of a vertex v can be defined as the length of the longest ≤-paths to v from a source vertex s of the TL-graph representing the "universal start time", times a rank distance increment k [3]. The special vertex s has no predecessor and its successors are all the vertices of the graph that have no other predecessor. As observed in [1,3], the use of the ranks can significantly speed up the search for a path from a vertex p to another vertex q: the search can be pruned whenever a vertex with a rank greater than or equal to the rank of q is reached.

A **timegraph** [3] is an acyclic ranked TL-graph partitioned into a set of *time chains*, such that each vertex is on one and only one time chain. A time chain is a ≤-path, plus possibly "transitive edges" connecting pairs of vertices on the ≤-path. Distinct chains of a timegraph can be connected by *cross-chain edges*. Vertices connected by cross-chain edges are called *metanodes*. Cross-chain edges and certain auxiliary edges connecting metanodes on the same chain are called *metaedges*. The auxiliary edges connect each metanode to the first (last) successor (predecessor) metanode on the same chain with an outgoing cross-edge, and to the first (last) successor (predecessor) metanode on the same chain with an incoming cross-edge. These auxiliary edges are called the *NextOut* (*PrevOut*) and *NextIn* (*PrevIn*) edges of a metanode. The metanodes and metaedges of a timegraph T form the **metagraph** of T.[2]

Figure 3 shows the timegraph built from the TL-graph of Figure 1. All vertices except d, e and s are metanodes. The edges connecting vertices a to i, i to c, b

[2] The purpose of the metagraph is not to be an autonomous structure independent of the rest of the graph, but a support structure to facilitate the graph search conducted during the construction of the timegraph data structures or at query time. Our implementation of the timegraph algorithms does handle the potential "pathological case" identified in [1]. This is done by considering as the successors of a metanode v on a chain c *all* successors of v on c with at least one outgoing cross-chain metaedge.

to g, h with f, are metaedges. Dotted edges are special links called *nextgreaters* that are computed during the construction of the timegraph and that indicate for each vertex v the nearest descendant v' of v on the same chain as v such that the represented CSP entails $v < v'$.

In a timegraph the main purpose of the ranks is to support the computation of the strongest entailed relation between two vertices on the same chain in constant time: given two vertices v_1 and v_2 on the same chain such that the rank of v_2 is greater than the rank of v_1, if the rank of the nextgreater of v_1 is less than or equal to the rank of v_2, then the timegraph entails $v_1 < v_2$, otherwise it entails $v_1 \leq v_2$. For example, the timegraph of Figure 3 entails $a < d$ because a and d are on the same chain, and the rank of the nextgreater of a is less than the rank of d.

Given a CSP C over PA, in order to build a timegraph representation of C, we start from a TL-graph $\mathcal{G}$ representing C. The construction of the timegraph from $\mathcal{G}$ consists of four main steps: checking the consistency of $\mathcal{G}$ (and C), ranking of the graph vertices, formation of the time chains and the metagraph, and making explicit the implicit $<$ relations. The total time complexity of building the timegraph for a CSP C consisting of c PA-constraints involving n point variables is [3]:

– $O(n + c + \hat{e} \cdot \hat{n})$, if C is over the convex PA,
– $O(n + c + \hat{e} \cdot \hat{n} + \hat{e}_{\neq} \cdot (\hat{e} + \hat{n}))$, if C is over the full PA,

where $\hat{n}$ is the number of metanodes in the timegraph, $\hat{e}$ is the number of metaedges and $\hat{e}_{\neq}$ is the number of metaedges labeled $\neq$. It is worth noting that typically $\hat{n}$ is smaller than n, $\hat{e}$ is smaller than c, and $\hat{e}_{\neq}$ is smaller than then the number of input $\neq$-constraints.

Concerning querying the strongest entailed relations between two point variables p_1 and p_2 represented in a timegraph, there are four cases in which this can be accomplished in constant time: (1) p_1 and p_2 are alternative names of the same vertex (the strongest entailed relation is "$=$"); (2) the vertices v_1 and v_2 corresponding to p_1 and p_2 are on the same time chain; (3) v_1 and v_2 are not on the same chain and have the same rank, and there is no $\neq$ edge between them (the strongest entailed relation is "$\top$"); (4) v_1 and v_2 are connected by a $\neq$-edge (the strongest entailed relation is $\neq$). In the remaining cases an explicit search on the metagraph needs to be performed. If there exists at least one $<$-path from v_1 to v_2, then the answer is $v_1 < v_2$. If there are only $\leq$-paths (but no $<$-paths) from v_1 to v_2, then the answer is $v_1 \leq v_2$ [3]. (Analogously for the paths from v_2 to v_1.) Such a graph search can be accomplished in $O(\hat{e} + \hat{n})$ time.

3 Chain Closure for Timegraphs

In this section we extend the timegraph representation with additional information that can be exploited to compute the strongest entailed relation (or minimal constraint) between *any* pair of variables in constant time. This information consists of two additional links for each metanode v with an outgoing cross-chain edge and each chain c:

- *ChainLess*(v, c), which is the first node w on c such that $v < w$ is entailed by the timegraph (there is a $<$-path from v to w);
- *ChainLeq*(v, c), which is the first node t on c such that $v \leq t$ is entailed by the timegraph (there is a $\leq$-path from v to t).

When one of these links is undefined, the corresponding link has value "*null*". We call the set of *ChainLess* and *ChainLeq* links the **chain closure** (or *metagraph closure*) of the timegraph.

3.1 Chain Closure Algorithm

The algorithm in Figure 4, ChainClosure, consists of three nested loops. The most external loop considers each chain c; the second nested loop considers each node v with outgoing cross-chain edge on c as a start node for a search; the third nested loop performs a complete search on the metagraph for computing the *ChainLess* and *ChainLeq* links for v and each time chain.

The first search starting from a metanode on a chain c starts from the last metanode $v =$ *LastOut*(v) on c with an outgoing cross-edge (step 3). Once the algorithm has found all paths from v to the metanodes on each chain $c' \neq c$, the *ChainLess* and *ChainLeq* links of v for all these chains have been computed, and the algorithm "moves back" to the previous metanode on c, $v =$ *PrevOut*(v), with an outgoing cross-chain edge (step 23) to initiate another search (step 5).

The search from v is conducted by maintaining a frontier of nodes to be visited (*Open*). Each time the search visits a metanode s *ChainLess*$(v,$ *Chain*$(s))$ and *ChainLeq*$(v,$ *Chain*$(s))$ are updated, where *Chain*(s) denotes the chain of s (steps 7–14). Since the order in which the chains are processed by the external loop corresponds to their increasing number, if *Chain*$(s) <$ *Chain*(v), then, for all metanodes on *Chain*(s), the *ChainLess* and *ChainLeq* links of s have already been computed, and so they can be used to update the *ChainLess* and *ChainLeq* of v (steps 7-8). For example, if *Rank*(*ChainLess*$(s, c')) <$ *Rank*(*ChainLess*$(v, c'))$, where $c \neq c'$, then *ChainLess*(v, c') is set to *ChainLess*(s, c'), and similarly for *ChainLeq*(v, c').[3] A similar updating is done when *Chain*$(s) =$ *Chain*(v) and s has an outgoing cross-chain edge; this propagates to v the *ChainLess* and *ChainLeq* information previously computed for s. Steps 9–14 consider all the other cases in which the *ChainLess* and *ChainLeq* links of v for *Chain*(s) need to be updated. The flag *Rel*$(s) \in \{<, \leq, null\}$ keeps track of the strongest path (relation) from v to s found by the search (*null* means "no path found" so far).

After visiting s, the frontier *Open* is extended with the child nodes of s (steps 15–20), provided that they satisfy certain conditions illustrated below. The purpose of these conditions is pruning the successor nodes for which we can anticipate that the current *ChainLess* and *ChainLeq* of v cannot be refined by continuing the search from them. The search from v terminates when $s =$ *Pop*(*Open*) is *null* (step 6), i.e., when *Open* becomes empty.

In order to make the search more efficient, not all child nodes of the current node s are added to *Open*. This pruning is performed by exploiting the chain

[3] We omit the details of this updating process, which is straightforward.

Algorithm: ChainClosure

Input: a timegraph T;
Output: T extended with chain closure (*ChainLeq* and *ChainLess* links);

```
1.  Open := empty list;
2.  for each chain c (processed according to their increasing number) do
3.    v := LastOut(c); Visited := empty list;
4.    while v ≠ null
5.      s := v; add s to Visited;
6.      while s ≠ null
7.        if Chain(s) ≤ Chain(v) and s ≠ v and s has outgoing metaedges then
8.          Update ChainLeq(v, c'), ChainLess(v, c') with ChainLeq(s, c') and
            ClainLess(s, c'), respectively, for each chain c' ≠ c;
9.        if Chain(v) ≠ Chain(s) and Rel(s) = < then
10.         if Rank(ChainLess(v, Chain(s))) > Rank(s) then
              ChainLess(v, Chain(s)) := s;
11.         if ChainLeq(v, Chain(s)) ≠ null and Rank(ChainLeq(v, Chain(s))) ≥ Rank(s)
              then ChainLeq(v, Chain(s)) := null;
12.       if Chain(v) ≠ Chain(s) and Rel(s) = ≤ then
13.         if Rank(ChainLess(v, Chain(s))) > Rank(s) and
              Rank(ChainLeq(v, Chain(s))) > Rank(s) then ChainLeq(v, Chain(s)) := s;
14.         if NG(s) ≠ null and Rank(ChainLess(v, Chain(s)) > Rank(NG(s)) then
              ChainLess(v, Chain(s)) := NG(s);
15.       if Chain(s) > Chain(v) or s = v or s has no outgoing cross-chain edges then
16.         S := set of metanodes to which s is connected by outgoing cross-chain edges
17.         if s = v or RelChain(s) = null or (RelChain(s) = ≤ and Rel(s) = <) then
              S := S ∪ {s' | s' is successor of s on Chain(s) through the NextOut links}
18.         for each w ∈ S do
19.           if Rel(s) = < or (s, <, w) ∈ Ê or (Chain(s) = Chain(w) and s < w)
                then update := < else update := ≤;
20.           if Rel(w) = null or (Rel(w) = ≤ and update = <) then
                Rel(w) := update; add w to Open (maintaining the list ordered by rank);
21.       if s = v then RelChain(s) := ≤ else RelChain(s) := Rel(s);
22.       s := Pop(Open); add s to Visited;
23.     v := PrevOut(v); RelChain(v) := null;
24. For each node n in Visited, set Rel(n) to null;
```

Fig. 4. Algorithm for computing the chain closure of a timegraph. We assume that $Rank(null) = +\infty$. $\hat{E}$ is the set of metaedges. $NG(s)$ abbreviates $Nextgreater(s)$. The *RelChain* and *Rel* flags, which we assume are initially set to *null*, are described in the text. Condition $s < w$ at step 19 can be checked in constant time by querying the timegraph because s and w belong to the same chain.

numbering, the *Rel* flag, and an additional information called *RelChain.* As mentioned above, when the search visits a node s with an outgoing metaedge on a chain already processed, i.e., $Chain(s) < Chain(v)$, there is no need to add the child nodes of s to *Open.* Similarly, when for a child node w we have $Rel(w) = <$, or $Rel(w) = \leq$ and $Rel(s) = \leq$, there is no need to add w to *Open.*

The meaning of the *RelChain* flag and its use for pruning the search at step 17 of the algorithm are slightly less intuitive. $RelChain(s) \in \{<, \leq, null\}$ indicates whether the chain of s has already been reached by the current search from v and, if $RelChain(s) \neq null$, it gives the strongest relation between v and *any* visited metanode on $Chain(s)$ that has been computed. When at step 17 the algorithm considers the s' nodes that are successors of s on the same chain as s, such nodes are added to *Open* only if $RelChain(s)$ is *null*, or $RelChain(s)$ is $\leq$ and $Rel(s)$ is $<$. In the other cases the s' nodes have already been considered by the search from v, and the current path from v to s' is not stronger than the one already found.

Finally, the elements in *Open* are maintained ordered by increasing rank, and the next visited node (step 22) is always one with the lowest rank in *Open*. This determines that, when a node s is visited, s cannot precedes any other node on the same chain as s that has already been visited by the current search; this property guarantees the correctness of the pruning described above.

The following theorem states the time complexity of ChainClosure.

Theorem 1. *Let T be a timegraph with $\hat{n}$ metanodes, $\hat{e}$ metaedges and n_c chains. The time complexity of Algorithm* ChainClosure *applied to T is $O(n_c \cdot \hat{e} + \hat{n}^2)$.*

Proof. The time complexity is determined by (1) the total number of metanodes and metaedges visited by all the searches from the metanodes with an outgoing cross-chain edge; (2) the total cost of maintaining *Open* ordered by the rank of its members.

Concerning (1), for each chain c, we have that the total number of metanodes entering into *Open* for *all* the searches from a metanode on c is $O(\hat{n})$. This is because, for each search from a metanode v on c, by exploiting the *Rel* flag (steps 19-20), a node s that has already been visited by the current or any previous search (from another metanode on c successor of v) enters into *Open* only if it is revisited with a stronger relation (step 20). It follows that, for each chain, the total number of visited metanodes is $O(\hat{n})$ and the total number of visited cross-chain edges is $O(\hat{e})$. Hence the total number of nodes and cross-chain edges visited by the algorithm is $O(n_c \cdot \hat{n} + n_c \cdot \hat{e}) = O(n_c \cdot \hat{e})$.

The other metaedges visited by the search are the *NextOut* links connecting two metanodes on the same chain. The total number of these edges in a timegraph is $O(\hat{n})$. By exploiting the *Rel* and *RelChain* flags (step 17), for each search, the algorithm visits each *NextOut* link at most twice. Hence, since the total number of searches performed by the algorithm is $O(\hat{n})$, the total number of visited *NextOut* links is $O(\hat{n}^2)$.

Concerning (2), consider the collection of the $O(\hat{n})$ nodes entering into *Open* for all searches from a start vertex on the same chain. By representing *Open* as a vector of metanodes indexed by their rank divided by the rank increment, and the fact that the nodes in *Open* are processed by increasing rank order, we can derive an efficient method for maintaining *Open* ordered in $O(\hat{n})$ total time. Hence, the total cost for maintaining *Open* ordered is $O(n_c \cdot \hat{n})$. It follows that the total time complexity of the algorithm is $O(n_c \cdot \hat{e} + \hat{n}^2)$. □

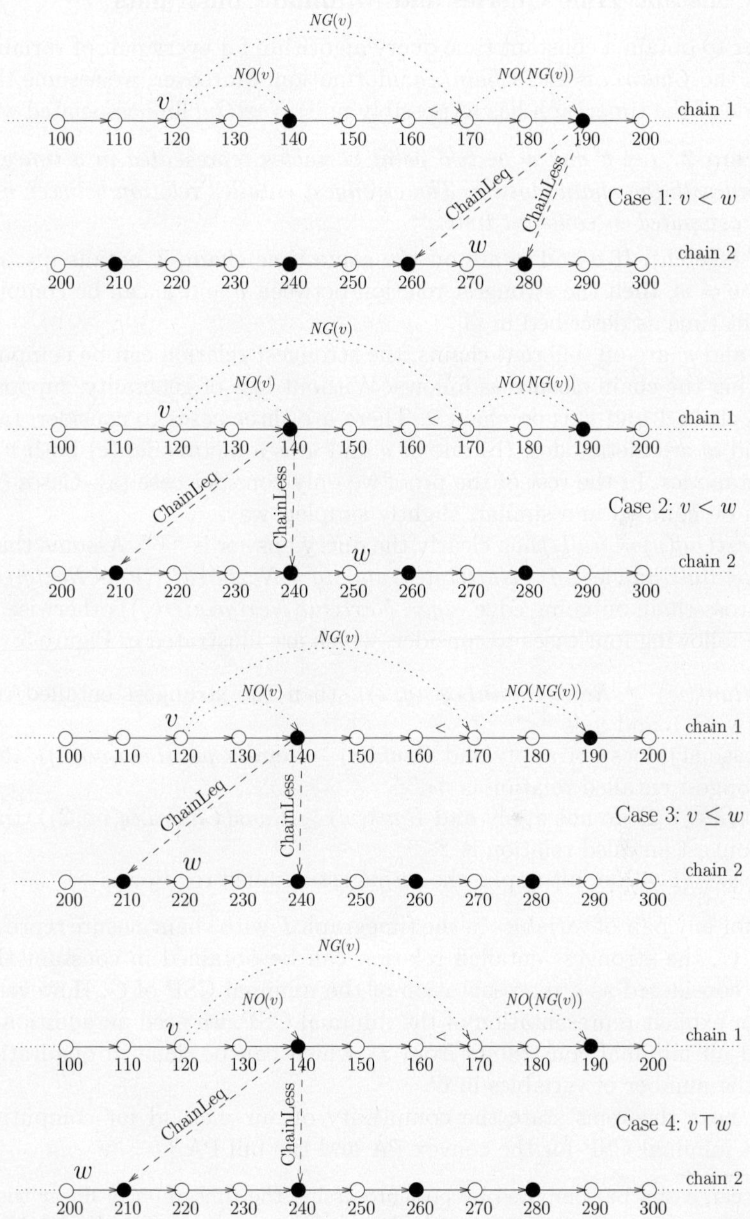

Fig. 5. Illustration of cases (1)–(4) in the constant time query algorithm outlined in the proof of Theorem 2. *NG* and *NO* abbreviate *Nextgreater* and *NextOut*, respectively. Edges on the same chain without a label are assumed to be $\leq$-edges.

3.2 Constant Time Queries and Minimal Constraints

In order to obtain a constant time query algorithm for every pair of variables, we exploit the *ChainLess* and *ChainLeq* information. Moreover, we assume that every node of the timegraph has a (possibly null) *NextOut* link associated with it.[4]

Theorem 2. *Let v and w be two point variables represented in a timegraph T extended with the chain closure. The strongest entailed relation between v and w can be computed in constant time.*

Proof (sketch)**.** If v and w are on the same time chain, T entails $v = w$ or T entails $v \neq w$, then the strongest relation between v and w can be computed in constant time as described in [3].

If v and w are on different chains, the strongest relation can be computed by exploiting the chain closure as follows. Without loss of generality, suppose that v is on chain 1 and w is on chain 2. There are three cases to consider: (a) none of v and w are metanodes, (b) one of v and w is a metanode, (c) both v and w are metanodes. In the rest of the proof we only consider case (a). Cases (b) and (c) can be handled in a similar, slightly simpler, way.

If $NextOut(v) = null$, then clearly the query answer is "⊤". Assume that $NextOut(v) \neq null$, and let $no = NextOut(v)$ and $ng = Nextgreater(v)$, if $Nextgreater(v)$ has a cross-chain outgoing edge, $ng = NextOut(Nextgreater(v))$ otherwise. There are the following four cases to consider, which are illustrated in Figure 5:

(1) if $Rank(w) \geq Rank(ChainLeq(ng, 2))$, then the strongest entailed relation between v and w is "<";
(2) if case (1) does not apply and $Rank(w) \geq Rank(ChainLess(no, 2))$, then the strongest entailed relation is "<";
(3) if cases (1-2) do not apply and $Rank(w) \geq Rank(ChainLeq(no, 2))$, then the strongest entailed relation is "≤";
(4) if cases (1–3) do not apply, the strongest entailed relation is "⊤". □

Since, for any pair of variables in the timegraph T with chain closure representing a CSP C, the strongest entailed relation can be obtained in constant time, T can be considered as a representation of the minimal CSP of C. However, if we want an explicit representation of the minimal CSP, we need an additional step to read all minimal constraints from T, which can be done in quadratic time w.r.t. the number of variables in C.

The next theorems state the complexity of our method for computing the explicit minimal CSP for the convex PA and the full PA.[5]

---

[4] This can easily be computed by post-processing the timegraph in linear time with respect to the number of nodes and edges in the timegraph. The *NextOut* links for a node that is not a metanode are used only to support constant time queries as described in the proof of Theorem 2; they are not part of the metagraph. In the original version of the timegraph only the metanodes can have a *NextOut* link.

[5] If we use the extended timegraph as the representation of the output minimal constraints, then the $O(n^2)$ term in the complexity bounds can be omitted, and we need to add the number of input constraints as an additional term; such a number is no greater than $O(n^2)$ and for sparse CSPs is less than quadratic.

Theorem 3. *Let C be a CSP over the convex Point Algebra involving n variables, the explicit minimal CSP of C can be computed in $O(\hat{n} \cdot \hat{e} + n^2)$ time, where $\hat{n}$ and $\hat{e}$ are the metanodes and metaedges, respectively, in the timegraph representing C.*

Proof. The total time complexity for constructing the timegraph for C is $O(n + |C| + \hat{n} \cdot \hat{e})$ [3], where $|C|$ is the number of constraints in C. By Theorem 2, computing the strongest relation entailed by a timegraph with chain closure for a pair of variables can be accomplished in constant time, and so all minimal constrains of C can be obtained in $O(n^2)$ time. By Theorem 1, the chain closure of the timegraph for C can be computed in $O(n_c \cdot \hat{e} + \hat{n}^2)$. It follows that the total time complexity of computing the minimal CSP of C is $O(\hat{n} \cdot \hat{e} + n^2)$. □

Theorem 4. *Let C be a CSP over the full Point Algebra involving n point variables, the explicit minimal CSP of C can be computed in $O(\hat{e} \cdot \hat{n} + \hat{e}_{\neq} \cdot (\hat{e} + \hat{n}) + n^2)$ time, where $\hat{n}$, $\hat{e}$ and $\hat{e}_{\neq}$ are the metanodes, metaedges and $\neq$-metaedges, respectively, in the timegraph representing C.*

Proof (sketch)**.** The proof is similar to the proof of Theorem 3, except that the time complexity of computing the timegraph for C is $O(n + |C| + \hat{e} \cdot \hat{n} + \hat{e}_{\neq} \cdot (\hat{e} + \hat{n}))$. □

Remark. We observe that the number of metanodes and metaedges in a timegraph can be significantly smaller than the number of variables n and constraints c in the input CSP. For this reason, in practice the time complexity of our approach can be lower than the complexity of the known techniques for computing the minimal CSP of a CSP over the convex PA ($O(n^3)$) and the full PA ($O(n^3 + c_{\neq} \cdot n^2)$), where $c_{\neq}$ is the number of input $\neq$-constraints [10,6]. Moreover, for a sparse input CSP, our method has a better worst-case time complexity. In particular, when c is linear with respect to n, the complexity of our method is $O(n^2)$, while the techniques in [10,6] require $O(n^3)$ time. This can be shown by considering a CSP with n variables forming a single time chain. The path-consistency algorithm in [10] revises the relation between $O(n^2)$ pairs of variables, and for each of these pairs it considers $O(n)$ triples of variables.

4 Experimental Analysis

We implemented (in C) all timegraph algorithms described in [3] and our new chain closure algorithm. We call the resulting temporal reasoner TGC. In order to evaluate the effectiveness of our approach in practice, we compared the performance of TGC with an implementation of

- the path-consistency algorithm given in [10] with the improvements proposed in [8], which we call PC,

– PC extended with van Beek's algorithm for removing the forbidden graphs in a path-consistent CSP over PA [6], which we call PC-FG.[6]

PC solves the problem of computing the minimal CSP for the convex PA [9], while PC-FG solves this problem for the full PA [4,6].

The output of PC and PC-FG is a matrix M such that each entry $M[i, j]$ contains a representation of the strongest entailed relation (minimal constraint) between the i-th and the j-th variables in the input CSP. The output of TGC is the collection of data structures representing a timegraph with chain closure. In both cases, the minimal constraint for a pair of variables can be read from the corresponding data structures in constant time. In our experimental comparison, for TGC we also consider the additional total CPU-time for making all possible queries, which for PC and PC-FG was not considered.

4.1 Experimental Settings and Test Domains

The experiments were aimed at evaluating the hypothesis that our approach works well in practice for chain-structured CSPs (common, e.g., in automated planning and story comprehension) as well as for randomly generated (sparse and dense) CSPs. The data sets were obtained by running three different generators, two of which are based on the available code of known generators [1,3]. Since we were mostly interested in testing the use of our closure algorithm, every generated CSP is consistent and does not contain or entail equality constraints.

In each plot with the experimental results, for the CPU-time of TGC we consider two series of experimental results: one includes the total time for performing all queries, the other does not. In both cases the CPU-time for TGC includes the construction of the timegraph and the chain closure. All tests were conducted on an Intel Xeon(tm) 3 GHz, 1 Gbytes of RAM. The CPU-time corresponding to each point on a curve is an average value over 100 CSPs.

We used six test domains. The CSPs in Domains A, B, C and E, were synthesized using DelGrande et al.'s generator [1], while Domain D using Gerevini & Schubert's generator [3]. For Domain F we used a new generator.

Domain A: randomly generated CSPs over the convex PA with equal numbers of $<$, $\leq$-constraints and no $\neq$-relation. For each considered number n of variables, 100 CSPs with $n \cdot \lfloor(\log_2(n))\rfloor$ constraints each are generated.

Domain B: this domain is the same as Domain A, except that the differences among the CSP instances concern the number c of constraints, rather than the number of variables, which is set to 1000. The generated CSPs range from sparse CSPs ($c = 3000$) to dense CSPs ($c = 449,850$).

---

6 We carefully checked the code of PC and PC-FG to make the implementation efficient and bug-free. The correctness of the three implemented systems was checked by comparing the corresponding minimal constraints obtained for the same CSP, using many randomly generated CSPs.

Domain C: randomly generated CSPs over the convex PA with a chain based structure. For each considered number n of variables, the procedure generates 100 CSPs as described in [1].

Domain D: randomly generated CSPs over the convex PA consisting of data sets that tend to fall into chains. For each considered number n of variables, the procedure generates 100 CSPs as described in [3], each of which contains $n \cdot \lfloor(\log_2(n))\rfloor$ constraints.

Domain E: this domain is the same as Domain A, except that the CSPs also contain $\neq$-constraints. For each considered number n of variables, the procedure generates 100 CSPs. Each generated CSP contains $n \cdot \lfloor(\log_2(n))\rfloor$ constraints, 10% of which are $\neq$-constraints.

Domain F: randomly generated CSPs over the full PA consisting of CSPs with a chain structure and many $\neq$-diamonds (forbidden graphs). For each considered number n of variables, the procedure generates 100 CSPs as follows. We partition the variables in three subsets, each of which containing $\lfloor n/3 \rfloor$ variables constrained to form a chain of $\leq$-constraints. The variables in each subset are constrained in a way that determine at least $\lfloor n/3 \rfloor - 1$ $\neq$-diamonds. In each generated CSP, the percentage of $\neq$-constraints is about 50.

4.2 Experimental Results

First we present the results for the convex PA and then those for the full PA. Figure 6 shows the performance of TGC and PC for Domains A and B. The results for Domain A (plot on the left side of the figure) indicate that for large CSPs TGC is up to about three orders of magnitude faster than PC. The results for Domain B (plot on the right side of the figure) indicate that the very good performance of TGC relative to PC does not depend on the sparseness of

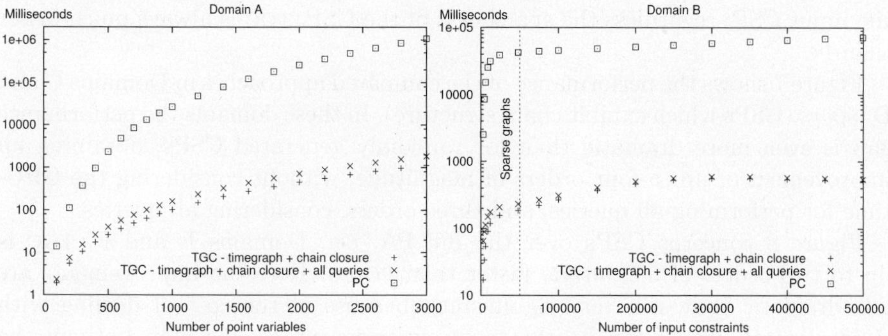

Fig. 6. Average CPU-times of TGC and PC in Domains A and B. For Domain A, on the x-axis we have the number of point variables, while for Domain B we have the number of edges (input constraints) in the timegraph. In both cases on the y-axis we have the CPU-milliseconds (logarithmic scale).

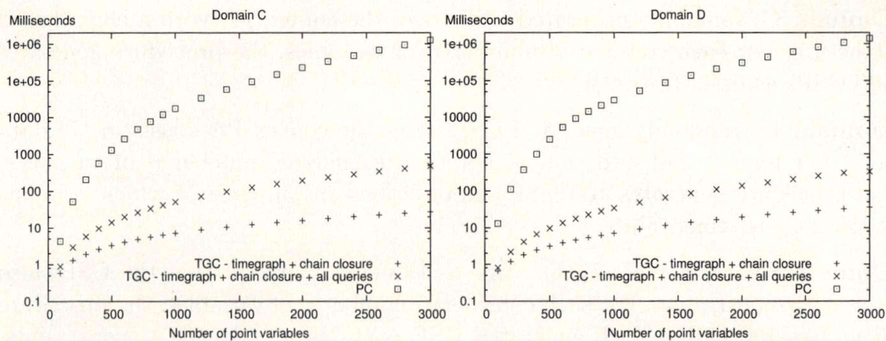

Fig. 7. Average CPU-times of TGC and PC in Domains C and D. On the x-axis we have the number of point variables, on the y-axis the CPU-milliseconds (logarithmic scale).

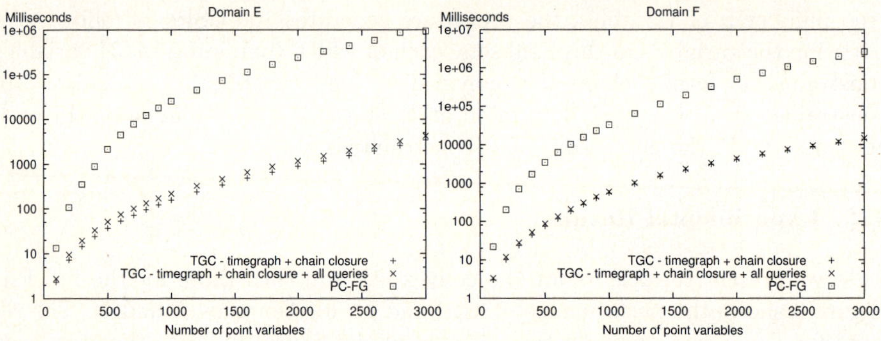

Fig. 8. Average CPU-times of TGC and PC-FG in Domains D and E. On the x-axis we have the number of point variables, on the y-axis we have the CPU-milliseconds (logarithmic scale).

the input CSP: regardless the sparseness of the CSP, TGC is always much faster than PC.

Figure 7 shows the performance of the compared approaches in Domains C and D (sparse CSPs which exhibit chain structure). In these domains the performance gap is even more dramatic than for randomly generated CSPs, obtaining an improvement of up to four orders of magnitude, without considering the CPU-time for performing all queries, and three orders, considering all queries.

Figure 8 concerns CSPs over the full PA, i.e., Domains E and F. TGC is up to two orders of magnitude faster than PC-FG. Here the improvements are less dramatic (but still very significant), because of the cost of dealing with $\neq$-constraints, which can be the most expensive processing step both in the construction of the timegraph with chain closure and in PC-FG.

Finally, we also tested a simple alternative method for computing the minimal CSP using the timegraph representation. Instead of computing the chain closure, we use the original data structures and query algorithms to compute, for every pair of variables, the corresponding strongest entailed relation. We compared the CPU-times of this simple approach and the one computing the chain closure using our test domains. The results of this experiment indicate that computing the chain closure is advantageous. Our method is up to 300 times faster than making all queries in the timegraph without chain closure. An exception to this behavior are particular CSPs that have a very strong chain structure (e.g., when the timegraph has only one chain), where an extremely high percentage of pair of nodes lie on the same chain. In these special cases the two timegraph-based approaches perform similarly.

5 Conclusions

We have presented a new efficient method for computing the minimal CSP of a CSP over the Point Algebra. For sparse CSPs the worst-case complexity of our method improves the complexity of known methods based on enforcing path consistency. In practice, an experimental analysis using various types of data sets shows that our approach is much faster than computing the minimal CSP using known techniques, both for CSPs with a chain structure and for general randomly generated (sparse and dense) CSPs. A price to pay for the efficiency gain is the more complex algorithms and implementation (however, the implementation used in our experiments will be made publicly available).

While the techniques presented in this paper build on the timegraph representation, we believe that our method can be applied to other graph-based representation, such as the metagraph of the SPMG system [1], which uses series-parallel graphs instead of chains. Future work includes investigating an algorithm for the metagraph closure in the context of SPMG and additional experiments.

Acknowledgments. We would like to thank Nicola Ferrari and Nicola Morotti for their help with the implementation of the timegraph algorithms.

References

1. Delgrande, J., Gupta, A., Van Allen, T.: A comparison of point-based approaches to qualitative temporal reasoning. Artificial Intelligence 131, 135–170 (2001)
2. Gerevini, A.: Processing qualitative temporal constraints. In: Handbook of Temporal Reasoning in Artificial Intelligence, pp. 247–276. Elsevier, Amsterdam (2005)
3. Gerevini, A., Schubert, L.: Efficient algorithms for qualitative reasoning about time. Artificial Intelligence 74, 207–248 (1995)
4. Gerevini, A., Schubert, L.: On computing the minimal labels in time point algebra networks. Computational Intelligence 11(3), 443–448 (1995)
5. Golumbic, C.M., Shamir, R.: Complexity and algorithms for reasoning about time: a graph-theoretic approach. Journal of the Association for Computing Machinery (ACM) 40(5), 1108–1133 (1993)
6. van Beek, P.: Reasoning about qualitative temporal information. Artificial Intelligence 58(1-3), 297–321 (1992)
7. van Beek, P., Cohen, R.: Exact and approximate reasoning about temporal relations. Computational Intelligence 6, 132–144 (1990)

8. van Beek, P., Manchak, D.W.: The design and experimental analysis of algorithms for temporal reasoning. Journal of Artificial Intelligence Research 4, 1–18 (1996)
9. Vilain, M., Kautz, H.A.: Constraint propagation algorithms for temporal reasoning. In: Proceedings of the Fifth National Conference of the American Association for Artificial Intelligence (AAAI-86), pp. 377–382. Morgan Kaufmann, San Francisco (1986)
10. Vilain, M., Kautz, H.A., van Beek, P.: Constraint propagation algorithms for temporal reasoning: a revised report. In: Weld, D.S., de Kleer, J. (eds.) Readings in Qualitative Reasoning about Physical Systems, pp. 373–381. Morgan Kaufmann, San Mateo, CA (1990)

MUST: Provide a Finer-Grained Explanation of Unsatisfiability

Éric Grégoire, Bertrand Mazure, and Cédric Piette

CRIL-CNRS & IRCICA
Université d'Artois
rue Jean Souvraz SP18
F-62307 Lens Cedex France
{gregoire,mazure,piette}@cril.fr

Abstract. In this paper, a new form of explanation and recovery technique for the unsatisfiability of discrete CSPs is introduced. Whereas most approaches amount to providing users with a minimal number of constraints that should be dropped in order to recover satisfiability, a finer-grained alternative technique is introduced. It allows the user to reason both at the constraints and tuples levels by exhibiting both problematic constraints and tuples of values that would allow satisfiability to be recovered if they were not forbidden. To this end, the Minimal Set of Unsatisfiable Tuples (MUST) concept is introduced. Its formal relationships with Minimal Unsatisfiable Cores (MUCs) are investigated. Interestingly, a concept of shared forbidden tuples is derived. Allowing any such tuple makes the corresponding MUC become satisfiable. From a practical point of view, a two-step approach to the explanation and recovery of unsatisfiable CSPs is proposed. First, a recent approach proposed by Hemery *et al.*'s is used to locate a MUC. Second, a specific SAT encoding of a MUC allows MUSTs to be computed by taking advantage of the best current technique to locate Minimally Unsatisfiable Sub-formulas (MUSes) of Boolean formulas. Interestingly enough, shared tuples coincide with protected clauses, which are one of the keys to the efficiency of this SAT-related technique. Finally, the feasibility of the approach is illustrated through extensive experimental results.

Keywords: CSP, constraint networks, explanation, unsatisfiability, MUC, MUS, MUST.

1 Introduction

In this paper, we are concerned with unsatisfiable finite CSPs, namely finite Constraint Satisfaction Problems for which no solution exists. Recent approaches to explain such a form of unsatisfiability have been defined at the constraints level. For example, Hemery *et al.* [1] have proposed an approach called `DC(wcore)` to detect Minimally Unsatisfiable Cores (MUCs) of CSPs, i.e. unsatisfiable subsets of constraints of the initial CSP that are such that dropping any one the constraints allows the resulting subset to become satisfiable. In this paper, a finer-grained alternative technique is introduced. Indeed, dropping constraints can be too much destructive. Finer-grained information could be provided to the user, allowing him (her) not only to pinpoint the causes of

C. Bessiere (Ed.): CP 2007, LNCS 4741, pp. 317–331, 2007.

unsatisfiability at the constraints level, but also detect the tuples of values that are forbidden by the constraints and that would lead to satisfiability if they were allowed by those constraints.

In this respect, the contribution of this paper is twofold. On the one hand, a *Minimally Unsatisfiable Set of Tuples* (MUST) concept is introduced: it is aimed at encompassing the aforementioned notion of tuples that can allow satisfiability to be regained. The formal relationships between MUSTs and MUCs are investigated. Interestingly, a concept of shared forbidden tuples is derived. Allowing any shared tuple makes the corresponding MUC become satisfiable. On the other hand, a two-step approach to the explanation and recovery of unsatisfiable CSPs is proposed. A specific SAT encoding of a MUC allows MUSTs to be computed by taking advantage of the best current technique to locate Minimally Unsatisfiable Sub-formulas (MUSes) of Boolean formulas. Interestingly enough, shared tuples coincide with protected clauses [2], which are one of the keys to the efficiency of this SAT-related technique.

Accordingly, the paper is organized as follows. First, some basic definitions about CSPs and MUCs are provided. In section 3, MUSTs are introduced and linked to MUCs in section 4. Next, an original two-step approach to explain and recover from unsatisfiable CSPs is described. In section 5, a SAT-related approach to compute MUSTs and shared forbidden tuples of a MUC is introduced. The feasibility of the approach is illustrated through extensive experimental results in section 6. Section 7 compares the contribution presented in this paper with the current existing works. In the conclusion, some interesting paths for future research are described.

2 Background: CSPs and MUCs

In this section, the reader is provided with basic concepts about CSPs and MUCs.

Definition 1. *A finite Constraint Satisfaction Problem (in short, CSP) is a pair* $P = \langle V,C \rangle$ *where*

1. V *is a finite set of* n *variables* $\{v_1, \ldots, v_n\}$ *s.t. each variable* $v_i \in V$ *has an associated finite instantiation domain, denoted* $dom(v_i)$*, which contains the set of possible values for* v_i*,*
2. C *is a finite set of* m *constraints* $\{c_1, \ldots, c_m\}$ *s.t. each constraint* $c_j \in C$ *involves a subset of variables of* V*, called scope and denoted* $Var(c_j)$*, and has an associated relation* $R(c_j)$*, which contains the set of tuples allowed for the variables of its scope.*

Definition 2. *Solving a CSP* $P = \langle V,C \rangle$ *consists in checking whether* P *admits at least one solution, i.e. an assignment of values for all variables of* V *s.t. all constraints of* C *are satisfied. If* P *admits at least one solution then* P *is called satisfiable else* P *is called unsatisfiable.*

In this paper, it will prove useful to adopt an alternative but equivalent definition for CSPs, expressed in terms of *forbidden* tuples of values.

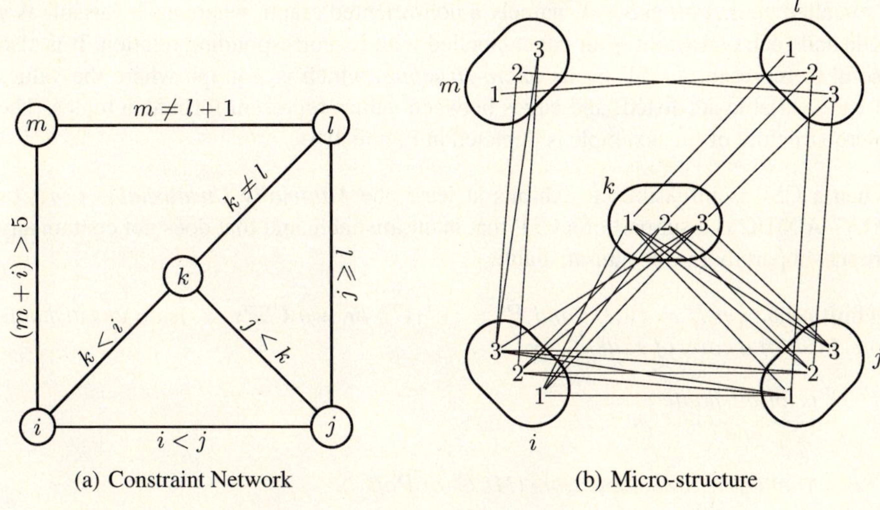

(a) Constraint Network (b) Micro-structure

Fig. 1. Graph-representations of Example 1

Definition 3. *Let $\langle V, C\rangle$ be a CSP and let $c \in C$ s.t. $Var(c) = \{v_c^1, \ldots, v_c^l\}$. A forbidden tuple of values is a member of $dom(v_c^1) \times \cdots \times dom(v_c^l)$ s.t. $R(c)$ is not satisfied. The set of forbidden tuples of values for a constraint c is denoted $T(c)$.*

Accordingly, CSPs can be redefined as follows.

Definition 4. *A finite CSP is a pair $P = \langle V, C\rangle$ where*

1. *V is a finite set of n variables $\{v_1, \ldots, v_n\}$ s.t. each variable $v_i \in V$ has an associated finite instantiation domain, denoted $dom(v_i)$, which contains the set of possible values for v_i,*
2. *C is a finite set of m constraints $\{c_1, \ldots, c_m\}$ s.t. each constraint $c_j \in C$ involves a subset of variables of V, called scope and denoted $Var(c_j)$, and is given a relation $T(c_j)$, which contains the set of tuples forbidden for the variables of its scope.*

Accordingly, P will also be denoted $\langle V, \{(Var(c_1), T(c_1)), (Var(c_2), T(c_2)), \ldots, (Var(c_n), T(c_n))\}\rangle$.

Definition 5. *A constraint $c \in C$ of the CSP $P = \langle\{v_1, \ldots, v_n\}, C\rangle$ is falsified by an assignment $A \in dom(v_1) \times \cdots \times dom(v_n)$ iff the projection of A on $Var(c)$ is included in $T(c)$.*

In the following, *(forbidden) tuple* will be a shorthand for *forbidden tuple of values*, and binary CSPs will be considered only, namely CSPs where constraints involve two variables. Using binary CSPs do not restrict the impact of our works, since it is well-known that every discrete CSP can be reduced into a binary one, in polynomial time.

Example 1. Let V be $\{i,j,k,l,m\}$ where each variable has the same domain $\{1,2,3\}$. Let C be a set of 7 constraints. In Figure 1(a), the CSP $P = \langle V, C\rangle$ is represented by a so-called *constraint network*, namely a non-oriented graph, where each variable is a node and each constraint is an edge, labelled with its corresponding relation. It is also useful to represent a CSP by its *micro-structure*, which is a graph where the values of each variable are listed, and edges between values represent forbidden tuples. The micro-structure of this example is depicted in Figure 1(b).

When a CSP is infeasible, it exhibits at least one *Minimally Unsatisfiable Core*, or MUC. A MUC is a subpart of a CSP that is unsatisfiable and that does not contain any proper subpart that is also unsatisfiable.

Definition 6. *Let $P = \langle V, C\rangle$ and $P' = \langle V', C'\rangle$ be two CSPs. P' is an unsatisfiable core, in short a core, of P iff*

1. *P' is unsatisfiable*
2. *$V' \subseteq V$ and $C' \subseteq C$*

P' is a Minimal Unsatisfiable Core (MUC) of P iff

1. *P' is a core of P*
2. *there does not exist any proper core of P'*

Example 2. In the previous example, P is unsatisfiable. Indeed, P contains the MUC $P' = \langle V, \{i < j, j < k, k < i\}\rangle$: no assignment of values for i, j and k can be found such that these three constraints are satisfied, and dropping any constraint leads to satisfiability.

Computing one MUC for an unsatisfiable CSP is an NP-hard problem. More precisely, checking whether a constraint belongs to a MUC or not is in Σ_2^p [3]. Moreover, the number of MUCs inside a CSP can be exponential in the worst-case; it is in $\mathcal{O}(C_m^{m/2})$, where m is the number of constraints in the CSP. It should be noted that MUCs can share non-empty intersections. Several techniques have been proposed in the literature to compute MUCs, the `DC(wcore)` approach introduced recently by Hemery *et al.* [1] is claimed by its authors to be the most efficient one, most often.

3 MUSTs

Restoring the satisfiability of a CSP can be achieved through restoring the satisfiability of each of its MUCs. A natural way to break the unsatisfiability of a MUC is to drop any of its constraints. However, dropping some constraints as a whole can appear too much destructive. On the contrary, we might prefer to *weaken* one or several constraints, instead of removing them. One way to do that is to provide the user with some forbidden tuples that should be allowed in order to recover satisfiability.

Let us introduce the following MUST concept and study to which extent it can be a first good step in that direction. A MUST (*Minimally Unsatisfiable Set of Tuples*) of an unsatisfiable CSP P is an unsatisfiable CSP P' that is such that the sets of forbidden tuples of its constraints are subsets of the corresponding sets w.r.t. P and such that allowing any of the tuples of P' will render P' satisfiable.

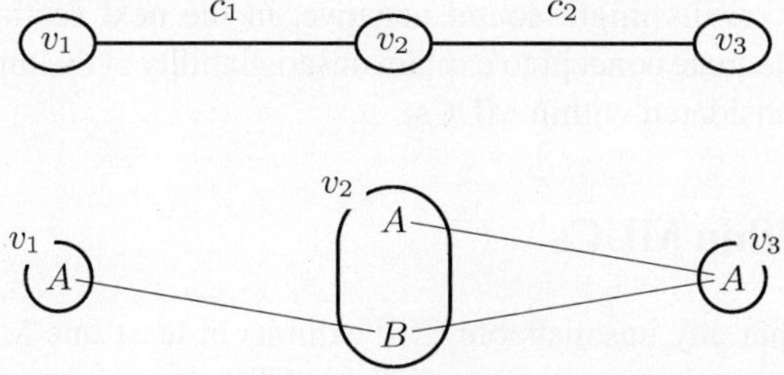

Fig. 2. Graphical representations of Example 3

Definition 7. *Let* $P = \langle V, \{(Var(c_1), T(c_1)), \ldots, (Var(c_m), T(c_m))\}\rangle$ *be an unsatisfiable CSP. The CSP* $P' = \langle V, \{(Var(c_1), T'(c_1)), \ldots, (Var(c_m), T'(c_m))\}\}\rangle$ *is a* MUST (Minimally Unsatisfiable Set of Tuples) *of P if and only if :*

1. P' *is unsatisfiable*
2. $\forall i$ *s.t.* $1 \leq i \leq m$, $T'(c_i) \subseteq T(c_i)$
3. $\forall i$ *s.t.* $1 \leq i \leq m$, $\forall\, T''(c_i) \subset T'(c_i)$,
$\langle V, \{(Var(c_1), T'(c_1)), ..., (Var(c_i), T''(c_i)), ..., (Var(c_m), T'(c_m))\}\rangle$ *is satisfiable*

Hence, a MUST can be interpreted as a tentative way to explain infeasibility at a lower level of abstraction than the constraints one does. At this point, it is important to note that this definition for a MUST of a CSP P does not require that allowing one of the forbidden tuples of the MUST will make P become satisfiable. Indeed, it is easy to prove that an unsatisfiable CSP can exhibit an exponential number of MUSTs in the worst case and that their set-theoretic intersection can be empty. Thus, the removal of *one* forbidden tuple might not be enough to regain satisfiability. Furthermore, as the following example shows, tuples contained in a MUST might even not take part into the actual cause of the infeasibility of the CSP.

Example 3

Let $P = \langle V, C\rangle$ s.t. $V = \{v_1, v_2, v_3\}$, with $dom(v_1) = dom(v_3) = \{A\}$, $dom(v_2) = \{A, B\}$, and $C = \{c_1 = (\{v_1, v_2\}, \{(A, B)\}), c_2 = (\{v_2, v_3\}, \{(A, A), (B, A)\})\}$. In Figure 2, both the graph and the micro-structure of this CSP are given. Clearly, P is unsatisfiable and exhibits only one MUC, made of the c_2 constraint, since this one prevents any assignment from being valid between v_2 and v_3. On the contrary, considering a lower level of abstraction, we see that P exhibits two MUSTs, namely:

– $P_{M_1} = \langle V, \{(\{v_1, v_2\}, \{(A, B)\}), \{(\{v_2, v_3\}, \{(A, A)\})\}\}\rangle$
– $P_{M_2} = \langle V, \{(\{v_2, v_3\}, \{(A, A), (B, A)\})\}\rangle$

P_{M_1} is a MUST that contains tuples from both constraints. It does not correspond to any MUC of P. P_{M_2} is a MUST that is also a MUC of P. Moreover, P_{M_1} contains the only forbidden tuple linking v_1 and v_2, which does not participate to the unsatisfiability of P.

Although these results might sound negative, in the next section it is shown that MUSTs form an adequate concept to explain unsatisfiability at the tuples level, provided that MUSTs are considered within MUCs.

4 MUSTs Within MUCs

It is well-known that any unsatisfiable CSP exhibits at least one MUC (which can be the CSP itself). Unsurprisingly, any unsatisfiable CSP also exhibits at least one MUST. Indeed, MUCs are unsatisfiable CSPs, which ensures that at least one MUST can be extracted from any MUC of a CSP.

Proposition 1. *At least one MUST can be extracted from any unsatisfiable CSP.*

Proof. *Let $P = \langle V, C\rangle$ be an unsatisfiable CSP. Assume that P does not contain any MUST. Thus, P itself is not a MUST: hence there exists a forbidden tuple of P s.t. allowing it gives rise to another unsatisfiable CSP containing no MUST, namely $\exists c \in C, \exists t \in T(c)$ such that $P^1 = \langle V, (C\backslash c) \cup (Var(c), T(c)\backslash t)\rangle$ is also unsatisfiable, and does not exhibit any MUST. Iterating this reasoning, it is easily proved by induction that this would lead to the existence of a CSP $P' = \langle V, \emptyset\rangle$ that should be unsatisfiable, whereas such a CSP is clearly satisfiable.* □

Moreover, stronger relations link MUCs and MUSTs, as shown by the following proposition.

Proposition 2. *Let P be a MUC that contains m constraints. There exists at least m tuples s.t. allowing any one of them makes P regain satisfiability. These tuples belong to all MUSTs of P.*

Proof. *Since $P = \langle V, C\rangle$ is a MUC, whenever any of its m constraints c_i is dropped, the resulting CSP is satisfiable. Let A be an assignment that satisfies $P' = \langle V, C\backslash c_i\rangle$. c_i is violated by A: indeed, in the opposite case, P would be satisfiable and would not be a MUC. The projection of A on $Var(c_i)$ is included in $T(c_i)$, according to definition 5. Thus, removing this forbidden tuple is sufficient to make P feasible. The same argument can be used for any of the m constraints of P. Thus, there exists at least m tuples such that omitting one of them makes the MUC regain feasibility. Clearly, these tuples necessarily belong to all the sources of unsatisfiability, and consequently to every MUST of the MUC. Hence, the set-theoretic intersection of all MUSTs of P contains at least m tuples.* □

In this respect, some tuples allow the unsatisfiability of the MUC to be "broken", simply by allowing any of them. These tuples necessarily belong to all sources of unsatisfiability of the MUC, and consequently to every MUST of the MUC. Accordingly, it is thus not possible to discover two MUSTs of a MUC with an empty set-theoretic intersection. Tuples belonging to every MUST of a MUC P will be called *shared tuples* of P.

Definition 8. *Let P be a MUC. The shared tuples of P are the forbidden tuples belonging to all MUSTs of P.*

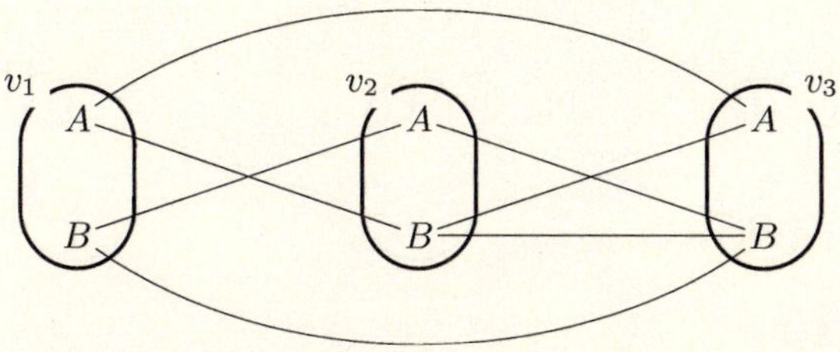

Fig. 3. Micro-structure of Example 4

Allowing any shared tuple allows the corresponding MUC to be broken. Moreover, computing a MUST of a MUC P delivers a super-set of the set of shared tuples.

Example 4. Let a CSP $P = \langle \{v_1, v_2, v_3\}, \{c_1, c_2, c_3\} \rangle$ s.t.

1. $\forall i \in \{1, 2, 3\}, dom(v_i) = \{A, B\}$
2. $c_1 = (\{v_1, v_2\}, \{(A, B), (B, A)\})$
3. $c_2 = (\{v_2, v_3\}, \{(A, B), (B, A), (B, B)\})$
4. $c_3 = (\{v_1, v_3\}, \{(A, A), (B, B)\})$

The micro-structure of P is given in Figure 3. Let us note that P is a MUC since P is unsatisfiable and dropping any of its constraints yields a satisfiable CSP. P exhibits two MUSTs; their micro-structures are given in Figure 4. By considering the set-theoretic intersection of those MUSTs, one can obtain the shared tuples of P. The shared tuples are represented using boldface edges in Figure 5, while the other tuples are represented using dotted lines. Clearly, allowing one shared tuple allows us to restore the satisfiability of both MUSTs and their corresponding MUC. However, allowing any other forbidden tuple of these MUSTs does not guarantee the satisfiability of the initial MUC to be restored. This example also shows us that the CSP formed with the shared tuples of a MUC is not necessarily unsatisfiable.

These last results plead for a two-step policy for the explanation of unsatisfiability in terms of MUCs, MUSTs and shared tuples. Indeed, looking for MUSTs in the general case does not seem the most promising approach since MUSTs can coincide with no MUC at all. On the contrary, an interesting approach would require to search for MUCs as a first step. MUCs provide explanations of unsatisfiability that are expressed in terms of a minimal number of constraints. The user can drop one such constraint to break the unsatisfiability of the MUC. Alternatively, he (she) could rather search for MUSTs corresponding to the discovered MUC. More precisely, if he (she) manages to discover shared tuples, the user would be provided with a set of forbidden tuples that is such that allowing just one such tuple is *enough* to break the unsatisfiability of the MUC. In such a way, the user would be given the ability to weaken problematic constraints instead of dropping one whole constraint. Such a policy is to be iterated until all (remaining) MUCs of the resulting CSP have been addressed.

Several algorithms have been proposed to compute one MUC. Thus, the next issue that is to be addressed is how both MUSTs and shared tuples could be computed within

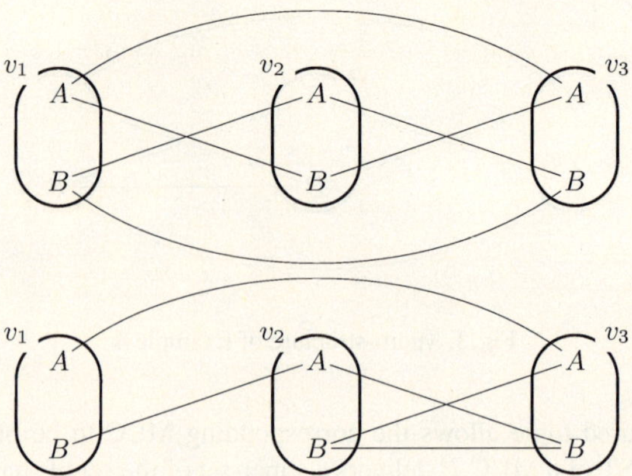

Fig. 4. Micro-structure of the two MUSTs of Example 4

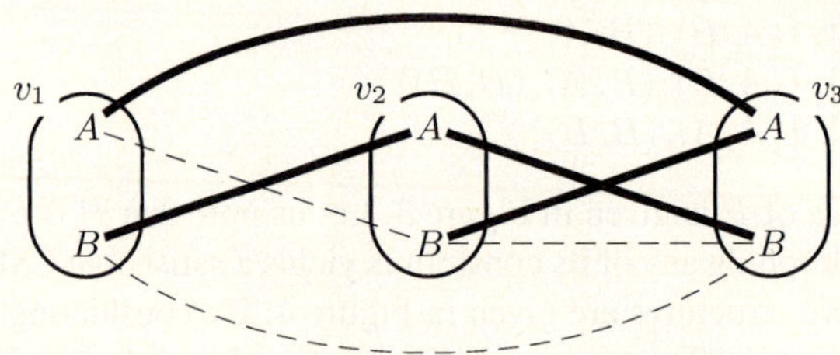

Fig. 5. Shared tuples of Example 4

a MUC. In the following, it is shown that, modulo a specific SAT encoding, shared tuples exactly coincide with so-called protected clauses [2], which play a central role in the efficiency of the currently most efficient technique to compute MUCs in the Boolean case, namely MUSes (Minimally Unsatisfiable Sub-formulas). In this respect, a Boolean translation of MUCs that allows us to benefit from the efficiency of this powerful computational technique will be provided.

5 Using OMUS to Compute MUSTs and Shared Tuples

Computing a MUST could be performed through several traditional techniques from the CSP and the operational research domains, such as the destructive, additive or dichotomic minimization procedures [4]. However, those approaches would deliver MUSTs, only. The computation of shared tuples would require either a linear number of additional step-by-step tests of satisfiability, or to consider all solutions of each relaxation obtained by removing one constraint from the computed MUC. On the contrary, an approach allowing both a MUST and shared tuples to be computed at the same time is introduced in this section.

When one MUC has been obtained trough e.g. Hemery *et al.*'s `DC(wcore)` technique [1], it is translated inside the Boolean framework in such a way that the computation of MUSTs and shared tuples of the MUC is achieved through the computation of MUSes, namely minimally unsatisfiable sets of clauses of a CNF formula. The selected translation schema is a form of *direct encoding* [5] that consists in encoding each domain value of each variable by a different Boolean variable C_{v_i}. Accordingly, the number of variables in the Boolean framework is given by the sum of the sizes of the domains of the variables of the MUC. Let $P = \langle V, C \rangle$ be a MUC, the following clauses are then created.

1. *at-Least-one clauses* ensure that at least one possible value for each variable v_i is selected in a solution
   $C_{v_1} \vee C_{v_2} \vee ... \vee C_{v_m}$ $\forall v \in V$ with $dom(v) = \{v_1, v_2, ..., v_m\}$
2. *at-Most-one clauses* ensure that at most one value is selected for each variable
   $\neg C_{v_a} \vee \neg C_{v_b}$ $\forall v \in V$ $\forall (v_a, v_b) \in dom(v) \times dom(v)$
3. *Conflict clauses* encode forbidden tuples
   $\neg C_{v_i} \vee \neg C_{v_j}$ $\forall c \in C$ $\forall (v_i, v_j) \in T(c)$

This form of encoding has been adopted because it allows a forbidden tuple to be translated into a unique clause. Moreover, the "at-Most-one clauses" are actually not added to the generated formula. Indeed, those clauses have been proved optional [6]; moreover, omitting them enables us to ensure that minimality is preserved in both frameworks. Thus, each MUS of the generated Boolean formula corresponds to a MUST of the infeasible CSP. Computing one MUST amounts to computing one MUS in this Boolean framework, provided that every *at-Least-one* clauses belong to the MUS.

More precisely, we make use of the `OMUS` technique by Grégoire *et al.* [2], which is currently one of the most efficient complete techniques to discover one MUS inside an unsatisfiable SAT instance. One key to the efficiency of this approach is the concept of *protected clauses*. Interestingly enough, protected clauses appear to encode shared tuples.

The `OMUS` technique is based on the so-called critical clause concept, which is a clause that is falsified under a given assignment of values and that is such that satisfying it by a minimal change of the assignment will always conduct at least another clause to be falsified in its turn. Roughly, the `OMUS` technique is a two-step approach. First, a superset of a MUS is computed by iterating the computation of the number of times each clause is critical during local search runs and by dropping clauses with the lowest scores. Second, a fine-tune process allows an exact MUS to be delivered. Interestingly, each time there is just one clause that is not satisfied w.r.t. some variables assignment during the local search run, it is marked and never be dropped from the formula. These clauses are called *protected*, and belong to all MUSes of the Boolean formula. According to this encoding, protected clauses coincide with shared tuples of the translated MUC. These tuples are thus delivered together with the MUST, without any computing overhead. Furthermore, the first step of this local-search-based algorithm sometimes delivers an unsatisfiable set of protected clauses, which forms a MUS, and the second step of the algorithm is avoided.

Algorithm 1. `direct_encode`

Input: a CSP: $\langle V, C\rangle$
Output: a set of clauses Σ viewed as a CNF formula
begin
  $\Sigma \longleftarrow \emptyset$;
  foreach $v_i \in V$ **do**
    $\Sigma \longleftarrow \Sigma \bigcup \{ \bigvee_{\forall j \in dom(v_i)} x_{ij}\}$; `/* "At-least-one" clauses */`
  foreach $c \in C$ **do**
    foreach $t \in T(c)$ **do**
      $\Sigma = \Sigma \bigcup \{ \bigvee_{\substack{\forall (v_i \in Var(c) \text{ and } j \in dom(v_i)) \\ \text{s.t. } j \text{ is the forbidden value of } v_i \text{ in } t}} \neg x_{ij}\}$;
  return Σ ;
end

Algorithm 2. `mus2must`

Input: a MUS: Σ and a MUC: $\langle V, \{(Var(c_1), T(c_1)), ..., (Var(c_m), T(c_m))\}\rangle$
Output: a MUST: $\langle V, \{(Var(c_1), T'(c_1)), ..., (Var(c_m), T'(c_m))\}\rangle$
begin
  foreach $c \in C$ *s.t.* $C = \{(Var(c_1), T(c_1)), ..., (Var(c_m), T(c_m))\}$ **do**
    $T'(c) \longleftarrow \emptyset$;
    foreach $t \in T(c)$ **do**
      if $((\bigvee_{\substack{\forall (v_i \in Var(c) \text{ and } j \in dom(v_i)) \\ \text{s.t. } j \text{ is the forbidden value of } v_i \text{ in } t}} \neg x_{ij}) \in \Sigma)$ **then**
        $T'(c) \longleftarrow T'(c) \cup \{t\}$;
  return $\langle V, \{(Var(c_1), T'(c_1)), ..., (Var(c_m), T'(c_m))\}\rangle$;
end

6 Experimental Studies

In order to assess the practical value of these techniques, an algorithm called `MUSTER` (MUST-ExtRaction) has been implemented and run on various benchmarks from the last CSP competition [7]. This software makes thus use of (a `C` variant of) Hemery *et al.*'s `DC(wcore)` technique to extract a MUC from the considered CSP. Then, the MUC is converted into a Boolean clausal formula according to the aforementioned *direct-encoding* described in Algorithm 1. A MUS is then computed thanks to Grégoire *et al.*'s `OMUS` procedure [2]. As described above, there is a one-to-one correspondence between this MUS and a MUST from the CSP; this latter one is delivered, together with detected shared tuples, using a simple translation procedure described in Algorithm 2. The `MUSTER` method is summarized in Algorithm 3.

All experiments have been conducted on a Pentium IV, 3Ghz under Linux Fedora Core 5. A significant sample of results are given on Table 1, which contains 3 main columns, namely *Instance*, *Extracted MUC* and *Extracted MUST*. The first column provides information about the considered unsatisfiable CSP: namely, the benchmark

Algorithm 3. MUSTER

Input: a CSP: $\langle V, C\rangle$
Output: a MUST: $\langle V, \{(Var(c'_1), T''(c'_1)), ..., (Var(c'_m), T''(c'_m))\}\rangle$
begin
  $\langle V, C'\rangle \longleftarrow$ DC(wcore)($\langle V, C\rangle$) ; /* $\langle V, C'\rangle$ is a MUC s.t. $C' \subseteq C$ */
  /* and $C' = \{(Var(c'_1), T(c'_1)), ..., (Var(c'_m), T(c'_m))\}$ */
  $\Sigma_{CNF} \longleftarrow$ direct_encode($\langle V, C'\rangle$) ;
  $\Sigma_{MUS} \longleftarrow$ OMUS(Σ_{CNF}) ; /* $\Sigma_{MUS} \subseteq \Sigma_{CNF}$ */
  $\langle V, \{(Var(c'_1), T''(c'_1)), ..., (Var(c'_m), T''(c'_m))\}\rangle \longleftarrow$ mus2must(Σ_{MUS}, $\langle V, C'\rangle$);
  /* $\forall\ 1 \leq i \leq m\ \ T''(c'_i) \subseteq T(c'_i)$ */
  return $\langle V, \{(Var(c'_1), T''(c'_1)), ..., (Var(c'_m), T''(c'_m))\}\rangle$;
end

name, the number of involved constraints and the number of forbidden tuples that the constraints represent. In the second one, the main information about the MUC computed by DC(wcore) is given: namely, the number of constraints of the MUC, the number of tuples that they represent, and the computing time in seconds that was spent. Finally, the third main column provides the main information about the computed MUST: namely, its number of tuples, the number of discovered shared tuples, and the computing time in seconds that was spent. A time-out was set to 3 hours of CPU time.

First, let us note that a MUST was extracted within a reasonable amount of time for most benchmarks, which represent hard to solve problems. For instance, a MUC made of 13 constraints is discovered for the composed-75-1-2-1 CSP, which contains 624 contraints. This MUC forbids 845 tuples. Actually, this set can be reduced to just 344 tuples, which form one MUST of the benchmark. Moreover, the user is provided with a set of 104 tuples such that if one of these latter tuples is allowed, then the unsatisfiable part of the CSP represented by the MUC is fixed. Similar results were obtained for e.g. scen11_f10, which is an instance of the famous Radio Link Frequency Assignment Problem (RLFAP). This latter benchmark involves almost 800,000 forbidden tuples. However, only some of these them really participate to the unsatisfiability of the CSP. Indeed, a MUC that contains less than 5,000 tuples is exhibited, and this one has been reduced into a MUST made of 3,077 tuples. In this MUST, allowing one tuple among the 2,728 discovered shared ones is enough to allow the MUC to regain feasibility.

Obviously enough, due to the high-level computational complexity of the addressed problem, we cannot expect our approach to solve all problems within a reasonable amount of time. For example, although a MUST was extracted for the Queen-Knight problem qk_8_8_5_add, MUSTER was not able to deliver any of its shared tuples, although we know that these latter tuples are contained in the 10149 tuples that form the computed MUST. Let us also note that the same MUC and MUST have been discovered for both qk_8_8_5_add and qk_8_8_5_mul problems. This is easily explained: those problems result from various combinations between the 8 queens problem and 5 knights one. Since the 5 knights problem is not feasible, a same explanation of unsatisfiability can be delivered for all combinations of this problem with other CSPs.

Table 1. Extracting a MUST

Instance			Extracted MUC			Extracted MUST		
name	#con	#tuples	#con	#tuples	time (s)	#tuples	#st[1]	time (s)
composed-25-1-2-0	224	4,440	14	910	10.72	354	119	13.08
composed-25-1-2-1	224	4,440	15	975	9.09	339	59	17.47
composed-25-1-25-8	247	4,555	9	585	8.85	259	116	6.25
composed-75-1-2-1	624	10,440	13	845	66.42	344	104	10.85
composed-75-1-2-2	624	10,440	14	910	66.74	376	48	14.44
composed-75-1-25-8	647	10,555	16	1,040	59.09	461	51	23.69
composed-75-1-80-6	702	10,830	11	715	61.48	278	55	8.17
composed-75-1-80-7	702	10,830	16	1,040	379.85	420	75	17.23
composed-75-1-80-9	702	10,830	12	780	86.16	306	89	9.01
qk_10_10_5_add	55	48,640	5	47,120	19.68	24,855	0	3081.1
qk_10_10_5_mul	105	49,140	5	47,120	1.29	24,855	0	2812.99
qk_8_8_5_add	38	19,624	5	18,800	3.33	10,149	0	544.7
qk_8_8_5_mul	78	19,944	5	18,800	0.66	10,149	0	531.24
graph2_f25	2,245	145,205	43	4,498	427.36	2470	1,516	426.05
qa_3	40	800	15	583	0.32	203	152	8.32
dual_ehi-85-297-14	4,111	102,234	40	1,145	3.35	311	142	40.26
dual_ehi-85-297-15	4,133	102,433	35	1,083	4.03	310	172	25.85
dual_ehi-85-297-16	4,105	102,156	36	1,032	4.68	301	159	29.05
dual_ehi-85-297-17	4,102	102,112	43	1,239	4.83	348	172	42.21
dual_ehi-85-297-18	4,120	102,324	33	972	3.48	271	141	30.4
dual_ehi-90-315-21	4,388	108,890	37	1,120	3.16	354	129	35
dual_ehi-90-315-22	4,368	108,633	41	1,218	4.57	410	187	43.69
dual_ehi-90-315-23	4,375	108,766	29	835	2.86	251	131	12.23
dual_ehi-90-315-24	4,378	108,793	31	974	4.57	315	167	25.42
dual_ehi-90-315-25	4,398	108,974	38	1,106	3.89	375	179	30.41
scen6_w2	648	513,100	7	8,020	53.78	4,872	2,953	1107.39
scen6_w1_f2	319	274,860	21	21,146	488.64	-	-	*time out*
scen11_f10	4,103	738,719	16	4,588	164.27	3,077	2,728	438.26
scen11_f12	4,103	707,375	16	4,588	122.12	3,053	2,728	419.83

Finally, let us comment on the number of shared tuples. Proposition 2 ensures that a MUC made of m constraints contains at least m shared tuples. However, the number of shared tuples is often larger in practice. For example, a MUC made of 43 constraints is extracted from `graph2_f25`: so, at least 43 shared tuples could have been expected. Actually, 1,516 such tuples were delivered, enabling the user to just select one constraint among 43 ones, and then just select and allow one tuple among an average of 35 candidate ones, to regain feasibility.

7 Related Works

The approach introduced in this paper can be interpreted as a refinement of explanation techniques that provide users with MUCs in case of unsatisfiability. There have been

[1] #st: #shared tuples.

only a few research results about extracting MUCs from CSPs, or MUSes in the Boolean case. In this respect, the approach in this paper takes advantage of one of the most often efficient technique to compute MUCs [1] and of the currently most efficient technique compute MUSes [2], in order to deliver MUSTs and shared tuples.

In the CSP framework, there have been several other works about the identification of (minimal) conflict sets of constraints (e.g. [8]) that are recorded during the search in order to perform various forms of intelligent backtracking, like dynamic backtracking [9] [10] or conflict-based backjumping [11]. In [12] a non-intrusive method was proposed to detect them. However, there have been few research works about the problem of extracting MUCs themselves. A method to find all MUCs from a given set of constraints has been presented in [13] and in [14], which corresponds to an exhaustive exploration of a so-called CS-tree but is limited by the combinatorial blow-up in the number of subsets of constraints. Other approaches are given in [15] and in [16], where an explanation that is based on the user's preferences is extracted. Also, the `PaLM` framework [17], implemented in the constraint programming system `Choco` [18], is an explanation tool that can answer for instance the question: why is there no solution that contains the value v_i for some variable A? Moreover, in case of unsatisfiability, `PaLM` is able to provide a core, but this one is not guaranteed to be minimal. The `DC(wcore)` approach that is used in this paper appears to improve a previous method introduced in [19] to extract a MUC, that was proposed in the specific context of model-based diagnosis. It also proves more competitive than the use of the `QuickXPlain` [12] method to compute MUCs.

In the Boolean framework, the problem of extracting a MUS from an unsatisfiable CNF formula has also received much attention. In [20], Bruni has proposed an approach that approximates MUSes by means of an adaptative search guided by clauses hardness. Zhang and Malik have described in [21] a way to extract MUSes by learning nogoods involved in the derivation of the empty clause by resolution. In [22], Lynce and Marques-Silva have proposed a complete and exhaustive technique to extract one smallest MUS of a SAT instance. Together with Mneimneh, Andraus and Sakallah [23], the same authors have also proposed an algorithm that makes use of iterative max-SAT solutions to compute such smallest unsatisfiable subsets of clauses. Oh and her co-authors have presented in [24] a Davis, Putnam, Logemann and Loveland DPLL-oriented approach that is based on a marked clause concept to allow one to approximate MUSes. Let us also mention a complete approach by Liffiton and Sakallah [25], recently improved by a non-standard use of local search [26], that attempts to compute the exhaustive set of MUSes of a propositional formula.

Finally, let us note that the problem of finding an *Irreductible Infeasible Subsystem* has also been the subject of specific research efforts in mathematical programming [4][27].

8 Conclusions and Perspectives

These results open many interesting research perspectives.

An unsatisfiable CSP can exhibit several MUCs that can share non-empty set-theoretic intersections. Regaining feasibility through permitting shared tuples thus requires the MUSTER process to be iterated until all remaining MUCs in the resulting CSP have been addressed. Clearly, the order according to which MUCs are addressed influences the tuples that are delivered to the users. In this respect, it could be fruitful to develop order-independent techniques that directly deliver sets of tuples that would make the CSP feasible if these latter tuples were allowed. In this respect, recent results by Grégoire *et al.* [28] that allows covers of MUSes to be computed, i.e. sets of MUSes that cover all basic infeasibility causes, could be exploited in that direction. The concept of shared tuples would have to be revised accordingly, and specific computational techniques would have to be devised in order to compute that.

Although it appears to be highly competitive in practice, our technique to compute shared tuples remains uncomplete since it does not guarantee that all shared tuples will be delivered. Another interesting path for future research would consist in developping complete techniques that guarantee, modulo a possible exponential blow-up, the computation of *all* shared tuples.

In this paper, basic formal results about MUSTs have been provided. Clearly, much more can be done in this respect. Variant definitions coud be provided, in particular variants that would not rely on the MUC concept to address infeasibility.

Also, several MUSTs can be inter-dependent within a CSP: studying the formal properties of their relationships is also a promising path for future research.

References

1. Hemery, F., Lecoutre, C., Saïs, L., Boussemart, F.: Extracting MUCs from constraint networks. In: ECAI'06. Proceedings of the 17th European Conference on Artificial Intelligence, pp. 113–117 (2006)
2. Grégoire, E., Mazure, B., Piette, C.: Extracting MUSes. In: ECAI'06. Proceedings of the 17th European Conference on Artificial Intelligence, pp. 387–391 (2006)
3. Eiter, T., Gottlob, G.: On the complexity of propositional knowledge base revision, updates and counterfactual. Artificial Intelligence 57, 227–270 (1992)
4. Chinneck, J.: Feasibility and Viability. In: Advances in Sensitivity Analysis and Parametric Programming, ch. 14, vol. 6. Kluwer Academic Publishers, Boston (USA) (1997)
5. de Kleer, J.: A comparison of ATMS and CSP techniques. In: Proceedings of the Eleventh International Joint Conference on Artificial Intelligence (IJCAI'89), pp. 290–296 (1989)
6. Walsh, T.: SAT v CSP. In: Dechter, R. (ed.) CP 2000. LNCS, vol. 1894, pp. 441–456. Springer, Heidelberg (2000)
7. CSPcomp: CSP competition, http://cpai.ucc.ie/06/competition.html
8. Petit, T., Bessière, C., Régin, J.: A general conflict-set based framework for partial constraint satisfaction. In: Rossi, F. (ed.) CP 2003. LNCS, vol. 2833, Springer, Heidelberg (2003)
9. Ginsberg, M.L.: Dynamic backtracking. Journal of Artificial Intelligence Research 1, 25–46 (1993)
10. Jussien, N., Debruyne, R., Boizumault, P.: Maintaining arc-consistency within dynamic backtracking. In: Principles and Practice of Constraint Programming, pp. 249–261 (2000)
11. Prosser, P.: Hybrid algorithms for the constraint satisfaction problems. Computational Intelligence 9(3), 268–299 (1993)
12. Junker, U.: QuickXplain: Conflict detection for arbitrary constraint propagation algorithms. In: IJCAI'01 Workshop on Modelling and Solving problems with constraints (CONS-1) (2001)

13. Han, B., Lee, S.: Deriving minimal conflict sets by CS-Trees with mark set in diagnosis from first principles. IEEE Transactions on Systems, Man, and Cybernetics 29, 281–286 (1999)
14. de la Banda, M., Stuckey, P.J., Wazny, J.: Finding all minimal unsatisfiable subsets. In: Proceedings of the Fifth ACM-SIGPLAN International Conference on Principles and Practice of Declarative Programming (PPDL'03), pp. 32–43 (2003)
15. Mauss, J., Tatar, M.M.: Computing minimal conflicts for rich constraint languages. In: Proceedings of the 15th European Conference on Artificial Intelligence (ECAI'02), pp. 151–155 (2002)
16. Junker, U.: QuickXplain: Preferred explanations and relaxations for over-constrained problems. In: Proceedings of the 19th National Conference on Artificial Intelligence (AAAI'04), pp. 167–172 (2004)
17. Jussien, N., Barichard, V.: The PaLM system: explanation-based constraint programming. In: Dechter, R. (ed.) CP 2000. LNCS, vol. 1894, pp. 118–133. Springer, Heidelberg (2000)
18. Laburthe, F., Team, T.O.P.: Choco: implementing a cp kernel. In: Dechter, R. (ed.) CP 2000. LNCS, vol. 1894, Springer, Heidelberg (2000), http://www.choco-constraints.net
19. Bakker, R.R., Dikker, F., Tempelman, F., Wognum, P.M.: Diagnosing and solving overdetermined constraint satisfaction problems. In: Proceedings of the 13th International Joint Conference on Artificial Intelligence (IJCAI'93), vol. 1, pp. 276–281. Morgan Kaufmann, San Francisco (1993)
20. Bruni, R.: Approximating minimal unsatisfiable subformulae by means of adaptive core search. Discrete Applied Mathematics 130(2), 85–100 (2003)
21. Zhang, L., Malik, S.: Extracting small unsatisfiable cores from unsatisfiable boolean formula. In: Giunchiglia, E., Tacchella, A. (eds.) SAT 2003. LNCS, vol. 2919. Springer, Heidelberg (2004)
22. Lynce, I., Marques-Silva, J.: On computing minimum unsatisfiable cores. In: International Conference on Theory and Applications of Satisfiability Testing (2004)
23. Mneimneh, M.N., Lynce, I., Andraus, Z.S., Marques Silva, J.P., Sakallah, K.A.: A branch-and-bound algorithm for extracting smallest minimal unsatisfiable formulas. In: Bacchus, F., Walsh, T. (eds.) SAT 2005. LNCS, vol. 3569, pp. 467–474. Springer, Heidelberg (2005)
24. Oh, Y., Mneimneh, M., Andraus, Z., Sakallah, K., Markov, I.: AMUSE: a minimally-unsatisfiable subformula extractor. In: Proceedings of the 41th Design Automation Conference (DAC 2004), pp. 518–523 (2004)
25. Liffiton, M., Sakallah, K.: On finding all minimally unsatisfiable subformulas. In: Bacchus, F., Walsh, T. (eds.) SAT 2005. LNCS, vol. 3569, pp. 173–186. Springer, Heidelberg (2005)
26. Grégoire, E., Mazure, B., Piette, C.: Boosting a complete technique to find MSSes and MUSes thanks to a local search oracle. In: Proceedings of the 20th International Joint Conference on Artificial Intelligence (IJCAI'07), vol. 2, pp. 2300–2305 (2007)
27. Atlihan, M., Schrage, L.: Generalized filtrering algorithms for infeasibility analysis. Computers and Operations Research (to appear, 2007)
28. Grégoire, E., Mazure, B., Piette, C.: Local-search extraction of MUSes. Constraints Journal: Special issue on Local Search in Constraint Satisfaction 12(3) (to appear, 2007)

An Integrated White+Black Box Approach for Designing and Tuning Stochastic Local Search

Steven Halim[1], Roland H.C. Yap[1], and Hoong Chuin Lau[2]

[1] School of Computing, National University of Singapore
{stevenha,ryap}@comp.nus.edu.sg

[2] School of Information Systems, Singapore Management University
hclau@smu.edu.sg

Abstract. Stochastic Local Search (SLS) is a simple and effective paradigm for attacking a variety of Combinatorial (Optimization) Problems (COP). However, it is often non-trivial to get good results from an SLS; the designer of an SLS needs to undertake a laborious and ad-hoc algorithm tuning and re-design process for a particular COP. There are two general approaches. Black-box approach treats the SLS as a black-box in tuning the SLS parameters. White-box approach takes advantage of humans to observe the SLS in the tuning and SLS re-design. In this paper, we develop an integrated white+black box approach with extensive use of visualization (white-box) and factorial design (black-box) for tuning, and more importantly, for designing arbitrary SLS algorithms. Our integrated approach combines the strengths of white-box and black-box approaches and produces better results than either alone. We demonstrate an effective tool using the integrated white+black box approach to design and tune variants of Robust Tabu Search (Ro-TS) for Quadratic Assignment Problem (QAP).

1 Introduction

Stochastic Local Search (SLS) algorithms, also called Metaheuristics (e.g. Tabu Search, Iterated Local Search, etc) [1], have been extensively used to tackle large-scale NP-hard Combinatorial (Optimization) Problems (COP), often with impressive results. However, algorithm designers usually need to spend substantial effort to design and tune the SLS implementations to get good results.

Real world COPs are often new problems or variants of classic COPs but may not be well studied or no algorithm is known. It is frustrating that even if the COP C' resembles a *classic* COP C for which a good SLS S is known, a direct application of SLS S on COP C' will usually not immediately yield good performance. Thus, it is necessary to adapt an existing or create a new SLS for COP C'. It is often said that it is easy to create a working SLS for a COP, but hard to tune the SLS to achieve good performance on problem instances [1,2,3,4,5].

Most research has *only* focused on the problem of fine-tuning the parameter values for SLS. Pure tuning assumes that the appropriate SLS components and

C. Bessiere (Ed.): CP 2007, LNCS 4741, pp. 332–347, 2007.

search strategies are already known and we just need to find the appropriate parameters for those components and strategies. In this paper, we consider the SLS *design and tuning* problem as a *holistic* problem of finding a suitable configuration including parameter values, choice of components, and search strategies for an SLS in order to give good results for the class of COP instances.

There are two general approaches for this SLS design and tuning problem [5]:

1. The *black-box approach* uses automatic fine-tuning. It aims to develop special 'tuning algorithms' to explore the SLS configuration space systematically and as efficient as possible. The human designs the SLS and specifies an initial configuration space to be explored by the automated tuning algorithm. The tuning algorithm finds the best configuration within the *given* configuration space and computational resource requirements. Examples of the black-box approaches are F-Race [3], CALIBRA [4], Search Parameter Optimization [6], and iMDF [7].
2. The *white-box approach* leverages the use of human intelligence and/or visual perception. It aims to create tools or methods to help analyze the performance of the SLS so that the algorithm designer has a basis for tweaking the SLS implementation. Thus, the SLS may be redesigned to extend beyond the initial configuration space. Examples of the white-box approaches are: Statistical Analysis (Fitness Distance Correlation, Run Time Distribution, etc) [1,8], Sequential Parameter Optimization [9], Viz [10], etc.

Neither approach addresses *all* aspects of the SLS design and tuning. Black-box approaches are simple to apply, but will not help if the best configuration happens to be 'outside the box' of the initial configuration space (e.g. instance A with size 30 requires configuration 1, instance B with size 50 requires configuration 2 but the best configuration is a function of the instance size rather choosing between configuration 1 or 2). White-box approaches can give the algorithm designer insights into the search process, but are less effective for fine-tuning.

In this paper, we propose an integrated white+black box approach to address the SLS design and tuning problem. The fitness landscape and search trajectory visualization [10,11] opens the SLS 'box' to allow better understanding of the current 'problem(s)' being faced by the SLS trajectory when searching in the fitness landscape of the COP instance. This allows the algorithm designer to narrow down the potentially huge set of SLS configuration space into a much smaller and focused configuration space. Black-box tuning then further fine-tunes the SLS on this focused configuration space using factorial design [12]. This process is iterated: use the visualization to verify the *new* SLS behavior, obtain more complete picture of the fitness landscape, generate new hypothesis or redesign the SLS if necessary, fine-tune the SLS with black-box tuning, and so on until the performance criteria are met.

Ideally our approach is valuable when facing new or not well understood problems. However, it would be more difficult to evaluate our approach on such problems since not enough may be known. As such, we evaluate our approach on classic COPs: the Traveling Salesman Problem (TSP) for illustration and the

Quadratic Assignment Problem (QAP). We demonstrate that one can combine the strengths of both white+black box approaches to get better results than either alone. Furthermore, we take into account the practical effort and resource requirements for industrial problems: we want to design and tune SLS for good results within *limited development time* and *limited running time*.

We have developed a tool Viz for our integrated white+black box approach. Viz can visualize the COP fitness landscape and the SLS trajectory on the fitness landscape. Black-box tuning is supported using factorial design on the given configuration space. The details of the tools are outside the scope of this paper, see [10,11]. The website `http://sls.visualization.googlepages.com` contains further details and also a video which complements the presentation here. The online PDF version of this paper is in color and can be magnified.

We remark that systematic search algorithms usually also employ heuristics. As an example, MULTI-TAC [13] configures search heuristics for backtracking search by learning configuration rules which are applied on backtracking search algorithm schemas. While our approach is not directly relevant to configure exact algorithms, combining human intelligence and searching in the algorithm configuration space is a promising avenue for further research.

2 The Basic Ideas

2.1 White-Box: Fitness Landscape and Search Trajectory Analysis

The notion of fitness landscape has been shown to be useful for understanding the behavior (search trajectory) of SLS algorithms [1,8,14].

Given a COP instance π, the *fitness landscape* of π, $FL(\pi)$, is defined as the tuple $\langle S(\pi), d(s_1, s_2), g(\pi)\rangle$ [8], where $S(\pi)$ is the set of solutions of the COP instance (the search space); $d(s_1, s_2) : S \times S \rightarrow \Re$ is a distance metric which is natural for the COP in question (e.g. bond distance for TSP, Hamming distance for QAP, etc); and $g(\pi) : S \rightarrow \Re$ is the objective function. One can think of the fitness landscape as a surface with solutions as points on the surface, points are separated according to their distance, and the height reflects the fitness (objective value) of that solution.

The *search trajectory* of an SLS algorithm on this $FL(\pi)$ is defined as a finite sequence $(s_0, s_1, \ldots, s_k)$ where $s_i \in S(\pi)$ and $\forall i \in \{1, 2, \ldots, k\}$, (s_{i-1}, s_i) is either a local move done by the SLS according to its neighborhood $N(\pi)$ or a stronger diversification move beyond $N(\pi)$ [1]. Note that in this definition, a solution s_i can be satisfiable or not.

Understanding the characteristics of the fitness landscape empowers the algorithm designer to tailor the SLS implementation so that the search performs a better trajectory on the fitness landscape [1,8,14]. However, matching an SLS algorithm to the fitness landscape(s) of an instance or class of instances of a COP is not easy:

1. Different problem instances of the same COP may have quite different fitness landscapes [1].

2. The SLS behavior depends on the fitness landscape [1,8,14]. SLS with the same configuration may behave differently on different fitness landscapes.
3. The selected configuration (parameters [3,4], heuristics components [2], and search strategies [5]), the implementation details, and any unexpected programming bugs, determine the *actual* SLS behavior. This behavior may be wrong, e.g. doing diversification when we expect the SLS to do intensification on the fitness landscape — the metaheuristic failure modes [15]).
4. Stochastic elements mean the SLS can take different search trajectories in replicated runs.

White-box techniques such as Fitness Distance Correlation (FDC) [1,8] for analyzing fitness landscape properties and Run Time Distribution (RTD) [1,16] for analyzing potential search stagnation, are commonly used to assist matching an SLS with the fitness landscape. However, while FDC and RTD are useful, they do not explain the *details* of the SLS behavior on the COP fitness landscape.

In [10,11], we show how the abstract fitness landscape and search trajectory visualization in Viz can enhance the understanding of the SLS behavior on the COP fitness landscape. The main visualization ideas embedded inside Viz are briefly explained below.

Viz uses a notion of *Anchor Point* (AP) set which is a fixed set of local optima found by SLS runs on a COP instance. The AP set are diverse, high quality, and important solutions in the search runs (e.g. best found, frequently visited). The visualization layouts the AP points in an abstract 2-D space according to their distance metric w.r.t other APs. This forms the landscape visualization. Next,

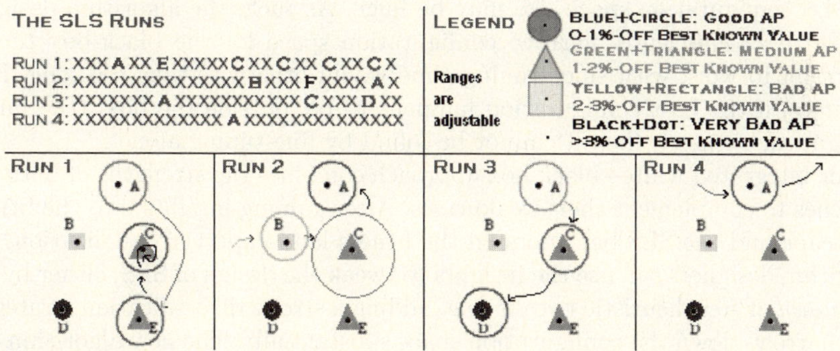

Fig. 1. An example of abstract fitness landscape and search trajectory visualization in Viz. The fitness landscape is represented by 5 APs {A,B,C,D,E} with quality labels shown in sub-figure 'Legend'. There are 4 SLS runs. **Run 1**→SLS starts from a very bad AP A, walks to a medium quality AP E, and then cycles around AP C. **Run 2**→SLS starts from a bad AP B, walks to a point *near* AP C (larger circle: assume blue point F in Run 2 is near AP C), then moves to a very bad AP A – a poor intensification. **Run 3**→SLS starts from a very bad AP A, gradually walks to a medium AP C, escapes from it, then arrives at a good AP D – a good intensification, better than Run 1 in escaping AP C. **Run 4**→The SLS trajectory bypasses a very bad AP A and is not near any other known APs – failure to navigate to promising region.

for each SLS run, we plot the positions of every solution or point in the search trajectory w.r.t its distance to AP points in the fitness landscape visualization. However, points that are too far from known APs are not visualized. See Fig 1 for the illustration of this visualization.

Our integrated white+black box approach uses Viz to first *understand* the characteristics of the fitness landscape of the COP (e.g. the fitness landscape is rugged). This helps the algorithm designer in *predicting* which search strategies will likely work well on the fitness landscape of the COP instance. The prediction can then be *verified* via visualization to see whether the SLS encounters any 'problem(s)' (e.g. stuck in a local optima as in Fig 1, Run 1). The algorithm designer uses these insights to think outside the box, make informed changes (e.g. adding a strong diversification strategy), and also narrow down the possible configuration space (e.g. avoid SLS configurations that make the SLS harder to escape from local optima such as lowering the tabu tenure in Tabu Search).

The white-box component leverages on the strengths of humans to analyze and learn from the visualizations. Although this is subjective and visualization is limited to points that have been visited, the process can be made intuitive and fruitful insights can be gained.

2.2 Black-Box Tuning: Factorial Design

Ideally, given an initial SLS configuration space, black-box tuning algorithms can be used to systematically find the most suitable configuration in the given configuration space to attack the COP at hand. However in practice, the size of the SLS configuration space size may be huge. As such, the algorithm designer must give a 'sufficiently narrow' configuration space for the black-box tuning algorithm to work with since tuning time would otherwise take too long. Furthermore, if the best configuration happens to be 'outside the box' (the initial configuration space), then it cannot be found by fine-tuning alone.

Our integrated white+black box approach combines the strengths of both approaches to complement their weaknesses. After gaining insights into the fitness landscape and the SLS behaviors on the fitness landscape via visualization, the algorithm designers can use the insights to tweak the design of SLS, either by using *known* or *new* heuristic tweaks (e.g. adding a strong diversification strategy). This narrows down the configuration space substantially. The new algorithm can then be more easily fine-tuned (e.g. precisely how much diversification).

While a white-box approach may be usable for designing good SLS algorithm, it is still tedious for humans to explore the narrowed configuration space manually. Automatic black-box tuning algorithms are best for this situation. We have chosen to implement a full factorial design [12] in Viz system since we can obtain smaller configuration spaces through the white-box visualization process. However, other black-box tuning tools such as F-Race [3], CALIBRA [4], or iMDF [7] can be used in this phase.

3 An Integrated White+Black Approach

The methodology of the integrated white+black box approach is summarized in Fig 2. While the general approach is not new (compared with [9]), what is novel here is how visualization has been integrated in the white-box steps 3–6, 8, and black-box tuning algorithm in the black-box step 7. As we will show, the use of automatic visualizations in Viz[1] makes it much easier to analyze the fitness landscapes and SLS behaviors. Viz also has integrated support for black-box tuning in step 7 and some other handy automation for running SLS experiments and computing statistical analysis in step 9.

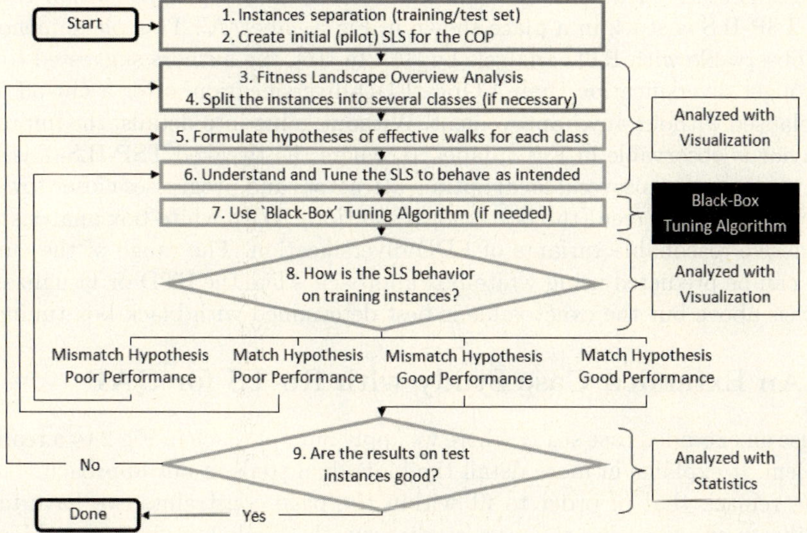

Fig. 2. Flow chart of the integrated white+black box approach

We first *briefly* illustrate some aspects of our integrated approach on the Traveling Salesman Problem (TSP). The chosen SLS is Iterated Local Search (TSP-ILS). It performs a 4-Opt perturbation, then the move operator swaps several pair of tour edges to reach a 2-Opt TSP local optimum. If the new local optimum is better, TSP-ILS will move to the new local optimum [16].

In Fig 3, we see that good quality (blue circle) and medium quality (green triangle) APs form one big cluster in the middle of the visualization (shown by the solid black arrows) and are close to each other when compared with the diameter of the fitness landscape (partially shown by the dashed red arrows). This shows a well known phenomenon called 'Big Valley'. We observe that outside this Big Valley region, we mostly see very bad (tiny black dot) APs. For such fitness landscape, it is suggested that the SLS should simply concentrate on the Big Valley region rather than wandering too far from it [1,8,16].

[1] Viz includes visualizations such as the fitness landscape and search trajectory (see Fig 1), objective value over time, FDC scatter plot visualization, etc.

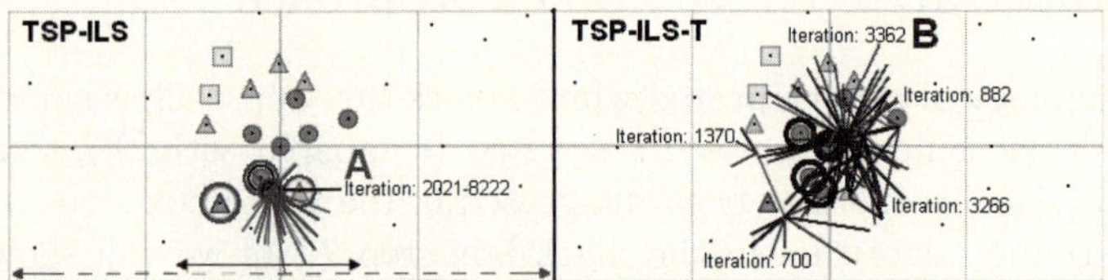

Fig. 3. Visualization of TSP fitness landscape and ILS behavior. See text for details.

TSP-ILS already uses this strategy. However, visualization shows that sometimes it is stuck in a local optimum and unable to escape. Animation reveals that TSP-ILS is stuck in a place shown in Fig 3, label 'A'. This phenomenon is also observable with RTD analysis by [16]. In [16], the authors suggested to use a stronger diversification than 4-Opt: 'FDD-diversification' after a cut-off time has elapsed without any improvement. Without going into details, the improved behavior is observable in Fig 3, label 'B' where the tweaked TSP-ILS-T is now able to escape from several local optima attractors and progresses closer towards the center of the screen (the best-known solution). With white-box analysis, one can derive reasonable variants of FDD-diversification. The range of the cut-off time can be predicted using white-box approaches like the RTD or visualization analysis above but the exact value is best determined with black-box tuning.

4 An Extended Case Study with Ro-TS for QAP

We use an extended case study where we apply our approach in Fig 2 to a realistic problem. It explains in more detail the individual steps in our approach.

We remark that in order to fit within the page constraints, we have taken the liberty of presenting this case study from the final step viewpoint. Most of the visualizations make use of the final AP set from good and bad runs from the entire development process. In the actual development process, we learn the fitness landscape structure and the search trajectory behavior incrementally via some pilot runs. For a discussion of incremental learning of fitness landscape and search trajectory with visualization, see [11].

4.1 Experiment Set-Up: QAP Instances and Baseline Algorithm

The COP used is the Quadratic Assignment Problem (QAP) with benchmark instances from QAPLIB [17]. We have picked tai30a/30b/35a/35b/50a/50b as training instances and tai40a/40b/60a/60b/sko42/ste36b as test instances.

We have intentionally chosen a classic COP for this experiment so that the reader can more easily appreciate the problem and results. The best known (BK) objective values for each QAP instance are in the benchmark library. We have defined the following solution quality measures: good ($<$ 1%-off BK), medium (1% – 2%-off BK), bad (2% – 3%-off BK), and very bad ($>$ 3%-off BK).

The initial baseline SLS for QAP in this case study is Robust Tabu Search (Ro-TS) [18] which has been shown to give good performance on QAP. We

Table 1. Initial Ro-TS-I Configuration

Component	Choice	Remark
Neighborhood	$O(n^2)$ 2-Opt	Natural (swap) move operation for QAP.
Objective Function	$O(1)$ delta	Measure delta as shown in [18]
Tabu Tenure (TT)	n	The default tabu tenure length
Tabu 'Table' [18]	pair $i - j$	Item i cannot be swapped with item j for TT steps
Aspiration Criteria	Better	Override tabu if move leads to a better solution
Search Strategy	'Ro-TS' [18]	Change TT within $[90\% * n, 110\% * n]$ after $2n$ steps

implemented a *variant* of Ro-TS called **Ro-TS-I** (Initial) which replicates the neighborhood and tabu mechanism in [18]. The details are in Table 1.

We do not expect to outperform the state-of-the-art algorithms on well studied and classic problems as they have been reached after extensive development efforts over a long period of time. For QAP, many good SLS algorithms, including Ro-TS, can find the BK objective value of many QAP instances in QAPLIB with long runs. Thus, to prevent the *ceiling effect*, we have fixed the number of iterations of every SLS run to be quite 'small': $5n^2$ iterations where n is the instance size. The experiment goal is to design and tune the best SLS+configuration for attacking the selected QAP instances within that *limited* $5n^2$ iteration bound.

4.2 Preliminary Analysis

The initial results of Ro-TS-I on training instances are shown in Table 2. We observe that within the limited iteration bound, the initial results are reasonably good for tai30a/35a/35b/50a but not for tai30b/50b (underlined). We want to investigate why we get these results and redesign an improved SLS.

We apply fitness landscape visualization on the QAP training instances. We observe a possible difference between tai35a (and tai30a/50a) with tai35b (and tai30b/50b). See Fig 4 text for details.

A working hypothesis from this observation is that there are *at least* **two classes of QAP instances**. By looking at the fitness landscape visualizations and/or data matrices of the QAP instances, we classify tai30a/35a/50a (training), tai40a/60a/sko42 (test) as QAP (type A) instances and tai30b/35b/50b (training), tai40b/60b/ste36b (test) as QAP (type B) instances. This is consistent with the characteristics of these classes which differ in the smoothness (type A) or ruggedness (type B) in the fitness landscape visualization and in the uniformity (type A) and non-uniformity (type B) of their data matrices.

In Table 2, we observe that Ro-TS-I already has reasonable performance on the type A instances. This may be because the gap among local optima is small — the quality of most APs are medium (green triangle). The animations of search trajectories of Ro-TS-I do not indicate any obvious sign of Ro-TS-I being stuck in a local optimum.

Since the QAP (type A) landscape is smoother, it is hard to decide where to navigate as 'everything' looks good. Diversifying too much may not be effective since the search will likely end up in another region with similar quality. We thus

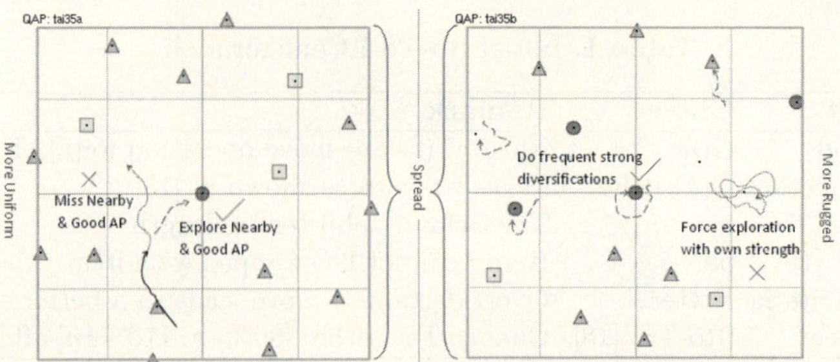

Fig. 4. Fitness landscape overview of tai35a and tai35b automatically generated from Viz. See Fig 1 sub-figure 'Legend' for the meaning of the shapes and colors. The best found solution is always in the center. APs in tai35a and tai35b are spread throughout the fitness landscape. However, the quality of the APs in tai35a seems to be more 'uniform' (most are green triangles) than tai35b (all types of AP quality exist). The actual Ro-TS-I behaviors on QAP (type A/B) instances are shown with red dotted lines. Our hypotheses on *ideal* good trajectories are shown with blue dashed lines.

formulate the hypothesis that it is better to reduce the possibility of missing the best solution within a close region where the SLS is currently in. Fig 4 (left) illustrates our hypothesis and shows the ideal desired trajectory (blue dashed lines) searches around nearby good local optima rather than Ro-TS-I trajectory (red dotted lines) which moves away from the good local optima region.

On the other hand, the performance of the same Ro-TS-I on the type B instances is very bad as seen in Table 2. In Fig 6 (left) we observe that Ro-TS-I is stuck in very bad APs (textual explanation of the visualization: the search trajectory enters a region near some APs, then until the last iteration, it is still near the same APs). If the quality of the solutions in that region happens to be bad, the final best found solution reported will also be bad.

The QAP (type B) landscape is more rugged, i.e. the local optima are deeper and more spread out. We thus hypothesize that within the limited iteration bound, rather than attempting to escape deep local optima with its own strength (e.g. via a tabu mechanism), it is better for the SLS to perform frequent strong diversification. Fig 4 (right) illustrates our hypothesis where the desired trajectory (blue dashed lines) only makes short runs in a region before jumping elsewhere rather than the trajectory of Ro-TS-I (red dotted lines) which struggles to escape a deep local optimum.

4.3 Tweaking Ro-TS-I to Ro-TS-A for QAP (type A) Instances

The search coverage[2] of Ro-TS-I on QAP (type A) instances is not good (see Fig 5, left). Visualization[3] shows that Ro-TS-I sometimes gets near to known good APs but does not in the end navigate to those APs.

---

[2] APs that are near any points in search trajectory are highlighted.

[3] In Viz, a circle drawn on an AP shows that the SLS trajectory pass through an area near that AP. The diameter of the enclosing circle shows the approximate distance.

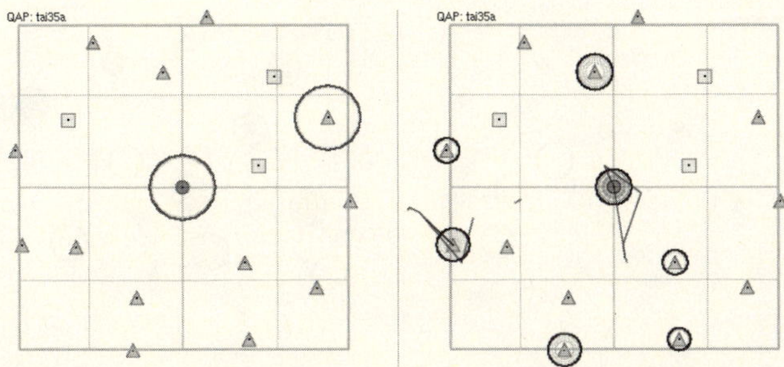

Fig. 5. Search coverage of Ro-TS-I (left) and Ro-TS-A (right) on QAP (type A) instance. Ro-TS-I (left) is already 'near' the best found AP but then wanders somewhere else (see the large red circles, animation not shown). On the other hand, a lower Tabu Tenure Range in Ro-TS-A (right) enables it to take different search trajectory which covers some medium and good quality APs (see the large blue circles).

Initially, we thought that in order to make Ro-TS-I focus on a particular region, we should increase the intensification from a 2-Opt into a **3-Opt** swap move neighborhood. Although this is more costly, it might allow better results from the region where the SLS is currently searching in. However, this idea turned out to be ineffective as no significant improvement in the search behavior was seen. To investigate, we added an algorithm specific visualization that shows a spike if 3-Opt code is executed. We were surprised that we almost never saw any spikes (only rarely when attacking tai35a). This may be because the smooth fitness landscape causes most moves that exchange 3 facilities at once in a QAP solution are worse than those that exchange 2 facilities at once. Also, the larger neighborhood slows down the SLS significantly. The results do not show significant improvement (see Table 2) so this configuration was not pursued.

We came up with another hypothesis for the SLS algorithm. During short runs, there may be some Ro-TS-I moves which lead to known good APs that are under tabu status and are not overridden by aspiration criteria.

The idea for robustness in Ro-TS [18] is to change tabu tenure randomly during the search within a defined Tabu Tenure Range (TTR) every Z*n steps. The TTR is defined as the interval $[TTL, TTL+TTD]$ which has two parameters: Tabu Tenure Low (TTL) and Tabu Tenure Delta (TTD). To encourage Ro-TS-I to do more intensification, we decrease its TTR from the recommendation in [18]: [90%*n, 110%n] into a lower range and changing the robust tabu tenure value more often — after n steps (Z=1), not $2n$ steps (Z=2) as in Table 1.

We do not know the best TTR for Ro-TS-I, except that it should be lower. We use systematic black-box tuning with *full factorial design* on TTL={40, 70} and TTD={20, 40} and obtain TTR=[40%*n, 80%*n] (TTL=40, TTD=40) as the TTR that works best on the training instances and also slightly but consistently outperforms the original Ro-TS-I (see Table 2).

We call Ro-TS-I with lower TTR as **Ro-TS-A**. We observed that although TTR is smaller, it is still enough to ensure Ro-TS-A avoids solution cycling

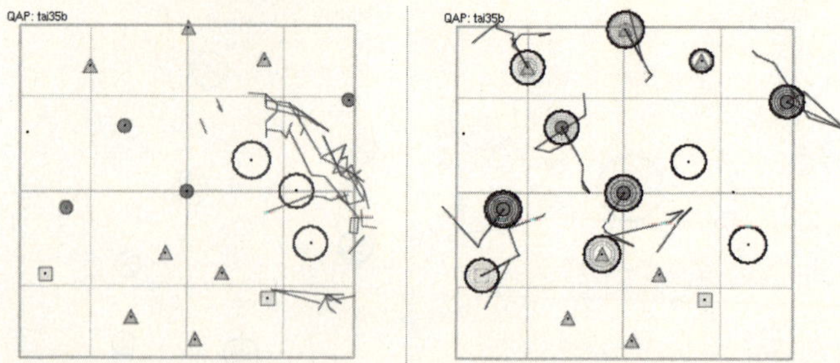

Fig. 6. Search coverage of Ro-TS-I (left) and Ro-TS-B (right) on QAP (type B) instance. Ro-TS-I (left) is stuck around very bad APs (see the large red circles). On the other hand, Ro-TS-B (right) employs frequent strong diversifications and we see that it visits several APs of varying qualities (see the large blue circles) that are (very) far from each other.

issues. This may be because it is quite easy to escape from any local optima of smooth fitness landscape of type A instances. Fig 5 (right) shows the search coverage of Ro-TS-A which seems better than the search coverage of Ro-TS-I.

4.4 Tweaking Ro-TS-I to Ro-TS-B for QAP (type B) Instances

Visualization reveals that Ro-TS-I is stuck near very bad APs. This leads to a very bad performance (see Fig 6, left). With the understanding that the fitness landscape of type B instances is rugged, we conclude that the inability of Ro-TS-I to escape those APs is because the APs are part of deep local optima regions.

To alleviate this situation, we add a strong diversification strategy into the Ro-TS-I. We consider Ro-TS-I to be stuck in a deep local optimum after n non-improving moves (Z=1). To escape, we employ a *strong* diversification mechanism which preserves $max(0, n\text{-}X)$ items and randomly permutates the assignment of the other $min(n, X)$ items in the current solution. The value of X is sufficiently large: close to n but not equal to n, otherwise it would be tantamount to random restart. The rationale for this *strong* diversification heuristic is that we see in the fitness landscape that good APs (blue circles) in type B instances are located quite far apart but *not* as far as the problem diameter n.

How should the diversification strength X be determined? One can manually experiment with different values of X on various training instances but it is better to do systematic black-box tuning. We automatically tune using 1-factor design on X=$\{5, 10, \ldots, n\}$. With tai30b and tai35b as training instances, we get good results when X=15. However, X=15 is not the best configuration for tai50b (see Table 2). We found that fixing the value of X to a constant (**Fixed-Diversification**) tends to make the Ro-TS-I overfit the training instances.

After fine-tuning the fixed-diversification strategy, we realized that X should not be *fixed* for all type B instances but rather be *robust* within a range correlated with the instance size. The value of X is randomly changed within this range after each diversification step. This helps maintaining the consistency of the performance quality across various QAP (type B) instances.

As the pilot runs using a fixed-diversification strategy yield reasonably good results when X is set around the half of the instance size n, we apply *full factorial design* on $X_{low}=\{\frac{4}{10}n, \frac{5}{10}n\}$ and $X_{high}=\{\frac{6}{10}n, \frac{7}{10}n\}$ to try various X within the interval $[X_{low}, X_{high}]$ settings systematically. We arrived at a good range for $X=[\frac{4}{10}n, \frac{6}{10}n]$ that works best on the training instances.

We call the revised SLS as **Ro-TS-B**. Animation shows that Ro-TS-B visits several far away APs of varied quality, where each AP is visited only in a brief period. However, some APs visited by Ro-TS-B have good quality and thus the overall performance is good. See Fig 6 (right) and Table 2.

4.5 Benchmarking on the Test Instances

We now compare the initial and final SLS algorithms on the test instances using the same iteration bound. The results are given in Table 2. We observe that on average Ro-TS-A performs slightly better than Ro-TS-I on type A instances while Ro-TS-B is significantly better than Ro-TS-I on type B instances. Note that for type A instances, since the fitness landscape is more smooth, any improvements will be small. The results here are also comparable with the updated Ro-TS results in [19].

We see that applying either Ro-TS-A or Ro-TS-B to its opposite instance class mostly gives no or negative improvements (underlined). This result shows that we have successfully tailored the SLS algorithm to match different fitness landscape of these instances.

5 Comparison with a Pure Black-Box Approach

We compared our integrated white+black approach with a pure black-box approach on several tuning scenarios. Note that we have not compared against a pure white-box approach as the comparison would be subjective.

We use CALIBRA [4] as the black-box tuning algorithm. CALIBRA works by iteratively trying different configurations from the given configuration space (using fractional factorial design) to set-up the SLS, run the SLS on training instances, and obtain results from the black-box SLS (e.g. best found solution quality). CALIBRA uses the results from the SLS runs to determine which configuration to try next.

For the experiments with CALIBRA, we chose the following *default* range of values for the initial configuration space {Z,Str,TTL,TTD,X} with size 1152 (3*2*8*6*4). The size of this configuration space is purposely larger and includes most of the configuration space used in Section 4. Note that this configuration would not be necessarily obvious from the initial Ro-TS-I configuration.

1. Execute strategy after **Z***n iterations without improvement, Z: {1, 2, 3},
2. Strategy (**Str**): {1: Lower-TTR, 2: Fixed-Diversification},
3. Tabu Tenure Low (**TTL**): {30, 40, ..., 100},

Table 2. The results of Ro-TS-I, Ro-TS-A, and Ro-TS-B on training and test instances — averaged over **10** runs per instance. The instance size n, Best Known (BK) objective value, maximum iteration bound ($5n^2$ iterations), run times (except column '3-Opt'), average percentage-off $\bar{x}$ and standard deviation σ from BK are given.

Training Instances

Instance	n	Best Known	Iters	Time	Ro-TS-I		> 3-Opt <		Ro-TS-A	
					$\bar{x}$	σ	$\bar{x}$	σ	$\bar{x}$	σ
tai30a	30	1818146	4500	3s	0.99	0.46	1.00	0.38	**0.85**	0.32
tai35a	35	2422002	6125	5s	1.24	0.22	1.14	0.16	**0.98**	0.29
tai50a	50	4938796	12500	18s	1.62	0.11	1.67	0.15	**1.42**	0.21
Instance	**n**	**Best Known**	**Iters**	**Time**	**Ro-TS-I**		**> X=15 <**		**Ro-TS-B**	
					$\bar{x}$	σ	$\bar{x}$	σ	$\bar{x}$	σ
tai30b	30	637117113	4500	3s	<u>16.18</u>	0.00	0.14	0.11	**0.17**	0.17
tai35b	35	283315445	6125	5s	2.90	1.06	0.20	0.14	**0.25**	0.26
tai50b	50	458821517	12500	18s	<u>7.58</u>	0.01	0.79	0.84	**0.15**	0.14

Test Instances

Instance	n	Best Known	Iters	Time	Ro-TS-I		Ro-TS-A		Ro-TS-B	
					$\bar{x}$	σ	$\bar{x}$	σ	$\bar{x}$	σ
tai40a	40	3139370	8000	8s	1.25	0.19	**1.22**	0.25	<u>1.63</u>	0.26
sko42	42	15812	8820	9s	0.21	0.08	**0.11**	0.06	0.16	0.09
tai60a	60	7205962	18000	34s	1.60	0.17	**1.53**	0.14	<u>2.12</u>	0.16
ste36b	36	15852	6480	6s	6.20	1.21	<u>7.28</u>	0.92	**0.65**	0.73
tai40b	40	637250948	8000	8s	9.01	0.00	<u>9.04</u>	0.09	**0.01**	0.02
tai60b	60	608215054	18000	35s	2.38	0.47	<u>2.93</u>	0.36	**0.17**	0.13

Table 3. CALIBRA results on tuning Ro-TS-I^C. The 1st column is the scenario ID. The 3rd column gives the selected configuration when CALIBRA is trained using training instances specified in the 2nd column. The 4th-9th columns give the percentage-off and standard deviation w.r.t BK values on the test instances — averaged over **10** runs.

Sc	Training Set	Configuration	tai40a	sko42	tai60a	ste36b	tai40b	tai60b
1.	tai30**a**/tai30**b** tai50**a**/tai50**b**	{3, 2, 40, 10, 20}	1.23 (0.29)	**0.09** (0.08)	1.59 (0.20)	0.90 (0.80)	1.86 (1.55)	1.70 (0.24)
2.	tai30**b**/tai35**b** tai50**b**	{3, 1, 90, 40, -}	1.26 (0.16)	0.28 (0.09)	1.55 (0.21)	5.12 (1.30)	8.93 (0.16)	2.09 (0.02)
3.	tai30**a**/tai35**a** tai50**a**	{3, 1, 40, 40, -}	1.25 (0.19)	0.16 (0.06)	**1.50** (0.15)	7.13 (1.01)	9.04 (0.09)	2.93 (0.33)
4.	tai30**b**/tai35**b** tai50**b**	{1, 2, 90, 40, 20}	1.81 (0.24)	0.16 (0.11)	1.70 (0.16)	0.93 (0.89)	0.05 (0.09)	0.94 (0.71)

4. Tabu Tenure Delta (**TTD**): {0, 10, ..., 50},
5. Diversification strength **X** (only used when Str=2), X: {20, 25, ..., 35}.

CALIBRA is used to configure our baseline algorithm Ro-TS-I for 20 minutes per scenario (that is, with $\approx$ 30 seconds for Ro-TS-I runs on QAP instances of size 30/35/50, this roughly allows CALIBRA to examine $\approx 20 * 60/30 \approx 40$ different configurations. This is sufficient for our experiments as CALIBRA seems to hit a local optimum of the configuration space after around 30 configurations. The various CALIBRA configured algorithms are called Ro-TS-I^C.

In scenario 1, we assume that we do not know that there are 2 different fitness landscape characteristics in QAP instances used. We see that CALIBRA chooses a 'balanced' configuration {3, Fixed-Diversification, 40, 10, 20} when trained with mixed type A and type B instances. This Ro-TS-I^C yields *balanced* performance on both types but poorer than the specialized Ro-TS-A or Ro-TS-B on type A or type B instances, respectively (compare with Table 2).

In scenario 2, we deliberately omitted Fixed-Diversification as the choice for the second parameter (Str). By doing so, CALIBRA is forced to choose the 'best' configuration: {3, Lower-TTR, 90, 40, -} in the smaller box with size 576 when given type B training instances. This Ro-TS-I^C produces very bad results for type B test instances (compare with Ro-TS-B results in Table 2) and shows that pure black-box tuning algorithm cannot find a good configuration outside the box by itself.

Scenario 3 and scenario 4 are similar to the full factorial design using Viz in Section 4 but now with bigger configuration space. Note that CALIBRA uses fractional factorial design.

In scenario 3, since CALIBRA is trained with type A instances, it converges to a configuration that works well for type A but works badly for type B instances. Ro-TS-I^C (compare with Z=1 in the configuration of Ro-TS-A) obtains better results for tai60a but not for tai40a and sko42. However, the performance of Ro-TS-I^C is more or less similar to Ro-TS-A in this scenario.

The opposite situation from scenario 3 occurs in scenario 4 where this time the configured Ro-TS-I^C performs much better on type B instances. Note that since a black-box tuning algorithm cannot think out of the box to correlate X with instance size, it selects the 'best' X given the training instances. We get X=20 which is good for tai40b but bad for ste36b and tai60b — a case of over-fitting. Ro-TS-I^C has worse performance than Ro-TS-B in this scenario.

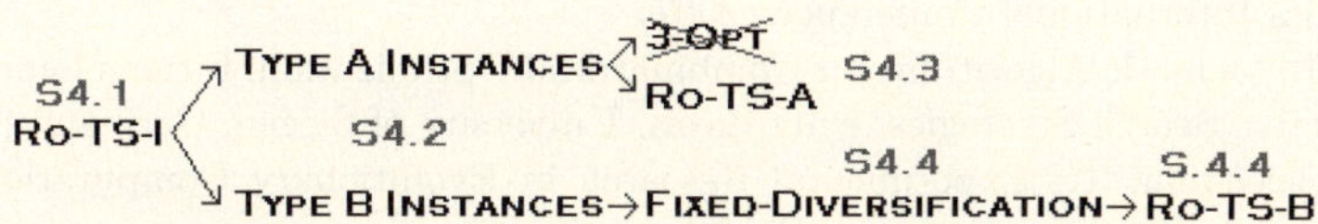

Fig. 7. The development of the two Ro-TS variants

6 Conclusion

In this paper, we have shown an integrated white+black box approach for designing and tuning SLS algorithms. We demonstrate that starting from a good baseline SLS, Robust Tabu Search, on a realistic problem, QAP, we are able to derive two algorithm variants with better performance. Fig 7 summarizes the development steps with reference to SLS algorithms devised and tuned in Section 4. The white-box steps are necessarily subjective. However, since Robust Tabu Search is already quite good on QAP and given that each major step in the SLS algorithm development is well supported by visualizations and tools, we believe that this gives evidence that our approach is both valuable and effective.

In practice, for real-life COPs, the goal is to design an SLS algorithm with good performance under limited resources. To reduce the development time, we would also need techniques and more importantly tools which can help in SLS design and tuning. Our integrated white+black box approach combines the strengths of leveraging the developer intuition by using generic automated visualization tools with generic automatic parameter tuning. The techniques presented here should be relevant to anyone designing a new SLS, particularly when dealing with new COPs.

References

1. Hoos, H.H., Stuetzle, T.: Stochastic Local Search: Foundations and Applications. Morgan Kaufmann, San Francisco (2005)
2. Charon, I., Hudry, O.: Mixing Different Components of Metaheuristics. In: Meta-Heuristics: Theory and Applications, pp. 589–603. Kluwer Academic Publishers, Dordrecht (1996)
3. Birattari, M.: The Problem of Tuning Metaheuristics as seen from a machine learning perspective. PhD thesis, Université Libre de Bruxelles (2004)
4. Adenso-Diaz, B., Laguna, M.: Fine-tuning of Algorithms Using Fractional Experimental Designs and Local Search. Operations Research 54(1), 99–114 (2006)
5. Halim, S., Lau, H.C.: Tuning Tabu Search Strategies via Visual Diagnosis. In: Meta-Heuristics: Progress as Complex Systems Optimization. Kluwer, Dordrecht (2007)
6. Hutter, F., Hamadi, Y., Hoos, H.H., Leyton-Brown, K.: Performance Prediction and Automated Tuning of Randomized and Parametic Algorithms. In: Principles and Practice of Constraint Programming, pp. 213 228 (2006)
7. Lau, H.C., Xiao, F.: Toward an Intelligent Metaheuristics Framework. In: Metaheuristics International Conference (2007)
8. Merz, P.: Memetic Algorithms for Combinatorial Optimization: Fitness Landscapes & Effective Search Strategies. PhD thesis, University of Siegen, Germany (2000)
9. Bartz-Beielstein, T.: Experimental Research in Evolutionary Computation: The New Experimentalism. Springer, Heidelberg (2006)
10. Halim, S., Yap, R.H.C., Lau, H.C.: Viz: A Visual Analysis Suite for Explaining Local Search Behavior. In: User Interface Software and Technology, pp. 57–66 (2006)
11. Halim, S., Yap, R.H.C.: Designing and Tuning SLS through Animation and Graphics - an extended walk-through. In: SLS: Stochastic Local Search Workshop (2007)
12. NIST: e-Handbook of Statistical Methods, `http://www.itl.nist.gov/div898/handbook`
13. Minton, S.: Automatically Configuring Constraint Satisfaction Programs: A Case Study. Constraints 1(1/2), 7–43 (1996)
14. Schneider, J.J., Kirkpatrick, S.: Stochastic Optimization. Springer, Heidelberg (2006)
15. Watson, J.P.: On Metaheuristics "Failure Modes". In: Metaheuristics International Conference, pp. 910–915 (2005)

16. Stuetzle, T., Hoos, H.H.: Analyzing the Run-Time Behavior of Iterated Local Search for the TSP. In: Essays and Surveys in Metaheuristics, pp. 449–453. Kluwer, Dordrecht (1999)
17. QAPLIB: Quadratic Assignment Problem Library, http://www.seas.upenn.edu/qaplib
18. Taillard, E.: Robust Tabu Search for Quadratic Assignment Problem. Parallel Computing 17, 443–455 (1991)
19. Taillard, E.: Comparison of Iterative Searches for the Quadratic Assignment Problem. Location Science 3, 87–105 (1995)

Limitations of Restricted Branching in Clause Learning

Matti Järvisalo and Tommi Junttila

Helsinki University of Technology (TKK)
Laboratory for Theoretical Computer Science
P.O. Box 5400, FI-02015 TKK, Finland
matti.jarvisalo@tkk.fi, tommi.junttila@tkk.fi

Abstract. The techniques for making decisions, i.e., branching, play a central role in complete methods for solving structured CSP instances. In practice, there are cases when SAT solvers benefit from limiting the set of variables the solver is allowed to branch on to so called input variables. Theoretically, however, restricting branching to input variables implies a super-polynomial increase in the length of the optimal proofs for DPLL (without clause learning), and thus input-restricted DPLL cannot polynomially simulate DPLL. In this paper we settle the case of DPLL with clause learning. Surprisingly, even with unlimited restarts, input-restricted clause learning DPLL cannot simulate DPLL (even without clause learning). The opposite also holds, and hence DPLL and input-restricted clause learning DPLL are polynomially incomparable. Additionally, we analyse the effect of input-restricted branching on clause learning solvers in practice with various structural real-world benchmarks.

1 Introduction

Modern complete satisfiability (SAT) solvers provide an efficient way of solving various real-world problems as propositional satisfiability. Typical SAT solvers aimed at solving such structured problems are based on the conjunctive normal form (CNF) level *Davis-Putnam-Logemann-Loveland* procedure (DPLL) [1,2] and incorporate techniques such as *intelligent branching heuristics*, *randomisation* and *restarts* [3], and *clause learning* [4] for boosting search efficiency.

In SAT based approaches to structured problems such as bounded model checking [5] and automated planning [6], the CNF encoding is often derived from a transition relation, where the behaviour of the underlying system is dependent on the *input*—initial state, nondeterministic choices, et cetera—of the system. Since irrelevant decisions may have an exponential effect on the running times of the solver, techniques for making decisions, i.e., branching, play a central role in complete SAT methods aimed at solving typically very large real-world problem instances. Empirical case studies [7,8,9,10] have shown that, in some cases, SAT solvers benefit from restricting the variables the solver is allowed to branch on to so called *input (*or *independent) variables*, corresponding to the input of the underlying system. Since the system behaviour is determined by its input, input-restricted branching DPLL remains complete. Intuitively, this drops the search space size from 2^N to 2^I with $I << N$, where I and N are the number of input variables and all variables in the CNF encoding, respectively.

C. Bessiere (Ed.): CP 2007, LNCS 4741, pp. 348–363, 2007.

From another point of view, one can investigate the *best-case* performance of SAT algorithms through *proof complexity* [11], by studying the relative power of their underlying inference systems (or *proof systems*) in terms of the shortest existing proofs in the systems. For two proof systems S,S', we say that S' *(polynomially) simulates* S if, for all infinite families $\{F_n\}$ of unsatisfiable CNF formulas, there is a polynomial that bounds for all F_n the length of the shortest proofs in S' w.r.t. the length of the shortest proofs in S. If S' simulates S and vice versa, then S and S' are *polynomially equivalent*. If S' cannot simulate S and vice versa, then S and S' are *incomparable*. From the practical point of view, if S' cannot simulate S, we know that any implementation of S' can suffer a notable decrease in efficiency compared to implementations of S. For example, through a formal characterisation CL of DPLL with clause learning, Beame et al. [12] show that CL can provide exponentially shorter proofs than DPLL, and thus DPLL cannot simulate CL.

Considering restricting branching in DPLL algorithms to input variables, a natural question to ask is *whether the power of the underlying inference systems of* DPLL *based solvers is affected by the input-restriction*. For DPLL without clause learning, this question is answered in [13]: input-restricted DPLL cannot simulate DPLL.

In this paper we settle the case of input-restricted CL: it turns out that input-restricted CL cannot simulate CL. This implies that all implementations of clause learning DPLL, even with optimal heuristics, have the potential of suffering a notable efficiency decrease if branching is restricted to input variables. In fact, we show that even with unlimited restarts and the ability to create conflicts at will, input-restricted CL cannot even simulate the basic DPLL *without clause learning*. This is surprising, since the unrestricted version of this variant of CL can efficiently simulate general resolution [12], being thus very powerful compared to DPLL. Additionally, we evaluate the effect of input-restricted branching on clause learning with various structural real-world benchmarks, and explain why branching restrictions are difficult to apply with typical clause learning search techniques.

As preliminaries, in Sect. 2 we define Boolean circuits, which we use for representing structural formulas, and discuss the close relation of circuits and CNF formulas. We then review the Resolution proof system and characterisations of DPLL and CL, and discuss known results concerning their relative efficiency (Sect. 3). The main theoretical and experimental contributions of this paper are presented in Sect. 4–5.

2 Boolean Circuits and Propositional Satisfiability

The correspondence between system input of a real-world problem and propositional variables in the flat CNF encoding is not evident. However, in SAT based approaches, direct CNF encodings of a problem domain are rarely used: the problem at hand is typically encoded with a general propositional formula ϕ, which is then translated into a CNF formula by introducing additional variables for the sub-formulas of ϕ. *Boolean circuits* (see e.g. [14]) offer a natural way of presenting propositional formulas in a compact DAG-like structure with *sub-formula sharing*, which helps in lowering the number of additional variables needed. The system input of the original problem is also reflected as *input gates* in Boolean circuits.

A Boolean circuit over a finite set G of *gates* is a set $\mathcal{C}$ of equations of the form $g := f(g_1, \ldots, g_n)$, where $g, g_1, \ldots, g_n \in G$ and $f : \{\mathbf{f}, \mathbf{t}\}^n \to \{\mathbf{f}, \mathbf{t}\}$ is a Boolean function, such that (i) each $g \in G$ appears at most once as the left hand side in the equations in $\mathcal{C}$, and (ii) the underlying graph $\langle G, E(\mathcal{C}) = \{\langle g', g\rangle \in G \times G \mid g := f(\ldots, g', \ldots) \in \mathcal{C}\}\rangle$ is acyclic. When convenient, we identify $\mathcal{C}$ with its underlying DAG. If $\langle g', g\rangle \in E(\mathcal{C})$, then g' is a *child* of g and g is a *parent* of g'. For any $g \in G$, if $g := f(g_1, \ldots, g_n)$ is in $\mathcal{C}$, then g is an f-gate (or of *type* f), otherwise it is an *input gate*. A gate with no parents is an *output gate*. A (partial) truth assignment for $\mathcal{C}$ is a (partial) function $\tau : G \to \{\mathbf{f}, \mathbf{t}\}$. A truth assignment τ is consistent with $\mathcal{C}$ if $\tau(g) = f(\tau(g_1), \ldots, \tau(g_n))$ for each $g := f(g_1, \ldots, g_n)$ in $\mathcal{C}$.

A *constrained Boolean circuit* $\mathcal{C}^\tau$ is a pair $\langle \mathcal{C}, \tau\rangle$, where $\mathcal{C}$ is a Boolean circuit and τ is a partial truth assignment for $\mathcal{C}$. With respect to a $\langle \mathcal{C}, \tau\rangle$, each $\langle g, v\rangle \in \tau$ is a *constraint*, and g is *constrained* to v if $\langle g, v\rangle \in \tau$. A truth assignment τ' *satisfies* $\mathcal{C}^\tau$ if (i) τ' is consistent with $\mathcal{C}$, and (ii) $\tau' \supseteq \tau$. If some truth assignment satisfies $\mathcal{C}^\tau$ then $\mathcal{C}^\tau$ is *satisfiable* and otherwise *unsatisfiable*.

For notational convenience, when well-defined, the *join* of constrained circuits $\mathcal{A}^\tau = \langle \mathcal{A}, \tau\rangle$ and $\mathcal{B}^\theta = \langle \mathcal{B}, \theta\rangle$ is $\mathcal{A}^\tau \cup \mathcal{B}^\theta := \langle \mathcal{A} \cup \mathcal{B}, \tau \cup \theta\rangle$. Without loss of generality, we restrict the set of Boolean functions available as gate types to

(i) $\text{NOT}(v)$ is $\mathbf{t}$ iff v is $\mathbf{f}$,

(ii) $\text{OR}(v_1, \ldots, v_n)$ is $\mathbf{t}$ iff at least one of $v_1, \ldots, v_n$ is $\mathbf{t}$,

(iii) $\text{AND}(v_1, \ldots, v_n)$ is $\mathbf{t}$ iff all $v_1, \ldots, v_n$ are $\mathbf{t}$, and

(iv) $\text{XOR}(v_1, v_2)$ is $\mathbf{t}$ iff exactly one of v_1, v_2 is $\mathbf{t}$.

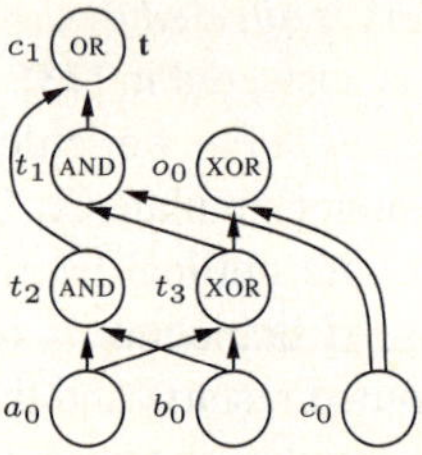

As an example, Fig. 1 shows a Boolean circuit for a full-adder with the carry-out bit c_1 constrained to $\mathbf{t}$. Formally, this constrained circuit is $\langle \mathcal{C}, \tau\rangle$, where $\mathcal{C} = \{c_1 := \text{OR}(t_1, t_2),\ t_1 := \text{AND}(t_3, c_0),\ o_0 := \text{XOR}(t_3, c_0),\ t_2 := \text{AND}(a_0, b_0),\ t_3 := \text{XOR}(a_0, b_0)\}$ and $\tau = \{\langle c_1, \mathbf{t}\rangle\}$.

Fig. 1. A constrained circuit

2.1 From Circuits to CNF, and CNF Formulas as Circuits

Given a Boolean variable x, there are two *literals*, the positive literal, denoted by x, and the negative literal, denoted by $\overline{x}$. As usual, we identify $\overline{\overline{x}}$ with x. A *clause* is a disjunction of distinct literals and a CNF formula is a conjunction of clauses. When convenient, we view a clause as a finite set of literals and a CNF formula as a finite set of clauses. The sets of variables appearing as positive and negative literals in a CNF F are denoted by $\mathsf{vars}^+(F)$ and $\mathsf{vars}^-(F)$, respectively, and the set of variables by $\mathsf{vars}(F)$; for a clause C, $\mathsf{vars}^+(C)$, $\mathsf{vars}^-(C)$, and $\mathsf{vars}(C)$ are defined similarly.

Given a CNF formula F, a (partial) *assignment* for F is a (partial) function $\tau : \mathsf{vars}(F) \to \{\mathbf{t}, \mathbf{f}\}$. With slight abuse of notation, if $\tau(x) = v$, then $\tau(\overline{x}) = \neg v$, where $\neg\mathbf{t} = \mathbf{f}$ and $\neg\mathbf{f} = \mathbf{t}$. A clause is satisfied by τ if it contains at least one literal l such that $\tau(l) = \mathbf{t}$. An assignment τ *satisfies* F if it satisfies every clause in F. A formula is *satisfiable* if there is an assignment that satisfies it, and *unsatisfiable* otherwise. We apply the stardard "Tseitin translation" to map each constrained Boolean circuit $\langle \mathcal{C}, \tau\rangle$ into an equi-satisfiable CNF formula $\mathsf{cnf}(\langle \mathcal{C}, \tau\rangle)$. To obtain a small CNF formula, the

Table 1. Translating a constrained Boolean circuit $\langle \mathcal{C}, \tau \rangle$ to the CNF formula $\mathsf{cnf}(\langle \mathcal{C}, \tau \rangle)$

circuit $\langle \mathcal{C}, \tau \rangle$	clauses in $\mathsf{cnf}(\langle \mathcal{C}, \tau \rangle)$
$g := \text{NOT}(g_1) \in \mathcal{C}$	$\{\bar{x}_g, \bar{x}_{g_1}\}, \{x_g, x_{g_1}\}$
$g := \text{OR}(g_1, \ldots, g_n) \in \mathcal{C}$	$\{\bar{x}_g, x_{g_1}, \ldots, x_{g_n}\}, \{x_g, \bar{x}_{g_1}\}, \ldots, \{x_g, \bar{x}_{g_n}\}$
$g := \text{AND}(g_1, \ldots, g_n) \in \mathcal{C}$	$\{\bar{x}_g, x_{g_1}\}, \ldots, \{\bar{x}_g, x_{g_n}\}, \{x_g, \bar{x}_{g_1}, \ldots, \bar{x}_{g_n}\}$
$g := \text{XOR}(g_1, g_2) \in \mathcal{C}$	$\{\bar{x}_g, \bar{x}_{g_1}, \bar{x}_{g_2}\}, \{\bar{x}_g, x_{g_1}, x_{g_2}\}, \{x_g, \bar{x}_{g_1}, x_{g_2}\}, \{x_g, x_{g_1}, \bar{x}_{g_2}\}$
$\langle g, \mathbf{t} \rangle \in \tau$	$\{x_g\}$
$\langle g, \mathbf{f} \rangle \in \tau$	$\{\bar{x}_g\}$

idea is to introduce a variable x_g for each gate g in the circuit, and then to describe the functionality of each gate with a linear number of clauses (Table 1).

Any CNF formula $F = \{C_1, \ldots, C_k\}$ can naturally be seen as a Boolean circuit. Basically, F is a Boolean circuit with an AND of ORs which represent the clauses. Formally, $\mathsf{circuit}(F) := \langle \mathcal{C}, \tau \rangle$ is defined by associating an input gate g_x with each $x \in \mathsf{vars}(F)$, a NOT-gate $g_{\bar{x}}$ with each $x \in \mathsf{vars}^-(F)$, an OR-gate g_{C_i} with each clause $C_i \in F$, an AND-gate g_F with F, and defining $\tau = \{\langle g_F, \mathbf{t} \rangle\}$ and

$$\mathcal{C} = \{g_F := \text{AND}(g_{C_1}, \ldots, g_{C_k})\} \cup \{g_{\bar{x}} := \text{NOT}(g_x) \mid x \in \mathsf{vars}^-(F)\} \cup \{g_{C_i} := \text{OR}(g_{l_{i,1}}, \ldots, g_{l_{i,n_i}}) \mid C_i = \{l_{i,1}, \ldots, l_{i,n_i}\} \in F\}.$$

3 Resolution, DPLL, and CL with Variants

We now review proof systems for CNF formulas, namely, *Resolution*, and characterisations of DPLL and CL [12] (DPLL with clause learning). We will apply these in Sect. 4.

3.1 Resolution

The well-known Resolution proof system (RES) is based on the *resolution rule*. Let C, D be clauses, and x a Boolean variable. The resolution rule lets us derive the clause $C \cup D$ from the clauses $\{x\} \cup C$ and $\{\bar{x}\} \cup D$ by *resolving on* x. A RES *proof (for the unsatisfiability) of a CNF formula* F is a sequence of clauses $\pi = (C_1, C_2, \ldots, C_m = \emptyset)$, where each C_i, $1 \leq i \leq m$, is either (i) a clause in F (an *initial clause*), or (ii) derived with the resolution rule from two clauses C_j, C_k where $1 \leq j, k < i$ (a *derived clause*). The *length* of π is m, the number of clauses occurring in it.

Many *refinements of* Resolution, in which the structure of RES proofs is restricted, have been proposed and studied. Here of particular interest is *Tree-like Resolution* (T-RES) that requires the refutations to be representable as trees. This implies that a derived clause, if subsequently used multiple times in the refutation, must be derived anew each time starting from initial clauses.

Superpolynomial lower bounds on proof length in RES have been shown for various families of CNF formulas. Among the most studied such families is the *pigeon-hole principle*, which states that there is no injective mapping from an m-element set into an n-element set if $m > n$ (i.e., m pigeons cannot sit in less than m holes so that every pigeon has its own hole). We consider the case $m = n + 1$ encoded as the CNF formula

$$\mathrm{PHP}_n^{n+1} := \bigwedge_{i=1}^{n+1} \Big(\bigvee_{j=1}^{n} p_{i,j} \Big) \wedge \bigwedge_{j=1}^{n} \bigwedge_{i=1}^{n} \bigwedge_{i'=i+1}^{n+1} (\bar{p}_{i,j} \vee \bar{p}_{i',j}),$$

where each $p_{i,j}$ is a Boolean variable with the interpretation "$p_{i,j}$ is **t** if and only if the ith pigeon sits in the jth hole".

Theorem 1 (Haken [15]). *There is no polynomial length* RES *proof of* PHP_n^{n+1}.

It is also known that T-RES is a *proper* refinement of RES. This originates from the facts that *regular resolution* cannot simulate RES [16], and T-RES in turn cannot simulate regular resolution [17].

Corollary 1 (of [16,17]). T-RES *cannot polynomially simulate* RES.

3.2 DPLL

Most modern complete SAT solvers are based on the DPLL procedure [1,2]. Given a CNF formula F as input, DPLL is a depth-first search procedure building a partial assignment τ on vars(F) through *branching* and *unit propagation* (UP). By branching the current partial assignment τ is extended with $\tau(x) = v$, $v \in \{\mathbf{f}, \mathbf{t}\}$, for some unassigned variable x. Unit propagation refers to the process of immediately applying the *unit clause rule* with which the current partial assignment τ is extended with $\tau(l) = \mathbf{t}$ if there is a clause $\{l_1, \ldots, l_k, l\} \in F$ such that $\tau(l_i) = \mathbf{f}$ for each $1 \leq i \leq k$. A branch is extended until (i) there is a clause $C \in F$ for which $\tau(l) = \mathbf{f}$ for each literal $l \in C$, or (ii) τ satisfies F. In case (i), τ is *conflicting* with the particular clause, and DPLL *backtracks* to the last branching decision whose other branch has not been tried yet, and flips the particular decision in τ. A DPLL search terminates when either a satisfying assignment is found, or when all possible branches have been covered, in which case F is determined as unsatisfiable.

As a proof system, the strength of DPLL does not depend on whether UP is applied. Any application of the unit clause rule on a clause C can be simulated by branching on the remaining unassigned literal $l \in C$; assigning l a conflicting value by branching causes immediately backtracking. It is well-known that DPLL and T-RES can polynomially simulate each other; one can show that for any unsatisfiable CNF formula, with UP seen as branching, the branches tried by DPLL correspond one-to-one with the paths of a T-RES proof with the conflicting clauses as leafs.

Fact 1. DPLL and T-RES are polynomially equivalent.

Considering the branch at an arbitrary stage of DPLL, the variables assigned by branching are called *decision variables* and those assigned values by UP are *implied variables*, with analogous definitions for *decision literals* and *implied literals*. The *decision level of a decision variable* x is one more than the number of decision variables in the branch before branching on x. The *decision level of an implied variable* x is the number of decision variables in the branch when x is assigned a value. The decision level of DPLL at any stage is the number of decision variables in the current branch.

Implication graphs capture naturally the ways of deriving all implied literals from decision literals by UP.

Definition 1. *The* implication graph *G at a given stage of* DPLL *is a directed graph with edges labeled with sets of clauses. An implication graph is constructed as follows.*

1. *Create a node for each decision literal, labeled with that literal.*
2. *While there is a clause $C = \{l_1, \ldots, l_k, l\}$ such that $\bar{l}_1, \ldots, \bar{l}_k$ label nodes in G,*
   (a) Add a node labeled l if not already in G.
   (b) Add edges $\langle l_i, l\rangle$ for $1 \leq i \leq k$, if not already present.
3. *Add a special node Λ to G. For any variable x with both labels x and $\bar{x}$ in G, add edges $\langle x, \Lambda\rangle$ and $\langle \bar{x}, \Lambda\rangle$. Any such $x, \bar{x}$ are* conflict literals, *and the variable x is a* conflict variable.

An implication graph contains a conflict if it contains a conflict variable; DPLL has a conflict at a given stage if the implication graph at the stage contains a conflict.

3.3 Clause Learning

Most state-of-the-art complete SAT solvers today apply DPLL enhanced with conflict analysis [4], resulting in Clause Learning (CL). Like the basic DPLL, CL performs branching and UP until a conflict is reached. If this happens without any branching, CL determines the formula F unsatisfiable. In other cases, the conflict is *analyzed*, and a *learned clause* (or *conflict clause*), which describes the "cause" of the conflict, is added to F. After this CL continues by backtracking as DPLL does, or can backjump to an earlier decision level that "caused" the conflict (as discussed in more detail below).

At a given stage of a CL search procedure, a clause is called *known* if it either appears in the original CNF formula or has been learned earlier during the search. Conflict analysis is based on a *conflict graph*, which captures one way of reaching the conflict at hand form the decision variables by using UP on known clauses.

Definition 2. *Given an implication graph G containg a conflict, a* conflict graph *$H = (V, E)$ based on G is any acyclic subgraph of G having the following properties.*

1. *H contains Λ and exactly one conflict literal pair $x, \bar{x}$.*
2. *All nodes in H have a path to Λ.*
3. *Every node $l \in V \setminus \{\Lambda\}$ either corresponds to a decision literal or has precisely the nodes $\bar{l}_1, \bar{l}_2, \ldots, \bar{l}_k$ as predecessors where $\{l_1, l_2, \ldots, l_k, l\}$ is a known clause.*

A conflict graph describes a single conflict and contains only decision and implied literals that can be used in reaching the conflict when applying the unit clause rule *in some order*. Hence the way of implementing unit propagation in a solver has an effect on the choice of the conflict graph.

Conflict clauses are associated with *cuts* in a conflict graph. Fix a conflict graph contained in an implication graph with a conflict. A *conflict cut* is any cut in the conflict graph with all the decision variables on one side (the *reason side*) and at least one conflict literal on the other side (the *conflict side*). Those nodes on the reason side with at least one edge going to the conflict side in a conflict cut form a cause of the conflict; with the associated literals set to **t**, UP can arrive at the conflict at hand. The negations of these literals from the *conflict clause associated with the conflict cut.* The strategy for fixing a conflict cut is called the *learning scheme*. A learning scheme which always learns a currently unknown clause is *non-redundant*.

A clause learning proof (or CL proof) under a learning scheme is a CL search tree using that learning scheme. The length of the proof is the number of branching decisions. The proof system CL consists of CL proofs under any learning scheme.

While the practical efficiency gains of implementing clause learning into DPLL based algorithms are well-established, the first formal study on the power of clause learning is [12]: CL can provide exponentially shorter proofs than T-RES, and thus

Corollary 2 (of Fact 1 and [12]). DPLL *cannot polynomially simulate* CL.

Typically implemented clause learning schemes are based on *unique implication points* (UIPs) [4]. A UIP of a conflict graph is a node u on the maximal decision level d such that all paths from the decision variable x at level d to Λ go through u. Such a u always exists, since x satisfies this condition; intuitively u is a *single* reason for the conflict at level d. Thus one can always choose a conflict cut that results in a conflict clause with a UIP as the only variable from the maximal decision level. Such a conflict clause causes the value of the UIP to be immediate flipped when backtracking. Furthermore, UIP learning enables *conflict-driven backtracking* (or *backjumping*), in which DPLL backtracks to the maximal decision level of the variables other than the UIP in the conflict clause. A popular version of UIP learning is the 1-UIP scheme, where the UIP closest to Λ is chosen. Different learning schemes are evaluated in [18].

Restarts are also often implemented in modern solvers. When a restart occurs, the decisions and unit propagations made so far are undone, and the search continues from decision level 0. The clauses learned so far remain known after the restart. Intuitively, restarts help in escaping from getting stuck in hard-to-prove subformulas. In practice, the choice of when and how often to restart is again part of the strategy of a solver. When any number of restarts are allowed during search, CL has *unlimited restarts*.

Beame et al. [12] define CL-- as CL with branching allowed also on literals already set at the current stage of DPLL. Although being non-typical in practice, this enables creating immediate conflicts at will. Although it is not known whether CL can simulate RES, it has been shown that this is true for CL-- using restarts.

Theorem 2 (Beame et al. [12]). RES *and* CL-- *with unlimited restarts and any non-redundant learning scheme are polynomially equivalent.*

In the following, we will explicitly mention when restarts are allowed.

3.4 Input-Restricted Branching DPLL and CL

In structural application domains of SAT solvers, such as planning and bounded model checking of hardware and software, Boolean circuits offer a natural presentation form for the problem descriptions. Typically, such problems are based on a transition relation, where the behaviour of the underlying system is dependent solely on the *input* of the system. In the Boolean circuit encoding $\langle \mathcal{C}, \tau \rangle$, the input is represented by the set of input gates (sometimes called *independent variables*) of the circuit, $\mathsf{inputs}(\mathcal{C})$. Since the circuit can be evaluated when all gates in $\mathsf{inputs}(\mathcal{C})$ have values, branching in DPLL *with unit propagation* can be restricted to the variables associated with $\mathsf{inputs}(\mathcal{C})$—denoted by $\mathsf{DPLL}_{\mathsf{inputs}}$ and $\mathsf{CL}_{\mathsf{inputs}}$ for clause learning—without losing completeness. Intuitively, the idea is that since $|\mathsf{inputs}(\mathcal{C})|$ is often much less than the total amount $|G|$

of gates in $\mathcal{C}$, search space size is reduced from $2^{|G|}$ to $2^{|\mathsf{inputs}(\mathcal{C})|}$, where $|\mathsf{inputs}(\mathcal{C})| << |G|$. From the view of proof complexity, however, in [13] a formal study on the effect of restricting branching in DPLL (without clause learning) to inputs reveals that this weakens the proof system considerably.

Theorem 3 (Järvisalo et al. [13]). $\mathsf{DPLL}_{\mathsf{inputs}}$ *cannot polynomially simulate* DPLL.

The rest of the paper is dedicated to investigating the effect of restricting branching to inputs in the case of clause learning, which is posed as an open question in [13].

4 Separating Input-Restricted and Unrestricted CL

We will now consider the relative power of input-restricted and unrestricted CL and DPLL. This will result in a refined relative efficiency hierarchy of DPLL and CL (Fig. 3).

Since the cnf translation associates a variable for each gate in a circuit, when appropriate we will use the term "(e.g., branch on, set value to) gate g" when referring to the variable x_g associated with g in the CNF translation of the circuit. Correspondingly, a DPLL or CL proof of a constrained circuit $\mathcal{C}^\tau$ means a proof of the translation $\mathsf{cnf}(\mathcal{C}^\tau)$.

Lemma 1. *There is an infinite family* $\{\mathcal{C}_n^\tau\}$ *of constrained Boolean circuits for which* DPLL *has exponentially longer minimal proofs than* $\mathsf{CL}_{\mathsf{inputs}}$.

Proof. Take any infinite family $\{F_n\}$ of CNF formulas that is a witness of Corollary 2. Define the family of Boolean circuits $\{\mathsf{circuit}(F) \mid F \in \{F_n\}\}$. The formula resulting from UP on $\mathsf{cnf}(\mathsf{circuit}(F))$ without branching corresponds to the result of unit propagation on F without branching. Thus DPLL will only branch on the variables in $\mathsf{cnf}(\mathsf{circuit}(F))$ that are associated with the input gates of $\mathsf{circuit}(F)$. Thus $\mathsf{CL}_{\mathsf{inputs}}$ can simulate CL on $\mathsf{cnf}(\mathsf{circuit}(F))$, and the claim follows by Corollary 2. □

Corollary 3. *Neither* DPLL *nor* $\mathsf{DPLL}_{\mathsf{inputs}}$ *can polynomially simulate* $\mathsf{CL}_{\mathsf{inputs}}$.

To highlight the strength of clause learning even when branching is restricted to input gates, we now give an example of a family $\{\text{XOR-UNSAT}_n\}$ of Boolean circuits on which $\mathsf{CL}_{\mathsf{inputs}}$ can simulate CL, although $\mathsf{DPLL}_{\mathsf{inputs}}$ cannot simulate DPLL on the family. The circuit $\text{XOR-UNSAT}_n := \text{UNSAT} \cup \langle \text{XOR}_n^a \cup \text{XOR}_n^b, \emptyset \rangle$ consists of two parts: (i) the constant size circuit $\text{UNSAT} := \mathsf{circuit}(\{\{a,b\},\{a,\bar{b}\},\{\bar{a},b\},\{\bar{a},\bar{b}\}\})$ and (ii) two copies (for a and b, $\rho \in \{a,b\}$) of the circuit structure

$$\text{XOR}_n^\rho := \{\rho := \text{XOR}(x_{1,1}^\rho, x_{1,2}^\rho)\} \cup \bigcup_{i=1}^{n-1} \bigcup_{j=1}^{i+1} \{x_{i,j}^\rho := \text{XOR}(x_{i+1,j}^\rho, x_{i+1,i+2}^\rho)\}.$$

XOR-UNSAT_2 is shown in Fig. 2. Now, since UP will result in a conflict in the UNSAT subcircuit for any value of the gate a, XOR-UNSAT_n yields a trivial (constant length) proof in DPLL. It is also easy to see that minimal length proofs of XOR-UNSAT_n are exponential w.r.t. n in $\mathsf{DPLL}_{\mathsf{inputs}}$. Due to the structure of XOR_n, in order to propagate a value for the gate a or b, $\mathsf{DPLL}_{\mathsf{inputs}}$ has to branch on all of the inputs in the corresponding XOR_n^ρ subcircuit. With the backtracking process of DPLL this implies that minimal length $\mathsf{DPLL}_{\mathsf{inputs}}$ proofs of XOR-UNSAT_n are exponential w.r.t. n.

However, $\mathsf{CL}_{\mathsf{inputs}}$ can produce linear length proofs on the family. Let $\mathsf{CL}_{\mathsf{inputs}}$ branch according to the sequence ($x^a_{n,1} =$ **f**, ..., $x^a_{n,n} =$ **f**). After this, UP cannot still propagate any values. Then branch with $x^a_{n,n+1} =$ **f**. Now UP sets values for all $x^a_{i,j}$, without a conflict. The values for $x^a_{1,1}$ and $x^a_{1,2}$ propagate a value for a, which then propagates a conflict at a gate in UNSAT. Notice that $x^a_{1,1}$ and $x^a_{1,2}$ are the *only* reasons for the value of a. In *any* conflict graph associated with the branching sequence ($x^a_{n,1} =$ **f**, ..., $x^a_{n,n+1} =$ **f**), a is an UIP, and, furthermore, constitutes a reason for the conflict on its own. Hence $\mathsf{CL}_{\mathsf{inputs}}$ can learn as a unit clause the opposite value of a, and backjump to the decision level zero. This opposite value will then propagate a contradiction without branching, and $\mathsf{CL}_{\mathsf{inputs}}$ terminates. It is interesting to notice how $\mathsf{CL}_{\mathsf{inputs}}$ can branch on ($x^a_{n,1} =$ **f**, ..., $x^a_{n,n+1} =$ **f**) and still avoid backtracking on these decisions since there is the *bottleneck* at gate a due to the construction of XOR-UNSAT$_n$. This shows the power of clause learning with conflict-driven backtracking due to its ability to backjump over an exponential size search space by detecting small locally inconsistent subformulas. With this intuition, it is evident that the results in [13] on the power $\mathsf{DPLL}_{\mathsf{inputs}}$ w.r.t. DPLL cannot be directly adopted for proving the analogous result for $\mathsf{CL}_{\mathsf{inputs}}$.

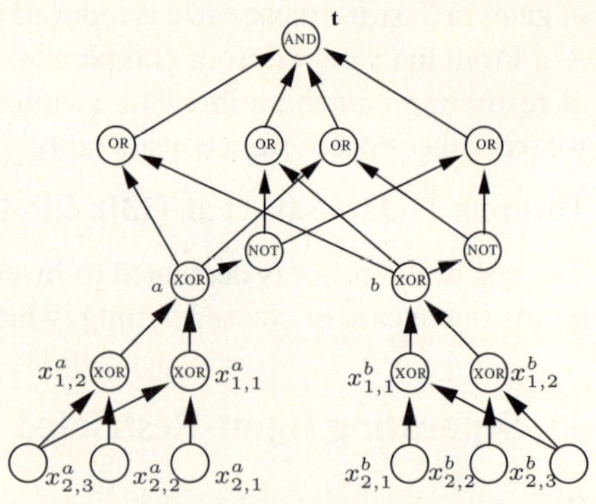

Fig. 2. XOR-UNSAT$_n$ for $n = 2$

Although $\mathsf{CL}_{\mathsf{inputs}}$ can simulate CL on this specific family, this is generally not the case. In fact, it turns out that $\mathsf{CL}_{\mathsf{inputs}}$ *cannot even simulate* DPLL, as detailed next. We will apply the concept of *redundant gates in constraint Boolean circuits.*

Definition 3. *A gate g in a constrained Boolean circuit $\langle\langle G, E\rangle, \tau\rangle$ is* redundant *if (i) g is unconstrained, and (ii) g is not a descendant of any constrained gate g' in $\langle G, E\rangle$.*

We will assume that circuits do not contain redundant input gates; such inputs can always be assigned an arbitrary truth value without affecting satisfiability.

Lemma 2. *Redundant gates do not occur in any conflict graph at any stage of* $\mathsf{CL}\text{--}_{\mathsf{inputs}}$ *whether or not restarts are allowed.*

Proof. For a constrained circuit $\langle\langle G, E\rangle, \tau\rangle$, a *subcircuit* $\langle\langle G', E'\rangle, \tau'\rangle$ induced by $G' \subseteq G$ is $E' = \{\langle g, g'\rangle \in E \cap (G' \times G')\}$ and $\tau' = \{\langle g, \epsilon\rangle \in \tau \mid g \in G'\}$.

Assume that the lemma holds at a stage where $\mathsf{CL}\text{--}_{\mathsf{inputs}}$ has made m conflicts. Consider the $(m + 1)$th conflict. We prove by induction on the structure of $\mathcal{C}^\tau$ that no redundant gates occur in the conflict graph at the $(m + 1)$th conflict. The base case, considering a subcircuit with $n = 1$ gates, is trivial. Assume that the claim holds for all subcircuits with at most n gates. Let $\mathcal{C}^\tau_{n+1}$ be any subcircuit of $\mathcal{C}^\tau$ induced by a set G_{n+1} of $n + 1$ gates. Remove an arbitrary output gate $g := f(g_1, \ldots, g_k)$ from $\mathcal{C}^\tau_{n+1}$ to obtain a subcircuit induced by $G_{n+1} \setminus \{g\}$ with n gates. Such a g cannot be an input gate, since else it would not be connected to the rest of the circuit $\mathcal{C}^\tau$. Thus g is not branchable.

The case that g is not redundant is trivial. Now assume that g is redundant. Since there are no known learned clauses containing redundant gates before the $(m+1)$th conflict, the only way to set a value for g is by UP from values set on (a subset of) $\{g_1, \ldots, g_k\}$. Any value for each g_i can be the result of UP on values for $G_{n+1} \setminus \{g\}$, or of branching in the case g_i is an input gate. For example, consider the case $g := \text{OR}(g_1, g_2)$. If g_1 has the value **t**, g is propagated the value **t**. After this, the value of g cannot propagate a value for g_2, nor can any value of g_2 propagate **f** for g. Other cases are similar. Thus the value of g cannot be used in propagating a value for any gate in C^{τ}_{n+1}, and therefore g cannot occur in any conflict graph for $\mathsf{CL\text{--}}_{\mathsf{inputs}}$. □

Redundant gates can be removed from any constrained Boolean circuit without affecting its satisfiability. However, they may have an effect on the length of minimal proofs. Cook [19] gives a way of introducing a polynomial number of clauses which can be interpreted as redundant gates to circuit(PHP^{n+1}_n) so that, contrarily to circuit (PHP^{n+1}_n), the extended circuit yields polynomial length proofs in RES. As a circuit structure, this *extension* is defined as $\text{EXT}_n := \bigcup_{l=1}^{n} \text{EXT}^l$, where

$$\text{EXT}^l := \bigcup_{i=1}^{l} \bigcup_{j=1}^{l-1} \{e^l_{i,j} := \text{OR}(e^{l+1}_{i,j}, o^l_{i,j}),\ o^l_{i,j} := \text{AND}(e^{l+1}_{i,l}, e^{l+1}_{l+1,j})\},$$

and each $e^n_{i,j}$ is the input gate $g_{p_{i,j}}$ associated with the variable $p_{i,j}$ in PHP^{n+1}_n. By [19] we immediately have a polynomial length RES proof [1] $\pi = (C_1, \ldots, C_m = \emptyset)$ of $\mathsf{cnf}(\mathsf{circuit}(\text{PHP}^{n+1}_n) \cup \langle \text{EXT}_n, \emptyset \rangle)$. Using π, we define the construct

$$\text{E}(\pi) := \bigcup_{i=2}^{m-1} \{h_i := \text{AND}(g_{C_i}, h_{i-1})\} \cup \bigcup_{i=1}^{m-1} \{\hat{g} := \text{NOT}(g) \mid x_g \in \mathsf{vars}^-(C_i)\}$$
$$\bigcup_{i=1}^{m-1} \{g_{C_i} := \text{OR}(\alpha(l_{i,1}), \ldots, \alpha(l_{i,k_i})) \mid C_i = \{l_{i,1}, \ldots, l_{i,k_i}\}\}$$

where h_1 is the gate g_{C_1}, $\alpha(x_g) = g$, and $\alpha(\bar{x}_g) = \hat{g}$. The construct encodes π in a way that allows polynomial length DPLL proofs of $\text{EPHP}_n = \mathsf{circuit}(\text{PHP}^{n+1}_n) \cup \langle \text{EXT}_n, \emptyset \rangle \cup \langle \text{E}(\pi), \emptyset \rangle$, while there is no polynomial length $\mathsf{CL\text{--}}_{\mathsf{inputs}}$ proof of EPHP_n. Intuitively this is because $\text{E}(\pi)$ allows DPLL to "verify" the resolution proof of PHP^{n+1}_n extended with EXT_n step-by-step, while $\mathsf{CL\text{--}}_{\mathsf{inputs}}$ cannot make use of the redundant gates of EXT_n and $\text{E}(\pi)$.

Lemma 3. *For the infinite family* $\{\text{EPHP}_n\}$ *of constrained Boolean circuits,* $\mathsf{CL\text{--}}_{\mathsf{inputs}}$ *with unlimited restarts has superpolynomially longer minimal proofs than* DPLL.

Proof. A polynomial length DPLL proof of EPHP_n is witnessed by the branching sequence $(h_1 = \mathbf{f}, h_2 = \mathbf{f}, \ldots, h_{m-1} = \mathbf{f})$, as detailed next. By induction on i, we will

[1] Due to space constraint, we do not give π explicitly. Intuitively, EXT^l allows reducing PHP^{l+1}_l to PHP^l_{l-1} with a polynomial number of resolution steps. For more details, see the report version [20].

show that, if $h_1 = \mathbf{t}, \ldots, h_{i-1} = \mathbf{t}$, then branching with $h_i = \mathbf{f}$ results in a conflict by UP, and hence immediately setting $h_i = \mathbf{t}$.

The base case. The gate $h_1 = g_{C_1}$ represents the first clause C_1 in π, and C_1 must belong to $\mathsf{cnf}(\mathsf{circuit}(\mathrm{PHP}_n^{n+1}) \cup \langle \mathrm{EXT}_n, \emptyset \rangle)$. As C_1 is a result of applying the cnf translation to a gate g in $\mathsf{circuit}(\mathrm{PHP}_n^{n+1}) \cup \langle \mathrm{EXT}_n, \emptyset \rangle$ (which is part of EPHP_n), setting $h_1 = \mathbf{f}$ will result in a conflict after UP because the functional definition or the constraint of the gate g is violated. For example, if $g := \mathrm{OR}(g_1, g_2)$ and $C_1 = \{x_g, \bar{x}_{g_1}\}$, then $h_1 = g_{C_1} := \mathrm{OR}(g, \hat{g_1})$, $\hat{g_1} := \mathrm{NOT}(g_1)$, and the assignment $h_1 = \mathbf{f}$ will propagate $g = \mathbf{f}$ and $g_1 = \mathbf{t}$, violating the definition of g and thus resulting in a conflict.

Now assume as the induction hypothesis that we have $h_{i'} = \mathbf{t}$ for all $1 \leq i' < i$. Recall that $h_i := \mathrm{AND}(g_{C_i}, h_{i-1})$. By branching with $h_i = \mathbf{f}$, UP sets $g_{C_i} = \mathbf{f}$ by the induction hypothesis. If the ith clause C_i in π belongs to $\mathsf{cnf}(\mathsf{circuit}(\mathrm{PHP}_n^{n+1}) \cup \langle \mathrm{EXT}_n, \emptyset \rangle)$, branching on $g_{C_i} = \mathbf{f}$ will result in a conflict after UP as in the base case. Otherwise C_i has been derived from two clauses, $C_j = C'_j \cup \{x_g\}$ and $C_k = C'_k \cup \{\bar{x}_g\}$, in π for $1 \leq j, k < i$, by resolving on a variable x_g. By the induction hypothesis we have $h_j = \mathbf{t}$ and $h_k = \mathbf{t}$, and thus $g_{C_j} = \mathbf{t}$ and $g_{C_k} = \mathbf{t}$ by UP. On the other hand, as $g_{C_i} = \mathbf{f}$, all the gates corresponding to the literals in $C'_j \cup C'_k$ are assigned to $\mathbf{f}$ by UP, implying that UP will assign both $g = \mathbf{t}$ and $g = \mathbf{f}$ as $g_{C_j} = g_{C_k} = \mathbf{t}$. Thus a conflict is reached, closing the branch $h_i = \mathbf{f}$, and $h_i = \mathbf{t}$ is set by backtracking.

Finally, since $C_m = \emptyset \in \pi$, there are unit clauses $C_j = \{x_g\}$ and $C_k = \{\bar{x}_g\}$ in π, where $1 \leq j, k < m$. W.l.o.g., assume $j < k$. By induction, at latest after branching with $h_k = \mathbf{f}$ and setting $h_k = \mathbf{t}$ by backtracking, we will have $g_{C_j} = g_{C_k} = \mathbf{t}$ in the branch, and thus both $g = \mathbf{t}$ and $g = \mathbf{f}$, a conflict. The result is a linear DPLL proof.

Now consider proofs of EPHP_n in CL--$_{\text{inputs}}$. The non-input gates in $\langle \mathrm{EXT}_n, \emptyset \rangle \cup \langle \mathrm{E}(\pi), \emptyset \rangle$ are all redundant in EPHP_n, and they cannot be part of a reason for any conflict in CL--$_{\text{inputs}}$ (Lemma 2). Thus any CL--$_{\text{inputs}}$ proof of EPHP_n contains a CL--$_{\text{inputs}}$ proof of PHP_n^{n+1}, which cannot be of polynomial length (Theorems 1 and 2). □

Directly by Lemmas 1 and 3 we have

Theorem 4. CL--$_{\text{inputs}}$ *(with or without restarts) and* DPLL *are incomparable.*

Corollary 4. CL--$_{\text{inputs}}$ *with unlimited restarts cannot polynomially simulate* CL.

Remark 1. We use redundant gates in the EPHP_n construction for simplicity of the proof of Lemma 3; by a simple modification of EPHP_n one can construct as a witness for Lemma 3 a constrained circuit with no redundant gates and a single output as the only constrained gate.

Remark 2. Since redundant gates can be removed from constrained Boolean circuits without affecting the sets of satisfying assignments, such gates are typically removed in practice before the CNF translation by so called *cone-of-influence reduction*. However, as witnessed by EPHP_n in Lemma 3, applying cone-of-influence can have a drastic negative effect on the minimal length proofs. It is especially interesting to notice that DPLL solvers with full one-step lookahead can detect the small proofs of EPHP_n witnessed by the branching sequence $(h_1 = \mathbf{f}, h_2 = \mathbf{f}, \ldots, h_{n-1} = \mathbf{f})$.

Figure 3 gives a refined relative efficiency hierarchy for the proof systems considered in this paper. An arrow without a slash from system S to S' means that S can polynomially

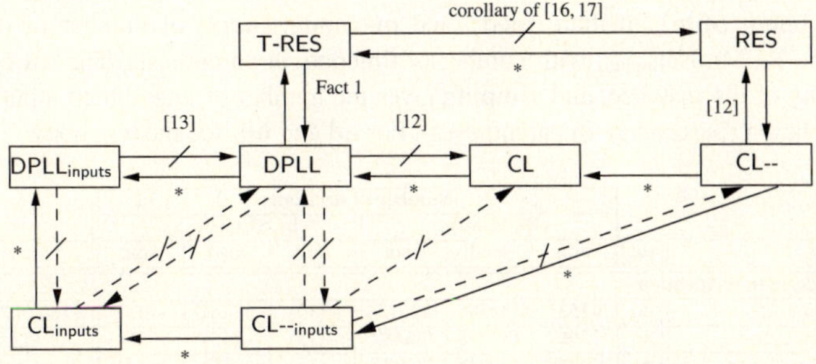

Fig. 3. A refined relative efficiency hierarchy for the proof systems considered in this paper

simulate S', and with a slash that S cannot simulate S'. Arrows labeled with $*$ are due to trivial subsumption. The new results, detailed in the following, are represented by dashed arrows. Disregarding transitivity of the results, missing arrows represent questions which are open to the best of our knowledge.

5 Experiments

We evaluate the effect of input-restriction on the functionality of modern clause learning solver techniques. The benchmark set used in the experiments consists of instances from various application domains, for which Boolean circuits offer a natural representation form: super-scalar processor verification [21], integer factorisation based on hardware multipliers [22], equivalence checking of hardware multipliers [23], bounded model checking (BMC) for deadlocks in asynchronous parallel systems as labelled transition systems (LTS) [24], and linear temporal logic (LTL) BMC of finite state systems with a linear encoding [25]. We use standard PCs with 2-GHz AMD 3200+ processors and 2 GBs of memory running Linux, with a timeout of 1 hour and a memory limit of 1 GB.

For solving the Boolean circuit instances, we apply BCMinisat[2] (version 0.26), which we have modified in order to restrict branching to input variables. BCMinisat is a Boolean circuit front-end for the successful clause learning SAT solver Minisat [26] (version 1.14). BCMinisat accepts as input Boolean circuits with various Boolean functions allowed as gate types, performs circuit-level preprocessing, including Boolean propagation, substructure sharing, and cone-of-influence reductions to the circuit, normalising the circuit into a form which can be translated into CNF applying a standard translation in the style of cnf defined in Table 1. BCMinisat feeds the resulting CNF translations and the input-restriction to Minisat, which then solves the CNF. For each circuit, we obtain 15 CNF instances by permuting the CNF variable numbering.

Minisat implements 1-UIP clause learning. After each conflict the heuristic value of each variable on the conflict side and in the conflict clause is incremented by one, and the values of all variables are decremented by 5%. To avoid hindering efficiency by learning massive amounts of clauses, the solver also uses a scheme for forgetting learned clauses that have not occurred on the conflict side in recent conflicts.

[2] Part of the BCTools package, `http://www.tcs.hut.fi/~tjunttil/bcsat/`

Table 2. Minimum (**min**), median (**med**), and maximum (**max**) of number of decisions for BCMinisat and BCMinisat$_{\text{inputs}}$, with number of timeouts in parenthesis. The **sat** column gives the satisfiability of the instance, and #inputs gives the number of unassigned input variables in the CNF translation (percentage in parentheses). For **ud** and **bb**, see the text body.

		Number of decisions								
		BCMinisat			BCMinisat$_{\text{inputs}}$					
Instance	**sat**	**min**	**med**	**max**	**min**	**med**	**max**	#inputs	**ud**	**bb**
Super-scalar processor verification										
fvp.2.0.3pipe.1	no	**61531**	**384386**	**1225134**	- (15)	- (15)	- (15)	186 (8.2)	-	-
fvp.2.0.3pipe_2_ooo.1	no	**75962**	**184798**	**426489**	- (15)	- (15)	- (15)	305 (11.7)	-	-
fvp.2.0.4pipe_1_ooo.1	no	**188992**	**209048**	**271982**	- (15)	- (15)	- (15)	544 (10.4)	-	-
fvp.2.0.4pipe_2_ooo.1	no	**1033607**	**2094617**	**5241781**	- (15)	- (15)	- (15)	547 (9.8)	-	-
fvp.2.0.5pipe_1_ooo.1	no	**336281**	**746231**	**1838599**	- (15)	- (15)	- (15)	845 (8.9)	-	-
Equivalence checking hardware multipliers										
eq-test.atree.braun.8	no	180449	285665	339805	**65785**	**73834**	**82372**	16 (2.3)	88.5	0.02
eq-test.atree.braun.9	no	898917	1055511	1317785	**323688**	**385398**	**389890**	18 (2.0)	106.6	0.02
eq-test.atree.braun.10	no	3755375	4540598	5089443	**1428957**	**1590390**	**1787295**	20 (1.8)	127.9	0.01
Integer factorisation										
atree.sat.34.0	yes	156733	228792	761620	**24820**	**208880**	**277896**	60 (0.6)	21.9	0.04
atree.sat.36.50	yes	**251218**	721474	937152	316590	**571533**	**788762**	64 (0.6)	18.4	0.04
atree.sat.38.100	yes	284980	1095192	- (1)	**190330**	**498092**	**1082729**	68 (0.6)	-	-
atree.unsat.32.0	no	141419	163508	180973	**123502**	**138797**	**162546**	57 (0.7)	15.3	0.04
atree.unsat.34.50	no	248371	287351	404418	**223130**	**244382**	**301464**	60 (0.6)	18.0	0.04
atree.unsat.36.100	no	527237	623889	915810	**431576**	**480469**	**578331**	64 (0.6)	19.4	0.03
braun.sat.32.0	yes	27480	82122	140150	**5675**	**81269**	**135093**	61 (2.2)	25.6	0.05
braun.sat.34.50	yes	**30717**	152224	353464	43924	**110614**	**223306**	65 (2.1)	25.3	0.05
braun.sat.36.100	yes	129771	447716	**589449**	**86134**	**374884**	752645	69 (2.0)	19.4	0.05
braun.unsat.32.0	no	107617	122550	156004	**96894**	**119437**	**150121**	60 (2.2)	10.4	0.06
braun.unsat.34.50	no	215624	263845	341855	**213199**	**258446**	**316819**	64 (2.0)	9.1	0.06
braun.unsat.36.100	no	**514725**	**623671**	807610	533575	640111	**674470**	68 (1.9)	8.9	0.06
BMC for deadlocks in LTSs										
dp_12.i.k10	no	**513935**	**639756**	**987595**	2497570	- (10)	- (10)	480 (16.0)	-	-
key_4.p.k28	no	**121552**	**147063**	**169386**	138361	184875	220107	967 (10.9)	3.7	0.53
key_4.p.k37	yes	56784	**321552**	**1549271**	**7574**	663152	- (1)	1507 (9.8)	-	-
key_5.p.k29	no	**193139**	**223867**	**310207**	230844	343255	405686	1212 (10.7)	3.9	0.54
key_5.p.k37	yes	104496	**421324**	**1540174**	**19027**	1041807	- (3)	1796 (9.8)	-	-
mmgt_4.i.k15	no	**210288**	**287599**	**457009**	582998	1105986	2170048	456 (10.9)	4.2	0.41
q_1.i.k18	no	**168156**	**353421**	**507246**	375493	929019	1349785	566 (13.1)	3.7	0.49
LTL BMC by linear encoding										
1394-4-3.p1neg.k10	no	141822	155295	164900	**138468**	**148545**	**156839**	1845 (5.6)	6.6	0.34
1394-4-3.p1neg.k11	yes	72988	128708	203647	**34619**	**55575**	**189434**	2023 (5.5)	9.0	0.32
1394-5-2.p0neg.k13	no	**125840**	**143928**	**158320**	146144	156527	186468	1940 (5.0)	6.7	0.32
brp.ptimonegnv.k23	no	**106338**	**130577**	**259025**	193839	302930	356313	461 (6.7)	4.1	0.28
brp.ptimonegnv.k24	yes	43013	96775	**162114**	**13699**	**74907**	260481	481 (6.7)	5.5	0.27
csmacd.p0.k16	no	**229192**	**316082**	**376280**	269520	341751	381248	1794 (2.9)	4.9	0.28
dme3.ptimo.k61	no	**314659**	**549686**	**1658757**	- (15)	- (15)	- (15)	6375 (26.3)	-	-
dme3.ptimo.k62	yes	**427100**	**688505**	**1545603**	- (15)	- (15)	- (15)	6506 (26.3)	-	-
dme3.ptimonegnv.k58	no	**324770**	**568864**	**962967**	- (15)	- (15)	- (15)	5982 (26.3)	-	-
dme3.ptimonegnv.k59	yes	**303921**	**480073**	**1136938**	- (15)	- (15)	- (15)	6113 (26.3)	-	-
dme5.ptimo.k65	no	**497190**	**735741**	**1839619**	- (15)	- (15)	- (15)	10750 (26.8)	-	-

5.1 Results

Table 2 gives the minimum, median, and maximum number of decisions for BCMinisat and input-restricted BCMinisat (BCMinisat$_{\text{inputs}}$) for each benchmark instance. For the instances based on hardware multiplication designs, for which the number of unassigned input variables is 2% or less out of all unassigned variables, BCMinisat$_{\text{inputs}}$ shows an advantage over BCMinisat w.r.t. the number of decisions. However for the hardware verification and BMC instances, the overall performance of BCMinisat$_{\text{inputs}}$

is much worse, with timeouts on all verification and half of the LTL BMC instances. The possible gains of input-restriction seems to correlate with a very low relative number of input variables. On the equivalence checking instances, we notice that the number of decision for BCMinisat$_{\mathsf{inputs}}$ *is more than the brute-force upper bound*, e.g., for `eq-test.atree.braun.10` around $1.4 - 1.8 \times 10^6$, compared to the brute-force bound $2^{20} \approx 1.0 \times 10^6$. Considering that we are using a state-of-the-art clause learning solver, this surprising result is most likely due to conflict clause forgetting; when forgetting a conflict clause C, the solver may have to re-examine the search space characterised as unsatisfiable by C.

Figure 4 gives a cumulative plot of the number of solved instances, showing a drastic decrease in performance for the input-restriction. The effect of input-restriction varies depending on whether unsatisfiable or satisfiable instances are considered (leftmost and middle plots in Fig. 5). For the unsatisfiable instances the plot correlates well with Corollary 4, with timed out runs on the horizontal line. For satisfiable instances, there seems to be no clear winner, although when selecting from the relative small set of input variables, the probability of choosing a satisfying assignment is intuitively greater. A noticeable point is that, while BCMinisat$_{\mathsf{inputs}}$ makes less decisions, e.g, on the equivalence checking instances, unrestricted BCMinisat is at least as efficient as BCMinisat$_{\mathsf{inputs}}$ w.r.t. running times. Interestingly, this is due to the fact that unrestricted BCMinisat often *manages more decisions per second* (on the right in Fig. 5).

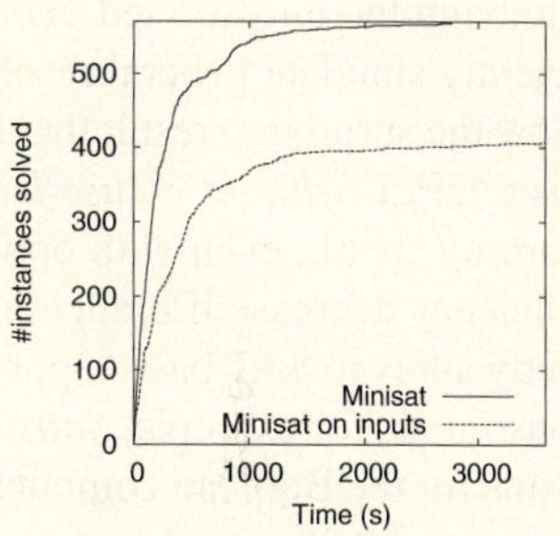

Fig. 4. Solved instances

We also observe that the VSIDS heuristic might not work as intended with the input-restriction. The number of unbranchable variables which have better heuristic values than the best branchable variable can be high per decision (median of averages: **ud** in Table 2), e.g., for `eq-test.atree.braun.10` on the average there are, per decision, over 100 unbranchable variables with better heuristic scores than the best branchable one. From another point of view, the fraction of increments on branchable variables from the number of all increments to heuristic values during search can be in some cases

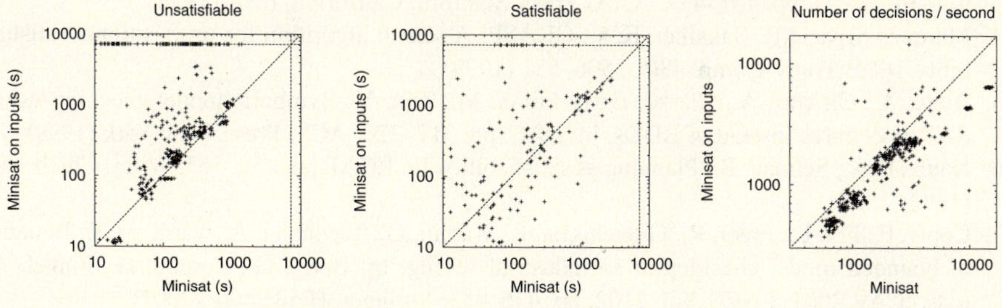

Fig. 5. Scatter plots: running times on unsatisfiable (left) and satisfiable (middle) instances; number of decisions / second (right)

even as low as 1% (median: **bb** in Table 2)—running the risk of VSIDS degenerating into a random heuristic. These observations imply that in order to incorporate branching restrictions in clause learning solvers, the restriction itself should be taken into account in developing suitable heuristics and learning schemes.

6 Conclusions

We investigate the effect of restricting branching in clause learning SAT solving on the efficiency of the underlying inference system from the view of proof complexity. Although the unrestricted version of the considered variant of clause learning can efficiently simulate general resolution, being thus very powerful compared to DPLL, we show the surprising result that input-restricted clause learning cannot even simulate the basic DPLL *without clause learning*. This implies that all implementations of clause learning DPLL, even with optimal heuristics, have the potential of suffering a notable efficiency decrease if branching is restricted to input variables. Notably, the results directly apply to SAT based approaches to solving Boolean combinations of more general constraints, for example, *Satisfiability Modulo Theories*, where the propagation mechanisms for the Boolean combinations can be seen as a form of unit propagation. The experimental evidence shows that by restricting branching the robustness of SAT solvers can decrease, and that input-branching does not go well with clause learning based heuristics of modern solvers.

Acknowledgements. The authors thank Ilkka Niemelä and Emilia Oikarinen for fruitful discussions. Järvisalo gratefully acknowledges the financial support of Helsinki Graduate School in Computer Science and Engineering, Academy of Finland (grant #211025), the Emil Aaltonen Foundation, and the Technological Foundation TES.

References

1. Davis, M., Putnam, H.: A computing procedure for quantification theory. JACM 7(3), 201–215 (1960)
2. Davis, M., Logemann, G., Loveland, D.: A machine program for theorem proving. CACM 5(7), 394–397 (1962)
3. Gomes, C.P., Selman, B., Kautz, H.A.: Boosting combinatorial search through randomization. In: AAAI, pp. 431–437. AAAI Press, Stanford, California, USA (1998)
4. Marques-Silva, J.P., Sakallah, K.A.: GRASP: A search algorithm for propositional satisfiability. IEEE Trans. Comp. 48(5), 506–521 (1999)
5. Biere, A., Cimatti, A., Clarke, E.M., Fujita, M., Zhu, Y.: Symbolic model checking using SAT procedures instead of BDDs. In: DAC, pp. 317–320. ACM Press, New York (1999)
6. Kautz, H.A., Selman, B.: Planning as satisfiability. In: ECAI, pp. 359–363. Wiley, Chichester (1992)
7. Copty, F., Fix, L., Fraer, R., Giunchiglia, E., Kamhi, G., Tacchella, A., Vardi, M.Y.: Benefits of bounded model checking at an industrial setting. In: Berry, G., Comon, H., Finkel, A. (eds.) CAV 2001. LNCS, vol. 2102, pp. 436–453. Springer, Heidelberg (2001)
8. Giunchiglia, E., Massarotto, A., Sebastiani, R.: Act, and the rest will follow: Exploiting determinism in planning as satisfiability. In: AAAI, pp. 948–953. AAAI Press, Stanford, California, USA (1998)

9. Strichman, O.: Tuning SAT checkers for bounded model checking. In: Emerson, E.A., Sistla, A.P. (eds.) CAV 2000. LNCS, vol. 1855. Springer, Heidelberg (2000)
10. Giunchiglia, E., Maratea, M., Tacchella, A.: Dependent and independent variables in propositional satisfiability. In: Flesca, S., Greco, S., Leone, N., Ianni, G. (eds.) JELIA 2002. LNCS (LNAI), vol. 2424, pp. 296–307. Springer, Heidelberg (2002)
11. Cook, S.A., Reckhow, R.: On the relative efficiency of propositional proof systems. J. Symb. Logic 44, 36–50 (1977)
12. Beame, P., Kautz, H.A., Sabharwal, A.: Towards understanding and harnessing the potential of clause learning. JAIR 22, 319–351 (2004)
13. Järvisalo, M., Junttila, T., Niemelä, I.: Unrestricted vs restricted cut in a tableau method for Boolean circuits. AMAI 44(4), 373–399 (2005)
14. Papadimitriou, C.H.: Computational Complexity. Addison-Wesley, Reading (1995)
15. Haken, A.: The intractability of resolution. TCS 39(2–3), 297–308 (1985)
16. Goerdt, A.: Regular resolution versus unrestricted resolution. SIAM J. Comp. 22(4), 661–683 (1993)
17. Urquhart, A.: The complexity of propositional proofs. B. Symb. Logic 1(4), 425–467 (1995)
18. Zhang, L., Madigan, C.F., Moskewicz, M.W., Malik, S.: Efficient conflict driven learning in boolean satisfiability solver. In: ICCAD, pp. 279–285 (2001)
19. Cook, S.A.: A short proof of the pigeon hole principle using extended resolution. SIGACT News 8(4), 28–32 (1976)
20. Järvisalo, M.: Impact of restricted branching on clause learning SAT solving. Research Report A107, Helsinki University of Technology, Laboratory for Theoretical Computer Science (2007), See
`http://www.tcs.hut.fi/Publications/`
21. Velev, M., Bryant, R.: Superscalar processor verification using efficient reductions of the logic of equality with uninterpreted functions to propositional logic. In: Pierre, L., Kropf, T. (eds.) CHARME 1999. LNCS, vol. 1703, pp. 37–53. Springer, Heidelberg (1999)
22. Pyhälä, T.: Factoring benchmarks for SAT-solvers (2004),
`http://www.tcs.hut.fi/Software/genfacbm/`
23. Järvisalo, M.: Equivalence checking multiplier designs, SAT Competition 2007 benchmark description (2007),
`http://www.tcs.hut.fi/~mjj/benchmarks/`
24. Jussila, T., Heljanko, K., Niemelä, I.: BMC via on-the-fly determinization. International Journal on Software Tools for Technology Transfer 7(2), 89–101 (2005)
25. Latvala, T., Biere, A., Heljanko, K., Junttila, T.A.: Simple bounded LTL model checking. In: Hu, A.J., Martin, A.K. (eds.) FMCAD 2004. LNCS, vol. 3312, pp. 186–200. Springer, Heidelberg (2004)
26. Eén, N., Sörensson, N.: An extensible SAT-solver. In: Giunchiglia, E., Tacchella, A. (eds.) SAT 2003. LNCS, vol. 2919, pp. 502–518. Springer, Heidelberg (2004)

Dynamic Management of Heuristics for Solving Structured CSPs

Philippe Jégou, Samba Ndojh Ndiaye, and Cyril Terrioux

LSIS - UMR CNRS 6168
Université Paul Cézanne (Aix-Marseille 3)
Avenue Escadrille Normandie-Niemen
13397 Marseille Cedex 20 (France)
{philippe.jegou,samba-ndojh.ndiaye,cyril.terrioux}@univ-cezanne.fr

Abstract. This paper deals with the problem of solving efficiently structured CSPs. It is well known that (hyper)tree-decompositions offer the best approaches from a theoretical viewpoint, but from the practical viewpoint, these methods do not offer efficient algorithms. Therefore, we introduce here a framework founded on coverings of CSP by acyclic hypergraphs. We study their properties and relations, and evaluate theoretically their interest with respect to the solving of structured problems. This framework does not define a new decomposition, but makes easier a dynamic management of the CSP structure during the search, and so an exploitation of dynamic variables ordering heuristics in the solving method. Thus, we provide a new complexity result which outperforms significantly the previous one given in the literature about heuristics for solving a decomposed problem. Finally, we present experimental results to assess the practical interest of these notions.

1 Introduction

In the past, the interest for the exploitation of structural properties of a problem was attested in various domains: for checking satisfiability in SAT [1,2,3], for solving CSP [4], in Bayesian or probabilistic networks [5,6], in relational databases [7,8], for constraint optimization [9,10]. Complexity results based on topological properties of the network structure have been proposed. Generally, these results rely on the properties of a tree-decomposition [11] or a hypertree-decomposition [12] of the network, which can be considered as an acyclic hypergraph (a hypertree) covering the network. If we consider tree-decomposition, the time complexity of the best structural methods is $O(exp(w+1))$, with w the width of the used tree-decomposition. If we consider hypertree-decomposition, the time complexity is then $O(exp(k))$, with k the width of the used hypertree-decomposition. It has been shown that hypertree-decomposition is better than tree-decomposition [12], while it is recently outperformed by a generalized hypertree-decomposition [13,14]. Note that these theoretical complexities can really outperform the classical one which is $O(exp(n))$ ($k < w < n$) with n the number of variables of the considered CSP.

C. Bessiere (Ed.): CP 2007, LNCS 4741, pp. 364–378, 2007.

However, while several methods and theoretical results have been proposed, the practical interests of such approaches have not been proved yet, except in some recent works around CSPs [15] or Valued CSPs [16,17,10]. This is due to the fact that the good complexity bounds are often reached to the detriment of the practical efficiency. Precisely, approaches based on hypertree-decompositions and their generalizations assume that relations associated to constraints are expressed by tables, what is unrealistic, in practice, for many real life problems. Moreover, to ensure complexity bounds, the decompositions perform joins of relations. For solving CSPs, such an approach is generally unrealistic due to the size of the generated relations. Indeed, solving structured CSPs sometimes requires to manage joins of relations defined on several tens of attributes (i.e. variables), which is clearly impossible in practice. On the other hand, the methods that have shown their feasibility and their practical interest are based on assignments of variables. These methods can exploit the practical efficiency of backtracking-based algorithms with filtering, while they ensure complexity bounds without problems related to practical space complexity, contrary to approaches based on management of relations as hypertree-decomposition. Yet, some methods exploiting the structure of the problem, based on heuristics guaranteeing no good complexity bound, have shown the interest of such an approach [3].

In this paper, we propose to make a trade-off between good theoretical complexity bounds and the peremptory necessity to exploit efficient heuristics as often as possible. From this viewpoint, this work can be considered as an extension of the works recently presented in [17] in the field of AND/OR Branch-and-Bound Search in Constraint Optimization, or in [18] in the field of tree-decomposition methods for CSPs. Our contribution is more precisely an extension of the approach presented in [18]. Furthermore, we propose a framework different from the previous one, better theoretical results and a practical validation of this approach. Actually, we prefer here the more general and useful concept of covering acyclic hypergraph to the concept of tree-decomposition. Note that we do not aim here to define a new decomposition method for solving CSPs, nor to propose new bounds for complexity. We introduce a framework that makes possible to implement decomposition methods which can be more efficient than previously, because they can exploit efficient heuristics. Note that generally, decomposition methods define a decomposition of the constraint network, and then solve the associated CSP exploiting statically this structure. Here, our goal is to exploit dynamically sets of structures induced by the considered decomposition.

Given a hypergraph $H = (X, C)$ related to the graphical representation of the considered problem, we consider a covering of this hypergraph by an acyclic hypergraph $H_A = (X, E)$: the set of vertices is the same while for each edge $C_i \in C$, there is an edge $E_i \in E$ covering C_i ($C_i \subset E_i$). Now, given H_A, we can define various classes of acyclic hypergraphs which cover H_A. These classes are defined on the basis of criteria related to the nature of coverings and the relations existing with the solving methods: bounding the value of parameters such as tree-width, preservation of the separators in H_A, merging of neighboring hyperedges or ability to implement effective heuristics, in particular dynamic ones. First, these coverings are studied theoretically in order to determine their characteristics and properties. After, we show that they permit to preserve already known complexity results and also to improve some of them. Moreover, we indicate how they offer a framework for a dynamic management of the structure: during a search, we can take into account not only one acyclic hypergraph covering, but a set of coverings in order to manage heuristics dynamically. Thanks to this formal framework, we present a new algorithm (called BDH for "Backtracking on Dynamic covering by acyclic Hypergraphs") for which it is easy to extend heuristics. For example, for dynamic variable ordering, we can add dynamically a set of Δ variables for the choices. Moreover, we show how an implementation is made possible easily, allowing us to show the practical interest of this approach.

In the next section, we recall some results on structural decompositions. Section 3 introduces various classes of acyclic hypergraph coverings and show their relations. The fourth section describes how these classes can be exploited on the algorithmic level and gives the theoretical complexity they guarantee. Finally, we presents an experimental analysis before concluding.

2 Decompositions Methods for Solving CSPs Efficiently

A *constraint satisfaction problem* (CSP) is defined by a tuple (X, D, C, R). X is a set of n variables which must be assigned in their respective finite domain from D, by satisfying a set C of constraints which are defined on a set of relations R. A solution is an assignment of every variable which satisfies all the constraints. Here a constraint $C_i \in C$ is defined by a subset of variables ($C_i \subset X$), while the associated relation R_i expresses a set of tuples of values defined on domains of variables belonging to C_i, all tuples in R_i satisfying the constraint C_i. The CSP structure can be represented by the hypergraph (X, C), called the *constraint hypergraph* (if all the constraints of a CSP are defined by pairs of variables, then we consider a *constraint graph*).

In this paper, we assume that the relations can be represented by tables, predicates, functions, or (in)equations. This remark is important in the field of decomposition methods. Indeed, several results assume that relations are represented by tables. From a theoretical viewpoint, this is possible since we consider finite domains, but from a practical viewpoint, this restriction can be unrealistic. Let us consider a constraint defined by the inequation $x_1 + x_2 + \ldots x_c > c$, with domains $D_i = \{1, \ldots 1000\}, i = 1, \ldots, c$. The memory size of the table for representing the associated relation is then $c.(1000^c - 1)$, which is clearly unrealistic even for small values of c.

The basic concept which interests us here is the acyclicity of networks. Often, this concept is expressed by considering the tree-decomposition of constraint graphs, hypertree-decomposition of constraint hypergraphs, or more generally, coverings of variables and constraints by acyclic hypergraphs. We recall these different decompositions.

Tree-decomposition is based on graphs. Nevertheless, given a constraint hypergraph, we can exploit it by considering its primal graph. Let $H = (X, C)$ be a hypergraph, with X a finite set of vertices and $C = \{C_1, C_2, \ldots C_m\}$ a set of edges (sometimes called hyperedges) which are nonempty subsets of X. Here we consider only reduced hypergraphs, that is hypergraphs such that for all edges C_i of H, C_i is not a proper subset of another edge of H. The primal graph of H is the graph $G = (X, A)$ where $A = \{\{x, y\} : \exists C_i \in C$ such that $\{x, y\} \subset C_i\}$.

Definition 1. *A tree-decomposition of a graph $G = (X, A)$ is a pair (E, T) where $T = (I, F)$ is a tree with nodes I and edges F and $E = \{E_i : i \in I\}$ a family of subsets of X, s.t. each subset (called cluster) E_i is a node of T and verifies:*

(i) $\cup_{i \in I} E_i = X$,
(ii) for each edge $\{x, y\} \in A$, there exists $i \in I$ with $\{x, y\} \subset E_i$, and
(iii) for all $i, j, k \in I$, if k is in a path from i to j in T, then $E_i \cap E_j \subset E_k$.

The width w of a tree-decomposition (E, T) is equal to $max_{i \in I}|E_i| - 1$. The tree-width w^* of G is the minimal width over all the tree-decompositions of G.

Assume that we have a tree-decomposition of width w for the constraint network. The best structural methods based on a tree-decomposition of a CSP have a time complexity in $O(exp(w + 1))$, while their space complexity can be reduced to $O(exp(s))$ where s is the size of the largest intersection $E_i \cap E_j$ (generally considered as minimal separators) between neighboring clusters of the tree-decomposition. Tree-Clustering (TC [4]) is based on this notion, but has never shown its efficiency for real life problems. This is due to the fact that TC runs in finding firstly all solutions of each subproblem induced by the variables in each E_i. An example of an efficient method exploiting tree-decomposition is BTD [15], which does not compute all solutions of subproblems. This method applies a backtracking driven by the tree-decomposition and preserves complexity bounds in $O(exp(w + 1))$. Note that this kind of methods can be considered as driven by the assignment of variables (or as "variables driven" methods). As a consequence, it does not need to represent relations in tables.

From a theoretical viewpoint, methods based on tree-decomposition are less interesting than those based on hypertree-decomposition and their generalizations [12].

Definition 2. *Given a hypergraph $H = (X, E)$, a hypertree for the hypergraph H is a triple (T, χ, λ) where $T = (N, F)$ is a rooted tree, and χ and λ are labelling functions which associate to each vertex $p \in N$ two sets $\chi(p) \subset X$ and $\lambda(p) \subset E$. If $T' = (N', F')$ is a subtree of T, we define $\chi(T') = \cup_{v \in N'} \chi(v)$. We denote the set of vertices N of T by vertices(T), and the root of T by root(T). Moreover, for any $p \in N$, T_p denotes the subtree of T rooted at p.*

Definition 3. *Given a hypergraph $H = (X, E)$, a hypertree-decomposition of H is a hypertree $HD = (T, \chi, \lambda)$ for H which satisfies all the following conditions:*

(i) for each edge $E_i \in E, \exists p \in vertices(T)$ such that $E_i \subset \chi(p)$,
(ii) for each vertex $x \in X$, the set $\{p \in vertices(T) : x \in \chi(p)\}$ induces a (connected) subtree of T,

(iii) for each $p \in vertices(T), \chi(p) \subset \cup_{E_i \in \lambda(p)} E_i$,
(iv) for each $p \in vertices(T), \cup_{E_i \in \lambda(p)} E_i \cap \chi(T_p) \subset \chi(p)$.

An edge $E_i \in E$ *is strongly covered in* HD *if there exists* $p \in vertices(T)$ *such that* $E_i \subset \chi(p)$ *and* $E_i \in \lambda(p)$. *A hypertree-decomposition* HD *is a complete decomposition of* H *if every edge of* H *is strongly covered in* HD. *The width* k *of a hypertree-decomposition* $HD = (T, \chi, \lambda)$ *is* $max_{p \in vertices(T)} |\lambda(p)|$. *The hypertree-width* k^* *of* H *is the minimum width over all its hypertree-decompositions.*

Remark that acyclic hypergraphs are precisely those hypergraphs having a hypertree width one.

While tree-decomposition consists in grouping the vertices in clusters (i.e. variables in subproblems), hypertree-decomposition consists in grouping the constraints (and so the relations) in nodes of the hypertree. Given a hypertree-decomposition of a CSP, the method exploiting it consists in solving first each node of T, and then solving the acyclic induced problem. Thus its time complexity is $O(|\mathcal{P}|^{k+1} log(|\mathcal{P}|))$ where $|\mathcal{P}|$ denotes the size of the CSP $\mathcal{P}$ and k the width of the considered hypertree-decomposition of $H = (X, C)$. This complexity can be limited to $O(r^{k+1} log(r))$ where r is the maximum size for all tables representing relations in the considered CSP. This cost is related to the cost of computing each node of the hypertree, which is bounded by the cost of joins between k relations, which is r^k. Now, if we consider complexity space, the complexity is related to the size of the largest relation induced for each node of the hypertree, that is also $O(r^k)$. This kind of methods can be considered as "relations driven" approaches. Indeed, the time complexity bounds of these approaches outperform those guaranteed by methods as TC or BTD. Nevertheless, the relations associated to constraints must be represented by tables, or at least, the relations associated to nodes of the hypertree must be represented by tables. This restriction can make these approaches unusable in practice. Moreover, like TC, they must compute first all the solutions in each node of the hypertree by joining relations in it. Consequently, as for TC, these methods will require a too expensive amount of memory space in practice making them unusable again. Thus, they are generally unrealistic to solve real instances of CSPs, and then, at the present time, the proof of their practical efficiency has never been shown.

So, while from a theoretical viewpoint, it appears that (generalized-)hypertree-decompositions should be considered, we prefer consider here "variables driven" decompositions. In this paper, we will refer to the covering of constraint networks by acyclic hypergraphs. Different definitions of acyclicity have been proposed. Here, we consider the classical definition called $\alpha - acyclicity$ in [7].

Definition 4. *Let* $H = (X, C)$ *be a hypergraph. A covering by an acyclic hypergraph (CAH) of the hypergraph* H *is an acyclic hypergraph* $H_A = (X, E)$ *such that for each edge* $C_i \in C$, *there exists* $E_j \in E$ *such that* $C_i \subset E_j$. *The width* α *of a CAH* (X, E) *is equal to* $max_{E_i \in E} |E_i|$. *The CAH-width* α^* *of* H *is the minimal width over all the CAHs of* H_A. *Finally,* $\mathcal{CAH}(H)$ *is the set of the CAHs of* H.

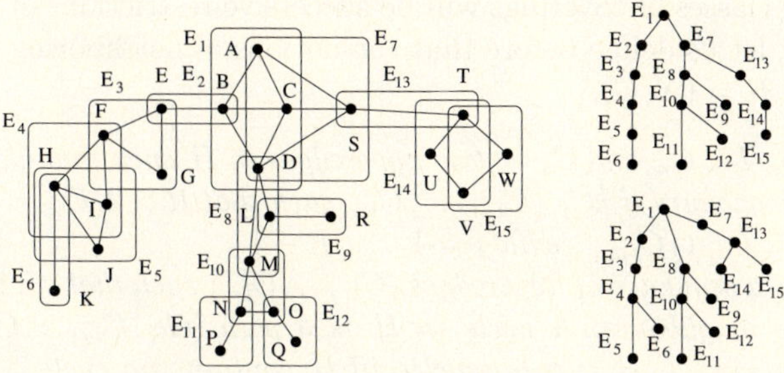

Fig. 1. A graph on 23 vertices under a covering by an acyclic hypergraph (of 15 edges) and 2 possible tree-decompositions

The notion of covering by acyclic hypergraph (called hypertree embedding in [19]) is very close to the one of tree-decomposition. Particularly, it is easy to see that for a tree-decomposition (E, T) of the primal graph of $H = (X, C)$, the pair (X, E) is a CAH of the hypergraph H. Moreover, the CAH-width α^* of H is equal to the *tree-width* of G plus one. However, the concept of CAH is less restrictive. Indeed, for a given (hyper)graph, it can exist a single CAH whose width is α, while it can exist several tree-decompositions of width w such that $\alpha = w + 1$. An example is given in figure 1, where for a constraint network, we have one CAH (with $\alpha = 4$) and two possible tree-decompositions (with $w = 3$). Given a CSP with a CAH of width α, the time complexity of better structural methods for solving it is $O(exp(\alpha))$ while its space complexity can be reduced to $O(exp(s))$ where s is the size of the largest intersection $E_i \cap E_j$ in H_A.

he next section presents different classes of covering acyclic hypergraphs.

3 Coverings by Classes of Acyclic Hypergraphs

In the sequel, given a hypergraph $H = (X, C)$ and one of its CAHs $H_A = (X, E)$, we study several classes of acyclic coverings of H_A. These coverings correspond to coverings of hyperedges (elements of E) by other hyperedges (larger but less numerous), which belong to a hypergraph defined on the same set of vertices and which is acyclic. In all the cases, these extensions are defined with respect to a particular CAH H_A, called *CAH of reference*. Here, we do not introduce a new decomposition of hypergraph. We study different ways for covering and so to solve a CSP by decomposition. Our objective is to formalize different classes of acyclic coverings, to manage dynamically, during search, acyclic coverings of the considered CSP. We hope by this mean, to manage dynamic heuristics to optimize backtrack search while preserving complexity results.

Definition 5. *The set of coverings of a CAH $H_A = (X, E)$ of a hypergraph $H = (X, C)$ is defined by $\mathcal{CAH}_{H_A} = \{(X, E') \in \mathcal{CAH}(H) : \forall E_i \in E, \exists E'_j \in E' : E_i \subset E'_j\}$.*

The following classes of coverings will be successive restrictions of this first class $\mathcal{CAH}_{H_A}$. But, let us define before that the notions of neighboring hyperedges in a hypergraph $H = (X, C)$.

Definition 6. *Let C_u and C_v be two hyperedges in H such that $C_u \cap C_v \neq \emptyset$. C_u and C_v are neighbours if $\nexists C_{i_1}, C_{i_2}, \ldots, C_{i_R}$ such that $R > 2, C_{i_1} = C_u, C_{i_R} = C_v$ and $C_u \cap C_v \subsetneq C_{i_j} \cap C_{i_{j+1}}$, with $j = 1, \ldots, R-1$.*
A path in H is a sequence of hyperedges $(C_{i_1}, \ldots C_{i_R})$ such that $\forall j, 1 \leq j < R, C_{i_j}$ and $C_{i_{j+1}}$ are neighbours. A cycle in H is a path $(C_{i_1}, C_{i_2}, \ldots C_{i_R})$ such that $R > 3$ and $C_{i_1} = C_{i_R}$. H is α − acyclic iff H contains no cycle.

The first restriction imposes that the edges E_i covered (even partially) by a same edge E'_j are connected in H_A, i.e. mutually accessible by paths. This class is called *set of connected-coverings of a CAH* $H_A = (X, E)$ and is denoted $\mathcal{CAH}_{H_A}[C^+]$. It is possible to restrict this class by restricting the nature of the set $\{E_{i_1}, E_{i_2}, \ldots E_{i_R}\}$. On the one hand, we can limit the considered set to paths (class of *path-coverings of a CAH* denoted $\mathcal{CAH}_{H_A}[P^+]$), and on the other hand by taking into account the maximum length of connection (class of *family-coverings of a CAH* denote $\mathcal{CAH}_{H_A}[F^+]$). We can also define a class (called *unique-coverings of a CAH* and denoted $\mathcal{CAH}_{H_A}[U^+]$) which imposes the covering of an edge E_i by a single edge of E'. Finally, it is possible to extend the class $\mathcal{CAH}_{H_A}$ in another direction (class of *close-coverings of a CAH* denoted $\mathcal{CAH}_{H_A}[B^+]$), ensuring neither connexity, nor unicity: we can cover edges with empty intersections but which have a common neighbor.

Definition 7. *Given a graph H and a CAH H_A of H:*

- $\mathcal{CAH}_{H_A}[C^+] = \{(X, E') \in \mathcal{CAH}_{H_A} : \forall E'_i \in E', E'_i \subset E_{i_1} \cup E_{i_2} \cup \ldots \cup E_{i_R}$ *with* $E_{i_j} \in E$ *and* $\forall E_{i_u}, E_{i_v}, 1 \leq u < v \leq R$, *there is a path in H between* E_{i_u} *and* E_{i_v} *defined on edges belonging to* $\{E_{i_1}, E_{i_2}, \ldots E_{i_R}\}\}$.
- $\mathcal{CAH}_{H_A}[P^+] = \{(X, E') \in \mathcal{CAH}_{H_A} : \forall E'_i \in E', E'_i \subset E_{i_1} \cup E_{i_2} \cup \ldots \cup E_{i_R}$ *with* $E_{i_j} \in E$ *and* $E_{i_1}, E_{i_2}, \ldots E_{i_R}$ *is a path in* $H\}$.
- $\mathcal{CAH}_{H_A}[F^+] = \{(X, E') \in \mathcal{CAH}_{H_A} : \forall E'_i \in E', E'_i \subset E_{i_1} \cup E_{i_2} \cup \ldots \cup E_{i_R}$ *with* $E_{i_j} \in E$ *and* $\exists E_{i_u}, 1 \leq u \leq R, \forall E_{i_v}, 1 \leq v \leq R$ *and* $v \neq u$, E_{i_u} *and* E_{i_v} *are neighbours* $\}$.
- $\mathcal{CAH}_{H_A}[U^+] = \{(X, E') \in \mathcal{CAH}_{H_A} : \forall E_i \in E, \exists! E'_j \in E' : E_i \subset E'_j\}$.
- $\mathcal{CAH}_{H_A}[B^+] = \{(X, E') \in \mathcal{CAH}_{H_A} : \forall E'_i \in E', E'_i \subset E_{i_1} \cup E_{i_2} \cup \ldots \cup E_{i_R}$ *with* $E_{i_j} \in E$ *and* $\exists E_k \in E$ *such that* $\forall E_{i_v}, 1 \leq v \leq R\ E_k \neq E_{i_v}$ *and* E_k *and* E_{i_v} *are neighbours* $\}$.

If $\forall E'_i \in E', E'_i = E_{i_1} \cup E_{i_2} \cup \ldots \cup E_{i_R}$, *these classes will be denoted* $\mathcal{CAH}_{H_A}[X]$ *for* $X = C, P, F, U$ *or* B.

The concept of separator is essential in the methods exploiting the structure, because space complexity directly depends on their size. This concept is introduced here to impose a new restriction. This one will make it possible to limit the separators to an existing subset of those in the hypergraph of reference:

Definition 8. *The set of separator-based coverings of a CAH* $H_A = (X, E)$ *is defined by* $\mathcal{CAH}_{H_A}[S] = \{(X, E') \in \mathcal{CAH}_{H_A} : \forall E'_i, E'_j \in E', i \neq j, \exists E_k, E_l \in E, k \neq l : E'_i \cap E'_j = E_k \cap E_l\}$.

In fact, this class imposes both the unicity and the connexity. It thus corresponds to restrictions of the two classes $[U]$ and $[C]$. One deduces from it that the unicity of covering and the connexity of the covered edges impose the conservation of the separators of H_A:

Theorem 1. $\mathcal{CAH}_{H_A}[S] = \mathcal{CAH}_{H_A}[U] \cap \mathcal{CAH}_{H_A}[C]$

By lack of place, we do not provide the proof of theorems 1-6.

Let us note that this classification is not exhaustive. We could consider additional classes but their interest and thus their study would probably be limited. Finally, the computation of an element of these various classes is easy in terms of complexity. For example, given H and H_A (H_A can be obtained as a tree-decomposition), we can compute $H'_A \in \mathcal{CAH}_{H_A}[S]$ by merging neighboring edges of H_A.

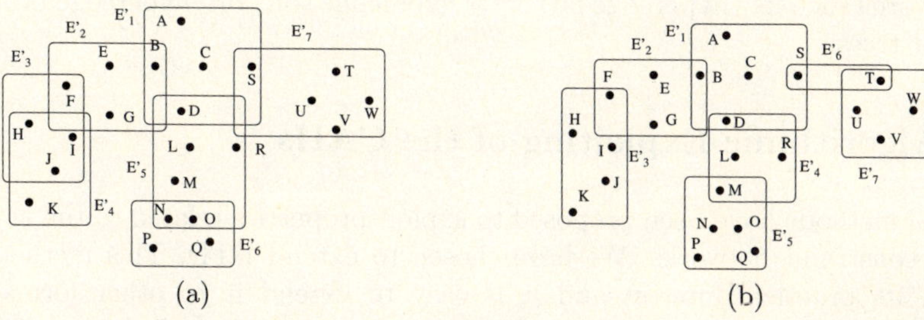

Fig. 2. (a) In this covering, neither connexity ($E'_6 = E_{11} \cup E_{12}$), nor unicity ($E_5 \subset E'_4 \cap E'_3$) and then separators (e.g. $E'_4 \cap E'_3$) are satisfied. This covering belongs to $\mathcal{CAH}_{H_A}[C^+]$. (b) This covering belongs to $\mathcal{CAH}_{H_A}[S]$.

In all the cases, one can observe that the value of the CAH-width increase inside these classes, and then is larger than α, the width associated to the hypergraph of reference H_A. In particular, for the classes of the type $\mathcal{CAH}_{H_A}[X^+]$, it is an additive increase:

Theorem 2. $\forall H'_A \in \mathcal{CAH}_{H_A}[X^+]$ *with* $X = C, P, F, U$ *or* B, $\exists \Delta \geq 0$ *such that* $\alpha' \leq \alpha + \Delta$.

Concerning the other classes, the increase is multiplicative. Indeed, in each case, covering is related to the merging of edges of (X, E):

Theorem 3. $\forall H'_A \in \mathcal{CAH}_{H_A}[C], \exists \delta \geq 1$ *such that* $\alpha' \leq \delta(\alpha - s^-) + s^-$, *where* s^- *is the minimum size of separators.*

For classes $\mathcal{CAH}_{H_A}[U]$ and $\mathcal{CAH}_{H_A}[B]$, edges can be deconnected and consequently with empty intersections. So, we cannot take into account the size of separators:

Theorem 4. *$\forall H'_A \in \mathcal{CAH}_{H_A}[U] \cup \mathcal{CAH}_{H_A}[B], \exists \delta \geq 1$ such that $\alpha' \leq \delta.\alpha$.*

These remarks are useful because they have consequences on the complexity of the algorithms which will exploit these coverings. They show in particular that classes $\mathcal{CAH}_{H_A}[C]$ (and then $[P]$, $[F]$ and $[S]$) must be privileged rather than classes $\mathcal{CAH}_{H_A}[U]$ or $\mathcal{CAH}_{H_A}[B]$. Concerning the size of the separators, one can observe that for the class $\mathcal{CAH}_{H_A}[S]$, the value s associated to H_A is an upper bound for any considered hypergraph H'_A. Formally:

Theorem 5. *$\forall H'_A \in \mathcal{CAH}_{H_A}[S], s' \leq s$.*

This study indicates us the most promising classes. From a theoretical viewpoint, it seems that a class as $\mathcal{CAH}_{H_A}[S]$ could be the most useful, on condition that we limit the size of the induced width.

In the sequel, we exploit these concepts at the algorithmic level. So, each CAH is thus now equipped of a privileged edge - the root - from which the search begins. Consequently, the connections between edges of the hypergraph will be oriented. Thus, certain concepts introduced before will be now expressed with words such as "hyperedge father", "hyperedge son" or "hyperedge brother" like for trees.

4 Algorithmic Exploiting of the CAHs

Several methods have been proposed to exploit properties related to the acyclicity of constraint networks. We have chosen to extend BTD. This method has shown its practical interest and it is easy to extend it to other formalisms [9,20,10]. It relies on the concept of tree-decomposition of graph, but its adaptation to acyclic hypergraphs is easy. BTD explores the search space by assigning the variables according to an order induced by a tree-decomposition (E, T). BTD initially chooses a node E_1 as the root of T. Thus, T is now directed. For a node E_i, $Father(E_i)$ denotes its father node, and $Sons(E_i)$ the set of its sons. BTD carries out a backtracking search, by using an induced order and maintaining an assignment $\mathcal{A}$ of the variables. During the search, BTD assigns the variables V_{E_i} of the current cluster E_i. Assume that it succeeds to extend the current assignment on these variables. If E_i is a leaf of T, the search continues on another part of the problem. If E_i has sons, BTD will continue the search on a son $E_j \in Sons(E_i)$. Note that the assignment $\mathcal{A}[E_i \cap E_j]$ allows in fact to disconnect the problem in two independent subproblems. One independent subproblem is the one located below E_i which is rooted in E_j. Then two possibilities arise. Either, $\mathcal{A}[E_i \cap E_j]$ has never been computed until now and then the search continues on the subproblem rooted in E_j; or, $\mathcal{A}[E_i \cap E_j]$ has been computed before. In case the subproblem rooted in E_j has a consistent extension of $\mathcal{A}[E_i \cap E_j]$, this information has been recorded as a *structural good of E_i with respect to E_j* (i.e. a consistent assignment on the separator $E_i \cap E_j$ which can be consistently extended on the subproblem rooted on E_j). Otherwise, the subproblem rooted in E_j has no consistent extension of $\mathcal{A}[E_i \cap E_j]$. This information has been recorded as *structural nogood of E_i with respect to E_j* (i.e. a consistent assignment on $E_i \cap E_j$ which cannot be extended consistently on the subproblem rooted on E_j). In these two cases, the search will be immediately stopped on this part of the problem, either by a success (good), or by a failure (nogood). The efficiency of BTD is based on these principles. The time complexity of BTD is $O(exp(w+1))$. Its space complexity can be limited to $O(exp(s))$, although this complexity is never reached in practice.

We propose an extension of BTD, called *BDH* (for "Backtracking on Dynamic covering by acyclic Hypergraphs"), and based on dynamic exploitation of the CAH. This approach will make it possible to effectively integrate more dynamic variable ordering heuristics. Such heuristics are necessary to ensure an effective practical solving. In order to make the implementation easier and to guarantee interesting time and space complexity bounds, we will only consider hypergraphs in $\mathcal{CAH}_{H_A}[S]$, with H the constraint hypergraph of the given problem and H_A its reference hypergraph.

Firstly, we must exploit an orientation of the hypergraph by considering edges as nodes and distinguishing an edge E_1 as the root. The neighbouring edges of E_1 are its sons and recursively the neighbouring edges of an edge E_i are its sons except the one on the path from the root to E_i, actually its father. Let E_i be a node, $Father(E_i)$ denotes its father node and $Sons(E_i)$ its son set. The descent of E_i is the set of variables in the edges contained in the acyclic sub-hypergraph rooted on E_i. The subproblem rooted on E_i is the subproblem induced by the variables in the descent in E_i.

BDH has 4 inputs: $\mathcal{A}$ the current assignment, E'_i the current edge, $V_{E'_i}$ the set of unassigned variables in E'_i and H'_A the current hypergraph. This hypergraph is computed recursively. The choice (heuristic) of a new covering hypergraph H''_A in $\mathcal{CAH}_{H_A}[S]$ is made before the beginning of the search on a subproblem. BDH solves recursively the subproblems rooted on E'_i and returns *true* if $\mathcal{A}$ can be consistently extended on this subproblem and *false* otherwise. At the first call, the assignment $\mathcal{A}$ is empty, the subproblem rooted on E_1 corresponds to the whole problem and H_A is the hypergraph of reference. Like in BTD, the order according to which variables are assigned is partially induced by the current hypergraph H'_A. During the search, the covering hypergraph is modified to take into account the evolutions of the problem. While $V_{E'_i}$ is not empty, BDH chooses a variable x in $V_{E'_i}$ (line 16) and a value in its domain (line 18) (if not empty) that verifies all the constraints (included those induced by the nogoods). Then $BDH(\mathcal{A} \cup \{x \leftarrow v\}, E'_i, V_{E'_i} \backslash \{x\}, H'_A)$ is called in the rest of the edge (line 19). When all the variables in E'_i are assigned, the algorithm chooses a son E'_j of the current edge (line 4) (if exists). If $\mathcal{A}[E'_i \cap E'_j]$ is a good (line 5), we know that $\mathcal{A}$ can be consistently extended on $Desc(E'_j)$ (descent of E'_j). Likewise, if E'_i contains a separator $s_k = E_{k_u} \cap E_{k_{u'}}$ of H_A, with $E_{k_{u'}}$ a son of E_{k_u}, such that the subproblem rooted on E'_j is included in the one rooted on $E_{k_{u'}}$ and if $\mathcal{A}[s_k]$ is a good (line 7), we know that $\mathcal{A}$ can be consistently extended on $Desc(E_{k_{u'}})$. So $\mathcal{A}$ can also be consistently extended on $Desc(E'_j)$. Thus a forward-jump is performed and the algorithm keeps on the search on the rest of the problem.

Algorithm 1. BDH($\mathcal{A}, E'_i, V_{E'_i}, H'_A$)

1 **if** $V_{E'_i} = \emptyset$ **then**
2 $\quad$ $Cons \leftarrow true$; $F \leftarrow Sons(E'_i)$
3 $\quad$ **while** $F \neq \emptyset$ **and** $Cons$ **do**
4 $\quad\quad$ Choose E'_j in F ; $F \leftarrow F \backslash \{E'_j\}$
5 $\quad\quad$ **if** $\mathcal{A}[E'_j \cap E'_i]$ *is a good* **then** $Cons \leftarrow true$
6 $\quad\quad$ **else**
7 $\quad\quad\quad$ **if** $\exists s_k = E_{k_u} \cap E_{k_{u'}}$ *in* H_A *s.t.* $E_{k_{u'}} \in Sons(E_{k_u}), s_k \subset E'_i, E'_j \subset Desc(E_{k_{u'}})$ *and* $\mathcal{A}[s_k]$ *is a good* **then** $Cons \leftarrow true$
8 $\quad\quad\quad$ **else**
9 $\quad\quad\quad\quad$ Choose H''_A induced by H'_A and E'_j with root E''_1
10 $\quad\quad\quad\quad$ $Cons \leftarrow BDH(\mathcal{A}, E''_1, E''_1 \backslash (E''_1 \cap E'_i), H''_A)$
11 $\quad\quad\quad\quad$ **if** $Cons$ **then** Record the good $\mathcal{A}[E''_1 \cap E'_i]$
12 $\quad\quad\quad\quad$ **else** Record the nogood $\mathcal{A}[E''_1 \cap E'_i]$
13 $\quad$ **if** $Cons$ **then** $\forall E_u \cap E_v \subset E'_i$, record the good $\mathcal{A}[E_u \cap E_v]$
14 $\quad$ **return** $Cons$
15 **else**
16 $\quad$ Choose $x \in V_{E'_i}$; $d_x \leftarrow D_x$; $Cons \leftarrow false$
17 $\quad$ **while** $d_x \neq \emptyset$ **and** $\neg Cons$ **do**
18 $\quad\quad$ Choose v in d_x ; $d_x \leftarrow d_x \backslash \{v\}$
19 $\quad\quad$ **if** $\mathcal{A} \cup \{x \leftarrow v\}$ *satisfies constraints and nogoods* **then** $Cons \leftarrow BDH(\mathcal{A} \cup \{x \leftarrow v\}, E'_i, V_{E'_i} \backslash \{x\}, H'_A)$
20 $\quad$ **return** $Cons$

Since the nogoods are used like constraints, the assignment $\mathcal{A}$ is stopped in E'_i if it contains a nogood. If E'_i contains no (no)good, then the search continues on the subproblem rooted on E'_j. If $\mathcal{A}$ admits a consistent extension on this subproblem, $\mathcal{A}[E'_i \cap E'_j]$ is recorded as a good (line 11) and *true* is returned, else $\mathcal{A}[E'_i \cap E'_j]$ is recorded as a nogood (line 12) and *false* is returned. If BDH fails to consistently extend $\mathcal{A}$ on E'_i then it returns *false*.

This extension of BTD brings several advantages. It makes it possible to propose a large number of heuristics since we are freed from the initial structure H_A (e.g. the next variable to assign is not necessarily chosen in one single edge E_j). Then BDH can exploit all the (no)goods recorded on all the separators of the reference CAH included separators which are currently included in a larger edge in the current CAH, while BTD with a class 5 order only exploits (no)goods on the intersection of two clusters of the current covering. The space complexity is not modified ($O(exp(s))$) because the search is based on the same set of separators that those of H_A. Finally, its implementation is straightforward because only hypergraphs of $\mathcal{CAH}_{H_A}[S]$ will be considered and these hypergraphs will be obtained by a simple merging of neighboring edges in H_A.

Theorem 6. *BDH is sound, complete and terminates.*

BDH uses a subset of hypergraphs in $\mathcal{CAH}_{H_A}[S]$. The theorem 2 states that there exists $\Delta \geq 0$ such that for all H'_A in this subset, $\alpha' \leq \alpha + \Delta$. The time complexity of the method depends on Δ. Besides, Δ can be parametrized : it is possible to bound the value of Δ and only consider covering hypergraphs in $\mathcal{CAH}_{H_A}[S]$ whose width is bounded by $\alpha + \Delta$. Anyway, the time complexity of BDH is given by the following theorem.

Theorem 7. *The time complexity of BDH is $O(exp(\alpha + \Delta + 1))$.*

Proof. Let (X, D, C, R) be a CSP, H_A the reference CAH of $H = (X, C)$. Let V be a set of $\alpha + \Delta + 1$ variables such that $\exists E_{u_1}, \ldots, E_{u_r}$, a path in H_A (with $r \geq 2$ since $|V| = \alpha + \Delta + 1$ and α is the maximum size of the edges of H_A), $V \subset E_{u_1} \cup \ldots \cup E_{u_r}$ and $E_{u_2} \cup \ldots \cup E_{u_{r-1}} \subsetneq V$ (resp. $E_{u_1} \cap E_{u_2} \subsetneq V$) if $r \geq 3$ (resp. $r = 2$). We will prove first that any assignment on V is computed only twice. $\forall H'_A \in \mathcal{CAH}_{H_A}[S], \exists E'_{i_1}, \ldots, E'_{i_{r'}}$, a path, (with $r' \geq 2$ since the maximum size of the edges in H'_A is $\alpha + \Delta$) such that $V \subset E'_{i_1} \cup \ldots \cup E'_{i_{r'}}$ and $E'_{i_2} \cup \ldots \cup E'_{i_{r'-1}} \subsetneq V$ (resp. $E'_{i_1} \cap E'_{i_2} \subsetneq V$) if $r' \geq 3$ (resp. $r' = 2$). Let $\mathcal{A}$ be an assignment to extend on V. The order in which the variables of $\mathcal{A}$ will be assigned is induced by $H'_A \in \mathcal{CAH}_{H_A}[S]$. We suppose in the following that the edges covering V are ordered w.r.t. the order they are assigned: E'_{i_j} is visited before $E'_{i_{j'}}$ if $j < j'$. Thus E_{u_1} is the first assigned edge among those of the path in H_A covering V and $s_1 = E_{u_1} \cap E_{u_2}$ is included in E'_{i_1} because $E_{u_1} \subset E'_{i_1}$.

If $E'_{i_1} \cap E'_{i_2} = s_1$, the solving of the subproblem rooted on E'_{i_2} with the assignment $\mathcal{A}$ leads to the recording of one (no)good on the separator s_1: $\mathcal{A}[s_1]$. Let $\mathcal{B}$ be a new assignment that we try to extend on V with the same values in $\mathcal{A}[V]$ and $H''_A \in \mathcal{CAH}_{H_A}[S]$ induce the order in which the variables of $\mathcal{B}$ were assigned. $\exists E''_{j_1}, \ldots, E''_{j_{r''}}, r'' \geq 2$, a path in H''_A such that $V \subset E''_{j_1} \cup \ldots \cup E''_{j_{r''}}$ and $E''_{j_2} \cup \ldots \cup E''_{j_{r''-1}} \subsetneq V$ (resp. $E''_{j_1} \cap E''_{j_2} \subsetneq V$) if $r'' \geq 3$ (resp. $r' = 2$). Since $s_1 \subset E''_{j_1}$, as soon as E''_{j_1} is totally assigned, $\mathcal{A}[s_1]$ stops the assignment on V. Thus $\mathcal{A}[V]$ is computed twice only on $\alpha + \Delta$ variables of V at worst.

Now we suppose $E'_{i_1} \cap E'_{i_2} \neq s_1$. If $\mathcal{A}[E'_{i_1} \cap E'_{i_2}]$ can be consistently extended on the subproblem rooted on E'_{i_2} then $\mathcal{A}[E'_{i_1} \cap E'_{i_2}]$ is recorded as a good. Since $s_1 \subset E'_{i_1}$, if this current assignment $\mathcal{A}$ can be consistently extended on the unassigned variables in the subproblem rooted on E'_{i_1} then $\mathcal{A}[s_1]$ is recorded as a good. Otherwise, this assignment cannot be consistently extended on at least one subproblem rooted on $E'_{t'}$ an edge of H'_A such that $E'_{t'} \neq E'_{i_l}, l = 1, \ldots, r'$ and $E'_{t'} \cap E'_{i_1} \neq \emptyset$. Thus $\mathcal{A}[E'_{i_1} \cap E'_{t'}]$ is recorded as a nogood. When we try to extend $\mathcal{B}$ on V, if $\mathcal{A}[s_1]$ is a good then for the same reasons as previously $\mathcal{A}[V]$ is computed twice only on $\alpha + \Delta$ variables of V at worst.

If $\mathcal{A}[s_1]$ is not a good then $\mathcal{A}[E'_{i_1} \cap E'_{t'}]$ is recorded as a nogood. Nevertheless, it is possible to compute $\mathcal{A}[V]$ twice if $(E'_{i_1} \cap E'_{i_2}) \cup (E'_{i_1} \cap E'_{t'}) \subset E''_{j_{r''}}$. If $\mathcal{B}[E''_{j_1} \cap E''_{j_2}]$ can be consistently extended on the subproblem rooted on E''_{j_2} then $\mathcal{B}[E''_{j_1} \cap E''_{j_2}]$ is recorded as a good. Since $s_1 \subset E''_{j_1}$, either $\mathcal{B}[s_1]$ is recorded as a good or $\mathcal{A}[E''_{j_1} \cap E''_{t''}]$ is recorded as a nogood, with $E''_{t''}$ an edge of H''_A such that $E''_{t''} \neq E''_{j_l}, l = 1, \ldots, r''$ and $(E''_{t''} \cap E''_{j_1}) \neq \emptyset$. If $\mathcal{B}[s_1]$ is a good then $\mathcal{B}[V]$ is computed again only on $\alpha + \Delta$ variables of V at worst.

If $\mathcal{B}[E''_{j_1} \cap E''_{t''}]$ is a nogood: two nogoods are recorded on two separators in V. As soon as the first one of these separators is totally assigned, the nogood related to this separator stops the assignment on V. Thus $\mathcal{A}[V]$ is not computed again.

If $\mathcal{B}[E''_{j_1} \cap E''_{j_2}]$ cannot be consistently extended on the subproblem rooted on E''_{j_2} then $\mathcal{B}[E''_{j_1} \cap E''_{j_2}]$ is recorded as a nogood. Since two nogoods are recorded, $\mathcal{A}[V]$ is not computed again.

If $\mathcal{A}[E'_{i_1} \cap E'_{i_2}]$ cannot be consistently extended on the subproblem rooted on E'_{i_2} then we use the same reasoning as in the first part of this proof to demonstrate that $\mathcal{A}[V]$ is computed only twice at worst.

e prove that any assignment on V is computed only twice at worst. Now, we suppose that H is covered by a set of V_i which verifies that V_i contains $\alpha+\Delta+1$ variables such that $\exists E_{u_1}, \ldots, E_{u_r}$, a branch in H (with $r \geq 2$), $V \subset E_{u_1} \cup \ldots \cup E_{u_r}$ and $E_{u_2} \cup \ldots \cup E_{u_{r-1}} \subsetneq V$ (resp. $E_{u_1} \cap E_{u_2} \subsetneq V$) if $r \geq 3$ (resp. $r = 2$). It is sufficient to cover each branch in H by some V_i (they can intersect). On each V_i covering H an assignment is computed twice at worst. The number of possible assignments on V_i is $d^{\alpha+\Delta+1}$. Thus the number of possible assignments on the variables of the problem is bounded by $number_{V_i}.d^{\alpha+\Delta+1}$, with $number_{V_i}$ the number of sets V_i covering H. Since the number of V_i is bounded, then the time complexity of BDH is in $O(exp(\alpha + \Delta + 1))$. □

5 Experimental Study

In this section, we assess the efficiency of BDH on benchmarks (structured random CSPs) presented in [18] with the same empirical protocol and PC. The reference hypergraph is computed thanks to the triangulation of the constraint graph H performed in [18]. We also use the best heuristics given in this paper for an efficient traversal of a hypergraph: *minexp*. Now, we define some heuristics for computing the covering hypergraphs dynamically. In order to reduce the space complexity, we merge edges in the following heuristics only if their intersection size is greater than 5 unless the size of the resulting edge is greater than 1.5α (Δ is bounded by 0.5α). According to the order edges are considered, different covering hypergraphs are computed. We define an order on edges based on the traversal heuristic *minexp*. *Br*: the current edge is merged with its first son (w.r.t. *minexp*), the first son of this one and so on, if the size of their separator is greater than 5 and while the size of the resulting edge is less than 1.5α. *Br + vp*: first, the reference hypergraph is modified such that edges with less than 3 variables not included in their parent are merged to it. Then the heuristic *Br* is used to compute dynamically covering hypergraphs. Table 1 shows the runtime of BDH with heuristics *Br*, *Br + vp*, as well as with heuristics based on *minexp* in the Classes 3 and 4 defined in [18] (with a hypergraph with maximum size of edge intersections bounded by 5 for the Class 4). The Class 4 obtains better results than the Class 3. The heuristic *Br* has very good results, close to Class 4 ones, and succeeds in solving all the instances in $(250, 20, 20, 99, 10, 25, 10)$ while two are not solved in the Class 4 within 1,800 s. Having a better reference hypergraph w.r.t. the solving allows the heuristic *Br + vp* to obtain generally the best results. These experiments highlight the great importance of a good reference hypergraph (w.r.t. the solving) for the search. Furthermore a dynamic exploitation of this hypergraph structure leads to significant improvements. Let us note that BDH with heuristics in Classes 3 and 4 is identical to BTD so it obtains similar results to BTD's ones in [18] for these classes. Moreover, the methods FC and MAC fail in solving most of these instances within 1,800 s. Likewise,

Table 1. Runtime (in s) on random partial structured CSPs: (a) Class 3, (b) Class Br, (c) Class $Br + vp$ and (d) Class 4

CSP (n, d, w, t, s, ns, p)	(a)	(b)	(c)	(d)
(150, 25, 15, 215, 5, 15, 10)	2.04	1.78	1.93	1.76
(150, 25, 15, 237, 5, 15, 20)	8.84	1.23	1.12	1.10
(150, 25, 15, 257, 5, 15, 30)	4.20	1.40	1.30	3.19
(150, 25, 15, 285, 5, 15, 40)	3.08	1.17	0.27	0.23
(250, 20, 20, 107, 5, 20, 10)	14.87	10.49	12.89	13.14
(250, 20, 20, 117, 5, 20, 20)	11.43	6.97	13.18	5.98
(250, 20, 20, 129, 5, 20, 30)	29.24	3.62	2.80	2.87
(250, 20, 20, 146, 5, 20, 40)	12.26	6.99	3.97	7.89
(250, 25, 15, 211, 5, 25, 10)	7.18	4.19	3.79	4.64
(250, 25, 15, 230, 5, 25, 20)	3.86	2.76	1.69	2.36
(250, 25, 15, 253, 5, 25, 30)	3.86	3.73	2.61	2.08
(250, 25, 15, 280, 5, 25, 40)	56.66	13.87	11.88	12.33
(250, 20, 20, 99, 10, 25, 10)	112.88	82.07	78.16	144.20
(500, 20, 15, 123, 5, 50, 10)	7.11	2.23	2.00	3.12
(500, 20, 15, 136, 5, 50, 20)	6.11	3.01	3.23	4.13

TC and so the hypertree-decomposition method do not succeed in solving most of these instances due to an expensive time and space consumption.

6 Conclusion

In this paper, we have proposed a framework based on an old concept: the covering of a problem by acyclic hypergraphs. We have shown that such an approach seems to be more useful than the tree-decomposition based one. In particular, this approach offers more flexibility to the variable ordering heuristic and obtains better theoretical and practical results. Moreover, it turns to be operational in practice, what is not the case for the hypertree-decomposition method and its generalizations.

Firstly, these coverings have been studied theoretically in order to determine their characteristics and properties. After, we have focused our study on a particular class of coverings that preserves time and space complexity results and also improves some of them. One of the major results presented in this paper is the theorem indicating that the addition of Δ variables to offer freedom in a dynamic variable ordering, induces a limited time complexity in $O(exp(\alpha+\Delta+1))$, which outperforms previous results significantly (namely $O(exp(2(w + \Delta + 1) - s^-))$ with s^- the minimum size of separators [18] and $\alpha = w + 1$). Furthermore, we have shown that our approach makes easier the implementation and permits to improve practical efficiency showing thus the practical interest of this approach. This work, introduced within the framework of CSPs, must now be extended to other formalisms like SAT, MAX-SAT, VCSP or probabilistic networks.

Acknowledgments. This work is supported by a "programme blanc" ANR grant (STAL-DEC-OPT project).

References

1. Rish, I., Dechter, R.: Resolution versus Search: Two Strategies for SAT. Journal of Automated Reasoning 24, 225–275 (2000)
2. Huang, J., Darwiche, A.: A structure-based variable ordering heuristic for SAT. In: Proceedings of IJCAI, pp. 1167–1172 (2003)
3. Li, W., van Beek, P.: Guiding Real-World SAT Solving with Dynamic Hypergraph Separator Decomposition. In: Proceedings of ICTAI, pp. 542–548 (2004)
4. Dechter, R., Pearl, J.: Tree-Clustering for Constraint Networks. Artificial Intelligence 38, 353–366 (1989)
5. Dechter, R.: Bucket Elimination: A Unifying Framework for Reasoning. Artificial Intelligence 113(1-2), 41–85 (1999)
6. Darwiche, A.: Recursive conditioning. Artificial Intelligence 126, 5–41 (2001)
7. Beeri, C., Fagin, R., Maier, D., Yannakakis, M.: On the desirability of acyclic database schemes. J. ACM 30, 479–513 (1983)
8. Gottlob, G., Leone, N., Scarcello, F.: Hypertree Decompositions and Tractable Queries. J. Comput. Syst. Sci. 64(3), 579–627 (2002)
9. Terrioux, C., Jégou, P.: Bounded backtracking for the valued constraint satisfaction problems. In: Rossi, F. (ed.) CP 2003. LNCS, vol. 2833, pp. 709–723. Springer, Heidelberg (2003)
10. de Givry, S., Schiex, T., Verfaillie, G.: Exploiting Tree Decomposition and Soft Local Consistency in Weighted CSP. In: Proceedings of AAAI, pp. 22–27 (2006)
11. Robertson, N., Seymour, P.D.: Graph minors II: Algorithmic aspects of tree-width. Algorithms 7, 309–322 (1986)
12. Gottlob, G., Leone, N., Scarcello, F.: A Comparison of Structural CSP Decomposition Methods. Artificial Intelligence 124, 282–343 (2000)
13. Cohen, D., Jeavons, P., Gyssens, M.: A Unified Theory of Structural Tractability for Constraint Satisfaction and Spread Cut Decomposition. In: Proc. of IJCAI, pp. 72–77 (2005)
14. Grohe, M., Marx, D.: Constraint solving via fractional edge covers. In: Proc. of SODA, pp. 289–298 (2006)
15. Jégou, P., Terrioux, C.: Hybrid backtracking bounded by tree-decomposition of constraint networks. Artificial Intelligence 146, 43–75 (2003)
16. Jégou, P., Terrioux, C.: Decomposition and good recording for solving Max-CSPs. In: Proc. of ECAI, pp. 196–200 (2004)
17. Marinescu, R., Dechter, R.: Dynamic Orderings for AND/OR Branch-and-Bound Search in Graphical Models. In: Proc. of ECAI, pp. 138–142 (2006)
18. Jégou, P., Ndiaye, S.N., Terrioux, C.: Dynamic Heuristics for Backtrack Search on Tree-Decomposition of CSPs. In: Proc. of IJCAI, pp. 112–117 (2007)
19. Dechter, R.: Constraint processing. Morgan Kaufmann, San Francisco (2003)
20. Sachenbacher, M., Williams, B.C.: Bounded Search and Symbolic Inference for Constraint Optimization. In: Proc. of IJCAI, pp. 286–291 (2005)

A Compression Algorithm for Large Arity Extensional Constraints*

George Katsirelos and Toby Walsh

NICTA and UNSW
{george.katsirelos,toby.walsh}@nicta.com.au

Abstract. We present an algorithm for compressing table constraints representing allowed or disallowed tuples. This type of constraint is used for example in configuration problems, where the satisfying tuples are read from a database. The arity of these constraints may be large. A generic GAC algorithm for such a constraint requires time exponential in the arity of the constraint to maintain GAC, but Bessière and Régin showed in [1] that for the case of allowed tuples, GAC can be enforced in time proportional to the number of allowed tuples, using the algorithm GAC-SCHEMA.

We introduce a more compact representation for a set of tuples, which allows a potentially exponential reduction in the space needed to represent the satisfying tuples and exponential reduction in the time needed to enforce GAC. We show that this representation can be constructed from a decision tree that represents the original tuples and demonstrate that it does in practice produce a significantly shorter description of the constraint. We also show that this representation can be efficiently used in existing algorithms and can be used to improve GAC-SCHEMA further. Finally, we show that this method can be used to improve the complexity of enforcing GAC on a table constraint defined in terms of forbidden tuples.

1 Introduction

The table constraint is an important constraint that is available in most constraint toolkits. With this, we are able to express directly a set of acceptable assignments to a set of variables. These constraints can be generated from data that has been read from a database in a configuration problem, or may encode users' preferences, among other applications. The table constraint is usually propagated using GAC-SCHEMA, an algorithm proposed in [1] and studied further in [9, 8, 4] among others.

In this paper, we introduce a compression algorithm for table constraints. This algorithm attempts to capture the structure that may exist in a table but

* NICTA is funded by the Australian Government's Department of Communications, Information Technology and the Arts and the Australian Research Council through Backing Australia's Ability and the ICT Centre of Excellence program. Thanks to Fahiem Bacchus and Nina Narodytska for their insightful comments.

C. Bessiere (Ed.): CP 2007, LNCS 4741, pp. 379–393, 2007.

is not explicitly encoded. In order to achieve this, we propose an alternative representation of tuples that may capture an exponential number of tuples in polynomial space, although each compressed tuple may be larger than the arity n of the constraint. GAC-SCHEMA can be adapted easily to work with such compressed tuples. Since the runtime of GAC-SCHEMA is proportional to the number of tuples in the table and we do not increase the cost of examining a single tuple significantly, we can reasonably expect it to perform better after we reduce the number of tuples in this way. The approach can also be extended from the sets of allowed tuples to work also on constraints that are expressed as sets of forbidden tuples. This can potentially deliver great improvements in runtime, as the complexity of GAC-SCHEMA+FORBIDDEN is exponential in the arity of the constraint, whereas with our approach it becomes proportional to the number of forbidden tuples.

The rest of the paper is organized as follows. We first present the necessary background in section 2, then we describe the compression algorithm in section 3. In section 4 we describe how GAC-SCHEMA can be modified to work on compressed tables. In section 5, we extend this approach to work on tables of forbidden tuples. Finally, in section 6 we present experimental confirmation that GAC-SCHEMA using compressed tuples is faster.

2 Background

A constraint satisfaction problem $\mathcal{P}$ is a tuple $(\mathcal{V}, \mathcal{D}, \mathcal{C})$, where $\mathcal{V}$ is a set of variables, $\mathcal{D}$ is a function mapping a variable to a domain of values and $\mathcal{C}$ is a set of constraints. Given $V \in \mathcal{V}$ and $x \in \mathcal{D}(V)$, we say that $V = x$ is an *assignment*, it assigns to V the value x. The goal is to find a set of assignments that *satisfy* the constraints, assigning exactly one value to each variable.

An **assignment set** is a set of assignments $\mathcal{A} = \{X_1 = a_1, \ldots, X_k = a_k\}$ such that no variable is assigned more than one value. We use $scope(\mathcal{A})$ to denote the set of variables assigned values in $\mathcal{A}$. A constraint C consists of an ordered set of variables, $scope(C)$, and a set of assignment sets. Each of these specifies an assignment to the variables of $scope(C)$ that satisfies C. We say that an assignment set $\mathcal{A}$ is **consistent** if it satisfies all constraints it covers: $\forall C. scope(C) \subseteq scope(\mathcal{A}) \Rightarrow \exists \mathcal{A}'.\mathcal{A}' \in C \wedge \mathcal{A}' \subseteq \mathcal{A}$. Thus, a **solution** to the CSP is a consistent assignment set containing all of the variables of the CSP.

We deal here with backtracking search algorithms. Constraint propagation is used during backtracking search to filter the domains of variables so that values that cannot be part of a solution are removed from the domains of unassigned variables. Most solvers maintain generalized arc consistency for the table constraint.

Definition 1 (Support). *A* support *of a constraint C is a set of assignments to exactly the variables in $scope(C)$ such that C is satisfied. A support of C that includes the assignment $V = x$ is called a support of $V = x$ in C.*

Definition 2 (Generalized arc consistency (GAC)). *A constraint C is GAC if there exists a support for all values in the current domains of the variables in $scope(C)$. A problem P is GAC if all of its constraints are GAC.*

Constraints can be defined in several ways, including as a set of satisfying assignments; as a set of non-satisfying assignments; as a predicate; or algebraically. In this paper, we deal with the first two (extensional) representations.

3 The Compression Algorithm

Representation. Let C be a constraint that is represented in extension as a set of satisfying tuples. Let $\mathcal{U}_C = \{U_1, \ldots, U_u\}$ be the set of satisfying tuples that define the constraint, $n = |scope(C)|$ and $d = max_{V \in scope(C)}|\mathcal{D}(V)|$.

The set of tuples $\mathcal{U}_C$ represents the propositional disjunction $c(U_1) \vee \ldots \vee c(U_u)$, where $c(U_i)$ is $V_1 = d_{i1} \wedge \ldots \wedge V_n = d_{in}$, the propositional form of the tuple $U_i = \langle d_{i1}, \ldots, d_{in} \rangle$. From now on, we refer to these as u-tuples. The compression scheme that we propose transforms the constraint into a conjunction of compressed tuples. Each compressed tuple C_i corresponds to a more compact propositional formula $c(C_i)$ of the form $(V_1 = d_{i,1,1} \vee \ldots \vee V_1 = d_{i,1,k_{i,1}}) \wedge \ldots \wedge (V_n = d_{i,n,1} \vee \ldots \vee V_n = d_{i,n,k_{i,n}})$. A compressed tuple can then be written $C_i = \langle (d_{i,1,1}, \ldots, d_{i,1,k_{i,1}}), \ldots, (d_{i,n,1}, \ldots, d_{i,n,k_{i,n}}) \rangle$. A compressed tuple C_i admits any set of assignments that assigns one of $d_{i,1,1}, \ldots, d_{i,1,k_{i,1}}$ to V_1, one of $d_{i,2,1}, \ldots, d_{i,2,k_{i,1}}$ to V_2 and so on. Note that a compressed tuple can represent a potentially exponential number of u-tuples. Specifically it will accept any combination of the $k_{i,1}$ values for V_1, $k_{i,2}$ values for V_2 and so on, so that it represents $k_{i,1}k_{i,2} \ldots k_{i,n}$ u-tuples. We refer to this representation as c-tuples. The set of u-tuples represented by a c-tuple c is written $u(c)$.

This compact representation is not new, as it has been used before in different contexts. Milano and Focacci[3] used it in the context of symmetry breaking, while Katsirelos and Bacchus[6] used it in the context of nogood learning.

Clearly not all sets of tuples can be compressed in this way. For any set of domains, there exist two maximum sets of tuples that cannot be compressed. We derive them by ordering all possible tuples lexicographically and choosing those with an even (odd) index in this ordering. In general, a set of tuples can be expressed more succinctly as c-tuples if there exist clusters of tuples with pairwise Hamming distance 1. For example, consider the set $U_1 = \{\langle 1, 1, 1 \rangle, \langle 1, 2, 2 \rangle\}$. Since the two tuples have Hamming distance 2, this cannot be expressed any more succinctly as a set of c-tuples. The set $U_2 = \{\langle 1, 1, 1 \rangle, \langle 1, 2, 1 \rangle, \langle 1, 2, 2 \rangle\}$ has two pairs of tuples with Hamming distance 1, while the other two have distance two, and can therefore be expressed either as $C_2 = \{\langle (1)(1, 2)(1) \rangle, \langle (1)(2)(2) \rangle\}$ or $C_2' = \{\langle (1)(1)(1) \rangle, \langle (1)(1)(1, 2) \rangle\}$. Finally, by adding one more tuple, the set $U_3 = \{\langle 1, 1, 1 \rangle, \langle 1, 1, 2 \rangle, \langle 1, 2, 1 \rangle, \langle 1, 2, 2 \rangle\}$, all tuples have pairwise Hamming distance 1 and can be expressed as the single c-tuple $\langle (1)(12)(12) \rangle$.

Note this representation cannot improve the efficiency of existing algorithms (e.g. AC-*[12]) for propagating binary constraints. Since the arity of these constraints is two, each compressed tuple can at best represent a quadratic number of uncompressed tuples. However, when AC-* examines a value to determine whether it still has a support, it will only examine the tuples that contain this value. There is a linear number of such tuples, which can each be checked in constant time. On the other hand checking the single compressed tuple is done in linear time also, so in the best case using compressed tuples for binary constraints yields no improvement.

The applicability of the representation is also reduced for tables where some of the variables are functionally dependent on some others. Consider for example the arithmetic constraint $X = Y + Z$. For every value of Y and Z, X is uniquely defined. Thus, we can only attempt to represent more compactly the set of values of Y and Z that yield a specific value of X. The functional dependency of X on Y and Z effectively partitions the space of possibly more compact representations among the different values of X and reduces the arity of the table by 1, as far as the compression scheme is concerned.

Decision trees. We derive a set of c-tuples from the original u-tuples by creating a decision tree $T(U)$ that describes the u-tuples and then deriving c-tuples from the decision tree.

A decision tree is a structure that can describe a Boolean function. Each non-leaf node v of the tree is labeled with a test $l(v)$. Each leaf is labeled with either 1 or 0. In order to evaluate the Boolean function $f(\boldsymbol{x})$, we start at the root and test x against $l(v)$. The left child of v is visited if the test succeeds and right child if it fails. When a leaf is reached, the value of $f(\boldsymbol{x})$ is determined to be the same as the label of the leaf. For convenience, we also label the edge to the left child of v with $l(v)$ and the edge to the right child of v with $\neg l(v)$.

Here we treat a set of tuples $\mathcal{U}_C$ as a function $f_{\mathcal{U}_C} : \{0,1\}^{dn} \rightarrow \{0,1\}$ where the tests are literals that correspond to all dn possible assignments. f evaluates to 1 if its arguments form a tuple in $\mathcal{U}_C$ and 0 otherwise. Let $T(\mathcal{U}_C)$ be a decision tree that describes $f_{\mathcal{U}_C}$. A u-tuple $u \in \mathcal{U}_C$ *agrees* with a node v if v is the root or if it agrees with the parent $P(v)$ of v and v is the left child of $P(v)$ and $l(P(v)) \in u$ or v is the right child of $P(v)$ and $l(P(v)) \notin u$. A tuple $u \in \mathcal{U}_C$ is associated with a node v if it agrees with it and the set of all such tuples is $U(v)$. By this definition, each u-tuple agrees with at most one of the child nodes of v. Additionally, we enforce that each tuple $u \in U(v)$ must agree with exactly one child of v[1] so all the nodes at a level of the tree describe a partition of $\mathcal{U}_C$. If $U(v) = \emptyset$ then the node is *empty*. A literal s (resp. $\neg s$) is *implied* in v iff $\forall u \in U(v)\ s \in u$ (resp. $\forall u \in U(v)\ s \notin u$.)

We can determine the set of tuples $poss(v)$ *described* by a node v by enumerating all the possible u-tuples that agree with v. A node v *completely describes* the set of tuples $U(v)$ associated with it if $poss(v) = U(v)$.

Finally, a c-tuple can be constructed from a node v. Let $S(v)$ be the set of literals that label the edges in the path from v to the root of the tree. $S(v, V)$ is the set of values of V that appear in a literal in $S(v)$ if $\nexists d | V = d \in S(v)$, else it is $\mathcal{D}(V) - \{d\}\,|V = d \in S(v)$. Then the c-tuple $c(v)$ that describes exactly the same tuples as v is $c(v) = \langle (d_1 \in \mathcal{D}(V_1) - S(v, V_1)) \ldots (d_n \in \mathcal{D}(V_n) - S(v, V_n))\rangle$. For example, if $S(v) = \{V_1 = 1, V_2 \neq 2, V_2 \neq 3, V_3 \neq 1, V_3 \neq 2, V_4 = 2\}$ and $\mathcal{D}(V_1) = \mathcal{D}(V_2) = \mathcal{D}(V_3) = \mathcal{D}(V_4) = \{1,2,3,4\}$, then $c(v) = \langle (1)(1,4)(3,4)(2)\rangle$. We see that $c(v)$ admits all u-tuples in $poss(v)$.

---

[1] If this is not true, then $T(\mathcal{U}_C)$ is not a decision tree for the function $f_{\mathcal{U}_C}$.

Proposition 1. *Let v be a node in the decision tree. The c-tuple $c(v)$ admits exactly the tuples $poss(v)$.*

Proof. Let u be a tuple in $poss(v)$. We only need to show that for each variable V, u assigns d to V if and only if $V = d$ is part of $c(v)$. Since $u(c(v))$ contains all combinations of assignments to each variable, this is enough to show $u \in u(c(v)) \iff u \in poss(v)$ for all u. Let u assign the value d to variable V. Since u agrees with v then either $V = d \in S(v)$ or $V \neq d \notin S(v)$. In the first case, $c(v)$ also assigns d to V. In the second case, $c(v)$ will contain all assignments to V in $D(V) - S(v, V)$. But since $V \neq d \notin S(v)$ then $d \in D(V) - S(v, V)$. Therefore $V = d \in c(v)$. □

If v completely describes $U(v)$, $c(v)$ also completely describes $U(v)$ and the u-tuples in $U(v)$ can be replaced by $c(v)$. This means that given a decision tree that represents a set of clauses, the set of c-tuples that are constructed from the non-empty leaves of the tree are exactly equivalent to the original u-tuples.

Example. Let $C_1(V_1, V_2)$ be a constraint such that $D(V_1) = D(V_2) = \{0, \ldots, d-1\}$ and $U(C_1) = \{\langle 0, 1\rangle, \ldots, \langle 0, d-1\rangle, \langle 1, 1\rangle\}$. This constraint allows every tuple where $V_1 = 0$ and the tuple $\langle 1, 1\rangle$. In figure 1(a) we show an optimal decision tree and the tuples associated with each leaf node. We also show in 1(b) and 1(c) the decision trees for $C_2(V_1, V_2)$ with $U(C_2) = \{\langle 0, 0\rangle, \ldots, \langle 0, d-2\rangle, \langle 1, 0\rangle, \ldots, \langle 1, d-2\rangle, \ldots, \langle d-2, 0\rangle, \ldots, \langle d-2, d-2\rangle\}$ and $C_3(V_1, V_2)$ with $U(C_3) = \{\langle 0, 0\rangle, \ldots, \langle 0, d-3\rangle, \langle 1, d-2\rangle, \langle 1, d-1\rangle\}$, respectively. In this figure, a round node v is an internal node of the decision tree and is labeled with the literal that we branch on at v. A square node v is a leaf node and is either labeled by $\emptyset$, in which case is empty, or it completely describes the tuples $U(v)$ and it is labeled with the corresponding c-tuple. The left child of a node that branches on s contains tuples that contain s and thus the edge to the parent is labeled with $=$, while the right child contains tuples that do not contain s and the edge to the parent is labeled with $\neq$.

Constructing decision trees. The problem of constructing a minimum decision tree (with minimum average branch length) is NP-hard [5]. We have tried to solve this problem to optimality using constraint programming techniques, but were unsuccessful in improving significantly over generate-and-test. Thus, we use a heuristic approach.

Algorithms that construct decision trees follow an outline similar to that of TableToDecisionTree, shown in figure 2 (see, for example [10]). This algorithm is straightforward. At each node it checks whether any implied literals exist and extends the tree with a node for each of them. If no implied literals exist, it selects a literal to branch on and then expands each of the child nodes. If it creates an empty node (where $|U(v)| = 0$) or a node that completely describes $U(v)$, it stops. After construction of the tree, a c-tuple is generated from each leaf v that completely describes $U(v)$.

The complexity of the algorithm depends on how much work the splitting heuristic needs to do to select a literal to branch on. Here, we only deal with

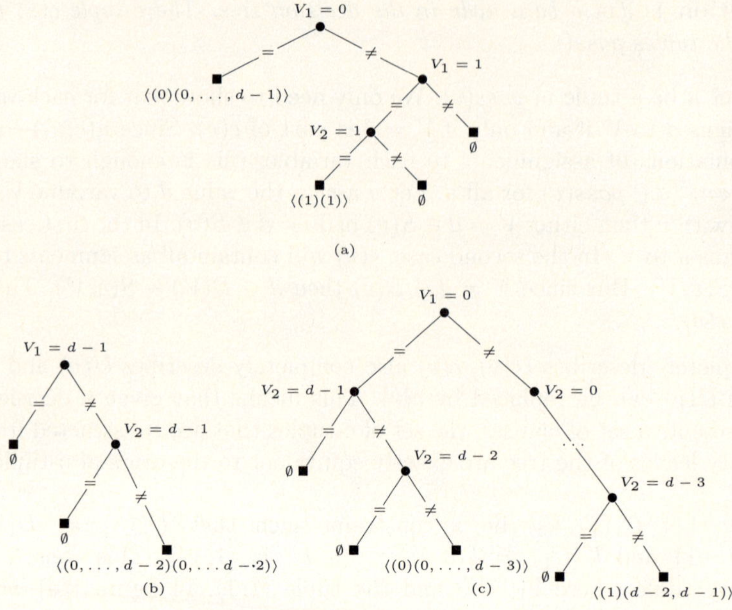

Fig. 1. Optimal decision trees for the constraints (a) C_1, (b) C_2 and (c) C_3. Each node is labeled with the literal on which to branch. Round nodes contain both tuples and non-tuples, while square nodes are leaves and are either empty and labeled with ∅ or contain tuples only and are labeled with a c-tuple.

```
TableToDecisionTree(U_C, v:Node)
    if v is empty ∨ v is complete
        return
    if ∃ s s.t. s is implied
        v' = {Parent:v, EdgeLiteral:s}
        TableToDecisionTree(U(v'), v')
    else
        s = ChooseLiteral(U(v))
        v1 = {Parent:v, EdgeLiteral:s}
        v2 = {Parent:v, EdgeLiteral:¬s}
        TableToDecisionTree(U(v1), v1)
        TableToDecisionTree(U(v2), v2)
```

Fig. 2. Compression algorithm

heuristics that examine the frequency with which literals appear in $U(v)$. If V_l is the set of nodes at level l of the binary tree, then we know that the sets $U(v), v \in V_l$ are a partition of $\mathcal{U}_C$, therefore at each level of the tree each tuple in $\mathcal{U}_C$ will be examined exactly once. Since all tuples have length n, the cost of choosing a literal to branch on for every node at a level is $O(|\mathcal{U}_C|n)$. The depth of the tree is bounded by the total number of literals nd, since a literal cannot be branched on more than once in the same branch. Thus the total cost of building the tree is $O(|\mathcal{U}_C|n^2d)$. Note however that this assumes that no compression can be achieved on the table. In practice the runtimes are often much lower.

Splitting heuristics. The splitting heuristics we will examine are based on counting the frequency with which literals appear in $U(v)$. We write $f(s,v)$ for the number of times s appears in a tuple in $U(v)$ and $f(\neg s,v) = |U(v)| - f(s,v)$. We describe the following heuristics.

- MaxFreq. This heuristic chooses the literal with maximum $f(s,v)$ (or minimum $f(\neg s,v)$). The reasoning is that the c-tuples that will be constructed in the subtree containing s have a better chance of representing more u-tuples, since s appears often. For example, consider the constraint C_1 discussed earlier, with $U(C_1) = \{\langle 0,0\rangle,\ldots,\langle 0,d\rangle,\langle 1,1\rangle\}$, with an optimal decision tree shown in figure 1(a). Since $V_1 = 0$ appears d times, MaxFreq will make the optimal choice at the root. The branch that contains $V_1 = 0$ completely describes all u-tuples for which $V_1 = 0$, thus the algorithm stops expanding at this point. The other branch only contains the tuple $\langle 1,1\rangle$ which will be left uncompressed. Thus this heuristic finds an optimal branching for this example. On the other hand, consider the constraint C_2 with $U(C_2) = \{\langle 0,0\rangle,\ldots,\langle 0,d-2\rangle,\langle 1,0\rangle,\ldots,\langle 1,d-2\rangle,\ldots,\langle d-2,0\rangle,\ldots,\langle d-2,d-2\rangle\}$, whose optimal decision tree is shown in figure 1(b). Each literal in this set of u-tuples appears exactly $d-1$ times, except for $V_1 = d-1$ and $V_2 = d-1$ which do not appear at all, so MaxFreq chooses one of those that appear $d-1$ times arbitrarily. Assume it chooses $V_1 = 0$. On the positive branch, each literal of V_2 appears once except for $V_2 = d-1$, so once again MaxFreq chooses one arbitrarily. This continues until each c-tuple containing $V_1 = 0$ is placed on a separate branch, therefore no compression occurs. On the negative branch of $V_1 = 0$, each literal of V_1 appears $d-1$ times and each literal of V_2 appears $d-2$ times, so another literal of V_1 is chosen and the process repeats so that no compression occurs. However, $U(C_2)$ is compressible to the single c-tuple $\langle (0,\ldots,d-2)(0,\ldots,d-2)\rangle$, so clearly MaxFreq does not perform optimally in every case.
- MinFreq. This chooses the literal with the minimum $f(s,v)$. If many u-tuples are similar but contain many different assignments to a single variable V, then branching on all the values of V that *do not* appear in the u-tuples will quickly lead to a subtree that contains these similar u-tuples that can hopefully be compressed efficiently. It is easy to see that for the constraint C_2 mentioned above MinFreq will find the optimal compression. On the other hand, it will not do so for the constraint C_1.
- MinMinFreq. This chooses the literal with the minimum $min(f(s,v), f(\neg s,v))$. This is an attempt to combine MinFreq and MaxFreq, by using $f(s,v)$ and $f(\neg s,v)$ respectively as *measures* of the fitness of a literal. At each node, the best literals chosen by both heuristics are compared against each other using this measure and the best one is branched on. We can see that both C_1 and C_2 are compressed optimally using MinMinFreq. However, for

the constraint C_3 with $U(C_3) = \{\langle 0,0\rangle, \ldots, \langle 0, d-3\rangle, \langle 1, d-2\rangle, \langle 1, d-1\rangle\}$ (decision tree in figure 1(c)), we have $f(V_1 = 0) = d-2, f(V_1 = 1) = 2$ and $f(V_2 = k) = 1$ for all k. In order to produce the optimum compression $\{\langle (0)(0, \ldots, d-3)\rangle, \langle (1)(d-2, d-1)\rangle\}$, the heuristic needs to branch either on the literal $V_0 = 0$ or on $V_0 = 1$. However, MinMinFreq will not choose either of these and neither will MinFreq. MaxFreq will choose the correct literal to branch on, but we showed that it performs worse in C_2.

- MinDiff. This chooses the literal with the minimum $|f(s, v) - f(\neg s, v)|$. This heuristic tries to create a more balanced tree, therefore a smaller one. MinDiff will perform optimally on C_1 and C_3 but not C_2.
- MaxGain. This is the heuristic used by ID3 [10] and C4.5 [11]. It calculates first the information content $I(v)$ for the current node. For each literal s, it calculates the expected information $E(s)$ of the subtree that will be created by branching on s and chooses s so that $I(v) - E(s)$ is maximum. This means that it chooses the literal that gains the most information. The decision tree under the node v is treated as a source of a message 'T' or 'N' for tuples that belong or do not belong, respectively, to $U(v)$. Then the information of that tree is

$$I(v) = -\frac{|U(v)|}{|poss(v)|}\log_2\frac{|U(v)|}{|poss(v)|} - \frac{|poss(v) - U(v)|}{|poss(v)|}\log_2\frac{|poss(v) - U(v)|}{|poss(v)|}$$

The expected information required if we branch on the literal s is

$$E(s) = \frac{|poss(v \cup \{s\}))|}{|poss(v)|} I(v \cup \{s\}) + \frac{|poss(v \cup \{\neg s\})|}{|poss(v)|} I(v \cup \{\neg s\})$$

where $n \cup \{s\}$ and $n \cup \{\neg s\}$ are the child nodes of v resulting by branching on s.

Since $I(v)$ is common to all literals, MaxGain chooses the literal that minimizes $E(s)$.

Empirical results. We implemented and tested this compression algorithm on all the instances from the 2005 CSP competition [13] that contain non-binary tables. We tested for compression efficiency and runtime performance. We omitted binary instances and binary table constraints in non-binary instances, because as we already pointed out, modern algorithms for maintaining arc consistency in binary constraints cannot benefit from compression.

In table 1 we show the compression achieved with three of the heuristics we mentioned (MinMinFreq, MinDiff and MaxGain) for some of the instances we tested. For each instance, we report the number of tables that were compressed, the average number of tuples t and the average number of literals l per table and for each splitting heuristic the ratios t/t_c, l/l_c and the average time to compress a table. The ratio t/t_c is the ratio of the number of tuple in the original table versus the number of tuples in the compressed table, while l/l_c is the ratio of the total number of literals in the expression. Note that for each constraint C, l is simply $t \cdot |scope(C)|$. The ratio t/t_c gives an indication to how

Table 1. Compression efficiency for instances from the 2005 CSP competition. The best ratios t/t_C and l/l_C are highlighted.

				MinMinFreq			MinDiff			MaxGain		
Instance	# Tables	Avg t	Avg l	t/t_c	l/l_c	time	t/t_c	l/l_c	time	t/t_c	l/l_c	time
Golomb-12-sat	4	2631.25	7893.75	**1.0**	**1.0**	1.16	**1.0**	**1.0**	2.24	**1.0**	**1.0**	2.72
Golomb-12-unsat	8	4776.88	14330.62	**1.0**	**1.0**	2.05	**1.0**	**1.0**	3.15	**1.0**	**1.0**	4.36
0-TSP-10	3	7651.0	22953.0	**1.0**	**1.0**	12.45	**1.0**	**1.0**	24.78	**1.0**	**1.0**	26.46
series10	1	90.0	270.0	1.0	1.0	0.0	**1.36**	**1.22**	0.0	**1.36**	**1.22**	0.0
cril_sat_nb_0	27	1482.11	15076.22	**19.65**	**13.14**	0.01	1.98	1.73	0.03	5.25	4.21	0.01
cril_unsat_nb_6	9	281.33	1125.33	**50.6**	**18.06**	0.0	29.03	9.6	0.0	38.36	12.76	0.0
cril_unsat_nb_7	9	292.67	1170.67	**61.61**	**20.04**	0.0	40.28	11.58	0.0	45.56	13.59	0.0
gr_55_11_a3	1.0	1540	4620.0	**1.0**	**1.0**	0.17	**1.0**	**1.0**	0.09	**1.0**	**1.0**	0.23
random-3-20-20-60-632-forced-1	60	2944.0	8832.0	3.14	1.9	0.06	6.85	2.32	0.04	**7.18**	**2.35**	0.06
random-3-24-24-76-632-forced-1	74	5001.28	15003.85	3.6	1.99	0.13	8.15	2.4	0.07	**8.48**	**2.42**	0.11
random-3-28-28-93-632-forced-1	91	7967.01	23901.03	4.13	2.08	0.25	9.56	2.47	0.15	**9.97**	**2.49**	0.21
renault-merged	89	2182.76	14455.07	7.32	4.08	0.04	**51.92**	**7.65**	0.01	14.34	5.53	0.04

efficient the compression was. l/l_c is an accurate representation of the memory savings that have been achieved.

We show only one representative instance from most families. The results tend to be the same for all instances of one family, as they tend to reuse the same tables. The exception to this is the Golomb ruler problem where the tables express arithmetic tables over domains that grow with the number of marks on the ruler, therefore the tables themselves grow as well. We show results for the largest satisfiable and largest unsatisfiable instance of the Golomb ruler problem. The `cril` family of problem also does not follow this pattern, because it is a collection of instances from different domains.

We see that not all domains are amenable to applying our technique. This is to be expected, as it is possible that the tuples cannot be more compactly represented. On the other hand, for three domains the technique works very well and for those we present results for more instances. In the domains where the technique achieves no reduction in the number of tuples, the overhead of attempting and failing to compress the tables is generally small. The only families where it is even noticeable are the Golomb ruler and travelling salesman problems, in which case it takes 20 seconds and 60 seconds, respectively, to examine all tables of the instance. Moreover, in many cases the tables are shared among many instances and therefore compression can be considered an offline procedure that can be performed once before solving a set of instances.

In the three domains where compression achieves improvement, we see that no splitting heuristic dominates. Moreover, the differences can be dramatic. In the `cril` family the heuristic MinMinFreq outperforms both the other ones and in the instance `cril_sat_nb_0` the ratio l/l_c is 7 times higher than for MinDiff and 3 times higher than for MaxGain. On the other hand, in the `renault` configuration problem, MinDiff performs best and in random problems MaxGain is the better choice.

In our experiments, we also tried to use the C4.5 algorithm [11]. Although the ideas for the construction of decision trees are similar, C4.5 was created with machine learning applications in mind, where the purpose is to improve the ability of the decision tree to correctly classify tuples that have not yet been seen. As a result, the software is not suitable for our purposes. We believe however that our use of the MaxGain heuristic captures the major ideas behind C4.5.

4 Modifying GAC-Schema

The GAC-Schema algorithm was proposed in three different variations: GAC-Schema+Allowed, GAC-Schema+Forbidden, GAC-Schema+Predicate. The first two are intended to work with constraints expressed in extension by satisfying or conflicting tuples, respectively. The third works with constraints defined by a predicate which succeeds for satisfying complete assignments. Here, we only deal with GAC-Schema+Allowed (to which we refer simply as GAC-Schema). In section 5, we will also deal with GAC-Schema+Forbidden.

GAC-Schema uses the procedure seekNextSupport to identify a support for a value $V = x$. seekNextSupport iterates over the tuples in the table that contain $V = x$ until it finds a support for $V = x$, i.e. a tuple such that none of its values have been pruned. In order to minimize the number of checks performed by seekNextSupport, GAC-Schema maintains a *current support* for each unpruned value. A current support for $X = a$ is a tuple that contains $X = a$ and is *valid*. In the context of uncompressed tuples, a tuple is valid if none of the values that it contains are pruned. It maintains this information in three data structures: $S(U)$ is the set of values that are currently supported by the tuple U; $S_C(X = a)$ is the set of tuples that contain $X = a$ and are currently supports for some values; $last_C(X = a)$ is the last support of value $X = a$ returned by seekNextSupport. When a value $X = a$ is pruned, new support has to be found for values that have lost their current support because of this pruning. These values are in the set $P = \bigcup_{U \in S_c(X=a)} S(U)$. For each value $Y = b \in P$, a new support is first sought among $S_c(Y = b)$ and then among tuples that contain $Y = b$ and have index higher than $last_C(Y = b)$. If no support is found by either procedure, the value is pruned. If a support U is found in $S_C(Y = b)$, then $Y = b$ is placed in $S(U)$. If a support σ is found by seekNextSupport, it becomes the new current support for $Y = b$ and the data structures are updated accordingly. Multidirectionality is exploited by placing the new support σ in $S_C(Z = c)$ for every other value in σ.

In order to work on a table of compressed tuples, we first modify the definition of a valid tuple, which is needed by seekNextSupport. A c-tuple is invalid when there exists a variable in the scope of the constraint such that all its values in the c-tuple are pruned. Note that this allows for a simple but significant optimization: if all values of a variable appear in a compressed tuple, we can simply avoid checking them altogether. However, the complexity of checking whether a c-tuple is valid is $O(nd)$, as a c-tuple can contain many values from each variable, as opposed to $O(n)$ for a u-tuple. On the other hand, the greater the length of the c-tuple, the more u-tuples it represents, so we can expect that the greater complexity of performing a single constraint check is balanced by the fact that we need to perform fewer of them.

In order to have GAC-Schema work with c-tuples, we need to note the following. First, when we prune a value $X = a$, it is not necessary that all tuples in $S_C(X = a)$ will be invalid, as they may contain other values of X that have not been pruned. Second, since a c-tuple is valid as long as one value from each variable is not pruned, it is not necessary to examine the tuple for validity every time one of the values it contains is pruned. We see that the structure $S_C(X = a)$ serves two purposes: it identifies tuples that may become invalid if $X = a$ is pruned and it identifies tuples that have already been found to support other values and may be a support for $X = a$. In the case of uncompressed tuples, the two are necessarily identical, as the pruning of a value $X = a$ will invalidate all tuples $X = a$ appears in. In the case of compressed tuples, we need to maintain two different structures for the two purposes. The first one is called W_C and the second S_C. W_C will always be a (not necessarily strict) subset of S_C. Every time a tuple σ is identified as a support for a variable, we choose one value $X = a \in \sigma$ from each variable in the scope of the constraint and place σ in $W_C(X = a)$. This optimization is similar in spirit to the watch literal technique used in SAT solvers to unit propagate propositional clauses.

5 GAC-Schema with Forbidden Tuples

Recall that in constructing a decision tree to compress a set of tuples, we view this set as a Boolean function that evaluates to 1 if its arguments form a tuple in U and 0 otherwise. If we were to use this method on a constraint that is represented as a set of forbidden tuples, we would have no useful way of using the compressed tuples to perform propagation, as the instantiation of the function seekNextSupport for GAC-Schema+Forbidden does not iterate over the tuples, but needs to check whether or not an arbitrary tuple is forbidden.

Note however that we can convert between the two equivalent representations of a constraint as a set of forbidden or allowed tuples. A constraint on variables $V_1, \ldots, V_n$ with domains $D_1, \ldots, D_n$ represented as the set of forbidden tuples U is equivalent to a constraint represented by the set of allowed tuples $D_1 \times \ldots \times D_n - U$. In terms of the corresponding Boolean function, this means that the function evaluates to 1 if its arguments form a tuple not in U and 0 otherwise. This suggests that we can use our compression method to compress the equivalent constraint that is expressed as a set of satisfying tuples, without actually generating the satisfying tuples. This is done by generating c-tuples from the leaves that are empty, as opposed to those that completely describe $U(v)$. These compressed tuples are allowed and can be used with GAC-Schema with c-tuples.

For example, consider the ternary table constraint $C(V_1, V_2, V_3)$, with $D(V_1) = D(V_2) = D(V_3) = \{1, 2, 3\}$ that disallows the tuples $\langle 1, 2, 3\rangle$ and $\langle 3, 2, 1\rangle$. The optimal decision tree for this table is shown in figure 3. In this decision tree, the leaves that would normally contain the two tuples are instead labeled with the empty set, while the leaves that would be empty are used to construct c-tuples. The resulting set of allowed c-tuples is $\{\langle (1,2,3)(1,3)(1,2,3)\rangle, \langle (1)(2)(1,2)\rangle, \langle (2)(2)(1,2,3)\rangle, \langle (3)(2)(2,3)\rangle\}$.

Even though the number of allowed tuples may be exponentially larger than the number of forbidden tuples, the number of allowed compressed tuples will not be significantly bigger than the number of forbidden tuples.

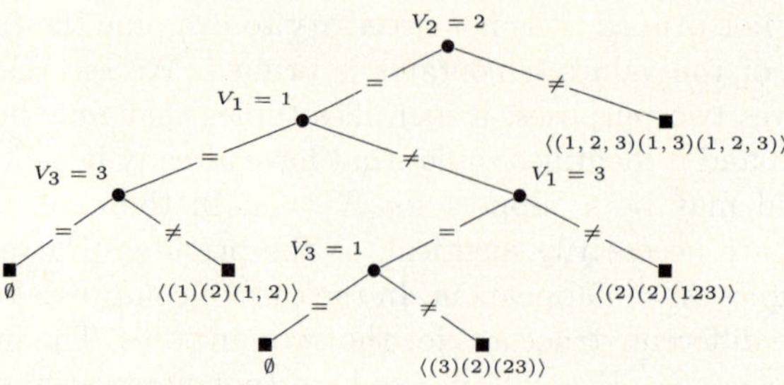

Fig. 3. Constructing a set of allowed c-tuples from a table constraint with forbidden tuples

Proposition 2. *Let C be a constraint on variables $V_1, \ldots, V_n$ with domains $D_1 = \ldots = D_n = D$ and $|D| = d$, represented as a set of forbidden tuples F. The size of the set C of compressed tuples generated from the empty leaves of the decision tree $T(F)$ is $O(nd|F|)$.*

Proof. Consider a leaf v that completely describes $F(n)$. Assume that at every node along this branch, following the alternative branch leads to an empty leaf. This is the maximum number of empty leaves that may correspond to each complete leaf. Since the maximum length of any branch is nd and there exist at most $|F|$ non-empty branches (in which case the set cannot be compressed), the maximum number of empty leaves is $O(nd|F|)$. □

Note that this upper bound is a worst case scenario, which assumes that the decision tree is maximal, thus the set of allowed u-tuples that represent the constraint cannot be compressed.

6 Empirical Results

We implemented the algorithm GAC3.1r [7] with and without compressed tuples. We compared the runtime for searching 100,000 nodes (for random problems) or 1 million nodes (for the rest) for table constraints with compressed and uncompressed tuples, in the subset of families from section 3 where our heuristic algorithms were able to produce a smaller representation. We present our findings for some representative instances in table 2. We used the best splitting heuristic for each instance, as determined by the results in table 1.

For each instance we present the number of variables, number of constraints, number of tables (which may differ from the number of constraints, as many constraint may share the same table,) the ratio t/t_c and l/l_c and finally the time needed to search 100,000 nodes and the number of constraint checks, in millions.

We see that in random problems using the compressed representation is uniformly better. The reduction in the number of constraint checks corresponds with the reduction in runtime over the simple version of the algorithm. In the `cril` instances, the picture is somewhat different. While the reduction in the

Table 2. CPU time and number of constraint checks needed to search 100,000 nodes (for random problems) or 1,000,000 (for the cril instances) using both the uncompressed and compressed representation for table constraints, in instances from the 2005 CSP competition

						w/compression		w/out compression	
Instance	#Vars	#Cons	#Tables	t/t_c	l/l_c	Time	#CC$\times 10^6$	Time	#CC$\times 10^6$
random-3-20-20-60-632-forced-1	20	60	60	6.85	2.32	**76.26**	994.90	182.32	2010.40
random-3-20-20-60-632-forced-8	20	58	58	6.74	2.30	**73.48**	945.76	164.42	1935.04
random-3-20-20-60-632-forced-9	20	59	59	6.78	2.31	**120.65**	1165.17	234.57	2339.77
random-3-24-24-76-632-forced-1	24	74	74	8.15	2.40	**158.87**	1661.22	407.64	3207.54
random-3-24-24-76-632-forced-8	24	76	76	8.28	2.42	**207.80**	2033.63	503.94	4659.31
random-3-24-24-76-632-forced-9	24	74	74	8.12	2.40	**97.79**	1132.62	288.58	2922.41
random-3-28-28-93-632-forced-1	28	91	91	9.56	2.47	**268.93**	2495.32	739.16	6297.27
random-3-28-28-93-632-forced-8	28	92	92	9.67	2.48	**245.00**	2375.20	560.28	5470.00
random-3-28-28-93-632-forced-9	28	91	91	9.59	2.48	**494.69**	4543.70	1046.52	6440.60
cril_sat_nb_0	108	35	27	19.65	13.14	**22.57**	127.14	159.57	362.49
cril_unsat_nb_6	36	153	9	50.60	18.06	**10.99**	11.25	11.77	66.89
cril_unsat_nb_7	36	153	9	61.61	20.04	**19.21**	25.76	20.08	130.79

number of constraint checks is significant, the difference in runtime does not reflect this. In the instance `cril_sat_nb_0`, the number of constraint checks is reduced by a factor of 13, but the runtime is only reduced by a factor of 7. In the other two instances, the number of constraint checks is reduced by a factor of 6, but the runtime is approximately the same with and without compression. Part of the reason for this is that these instances contain other constraints, so the improvement in speed is not apparent. For example, we found by profiling, that propagating the table constraints for the `cril_unsat_nb_6` only took approximately 15% of the total runtime for the uncompressed problem, therefore the improvement of .8 seconds actually corresponds to a 55% improvement in the time spent propagating the table constraints. This is still less than expected based on the number of constraint checks performed, however.

Finally, we also ran the `renault` configuration problem with both compressed and uncompressed tuples. In that problem, propagation takes too little time and thus in tests to find the first 2 million solutions, both algorithms performed identically. In profiling the programs, we found that propagation takes less 1% of the total runtime and the majority of the time is instead spent on other aspects of backtracking search.

7 Related Work

Our work on constructing small decision trees overlaps with similar work that has been performed in machine learning [10, 11]. As we mentioned earlier, the decision trees constructed for machine learning applications are intended to be used to classify as yet unseen tuples. Misclassification of some tuples is acceptable if it means keeping the size of the decision tree smaller. In our case, all tuples are known and we cannot accept any error in the classification.

GAC-Schema has been studied extensively. The work however has focused on more efficient search of the set of supporting tuples. Lhomme and Régin proposed the holotuple data structure [9] to avoid checking some tuples. Lecoutre and Szymanek proposed using binary search to locate a valid support [8]. Both these techniques are essentially orthogonal to using compressed tuples and can be used in conjunction with them.

In [4], it is proposed to use tries to represent the set of satisfying tuples. The tries can be viewed as a way to compress the shared prefixes of tuples. Even though tries have one leaf per tuple, finding a support may skip up to d^{n-m} invalid tuples if it encounters a pruned value at level $m < n$ of the trie. However, tries are restricted to having the same ordering along every branch, while our method of constructing decision trees is not restricted in this way. Moreover, in our method many branches may be combined (as we perform binary branching on the decision trees.) Thus, the reduction in the number of constraint checks that can be achieved using our method may be significantly better.

Finally, in [2] it is proposed to build a DAG where each node represents a range of values for a variable. A path from the root to a leaf in the DAG is equivalent to one c-tuple. However, no method is proposed to derive this DAG from an arbitrary set of tuples.

As far as we are aware, we are also the first to propose using this technique to propagate table constraints with sets of forbidden tuples.

8 Conclusions

We have presented an algorithm for compressing table constraints, for both the case when the table consists of allowed tuples and when the table consists of forbidden tuples. The representation produced contains c-tuples, each of which may correspond to exponentially many uncompressed tuples. Existing algorithms that enforced GAC on tables with allowed tuples can be adapted to work with c-tuples while maintaining the central structure of the algorithm that involves examining (c-)tuples for validity. As a result, compression can also deliver exponential time savings. Moreover, compression allows us to enforce GAC on tables with forbidden tuples in time polynomial in the number of forbidden tuples, while the best result so far has been exponential in the arity of the constraint. Finally, we demonstrated that this technique works in practice, using instances from the 2005 CSP Competition. Moreover, instances where compression does not work can be detected relatively quickly.

Besides improving table constraint propagation, this work raises some questions. First, it appears that the heuristics developed in machine learning for creating small decision trees are not necessarily better than simpler alternatives. It would be interesting to develop better heuristics to create smaller trees. Alternatively, more effort could be put into finding better solutions to this NP-hard problem by utilizing constraint programming techniques. Finally, we intend to evaluate our methods on table constraints with forbidden tuples and integrate with other improvements to the GAC-Schema algorithm, such as the holotuples data structure of [9].

References

[1] Bessière, C., Régin, J.-C.: Arc consistency for general constraint networks: Preliminary results. In: Proceedings of the Sixteenth International Joint Conference on Artificial Intelligence, Nagoya, Japan, pp. 398–404 (1997)

[2] Carlsson, M.: Filtering for the case constraint. Talk given at Advanced School on Global Constraints, Samos, Greece (2006)

[3] Focacci, F., Milano, M.: Global cut framework for removing symmetries. In: Walsh, T. (ed.) CP 2001. LNCS, vol. 2239. Springer, Heidelberg (2001)

[4] Gent, I.P., Jefferson, C., Miguel, I., Nightingale, P.: Data structures for generalised arc consistency for extensional constraints. In: Proceedings of the Twenty Second Conference on Artificial Intelligence (to appear 2007)

[5] Hyafil, L., Rivest, R.L.: Constructing optimal binary decision trees is np-complete. Information Processing Letters 5(1), 15–17 (1976)

[6] Katsirelos, G., Bacchus, F.: Generalized nogoods in CSPs. In: Proceedings of the Twentieth National Conference on Artificial Intelligence (2005)

[7] Lecoutre, C., Hemery, F.: A study of residual supports in arc consistency. In: Proceedings of the Twentieth International Joint Conference on Artificial Intelligence, pp. 125–130 (2007)

[8] Lecoutre, C., Szymanek, R.: Generalized arc consistency for positive table constraints. In: Benhamou, F. (ed.) CP 2006. LNCS, vol. 4204. Springer, Heidelberg (2006)

[9] Lhomme, O., Régin, J.-C.: A fast arc consistency algorithm for n-ary constraints. In: Proceedings of the Twentieth National Conference on Artificial Intelligence (AAAI-05) (2005)

[10] Quinlan, J.: Induction of decision trees. Machine Learning 1, 81–106 (1986)

[11] Quinlan, J.: Programs for Machine Learning. Morgan Kaurmann Publishers, San Francisco (1993)

[12] Régin, J.-C.: AC-*: A configurable, generic and adaptive arc consistency algorithm. In: van Beek, P. (ed.) CP 2005. LNCS, vol. 3709, pp. 505–519. Springer, Heidelberg (2005)

[13] van Dongen, M., Lecoutre, C., Wallace, R., Zhang, Y.: 2005 CSP solver competition. In: van Dongen, M. (ed.) Second International Workshop on Constraint Propagation and Implementation (2005)

Valid Inequality Based Lower Bounds for WCSP

Mohand Ou Idir Khemmoudj and Hachemi Bennaceur

LIPN - UMR 7030 CNRS - Université Paris 13 F-93430 Villetaneuse, France*
{MohandOuIdir.Khemmoudj,Hachemi.Bennaceur}@lipn.univ-paris13.fr

Abstract. Most of efficient WCSP solving methods are based on arc consistency notion used to transform a WCSP into an equivalent one easier to solve. There are several forms of arc consistency : AC* [9], DAC* [8], FDAC* [8], EDAC* [4]. Recently, an Optimal Soft Arc Consistency (OSAC) was proposed [2]. But this technique requires much computing time since it is based on a large linear program. We propose in this work a new valid transformation based on modeling of the WCSP as a linear program easier to solve than the computing of OSAC. Preliminary experiments on random and structured problems are presented, showing the advantage of our technique.

1 Introduction

The WCSP problem (*Weighted Constraint Satisfaction Problem*) consists in satisfying in an optimal way a set of weighted constraints. Most of WCSP solving methods are based on arc consistency notion used to transform a WCSP to an equivalent one easier to solve. In this purpose, several forms of arc consistency were proposed : AC* [9], DAC* [8], FDAC* [8], EDAC* [4]. Recently, an Optimal Soft Arc Consistency (OSAC) [2] was proposed. Its disadvantage is that it requires much computing time since it is based on a large linear program.

We present in this paper a new equivalence preserving transformation for binary WCSP. Our technique is based on valid inequality notion. We will say that a system of inequalities is valid if its optimal value is lower than the cost of an optimal solution of the WCSP. We demonstrate that it is always possible to build a valid system, composed from one inequality per constraint of the WCSP, whose value is equal to the OSAC lower bound. The construction of such optimal system being expensive in computing time, we propose then another way to build a good valid system and not necessarily optimal. It is obtained by solving the continuous relaxation of an Integer Linear Program equivalent to the WCSP, itself based on valid inequalities.

We empirically evaluated our technique on instances of the Radio Link Frequency Assignment Problem and on random Max-CSPs. The results show clearly the practical advantage of this technique. In addition to these interesting practical results, we present theoretical results establishing links between arc consistency techniques and Linear Programming. This leads to open new research prospects to develop WCSP solving methods combining local consistency techniques and Linear Programming.

* This work is supported in part by the French Electricity Board (EDF).

C. Bessiere (Ed.): CP 2007, LNCS 4741, pp. 394–408, 2007.

2 Preliminaries

In this section, we present the WCSP formalism and its graphic representation used in this paper. Then, we describe a mathematical formulation of a WCSP known in the CSP literature.

2.1 WCSP Formalism

Formally, a binary WCSP is defined by a quadruplet (X, D, C, Sv) where :

1. $Sv = (\{0, 1, ..., h\}, \oplus, \leq)$ is a *valuation structure* :
   - $\leq$ is the usual order relation among integers;
   - h is an integer (it is an upper bound);
   - $\oplus$ is an operation used to combine costs :
     - $a \oplus b = \min(a + b, h)$;
     - $a \ominus b = \begin{cases} a - b \text{ if } a \neq h; \\ h \quad \text{otherwise} \end{cases}$
2. $X = \{X_1, X_2, \ldots, X_n\}$ is a set of n variables;
3. $D = \{D_1, D_2, \ldots, D_n\}$ is a set of n domains where each D_i is the set of $d_i \leq d$ possible values for the variable X_i;
4. C is a set composed from a constant constraint $c_\emptyset$, n unary weighted constraints $c_1, c_2, ..., c_n$ and e weighted binary constraints[1]. The unary and binary constraints are cost functions : a unary constraint c_i associates a cost $c_i(k) \in \{0, 1, ..., h\}$ for each value $k \in D_i$ of the variable X_i. A binary constraint c_{ij} associates a cost $c_{ij}(k, l) \in \{0, 1, ..., h\}$ for each pair $(k, l) \in D_i \times D_j$. When a constraint $c \in C$ assigns cost h, it means that c forbids the corresponding assignment, otherwise it is permitted by c with the corresponding cost.

The cost of an assignment $I = (v_1, v_2, ..., v_n) \in \prod_{X_i \in X} D_i$, denoted $V(I)$, is the sum of all costs : $V(I) = c_\emptyset \oplus \sum_{X_i \in X} c_i(v_i) \oplus \sum_{c_{ij} \in C} c_{ij}(v_i, v_j)$.

An assignment I is consistent if $V(I) < h$. The problem is to find a consistent assignment with minimum cost, which is NP-hard.

In this paper we assume that h is infinite. In this case, the laws $\oplus$ and $\ominus$ are equivalent to the usual laws of addition and subtraction.

2.2 Graphic Representation of a WCSP

The WCSP can be represented by a graph $G(V, A)$ where V is the set of its vertices and A is the set of its edges. The set V is composed from n subsets $V_1, V_2, ..., V_n$. Each subset V_i contains a vertex (i, k) for each value $k \in D_i$ ($V_i = \{(i, k) : k = 1, ..., d_i\}$). The vertex (i, k) is labeled by $c_i(k)$ if $c_i(k) > 0$. There exists an edge in A between two vertices (i, k) and (j, l) if $c_{ij} \in C$ and $c_{ij}(k, l) > 0$. We denote $< (i, k), (j, l) >$ the edge between the vertices (i, k) and (j, l). The edge $< (i, k), (j, l) >$ is labeled by $c_{ij}(k, l)$ if $c_{ij}(k, l) > 1$.

[1] We assume the existence of the constraints $c_\emptyset, c_1, c_2, ..., c_n$. If no such constraint is defined, we can always define *dummy* ones $c_\emptyset = 0$ and $c_i(k) = 0, \forall k \in D_i$.

2.3 Mathematical Formulation of a WCSP

In [7], a 0-1 linear formulation is proposed for WCSP. Let IPK denotes this formulation. It introduces for each variable $X_i \in X$, d_i binary variables $x_i(1), x_i(2), ..., x_i(d_i)$ constrained to satisfy the following system :

$$(S) \begin{cases} \sum_{k \in D_i} x_i(k) = 1 \ \forall X_i \in X \\ x_i(k) \in \{0,1\} \ \forall X_i \in X, \ \forall k \in D_i \end{cases}$$

The system (S) expresses all the possible complete assignments of the WCSP.

Remark 1. *The constraints* $X_i = \sum_{k \in D_i} kx_i(k) \ \ \forall X_i \in X$ *may be added to the system* (S) *to explicitly express the link between the introduced binary variables and the finite domain variables of the WCSP.*

In IPK, a binary variable $y_{ij}(k,l)$ is introduced for each constraint $c_{ij} \in C$ and each pair $(k,l) \in D_i \times D_j$. So, the WCSP is expressed as follows :

$$IPK \begin{cases} \min c_\emptyset + \sum_{i=1}^{n} \sum_{k \in D_i} c_i(k)x_i(k) + \sum_{c_{ij} \in C} \sum_{k \in D_i} \sum_{l \in D_j} c_{ij}(k,l)y_{ij}(k,l) \\ s.c \quad x_i(k) = \sum_{l \in D_j} y_{ij}(k,l) \ \forall c_{ij} \in C, \forall k \in D_i \\ \qquad x_j(l) = \sum_{k \in D_i} y_{ij}(k,l) \ \forall c_{ij} \in C, \forall l \in D_j \\ \qquad x \in S \end{cases}$$

where x is the vector of the binary variables $x_i(k)$, $\forall X_i \in X, \forall k \in D_i$; the objective expresses complete assignements total costs and the constraints force each $y_{ij}(k,l)$ variable to take the value 1 iff $x_i(k) = 1$ and $x_j(l) = 1$. The disadvantage of this model is its large size : $O(nd+ed^2)$ variables and $O(2ed+n)$ constraints.

Let LPK denotes the continuous relaxation of IPK. Recently, an interesting result is presented in [2]. In this paper, the authors proposed a linear program with continuous variables and show that its solving allows to compute a lower bound (OSAC, Optimal Soft Arc Consistency) better than those computed by techniques based on arc consistency such as FDAC* and EDAC*. The linear program they propose is the dual of LPK.

3 The Main Objective

The main objective of our work is to transform a WCSP into an equivalent[2] one increasing the lower bound $c_\emptyset$. The following example will be used to present our motivations and to illustrate the equivalence preserving transformation proposed in this paper.

[2] Two WCSP are equivalent iff they associate the same cost to each complet assignment.

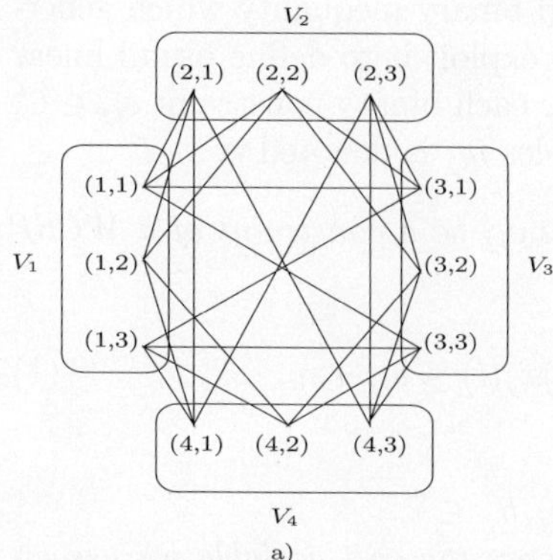

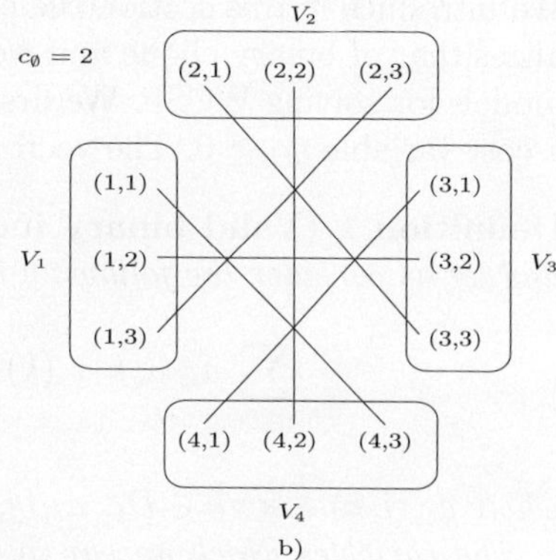

Fig. 1. Two equivalent WCSP

Example 1. *Figure 1 shows two equivalent WCSPs. The graph a) represents an example of Max-CSP with 4 variables ($X = \{X_1, X_2, X_3, X_4\}$) having the same domain $\{1, 2, 3\}$, and 6 constraints ($C = \{c_{12}, c_{13}, c_{14}, c_{23}, c_{24}, c_{34}\}$). This example of Max-CSP is completely arc consistent (it is FAC* since $\forall X_i \in X, \forall k \in D_i, \forall c_{ij} \in C, \exists l \in D_j : c_j(l) + c_{ij}(k,l) = 0$). Thus, all the based on arc consistency methods compute the trivial lower bound 0. The technique proposed in [2] leads to transform this example of WCSP to the equivalent WCSP on the graph b) with $c_\emptyset = 2$. However, in general, this technique is very expensive in computing time since it is based on the solving of the dual of the continuous relaxation LPK of IPK.*

Our transformation approach leads to compute lower bounds closer to the OSAC lower bound. However, it is less time consuming than OSAC. This approach is based on the notion of valid binary inequality introduced below.

4 Linear Models Based on Valid Inequalities

In our previous works [5,6], we introduced the concept of binary clique and we showed how to exploit it for solving Max-CSP. Recall that a binary clique Γ_{ij} associated to a constraint c_{ij} is a union of two subsets E_i and E_j of V_i and V_j respectively such that $(i,k) \notin E_i \vee (j,l) \notin E_j, \forall (k,l) \in D_i \times D_j : c_{ij}(k,l) = 0$.

A binary clique Γ_{ij} is maximal if there is not another binary clique Γ'_{ij} such that $\Gamma_{ij} \subset \Gamma'_{ij}$. In the Max-CSP framework, a set Γ of binary cliques is said complete if and only if for each constraint c_{ij} and for each pair $(k,l) \in D_i \times D_j$: $c_{ij}(k,l) \neq 0$, the set Γ contains at least one binary clique Γ_{ij} associated to c_{ij} such that $(i,k) \in \Gamma_{ij}$ and $(j,l) \in \Gamma_{ij}$.

Example 2. *In the graph a) of figure 1, $\Gamma_{12} = \{(1,1), (1,2), (2,1), (2,2)\}$ is a maximal binary clique relatively to the constraint c_{12}. In the CSP context, this clique may be formulated by the linear inequality $x_1(1) + x_1(2) + x_2(1) + x_2(2) \leq 1$.*

We introduce in this section the concept of valid binary inequality which generalizes that of binary clique and we show how to exploit it to define useful linear models for solving WCSP. We first introduce for each binary constraint $c_{ij} \in C$, a cost variable $\eta_{ij} \geq 0$. The vector of the variables η_{ij} is denoted η.

Definition 1 (Valid binary inequality). *Let c_{ij} be a constraint of a WCSP and let us consider the following inequality :*

$$\sum_{k \in D_i} a_{ij}(i,k)x_i(k) + \sum_{l \in D_j} a_{ij}(j,l)x_j(l) \leq b_{ij} + \eta_{ij} \qquad (1)$$

where $a_{ij}(i,k) \in \mathbb{R}\,\forall k \in D_i$, $a_{ij}(j,l) \in \mathbb{R}\,\forall l \in D_j, b_{ij} \in \mathbb{R}$.

*The variables which appear in this inequality are the cost variable η_{ij} associated to the constraint c_{ij} and the binary variables associated to the values of the **two** variables X_i and X_j. We say that it is a **binary** inequality associated to c_{ij}. It is **valid** if and only if it can be always satisfied with a cost η_{ij} lower than the cost induced by the constraint c_{ij}. That is,*

$$a_{ij}(i,k) + a_{ij}(j,l) \leq b_{ij} + c_{ij}(k,l) \;\; \forall (k,l) \in D_i \times D_j.$$

An inequality of type (1) is a weighted clique if its coefficients ($a_{ij}(i,k)\,\forall k \in D_i$, $a_{ij}(j,l)\,\forall l \in D_j$, b_{ij}) are integers and such that :

$$a_{ij}(i,k) = 0 \vee a_{ij}(j,l) = 0 \qquad \forall (k,l) \in D_i \times D_j : c_{ij}(k,l) = 0.$$

Example 3. *The two valid inequalities $2x_1(1) + x_1(2) + x_2(1) + 2x_2(2) \leq 2 + \eta_{12}$ and $3x_1(1) + \frac{3}{2}x_1(2) + \frac{3}{2}x_2(1) + 3x_2(2) \leq 3 + \eta_{12}$ can be associated to the constraint represented by the graph a) on figure 2. Both these two inequalities are not weighted binary cliques since the vertices $(1,2)$ and $(2,1)$ are not linked and the variables $x_1(2)$ and $x_2(1)$ occur with non null coefficients in the two inequalities. The fact that the coefficients of the last inequality are not all integers is another reason which makes that it is not regarded as being a weighted binary clique.*

For each constraint of the WCSP, it is possible to associate several binary valid inequalities. In the following, we say that a system $Ax \leq b + \eta$ is valid if it is composed from binary inequalities all valid.

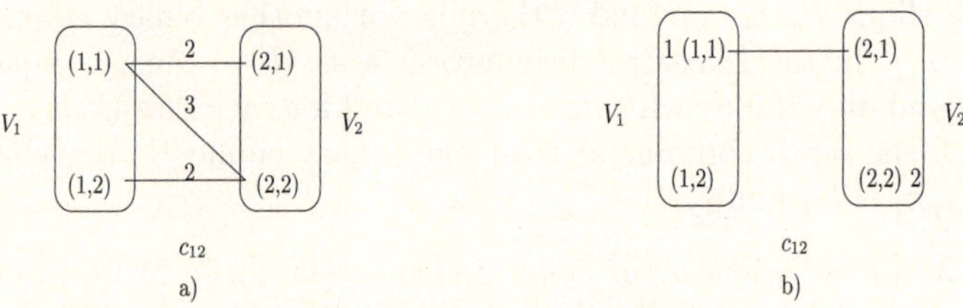

Fig. 2. Two equivalent weighted constraints

Theorem 1. *If $Ax \leq b + \eta$ is a linear system whose all constraints are valid inequalities of type (1) then each lower bound of the linear program*

$$IP(A,b)\begin{cases}\min c_\emptyset + \sum_{i=1}^{n}\sum_{k\in D_i} c_i(k)x_i(k) + \sum_{c_{ij}\in C}\eta_{ij}\\ s.c: Ax \leq b+\eta, x\in S, \eta\geq 0\end{cases}$$

is also a lower bound of the WCSP.

Proof. Since the system $Ax \leq b+\eta$ is valid then we can associate to any optimal solution $I = (v_1, v_2, ..., v_n)$ of the WCSP the solution (x, η) of $IP(A,b)$ where $x_i(v_i) = 1\,\forall X_i \in X; x_i(k) = 0\,\forall X_i \in X, \forall k \in D_i\backslash\{v_i\}$ and $\eta_{ij} = c_{ij}(v_i, v_j)\,\forall c_{ij} \in C$. The solution (x, η) is not necessarily optimal and its cost $V(x, \eta)$ is by construction equal to the cost $V(I)$ of I. The optimal value of $IP(A,b)$ is then a lower bound of the WCSP. Thus, any lower bound of $IP(A,b)$ is also a lower bound of the WCSP.

Corollary 1. *If $Ax \leq b + \eta$ is valid and if for each constraint c_{ij} of the WCSP and for each pair $(k,l) \in D_i \times D_j$, the system $Ax \leq b + \eta$ contains at least one inequality associated to c_{ij} such as $a_{ij}(i,k) + a_{ij}(j,l) = b_{ij} + c_{ij}(k,l)$ then $IP(A,b)$ is equivalent to the WCSP.*

5 Using Valid Inequalities for Preprocessing WCSP

We propose in this section a technique exploiting valid inequalities for preprocessing WCSP. We first present the valid operations used to transform a WCSP to an equivalent one. Then, we show how to build good linear systems in order to benefit as well as possible from these operations.

5.1 Equivalence Preserving Transformation

Let $Ax \leq b + \eta$ be a system containing **one** valid inequality of type (1) per constraint $c_{ij} \in C$ of the WCSP and let us consider the following operations :

op1 $c_{ij}(k,l) \leftarrow c_{ij}(k,l) + b_{ij} - a_{ij}(i,k) - a_{ij}(j,l)\ \forall c_{ij} \in C,\ \forall (k,l) \in D_i \times D_j$;
op2 $c_i(k) \leftarrow c_i(k) + \sum_{j:c_{ij}\in C} a_{ij}(i,k)\ \forall X_i \in X,\ \forall k \in D_i$;
op3 $u_i \leftarrow \min_{k\in D_i} c_i(k)\ \forall X_i \in X$;
op4 $c_i(k) \leftarrow c_i(k) - u_i\ \forall X_i \in X,\ \forall k \in D_i$;
op5 $c_\emptyset \leftarrow c_\emptyset + \sum_{i=1}^{n} u_i - \sum_{c_{ij}\in C} b_{ij}$.

These operations can be seen as a succession of classical projections directed by the linear system $Ax \leq b + \eta$ of valid inequalities. Note that, for every variable $X_i \in X$ and for each binary constraint $c_{ij} \in C$, u_i is the amount of cost projected from c_i to $c_\emptyset$, b_{ij} is the amount of cost projected from $c_\emptyset$ to c_{ij} and the amounts $a_{ij}(i,k)$ and $a_{ij}(j,l)$ are projected from c_{ij} to $c_i(k)$ and $c_j(l)$ respectively.

Theorem 2. *The above operations (op1, op2, op3, op4 and op5) are valid : they transform the WCSP into another equivalent one.*

Proof. We show that the cost of any complete assignment $I = (v_1, v_2, ..., v_n)$ remains the same after achieving this transformation:

$$c_\emptyset + \sum_{i=1}^{n} u_i - \sum_{c_{ij}\in C} b_{ij} + \sum_{i=1}^{n}\left(c_i(v_i) + \sum_{j:c_{ij}\in C} a_{ij}(i,v_i) - u_i\right)$$
$$+ \sum_{c_{ij}\in C} (c_{ij}(v_i,v_j) + b_{ij} - a_{ij}(i,v_i) - a_{ij}(j,v_j))$$
$$=$$
$$c_\emptyset + \sum_{i=1}^{n} c_i(v_i) + \sum_{c_{ij}\in C} c_{ij}(v_i,v_j)$$
$$+ \sum_{i=1}^{n} u_i - \sum_{i=1}^{n} u_i - \sum_{c_{ij}\in C} b_{ij} + \sum_{c_{ij}\in C} b_{ij} + \sum_{i=1}^{n}\sum_{j:c_{ij}\in C} a_{ij}(i,v_i) - \sum_{c_{ij}\in C} (a_{ij}(i,v_i) + a_{ij}(j,v_j))$$
$$=$$
$$c_\emptyset + \sum_{i=1}^{n} c_i(v_i) + \sum_{c_{ij}\in C} c_{ij}(v_i,v_j).$$

Remark 2. *The value of $c_\emptyset$ obtained after performing the transformation is a lower bound. This is guaranteed by the fact that $Ax \leq b + \eta$ is valid : after achieving the transformation, we have $c_i(k) \geq 0\ \forall X_i \in X, \forall k \in D_i$ and $c_{ij}(k,l) \geq 0\ \forall c_{ij} \in C, \forall (k,l) \in D_i \times D_j$. The resulting WCSP may contain fractional valuations when the coefficients of A and b are not all integers.*

Remark 3. *We can consider individually the constraints and use the corresponding valid inequalities to perform the five operations. In this case, if $b_{ij} > 0$ then the value of $c_\emptyset$ may be decreased after considering the constraint c_{ij}. This possibility ($b_{ij} > 0$), which is not allowed in previous based on arc consistency techniques, can be exploited to develop local search techniques based on arc consistency authorizing temporary decreasing of the lower bound in order to escape from local consistency closures.*

5.2 Optimal System of Valid Inequalities

Any system of valid inequalities can be used to transform a WCSP into an equivalent one. It can be interesting to choose the system which allows the computing of the largest lower bound, i.e. the system leading to maximize the quantity $\sum_{i=1}^{n} u_i - \sum_{c_{ij}\in C} b_{ij}$ without producing negative valuations.

For this aim, the following linear program can be solved :

$$LP^* \begin{cases} \max \sum_{i=1}^{n} u_i - \sum_{c_{ij}\in C} b_{ij} \\ a_{ij}(i,k) + a_{ij}(j,l) \leq b_{ij} + c_{ij}(k,l)\ \forall c_{ij} \in C,\ \forall (k,l) \in D_i \times D_j \\ u_i - \sum_{j:c_{ij}\in C} a_{ij}(i,k) \leq c_i(k)\ \forall X_i \in X, \forall k \in D_i \end{cases}$$

The constraints of this linear program express the condition that nonnegative valuations will be produced at the end of the transformation, otherwise the obtained value of $c_\emptyset$ is not guaranteed to be a lower bound.

Theorem 3. *The value $V(LP^*)$ of the linear program LP^* is equal to the lower bound of $OSAC$.*

Proof. Since we must satisfy the assignment constraints $\sum_{k \in D_i} x_i(k) = 1$ and $\sum_{l \in D_j} x_j(l) = 1$, the following set

$$\{\sum_{k \in D_i} (M + a_{ij}(i,k))x_i(k) + \sum_{l \in D_j} (M + a_{ij}(j,l))x_j(l) \leq 2M + b_{ij} + \eta_{ij} : M \in \mathbb{R}\}$$

is composed from inequalities all equivalents. So, if the coefficient b_{ij} is not null in a valid inequality associated to the constraint $c_{ij} \in C$ then we can choose $M = -\frac{bij}{2}$ to form an equivalent valid inequality with $b_{ij} = 0$. We deduce that if all b_{ij} in LP^* are set equal to 0 then the optimal value remains the same. The linear program LP^* with all b_{ij} equal to 0 corresponds exactly to the dual of LPK used in [2] to compute the $OSAC$ lower bound.

Remark 4. *The constraints $a_{ij}(i,k) + a_{ij}(j,l) \leq b_{ij} + c_{ij}(k,l)$ of LP^* express the validity of the inequalities used for the transformation. Note that if we consider individually the constraints, then we can choose nonnegative the coefficients of the valid inequalities in order to be sure that during all the transformation process, the valuations are always nonnegative. This is not a restriction since the coefficients b_{ij} ($\forall c_{ij} \in C$) are not necessarily all nulls as in $OSAC$ [2]. Indeed, it is always possible to choose a sufficiently large constant M in order to transform a valid inequality of type (1) to an equivalent one with only nonnegative conefficients.*

The disadvantage of LP^* is that it requires much computing time since it is of a large size : $O(ed + n)$ variables and $O(ed^2 + nd)$ constraints.

5.3 Heuristic Approach to Build Valid Inequality Systems

The solving of LP^* allows the determination of an optimal system among all systems containing one valid inequality per constraint of the WCSP : it is a system which can be used to transform the WCSP into an equivalent one and to increase to the maximum the lower bound $c_\emptyset$. However, the solving of LP^* is expensive in computing time. To attenuate this disadvantage, we propose to use another valid inequality system which is not necessarily optimal to transform the WCSP.

The system that we propose is obtained by solving the continuous relaxation of an Integer Linear Program (ILP) equivalent to the WCSP. All the inequalities of this ILP are weighted cliques. In order to form them, each constraint $c_{ij} \in C$ of the WCSP is first decomposed into several constraints, each one associates to each pair of $D_i \times D_j$ the same cost or the cost 0. This decomposition is done by the algorithm 1.

Algorithm 1. Constraint decomposition

Require: a constraint c_{ij}

Ensure: p_{ij} binary constraints $c_{ij}^1, c_{ij}^2, ..., c_{ij}^{p_{ij}} : c_{ij}(k,l) = \sum_{q=1}^{p_{ij}} c_{ij}^q(k,l)\ \forall(k,l) \in D_i \times D_j$

STOP $\leftarrow$ false, $q \leftarrow 0$
while STOP = false **do**
  if $\exists(k,l) \in D_i \times D_j : c_{ij}(k,l) > 0$ **then**
    $\alpha \leftarrow \min\{c_{ij}(k,l) : c_{ij}(k,l) > 0,\ (k,l) \in D_i \times D_j\}$
    $q \leftarrow q + 1$
    $c_{ij}^q(k,l) \leftarrow \min(c_{ij}(k,l), \alpha), \forall(k,l) \in D_i \times D_j$
    $c_{ij}(k,l) \leftarrow \max(0, c_{ij}(k,l) - \alpha), \forall(k,l) \in D_i \times D_j$
  else
    STOP $\leftarrow$ true, $p_{ij} \leftarrow q$
  end if
end while

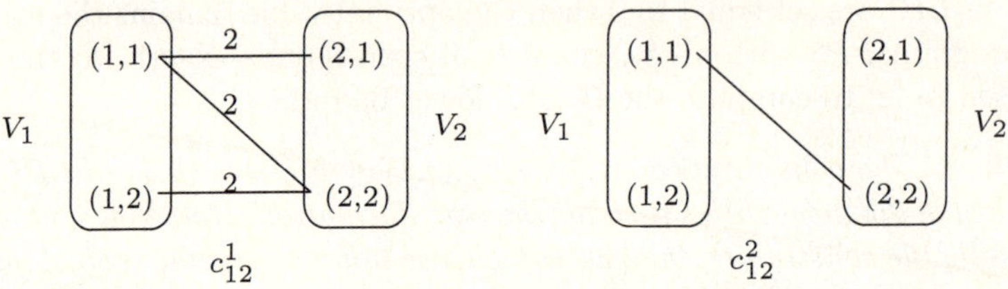

Fig. 3. Decomposition result of the constraint given by the graph a) on figure 2

Example 4. *The constraints represented by figure 3 are the result of the decomposition of the constraint represented by the graph a) on figure 2.*

Remark 5. *The algorithm 1 produces at most $O(d^2)$ constraints.*

After the decomposition of all the constraints, a complet set of weighted cliques Γ_c [6] is built : we associate for each constraint c_{ij}^q, produced by the decomposition, $d_i + d_j$ maximal weighted cliques (one for each value of the two variables X_i and X_j). Namely, for any value k of X_i and for any constraint c_{ij}^q involving the variable X_i we associate the maximal weighted clique $MC(\{(i,k)\}, j, q)$ built as follows:

1. $E_j = \{(j,l) : l \in D_j, c_{ij}^q(k,l) \neq 0\}$;
2. $E_i = \{(i,k') : k' \in D_i, c_{ij}^q(k',l) \neq 0\,\forall(j,l) \in E_j\}$;
3. $MC(\{(i,k)\}, j, q) = E_i \cup E_j$.

In the same way, for any value l of X_j and for any constraint c_{ij}^q involving the variable X_j we associate the maximal weighted clique $MC(\{(j,l)\}, i, q)$ built as follows :

1. $E_i = \{(i,k) : k \in D_i, c_{ij}^q(k,l) \neq 0\}$;
2. $E_j = \{(j,l') : l' \in D_j, c_{ij}^q(k,l') \neq 0\,\forall(i,k) \in E_i\}$;
3. $MC(\{(j,l)\}, i, q) = E_i \cup E_j$.

For each constraint c^q_{ij} we associate a cost variable η^q_{ij} and we formulate by an inequality of type (1) each weighted clique $\Gamma_{ij} \in \Gamma_c$ associated to c^q_{ij} as follows:

- $b_{ij} = \max_{(k,l)\in D_i\times D_j} c^q_{ij}(k,l)$;
- $a_{ij}(i,k) = b_{ij}$ if $(i,k) \in \Gamma_{ij}$, $a_{ij}(i,k) = 0$ otherwise;
- $a_{ij}(j,l) = b_{ij}$ if $(j,l) \in \Gamma_{ij}$, $a_{ij}(j,l) = 0$ otherwise.

Example 5. *The formulation of the weighted cliques which we associate to the constraints* c^1_{12} *and* c^2_{12} *given by figure 3 is as follows:*

$$\begin{aligned}
&2x_1(1) + 2x_2(1) + 2x_2(2) \le 2 + \eta^1_{12}\\
&2x_1(2) + 2x_2(2) \le 2 + \eta^1_{12}\\
&2x_1(1) + 2x_2(1) \le 2 + \eta^1_{12}\\
&2x_1(1) + 2x_1(2) + 2x_2(2) \le 2 + \eta^1_{12}\\
&x_1(1) + x_2(2) \le 1 + \eta^2_{12}\\
&x_1(2) \le 1 + \eta^2_{12}\\
&x_2(1) \le 1 + \eta^2_{12}\\
&x_1(1) + x_2(2) \le 1 + \eta^2_{12}
\end{aligned}$$

Let $IP(\Gamma_c)$ denotes the complete linear system which consists in determining a solution in S minimizing the objective $\sum_{i=1}^{n} \sum_{k\in D_i} c_i(k)x_i(k) + \sum_{c_{ij}\in C} \sum_{q=1}^{p_{ij}} \eta^q_{ij}$ and satisfying the valid inequalities corresponding to the set Γ_c of weighted cliques, where p_{ij} is the number of constraints produced by the decomposition of c_{ij}. The $IP(\Gamma_c)$ system is an Integer Linear Program of type $IP(A, b)$ where all its inequalities are weighted cliques. It is equivalent to the WCSP.

Once $IP(\Gamma_c)$ is built, its continuous relaxation $LP(\Gamma_c)$ is solved and the obtained dual variable values are used to aggregate its inequalities in order to produce only one inequality for each initial constraint of the WCSP.

Example 6. *Suppose that the constraint* c_{12} *given by the graph a) on figure 2 is one of the e binary constraints of a WCSP,* $IP(\Gamma_c)$ *is the linear system constructed after the decomposition of these e constraints and* λ *is an optimal dual solution of the continuous relaxation* $LP(\Gamma_c)$*. The vector* λ *contains one component for each inequality in* $LP(\Gamma_c)$*. Let* $(\frac{1}{2}, 0, 0, 1, 0, 0, 0, 0)$ *be the components which correspond to the inequalities associated to* c_{12}*. These inequalities are then aggregated as follows :*

$$\begin{aligned}
&\tfrac{1}{2}.\ (2x_1(1) + 2x_2(1) + 2x_2(2) \le 2 + \eta^1_{12})\\
&+ 0.\ (2x_1(2) + 2x_2(2) \le 2 + \eta^1_{12})\\
&+ 0.\ (2x_1(1) + 2x_2(1) \le 2 + \eta^1_{12})\\
&+ 1.\ (2x_1(1) + 2x_1(2) + 2x_2(2) \le 2 + \eta^1_{12})\\
&+ 0.\ (x_1(1) + x_2(2) \le 1 + \eta^2_{12})\\
&+ 0.\ (x_1(2) \le 1 + \eta^2_{12})\\
&+ 0.\ (x_2(1) \le 1 + \eta^2_{12})\\
&+ 0.\ (x_1(1) + x_2(2) \le 1 + \eta^2_{12})\\
\hline
&= 3x_1(1) + 2x_1(2) + x_2(1) + 3x_2(2) \le 3 + \eta^1_{12} + \eta^2_{12}
\end{aligned}$$

The obtained inequality is simplified by replacing $\eta_{12}^1 + \eta_{12}^2$ *by* η_{12}. *We obtain :* $3x_1(1) + 2x_1(2) + x_2(1) + 3x_2(2) \leq 3 + \eta_{12}$.

Now, we dispose from a system[3] with one valid inequality per initial constraint (before the decomposition) which can be used to transform the WCSP.

Example 7. *If we use the valid inequality* $3x_1(1) + 2x_1(2) + x_2(1) + 3x_2(2) \leq 3 + \eta_{12}$ *to perform the five operations op1, op2,..., op5 on the constraint* c_{12} *given by the graph a) on the figure 2 then we obtain the equivalent constraint given by the graph b) on the same figure.*

Example 8. *Let us consider the WCSP on the graph a) of figure 1 again. The corresponding* Γ_c *contains 36 maximal cliques. The solving of* $LP(\Gamma_c)$ *supplies an optimal dual solution which we use to aggregate the cliques in order to produce the following complete system of one inequality per constraint of the WCSP :*

$$\begin{cases} \min \eta_{12} + \eta_{13} + \eta_{14} + \eta_{23} + \eta_{24} + \eta_{34} \\ t.q \quad x_1(1) + x_1(2) + x_2(1) + x_2(2) \leq 1 + \eta_{12} \\ \qquad x_1(1) + x_1(3) + x_3(1) + x_3(3) \leq 1 + \eta_{13} \\ \qquad x_1(2) + x_1(3) + x_4(1) + x_4(2) \leq 1 + \eta_{14} \\ \qquad x_2(2) + x_2(3) + x_3(1) + x_3(2) \leq 1 + \eta_{23} \\ \qquad x_2(1) + x_2(3) + x_4(1) + x_4(3) \leq 1 + \eta_{24} \\ \qquad x_3(2) + x_3(3) + x_4(2) + x_4(3) \leq 1 + \eta_{34} \\ \qquad x \in S, \eta \geq 0 \end{cases}$$

This system is then used to transform the initial Max-CSP to the equivalent WCSP given by the graph b). Note that, the performing of the five operations (op1, op2, ..., op5) directed by the first inequality decreases temporary the lower bound from 0 to -1 (see remark 3). The transformation directed by the 5 other inequalities leads to increase the lower bound from -1 to 2. During the transformation process, since the coefficients in the valid system used are all nonnegative, the valuations are always nonnegative and not only at the end of the transformation (see remark 4). So we believe, as this example shows, that valid inequalities with nonnegative integer coefficients can be exploited to develop local search techniques based on arc consistency authorizing the temporary decreasing of the lower bound in order to escape from local consistency closures.

For this example, our approach and the OSAC technique [2] lead to the same result.

Remark 6. *Each valid inequality can be transformed into another valid inequality with integer coefficients as follows :*

1. $b_{ij} \leftarrow \lceil b_{ij} \rceil$;
2. $a_{ij}(j,l) \leftarrow \min\{b_{ij}, \lceil a_{ij}(j,l) \rceil\}\ \forall l \in D_j$;
3. $a_{ij}(i,k) \leftarrow b_{ij} + \min\{c_{ij}(k,l) - a_{ij}(j,l), l \in D_j\}\ \forall k \in D_i$.

[3] This system can be not optimal since it is not selected among all the systems of one inequality per constraint. An optimal system of one inequality per constraint can be computed by solving LP^*.

Thus, if $Ax \leq b + \eta$ *is a system of valid inequalities with fractional coefficients and if we perform the above instructions to each inequality then we will obtain a new system which we can use*[4] *to transform the WCSP into an equivalent one with integer valuations. Such transformation is necessary if the solving method is not adapted to the case of WCSP with fractional valuations.*

5.4 Recapitulation

The following algorithm summarizes steps to be followed in order to benefit as much as possible from the preprocessing we propose :

Algorithm 2. $LP(\Gamma_c) + MEDAC$

1: multiply by a sufficiently large constant M the valuations of the WCSP (see remark 6);
2: use algorithm 1 to decompose all constraints of the WCSP;
3: construct a complete set Γ_c of weighted cliques;
4: use an optimal dual solution of $LP(\Gamma_c)$ to aggregate its cliques in order to produce a new system of one valid inequality per constraint of the initial WCSP;
5: transform these inequalities into inequalities with integer coefficients (see remark 6);
6: use the obtained valid inequalities to transform the WCSP into an equivalent WCSP;
7: solve the obtained WCSP by MEDAC and divide by M the cost of the obtained solution in order to give its cost in the initial WCSP.

6 Experiments

6.1 Lower Bounds

We have compared the bounds $V(LP(\Gamma_c)), OSAC$ and $EDAC^*$. The former two bounds were computed by using ILOG CPLEX (using the barrier algorithm). The bound $EDAC^*$ is computed by using the solver *toolbar* [3].

The first set of instances processed are six classes of random Max-CSP with domain size 10 created by a random generator following the protocol defined in [8] : sparse loose (SL, 40 var), dense loose (DL, 30 var), complete loose (CL, 25 var), sparse tight (ST, 25 var), dense tight (DT, 25 var) and complete tight (CT, 15 var) (see http://carlit.toulouse.inra.fr/cgi-bin/awki.cgi/softCSP for more details). For each class, 50 different problems were considered.

The left table on figure 4 shows the average values of the three lower bounds on tight problems (on loose problems, the three techniques compute the trivial lower bound 0). The right table shows the average time in seconds to compute the bounds OSAC and $V(LP(\Gamma_c))$. The necessary time to compute $EDAC^*$ is in order of microseconds[5].

[4] The disadvantage of restricting to use inequalities with integer coefficients can be attenuated by multiplying all the valuations by a same sufficiently large integer M and by solving the new obtained WCSP.

[5] The machine used is a 2,80GHz Pentium with 2GB of RAM and a Linux operating system.

Binf	ST	DT	CT
$V(LP(\Gamma_c))$	11	18.30	53.89
$OSAC$	12.30	19.80	54.75
$EDAC^*$	4.26	9.96	44.46

cpu-time (s)	SL	DL	CL	ST	DT	CT
$V(LP(\Gamma_c))$	0.29	0.1	0.15	0.09	0.10	0.12
$OSAC$	1.97	0.84	11.80	0.34	0.55	1.63
$EDAC^*$	0	0	0	0	0	0

Fig. 4. Lower bounds comparison on random Max-CSP

	scen07		scen08		graph11		graph13	
	Binf	cpu-time (s)	Binf	cpu-time (s)	Binf	cpu-time (s)	Binf	cpu-time (s)
$V(LP(\Gamma_c))$	30346.7	118.66	44.1278	167.88	2952.34	50.94	9797.5	147.01
$OSAC$	31453.1	1461.94	48.3225	1999.21	2957	109.87	9797.5	2031.51
$EDAC^*$	10000	0.01	6	0.04	2710	0.01	8722	0.03

Fig. 5. Lower bounds comparison on structured WCSP

The bounds $V(LP(\Gamma_c)), OSAC$ and $EDAC^*$ are also compared on 4 instances of the Radio Link Frequency Assignment Problem of the CELAR [1]. The problem considered are the scen0{7,8}reduc.wcsp and graph1{1,3}reducemore.wcsp (see the Benchmarks section in [3]).

As the tables on figures 4 and 5 show, the bounds $OSAC$ and $V(LP(\Gamma_c))$ are extremely powerful, providing lower bounds which are much better than $EDAC^*$. However, these two bounds require much more computing time than the computing of $EDAC^*$. The bounds $OSAC$ and $V(LP(\Gamma_c))$ are close but $V(LP(\Gamma_c))$ requires much less computing time than $OSAC$.

6.2 Preprocessing

To evaluate the preprocessing which we propose, we have solved the random Max-CSP presented in the previous subsection by the two methods $MEDAC$ and $LP(\Gamma_c) + MEDAC$. The constant M used by $LP(\Gamma_c) + MEDAC$ is chosen equal to 1000 and as in [2], the code of toolbar has been modified accordingly[6].

The table on the figure 6 reports the average size of the tree search and the average cpu-time required by the two methods to solve the problems considered.

On the loose problems, the preprocessing proposed does not yield any improvement. This is due to the lower bound $V(LP(\Gamma_c))$ which is equal to 0 for these problems. However, it is worth noting that the computing time of the preprocessing is insignificant comparatively to the global solving time.

On the tight problems, the preprocessing that we propose is very effective especially on the class DT where the number of nodes explored and the global solving time were significantly reduced.

[6] If a solution of cost $3M$ is found for example then, since the cost solutions are multiples of M, the upper bound is fixed to $2M + 1$ in order to eliminate solutions of cost higher than $2M$.

	MEDAC		$LP(\Gamma_c) + MEDAC$	
	#nodes	cpu-time (s)	#nodes	cpu-time (s)
SL	24872.1	2.605	24872.1	2.762
DL	14706	1.376	14706	1.467
CL	202132	25.515	202132	25.741
ST	7993.38	0.774	2440.88	0.601
DT	22025	2.374	5856.34	1.601
CT	156588	16.751	67036.5	16.730

Fig. 6. Preprocessing evaluation

7 Conclusion

In this paper, we have introduced the valid inequality notion and have shown how it can be exploited to solve binary Max-CSP and WCSP problems.

We proposed an equivalence preserving transformation based on valid inequality notion and demonstrated that it is always possible to construct an optimal system of one valid inequality per constraint of the WCSP, on which the transformation can be based. The computing time necessary to search for a such optimal system is disadvantageous. Thus, we proposed an heuristic to search for a good (not necessarily optimal) system of one valid inequality per constraint of the WCSP. The proposed technique is based on continuous relaxation $LP(\Gamma_c)$ of an integer linear system $IP(\Gamma_c)$ equivalent to the WCSP.

The lower bound produced by solving $LP(\Gamma_c)$ is compared with the bound produced by the best known heuristic technique ($EDAC^*$) based on arc consistency and with the bound produced by the optimal soft arc consistency (OSAC). The obtained results show that the value of $LP(\Gamma_c)$ is very close to the bound produced by OSAC and much higher than the bound produced by $EDAC^*$.

Despite the relatively high necessary time to solve $LP(\Gamma_c)$, we have shown that it is useful to exploit it in a preprocessing phase. Indeed, our experiments show that this preprocessing is effective for tight problems and for loose problems, the necessary computing time to solve $LP(\Gamma_c)$ is insignificant comparatively to the global solving time.

Furthermore, this article presents new interesting research prospects. Our prospects are :

1. the study of the possible enhancement of heuristic based on arc consistency such as $EDAC^*$ by using techniques based on valid inequality notion to escape from local consistency closures;
2. the extension of our study to WCSP with n-ary constraints.

References

1. Cabon, B., de Givry, S., Lobjois, L., Schiex, T., Warners, J.P.: Radio Link Frequency Assignment. Constraints 4(1), 79–89 (1999)
2. Cooper, M., de Givry, S., Schiex, T.: Optimal soft arc consistency. In: IJCAI, pp. 68–73 (2007)

3. de Givry, S., Heras, F., Larrosa, J., Rollon, T., Schiex, T.: The SoftCSP and Max-SAT benchmarks and algorithm web site (2006), `http://carlit.toulouse.inra.fr/cgi-bin/awki.cgi/softcsp`
4. de Givry, S., Zytnicki, M., Larrosa, J.: Existential arc consistency: Getting closer to full arc consistency in weighted CSPs. In: IJCAI, pp. 84–89 (2005)
5. Khemmoudj, M.O.I., Bennaceur, H.: Clique Inference Process for Solving Max-CSP. In: Benhamou, F. (ed.) CP 2006. LNCS, vol. 4204, pp. 746–750. Springer, Heidelberg (2006)
6. Khemmoudj, M.O.I., Bennaceur, H.: Clique Based Lower Bounds for Max-CSP. Technical report 2006-02, LIPN (2006)
7. Koster, A.: Frequency Assignment: Models and Algorithms. PhD Thesis. UM (Maastricht, The Netherlands) (1999)
8. Larrosa, J., Schiex, T.: In the quest of the best form of local consistency for Weighted CSP. In: IJCAI, pp. 239–244 (2003)
9. Schiex, T.: Arc Consistency for Soft Constraints. In: Dechter, R. (ed.) CP 2000. LNCS, vol. 1894, pp. 411–424. Springer, Heidelberg (2000)

Advisors for Incremental Propagation

Mikael Z. Lagerkvist and Christian Schulte

School of Information and Communication Technology
KTH - Royal Institute of Technology, Sweden
{zayenz,cschulte}@kth.se

Abstract. While incremental propagation for global constraints is recognized to be important, little research has been devoted to how propagator-centered constraint programming systems should support incremental propagation. This paper introduces advisors as a simple and efficient, yet widely applicable method for supporting incremental propagation in a propagator-centered setting. The paper presents how advisors can be used for achieving different forms of incrementality and evaluates cost and benefit for several global constraints.

1 Introduction

Global constraints are essential in constraint programming as they are useful for modeling and crucial for efficient and powerful propagation. For many propagators implementing global constraints, incrementality is important for efficiency.

The key features to support incremental propagation are state for propagators (to store datastructures for incremental propagation) and modification information (which variables have been modified and how have their domains changed). Without state, incrementality is impossible. Without modification information, the asymptotic complexity of a propagator is at least linear in the number of variables: a propagator must scan all its variables for modification.

Propagation comes in two flavors: variable- or propagator-centered. Variable-centered propagation is controlled by the set of modified variables with some additional information (for example, variable and constraint in AC3 [17], variable and value in AC4 [18]). Propagator-centered propagation is controlled by the set of propagators still to be propagated, see for example [2].

Providing modification information to a propagator is straight-forward with variable-centered propagation, and is used in systems such as Choco [15], ILOG Solver [13], and Minion [10]. This is not true for propagator-centered propagation which is for example used in CHIP [8], SICStus [7], and Gecode [9,23]. While propagator-centered propagation typically lacks support for modification information, it is simple and has important advantages such as fixpoint reasoning, priorities, and priority-based staging [23].

This paper presents *advisors* as a simple, efficient, yet widely applicable method for supporting incremental propagation in a propagator-centered setting. The idea for advisors is not new; similar concepts called demons are used in CHIP [8] and SICStus [6]. This paper, however, is the first attempt to define a model, to describe an implementation, and to analyze advisors.

C. Bessiere (Ed.): CP 2007, LNCS 4741, pp. 409–422, 2007.

Basic requirements and approach. For propagator-centered propagation, it is not too difficult to record for a propagator its modified variables. However, information about modified variables is often not what a propagator needs. For example, when a variable x is modified, a propagator might need to know the position of x in an array, or the node in a variable-value graph corresponding to x. That is, a propagator requires propagator-specific information.

Providing information on domain change is difficult in a propagator-centered setting: the information is specific to each propagator, in contrast to variable-centered propagation where the information is the same for all constraints. Moreover, domain change information should be computed on demand: the overall efficiency of a system should not be compromised.

Taking these issues into account, advisors are programmed for a particular propagator to support propagator-specific modification information. Like propagators, advisors are generic in that they can be used with arbitrary variable domains. Advisors are second-class citizens compared to propagators: advisors cannot propagate, they can only advise propagators to achieve incremental and more efficient propagation. The second-class citizen status is deliberate: advisors are designed to be the simplest possible extension to support incremental propagation while introducing close to no overhead.

Contributions. The contributions of the paper are as follows:

- a simple, general, and implementation-independent model for propagation with advisors in a propagator-centered setup;
- a description of essential properties to make advised propagation well-behaved;
- implementation aspects and design decisions for advisors;
- examples of how to use advisors for global constraints.

Plan of the paper. The next section reviews propagator-based propagation in a setup that is extended to advised propagation in Sect. 3. Implementation aspects and an assessment of cost and potential benefit follow in Sect. 4. Section 5 demonstrates how advisors can be used in practice. The following section concludes the paper.

2 Simple Propagation

This section introduces the basic notions for constraint propagation with propagators. The setup is slightly uncommon: a propagator is a function that takes a domain and a state as input and returns a log as a sequence of tell operations and a new state, where the log describes the domain obtained by propagation. State and log will be essential for propagation with advisors. This paper focuses entirely on propagators. Information on how a propagator faithfully implements a constraint can for example be found in [22].

Domains. A *domain* d is a complete mapping from a finite set of variables $\mathcal{V}$ into the set of subsets of a finite subset of the integers. A domain d_1 is *stronger* than a domain d_2, written $d_1 \leq d_2$, if $d_1(x) \subseteq d_2(x)$ for all $x \in \mathcal{V}$. A domain d_1 is *strictly stronger* than a domain d_2, written $d_1 < d_2$, if $d_1 \leq d_2$ and $d_1 \neq d_2$. The *disagreement set* $\text{dis}(d_1, d_2)$ of domains d_1 and d_2 is $\{x \in \mathcal{V} \mid d_1(x) \neq d_2(x)\}$. Domains d_1 and d_2 are *equal* with respect to a set of variables $X \subseteq \mathcal{V}$, written $d_1 =_X d_2$, if $d_1(x) = d_2(x)$ for all $x \in X$.

Tells and logs. A *tell* $x \sim n$ describes how to update a domain, where $x \in \mathcal{V}$ and $n \in \mathbb{Z}$ and $\sim$ is one of the relation symbols $\leq, \geq, \neq$. The *domain update* $d[x \sim n]$ of a domain d by a tell $x \sim n$ is as follows: $d[x \sim n]\,(x) = \{m \in d(x) \mid m \sim n\}$ and $d[x \sim n]\,(y) = d(y)$ if $x \neq y$. Note that $d[t] \leq d$ for any tell t and domain d. A tell t is *pruning* for a domain d, if $d[t] < d$. The relation symbols in a tell capture domain updates typically found in systems.

Propagators describe the result of propagation by a tuple of tells, called *log*. The *domain update* $d[l]$ of a domain d by a log l successively applies the updates from l to d. The update $d[\langle\rangle]$ by the empty log is d itself. For a non-empty log $\langle t_1, \ldots, t_n \rangle$ with $n > 0$, the update $d[\langle t_1, \ldots, t_n \rangle]$ is defined as $(d[t_1])[\langle t_2, \ldots, t_n \rangle]$. Clearly, $d[l] \leq d$ for any log l and domain d.

A log $\langle t_1, \ldots, t_n \rangle$ is *pruning* for a domain d, if $n = 0$, or t_1 is pruning for d and $\langle t_2, \ldots, t_n \rangle$ is pruning for $d[t_1]$. Note that the empty log is pruning and that a pruning log can contain multiple tells for the same variable.

Propagators. A propagator can use state for incremental propagation where the exact details are left opaque. A *propagator* is a function p that takes a domain d and a state s as input and returns a pair $\langle l, s' \rangle$ of a log l and a new state s'. The domain obtained by propagation is the update $d[l]$ of d by l. It is required that l is pruning for d (capturing that a propagator only returns pruning and hence relevant tells but not necessarily a minimal log).

As a simplifying assumption, the result of propagation is independent of state: for a propagator p and a domain d for any two states s_i with $p(d, s_i) = \langle l_i, s'_i \rangle$ $(i = 1, 2)$ it holds that $d[l_1] = d[l_2]$. Hence, the *result* of propagation $p[\![d]\!]$ is defined as $d[l]$ where $p(d, s) = \langle l, s' \rangle$ for an arbitrary state s.

A propagator p is *contracting*: by construction of a log, $p[\![d]\!] \leq d$ for all domains d. A propagator p must also be *monotonic*: if $d_1 \leq d_2$ then $p[\![d_1]\!] \leq p[\![d_2]\!]$ for all domains d_1 and d_2. A domain d is a *fixpoint* of a propagator p, if $p[\![d]\!] = d$ (that is, if $p(d, s) = \langle l, s' \rangle$ for states s, s', the log l is empty).

Variable dependencies. A set of variables $X \subseteq \mathcal{V}$ is *sufficient* for a propagator p, if it satisfies the following properties. First, no output on other variables is computed, that is, $d =_{\mathcal{V}-X} p[\![d]\!]$ for all domains d. Second, no other variables are considered as input: if $d_1 =_X d_2$, then $p[\![d_1]\!] =_X p[\![d_2]\!]$ for all domains d_1, d_2.

For each propagator p a sufficient set of variables, its *dependencies*, $\text{var}[p] \subseteq \mathcal{V}$ is defined. Dependencies are used in propagation as follows: if a domain d is a fixpoint of a propagator p, then any domain $d' \leq d$ with $\text{var}[p] \cap \text{dis}(d, d') = \emptyset$ is also a fixpoint of p. To better characterize how propagators and variables are organized in an implementation, the set of propagators $\text{prop}[x]$ depending on a variable x is defined as: $p \in \text{prop}[x]$ if and only if $x \in \text{var}[p]$.

$N \leftarrow P$;
while $N \neq \emptyset$ **do**
  remove p from N;
  $\langle l, s \rangle \leftarrow p(d, \text{state}[p])$;
  $d' \leftarrow d[l]$; $\text{state}[p] \leftarrow s$;
  $N \leftarrow N \cup \bigcup_{x \in \mathtt{dis}(d,d')} \text{prop}[x]$;
  $d \leftarrow d'$;
return d;

Algorithm 1. Simple propagation

Propagation. Propagation is shown in Algorithm 1. It is assumed that all propagators are contained in the set P and that $\text{state}[p]$ stores a properly initialized state for each propagator $p \in P$.

The set N contains propagators not known to be at fixpoint. The remove operation is left unspecified, but a realistic implementation bases the decision on priority or cost, see for example [23]. Computing the propagators to be added to N does not depend on the size of the log l. While the log can have multiple occurrences of a variable, each variable from $\text{dis}\,(d, d')$ is considered only once.

Algorithm 1 does not spell out some details. Failure is captured by computing a failed domain (a domain d with $d(x) = \emptyset$ for some $x \in \mathcal{V}$) by propagation. A real system will also pay attention to entailment or idempotency of propagators. Propagation events describing how domains change are discussed in Sect. 4.

The result computed by Algorithm 1 is well known: the weakest simultaneous fixpoint for all propagators $p \in P$ stronger than the initial domain d. For a proof of this fact in a related setup, see for example [1, page 267].

3 Advised Propagation

Advised propagation adds advisors to the model to enable a broad and interesting range of techniques for incremental propagation while keeping the model simple. Simplicity entails in particular that capabilities of propagators are not duplicated, that the overhead for advisors is low, and that the essence of Algorithm 1 is kept. Ideally, a system with advisors should execute propagators not using advisors without any performance penalty.

The design of advisors takes two aspects into account: how an advisor gives advice to propagators (output) and what information is available to an advisor (input). Advisors are functions, like propagators are functions. From the discussion in the introduction it is clear that the input of an advisor must capture which variable has been changed by propagation and how it has been changed.

Based on the input to an advisor function, the only way an advisor can give advice is to modify propagator state and to decide whether a propagator must be propagated ("scheduled"). Modifying the state of a propagator enables the propagator to perform more efficient propagation. Deciding whether a propagator must be propagated enables the advisor to avoid useless propagation.

The model ties an advisor to a single propagator. This decision is natural: the state of a propagator should only be exposed to advisors that belong to that particular propagator. Additionally, maintaining a single propagator for an advisor simplifies implementation.

Advisors. An *advisor* a is a function that takes a domain d, a tell t, and a state s as input and returns a pair $a(d, t, s) = \langle s', Q\rangle$ where s' is a state and Q a set of propagators. An advisor a gives advice to a single propagator p, written as $\text{prop}[a] = p$ where p is referred to as a's propagator (not to be confused with the propagators $\text{prop}[x]$ depending on a variable x). The set of propagators Q returned by a must be either empty or the singleton set $\{p\}$. The intuition behind the set Q is that an advisor can suggest whether its propagator p requires propagation ($Q = \{p\}$) or not ($Q = \emptyset$). To ease presentation, $\text{adv}[p]$ refers to the set of advisors a such that $\text{prop}[a] = p$.

As for propagators, the model does not detail how advisors handle state: if $a(d, t, s_i) = \langle s'_i, Q_i\rangle$ $(i = 1, 2)$ then $Q_1 = Q_2$. In contrast to propagators, advisors have no own state but access to their propagators' state (an implementation most likely will decide otherwise).

Dependent advisors. Like propagators, advisors depend on variables. An advisor a, however, depends on a single variable $\text{var}[a] \in \mathcal{V}$. This restriction is essential: whenever an advisor a is executed, it is known that $\text{var}[a]$ has been modified. Similar to propagators, the set of advisors $\text{adv}[x]$ depending on a variable x is: $a \in \text{adv}[x]$ if and only if $x = \text{var}[a]$ (not to be confused with the advisors $\text{adv}[p]$ for a propagator p).

Variables of a propagator p and variables of its advisors are closely related. One goal with advised propagation is to make informed decisions by an advisor when a propagator must be re-executed. The idea is to trade variables on which the propagator depends for advisors that depend on these variables.

The set of *advised variables* $\text{avar}[p]$ of a propagator is defined as $\{x \in \mathcal{V} \mid \text{exists } a \in \text{adv}[p] \text{ with } \text{var}[a] = x\}$. For a propagator p, the set of dependent variables and advisors $\text{var}[p] \cup \text{avar}[p]$ must be *sufficient* for p: if a domain d is not a fixpoint of p (that is, $p[\![d]\!] < d$), then for all pruning tells $x \sim n$ for d' such that $d'[x \sim n] = d$ holds, $x \in \text{var}[p]$ or $a(d, x \sim n, s) = \langle s', \{p\}\rangle$ for some advisor $a \in \text{adv}[x] \cap \text{adv}[p]$.

Propagation. Algorithm 2 performs advised propagation. The only difference to simple propagation is that the update by the log computed by a propagator executes advisors.

Advisors are executed for each tell t in the order of the log l. Each advisor can schedule its propagator by returning it in the set Q and potentially modify the state of its propagator. Note the difference between variables occurring in the log l and variables from $\text{dis}(d, d')$: if a variable x occurs multiply in l, also all advisors in $\text{adv}[x]$ are executed multiply. Variables in $\text{dis}(d, d')$ are processed only once. The reason for processing the same variable multiply is to provide each tell $x \sim n$ as information to advisors.

Again, the propagation loop computes the weakest simultaneous fixpoint for all propagators in P. Consider the loop invariant: if $p \in P - N$, then d is a fixpoint of p. Since the set of advised variables and dependencies of a propagator

```
N ← P;
while N ≠ ∅ do
    remove p from N;
    ⟨l, s⟩ ← p(d, state[p]);
    d' ← d; state[p] ← s;
    foreach x ∼ n ∈ l do
        d' ← d'[x ∼ n];
        foreach a ∈ adv[x] do
            ⟨s, Q⟩ ← a(d', x ∼ n, state[prop[a]]);
            state[prop[a]] ← s; N ← N ∪ Q;
    N ← N ∪ ⋃_{x∈dis(d,d')} prop[x];
    d ← d';
return d;
```

Algorithm 2. Advised propagation

is sufficient for a propagator and an advisor always provides sufficient advice, the loop invariant holds. Hence, the result of advised propagation is as before.

The algorithm makes a rather arbitrary choice of how to provide tell information to an advisor: it first updates the domain d' by $x \sim n$ and then passes the updated domain $d'[x \sim n]$ together with $x \sim n$ to the advisor. It would also be possible to pass the not-yet updated domain d' and $x \sim n$. This decision is discussed in more detail in Sect. 4.

An essential aspect of advised propagation is that it is *domain independent*: the only dependencies on the domain of the variables are the tells. All remaining aspects readily carry over to other variable domains.

The algorithm reveals the benefit of making advisors second-class citizens without propagation rights. Assume that an advisor could also perform propagation (by computing a log). Then, after propagation by an advisor, all advisors would need to be reconsidered for execution. That would leave two options. One option is to execute advisors immediately, resulting in a recursive propagation process for advisors. The other is to organize advisors that require execution into a separate datastructure. This would clearly violate our requirement of the extension to be small and to not duplicate functionality. Moreover, both approaches would have in common that it would become very difficult to provide accurate information about domain changes of modified variables.

Dynamic dependencies. One simplifying assumption in this paper is that propagator dependencies and advised variables are static: both sets must be sufficient for all possible variable domains. Some techniques require dynamically changing dependencies, such as watched literals in constraint propagation [11]. The extension for dynamic dependencies is orthogonal to advisors, for a treatment of dynamic dependency sets see [24].

4 Implementation

This section discusses how advisors can be efficiently implemented: it details the model and assesses the basic cost and the potential benefit of advisors. Advisors will be included in Gecode 2.0.0 [9].

Advisors. Advisors are implemented as objects. Apart from support for construction, deletion, and memory managment, an advisor object maintains a pointer to its propagator object. The actual code for an advisor is implemented by a runtime-polymorphic method `advise` of the advisor's propagator. The call of `advise` corresponds to the application of an advisor in the model. Both advisor and modification information are passed as arguments to `advise`. As an advisor's propagator implements `advise`, the advisor does not require support for runtime polymorphism and hence uses less memory.

Advisors are attached to variables in the same way as propagators are. Systems typically provide one entry per propagation event where dependent propagators are stored (corresponding to $\text{prop}[x]$ for a variable x). Typically, the propagators are organized in a suspension list, whereas in Gecode they are stored in an array. To accommodate for advisors, a variable x provides an additional entry where dependent advisors $\text{adv}[x]$ are stored. This design in particulars entails that advisors do not honor events (to be discussed below).

Logs. The log in the model describes how propagation by a propagator should modify the domain of its variables. Most systems do not implement a log but perform the update by tells immediately. This is also the approach taken in Gecode. A notable exception is SICStus Prolog, which uses a datastructure similar to logs for implementing global constraints [14].

Performing updates immediately also executes advisors immediately. This differs from the model: the model separates propagator and advisor execution. In an implementation with immediate updates, the advisors of a propagator will be run while the propagator is running itself. When designing advisors and propagators this needs to be taken into account, in particular to guarantee consistent management of the propagator's state.

Modification information. During propagation, the domain and the tell provide information to an advisor which variable has changed and how it has changed. This information, provided as a suitable data structure, is passed as an argument to the advise function of an advisor object.

As discussed in Sect. 3, there are two options: either first modify the domain and then call the advisor, or the other way round. We chose to first modify the domain as in Algorithm 2: many advisors are only interested in the domain after update and not in how the domain changed.

There is an obvious tradeoff between information accuracy and its cost. The most accurate information is $\Delta(x) = d'(x) - d'[x \sim n]\,(x)$ as the set of values removed by $x \sim n$ from d'. Accuracy can be costly: whenever a variable x is modified by a tell, $\Delta(x)$ must be computed regardless of whether advisors actually use the information.

As a compromise between accuracy and cost, our implementation uses the smallest interval $I(x) = \{\min \Delta(x), \ldots, \max \Delta(x)\}$ as approximation. Hence, for a domain d' the interval for the pruning tell $x \leq n$ is $\{n+1, \ldots, \max d'(x)\}$, for $x \geq n$ is $\{\min d'(x), \ldots, n-1\}$, and for $x \neq n$ is $\{n\}$. For other domain operations, such as the removal of arbitrary values, $\emptyset$ can be passed to signal that anything might have changed.

Propagation events. Systems typically use propagation events to characterize changes to domains by tells. For finite domain systems, common propagation events are: the domain becomes a singleton, the minimum or maximum changes, or the domain changes. Sets of dependent variables for propagators are then replaced by event sets: only when an event from a propagator's event set occurs, the propagator is considered for re-execution.

The same approach can be taken for advisors: using sets of advised events rather than sets of advised variables. In our implementation, advisors do not use propagation events for the following reasons. Events are not essential for a system where propagator execution has little overhead [23,24]. Per event type additional memory is required for each variable. Events for advisors would increase the memory overhead even in cases no advisors are being used. The domain change information available to an advisor subsumes events, albeit not with the same level of efficiency.

Performance assessment. Advisors come at a cost. For memory, each variable x requires an additional entry for $\mathrm{adv}[x]$ regardless of whether advisors are used or not. If an advisor for a variable x and a propagator p is used rather than using x as a dependency of p (that is, $x \in \mathrm{var}[p]$), additional memory for an advisor is required (this depends on the additional information an advisor stores, in our implementation the minimal overhead is 8 bytes on a 32-bit machine). For runtime, each time a variable x is modified by a tell, the tell information must be constructed and the advise function of all advisors in $\mathrm{adv}[x]$ must be called.

Table 1. Performance assessment: runtime

Example	base	a-none	a-run	a-avoid
`stress-exec-1`	45.38	+0.2%	+55.1%	+63.5%
`stress-exec-10`	114.93	+0.9%	+88.7%	+98.7%
`queens-n-400`	519.14	±0.0%	+1316.7%	+634.5%
`queens-s-400`	14.57	+0.7%	+28.6%	+12.2%

Table 1 shows the runtime for systems using advisors compared to a system without advisors (`base`, runtime given in milliseconds). The system `a-none` provides advisors without using them, `a-run` uses advisors that always schedule their propagators (fully replacing propagator dependencies by advised variables), whereas advisors for `a-avoid` decide whether the execution of a propagator can be avoided. All runtime are relative to `base`.

All examples have been run on a Laptop with a 2 GHz Pentium M CPU and 1024 MB main memory running Windows XP. Runtimes are the average of 25 runs, the coefficient of deviation is less than 5% for all benchmarks.

The example `stress-exec-1` posts two propagators for $x < y$ and $y > x$ with $d(x) = d(y) = \{0, \ldots, 1000000\}$, whereas `stress-exec-10` posts the same propagators ten times. The advisor for avoiding propagation (system `a-avoid`) checks by $\max d(x) < \max d(y)$ and $\min d(x) > \min d(y)$ whether its propagator is already at fixpoint. `queens-n-400` uses $O(n^2)$ binary disequality propagators,

Table 2. Performance assessment: memory

Example	base	a-none	a-run	a-avoid
`queens-n-400`	24 656.0	±0.0%	+67.6%	+67.6%
`queens-s-400`	977.0	±0.0%	+5.6%	+5.6%

whereas `queens-s-400` uses 3 alldifferent propagators to solve the 400-Queens problem.

These analytical examples clarify that the overhead of a system with advisors without using them is negligible and does not exceed 1%. Advisors for small and inexpensive propagators as in `stress-exec-*` and `queens-n-400` are too expensive, regardless of whether propagation can be avoided. Only for sufficiently large propagators (such as in `queens-s-400`), the overhead suggests that advisors can be beneficial. Exactly the same conclusions can be drawn from the memory overhead shown in Table 2, where memory is given as peak allocated memory in KB.

Table 3. Performance assessment: break-even

Example	base	a-none	a-avoid
`bool-10`	0.01	+0.2%	−16.6%
`bool-100`	0.09	+7.6%	−22.3%
`bool-1000`	1.43	+33.0%	−30.2%
`bool-10000`	238.23	+20.6%	−94.7%

Table 3 gives a first impression that advisors can actually be useful. `bool-`n has a single propagator propagating that the sum of $4n+1$ Boolean variables is at least $2n$ where $2n$ variables are successively assigned to 0 and then propagated. System `a-avoid` uses $2n+1$ advisors (constant runtime) where the other systems use a single propagator (linear runtime) with $2n+1$ dependencies (using techniques similar to those from [10]). As the number of variables increases, the benefit of advisors truly outweigh their overhead.

5 Using Advisors

This section demonstrates advisors for implementing incremental propagation. Central issues are to *avoid* useless propagation, to *improve* propagation efficiency, and to *simplify* propagator construction.

Extensional constraints. We consider two algorithms for implementing n-ary extensional constraints, GAC-2001 [5] and GAC-Schema [4]. Implementing GAC-Schema with advisors is straightforward. If a variable is modified, support for the deleted values is removed from the support lists. If a value loses a support, a new support is found. If no support can be found, the value is deleted. Advisors remove supports, while the propagator deletes values. However, advisors as well as the propagator can potentially find new supports.

Table 4. Runtime and propagation steps for extensional propagation

Example	base		cheap		expensive	
rand-10-20-10-0	4 010.33	16 103	−11.4%	−24.3%	+164.0%	−57.9%
rand-10-20-10-1	64 103.00	290 163	−23.1%	−37.1%	+163.7%	−63.0%
rand-10-20-10-2	68 971.00	257 792	−16.0%	−18.3%	+239.5%	−56.6%
rand-10-20-10-3	7 436.80	34 046	−20.8%	−36.5%	+165.5%	−63.2%
rand-10-20-10-4	4 362.33	16 988	−1.6%	−29.7%	+168.6%	−65.4%
rand-10-20-10-5	28 009.20	84 805	−16.3%	−7.4%	+224.5%	−53.8%
crowded-chess-5	1.44	586	−1.1%	+0.7%	+7.4%	+0.5%
crowded-chess-6	468.29	2 720	−17.1%	−2.7%	+273.7%	−3.1%

Table 4 compares runtime (left in a table cell) and number of propagator executions (right in a table cell) for different extensional propagators. `base` is the GAC-2001 propagator, `cheap` is a GAC-Schema propagator where the propagator searches for new supports, and `expensive` is a GAC-Schema propagator where advisors search for new supports.

Examples `rand-10-20-10-`n are random instances from the Second International CSP Solver Competition, and are originally from [16]. `crowded-chess-`n is a structured problem where several different chess pieces are placed on an $n \times n$ chess board. The placement of bishops and knights is modeled by two n^2-ary extensional constraints on 0/1 variables.

Table 4 clarifies that using an incremental approach to propagate extensional constraints reduces the number of propagator executions. Using advisors to remove supports also reduces runtime. Finding new supports by advisors reduces the number of propagations the most, but is also consistently slowest: many more supports are entered into the support-lists as new supports are searched for eagerly. In contrast, searching for a new support in the propagator is done on demand. There is also a problem with priority inversion, where expensive advisors are run before cheap propagators.

As for memory, GAC-Schema will naturally use more memory than GAC-2001 since it uses an additional large datastructure. For the random problems, the memory overhead is around 5 to 6 times.

Regular. The regular constraint, introduced by Pesant in [19], constrains the values of a variable sequence to be a string of a regular language. The propagator for the regular constraint is based on a DFA for a regular language. The propagator's state maintains all possible DFA transitions for the values of the variables: values are pruned if they are no longer supported by a state reachable via a chain of possible transitions. The algorithm used in our experiments deviates slightly from both variants presented in [19]: it is less incremental in that it rescans all support information for an entire variable, if one of the predecessor or successor states for a variable is not any longer reachable.

Advisors for regular store the index of the variable in the variable sequence. When an advisor is executed, it updates the supported values taking the information on removed values into account. If a predecessor or a successor state changes reachability after values have been updated, the advisor can avoid scheduling the propagator. This can potentially reduce the number of propagator invocations. Besides improving propagator execution, advisors lead to a considerably simpler architecture of the propagator: advisors are concerned with how supported values are updated, while the propagator is concerned with analyzing reachability of states and potentially telling which variables have lost support.

Table 5. Runtime and propagation steps for regular

Example	base		advise		domain	
`nonogram`	803.13	122 778	+11.6%	+3.1%	+11.9%	+3.1%
`placement-1`	214.35	2 616	±0.0%	−44.8%	−0.5%	−44.8%
`placement-2`	7 487.81	91 495	−4.4%	−50.4%	−4.8%	−50.4%

Table 5 compares runtime (left in a table cell) and number of propagator executions (right in a table cell) not using advisors (`base`), using advisors but ignoring domain change information (`advise`), and using advisors and domain change information (`domain`). The memory requirements are the same for all examples. `nonogram` uses regular over 0/1 variables to solve a 25×25 nonogram puzzle, `placement-*` uses regular to place irregularly shaped tiles into a rectangle (8×8 with 10 tiles, 10×6 with 12 tiles).

The advisor-based propagators reduce the number of propagation steps by half in case there is little propagation (propagation for `nonogram` is rather strong due to its 0/1 nature). But the reduction in propagation steps does not translate directly into a reduction in runtime: executing the regular propagator in vain is cheap. With larger examples a bigger improvement in runtime can be expected, suggested by the improvement for `placement-2` compared to `placement-1`.

Alldifferent. The propagator used for domain-consistent alldifferent follows [21]. The key to making it incremental is how to compute a maximal matching in the variable-value graph: only if a matching edge (corresponding to a value) for a variable x is removed, a new matching edge must be computed for x. An observation by Quimper and Walsh [20] can be used to avoid propagation: if a variable domain changes, but the number of values left still exceeds the number of variables of the propagator, no propagation is possible.

Table 6. Runtime and propagation steps for alldifferent

Example	base		avoid		advise		domain	
`golomb-10`	1 301.80	3 359 720	+5.6%	±0.0%	+12.9%	−18.6%	+11.2%	−18.6%
`graph-color`	191.90	150 433	+1.7%	−3.4%	+3.1%	−8.1%	+4.9%	−7.3%
`queens-s-400`	3 112.13	2 397	−0.1%	−0.1%	+27.4%	−0.3%	+23.3%	−0.3%

Table 6 shows the number of propagator executions and runtimes for examples using the domain-consistent alldifferent constraint. `base` uses no advisors, for `avoid` advisors use the above observation to check whether the propagator can propagate, for `advise` advisors maintain the matching and use the observation, and for `domain` advisors maintain the matching by relying entirely on domain change information. For `domain`, the observation is not used to simplify matching maintenance by advisors. `golomb-10` finds an optimal Golomb ruler of size 10, `graph-color` colors a graph with 200 nodes based on its cliques, and `queens-s-400` is as above.

While the number of propagator invocations decreases, runtime never decreases. Using the observation alone is not beneficial as it does not outweigh the overhead of advisors. The considerable reduction in propagator executions for `advise` and `domain` is due to early detection of failure: advisors fail to find a matching without executing their propagator. The increase in runtime is not surprising: edges are matched eagerly on each advisor invocation. This is wasteful as further propagation can remove the newly computed matching edge again before the propagator runs. Hence, it is beneficial to wait until the propagator actually runs before reconstructing a matching. Another problem with eager matching is similar to the observations for extensional constraints: prioritizing matching by advisors over cheaper propagators leads to priority inversion between cheap propagators and expensive advisors.

Advisors again lead to an appealing separation of concerns, as matching becomes an orthogonal issue. However, the examples clarify another essential aspect of incremental propagation: even if a propagator does not use advisors, it can perform incremental propagation (such as matching incrementally). And for some propagators, it can be important to defer computation until perfect information about all variables is available when the propagators is actually run. Being too eager by using advisors can be wasteful.

Summary. The above experiments and the observations in Sect. 4 can be summarized as follows. Advisors are essential to improve asymptotic complexity for some propagators (in particular for propagators with sub-linear complexity, such as Boolean or general linear equations [12]). Advisors help achieving a good factorization of concerns for implementing propagators. However, the effort spent by an advisor must comply with priorities and must not be too eager. Efficiency improvements might only be possible for propagators with many variables.

6 Conclusions

This paper has added advisors to a propagator-centered setup for supporting more efficient propagation. Advisors are simple and do not duplicate functionality from propagators (no propagation and immediate execution). In particular, advisors satisfy the key requirement to not slow down propagation when not being used. That makes advisors a viable approach also for other propagator-centered constraint programming systems.

Advisors are shown to be useful for: increasing efficiency, in particular improving asymptotic complexity, and achieving a better factorization of concerns in the implementation of propagators (relying on the fact that advisors are programmable). The paper has clarified two other issues. First, advisors must comply with priorities in a propagator-centered approach with priorities. Second, for some propagators it is more important that an incremental algorithm is used rather than running the algorithm eagerly on variable change.

Advisors, like propagators, are generic. It can be expected that for variable domains with expensive domain operations (such as sets), the domain change information provided to an advisor can be more useful than for finite domain propagators. Adapting advisors for a particular variable domain only needs to define which domain change information is passed to an advisor by a tell.

Acknowledgments. We are grateful to Guido Tack and the anonymous reviewers for helpful comments. The authors are partially funded by the Swedish Research Council (VR) under grant 621-2004-4953.

References

1. Apt, K.: Principles of Constraint Programming. Cambridge University Press, Cambridge, United Kingdom (2003)
2. Benhamou, F.: Heterogeneous constraint solving. In: Hanus, M., Rodríguez-Artalejo, M. (eds.) ALP 1996. LNCS, vol. 1139, pp. 62–76. Springer, Heidelberg (1996)
3. Benhamou, F. (ed.): CP 2006. LNCS, vol. 4204. Springer, Heidelberg (2006)
4. Bessière, C., Régin, J.-C.: Arc consistency for general constraint networks: Preliminary results. In: IJCAI, vol. 1, pp. 398–404 (1997)
5. Bessière, C., Régin, J.-C., Yap, R.H.C., Zhang, Y.: An optimal coarse-grained arc consistency algorithm. Artificial Intelligence 165(2), 165–185 (2005)
6. Carlsson, M.: Personal communication (2006)
7. Carlsson, M., Ottosson, G., Carlson, B.: An open-ended finite domain constraint solver. In: Hartel, P.H., Kuchen, H. (eds.) PLILP 1997. LNCS, vol. 1292, pp. 191–206. Springer, Heidelberg (1997)
8. Dincbas, M., Van Hentenryck, P., Simonis, H., Aggoun, A., Graf, T., Berthier, F.: The constraint logic programming language CHIP. In: Proceedings of the International Conference on Fifth Generation Computer Systems FGCS-88, Tokyo, Japan, pp. 693–702 (December 1988)
9. Gecode Team. Gecode: Generic constraint development environment (2006), Available from `http://www.gecode.org`
10. Gent, I.P., Jefferson, C., Miguel, I.: Minion: A fast scalable constraint solver. In: Brewka, G., Coradeschi, S., Perini, A., Traverso, P. (eds.) ECAI, pp. 98–102. IOS Press, Amsterdam (2006)
11. Gent, I.P., Jefferson, C., Miguel, I.: Watched literals for constraint propagation in Minion. In: Benhamou [3], pp. 284–298.
12. Harvey, W., Schimpf, J.: Bounds consistency techniques for long linear constraints. In: Beldiceanu, N., Brisset, P., Carlsson, M., Laburthe, F., Henz, M., Monfroy, E., Perron, L., Schulte, C. (eds.) Proceedings of TRICS: Techniques foR Implementing Constraint programming Systems, a workshop of CP 2002, number TRA9/02, pp. 39–46, 55 Science Drive 2, Singapore 117599 (September 2002)

13. ILOG Inc., Mountain View, CA, USA. ILOG Solver 6.3 reference Manual (2006)
14. Intelligent Systems Laboratory: SICStus Prolog user's manual, 4.0.0. Technical report, Swedish Institute of Computer Science, Box 1263, 164 29 Kista, Sweden (2007)
15. Laburthe, F.: CHOCO: implementing a CP kernel. In: Beldiceanu, N., Harvey, W., Henz, M., Laburthe, F., Monfroy, E., Müller, T., Perron, L., Schulte, C. (eds.) Proceedings of TRICS: Techniques foR Implementing Constraint programming Systems, a post-conference workshop of CP 2000, number TRA9/00, pp. 71–85, 55 Science Drive 2, Singapore 117599 (September 2000)
16. Lecoutre, C., Szymanek, R.: Generalized arc consistency for positive table constraints. In: Benhamou [3], pp. 284–298.
17. Mackworth, A.K.: Consistency in networks of relations. Artificial Intelligence 8(1), 99–118 (1977)
18. Mohr, R., Masini, G.: Good old discrete relaxation. In: Kodratoff, Y. (ed.) Proceedings of the 8th European Conference on Artificial Intelligence, Munich, Germany, pp. 651–656. Pitmann Publishing (1988)
19. Pesant, G.: A regular language membership constraint for finite sequences of variables. In: Wallace [25], pp. 482–495.
20. Quimper, C.-G., Walsh, T.: The all different and global cardinality constraints on set, multiset and tuple variables. In: Hnich, B., Carlsson, M., Fages, F., Rossi, F. (eds.) CSCLP 2005. LNCS (LNAI), vol. 3978, pp. 1–13. Springer, Heidelberg (2006)
21. Régin, J.-C.: A filtering algorithm for constraints of difference in CSPs. In: Proceedings of the Twelfth National Conference on Artificial Intelligence, Seattle, WA, USA, vol. 1, pp. 362–367. AAAI Press, Stanford, California, USA (1994)
22. Schulte, C., Carlsson, M.: Finite domain constraint programming systems. In: Rossi, F., van Beek, P., Walsh, T. (eds.) Handbook of Constraint Programming. Foundations of Artificial Intelligence, ch. 14, pp. 495–526. Elsevier Science Publishers, Amsterdam, The Netherlands (2006)
23. Schulte, C., Stuckey, P.J.: Speeding up constraint propagation. In: Wallace [25], pp. 619–633. An extended version is available as [24]
24. Schulte, C., Stuckey, P.J.: Efficient constraint propagation engines (2006), Available from `http://arxiv.org/abs/cs.AI/0611009`
25. Wallace, M. (ed.): CP 2004. LNCS, vol. 3258. Springer, Heidelberg (2004)

Breaking Symmetry of Interchangeable Variables and Values*

Y.C. Law[1], J.H.M. Lee[1], Toby Walsh[2], and J.Y.K. Yip[1]

[1] Deparment of Computer Science and Engineering, The Chinese University of Hong Kong, Shatin, N.T., Hong Kong
{yclaw,jlee,ykyip}@cse.cuhk.edu.hk

[2] National ICT Australia and School of CSE, University of New South Wales, Sydney, Australia
tw@cse.unsw.edu.au

Abstract. A common type of symmetry is when both variables and values partition into interchangeable sets. Polynomial methods have been introduced to eliminate all symmetric solutions introduced by such interchangeability. Unfortunately, whilst eliminating all symmetric solutions is tractable in this case, pruning all symmetric values is NP-hard. We introduce a new global constraint called SIGLEX and its GAC propagator for pruning some (but not necessarily all) symmetric values. We also investigate how different postings of the SIGLEX constraints affect the pruning performance during constraint solving. Finally, we test these static symmetry breaking constraints experimentally for the first time.

1 Introduction

When solving complex real-life problems like staff rostering, symmetry may dramatically increase the size of the search space. A simple and effective mechanism to deal with symmetry is to add static symmetry breaking constraints to eliminate symmetric solutions [1,2,3,4]. Alternatively, we can modify the search procedure so that symmetric branches are not explored [5,6,7]. Unfortunately, eliminating all symmetric solutions is NP-hard in general. In addition, even when all symmetric solutions can be eliminated in polynomial time, pruning all symmetric values may be NP-hard [8]. One way around this problem is to develop polynomial methods for special classes of symmetries.

One common type of symmetry is when variables and/or values are interchangeable. For instance, in a graph colouring problem, if we assign colours (values) to nodes (variables), then the colours (values) are fully interchangeable. That is, we can permute the colours throughout a solution and still have a proper colouring. Similarly, variables may be interchangeable. For example, if two nodes (variables) have the same set of neighbours, we can permute them and keep a proper colouring. We call this *variable and value interchangeability*. It has also been called *piecewise symmetry* [9] and *structural symmetry* [10]. Recent results show that we can eliminate all symmetric solutions due

* We thank the anonymous referees for their constructive comments. The work described in this paper was substantially supported by grants (Project no. CUHK4131/05 and CUHK4219/04E) from the Research Grants Council of the Hong Kong SAR. NICTA is funded by DCITA and ARC through Backing Australia's Ability and the ICT Centre of Excellence program.

C. Bessiere (Ed.): CP 2007, LNCS 4741, pp. 423–437, 2007.

to variable and value interchangeability in polynomial time. Sellmann and Van Hentenryck gave a polynomial time dominance detection algorithm for dynamically breaking such symmetry [10]. Subsequently, Flener, Pearson, Sellmann and Van Hentenryck identified a set of static symmetry breaking constraints to eliminate all symmetric solutions [9]. In this paper, we propose using a linear number of the new SIGLEX constraint for breaking such symmetry. A SIGLEX constraint orders the interchangeable variables as well as the interchangeable values. Its propagator is based on a decomposition using REGULAR constraints [11].

2 Background

A *constraint satisfaction problem* (CSP) consists of a set of n *variables*, each with a finite *domain* of possible values, and a set of *constraints* specifying allowed combinations of values for given subsets of variables. A constraint restricts values taken by some subset of variables to a subset of the Cartesian product of the variable domains. Without loss of generality, we assume that variables initially share the same domain of m possible values, d_1 to d_m. Each finite domain variable takes one value from this domain. We also assume an ordering on values in which $d_i < d_j$ iff $i < j$. A *solution* is an assignment of values to variables satisfying the constraints.

A global constraint has a parameterised number of variables. We will use four common global constraints. The first, $\text{AMONG}([X_1, .., X_n], v, M)$, holds iff $|\{i \mid X_i \in v\}| = M$. That is, M of the variables from X_1 to X_n take values among the set v. Combining together multiple AMONG constraints gives the global cardinality constraint [12]. $\text{GCC}([X_1, .., X_n], [d_1, .., d_m], [O_1, .., O_m])$ holds iff $|\{i \mid X_i = d_j\}| = O_j$ for $1 \leq j \leq m$. That is, O_j of the variables from X_1 to X_n take the value d_j. If $O_j \leq 1$ for all j then no value occurs more than once and we have an all different constraint. $\text{ALLDIFF}([X_1, \ldots, X_n])$ holds iff $X_i \neq X_j$ for $1 \leq i < j \leq n$. Finally, a global constraint that we will use to encode other global constraints is the REGULAR constraint [11]. Let $\mathcal{M} = (Q, \Sigma, \delta, q_0, F)$ denote a *deterministic finite automaton* (DFA) where Q is a finite set of states, Σ an alphabet, $\delta : Q \times \Sigma \rightarrow Q$ a partial transition function, q_0 the initial state and $F \subseteq Q$ the set of final states. $\text{REGULAR}([X_1, \ldots, X_n], \mathcal{M})$ holds iff the string $[X_1, \ldots, X_n]$ belongs to the regular language recognised by $\mathcal{M}$. Quimper and Walsh encode a linear time GAC propagator for the REGULAR constraint using ternary constraints [13]. They introduce variables for the state of the DFA after each character, and post ternary constraints ensuring that the state changes according to the transition relation. One advantage of this encoding is that we have easy access to the states of the DFA. In fact, we will need here to link the final state to a finite domain variable.

Systematic search constraint solvers typically explore partial assignments using backtracking search, enforcing a local consistency at each search node to prune values for variables which cannot be in any solution. We consider a well known local consistency called generalized arc consistency. Given a constraint C on finite domain variables, a *support* is an assignment to each variable of a value in its domain which satisfies C. A constraint C on finite domain variables is *generalized arc consistent* (GAC) iff for each variable, every value in its domain belongs to a support.

3 Variable and Value Interchangeability

We suppose that there is a partition of the n finite domain variables of our CSP into a disjoint sets, and the variables within each set are interchangeable. That is, if we have a solution $\{X_i = d_{sol(i)} \mid 1 \leq i \leq n\}$ and any bijection σ on the variable indices which permutes indices within each partition, then $\{X_{\sigma(i)} = d_{sol(i)} \mid 1 \leq i \leq n\}$ is also a solution. We also suppose that there is a partition of the m domain values into b disjoint sets, and the values within each set are interchangeable. That is, if we have a solution $\{X_i = d_{sol(i)} \mid 1 \leq i \leq n\}$ and any bijection σ on the value indices which permutes indices within each partition, then $\{X_i = d_{\sigma(sol(i))} \mid 1 \leq i \leq n\}$ is also a solution. If $n = a$ we have just interchangeable values, whilst if $m = b$ we have just interchangeable variables. We will order variable indices so that $X_{p(i)}$ to $X_{p(i+1)-1}$ is the ith variable partition, and value indices so that $d_{q(j)}$ to $d_{q(j+1)-1}$ is the jth value partition where $1 \leq i \leq a$, $1 \leq j \leq b$. In other words, $p(i)$ and $q(j)$ give the starting indices of the ith variable partition and the jth value partition respectively.

Example 1. *Consider a CSP problem representing 3-colouring the following graph:*

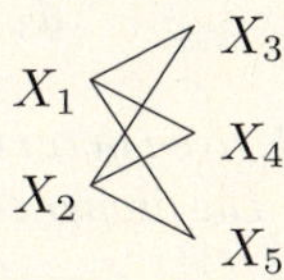

Nodes are labelled with the variables X_1 to X_5. Values correspond to colours. X_1 and X_2 are interchangeable as the corresponding nodes have the same set of neighbours. If we have a proper colouring, we can permute the values assigned to X_1 and X_2 and still have a proper colouring. Similarly, X_3, X_4 and X_5 are interchangeable. The variables thus partition into two disjoint sets: $\{X_1, X_2\}$ and $\{X_3, X_4, X_5\}$. In addition, we can uniformly permute the colours throughout a solution and still have a proper colouring. Thus, the values partition into a single set: $\{d_1, d_2, d_3\}$. In graph colouring, variable partitions can be identified by checking whether two nodes have the same set of neighbours, while in general problems, the underlying symmetry can be discovered automatically [14].

Flener *et al.* [9] show that we can eliminate all solutions which are symmetric due to variable and value interchangeability by posting the following constraints:

$$X_{p(i)} \leq .. \leq X_{p(i+1)-1} \qquad \forall\, i \in [1,a] \tag{1}$$

$$\text{GCC}([X_{p(i)}, .., X_{p(i+1)-1}], [d_1, .., d_m], [O_1^i, .., O_m^i]) \quad \forall\, i \in [1,a] \tag{2}$$

$$(O_{q(j)}^1, .., O_{q(j)}^a) \geq_{\text{lex}} .. \geq_{\text{lex}} (O_{q(j+1)-1}^1, .., O_{q(j+1)-1}^a) \;\; \forall\, j \in [1,b] \tag{3}$$

$(O_k^1, .., O_k^a)$ is called the *signature* of the value d_k, which gives the number of occurrences of the value d_k in each variable partition. Note that the signature is invariant to the permutation of variables within each equivalence class. By ordering variables within each equivalence class using (1), we rule out permuting interchangeable variables. Similarly, by lexicographically ordering the signatures of values within each equivalence class using (3), we rule out permuting interchangeable values.

Example 2. *Consider again the 3-colouring problem in Example 1. There are 30 proper colourings of this graph. When we post the above symmetry breaking constraints, the number of proper colourings reduces from 30 to just 3:*

(a) d_1, d_1 — d_2, d_2, d_2 (b) d_1, d_1 — d_2, d_2, d_3 (c) d_1, d_2 — d_3, d_3, d_3

Each colouring is representative of a different equivalence class. In fact, it is the lexicographically least member of its equivalence class. On the other hand, the following colourings are eliminated by the above symmetry breaking constraints:

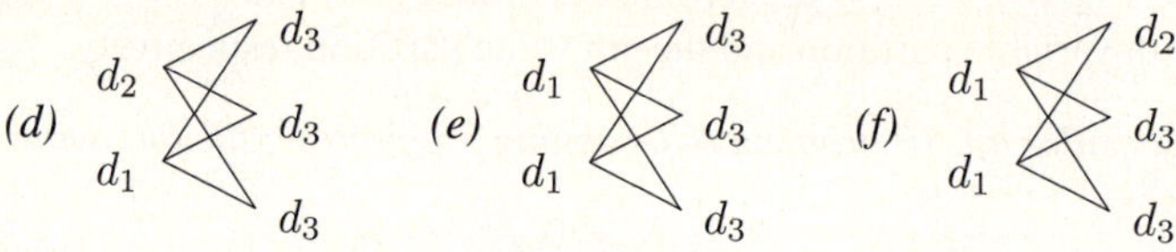

For instance, the proper colouring given in (e) is symmetric to that in (a) since if we permute d_2 with d_3 in (e), we get (a). The proper colouring given in (e) is eliminated by the symmetry breaking constraint $(O_2^1, O_2^2) \geq_{\text{lex}} (O_3^1, O_3^2)$ since $O_2^1 = O_3^1 = 0$ (neither d_2 nor d_3 occur in the first equivalence class of variables) but $O_2^2 = 0$ and $O_3^2 = 3$ (d_2 does not occur in the second equivalence class of variables but d_3 occurs three times).

Suppose BREAKINTERCHANGEABILITY$(p, q, [X_1, .., X_n])$ is a global constraint that eliminates all symmetric solutions introduced by interchangeable variables and values. That is, BREAKINTERCHANGEABILITY orders the variables within each equivalence class, as well as lexicographically orders the signatures of values within each equivalence class. It can be seen as the conjunction of the ordering, GCC and lexicographic ordering constraints given in Equations (1), (2) and (3). Enforcing GAC on such a global constraint will prune all symmetric values due to variable and value interchangeability. Not surprisingly, decomposing this global constraint into separate ordering, GCC and lexicographic ordering constraints may hinder propagation.

Example 3. *Consider again the 3-colouring problem in Example 1. Suppose X_1 to X_5 have domains $\{d_1, d_2, d_3\}$, the signature variables O_1^1, O_2^1, O_3^1 have domains $\{0, 1, 2\}$, whilst O_1^2, O_2^2, O_3^2 have domains $\{0, 1, 2, 3\}$. Flener et al.'s decomposition and the binary not-equals constraints between variables representing neighbouring nodes are GAC. However, by considering (a), (b) and (c), we see that GAC on* BREAKINTERCHANGEABILITY *and the binary not-equals constraints ensures $X_1 = d_1$, $X_2 \neq d_3$, $X_3 \neq d_1$, $X_4 \neq d_1$ and $X_5 \neq d_1$.*

As decomposing BREAKINTERCHANGEABILITY hinders propagation, we might consider a specialised algorithm for achieving GAC that prunes all possible symmetric values. Unfortunately enforcing GAC on such a global constraint is NP-hard [8].

4 A New Decomposition

We propose an alternative decomposition of BREAKINTERCHANGEABILITY. This decomposition does not need global cardinality constraints which are expensive to propagate. In fact, Flener *et al.*'s decomposition requires a propagator for GCC which prunes the bounds on the number of occurrence of values. The decomposition proposed here uses just REGULAR constraints which are available in many solvers or can be easily added using simple ternary transition constraints [13]. This new decomposition can be efficiently and incrementally propagated.

The results in Table 5 of [15] suggest that propagation is rarely hindered by decomposing a chain of lexicographic ordering constraints into individual lexicographic ordering constraints between neighbouring vectors. Results in Table 1 of [16] also suggest that propagation is rarely hindered by decomposing symmetry breaking constraints for interchangeable values into symmetry breaking constraints between neighbouring pairs of values in each equivalence class. We therefore propose a decomposition which only considers the signatures of neighbouring pairs of values in each equivalence class.

This decomposition replaces BREAKINTERCHANGEABILITY by a linear number of symmetry breaking constraints, SIGLEX. These lexicographically order the signatures of *neighbouring* pairs of values in each equivalence class, as well as order variables within each equivalence class. We decompose BREAKINTERCHANGEABILITY into SIGLEX$(k, p, [X_1, .., X_n])$ for $q(j) \leq k < q(j+1) - 1, 1 \leq j \leq b$. The global constraint SIGLEX$(k, p, [X_1, .., X_n])$ itself holds iff:

$$X_{p(i)} \leq .. \leq X_{p(i+1)-1} \quad \forall\, i \in [1, a] \tag{4}$$

$$\text{AMONG}([X_{p(i)}, .., X_{p(i+1)-1}], \{d_k\}, O_k^i) \quad \forall\, i \in [1, a] \tag{5}$$

$$\text{AMONG}([X_{p(i)}, .., X_{p(i+1)-1}], \{d_{k+1}\}, O_{k+1}^i) \quad \forall\, i \in [1, a] \tag{6}$$

$$(O_k^1, .., O_k^a) \geq_{\text{lex}} (O_{k+1}^1, .., O_{k+1}^a) \tag{7}$$

SIGLEX orders the variables within each equivalence class and lexicographically orders the signatures of two interchangeable and neighbouring values. To propagate each SIGLEX constraint, we give a decomposition using REGULAR constraints which does not hinder propagation.

Theorem 1. *GAC can be enforced on* SIGLEX$(k, p, [X_1, .., X_n])$ *in* $O(n^2)$ *time.*

Proof: We first enforce the ordering constraints $X_{p(i)} \leq .. \leq X_{p(i+1)-1}$ on each variable partition. We then channel into a sequence of four valued variables using the constraints: $Y_i^k = (X_i > d_{k+1}) + (X_i \geq d_{k+1}) + (X_i \geq d_k)$. That is, $Y_i^k = 3$ if $X_i > d_{k+1}$, $Y_i^k = 2$ if $X_i = d_{k+1}$, $Y_i^k = 1$ if $X_i = d_k$, and $Y_i^k = 0$ if $X_i < d_k$.

Within the ith variable partition, we enforce GAC on a REGULAR constraint on $Y_{p(i)}^k$ to $Y_{p(i+1)-1}^k$ to compute the difference between O_k^i and O_{k+1}^i and assign this difference to a new integer variable D_k^i. The automaton associated with this REGULAR constraint has state variables $Q_{p(i)}^k$ to $Q_{p(i+1)-1}^k$ whose values are tuples containing the difference between the two counts seen so far as well as the last value seen (so that we can ensure that values for Y_i^k are increasing). From (δ, y), the transition function on seeing Y_i^k moves to the new state $(\delta + (Y_i^k = 2) - (Y_i^k = 1), \max(y, Y_i^k))$ if and only if $Y_i^k \geq y$.

The initial state is $(0, 0)$. We set the difference between the two counts in the final state variable equal to the new integer variable D^i_k (which is thus constrained to equal $O^i_{k+1} - O^i_k$) Finally, we ensure that the vectors, $(O^1_k, .., O^a_k)$ and $(O^1_{k+1}, .., O^a_{k+1})$ are ordered using a final REGULAR constraint on the difference variables, D^1_k to D^a_k. The associated automaton has 0/1 states, a transition function which moves from state b to $b \vee (D^i_k < 0)$ provided $D^i_k \leq 0$ or $b = 1$, an initial state 0 and 0 or 1 as final states.

The constraint graph of all the REGULAR constraints is Berge-acyclic. Hence enforcing GAC on these REGULAR constraints achieves GAC on the variables Y^k_i [17]. Consider a support for the Y^k_i variables. We can extend this to a support for the X_i variables simply by picking the smallest value left in their domains after we have enforced GAC on the channelling constraints between the X_i and Y^k_i variables. Support for values left in the domains of the X_i variables can be constructed in a similar way. Enforcing GAC on this decomposition therefore achieves GAC on SIGLEX$(k, p, [X_1, .., X_n])$.

Assuming bounds can be accessed and updated in constant time and a constraint is awoken only if the domain of a variable in its scope has been modified, enforcing GAC on the ordering constraints takes $O(n)$ time, on the channelling constraints between X_i and Y^k_i takes $O(n)$ time, on the first set of REGULAR constraints which compute D^i_k takes $O(n^2)$ time, and on the final REGULAR constraint takes $O(na)$ time. As $a \leq n$, enforcing GAC on SIGLEX takes $O(n^2)$ time. ⋄

We compare this with the GCC decomposition in [9]. This requires a GCC propagator which prunes the bounds of the occurrence variables. This will take $O(mn^2 + n^{2.66})$ time [12]. To break the same symmetry, we need to post up to $O(m)$ SIGLEX constraints, which take $O(mn^2)$ time in total to propagate. In the best case for this new decomposition, m grows slower than $O(n^{0.66})$ and we are faster. In the worst case, m grows as $O(n^{0.66})$ or worse and both propagators take $O(mn^2)$ time. The new decomposition is thus sometimes better but not worse than the old one. We conjecture that the two decompositions are incomparable. The GCC decomposition reasons more globally about occurrences, whilst the SIGLEX decomposition reasons more globally about supports of increasing value. Indeed, we can exhibit a problem on which the SIGLEX decomposition gives exponential savings. We predict that the reverse is also true.

Theorem 2. *On the pigeonhole problem $PHP(n)$ with n interchangeable variables and $n+1$ interchangeable values, we explore $O(2^n)$ branches when enforcing GAC and breaking symmetry using the* GCC *decomposition irrespective of the variable and value ordering, but we solve in polynomial time when enforcing GAC using* SIGLEX.

Proof: The problem has $n+1$ constraints of the form $\bigvee_{i=1}^n X_i = d_j$ for $1 \leq j \leq n+1$, with $X_i \in \{d_1, .., d_{n+1}\}$ for $1 \leq i \leq n$. The problem is unsatisfiable by a simple pigeonhole argument. Enforcing GAC on SIGLEX$(i, [X_1, \dots, X_n])$ for $i > 0$ prunes d_{i+1} from X_1. Hence, X_1 is set to d_1. Enforcing GAC on SIGLEX$(i, p, [X_1, \dots, X_n])$ for $i > 1$ now prunes d_{i+1} from X_2. The domain of X_2 is thus reduced to $\{d_1, d_2\}$. By a similar argument, the domain of each X_i is reduced to $\{d_1, \dots d_i\}$. The SIGLEX constraints are now GAC. Enforcing GAC on the constraint $\bigvee_{i=1}^n X_i = d_{n+1}$ then proves unsatisfiability. Thus, we prove that the problem is unsatisfiable in polynomial time. On the other hand, using the GCC decomposition, irrespective of the variable and value ordering, we will only terminate each branch when $n-1$ variables have been assigned (and the last variable is forced). A simple calculation shows that the size of the search tree as least doubles as we increase n by 1. Hence we will visit $O(2^n)$ branches before declaring the problem unsatisfiable. ◇

5 Some Special Cases

Variables are not Interchangeable

Suppose we have interchangeable values but no variable symmetries (i.e. $a = n$ and $b < m$). To eliminate all symmetric solutions in such a situation, Law and Lee introduced value precedence [4]. This breaks symmetry by constraining when a value is first used. More precisely, $\text{PRECEDENCE}(k, [X_1, .., X_n])$ holds iff $\min\{i \mid X_i = d_k \vee i = n+1\} < \min\{i \mid X_i = d_{k+1} \vee i = n+2\}$. That is, the first time we use d_k is before the first time we use d_{k+1}. This prevents the two values being interchanged. It is not hard to show that the SIGLEX constraint is equivalent to value precedence in this situation.

Theorem 3. *$\text{PRECEDENCE}(k, [X_1, .., X_n])$ is equivalent to $\text{SIGLEX}(k, p, [X_1, .., X_n])$ when $n = a$ (i.e., $p(i) = i$ for $i \in [1, n]$).*

Proof: If $n = a$ then the vectors computed within SIGLEX, namely $(O_k^1, .., O_k^a)$ and $(O_{k+1}^1, .., O_{k+1}^a)$, are n-ary 0/1 vectors representing the indices at which d_k and d_{k+1} appear. Lexicographically ordering these vectors ensures that either d_k is used before d_{k+1} or neither are used. This is equivalent to value precedence. ◇

In this case, the propagator for SIGLEX mirrors the work done by the propagator for PRECEDENCE given in [16]. Although both propagators have the same asymptotic cost, we might prefer the one for PRECEDENCE as it introduces fewer intermediate variables.

All Variables and Values are Interchangeable

Another special case is when all variables and values are fully interchangeable (i.e. $a = b = 1$). To eliminate all symmetric solutions in such a situation, Walsh introduced a global constraint which ensures that the sequence of values is increasing but the number of their occurrences is decreasing [16]. More precisely, $\text{DECSEQ}([X_1, .., X_n])$ holds iff $X_1 = d_1$, $X_i = X_{i+1}$ or ($X_i = d_j$ and $X_{i+1} = d_{j+1}$) for $1 \leq i < n$ and $|\{i \mid X_i = d_k\}| \geq |\{i \mid X_i = d_{k+1}\}|$ for $1 \leq k < m$. Not surprisingly, the SIGLEX constraint ensures such an ordering of values.

Theorem 4. *$\text{DECSEQ}([X_1, .., X_n])$ is equivalent to $\text{SIGLEX}(k, p, [X_1, .., X_n])$ for $1 \leq k < m$ when $a = b = 1$ (i.e., $p : \{1\} \to \{1\}$).*

Proof: Suppose $\text{SIGLEX}(k, p, [X_1, .., X_n])$ holds for $1 \leq k < m$. Then $O_k^1 \geq O_{k+1}^1$ for $1 \leq k < m$. Now $O_k^1 = |\{i \mid X_i = d_k\}|$. Hence $|\{i \mid X_i = d_k\}| \geq |\{i \mid X_i = d_{k+1}\}|$ for $1 \leq k < m$. Suppose $O_1^1 = 0$. Then $O_k^1 = 0$ for $1 \leq k \leq m$ and no values can be used. This is impossible. Hence $O_1^1 > 0$ and d_1 is used. As $X_1 \leq .. \leq X_n$, $X_1 = d_1$. Suppose that d_k is the first value not used. Then $O_k^1 = 0$. Hence $O_j^1 = 0$ for all $j > k$. That is, all values up to d_k are used and all values including and after d_k are not used. Since $X_i \leq X_{i+1}$, it follows that $X_i = X_{i+1}$ or ($X_i = d_j$ and $X_{i+1} = d_{j+1}$) for $1 \leq i < n$. Thus, $\text{DECSEQ}([X_1, .., X_n])$ holds. The proof reverses easily. ◇

6 Variable Partition Ordering

Suppose there are two variable partitions $\{X_1, X_2\}$ and $\{X_3, X_4, X_5\}$, and all domain values $d_1, \ldots, d_5$ are interchangeable. Section 4 suggests that we can break the symmetry using SIGLEX$(k, p, \boldsymbol{X})$ for $1 \le k < 5$, where $\boldsymbol{X} = [X_1, \ldots, X_5]$, $p(1) = 1$ and $p(2) = 3$. In fact, the symmetry can be also broken by posting the SIGLEX constraints in another way: SIGLEX$(k, p', \boldsymbol{X}')$ for $1 \le k < 5$, where $\boldsymbol{X}' = [X'_1, X'_2, X'_3, X'_4, X'_5] = [X_3, X_4, X_5, X_1, X_2]$, $p'(1) = 1$ and $p'(2) = 4$. The former posting places the partition $\{X_1, X_2\}$ in front of $\{X_3, X_4, X_5\}$ in SIGLEX, and vice versa for the latter. The two postings eliminate different symmetric solutions, i.e., the solutions of the two postings are different. We observe that in the presence of ALLDIFF constraints, the order of the variable partitions placed in the SIGLEX constraints affects propagation. In the following, we study the issue of variable partition ordering in details.

In the above example, suppose that we also have ALLDIFF$([X_1, X_2])$ and ALLDIFF$([X_3, X_4, X_5])$, and we enforce GAC on these constraints. GAC on the former set of SIGLEX constraints alone removes $d_2, \ldots, d_5$ from the domain of X_1 (due to the lexicographic ordering on the signatures), making X_1 grounded. This triggers propagation on ALLDIFF$([X_1, X_2])$ that removes d_1 from the domain of X_2. Further propagation on the constraints results in $X_1 \in \{d_1\}$, $X_2 \in \{d_2\}$, $X_3 \in \{d_1, d_3\}$, $X_4 \in \{d_1, d_2, d_3, d_4\}$ and $X_5 \in \{d_1, d_2, d_3, d_4, d_5\}$. Note that all variables in the partition $\{X_1, X_2\}$ are grounded.

On the other hand, if we use the constraints SIGLEX$(k, p', \boldsymbol{X}')$ for $1 \le k < 5$, then enforcing GAC on these constraints and the two ALLDIFF constraints results in $X_1 \in \{d_1, d_4\}$, $X_2 \in \{d_1, d_2, d_4, d_5\}$, $X_3 \in \{d_1\}$, $X_4 \in \{d_2\}$ and $X_5 \in \{d_3\}$. This time, all variables in the partition $\{X_3, X_4, X_5\}$ are grounded.

In general, not every variable partition would contain an ALLDIFF constraint. If, however, all domain values are interchangeable and the *first* variable partition placed in the SIGLEX constraints contains an ALLDIFF, GAC on the SIGLEX and ALLDIFF constraints will either cause a domain wipe-out or ground *all* variables in the first partition.

Theorem 5. *Enforcing GAC on* ALLDIFF$([X_{p(1)}, \ldots, X_{p(2)-1}])$ *and the set of* SIGLEX *constraints decomposed from* BREAKINTERCHANGEABILITY *causes either domain wipe-out or* $X_i = d_i$ *for* $p(1) \le i \le \min(p(2) - 1, m)$ *if* $b = 1$.

Proof: Consider two cases $m < p(2) - 1$ or $m \ge p(2) - 1$. The former causes a domain wipe-out, as there are fewer domain values than variables in the ALLDIFF constraint.

For the latter case, we first prove by induction that $X_i \notin \{d_{i+1}, \ldots, d_m\} \forall p(1) \le i \le p(2) - 1$. When $i = p(1) = 1$, suppose conversely $X_1 = d_k$ for any $1 < k \le m$. As SIGLEX implies $X_1 \le \ldots \le X_{p(2)-1}$, we get $O^1_k \ge 1$ and $O^1_1 = 0$. But $O^1_k > O^1_1$ violates the lexicographic order on the signatures. Hence, $X_1 \ne d_k$ for $1 < k \le m$, i.e., $X_1 = d_1$. Assume the cases are true $\forall 1 \le i' < i$. Suppose conversely $X_i = d_k$, for any $i < k \le m$. Since $\forall i' < i, X_{i'} \notin \{d_{k-1}, d_k\}$, we get $O^1_k \ge 1$ and $O^1_{k-1} = 0$, which contradicts with the lexicographic order. This completes the induction.

We can now prove that for $p(1) \le i < p(2)$, either $X_i = d_i$ or X_i has empty domain. Since $X_1 \notin \{d_2, \ldots, d_m\}$, obviously either $X_1 = d_1$ or X_1 has empty domain. Suppose $X_1 = d_1$, enforcing GAC on ALLDIFF$([X_{p(1)}, \ldots, X_{p(2)-1}])$ will remove d_1 from the domains of $X_2, \ldots, X_{p(2)-1}$. Now, $X_2 \ne d_1$ and $X_2 \notin \{d_3, \ldots, d_m\}$. Then we have $X_2 = d_2$ or X_2 has empty domain. We can repeat the process of enforcing GAC on ALLDIFF($[X_{p(1)}, \ldots, X_{p(2)-1}]$) to consequently make either $X_i = d_i$ or domain wipe-out for $p(1) \leq i < p(2)$. $\diamond$

Therefore, if more than one variable partition contains an ALLDIFFconstraint, then placing the largest variable partition at the front in the SIGLEX constraints ensures the most variables are grounded, and therefore the most simplification of the problem. This can be seen from the above example, in which the first posting grounds only two variables, while the second posting grounds three. Furthermore, in the ALLDIFF constraints, a grounded variable in a larger partition triggers more prunings than one in a smaller partition, and enforcing GAC on SIGLEX tends to prunes values from variables earlier in the variable sequence, due to the $\geq_{\text{lex}}$ ordering on the signatures. Therefore, it is a good idea to place larger variable partitions at the front in the SIGLEX constraints to increase the chance of more prunings due to a grounded variable. This gives us a heuristic to rearrange the variables in the SIGLEX constraints so that *(1) variable partitions with* ALLDIFF *constraints are ordered before those without* ALLDIFF, *and (2) among those variable partitions with* ALLDIFF *constraints, order them in decreasing partition size.*

Theorem 5 applies to problems where all domain values are interchangeable. When there is more than one value partition ($b > 1$), enforcing GAC on the SIGLEX constraints does not necessarily ground the first variable in the first partition, since the first value $d_{q(j)}$ in every partition j can remain in its domain, making no subsequent groundings of the other variables in the partition by the SIGLEX and ALLDIFF constraints. Nonetheless, propagation by other problem constraints or variable instantiations during search can eventually ground variables and trigger the prunings by the ALLDIFF constraints. Therefore, in the case of $b > 1$, it is still worthwhile to reorder the variables using this heuristic. Note that this variable partition ordering heuristic helps improve the amount of pruning for the SIGLEX decomposition. Although it can be applied also to the GCC decomposition, the heuristic may not help here.

The discussion brings out an interesting question about posting symmetry breaking constraints. Ideally, symmetry breaking constraints remove all but one solution from each equivalence class of solutions. Different postings of the symmetry breaking constraints can leave a different solution. This is true for SIGLEX and also other symmetry breaking constraints. In terms of eliminating symmetric solutions, it does not matter which solution we leave. However, in terms of propagation, apparently the different postings give different behaviour. This is one of the first times it has been shown that breaking symmetry to leave a particular distinguished element of a symmetry class can reduce search. It would be interesting to study this systematically and formally in the future.

7 Implementation Notes

The proof of Theorem 1 already gives an overview of the implementation of the SIGLEX global constraint, which involves enforcing the $\leq$ ordering of the X_i variables, the channelling between the X_i and Y_i^k variables, and $a + 1$ REGULAR constraints, where a is the number of variable partitions. The first a REGULAR constraints are used to do the counting, while the last one enforces the $\geq_{\text{lex}}$ ordering using the final state information associated with the automata in the first a REGULAR constraints. The maintenance of the $\leq$ ordering and the channeling is straightforward. The REGULAR constraint, however, has to be slightly modified to fit the requirement of our implementation. In particular, we introduce an extra finite domain variable F_s to the REGULAR constraint so that REGULAR$([X_1, \ldots, X_n], F_s, \mathcal{M})$ means F_s is the final state of the string $[X_1, \ldots, X_n]$ admissible by the DFA $\mathcal{M} = (Q, \Sigma, \delta, q_0, F)$, where Q is the set of all states, Σ is the alphabet, δ is the state transition, q_0 is the initial state, and F is the set of final states.

Pesant [11] proposes a GAC propagator for the original REGULAR constraint by maintaining an associated layered directed multigraph $(N^1, \ldots, N^{n+1}, A)$, where n is the number of variables in the constraint. Let $\Sigma = \{v_1, \ldots, v_n\}$. Each layer $N^i = \{q_0^i, \ldots, q_{|Q|-1}^i\}$ contains a node q_l^i for each state $q_l \in Q$ and directed arcs in A appear only between two consecutive layers. The graph is acyclic by construction. There exists an arc from q_k^i to q_l^{i+1} iff there exists some v_j in the domain of X_i such that $\delta(q_k, v_j) = q_l$. The arc is labelled with the value v_j allowing the transition between the two states.

The multigraph is *consistent* if each node has a non-zero in-degree and a non-zero out-degree. Suppose a multigraph is inconsistent, i.e., there exists a node with either in-degree or out-degree being zero. We can make the multigraph consistent again by removing the node together with all its incoming or outgoing arcs from the graph. When the arc from q_k^i to q_l^{i+1} is removed, we check if the out-degree of q_k^i become zeros and if the in-degree of q_l^{i+1} becomes zero to ensure consistency of the multigraph. Pesant [11] gives a theorem stating that REGULAR$([X_1, \ldots, X_n], \mathcal{M})$ is GAC iff the domain of X_i is equal to the set of all labels from the outgoing arcs originating from nodes in layer N^i of a consistent multigraph associated with $\mathcal{M}$.

In the original constraint REGULAR$([X_1, \ldots, X_n], \mathcal{M})$, propagation is triggered when some values are deleted from the domain of some variable X_i. This corresponds to removing arcs from the associated multigraph of $\mathcal{M}$. In the new constraint REGULAR$([X_1, \ldots, X_n], F_s, \mathcal{M})$, we have to allow *also* triggerings caused by value deletions from the domain of F_s. This corresponds to removing a node in layer N^{n+1} of the associated multigraph of $\mathcal{M}$. If such a removal causes inconsistency in the multigraph, Pesant's procedure is still able to restore consistency. We can easily verify that REGULAR is GAC iff the domain of X_i is equal to the set of all labels from the outgoing arcs originating from nodes in layer N^i of a consistent multigraph associated with $\mathcal{M}$, and the domain of F_s is the set of nodes (states) in layer N^{n+1}.

We show in the proof of Theorem 1 that a SIGLEX constraint can be decomposed into several REGULAR constraints without hindering propagation, since the constraint graph of the decomposition is Berge-acyclic. However, we provide a global constraint implementation for SIGLEX as it provides opportunities for efficiencies. In our implementation, we achieved GAC on SIGLEX using a two-pass iteration. In the first pass, we enforce GAC on the decomposed constraints in a forward manner, from the $\leq$ ordering constraints on the X_i variables to the final REGULAR constraint for the $\geq_{\text{lex}}$ ordering. In the second pass, the constraints are propagated again but in the reverse order. This two-pass iteration guarantees that each constraint in the decomposition is propagated at most twice but GAC is still enforced on one SIGLEX constraint as a whole.

8 Experiments

To test the efficiency and effectiveness of the SIGLEX constraints, we perform experiments on the graph colouring and concert hall scheduling problems. We compare the SIGLEX constraints against (1) the GCC decomposition (GCC) and (2) PRECEDENCE constraints with $\leq$ ordering constraints (ValPrec). All three methods break both the variable and value interchangeability. When using SIGLEX constraints, we consider two variable partition orderings: the data file ordering (SigLex) and the decreasing partition size ordering (SigLex-dec) introduced in Section 6. The experiments are run on a Sun Blade 2500 ($2 \times$ 1.6GHz US-IIIi, 2GB RAM) using ILOG Solver 4.4. The time limit is 1 hour. The variable ordering heuristic is to choose first a variable with the smallest domain. Both benchmark problems are optimisation problems, and we report the number of fails and CPU time to find and prove the optimum in the results.

8.1 Graph Colouring

In graph colouring, nodes having the same set of neighbours form a partition and are interchangeable. We generate random graphs using four parameters $\langle n, r, p, q \rangle$, where n is the number of nodes and r is the maximum node partition size. We start from an independent graph (graph with no arcs) with n nodes and ensure node interchangeability while adding arcs to the graph in two steps. First, the subgraph containing nodes of two partitions must be either a complete bipartite or independent graph. In Example 1, the graph between partitions $\{X_1, X_2\}$ and $\{X_3, X_4, X_5\}$ is complete bipartite. The parameter p is the proportion of complete bipartite subgraphs between pairs of partitions. Second, the subgraph in one partition must also be either complete or independent. In Example 1, both subgraphs of the two partitions are independent. The parameter q is the proportion of complete subgraphs among the partitions. A complete subgraph in a partition is modelled using an ALLDIFF constraint on the variable partition.

With the four parameters, we generate two types of random graphs using different distributions on the variable partition size. In the first type, the number of nodes n_i in the ith partition is *uniformly* distributed in $[1, r]$. Since n is initially fixed, if the generated value of a particular n_i makes the total number of nodes exceed n, then the ith partition will be the final partition and its size n_i will be chosen such that the total number of nodes is exactly n. The second type has a *biased* distribution. The size of the first $\lfloor \frac{n}{2} \rfloor$ partitions are preset to 1, i.e., $\lfloor \frac{n}{2} \rfloor$ of the nodes are not interchangeable at all. The remaining nodes are then partitioned using a uniform distribution like in the first type. The latter type of graphs models a common scenario in real life problems where variable interchangeability occurs in only a subset of the variables. We test with various values of n, $r = 8$, $p = 0.5$ and $q \in \{0.5, 1\}$, and 20 instances are generated for each set of parameters. Fig. 1(a) and (b) show the experimental results for the uniform and biased distributions respectively. A data point is plotted only when at least 90% of the instances are solved within the time limit. All graphs are plotted in the log-scale.

At the same parameter setting, the instances of biased distribution are more difficult to solve than those of uniform distribution, since the former instances have fewer symmetries than the latter and thus fewer symmetry breaking constraints can be posted to reduce the search space. Nevertheless, for both distributions, SigLex and SigLex-dec

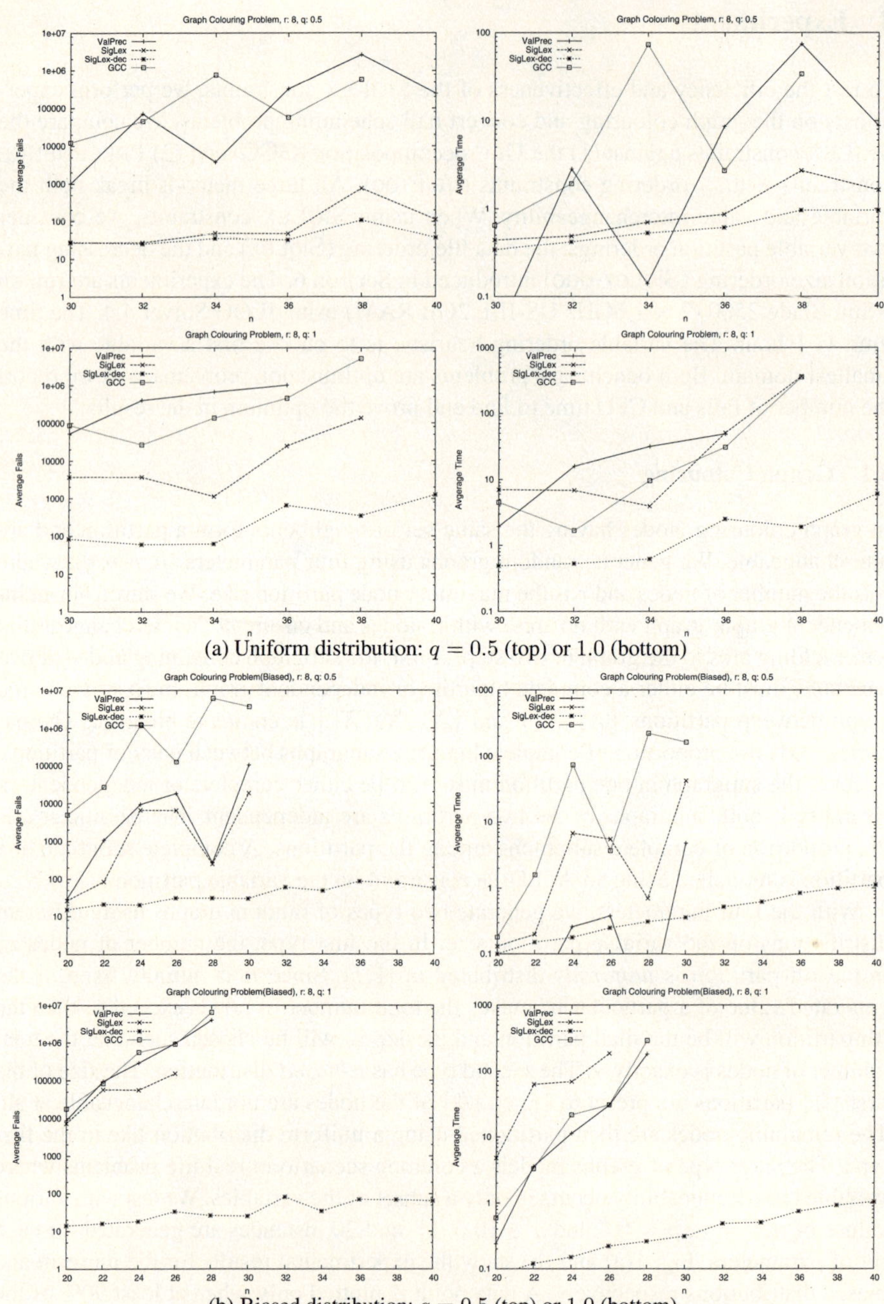

(a) Uniform distribution: $q = 0.5$ (top) or 1.0 (bottom)

(b) Biased distribution: $q = 0.5$ (top) or 1.0 (bottom)

Fig. 1. Graph colouring: average number of fails (left) and time (right)

took fewer number of fails than GCC and ValPrec in almost all parameter settings. The fewer number of fails, however, does not always lead to better run times, due to the overhead incurred by the introduction of intermediate variables inside the implementation of the SIGLEX constraint. ValPrec is competitive only for small values of n. The relative performance of SigLex and SigLex-dec over GCC and ValPrec increases as q increases. Among the two variable partition orderings in SIGLEX, SigLex-dec has much better performance than SigLex in both number of fails and run time, confirming the effectiveness of our proposed heuristic. The performance advantage of SigLex-dec over the other models becomes larger as both n and q increases.

8.2 Concert Hall Scheduling

A concert hall director receives n applications to use the k identical concert halls. Each application specifies a period and an offered price to use a hall for the whole period. The concert hall scheduling problem [18] is to decide which applications to accept in order to maximise the total income. Each accepted application should be assigned the same hall during its whole applied period. We use a variable to represent each application whose domain is $\{1, \ldots, k+1\}$ in two value partitions. Values $1, \ldots, k$ represent the k interchangeable halls, while the value $k+1$ represents a rejected application. Variables representing identical applications (same period and offered price) are interchangeable and form a partition. We generate problem instances with a maximum of $r = 8$ identical applications, and the size of each partition is generated uniformly. We test with n from 20 to 40 in steps of 2, $r = 8$ and $k \in \{10, 14\}$. Experimental results are shown in Fig. 2.

Regarding the number of fails, SigLex-dec achieves the best result and ValPrec performs the worst. Regarding the run time, SigLex-dec also achieves the best for almost all cases. SigLex has a slower run-time on this problem, despite a better number of fails than ValPrec and GCC. This is again due to the implementation overhead in the SIGLEX constraint. The decreasing variable partition ordering heuristic helps hugely to improve the pruning performance and hence outweigh the overhead to reduce the run time. We also generated instances using a biased distribution like in graph colouring and obtained similar experimental results. Due to space limitation, we skip the details.

Note that the concert hall scheduling problem does not really have ALLDIFF constraints in the variable partitions. However, the problem constraints are very similar to ALLDIFF: two variables X_i and X_j representing two interchangeable applications cannot take the same value (hall) *if* the two applications are not rejected. That is, $X_i \neq X_j$ if $X_i \neq k+1$ and $X_j \neq k+1$. The propagation behaviour of such kind of constraint is still similar to that of ALLDIFF. Thus, the decreasing size variable partition ordering can still help improve the pruning performance.

9 Related Work

Puget proved that symmetries can always be eliminated by the additional of suitable constraints [1]. Crawford *et al.* presented the first general method for constructing such symmetry breaking constraints, which are so-called “lex-leader” constraints [2]. They also argued that it is NP-hard to eliminate all symmetric solutions in general. The full set of lex-leader constraints can often be simplified. For example, when variables are

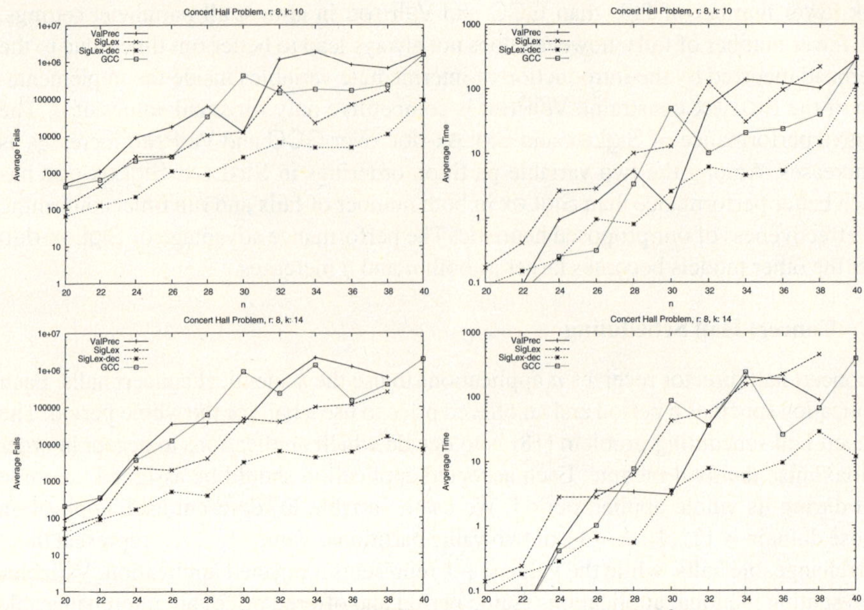

Fig. 2. Concert hall scheduling (uniform distribution): average number of fails (left) and time (right), $k = 10$ (top) or 14 (bottom)

interchangeable and must take all different values, Puget showed that the lex-leader constraints simplify to a linear number of binary inequality constraints [19]. To break value symmetry, Puget introduced one variable per value and a linear number of binary constraints [20]. Law and Lee formally defined value precedence and proposed a specialised propagator for breaking the special type of value symmetry between two interchangeable values [4]. Walsh extended this to a propagator for any number of interchangeable values [16]. Finally, an alternative way to break value symmetry statically is to convert it into a variable symmetry by channelling into a dual viewpoint and using lexicographic ordering constraints on this dual view [3,18]. Different postings of symmetry breaking constraints can leave a different solution from each equivalence class of solutions and affect search performance. Frisch *et al.* discussed choosing a good posting to give the best propagation and allow new implied constraints [21]. Smith presented experiments with different symmetry breaking constraints using the graceful graph problem, but did not give heuristics for choosing a good posting [22].

10 Conclusions

We have considered breaking the symmetry introduced by interchangeable variables and values. Whilst there exist polynomial methods to eliminate all symmetric solutions, pruning all symmetric values is NP-hard. We have introduced a new propagator called SIGLEX for pruning some (but not necessarily all) symmetric values. The new propagator is based on a decomposition using REGULAR constraints. We have also introduced a heuristic for ordering the variable partitions when posting SIGLEX constraints that improves pruning. Finally, we have tested these symmetry breaking constraints experimentally for the first time and shown that they are effective in practice.

References

1. Puget, J.F.: On the satisfiability of symmetrical constrained satisfaction problems. In: Proc. of ISMIS'93, pp. 350–361 (1993)
2. Crawford, J., Luks, G., Ginsberg, M., Roy, A.: Symmetry breaking predicates for search problems. In: Proc. of KR'96, pp. 148–159 (1996)
3. Flener, P., Frisch, A., Hnich, B., Kiziltan, Z., Miguel, I., Pearson, J., Walsh, T.: Breaking row and column symmetry in matrix models. In: Van Hentenryck, P. (ed.) CP 2002. LNCS, vol. 2470, pp. 462–476. Springer, Heidelberg (2002)
4. Law, Y.C., Lee, J.: Global constraints for integer and set value precedence. In: Wallace, M. (ed.) CP 2004. LNCS, vol. 3258, pp. 362–376. Springer, Heidelberg (2004)
5. Fahle, T., Schamberger, S., Sellmann, M.: Symmetry breaking. In: Walsh, T. (ed.) CP 2001. LNCS, vol. 2239, pp. 93–107. Springer, Heidelberg (2001)
6. Gent, I., Smith, B.: Symmetry breaking in constraint programming. In: Proc. of ECAI'00, pp. 599–603 (2000)
7. Roney-Dougal, C., Gent, I., Kelsey, T., Linton, S.: Tractable symmetry breaking using restricted search trees. In: Proc. of ECAI'04, pp. 211–215 (2004)
8. Walsh, T.: Breaking value symmetry. In: Proc. of CP'07 (2007)
9. Flener, P., Pearson, J., Sellmann, M., Van Hentenryck, P.: Static and dynamic structural symmetry breaking. In: Benhamou, F. (ed.) CP 2006. LNCS, vol. 4204, pp. 695–699. Springer, Heidelberg (2006)
10. Sellmann, M., Van Hentenryck, P.: Structural symmetry breaking. In: Proc. of IJCAI'05, pp. 298–303 (2005)
11. Pesant, G.: A regular language membership constraint for finite sequences of variables. In: Wallace, M. (ed.) CP 2004. LNCS, vol. 3258, pp. 295–482. Springer, Heidelberg (2004)
12. Quimper, C., van Beek, P., Lopez-Ortiz, A., Golynski, A.: Improved algorithms for the global cardinality constraint. In: Wallace, M. (ed.) CP 2004. LNCS, vol. 3258, pp. 542–556. Springer, Heidelberg (2004)
13. Quimper, C., Walsh, T.: Global grammar constraints. In: Benhamou, F. (ed.) CP 2006. LNCS, vol. 4204, pp. 751–755. Springer, Heidelberg (2006)
14. Puget, J.F.: Automatic detection of variable and value symmetries. In: van Beek, P. (ed.) CP 2005. LNCS, vol. 3709, pp. 475–489. Springer, Heidelberg (2005)
15. Frisch, A., Hnich, B., Kiziltan, Z., Miguel, I., Walsh, T.: Propagation algorithms for lexicographic ordering constraints. Artificial Intelligence 170, 803–908 (2006)
16. Walsh, T.: Symmetry breaking using value precedence. In: Proc. of ECAI'06, pp. 168–172 (2006)
17. Beeri, C., Fagin, R., Maier, D., Yannakakis, M.: On the desirability of acyclic database schemes. J. ACM 30, 479–513 (1983)
18. Law, Y.C., Lee, J.: Symmetry breaking constraints for value symmetries in constraint satisfaction. Constraints 11, 221–267 (2006)
19. Puget, J.F.: Breaking symmetries in all different problems. In: Proc. of IJCAI'05, pp. 272–277 (2005)
20. Puget, J.F.: Breaking all value symmetries in surjection problems. In: van Beek, P. (ed.) CP 2005. LNCS, vol. 3709, pp. 490–504. Springer, Heidelberg (2005)
21. Firsch, A., Jefferson, C., Miguel, I.: Symmetry breaking as a prelude to implied constraints: A constraint modelling pattern. In: Proc. of ECAI'04, pp. 171–175 (2004)
22. Smith, B.: Sets of symmetry breaking constraints. In: Proc. of SymCon'05. (2005)

Path Consistency by Dual Consistency

Christophe Lecoutre, Stéphane Cardon, and Julien Vion

CRIL – CNRS FRE 2499,
rue de l'université, SP 16
62307 Lens cedex, France
{lecoutre,cardon,vion}@cril.univ-artois.fr

Abstract. Dual Consistency (DC) is a property of Constraint Networks (CNs) which is equivalent, in its unrestricted form, to Path Consistency (PC). The principle is to perform successive singleton checks (i.e. enforcing arc consistency after the assignment of a value to a variable) in order to identify inconsistent pairs of values, until a fixpoint is reached. In this paper, we propose two new algorithms, denoted by sDC2 and sDC3, to enforce (strong) PC following the DC approach. These algorithms can be seen as refinements of Mac Gregor's algorithm as they partially and totally exploit the incrementality of the underlying Arc Consistency algorithm. While sDC3 admits the same interesting worst-case complexities as PC8, sDC2 appears to be the most robust algorithm in practice. Indeed, compared to PC8 and the optimal PC2001, sDC2 is usually around one order of magnitude faster on large instances.

1 Introduction

Constraint Networks (CNs) can naturally represent many interesting problems raised by real-world applications. To make easier the task of solving a CN (i.e. the task of finding a solution or proving that none exists), one usually tries to simplify the problem by reducing the search space. This is called inference [7].

Consistencies are properties of CNs that can be exploited (enforced) in order to make inferences. *Domain filtering consistencies* [6] allow to identify inconsistent values while *relation filtering consistencies* allow to identify inconsistent tuples (pairs when relations are binary) of values. For binary networks, Arc Consistency (AC) and Path Consistency (PC) are respectively the most studied domain and relation filtering consistencies. Many algorithms have been proposed to enforce PC on a given CN, e.g. PC3 [18], PC4 [9], PC5 [21], PC8 [5] and PC2001 [2].

Recently, a new relation filtering consistency, called Dual Consistency (DC) has been introduced [12]. The principle is to record inconsistent pairs of values identified after any variable assignment followed by an AC enforcement. Just like SAC (Singleton Arc Consistency), a domain filtering consistency, DC is built on top of AC. Interestingly, when applied on all constraints of a binary instance (including the implicit universal ones), DC is equivalent to PC, but when it is applied conservatively (i.e. only on explicit constraints of the binary network), Conservative DC (CDC) is stronger than Conservative PC (CPC). In [12], CDC is investigated: in particular, its relationship with other consistencies is studied and a cost-effective algorithm, called sCDC1, is proposed.

C. Bessiere (Ed.): CP 2007, LNCS 4741, pp. 438–452, 2007.

In this paper, we focus on DC and propose two new algorithms to enforce (strong) PC by following the principle underlying DC. It means that we establish (strong) PC by performing successive singleton checks (enforcing AC after a variable assignment) as initially proposed by Mac Gregor [16]. These two algorithms, denoted by sDC2 and sDC3, correspond to refined versions of the algorithm sCDC1, as they partially and totally exploit the incrementality of the underlying AC algorithm, respectively.

In terms of complexity, sDC2 admits a worst-case time complexity in $O(n^5d^5)$ and a worst-case space complexity in $O(n^2d^2)$ where n is the number of variables and d the greatest domain size. On the other hand, by its full exploitation of incrementality, sDC3 admits an improved worst-case time complexity in $O(n^3d^4)$ while keeping a worst-case space complexity in $O(n^2d^2)$. It makes sDC3 having the same (worst-case) complexities as PC8, the algorithm shown to be the fastest to enforce PC so far [5].

The paper is organized as follows. First, we introduce constraint networks and consistencies. Then, we describe two new algorithms to enforce strong path consistency, following the dual consistency approach, and establish their worst-case complexities. Finally, before concluding, we present the results of an experimentation we have conducted.

2 Constraint Networks and Consistencies

A Constraint Network (CN) P is a pair $(\mathscr{X}, \mathscr{C})$ where $\mathscr{X}$ is a finite set of n variables and $\mathscr{C}$ a finite set of e constraints. Each variable $X \in \mathscr{X}$ has an associated domain, denoted $dom^P(X)$, which represents the set of values allowed for X. Each constraint $C \in \mathscr{C}$ involves an ordered subset of variables of $\mathscr{X}$, called scope and denoted $scp(C)$, and has an associated relation denoted $rel^P(C)$, which represents the set of tuples allowed for the variables of its scope. When possible, we will write $dom(X)$ and $rel(C)$ instead of $dom^P(X)$ and $rel^P(C)$. X_a denotes a pair (X, a) with $X \in \mathscr{X}$ and $a \in dom(X)$ and we will say that X_a is a value of P. d will denote the size of the greatest domain, and λ the number of allowed tuples over all constraints of P, i.e. $\lambda = \sum_{C \in \mathscr{C}} |rel(C)|$. If P and Q are two CNs defined on the same sets of variables $\mathscr{X}$ and constraints $\mathscr{C}$, then we will write $P \leq Q$ iff $\forall X \in \mathscr{X}$, $dom^P(X) \subseteq dom^Q(X)$ and $\forall C \in \mathscr{C}$ $rel^P(C) \subseteq rel^Q(C)$. $P < Q$ iff $P \leq Q$ and $\exists X \in \mathscr{X} \mid dom^P(X) \subset dom^Q(X)$ or $\exists C \in \mathscr{C} \mid rel^P(C) \subset rel^Q(C)$. A binary constraint is a constraint which only involves two variables. In the following, we will restrict our attention to binary networks, i.e., networks that only involve binary constraints. Further, without any loss of generality, we will consider that the same scope cannot be shared by two distinct constraints. The density D of a binary CN is then defined as the ratio $2e/(n^2 - n)$.

A solution to a constraint network is an assignment of values to all the variables such that all the constraints are satisfied. A constraint network is said to be satisfiable iff it admits at least one solution. The Constraint Satisfaction Problem (CSP) is the NP-complete task of determining whether a given constraint network is satisfiable. Constraint networks can be characterized by properties called consistencies. The usual way to exploit them is to enforce them on a CN, while preserving the set of solutions. It then consists in identifying and removing some inconsistent values (e.g. with arc consistency), inconsistent pairs of values (e.g. with path consistency), etc. Here, "inconsistent" means that the identified values, pairs of values, etc. correspond to *nogoods*, i.e. cannot participate to any solution. We start introducing the consistencies we are interested in at the level of pairs of values. From now on, we will consider a binary constraint network $P = (\mathscr{X}, \mathscr{C})$.

Definition 1. *A pair (X_a, Y_b) of values of P such that $X \neq Y$ is:*

- *arc-consistent (AC) iff either $\nexists C \in \mathscr{C} \mid scp(C) = \{X,Y\}$ or $(X_a, Y_b) \in rel(C)$;*
- *path-consistent (PC) iff (X_a, Y_b) is AC and $\forall Z \in \mathscr{X} \mid Z \neq X \wedge Z \neq Y$, $\exists c \in dom(Z)$ such that (X_a, Z_c) is AC and (Y_b, Z_c) is AC.*

We can now introduce Arc Consistency (AC) and Path Consistency (PC) with respect to a CN.

Definition 2. *A value X_a of P is AC iff $\forall Y (\neq X) \in \mathscr{X}$, $\exists b \in dom(Y) \mid (X_a, Y_b)$ is AC. P is AC iff $\forall X \in \mathscr{X}$, $dom(X) \neq \emptyset$ and $\forall a \in dom(X)$, X_a is AC.*

Definition 3. *A pair (X,Y) of distinct variables of $\mathscr{X}$ is PC iff $\forall a \in dom(X)$, $\forall b \in dom(Y)$, (X_a, Y_b) is PC. P is PC iff any pair of distinct variables of $\mathscr{X}$ is PC.*

AC admits the following property: for any network P, there exists a greatest subnetwork of P which is arc-consistent, denoted by $AC(P)$. Remark that if any variable in $AC(P)$ has an empty domain, P is unsatisfiable. We will denote this by $AC(P) = \bot$. For any value X_a, we will write $X_a \in AC(P)$ iff $a \in dom^{AC(P)}(X)$ (we will consider that $X_a \notin \bot$). Finally, $P|_{X=a}$ represents the network obtained from P by restricting the domain of X to the singleton $\{a\}$. The singleton check of a pair (X,a) corresponds to determine whether or not $AC(P|_{X=a}) = \bot$. When the check is positive, we say that (X,a) is singleton arc inconsistent. We can now introduce Dual Consistency (DC) [12].

Definition 4. *A pair (X_a, Y_b) of values of P such that $X \neq Y$ is dual-consistent (DC) iff $Y_b \in AC(P_{|X=a})$ and $X_a \in AC(P_{|Y=b})$. A pair (X,Y) of distinct variables of $\mathscr{X}$, is DC iff $\forall a \in dom(X)$, $\forall b \in dom(Y)$, (X_a, Y_b) is DC. P is DC iff any pair of distinct variables of $\mathscr{X}$ is DC.*

Surprisingly, DC appears to be equivalent to PC although it was predictable since McGregor had already proposed an AC-based algorithm to establish sPC [16]. A proof can be found in [12].

Proposition 1. *DC = PC*

Finally, from any relation filtering consistency, it is possible to obtain a new consistency by additionally considering Arc Consistency. Classically, a network is strong path-consistent, denoted sPC, iff it is both arc-consistent and path-consistent. We can remark that enforcing AC (only once) on a PC network is sufficient to obtain an sPC network.

3 New Algorithms to Enforce Strong Path Consistency

The two algorithms that we propose to establish sPC are called sDC2 and sDC3. Before describing them, we need to quickly introduce a basic AC algorithm, FC and a direct adaptation of sCDC1. Remember that the general principle is to perform successive singleton checks until a fix-point is reached.

3.1 AC and FC

The description of the sDC algorithms (which enforce sPC since DC = PC) is given in the context of using an underlying coarse-grained AC algorithm, such as AC3 [15], AC2001/3.1 [2] or AC3^{rm} [13], with a variable-oriented propagation scheme. If $P = (\mathscr{X}, \mathscr{C})$ is a CN, then $AC(P, Q)$ with $Q \subseteq \mathscr{X}$ means enforcing arc consistency on P from the given propagation set Q. Q contains all variables that can be used to detect arc-inconsistent values in the domain of other variables.

The description is given by Algorithm 1. As long as there is a variable in Q, one is selected and the revision of any variable connected to it (via a constraint) is performed. A revision is performed by a call to the function $revise$ (e.g. see [2]) specific to the chosen coarse-grained arc consistency algorithm, and entails removing values in the domain of the given variable that have become inconsistent with respect to the given constraint. When a revision is effective (at least one value has been removed), the set Q is updated. We will not discuss here about potential optimizations.

Algorithm 1. AC (P = $(\mathscr{X}, \mathscr{C})$: Constraint Network, Q: Set of Variables)

while $Q \neq \emptyset$ **do**
  pick and delete X from Q
  foreach $C \in \mathscr{C} \mid X \in scp(C)$ **do**
    let Y be the second variable involved in C
    if $revise(C, Y)$ **then**
      $Q \leftarrow Q \cup \{Y\}$

In the sequel, we will also refer to Forward Checking (FC) [10] which is an algorithm that maintains a partial form of arc consistency. More precisely, whenever a variable is assigned during search, only unassigned variables connected to it are revised. This is described by Algorithm 2. Remark that the worst-case time complexity of a call to FC is $O(nd)$ since there are at most $n - 1$ revisions and the revision of a variable against an assigned variable is $O(d)$.

Algorithm 2. FC (P = $(\mathscr{X}, \mathscr{C})$: Constraint Network, X: Variable)

foreach $C \in \mathscr{C} \mid X \in scp(C)$ **do**
  let Y be the second variable involved in C
  $revise(C, Y)$

3.2 Algorithm sDC1

Here, our purpose is to establish sPC (strong PC). As we know that CDC (i.e. DC only considered between variables connected by a constraint) is equivalent to PC when the constraint graph is complete, we can slightly adapt the algorithm sCDC1 introduced in [12]. We quickly describe this algorithm (in order to make this paper self-contained as much as possible), called sDC1, before proposing some improvements to it.

In Algorithm 3, AC is enforced first (line 1), and then, at each iteration of the main loop, a different variable is considered (let us call it the current variable). Assuming here that $\mathscr{X}$ is ordered, $first(\mathscr{X})$ returns the first variable of $\mathscr{X}$, and $next\text{-}modulo(\mathscr{X}, X)$ returns the variable that follows X in $\mathscr{X}$, if it exists, or $first(\mathscr{X})$ otherwise. Calling $checkVar1$ at line 6 enables us to make all possible inferences from X (this is depicted below). If any inference is performed, $true$ is returned and arc consistency is re-established (line 7). Remark that, when the domain of the current variable is singleton, no inference can be made anymore since the network is always maintained arc-consistent. This is the reason of the test at line 5 (not present in sCDC1).

Algorithm 3. sDC1($P = (\mathscr{X}, \mathscr{C})$: CN)

```
1  P ← AC(P, 𝒳)
2  X ← first(𝒳)
3  marker ← X
4  repeat
5      if |dom(X)| > 1 then
6          if checkVar1(P, X) then
7              P ← AC(P, {X})
8              marker ← X
9      X ← next-modulo(𝒳, X)
10 until X = marker
```

Performing all inferences with respect to a variable X is achieved by calling the function $checkVar1$ (Algorithm 4). For each value a in the domain of X, AC is enforced on $P|_{X=a}$. If a is singleton arc-inconsistent, then a is removed from the domain of X (line 5). Otherwise (lines 8 to 12), for any value Y_b present in P and absent in P', the tuple (X_a, Y_b) is removed from $rel(C)$.

In [12], it is proved that sCDC1 always terminates, enforces sCDC and admits a worst-case time complexity of $O(\lambda end^3)$. A direct consequence is that sDC1 enforces sPC and admits a worst-case time complexity of $O(\lambda n^3 d^3)$.

3.3 Algorithm sDC2

The algorithm sDC2 can be seen as a refinement of sDC1. The idea is to limit the cost of enforcing AC each time we have to perform a singleton check. In sDC1, we apply $AC(P|_{X=a}, \{X\})$. This is strictly equivalent to $AC(FC(P|_{X=a}, X), Q)$ where Q denotes the set of variables of P whose domain has been reduced by $FC(P|_{X=a}, X)$. Indeed, when applying $AC(P|_{X=a}, \{X\})$, we first start by revising each variable $Y \neq X$

Algorithm 4. checkVar1($P = (\mathscr{X}, \mathscr{C})$: CN, X: Variable): Boolean

```
modified ← false
foreach a ∈ dom^P(X) do
    P' ← AC(P|X=a, {X})
    if P' = ⊥ then
        remove a from dom^P(X)
        modified ← true
    else
        foreach Y ∈ 𝒳 | Y ≠ X do
            let C ∈ 𝒞 | scp(C) = {X, Y}
            foreach b ∈ dom^P(Y) | b ∉ dom^P'(Y) do
                remove (X_a, Y_b) from rel^P(C)
                modified ← true
return modified
```

against X, and put this variable in the propagation queue if some value(s) of its domain has been removed. The first pass of AC enforcement is then equivalent to forward checking. Except for the first singleton check of (X, a), in sDC2, we will apply $AC(FC(P|_{X=a}, X), Q')$ where Q' is a set of variables built from some information recorded during propagation. The point is that necessarily $Q' \subseteq Q$, which means that sDC2 is less expensive than sDC1 (since some useless revisions may be avoided, and, as we will see, the cost of managing the information about propagation is negligible). Roughly speaking, we partially exploit the incrementality of the underlying arc consistency algorithm in sDC2. An arc consistency algorithm is said incremental if its worst-case time complexity is the same when it is applied one time on a given network P and when it is applied up to nd times on P where, between two consecutive executions, at least one value has been deleted. All current arc consistency algorithms are incremental.

To enforce sPC on a given network P, one can then call the second algorithm we propose, sDC2 (see Algorithm 5). This algorithm differs from sDC1 by the introduction of a counter and a data structure, denoted $lastModif$, which is an array of integers. The counter is used to count the number of turns of the main loop (see lines 4 and 6). The use of $lastModif$ is defined as follows: for each variable X, $lastModif[X]$ indicates the number of the last turn where one inference concerning X has been performed. Such an inference can be the removal of a value in $dom(X)$ or the removal of a tuple in the relation associated with a constraint involving X. When the function $checkVar2$ returns $true$, it means that at least one inference concerning X has been performed. This is why $lastModif[X]$ is updated (line 10). Then, AC is maintained (line 11), and if at least one value has been removed since X is the current variable ($nbValues(P)$ indicates the cumulated number of values in P), we consider that each variable has been "touched" at the current turn. Of course, a more subtle update of the array $lastModif$ can be conceived (looking for variables really concerned by the inferences performed when maintaining AC). From experience, it just bloats the algorithm without any noticeable benefit.

Algorithm 5. sDC2($P = (\mathscr{X}, \mathscr{C})$: CN)

1 $P \leftarrow AC(P, \mathscr{X})$
2 $X \leftarrow first(\mathscr{X})$
3 $marker \leftarrow X$
4 $cnt \leftarrow 0$
5 **repeat**
6     $cnt \leftarrow cnt + 1$
7   **if** $|dom(X)| > 1$ **then**
8         $nbValuesBefore \leftarrow nbValues(P)$
9   **if** $checkVar2(P, X, cnt)$ **then**
10             $lastModif[X] \leftarrow cnt$
11             $P \leftarrow AC(P, \{X\})$
12   **if** $nbValues(P) \neq nbValuesBefore$ **then**
13                 $lastModif[Y] \leftarrow cnt, \forall Y \in \mathscr{X}$
14             $marker \leftarrow X$
15     $X \leftarrow next\text{-}modulo(\mathscr{X}, X)$
16 **until** $X = marker$

All inferences, if any, concerning a given variable X, are achieved by calling the function $checkVar2$ (Algorithm 6). For each value a of $dom(X)$, if this is the first call to $checkVar2$ for X (line 3), then we proceed as usually. Otherwise, incrementality is partially exploited by removing first at least all values that were removed by the last AC enforcement of (X, a). This is done by calling FC. Then, we apply AC from a propagation queue composed of all variables that were concerned by at least one inference during the last $|\mathscr{X}| - 1$ calls to $checkVar2$. The remaining of the function is identical to $checkVar1$, except for the update of $lastModif$ (line 13) whenever a tuple is removed ($lastModif[X]$ is not updated since done at line 10 of Algorithm 5).

Proposition 2. *The algorithm sDC2 enforces sPC.*

Proof. First, it is immediate that any inference performed by sDC2 is correct. Completeness is guaranteed by the following invariant: when $P' \leftarrow AC(FC(P|_{X=a}, X), Q)$ with $Q = \{Y \mid cnt - lastModif[Y] < |\mathscr{X}|\}$ is performed at line 4 of Algorithm 6, we have $P' = AC(P|_{X=a}, \mathscr{X})$. It simply means that P' is either arc-consistent or equal to $\bot$. The reason is that the network P is maintained arc-consistent whenever a modification is performed (line 11 of Algorithm 5) and that any inference performed with respect to a value X_a has no impact on $P|_{X=b}$, where b is any other value in the domain of the variable X. The invariant holds since, whenever an inference is performed, it is recorded in $lastModif$. □

Proposition 3. *The worst-case time complexity of sDC2 is $O(\lambda n^3 d^3)$ and its worst-case space complexity is $O(n^2 d^2)$.*

Proof. Remember that the worst-case time and space complexities of sDC1 are respectively $O(\lambda n^3 d^3)$ and $O(n^2 d^2)$. Hence, to obtain the same result for sDC2, it suffices to remark that the cumulated worst-case time complexity of line 13 of Algorithm 5 is $O(n^2 d)$, and that the space complexity of the new structure $lastModif$ is $\theta(n)$. □

Algorithm 6. checkVar2($P = (\mathscr{X}, \mathscr{C})$: CN, X: Variable, cnt: integer): Boolean

```
modified ← false
foreach a ∈ dom^P(X) do
    if cnt ≤ |𝒳| then P' ← AC(P|X=a, {X})
    else P' ← AC(FC(P|X=a, X), {Y | cnt − lastModif[Y] < |𝒳|})
    if P' = ⊥ then
        remove a from dom^P(X)
        modified ← true
    else
        foreach Y ∈ 𝒳 | Y ≠ X do
            let C ∈ 𝒞 | scp(C) = {X, Y}
            foreach b ∈ dom^P(Y) | b ∉ dom^P'(Y) do
                remove (X_a, Y_b) from rel^P(C)
                lastModif[Y] ← cnt
                modified ← true
return modified
```

3.4 Algorithm sDC3

To fully exploit the incrementality of an AC algorithm such as AC3[1] when enforcing strong path consistency, we simply need to introduce the specific data structure of AC3 with respect to each value (it is then related to the approach used in [1] for the algorithm SAC-OPT). The set Q_{X_a}, which denotes this structure, represents the propagation queue dedicated to the problem $P|_{X=a}$. The principle used in sDC3 is the following: If P_1 corresponds to $AC(P|_{X=a}, \mathscr{X})$, and P_i with $i > 1$ denotes the result of the ith AC enforcement wrt X_a, then P_{i+1} corresponds to $AC(P'_i, Q_{X_a})$ where P'_i is a network such that $P'_i < P_i$ and $Q_{X_a} = \{X \in \mathscr{X} \mid dom^{P'_i}(X) \subset dom^{P_i}(X)\}$. The cumulated worst-case time complexity of making these successive AC enforcements wrt X_a is clearly $O(ed^3) = O(n^2d^3)$ since AC3 is incremental and from one call to another, at least one value has been removed from one domain.

To enforce sPC on a given network P, sDC3 (see Algorithm 7) can then be called. As mentioned above, a propagation queue Q_{X_a} is associated with any value X_a. We also introduce a queue Q to contain the set of values for which a singleton check must be performed. Note that $X_a \in Q$ iff $Q_{X_a} \neq \emptyset$. Initially, AC is enforced on P, all dedicated queues are initialized with a special value denoted $\top$ (which is equivalent to $\mathscr{X}$, although considered as being different) and Q is filled up. Then, as long as Q is not empty, one value is selected from Q, a singleton check is performed with respect to this value and potentially some tuples are removed.

When *checkValue* (see Algorithm 8) is called, it is possible to determine whether or not this is the first call for the given value X_a. Indeed, if $Q_{X_a} = \top$, this is the case, and then we just have to make a classical AC enforcement on $P|_{X=a}$. Otherwise, we enforce AC by using FC and the dedicated propagation queue Q_{X_a}. If a is detected as singleton arc inconsistent, it is removed and we look for any value Y_b being compatible

[1] To establish our complexity results for sDC3, we do not need to use an optimal AC algorithm.

Algorithm 7. sDC3($P = (\mathscr{X}, \mathscr{C})$: CN)

$P \leftarrow AC(P, \mathscr{X})$
$Q_{X_a} \leftarrow \top, \forall X \in \mathscr{X}, \forall a \in dom(X)$
$Q \leftarrow \{X_a \mid X \in \mathscr{X} \wedge a \in dom^P(X)\}$
while $Q \neq \emptyset$ **do**
  pick and remove an element X_a from Q
  $R \leftarrow checkValue(P, X_a)$
  $removeTuples(P, R)$

Algorithm 8. checkValue($P = (\mathscr{X}, \mathscr{C})$: CN, X_a: Value): Set of Tuples

$R \leftarrow \emptyset$
if $Q_{X_a} = \top$ **then** $P' \leftarrow AC(P|_{X=a}, \{X\})$
else $P' \leftarrow AC(FC(P|_{X=a}, X), Q_{X_a})$
$Q_{X_a} \leftarrow \emptyset$
if $P' = \bot$ **then**
  remove a from $dom^P(X)$
  foreach $Y \in \mathscr{X} \mid Y \neq X$ **do**
    foreach $b \in dom^P(Y) \mid (X_a, Y_b)$ *is AC* **do**
      add Y_b to Q ; add X to Q_{Y_b}
else
  foreach $Y \in \mathscr{X} \mid Y \neq X$ **do**
    foreach $b \in dom^P(Y) \mid b \notin dom^{P'}(Y)$ **do**
      add (X_a, Y_b) to R
return R

Algorithm 9. removeTuples($P = (\mathscr{X}, \mathscr{C})$: CN, R: Set of Tuples)

$initsize \leftarrow |R|$
$cnt \leftarrow 0$
while $R \neq \emptyset$ **do**
  $cnt \leftarrow cnt + 1$
  pick and delete the first element (X_a, Y_b) of R
  remove (X_a, Y_b) from $rel^P(C)$ where $C \in \mathscr{C} \mid scp(C) = \{X, Y\}$
  if $cnt > initsize$ **then**
    add X_a to Q ; add Y to Q_{X_a}
  add Y_b to Q ; add X to $Q_{Y,b}$
  foreach $Z \in \mathscr{X} \mid Z \neq X \wedge Z \neq Y$ **do**
    foreach $c \in dom^P(Z) \mid (Z_c, X_a)$ *is AC* $\wedge$ (Z_c, Y_b) *is AC* **do**
      if $\nexists d \in dom^P(X) \mid (Z_c, X_d)$ *is AC* $\wedge$ (X_d, Y_b) *is AC* **then**
        add (Z_c, X_a) to the end of R
      if $\nexists d \in dom^P(Y) \mid (Z_c, Y_d)$ *is AC* $\wedge$ (X_a, Y_d) *is AC* **then**
        add (Z_c, Y_b) to the end of R

with X_a. For each such value, we add X to Q_{Y_b} (and Y_b to Q) since the next time we will make an AC enforcement wrt Y_b, the value X_a which was present so far will have disappeared. We then need to take this into account, thanks to $X \in Q_{Y_b}$, in order to guarantee that AC is really enforced. If a is not detected as singleton arc inconsistent, we look for tuples that can be removed. Here, they are simply put in a set R.

When $removeTuples$ (see Algorithm 9) is called, each tuple (X_a, Y_b) is considered in turn in order to remove it (line 6). Then, we add Y to Q_{X_a} (and Y_b to Q): the next time we will make an AC enforcement wrt Y_b, the value X_a which was present so far (otherwise, the tuple will have already been removed) will have disappeared. Adding X to Q_{Y_b} is not necessary if the tuple (X_a, Y_b) has been put in R during the execution of $checkValue$ (by recording the initial size of the set R and using a counter, we can simply determine that). Indeed, if this is the case, it means that Y_b was removed during the last AC enforcement wrt X_a. Finally, we have to look for any value Z_c which is both compatible with X_a and Y_b. If there is no value X_d compatible with both Z_c and Y_b, it means that the tuple Z_c, X_a can be removed. Similarly, if there is no value Y_d compatible with both Z_c and X_a, it means that the tuple Z_c, Y_b can be removed.

Proposition 4. *The algorithm sDC3 enforces sPC.*

Sketch of proof. The following invariant holds: when $P' \leftarrow AC(FC(P|_{X=a}, X), Q_{X_a})$ is performed at line 3 of Algorithm 8, we have $P' = AC(P|_{X=a}, \mathscr{X})$. □

Proposition 5. *The worst-case time complexity of sDC3 is $O(n^3d^4)$ and its worst-case space complexity is $O(n^2d^2)$.*

Proof. The worst-case time complexity of sDC3 can be computed from the cumulated worst-case time complexity of $checkValue$ and the cumulated worst-case time complexity of $removeTuples$. First, it is easy to see that, in the worst-case, the number of calls to $checkValue$, for a given value X_a, is $O(nd)$. Indeed, between two calls, at least one tuple t of a relation, associated with a constraint involving X and another variable, such that $t[X] = a$ is removed. The cumulated worst-case time complexity of making the network FC, wrt X_a, is then $O(nd \times nd) = O(n^2d^2)$ whereas the cumulated worst-case time complexity of enforcing AC, wrt X_a, is $O(ed^3) = O(n^2d^3)$ if we use AC3 due to its incrementality. Lines 6 to 9 can only be executed once for X_a (it is only $O(nd)$) and the cumulated worst-case time complexity of executing lines 11 to 13, wrt X_a, is $O(n^2d^2)$. As a result, we obtain a cumulated worst-case time complexity of $checkValue$ with respect to any value in $O(n^2d^3)$ and then a cumulated worst-case time complexity of $checkValue$ in $O(n^3d^4)$ since there are $O(nd)$ values.

On the other hand, the cumulated number of turns of the main loop of $removeTuples$ is $O(n^2d^2)$ since the number of tuples in the constraint network is $O(n^2d^2)$ and since, at each turn, one tuple is removed (see line 6 of Algorithm 9). As the worst-case time complexity of one turn of the main loop of $removeTuples$ is $O(nd^2)$, we can deduce that the cumulated worst-case time complexity of $removeTuples$ is then $O(n^3d^4)$. From those results, we deduce that the worst-case time complexity of $sDC3$ is $O(n^3d^4)$. In terms of space, remember that representing the instance is $O(n^2d^2)$. The data structures introduced in sDC3 are the sets Q_{X_a} which are $O(n^2d)$, the set Q which is $O(nd)$ and the set R which is $O(n^2d^2)$. We then obtain $O(n^2d^2)$. □

Remark that if we use an optimal AC algorithm such as AC2001, the worst-case time complexity of sDC3 remains $O(n^3d^4)$ but the worst-case space complexity becomes $O(n^3d^2)$ since the *last* structure, in $O(n^2d)$ of AC2001 must be managed independently for each value. It can also be shared but, contrary to [1], the interest is limited here. On the other hand, one can easily adopt AC3^{rm} since the specific structure of AC3^{rm}, in $O(n^2d)$, can be naturally shared between all values.

3.5 Complexity Issues

As λ is bounded by $O(n^2d^2)$, sDC1 and sDC2 may be up to $O(n^5d^5)$. This seems to be rather high (this is the complexity of PC1), but our opinion is that, similarly to sCDC1, both algorithms quickly reach a fix-point (i.e. the number of times the function $checkVar1$ or $checkVar2$ is called for a given variable is small in practice) because inferences about inconsistent values and, especially pairs of values, can be immediately taken into account. Besides, sDC2 partially benefits from incrementality, and so is close to sDC3 which admits a nice worst-case time complexity in $O(n^3d^4)$.

On the other hand, the following proposition indicates that the time wasted to apply one of the three introduced algorithms on a network which is already sPC is quite reasonable. The three algorithms have essentially the same behaviour.

Proposition 6. *Applied to a constraint network which is sPC, the worst-case time complexity of sDC1, sDC2 and sDC3 is $O(n^3d^3)$.*

Proof. If the network is sPC, the number of singleton checks will be $O(nd)$. As a singleton check is $O(ed^2) = O(n^2d^2)$ if we use an optimal AC algorithm, we obtain $O(n^3d^3)$. □

Proposition 7. *The best-case time complexity of sDC1, sDC2 and sDC3 is $O(n^2d^2)$.*

Proof. The best case is when all constraints are universal (i.e. when all tuples are allowed). Indeed, in this case, enforcing AC corresponds to calling FC since we just need to check that any value of any variable is compatible with the current assignment. A singleton check is then $O(nd)$, and the overall complexity is $O(n^2d^2)$. □

There is another interesting case to be considered. This is when after the first pass of AC (actually, FC), many revisions can be avoided by exploiting Proposition 1 of [3]. Considering a network that is sPC and assuming that all revisions can be avoided by using this *revision condition* [17], the worst-case time complexity becomes $O(nd.(nd+n^2)) = O(n^2d.max(n,d))$ as for each singleton check the number of revisions which comes after FC is $O(n^2)$, each one being $O(1)$ since the revision effort is avoided. This has to be compared with the cost of the initialization phase of PC8 and PC2001 which is $O(n^3d^2)$ in the same context. It means that one can expect here an improvement by a factor $O(min(n,d))$.

4 Experiments

In order to show the practical interest of the approach described in this paper, we have conducted an experimentation on a i686 2.4GHz processor equipped with 1024 MiB

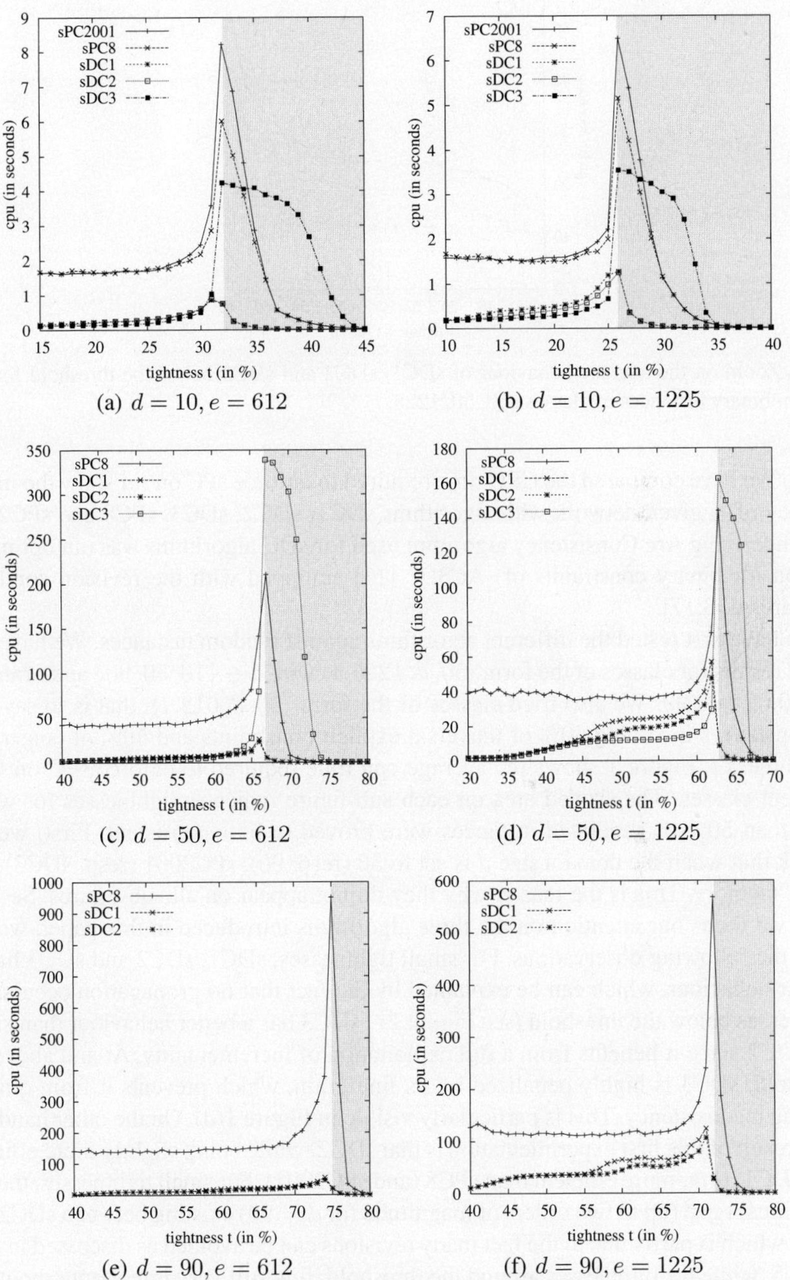

Fig. 1. Average results obtained for 100 random binary instances of classes $\langle 50, d, e, t \rangle$

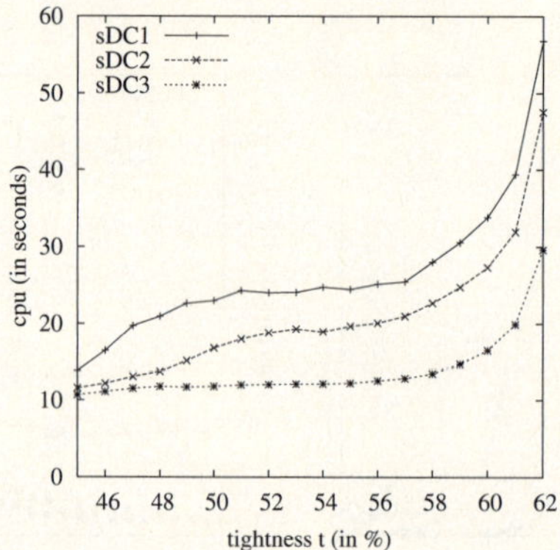

Fig. 2. Zoom on the average behaviour of sDC1, sDC2 and sDC3 below the threshold for 100 random binary instances of classes $\langle 50, 50, 1225, t\rangle$

RAM. We have compared the CPU time required to enforce sPC on (or show the inconsistency of) a given network with algorithms sDC1, sDC2, sDC3, sPC8 and sPC2001. The underlying Arc Consistency algorithm used for sDC algorithms was (an optimized version for binary constraints of) AC3^{rm} [13] equipped with the revision condition mechanism [3,17].

We have first tested the different algorithms against random instances. We have collected results for classes of the form $\langle 50, d, 1225, t\rangle$ with $d \in \{10, 50, 90\}$ and t ranging from 0.01 to 0.99. We also tried classes of the form $\langle 50, d, 612, t\rangle$, that is to say random instances involving 50% of universal explicit constraints and 50% of constraints of tightness t. Figure 1 shows the average cpu time required to enforce sPC on these different classes. The shaded area on each sub-figure indicates tightnesses for which more than 50% of generated instances were proved to be inconsistent. First, we can remark that when the domain size d is set to 50 (resp. 90), sPC2001 (resp. sDC3) runs out of memory. This is the reason why they do not appear on all sub-figures. Second, when we focus our attention on the three algorithms introduced in this paper, we can make the following observations. For small tightnesses, sDC1, sDC2 and sDC3 have a similar behaviour, which can be explained by the fact that no propagation occurs. For tightnesses below the threshold (see Figure 2) , sDC3 has a better behaviour than sDC1 and sDC2 since it benefits from a full exploitation of incrementality. At and above the threshold, sDC3 is highly penalized by its fine grain, which prevents it from quickly proving inconsistency. This is particularly visible in Figure 1(d). On the other hand, the main result of this first experimentation is that sDC2, while being slightly more efficient than sDC1, is far more efficient than sPC8 (and sPC2001). For small tightnesses, there is a significant gap (up to two orders of magnitude for $d = 90$) existing between sDC2 and sPC8, which is partly due to the fact many revisions can be avoided as discussed in Section 3.5, while for tightnesses around the threshold, it is still very important (about one order of magnitude for $d = 90$). We can even observe that the gap increases when the density decreases, which is not surprising since the number of allowed tuples increases with the number of universal constraints and the fact that classical PC algorithms deal with allowed tuples.

Table 1. Results obtained on academic queens and langford instances; cpu in seconds and mem(ory) in MiB

Instances		*sPC8*	*sPC2001*	*sDC1*	*sDC2*	*sDC3*
queens-30	*cpu*	5.06	5.37	2.22	2.28	2.60
	mem	17	76	17	17	37
queens-50	*cpu*	50.9	–	4.6	4.5	5.3
	mem	30		22	22	149
queens-80	*cpu*	557.9	–	26.8	24.7	–
	mem	97		44	44	
queens-100	*cpu*	1549	–	62	58	–
	mem	197		73	73	
langford-3-16	*cpu*	45.45	66.66	4.91	4.44	57.8
	mem	27	612	21	21	129
langford-3-17	*cpu*	63.48	–	6.06	6.07	76.79
	mem	34		22	22	157
langford-3-20	*cpu*	140	–	11	9.7	198
	mem	43		26	26	250
langford-3-30	*cpu*	1247	–	60	50	–
	mem	138		56	56	

Table 1, built from two series of academic instances, confirms the results obtained for random instances. Indeed, on such structured instances, sDC2 is about 20 times more efficient than sPC8 for large ones, whatever inference occurs or not. The *queens* instances are already sPC, which is not the case of the *langford* instances.

5 Conclusion

In this paper, we have introduced two algorithms to enforce strong path consistency. The algorithm sDC2 has been shown to be a good compromise between the basic sDC1 and the more refined sDC3. Even if the worst-case time complexity of sDC2 seems rather high, its close relationship with sDC3, which admits a complexity close to the optimal, suggests its practical efficiency. In practice, on random instances, sDC2 is slightly slower than sDC3 when the number of inferences is limited, but far faster at the phase transition of path consistency. Compared to sPC8 and the optimal sPC2001, sDC2 is usually around one order of magnitude faster on large instances.

Maybe, one can wonder about the interest of PC algorithms when the constraint graph is not complete. Indeed, when a pair of values is identified as not being PC, it has to be removed from the network. When no constraint binding the two involved variables exists in the CN, a new one has to be inserted (consequently, changing the constraint graph). To avoid this drawback, it is possible to enforce relation filtering consistencies in a conservative way, i.e. without adding new constraints, This gives rise to consistencies such as CDC and CPC. Of course, some pairs of values identified as inconsistent must be ignored, and consequently, some information is lost. However, there exists an alternative to inserting new constraints: recording nogoods, especially as this approach [8,20] has been recently re-investigated by the CSP community [11,4,19,14]. As a perspective of this work, we project to enforce strong path consistency by combining nogood recording with an adaptation of sDC2. Interestingly, it could be applied to any constraint network (even one involving non binary constraints).

References

1. Bessiere, C., Debruyne, R.: Optimal and suboptimal singleton arc consistency algorithms. In: Proceedings of IJCAI'05, pp. 54–59 (2005)
2. Bessiere, C., Régin, J.C., Yap, R.H.C., Zhang, Y.: An optimal coarse-grained arc consistency algorithm. Artificial Intelligence 165(2), 165–185 (2005)
3. Boussemart, F., Hemery, F., Lecoutre, C., Sais, L.: Support inference for generic filtering. In: Wallace, M. (ed.) CP 2004. LNCS, vol. 3258, pp. 721–725. Springer, Heidelberg (2004)
4. Boutaleb, K., Jégou, P., Terrioux, C.: (no)good recording and robdds for solving structured (v)csps. In: Proceedings of ICTAI'06, pp. 297–304 (2006)
5. Chmeiss, A., Jégou, P.: Efficient path-consistency propagation. International Journal on Artificial Intelligence Tools 7(2), 121–142 (1998)
6. Debruyne, R., Bessiere, C.: Domain filtering consistencies. Journal of Artificial Intelligence Research 14, 205–230 (2001)
7. Dechter, R.: Constraint processing. Morgan Kaufmann, San Francisco (2003)
8. Frost, D., Dechter, R.: Dead-end driven learning. In: Proceedings of AAAI'94, pp. 294–300 (1994)
9. Han, C.C., Lee, C.H.: Comments on Mohr and Henderson's path consistency. Artificial Intelligence 36, 125–130 (1988)
10. Haralick, R.M., Elliott, G.L.: Increasing tree search efficiency for constraint satisfaction problems. Artificial Intelligence 14, 263–313 (1980)
11. Katsirelos, G., Bacchus, F.: Generalized nogoods in CSPs. In: Proceedings of AAAI'05, pp. 390–396 (2005)
12. Lecoutre, C., Cardon, S., Vion, J.: Conservative dual consistency. In: Proceedings of AAAI'07, pp. 237–242 (2007)
13. Lecoutre, C., Hemery, F.: A study of residual supports in arc consistency. In: Proceedings of IJCAI'07, pp. 125–130 (2007)
14. Lecoutre, C., Sais, L., Tabary, S., Vidal, V.: Nogood recording from restarts. In: Proceedings of IJCAI'07, pp. 131–136 (2007)
15. Mackworth, A.K.: Consistency in networks of relations. Artificial Intelligence 8(1), 99–118 (1977)
16. McGregor, J.J.: Relational consistency algorithms and their application in finding subgraph and graph isomorphisms. Information Sciences 19, 229–250 (1979)
17. Mehta, D., van Dongen, M.R.C.: Reducing checks and revisions in coarse-grained MAC algorithms. In: Proceedings of IJCAI'05, pp. 236–241 (2005)
18. Mohr, R., Henderson, T.C.: Arc and path consistency revisited. Artificial Intelligence 28, 225–233 (1986)
19. Richaud, G., Cambazard, H., O'Sullivan, B., Jussien, N.: Automata for nogood recording in constraint satisfaction problems. In: Benhamou, F. (ed.) CP 2006. LNCS, vol. 4204. Springer, Heidelberg (2006)
20. Schiex, T., Verfaillie, G.: Nogood recording for static and dynamic constraint satisfaction problems. International Journal of Artificial Intelligence Tools 3(2), 187–207 (1994)
21. Singh, M.: Path consistency revisited. International Journal on Artificial Intelligence Tools 5, 127–141 (1996)

Exploiting Past and Future: Pruning by Inconsistent Partial State Dominance

Christophe Lecoutre, Lakhdar Sais, Sébastien Tabary, and Vincent Vidal

CRIL – CNRS FRE 2499,
rue de l'université, SP 16
62307 Lens cedex, France
{lecoutre,sais,tabary,vidal}@cril.univ-artois.fr

Abstract. It has recently been shown, for the Constraint Satisfaction Problem (CSP), that the state associated with a node of the search tree built by a backtracking algorithm can be exploited, using a transposition table, to prevent the exploration of similar nodes. This technique is commonly used in game search algorithms, heuristic search or planning. Its application is made possible in CSP by computing a partial state – a set of meaningful variables and their associated domains – preserving relevant information. We go further in this paper by providing two new powerful operators dedicated to the extraction of inconsistent partial states. The first one eliminates any variable whose current domain can be deduced from the partial state, and the second one extracts the variables involved in the inconsistency proof of the subtree rooted by the current node. Interestingly, we show these two operators can be safely combined, and that the pruning capabilities of the recorded partial states can be improved by a dominance detection approach (using lazy data structures).

1 Introduction

Backtracking search is considered as one of the most successful paradigm for solving instances of the Constraint Satisfaction Problem (CSP). Many improvements have been proposed over the years. They mainly concern three research areas: search heuristics, inference and conflict analysis. To prevent future conflicts, many approaches have been proposed such as intelligent backtracking (e.g. Conflict Based Backjumping [19]), and nogood recording or learning [11].

In the context of satisfiability testing (SAT), studies about conflict analysis have given rise to a new generation of efficient conflict driven solvers called CDCL (Conflict Driven Clause Learning), e.g. Zchaff [22] and Minisat [8]. This has led to a breakthrough in the practical solving of real world instances. The progress obtained within the SAT framework has certainly contributed to a renewed interest of the CSP community to learning [15,4,16].

In [17], a promising approach, called state-based search, related to learning, has been proposed. The concept of transposition table, widely used in game search algorithms and planning, has been adapted to constraint satisfaction.

C. Bessiere (Ed.): CP 2007, LNCS 4741, pp. 453–467, 2007.

More precisely, at each node of the search tree proved to be inconsistent, a partial snapshot of the current state (a set of meaningful variables and their associated domains) is recorded, in order to avoid a similar situation to occur later during search. To make this approach quite successful, two important issues must be addressed: limiting the space memory required, and improving the pruning capabilities of recorded partial states. Extracting partial states as small as possible (in terms of variables) is the answer to both issues. Different state extraction operators, which have yielded promising practical results, have been proposed in [17].

In this paper, we go further by providing two new powerful extraction operators. The first one eliminates any variable whose current domain can be deduced from the partial state, and the second one extracts the variables involved in the inconsistency proof of the subtree rooted by the current node. Interestingly, we show that these two operators can be combined. Also, we improve the pruning capabilities of the recorded inconsistent partial states using an advanced data structure based on the SAT well-known watched literal technique, and dominance detection (only equivalence detection was addressed in [17]).

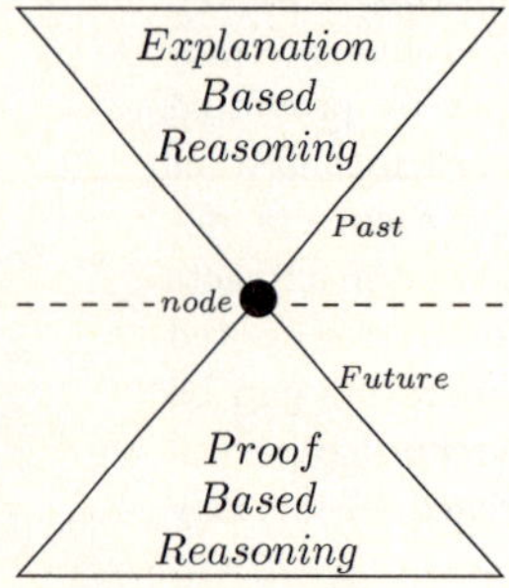

Fig. 1. Partial state extraction from past and future

Figure 1 illustrates our approach. At each node of the search tree, past and future can be exploited. On the one hand, by collecting information from the past, i.e. on the path leading from the root to the current node, redundant variables of any identified partial state (extracted using any other operator) can be removed. This is called explanation-based reasoning. On the other hand, by collecting information from the future, i.e during the exploration of the subtree, variables not involved in the proof of unsatisfiability can be removed. This is called proof-based reasoning. Pruning by inconsistent state dominance is made more efficient through the combination of both reasonings.

2 Technical Background

A Constraint Network (CN) P is a pair $(\mathscr{X}, \mathscr{C})$ where $\mathscr{X}$ is a finite set of n variables and $\mathscr{C}$ a finite set of e constraints. Each variable $X \in \mathscr{X}$ has an associated domain, denoted $dom^P(X)$ or simply $dom(X)$, which contains the set of values allowed for X. The set of variables of P will be denoted by $vars(P)$. A pair (X, a) with $X \in \mathscr{X}$ and $a \in dom(X)$ will be called a value of P. An instantiation t of a set $\{X_1, ..., X_q\}$ of variables is a set $\{(X_i, v_i) \mid i \in [1, q]$ and $v_i \in dom(X_i)\}$. The value v_i assigned to X_i in t will be denoted by $t[X_i]$. Each constraint $C \in \mathscr{C}$ involves a subset of variables of $\mathscr{X}$, called scope and denoted $scp(C)$, and has an associated relation, denoted $rel(C)$, which represents the set of instantiations allowed for the variables of its scope. A constraint $C \in \mathscr{C}$ with $scp(C) = \{X_1, \ldots, X_r\}$ is universal in P iff $\forall v_1 \in dom(X_1), \ldots, \forall v_r \in dom(X_r), \exists t \in rel(C)$ such that $t[X_1] = v_1, \ldots, t[X_r] = v_r$. If P and Q are two

CNs defined on the same sets of variables $\mathscr{X}$ and constraints $\mathscr{C}$, we will write $P \preceq Q$ iff $\forall X \in \mathscr{X}$, $dom^P(X) \subseteq dom^Q(X)$. A solution to P is an instantiation of $vars(P)$ such that all the constraints are satisfied. The set of all the solutions of P is denoted $sol(P)$, and P is satisfiable iff $sol(P) \neq \emptyset$.

The Constraint Satisfaction Problem (CSP) is the NP-complete task of determining whether or not a given CN is satisfiable. A CSP instance is then defined by a CN, and solving it involves either finding one (or more) solution or determining its unsatisfiability. To solve a CSP instance, one can modify the CN by using inference or search methods. Usually, domains of variables are reduced by removing inconsistent values, i.e. values that cannot occur in any solution. Indeed, it is possible to filter domains by considering some properties of constraint networks. Generalized Arc Consistency (GAC) remains the central one. It is for example maintained during search by the algorithm MGAC, called MAC in the binary case.

From now on, we consider a backtracking search algorithm (e.g. MGAC) using a binary branching scheme, in order to solve a given CN P. This algorithm builds a tree search and employs an inference operator ϕ that enforces a domain filtering consistency [6] at any step of the search called ϕ-search. We assume that ϕ satisfies some usual properties such as monotony and confluence. $\phi(P)$ is the CN derived from P obtained after applying the inference operator ϕ. If there exists a variable with an empty domain in $\phi(P)$ then P is clearly unsatisfiable, denoted $\phi(P) = \bot$. Given a set of decisions Δ, $P|_\Delta$ is the CN derived from P such that, for any positive decision $(X = v) \in \Delta$, $dom(X)$ is restricted to $\{v\}$, and, for any negative decision $(X \neq v) \in \Delta$, v is removed from $dom(X)$.

We assume that any inference is performed locally, i.e. at the level of a single constraint C, during the propagation achieved by ϕ. The inference operator ϕ can be seen as a collection of local propagators associated with each constraint, called ϕ-propagators. These propagators can correspond to either the generic revision procedure of a coarse-grained GAC algorithm called for a constraint, or to a specialized filtering procedure (e.g. in the context of global constraints).

3 Inconsistent Partial States

In this section, we introduce the central concept of partial state of a constraint network P. It corresponds to a set of variables of P with their potentially reduced associated domains.

Definition 1. *Let $P = (\mathscr{X}, \mathscr{C})$ be a CN, a partial state Σ of P is a set of pairs (X, D_X) with $X \in \mathscr{X}$ and $D_X \subseteq dom^P(X)$ such that any variable of $\mathscr{X}$ appears at most once in Σ.*

The set of variables occurring in a partial state Σ is denoted by $vars(\Sigma)$, and for any $(X, D_X) \in \Sigma$, $dom^\Sigma(X)$ denotes D_X. At a given step of a backtracking search, a partial state can be associated with the corresponding node of the search tree. This partial state is naturally built by taking into account all variables and their current domains, and will be called the current state.

A network can be restricted over one of its partial state Σ by replacing in P the domain of each variable occurring in Σ with its corresponding domain in Σ. The restricted network is clearly smaller ($\preceq$) than the initial network.

Definition 2. *Let $P = (\mathscr{X}, \mathscr{C})$ be a CN and Σ be a partial state of P. The restriction $\psi(P, \Sigma)$ of P over Σ is the CN $P' = (\mathscr{X}, \mathscr{C})$ such that $\forall X \in \mathscr{X}$, $dom^{P'}(X) = dom^{\Sigma}(X)$ if $X \in vars(\Sigma)$, and $dom^{P'}(X) = dom^{P}(X)$ otherwise.*

A partial state Σ of a CN P is said to be inconsistent with respect to P when the network defined as the restriction of P over Σ is unsatisfiable.

Definition 3. *Let P be a CN and Σ be a partial state of P. Σ is an inconsistent partial state of P (IPS_P for short), iff $\psi(P, \Sigma)$ is unsatisfiable.*

A partial state Σ is said to dominate a CN P if each variable of Σ occurs in P with a smaller domain.

Definition 4. *Let P and P' be two CNs such that $P' \preceq P$, and Σ be a partial state of P. Σ dominates P' iff $\forall X \in vars(\Sigma)$, $dom^{P'}(X) \subseteq dom^{\Sigma}(X)$.*

The following proposition is at the core of state-based reasoning by dominance detection.

Proposition 1. *Let P and P' be two CNs such that $P' \preceq P$, and Σ be an IPS_P. If Σ dominates P', P' is unsatisfiable.*

Proof. It is immediate since we can easily deduce that $\psi(P', \Sigma) \preceq \psi(P, \Sigma)$ from $P' \preceq P$ and the definition of ψ. □

In the context of solving a constraint network P using a backtracking search, this proposition can be exploited to prune nodes dominated by previously identified IPS_P. An IPS_P can be extracted from a node proved to be the root of an unsatisfiable subtree. Although the current state associated to such a node is an IPS_P itself, it cannot obviously be encountered later during search: to be useful, it must be reduced. That is why in what follows, we propose two new operators (and adapt an existing one) which eliminate some variables from a state proved unsatisfiable, while preserving its status of IPS_P.

Finally, it is important to relate the concept of (inconsistent) partial state with those of Global Cut Seed [10] and pattern [9]. The main difference is that a partial state can be defined from a subset of variables of the CN, whereas GCS and patterns, introduced to break global symmetries, contain all variables of the CN. On the other hand, it is close to the notion of nogood as introduced in [20], where it is shown that a nogood can be reduced to a subset of variables, those involved in the decisions taken along the current branch leading to an inconsistent node. In our context, we will show that it is possible to build a partial state by removing variables involved or not in taken decisions.

4 Universality-Based Extraction

In [17], three different operators have been introduced to extract *constraint subnetworks* whose state can be recorded in a transposition table. These operators allow to remove so-called s-eliminable (ρ^{sol}), u-eliminable (ρ^{uni}) and r-eliminable (ρ^{red}) variables. The principle is to determine whether or not the subnetwork corresponding to the current node of the search tree is equivalent to one already recorded in the table. If this is the case, this node can be safely discarded.

In this paper, we apply this approach to state dominance detection and propose new advanced operators. Only, the ρ^{uni} operator will be considered in our context, as s-eliminable variables are also u-eliminable (ρ^{sol} is interesting to count solutions), and the removal of r-eliminable variables is immediate when considering dominance detection. We propose a new formulation of this operator.

Definition 5. *Let $P = (\mathscr{X}, \mathscr{C})$ be a CN. The operator $\rho^{uni}(P)$ denotes the partial state $\Sigma = \{(X, dom^P(X)) \mid X \in \mathscr{X}$ and $\exists C \in \mathscr{C} \mid X \in scp(C)$ and C is not universal in $P\}$. A variable $X \in \mathscr{X} \setminus vars(\Sigma)$ is called an u-eliminable variable of P.*

The following proposition establishes that ρ^{uni} can extract inconsistent partial states at any node of a search tree proved to be the root of an unsatisfiable subtree.

Proposition 2. *Let P and P' be two CNs such that $P' \preceq P$. If P' is unsatisfiable then $\rho^{uni}(P')$ is an IPS_P.*

Proof. As shown in [17], the constraint subnetwork defined from the variables of $\Sigma = \rho^{uni}(P')$ is unsatisfiable. Its embedding in any larger constraint network entails its unsatisfiability. □

5 Proof-Based Extraction

Not all constraints of an unsatisfiable constraint network are necessary to prove its unsatisfiability. Some of them form (Minimal) Unsatisfiable Cores (MUCs) and different methods have been proposed to extract them. Indeed, one can iteratively identify the constraints of a MUC following a constructive [5], a destructive [1] or a dichotomic approach [14,13]. More generally, an unsatisfiable core can be defined as follows:

Definition 6. *Let $P = (\mathscr{X}, \mathscr{C})$, $P' = (\mathscr{X}', \mathscr{C}')$ be two CNs. P' is an unsatisfiable core of P if P' is unsatisfiable, $\mathscr{X}' \subseteq \mathscr{X}$, $\mathscr{C}' \subseteq \mathscr{C}$ and $\forall X' \in \mathscr{X}', dom^{P'}(X') = dom^P(X')$.*

Interestingly, it is possible to associate an IPS_P with any unsatisfiable core extracted from a network $P' \preceq P$. This is stated by the following proposition.

Proposition 3. *Let P and P' be two CNs such that $P' \preceq P$. For any unsatisfiable core P'' of P', $\Sigma = \{(X, dom^{P''}(X)) \mid X \in vars(P'')\}$ is an IPS_P.*

Proof. If Σ is not an IPS$_P$, i.e. if $\psi(P, \Sigma)$ is satisfiable, there exists an assignment of a value to all variables of $vars(\Sigma)$ such that all constraints of P are satisfied. As any constraint of P'' is included in P', and so in P, this contradicts our hypothesis of P'' being an unsatisfiable core. □

As an inconsistent partial state can be directly derived from an unsatisfiable core, one can be interested in extracting such cores from any node proved to be the root of an unsatisfiable subtree. Computing a posteriori a MUC from scratch using one of the approaches mentioned above seems very expensive since even the dichotomic approach is in $O(log(e).k_e)$ [13] where k_e is the number of constraints of the extracted core. However, it is possible to efficiently identify an unsatisfiable core by keeping track of all constraints involved in the proof of unsatisfiability [1]. Such constraints are the ones used during search to remove, through their propagators, at least one value in the domain of one variable. We adapt this "proof-based" approach to extract an unsatisfiable core from any node of the search tree by incrementally collecting relevant information.

Algorithm 1 depicts how to implement our method inside a backtracking ϕ-search algorithm. The recursive function *solve* determines the satisfiability of a network P and returns a pair composed of a Boolean (that indicates if P is satisfiable or not), and a set of variables. This set is either empty (when P is satisfiable) or represents a proof of unsatisfiability. A proof is composed of the variables involved in the scope of the constraints that triggered at least one removal during ϕ-propagation.

At each node, a proof, initially empty, is built from all inferences produced when enforcing ϕ and the proofs (lines 6 and 8) associated with the left and right subtrees (once a pair (X, a) has been selected). When the unsatisfiability of a node is proved after having considered two branches (one labelled with $X = a$ and the other with $X \neq a$), one obtains a proof of unsatisfiability (line 10) by simply merging the proofs associated with the left and right branches. Remark that the worst-case space complexity of managing the different local proofs of the search tree is in $O(n^2 d)$ since storing a proof is $O(n)$ and there are at most $O(nd)$ nodes per branch.

Using Algorithm 1, we can introduce a new advanced extraction operator that only retains variables involved in a proof of unsatisfiability. This operator can

Algorithm 1. $solve(P = (\mathscr{X}, \mathscr{C})$: CN): (Boolean, Set of Variables)

1 $localProof \leftarrow \emptyset$
2 $P' = \phi(P)$ // localProof updated according to ϕ
3 **if** $P' = \bot$ **then return** $(false, localProof)$
4 **if** $\forall X \in \mathscr{X}, |dom(X)| = 1$ **then return** $(true, \emptyset)$
5 select a pair (X, a) with $|dom(X)| > 1 \wedge a \in dom(X)$
6 $(sat, leftProof) \leftarrow solve(P'|_{X=a})$
7 **if** sat **then return** $(true, \emptyset)$
8 $(sat, rightProof) \leftarrow solve(P'|_{X \neq a})$
9 **if** sat **then return** $(true, \emptyset)$
10 // $leftProof \cup rightProof$ is a proof of inconsistency for P'
11 **return** $(false, localProof \cup leftProof \cup rightProof)$

be incrementally used at any node of a search tree proved to be the root of an unsatisfiable subtree.

Definition 7. *Let P be a CN such that $solve(P) = (false, proof)$. The operator $\rho^{prf}(P)$ denotes the partial state $\Sigma = \{(X, dom^P(X)) \mid X \in proof\}$. A variable $X \in vars(P) \setminus vars(\Sigma)$ is called a p-eliminable variable of P.*

Proposition 4. *Let P and P' be two CNs such that $P' \preceq P$. If P' is unsatisfiable then $\rho^{prf}(P')$ is an IPS_P.*

Proof. Let $P = (\mathscr{X}, \mathscr{C})$ and $solve(P') = (false, proof)$. Clearly, $P'' = (proof, \{C \in \mathscr{C} \mid scp(C) \subseteq proof\})$ is an unsatisfiable core of P'. $\rho^{prf}(P')$ is equal to $\{(X, dom^{P'}(X)) \mid X \in proof\}$ which is proved to be an IPS_P by Prop. 3. □

In practice, in Algorithm 1, one can call the ρ^{prf} operator to extract an IPS_P at line 10. Interestingly enough, the following proposition establishes that ρ^{prf} is stronger than ρ^{uni} (i.e. allows to extract partial states representing larger portions of the search space).

Proposition 5. *Let P be an unsatisfiable CN. $\rho^{prf}(P) \subseteq \rho^{uni}(P)$.*

Proof. An universal constraint cannot occur in an unsatisfiability proof. An u-eliminable variable only occurs in universal constraints, so is p-eliminable. □

It must be noted that, unlike ρ^{uni}, extracting an inconsistent partial state using ρ^{prf} can only be performed when the subtree has been completely explored. As a consequence, it is not possible to use this operator for pruning equivalent states using a transposition table whose keys correspond to partial states. Nevertheless, ρ^{prf} can be fully exploited in the context of dominance detection.

6 Explanation-Based Extraction

In this section, we propose a second advanced extraction operator of (inconsistent) partial states. Unlike the proof-based extraction operator, this new one can be applied each time we reach a new node by analyzing all propagation performed so far. The principle of this operator is to build a partial state by eliminating the variables whose domains can be inferred from the other ones. This is made possible by keeping track, for any value removed from the initial network, of the constraint at the origin of its removal. This kind of original explanations can be related to the concept of implication graphs used in the SAT community. In the context of achieving arc consistency for dynamic CSPs [2], such explanations were also exploited to put values back into domains when constraints are retracted.

In constraint satisfaction, eliminating explanations are classically decision-based, which means that each removed value is explained by a set of positive decisions, i.e. a set of variable assignments. This is usually exploited to perform some kind of intelligent backtracking (e.g. [7,19,12]). Interestingly, it is possible to define explanations in a more general way by taking into account not only some decisions taken during search but also some constraints of the original network.

Explanations recorded for each removal can be represented using an implication graph as used in the satisfiability context [22]. Given a set of decisions (the current partial instantiation), the inference process can be modelled using a fine-grained implication graph. More precisely, for each removed value, one can record positive and negative decisions implying this removal (through clauses). For our purpose, we can simply reason using a coarse-grained level of the implication graph. Whenever a value (X, a) is removed during the propagation associated with a constraint C, the (local) eliminating explanation of (X, a) is simply given by C. In other words, as our aim is to circumscribe a partial state (smaller than the current state in terms of variables), we only need to know for each removed value (X, a), the variables (in fact, those involved in C) responsible of its removal. From this information, it is possible to build a directed graph G where nodes correspond to variables and arcs to dependencies between variables. More precisely, an arc exists in G from a variable Y to a variable X if there exists a removed value (X, a) such that its local explanation is a constraint involving Y. Also, a special node denoted by *nil* is considered, and an arc exists from *nil* to a variable X if this variable is involved in a (positive or negative) decision. The implication graph can then be used to extract an inconsistent partial state from a subset of variables S (that already represents an inconsistent partial state) by eliminating any variable with no incoming arc from a variable outside S. Of course, such an extraction is not interesting if S is $\mathscr{X}$ since it necessary produces a set of variables corresponding to all decisions.

Important: For all definitions and propositions below, we consider given two CNs $P = (\mathscr{X}, \mathscr{C})$ and P' such that P' corresponds to a node of the ϕ-search tree of P. We obviously have $P' \preceq P$.

Definition 8. *For any (X, a) such that $X \in \mathscr{X}$ and $a \in dom^P(X) \setminus dom^{P'}(X)$, the local eliminating explanation of (X, a), denoted by $exp(X, a)$ is, if it exists, the constraint C whose associated ϕ-propagator has removed (X, a) along the path leading from P to P', and nil otherwise.*

These explanations can be used to extract a partial state from a CN wrt P and a set of variables S. This partial state contains the variables of S that cannot be "explained" by S.

Definition 9. *$\forall S \subseteq \mathscr{X}$, $\rho^{exp}_{P,S}(P')$ is the partial state $\Sigma = \{(X, dom^{P'}(X)) \mid X \in S$ and $\exists a \in dom^P(X) \setminus dom^{P'}(X)$ such that ($exp(X, a) = nil$ or $\exists Y \in scp(exp(X, a))$ such that $Y \notin S$). A variable $X \in S \setminus vars(\Sigma)$ is called an i-eliminable variable of P' wrt P and S.*

Proposition 6. *Let Σ be a partial state of P' and $\Sigma' = \rho^{exp}_{P,vars(\Sigma)}(P')$. We have: $\phi(\psi(P, \Sigma')) = \phi(\psi(P, \Sigma))$.*

Proof sketch. The only variables whose domain may differ between $\psi(P,\Sigma')$ and $\psi(P,\Sigma)$ are the i-eliminable variables of the set $\Delta = vars(\Sigma) \setminus vars(\Sigma')$. We also have $\forall X \in vars(\Sigma'), dom^{\psi(P,\Sigma')}(X) = dom^{\psi(P,\Sigma)}(X) = dom^{P'}(X)$ and $\forall X \in \Delta, dom^{\psi(P,\Sigma')}(X) = dom^{P}(X)$. This means that the domains of the variables in Σ' are in the state they were after performing all decisions and propagations that lead to P', and the domains of the variables of Δ are reset to the state they were in P. Also, every variable $X \in vars(P) \setminus vars(\Sigma)$ is such that $dom^{\psi(P,\Sigma')}(X) = dom^{\psi(P,\Sigma)}(X)$.

Let $R_\Delta = \{(X,a) \mid X \in \Delta \wedge a \in dom^P(X) \setminus dom^{P'}(X)\}$ be the set of values removed for the variables of Δ on the branch leading from P to P'. For any $(X,a) \in R_\Delta$, we have an explanation $C = exp(X,a)$ such that $C \neq nil$ and $scp(C) \subseteq vars(\Sigma)$ since X is i-eliminable. In other words, the removal of values from R_Δ were triggered along the path leading to P' by constraints (the explanations) only involving variables of Σ, that is variables of Σ' and Δ itself.

In $\psi(P,\Sigma')$, we can trigger the removal of all values in R_Δ in the order they were performed along the path leading to P'. Indeed, following the same order, the explanation associated with each value of R_Δ can trigger its removal again as (1) the domains of the variables of Σ' are kept after their reduction in the branch leading to P' ($\forall X \in \Sigma', dom^{\psi(P,\Sigma')}(X) = dom^{P'}(X)$), (2) variables of Δ are reset to their state in P ($\forall X \in \Delta, dom^{\psi(P,\Sigma')}(X) = dom^{P}(X)$) and (3) the explanation of any removal only involves variables of Σ. This can be shown by a recurrence on the order values are removed in the branch leading to P'. Finally, as the removed values represent the only difference between $\psi(P,\Sigma')$ and $\psi(P,\Sigma)$, by confluence of ϕ, we can conclude that $\phi(\psi(P,\Sigma')) = \phi(\psi(P,\Sigma))$. □

The following corollary (whose proof is a direct consequence of Proposition 6) is particularly interesting since it states that we can safely use ρ^{exp} after any other one which produces an IPS_P.

Corollary 1. *Let Σ be a partial state of P' and $\Sigma' = \rho^{exp}_{P,vars(\Sigma)}(P')$. If Σ is an IPS_P then Σ' is an IPS_P.*

It follows that the next two operators are guaranteed to produce an IPS_P.

Definition 10. $\rho^{prex}_P(P') = \rho^{exp}_{P,vars(\Sigma)}(P')$ *with* $\Sigma = \rho^{prf}(P')$. $\rho^{unex}_P(P') = \rho^{exp}_{P,vars(\Sigma)}(P')$ *with* $\Sigma = \rho^{uni}(P')$.

The ρ^{exp} operator can be implemented with a two-dimensional array *exp* such that for any pair (X,a) removed from P during a ϕ-search, $exp[X,a]$ represents its local eliminating explanation. When a positive decision $X = a$ is taken, $exp[X,b] \leftarrow nil$ for all remaining values $b \in dom(X) \mid b \neq a$, and when a negative decision $X \neq a$ is taken, $exp[X,a] \leftarrow nil$. The space complexity of *exp* is $O(nd)$ while the time complexity of managing this structure is $O(1)$ whenever a value is removed or restored during search. The worst-case time complexity of ρ^{exp} is $O(ndr)$ where r denotes the greatest constraint arity. Indeed, there are at most $O(nd)$ removed values which admit a local eliminating explanation.

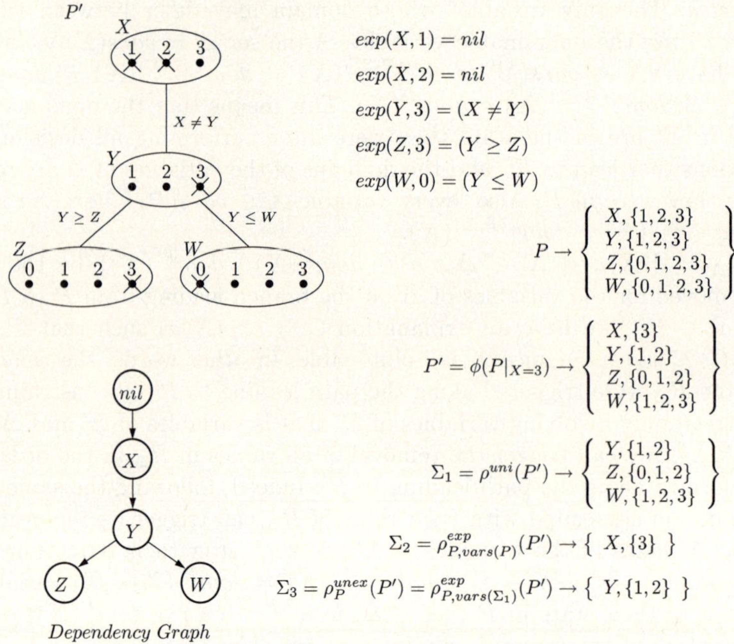

Fig. 2. Extracting partial states using ρ^{uni}, ρ^{exp} and ρ^{unex}

Figure 2 illustrates (on consistent partial states) the behavior of ρ^{uni}, ρ^{exp} and their combination ρ^{unex}. The problem at hand involves four variables (X, Y, Z, W) and three constraints ($X \neq Y$, $Y \geq Z$, $Y \leq W$). When the decision $X = 3$ is taken, the explanation associated with the removal of 1 and 2 from $dom(X)$ is set to *nil*. These removals are propagated to Y through the constraint $X \neq Y$, yielding the removal of 3 from $dom(Y)$. The explanation of this removal is thus set to $X \neq Y$. This removal is then propagated to Z and W: 3 is removed from $dom(Z)$ through the propagation of $Y \geq Z$ which constitutes its explanation, and 0 is removed from $dom(W)$ through the propagation of $Y \leq W$. No more propagation is possible, and the resulting network is denoted by P'. The dependency graph exploited later by ρ^{exp} is then built from these explanations.

Applying ρ^{uni} to P' leads to the elimination of X yielding the partial state Σ_1, as X is now only involved in universal constraints. Indeed, the remaining value 3 in $dom(X)$ is compatible with the two remaining values 1 and 2 in $dom(Y)$ within the constraint $X \neq Y$. The three other variables are involved in constraints which are not universal.

Applying ρ^{exp} to P' and $S = vars(P)$ leads to the elimination of Y, Z and W, yielding the partial state $\Sigma_2 = \{(X, \{3\})\}$. Indeed, X is the only variable from which a removal is explained by *nil* (S being all variables of P', this is the only relevant condition for determining variables of interest). This illustrates the fact that applying ρ^{exp} to all variables of a constraint network has no interest: as we obtain the set of decisions of the current branch, the partial state can never be encountered (or dominated) again without restarts. Note that we would have obtained the same result with a classical decision-based explanation scheme.

More interesting is the application of ρ^{unex}. Once ρ^{uni} has been applied, giving the partial state Σ_1 whose variables are $\{Y, Z, W\}$, ρ^{exp} is applied to determine which variables of Σ_1 have domains that can be determined by other variables of Σ_1. The variable Y is the only one for which all removals cannot be explained by constraints whose scope involve variables *inside* Σ_1 only, as the explanation $X \neq Y$ of the removal $(Y, 3)$ involves now a variable *outside* the variables of interest. This yields the partial state $\Sigma_3 = \{(Y, \{1, 2\})\}$, that contains a variable which is not a decision, and which can then be exploited later during search.

7 Dominance State Detection

In the context of a ϕ-search algorithm, we give now some details about the exploitation of the reduction operators. At each node associated with an unsatisfiable network, one can apply one (or a combination) of the operators to extract an inconsistent partial state, and record it in an IPS_P base. The IPS_P can then be exploited later during search either to prune nodes of the search tree, or to make additional inferences.

Equivalent nodes can be pruned using transposition tables as proposed in [17], but ρ^{prf} cannot be exploited this way. Indeed, when a node is opened, computing a key for it (to be used in the transposition table) is impossible: it requires the complete exploration of the subtree rooted by this node. As such, equivalence detection through the transposition table cannot be performed. However, a node dominated by an IPS_P stored in the base can be safely pruned.

One can go further, by identifying the values whose presence would lead to expand nodes dominated by an IPS_P. Similarly to [16], such inferences can be done thanks to the lazy data structure of watched literals [18] used to manage the IPS_P base. A watched literal of an IPS_P Σ is a pair (X, a) such that $X \in vars(\Sigma)$ and $a \in dom^{\Sigma}(X)$. It is said to be valid when $a \in dom(X) \setminus dom^{\Sigma}(X)$. Two watched literals are associated with each inconsistent partial state Σ. Σ is valid if its two watched literals are valid. When a value a is removed from $dom(X)$, the set of the IPS_P where (X, a) is watched is not valid anymore. To maintain the validity of these inconsistent partial states, we must for each of them, either find another valid watched literal, or remove the values in $dom(Y) \cap dom^{\Sigma}(Y)$ where (Y, b) is the second watched literal. Exploiting this structure, we have the guarantee that the current node cannot be dominated by an IPS_P.

Note that, when using the ρ^{prf} operator, inferences must be performed with caution. Indeed, the IPS_P Σ responsible of an inference participates to the proof of unsatisfiability of the current node. Σ can be seen as an additional constraint of the initial network: each variable occurring in $vars(\Sigma)$ must then also occur in the proof. Finally, whatever the operators are used, variables whose current domain has never been reduced on the current branch can be safely eliminated. Indeed, the dominance for such variables is guaranteed to hold.

Table 1. Number of solved instances per series (1, 800 seconds allowed per instance).

Series	*#Inst*	*brelaz*			*dom/ddeg*			*dom/wdeg*		
		$\neg\rho$	ρ^{uni}	ρ^{prex}	$\neg\rho$	ρ^{uni}	ρ^{prex}	$\neg\rho$	ρ^{uni}	ρ^{prex}
aim	48	32	25 (29)	39	32	25 (29)	38	48	43 (47)	48
dubois	13	4	0 (2)	13	4	1 (2)	13	5	13 (3)	11
ii	41	10	10 (10)	13	10	9 (10)	16	20	18 (19)	31
os-taillard-10	30	5	5 (5)	5	4	4 (4)	4	10	10 (10)	13
pigeons	25	13	17 (19)	13	13	17 (19)	13	13	16 (18)	10
pret	8	4	4 (4)	8	4	4 (4)	8	4	8 (4)	8
ramsey	16	3	3 (3)	6	5	3 (5)	5	6	5 (6)	6
scens-11	12	0	0 (0)	0	0	0 (0)	4	9	7 (8)	9
	193	71	64 (72)	92	73	63 (73)	105	115	120 (115)	136

8 Experiments

In order to show the practical interest of the new operators introduced for dominance detection, we have conducted an experimentation on a Xeon processor cadenced at 3 GHz and 1GiB RAM. We have used benchmarks from the second CSP solver competition (`http://cpai.ucc.ie/06/Competition.html`) including binary and non binary constraints expressed in extensional and intentional form. We have used MGAC (in our solver Abscon[1]) with various combinations of extraction operators and variable ordering heuristics. Performance is measured in terms of cpu time in seconds (*cpu*), number of visited nodes (*nodes*), memory in MiB (*mem*) and average number of variables eliminated when building inconsistent partial states (*elim*). For ρ^{uni}, we considered the same restriction as the one mentioned in [17]: only the variables with a singleton domain involved in constraints binding at most one non singleton-domain variable are removed (to avoid checking the universality of constraints). We also experimented equivalence detection (using a transposition table) with the operator ρ^{red} proposed in [17]: as ρ^{red} is related to ρ^{uni} since they have the same behaviour for dominance detection, the obtained results are given between brackets in the columns of ρ^{uni}.

Table 1 presents the results obtained on some series of structured instances. We do not provide any results on random instances as, unsurprisingly, our learning approach is not adapted to them. The tested configurations are labelled $\neg\rho$ (MGAC without state-based reasoning), ρ^{uni} and ρ^{prex}, each one being combined with the three heuristics *brelaz*, *dom/ddeg* and *dom/wdeg* [3]. The first thing that we can observe is that, whatever the heuristic is used, more instances are solved using ρ^{prex}. Also, note that the performance of the dominance detection approach can be damaged when ρ^{uni} is used: more instances are solved with *brelaz* and *dom/ddeg* using equivalence detection (results between brackets). Indeed, for ρ^{uni}, the size of the IPS_P can often be quite high, which directly affects dominance checking; whereas equivalence detection can be performed in nearly constant time using a hash table.

Table 2 focuses on some instances with the same tested configurations (*brelaz* is omitted, as similar results are obtained with *dom/ddeg*). One can first observe a drastic reduction in the number of expanded nodes using dominance detection, especially with ρ^{prex}. This is mainly due to the high average percentage of eliminated

[1] `http://www.cril.univ-artois.fr/~lecoutre/research/tools/abscon.html`

Table 2. Results on some structured instances (1, 800 seconds allowed per instance)

		dom/ddeg			*dom/wdeg*		
		$\neg\rho$	ρ^{uni}	ρ^{prex}	$\neg\rho$	ρ^{uni}	ρ^{prex}
	cpu	2.39	2.31 (1.9)	2.36	2.3	3.07 (2.25)	3.37
BlackHole-4-4-e-0	*nodes*	6, 141	1, 241 (1, 310)	931	6, 293	3, 698 (4, 655)	5, 435
(#V = 64)	*elims*	0	13.61 (14.16)	58.88	0	14.35 (14.84)	58.02
	cpu	11.54	65.16 (19.2)	2.45	2.14	2.45 (2.34)	2.2
aim-100-1-6-1	*nodes*	302K	302K (302K)	737	987	998 (909)	616
(#V = 200)	*elims*	0	161.80 (161.78)	190.22	0	174.94 (176.18)	189.78
	cpu	–	– (–)	4.059	3.4	4.44 (6.56)	3.18
aim-200-1-6-1	*nodes*			6, 558	9, 063	7, 637 (26, 192)	1, 814
(#V = 400)	*elims*			382.73	0	356.39 (348.35)	388.63
	cpu	7.39	6.02 (6.95)	2.65	2.56	2.77 (2.56)	2.47
composed-25-10-20-9	*nodes*	75, 589	20, 248 (54, 245)	184	323	315 (323)	164
(#V = 105)	*elims*	0	48.90 (48.95)	87.75	0	67.02 (65.91)	89.25
	cpu	422.2	189.71 (378.87)	83.85	13.69	14.61 (13.13)	12.25
driverlogw-09-sat	*nodes*	118K	37, 258 (98, 320)	17, 623	12, 862	8, 592 (11, 194)	6, 853
(#V = 650)	*elims*	0	511.69 (514.14)	541.81	0	513.21 (523.26)	544.05
	cpu	183.38	110.71 (78.94)	1.4	65.95	1.62 (47.72)	1.96
dubois-20	*nodes*	24M	787K (2, 097K)	379	8, 074K	1, 252 (1, 660K)	2, 133
(#V = 60)	*elims*	0	42.00 (48.50)	56.63	0	52.25 (45.93)	51.17
	cpu	–	– (–)	1.7	–	2.41 (–)	3.39
dubois-30	*nodes*			724		4, 267	12, 190
(#V = 90)	*elims*			86		81.2	78.5
	cpu	16.87	– (44.23)	4.09	3.08	3.99 (3.69)	2.99
ii-8a2	*nodes*	214K	(214K)	5, 224	4, 390	4, 391 (4, 390)	1, 558
(#V = 360)	*elims*	0	(276.08)	317.04	0	291.67 (291.90)	316.98
	cpu	–	– (–)	7.92	9.16	26.86 (22.48)	6.71
ii-8b2	*nodes*			2, 336	11, 148	11, 309 (11, 148)	3, 239
(#V = 1, 152)	*elims*			1, 090	0	979.59 (980.08)	1, 050
	cpu	–	– (–)	–	–	– (–)	467.26
os-taillard-10-100-3	*nodes*						134K
(#V = 100)	*elims*						66.90
	cpu	–	53.34 (5.63)	–	–	882.41 (23.62)	–
pigeons-15	*nodes*		106K (115K)			517K (900K)	
(#V = 15)	*elims*		6.99 (7.49)			8.13 (8.63)	
	cpu	–	– (–)	3.11	–	59.66 (6.32)	4.4
pret-150-25	*nodes*			9, 003		203K (97, 967)	17, 329
(#V = 150)	*elims*			135.72		132.62 (133.71)	137.67
	cpu	66.71	3.17 (3.38)	1.79	76.57	1.97 (1.94)	2.0
pret-60-25	*nodes*	7, 822K	17, 530 (47, 890)	1, 503	7, 752K	2, 631 (4, 080)	2, 501
(#V = 60)	*elims*	0	45.56 (45.71)	52.32	0	51.47 (52.46)	51.98
	cpu	72.72	– (108.41)	18.25	–	– (–)	–
ramsey-16-3	*nodes*	1, 162K	(1, 162K)	46, 301			
(#V = 120)	*elims*	0	(84.44)	105.49			
	cpu	3.86	4.18 (4.11)	4.15	3.81	4.17 (4.14)	4.04
ramsey-25-4	*nodes*	591	591 (591)	570	590	(591) (590)	537
(#V = 300)	*elims*	0	191.62 (191.40)	274.72	0	159.81 (159.73)	269.36
	cpu	–	– (–)	371.02	42.15	13.15 (10.17)	5.56
scen11-f6	*nodes*			110K	217K	16, 887 (18, 938)	2, 585
(#V = 680)	*elims*			655.80	0	22.72 (22.17)	654.81

variables from IPS_P (around 90% for ρ^{prex}, much less for ρ^{uni}), which compensates the cost of managing the IPS_P base. The bad results with ρ^{prex} on *pigeons* instances can be explained by the fact that many positive decisions are stored in unsatisfiability proofs when propagating the IPS_P base.

Table 3 exhibits some results obtained for hard RLFAP instances. We only consider *dom/wdeg* here, but with all extraction operators mentioned in this paper. Clearly, the dominance detection approach with ρ^{uni} suffers from memory consumption: due to the size of the IPS_P, two instances remain unsolved.

Table 3. Results on hard RLFAP instances using *dom/wdeg* (1,800 seconds allowed)

Instance		$\neg\rho$	ρ^{uni}	ρ^{unex}	ρ^{prf}	ρ^{prex}
	cpu	9.0	10.4 (8.54)	12.3 (9.6)	5.7	5.5
*scen*11-*f*8	*mem*	29	164 (65)	49 (37)	33	33
(#V = 680)	*nodes*	15,045	13,319 (13,858)	13,291 (13,309)	1,706	1,198
	elim		39.0 (38.1)	590.2 (590.2)	643.3	656.0
	cpu	26.0	11.1 (9.23)	10.4 (10.06)	5.5	5.6
*scen*11-*f*7	*mem*	29	168 (73)	49 (37)	33	33
(#V = 680)	*nodes*	113K	13,016 (14,265)	12,988 (13,220)	2,096	1,765
	elim		25.2 (25.4)	584.1 (584.7)	647.5	654.8
	cpu	41.2	15.0 (10.61)	15.5 (10.14)	6.4	6.8
*scen*11-*f*6	*mem*	29	200 (85)	53 (37)	33	33
(#V = 680)	*nodes*	217K	16,887 (18,938)	16,865 (17,257)	2,903	2,585
	elim		22.7 (22.1)	588.6 (589.3)	648.8	654.8
	cpu	202	– (72.73)	195 (98.16)	31.5	12.2
*scen*11-*f*5	*mem*	29	256	342 (152)	53	41
(#V = 680)	*nodes*	1,147K	257K	218K (244K)	37,309	14,686
	elim		24.1	592.6 (583.36)	651.6	655.7
	cpu	591	– (–)	555 (261.67)	404	288
*scen*11-*f*4	*mem*	29		639 (196)	113	93
(#V = 680)	*nodes*	3,458K		365K (924K)	148K	125K
	elim			586.6 (593.1)	651.7	655.0

Combining ρ^{uni} with ρ^{exp} (i.e. ρ^{unex}) allows to save memory (between brackets, we have the results for ρ^{red} combined with ρ^{exp}). However, the best performance is obtained when combining explanation-based and proof-based reasoning, i.e. with ρ^{prex}. Note that the average size of the inconsistent partial states recorded in the base is very small: they involve about $680 - 655 = 25$ variables.

To summarize, the results that we have obtained with the new extraction operators and the dominance detection approach outperform, both in space and time, those obtained with the operator ρ^{red} which is dedicated to equivalence detection (ρ^{red} combined with ρ^{exp} gives similar results as ρ^{red} alone, except a memory reduction for a few instances). Besides, it allowed to solve more instances in a reasonable amount of time. We believe the results can still be improved since we did not control the partial states recorded in the base (and this has a clear impact when the resolution is difficult, as e.g. for the instance *scen*11-*f*4).

9 Conclusion

In this paper, we have introduced two operators that enable the extraction of an (inconsistent) partial state at each node of a search tree. Whereas the former collects information above the current node (propagation analysis from the root to the node) to perform an explanation-based extraction, the latter collects it below (subtree analysis) to perform a proof-based extraction – making these two approaches complementary. Next, we have shown that inconsistent partial states can be efficiently exploited to prune the search space by dominance detection.

State-based search as studied in [17] and in this paper can be seen as an approach to automatically break some form of local symmetries. A direct perspective of this new paradigm is to combine it with SBDD (Symmetry Breaking by Dominance Detection) [9,10,20,21].

Acknowledgments

This paper has been supported by the CNRS and the ANR "Planevo" project n^{o}JC05_41940.

References

1. Baker, R.R., Dikker, F., Tempelman, F., Wognum, P.M.: Diagnosing and solving over-determined constraint satisfaction problems. In: Proceedings of IJCAI'93, pp. 276–281 (1993)
2. Bessière, C.: Arc-consistency in dynamic constraint satisfaction problems. In: Proceedings of AAAI'91, pp. 221–226 (1991)
3. Boussemart, F., Hemery, F., Lecoutre, C., Sais, L.: Boosting systematic search by weighting constraints. In: Proceedings of ECAI'04, pp. 146–150 (2004)
4. Boutaleb, K., Jégou, P., Terrioux, C.: (no)good recording and robdds for solving structured (v)csps. In: Proceedings of ICTAI'06, pp. 297–304 (2006)
5. de Siqueira, J.L., Puget, J.F.: Explanation-based generalisation of failures. In: Proceedings of ECAI'88, pp. 339–344 (1988)
6. Debruyne, R., Bessiere, C.: Domain filtering consistencies. Journal of Artificial Intelligence Research 14, 205–230 (2001)
7. Dechter, R., Frost, D.: Backjump-based backtracking for constraint satisfaction problems. Artificial Intelligence 136, 147–188 (2002)
8. Eén, N., Sorensson, N.: An extensible sat-solver. In: Giunchiglia, E., Tacchella, A. (eds.) SAT 2003. LNCS, vol. 2919. Springer, Heidelberg (2004)
9. Fahle, T., Schamberger, S., Sellman, M.: Symmetry breaking. In: Walsh, T. (ed.) CP 2001. LNCS, vol. 2239, pp. 93–107. Springer, Heidelberg (2001)
10. Focacci, F., Milano, M.: Global cut framework for removing symmetries. In: Walsh, T. (ed.) CP 2001. LNCS, vol. 2239, pp. 77–92. Springer, Heidelberg (2001)
11. Frost, D., Dechter, R.: Dead-end driven learning. In: Proceedings of AAAI'94, pp. 294–300 (1994)
12. Ginsberg, M.: Dynamic backtracking. Artificial Intelligence 1, 25–46 (1993)
13. Hemery, F., Lecoutre, C., Sais, L., Boussemart, F.: Extracting MUCs from constraint networks. In: Proceedings of ECAI'06, pp. 113–117 (2006)
14. Junker, U.: QuickXplain: preferred explanations and relaxations for over-constrained problems. In: Proceedings of AAAI'04, pp. 167–172 (2004)
15. Katsirelos, G., Bacchus, F.: Generalized nogoods in CSPs. In: Proceedings of AAAI'05, pp. 390–396 (2005)
16. Lecoutre, C., Sais, L., Tabary, S., Vidal, V.: Recording and minimizing nogoods from restarts. Journal on Satisfiability, Boolean Modeling and Computation (JSAT) 1, 147–167 (2007)
17. Lecoutre, C., Sais, L., Tabary, S., Vidal, V.: Transposition Tables for Constraint Satisfaction. In: Proceedings of AAAI'07, pp. 243–248 (2007)
18. Moskewicz, M.W., Madigan, C.F., Zhao, Y., Zhang, L., Malik, S.: Chaff: Engineering an Efficient SAT Solver. In: Proceedings of DAC'01, pp. 530–535 (2001)
19. Prosser, P.: Hybrid algorithms for the constraint satisfaction problems. Computational Intelligence 9(3), 268–299 (1993)
20. Puget, J.F.: Symmetry breaking revisited. Constraints 10(1), 23–46 (2005)
21. Sellmann, M., Van Hentenryck, P.: Structural symmetry breaking. In: Proceedings of IJCAI'05, pp. 298–303 (2005)
22. Zhang, L., Madigan, C.F., Moskewicz, M.W., Malik, S.: Efficient conflict driven learning in a Boolean satisfiability solver. In: Proceedings of ICCAD'01, pp. 279–285 (2001)

Scheduling Conditional Task Graphs

Michele Lombardi and Michela Milano

DEIS, University of Bologna
V.le Risorgimento 2, 40136, Bologna, Italy

Abstract. This paper describes a complete and efficient solution to the scheduling of conditional task graphs whose nodes are activities and whose arcs can be labelled with a probability distribution. Tasks are executed if a set of conditions hold at scheduling execution time. The model is therefore stochastic. The minimization of the expected makespan implies an exponential-sized description of the objective function. We propose an analytic formulation of the stochastic objective function based on the task graph analysis, and a conditional constraint that handles it efficiently. Experimental results show the effectiveness of our approach in comparison with (1) an approach using a deterministic objective function and (2) scenario based constraint programming taking into account all scenarios or only a part of them.

1 Introduction

We propose an original approach to the scheduling of conditional task graphs in presence of unary and cumulative resources, minimizing the expected makespan. Conditional Task Graphs (CTG) are directed acyclic graphs containing activities, linked by precedence relations. Some of the activities represent branches: at run time, only one of the successors of a branch is chosen for execution, depending on the occurrence of a condition labelling the corresponding arc. Since the truth or the falsity of those conditions is not known a priori, the problem is stochastic. Therefore, we have to take into account all possible scenarios during the schedule construction.

CTGs are ubiquitous to a number of real life problems. In compilation of computer programs [5], for example, CTGs are used to explicitly take into account the presence of conditional instructions. Similarly, in the field of system design [17] CTGs are used to describe applications with if-then-else statements; in this case tasks represent processes and arcs are data communications. Once a hardware platform and an application is given, to design a system amounts to allocate platform resources to processes and to compute a schedule: in this context, taking into account branches allows better resource usage, and thus lower costs. In the conditional planning approach [10,14], plans are generated prior to execution, but they include both observation actions and conditional branches which may or may not be executed depending on the execution time result of certain observations.

While a number of incomplete approaches have been proposed for this problem [16], [12], [17], to our knowledge, the only complete approaches working on conditional task graphs are described in [6] [11], and [8]; the first two papers only take into account unary resources (or, equivalently, disjunctive constraints), while in the latter unary and

C. Bessiere (Ed.): CP 2007, LNCS 4741, pp. 468–482, 2007.

cumulative resources are considered in a system design application under the minimization of the expected communication cost. The objective function we consider in this paper is far more complicated since it implies a declarative exponential-sized description.

We propose an efficient way to overcome this problem by defining an expected makespan constraint that uses an analytic formulation of the stochastic objective function. This constraint and all the problem constraints considering conditional activities rely on two data structures: the Branch Fork Graph (BFG) that compactly represents all possible scenarios and the ω-tree, a BFG subgraph selecting a set of scenarios which include or exclude a specified group of nodes. If a condition named Control Flow Uniqueness (CFU) holds, the algorithms working on the BFG are polynomial. CTGs satisfying CFU are common to a number of application. The BFG and the ω-tree provide a general and powerful tool for defining other conditional global constraints such as the conditional edge finder, the conditional precedence graph. This is subject of current research.

Experimental results are very promising. We have evaluated the approach on a set of 600 instances measuring the time to compute a solution, and compared the quality of the schedule to an approach using a deterministic objective function. In addition we have compared our methods with scenario based constraint programming [13] considering either all scenarios, or a fraction of them. In all comparisons our approach wins, outperforming the scenario based constraint programming both considering all scenarios or only a part of them.

In the literature other sources of uncertainty are taken into account: for example in stochastic scheduling [2] stochastic activity durations are considered, in simple temporal network with uncertainty again unknown durations are considered. Other papers deal with so called alternative activities (see [1,3]) whose execution is decided by the user at scheduling construction time.

The paper is organized as follows: we first describe the problem considered and the corresponding model in section 2; then the expected makespan constraint is proposed in section 3 along with the branch fork graph used for computing task probabilities, and the filtering algorithm used to prune end variables. Experimental results follow in section 4. Conclusion and current research description conclude the paper.

2 Problem Description and Model

The problem we tackle is the scheduling of Conditional Task Graphs (CTG) in presence of unary and cumulative resources. A CTG (figure 1A) is a triple $\langle T, A, C\rangle$, where T is the set of nodes modelling generic tasks, A is the set of arcs modelling precedence constraints, and C is a set of conditions, each one associated to an arc, modelling what should be true in order to choose that branch during execution (e.g. the condition of an if-then-else construct). A node with more than one outgoing arc is said to be a *branch* if all arcs are conditional (e.g., t_1 in figure 1A), a *fork* if all arcs are not conditional (e.g., t_0 in figure 1A); mixed nodes are not allowed. A node with more than one ingoing arc is an *or-node* (e.g., t_{15} in figure 1A) if all arcs are mutually exclusive, it is instead an *and-node* (e.g., t_{21} in figure 1A) if all arcs are not mutually exclusive; again, mixed nodes are not allowed.

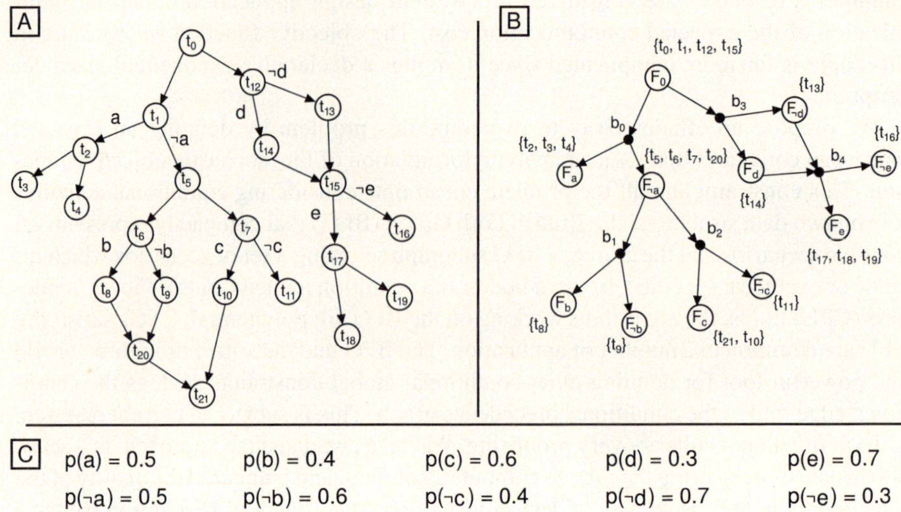

Fig. 1. A: Example of CTG; B: Mapping between CTG and the corresponding BFG

Since the truth or the falsity of conditions is known at scheduling execution time and the scheduler has no control on it, the problem is stochastic. In particular, we can associate to each branch a stochastic variable $\mathcal{B}$ with probability space $\langle C, \mathcal{A}, p\rangle$, where C is the set of possible branch exit conditions c, $\mathcal{A}$ the set of events (one for each condition) and p the branch probability distribution; we compactly denote as c the event $\{\mathcal{B} = c\}$, and therefore $p(c) = p(\{\mathcal{B} = c\})$ is the probability that condition c is true (see figure 1C).

We can associate to each node t_i an activation function $f(t_i)$ expressed as a boolean composition of branch outcome events (compactly denoted as conditions) that trigger the execution of the corresponding activity. For example in the graph of figure 1A $f(t_2) = a$, $f(t_8) = \neg a \wedge b$, $f(t_{17}) = (\neg d \wedge e) \vee (d \wedge e)$. Each activation function $f(t_i)$ also implicitly identifies a set of paths in the CTG sufficient for t_i to execute.

In the CTG each node represents a task (also called activity). Tasks are non preemptive, have fixed duration, and execute within a specified time window (defined by the earliest start time and the latest end time) and require for their execution either unary or cumulative resources. The objective function we consider is the minimization of the expected makespan. For this purpose we propose an expected makespan constraint, described in section 3. The solution of the CTG scheduling problem can be given either in terms of a scheduling table [16] or as a unique schedule. In the first case each task is assigned to a different start time, depending on the scenario. Unluckily, the size of such table grows exponentially as the number of branches increases. We therefore chose to provide a single schedule, where each task is assigned a unique start time, regardless it executes or not. All constraints should be satisfied whatever scenario appears at execution time. For example, in figure 2 we show a small CTG and the corresponding solution. If conditions $\neg a$ and b will be true at run time, only tasks t_0, t_1, t_3, t_4 and t_6 will actually execute.

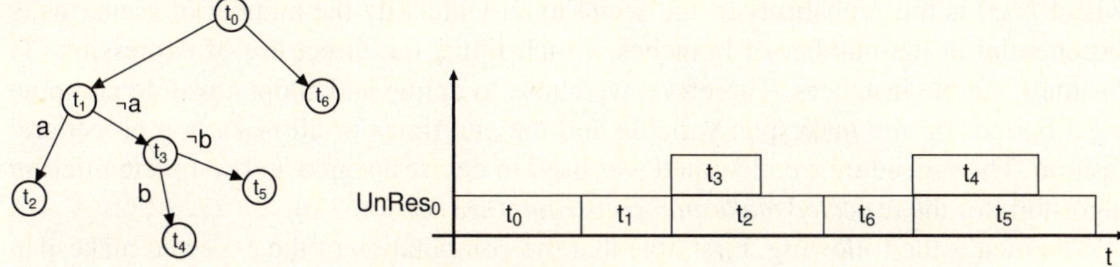

Fig. 2. Temporal task grouping

This choice goes in the line of the notion of strong consistency and controllability defined in [11]. In addition, for some classes of problems such as compilation of computer programs, this is the only kind of solution which can be actually executed ([12]). Resource constraints have to be modified to take into account the presence of mutually exclusive tasks. Two tasks t_i and t_j are said to be mutually exclusive (*mutex*(t_i,t_j)) if they never appear in the same scenario, so that they can access the same resource without competition. For example tasks t_2 and t_3 (or tasks t_4 and t_5) in figure 2 can overlap on the same unary resource since they are mutually exclusive. In fact tasks t_2 and t_3 are respectively triggered by conditions a and $\neg a$, which are never true in the same scenario.

A unary resource, can be implemented by means of a conditional disjunctive constraint [6], which enforces:

$\forall t_i, t_j \quad mutex(t_i, t_j) \vee end(t_i) \leq start(t_j) \vee end(t_j) \leq start(t_i)$

We model cumulative resources by means of conditional timetable constraints, proposed in [8]; the filtering algorithm is based on the branch/fork graph, described in section 3.1. We substantially adopted the same algorithm, but we reduced the worst case complexity from $O(n_a^2 n_c)$ to $O(n_a^2 \log(n_c))$, where n_a, n_c are the number of activities and conditions respectively.

Conditional constraints for unary and cumulative resources, as well as the new makespan constraint we propose, integrate well with a standard branch and bound procedure (which we use in this paper), as well as in many other CP search methods.

3 Expected Makespan Constraint

For a deterministic task graph, the makespan is simply the end time of the last task; it can be expressed as:

$$makespan = \max_i \{end(t_i)\}$$

If the task graph is conditional the last task depends on the occurring scenario. In a conditional task graph, each scenario ω contains a specific set of tasks (say $tasks(\omega)$); for each scenario the makespan is $\max\{end(t_i) \mid t_i \in tasks(\omega)\}$. Thus, the most natural declarative expression for the expected makespan would be:

$$E(makespan) = \sum_\omega p(\omega) \max\{end(t_i) \mid t_i \in tasks(\omega)\} \tag{1}$$

where $p(\omega)$ is the probability of the scenario ω. Unluckily the number of scenarios is exponential in the number of branches, which limits the direct use of expression (1) to small, simple instances. Therefore, we chose to define and adopt a way to compute legal bounds on the makespan variable and the end times of all tasks in a procedural fashion. The procedure we identified was used to devise a sound and complete filtering algorithm for the *expected makespan constraint* (see section 3.6).

The idea is the following. First note that the computation of the expected makespan is tractable when the order of the end variables of tasks is known.

Consider the example in figure 2: note that, since t_5 is the last task, the makespan of all scenarios containing t_5 is $end(t_5)$. Similarly, since t_4 is the last but one task, $end(t_4)$ is the makespan value of all scenarios containing t_4 and not containing t_5, and so on.

In general, let $t_0, t_1, \ldots, t_{n_a-1}$ be the sequence of CTG tasks ordered by increasing end time; let the order be completely specified, then:

$$E(makespan) = \sum_i p(t_i \wedge \neg t_{i+1} \wedge \ldots \wedge \neg t_{n_a-1})\ end(t_i) \tag{2}$$

The sum contains n_a terms, where n_a is the number of activities. Note that this number can be decreased by considering tail tasks only (i.e. tasks with no successor) Once the end order of tasks is fixed, we can thus compute the expected makespan in polynomial time, provided we are able to efficiently compute the probability weights in expression (2). In general, during search, the order of tasks is not fixed. It is always possible, however, to identify minimum and maximum length task sequences (note that they are possibly infeasible), compute their makespan with expression (2) and prune the task end variables accordingly.

Expression (2) can be used to devise a filtering algorithm to prune the makespan and the end variables during search and embed it in a new expected makespan constraint: $emakespan(mkspan, ends, mappings, graph)$ where $mkspan$ is the makespan variable, $ends$ is an array with the end variables, $mappings$ is an array which tells for each task the CTG node it is mapped to. Finally, the graph must be known in order to compute the associate BFG. Note that, in order to improve efficiency, one could build the constraint by specifying the end variables of tail tasks only.

In the next sections we will first show how to efficiently compute probabilities in expression 2. We propose to use a structure called Branch/Fork graph that compactly represents all scenarios, and a way to query it to obtain the needed probabilities. In section 3.6 we will present the filtering algorithms for the makespan and the end variables.

3.1 Branch/Fork Graph

A Branch/Fork Graph (BFG) intuitively represents the skeleton of all possible control flows and compactly encodes all scenarios of the corresponding CTG.

A BFG is a bichromatic acyclic directed graph. Nodes are either branch ("B", the solid dots in figure 1B) or fork ("F", the circles in figure 1B). There is a branch node in the BFG for each branch node in the CTG. F nodes instead group CTG nodes that belong to the same scenarios. Therefore, a BFG can be built from its associated CTG, provided we know the activation functions $f(t_i)$ of the tasks. All functions are supposed to be in disjunctive normal form, i.e. as disjunction of minterms, where a minterm is a conjunction of one or more conditions ($f(t_i) = m_0 \vee m_1 \vee \ldots$ and $m_j = c_{j_0} \wedge c_{j_1} \wedge \ldots$).

There is a mapping between CTG nodes and BFG nodes. For example, in figure 1, tasks t_2, t_3 and t_4 are CTG nodes mapped to the same F node F_a in the BFG. They in fact, belong to the same scenario and have the same activation function. Figure 1B shows the CTG and the corresponding BFG along with the task mappings.

Let $F(t_i)$ be the set of F nodes the task t_i is mapped to: if $F(t_i)$ contains an F node F_j and all its descendants, we can remove all of them from $F(t_i)$ and keep only F_j to compact the representation. For instance t_5 should be mapped to $F_{\neg a}$, F_b, $F_{\neg b}$, F_c, $F_{\neg c}$, but it is actually mapped only to $F_{\neg a}$.

Some structural properties of the BFG follow:

1. B node parents are always F nodes
2. B node parents represent mutually exclusive minterms/paths
3. outgoing arcs of B nodes originate mutually exclusive minterms/paths
4. F node parents represent non mutually exclusive minterms/paths
5. outgoing arcs of F nodes originate non mutually exclusive minterms/paths

We have defined a BFG construction procedure described in [9] that we skip here for lack of space. The construction procedure we outlined has exponential time complexity; in practice it can be replaced by a polynomial one, if a property named control flow uniqueness holds.

3.2 Control Flow Uniqueness

We are interested in conditional graphs satisfying *Control Flow Uniqueness* (CFU) a condition introduced in [8]. CFU is satisfied if for each non head task t_i there is at least a predecessor t_j such that: $f(t_j) \wedge c_{ji} \Rightarrow f(t_i)$, where c_{ji} is the condition possibly labeling arc (j, i); if there is no such condition $c_{ji} = \texttt{true}$. Note that if two predecessor tasks t_j and t_k both satisfy the expression above, then they are mutually exclusive. Tasks with a single predecessor trivially satisfy the expression above; the same holds for or-nodes since all their predecessors are mutually exclusive, therefore CFU translates into a restriction on and-nodes only. In particular CFU requires each and-node to be triggered by a single "main" predecessor, or, in other words, that every and-node must be on a single control path. For example in figure 3A, task t_5 is sufficient to trigger the execution of t_8 (since t_7 executes in all scenarios) and thus CFU holds. On the opposite, in figure 3B, neither t_4 nor t_5 alone are sufficient to activate t_7 and CFU is not satisfied. In many practical cases CFU is not restrictive assumption: for example, when the graph results from the parsing of a computer program written in a high level language (such as C++, Java, C#) CFU is naturally enforced by the scope rules of the language.

Control flow uniqueness translates into some additional structural properties for the BFG (proofs are omitted due to lack of space but can be found in [9]):

- If CFU holds, every F node has a single parent and it is always a B node
- If CFU holds, every F node splits its descendants into separated subgraphs

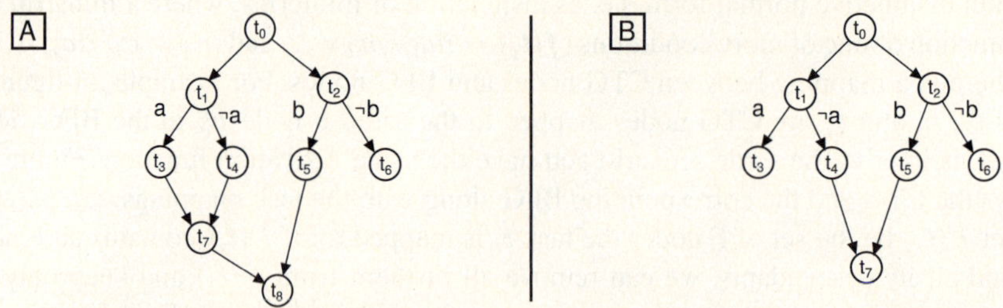

Fig. 3. A: a CTG which satisfies; CFU B: a CTG which does not satisfy CFU

From these properties, we deduce that if CFU holds the BFG is a bichromatic *alternate* graph. Moreover, since every branch node with m outgoing arcs originates exactly m F nodes, the BFG has exactly $n_c + 1$ F nodes, where n_c is the number of conditions.

CFU is also a necessary condition for the two structural properties listed above to hold; therefore we can check CFU by trying to build a BFG with a single parent for each F node: if we cannot make it, then the original graph does not satisfy the condition.

3.3 BFG and Scenarios

The most interesting feature of a BFG is that it can be used to select and encode groups of scenarios in which arbitrarily chosen nodes execute/do not execute. If we have algorithms to extract interesting features of these scenario groups, such as their maximum/minimum weight (see [8]) or their probability (algorithm devised further on), we can turn the BFG into a powerful tool to build many useful conditional constraints, for example the expected makespan constraint we develop in this work.

Groups of scenarios are encoded in the BFG as sets of ω-trees:

Definition 1 (**ω-tree**). *An ω-tree is any subgraph of the BFG satisfying the following properties:*

1. *the subgraph includes the root node*
2. *if the subgraph includes an F node, it includes also all its children*
3. *if the subgraph includes an F node, it includes also all its parents*
4. *if the subgraph includes a B node, it includes also one and only one of its children*

Note that, despite its name, an ω-tree is not necessarily a tree: this is always the case only if CFU (which is not required by definition 1) is satisfied (figure 4B). Any ω-tree translates to a single scenario where all and only the conditions it includes are true. By relaxing condition 4 in definition (1) we get subsets of the BFG representing sets of omega trees, and thus sets of scenarios (see figure 4C).

3.4 Querying the BFG

We now need a way to select subgraphs representing sets of scenarios which include or exclude a specified group of nodes. We consider selection rules specified by means of boolean queries in Conjunctive Normal Form (CNF). Each basic term of the query

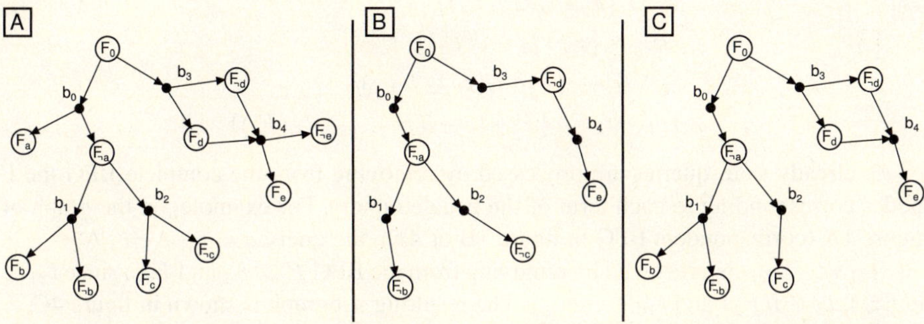

Fig. 4. (A) BFG for the graph in figure 1A - (B) an ω-tree - (C) a subgraph representing a set of ω-trees

can be t_i (with meaning "task t_i executes") or $\neg t_i$ (with meaning "task t_i does not execute"). Some examples of valid queries are:

$$q_0 = t_i \wedge t_j \qquad q_1 = t_i \wedge \neg t_j \wedge \neg t_k \qquad q_2 = (t_i \vee t_j) \wedge t_k$$

The idea at the base of the query processing procedure is that, since the complete BFG represents all possible scenarios, we can select a subset of them by removing F nodes which do not satisfy the boolean query. Thus, in order to be processed, queries are negated and translated in Disjunctive Normal Form (DNF):

$$\neg q_0 = \neg t_i \vee \neg t_j \qquad \neg q_1 = \neg t_i \vee t_j \vee t_k \qquad \neg q_2 = (\neg t_i \wedge \neg t_j) \vee \neg t_k$$

Each element in the negated disjunction now has to be mapped to a set of F nodes to be removed from the BFG. This requires to compute for each F and B node an *inclusion label* and an *exclusion label*:

1. Inclusion labels: A CTG task t_i is in the *inclusion label* $i(F_j)$ of a F node F_j if $F_j \in F(t_i)$ or if t_i is in the inclusion label of any of its parents (that are B nodes). A CTG task t_i is in the *inclusion label* $i(B_j)$ of a B node B_j if t_i is in the inclusion label of all of its parents. In practice $t_i \in i(F_j)$ (resp. $i(B_j)$) if it *does* execute in any ω-tree containing F_j (resp. B_j).

2. Exclusion labels: A CTG task t_i is in the *exclusion label* $e(F_j)$ of an F node F_j if t_i is in the exclusion label of any parent, or if parent of F_j is a B node and it exists a brother F node F_k such that t_i is mapped on a descendant of F_k and t_i is not mapped on a descendant of F_j. A CTG task t_i is in the *exclusion label* $e(B_j)$ of a B node B_j if t_i is in the exclusion label of all its parents. In practice $t_i \in e(F_j)$ (resp. $e(B_j)$) if it *cannot* execute in an ω-tree containing F_j (resp. B_j).

Note that we are interested only in F node labels; B nodes labels are used only in the building process. Once inclusion and exclusion labels are computed, each term of the disjunctions can be mapped to a set of F nodes. For example:

$$t_i \rightarrow \{F_j \mid t_i \in i(F_j)\}$$
$$\neg t_i \rightarrow \{F_j \mid t_i \in e(F_j)\}$$
$$t_i \wedge t_k \rightarrow \{F_j \mid t_i, t_k \in i(F_j)\}$$
$$t_i \wedge \neg t_k \rightarrow \{F_j \mid t_i \in i(F_j),\ t_k \in e(F_j)\}$$

As already said, queries are processed by removing from the complete BFG the F nodes corresponding to each term of the negated query. For example, on the graph of figure 1A (correspondent BFG in figure 1B or 4A), the query $q = t_{21} \wedge \neg t_3 \wedge \neg t_{16} = \neg(\neg t_{21} \vee t_3 \vee t_{16})$ is processed by removing from the BFG $F_{\neg c}$, F_a and $F_{\neg e}$, since $t_{21} \in e(F_{\neg c})$, $t_3 \in i(F_a)$ and $t_{16} \in i(F_{\neg e})$. The resulting subgraph is shown in figure 4C.

If during the process a B node loses all children the output of the query is an empty subgraph. Once the inclusion and exclusion labels are computed, a query is always processed in linear time.

3.5 Computing Subgraph Probabilities

Querying the BFG provides us with a first set of tools needed to achieve our primary objective, i.e. computing weights in expression (2) in polynomial time. Remember a weight is in the form: $w(t_i) = p(t_i \wedge \neg t_{i+1} \wedge \ldots \neg t_{n_a - 1})$

Since the BFG can be queried for identifying a subgraph satisfying condition $t_i \wedge \neg t_{i+1} \wedge \ldots \neg t_{n_a - 1}$, then in order to compute a weight we only need to extract the probability of a given subgraph. In the following we show a probability computation algorithm for BFGs derived from graphs satisfying Control Flow Uniqueness; we also assume branch probabilities are independent.

Statement 1: Since every F node with m children splits the set of possible branch combinations $\mathcal{E} = \mathcal{B}_0 \times \mathcal{B}_1 \times \ldots \times \mathcal{B}_{b-1}$ into m partial sets $\mathcal{E}_0, \mathcal{E}_1, \ldots \mathcal{E}_{m-1}$ such that: $P(\mathcal{E}) = \prod_i P(\mathcal{E}_i)$ That means, the partial set of combinations are independent, since they share no branch variable.

Statement 2: Every branch node with m children splits the set of scenarios Ω in a family $\{\Omega_0, \Omega_1, \ldots\}$ such that $\Omega = \bigcup_i \Omega_i$ and $\Omega_i \cap \Omega_j = \emptyset$. Thus: $P(\Omega) = \sum_i P(\Omega_i)$

Again the probabilities of sets Ω_i can be computed in an independent fashion.

Relying on those observations, the probability of a subgraph can be computed via a backward visit as show in algorithm 1, which runs in linear time.

As an example, consider the subgraph of figure 4C (condition probabilities are in figure 1C). The computation starts from the leaves (we consider $F_b, F_{\neg b}, F_c$): at the beginning $p(F_b) = 1$, $p(F_{\neg b}) = 1$, $p(f_c) = 1$ (line 2 in the algorithm). Then, probabilities of B nodes are the weighted sum of those of their children (line 6); for example $p(b_1) = p(b)p(F_b) + p(\neg b)p(F_{\neg b}) = 0.4 \times 1 + 0.6 \times 1 = 1$ and $p(b_2) = p(c)p(F_c) = 0.6 \times 1 = 0.6$. Probabilities of F nodes are instead the product of those of their children (line 8), and so $p(F_{\neg a}) = p(b_1)p(b_2) = 1 \times 0.6 = 0.6$. The visit proceeds backwards until $p(F_0)$ is computed, which is also the probability of the subgraph.

3.6 Filtering Algorithm

We now have sufficient tools to efficiently compute weights in the makespan expression (2) and to prune the makespan variable and the end time variables of each task.

Algorithm 1. Subgraph probability

let L be the set of nodes to visit and V the one of visited nodes. Initially L contains all subgraph leaves and $V = \emptyset$
for each F and B node keep a probability value $p(n)$. Initially $p(n) = 1$ for all F nodes, $p(n) = 0$ for all B nodes
while $L \neq \emptyset$ **do**
  pick a node $n \in L$
  if n is an F node with parent n_p and $a_p = (n_p, n)$ **then**
    $p(n_p) = p(n_p) + p(n)p(a_p)$
  else if n is a B node with parent n_p **then**
    $p(n_p) = p(n_p)p(n)$
  end if
  $V = V \cup \{n\}$
  $L = L \setminus \{n\}$
  if all children of n_p are in V **then**
    $L = L \cup \{n_p\}$
  end if
end while
return $p(root)$

As far as the makespan variable is concerned, its minimum value is achieved for the (possibly not feasible) configuration where all end variables assume their minimal value. Similarly, the maximum makespan corresponds to the configuration where all task ends are set to their maximal value. Note that in both situation the order of tasks is completely specified: we refer to their sequence in the two configurations as S_{min} and S_{max}. Sequence S_{min} is sorted by increasing $min(end(t_i))$, S_{max} by increasing $max(end(t_i))$. We can prune the makespan variable by enforcing:

$$mkspan(S_{min}) \leq mkspan \leq mkspan(S_{max}) \tag{3}$$

where $mkspan(S_{min})$ and $mkspan(S_{max})$ are the makespan values of configurations S_{min}, S_{max} computed by means of expression (2).

In order to improve computational efficiency, we can use F nodes instead of tasks in the computation of $mkspan(S_{min})$ and $mkspan(S_{min})$. Remember that there is a mapping between tasks (CTG nodes) and F nodes. Each F node is assigned a min and a max end value computed as follows:

$$\text{maxend}(F_j) = \max\{\max(end(t_i)) \mid t_i \text{ is mapped to } F_j\}$$
$$\text{minend}(F_j) = \max\{\min(end(t_i)) \mid t_i \text{ is mapped to } F_j\}$$

Therefore, the two sequences S_{min}, S_{max} can store F nodes (sorted by minend and maxend) instead of activities and their size can be reduced to at most n_c+1 (where n_c is the number of conditions). For example, suppose we have the bounds for the following F nodes: minend$(F_0) = 10$, maxend$(F_0) = 40$, minend$(F_1) = 12$, maxend$(F_1) = 80$, minend$(F_2) = 30$, maxend$(F_2) = 60$, and minend$(F_3) = 50$, maxend$(F_3) = 70$. The sequence S_{min} is $\{F_0 \rightarrow F_1 \rightarrow F_2 \rightarrow F_3\}$, while S_{max} is $\{F_0 \rightarrow F_2 \rightarrow F_3 \rightarrow F_1\}$.

Each time a variable $end(t_i)$ mapped to $F_j$changes, values maxend and minend of F_j are updated and possibly some nodes are swapped in the sequences S_{min}, S_{max}.

If $\text{maxend}(F_1)$ changes to 65, F_1 and F_3 are swapped in S_{max}. These updates can be done with complexity $O(n_a + n_c)$, where n_a is the number of tasks.

The makespan bound calculation of constraints (3) can be done by substituting tasks with F nodes in expression (2):

$$E(makespan) = \sum_i p(F_i \wedge \neg F_{i+1} \wedge \ldots \wedge \neg F_{n_c-1})\ end(F_i) \quad (4)$$

where $end(F_i) \in [minend(F_i), maxend(F_i)]$ and probabilities can be computed again by querying the BFG. The overall worst case complexity for the pruning of the makespan variable is $O(c^2 \log(c))$.

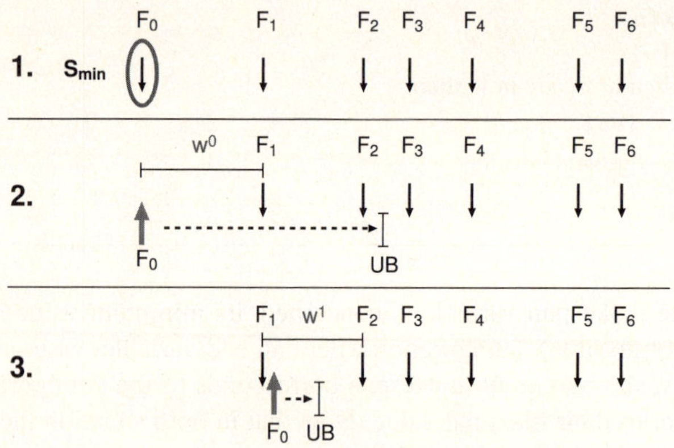

Fig. 5. Upper bound on end variables

Since we are dealing with a makespan minimization problem, it is crucial for the efficiency of the search process to exploit makespan domain updates to filter the end variables.

Bounds for $end(F_i)$ (and thus for the end variables of tasks) can be computed again with expression (4); for example to compute the upper bound we have to subtract from the maximum makespan value ($\max(mkspan)$) the minimum contribution of all F nodes other than F_i:

$$UB(end(F_i)) = \frac{\max(mkspan) - \sum_{j \neq i} p(F_j \wedge \neg F_{j+1} \wedge \ldots)\text{minend}(F_j)}{p(F_i \wedge \neg F_{i+1} \wedge \ldots)} \quad (5)$$

where $F_0, \ldots, F_{i-1}, F_i, F_{i+1}, \ldots$ is the sequence where the contribution of $F_j, j \neq i$ is minimized. Unfortunately, this computation is affected by the position of F_i. In principle, we should compute a bound for all possible assignments of $end(F_i)$, while keeping the contribution of other F nodes minimized. The configuration where the contribution of *all* F nodes is minimized is S_{min}: we can compute a set of bounds for $end(F_i)$ by "sweeping" its position in the sequence, and repeatedly applying formula (5). An example is shown in figure 5, where a bound is computed for F_0 (step 1 in figure 5). We start by computing a bound based on the current position of F_0 in the sequence (step 2 in figure 5); if such a bound is less than $\text{endmin}(F_1)$, then $\text{maxend}(F_0)$ is pruned, otherwise we swap F_0 and F_1 in the sequence and update the probabilities (or weights) accordingly in expression (4). The process continues by comparing F_0 with F_2 and so on until $\text{maxend}(F_0)$ is pruned or the end of S_{min} is reached. Lower bounds for $\text{minend}(F_i)$ can be computed similarly, by reasoning on S_{max}.

A detailed description of the filtering procedure is given in Algorithm 2. The F nodes are processed as listed in S_{min} (line 2); for each F_j the algorithm starts to scan the next intervals (line 6). For each interval we compute a bound (lines 7 to 11) based on the maximum makespan value ($\max(mkspan)$), the current F node probability/weight (wgt) and the contribution of all other F nodes to the makespan lower bound ($rest$).

If the end of the list is reached or the bound is within the interval (line 12) we prune all end variables of tasks mapped on F_j (line 13) and the next F node is processed. If the bound exceeds the current interval, we move to the next one. In the transition the current F node possibly gains weight by "stealing" it from the activity just crossed (lines 15 to 18): wgt and $rest$ are updated accordingly.

Algorithm 2. End variables pruning (upper bound)

1: let $S_{min} = F_0, F_1, \ldots, F_{k-1}$
2: **for** $j = 0$ to $k - 1$ **do**
3: compute result of query $q = F_j \wedge \neg F_{j+1} \wedge \ldots \wedge F_{k-1}$ and probability $p(q)$
4: $wgt = p(q)$
5: $rest = mkLB - \text{minend}(F_j)wgt$
6: **for** $h = j$ to $k - 1$ **do**
7: **if** $wgt > 0$ **then**
8: $UB = \dfrac{\max(mkspan) - rest}{wgt}$
9: **else**
10: $UB = \infty$
11: **end if**
12: **if** $h = (k - 1)$ or $UB \leq \text{minend}(F_{h+1})$ **then**
13: set UB as upper bound for all tasks mapped on F_j
14: **else**
15: remove element $\neg F_{h+1}$ from query q and update $p(q)$
16: $newwgt = p(q)$
17: $rest = rest - (newwgt - wgt)\text{minend}(F_{h+1})$
18: $wgt = newwgt$
19: **end if**
20: **end for**
21: **end for**

The algorithm takes into account all the F nodes (complexity $O(c)$), for each of them analyzes the subsequent intervals (compl. $O(c)$) and update weights at each transition (compl. $O(\log(c))$). The overall complexity is thus $O(c^2 \log(c))$.

4 Experimental Results

Our approach has been implemented using the state of the art solvers ILOG Solver 6.3 and Scheduler 6.3. We tested the approach on 600 randomly generated instances

Table 1. Performance tests

acts	URes	T(C)	F(C)	> TL	$\frac{C}{W}$	stc $\frac{C}{W}$
37-45	3-4	1.54	3115	0	0.83	0.80
45-50	3-5	2.67	4943	0	0.88	0.84
50-54	3-5	9.00	17505	0	0.88	0.85
54-57	4-5	25.68	52949	1	0.88	0.85
57-60	4-5	29.78	77302	1	0.94	0.90
60-65	4-6	24.03	28514	0	0.85	0.80
65-69	4-6	32.12	47123	2	0.90	0.84
69-76	4-6	96.45	101800	14	0.86	0.82
76-81	5-6	144.67	134235	21	0.90	0.86
81-86	5-6	143.31	130561	17	0.84	0.75
86-93	5-6	165.74	119930	25	0.93	0.87
93-109	5-6	185.56	127321	28	0.93	0.87

representing a hardware design problem, where a multi task application (described by means of a CTG) has to be scheduled on a multiprocessor hardware platform. The problem features complex precedence relations, unary resources (the processors) and a single cumulative resource (modelling a shared bus). Instances range from 37 to 109 tasks, 2 to 5 "heads" (tasks with no predecessor), 3 to 11 "tails" (tasks with no successor), 1 to 135 scenarios. The number of unary resources ranges from 3 to 6. Duration and resource usage parameters are randomly generated, but based on real values. Of course all instances satisfy the control flow uniqueness. We ran experiments with a time limit of 300 seconds; all tests were executed on a AMD Turion 64, 1.86 GHz.

We performed a first group of tests to evaluate the efficiency of the expected makespan conditional constraint and the quality of the solutions provided, and a second group to compare the performances of our solver with the scenario-based one. Table 1 shows the results for the first group of tests; here we evaluate the performance of the solver using conditional constraints (referred to as C) and compare the quality of the computed schedules versus an identical model where the deterministic makespan is minimized (referred to as W). In this last case, no expected makespan constraint is used and the objective function is deterministic. Each row identifies a group of 50 instances. For each group we report the minimum and maximum number of activities (acts), the minimum and maximum number of unary resources (URes), the average solution time (T(C)), the average number of fails (F(C)) and the number of instances which could not be solved within the time limit (> TL). The computing time of the two approaches is surprisingly roughly equivalent for all instances.

In column C/W we report the makespan value ratio which shows an average improvement of 12% over the deterministic objective. The gain is around 16% if we consider only the instances where the makespan is actually improved (column stc C/W).

Table 2 compares the conditional model with the scenario-based solver, where cumulative resources are implemented with one constraint per scenario and the expected makespan is expressed with the declarative formula (1). In both models unary resources are implemented with conditional constraints.

Table 2. Comparison with the scenario-based solver

scens	T(C)	F(C)	> TL	$\frac{T(S)}{T(C)}$	> TL	$\frac{T(S_{80})}{T(C)}$	> TL	$\frac{S_{80}}{C}$	$\frac{T(S_{50})}{T(C)}$	> TL	$\frac{S_{50}}{C}$
1-2	41.00	49517	5	22.60	5	22.66	5	1.00	0.58	3	0.77
2-3	66.02	97928	8	19.85	10	19.93	10	1.00	1.69	7	0.80
3-4	43.80	54744	5	35.05	8	35.12	8	1.00	9.19	5	0.79
4-5	49.94	51179	6	73.75	9	73.63	9	1.00	57.03	8	0.80
5-6	66.39	58223	9	48.74	12	16.64	12	0.98	0.77	8	0.82
6-6	51.26	85611	5	6.52	8	6.11	8	0.96	41.99	8	0.80
6-8	38.85	34572	5	82.21	11	71.09	9	0.98	84.41	3	0.80
8-9	57.78	58636	9	66.32	10	63.70	10	0.98	26.76	9	0.85
9-12	52.96	51126	5	89.52	13	86.97	13	0.98	40.43	6	0.85
12-14	117.93	86954	17	45.60	22	43.02	22	0.97	37.35	18	0.84
14-20	95.74	81721	11	32.62	22	31.85	21	0.99	28.76	15	0.90
20-135	178.88	135086	24	66.19	37	65.56	37	1.00	22.09	35	0.912

Again, rows of table 2 report average results for groups of 50 instances; groups are sorted by increasing number of scenarios. The table reports the solution time and fails of the conditional solver (T(C), F(C)) and the performance ratios w.r.t the scenario based solver with 100% (S), 80% (S_{80}) and 50% (S_{50}) of the most likely scenarios. The four columns "> TL" show the number of instances not solved within the time limit for each approach. Finally, columns S_{50}/C and S_{80}/C show the accuracy of the solution provided by S_{50} and S_{80} solvers.

As it can be seen the conditional model outperforms the scenario based one by an average factor of 49.08. By reducing the number of considered scenarios the performance gap decreases; nevertheless, the conditional solver remains always better than S_{80}; it is outperformed by S_{50} when the number of scenarios is low, but the solution provided has an average 17% inaccuracy. Moreover, neither S_{50} nor S_{80} guarantee feasibility in all cases.

5 Conclusion

In this paper we have proposed an efficient way to schedule conditional task graphs minimizing the expected makespan. The approach is based on the analysis of the conditional task graph and on the extraction of scenario probability. We show that the approach has similar performances with an approach using a deterministic objective function and outperforms the scenario based constraint programming even if not all scenarios are considered. The current research is aimed at implementing other global conditional constraints such as the edge finder and the precedence graph by exploiting the BFG and the ω-tree structures.

References

1. Barták, R., Čepek, O.: Temporal Networks with Alternatives: Complexity and Model. In: Proceedings of the Twentieth International Florida AI Research Society Conference (FLAIRS), pp. 641–646. AAAI Press, Stanford, California, USA (2007)

2. Beck, J.C., Wilson, N.: Proactive Algorithms for Scheduling with Probabilistic Durations. In: Proceedings of the Nineteenth International Joint Conference on Artificial Intelligence (IJCAI05) (2005)
3. Beck, J.C., Fox, M.S.: Scheduling Alternative Activities, pp. 680–687. AAAI/IAAI (1999)
4. Benini, L., Bertozzi, D., Guerri, A., Milano, M.: Allocation and scheduling for MPSOCs via decomposition and no-good generation. In: Proceedings of the International Conference in Principles and Practice of Constraint Programming (2005)
5. Faraboschi, P., Fisher, J.A., Young, C.: Instruction scheduling for instruction level parallel processors. Proceedings of the IEEE 89, 1638–1659 (2001)
6. Kuchcinski, K.: Constraints-driven scheduling and resource assignment. ACM Transactions on Design Automation of Electronic Systems 8 (2003)
7. Laborie, P.: Algorithms for propagating resource constraints in ai planning and scheduling: Existing approaches and new results. Journal of Artificial Intelligence 143, 151–188 (2003)
8. Lombardi, M., Milano, M.: Stochastic Allocation and Scheduling for Conditional Task Graphs in MPSoCs. In: Proceedings of the International Conference in Principles and Practice of Constraint Programming (2006)
9. Lombardi, M., Milano, M.: Scheduling Conditional Task Graphs LIA Technical Report LIA-005-97 (2007), `http://www-lia.deis.unibo.it/research/TechReport.html`
10. Kim, P., Williams, B., Abramson, M.: Executing Reactive, Model-based Programs through Graph-based Temporal Planning. In: Proceedings of the International Joint Conference on Artificial Intelligence (IJCAI) (2001)
11. Vidal, T., Fargier, H.: Handling Contingencies in temporal constraint network: from consistency to controllability. Journal of Experimental and Theoretical Artificial Intelligence 11, 23–45 (1999)
12. Shin, D., Kim, J.: Power-aware scheduling of conditional task graphs in real-time multiprocessor systems. In: Proceedings of the International Symposium on Low Power Electronics and Design (ISLPED). ACM, New York (2003)
13. Tarim, A., Manandhar, S., Walsh, T.: Stochastic constraint programming: A scenario-based approach. Constraints 11, 53–80 (2006)
14. Tsamardinos, I., Vidal, T., Pollack, M.: CTP: A New Constraint-Based Formalism for Conditional, Temporal Planning. Constraints 8, 365–388 (2003)
15. Walsh, T.: Stochastic constraint programming. In: Proceedings of the European Conference on Artificial Intelligence, ECAI (2002)
16. Wu, D., Al-Hashimi, B., Eles, P.: Scheduling and mapping of conditional task graph for the synthesis of low power embedded systems. Computers and Digital Techniques, IEE Proceedings 150(5), 262–273 (2003)
17. Xie, Y., Wolf, W.: Allocation and scheduling of conditional task graph in hardware /software co-synthesis. In: Proc. of Design, Automation and Test in Europe Conf. (2001)

Towards Robust CNF Encodings of Cardinality Constraints

Joao Marques-Silva[1] and Inês Lynce[2]

[1] School of Electronics and Computer Science, University of Southampton, UK
jpms@ecs.soton.ac.uk
[2] IST/INESC-ID, Technical University of Lisbon, Portugal
ines@sat.inesc-id.pt

Abstract. Motivated by the performance improvements made to SAT solvers in recent years, a number of different encodings of constraints into SAT have been proposed. Concrete examples are the different SAT encodings for $\leq 1\ (x_1, \ldots, x_n)$ constraints. The most widely used encoding is known as the pairwise encoding, which is quadratic in the number of variables in the constraint. Alternative encodings are in general linear, and require using additional auxiliary variables. In most settings, the pairwise encoding performs acceptably well, but can require unacceptably large Boolean formulas. In contrast, linear encodings yield much smaller Boolean formulas, but in practice SAT solvers often perform unpredictably. This lack of predictability is mostly due to the large number of auxiliary variables that need to be added to the resulting Boolean formula. This paper studies one specific encoding for $\leq 1\ (x_1, \ldots, x_n)$ constraints, and shows how a state-of-the-art SAT solver can be adapted to overcome the problem of adding additional auxiliary variables. Moreover, the paper shows that a SAT solver may essentially ignore the existence of auxiliary variables. Experimental results indicate that the modified SAT solver becomes significantly more robust on SAT encodings involving $\leq 1\ (x_1, \ldots, x_n)$ constraints.

1 Introduction

In recent years SAT solvers have increasingly been used in practical applications, including planning, hardware and software model checking, among many others. The encoding of an increasing number of computational problems into SAT raises the challenge of encoding different constraints into SAT. Among the constraints for which dedicated CNF encodings have been proposed, a special emphasis has been given to cardinality constraints [2,3]. In addition, past work addressed special forms of cardinality constraints, including $\leq 1\ (x_1, \ldots, x_n)$ constraints [11,13,1]. Observe that, given the straightforward CNF encoding of $\geq 1\ (x_1, \ldots, x_n)$ constraints, the encoding of $\leq 1\ (x_1, \ldots, x_n)$ constraints also serves for encoding $= 1\ (x_1, \ldots, x_n)$ constraints. In practice, the constraints $\geq 1\ (x_1, \ldots, x_n)$, $\leq 1\ (x_1, \ldots, x_n)$ and $= 1\ (x_1, \ldots, x_n)$ find a large number of applications.

A number of alternative encodings have been proposed for $\leq 1\ (x_1, \ldots, x_n)$ constraints. Encodings can be linear, logarithmic or quadratic, in the number

C. Bessiere (Ed.): CP 2007, LNCS 4741, pp. 483–497, 2007.

of variables, and may or may not guarantee arc-consistency. The most widely used encoding, that is often referred to as the pairwise encoding, is quadratic in the number of variables in the constraint and guarantees arc-consistency. Interestingly, most available benchmarks containing $\leq 1\ (x_1, \ldots, x_n)$ constraints use the pairwise encoding.

In most settings, the pairwise encoding performs acceptably well, but can require unacceptably large Boolean formulas. In contrast, linear encodings yield much smaller Boolean formulas, but in practice SAT solvers often perform unpredictably. This lack of predictability is mostly due to the large number of auxiliary variables that need to be added to the resulting Boolean formula.

This paper addresses one concrete linear encoding for $\leq 1\ (x_1, \ldots, x_n)$ constraints which guarantees arc-consistency [21], and identifies several properties associated with the auxiliary variables used. One consequence is that a SAT solver may essentially ignore the existence of auxiliary variables, and so this indirectly overcomes the problem of adding additional auxiliary variables. Experimental results indicate that a SAT solver that filters auxiliary variables becomes significantly more robust.

The paper is organized as follows. The next section surveys encodings for $\leq 1\ (x_1, \ldots, x_n)$ constraints. Section 3 provides a brief perspective of recent backtracking SAT solvers, referred to as conflict-driven clause-learning (CDCL) SAT solvers. Section 4 outlines some of the properties of the sequential counter encoding of [21]. Experimental results are analyzed in section 5. The paper concludes in section 6, by analyzing how some of the results proposed in the paper can be extended to other cardinality constraints and encodings, and by outlining directions for future research.

2 Related Work

A large body of research exists on encoding constraints into CNF [16,23,22,11,13] [12,6,1,10,4]. In addition, dedicated encodings have been proposed for specific types of constraints, including cardinality constraints [2,3].

A special case of cardinality constraints are those of the form $\leq 1\ (x_1, \ldots, x_n)$, which are widely used in practice. The most often used CNF encoding for $\leq 1\ (x_1, \ldots, x_n)$ constraints is referred to as the pairwise encoding. Given a $\leq 1\ (x_1, \ldots, x_n)$ constraint, the pairwise encoding is formulated as follows:

$$\bigwedge_{\substack{S \subseteq \{1,...,n\} \\ |S| = 2}} \left(\bigvee_{j \in S} \neg x_j \right) \tag{1}$$

This encoding introduces no additional auxiliary variables, but grows quadratically with the number of variables in the constraint.

An alternative is to use additional variables, thus obtaining asymptotically more efficient encodings. A number of linear encodings has been proposed over the years [11,13,12,1,21,23]. Some of these encodings do not guarantee arc-consistency (e.g. [23]) whereas others do [11,21].

One recent CNF encoding for cardinality constraints $\leq k\ (x_1, \ldots, x_n)$ is based on sequential counters [21]. The resulting CNF encoding is denoted by $LT_{SEQ}^{n,k}$. A special case of cardinality constraints is considered, namely $\leq 1\ (x_1, \ldots, x_n)$ constraints. The associated encoding will be denoted by $LT_{SEQ}^{n,1}$.

An arbitrary number of $\leq 1\ (x_1, \ldots, x_n)$ constraints is assumed, each being represented by an index k. Hence, each constraint is of the form:

$$\sum_{i=1}^{n_k} x_i^k \leq 1 \tag{2}$$

Where n_k is the number of variables in the constraint. From [21], the CNF encoding for the above constraint becomes:

$$(\neg x_1^k \vee s_1^k) \wedge (\neg x_n^k \vee \neg s_{n-1}^k) \bigwedge_{1<i<n_k} ((\neg x_i^k \vee s_i^k) \wedge (\neg s_{i-1}^k \vee s_i^k) \wedge (\neg x_i^k \vee \neg s_{i-1}^k)) \tag{3}$$

Where s_i^k, $1 \leq k \leq n-1$, are auxiliary variables. When clear from context, the index k is dropped, and so the $LT_{SEQ}^{n,1}$ encoding becomes:

$$(\neg x_1 \vee s_1) \wedge (\neg x_n \vee \neg s_{n-1}) \bigwedge_{1<i<n} ((\neg x_i \vee s_i) \wedge (\neg s_{i-1} \vee s_i) \wedge (\neg x_i \vee \neg s_{i-1})) \tag{4}$$

The remainder of the paper focus on the sequential counter CNF encoding and shows that this encoding has a number of interesting properties that can be exploited by a clause learning SAT solver. Before, however, the organization of backtracking SAT solvers is briefly overviewed.

3 CDCL SAT Solvers

This section provides a necessarily brief perspective of modern CDCL SAT solvers. CDCL SAT solvers follow the organization of the DPLL algorithm [8,7], but integrate a number of effective techniques, including clause learning [17,5], lazy data structures [18] and search restarts [15]. CDCL SAT solvers have evolved from the original solvers [17,5,24], which essentially proposed clause learning, to the more recent CDCL SAT solvers, that also integrate lazy data structures and search restarts [18,14,9].

In the following sections, a number of concepts associated with CDCL SAT solvers will be used. These concepts are briefly reviewed below (see [17,18,14,9] for additional detail).

A CDCL SAT solver is usually organized into three main engines [17,18,9]: the decision engine, used for branching; the deduction engine, used for unit propagation and identification of unsatisfied clauses (or *conflicts*); and the diagnosis engine, used for clause learning.

A *decision level* is associated with each assigned variable. Decision levels measure the depth of the search tree in terms of the number of variables the SAT algorithm has branched on. Variables can be assigned a Boolean value, either resulting from a decision (or branching step), or as the result of unit propagation [8]. Variables assigned as the result of unit propagation are said to be *implied.* With each implied variable the SAT algorithm also associates a *reason* or *antecedent*, representing the clause that explains why the variable is implied. The set of assigned variables and associated reasons implicitly represent the *implication graph* [17].

The process of *clause learning* consists of traversing the implication graph from a given unsatisfied clause by using the reasons of implied variable assignments, and recording unsatisfied literals assigned at decision levels less than the current one. The resulting set of recorded literals is then used to create a new clause, which serves for backtracking non-chronologically, and for preventing the same conflict from occurring again during the search process.

Moreover, all effective CDCL solvers use unique implication points (UIPs) [17,25]. UIPs represent dominators in the implication graph of unsatisfied clauses with respect to the most recent decision variable. Whereas some of the early CDCL SAT solvers would use UIPs to learn more clauses [17], more recent CDCL SAT solvers stop clause learning at the first UIP [25]. Albeit stopping at the first UIP usually yields a larger number of decision steps, it is also an observed fact that a smaller number of learnt clauses results in faster execution, and most often this results in smaller run times [25].

Finally, and besides the hallmarks of all CDCL SAT solvers, a number of additional techniques have been quite successfully used in recent solvers. These include deletion policies for learnt clauses [14,9,20], techniques for organization of literals in learnt clauses [19], and the representation of binary clauses as direct implications [20].

4 Filtering Auxiliary Variables

This section revisits the $LT_{SEQ}^{n,1}$ CNF encoding (see section 2), and introduces a number of its properties. Some of these properties allow eliminating most (or even all) of the auxiliary variables for branching purposes. Moreover, this section also outlines how to adapt a SAT solver for filtering auxiliary variables.

4.1 Analysis of the $\leq 1\ (x_1, \ldots, x_n)$ Encoding

This section identifies a number of properties of the $LT_{SEQ}^{n,1}$ encoding. These properties essentially allow a SAT solver to ignore all (or at least most) of the auxiliary variables.

The first property is used throughout this section, for proving additional properties of the $LT_{SEQ}^{n,1}$ encoding.

Proposition 1. *Consider the CNF encoding* $LT_{SEQ}^{n,1}$ *of constraint* $\leq 1\ (x_1, \ldots, x_n)$. *Furthermore, assume that all* x *and* s *variables are unassigned, and that a given variable* x_i *is assigned value 1. Then, the following holds:*

1. *All s_j variables, with $1 \leq j < i$, are implied to value 0.*
2. *All s_j variables, with $i \leq j \leq n-1$, are implied to value 1.*
3. *All x_j variables, with $j \neq i$, are implied to value 0;*

Proof. The result follows from the analysis of (4). The third clause guarantees that s_i is implied value 1. Subsequently, the fourth clause implies that every s_j, with $n-1 \geq j > i$, is implied value 1. The fifth clause guarantees that s_{i-1} is implied value 0. Subsequently, the fourth clause implies that every s_j, with $i > j \geq 1$, is implied value 0. Analysis of the first and last case is also straightforward. Finally, the third and fourth clauses ensure that every x_j, with $j \neq i$, is implied value 0. Again, analysis of the first and last case is straightforward. □

The next step is to evaluate the role of the auxiliary variables used in the $LT_{SEQ}^{n,1}$ encoding.

Proposition 2. *For any complete satisfying assignment to the variables x_1, $\ldots, x_n$ of (2), the following holds:*

1. *All clauses of (4) containing literals of x variables are satisfied.*
2. *There exist assignments to the auxiliary variables $s_1, \ldots s_n$ that satisfy the clauses of (4) containing no literals of x variables.*

Proof. If (2) is satisfied, then at most one of the x_i variables is assigned value 1. Hence, two cases need to be considered: either all x_i variables are assigned value 0, or exactly one variable x_i is assigned value 1 and the remaining x variables are assigned value 0. Now consider the $LT_{SEQ}^{n,1}$ (4) encoding of (2). For the first case, the x_i variables satisfy all clauses that contain a literal in an x variable. Hence, only the clauses $(\neg s_{i-1} \vee s_i)$ need to be satisfied, and this can be achieved by assigning value 0 to all s_i variables. For the second case, exactly one variable x_i is assigned value 1. (4) ensures that all auxiliary variables are assigned a given value. This is immediate from proposition 1. □

The previous result guarantees that by branching only of non-auxiliary variables, either a satisfying assignment exists, in which case it is simple to find consistent assignments to the auxiliary variables, or no satisfying assignment exists, in which case it is unnecessary to branch on the auxiliary variables.

It is possible to extend the previous result further, by analyzing the clause learning process of a SAT solver, when branching is restricted to the non-auxiliary variables. As a result, in what follows, the SAT solver is assumed to branch *only* on non-auxiliary variables.

The following results assert that, when branching is restricted *only* to non-auxiliary variables, the participation of auxiliary variables in conflicts is fairly constrained. This allows effectively discarding auxiliary variables from learnt clauses.

Proposition 3. *For the CNF encoding $LT_{SEQ}^{n,1}$ of constraint ≤ 1 $(x_1, \ldots, x_n)$, if the value of an auxiliary variable s_i is implied at decision level l, then all other auxiliary variables associated with the same constraint are implied at the same decision level, or a conflict is identified.*

Proof. From (4), the value of an auxiliary variable s is implied by the value of an x variable only when the x variable is assigned value 1. Without loss of generality, let x_i be the variable that is assigned value 1. Then, all s variables with index no less than i are assigned value 1, and all s variables with index less than i are assigned value 0 (see proposition 1). If more than one x variable is assigned value 1, then a conflict is identified. □

Proposition 4. *For the CNF encoding $LT_{SEQ}^{n,1}$ of constraint ≤ 1 $(x_1, \ldots, x_n)$, auxiliary variables can only be implied by single implication paths from non-auxiliary variables.*

Proof. For any CNF encoding $LT_{SEQ}^{n,1}$ of constraint 1 $(x_1, \ldots, x_n)$, all auxiliary variables are assigned by unit propagation on binary clauses. Hence, the result follows. □

Proposition 5. *For the CNF encoding $LT_{SEQ}^{n,1}$ of constraint ≤ 1 $(x_1, \ldots, x_n)$, learnt clauses can contain a single auxiliary variable s_i, which is a UIP variable.*

Proof. (Sketch)[1] The clause learning algorithm used by most SAT solvers [17,18] [14,9] records literals from clauses traced during the conflict analysis procedure. These literals must be assigned at decision levels less than the current decision level, or otherwise the literal corresponds to the UIP variable.
Since all auxiliary variables are assigned by unit propagation on binary clauses, and all must be assigned at the most recent decision level, then the conflict analysis procedure cannot record literals associated with auxiliary variables, unless variable tracing stops at a UIP corresponding to an auxiliary variable. □

Proposition 6. *For the CNF encoding $LT_{SEQ}^{n,1}$ of constraint ≤ 1 $(x_1, \ldots, x_n)$, and during clause learning, if a s_i variable is a UIP, then it can be replaced by a single non-auxiliary variable x_k.*

Proof. (Sketch) Proposition 4 guarantees that auxiliary variables are implied as the result of a single implication path. Hence, it suffices to trace this single implication path to eventually reach a single non-auxiliary variable. □

Proposition 7. *For the CNF encoding $LT_{SEQ}^{n,1}$ of constraint ≤ 1 $(x_1, \ldots, x_n)$, any learnt clause ω can be replaced by a learnt clause of the same size that only contains non-auxiliary variables.*

Proof. From proposition 5, auxiliary variables can occur in learnt clauses only if they are traced as a UIP. From proposition 6 this traced variable can be replaced by a single non-auxiliary variable. Hence the result follows. □

As a result, the main conclusion is that by branching only on non-auxiliary variables, then a satisfying assignment can be identified, if it exists. Otherwise, by branching only on non-auxiliary variables, unsatisfiability can be proved.

Moreover, by analyzing the clause learning process of a CDCL SAT solver, it is possible to conclude that learnt clauses need not contain auxiliary variables.

[1] A detailed proof would require a more formal definition of the organization of a CDCL SAT solver.

Hence, the SAT solver can effectively only consider non-auxiliary variables for branching and clause learning purposes.

In practice, branching only on non-auxiliary variables may not be the most effective strategy. As a result, one challenge is to evaluate which auxiliary variables can be deemed more effective for branching purposes.

Proposition 8. *For the CNF encoding $LT_{SEQ}^{n,1}$ of constraint $\leq 1\ (x_1, \ldots, x_n)$, and such that all auxiliary variables are unassigned, then the assignments $s_0 = 1$ and the assignment $s_{n-1} = 0$ originate the largest number of implied assignments, or a conflict is identified.*

Proof. Assume a conflict is not identified. A simple inductive argument suffices. $s_1 = 1$ implies $s_2 = 1$, and the same holds true for all i, $1 \leq i \leq n-2$, $s_i = 1$ implies $s_{i+1} = 1$. In addition, all variables x_i, $1 < i \leq n$, are assigned value 0. Similarly, $s_{n-1} = 0$ implies $s_{n-2} = 0$, and the same holds true for all i, $2 \leq i \leq n-1$, $s_i = 0$ implies $s_{i-1} = 0$. In contrast with the previous case, all variables x_i, $1 \leq i < n$, are assigned value 0.

Clearly, all the other auxiliary variables yield no more implied assignments than these auxiliary variables. □

Hence, a possible approach for deciding which auxiliary variables to consider for branching purposes is to select the first and last auxiliary variables of each $LT_{SEQ}^{n,1}$ encoding, the first variable is preferred to be assigned value 1, and the last is preferred to be assigned value 0.

Motivated by the previous results, a number of possible variable branching heuristics can thus be devised:

1. Branch on all variables, both non-auxiliary and auxiliary. This branching heuristic will be implemented by any existing CDCL SAT solver.
2. Branch only on non-auxiliary variables. This branching heuristic attempts to replicate the branching steps in the pairwise encoding.
3. Branch only on non-auxiliary variables, and on the auxiliary variables for which one of the value assignments guarantees the largest number of implied assignments. The rationale is that if branching on some auxiliary variables is useful, then these should be the preferred variables to branch on.

In order to implement the last two branching heuristics, a CDCL SAT solver needs to be adapted to accept branching directives from the CNF formula description. This can be achieved by specifying these directives as comments in the standard input format for SAT solvers. Section 5 evaluates these branching heuristics.

4.2 Modifications to a CDCL SAT Solver

This section focus on CDCL SAT solvers, and shows how the SAT solver can be modified to allow filtering auxiliary variables for branching purposes, as outlined in the previous section. The MiniSat [9] SAT solver is assumed, since the proposed modifications are straightforward to implement in MiniSat. Regarding the three main engines of a CDCL SAT solver, the deduction engines requires no modification, the decision engine needs to filter variables not used for branching purposes, and the diagnosis engine needs to exchange learnt literals on non-branching variables by literals on branching variables. A more detailed description of the modifications to the CDCL SAT solver is given below.

Internal Data Structures. When creating new variables, the SAT solver is informed of whether a variable is non-auxiliary, and so needs to be considered for variable branching purposes, or whether it is auxiliary, and so needs not be considered for variable branching purposes. For the auxiliary variables, the first and last auxiliary variables of each $LT^{n,1}_{SEQ}$ encoding can also be optionally considered for branching purposes. In addition to specifying the variables that can serve for branching purposes, with each such variable the preferred value can also be specified. In these cases, the preferred value is always used when the SAT solver branches on that variable.

The Decision Engine. When selecting a variable for branching, the SAT solver is modified to only consider variables that can serve as branching variables. Hence, the decision engine only branches on variables that were initially declared to be eligible as branching variables. Moreover, if a preferred value is associated with a given variable, then the decision engine uses the preferred value when branching on that variable.

The Diagnosis Engine. When learning a conflict clause, if the UIP condition holds and if the current variable is auxiliary, then the clause learning process continues. The results of the previous section (see Propositions 6 and 7) guarantee that the UIP condition will remain valid until a non-auxiliary UIP variable is identified or until a auxiliary branching variable is identified. As shown earlier, the size of learnt clauses is unchanged by filtering auxiliary variables.

5 Experimental Results

The ideas described above have been implemented in the most recent version of the MiniSat SAT solver [9] - MiniSat2, a cleaned up version of the winning entry of SAT-Race 2006. MiniSat is a CDCL solver, containing all the features of the current state-of-the-art solvers: conflict-clause learning, conflict-driven backjumping, dynamic variable ordering heuristic and two watched-literal scheme.

We have considered two different encodings:

1. The *pairwise encoding* (`pw`), which has a quadratic number of clauses but no additional variables.
2. The *sequential counter encoding* (`sc`), representing $LT^{n,1}_{SEQ}$, which has a linear number of clauses and also a linear number of auxiliary variables.

The sequential counter encoding has been evaluated for two additional configurations of the MiniSat SAT solver:

1. `sc-d`: for this configuration the *decision* variables are selected from the non-auxiliary variables only (and therefore auxiliary variables cannot be selected).

2. sc-dh: for this configuration the decision variables are selected from the non-auxiliary variables and also from two auxiliary variables: s_1 and s_{n-1} (again the remaining auxiliary variables cannot be selected). In case any of these two auxiliary variables are selected, *hints* are given for the value to assign to these variables: if variable s_1 is selected then it is assigned value 1, and if variable s_{n-1} is selected then it is assigned value 0. These assignments originate the largest number of implied assignments.

For the results given below, the main goal is to evaluate (1) the performance of the pairwise encoding against the sequential encoding in terms of the CPU time and the memory required and (2) the improvements achieved by the filtering of auxiliary variables. All the results were obtained on an Intel Xeon 5160 (3.0GHz with 4GB of RAM) and a timeout (TO) of 1000s.

5.1 Problem Instances

A number of problems were evaluated, all containing many $\leq 1\ (x_1, \ldots, x_n)$ constraints. These problems were the following: the n-queens problem, the pigeon hole problem, the round-robin problem, the all-interval series problem, the graph coloring problem and the Latin squares problem extended with constraints on (broken) diagonals [2]. The analysis of results is divided into two classes: instances for the n-queens problem, which modern SAT solvers can tackle, and instances from the other problems considered, since for these problems modern SAT solvers can solve only a few instances.

5.2 Results for the N-Queens Problem

The n-queens problem is the problem of placing n chess queens on an $n \times n$ chessboard such that no two queens share the same row, column, or diagonal, i.e. there is at most one queen in each row, column or diagonal. We may represent this problem with $n \times n$ Boolean variables, where each variable corresponds to one entry in the chess board. We then require $2 \times n$ constraints $\leq 1\ (x_1, \ldots, x_n)$ to guarantee that there is only one queen per row and one queen per column. In addition, we require $4n - 6$ constraints to guarantee that there is at most one queen per diagonal. We have generated n-queens problems ranging from $n = 100$ to $n = 300$ using both the pairwise (pw) and the sequential counter (sc) encoding. CNF formulas generated by both encodings were solved using the MiniSat SAT solver. In addition, two modified versions of MiniSat (sc-d and sc-dh) were evaluated for the sequential encoding.

Figure 1 gives the CPU time (in seconds) for solving the n-queens problems using the four different approaches. From this figure a few conclusions can be drawn:

[2] The quasigroup completion problem was also evaluated near the phase transition. For this problem the number of literals in the sequential encoding is in general larger than the number of literals in the pairwise encoding. Given that some entries in the quasigroup are already defined, the number of entries to be distinct is reduced.

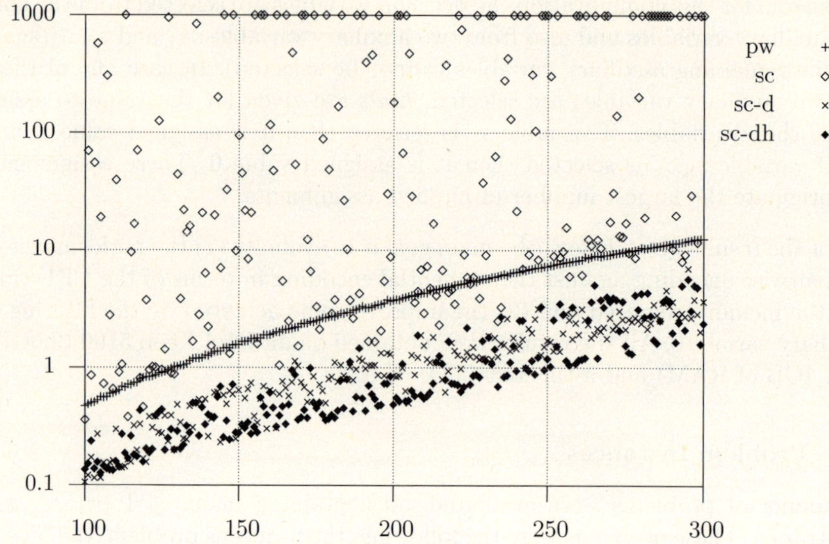

Fig. 1. Results on run times

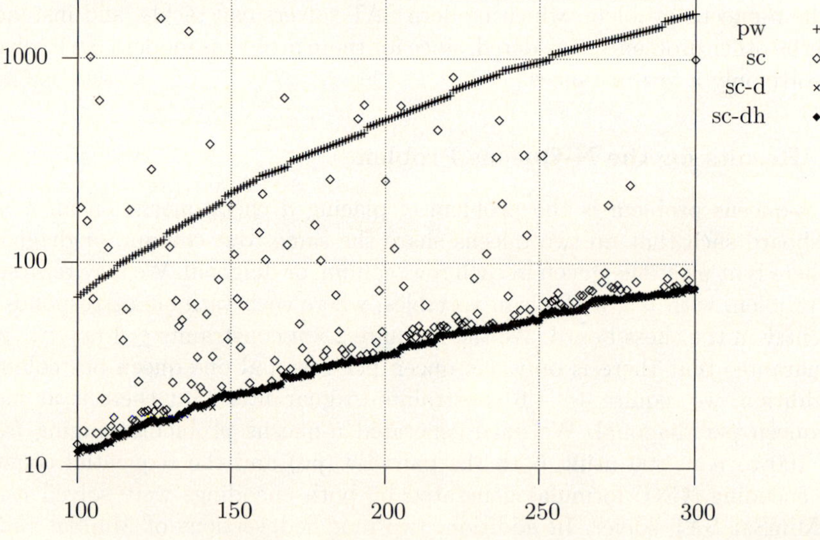

Fig. 2. Results on memory used

- The sequential encoding, when used with the plain MiniSat solver (`sc`) is quite unstable and in general takes more time than any other approach. Also, it is not able to solve 51 problem instances within the allowed CPU time (1000s).
- The pairwise encoding (`pw`) although being stable requires in general up to one order of magnitude more time than the two other approaches using the sequential encoding (`sc-d` and `sc-dh`).

– Both `sc-d` and `sc-dh` are more competitive than the `pw` approach. This contrasts with the `sc` approach. Not only the size of the search space in `sc` is larger but also the search *gets lost* recording useless clauses and being unable to find a solution.

Figure 2 evaluates the memory consumed by MiniSat (in MB) for solving a given problem instance following one of the four approaches. Again, from this figure a few conclusions can be drawn:

– The pairwise encoding (`pw`) requires more memory than both the `sc-d` and `sc-dh` approaches. The memory difference most often exceeds one order of magnitude. This difference is significant in practice: the `pw` requires around 1600 MB for the larger problem instances, whereas 75 MB suffice for the `sc-d` and `sc-dh` approaches.
– Although the CNF formula is exactly the same for `sc`, `sc-d` and `sc-dh`, the amount of memory required by `sc` is significantly larger. This is due to the clauses recorded during the search, resulting from the conflicts.

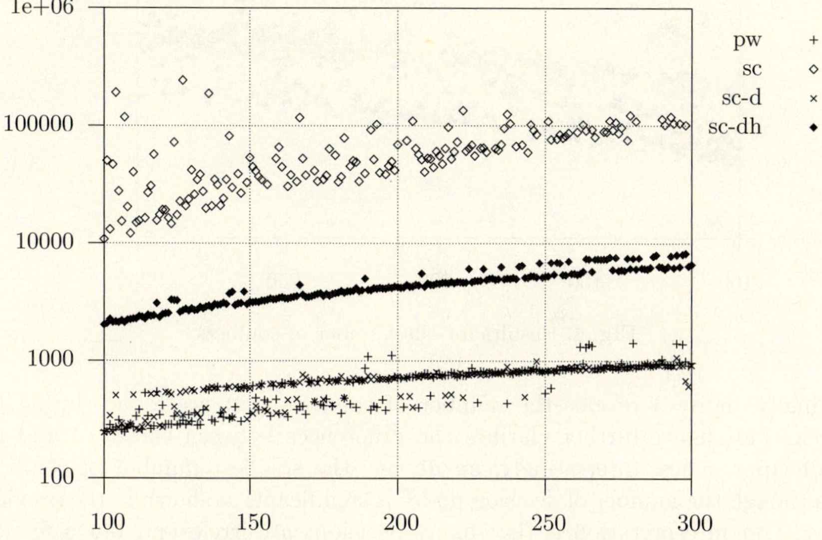

Fig. 3. Results for the number of decisions.

Figure 3 gives the number of decisions, corresponding to the number of nodes in the search tree, required by each of the approaches for solving a given problem instance.

– The `sc` approach explores by far the largest number of nodes. This is in part due to the larger search space. Moreover, it is also clear that the heuristic used is far from being accurate for this encoding.
– Both `sc-d` and `pw` approaches explore the smallest number of nodes. Given that `sc-d` only branches on non-auxiliary variables, both approaches may explore the same search space. This means that each one of the heuristics used by each one of the approaches is very effective for that specific approach.

– The sc-dh approach explores more nodes than sc-d and pw. This comes as no surprise given that the search space is larger. For each ≤ 1 $(x_1, \ldots, x_n)$ constraint we may have two more decision variables. However, given the CPU times, these variables when taken as decisions are not as harmful as the other auxiliary variables when taken as decisions in the sc approach. This is probably due to the *hints* on the values to be assigned to the auxiliary variables.

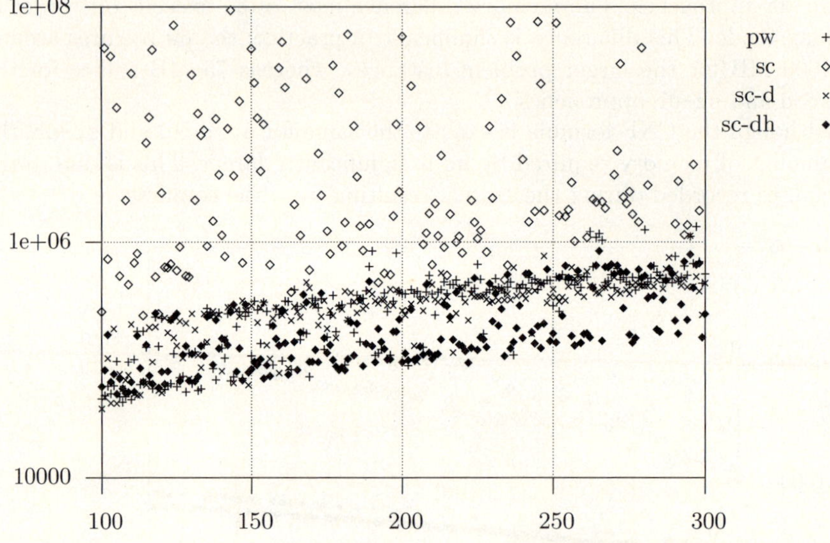

Fig. 4. Results for the number of conflicts

Finally, figure 4 reveals the number of conflicts that are found during the search. This figure further clarifies the differences between the sc-d and the sc-dh approaches. Interestingly, sc-dh has the smallest number of conflicts, even though the number of decision nodes is significant, as shown in the previous figure. Our interpretation is that many decisions are irrelevant, but a few are extremely useful. This makes the conflict clauses in general shorter and therefore able to prune more effectively the search space.

5.3 Results for Other Problems

This section presents results for a number of other instances which are also encoded with ≤ 1 $(x_1, \ldots, x_n)$ constraints. Example instances from the all-interval series, pigeon-hole, Latin squares and round-robin problems are considered. For these problems only a few instances are considered. Other instances are not considered, either because run times are negligible or because modern SAT solvers exceed the allowed CPU time limit.

The results are summarized in Table 5.3. As observed for the n-queens problem, the approaches sc, sc-dh and sc-d tend to perform more robustly than the

Table 1. Results on additional instances

Bench	pw		sc		sc-d		sc-h	
	mem	time	mem	time	mem	time	mem	time
ais16	6.74	5.12	3.68	0	8.06	45.12	7.29	24.57
ais17	13.27	77.33	3.8	0	6.51	8.24	9.28	53.95
ais18	—	TO	15.57	550.02	18.56	860.78	16.12	401.24
php9	3.54	2.4	3.54	1.6	3.54	4.76	3.54	4.18
php10	4.06	31.73	3.66	15.74	3.79	43.26	3.78	45.75
php11	5.45	526.03	4.41	189.51	4.52	652.91	4.53	741.6
ls8	7.45	40.51	7.31	64.58	6.71	33.51	6.61	34.56
rr10	17.28	1.03	13.11	1.83	12.91	1.74	8.77	0.39
rr12	41.23	4.28	90.85	50.26	20.21	3.71	106.79	50.79
gc-anna	9.93	18.87	10.71	39.98	9.98	27.56	10.52	42.05
gc-david	9.47	29.66	9.3	30.64	9.59	41.64	9.41	33.17
gc-huck	8.77	32.71	7.66	25.01	8.23	33.14	8.48	30.69

pw approach, with a few outliers. In terms of memory used, no concrete pattern was identified in the results, in part because of the small number of instances that can be considered. For instances with similar run times, the sc encodings use significantly less memory than the pw encoding (e.g. *rr10* and *php10*).

6 Conclusions

This paper studies techniques for improving the robustness of linear size encodings of $\leq 1\ (x_1, \ldots, x_n)$ constraints. The sequential counter ($LT^{n,1}_{SEQ}$) encoding of [21] is considered. For this encoding, the additional auxiliary variables used for encoding $\leq 1\ (x_1, \ldots, x_n)$ constraints can essentially be ignored by the SAT solver. A related result is that auxiliary variables can be discarded from learnt clauses, without affecting the number of literals of each learnt clause. An additional result is that auxiliary variables are guaranteed to yield different numbers of implied variables, and so this yields a natural ranking of auxiliary variables for branching purposes.

A number of different strategies for selecting branching variables are outlined and experimentally evaluated. Experimental results indicate that filtering most of the auxiliary variables is an effective technique, yielding significantly more robust CDCL SAT solvers, and may represent a valid alternative to the space-consuming pairwise encoding.

A future line of research is to devise techniques for extending the work in this paper, by being more precise at filtering auxiliary variables that are not effective for branching purposes. The properties identified for the $LT^{n,1}_{SEQ}$ encoding also suggest a family of branching heuristics, besides the ones outlined in the paper. These heuristics allow increasing number of decision variables ranked by the number of guaranteed implied assignments. One possible application of these heuristics would be to instruct SAT solvers to switch between branching heuristics after each search restart.

Finally, another line of research is to extend the results in the paper to other cardinality constraints. Results equivalent to the ones proposed in this paper, namely Proposition 2, are expected to exist for most linear encodings of constraint $\leq 1\ (x_1, \ldots, x_n)$, and for encodings of general cardinality constraints $\leq k\ (x_1, \ldots, x_n)$. A more challenging question is how some of the other results proposed in the paper, namely the ones related with clause learning, can be adapted either to other encodings of constraint $\leq 1\ (x_1, \ldots, x_n)$ or to general cardinality constraints $\leq k\ (x_1, \ldots, x_n)$.

Acknowledgments. This work is partially supported by Fundação para a Ciência e Tecnologia under research projects POSC/EIA/61852/2004 and POSI/SRI/41926/01, EPSRC grant EP/E012973/1, and EU project IST/033709.

References

1. Ansótegui, C., Manyá, F.: Mapping problems with finite-domain variables to problems with boolean variables. In: Proceedings of the International Conference on Theory and Applications of Satisfiability Testing, pp. 1–15 (2004)
2. Bailleux, O., Boufkhad, Y.: Efficient CNF encoding of boolean cardinality constraints. In: Proceedings of the International Conference on Principles and Practice of Constraint Programming, pp. 108–122 (2003)
3. Bailleux, O., Boufkhad, Y.: Full CNF encoding: The counting constraints case. In: Proceedings of the International Conference on Theory and Applications of Satisfiability Testing (2004)
4. Bailleux, O., Boufkhad, Y., Roussel, O.: A translation of pseudo Boolean constraints to SAT. Journal on Satisfiability, Boolean Modeling and Computation 2 (March 2006)
5. Bayardo Jr., R., Schrag, R.: Using CSP look-back techniques to solve real-world SAT instances. In: Proceedings of the National Conference on Artificial Intelligence, pp. 203–208 (July 1997)
6. Béjar, R., Hähnle, R., Manyà, F.: A modular reduction of regular logic to classical logic. In: Proceedings of the International Symposium on Multiple-Valued Logics, pp. 221–226 (2001)
7. Davis, M., Logemann, G., Loveland, D.: A machine program for theorem-proving. Communications of the Association for Computing Machinery 5, 394–397 (1962)
8. Davis, M., Putnam, H.: A computing procedure for quantification theory. Journal of the Association for Computing Machinery 7, 201–215 (1960)
9. Eén, N., Sörensson, N.: An extensible SAT solver. In: Proceedings of the International Conference on Theory and Applications of Satisfiability Testing, pp. 502–518 (May 2003)
10. Eén, N., Sörensson, N.: Translating pseudo-Boolean constraints into SAT. Journal on Satisfiability, Boolean Modeling and Computation 2 (March 2006)
11. Gent, I.P.: Arc consistency in SAT. In: Proceedings of the European Conference on Artificial Intelligence, pp. 121–125 (2002)
12. Gent, I.P., Nightingale, P.: A new encoding of AllDifferent into SAT. In: Proceedings 3rd International Workshop on Modelling and Reformulating Constraint Satisfaction Problems, pp. 95–110 (September 2004)

13. Gent, I.P., Prosser, P.: An empirical study of the stable marriage problem with ties and incomplete lists. In: Proceedings of the European Conference on Artificial Intelligence, pp. 141–145 (2002)
14. Goldberg, E., Novikov, Y.: BerkMin: a fast and robust SAT-solver. In: Proceedings of the Design Automation and Test in Europe Conference, pp. 142–149 (March 2002)
15. Gomes, C.P., Selman, B., Kautz, H.: Boosting combinatorial search through randomization. In: Proceedings of the National Conference on Artificial Intelligence, pp. 431–437 (July 1998)
16. Kasif, S.: On the parallel complexity of discrete relaxation in constraint satisfaction networks. Artificial Intelligence 45(3), 275–286 (1990)
17. Marques-Silva, J., Sakallah, K.: GRASP: A new search algorithm for satisfiability. In: Proceedings of the International Conference on Computer-Aided Design, pp. 220–227 (November 1996)
18. Moskewicz, M., Madigan, C., Zhao, Y., Zhang, L., Malik, S.: Engineering an efficient SAT solver. In: Design Automation Conference, pp. 530–535 (June 2001)
19. Nadel, A.: Backtrack search algorithms for propositional logic satisfiability: Review and innovations. Master's thesis, Hebrew University of Jerusalem (November 2002)
20. Ryan, L.: Efficient algorithms for clause-learning SAT solvers. Master's thesis, Simon Fraser University (February 2004)
21. Sinz, C.: Towards an optimal CNF encoding of boolean cardinality constraints. In: Proceedings of the International Conference on Principles and Practice of Constraint Programming, pp. 827–831 (October 2005)
22. Walsh, T.: SAT *v* CSP. In: Proceedings of the International Conference on Principles and Practice of Constraint Programming, pp. 441–456 (September 2000)
23. Warners, J.P.: A linear-time transformation of linear inequalities into conjunctive normal form. Information Processing Letters 68(2), 63–69 (1998)
24. Zhang, H.: SATO: An efficient propositional prover. In: Proceedings of the International Conference on Automated Deduction, pp. 272–275 (July 1997)
25. Zhang, L., Madigan, C.F., Moskewicz, M.W., Malik, S.: Efficient conflict driven learning in boolean satisfiability solver. In: Proceedings of the International Conference on Computer-Aided Design, pp. 279–285 (2001)

AND/OR Multi-valued Decision Diagrams for Constraint Optimization

Robert Mateescu, Radu Marinescu, and Rina Dechter

Donald Bren School of Information and Computer Science
University of California, Irvine, CA 92697-3425
{mateescu,radum,dechter}@ics.uci.edu

Abstract. We propose a new top down search-based algorithm for compiling AND/OR Multi-Valued Decision Diagrams (AOMDDs), as representations of the optimal set of solutions for constraint optimization problems. The approach is based on AND/OR search spaces for graphical models, state-of-the-art AND/OR Branch-and-Bound search, and on decision diagrams reduction techniques. We extend earlier work on AOMDDs by considering general weighted graphs based on cost functions rather than constraints. An extensive experimental evaluation proves the efficiency of the weighted AOMDD data structure.

1 Introduction

The compilation of graphical models, including constraint and probabilistic networks, has recently been under intense investigation. Compilation techniques are useful when an extended off-line computation can be traded for fast real-time answers. Typically, a tractable compiled representation of the problem is desired. Since the tasks of interest are in general NP-hard, this is not always possible in the worst case. In practice, however, it is often the case that the compiled representation is much smaller than the worst case bound, as was observed for Ordered Binary Decision Diagrams (BDDs) [1] which are extensively used in hardware and software verification.

In the context of constraint networks, compilation schemes are very useful for interactive solving or product configuration type problems [2,3]. These are combinatorial problems where a compact representation of the feasible set of solutions is necessary. The system has to be *complete* (to represent all solutions), *backtrack-free* (to never encounter dead-ends) and *real-time* (to provide fast answers).

In this paper we present a compilation scheme for constraint optimization, which has been of interest recently in the context of post-optimality analysis [4]. Our goal is to obtain a compact representation of the set of optimal solutions, by employing techniques from search, optimization and decision diagrams. Our approach is based on three main ideas: (1) AND/OR search spaces for graphical models [5]. Their key feature is the exploitation of problem structure during search, sometimes yielding exponential improvement over structure-blind search methods. (2) Branch-and-Bound search for optimization, applied to AND/OR search spaces [6]. (3) Reduction rules similar to OBDDs, that lead to the compilation of the search algorithm trace into an AND/OR Multi-Valued Decision Diagram (AOMDD) [7]. The novelty over previous results consists in: (1) the

C. Bessiere (Ed.): CP 2007, LNCS 4741, pp. 498–513, 2007.

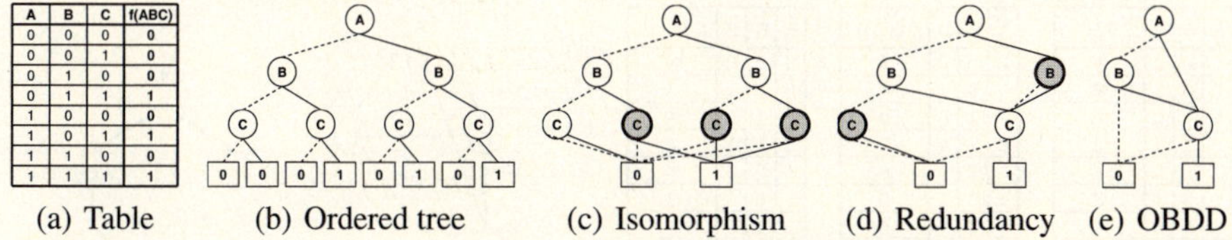

A	B	C	f(ABC)
0	0	0	0
0	0	1	0
0	1	0	0
0	1	1	1
1	0	0	0
1	0	1	1
1	1	0	0
1	1	1	1

(a) Table (b) Ordered tree (c) Isomorphism (d) Redundancy (e) OBDD

Fig. 1. Boolean function representations

treatment of general weighted graphs based on cost functions, rather than constraints. (2) a top down search based approach for generating the AOMDD, rather than Variable Elimination based as in [7]. (3) Extensive experimental evaluation that proves the efficiency of the weighted AOMDD. We show that the compilation scheme can often be accomplished relatively efficiently and that we sometimes get a substantial reduction beyond the initial trace of state-of-the-art search algorithms.

2 Background

2.1 Constraint Optimization Problems

A finite *Constraint Optimization Problem* (COP) is a triple $\mathcal{P} = \langle \mathbf{X}, \mathbf{D}, \mathbf{F} \rangle$, where $\mathbf{X} = \{X_1, ..., X_n\}$ is a set of variables, $\mathbf{D} = \{D_1, ..., D_n\}$ is a set of finite domains and $\mathbf{F} = \{f_1, ..., f_r\}$ is a set of cost functions. Cost functions can be either *soft* or *hard* (constraints). Without loss of generality we assume that hard constraints are represented as (bi-valued) cost functions. Allowed and forbidden tuples have cost 0 and ∞, respectively. The scope of function f_i, denoted $scope(f_i) \subseteq \mathbf{X}$, is the set of arguments of f_i. The goal is to find a complete value assignment to the variables that minimizes the global cost function, namely to find $x = \arg\min_{\mathbf{X}} \sum_{i=1}^{r} f_i$.

Given a COP instance, its *primal graph* G has a node for each variable and connects any two nodes whose variables appear in the scope of the same function. The *induced graph* of G relative to an ordering d of its variables is obtained by processing the nodes in reverse order of d. For each node all its earlier neighbors are connected, including neighbors connected by previously added edges. The *width* of a node is the number of edges connecting it to nodes lower in the ordering. The *induced width* (also equal to the *treewidth*) of a graph along d, denoted $w^*(d)$, is the maximum width of nodes in the induced graph. The *pathwidth* of a graph along d, $pw^*(d)$, is equal to the induced width of the graph with extra edges added between any node and its successor in d.

2.2 Binary Decision Diagrams

Decision diagrams are widely used in many areas of research to represent decision processes. In particular, they can be used to represent functions. Due to the fundamental importance of Boolean functions, a lot of effort has been dedicated to the study of *Binary Decision Diagrams* (BDDs), which are extensively used in formal verification.

A BDD is a representation of a Boolean function. Given $\mathbf{B} = \{0, 1\}$, a Boolean function $f : \mathbf{B}^n \to \mathbf{B}$, has n arguments, $X_1, \cdots, X_n$, which are Boolean variables,

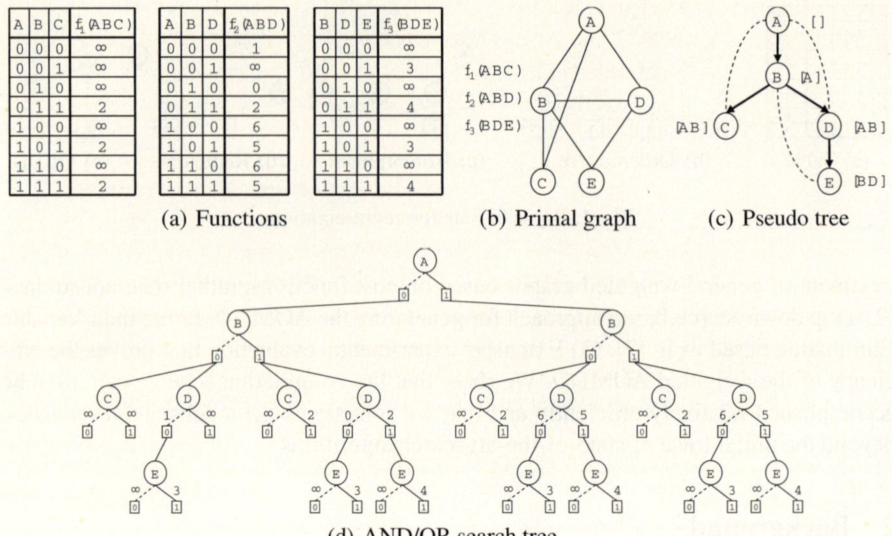

A	B	C	$f_1(ABC)$
0	0	0	∞
0	0	1	∞
0	1	0	∞
0	1	1	2
1	0	0	∞
1	0	1	2
1	1	0	∞
1	1	1	2

A	B	D	$f_2(ABD)$
0	0	0	1
0	0	1	∞
0	1	0	0
0	1	1	2
1	0	0	6
1	0	1	5
1	1	0	6
1	1	1	5

B	D	E	$f_3(BDE)$
0	0	0	∞
0	0	1	3
0	1	0	∞
0	1	1	4
1	0	0	∞
1	0	1	3
1	1	0	∞
1	1	1	4

(a) Functions (b) Primal graph (c) Pseudo tree

(d) AND/OR search tree

Fig. 2. AND/OR search tree for COP

and takes Boolean values. A Boolean function can be represented by a table (see Figure 1(a)), but this is exponential in n, and so is the binary tree representation in Figure 1(b). OBDDs [1] provide a more compact representation, that also supports efficient operations, by imposing the same order to the variables along each path in the binary tree, and then applying the following two reduction rules exhaustively: (1) *isomorphism*: merge nodes that have the same label and the same respective children (Figure 1(c)); (2) *redundancy*: eliminate nodes whose low (zero) and high (one) edges point to the same node (see Figure 1(d)). The resulting OBDD is shown in Figure 1(e).

2.3 AND/OR Search Spaces for COP

The AND/OR search space [5] is a unifying framework for advanced algorithmic schemes for graphical models, including constraint networks and cost networks. Its main virtue consists in exploiting independencies between variables during search, which can provide exponential speedups over traditional structure-blind search methods. The search space is defined using a backbone *pseudo-tree* [8].

Definition 1 (pseudo-tree). *Given an undirected graph $G = (\mathbf{X}, E)$, a directed rooted tree $\mathcal{T} = (\mathbf{X}, E')$ defined on all its nodes is called* pseudo-tree *if any edge of G that is not included in E' is a back-arc in $\mathcal{T}$, namely it connects a node to an ancestor in $\mathcal{T}$.*

AND/OR Search Trees Given a COP instance $\mathcal{P}$, its primal graph G and a pseudo tree $\mathcal{T}$ of G, the associated AND/OR search tree, $S_\mathcal{T}$, has alternating levels of OR and AND nodes. The OR nodes are labeled X_i and correspond to the variables. The AND nodes are labeled $\langle X_i, x_i\rangle$ (or just x_i) and correspond to value assignments of the variables. The structure of the AND/OR search tree is based on the underlying pseudo tree $\mathcal{T}$.

The root of the AND/OR search tree is an OR node labeled with the root of $\mathcal{T}$. The children of an OR node X_i are AND nodes labeled with assignments $\langle X_i, x_i \rangle$ that are consistent with the assignments along the path from the root. The children of an AND node $\langle X_i, x_i \rangle$ are OR nodes labeled with the children of variable X_i in $\mathcal{T}$. The AND/OR search tree can be traversed by a depth first search (DFS) algorithm, thus using linear space to compute the value of the root node. It was shown [8,9]:

Theorem 1. *Given a COP instance $\mathcal{P}$ and a pseudo tree $\mathcal{T}$ of depth m, the size of the AND/OR search tree based on $\mathcal{T}$ is $O(n \cdot k^m)$, where k bounds the domains of variables. A COP having treewidth w^* has a pseudo tree of depth at most $w^* \log n$, therefore it has an AND/OR search tree of size $O(n \cdot k^{w^* \log n})$.*

Weighted AND/OR Search Trees. The OR-to-AND arcs from nodes X_i to x_i in an AND/OR search tree are annotated by *weights* derived from the cost functions in $\mathbf{F}$.

Definition 2 (weight). *The* weight $w(X_i, x_i)$ *of the arc from the OR node X_i to the AND node x_i is the sum of all the cost functions whose scope includes X_i and is fully assigned along the path from the root to x_i, evaluated at the values along the path.*

The AND/OR search tree in Figure 2(d) shows the weights on the OR-to-AND arcs. Given a weighted AND/OR search tree, each node can be associated with a *value*:

Definition 3 (value). *The* value $v(n)$ *of a node n in a weighted AND/OR tree is defined recursively as follows (where $succ(n)$ are the children of n):*
(i) $v(n) = 0$, if $n = x_i$ is a terminal AND node;
(ii) $v(n) = \sum_{n' \in succ(n)} v(n')$, if $n = x_i$ is an internal AND node;
(iii) $v(n) = min_{n' \in succ(n)}(w(n, n') + v(n'))$, if $n = X_i$ is an OR node.

It is easy to see that the value $v(n)$ of a node in the AND/OR search tree $S_{\mathcal{T}}$ is the minimal cost solution to the subproblem rooted at n, subject to the current variable instantiation along the path from the root to n. If n is the root of $S_{\mathcal{T}}$, then $v(n)$ is the minimal cost solution to the initial problem [6,5].

Example 1. Figure 2 shows an example of AND/OR search tree for a COP with binary variables. The cost functions are given in Figure 2(a). The value ∞ indicates a hard constraint. The primal graph is given in Figure 2(b), and the pseudo tree in Figure 2(c). The square brackets indicate the context of the variables, a notion explained below. The AND/OR search tree is given in Figure 2(d). The numbers on the OR-to-AND arcs are the weights corresponding to the function values. Note that the tree is pruned whenever a weight shows inconsistency (e.g., for $A = 0, B = 0, D = 1$).

AND/OR Search Graphs. The AND/OR search tree may contain nodes that root identical conditioned subproblems. These nodes are said to be *unifiable*. When unifiable nodes are merged, the search space becomes a graph. Its size becomes smaller at the expense of using additional memory by the search algorithm. The depth first search algorithm can therefore be modified to cache previously computed results, and retrieve them when the same nodes are encountered again. Some unifiable nodes can be identified based on their *contexts*. We can define graph based contexts for both OR nodes

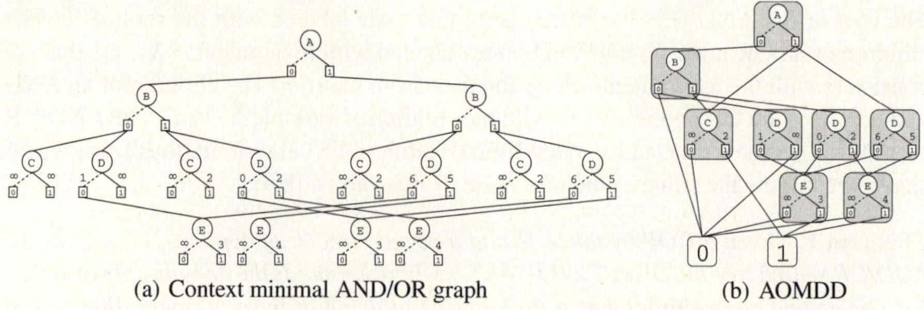

(a) Context minimal AND/OR graph (b) AOMDD

Fig. 3. AND/OR graphs for COP

and AND nodes, just by expressing the set of ancestor variables in $\mathcal{T}$ that completely determine a conditioned subproblem. It can be shown that using caching based on OR contexts makes caching based on AND contexts redundant, so we only use *OR caching*.

Given a pseudo tree $\mathcal{T}$ of an AND/OR search space, the *context* of an OR node X, denoted by $context(X) = [X_1 \dots X_p]$, is the set of ancestors of X in $\mathcal{T}$ ordered descendingly, that are connected in the primal graph to X or to descendants of X. The context of X separates the subproblem below X from the rest of the network.

Definition 4 (context minimal AND/OR graph). *Given a COP instance $\mathcal{P}$ and a pseudo-tree $\mathcal{T}$, the* context minimal *AND/OR graph, denoted by $C_\mathcal{T}$ is obtained from the AND/OR search tree of $\mathcal{P}$ along $\mathcal{T}$ by merging all the context unifiable OR nodes.*

Theorem 2 ([9,5]). *Given a COP $\mathcal{P}$, its primal graph G and a pseudo tree $\mathcal{T}$, the size of the context minimal AND/OR search graph $C_\mathcal{T}$ is $O(n \cdot k^{w^*_\mathcal{T}(G)})$, where $w^*_\mathcal{T}(G)$ is the induced width of G over the DFS traversal of $\mathcal{T}$, and k bounds the domain size.*

Example 2. Figure 2(c) shows a pseudo tree and the context of each variable in square brackets. The context minimal AND/OR graph is given in Figure 3(a). Note that only the cache table of E will get cache hits during the depth first search traversal (E is the only level of OR nodes that has more than one incoming arc). It can be determined from the pseudo tree inspection that all variables except for E generate *dead-caches* [5,10] (also explained in following section), and their cache tables need not be stored.

3 Weighted AND/OR Multi-valued Decision Diagrams

The context minimal AND/OR graph offers an effective way of identifying some unifiable nodes. However, merging based on context is not complete, i.e. there may still be unifiable nodes in the search graph that do not have identical contexts. The context-based merging uses only information available from the ancestors in the pseudo tree. If all the information from the descendants would also be available, it could lead to the identification of more unifiable nodes. This comes at a higher cost, however, since information from descendants in the pseudo tree means that the entire associated subproblem has to be solved. Orthogonal to the problem of unification, some of the nodes in an AND/OR search graph may be redundant, for example when the set of solutions rooted at variable X_i is not dependent on the specific value assigned to X_i.

The above criteria suggest that once an AND/OR search graph is available (e.g., after search terminates, and its trace is saved) reduction rules based on *isomorphism* and *redundancy* (similar to OBDDs) can be applied further, reducing the size of the AND/OR search graph that was explicated by search. In order to apply the reduction rules, it is convenient to group each OR node and its children into a *meta-node*:

Definition 5 (meta-node). *A meta-node v in a weighted AND/OR search graph consists of an OR node labeled $var(v) = X_i$ and its k_i AND children labeled $x_{i_1}, ..., x_{i_{k_i}}$ that correspond to its value assignments. Each AND node labeled x_{i_j} points to a list of child meta-nodes, $u.children_j$, and also stores the weight $w(X_i, x_{i_j})$.*

The reduction rules are straightforward. Two meta-nodes are *isomorphic* if they have the same variable label and the same respective lists of children and weights. A meta-node is *redundant* if all its lists of children and weights are respectively identical.

When reduction rules are applied exhaustively to an AND/OR search graph, the result is an AND/OR Multi-Valued Decision Diagram (AOMDD). The AOMDD data structure for constraint networks (where weights are all 1) was introduced in [7], along with a Variable Elimination type algorithm to generate it, based on the *apply* operator, similar to the OBDD case.

An example of a AOMDD appears in Figure 3(b), representing the exhaustive reduction of the context minimal AND/OR graph in Figure 3(a). The terminal nodes labeled with **0** and **1** denote inconsistent and consistent assignments, respectively. Note that when $A = 1$, B is redundant and its common list of children becomes the list of children for $A = 1$, namely the problem already splits into two independent components after $A = 1$, even though this can not be read from the pseudo tree in Figure 2(c).

4 Compiling COPs into AOMDDs

We next define the AOMDD describing the set of optimal solutions to a COP and present a general scheme for generating these compiled data structures.

Definition 6. *Given a set of tuples S over variables $\mathbf{X}$ and a tree $\mathcal{T}$ over $\mathbf{X}$, $\mathcal{T}$ expresses S iff there exists an AND/OR tree guided by $\mathcal{T}$ that expresses all and only tuples in S.*

Proposition 1. *If $\mathcal{T}$ is a pseudo-tree of a COP $\mathcal{P}$, then $\mathcal{T}$ can be used to express S^{opt}, the set of optimal solutions of $\mathcal{P}$.*

Definition 7. *Given a COP $\mathcal{P}$, its set of optimal solutions S^{opt} and a pseudo tree $\mathcal{T}$ of $\mathcal{P}$, its AOMDD$_{\mathcal{T}}^{opt}$ is the AOMDD that expresses all and only S^{opt} relative to $\mathcal{T}$.*

The target is to generate AOMDD$_{\mathcal{T}}^{opt}$ of a COP. The idea is to use a pseudo tree $\mathcal{T}$ that can express all solutions and explore a subset of its context minimal AND/OR graph, $C_{\mathcal{T}}$ that contains all the optimal solutions and then process it so that it will represent only optimal solutions and be completely reduced relative to isomorphism and redundancy. Therefore, any search algorithm for optimal solutions that explores the context minimal graph can be used to generate the initial trace. The better the algorithm we use, the more efficient the procedure would be because the initial trace will be tight around the context minimal graph that is restricted to the optimal solutions.

In recent years several Branch-and-Bound and Best-First search algorithms were developed to search the context minimal AND/OR graph for solving COPs [6,10,11]. In this paper we use a depth-first AND/OR Branch-and-Bound (AOBB) algorithm.

4.1 AND/OR Branch-and-Bound Search

AOBB traverses the context minimal AND/OR search graph in a depth-first manner via full caching. It interleaves forward expansion of the current partial solution subtree with a backward cost revision step that updates node values, until search terminates. The efficiency of the algorithm also depends on the strength of its heuristic evaluation function (i.e., lower bound). Specifically, each node n along the path from the root has an associated *static* heuristic function $h(n)$ underestimating $v(n)$ that can be computed efficiently when the node n is first expanded. The algorithm then improves the heuristic function dynamically during search. The *dynamic heuristic function* $f_h(n)$ is computed based on the search space below n that has already been explored [6], and is used to prune irrelevant portions of the search space, based on the Branch-and-Bound principle.

In the forward step the algorithm expands alternating levels of OR and AND nodes. Since we are using OR caching, before expanding an OR node, its cache table is checked. If the same context was encountered before, it is retrieved from the cache, and its successors set is set to empty which will trigger the cost revision step. If an OR node is not found in the cache, it is expanded in the usual way. Before expanding an AND node n, the algorithm updates the heuristic function $f_h(a)$ for every ancestor a of n along the current path, and discontinues search below n if, for some a, $f_h(a)$ is greater or equal than the best cost solution found at a (the upper bound).

The backward cost revision step is triggered when a closed node has an empty set of successors. This means that all its children have been evaluated, and its final value can now be computed. If the current node is the root, then the search terminates with its value. OR nodes update their values by minimization, while AND nodes combine their children values by summation.

4.2 The Compilation Algorithm

The compilation algorithm, called AOBB-COMPILE, is described in Algorithm 1. It extends the AND/OR Branch-and-Bound algorithm described above by compiling the trace of the search into an AND/OR Multi-Valued Decision Diagram representing all optimal solutions to the input COP instance.

The algorithm is based on two mutually recursive steps, similar to AOBB: EXPAND and REVISE which call each other until the search terminates. The fringe of the search is maintained on a stack called OPEN. The current node is n, its parent p, and the current path π_n. The children of the current node in the AND/OR search graph are denoted by $succ(n)$. The AND/OR decision diagram being constructed is denoted by AOMDD. Each node u in the AND/OR search graph has a pointer, denoted by $u.metanode$, to the corresponding meta-node in AOMDD.

In the EXPAND step, when the current OR node n is expanded, AOBB-COMPILE creates a new meta-node corresponding to n and adds it to AOMDD. If n is already present in cache, then AOBB-COMPILE ensures that the meta-node corresponding to n's parent in the context minimal search graph points to the meta-node that was created when n was first expanded.

In the REVISE step when node values are propagated backwards, the algorithm also attempts to reduce the diagram by removing isomorphic meta-nodes. Specifically, if n is the current OR node being evaluated and if there exists a meta-node m which is isomorphic with $n.metanode$, then the parents of $n.metanode$ in the AOMDD are updated to point to m instead of $n.metanode$, which is then removed from the diagram.

The compiled AOMDD may contain sub-optimal solutions that were visited during the Branch-and-Bound search but were not pruned. Therefore, a second pass over the decision diagram is necessary to remove any path which does not appear in any optimal solution (omitted from the algorithm due to space limitations). Specifically, in the second pass AOBB-COMPILE traverses the AOMDD in a depth-first manner for every meta-node u along the current path from the root, it prunes $u.children_j$ from the diagram if $(\sum_{u' \in u.children_j} v(u') + w(X_i, x_{i_j})) > v(u)$, namely the optimal cost solution to the problem below the j child of u is not better than the optimal cost solution at u.

Theorem 3. *Given a COP instance $\mathcal{P} = \langle \mathbf{X}, \mathbf{D}, \mathbf{F} \rangle$ and a pseudo tree $\mathcal{T}$ of $\mathcal{P}$, the AOMDD generated by AOBB-COMPILE along $\mathcal{T}$ is AOMDD$_{\mathcal{T}}^{opt}$.*

The complexity of AOBB-COMPILE is bounded time and space by the trace generated, which is $O(n \cdot exp(w^*))$. However, the heuristic evaluation function used by AOBB typically restricts the trace far below this complexity bound.

5 Experiments

In this section we evaluate empirically the compilation scheme on two common classes of optimization problems: Weighted CSPs (WCSP) [12] and 0/1 Integer Linear Programs (0/1 ILP) [13]. In our experiments we compiled the search trace relative to isomorphic meta-nodes only, without removing redundant nodes. Also we did not perform the second top-down pass over the diagram to remove additional sub-optimal solutions.

5.1 Weighted CSPs

Weighted CSP [12] extends the classic CSP formalism with *soft constraints* which assign positive integer costs to forbidden tuples (allowed tuples have cost 0). The goal is to find a complete assignment with minimum aggregated cost. The model has numerous applications in domains such as resource allocation, scheduling or planning.

We consider the compilation algorithm based on the AND/OR Branch-and-Bound algorithm with pre-compiled mini-bucket heuristics and full caching introduced by [10] and denoted by AOBB(i). The parameter i represents the mini-bucket i-bound and controls the accuracy of the heuristic.

For each test instance we report the number of OR nodes in the context minimal AND/OR search graph (#cm) visited by AOBB(i), and the number of meta-nodes in

Algorithm 1. AOBB-COMPILE

```
Data: A COP instance P = ⟨X, D, F⟩, pseudo-tree T, root s, heuristic function f_h.
Result: AOMDD containing the optimal solutions to P.
v(X_1) ← ∞; OPEN ← {X_1}; AOMDD ← ∅;                                   // Initialize
while OPEN ≠ ∅ do
    n ← top(OPEN); remove n from OPEN
    let π_n be the assignment along the path from the root to n
    if n is an OR node, labeled X_i then                                  // EXPAND
        if Cache(n, context(X_i)) ≠ ∅ then
            v(n) ← Cache(n, context(X_i))
            succ(n) ← ∅
            let p = ⟨X_j, x_j⟩ be the AND parent of n in the AND/OR search graph
            p.metanode.children_{x_j} ← p.metanode.children_{x_j} ∪ {n.metanode}
        else
            succ(n) ← {⟨X_i, x_i⟩ | ⟨X_i, x_i⟩ is consistent with π_n}
            for ⟨X_i, x_i⟩ ∈ succ(n) do
                v(⟨X_i, x_i⟩) ← 0; h(⟨X_i, x_i⟩) ← heuristic(X_i, x_i)
                w(X_i, x_i) ← Σ_{f∈F, X_i∈scope(f)} f(π_n)
            create a new meta-node m for X_i and add it to AOMDD
            let p = ⟨X_j, x_j⟩ be the AND parent of n in the AND/OR search graph
            p.metanode.children_{x_j} ← p.metanode.children_{x_j} ∪ {m}
        Add succ(n) on top of OPEN
    else if n is an AND node, labeled ⟨X_i, x_i⟩ then
        for a ∈ ancestors(X_i, x_i) do
            if (a is OR) and (f_h(a) > v(a)) then
                n.deadend ← true
                n.metanode.children_{x_i} ← UNSOLVED
                break
        if n.deadend == false then
            succ(n) ← {X_j | X_j ∈ children_T(X_i)}
            v(X_j) ← ∞; h(X_j) ← heuristic(X_j)
            Add succ(n) on top of OPEN
            if succ(n) == ∅ then
                n.metanode.children_{x_i} ← SOLVED
    while succ(n) == ∅ do                                                 // REVISE
        let p be the parent of n
        if n is an OR node, labeled X_i then
            if X_i == X_1 then                                            // Search is complete
                return AOMDD
            Cache(n, context(X_i)) ← v(n)
            v(p) ← v(p) + v(n)
            n.metanode.value ← v(n)
            if findIsomorphism(n.metanode) == true then
                let m be the meta-node isomorphic with n.metanode
                redirect the links of n.metanode's parents in AOMDD to point to m
                AOMDD ← AOMDD − {n.metanode}
        if n is an AND node, labeled ⟨X_i, x_i⟩ then
            v(p) ← min(v(p), w(X_i, x_i) + v(n))
        remove n from succ(p)
        n ← p
```

the resulting AND/OR decision diagram (#aomdd), as well as their ratio defined as $ratio = \frac{\#cm}{\#aomdd}$. In some cases we also report the compilation time. We record the number of variables (n), the number of constraints (c), the depth of the pseudo-trees (h) and the induced width of the graphs (w^*) obtained for the test instances. The pseudo-trees were generated using the min-fill heuristic, as described in [6].

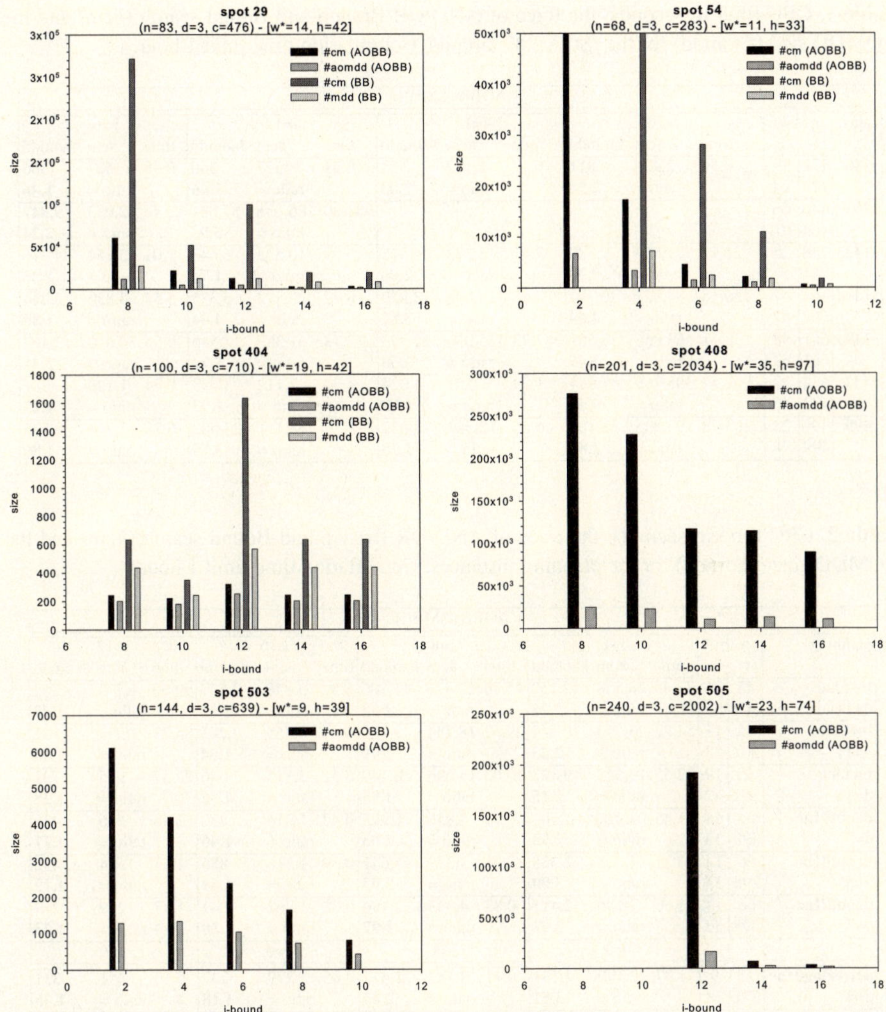

Fig. 4. The trace of AND/OR Branch-and-Bound search (nodes) versus the AOMDD size (aomdd) for the SPOT5 networks. Compilation time limit 1 hour.

Earth Observing Satellites. The problem of scheduling an Earth observing satellite is to select from a set of candidate photographs, the best subset such that a set of imperative constraints are satisfied and the total importance of the selected photographs is maximized. We experimented with problem instances from the SPOT5 benchmark [14] which can be formulated as non-binary WCSPs. For our purpose we considered a simplified MAX-CSP version of the problem where the goal is to minimize the number of imperative constraints violations (i.e., we ignored the importance of the photographs).

Figure 4 displays the results for experiments with 6 SPOT5 networks. Each subgraph depicts the trace of AOBB(i) and the size of the resulting AND/OR decision diagram as a function of the i-bound of the mini-bucket heuristic. For comparison, we also include

Table 1. CPU time in seconds, the trace of AND/OR Branch-and-Bound search (#cm) and the AOMDD size (#aomdd) for the ISCAS'89 circuits. Compilation time limit 1 hour.

			AOBB+SMB(i)											
iscas	n	w*		i=10			i=12			i=14			i=16	
	c	h	time	#cm	#aomdd	time	#cm	#aomdd	time	#cm	#aomdd	time	#cm	#aomdd
s386	172	19	0.50	2,420	811	0.17	1,132	558	0.21	527	360	0.38	527	360
	172	44		ratio =	**2.98**		ratio =	**2.03**		ratio =	**1.46**		ratio =	**1.46**
s953	440	66		-			-		981.20	186,658	37,084	22.46	22,053	9,847
	464	101								ratio =	**5.03**		ratio =	**2.24**
s1423	748	24	21.12	21,863	9,389	7.47	13,393	6,515	5.09	10,523	6,043	2.01	5,754	4,316
	751	54		ratio =	**2.33**		ratio =	**2.06**		ratio =	**1.74**		ratio =	**1.33**
s1488	667	47	250.18	83,927	20,774	4.48	15,008	3,929	10.72	23,872	5,375	5.54	5,830	3,246
	667	67		ratio =	**4.04**		ratio =	**3.82**		ratio =	**4.44**		ratio =	**1.80**
s1494	661	48	138.61	63,856	18,501	387.73	125,030	22,393	37.78	31,355	11,546	39.75	30,610	12,467
	661	69		ratio =	**3.45**		ratio =	**5.58**		ratio =	**2.72**		ratio =	**2.46**
c432	432	27	1867.49	395,766	41,964	1.29	7,551	4,024	1.30	7,112	3,693	0.74	1,120	881
	432	45		ratio =	**9.43**		ratio =	**1.88**		ratio =	**1.93**		ratio =	**1.27**
c499	499	23	363.78	93,936	33,157	6.66	12,582	7,051	271.26	88,131	23,502	16.75	17,714	9,536
	499	74		ratio =	**2.83**		ratio =	**1.78**		ratio =	**3.75**		ratio =	**1.86**

Table 2. CPU time in seconds, the trace of AND/OR Branch-and-Bound search (#cm) and the AOMDD size (#aomdd) for the planning instances. Compilation time limit 1 hour.

			AOBB+SMB(i)											
planning	n	w*		i=6			i=8			i=10			i=12	
	c	h	time	#cm	#aomdd	time	#cm	#aomdd	time	#cm	#aomdd	time	#cm	#aomdd
bwt3ac	45	16	77.45	28,558	12,152	45.76	22,475	11,106	8.92	3,878	2,537	99.00	1,775	1,252
d=11	301	34		ratio =	**2.35**		ratio =	**2.02**		ratio =	**1.53**		ratio =	**1.42**
bwt3bc	45	11	54.22	23,560	10,544	29.62	18,734	9,422	8.61	3,455	2,243	85.73	1,599	1,141
d=11	301	33		ratio =	**2.23**		ratio =	**1.99**		ratio =	**1.54**		ratio =	**1.40**
bwt3cc	45	19	32.55	19,643	9,122	20.03	15,696	8,149	8.51	3,113	2,046	85.57	935	731
d=11	301	42		ratio =	**2.15**		ratio =	**1.93**		ratio =	**1.52**		ratio =	**1.28**
depot01ac	66	14	1.45	7,420	2,504	0.73	4,056	1,995	0.42	1,214	830	1.48	506	432
d=5	298	33		ratio =	**2.96**		ratio =	**2.03**		ratio =	**1.46**		ratio =	**1.17**
depot01bc	66	14	1.31	7,068	2,358	0.55	3,333	1,641	0.39	1,316	886	1.47	514	432
d=5	298	33		ratio =	**3.00**		ratio =	**2.03**		ratio =	**1.49**		ratio =	**1.19**
depot01cc	66	14	1.36	7,156	2,411	0.82	4,333	2,196	0.38	1,262	841	1.47	269	219
d=5	298	33		ratio =	**2.97**		ratio =	**1.97**		ratio =	**1.50**		ratio =	**1.23**
				i=2			i=4			i=6			i=8	
driverlog01ac	71	9	1.37	7,490	2,134	0.41	3,143	1,412	0.05	279	237	0.10	451	331
d=4	271	38		ratio =	**3.51**		ratio =	**2.23**		ratio =	**1.18**		ratio =	**1.36**
driverlog01bc	71	9	1.36	7,447	2,128	0.42	3,098	1,389	0.04	231	210	0.07	247	212
d=4	271	38		ratio =	**3.50**		ratio =	**2.23**		ratio =	**1.10**		ratio =	**1.17**
driverlog01cc	71	9	1.61	7,741	2,185	0.10	883	622	0.04	279	237	0.07	295	239
d=4	271	38		ratio =	**3.54**		ratio =	**1.42**		ratio =	**1.18**		ratio =	**1.23**
mprime03ac	49	9	2.12	7,172	1,562	0.66	3,343	863	0.11	595	386	0.16	111	94
d=10	185	23		ratio =	**4.59**		ratio =	**3.87**		ratio =	**1.54**		ratio =	**1.18**
mprime03bc	49	9	2.07	7,266	1,573	0.68	3,486	849	0.12	641	396	0.10	111	94
d=10	185	23		ratio =	**4.62**		ratio =	**4.11**		ratio =	**1.62**		ratio =	**1.18**
mprime03cc	49	9	1.47	5,469	1,391	0.45	2,336	721	0.12	534	366	0.10	111	94
d=10	185	23		ratio =	**3.93**		ratio =	**3.24**		ratio =	**1.46**		ratio =	**1.18**

the results obtained with the OR version of the compilation scheme that explores the traditional OR search space.

We observe that the resulting AOMDD is substantially smaller than the context minimal AND/OR graph traversed by `AOBB(i)`, especially for relatively small i-bounds that generate relatively weak heuristic estimates. For instance, on the `408` network, we were able to compile an AOMDD 11 times smaller than the AND/OR search graph explored by AOBB(8). As the i-bound increases, the heuristic estimates become stronger and they are able to prune the search space significantly. In consequence, the difference in size between the AOMDD and the AND/OR graph explored decreases. When looking at the OR versus the AND/OR compilation schemes, we notice that AOMDD is smaller than the OR MDD, for all reported i-bounds. On some of the harder instances, the OR compilation scheme did not finish within the 1 hour time limit (e.g., 408, 505).

ISCAS'89 Benchmark Circuits. ISCAS'89 circuits are a common benchmark used in formal verification and diagnosis (*http://www.fm.vslib.cz/ kes/asic/iscas/*). For our purpose, we converted each of these circuits into a non-binary WCSP instance by removing flip-flops and buffers in a standard way, creating hard constraints for gates and uniform unary cost functions for the input signals. The penalty costs were distributed uniformly randomly between 1 and 10.

Table 1 shows the results for experiments with 7 circuits. The columns are indexed by the mini-bucket i-bound. We observe again that the difference in size between the resulting AOMDD and the AND/OR search graph explored by AOBB(i) is more prominent for relatively small i-bounds. For example, on the c432 circuit and at $i = 10$, the AOMDD is about 9 times smaller than the corresponding AND/OR graph.

Planning. We also experimented with problems from planning in temporal and metric domains (*http://carlit.toulouse.inra.fr/cgi-bin/awki.cgi/BenchmarkS*). These instances were converted into binary WCSPs as follows: each fluent of the planning graph is represented by a variable with domain values representing possible actions to produce this fluent. Hard binary constraints represent mutual exclusions between fluents and actions, and activity edges in the graph. Soft unary constraints represent action costs. The goal is to find a valid plan which minimizes the sum of the action costs.

Table 2 shows the results for experiments with 12 planning networks. On this domain we only observe minor differences between the size of the compiled AOMDD and the corresponding AND/OR search graph. This is due to very accurate mini-bucket heuristics which cause the AND/OR Branch-and-Bound to avoid expanding nodes that correspond to solutions whose cost is above the optimal one.

5.2 0/1 Integer Linear Programs

A *0/1 Integer Linear Programming* (0/1 ILP) [13] consists of a set of integer decision variables (restricted to values 0 or 1) and a set of linear constraints (equalities or inequalities). The goal is to minimize a global linear cost function subject to the constraints. 0/1 ILPs can formulate many practical problems such as capital budgeting, cargo loading, combinatorial auctions or maximum satisfiability problems.

We consider the AND/OR Branch-and-Bound algorithm developed in [15] and denoted by AOBB, as the basis for our AND/OR compilation scheme. The heuristic evaluation function used by AOBB is computed by solving the linear relaxation of the current subproblem with the SIMPLEX method [16] (our code used the implementation from the open source library lp_solve 5.5 available at http://lpsolve.sourceforge.net/5.5/).

MIPLIB Instances. MIPLIB is a library of Mixed Integer Linear Programming instances that is commonly used for benchmarking integer programming algorithms. For

Table 3. The trace of AND/OR Branch-and-Bound search (#cm) versus the AOMDD size (#aomdd) for the MIPLIB instances. Compilation time limit 1 hour.

miplib	(n, c)	(w*, h)	time	#cm	#aomdd	ratio
p0033	(33, 15)	(19, 21)	0.52	441	164	**2.69**
p0040	(40, 23)	(19, 23)	0.36	129	77	**1.66**
p0201	(201, 133)	(120, 142)	89.44	12,683	5,499	**2.31**
lseu	(89, 28)	(57, 68)	454.79	109,126	21,491	**5.08**

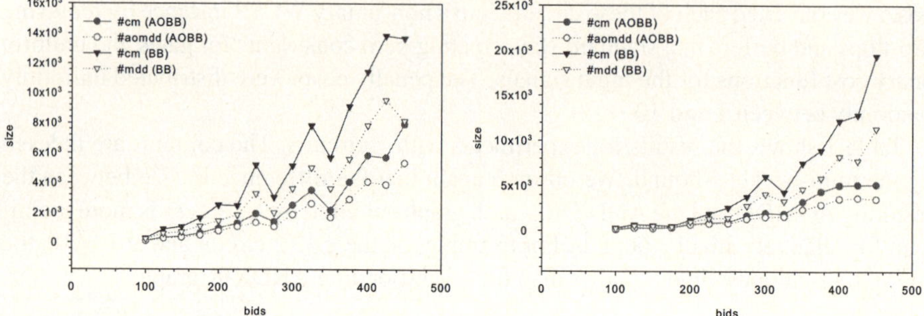

Fig. 5. The trace of AND/OR Branch-and-Bound search versus the AOMDD size for the `regions-upv` and `regions-npv` combinatorial auctions

our purpose we selected four 0/1 ILP instances of increasing difficulty. Table 3 reports a summary of the experiment. We observe that the AOMDD is smaller than the corresponding AND/OR search graph, especially for harder problems where the heuristic function generates relatively weak estimates. Results on these instances have been reported in [4], but we note that they are only for optimal solutions, while we also include suboptimal ones here. Also, in [4] they use of-the-shelf optimized BDD packages, while we use our own far-from-optimized implementation, and in particular we do not use redundancy reduction in these experiments. Moreover, the order of variables plays an enormous part in compilation and it may be the case that the ordering selected by the BDD tools is far superior (albeit OR ordering).

Combinatorial Auctions. In combinatorial auctions, an auctioneer has a set of goods, $M = \{1, 2, ..., m\}$ to sell and the buyers submit a set of bids, $\mathcal{B} = \{B_1, B_2, ..., B_n\}$. A bid is a tuple $B_j = \langle S_j, p_j \rangle$, where $S_j \subseteq M$ is a set of goods and $p_j \geq 0$ is a price. The winner determination problem is to label the bids as winning or loosing so as to maximize the sum of the accepted bid prices under the constraint that each good is allocated to at most one bid. We used the 0/1 ILP formulation described in [17].

Figure 5 shows results for experiments with combinatorial auctions drawn from the `regions` distribution of the CATS 2.0 test suite [17]. The suffixes `npv` and `upv` indicate that the bid prices were drawn from either a normal or uniform distribution. These problem instances simulate the auction of radio spectrum in which a government sells the right to use specific segments of spectrum in different geographical areas. We looked at auctions with 100 goods and increasing number of bids. Each data point

Table 4. The trace of AND/OR Branch-and-Bound search (#cm) versus the AOMDD size (#aomdd) for MAX-SAT `pret` instances

pret	(w*, h)	time	#cm	#aomdd	ratio
pret60-25	(6, 13)	2.74	593	255	**2.33**
pret60-40	(6, 13)	3.39	698	256	**2.73**
pret60-60	(6, 13)	3.31	603	222	**2.72**
pret60-75	(6, 13)	2.70	565	253	**2.23**
pret150-25	(6, 15)	18.19	1,544	851	**1.81**
pret150-40	(6, 15)	29.09	2,042	922	**2.21**
pret150-60	(6, 15)	30.09	2,051	877	**2.34**
pret150-75	(6, 15)	29.08	2,033	890	**2.28**

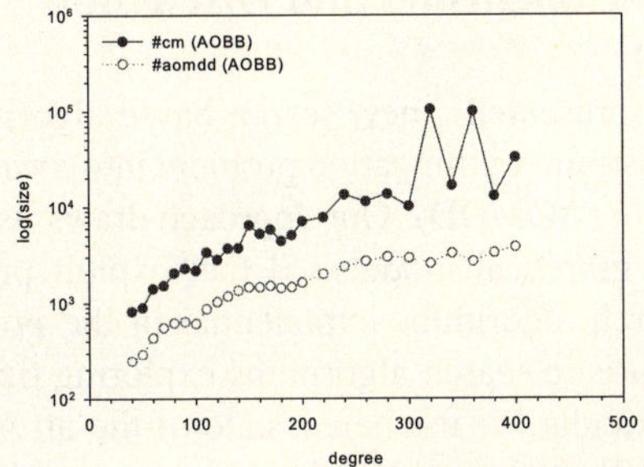

Fig. 6. The trace of AND/OR Branch-and-Bound search (#cm) versus the AOMDD size (#aomdd) for MAX-SAT `dubois` instances

represents an average over 10 random instances. For comparison, we also included results obtained with the OR compilation scheme. On this domain, we observe that the compiled AOMDD improves only slightly over the size of the AND/OR search graph. This is because the context minimal AND/OR graph is already compact enough due to very accurate heuristic estimates.

Maximum Satisfiability (MAX-SAT). Given a set of Boolean variables the goal of MAX-SAT is to find a truth assignment to the variables that violates the least number of clauses. The MAX-SAT problem can be formulated as a 0/1 ILP [18]. We experimented with problem classes `pret` and `dubois` from the SATLIB (*http://www.satlib.org/*) library, which were previously shown to be difficult for 0/1 ILP solvers (CPLEX) [19].

Table 4 shows the results for experiments with 8 `pret` instances. These are unsatisfiable instances of graph 2-coloring with parity constraints. The size of these problems is relatively small (60 variables with 160 clauses for `pret60` and 150 variables with 400 clauses for `pret150`, respectively). However, they have a very small context with size 6 and a shallow pseudo-tree with depths between 13 and 15. For this problem class we observe that the AND/OR decision diagrams have about 2 times fewer nodes than the AND/OR search graphs explored by `AOBB`. This is because the respective search spaces are already small enough, and this does not leave much room for additional merging of isomorphic nodes in the diagram.

Figure 6 displays the results for experiments with random `dubois` instances with increasing number of variables. These are 3-SAT instances with $3 \times degree$ variables and $8 \times degree$ clauses, each of them having 3 literals. As in the previous test case, the `dubois` instances have very small contexts of size 6 and shallow pseudo-trees with depths ranging from 10 to 20. The AND/OR decision diagrams compiled for these problem instances are far smaller than the corresponding AND/OR search graphs, especially for some of the larger instances. For example, at degree 320, the corresponding AOMDD is 40 times smaller than the trace of `AOBB`.

6 Conclusion and Discussion

We presented a new search based algorithm for compiling the optimal solutions of a constraint optimization problem into a weighted AND/OR Multi-Valued Decision Diagram (AOMDD). Our approach draws its efficiency from: (1) AND/OR search spaces for graphical models [5] that exploit problem structure, yielding memory intensive search algorithms exponential in the problem's *treewidth* rather than *pathwidth*. (2) Heuristic search algorithms exploring tight portions of the AND/OR search space. In particular, we use here a state-of-the-art AND/OR Branch-and-Bound search algorithm [6,10], with very efficient heuristics (mini-bucket, or simplex-based), that in practice traverses only a small portion of the context minimal graph by exploiting the pruning power of the cost function. (3) Reduction techniques similar to OBDDs further reduce the trace of the search algorithm.

The paper extends earlier work on AOMDDs [7] by considering weighted AOMDDs based on cost functions, rather than constraints. This can now easily be extended to any weighted graphical model, for example to probabilistic networks. Finally, using an extensive experimental evaluation we show the efficiency and compactness of the weighted AOMDD data structure.

For future work, we mention the possibility of using best-first AND/OR search for the compilation task, whose virtue is that it does not expand nodes whose heuristic evaluation function is larger than the optimal cost.

References

1. Bryant, R.E.: Graph-based algorithms for boolean function manipulation. IEEE Transaction on Computers 35, 677–691 (1986)
2. Fargier, H., Vilarem, M.: Compiling CSPs into tree-driven automata for interactive solving. Constraints 9(4), 263–287 (2004)
3. Hadzic, T., Andersen, H.R.: A BDD-based polytime algorithm for cost-bounded interactive configuration. In: National Conference on Artificial Intelligence (AAAI-2006) (2006)
4. Hadzic, T., Hooker, J.: Cost-bounded binary decision diagrams for 0-1 programming. In: International Conference on Integration of AI and OR Techniques (CPAIOR-2007) (2007)
5. Dechter, R., Mateescu, R.: AND/OR search spaces for graphical models. Artificial Intelligence 171, 73–106 (2007)
6. Marinescu, R., Dechter, R.: AND/OR branch-and-bound for graphical models. In: International Joint Conferences on Artificial Intelligence (IJCAI-2005), pp. 224–229 (2005)
7. Mateescu, R., Dechter, R.: Compiling constraint networks into AND/OR multi-valued decision diagrams (AOMDDs). In: Benhamou, F. (ed.) CP 2006. LNCS, vol. 4204, pp. 329–343. Springer, Heidelberg (2006)
8. Freuder, E.C., Quinn, M.J.: Taking advantage of stable sets of variables in constraint satisfaction problems. In: International Joint Conferences on Artificial Intelligence (IJCAI-1985), pp. 1076–1078 (1985)
9. Bayardo, R., Miranker, D.: A complexity analysis of space-bound learning algorithms for the constraint satisfaction problem. In: National Conference on Artificial Intelligence (AAAI-1996), pp. 298–304 (1996)
10. Marinescu, R., Dechter, R.: Memory intensive branch-and-bound search for graphical models. In: National Conference on Artificial Intelligence (AAAI-2006) (2006)

11. Marinescu, R., Dechter, R.: Best-first AND/OR search for graphical models. In: National Conference on Artificial Intelligence (AAAI-2007) (2007)
12. Bistarelli, S., Montanari, U., Rossi, F.: Semiring based constraint solving and optimization. Journal of ACM 44, 309–315 (1997)
13. Nemhauser, G., Wolsey, L.: Integer and combinatorial optimization. Wiley, Chichester (1988)
14. Bensana, E., Lemaitre, M., Verfaillie, G.: Earth observation satellite management. Constraints 4, 293–299 (1999)
15. Marinescu, R., Dechter, R.: AND/OR branch-and-bound search for pure 0/1 integer linear programming problems. In: International Conference on Integration of AI and OR Techniques (CPAIOR-2006), pp. 152–166 (2006)
16. Dantzig, G.: Maximization of a linear function of variables subject to linear inequalities. Activity Analysis of Production and Allocation (1951)
17. Leyton-Brown, K., Pearson, M., Shoham, Y.: Towards a universal test suite for combinatorial auction algorithms. ACM Electronic Commerce, 66–76 (2000)
18. Joy, S., Mitchell, J., Borchers, B.: A branch and cut algorithm for max-SAT and weighted max-SAT. Satisfiability Problem: Theory and Applications, 519–536 (1997)
19. de Givry, S., Larrosa, J., Schiex, T.: Solving max-SAT as weighted CSP. In: Rossi, F. (ed.) CP 2003. LNCS, vol. 2833. Springer, Heidelberg (2003)

Parallelizing Constraint Programs Transparently

Laurent Michel[1], Andrew See[1], and Pascal Van Hentenryck[2]

[1] University of Connecticut, Storrs, CT 06269-2155
[2] Brown University, Box 1910, Providence, RI 02912

Abstract. The availability of commodity multi-core and multi-processor machines and the inherent parallelism in constraint programming search offer significant opportunities for constraint programming. They also present a fundamental challenge: how to exploit parallelism transparently to speed up constraint programs. This paper shows how to parallelize constraint programs transparently without changes to the code. The main technical idea consists of automatically lifting a sequential exploration strategy into its parallel counterpart, allowing workers to share and steal subproblems. Experimental results show that the parallel implementation may produces significant speedups on multi-core machines.

1 Introduction

Recent years have witnessed a transition in processor design from improvements in clock speed to parallel architectures. Multi-core and multiprocessor machines are now commodity hardware, a striking example of which is the recent announcement of the 80 core prototype developed by Intel [3]. Constraint programming (CP) search naturally offers significant opportunities for parallel computing, yet very little research has been devoted to parallel constraint programming implementations. Notable exceptions include CHIP/PEPSys [12] and its successors ECLiPSe [6], Parallel Solver [7], and Mozart [10].

The paper tackles the challenge eloquently stated by Schulte and Carlsson [11]: *how to exploit the resources provided by parallel computers and making their useful exploitation simple.* One of the difficulties here is the rich search languages typically supported by modern constraint programming languages (e.g., [9,7,13]). Indeed, CP search is best described by the equation

CP Search = Nondeterministic Program + Exploration Strategy

indicating that a CP search procedure consists of a nondeterministic program implicitly describing the search tree and an exploration strategy specifying how to explore the search space. For instance, in COMET, the nondeterministic program is expressed using high-level nondeterministic instructions such as `tryall`, while the exploration strategy is specified by a search controller, i.e.,

CP Search in COMET = Nondeterministic Program + Search Controller.

This research shows how to transparently parallelize such rich and expressive search procedures. The parallelization is purely built on top of the COMET system and involves no modification to its runtime. The key technical idea is to

C. Bessiere (Ed.): CP 2007, LNCS 4741, pp. 514–528, 2007.

```
1  CPSolver cp();
2  LDS lds(cp);
3  range S = 1..8;
4  var<CP>{int} q[S](m,S);
5  m.post(allDifferent(all(i in S) q[i] + i));
6  m.post(allDifferent(all(i in S) q[i] - i));
7  m.post(allDifferent(q));
8  exploreall<cp> {
9   forall(i in S) by q[i].getSize()
10   tryall<cp>(v in S : q[i].memberOf(v))
11     label(q[i],v);
12 }
```

Fig. 1. A Constraint Program for the N-Queens Problem

automatically lift the search controller of a constraint program into a parallel controller implementing the same exploration strategy in parallel. This parallelization does not require any change to the CP program and reuses the very same nondeterministic program and search controller. More precisely, the parallelization creates a number of workers, each of which executes the original constraint program with the generic parallel controller instead of the original search controller. The generic parallel controller, which encapsulates the original search controller, implements a work-stealing strategy in which an idle worker steals CP subproblems from other workers. Experimental results show that such a transparent parallelization may produce significant speedups compared to the sequential implementation.

The paper briefly reviews the concepts of nondeterministic programs and search controllers from the COMET system, since these are at the core of the parallel implementation. The paper then presents the transparent parallelization of a constraint program and its implementation. It reports experimental results showing the benefits of the approach and contrasts this implementation with earlier work, emphasizing the transparency and genericity of the approach.

2 Nondeterministic Programs and Search Controllers

Nondeterministic Programs COMET features high-level abstractions for nondeterministic search such as `try` and `tryall`, preserving an iterative programming style while making nondeterminism explicit. Figure 1 shows a constraint program for finding all solutions to the queens problem, illustrating some of the nondeterministic abstractions. Line 1 declares a CP solver and line 4 defines the decision variables. Lines 5–7 state the problem constraints, while lines 8–12 specify the nondeterministic search. The `exploreall` instruction in line 8 specifies that all solutions are required. The search procedure iterates over all variables ordered by smallest domains (line 9), nondeterministically chooses a value for the selected variable (line 10), and assigns the value to the variable (line 11).

```
interface SearchController {
  void start(Continuation s,Continuation e);
  void addChoice(Continuation c);
  void fail();
  void startTry();
  void label(var<CP>{int} x,int v);
  ...
}
```

Fig. 2. Interface of Search Controllers

The nondeterministic choice is expressed using a `tryall` instruction. Note that lines 8–12 specify a nondeterministic program that describes the search tree to explore. The nondeterministic instructions are concerned with the control flow only and are implemented using continuations.

Search Controllers. It is the role of the search controller to implement the exploration strategy (i.e., in which order to explore the search nodes), as well as how to save and restore search nodes. In Figure 1, the search controller is declared in line 2 and implements an LDS strategy. It is then used (through the CP solver) in the nondeterministic instructions in lines 8 and 10. The interface of search controllers is partially specified in Figure 2 and it is useful to review the semantics of some of its methods. Method `start` is called by instructions starting a nondeterministic search (e.g., the `exploreall` or `minimize` instructions). It receives two continuations `s` and `e` as parameters. Continuation `e` (for exit) is called when the search is complete. Continuation `s` (for start) can be called each time a restart is executed: When called, it restarts execution at the beginning of the nondeterministic search. Method `addChoice` adds a new choice point (described by a continuation) and method `fail` is called upon failure. Method `startTry` is called when a `try` or a `tryall` instruction is executed. Finally, method `label` is called to instantiate a variable to a specific value.

The connection between nondeterministic programs and controllers relies on source-to-source rewritings. For instance, the rewriting for the `try` instruction

```
                           →    sc.startTry();
try<sc> LEFT | RIGHT            bool rightBranch = true;
                                continuation c { rightBranch=false;
                                                 sc.addChoice(c);
                                                 LEFT; }
                                if (rightBranch) RIGHT;
```

first invokes the `startTry` method of the controller. It then creates a continuation c to represent the right choice, adds the choice point to the controller, and executes the left branch. When the system wishes to return to the right choice, it calls the continuation `c`, executing the conditional statement. Since `rightBranch` is true in the continuation, the body `RIGHT` is executed.

An LDS Controller. The LDS controller is shown in Figure 3 and is organized around a queue of search node. A search node is represented by a pair (c, p), where c is the continuation produced by the nondeterministic program and p is a semantic path [2,4], i.e., the sequence of constraints added on the path from the root to the search node. The most significant methods are `addChoice` (lines 7–9) and `fail` (lines 10–17). Method `addChoice` enqueues a search node composed of the continuation and a *checkpoint* which encapsulates the semantic path from the root to the node. Method `fail` calls the exit continuation if the queue is empty (line 11). Otherwise, it dequeues a search node (line 13), restores the search state (line 14), and calls the continuation (line 15) to resume execution. To restore a search state j from node i, the implementation finds the longest common prefix k in the sequence of i and j, backtracks to k, and posts all the remaining constraints of j. Note that the state restoration may fail in optimization applications when new bounds have been found elsewhere in the tree, in which case the `fail` method is called recursively.

```
1  class LDS implements SearchController {
2     CPSolver _cp; Continuation _exit; CPNodeQueue _Q;
3     LDS(CPSolver cp) { _cp = cp; _Q = new CPNodeQueue(); }
4     void start(Continuation s,Continuation e) { _exit = e; }
5     void exit() { call(_exit);}
6     void startTry() {}
7     void addChoice(Continuation c) {
8       _Q.enQueue(new CPNode(new CheckPoint(_cp),c));
9     }
10    void fail() {
11      if (_Q.emtpy()) exit();
12      else {
13         CPNode next = _Q.deQueue();
14         if (next.restore(_cp)==Failure) fail();
15         else call(next.getContinuation());
16      }
17    }
18    void label(var<CP>{int} x,int v) {
19      if (_m.label(x,v)==Failure) fail();
20    }
21 }
```

Fig. 3. The Controller for Limited Discrepancy Search

3 Transparent Parallelization of Constraint Programs

The parallelization of constraint programs is illustrated in Figure 4, which shows a parallel constraint program to solve the n-queens problem with 4 workers. It features a `ParallelCPSolver` instruction specifying the number of workers and enclosing the constraint program. Observe that the parallelization is entirely transparent and does not require any modification to the constraint program besides replacing the sequential CP solver by its parallel counterpart. In this program, all the workers use an LDS exploration strategy. It is also possible to design a similar parallelization in which different workers implement different exploration strategies by using, say, a factory to create search controllers. The next two sections describes the implementation, starting with the high-level architecture before diving into the implementation.

```
ParallelCPSolver cp(4) {
  LDS lds(cp);
  range S = 1..8;
  var<CP>{int} q[S](m,S);
  m.post(allDifferent(all(i in S) q[i] + i));
  m.post(allDifferent(all(i in S) q[i] - i));
  m.post(allDifferent(q));
  exploreall<cp> {
    forall(i in S) by q[i].getSize()
      tryall<cp>(v in S : q[i].memberOf(v))
        label(q[i],v);
  }
}
```

Fig. 4. Parallelizing the Constraint Program for the N-Queens Problem

4 High-Level Description of The Parallel Architecture

Each worker is associated with a thread and executes its own version of the constraint program. The workers collaborate by sharing subproblems, naturally leveraging the semantic paths used in the underlying search controllers. The collaboration is based on work stealing: When a worker is idle, it steals subproblems from active workers. Work stealing has some strong theoretical guarantees [1] and was successfully used in parallel (constraint) logic programming systems as early as in the 1980s (e.g., [14,12]) and in recent systems. Figure 5 illustrates work stealing. The left part depicts the search tree explored by a busy worker. The right part shows the new search tree after a steal operation: The stolen subproblems 4, 5, and 6 are placed in a problem pool (top right) and the search tree of the active worker is updated accordingly (bottom right).

In a continuation-based implementation of nondeterminism, the search nodes corresponding to open subproblems (e.g., subproblems 4–6 and 7–9 in Figure 5) have not been created yet: for instance, these nodes are created by lines 13–15 using continuation C_1 in the LDS controller in Figure 3. This lazy creation of search nodes is important for efficiency reasons. However, when an idle worker wants to steal these nodes, the busy worker has to generate them itself (since the continuation references its own stack). As a result, each worker is organized as a simple finite state machine, alternating the exploration of its search tree and the generation of subproblems to be stolen (see Figure 6). The transition from exploration to generation occurs when an idle worker requests a node, in which case the busy worker explicitly generates the top-level subproblems and

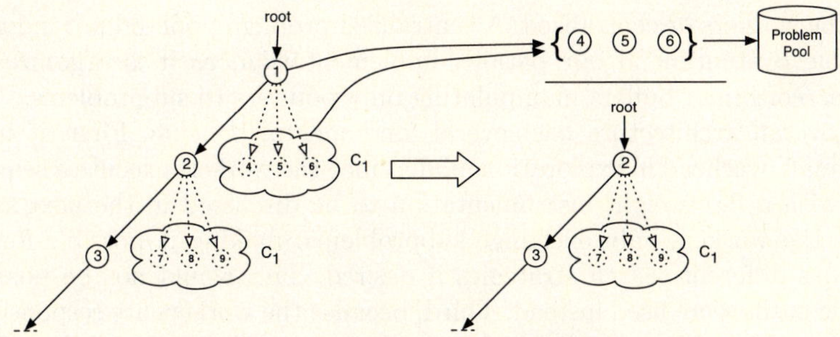

Fig. 5. Work Stealing in the Parallel Architecture

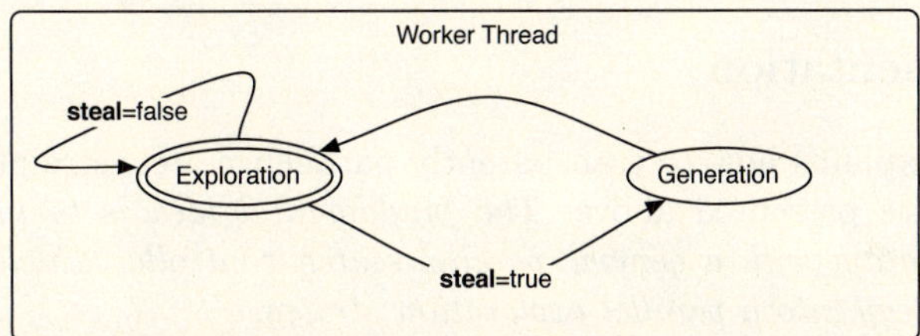

Fig. 6. The Finite State Machine for Workers

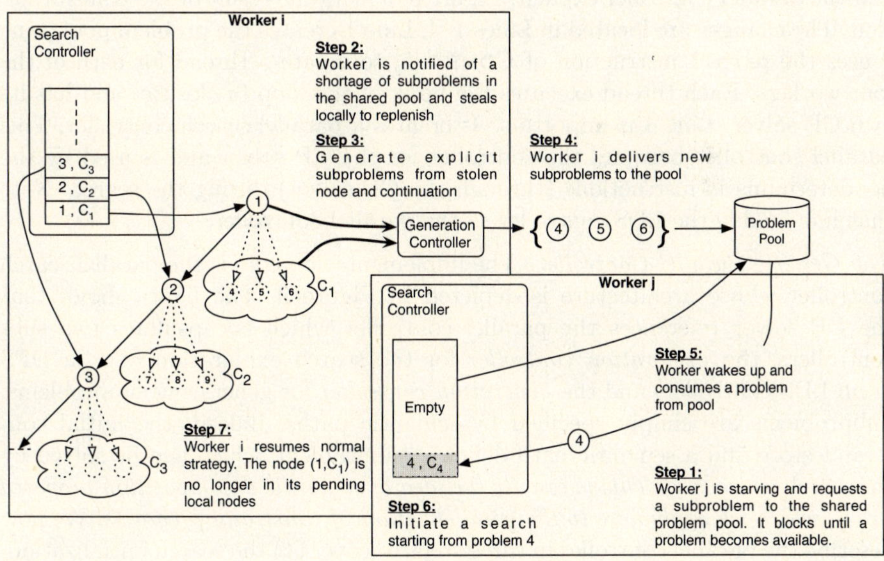

Fig. 7. The Work-Stealing Protocol

returns to its exploration. The work-stealing protocol is depicted in Figure 7 which describes all the steps in detail. The workers interact through a problem pool which store subproblems available for stealing. The pool may be distributed across the workers or centralized. A centralized problem pool did not induce any noticeable contention in our parallel implementation, as it is organized as a producer/consumer buffers manipulating only pointers to subproblems.

The overall architecture has several fundamental benefits. First, it induces only a small overhead in exploration mode, since the workers execute a sequential engine with a lightweight instrumentation to be discussed in the next section. Second, the workers only exchange subproblems, making it possible for them to execute different search strategies if desired. This would not be possible if syntactic paths were used instead. Third, because the workers are responsible for generating subproblems available for stealing, the architecture applies directly to any exploration strategy: the strategy is encapsulated in the search controller and not visible externally.

5 Implementation

This section explains how to transparently parallelize a constraint program for the architecture presented above. *The fundamental idea is to instrument the constraint program with a generic parallel search controller which lifts any exploration strategy into a parallel exploration strategy.*

The Source to Source Transformation. The first step consists of rewriting the `ParallelCPSolver cp(4)` instruction to make the threads, the problem pool, and the parallel controller explicit. Figure 8 depicts the result of the transformation. The changes are located in Lines 1–4. Line 1 creates the problem pool. Line 2 uses the `parall` instruction of COMET [5] to create a thread for each of the four workers. Each thread executes the body of the loop (a closure) and has its own CP solver. Line 4 is important: It creates a parallel search controller. This parallel controller becomes the controller for the CP solver and is used by the nondeterministic instructions (through the CP solver) during the search. Note that line 5 adds the LDS controller to the parallel controller.

The Generic Parallel Controller. The implementation core is the parallel search controller whose architecture is depicted in Figure 9. The figure shows that the CP solver references the parallel controller which encapsulates two subcontrollers: the *exploration controller* for the search exploration (e.g., a DFS or an LDS controller) and the *generation controller* for generating subproblems. Subproblems are simply specified by semantic paths. Indeed, the initial constraint store and a semantic path define a subproblem, which can be solved by the search procedure. *This is exactly the idea of semantic decomposition proposed in [4], which we apply here to the parallelization of constraint programs.* We now describe the parallel controller in three steps to cover (1) the search initialization, (2) the transition between exploration and generation, and (3) subproblem generation. Observe that workers execute their own parallel controller: They only share the problem pool which is synchronized.

The Search Initialization. Figure 10 illustrates the two methods at the core of the initialization process. Recall that method `start` is called at the beginning

```
ProblemPool pool();
parall(i in 1..4) {
  CPSolver cp();
  ParallelController par(cp,pool);
  LDS lds(cp);
  range S = 1..8;
  var<CP>{int} q[S](cp,S);
  m.post(allDifferent(all(i in S) q[i] + i));
  m.post(allDifferent(all(i in S) q[i] - i));
  m.post(allDifferent(q));
  exploreall<cp> {
    forall(i in S) by q[i].getSize()
      tryall<cp>(v in S : q[i].memberOf(v))
        label(q[i],v);
  }
}
```

Fig. 8. The Parallel Constraint Program after Source to Source Transformation

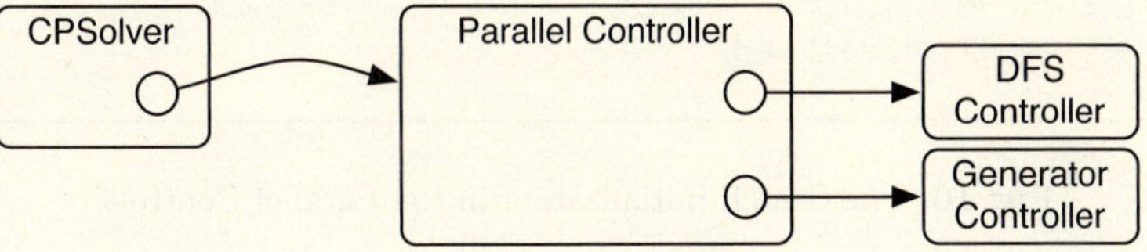

Fig. 9. The Architecture of the Parallel Controller

of the search (e.g., when the `exploreall` or `minimize` instructions are called). The `start` method of the generic parallel controller has two functionalities: (1) it must ensure that a single worker starts its exploration to avoid redundant computation; (2) it must allow all workers to steal work once they have completed their current execution. The `start` method solves the second problem by creating a continuation `steal` (lines 3–6) used to initialize the exploration controller in line 5. This means that the exploration controller, when calling its `exit` continuation, will now execute the instruction in line 7 to steal work instead of leaving the search. The first problem mentioned above is solved by the instruction in line 7. The problem pool is used to synchronize all the workers. A single worker is allowed to start exploring; the others start stealing. Note also that, when the first worker has finished its first exploration, it will also return to line 7 and start stealing work, since the test in line 7 succeeds exactly once.

Stealing work is depicted in lines 9–17. The worker requests a problem from the pool (line 10), i.e., it tries to steal problems from other workers. This call to a method of the problem pool only returns when the worker has found a subproblem or when all the workers are looking for work. When a subproblem is available, the parallel controller uses *semantic decomposition*: It restores the subproblem for its worker and restarts an entirely new search. That means (1) executing the `start` method on the subcontroller (line 13) and (2) restarting the search by calling the `_start` continuation received by the `start` method (line 14) to restart execution from scratch. If no search problem is available, no work can be stolen anywhere and the worker exits (which means that its thread waits on a barrier to meet all the other threads in the `parall` instruction [5]).

```
1  void ParallelController::start(Continuation s,Continuation e) {
2     _start = s; _exit = e;
3     continuation steal {
4        _steal = steal;
5        _explorationController.start(null,_steal);
6     }
7     if (!_pool.firstWorker()) stealWork();
8  }
9  void ParallelController::stealWork() {
10    Checkpoint nextProblem = _pool.getProblem();
11    if (nextProblem != null) {
12       nextProblem.restore(_cp);
13       _explorationController.start(null,_steal);
14       call(_start);
15    }
16    else call(_exit);
17 }
```

Fig. 10. The Search Initialization in the Parallel Controller

```
void ParallelController::startTry() {
  if (_generatingMode)     _generationController.startTry();
  else if (!_stealRequest) _explorationController.startTry();
  else                     transition();
 }
 void ParallelController::transition() {
    CPNode node = _explorationController.steal();
    if (node != null) {
      _generatingMode = true;
      Checkpoint currentState = new Checkpoint(_cp);
      continuation resume {
         node.restore(_cp);
         _generationController.start(null,resume);
         call(node.getContinuation());
      }
      currentState.restore(_cp);
      _generatingMode = false;
    }
    _explorationController.startTry();
 }
```

Fig. 11. Mode switching in the Parallel Controller

The Transition Between Exploration and Generation. The transition between exploration and generation, as well as method delegation to the appropriate subcontroller, is depicted in Figure 11. Method **startTry** explains what happens at the beginning of every nondeterministic instruction. In generation mode, the parallel controller delegates to the generation controller (line 2); in exploration mode, as long as there are no stealing request, it delegates to the exploration controller (line 3). Otherwise, the parallel controller transitions to generation mode (line 4). To transition, the parallel controller first tests whether there is something to steal, in which case the instructions in lines 9–15 are executed. These instructions are responsible to start the generation of the nodes as discussed in Section 4. The parallel controller first steals the local node (line 10) (e.g., checkpoint 1 and continuation C_1 in Figure 7), restores the subproblem (line 12), calls the **start** method on the generation controller to initiate the generation process (line 13), and executes the continuation to produce the subproblems (line 14). Observe that the generation controller is called with a new exit continuation **resume**; upon exiting, the generation controller executes this continuation to return to line 16 allowing the worker to return to exploration mode. Indeed, line 16 restores the current state, while line 17 indicates that the parallel controller is in exploration mode. Finally, line 19 is executed to delegate the **startTry** call to the exploration controller.

```
1  void GenerationController::label(var<CP>{int} x,int val) {
2    if (_store.label(x,val)==Failure)
3      fail();
4    else {
5      _pool.add(new CheckPoint(_cp));
6      fail();
7    }
8  }
```

Fig. 12. The Implementation of the Generation Controller

The Generation Controller. The generation controller explores the children of a node, sending their subproblems to the problem pool. It can be viewed as a simple DFS controller failing each time a new subproblem is created. For instance, Figure 12 depicts the implementation of method **label** for the generation controller. Compared to the LDS controller in Figure 3, it adds lines 4–7 to produce the child subproblem to the problem pool and then fails immediately.

Optimization. In the description so far, workers only exchange subproblems. In optimization applications, it is critical for the workers to communicate new bounds on the objective function. The parallel workers use events to receive new bounds asynchronously. The instruction

```
whenever _pool@newBound(int bound)
   _bestFound = min(_bestFound,bound);
```

```
void ParallelController::addChoice(Continuation f) {
   if (!_cp.setBound(_bestBound)) fail();
   if (_generatingMode) _generationController.addChoice(f);
   else                 _explorationController.addChoice(f);
}
```

Fig. 13. Using Bounds in the Parallel Controller

updates the best found solution in the parallel controller. The bound can then be used in the `addChoice` method to fail early as shown in Figure 13.

6 Experimental Results

We now describe the experimental results showing the feasibility of transparent parallelization. Before presenting the results, it is important to point out some important fact of parallel implementations. First, optimization applications may exhibit interesting behaviors. Some are positive: *superlinear* speedups may occur because the parallel version finds better solutions quicker and thus prunes the search space earlier. Some are negative: the parallel implementation may explore some part of the search tree not explored by the sequential implementation, reducing the speed-up. Typically, in optimization applications, we also give results factoring these behaviors by reporting the time to prove optimality given an optimal solution at the start of the search. Second, the parallel implementation of a search strategy produces a different search strategy because of work stealing. This strategy may be less or more effective on the problem at hand.

Experimental Setting. The results use an Apple PowerMac with two dual-core Intel Xeon 2.66 GHz processors (4 cores total), 4MB L2 Cache per processor, and 2GB of RAM running Mac OSX 10.4.9. Our implementation links our own in-house dynamic library for finite domains to the COMET system and implements the parallel controller in COMET itself. No change to the COMET runtime system were requested from its implementors. Results are the average of 10 runs. It is important to mention that parallel threads are in contention for the cache and for memory on multicore machines, which may have adverse effects on runtime.

Table 1. Experimental Results on the Queens Problem using DFS and LDS

			Runtime (s)				Speedup (vs. seq)				Speedup (vs. 1w)		
	N	seq	1w	2w	3w	4w	1w	2w	3w	4w	2w	3w	4w
DFS	12	1.25	1.46	0.81	0.57	0.47	0.85	1.55	2.19	2.67	1.81	2.56	3.11
DFS	14	36.6	41.9	22.8	16.6	13.5	0.87	1.60	2.19	2.70	1.84	2.52	3.09
DFS	16	1421	1611.7	863.19	653.88	488.22	0.88	1.65	2.17	2.91	1.87	2.46	3.30
LDS	12	2.12	2.33	1.47	1.15	0.91	0.91	1.45	1.84	2.33	1.59	2.02	2.56
LDS	14	178	73.05	42.46	39.26	33.06	2.4	4.2	4.5	5.3	1.72	1.86	2.21

Table 2. Experimental Results on a Scene Allocation Problem

	Runtime (s)					Speedup (vs. seq)				Speedup (1w)		
	seq	1w	2w	3w	4w	1w	2w	3w	4w	2w	3w	4w
DFS	257	267	138	96	74	0.96	1.86	2.70	3.49	1.94	2.80	3.62
DFS-P	248	264	138	94	72	0.94	1.80	2.64	3.45	1.92	2.82	3.68
LDS	435	376	200	164	121	1.16	2.18	2.66	3.60	1.88	2.30	3.11
LDS-P	388	362	190	160	115.7	1.07	2.04	2.43	3.35	1.90	2.27	3.13

Table 3. Experimental Results on Graph Coloring using DFS

Runtime						Speedup (seq)				Speedup (1w)		
	seq	1w	2w	3w	4w	1w	2w	3w	4w	2w	3w	4w
0	18.0	21.4	16.7	8.3	7.7	.84	1.07	2.16	2.33	1.28	2.57	2.78
1	39.8	46.9	16.3	12.3	10.5	.85	2.44	3.23	3.79	2.87	3.8	4.46
2	148.5	176.0	93.2	65.3	51.3	.84	1.59	2.27	2.89	1.89	2.70	3.40
3	323.8	385.6	198.1	141.9	111.1	.84	1.63	2.28	2.91	1.94	2.72	3.47
0-P	9.7	11.6	6.1	4.4	3.4	.84	1.60	2.20	2.85	1.9	2.63	3.41
1-P	22.6	26.9	14.1	10.0	7.9	.84	1.60	2.26	2.86	1.9	2.69	3.40
2-P	147.9	178.2	92.7	64.9	51.1	.83	1.60	2.28	2.89	1.92	2.75	3.49
3-P	324.0	390.0	199.1	141.2	111.0	.83	1.62	2.29	2.91	1.95	2.76	3.51

The Queens Problem. Table 1 depicts the results for finding all solutions to the queens problem using DFS. The table reports the times in seconds for the sequential program and for the parallel version with 1–4 workers. Columns 7–10 give the speedups with respect to the sequential version and columns 11–13 with respect to a single worker. The results show that the speedups increase with the problem sizes, reaching almost a speedup of 3 with 4 processors over the sequential implementation and 3.30 over a single worker. The overhead of a single worker compared to the sequential implementation is reasonable (about 13% for 16-queens). The last two lines depict the results for LDS: these results were surprising and show superlinear speedups for 14 queens due to the different exploration strategy induced by work stealing. Indeed, each time a node is stolen, a new LDS search is restarted with a smaller problem generating fewer waves. As a result, the size of the LDS queue is smaller, inducing time and space benefits.[1]

Scene Allocation. Table 2 reports experimental results on a scene allocation problem featuring a global cardinality constraint and a complex objective function. The search procedure does not use symmetry breaking and the instance features 19 scenes and 6 days. The first two lines report results on DFS and the last two on LDS. The second and fourth lines report times for the optimality proof. DFS exhibits nice speedups reaching 3.45 for the proof and 3.49 overall. Observe also the small overhead of 1 worker over the sequential implementation. LDS exhibits superlinear speedups for 1 and 2 workers and nice speedups overall.

[1] The first worker always generates some problems in the pool (its steal request flag is initialized to true) which explains the superlinear speedup even with one worker.

Table 4. Experimental Results on Golomb Rulers

	N	seq	1w	2w	3w	4w
DFS	12	209/305	217/313 (0.97)	35/99 (3.08)	35/76 (4.01)	35/64 (4.76)
DFS	13	2301/5371	2354/5421 (0.99)	254/2228 (2.41)	254/1536 (3.49)	254/1195 (4.49)
LDS	12	575/1494	411/757 (1.97)	135/427 (3.49)	129/379 (3.94)	131/334 (4.47)

Graph Coloring. Table 3 illustrates results on four different instances of graph coloring with 80 vertices and edge density of 40%. The search procedure uses symmetry breaking. The overhead of the single worker is more significant here (about 20%) since there is little propagation and the cost of maintaining the semantic paths is proportionally larger. The top half of the table shows the total execution time, while the bottom part shows the time for proving optimality (given the optimal solution). Once again, the parallel implementation shows good speedups for a problem in which maintaining semantic paths is costly.

Golomb Rulers. The Golomb rulers problem is to place N marks on a ruler such that the distances between any two marks are unique. The objective is to find the shortest such ruler for N marks. The propagation is more time-consuming on this benchmark. Table 4 shows the speedups for Golomb 12–13 using DFS and Golomb 12 using LDS. The table reports, for each entry, the time to find the optimal solution, the total time, and the speedup. The speedups are always superlinear in this benchmark and the overhead of a single worker is small compared to the sequential implementation. Moreover, for DFS which dominates LDS here, the speedups scale nicely, moving from 3.49 with three processors to 4.49 with 4 processors (N=13), although the optimal solution is found after about 254 seconds in both. This is particularly satisfying since complex applications are likely to spend even more time in propagation than this program, showing (again) the potential of parallel computing for constraint programming. It is also important to mention that the sequential implementation is only about 20% slower than GECODE for the same number of choice points on this benchmark, although COMET is a very high-level garbage-collected language which imposes some overhead on our finite-domain library.

7 Related Work

The main novelty of this paper is the transparent parallelization of advanced constraint programming searches. To our knowledge, no other systems feature a similar functionality which addresses the challenge recently formulated by Schulte and Carlsson [11]. We review related work in constraint programming to emphasize the originality of our proposal.

Parallel constraint logic programming was pioneered by the CHIP/PEPSys system [12] and elaborated in its successors [6]. These systems offer transparent parallelization. However, they were implemented at a time when there was no clean separation between the nondeterministic program and the exploration strategy (DFS was the exploration strategy). Moreover, these systems induce a performance penalty when parallelism is not used, since they must use advanced data structures (hash-windows, binding arrays, enhanced trailing) to support parallelism transparently [12]. *The proposal in this paper is entirely implemented on top of* COMET *and requires no change to its runtime system.*

Perron describes Parallel Solver in [7] and reports experimental results in [8], but he gives almost no detail on the architecture and implementation. Parallel Solver builds on Ilog Solver which supports exploration strategies elegantly through node evaluators and limits [7]. However, Ilog Solver uses syntactic paths which induce a number of pitfalls when, say, global cuts and randomization are used. It is not clear how work is shared and what is involved in parallelizing a search procedure, since no code or details are given.

Oz/Mozart was a pioneering system in the separation of nondeterministic programs and exploration strategies, which are implemented as search engines [9]. Schulte [10] shows how to exploit parallelism in Oz/Mozart using a high-level architecture mostly similar to ours. At the implementation level, workers are implemented as search engines and can generate search nodes available for stealing from a master. The actual implementation, which consists of about 1,000 lines of code, is not described in detail. It seems that syntactic paths are used to represent subproblems. Moreover, since search engines implement an entire search procedure, the worker cannot transparently lift another engine into a parallel search engine without code rewriting. In contrast, search controllers in COMET do not implement the complete search procedure: they just encapsulate the exploration order (through the `addNode` and `fail` methods) and save/restore search nodes. *It is the conjunction of the nondeterministic program (control flow through continuation) and search controllers (exploration order and node management) which implements the search procedure and makes transparent parallelization possible.* Note also that the code of the parallel controller is very short.

8 Conclusion

This paper showed how to transparently parallelize constraint programs addressing a fundamental challenge for CP systems. The key technical idea is to lift a search controller into a parallel controller supporting a work-stealing architecture. Experimental results show the practicability of the approach which produces good speedups on a variety of benchmarks. The parallel controller is built entirely on top of the COMET system and hence the approach induces no overhead when parallelism is not used. The architecture also allows different workers to use different strategies. Advanced users can write their own parallel controllers for specific applications, as the architecture is completely open. Future research will be concerned with a distributed controller: This requires distributing the problem pool which must become a shared object and replacing threads by processes, but these abstractions are also available in COMET.

Acknowledgments. This research is partially supported by NSF awards DMI-0600384 and IIS-0642906 and ONR Award N000140610607.

References

1. Blumhofe, R.D., Leiserson, C.E.: Scheduling Multithreaded Computations by Work Stealing. In: FOCS '94 (1994)
2. Choi, C.W., Henz, M., Ng, K.B.: Components for State Restoration in Tree Search. In: Walsh, T. (ed.) CP 2001. LNCS, vol. 2239. Springer, Heidelberg (2001)
3. Intel Corp.: Teraflops research chip (2007)
4. Michel, L., Van Hentenryck, P.: A Decomposition-Based Implementation of Search Strategies. ACM Transactions on Computational Logic 5(2) (2004)
5. Michel, L., Van Hentenryck, P.: Parallel Local Search in Comet. In: van Beek, P. (ed.) CP 2005. LNCS, vol. 3709. Springer, Heidelberg (2005)
6. Mudambi, S., Schimpf, J.: Parallel CLP on Heterogeneous Networks. In: ICLP-94 (1994)
7. Perron, L.: Search Procedures and Parallelism in Constraint Programming. In: Jaffar, J. (ed.) Principles and Practice of Constraint Programming – CP'99. LNCS, vol. 1713. Springer, Heidelberg (1999)
8. Perron, L.: Practical Parallelism in Constraint Programming. In: CP-AI-OR'02 (2002)
9. Schulte, C.: Programming Constraint Inference Engines. In: Smolka, G. (ed.) Principles and Practice of Constraint Programming - CP97. LNCS, vol. 1330. Springer, Heidelberg (1997)
10. Schulte, C.: Parallel Search Made Simple. In: TRICS'2000 (2000)
11. Schulte, C., Carlsson, M.: Finite Domain Constraint Programming Systems. In: Handbook of Constraint Programming. Elsevier, Amsterdam (2006)
12. Van Hentenryck, P.: Parallel Constraint Satisfaction in Logic Programming: Preliminary Results of CHIP within PEPSys. In: ICLP'89 (1989)
13. Van Hentenryck, P., Michel, L.: Nondeterministic Control for Hybrid Search. In: CP-AI-OR'05 (2005)
14. Warren, D.H.D.: The SRI Model for Or-Parallel Execution of Prolog. Abstract Design and Implementation Issues. In: ISLP-87 (1987)

MiniZinc: Towards a Standard CP Modelling Language

Nicholas Nethercote[1], Peter J. Stuckey[1], Ralph Becket[1], Sebastian Brand[1], Gregory J. Duck[1], and Guido Tack[2]

[1] National ICT Australia and the University of Melbourne, Victoria, Australia
{njn,pjs,rafe,sbrand,gjd}@csse.unimelb.edu.au

[2] Programming Systems Lab, Saarland University, Saarbrücken, Germany
tack@ps.uni-sb.de

Abstract. There is no standard modelling language for constraint programming (CP) problems. Most solvers have their own modelling language. This makes it difficult for modellers to experiment with different solvers for a problem.

In this paper we present MiniZinc, a simple but expressive CP modelling language which is suitable for modelling problems for a range of solvers and provides a reasonable compromise between many design possibilities. Equally importantly, we also propose a low-level solver-input language called FlatZinc, and a straightforward translation from MiniZinc to FlatZinc that preserves all solver-supported global constraints. This lets a solver writer support MiniZinc with a minimum of effort—they only need to provide a simple FlatZinc front-end to their solver, and then combine it with an existing MiniZinc-to-FlatZinc translator. Such a front-end may then serve as a stepping stone towards a full MiniZinc implementation that is more tailored to the particular solver.

A standard language for modelling CP problems will encourage experimentation with and comparisons between different solvers. Although MiniZinc is not perfect—no standard modelling language will be—we believe its simplicity, expressiveness, and ease of implementation make it a practical choice for a standard language.

1 Introduction

Many constraint satisfaction and optimisation problems can be solved by CP solvers that use finite domain (FD) and linear programming (LP) techniques. There are many different solving techniques, and so there are many solvers. Examples include Gecode [1], ECLiPSe [2], ILOG Solver [3], Minion [4], and Choco [5].

However, these solvers use different, incompatible modelling languages that express problems at varying levels of abstraction. This makes life difficult for modellers—if they wish to experiment with different solvers, they must learn new modelling languages and rewrite their models. A standard CP modelling language supported by multiple solvers would mitigate this problem.

C. Bessiere (Ed.): CP 2007, LNCS 4741, pp. 529–543, 2007.

A standard CP modelling language could also make solver benchmarking simpler. For example, if the CSPlib benchmark library problems [6] had their natural language specifications augmented with standard machine-readable descriptions, it could stimulate competition between solver writers and lead to improvements in solver technology.

For these reasons, we believe a standard CP modelling language is desirable. The main challenges in proposing such a language are (a) finding a reasonable middle ground when different solvers have such a wide range of capabilities—particularly different levels of support for global constraints—and (b) encouraging people to use the language. In this paper we make the following two contributions that we believe solve these two problems.

A CP modelling language suitable as a standard. Section 2 introduces MiniZinc, a medium-level declarative modelling language.[1] MiniZinc is high-level enough to express most CP problems easily and in a largely solver-independent way; for example, it supports sets, arrays, and user-defined predicates, some overloading, and some automatic coercions. However, MiniZinc is low-level enough that it can be mapped easily onto many solvers. For example, it is first-order, and it only supports decision variable types that are supported by most existing CP solvers: integers, floats, Booleans and sets of integers. Other MiniZinc features include: it allows separation of a model from its data; it provides a library containing declarative definitions of many global constraints; and it also has a system of annotations which allows non-declarative information (such as search strategies) and solver-specific information (such as variable representations) to be layered on top of declarative models.

A simple way to implement MiniZinc. Solver writers (who may not have language implementation skills) will not want to do a large amount of work to support a modelling language. Therefore we provide a way for solver writers to provide reasonable MiniZinc support with a minimum of effort. Section 3 introduces FlatZinc, a low-level solver input language that is the target language for MiniZinc. FlatZinc is designed to be easy to translate into the form required by a CP solver. Section 4 then defines a standard translation from MiniZinc to FlatZinc, which involves only well-understood transformations such as predicate inlining and reification. Importantly it allows a solver to use native definitions of any global constraints it supports, while decomposing unsupported ones into lower-level constraints. Even though this transformation will not be ideal for all solvers, it provides an excellent starting point for an implementation.

At the paper's end, Section 5 describes our supporting tool set and presents some experimental results, Section 6 presents related work, and Section 7 discusses future work and concludes.

---

[1] Modelling is sometimes divided into "conceptual" and "design" modelling. But these are just two points on a spectrum of "how many modelling decisions have been made" that spans from the highest level (e.g. natural language) to the lowest level (e.g. solver input formats). For this reason we follow the simpler programming language terminology and talk about high-, medium- and low-level languages.

The core MiniZinc language is not particularly novel, as is appropriate for a standard language—it incorporates ideas from many existing modelling languages. The novel features are: (a) the use of predicates to allow more extensible modelling, (b) the use of annotations to provide non-declarative and solver-specific information, (c) the use of a lower-level language and a standard translation to make it easy to connect the language to existing solvers, and (d) the preservation of calls to supported global constraints in that translation.

We believe that MiniZinc's characteristics—simplicity, expressiveness, and ease of initial support—make it a practical choice for a standard language.

2 MiniZinc

2.1 Specifying a Problem

A MiniZinc problem specification has two parts: (a) the *model*, which describes the structure of a class of problems; and (b) the *data*, which specifies one particular problem within this class. The pairing of a model with a particular data set is a *model instance* (sometimes abbreviated to *instance*).

The model and data may be in separate files. Data files can only contain assignments to parameters declared in the model. A user specifies data files on the command line, rather than naming them in the model file, so that the model file is not tied to any particular data file.

2.2 A MiniZinc Example

Each MiniZinc model is a sequence of *items*, which may appear in any order. Consider the MiniZinc model and example data for a restricted job shop scheduling problem in Figures 1 and 2.

Line 0 is a comment, introduced by the '`%`' character.

Lines 1–5 are *variable declaration items*. Line 1 declares `size` to be an integer *parameter*, i.e. a variable that is fixed in the model. Line 20 (in the data file) is an *assignment item* that defines the value of `size` for this instance. Variable declaration items can include assignments, as in line 3. Line 4 declares `s` to be a 2D array of *decision variables*. Line 5 is an integer variable with a restricted range. Decision variables are distinguished by the `var` prefix.

Lines 7–8 show a user-defined *predicate item*, `no_overlap`, which constrains two tasks given by start time and duration so that they do not overlap in time.

Lines 10–17 show a *constraint item*. It uses the built-in `forall` to loop over each job, and ensure that: (line 12) the tasks are in order; (line 13) they finish before `end`; and (lines 14–16) that no two tasks in the same column overlap in time. Multiple constraint items are allowed, they are implicitly conjoined.

Line 19 shows a *solve item*. Every model must include exactly one solve item. Here we are interested in minimising the end time. We can also maximise a variable or just look for any solution ("`solve satisfy`").

There is one kind of MiniZinc item not shown by this example: *include items*. They facilitate the creation of multi-file models and the use of library files.

```
% (square) job shop scheduling in MiniZinc
int: size;                                          % size of problem
array [1..size,1..size] of int: d;                  % task durations
int: total = sum(i,j in 1..size) (d[i,j]);          % total duration
array [1..size,1..size] of var 0..total: s;         % start times
var 0..total: end;                                  % total end time

predicate no_overlap(var int:s1, int:d1, var int:s2, int:d2) =
    s1 + d1 <= s2 \/ s2 + d2 <= s1;

constraint
    forall(i in 1..size) (
        forall(j in 1..size-1) (s[i,j] + d[i,j] <= s[i,j+1]) /\
        s[i,size] + d[i,size] <= end /\
        forall(j,k in 1..size where j < k) (
            no_overlap(s[j,i], d[j,i], s[k,i], d[k,i])
        )
    );

solve minimize end;
```

Fig. 1. MiniZinc model (`jobshop.mzn`) for the job shop problem.

```
size = 2;
d = [ 2,5,
      3,4 ];
```

Fig. 2. MiniZinc data (`jobshop2x2.data`) for the job shop problem

There is currently no way to control the output produced at run-time. We plan to add such control in the near future (see Section 7).

2.3 Types and Insts

MiniZinc provides three scalar types: Booleans, integers, and floats; and two compound types: sets, and arrays. There are no user-defined types, however we will see shortly that restricted types such as integer and float ranges are allowed. Scalars and sets have a built-in (lexicographical) ordering.

As well as having a type, each variable has an *instantiation* (often abbreviated to *inst*), which indicates if it is fixed in the model to a known value (a parameter, shortened to *par*) or not (a decision variable, shortened to *var*). A pairing of a type and an inst is called a *type-inst*.

Booleans, integers and floats may be parameters or decision variables. Example syntax for scalars: `par bool`, `var int`, `float`; if the inst is omitted it defaults to `par`. There is no automatic coercion of integers to floats.

Sets can only contain *par* scalars. Sets of integers can be *par* or *var*, but all other sets must be *par*. For example: `var set of int` is legal, but `var set of bool` and `set of var int` are illegal.

Arrays must be *par*, i.e. of fixed length. They can be multi-dimensional. Each dimension's index set is a contiguous range of integers. Arrays may contain *par* or *var* scalars or sets of integers. For example, `array[0..9,5..10] of var int` is a 2D array of integer decision variables.

The following set expressions can be used as types: set ranges, set literals, and *par* set variables. Float ranges can also be used as types. The meaning is as if the type was declared as a normal type and then constrained, for example:

```
0..3:          v1;      %     int: v1;  constraint v1 in 0..3;
var {1,3,5}: v2;        % var int: v2;  constraint v2 in {1,3,5};
var 0.1 .. 9.5: v4;     % var float: v4;
                        %   constraint 0.1 <= v4 /\ v4 <= 9.5;
```

MiniZinc has some polymorphism: some operations are overloaded to work with multiple type-insts (see Section 2.5); certain arrays are automatically coerced, and the type of each anonymous variable '`_`' (see Section 2.4) is inferred; and *par* values are automatically coerced to *var* values as necessary.

2.4 Expressions

MiniZinc has several kinds of expression.

Variable names can serve as expressions. Also, there is a special identifier '`_`' that represents an unconstrained, anonymous decision variable (of any type). It is particularly useful when partially initialising arrays, e.g. in a Sudoku puzzle.

Scalar literals are written in standard ways, for example: `true`, `false`, `23`, `-44.5`, `2.3e-05`.

Sets are written using set literals or set comprehensions. For example: `{1,2,3}` or `{ i * j | i,j in 1..10 where i != j }`. Comprehensions can have multiple variables per generator, multiple generators, and each generator can have a filtering `where` clause.

Arrays are written similarly, using array literals or array comprehensions. For example: `[2,_,3,_]` or `[ 2*i | i in 1..5 ]`. Array literals are automatically coerced to different index ranges so long as the element type and lengths match; lines 21 and 22 of the job shop model shows an example with a 2D array.

If-then-else expressions (e.g. `if C1 then A else B endif`) and let expressions (e.g. `let { int: x = 1, int: y = 2 } in x + y`) are supported; the latter are used within predicates to declare local variables (see Section 2.6). The condition of an if-then-else must be *par*.

Most predicate and function calls use the usual syntax, e.g. `even(n)`. Some built-in functions, such as '+', are *operators*—their names are non-alphanumeric, and calls to them are written using infix or prefix notation. There is also special syntax for combining an array comprehension with a call—a *generator call* `P(Gs)(E)` is equivalent to `P([E | Gs])`; the parentheses around the `E` are mandatory so as to avoid possible ambiguity when the generator call is part of a larger expression. Figure 1 includes an example, `sum(i,j in 1..size)(d[i,j])`, which is syntactic sugar for `sum([d[i,j] | i,j in 1..size])`.

2.5 Built-in Operations

MiniZinc has many useful built-in operators, predicates and functions. They include: comparisons (e.g. `<`, `==`), arithmetic operations (e.g. `+`, `*`, `sum`, `min`), logical operations (e.g. `/\`, `xor`, `forall`), set operations (e.g. `union`, `subset`, `in`, `card`), array operations (e.g. `length`, `index_set`), coercions (e.g. `round`, `int2float`, `bool2int`), and bounds operations (`ub`, `lb`, `dom`).

Most are overloaded to work with parameters and decision variables. Some are overloaded to work with multiple types, e.g. arithmetic operations work with both integers and floats, and comparisons support all types.

2.6 Predicates

Users can define their own predicates in MiniZinc. The job shop model shows an example, `no_overlap`. Predicates may not be recursive, but can call other predicates. Predicates implicitly return a Boolean value. Predicates may have local variables; they are introduced via let expressions. For example:

```
predicate even(var int:x) = let { var int: y } in x == 2 * y;
```

Any predicate containing a non-*par* local variable cannot be called in a possibly-negated context (e.g. inside a `not`, or `<->`), because the local variable(s) would be effectively universally quantified, which most solvers do not support.

2.7 Global Constraints

MiniZinc has a global constraints library. It can be used in models via an include item: `include "globals.mzn"`. The default version of this library contains predicate definitions of many global constraints, such as `all_different`, `cumulative`, etc.

Crucially, this library can be tailored by solver writers for use with individual solvers. All global constraints that are not supported by the solver should be left untouched, so calls to them can be inlined during the MiniZinc-to-FlatZinc translation. For example:

```
predicate disjoint(var set of int:S, var set of int:T) =
    S intersect T == {};
```

In contrast, global constraints that are supported by a solver can have their definition removed (but not their declaration). Calls to these global constraints will be left untouched by the MiniZinc-to-FlatZinc conversion.

Type-overloaded global constraints that are supported by the solver can be defined separately for each type. For example, the overloaded `all_different` might be defined as:

```
predicate all_different(array[int] of var float:x) =
    forall(i,j in index_set(x) where i < j)(x[i] != x[j]);
predicate all_different(array[int] of var int:x) =
    gecode_all_different(x);  % native Gecode version for ints
```

Finally, although MiniZinc provides a standard definition for each global constraint, a solver writer can arbitrarily replace each definition with an alternative definition in MiniZinc that may suit their solver better, if that is easier than providing a native implementation.

2.8 Modelling Techniques

MiniZinc is deliberately small to make it easier to translate. Some common CP modelling techniques need to be indirectly modelled in MiniZinc.

Enumerated types can be modelled using named sets of integers, for example:

```
set of int: Colour = 1..3;
Colour: Red = 1;  Colour: Green = 2;  Colour: Blue = 3;
array[Colour,Colour] of var int: clashing;
```

Extensional relations can be modelled using multiple arrays with the same indices, e.g. $(x, y) \in \{(1, 2.0), (-2, 3.4), (6, -1000.0)\}$ is modelled as:

```
array[1..3] of int:   r1 = [1,   -2,    6];
array[1..3] of float: r2 = [2.0, 3.4, -1000.0];
var 1..3: i;  var int: x;  var int: y;
constraint x == r1[i] /\ y == r2[i];
```

However this does not allow negatively defined relations such as $(x, y) \notin \{(5, 6), (8, 9)\}$.

2.9 Adding Non-declarative and Solver-Specific Information

MiniZinc (as described so far) includes no information about how models should be solved. In practice we need a way to attach such non-declarative and solver-specific information to the model to support efficient solving.

Our solution is to use *annotations*. MiniZinc defines some standard annotations that should be supported by most solvers. Also, because a solver is free to ignore annotation information, more solver-specific annotations can be used.

Annotations consist of an identifier, with optional arguments appearing in parentheses. We use string literals for many annotation arguments. Annotations are attached to variable declarations, expressions, and solve items using the (left-associative) operator `::` which binds tighter than all other operators, as illustrated by the examples in Figure 3.

Line 30 shows a variable annotations. Here we assume that `bounds` instructs the solver to use a special implementation that only maintains bounds.

Line 31 shows two constraint annotations: the first (`domain`) instructs the solver to use a domain-consistent (GAC) version of the `all_different` constraint; the second (`priority`) assigns the constraint a priority equal to the size of its argument array. Another constraint annotation is `bounds`, which indicates that bounds propagation should be used for the constraint.

Lines 32–34 give an example of an annotated solve item, where the search strategy is specified for an FD solver. Solve annotations are based on the `search`

```
array [1..size,1..size] of var 0..total: a :: bounds;
constraint all_different(a) :: domain :: priority(length(a));
solve :: int_search([end],"input_order","indomain_min","complete")
      :: int_search(a,"smallest","indomain_min","lds(3)")
   minimize end;
```

Fig. 3. Example annotations on variables, constraints and solve items

predicate of ECLiPSe. The parameters to the `int_search` annotation indicate: (a) the variables being fixed via the strategy, (b) the variable selection strategy, (c) the value choice method, and (d) the exploration strategy. Combinations of strategies can be specified in order. The strategy in the example is: first set `end` to its least value and then try setting start times by setting the variable with the smallest possible value to this value, and only consider limited discrepancy search with a limit of 3 discrepancies.

3 FlatZinc

FlatZinc is mostly a subset of MiniZinc. We wait until Section 4 before giving a FlatZinc example, in order to show how MiniZinc-to-FlatZinc translation works.

Model structure. Unlike MiniZinc, FlatZinc has no model/data separation, nor multi-file models—a FlatZinc model instance must be in a single file.

Items. Some of the MiniZinc items are supported: constraint items, variable declarations (with optional assignments) and solve items. The rest are not: include items, stand-alone assignment items, and user-defined predicates. Unlike MiniZinc, in FlatZinc variables must be defined before they are used.

Types and type-insts. Some MiniZinc types (and their insts) are supported: Booleans, integers and floats (including range-restricted ones), and sets. Arrays are supported but must be one-dimensional, and they are always indexed from $0..length - 1$. Also, there is no type or type-inst polymorphism—for example, the built-in `int_plus` is distinct from `float_plus`. Implicit *par*-to-*var* coercions are supported, as in MiniZinc.

Expressions. Some of MiniZinc's expressions are supported: identifiers, scalar literals, set literals, array literals, predicate calls, and array accesses with a *par* index. Expressions not supported are: anonymous variables, set and array comprehensions, if-then-else expressions, let expressions, generator calls, and array accesses with a *var* index (which must be done via `element` constraints). Also, no operators are supported (but negative numbers such as `-1` are allowed—the '`-`' is considered part of the numeric literal.)

Built-ins. The main way in which FlatZinc is not a subset of MiniZinc is that it has different built-in operations. These are operations that a CP solver is expected to support natively. Most of them correspond directly to a MiniZinc operation, although the names are different because FlatZinc has no operators

```
40 array[0..3] of var 0..14: s;
41 var 0..14: end;
42 var bool: b1;
43 var bool: b2;
44 var bool: b3;
45 var bool: b4;
46 constraint int_lin_le      ([1,-1], [s[0], s[1]], -2);
47 constraint int_lin_le      ([1,-1], [s[2], s[3]], -3);
48 constraint int_lin_le      ([1,-1], [s[1], end ], -5);
49 constraint int_lin_le      ([1,-1], [s[3], end ], -4);
50 constraint int_lin_le_reif([1,-1], [s[0], s[2]], -2, b1);
51 constraint int_lin_le_reif([1,-1], [s[2], s[0]], -3, b2);
52 constraint bool_or(b1, b2, true);
53 constraint int_lin_le_reif([1,-1], [s[1], s[3]], -5, b3);
54 constraint int_lin_le_reif([1,-1], [s[3], s[1]], -4, b4);
55 constraint bool_or(b3, b4, true);
56 solve minimize end;
```

Fig. 4. FlatZinc translation of the MiniZinc job shop model

or overloading. They include: comparison constraints (e.g. `int_eq`, `float_gt`), linear (in)equalities (e.g. `int_lin_eq`), arithmetic constraints (e.g. `int_plus`), logical constraints (e.g. `bool_or`, `bool_not`), set constraints (e.g. `set_subset`, `set_card`), element constraints (e.g. `array_int_element`), and coercion constraints (e.g. `bool2int`). There are also reified versions of many constraints which take an additional Boolean argument, e.g. `int_eq_reif`, `set_subset_reif`.

Also, a FlatZinc model instance may include calls to any global constraints that the target solver supports natively, as Section 2.7 explained.

Annotations. FlatZinc's annotations are the same as MiniZinc's, although any expressions within them must of course be valid FlatZinc expressions.

Writing a FlatZinc front-end. A FlatZinc front-end for a solver must parse the FlatZinc, and translate declarations and constraints into whatever form the solver requires. The grammar can be expressed in a way that most type and inst errors manifest as syntax errors, which reduces the work that must be done by the FlatZinc front-ends. Any FlatZinc constraints not handled by the solver can be converted into run-time aborts. These steps are easy by language implementation standards, because FlatZinc is so simple. Section 5 describes how our existing tools help further with this task. A solver writer must also specialise `globals.mzn`, which is a trivial exercise in removing predicate bodies.

4 Translating MiniZinc to FlatZinc

The translation from MiniZinc to FlatZinc has two parts: flattening, and the rest. We use the FlatZinc translation in Figure 4 of the MiniZinc model instance from Section 2.2 as an example. Line 40 is the original 2D array of decision variables, mapped to a zero-indexed 1D array. Line 41 is the original `end` variable. Lines 42–45 are variables introduced by Boolean decomposition. Lines 46–55 are the constraints. Lines 46 and 47 result from line 12, lines 48 and 49 result from line 13, and lines 50–55 result from lines 14–15 and 7–8.

4.1 Flattening

Flattening involves the following simple steps that statically reduce the model and data as much as possible. There is no fixed order to the steps because some enable others, which can then enable further application of previously applied steps. Therefore, they must be repeated, e.g. by iterating until a fixpoint is reached, or by re-flattening child nodes of expressions that have been flattened.

Parameter substitution. This step substitutes any atomic literal value assigned to a global or let-local scalar parameter throughout the model, and removes the declaration and assignment. For example, with `size = 2` we substitute 2 for `size`, but `size = 2 + y` would not be substituted until fully reduced.

Built-ins evaluation. This step evaluates all calls to built-ins that have fixed, atomic literal arguments. For example, `2-1` (from `size-1`, after parameter substitution) in the jobshops example becomes `1`.

Comprehension unrolling. This step unrolls all set and array comprehensions, once the generator ranges are fully reduced.

Compound built-in unrolling. This step unrolls compound built-ins (those that involve the folding of an operation over an array of elements, such as `sum` and `forall`) by replacing them with multiple lower-level operations.

We will use lines 11, 14 and 15 of Figure 1 as the starting point of a running example. They unroll to give the following conjunction (the first conjunct has `i=1`, `j=1` and `k=2`; the second has `i=2`, `j=1` and `k=2`).

```
no_overlap(s[1,1], d[1,1], s[2,1], d[2,1]) /\
no_overlap(s[1,2], d[1,2], s[2,2], d[2,2])
```

Fixed array access replacement. This step replaces all array accesses involving fixed indices and fixed elements with the appropriate value. Once all the accesses of an array have been replaced, its declaration and assignment can be removed. For example, our running example becomes:

```
no_overlap(s[1,1], 2, s[2,1], 3) /\
no_overlap(s[1,2], 5, s[2,2], 4)
```

If-then-else evaluation. This step evaluates each if-then-else expression, once its condition is fully reduced. This is always possible because if-then-else conditions must be fixed.

Predicate inlining. This step replaces each call to a defined predicate with its body, substituting actual arguments for formal arguments. This is easy because predicates cannot be recursive, either directly or mutually. Calls to predicates lacking a definition (such as those in the MiniZinc globals library) are left as-is. For example, the first conjunct from our running example becomes:

```
s[1,1] + 2 <= s[2,1] \/ s[2,1] + 3 <= s[1,1]
```

4.2 Post-flattening

After flattening, we apply the following steps once each, in the given order.

Stand-alone assignment removal. This step removes each stand-alone assignment by merging it with the appropriate variable declaration.

Let floating. This step moves let-local decision variables to the top-level and renames them appropriately.

Boolean decomposition. This step decomposes all Boolean expressions that are not top-level conjunctions. It replaces each sub-expression with a new Boolean variable (also adding a declaration for each variable), and adds conjuncts equating these new variables with the sub-expressions they replaced. This facilitates the later introduction of reified constraints. For example, our running example becomes:

```
((b1 \/ b2) <-> true) /\
((s[1,1] + 2 <= s[2,1]) <-> b1) /\
((s[2,1] + 3 <= s[1,1]) <-> b2)
```

Declarations are also added for the new Boolean variables `b1` and `b2`.

Numeric decomposition. This step decomposes numeric equations or inequations in a manner similar to Boolean decomposition, by renaming each non-linear sub-expression with a new variable.

Set decomposition. This step decomposes compound set expressions into primitive set constraints in a manner similar to Boolean/numeric decomposition.

(In)equality normalisation. This step normalises (in)equations, e.g. it converts `>=` into `<=`, moves sub-expressions so the right-hand side is constant, and replaces negations with multiplications by -1. This facilitates the later introduction of linear (in)equality constraints. For example, the second conjunct from our running example becomes:

```
(s[1,1] + (-1)*s[2,1] <= -2) <-> b1
```

Array simplification. This step simplifies all arrays to one-dimensional, zero-indexed arrays. It also updates any remaining array accesses accordingly. For example, our running example becomes:

```
(s[0] + (-1)*s[2] <= -2) <-> b1
```

Anonymous variable naming. This step replaces each anonymous variable ('_') with a newly introduced variable of the appropriate type.

Conversion to FlatZinc built-ins. This step converts the remaining MiniZinc built-ins and array accesses (which all must have at least one non-*par* argument) into FlatZinc built-ins. The FlatZinc built-ins may be type-specialised, and will be reified if the MiniZinc built-in occurs inside a Boolean expression (other than conjunction).

The most complex case involves linear (in)equalities. Each one is replaced with a (type-specific, possibly reified) linear predicate, unless it can be replaced with a simpler arithmetic constraint. For example, our running example becomes:

```
int_lin_le_reif([1,-1], [s[0], s[2]], -2, b1)
```

The next case is that array accesses involving non-fixed indices are replaced with FlatZinc element constraints such as `array_int_element`.

The remaining cases are simpler, as each remaining MiniZinc operation has a corresponding FlatZinc operation. For example, `(b1 \/ b2) <-> true` becomes `bool_or(b1, b2, true)`, and `x * y = z` becomes `int_times(x, y, z)`.

Top-level conjunction splitting. This step splits top-level conjunctions into multiple constraint items, e.g. `constraint a /\ b;` becomes two items.

4.3 Annotations

Most annotations are maintained during the translation. Fixed expressions within annotations are evaluated like other expressions. When annotated expressions are unrolled, the annotation is copied to the resulting operations. When expressions are reified, their annotations are lost.

4.4 Summary

The translation above provides much of what a solver writer would want. But it is clearly not ideal for every underlying solver. For example, solvers may be more efficient on the undecomposed versions of Boolean constraints [7] or non-linear constraints. We plan to investigate methods to control which transformations should be applied for a particular solver when we have more experience.

5 Tool Set and Experiments

We have a MiniZinc front-end that parses, checks types and instantiations, and converts to FlatZinc. It has two different MiniZinc-to-FlatZinc converters: one written using the term-rewriting system Cadmium [8] (which produced Figure 4 as shown, modulo some variable renaming and item reordering), and the other written in Mercury. The Cadmium implementation allows us to omit various steps of the translation.

Our MiniZinc global constraints library includes around a dozen global constraints, all less than 20 lines of code. Clearly there are many more to be included.

We have several FlatZinc front-ends. The first one, FlatZinc/G12, is a FlatZinc interpreter for the G12 constraint platform. It uses FD and FD set solvers written in Mercury, and one of several LP solvers such as CPLEX and GLPK. The second front-end, FlatZinc/Gecode, is a FlatZinc interpreter for Gecode [1]. It was implemented from scratch in less than one week by one of the authors (a

	Size (LOC)			Trans. time (s)		Solve time (s)			
Benchmark	MZ	FZ	Ge	Merc	Cd	Ge	FZ/Ge	FZ/G12	FZ/Ecl
alpha	54	55	65	0.05	0.70	0.22	0.23	0.35	0.67
eq20	66	82	61	0.12	0.68	0.00	0.00	0.01	0.02
packing2	41	1145	138	0.12	0.73	0.02	0.14	0.15	0.52
warehouses	47	517	100	0.14	0.98	0.00	0.02	0.79	0.04

Fig. 5. Experimental Results. Column 1 gives the benchmark names. Columns 2–4 give the code sizes of the MiniZinc, FlatZinc and native-Gecode versions. Column 5–6 give the translation times for the Mercury and Cadmium MiniZinc-to-FlatZinc translators. Columns 7–10 give the solve times for the native Gecode, FlatZinc/Gecode, FlatZinc/G12 and FlatZinc/Eclipse versions.

Gecode developer) with no prior knowledge of FlatZinc. Reuse of the lex and yacc parser he developed should further reduce development time for other solver writers. The third front-end, FlatZinc/Eclipse, is a prototype front-end for ECLiPSe that plugs into FlatZinc/G12; it was written in one afternoon using Cadmium. Finally, we also have a translator from FlatZinc to the Minion format [4], but we do not present results for it. Although Minion's file format appears similar to FlatZinc, the conversion is non-trivial: Minion offers various tuning options (notably a choice of operationally different variable types and constraint propagators), and it allows only basic control over search.

Figure 5 shows some results comparing native Gecode (v1.3.1) to FlatZinc/Gecode and FlatZinc/G12. The benchmarks were taken from the Gecode examples suite and ported to MiniZinc. All implementations use the same search strategy for each benchmark. The test machine was a 2.0 GHz Pentium M with 2GB of RAM and 2MB L2 cache running Fedora Core 4 (Linux kernel 2.6.15). All Mercury code was compiled with Mercury rotd-2007-02-05, and C and C++ code was compiled with GCC 4.0.2. All timings are the best of five runs.

The code sizes show that MiniZinc models are compact, much more so than native Gecode programs—Gecode is not a modelling language, its constraints are written as low-level C++ calls to the Gecode library, and a Gecode model is thus a C++ program. The code sizes also show that FlatZinc models are (unsurprisingly) bigger than MiniZinc models, sometimes greatly so; this is due to FlatZinc's lack of looping constructs.

The translation times show that the MiniZinc-to-FlatZinc translation is fast in Mercury, but slower in Cadmium. Note that the translation step itself only accounts for part of the time taken—these numbers include the overhead of parsing, topological sorting and type-checking of the MiniZinc code, as well as printing of the FlatZinc. Also, these programs have not been tuned and so there is scope for further speed improvement.

The FlatZinc/Gecode solve time results show that FlatZinc models are competitive with the native Gecode models, and thus that the MiniZinc-to-FlatZinc translation is reasonable.

Although there is clearly more work to be done with other benchmarks and other front-ends, these results provide some evidence that MiniZinc and FlatZinc provide a way to write reasonably efficient models. It was difficult to ensure that the native Gecode versions were equivalent to the MiniZinc versions, because Gecode's search specifications are subtly different to MiniZinc's. This is more evidence that having a standard language would help with benchmarking.

The Gecode front-end is available at `www.gecode.org/flatzinc.html`. The other tools, the MiniZinc benchmarks, and a full specification of MiniZinc and FlatZinc are available at `www.g12.csse.unimelb.edu.au/minizinc/`.

6 Related Work

MiniZinc is (mostly) a subset of Zinc [9], a solver-independent modelling language designed to allow very high-level modelling and user-controlled translation of each high-level model to an appropriate solver-level model. Although we believe Zinc would be an excellent standard CP modelling language, the language is large enough that implementing it is a serious challenge. MiniZinc removes much of the complexity of Zinc—particularly user-defined types, various coercions, and user-defined functions—in order to make compilation simpler. Essence [10] and ESRA [11] are two other high-level, solver-independent modelling languages. MiniZinc should provide a good target language for them (as well as for Zinc).

MiniZinc is closely related to OPL [12]. Indeed, a cut-down version of OPL was proposed some time ago as a basis for a standard CP modelling language [13]. Compared to OPL, MiniZinc lacks complex types, resources, and programmable search specifications, among other things. The advantages of MiniZinc over OPL are its simplicity, the independence of models from global constraints supported by the solver, and the ease with which solver writers can utilise it (thanks to FlatZinc). Thus it should be easier to support as a proposed standard.

FlatZinc is similar to several low-level solver formats. The most significant of these is the verbose, XML format used by the CSP solver competitions [14]. Important differences with MiniZinc are: it has no separation of model and data, it is restricted to integers, it lacks arrays and looping constructs, and it has no solution to the problem of varied global constraints. Compared to this format, MiniZinc is more expressive and concise, and FlatZinc allows a similarly easy implementation for solver writers.

7 Conclusion and Future Work

Our main goal with MiniZinc was to define a language that is not too big but expressive enough to succinctly capture most CP problems. Our hope is that by providing simple-to-use tools for manipulating MiniZinc and FlatZinc it will be easy for solver writers to support this proposed standard, which will lead to benefits for both solver users and solver writers.

There are some obvious ways to extend MiniZinc which could be contemplated. Some of these are features of Zinc, for example: more type and instance polymorphism, user-defined functions, tuple types, and output items that allow control of the output from the solver. All involve a trade-off between modelling ease and implementation complexity. Other possible extensions include: a module system; a way of selectively applying parts of the MiniZinc-to-FlatZinc translation (e.g. omitting Boolean decomposition for solvers that handle Boolean constraints more directly); and the application of common sub-expression elimination to the MiniZinc-to-FlatZinc translation. Experience will guide the introduction of such extensions.

Finally, we intend to write FlatZinc translators to SAT and MIP solver input languages to further ease comparisons between different solving technologies.

Acknowledgments

Thanks to Christian Schulte, Mikael Lagerkvist, Joachim Schimpf, Kim Marriott and Mark Wallace for helpful discussions about MiniZinc and FlatZinc, and the anonymous reviewers for feedback on earlier versions of this paper.

References

1. Schulte, C., Lagerkvist, M., Tack, G.: Gecode, `http://www.gecode.org/`
2. Apt, K., Wallace, M.: Constraint Logic Programming using Eclipse. Cambridge University Press, Cambridge (2006)
3. ILOG: ILOG Solver, `http://www.ilog.com/products/solver/`
4. Gent, I.P., Jefferson, C., Miguel, I.: Minion: A fast, scalable constraint solver. In: Proceedings of ECAI 2006, Riva del Garda, Italy (August 2006)
5. Laburthe, F.: CHOCO: implementing a CP kernel. In: Proceedings of TRICS 2000, Singapore, pp. 71–85 (2000)
6. Gent, I.P., Walsh, T.: CSPLIB: a benchmark library for constraints. In: Jaffar, J. (ed.) Principles and Practice of Constraint Programming – CP'99. LNCS, vol. 1713, pp. 480–481. Springer, Heidelberg (1999)
7. Brand, S., Yap, R.H.: Towards "Propagation = Logic + Control". In: Etalle, S., Truszczyński, M. (eds.) ICLP 2006. LNCS, vol. 4079, pp. 102–116. Springer, Heidelberg (2006)
8. Duck, G., Stuckey, P., Brand, S.: ACD term rewriting. In: Etalle, S., Truszczyński, M. (eds.) ICLP 2006. LNCS, vol. 4079, pp. 117–131. Springer, Heidelberg (2006)
9. Garcia de la Banda, M., Marriott, K., Rafeh, R., Wallace, M.: The modelling language Zinc. In: Benhamou, F. (ed.) CP 2006. LNCS, vol. 4204, pp. 700–705. Springer, Heidelberg (2006)
10. Frisch, A.M., Grum, M., Jefferson, C., Hernandez, B.M., Miguel, I.: The design of ESSENCE: A constraint language for specifying combinatorial problems. In: Proceedings of IJCAI-07, Hyderabad, India (January 2007)
11. Flener, P., Pearson, J., Ågren, M.: Introducing ESRA, a relational language for modelling combinatorial problems. In: Proceedings of LOPSTR 2003, Uppsala, Sweden, pp. 214–232 (August 2003)
12. Van Hentenryck, P.: The OPL Optimization Programming Language. MIT Press, Cambridge (1999)
13. Wallace, M.: Personal communication (January 2007)
14. van Dongen, M., et al.: Second international CSP solver competition, `http://cpai.ucc.ie/06/Competition.html`

Propagation = Lazy Clause Generation

Olga Ohrimenko[1], Peter J. Stuckey[1], and Michael Codish[2]

[1] NICTA Victoria Research Lab, Department of Comp. Sci. and Soft. Eng. University of Melbourne, Australia

[2] Department of Computer Science, Ben-Gurion University, Israel

Abstract. Finite domain propagation solvers effectively represent the possible values of variables by a set of choices which can be naturally modelled as Boolean variables. In this paper we describe how we can mimic a finite domain propagation engine, by mapping propagators into clauses in a SAT solver. This immediately results in strong nogoods for finite domain propagation. But a naive static translation is impractical except in limited cases. We show how we can convert propagators to lazy clause generators for a SAT solver. The resulting system can solve scheduling problems significantly faster than generating the clauses from scratch, or using Satisfiability Modulo Theories solvers with difference logic.

1 Introduction

Propagation is an essential aspect of finite domain constraint solving which tackles hard combinatorial problems by interleaving search and restriction of the possible values of variables (propagation). The propagators that make up the core of a finite domain propagation engine represent tradeoffs between the speed of inference of information versus the strength of the information inferred. Good propagators represent a good tradeoff at least for some problem classes. The success of finite domain propagation in solving hard combinatorial probles arises from these good tradeoffs, and programmable search.

Propositional satisfiability (SAT) solvers are becoming remarkably powerful and there is an increasing number of papers which propose encoding hard combinatorial (finite domain) problems in SAT. The success of modern SAT solvers is largely due to a combination of techniques including: watch literals, 1UIP nogoods and the VSIDS variable ordering heuristic [13].

In this paper we propose modelling combinatorial problems in SAT, not by modelling the constraints of the problem, but by modelling/mimicking the propagators used in a finite domain model of the problem. Variables are modelled in terms of the changes in domain that occur during the execution of propagation. We can then model the domain changing behaviour of propagators as clauses.

Encoding finite domain propagation uncovers an Achilles' heel of SAT solvers. While modern SAT solvers can often handle problems with millions of constraints and hundreds of thousands of variables, many problems are difficult to encode into SAT without breaking these implicit limits. We propose a hybrid approach.

C. Bessiere (Ed.): CP 2007, LNCS 4741, pp. 544–558, 2007.

Instead of introducing clauses representing propagators *a priori*, we execute the original (finite domain) propagators as lazy clause generators inside the SAT solver. Propagators introduce their propagation clauses precisely when they are able to trigger new unit propagation. The resulting hybrid combines the advantages of SAT solving, in particular powerful and efficient nogood learning and backjumping, with the advantages of finite domain propagation, simple and powerful modelling and specialized and efficient propagation of information.

This paper contributes a hybrid system for implementing propagation-based finite domain solving with a SAT solver and demonstrates its successful application to hard open-shop scheduling benchmarks. We compare the hybrid solver with a static approach that introduces the propagation clauses a priori, and with Satisfiability Modulo Theories (SMT) [14] solving using difference logic. Our prototype implementation can significantly improve on the carefully engineered SAT and SMT solvers.

In the remainder of the paper we first introduce terminology, and then propagation rules, a method of understanding propagator behaviour. We show how these can be expressed as CNF formulae, and introduce the lazy clause generation approach. After experiments we compare with related work and conclude.

2 Propagation-Based Constraint Solving

We consider a typed set of variables $\mathcal{V} = \mathcal{V}_I \cup \mathcal{V}_S$ made up of *integer* variables, $\mathcal{V}_I$, and *sets of integers* variables, $\mathcal{V}_S$. We use lower case letters such as x and y for integer variables and upper case letters such as S and T for sets of integers. A *domain* D is a complete mapping from $\mathcal{V}$ to finite sets of integers (for the variables in $\mathcal{V}_I$) and to finite sets of finite sets of integers (for the variables in $\mathcal{V}_S$). We can understand a domain D as a formula $\wedge_{v \in \mathcal{V}}(v \in D(v))$ stating for each variable v that its value is in its domain.

Let D_1 and D_2 be domains and $V \subseteq \mathcal{V}$. We say that D_1 is *stronger* than D_2, written $D_1 \sqsubseteq D_2$, if $D_1(v) \subseteq D_2(v)$ for all $v \in \mathcal{V}$ and that D_1 and D_2 are *equivalent modulo* V, written $D_1 =_V D_2$, if $D_1(v) = D_2(v)$ for all $v \in V$. The *intersection* of D_1 and D_2, denoted $D_1 \sqcap D_2$, is defined by the domain $D_1(v) \cap D_2(v)$ for all $v \in \mathcal{V}$.

We use *range* notation: For integers l and u, $[\,l\,..\,u\,]$ denotes the set of integers $\{d \mid l \leqslant d \leqslant u\}$, while for sets of integers L and U, $[\,L\,..\,U\,]$ denotes the set of sets of integers $\{A \mid L \subseteq A \subseteq U\}$. A *convex* domain D is where $D(T)$ is a range for all $T \in \mathcal{V}_S$. We restrict attention to convex domains. We assume an *initial domain* D_{init} which is convex such that all domains D that occur will be stronger i.e. $D \sqsubseteq D_{init}$.

A *valuation* θ is a mapping of integer and set variables to correspondingly typed values, written $\{x_1 \mapsto d_1, \ldots, x_n \mapsto d_n, S_1 \mapsto A_1, \ldots, S_m \mapsto A_m\}$. We extend the valuation θ to map expressions or constraints involving the variables in the natural way. Let *vars* be the function that returns the set of variables appearing in an expression, constraint or valuation. In an abuse of notation, we define a valuation θ to be an element of a domain D, written $\theta \in D$, if $\theta(v) \in D(v)$ for all $v \in vars(\theta)$.

A constraint is a restriction placed on the allowable values for a set of variables. We define the *solutions* of a constraint c to be the set of valuations θ that make that constraint true, i.e. $solns(c) = \{\theta \mid (vars(\theta) = vars(c)) \wedge (\models \theta(c))\}$.

We associate with every constraint c a set of *propagators*, $prop(c)$. A propagator $f \in prop(c)$ is a monotonically decreasing function on domains such that for all domains $D \sqsubseteq D_{init}$: $f(D) \sqsubseteq D$ and $\{\theta \in D \mid \theta \in solns(c)\} = \{\theta \in f(D) \mid \theta \in solns(c)\}$. This is a weak restriction since, for example, the identity mapping is a propagator for any constraint. In this paper we restrict ourselves to *set bounds propagators* that map convex domains to convex domains.

The *output* variables $output(f) \subseteq \mathcal{V}$ of a propagator f are the variables changed by the propagator: $v \in output(f)$ if $\exists D \sqsubseteq D_{init}$ such that $f(D)(v) \neq D(v)$. The *input* variables $input(f) \subseteq \mathcal{V}$ of a propagator f is the smallest subset $V \subseteq \mathcal{V}$ such that for each $D \sqsubset D_{init}$: $D =_V D'$ implies that $f(D) \sqcap D' =_{output(f)} f(D') \sqcap D$. Only the input variables are useful in computing the application of the propagator to the domain.

Example 1. For the constraint $c \equiv x_1 + 1 \leqslant x_2$ the function f defined by $f(D)(x_1) = \{d \in D(x_1) \mid d \leqslant \max D(x_2) - 1\}$ and $f(D)(v) = D(v), v \neq x_1$ is a propagator for c. Its output variables are $\{x_1\}$ and its input variables are $\{x_2\}$. Let $D_1(x_1) = \{3, 4, 6, 8\}$ and $D_1(x_2) = \{1, 5\}$, then $f(D_1)(x_1) = \{3, 4\}$ and $f(D_1)(x_2) = \{1, 5\}$. □

A *propagation solver* for a set of propagators F and current domain D, $solv(F, D)$, repeatedly applies all the propagators in F starting from domain D until there is no further change in resulting domain. $solv(F, D)$ is the weakest domain $D' \sqsubseteq D$ which is a fixpoint (i.e. $f(D') = D'$) for all $f \in F$. In other words, $solv(F, D)$ returns a new domain defined by

$$solv(F, D) = \text{gfp}(\lambda d.iter(F, d))(D) \qquad iter(F, D) = \sqcap_{f \in F} f(D).$$

where gfp denotes the greatest fixpoint w.r.t $\sqsubseteq$ lifted to functions.

3 SAT and Unit Propagation

A *proposition* p is a Boolean variable from a universe of Boolean variables, $\mathcal{P}$. A *literal* l is either: a proposition p, its negation $\neg p$, the false literal $\bot$, or the true literal $\top$. The *complement* of a literal l, $\neg l$ is $\neg p$ if $l = p$ or p if $l = \neg p$, while $\neg\bot = \top$ and $\neg\top = \bot$. A *clause* C is a disjunction of literals. An *assignment* is either a set of literals A excluding $\bot$ such that $\forall p \in \mathcal{P}.\{p, \neg p\} \not\subseteq A$, or the failed assignment $\{\bot\}$. We define $A \sqsubseteq \{\bot\}$, and $A \sqcup A' = A \cup A$ unless the union contains $\bot$ or $\{p, \neg p\}$ for some literal p in which case $A \sqcup A' = \{\bot\}$.

An assignment A *satisfies* a clause C if one of the literals in C appears in A. A *theory* T is a set of clauses. An assignment is a *solution* to theory T if it satisfies each $C \in T$.

A SAT solver takes a theory T and determines if it has a solution. Complete SAT solvers typically involve some form of the DPLL algorithm which combines search and propagation by recursively fixing the value of a proposition to either $\top$ (true) or

$\bot$ (false) and using unit propagation to determine the logical consequences of each decision made so far. The unit propagation algorithm finds all unit resolutions of an assignment A with the theory T. It can be defined as follows where C denotes a clause:

$$up(A, C) = \begin{cases} \{\bot\} & \forall l \in C . \neg l \in A \\ A \sqcup \{l\} & \exists l \in C, , \neg l \notin A, \forall l' \in (C \setminus \{l\}). \neg l' \in A \\ A & \text{otherwise} \end{cases}$$
$$UP(A, T) = \text{lfp}.(\lambda a. \textstyle\bigsqcup_{C \in T} up(a, C))(A)$$

4 Atomic Constraints and Propagation Rules

Atomic constraints and propagation rules were originally devised for reasoning about propagation redundancy [1]. They provide a way of describing the behaviour of propagators.

An *atomic constraint* represents the basic changes in domain that occur during propagation. For integer variables, the atomic constraints represent the elimination of values from an integer domain, i.e. $x_i \leqslant d$, $x_i \geqslant d$, $x_i \neq d$ or $x_i = d$ where $x_i \in \mathcal{V}_I$ and d is an integer. For set variables, the atomic constraints represent the addition of a value to a lower bound set of integers or the removal of a value from an upper bound set of integers, i.e. $e \in S_i$ or $e \notin S_i$ where e is an integer and $S_i \in \mathcal{V}_S$. We also consider the atomic constraint *false* which indicates that unsatisfiabity is the direct consequence of propagation.

Define a *propagation rule* as $C \rightarrowtail c$ where C is a conjunction of *atomic constraints*, and c is a single atomic constraint such that $\not\models C \rightarrow c$. A propagation rule $C \rightarrowtail c$ defines a propagator (for which we use the same notation) in the obvious way.

$$(C \rightarrowtail c)(D)(v) = \begin{cases} \{\theta(v) \mid \theta \in D \cap solns(c)\} & \text{if } vars(c) = \{v\} \text{ and } \models D \rightarrow C \\ D(v) & \text{otherwise.} \end{cases}$$

In another words, $C \rightarrowtail c$ defines a propagator that removes values from D based on c only when D implies C. We can characterize an arbitrary propagator f in terms of the propagation rules that it implements. A propagator f *implements* a propagation rule $C \rightarrowtail c$ iff $\models D \rightarrow C$ implies $\models f(D) \rightarrow c$ for all $D \sqsubseteq D_{init}$.

Example 2. A common propagator f for the constraint $x_1 = x_2 \times x_3$ [11] is

$$\begin{aligned} f(D)(x_1) = {} & D(x_1) \cap [\min S \,..\, \max S] \\ & \text{where } S = \{(\min D(x_2)) \times (\min D(x_3)), (\min D(x_2)) \times (\max D(x_3)), \\ & (\max D(x_2)) \times (\min D(x_3)), (\max D(x_2)) \times (\max D(x_3))\} \\ f(D)(x_2) = {} & D(x_2) \text{ if } \min D(x_3) < 0 \wedge \max D(x_3) > 0 \\ & D(x_2) \cap [\min S \,..\, \max S] \text{ otherwise} \\ & \text{where } S = \{(\min D(x_1))/(\min D(x_3)), (\min D(x_1))/(\max D(x_3)), \\ & (\max D(x_1))/(\min D(x_3)), (\max D(x_1))/(\max D(x_3))\} \end{aligned}$$

and symmetrically for x_3.[1] Note that f does not enforce any notion of consistency.

[1] Division by zero has to be treated carefully here, see [11] for details.

The propagator f implements the following propagation rules (among many others) for $D_{init}(x_1) = D_{init}(x_2) = D_{init}(x_3) = [-20..20]$.

$$x_1 \leqslant 10 \wedge x_2 \geqslant 6 \rightarrowtail x_3 \leqslant 1$$
$$x_1 \leqslant 10 \wedge x_2 \geqslant 9 \rightarrowtail x_3 \leqslant 1$$
$$x_2 \geqslant -1 \wedge x_2 \leqslant 1 \wedge x_3 \geqslant -1 \wedge x_3 \leqslant 1 \rightarrowtail x_1 \leqslant 1$$

□

Let *rules*(f) be the set of all possible propagation rules implemented by f. This definition of *rules*(f) is usually unreasonably large, and full of redundancy. For example the second propagation rule in Example 2 is clearly weaker than the first.

A set of propagation rules $F \subseteq rules(f)$ *implements* f iff $solv(F, D) = f(D)$, for all $D \sqsubseteq D_{init}$.

In order to reason more effectively about propagation rules for a given propagator f, we want to have a concise representation *rep*(f) such that *rep*(f) implements f.

A propagation rule $C' \rightarrowtail c'$ is *directly redundant* with respect to another rule $C \rightarrowtail c$ if $D_{init} \models C' \rightarrow C \wedge c \rightarrow c'$ and not $D_{init} \models C \rightarrow C' \wedge c' \rightarrow c$. A propagation rule r for propagator f is *tight* if it is not directly redundant with respect to any rule in *rules*(f). Obviously we would prefer to only use tight propagation rules in *rep*(f) if possible.

Example 3. Consider the reified difference inequality $c \equiv x_0 \Leftrightarrow x_1 + 1 \leqslant x_2$ where $D_{init}(x_0) = \{0,1\}$, $D_{init}(x_1) = \{0,1,2\}$, $D_{init}(x_2) = \{0,1,2\}$. Then a set of tight propagation rules *rep*(f) implementing the domain propagator f for c is

$$x_1 \leqslant 0 \wedge x_2 \geqslant 1 \rightarrowtail x_0 = 1 \qquad x_1 \geqslant 2 \rightarrowtail x_0 = 0$$
$$x_1 \leqslant 1 \wedge x_2 \geqslant 2 \rightarrowtail x_0 = 1 \qquad x_1 \geqslant 1 \wedge x_2 \leqslant 1 \rightarrowtail x_0 = 0$$
$$x_0 = 1 \rightarrowtail x_2 \geqslant 1 \qquad x_2 \leqslant 0 \rightarrowtail x_0 = 0$$
$$x_0 = 1 \wedge x_1 \geqslant 1 \rightarrowtail x_2 \geqslant 2 \qquad x_0 = 0 \wedge x_1 \leqslant 1 \rightarrowtail x_2 \leqslant 1$$
$$x_0 = 1 \rightarrowtail x_1 \leqslant 1 \qquad x_0 = 0 \wedge x_1 \leqslant 0 \rightarrowtail x_2 \leqslant 0$$
$$x_0 = 1 \wedge x_2 \leqslant 1 \rightarrowtail x_1 \leqslant 0 \qquad x_0 = 0 \wedge x_2 \geqslant 1 \rightarrowtail x_1 \geqslant 1$$
$$x_0 = 0 \wedge x_2 \geqslant 2 \rightarrowtail x_1 \geqslant 2$$

For constraints of the form $x_0 \Leftrightarrow x_1 + d \leqslant x_2$ we can build *rep*(f) linear in the domain sizes of the variables involved. □

5 Clausal Representations of Propagators

Propagators can be understood simply as a collection of propagation rules. This gives the key insight for understanding them as conjunctions of clauses, since we can translate propagation rules to clauses straightforwardly.

5.1 Atomic Constraints and Boolean Variables

Changes in domains of variables are the information recorded by a propagation solver. In this sense they are the "decisions" made or stored representing the sub-problem. In translating propagation to Boolean reasoning these decisions become the Boolean variables. We introduce a, novel to our knowledge, encoding of integer domains as Booleans, combining the DIMACS encoding (see e.g. [18]) with that of [2]. It uses Boolean variables $[\![x = d]\!], d \in D_{init}(x)$, $[\![x \leqslant d]\!], \min D_{init}(x) \leqslant d < \max D_{init}(x)$. Set bounds domains are encoded as usual with the Boolean variables $[\![e \in S_i]\!], e \in \max D_{init}(S_i)$.

The Boolean variables directly represent changes to domains made by atomic constraints. Let *lit* be the mapping of atomic constraints to Boolean literals. We define

$$\begin{aligned} lit(false) &= \bot \\ lit(x_i = d) &= [\![x_i = d]\!] \\ lit(x_i \neq d) &= \neg[\![x_i = d]\!] \\ lit(e \in S_i) &= [\![e \in S_i]\!] \\ lit(e \notin S_i) &= \neg[\![e \in S_i]\!] \end{aligned} \qquad lit(x_i \leqslant d) = \begin{cases} \top & d = \min D_{init}(x_i) \\ [\![x_i \leqslant d]\!] & \text{otherwise} \end{cases}$$

$$lit(x_i \geqslant d) = \begin{cases} \top & d = \max D_{init}(x_i) \\ \neg[\![x_i \leqslant d-1]\!] & \text{otherwise} \end{cases}$$

where $\min D_{init}(x_i) \leqslant d \leqslant \max D_{init}(x_i)$ and $e \in \max D_{init}(S_i)$. Note that *lit* is a bijection except where the result is $\top$, hence $lit^{-1}(l)$ is defined as long as $l \neq \top$. Note also that for "Boolean" integers where $D_{init}(x) = [\,0\,..\,1\,]$ we have that $[\![x = 1]\!] \leftrightarrow \neg[\![x = 0]\!] \leftrightarrow \neg[\![x \leqslant 0]\!]$ so we can just use a single Boolean variable to represent the integer.

There is a mapping from the domain of a variable v to an assignment on the Boolean variables $[\![x_i \leqslant d]\!]$, $[\![x_i = d]\!]$, and $[\![e \in S_i]\!]$ defined as:

$$assign(D, v) = \{lit(c) \mid v \in D(v) \models c, v \in vars(c)\}$$

$$assign(D) = \begin{cases} \{\bot\} & \exists v \in \mathcal{V}.D(v) = \varnothing \\ \bigcup_{v \in \mathcal{V}} assign(D, v) & \text{otherwise} \end{cases}$$

5.2 Consistency of Domains

Representations of set variables are automatically consistent with respect to a set of literals, but this is not the case for representations of integer variables, since we could assert for example $[\![x = 3]\!]$ and $[\![x \leqslant 2]\!]$ simultaneously. For a variable x where $D_{init}(x) = [\,l\,..\,u\,]$ we maintain the consistency of assignment by adding the clauses $DOM(x)$:

$$\begin{aligned} \neg[\![x \leqslant d]\!] \vee [\![x \leqslant d+1]\!] &\quad l \leqslant d < u-1 \\ \neg[\![x = d]\!] \vee [\![x \leqslant d]\!] &\quad l \leqslant d < u \\ \neg[\![x = d]\!] \vee \neg[\![x \leqslant d-1]\!] &\quad l < d \leqslant u \\ [\![x = l]\!] \vee \neg[\![x \leqslant l]\!] &\quad \\ [\![x = d]\!] \vee \neg[\![x \leqslant d]\!] \vee [\![x \leqslant d-1]\!] &\quad l < d < u \\ [\![x = u]\!] \vee [\![x \leqslant u-1]\!] &\quad \end{aligned}$$

which encode $[\![x \leqslant d]\!] \rightarrow [\![x \leqslant d+1]\!]$ and $[\![x = d]\!] \leftrightarrow ([\![x \leqslant d]\!] \wedge \neg[\![x \leqslant d-1]\!])$. For a set variable S, we define $DOM(S) = \{\}$, and then for all variables, $DOM = \cup\{DOM(v) \mid v \in \mathcal{V}\}$.

With these domain clauses, unit propagation on a translated set of atomic constraints generates all the consequences of the atomic constraints, i.e. faithfully represents a domain.

Theorem 1. *Let C be a set of atomic constraints on variable v, and $D = solv(\{true \rightarrowtail c | c \in C\}, D_{init})$ then $assign(D, v) = UP(\{\}, \{lit(c) \mid c \in C\} \cup DOM(v))$.*

The usual encoding of finite domains into SAT is the so called DIMACS encoding using only the variables $[\![x = d]\!]$ (see e.g. [18]). It enforces consistency of domains for $D_{init}(x) = [\,l\,..\,u\,]$ with the clause $\vee_{d=l}^{u}[\![x = d]\!]$ and the $O(n^2)$ clauses $\wedge_{l \leqslant d_1 < d_2 \leqslant u} \neg[\![x = d_1]\!] \vee \neg[\![x = d_2]\!]$. Note our encoding is linear and has equally strong unit propagation.

If for a variable x we are only interested in the atomic constraints $x \leqslant d$ and $x \geqslant d$ (i.e. bounds propagation on x) then we can omit the propositions $[\![x = d]\!]$ and the corresponding clauses from $DOM(x)$.

We can map unit propagation fixpoints of $DOM(v)$ to domains $D(v)$. Suppose $A = UP(A, DOM(v))$, then define $domain(A, v) = \{d \mid \forall l \in A.l$ involves $v, v = d \models l\}$.

We will be interested in minimal assignments that model a domain D. Let $A = UP(A, DOM(v))$, then an information equivalent assignment is any A' where $A = UP(A', DOM(v))$. Define $minassign(A, v)$ as the set A' of minimal cardinality where $A = UP(A', DOM(v))$, and preferring positive equational literals, over inequality literals, over negative equational literals.

Example 4. The set $A = \{[\![x = 1]\!], [\![x \leqslant 1]\!], \neg[\![x \geqslant 2]\!], \neg[\![x = 0]\!], \neg[\![x = 2]\!]\}$ is a fixpoint of $DOM(x)$ assuming $D_{init}(x) = [\,0\,..\,2\,]$. $minassign(A, x) = \{[\![x = 1]\!]\}$, since $A = UP(\{[\![x = 1]\!]\}, DOM(x))$.

The set $A' = \{[\![x \leqslant 1]\!], \neg[\![x = 2]\!]\}$ is also a fixpoint of $DOM(x)$. Here $minassign(A, x) = \{[\![x \leqslant 1]\!]\}$ even though $A' = UP(\{\neg[\![x = 2]\!]\}$ is information equivalent, because inequalities are preferred over negated equality literals. □

5.3 Propagation Rules to Clauses

The translation from propagation rules to clauses is straightforward:

$$cl(C \rightarrowtail c) = \vee_{c' \in C}(\neg\, lit(c')) \vee lit(c)$$

Example 5. The translation of the propagation rule:

$$x_2 \geqslant -1 \wedge x_2 \leqslant 1 \wedge x_3 \geqslant -1 \wedge x_3 \leqslant 1 \rightarrowtail x_1 \leqslant 1$$

is the clause $C_0 \equiv [\![x_2 \leqslant -2]\!] \vee \neg[\![x_2 \leqslant 1]\!] \vee [\![x_3 \leqslant -2]\!] \vee \neg[\![x_3 \leqslant 1]\!] \vee [\![x_1 \leqslant 1]\!]$ The advantage of the inequality literals is clear here: to define this clause using only $[\![x = d]\!]$ propositions for the domains given in Example 2 requires a clause of ≈100 literals. □

The translation of propagation rules to clauses gives a system of clauses where unit propagation is at least as strong as the original propagators.

Theorem 2. *Let R be a set of propagation rules such that $D' = solv(R, D)$. Let $A = UP(assign(D), DOM \cup \bigcup\{cl(r) \mid r \in R\})$ then $A = \{\bot\}$ or $A \supseteq assign(D')$.*

In particular if we have clauses representing all the propagators F then unit propagation is guaranteed to be at least as strong as finite domain propagation.

Corollary 1. *Let $rep(f)$ be a set of propagation rules implementing propagator f. Let $A = UP(assign(D), DOM \cup \bigcup\{cl(r) \mid f \in F, r \in rep(f)\})$. Then $A = \{\bot\}$ or $A \supseteq assign(solv(F, D))$.*

Example 6. Notice that the clausal representation may be "stronger" than the propagator. Consider the propagator f for $x_1 = x_2 \times x_3$ defined in Example 2. Then the clause C_0 defined in Example 5 is in the Boolean representation of the propagator. Given $\neg[\![x_2 \leqslant -2]\!], [\![x_2 \leqslant 1]\!], \neg[\![x_3 \leqslant -2]\!], \neg[\![x_1 \leqslant 1]\!]$ we infer $\neg[\![x_3 \leqslant 1]\!]$. But given the domain $D(x_1) = [2\,..\,20]$, $D(x_2) = [-1\,..\,1]$, and $D(x_3) = [-1\,..\,20]$ then $f(D)(x_3) \neq [2\,..\,20]$. In fact the propagator f can determine no new information. □

Given the Corollary above it is not difficult to see that, if it uses the same search strategy as a propagation based solver for propagators F, a SAT solver using clauses $\bigcup\{cl(r) \mid f \in F, r \in rep(f)\})$ needs no more search space to find the same solution(s).

But there is a difficulty in this approach. Typically $rep(f)$ is extremely large. The size of $rep(f)$ for the propagator f for $x_1 = x_2 \times x_3$ of Example 2 is around 100,000 clauses. But clearly most of the clauses in $rep(f)$ must be useless in any computation, otherwise the propagation solver would make an enormous number of propagation steps, and this is almost always not the case. This motivates the fundamental approach of this paper which is to represent propagators lazily as clauses, only adding a clause to its representation when it is able to propagate new information.

6 Lazy Clause Generation

The key idea is rather than apriori representing a propagator f by a set of clauses, we execute the propagator during the SAT search and record what propagation rules actually fired as clauses.

We execute a SAT solver over theory $T \supseteq DOM$. At each fixpoint of unit propagation we have an assignment A. This corresponds to a domain $D = domain(A)$. We then execute (individually) each propagator $f \in F$ on this domain obtaining new domain $D' = f(D)$. We then select a set of propagation rules R implemented by f such that $solv(R, D) = D'$ and add the clauses $\{cl(r) \mid r \in R\}$ to the theory T in the SAT solver.

We do not execute the propagation solver to fixpoint (although this is possible) because adding a single new clause may cause failure which means the work is wasted.

Given the above discussion we need to modify our propagators, so that rather than returning a new domain they return a set of propagation rules that would fire adding new information to the domain.

Let $lazy(f)$ be the function from domains to sets of propagation rules $R \subseteq rules(f)$ such that if $f(D) = D'$ then $lazy(f)(D) = R$ where $solv(R, D) = D'$, and for each $C \rightarrowtail c \in R$ not $D \models c$ (that is they generate new information). Ideally $R \subseteq \mathit{rep}(f)$ for some concise representation $\mathit{rep}(f)$ of the propagator f, but this may be difficult to achieve.

We can automatically create $\mathit{lazy}(f)$ from f as follows. Let $f(D) = D'$ and let $C_v = \mathit{minassign}(D', v) - \mathit{assign}(D, v)$ be the new information (propositions) about v determined by propagating f on domain D. Then a correct set of rules $R = \mathit{lazy}(f)(D)$ is the set of propagation rules

$$\wedge_{v \in \mathit{input}(f)} \{\mathit{lit}^{-1}(l') \mid l' \in \mathit{minassign}(D, v)\} \rightarrowtail \mathit{lit}^{-1}(l)$$

for each $v \in \mathit{output}(f)$ and each $l \in C_v$

We can almost certainly do better than this. Usually a propagator is well aware of the reasons why it discovered some new information.

Example 7. Consider the propagator f for $x_1 = x_2 \times x_3$ defined in Example 2. Applied to $D(x_1) = [-10\,..\,18]$, $D(x_2) = \{3, 5, 6\}$, $D(x_3) = [1\,..\,3]$ it determines $f(D)(x_1) = [3\,..\,18]$. The new information is $\neg[\![x_1 \leqslant 2]\!]$. The naive propagation rule defined above is

$$x_1 \geqslant -10 \wedge x_1 \leqslant 18 \wedge x_2 \geqslant 3 \wedge x_2 \neq 4 \wedge x_2 \leqslant 6 \wedge x_3 \geqslant 1 \wedge x_3 \leqslant 3 \rightarrowtail x_1 \geqslant 3$$

It is easy to see from the definition of the propagator, that the bounds of x_1 and the missing values in x_2 are irrelevant, so the propagation rule could be

$$x_2 \geqslant 3 \wedge x_2 \leqslant 6 \wedge x_3 \geqslant 1 \wedge x_3 \leqslant 3 \rightarrowtail x_1 \geqslant 3$$

but in fact it could also correctly simply be $x_2 \geqslant 3 \wedge x_3 \geqslant 1 \rightarrowtail x_1 \geqslant 3$ but this is not so obvious from the definition of f. The final rule is tight. □

Example 8. Consider the propagator f for $x_0 \leftrightarrow x_1 + 1 \leqslant x_2$ from Example 3 When applied to the domain $D(x_0) = \{0, 1\}$, $D(x_1) = \{1, 2\}$, $D(x_2) = \{0\}$ it determines $f(D)(x_0) = \{0\}$. We can define $\mathit{lazy}(f)$ to return propagation rules in $\mathit{rep}(f)$ as defined in Example 3. For this case $\mathit{lazy}(f)(D)$ could return either $\{x_1 \geqslant 1 \wedge x_2 \leqslant 1 \rightarrowtail x_0 = 0\}$ or $\{x_2 \leqslant 0 \rightarrowtail x_0 = 0\}$. □

Given we understand the implementation of propagator f, it is usually straightforward to see how to implement $\mathit{lazy}(f)$.

Example 9. Let $c \equiv \sum_{i=1}^{n} a_i x_i - \sum_{i=n+1}^{m} b_i x_i \leqslant d$ be a linear constraint where $a_i > 0, b_i > 0$. The bounds propagator f for c is defined as

$$\begin{aligned} f(D)(x_i) &= D(x_i) \cap \left[-\infty\,..\,\lfloor \tfrac{S - a_i \min D(x_i)}{a_i} \rfloor\right] & 1 \leqslant i \leqslant n \\ f(D)(x_i) &= D(x_i) \cap \left[\lceil \tfrac{S - b_i \max D(x_i)}{b_i} \rceil\,..\,+\infty\right] & n+1 \leqslant i \leqslant m \end{aligned}$$

where $S = d - \sum_{i=1}^{n} a_i \min D(x_i) + \sum_{i=n+1}^{m} b_i \max D(x_i)$. If the bounds changes for some $x_i, 1 \leqslant i \leqslant n$, so $u_i = \max f(D)(x_i) < \max D(x_i)$ then the propagation rule $\mathit{lazy}(f)$ generates is

$$\bigwedge_{j=1, j \neq i}^{n} x_i \geqslant \min D(x_i) \wedge \bigwedge_{j=n+1}^{m} x_i \leqslant \max D(x_i) \rightarrowtail x_i \leqslant u_i$$

similarly for $x_i, n+1 \leqslant i \leqslant m$. Note that this is not necessarily tight.

We claim extending a propagator f to create $lazy(f)$ is usually straightforward. For example, Katsirelos and Bacchus [9] explain how to create $lazy(f)$ (or the equivalent in their terms) for the `alldifferent` domain propagator f by understanding the algorithm for f. For a propagator f defined by indexicals [17], we can straightforwardly construct $lazy(f)$ since the indexical definition illustrates directly which atomic constraints contributed to the result. Direct constructions of $lazy(f)$ may not necessarily be tight. For propagators implemented using Binary Decision Diagrams we can automatically generate tight propagation rules using BDD operations [7]. If we want to generate tight propagation rules from arbitrary propagators f then we may need to modify the algorithm for f more substantially to obtain $lazy(f)$.

Example 10. We can make the propagation rules of Example 9 tight by weakening the bounds on some other variables. Let $r = a_i(u_i+1)-(S-a_i \min D(x_i))-1$ be the remainder before rounding down will increase the bound. If there exists $a_j \leqslant r$ where $\min D(x_j) > \min D_{init}(x_j)$ then we can weaken the propagation rule replacing the atomic constraint $x_j \geqslant \min D(x_j)$ by $x_j \geqslant \min D(x_j) - r_j$ where $r_j = \min\{\lfloor \frac{r}{a_j} \rfloor, \min D(x_j) - \min D_{init}(x_j)\}$. This reduces the remainder r by $a_j r_j$. Similarly if there exists $b_j \leqslant r$. We can repeat the process until $r < a_j$ and $r < b_j$ for all j. The result is tight.

For example given $100x_1 + 50x_2 + 10x_3 + 9x_4 \leqslant 100$ where $D_{init}(x_1) = D_{init}(x_2) = D_{init}(x_3) = D_{init}(x_4) = [-3\,..\,10]$ where $D(x_1) = D(x_2) = D(x_3) = D(x_4) = [0\,..\,10]$ then the propagation gives $S = 100$. The new upper bound on x_1 is $u_1 = 1$, and $r = 100 \times 2 - (100 - 100 \times 0) - 1 = 99$. The initial propagation rule is

$$x_2 \geqslant 0 \wedge x_3 \geqslant 0 \wedge x_4 \geqslant 0 \rightarrowtail x_1 \leqslant 1$$

We have $a_2 < r$ so we can decrease the coefficient of x_2 by $\min\{\lfloor \frac{99}{50} \rfloor, 3\} = 1$. There is still a remainder of $r = 99 - 1 \times 50 = 49$. We can reduce the coefficient of x_3 by 3 (the maximum since this takes it to the initial lower bound). This still leaves $r = 49 - 3 \times 10 = 19$. We can reduce the coefficient of x_4 by 2, the remainder is now 1, and less than any coefficient. The final tight propagation rule is

$$x_2 \geqslant -1 \wedge x_3 \geqslant -3 \wedge x_4 \geqslant -2 \rightarrowtail x_1 \leqslant 1 \qquad \square$$

Regardless of the tightness of propagation rules, the lazy clause generation approach ensures that the unit propagation that results is at least as strong as applying the propagators themselves.

Theorem 3. *Let* $A = UP(assign(D), DOM \cup \{cl(r) \mid r \in \cup_{f \in F} lazy(f)(D), \}$ *then* $A = \{\bot\}$ *or* $A \supseteq assign(iter(F, D))$.

Because we only execute the propagators at a fixpoint of unit propagation, generating a propagation rule whose right hand side gives new information means the clause cannot previously occur. The advantage of tight propagators is that, if the set of propagation rules R generated by $lazy(f)$ is tight, over the lifetime of a search it will not involve any direct redundancy.

7 Building a Lazy Clause Generator System

We construct a lazy clause generator, by adding a cut-down propagation engine into a SAT solver. The interface between the propagators and the SAT solver is managed as follows. Each Boolean variable is associated with an integer or set atomic constraint. After the SAT solver reaches a fixpoint of unit propagation, we run over the newly fixed Boolean literals. For each Boolean literal l which is decided or inferred, we make the corresponding change to the domain defined by the atomic constraint $lit^{-1}(l)$. We queue the propagators possibly effected by the change, and then execute them. If we find a propagation that modifies the domain of some integer or set variable, we construct the propagation rule that explains it and add this as a clause permanently[2] to the SAT solver, and add its unit consequence to the SAT solvers literal queue (queue of decisions and unit consequences). If we find a clause that causes failure we immediately invoke the SAT solvers conflict resolution procedure. Otherwise when the queue is empty, we invoke the SAT solver on the new literals discovered by propagation, and the process repeats.

On failure for each Boolean literal l which is removed from the current assignment, we undo the change of atomic constraint $lit^{-1}(l)$. Note that since all individual domain changes are reflected in Boolean literals this is sufficient. For example suppose $[\![x \leqslant 5]\!]$ was inferred at an earlier point in execution so $\max D(x) = 5$. Then suppose $[\![x \leqslant 2]\!]$ is inferred. In forward execution we will modify $\max D(x) = 2$, but unit propagation will also infer $[\![x \leqslant 3]\!]$ and $[\![x \leqslant 4]\!]$. On backtracking we walk up the trail of decided and inferred variables. When we unset $[\![x \leqslant 4]\!]$ we reset $\max D(x) = 5$, and then when unsetting $[\![x \leqslant 3]\!]$ and $[\![x \leqslant 2]\!]$ we do not change it further.

8 Experiments

We have built a prototype lazy clause generator system using MiniSat [12] version 2.0 beta as the starting point. We give experiments using open-shop scheduling problems from [3]. The experiments are run on a 3GHz Intel Pentium D with 4Gb RAM running Debian Linux 3.1. Each of the constraints in these problems is of the form $x_1 \vee x_2$, $x_1 + d \leqslant x_2$ or $x_0 \Leftrightarrow x_1 + d \leqslant x_2$ where d is a constant. These problems are also amenable to solving using SAT modulo difference logic. All of the propagators we use are tight bounds propagators so we only use Boolean variables of the form $[\![x \leqslant d]\!]$ and the first class of clause for $DOM(x)$. Using the full domain representation approximately doubles the computation time of the lazy approach. We use static translations for the first two kinds of constraints and lazy propagators for the reified difference inequalities.

We compare our lazy clause generation approach versus the static approach of [16] using MiniSat version 2.0 beta as the SAT solver, and versus the Barcelogic DPLL(T) solver version 1.1 using its difference logic theory solver [5]. We do not compare against other finite domain propagation solvers, because without very

[2] We do not currently allow nogood minimzation to remove these clauses, though perhaps we should.

Table 1. Open shop scheduling suite gp (80 instances)

Benchmark	Time(sec)				Conflict number			Clause ratio	
	cut_sat	csp2sat	sat	smt	cut_sat	csp2sat	smt	ave	min
gp04-09	0.38	6.84	1.31	0.17	32	21	39	5.15	5.15
gp05-01	1.41	27.32	6.53	0.27	39	19	61	5.67	5.67
gp08-09	5.09	136.62	32.25	0.86	129	53	121	9.05	9.05
gp10-07	16.25	347.60	99.30	9.53	622	622	1400	11.05	10.97
gp10-10	21.68	410.34	115.79	7.80	995	857	1371	10.85	10.82
Arith. mean	6.04	113.46	30.05	2.59	311	242	492	7.43	7.40
Geom. mean	2.49	47.43	11.14	0.59	100	48	94	7.03	7.02

sophisticated encodings and search strategies [10], they are not competitive on these problems, since they lack nogoods.

These scheduling problems are optimization problems. we search for the minimal makespan (completion time for all jobs). The minimization is conducted by dichotomic search over the space of possible makespans, see [16] for details. We note that dichtomic optimization search is in a sense advantageous to the static approach since it generates clauses once which are effectively used in solving multiple (linked) satisfaction subproblems.

Since these are large suites of benchmarks, we show summary results as well as a few individual instances to illustrate the spread of results. In each table we show the user time to find and prove the optimal solution for: the lazy approach **cut_sat**, the static approach **csp2sat** (and just the time spend in the SAT solver for the static approach **sat**), and the SMT approach **smt**. We also give the number of conflicts for each approach, and the average and minimum across all subproblems in the dichotomic search of the ratio of clauses for the static approach divided by the total created by the lazy approach.

The open-shop scheduling suite gp shown in Table 1 is easy for all approaches. For these problems csp2sat spends most of its time just generating the clauses. While clearly SMT requires more search to find the solution, given the tiny description of the problem for SMT it is very rapid. Note that some of these problems were only closed in 2005 [10], so they are not considered easy for technologies without nogoods.

The open-shop scheduling suite tai shown in Table 2 is more difficult. As the problem size grows the advantage of the lazy and static approaches grows over the SMT approach. The search space explored by the lazy approach is around twice that of the static approach, but it is still uniformly faster. Note also that the larger the example the smaller the percentage of clauses generated by the lazy approach.

The open-shop scheduling suite j shown in Table 3 is much harder. The three hardest problems j7-per0-0, j8-per0-1, and j8-per10-2 which were closed recently [16] are examined separately. The lazy approach is better than the static approach except for j7-per10-2, and better than SMT on the larger problems. To save experimental time for the three hardest problems we only try to find a solution with optimal makespan (a single subproblem) (dichotomic search for the

Table 2. Open shop scheduling suite tai (60 instances)

Benchmark	Time(sec)				Conflict number			Clause ratio	
	cut_sat	csp2sat	sat	smt	cut_sat	csp2sat	smt	ave	min
tai_5x5_1	0.42	4.64	1.08	0.95	887	774	1679	6.33	5.53
tai_7x7_6	16.23	23.75	10.37	452.15	12722	4397	264167	7.38	5.38
tai_10x10_1	7.52	78.76	18.65	674.99	3614	1599	108764	12.90	10.63
tai_10x10_10	3.80	79.32	17.97	33.34	1431	2675	7848	13.21	12.66
tai_20x20_4	269.89	1361.31	369.42	601.35	11247	3782	39831	26.23	24.42
tai_20x20_8	424.78	1420.77	428.60	6035.09	56092	15891	345876	24.42	20.51
Arith. mean	62.42	317.95	88.39	631.78	6611	3597	43231	13.17	12.03
Geom. mean	4.02	42.47	9.98	21.12	1783	1231	5565	11.20	10.14

Table 3. Open shop scheduling suite j (48+3 instances)

Benchmark	Time(sec)				Conflict number			Cl. ratio	
	cut_sat	csp2sat	sat	smt	cut_sat	csp2sat	smt	ave	min
j3-per0-2	0.29	4.02	0.89	0.15	57	20	31	3.46	3.46
j6-per0-0	500.68	703.66	638.23	277.67	158117	137911	212512	6.22	5.35
j7-per10-1	25.45	84.75	36.84	47.83	8967	5019	23478	8.23	7.75
j7-per10-2	1451.79	1437.52	1379.42	3136.69	303011	250942	1625354	6.90	5.04
j8-per20-0	19.02	104.56	36.57	552.40	5493	3138	186300	9.36	8.55
Arith. mean	113.48	252.97	226.08	298.71	25430	29877	110525	6.51	6.21
Geom. mean	3.19	29.37	8.96	2.66	780	559	937	6.30	6.04
j7-per0-0-sat	8443	5246	5210	11470	991907	533852	4328222	3.92	3.92
j8-per0-1-sat	19031	34322	34246	32413	1828054	1452649	8539727	5.90	5.90
j8-per10-2-sat	2205	1395	1322	3846	209822	160075	1316112	5.52	5.52

largest problem takes over 2 days for **csp2sat**). Surprisingly **csp2sat** improves on **cut_sat** for two of these problems, showing that having all the clause information from the beginning can be advantageous. The main extra cost appears to be the size of nogoods generated.

Overall, **cut_sat** solves faster than **csp2sat** except for `j7-per0-0`, `j8-per10-2` and `j7-per10-2`. While it requires more search than **csp2sat**, the massive reduction in clauses pays off. The lowest clause ratio that occurs in any instance is 3.46. Overall **cut_sat** generally improves upon **smt** the harder the examples become.

Finally we also experimented with some well-known problems using (non-tight) bounds propagators for large linear equations (see Example 9). For none of these problems could the static approach generate the clauses within hours, and SMT modulo difference logic is not applicable, so we compare with Gecode 1.3.1 [6] a highly optimized propagation solver. The lazy approach uses an **alldifferent** propagator equivalent to bounds propagation on disequations ($x_1 \neq x_2$) and SAT VSIDS search, while Gecode uses its native `distinct` propagator and default labelling. Both solvers look for all solutions. The results are shown in Table 4. Clearly nogoods can substantially reduce the search for these problems, and the lazy approach is at least competitive with Gecode.

Table 4. Linear equations examples (average of 100 runs)

Benchmark	Time(sec)		Conflicts/Failures	
	cut_sat	gecode	cut_sat	gecode
eq10	0.010	0.070	28	94
eq20	0.011	0.070	18	54
alpha	0.089	0.263	180	7435
money	0.010	0.069	68	3

9 Related Work and Conclusion

The paper [16] explains how to statically encode linear arithmetic constraints into CNF (to give tight clauses) using the propositions $[\![x \leqslant d]\!]$. They closed three very hard open-shop scheduling problems using their static approach, but the approach is manifestly impractical when the linear constraint involves a significant number of variables. Our lazy approach makes the encoding of linear arithmetic possible for large linear constraints, and allows encoding of arbitrary propagators.

The closest related work to this paper is the hybrid BDD and SAT bounds propagation set solver described in [7]. There a BDD-based set solver and a SAT solver are integrated and the BDD set solver passes clauses describing its propagations to the SAT solver in order to make use of the nogood capabilities of the SAT solver. Using BDD propagators, the construction of tight propagation rules can be automatic. Here we extend the approach beyond set variables to support integer variables, eliminate the propagation solver by embedding the minimal amount of machinery required into the SAT solver.

There is a substantial body of work on look back methods in constraint satisfaction (see e.g. [4], chapter 6), but there was little evidence until recently of success for look back methods that combine with propagation. The work of Katsirelos and Bacchus [8] showed that one could use nogood technology derived from SAT for storing and managing nogoods in a CSP system using FC-CBJ. In further work [9] they consider how to generate explanations (which are effectively clauses) of propagation for a number of global constraints, in order to support nogoods in a CP solver. They consider the usual DIMACS encoding of integers $\{[\![x = d]\!]\}$ and hence do not consider bounds propagation.

Roussel [15] gave a linear encoding of domains (not including inequality literals) which has the same unit propagation strength as our new encoding, but requires more variables and literals.

The lazy propagation approach can be viewed as a special form of Satisfiability Modulo Theories [14] solver, where each propagator is considered as a separate theory, and theory propagation is used to learn clauses.

In conclusion, we have constructed a hybrid SAT finite domain propagation solver using lazy clause generation that captures some of the advantages of both paradigms. It can tackle hard scheduling problems efficiently without complex search strategies. Where large amounts of search are required we expect it to be more effective than propagation based solvers because it includes nogoods and conflict directed backjumping. But we have only really scratched the surface of the possibilities of the lazy approach.

References

1. Choi, C.W., Lee, J.H.M., Stuckey, P.J.: Propagation redundancy in redundant modelling. In: Rossi, F. (ed.) CP 2003. LNCS, vol. 2833, pp. 229–243. Springer, Heidelberg (2003)
2. Crawford, J., Baker, A.: Experimental results on the application of satisfiability algorithms to scheduling problems. In: Procs. AAAI-94, pp. 1092–1097 (1994)
3. CSP2SAT: (December 2006), `http://bach.istc.kobe-u.ac.jp/csp2sat/`
4. Dechter, R.: Constraint Processing. Morgan Kaufmann, San Francisco (2003)
5. Barcelogic for SMT: (February 2007), `http://www.lsi.upc.es/~oliveras/bclt-main.html`
6. GECODE: (February 2007), `http://www.gecode.org`
7. Hawkins, P., Stuckey, P.J.: A Hybrid BDD and SAT Finite Domain Constraint Solver. In: Van Hentenryck, P. (ed.) PADL 2006. LNCS, vol. 3819, pp. 103–117. Springer, Heidelberg (2005)
8. Katsirelos, G., Bacchus, F.: Unrestricted nogood recording in CSP search. In: Rossi, F. (ed.) CP 2003. LNCS, vol. 2833, pp. 873–877. Springer, Heidelberg (2003)
9. Katsirelos, G., Bacchus, F.: Generalized nogoods in CSPs. In: The Twentieth National Conference on Artificial Intelligence (AAAI-05), pp. 390–396 (2005)
10. Laborie, P.: Complete MCS-Based Search: Application to Resource Constrained Project Scheduling. In: Proceedings IJCAI 2005, pp. 181–186 (2005)
11. Marriott, K., Stuckey, P.J.: Programming with Constraints: an Introduction. MIT Press, Cambridge (1998)
12. MiniSat: (December 2006), `http://www.cs.chalmers.se/Cs/Resarch/FormalMethods/MiniSat/`
13. Moskewicz, M., Madigan, C., Zhao, Y., Zhang, L., Malik, S.: Chaff: Engineering an efficient SAT solver. In: Proceedings of DAC-2001 (2001)
14. Niewenhuis, R., Oliveras, A., Tinelli, C.: Abstract DPLL and abstract DPLL modulo theories. In: Baader, F., Voronkov, A. (eds.) LPAR 2004. LNCS (LNAI), vol. 3452, pp. 36–50. Springer, Heidelberg (2005)
15. Roussel, O.: Some notes on the implementation of csp2sat+zchaff, a sim- ple translator from CSP to SAT. In: Proceedings of the 2nd International Workshop on Constraint Propagation and Implementation, pp. 83–88 (2005)
16. Tamura, N., Taga, A., Kitagawa, S., Banbara, M.: Compiling finite linear CSP to SAT. In: Benhamou, F. (ed.) CP 2006. LNCS, vol. 4204, pp. 590–603. Springer, Heidelberg (2006)
17. Van Hentenryck, P., Saraswat, V., Deville, Y.: Design, implementation and evaluation of the constraint language cc(FD). JLP 37(1–3), 139–164 (1998)
18. Walsh, T.: SAT v CSP. In: Dechter, R. (ed.) CP 2000. LNCS, vol. 1894, pp. 441–456. Springer, Heidelberg (2000)

Boosting Probabilistic Choice Operators

Matthieu Petit* and Arnaud Gotlieb

IRISA – INRIA, Campus Beaulieu, 35042 Rennes Cedex, France
{Matthieu.Petit,Arnaud.Gotlieb}@irisa.fr

Abstract. Probabilistic Choice Operators (PCOs) are convenient tools to model uncertainty in CP. They are useful to implement randomized algorithms and stochastic processes in the concurrent constraint framework. Their implementation is based on the random selection of a value inside a finite domain according to a given probability distribution. Unfortunately, the probabilistic choice of a PCO is usually delayed until the probability distribution is completely known. This is inefficient and penalizes their broader adoption in real-world applications. In this paper, we associate to PCO a filtering algorithm that prunes the variation domain of its random variable during constraint propagation. Our algorithm runs in $O(n)$ where n denotes the size of the domain of the probabilistic choice. Experimental results show the practical interest of this approach.

1 Introduction

Motivations. Reasoning with uncertainty is an important issue in Constraint Programming as many real-world problems (resource management, network traffic analysis, energy trading) invariably include incomplete or unknown parameters. Besides the original probabilistic extension of Constraint Satisfaction Problems proposed by Fargier and Lang [4], these last years have seen the development of several frameworks that offer capabilities to model uncertainty with probabilities. In 2000, Walsh proposed Stochastic Constraint Programming that extends CP by including both decision variables, that can be set, and stochastic variables that follow a given probability distribution [16,14]. In the concurrent constraint framework, Di Pierro and Wiklicky [2] and Gupta, Jagadeesan and Saraswat [6] introduced Probabilistic Choice Operators (PCOs) in concurrent constraint processes to implement randomized algorithms [3] and stochastic processes [5]. In all these frameworks, random draws have to be performed over completely known probability distributions. But, as noted by Yorke-Smith and Gervet [17], for many real-world problems, exact probability distributions are unknown or just implicitly defined via some additional constraints. For example, in resources assignment problems, one often knows that the probability to sell an item during summer time is five times lower than the probability to sell it during winter but we don't know the exact probability distribution to sell it over the year. In some

* This work is part of the GENETTA project granted by the Brittany region.

C. Bessiere (Ed.): CP 2007, LNCS 4741, pp. 559–573, 2007.

problems, the probability distribution itself is what we are looking for. Typical examples include biased games models, hardware and software constraint-based verification. For example, consider the Statistical Structural Testing technique [15] in Software Engineering. The problem aims at finding a distribution probability over the input domain of a program, that maximizes the coverage of some structural criteria, such as all_statements or all_paths. Up to know, there is no satisfactory automated technique for biasing the choice of test data that meet this objective. It has been shown in [9] that this problem can be modelled as a stochastic constraint solving problem for which the solution is the probability distribution. In order to model accurately such problems, probabilistic choices are currently delayed until complete information over the probability distribution is available. In terms of constraint modelling, this corresponds to enumerate the possible probability distributions and to solve each of the corresponding stochastic constraint system. This is inefficent and penalizes the broader adoption of PCOs in real-world applications.

Contributions. In this paper, we associate to PCOs a filtering algorithm that prunes the domain of the stochastic variable of the probabilistic choice. Our purpose is to boost the probabilistic decision even if the probability distribution is unknown or just known via some additional constraints. The main idea is to benefit from the early random draw of an auxiliary stochastic variable in order to prune the variation domain of the probability distribution during constraint propagation. Thanks to the availability of this random value, our filtering algorithm can eliminate the values of the probabilistic choice that are incompatible with current state of the PCO. Interestingly, this algorithm runs in $O(n)$ where n denotes the size of the domain of the probabilistic choice.

As a basic example, consider the stochastic optimization problem of Fig.1 inspired from a production planning problem. The problem aims at finding a value for X that minimizes $X - Y$ where Y is a stochastic variable, the value of which is given by the random draw of a biased die. Suppose we ignore the exact bias of the die and we just know that the 6-face of the die is two times more overloaded than the 1-face, the 5-face is two times more overloaded than the 2-face, and the 4-face is two times more overloaded than the 3-face. The PCO `choose` picks up at random a value of the die according to the unknown distribution probability $[1, 2, 3, 4, 5, 6] - [W1, W2, W3, W4, W5, W6]$ where Wi denotes the weight associated to face i of the die.

The simplest approach to solve this problem consists in labeling first on the possible distribution probabilities in order to allow the random draw of Y (option `no_filtering` in Fig.1). Unfortunately, this approach rapidely becomes intractable. `R` denotes the mean CPU time (in sec.) obtained by launching 2000 times the solving process. When our filtering algoithm is used (option `domain_bound`), the possible probability distributions are pruned before labelling. On this example, our gain is more than one order of magnitude in average.

```
s_optim(Opt) :-
        X in 1..6,
        domain([W1,W2,W3,W4,W5,W6], 1, 10),
        choose(Y,[1,2,3,4,5,6]-[W1,W2,W3,W4,W5,W6],[],Opt), % PCO call
        X #>= Y,
        2*W1 #= W6, % 6-face is two times more overloaded than 1-face
        2*W2 #= W5,
        2*W3 #= W4,
        labeling([minimize(X-Y)],[X,W1,W2,W3,W4,W5,W6]).

?- bench([s_optim([no_filtering]), 2000, R).
R = 9.479 ?

?- bench([s_optim([domain_bound]), 2000, R). % filtering on choose
R = 0.646 ?
```

Fig. 1. A stochastic optimization problem on SICStus 3.11, Intel-Pentium 2Ghz, 1Go RAM, WinXP

We implemented our filtering algorithm in several PCOs of the SICStus Prolog library PCC(FD). Experimental results show the practical interest of our approach.

Organization. The paper is organized as follows : Section 2 briefly describes the theoretical background on PCOs required to understand the rest of the paper. Section 3 presents the principles of filtering associated to PCO. Section 4 describes our implementation of several PCOs in SICStus Prolog, while section 5 presents the experimental results. Finally, Section 6 indicates several perspectives to this work.

2 Background on Probabilistic Choice Operators

Probabilistic Choice Operators have been introduced originally within the Concurrent Constraint framework of Saraswat. In the first subsection, we start by briefly recalling the principles of the theoretical scheme: Probabilistic Concurrent Constraint Programming (PCCP). In the second subsection, we focus on Finite Domains which form a computational domain of the generic scheme PCCP.

2.1 Probabilistic Concurrent Constraint Programming

Concurrent Constraint Programming (CCP)

We start by recalling some syntax and semantics elements of CCP. In CCP, processes are executed concurrently and can interact with each other through a common constraint store. A CCP language is parameterized by a constraint system [12], which is composed of a set of primitive constraints and an entailment relation. The syntax of a CCP language is given by the following grammar:

$$\begin{aligned} Process ::= &\ tell(C) \,|\, if\ C\ then\ Process \,| \\ &\ new\, X\, in\, Process \,|\, Process \| Process. \end{aligned}$$

where $tell(C)$ adds the constraint C to the constraint store, $if\ C\ then\ Process$ asks whether C is entailed by the current constraint store and adds the constraints of $Process$ if C is entailed, $new\ X\ in\ Process$ adds the constraints of $Process$ to the store while hiding the variable X from other processes, and finally, $\|$ represents the parallel composition that can be interpreted as a logical conjunction in a Logic Programming environment. Well known examples of CCP languages include cc(FD)[7], AKL[8] or Oz/Mozart[13] just to name a few.

Probabilistic Choice Operators

A few years ago, Gupta et al. [6,5] and Di Pierro and Wiklicky [2,3] proposed to add probabilistic choice operators to CCP. In our presentation, we will confine ourselves to the PCO *choose* [6]. Formally, the operator $choose(X, Law_X, Process)$ injects a stochastic variable X along with a probabilistic law Law_X into a concurrent process $Process$. For the sake of simplicity, we suppose that Law_X takes the form of a pair $[v_1, \ldots, v_n] - [w_1, \ldots, w_n]$ where $[v_1, \ldots, v_n]$ denotes the list of possible (distinct) values for X, called the *domain* of the probabilistic choice, while $[w_1, \ldots, w_n]$ denotes the list of non-negative weights associated to the v_i, called the *probability distribution* of the probabilistic choice. In the rest of the paper, $dom(X) = [v_1, \ldots, v_n]$ denotes a sorted finite set of integer values associated to variable X. $min(X)$ (resp. $max(X)$) denotes the minimum (resp. maximum) of $dom(X)$.

Operationally, $choose(X, [v_1, \ldots, v_n] - [w_1, \ldots, w_n], Process)$ executes $Process_{X \leftarrow v_i}$ with a probability p_i. $Process_{X \leftarrow v_i}$ denotes the concurrent process P where X has been substituted by v_i and p_i denotes the probability of the event $X = v_i$ which is computed by the following formula:

$$p_i = \frac{w_i}{\sum_{j=1}^{n} w_j}.$$

Just to make things more concrete, we illustrate the processing of a PCCP request on a basic example extracted from [5]:

Example 1.

$$\begin{aligned} P = {} & choose(X, [0,1] - [1,1], tell(X = Z)) \parallel \\ & choose(Y, [0,1] - [1,1], if\ Z = 1\ then\ tell(Y = 1)). \end{aligned}$$

Roughly speaking, three possible terminal configurations can be obtained: Z is constrained to 0 with the probability $\frac{1}{2}$ (event $X = 0$), Z is constrained to 1 with the probability $\frac{1}{4}$ (event $X = 1 \wedge Y = 1$) and $false$ is obtained with the probability $\frac{1}{4}$ (event $X = 1 \wedge Y = 0$).

2.2 Probabilistic Choice Operator over Finite Domains

PCCP is parameterized by a computational domain over which the constraints are interpreted. In this paper, we focus on Finite Domains and we provide an operational semantics for PCO onto Finite Domains.

Uncertainty on the Probabilistic Choice

The simulation (random draw) of values for the stochastic variable X in a PCO is always possible when Law_X is fully instantiated. On the contrary, when there is some uncertain data within the probabilistic choice, the simulation is delayed until all the parameters (domain, probability distribution) become instantiated. The set of uncertain data is characterized by the following definition.

Definition 1. *Let X be a stochastic variable, let $Law_X = [v_1, \ldots, v_n]-[W_1, \ldots, W_n]$ be its probabilistic choice where $W_1, \ldots, W_n$ are Finite Domains variables, then the set of the possible probability distributions, called SL_X associated to X is defined as follows:*

$$\mathcal{SL}_X \triangleq \{[v, \ldots, v_n] - [w_1, \ldots, w_n] | w_1 \in dom(W_1), \ldots, w_n \in dom(W_n)\}$$

This definition will be useful when we will introduce our filtering algorithm to prune the domain of the stochastic variable X. The filtering algorithm will be illustrated on the following example.

Example 2. Consider the example of a biased die where the 6-face is two times overloaded than the 1-face.

$$W_6 = 2 * W_1 \wedge choose(X, [1,2,3,4,5,6] - [W_1, W_2, W_3, W_4, W_5, W_6], X = Die)$$

Suppose that $dom(W_1) = 1..2$, $dom(W_2) = 2..2$, $dom(W_3) = 2..2$, $dom(W_4) = 2..2$, $dom(W_5) = 2..2$ and $dom(W_6) = 2..4$, then uncertainty on the unknown bias of the die is given by the following set:

$$\begin{aligned}\mathcal{SL}_X = \{ & [1,2,3,4,5,6] - [1,2,2,2,2,2], [1,2,3,4,5,6] - [1,2,2,2,2,3],\\ & [1,2,3,4,5,6] - [1,2,2,2,2,4], [1,2,3,4,5,6] - [2,2,2,2,2,2],\\ & [1,2,3,4,5,6] - [2,2,2,2,2,3], [1,2,3,4,5,6] - [2,2,2,2,2,4]\}.\end{aligned}$$

PCOs as Constraint Combinators

As said above, in the presence of uncertainty, the simulation of PCO should be delayed. Then, we considered PCOs as constraint combinators. This allows to reason on probabilistic choices that are only partially known and opens the door to apply constraint reasoning on PCOs. In this view, the probability distribution associated to a PCO is just constrained by a set of constraints on its possible values.

Base on that, constraint propagation over the *choose* operator can be defined. When *choose* is equipped with a filtering algorithm, one speak of the constraint combinator *choose*. $choose(X, Law_X, Process)$ succeeds whenever X is valuated and *Process* succeeds. When the probabilistic choice is only partially instantiated, *choose* is introduced into the propagation queue of the constraint solver and then, a filtering algorithm that is detailed below is launched to prune the domain of values for X. When no more pruning can be performed, the combinator falls asleep. It is awoken whenever the domain of at least one variable of the distribution probability is modified and then the combinator is reintroduced in the propagation queue. This process iterates until a fix point is reached, i.e. a state where no more deduction on the domain of X is obtained.

3 Principle of the Filtering on *choose*

In this section, we introduce the principles of the filtering on the *choose* combinator. This filtering algorithm permits to prune early the domain of the probabilistic choice. The main idea is to benefit from the early random draw of an auxiliary variable, the value of which is exploited within the filtering algorithm. First subsection is devoted to recall the principle of simulating random choice over Finite Domains. This principle is the basis of our filtering algorithm. Second subsection presents the correction properties on the *choose* combinator, while the third subsection presents the filtering algorithm. In this subsection, we prove correctness and termination of our algorithm and also give its complexity.

3.1 Simulation of a Stochastic Variable over Finite Domains

Stochastic variables over Finite Domains are usually simulated with the values of a uniform stochastic variable over $[0;1]$. This uniform stochastic variable is noted U. Our filtering algorithm for $choose(X, Law_X, Process)$ exploits an *a priori* random value of U to prune $dom(X)$.

Definition 2 (Distribution function). *Let X be a stochastic variable, let $Law_X = [v_1, \ldots, v_n] - [w_1, \ldots, w_n]$ be its probabilistic choice and U an uniform stochastic variable over $[0;1]$, then a distribution function is a function f that maps a random value of U to a value of X, as follows:*

$$f : [0;1] \rightarrow Dom(X)$$
$$u \quad \mapsto \begin{cases} v_1 & \textit{if } u \in \left[0, \frac{w_1}{\sum_{i=1}^{n} w_i}\right[\\ \vdots & \vdots \\ v_n & \textit{if } u \in \left[\frac{\sum_{i=1}^{n-1} w_i}{\sum_{i=1}^{n} w_i}, 1\right[\end{cases}.$$

It is trivial to see that the probability of the event $X = v_i$ is equal to $P(u \in [pr_1 + \ldots + pr_{i-1}, pr_1 + \ldots + pr_i]) = (pr_1 + \ldots + pr_i) - (pr_1 + \ldots + pr_{i-1}) = pr_i$, as expected.

For example, consider the distribution function f associated to a non-biased die, given by FIG. 2. Here, the distribution probability is given by $[1,2,3,4,5,6] - [1,1,1,1,1,1]$ and $u = 0.6$. As a result, $X = f(0.6) = 4$.

Associated to each probability distribution of $\mathcal{SL}_X$, a distribution function f is defined. The set of distribution functions associated to $\mathcal{SL}_X$ is noted $\mathcal{F}_X$. For example, the set $\mathcal{F}_X$ of Example 2 is represented by FIG.3.

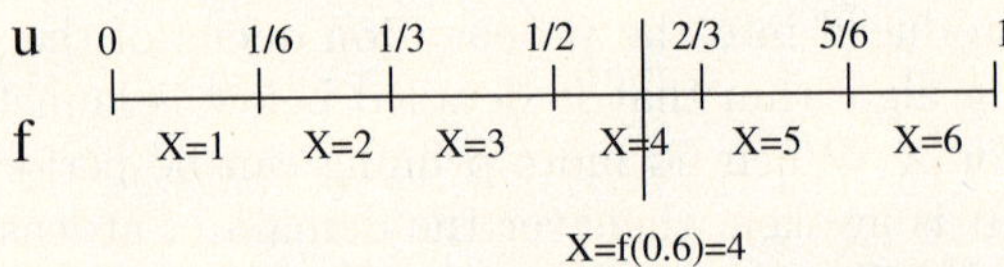

Fig. 2. Simulation of the stochastic variable X with a uniform probability distribution on $\{1, 2, 3, 4, 5, 6\}$

3.2 Stochastic Consistencies on the *choose* Combinator

We propose to characterize the consistency level achieved by our filtering combinator by using the notion of stochastic consistency. Stochastic consistency is a local consistency parameterized by an uniform random value u. In our framework, we define two stochastic consistencies on the $choose(X, Law_X, Process)$ combinator.

Definition 3. *(Stochastic domain consistency)*
Let u be a uniform random value and $\mathcal{F}_X$ be the set of distribution functions associated to Law_X, then the combinator $choose(X, Law_X, Process)$ is stochastic domain consistent iff

$$\forall v_i \in dom(X), \exists f \in \mathcal{F}_X \textit{ such that } f(u) = v_i$$

Definition 4. *(Stochastic bound consistency)*
Let u be a uniform random value and $\mathcal{F}_X$ be the set of distribution functions associated to Law_X, then the combinator $choose(X, Law_X, Process)$ is stochastic bound consistent iff

$$\exists f_1, f_2 \in \mathcal{F}_X \textit{ such that } f_1(u) = min(X) \textit{ and } f_2(u) = max(X)$$

From the definitions, it is clear that *stochastic domain consistency* implies *stochastic bound consistency.*

3.3 Filtering on $dom(X)$

Given an uniform random value, the principle of the filtering algorithm is to detect values for the stochastic variable than cannot be randomly chosen.

The Algorithm
For a given u, reasoning on the set of possible probability distributions $\mathcal{F}_X$ and the set of probability distributions $\mathcal{SL}_X$ yields to prune $dom(X)$. For each value v of $dom(X)$, we compute a support for the event $X = v$, i.e the set of values for u such as v can be randomly chosen. Formally, this support is defined as follows.

Definition 5. *(Support of $X = v$)*
Let i be the indice of v in $[v_1, \ldots, v_n]$

$$\forall i \in [1, \ldots, n],\ Supp_{\{X=v\}} = \bigcup_{[v_1 \ldots, v_n]-[w_1, \ldots, w_n] \in \mathcal{SL}_X} \left[\frac{\sum_{j=1}^{i-1} w_j}{\sum_{j=1}^{n} w_j}, \frac{\sum_{j=1}^{i} w_j}{\sum_{j=1}^{n} w_j} \right[$$

Our filtering algorithm is based on the following property:

$$\forall v \in [v_1, \ldots, v_n],\ u \notin Supp_{\{X=v\}} \Rightarrow X \neq v$$

However, the computation of $Supp_{\{X=v\}}$ is based on the labelling of each element of $\mathcal{SL}_X$ and in the worst case, the number of elements of $\mathcal{SL}_X$ is exponential with the size of the probabilistic choice. Indeed, this is the cardinality of the Cartesian product of the domains of the weight variables. As a consequence, we propose to approximate the computation of $Supp_{\{X=v\}}$ using only the bounds of this union of intervals. This is shown on Algorithm 1 that presents our filtering algorithm. It takes as inputs X, Law_X and u and removes values from $dom(X)$ that cannot be randomly chosen. For each value $v \in dom(X)$, the bounds of $Supp_{\{X=v\}}$, noted $Min\_Sup_{\{X=v\}}$ and $Max\_Sup_{\{X=v\}}$, are computed by the function INTPROBA. If $u \notin [Min\_Supp_{\{X=v\}}; Max\_Supp_{\{X=v\}}]$, then v is removed from $dom(X)$.

The efficiency of the filtering algorithm relies directly on the efficient computation of the bounds of each support $Supp_{\{X=v\}}$. Fortunately, theses bounds can be computed from the result of an analytical study that is described below.

Algorithm 1. FILTERALGO

```
Input  : X,Law_X and u

forall v ∈ dom(X) do
    [Min_Sup{X=v}; Max_Sup{X=v}] ← IntProba(v, Law_X);
    if u ∉ [Min_Sup{X=v}; Max_Sup{X=v}] then
        v is removed from dom(X)
    end
end
```

A Method to Compute an Approximation of $Supp_{\{X=v\}}$

The method aims at computing the two elements of $\mathcal{SL}_X$ such that $Supp_{\{X=v\}}$ is minimized and maximized. For that, we compute the minimum (resp. maximum) value of $\frac{\sum_{j=1}^{i-1} w_j}{\sum_{j=1}^{n} w_j}$ (resp. $\frac{\sum_{j=1}^{i} w_j}{\sum_{j=1}^{n} w_j}$) for each distribution probability of $\mathcal{SL}_X$ where i denotes the indice of v in $[v_1, \dots, v_n]$. Computing $\min_{[v_1 \dots, v_n]-[w_1, \dots, w_n] \in \mathcal{SL}_X} \left(\frac{\sum_{j=1}^{i-1} w_j}{\sum_{j=1}^{n} w_j}\right)$ and $\max_{[v_1 \dots, v_n]-[w_1, \dots, w_n] \in \mathcal{SL}_X} \left(\frac{\sum_{j=1}^{i} w_j}{\sum_{j=1}^{n} w_j}\right)$ is efficient by using the two following analytical results.

Without any loss of generality, we suppose that $\sum_{j=1}^{n} min(W_j) > 0$. Then,

$\forall i \in [1, \dots, n]$,

$$\min_{[v_1 \dots, v_n]-[w_1, \dots, w_n] \in \mathcal{SL}_X} \left(\frac{\sum_{j=1}^{i-1} w_j}{\sum_{j=1}^{n} w_j}\right) = \frac{\sum_{j=1}^{i-1} \min(W_j)}{\sum_{j=1}^{i-1} \min(W_j) + \sum_{j=i}^{n} \max(W_j)}$$

and

$\forall i \in [1, \dots, n]$,

$$\max_{[v_1 \dots, v_n]-[w_1, \dots, w_n] \in \mathcal{SL}_X} \left(\frac{\sum_{j=1}^{i-1} w_j}{\sum_{j=1}^{n} w_j}\right) = \frac{\sum_{j=1}^{i} \max(W_j)}{\sum_{j=1}^{i} \max(W_j) + \sum_{j=i+1}^{n} \min(W_j)}$$

The complete proofs of these equations can be done by refutation and is available in [11].

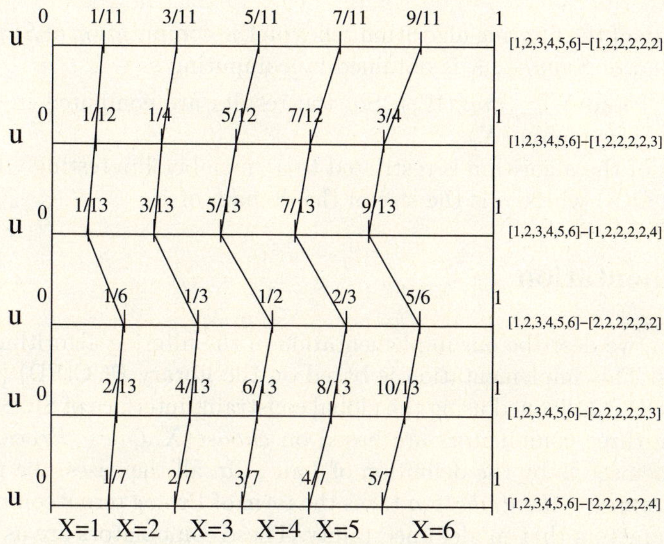

Fig. 3. Set of the distribution functions of the example 2 die

Consider again the example 2 and the set $\mathcal{F}_X$ given in FIG. 3. The values of $Supp_{\{X=v\}}$ are computed by our algorithm and are shown below.

$Supp_{\{X=1\}} = [0\ ;\frac{1}{6}[$	$Supp_{\{X=4\}} = [\frac{5}{13}\ ;\frac{2}{3}[$
$Supp_{\{X=2\}} = [\frac{1}{13}\ ;\frac{1}{3}[$	$Supp_{\{X=5\}} = [\frac{7}{13}\ ;\frac{5}{6}[$
$Supp_{\{X=3\}} = [\frac{3}{13}\ ;\frac{1}{2}[$	$Supp_{\{X=6\}} = [\frac{9}{13}\ ;1[$

$X = 1$ is removed from $dom(X)$ by the filtering algorithm when $u \notin [0; \frac{1}{6}[$, $X = 2$ is removed from $dom(X)$ when $u \notin [\frac{1}{13}\ ; \frac{1}{3}[$ and so on.

Termination and Correction

The filtering algorithm iterates over the possible values of $dom(X)$ then its termination is trivially demonstrated, as the set $dom(X)$ is finite.

Correction of the algorithm can be proved by showing that it permits to achieve a chosen level of consistency. Based on our definition 3 and 4 of stochastic consistencies , we show that FILTERALGO achieves only *stochastic bound consistency*. Due to the approximation of $Supp_{\{X=v\}}$, *stochastic domain consistency* cannot be achieved by our algorithm.

We only give a sketch of the proof that is available in [11]. We have to prove that after the execution of FILTERALGO, there exist two distribution functions f_1 and f_2 of $\mathcal{F}_X$ such that $f_1(u) = min(X)$ and $f_2(u) = max(X)$. Given a value v_j for the minimum (resp. the maximum) of $dom(X)$ in $[v_1, \ldots, v_n]$, the proof consists in finding an element of $\mathcal{SL}_X$ $[w_1, \ldots, w_{j-1}, w_j, \ldots, w_n]$ such that $u \in \left[\frac{\sum_{i=1}^{j-1} w_j}{\sum_{i=1}^{n} w_j}, \frac{\sum_{i=1}^{j} w_j}{\sum_{i=1}^{n} w_j}\right[$. A case-based reasoning on the distinct values of $min(X)$ and $max(X)$ in $[v_1, \ldots, v_n]$ completes the proof.

Complexity

The complexity of the filtering algorithm relies on the computation of $Supp_{\{X=v\}}$ and each bound of $Supp_{\{X=v\}}$ is obtained by computing $\forall i \in 1 \dots n$, $\sum_{j=1}^{i} min(W_j)$ and $\sum_{j=1}^{i} max(W_j)$. So, the results are computed in a linear time w.r.t. the size of $dom(X)$.

As the rest of the algorithm is restricted to a "membership testing", FILTERALGO runs in $O(n)$ where n is the size of the domain of X.

4 Implementation

In this section, we describe our implementation of the filtering algorithm within several PCOs. This implementation is based on the library PCC(FD) [10] that contains three PCOs defined using the global constraint interface of SICStus Prolog [1]. These three combinators are based on $choose(X, Law_X, Process)$, but distinguish themselves by the definition of Law_X. In all the cases, the probabilistic choice *Domain – Distribution* takes the form of Prolog terms compound of unbound parameters that model uncertainty. These combinators are as follows:

- `choose`, where *Domain* is a list of values and *Distribution* is a list of finite domain variables that represent weights;
- `choose_range`, where *Domain* is a range represented with two distinct FD variables Min and Max, and *Distribution* is a list of finite domain variables that represent weights;
- `choose_decision`, where *Domain* is the boolean domain $\{0, 1\}$ and *Distribution* is a pair of distinct finite domain variables that represent weights.

When a PCO is posted in the constraint store, the predicate `random/1` allows to obtain a uniform pseudo-random value for U. During the constraint propagation, PCOs `choose`, `choose_range` and `choose_decision` are awoken when the domain of the stochastic variable X or the domain of weight variables are pruned. Then, the filtering algorithm is launched as soon as new information on the probabilistic choice is available.

Some options are available to parameterize the filtering capabilities of the algorithm. The `domain_bound` option is used to launch our implementation of FILTERALGO, while the `no_filtering` option permits to switch off the filtering algorithm. The `inconsistency_check` option checks whether *Process* is partially consistent w.r.t. $dom(X)$. This option is useful to improve the pruning capabilities of the filtering algorithm but is also more costly.

5 Experimental Validation

In this section, we present the experimental results we obtained on two applications of PCOs. The first one concerns biased games models that play a prevalent role in many applications. The second one is a resource planning application adapted from [16].

5.1 Biased Games Model

In this subsection, we consider two dice games: 421 and *less than* 8. We start by briefly describing the models of the games and then we present the experimental results.

Models

421. The 421 game consists in drawing three N-face dice. The game is won when faces 4, 2 and 1 are drawn without considering the valuation order of the dice. The problem we adress here is to play 421 with a biased die for which the exact bias is unknown.

A model that considers only a 6-face die is given below by the predicate `four_two_one/3`. In the model, the unknown bias is formalized via the Finite Domains variables $[W1, .., W6]$ representing the weights of the probability distribution. Each weight has a value in 1..10 and additionnal constraints on the bias are given by the constraints `2*W1#=W6, 2*W2#=W5 ,2*W4#=W3`.

```
four_two_one([D1,D2,D3],[W1,W2,W3,W4,W5,W6],Opt) :-
        domaine([W1,W2,W3,W4,W5,W6],1,10),
        2*W1=W6, 2*W2=W5 ,2*W4=W3,
        choose(D1, [1,2,3,4,5,6]-[W1,W2,W3,W4,W5,W6],[],Opt),
        choose(D2, [1,2,3,4,5,6]-[W1,W2,W3,W4,W5,W6],[],Opt),
        choose(D3, [1,2,3,4,5,6]-[W1,W2,W3,W4,W5,W6],[],Opt),
        all_different([D1,D2,D3]),
        D1+D2+D3#=7.
```

The predicate `four_two_one([D1,D2,D3],Distribution,Opt)` is true iff `D1`, `D2` and `D3` have been valuated to 4, 2 and 1, which is modelled by the two latter constraints.

Less Than 8. This game consists in drawing five N-face dice. The game is won when the sum of the values of the dice are less or equal than 8. The game with 6-face dice is modelled by `less_than_8/2` predicate.

```
less_than_8([D1,D2,D3,D4,D5],[W1,W2,W3,W4,W5,W6],Opt) :-
        domain[W1,W2,W3,W4,W5,W6],1,10),
        4*W6 #= W1,3*W5 #= W2,2*W4 #= W3,
        choose(D1, [1,2,3,4,5,6]-[W1,W2,W3,W4,W5,W6],[],Opt),
        choose(D2, [1,2,3,4,5,6]-[W1,W2,W3,W4,W5,W6],[],Opt),
        choose(D3, [1,2,3,4,5,6]-[W1,W2,W3,W4,W5,W6],[],Opt),
        choose(D4, [1,2,3,4,5,6]-[W1,W2,W3,W4,W5,W6],[],Opt),
        choose(D5, [1,2,3,4,5,6]-[W1,W2,W3,W4,W5,W6],[],Opt),
        D1+D2+D3+D4+D5 #=<8.
```

Results

Our experiment seeks for a valuation of `Distribution` (the bias of the die) such as the game is always won by the player. We parameterized our model with N, the number of the faces of the die in order to evaluate the boosting of our filtering algorithm. For both games, the request was iterated 2000 times in order to avoid the factor of good luck due the choice of the uniform random value. A large number of iterations has been chosen in order to get a significant sampling of request. Experimental results were obtained on a Win XP machine powered by a 2GHz Intel Pentium with 1Go memory running SICStus 3.11. We compare two approaches: in the first one, no filtering was launched during constraint propagation (no_filtering) while in the second one, our filtering algorithm was applied (domain_bound).

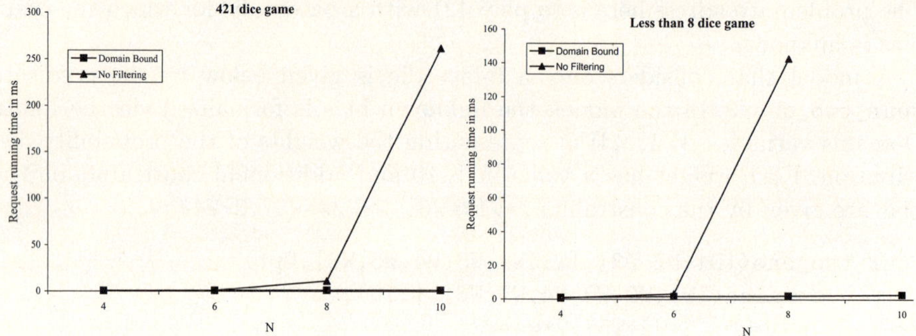

Fig. 4. Experimental results on 421 and *less than* 8

The results are given in FIG.4. Both curves with the no_filtering option present a combinatorial explosion when N grows while they remain proportional when option domain_bound is selected. This confirms that our filtering algorithms boosts combinators when additional constraints on the probabilistic choice are available. Note that the overhead due to our algorithm during constraint propagation remains modest. Note also that our results are nearly the same regardless the labelling heuristic that is used. This comes from the symmetry of the problems.

5.2 Books Production Planning

Models

Our books production planning constraint model is adapted from the classical M quarter production planning problem of [16]. In our model, the demand of books is modelized by the PCO $choose(Demand, [100, 101, 102, 103, 104, 105] - [W_{100}, W_{101}, W_{102}, W_{103}, W_{104}, W_{105}], [], Opt)$ where the weights W_i denote the unknown probability distribution. So, we solve the problem with an unknown probability distribution but we don't solve the original stochastic constraint system aiming at satisfying the clientele eighty percent of the time. Additional constraints on W_i come from the variability on book demands over the year. For example, during winter, the book editor expects that the demand would be greater and then the probability of sold 105 books is 2 times greater than the probability of sold 100 (`2*W100#=W105`).

```
book_production(M,Opt) :-
    domain([W100,W101,W102,W103,W104,W105],1,10),
    2*W100#=W105,2*W101#=W104,2*W102#=W103,
    choose(Demand,[100,101,102,103,104,105]-
                            [W100,W101,W102,W103,W104,W105],[],Opt),
    Prod#>=Demand, Surplus #= Prod-Demand,
    Cost #= Surplus+Cost_Rest,
    M1 is M-1,
    book_production_rec(M1,Prod_Rest,Surplus,Cost_Rest,Opt),
    append([Prod|Prod_Rest],[W100,W101,W102,W103,W104,W105],Lab_List),
    labeling([minimize(Cost)],Lab_List).

book_production_rec(0,[],_Surplus,0,_Opt).

book_production_rec(M,[Prod|Prod_Rest],Surplus,Cost,Opt) :-
    choose(Demand,[100,101,102,103,104,105]-
                            [W100,W101,W102,W103,W104,W105],[],Opt),
    Prod#>=Demand-Surplus,
    Surplus2 #= Prod-Demand+Surplus,
    Cost #= Prod-Demand+Surplus+Cost_Rest,
    M1 is M-1,
    book_production_rec(M1,Production_Rest,Surplus2,Cost_Rest).
```

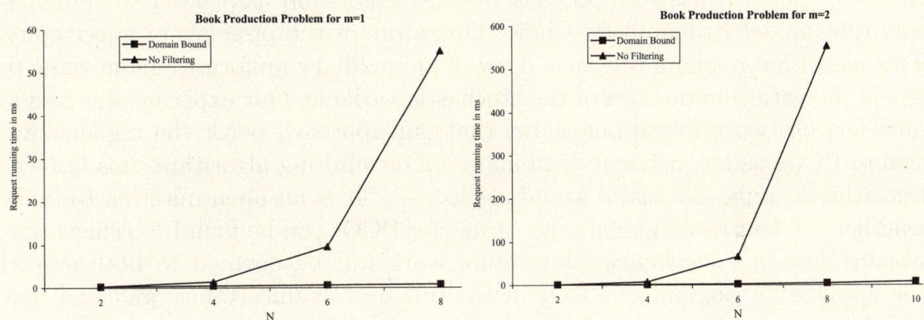

Fig. 5. Results on Book Production assignment for $M = 1$ and $M = 2$

Results

In our experiments, two parameters are used to control the model: the variation domain of the book demand N and the number of considered quarters M. The experimental results are given by FIG.5. They present a similar profile than the results we got on biased games models. In fact, this is explained by the similar constraints that we use on the weights. However, when changing these constraints in the experiment (removing `2*W1#=W6,2*W2#=W5,2*W3#=W4` and adding `W1+W6#=5`, `W1-W6#=3`,`W2+W5#=5`,`W2-W5=3`,`W3+W4#=5` and `W3-W4#=3`), we got different results that are shown in Fig.6. In this case where the underlying problem is more constrained, the CPU time elapsed in labelling is less important as constraint propagation becomes more efficient. Hence, we suggest

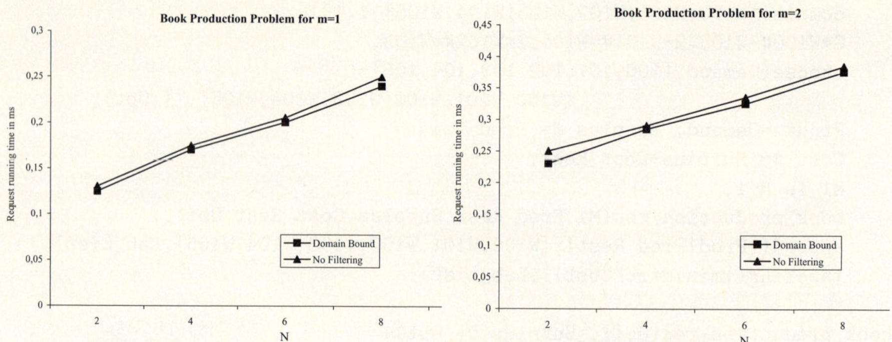

Fig. 6. Results on Book Production assignment for a new model of the demand

to use our filtering algorithm in priority for problems where the probability distribution is weakly constrained and it is difficult to find a bias such as the constraints systems are satisfied.

6 Conclusions

In this paper, we have proposed a filtering algorithm associated to combinators that model Probabilistic Choice Operators in the presence of uncertainty. This algorithm exploits the early draw of an auxiliary uniform random value to prune the variation domain of the stochastic variable. Our experimental results obtained on two applications shows that our approach boost the implementation of PCOs as a constraint combinators. Our filtering algorithm runs in $O(n)$ but achieves only *stochastic bound consistency*. It is an open question to know whether efficient (polynomial) algorithms for PCOs can be found to achieve *stochastic domain consistency*. Our future work will be devoted to both extend the application domain of PCOs in the presence of uncertainty and find new algorithms to achieve better level of consistency.

References

1. Carlsson, M., Ottosson, G., Carlson, B.: An Open–Ended Finite Domain Constraint Solver. In: Proceedings of Programming Languages: Implementations, Logics, and Programs (1997)
2. Di Pierro, A., Wiklicky, H.: On probabilistic CCP. In: APPIA-GULP-PRODE, Grado, Italy, pp. 225–234 (1997)
3. Di Pierro, A., Wiklicky, H.: Implementing randomised algorithms in constraint logic programming. In: Proceedings of the ERCIM/Compulog Workshop on Constraints (2000)
4. Fargier, H., Lang, J.: Uncertainty in constraint satisfaction problems: A probabilistic approach. In: Proceedings of the European Conference on Symbolic and Quantitative Approaches to Reasoning and Uncertainty, Grenada, pp. 97–104. Springer, Heidelberg (1993)

5. Gupta, V., Jagadeesan, R., Panangaden, P.: Stochastic processes as concurrent constraint programs. In: Proceedings of Symposium on Principles of Programming Languages (1999)
6. Gupta, V., Jagadeesan, R., Saraswat, V.A.: Probabilistic concurrent constraint programming. In: Proceedings of the International Conference Conference on Concurrency Theory, pp. 243–257. Springer, Heidelberg (1997)
7. Van Hentenryck, P., Saraswat, V., Deville, Y.: Design, implementation, and evaluation of the constraint language cc(fd). Technical Report CS-93-02, Brown University (1993)
8. Janson, S., Haridi, S.: Programming paradigms of the Andorra kernel language. In: Proceedings of the International Symposium on Logic Programming, San Diego, USA, pp. 167–186 (1991)
9. Petit, M., Gotlieb, A.: Probabilistic choice operators as global constraints: application to statistical software testing. In: Proceedings of International Conference on Logic Programming – Poster Presentation. LNCS, pp. 471–472 (2004)
10. Petit, M., Gotlieb, A.: Library of probabilistic constraint combinators over finite domain (May 2006), available at `http://www.irisa.fr/lande/petit/tools.html`
11. Petit, M., Gotlieb, A.: Constraint-based reasoning on probabilistic choice operators. Research Report 6165, INRIA, 04 (2007)
12. Saraswat, V.A., Rinard, M., Panangaden, P.: Semantic foundations of concurrent constraint programming. In: Proceedings of Symposium on Principles of Programming Languages, Orlando, Florida, pp. 333–352 (1991)
13. Smolka, G.: The Oz programming model. In: van Leeuwen, J. (ed.) Computer Science Today. LNCS, vol. 1000, pp. 324–343. Springer, Heidelberg (1995)
14. Tarim, S.A., Manandhar, S., Walsh, T.: Stochastic constraint programming: A scenario-based approach. Constraints 11(1), 53–80 (2006)
15. Thévenod-Fosse, P., Waeselynck, H.: An investigation of statistical software testing. Journal of Sotware Testing, Verification and Reliability 1(2), 5–25 (1991)
16. Walsh, T.: Stochastic constraint programming. In: Proceedings of the 15th European Conference on Artificial Intelligence, Lyon, France, pp. 111–115. IOS Press, Amsterdam, Trento, Italy (2002)
17. Yorke-Smith, N., Gervet, C.: Certainty closure: A framework for reliable constraint reasoning with uncertainty. In: Proceedings of the International Conference on Principles and Practice of Constraint Programming, Kinsale, Ireland. LNCS, pp. 769–783. Springer, Heidelberg (2003)

A Multi-engine Solver for Quantified Boolean Formulas

Luca Pulina and Armando Tacchella*

DIST, Università di Genova, Viale Causa, 13 – 16145 Genova, Italy
{Luca.Pulina,Armando.Tacchella}@unige.it

Abstract. In this paper we study the problem of yielding robust performances from current state-of-the-art solvers for quantified Boolean formulas (QBFs). Building on top of existing QBF solvers, we implement a new multi-engine solver which can inductively learn its solver selection strategy. Experimental results confirm that our solver is always more robust than each single engine, that it is stable with respect to various perturbations, and that such results can be partially explained by a handful of features playing a crucial role in our solver.

1 Introduction

The problem of evaluating quantified Boolean formulas (QBFs) is one of the cornerstones of Complexity Theory. In its most general form, it is the prototypical PSPACE-complete problem, also known as QSAT [1]. Introducing limitations on the number and the placement of alternating quantifiers, QSAT is complete for each class in the polynomial hierarchy (see, e.g., [2]). Therefore, QBFs can be seen as a low-level language in which high-level descriptions of several hard combinatorial problems can be encoded to find a solution by means of a QBF solver. The quantified constraint satisfaction problem is one relevant example of such classes (see, e.g., [3]), and it has been shown that QBFs can provide compact propositional encodings in many automated reasoning tasks (see, e.g., [4,5,6]). To make such approach effective, QBF solvers ought to be robust, i.e., able to perform well across different problem classes. The results of the yearly QBF solvers competitions [7] show, on the contrary, that QBF solvers are rather brittle. This is to be expected, since every heuristic algorithm will occasionally find problem instances that are exceptionally hard to solve, while the same instances can easily be tackled by resorting to another algorithm, or by using a different heuristic (see, e.g., [8]).

In this paper we study the problem of yielding robust performances from current state-of-the-art QBF solvers. We start by considering syntactic features of QBFs, e.g., the number of variables, the number of quantifier alternations and other inexpensively computable parameters. We focus on the results of the last QBF solvers competition (QBFEVAL'06) [7], and show that the above features are sufficient to hint the best solver to run on each formula. To empirically validate our conclusions, we implement AQME (Adaptive QBF Multi-Engine), a new QBF solver which is based on existing state-of-the-art systems, and which can learn its engine selection strategy using different inductive models. We validate AQME performances against its engines using

* The authors wish to thank the Italian Ministry of University and Research for its financial support, and the anonymous reviewers who helped to improve the original manuscript.

C. Bessiere (Ed.): CP 2007, LNCS 4741, pp. 574–589, 2007.

QBFEVAL'06 formulas, and a sample of QBFEVAL'07 formulas that have been used neither in the design of AQME, nor in previous validations. Our experiments confirm that AQME is more robust than each single engine. Considering various perturbations of the QBFEVAL'06 dataset, we show that AQME is also stable, i.e., its performances are fairly independent of the dataset on which its engine selection strategy is learned. Finally, we show that these results can be partially explained by a handful of features which play a crucial role in AQME. Such features can be related to differences among the engines of AQME, and thus they bring supporting evidence to our design.

Our approach is inspired by the literature on algorithm portfolios [8,9], and it is related also to [10], wherein the implementation of the SATZILLA solver portfolio for propositional satisfiability (SAT) is described. However, both [8] and [9] do not consider Machine Learning techniques in order to learn and adapt the engine selection policy, whilst the results of [10] are limited to SAT. Since QSAT is a generalization of SAT, our work considers problem classes in PSPACE that extend beyond NP, and provides results that are typical of such classes. An independent contribution along the same way of ours is [11], wherein the problem of dynamically adapting the heuristics of a solver is also considered.

The paper is structured as follows. In Section 2 we review the syntax of QBFs, the features that we consider, and the essentials of the datasets from QBFEVAL'06/07. In Section 3 we discuss the design of AQME, and in Section 4 we present the experimental validation of AQME on the QBFEVAL'06/07 datasets. In Section 5 we present results about the stability of AQME under different point of views, and the experiments aimed at isolating the features playing a crucial role in AQME. We conclude the paper in Section 6 with some final remarks.

2 Preliminaries

The syntax of QBFs Consider a set P of propositional letters. A *variable* is an element of P. A *literal* is a variable or the negation of a variable. In the following, for any literal l, $|l|$ is the variable occurring in l, and $\bar{l}$ is $\neg l$ if l is a variable, and is $|l|$ otherwise. A literal is *positive* if $|l| = l$ and *negative* otherwise. A *clause* C is an n-ary $(n \geq 0)$ disjunction of literals such that, for any two distinct disjuncts l, l' in C, it is not the case that $|l| = |l'|$. A *propositional formula* is a k-ary $(k \geq 0)$ conjunction of clauses. A *QBF* is an expression of the form

$$Q_1 Z_1 ... Q_k Z_k \Phi \qquad k \geq 0 \tag{1}$$

where, for each $1 \leq i \leq k$, Q_i is a quantifier, either existential $Q_i = \exists$ or universal $Q_i = \forall$, such that $Q_i \neq Q_{i+1}$, and the set of variables $Z_i = z_{i,1}, \ldots z_{i,m_i}$ is a *quantified set*. The expression $Q_i Z_i$ stands for $Q_i z_{i,1} \ldots Q_i z_{i,m_i}$, and Φ is a propositional formula in the variables $Z_1, \ldots, Z_k$. The expression $Q_1 Z_1 \ldots Q_k Z_k$ is the *prefix* and Φ is the *matrix* of (1). A literal l is *existential* if $|l| \in Z_i$ for some $1 \leq i \leq k$ and $\exists Z_i$ belongs to the prefix of (1), and it is *universal* otherwise. In the prefix, $k - 1$ is the number of *alternations*, and $k - i + 1$ is the *level* of all the variables contained in the set Z_i $(1 \leq i \leq k)$; the level of a literal l is the same as $|l|$. Similarly to variables, if $Q_i = \exists$ then the quantifier set Z_i is existential, and universal otherwise.

Representing QBFs In order to perform inductive inference on QBFs, we transform them into vectors of numeric values, where each value represents a specific feature. In particular, we consider the following basic features:

- c, total number of clauses; c_1, c_2, c_3 total number of clauses with 1, 2 and more than two existential literals, respectively; c_h, c_{dh} total number of Horn and dual-Horn clauses, respectively;
- v, total number of variables; $v_\exists$, $v_\forall$, total number of existential and universal variables, respectively; l_{tot}, total number of literals; vs, $vs_\exists$, $vs_\forall$, distribution of the number of variables per quantifier set, considering all the variables, and focusing on existential and universal variables, respectively; s, $s_\exists$, $s_\forall$, number of total, existential and universal, quantifier sets;
- l, distribution of the number of literals in each clause; l_+, l_-, $l_\exists$, $l_{\exists+}$, $l_{\exists-}$, $l_\forall$, $l_{\forall+}$, $l_{\forall-}$, distribution of the number of positive, negative, existential, positive existential, negative existential, universal, positive universal, negative universal number of literals in each clauses, respectively.
- r, distribution of the number of variable occurrences r_+, r_-, $r_\exists$, $r_{\exists+}$, $r_{\exists-}$, $r_\forall$, $r_{\forall+}$, $r_{\forall-}$, distribution of the number of positive, negative, existential, positive existential, negative existential, universal, positive universal, negative universal variable occurrences, respectively; wr, wr_+, ... (as above), distributions of the number of variable occurrences weighted according to the level in the prefix.

We also consider the following combined features:

- p, distribution of the values of the products, computed for each existential variable x, between the number of occurrences of x and the number of occurrences of $\neg x$; wp, the same as p, where each product is weighted according to the prefix level.
- $\frac{c}{v}$, the classic clauses-to-variables ratio, and for each $x \in \{l, r, wr\}$ the following ratios (on mean values):
  - $\frac{x_+}{x}$, $\frac{x_-}{x}$, $\frac{x_+}{x_-}$, balance ratios;
  - $\frac{x_\exists}{x}$, $\frac{x_{\exists+}}{x}$, $\frac{x_{\exists-}}{x}$, $\frac{x_{\exists+}}{x_\exists}$, $\frac{x_{\exists-}}{x_\exists}$, $\frac{x_{\exists+}}{x_{\exists-}}$, $\frac{x_{\exists+}}{x_+}$, $\frac{x_{\exists-}}{x_-}$, balance ratios (existential part);
  - $\frac{x_\forall}{x}$, $\frac{x_{\forall+}}{x}$, $\frac{x_{\forall-}}{x}$, $\frac{x_{\forall+}}{x_+}$, $\frac{x_{\forall-}}{x_-}$, $\frac{x_{\forall+}}{x_\forall}$, $\frac{x_{\forall-}}{x_\forall}$, $\frac{x_{\forall+}}{x_{\forall-}}$, balance ratios (universal part);
- $\frac{c_1}{c}$, $\frac{c_2}{c}$, $\frac{c_3}{c}$, $\frac{c_h}{c}$, $\frac{c_{dh}}{c}$, $\frac{c_h}{c_{dh}}$, i.e., balance ratios between different kinds of clauses.

The choice of the above features is dictated by several factors, including previous related work (see, e.g. [10]), inexpensiveness, and, in the case of $(w)r$ and $(w)p$, also specific considerations about the nature of QBFs. Notice that totals such as, e.g., c or v, yield a very abstract representation of QBFs, i.e., specific values of such features may correspond to several – possibly diverse – QBFs. On the other hand, distributions such as, e.g., l or r, give a more detailed representation of the underlying QBF, at the expense of an increased complexity. For each distribution we consider only its mean and its standard deviation from the mean, measuring the center and the spread of the distribution, respectively. Overall, for each QBF we compute 141 features, which is a fairly large number compared to previous related work (e.g., SATZILLA [10] computes "only" 83 features). However, the median CPU time spent to compute all the 141 features, e.g., on the QBFEVAL'06 formulas, is 0.04s (min. 0.00s, max. 2.04s), so we can afford to keep all of them and avoid missing something important, at least in the preliminary stages.

The QBF solvers competition. QBFEVAL'06 [7] is the first competition of QBF solvers, and the fourth event in a series dating back to 2003. The data used in this paper are

Table 1. QBFEVAL'06/07 datasets synopses: "#" is the number of formulas per suite, and the remaining columns are the statistics – (Min)imum, (Med)ian, and (Max)imum – regarding the number of existential ($v_\exists$), and universal ($v_\forall$) variables, the number of quantified sets (s), the number of clauses (c) and the total number of literals (l_{tot}).

QBFEVAL'06 Suite	#	$v_\exists$			$v_\forall$			s			c			l_{tot}		
		Min	Med	Max	Min	Med	Max	Min	Med	Max	Min	Med	Max	Min	Med	Max
Ansotegui	10	1931	3404.5	8797	16	31	48	5	10	17	12973	28140	78971	48613	108335	314239
Ayari	18	162	2348	27767	48	256	1080	2	4	7	530	4480.5	34659	3110	16981.5	90169
Biere	74	14	970	4497	1	25.5	440	3	3	17	37	2764	13063	85	6448	30479
Gent-Rowley	3	3949	4629	8038	50	50	90	21	21	31	12868	15588	27363	45367	55567	96780
Herbstritt	28	1145	3904	6728	41	139	189	7	9	11	3091	10648	18742	7211	24844	43730
Ling	6	63	65	102	7	7.5	10	3	3	3	446	560.5	1832	2805	3742	16884
Mneimneh-Sakallah	11	94	819	2107	23	153	437	3	3	3	254	2665	6967	647	6850	18165
Pan	85	32	904	5254	8	37	264	2	27	133	743	3274	131072	1784	8840	1310720
Rintanen	77	184	1052	4017	1	9	896	2	3	3	601	3568	178750	1505	9557	362756
Scholl-Becker	6	273	1058	1113	1	2.5	11	3	3	23	746	3646.5	3877	1762	8918.5	9500

QBFEVAL'07 Suite	#	$v_\exists$			$v_\forall$			s			c			l_{tot}		
		Min	Med	Max	Min	Med	Max	Min	Med	Max	Min	Med	Max	Min	Med	Max
Biere	47	105	7642	48097	2	101	1172	3	3	3	304	21538	143239	708	50254	334223
Herbstritt	39	472	3219	33803	0	13	170	1	3	341	1120	7428	95242	2546	16528	221130
Mangassarian-Veneris	7	2280	5548	68488	1	4	4	3	3	3	6263	16664	182894	14767	59412	517102
Palacios	7	171	1320	4191	4	7	11	3	3	3	1026	51076	67530	3477	152916	589575

obtained by running 16 versions of 11 solvers, namely OPENQBF, QBFL, QUAFFLE, QUBE, SSOLVE, YQUAFFLE, 2CLSQ, PREQUANTOR, QUANTOR, SKIZZO and SQBF. The first six solvers above are pure search-based engines, i.e., they are an extension to QSAT of the DLL algorithm for SAT [12], while the other ones are based on techniques such as Q-resolution [13], skolemization (see, e.g., [14]), variable expansion (see, e.g., [15]), or a combination thereof, possibly including also search as in 2CLSQ[1] and SKIZZO. Formulas used in QBFEVAL'06 were submitted to the competition and picked from QBFLIB [16]. In this paper we consider fixed structure formulas (FSFs for short) used in QBFEVAL'06. Intuitively, FSFs are resulting from encodings and/or artificial generators where a setting of the problem parameters yields a unique instance (see [17]). The competition ran in two tracks: the *short track*, where the solvers were limited to 600 CPU seconds, and the *marathon track*, where we alloted a time limit of 6000 CPU seconds. The memory was limited to 900MB in both tracks. Considering the results of the marathon track, out of 427 FSFs, 371 were solved (87% of the initial selection), 234 (55%) were declared satisfiable and 137 (32%) were declared unsatisfiable. The top-five solvers were: 2CLSQ, PREQUANTOR, SQBF, SKIZZO-0.9-ABS and QUANTOR. QUBE5.0, running hors-concours, was the best search-based solver, and it would have ranked fifth if running as a regular competitor. In the following, when speaking of the "QBFEVAL'06 dataset" we refer to a subset of 318 formulas obtained by discarding those that were easily solved by most of the competitors. A synopsis of such dataset is provided in Table 1 (top). For testing AQME against its engines, we also harness a random sample of 100 formulas from the QBFEVAL'07 [7] dataset such that no formula in this dataset is part of the QBFEVAL'06 dataset as well. A synopsis of the "QBFEVAL'07 dataset" is also shown in Table 1 (bottom), and a complete description of the problems in each suite for QBFEVAL'06/07 datasets can be found in [16].

[1] 2CLSQis indeed a multi-stage solver: a preprocessor is run in the first stage, and the solver QUANTOR is run in the second stage; if the second stage is not successful within a short time limit, a third stage based on a search-based decision procedure is accomplished.

Table 2. Classification of formulas according to their features and correspondence with solvers

Cluster ID	**1**	**2**	**3**	**4**	**5**	**6**	**7**	**8**	**9**	**10**	**11**
Formulas	6	3	30	15	28	7	1	2	4	2	26
Search	100%	67%	83%	100%	100%	–	–	–	–	–	–
Hybrid	–	33%	17%	–	–	100%	100%	100%	100%	100%	100%
2CLSQ	–	–	50%	–	–	43%	100%	50%	50%	100%	96%
OPENQBF	100%	–	–	–	–	–	–	–	–	–	–
PREQUANTOR	–	–	13%	–	–	29%	100%	50%	50%	100%	96%
QUAFFLE	–	–	–	–	–	–	–	–	–	–	–
QUANTOR	–	–	10%	–	–	29%	100%	50%	50%	100%	96%
QUBE	100%	–	77%	100%	100%	–	–	–	–	–	–
SQBF	–	–	–	–	–	29%	100%	50%	50%	100%	96%
SKIZZO	–	33%	10%	–	–	100%	100%	100%	100%	100%	77%
SSOLVE	100%	67%	17%	–	–	–	–	–	–	–	–
YQUAFFLE	–	–	–	40%	–	–	–	–	–	–	–

3 Designing a Multi-engine Solver for QBFs

The first and foremost design issue when developing AQME is whether the features described previously are sufficient to determine the best engine to run on each formula. We would like our features to be at least as descriptive as to discriminate between search-based solvers and the remaining ones, that we call "hybrid" in the following. Considering the QBFEVAL'06 dataset, we remove 194 formulas that were solved both by search and hybrid solvers, to end up with 124 formulas that are solved either by search solvers or hybrid ones, but not by both. We apply partition around medoids (PAM), a classical divisive clustering algorithm [18], to classify the formulas. We estimate the number of clusters using the silhouette coefficient of clustering quality [18], where the silhouette value is computed for each element of a cluster, ranging from -1 (bad) to 1 (good). We consider optimal the clustering such that the *average* silhouette is maximized, and we choose the number of clusters accordingly. In our experiments, eleven clusters yielded the maximum average silhouette value of 0.9. Finally, we compare the clusters with the percentage of formulas solved by search and hybrid solvers respectively. If the initial choice of features was a good one, then we expect to find a clear correlation between cluster membership and the likelihood of being solved by a particular kind of solver.

In Table 2 we present the results of the above analysis. In the table, each column corresponds to a cluster (**Cluster ID**) where we detail the number of formulas in the cluster (**Formulas**), the percentage of such formulas that were solved by search solvers (**Search**), and by hybrid solvers (**Hybrid**), respectively. For the sake of completeness, we report also the data about individual solvers or families thereof – QUBE, SKIZZO and SSOLVE data are the cumulative numbers considering the three versions of each solver as one. With the only exception of clusters #2 and #3, the features described in Section 2 enable us to automatically partition QBFs into classes such that we can predict with reasonable accuracy whether the best solver in each class is search-based or not. This is an indication that the features we consider are good candidates to hint the best engine to run on each formula. As a side effect, we can also see that our distinction between search and hybrid solvers does make sense, at least on the QBFEVAL'06 dataset. Indeed, search solvers perform badly on the clusters #6 – #11 dominated by hybrid solvers, while on the other clusters, either search solvers dominate, or there is always at least one search solver that performs better than any hybrid one.

The second design issue concerns the inductive models to implement in AQME. An inductive model is comprised of a *classifier*, i.e., a function that maps an unlabeled instance (a QBF) to a label (a solver), and an *inducer*, i.e., an algorithm that builds the classifier. In the following, we call *training set* the dataset on which inducers are trained, and *test set* the dataset on which classifiers are tested. While there is an overwhelming number of inductive models in the literature (see, e.g., [19]), we can somewhat limit the choice considering that AQME has to deal with numerical attributes (QBF features) and multiple class labels (engines). Moreover, we would like to avoid formulating specific hypotheses about the features, and thus we prefer inducers that are not based on hypotheses of normality or (in)dependence among the features. Finally, we also prefer inducers that do not require complex ad-hoc parameter tuning. Considering all the above, we chose to implement four inductive models in AQME, namely:

Decision trees (AQME-C4.5). A classifier arranged in a tree structure, wherein each inner node contains a test on some attributes, and each leaf node contains a label; we use C4.5 [20] to induce decision trees.

Decision rules (AQME-RIPPER). A classifier providing a set of "if-then-elsif" constructs, wherein the "if" part contains a test on some attributes and the "then" part contains a label; we use RIPPER [21] to induce decision rules.

Logistic regression (AQME-MLR). A classifier providing a linear estimation, i.e., a hyperplane, of the hypersurfaces that separate the class labels in the feature space; we use the multinomial logistic regression (MLR) inducer described in [22].

1-nearest-neighbor (AQME-1NN). A classifier yielding the label of the training instance which is closer to the given test instance, whereby closeness is evaluated using some proximity measure, e.g. Euclidean distance; we use the method described in [23] to store the training instances for fast lookup.

The above methods are fairly robust, efficient, they are not subject to stringent hypotheses[2] on the training data, and they do not need complex parameter tuning. They are also "orthogonal", as they use algorithms based on radically different approaches.

One final remark concerns the solvers that should be used as the basic engines in AQME. While it is clear that at least one search and one hybrid solver should be selected, some preliminary experiments showed that choosing only the best search (QuBE5.0) and hybrid (2CLSQ) solvers is not rewarding. On the other hand, using all the sixteen competitors altogether rises the chance of getting a bad prediction because of aliasing. We opted for an intermediate solution based on our knowledge of the solvers, wherein we include five search solvers, namely QuBE3.0, QuBE5.0, SSOLVE+UT, QUAFFLE, and YQUAFFLE, and three hybrid ones, namely 2CLSQ, QUANTOR, and SKIZZO-0.9-STD. In the following, we will refer to SKIZZO-0.9-STD as SKIZZO, and to SSOLVE-UT as SSOLVE.

4 Experimental Evaluation

All the experiments that we performed ran on a farm of 10 identical rack-mount PCs, equipped with 3.2GHz PIV processors, 1GB of RAM and running Ubuntu/GNU Linux

[2] MLR is guaranteed to yield optimal discriminants – in the least squares sense – only when the dataset is partitioned into classes characterized by a multivariate normal distribution. If this is not the case, MLR can still provide us with a reasonable, albeit suboptimal, classification.

Table 3. Estimating the accuracy of various versions of AQME using cross validation

		AQME-C4.5				AQME-MLR				AQME-1NN				AQME-RIPPER				Best Engine	
CV	**N**	**#**	**Time**	α_1	α_2	**#**	**Time**	α_1	α_2	**#**	**Time**	α_1	α_2	**#**	**Time**	α_1	α_2	**#**	**Time**
1	32	30	12723	0.93	0.97	30	12723	0.93	0.97	29	18724	0.90	0.97	31	6740	0.96	0.97	25	43565
2	32	32	201	0.99	1	32	201	0.99	1	31	6196	0.97	0.97	32	658	0.99	0.98	25	42630
3	31	31	60	0.99	1	31	60	0.99	1	31	153	0.99	0.99	30	6060	0.97	0.97	20	66668
4	32	32	4098	0.98	1	32	4098	0.98	1	31	10095	0.95	0.98	29	22087	0.88	0.97	25	51609
5	32	30	12832	0.93	0.97	30	12832	0.93	0.97	32	955	0.99	1	30	12959	0.93	0.97	22	60601
6	32	31	10543	0.94	0.98	31	10543	0.94	0.98	31	10278	0.95	0.98	28	28294	0.84	0.97	22	64267
7	32	31	6156	0.97	0.97	31	6156	0.97	0.97	32	158	1	1	30	13515	0.93	0.97	21	67569
8	31	31	1030	0.99	1	31	1030	0.99	1	29	12954	0.93	0.97	27	24375	0.87	0.97	22	55954
9	32	32	2990	0.98	0.98	32	2990	0.98	0.98	32	1074	0.99	0.99	32	1071	0.99	0.99	24	50055
10	32	32	1509	0.99	1	32	1509	0.99	1	30	13426	0.93	0.97	31	7509	0.96	0.97	25	47211
Median			3544	0.98	0.99		3544	0.98	0.99		8146	0.96	0.98		10234	0.94	0.97		53782

(distribution `Edgy 6.10`). We evaluated the performances of AQME[3] in two rounds of experiments. In the first round, we wish to estimate its performances on the QBFEVAL'06 dataset. To this end, we consider *accuracy*, usually defined as the ratio of correctly predicted instances versus the total number of instances in the test set (see, e.g., [19]). Such definition is not adequate in our case, since it assumes that all the wrong predictions have the same – unitary – cost. Indeed, in AQME a wrong prediction has a cost which depends on the performances of the solver predicted in place of the best one. Therefore, we consider different kind of accuracies defined as:

$$\alpha_1 := 1 - \frac{\sum_{\varphi \in \Gamma} t(\varphi)}{L|\Gamma|} \qquad \alpha_2 := 1 - \frac{1}{|\Gamma|} \sum_{\varphi \in \Gamma} \frac{t(\varphi) - t^*(\varphi)}{t(\varphi)} \tag{2}$$

where Γ is a set of formulas, $t(\varphi)$ is the time spent by the selected engine evaluating φ, L is the time limit imposed on the engines, and $t^*(\varphi)$ is the time spent by the best engine on φ. The parameter α_1 is close to 1 when AQME solves most of the formulas in Γ without getting close to the time limit L. The parameter α_2 does not depend on L: if α_2 is close to 1, then the time spent by AQME on most formulas is close to the ideal solver always faring the best time among the engines. Both α_1 and α_2 are valid for our purposes, but α_1 turns out to be slightly more conservative as we show in the following.

We estimate the accuracy of AQME on the QBFEVAL'06 dataset using cross-validation (see, e.g., [19]), described in [24] to be one of the most reliable methods for our purposes. In particular, as suggested in [24], we use a ten-times ten-fold stratified cross-validation, whereby the original dataset is divided into ten subsets, or folds, such that each subset is a stratified sample, i.e., it contains exactly the same proportions of class labels that are present in the original dataset. Once the folds are computed, nine out of ten are used for training an inducer, and the remaining one is used to test the classifier. The process is repeated ten times, each time using a different fold for testing, and thus yielding ten different samples of the accuracy value. We can then compute some statistic, e.g., the median, to reach our final estimate of the accuracy.

In Table 3 we show the detailed results of cross-validation. In the table (going from left to right), the first column (**CV**) denotes the i-th fold being used as test set ($1 \leq i \leq 10$); the second column (**N**) contains the number of formulas in each fold; the five

[3] The working implementation of AQME is freely available upon request to the authors.

Table 4. AQME vs. its engines on the QBFEVAL'07 dataset

Solver	AQME-C4.5	AQME-MLR	QUBE5.0	AQME-RIPPER	QUBE3.0	SKIZZO
#	66	65	61	60	57	57
Time	983	1109	1076	868	291	1379
Solver	AQME-1NN	2CLSQ	SSOLVE	YQUAFFLE	QUANTOR	QUAFFLE
#	54	53	53	51	45	42
Time	1008	108	1251	84	42	253

groups of columns contain the results of AQME (labeled after the model), and the performances of the best single engine on each fold (**Best engine**). In each group, except the fifth, four columns report, respectively, the number of formulas solved (#), the cumulative CPU seconds to solve them (**Time**) – *including* the default time limit value (6000s) for the instances that were not solved – and the accuracy obtained by AQME on the fold according to the definitions (2) (α_1 and α_2); in the fifth group, the columns "#" and "**Time**" have the same meaning, and we do not report an accuracy value. The last row of Table 3, reports the median cumulative CPU time, and the median accuracy for all the versions of AQME. Notice that we do not report the time spent to train the inducer, to compute the features and to classify the instances, since it is negligible with respect to the time spent to evaluate QBFs.

As we can see from Table 3, AQME is more efficient and robust than the best engine on each fold. Overall, even AQME-RIPPER, the weakest version of AQME according to these experiments, is cumulatively much faster than an *ideal* solver yielding top performances on each fold.[4] The accuracy estimate tells us that both AQME-C4.5 and AQME-MLR have a very thin chance of missing the best solver for a given QBF. Incidentally, these models turn out to yield exactly the same predictions on this dataset. Notice that the overall accuracy is never less than the 0.85 threshold, even under unfavorable conditions. As we anticipated, α_1 is slightly more conservative than α_2, so we view the the former as a more realistic estimator for the real (unknown) accuracy.

In the second round of experiments, we train AQME on the whole QBFEVAL'06 dataset, and we run it against its engines on the QBFEVAL'07 dataset. This is a typical deployment scenario, wherein the classifiers are used to predict the best solver on previously unseen QBFs. In Table 4 we show the results of the above experiment. The table is split in two parts, the one on top reporting the results of the best six solvers, and the one at the bottom reporting the remaining ones. Each part has three rows, including the name of the solver and the performance data, with the same meaning as in Table 3.

Looking at Table 4, and considering that 27 formulas out of 100 were not solved by any engine within a time limit of 600 seconds, we can see that AQME mostly confirms the results obtained on the QBFEVAL'06 dataset. In particular, the accuracy of C4.5 and MLR is almost the same, and it is higher than RIPPER and 1NN. C4.5 and MLR also yield the best solvers on this dataset, with 66 and 65 formulas solved, respectively. The best engine (QUBE5.0) ranks only third-best since it cannot solve 5 formulas from the "Biere" suite: C4.5 and MLR solve them by picking QUANTOR and 2CLSQ instead. On the other hand, notice that 1NN is ranking below all the other AQME versions *and* three of its engines, namely QUBE5.0, QUBE3.0, and SKIZZO. The cause of 1NN

[4] The fact that the cumulative median time of the "Best engine" is that of an ideal solver, stems from the fact that the best solver on each of the folds shown in Table 3 is not always the same.

behavior can be ascribed to the fact that this method is quite prone to overfitting the training data, and thus generalize poorly, but in this case it is also linked to a dimensionality problem, since the training set contains formulas whose features have relatively small values compared to the ones in the test set. Therefore, the distance between the test formulas and the training formulas computed by 1NN could be pretty much the same for all the test formulas, thus resulting in a substantial aliasing. Another factor to be considered, which explains also the weak performances of RIPPER, is that the QBFEVAL'07 test set is quite challenging for AQME trained on QBFEVAL'06 dataset, since the former favors search solvers over hybrid ones – QUBE5.0 and QUBE3.0 perform as well as or better than, e.g., SKIZZO – while the contrary is true for the latter – the top-five solvers in QBFEVAL'06 are all hybrid, with the exception of QUBE5.0. As we will see in Section 5.1, a training set biased in favor of a given solver may hurt the performances of AQME more than other kinds of perturbations. However, in spite of the unfavorable scenario, at least two versions of AQME are able to stand out and guarantee a a more robust behavior than any of the engines.

5 Validating the Multi-engine Approach

The results presented in Section 4 are very positive. However, there are at least two questions of interest that remain unanswered. The first is whether the results that we obtained are valid only within the context of QBFEVAL'06. Since any classifier learned in AQME will always be dependent on the training data – as any approach based on inductive inference (see, e.g., [19]) – the real question is *how strong* is such dependence. In Section 5.1 we study this problem by investigating the stability of AQME in the face of perturbations that can affect the dataset used for training/testing. Since the features described in Section 2 have shown interesting properties, the second question is whether only some of them are important, and whether we can find any relationships between such features and the basic engines. We devote Section 5.2 to study this problem.

5.1 Assessing (in)Dependence from the QBFEVAL'06 Dataset

The first experiment that is aimed at understanding the effect of random changes in the composition of the dataset used for training/testing. We compute several pairs of training/test sets by removing instances uniformly at random without repetition from the QBFEVAL'06 dataset. The removed instances are used to build test sets, while the remaining instances are used for training. By increasing the percentage of removed instances, we can increase the level of departure with respect to the original dataset, and thus we can assess the stability of our results with respect to an increasing perturbation. We remove 10% to 50% of the original instances, in increments of 10%, and we randomly generate 50 training/testing sets for each percentage of removed instances.

In Table 5 we show the results of our experiments. The first column contains the solver names, and it is followed by five groups of columns, one for each percentage of removed instances, with an indication of the cardinality of the test set; the two subgroups "**B**" (resp. "**W**") show the best (resp. worst) case performances of each solver across 50 sampled test sets. The columns "#" and "Time" contain the number of instances solved

Table 5. Results obtained by randomly choosing increasingly smaller datasets for training

	10% (32)				20% (63)				30% (95)				40% (126)				50% (159)			
	B		W		B		W		B		W		B		W		B		W	
	#	Time	#	Time	#	Time	#	Time	#	Time	#	Time	#	Time	#	Time	#	Time	#	Time
AQME-1NN	**32**	**162**	**28**	**616**	**63**	**995**	**57**	**928**	**95**	**1049**	**88**	**4757**	**126**	**6542**	**116**	**9049**	**158**	**4713**	**147**	**11707**
AQME-C4.5	**32**	**164**	**30**	**2312**	**63**	**324**	**59**	**933**	**95**	**1843**	**90**	**7028**	**126**	**2427**	**119**	**7178**	**158**	**7202**	**149**	**5977**
AQME-RIPPER	**32**	**171**	28	1012	**63**	**1595**	54	6422	93	1122	84	9342	123	7250	107	12868	**156**	**7588**	131	9702
AQME-MLR	32	182	**28**	**134**	62	271	**56**	**1537**	**93**	**972**	**87**	**2338**	**123**	**2686**	**110**	**5487**	156	11791	**140**	**5820**
2CLSQ	27	2021	18	261	50	5351	38	2773	77	15655	62	9495	95	11752	81	8431	121	13329	102	7384
SKIZZO	24	1644	16	5036	47	3414	36	5701	73	13274	57	6666	91	15763	78	17965	114	16903	100	33631
QUBE5.0	24	3298	14	3352	44	6140	33	5695	68	18318	49	9253	87	21702	72	5929	107	20244	89	19293
SSOLVE	23	10847	13	3666	41	18574	28	18335	61	27736	43	6760	67	23668	60	16443	96	39064	77	32658
QUANTOR	21	156	12	86	42	45	30	3265	64	408	47	3544	79	3940	66	3806	101	776	79	359
QUBE3.0	20	6563	8	4471	32	7530	17	10959	46	7867	29	11971	57	19515	36	10325	75	18256	49	11792
YQUAFFLE	19	1097	5	499	29	3233	16	893	43	11110	24	8867	53	11109	35	9597	72	21023	47	10133
QUAFFLE	16	980	6	5869	29	5453	15	1491	43	8481	25	7646	53	9090	37	8592	66	14927	47	4936

and the cumulative CPU seconds to solve them, respectively. The top-three performers in each subgroup are highlighted with bold text.[5]

Looking at Table 5, we can conclude that the performances of AQME are substantially stable and fairly independent of the relative composition of the training vs. the test sets. Notice that, considering the best case scenarios, and with the only exception of the "**50%**" group, at least one version of AQME is able to solve all the instances in the test set. Moreover, the ratio between the number of instances solved in the best case scenario and in the worst case scenario for AQME is closer to 1 than all its engines. This indicates that AQME is more robust than its components for all but substantial departures from the QBFEVAL'06 dataset.

The second experiment that we describe is aimed at understanding how much AQME is sensitive to perturbations that diminish the maximum amount of CPU time granted to the solvers. The time limit in QBFEVAL'06 is 6000s. For this experiment, we considered four datasets extracted from QBFEVAL'06 by setting the time limit to 10, 5, 1 and 0.5 seconds, and then considering all the formulas that were solved by at least one competitor within each given time limit. We used the time-capped datasets as training sets, and the remaining instances as test sets. Notice that the size of the sets increases as the time limit decreases, so this experiment explores the possibility of training AQME with a small number of easy-to-solve formulas, and then deploying it on a large number of hard-to-solve ones.

In Table 6 we show the results of the above experiment. The table is arranged similarly to Table 5, modulo the fact that best- and worst-case performances coincide, since the test sets are obtained deterministically. Looking at Table 6, we can see that even when training on relatively easy formulas (the **0.5** group), the four AQME versions perform substantially better than every other engine. This result confirms that AQME models are relatively immune to changes in the training set that have an impact on the time resources alloted to the solvers.

Our third experiment aims to establish how much AQME is sensitive to a training set that is biased in favor of a given solver. For each engine, we consider all the formulas that it can evaluate within the time limit as the training set, and the remaining formulas as the test set. In Table 7 we show the results of the above experiment. The first column contains the solver names, and it is followed by eight group of columns, one for each

[5] In case of ties on the number of problems solved, the solver yielding the smallest time is preferred.

Table 6. Results obtained by choosing increasingly easier datasets for training

	10s (49)		5s (61)		1s (110)		0.5s (140)	
	#	Time	#	Time	#	Time	#	Time
AQME-C4.5	**46**	**14501**	**56**	**14569**	**100**	**14893**	**130**	**16013**
AQME-1NN	**45**	**14451**	**55**	**14476**	**96**	**22807**	**129**	**17769**
AQME-MLR	**37**	**12798**	39	7322	**92**	**8094**	**115**	**12985**
AQME-RIPPER	34	9397	**49**	**12271**	91	10125	114	9652
QuBE5.0	25	16622	29	16653	55	18354	80	23496
2CLSQ	13	2238	20	2334	52	7961	66	17781
sKizzo	13	11780	21	14341	52	22956	65	23554
QuBE3.0	12	8503	12	8503	21	9505	30	10554
QUANTOR	11	3542	18	3634	45	4156	56	4409
SSOLVE	11	6178	12	8124	27	17329	36	19653
YQUAFFLE	5	3011	5	3011	14	4381	24	13424
QUAFFLE	2	87	2	87	17	3689	24	4305

Table 7. Results obtained by biasing the dataset used for training

	2CLSQ		QUAFFLE		QUANTOR		QuBE3.0		QuBE5.0		sKizzo		SSOLVE		YQUAFFLE	
	#	Time	#	Time	#	Time	#	Time	#	Time	#	Time	#	Time	#	Time
AQME-1NN	**75**	**19859**	**155**	**21624**	57	11741	**178**	**5519**	**106**	**4890**	**82**	**15276**	79	13205	**153**	**14631**
AQME-C4.5	**81**	**13493**	118	2309	**80**	**12896**	**174**	**9816**	88	4893	**87**	**15632**	**80**	**13681**	**147**	**10319**
AQME-RIPPER	70	16441	**148**	**14640**	**96**	**22764**	130	4214	99	4944	57	14636	**118**	**14565**	**149**	**10699**
AQME-MLR	58	14812	**159**	**25304**	61	16585	**166**	**4099**	93	4754	71	14511	80	17981	143	8942
2CLSQ	–	–	112	14509	50	19759	118	2762	**99**	**885**	33	16888	71	14115	116	3877
QUAFFLE	6	246	–	–	22	870	28	6088	17	4737	13	651	27	3455	26	4833
QUANTOR	8	3655	86	4348	–	–	106	4450	86	647	14	311	61	1182	100	4396
QuBE3.0	17	6851	33	7043	47	12586	–	–	4	4299	33	8742	35	8151	20	11131
QuBE5.0	**74**	**15225**	98	16723	**103**	**17567**	80	10069	–	–	**88**	**17368**	**93**	**15399**	94	19687
sKizzo	25	11571	111	25276	48	19581	126	29832	**105**	**27100**	–	–	64	20431	121	21946
SSOLVE	21	13197	83	35501	53	35980	86	28130	68	25035	22	23094	–	–	92	37296
YQUAFFLE	8	649	24	5239	34	4913	13	10664	11	7379	21	3293	34	9899	–	–

engine of AQME whereupon the training set is biased. The number of instances in each of the eight test sets is (from left to right): 96, 202, 138, 197, 121, 104, 146, and 204. The table is then arranged as Table 6. When the training set is biased in favor of a given solver, a dash indicates that the corresponding test set does not contain any formula that can be evaluated by such solver within the time limit.

Looking at the results of Table 7, we can see that a biased training set poses a serious challenge to AQME, but, with the exception of the training set biased on QUANTOR, at least one of its versions is always the best solver in each group. According to the specific bias, a different version of AQME, if any, is best. In particular, AQME-1NN is the best solver when the bias is in favor of QuBE3.0, QuBE5.0 and YQUAFFLE; AQME-C4.5, AQME-RIPPER and AQME-MLR are the best solvers when the bias is in favor of 2CLSQ, SSOLVE, and QUAFFLE, respectively. Notice that when the bias is in favor of 2CLSQ, QuBE5.0, sKizzo, and SSOLVE, then the solvers QuBE5.0, and sKizzo are very close to the performances of AQME. These results can be explained if we consider that removing a specific solver may substantially alter the proportion of formulas in the training/test sets that are more likely to be solved by search rather than hybrid solvers. For instance, since QuBE5.0 is the best search solver, the test set corresponding to the training set biased on QuBE5.0 will be comprised almost completely by formulas that are more likely to be solved by hybrid solvers, which explains the good performances of sKizzo in this case.

	RIPPER	**C4.5**	**MLR**
1NN	$\frac{wr_{\forall-}}{wr_-}$ * $\frac{wr_{\forall+}}{wr}$ * $\frac{r_{\forall+}}{r}$ $\frac{r_{\forall-}}{r}$ $\frac{r_{\forall-}}{r_-}$ $\frac{wr_{\forall}}{wr}$ $\frac{wr_{\forall-}}{wr}$	$\frac{wr_{\forall-}}{wr_-}$ * $\frac{wr_{\forall}}{wr}$ * $\frac{r_{\forall+}}{r}$ $\frac{wr_{\forall+}}{wr}$ $\frac{wr_{\forall-}}{wr}$ $\frac{r_{\forall}}{r}$ $\frac{r_{\forall-}}{r}$ $\frac{r_{\forall-}}{r_-}$	–
RIPPER		l^* $r_{\exists}^*$ p^* $\frac{wr_{\forall}}{wr}$ * $\frac{wr_{\forall+}}{wr}$ * l_-, $r_{\exists+}$ r_+ r_- $\frac{c}{v}$ $\frac{r_{\forall+}}{r}$ $\frac{r_{\forall}}{r}$ $\frac{r_{\forall-}}{r}$ $\frac{r_{\forall-}}{r_-}$ $\frac{wr_{\forall-}}{wr}$ $\frac{wr_{\forall-}}{wr_-}$	l^* l_-^* p^* $r_{\exists}^*$ $r_{\exists-}$ $\frac{c}{v}$
C4.5			l^* l_-^* $r_{\exists}^*$ p $r_{\exists-}$ $\frac{c}{v}$

	FS		M		FS+M	
Solver	**#**	**Time**	**#**	**Time**	**#**	**Time**
QUBE5.0	**61**	**1076**	**61**	**1076**	**61**	**1076**
AQME-RIPPER	**58**	**335**	54	712	53	1426
SKIZZO	**57**	**1379**	**57**	**1379**	**57**	**1379**
QUBE3.0	57	291	**57**	**291**	57	291
AQME-MLR	53	1274	53	1219	53	1013
SSOLVE	53	1251	53	1251	53	1251
2CLSQ	53	108	53	108	53	108
YQUAFFLE	51	84	51	84	51	84
AQME-1NN	46	614	51	625	51	1176
AQME-C4.5	45	75	55	1083	**58**	**1096**
QUANTOR	45	42	45	42	45	42
QUAFFLE	42	253	42	253	42	253

Fig. 1. Relevant features common to various models implemented in AQME (left) and AQME vs. its engines on the QBFEVAL'07 dataset considering only subsets of features (right)

5.2 Assessing the Relevant Features

In all the experiments presented so far, we train and test AQME considering the whole set of features, and the results are rewarding. Now we are interested to know (i) whether a *subset* of the features considered still enables AQME to reach acceptable performances and (ii) whether such features have some relationship with algorithmic differences among its engines. Our main task is thus to isolate a subset of features that are *relevant*, i.e., such that AQME restricted to these features can reach, or at least get close to, the same performances obtained using the whole set of features. We would like the features in such a set to be *model-independent*, i.e., relevant for all the models implemented in AQME. Clearly, since different features may be relevant for different models, model-independent features should hint more clearly to the relationships, if any, between properties of QBFs and differences among the engines of AQME.

The question then becomes how to find the relevant features, since exhaustive search over 2^k subsets of k features is impractical. We consider feature forward selection (FS), a greedy search in the space of possible subsets of features (see, e.g., [19]). FS starts with an empty subset of features. Each feature that is not already in the current subset is tentatively added to it, and the resulting set of features is evaluated using, e.g., cross validation. The effect of adding each feature in turn is quantified, the best one is chosen, and the procedure continues. If no feature produces an improvement, the search ends. Since FS guarantees to find a *locally* optimal set of features, we compensate for this by considering the sets computed by FS augmented by all the features that are highly correlated with the elements of such sets. We assess correlation using Kendall τ, a coefficient that tests how much the trend of a feature is related to the trend of another. We consider two features to be significantly correlated whenever $|\tau| \geq 0.9$.

Figure 1 (left) contains the results of the above analysis arranged in a matrix, where each cell corresponds to a set obtained by intersecting the subsets of relevant features for any two models implemented in AQME. In each cell, the features marked with a

"*" are the ones originally spotted by FS, and mean values are considered for features corresponding to a distribution of values. According to our experiments there are no common relevant features between AQME-MLR and AQME-1NN, and thus no model-independent ones. However, non-empty intersections can be found across RIPPER, C4.5, and 1NN, as well as across RIPPER, C4.5, and MLR. We denote such intersections with F_1 and F_2:

$$\begin{array}{l} F_1 = \{\frac{wr_\forall}{wr}, \frac{wr_{\forall+}}{wr}, \frac{wr_{\forall-}}{wr}, \frac{wr_{\forall-}}{wr_-}, \frac{r_{\forall+}}{r}, \frac{r_{\forall-}}{r}, \frac{r_{\forall-}}{r_-}\} \\ F_2 = \{l, l_-, p, r_\exists, r_{\exists-}, \frac{c}{v}\} \end{array} \quad (3)$$

The features in F_1 are all variations of the ratio between the average (weighted) number of universal variable occurrences vs. the average (weighted) number of variable occurrences ($\frac{r_\forall}{r}$). Small (resp. large) values of this ratio indicate that the universal variables tend to occur less (resp. more) than the average. If we consider the runtime distribution of search vs. hybrid solvers on the QBFEVAL'06 dataset, we have that search solvers tend to perform better on small values of $\frac{r_\forall}{r}$, while the contrary is true for hybrid solvers. This is probably related to the fact that (a) the QBFEVAL'06 dataset is biased in favor of satisfiable formulas, and (b), for such formulas search solvers tend to spend a lot of time in checking all the combinations of universal variables. Solvers that are not based on search, on the other hand, do perform better on these kind of formulas, as long as they do not apply expansion of universal variables. In the case of weighted occurrences, since outer variables in the prefix have higher weight, either the number of levels is small, or the bulk of existential variables occurrences concerns variables appearing in the outer level of the prefix. Since the median number of quantifier sets in the QBFEVAL'06 dataset is 3 (min. 2, max. 133)[6] the first explanation is the one that applies to our results.

The features in F_2 are related to the distribution of the number of literals per clause (l, and l_-), the distribution of the values of the products between negative and positive occurrences of existential variables (p, and the related $r_\exists$ and $r_{\exists-}$), and the clauses-to-variables ratio ($\frac{c}{v}$). If we consider the runtime distribution of search vs. hybrid solvers, we have that search solvers tend to perform better for small values of the above parameters. For l (and l_-), we conjecture that this is related to the fact that in search solvers the number of steps, i.e., variable assignments, required to falsify a clause is proportional to the number of its literals, and thus longer clauses can hurt performances of search solvers. In the case of p, search solvers should be relatively insensitive to this parameter, while for solvers based, e.g., on variable elimination by Q-resolution, this parameter gives a rough estimate of the effort required to eliminate a variable. While it is somewhat peculiar that large values of p favor hybrid solvers in the QBFEVAL'06 dataset, considering also the results about $\frac{c}{v}$ and other features, we conjecture that this is due to the fact that hybrid solvers are able to solve some of the largest formulas in the dataset, and that this effect may be prevalent over others.

In order to check the significance of the features in the subsets F_1 and F_2 with respect to the whole set of features, we use the QBFEVAL'06 and QBFEVAL'07 datasets to

[6] The corresponding distribution is right-skewed, i.e., it has a long tail on the right, but most formulas have a fairly small number of quantifier sets.

train and test AQME, respectively. We consider $F_1 \cup F_2$ features, as well as others that may discriminate between search and hybrid solvers, and precisely:

- The number of quantifier sets s, a rough indicator of complexity.
- The mean value of $v_{s\exists}$ and $v_{s\forall}$, which are related to (i) the number of different Skolem functions, and the size of the parameters of a Skolem function, respectively, as well as (ii) the number of variables to be resolved away with Q-resolution or expanded, respectively (see [15,14]).
- $\frac{l_\exists}{l}$ and $\frac{l_\forall}{l}$ which are related to the mean number of variables that could be transformed to a Skolem function, and the mean number of variables that could be expanded with respect to the total variables in a clause;
- $\frac{l_-}{l}$ and $\frac{l_+}{l}$ which are related to the size of the antecedent and of the consequent, respectively, looking at each clause as an implication.

The results of the above experiment are shown in the table on Figure 1 (right). The organization of the table is the same used for the experiments of Section 5.1. The three groups of columns correspond to considering the features in $F_1 \cup F_2$ alone (**FS**), the features outlined above (**M**), or both subsets of features (**FS+M**). Looking at the table, we can see that in the case of the "**FS**" selection, only AQME-RIPPER is able to keep up with the best performers in the dataset, namely QUBE5.0, SKIZZO and QUBE3.0, while AQME-MLR ranks only fourth best, and AQME-1NN and AQME-C4.5 performances are quite weak. Still, at least for AQME-RIPPER, most of the performances in Table 4, can be explained in terms of $F_1 \cup F_2$ only. In the "**M**" selection, even if AQME ranks fourth at most, the performances of its four inductive models are more consistent than in the "**FS**" selection: C4.5, RIPPER, MLR and 1NN solve 55, 54, 53 and 51 problems, respectively. From this, we can see that features that are supposedly linked to the engine internals are more likely to behave in a model-independent fashion. Looking at the "**FS+M**" selection, we can see that the performances of AQME with the combination of automatic and manual feature selection are very close to the performances that can be obtained using the whole set of features. Even if the performances are still weaker than in Table 4, we are now considering only 20 features out of 141, so it is fair to say that these are the features that matter most in the performances of AQME. In particular, with respect to the results of Table 4, AQME-C4.5 and AQME-1NN have a negative gap of three instances (58 vs. 61 and 51 vs. 54, respectively), while AQME-MLR and AQME-RIPPER have a negative gap of 12 and 7 instances, respectively. It is also interesting to notice that while RIPPER, C4.5 and MLR are quite sensitive to changes in the feature space, 1NN performances are not, possibly because of a floor effect.

6 Conclusions

In this paper we have shown that a set of inexpensive syntactic features can hint the choice of the best engine to run on a given QBF. We have provided experimental evidence that our multi-engine solver AQME is a robust alternative to current state-of-the-art QBF solvers. We have also shown that AQME is stable with respect to perturbations that may affect the QBFEVAL'06 dataset on which it is engineered. Finally, we have provided some experimental evidence about the significant features leveraged by AQME and their connection with algorithmic differences among its engines. The validation of AQME is still in progress, and further work will include broadening the set of formulas whereon we validate the performances of AQME, the study of dynamic adaptive mechanisms, and a deeper study of the features guiding the choice of the best engine to run on each formula.

References

1. Stockmeyer, L.J., Meyer, A.R.: Word problems requiring exponential time. In: 5th Annual ACM Symposium on the Theory of Computation (1973)
2. Papadimitriou, C.H.: Computational Complexity. Addison-Wesley, Reading (1994)
3. Gent, I.P., Nightingale, P., Rowley, A.: Encoding Quantified CSPs as Quantified Boolean Formulae. In: Proceedings of the 16th European Conference on Artificial Intelligence (ECAI 2004) (2004)
4. Jussila, T., Biere, A.: Compressing BMC encodings with QBF. In: Proc. 4th Intl. Workshop on Bounded Model Checking (BMC'06) (2006)
5. Ansotegui, C., Gomes, C.P., Selman, B.: Achille's heel of QBF. In: Proc. of AAAI (2005)
6. Egly, U., Eiter, T., Tompits, H., Woltran, S.: Solving Advanced Reasoning Tasks Using Quantified Boolean Formulas. In: Seventeenth National Conference on Artificial Intelligence (AAAI 2000), pp. 417–422. MIT Press, Cambridge (2000)
7. Narizzano, M., Pulina, L., Taccchella, A.: QBF solvers competitive evaluation (QBFEVAL) (2003-2007), http://www.qbflib.org/qbfeval
8. Huberman, B.A., Lukose, R.M., Hogg, T.: An economics approach to hard computational problems. Science 3 (1997)
9. Gomes, C.P., Selman, B.: Algorithm portfolios. Artificial Intelligence 126 (2001)
10. Nudelman, E., Leyton-Brown, K., Devkar, A., Shoham, Y., Hoos, H.: SATzilla: An Algorithm Portfolio for SAT. In: Hoos, H.H., Mitchell, D.G. (eds.) SAT 2004. LNCS, vol. 3542, pp. 13–14. Springer, Heidelberg (2005)
11. Samulowitz, H., Memisevic, R.: Learning to Solve QBF. In: AAAI'07. Proc. of 22nd Conference on Artificial Intelligence (2007)
12. Davis, M., Logemann, G., Loveland, D.: A machine program for theorem proving. Communications of the ACM 5(7), 394–397 (1962)
13. Kleine-Büning, H., Karpinski, M., Flögel, A.: Resolution for Quantified Boolean Formulas. Information and Computation 117(1), 12–18 (1995)
14. Benedetti, M.: sKizzo: a Suite to Evaluate and Certify QBFs. In: Nieuwenhuis, R. (ed.) Automated Deduction – CADE-20. LNCS (LNAI), vol. 3632. Springer, Heidelberg (2005)
15. Biere, A.: Resolve and Expand. In: Hoos, H.H., Mitchell, D.G. (eds.) SAT 2004. LNCS, vol. 3542. Springer, Heidelberg (2005)
16. Giunchiglia, E., Narizzano, M., Tacchella, A.: Quantified Boolean Formulas satisfiability library (QBFLIB) (2001), www.qbflib.org
17. Narizzano, M., Pulina, L., Tacchella, A.: The third QBF solvers comparative evaluation. Journal on Satisfiability, Boolean Modeling and Computation 2, 145–164 (2006), http://jsat.ewi.tudelft.nl/
18. Kaufman, L., Rousseeeuw, P.J.: Finding Groups in Data. Wiley, Chichester (1990)
19. Witten, I.H., Frank, E.: Data Mining, 2nd edn. Morgan Kaufmann, San Francisco (2005)
20. Quinlan, J.R.: C4.5: Programs for Machine Learning. Morgan Kaufmann, San Francisco (1993)
21. Cohen, W.W.: Fast effective rule induction. In: Twelfth International Conference on Machine Learning, pp. 115–123 (1995)

22. Le Cessie, S., van Houwelingen, J.C.: Ridge estimators in logistic regression. Applied Statistics 41, 191–201 (1992)
23. Aha, D., Kibler, D.: Instance-based learning algorithms. Machine Learning, 37–66 (1991)
24. Kohavi, R.: A study of cross-validation and bootstrap for accuracy estimation and model selection. In: Proc. of Intl. Joint Conference on Artificial Intelligence (IJCAI) (2005)

Decomposing Global Grammar Constraints

Claude-Guy Quimper[1] and Toby Walsh[2]

[1] Omega Omptimization
[2] NICTA and UNSW

Abstract. A wide range of constraints can be specified using automata or formal languages. The GRAMMAR constraint restricts the values taken by a sequence of variables to be a string from a given context-free language. Based on an AND/OR decomposition, we show that this constraint can be converted into clauses in conjunctive normal form without hindering propagation. Using this decomposition, we can propagate the GRAMMAR constraint in $O(n^3)$ time. The decomposition also provides an efficient incremental propagator. Down a branch of the search tree of length k, we can enforce GAC k times in the same $O(n^3)$ time. On specialized languages, running time can be even better. For example, propagation of the decomposition requires just $O(n|\delta|)$ time for regular languages where $|\delta|$ is the size of the transition table of the automaton recognizing the regular language. Experiments on a shift scheduling problem with a constraint solver and a state of the art SAT solver show that we can solve problems using this decomposition that defeat existing constraint solvers.

1 Introduction

Many problems in areas like planning, scheduling, routing, and configuration can be naturally expressed and efficiently solved using constraint programming (CP). One reason for the success of CP is that it provides a simple and declarative method for solving a wide range of difficult combinatorial problems. However, we are still some way from the "model and run" capability of solvers for mixed integer programming (MIP) and propositional satisfiability (SAT). A major direction of research in CP is therefore directed towards developing new ways for the user to state their problem constraints that can then be efficiently reasoned about.

One very promising method for rostering and other domains is to specify constraints via grammars or automata that accept some language. With the REGULAR constraint [1], we can specify the acceptable assignments to a sequence of variables by means of a deterministic finite automaton. For instance, we might want no more than two consecutive shift variables to be assigned to night shifts. One limitation of the REGULAR constraint is that we cannot compactly specify everything we might like using just deterministic finite automaton. For example, there are regular languages which can only be defined by a deterministic automaton with an exponential number of states. One extension is to consider regular languages specified by non-deterministic automata, as such automata can be exponentially smaller [2].

Researchers have considered moving above regular languages in the Chomsky hierarchy. For example, the GRAMMAR constraint [3,2] permits us to specify constraints

C. Bessiere (Ed.): CP 2007, LNCS 4741, pp. 590–604, 2007.

using any context-free grammar. However, this generalization has appeared till now to be mostly of theoretical interest, given the high cost of propagating the GRAMMAR constraint. The aim of this paper is to show that the global GRAMMAR constraint has practical promise. Context-free grammars can provide compact specifications for complex constraints, making it easier both to specify the problem as well as to reason with the constraints. For example, in the shift-scheduling benchmarks reported in this paper, we used a grammar with a dozen or so productions, whilst the corresponding automaton has thousand of states. The grammar is thus arguably much simpler to specify than the automaton. In addition, we argue that, using a simple decomposition of the GRAMMAR constraint, we can propagate such a specification efficiently and effectively.

We will show that the global GRAMMAR constraints be implemented using a simple AND/OR decomposition based on the well known CYK parser. We prove that this decomposition does not hinder propagation; unit propagation on the decomposition prunes all possible values. Decomposing global constraints in this way brings several advantages. First, we can easily add this global constraint to any constraint solver. Here, for example, we use the decomposition to add the GRAMMAR constraint to both a constraint toolkit and a state of the art SAT solver. Second, decomposition gives an efficient incremental propagator. The solver can simply wake up just those constraints containing variables whose domains have changed, ignoring those parts of the decomposition that do not need to be propagated. This gives a propagator whose worst case cost down a whole branch of the search tree is just the same as calling it once. Third, decomposition gives a propagator which we can backtrack over efficiently. Modern SAT and CP solvers use watch literals so that we can backtrack one level up the search tree in constant time. This decomposition provides us with this efficiency.

2 Background

A constraint satisfaction problem (CSP) consists of a set of variables, each with a finite domain of values, and a set of constraints. The domain of the variable X will be written $\text{dom}(X)$. A constraint restricts values taken by some subset of variables to a subset of the Cartesian product of their domains. A solution is an assignment of one value to each variable satisfying all the constraints. Systematic constraint solvers typically construct partial assignments using backtracking search, enforcing a local consistency to prune values for variables which cannot be in any solution. We consider one of the most common local consistencies: generalized arc consistency. A *support* for a constraint C is an assignment to each variable of a value in its domain which satisfies C. A constraint C is *generalized arc consistent* (*GAC*) iff for each variable, every value in its domain belongs to a support. Finally, a CSP is GAC iff each constraint is GAC.

We will consider global constraints which are specified in terms of a grammar or automaton which accepts just valid assignments for a sequence of n variables. Such constraints are useful in a wide range of scheduling, rostering and sequencing problems to ensure certain patterns do or do not occur over time. For example, we may wish to ensure that anyone working three night shifts then has two or more days off. Such a constraint can easily be expressed using a context-free language. Context-free languages are exactly those accepted by non-deterministic push-down automaton. A context-free language can be specified by a set of productions in Chomsky normal form in which the left-hand side has just one non-terminal, and the right-hand have just one terminal or two non-terminals. We will use capital letters for non-terminals and lower-case letters for terminals. We shall also assume that S is the unique non-terminal start symbol. Even though the production $A \rightarrow Bc$ is not in the Chomsky normal form since the symbol c is not a non-terminal, we will consider this production as a shorthand for the productions $A \rightarrow BZ$ and $Z \rightarrow c$ which are both in the Chomsky normal form.

A sequence belongs to a context-free language iff there exists a parsing tree whose root is the start symbol S, and whose leaves in order reproduce the sequence. A parsing tree for a non-terminal is a tree whose root is labelled with the given non-terminal, whose leaves are labelled with terminals and whose inner-nodes are labelled with other non-terminals. When the productions are in the Chomsky normal form, a node A in the parsing tree either has two children B and C where $A \rightarrow BC$ is a production in the grammar, or has one child t where $A \rightarrow t$ is again a production in the grammar and t is a terminal. Given a grammar defining a context-free language, the GRAMMAR constraint accepts just those assignments to a sequence of n variables which are strings in the given context-free language [2,3].

Example 1. Consider the following context-free grammar, $\mathcal{G}$

$$A \rightarrow aA \mid a \qquad\qquad B \rightarrow bB \mid b \qquad\qquad S \rightarrow AB$$

Suppose X_1, X_2 and $X_4 \in \{a, b\}$. Then enforcing GAC on GRAMMAR($\mathcal{G}, [X_1, X_2, X_3]$) prunes b from X_1 and a from X_3 as the only supports are the sequences aab and abb.

The REGULAR constraint [1] is a special case of the GRAMMAR constraint. This accepts just those assignments which come from a regular language. Regular languages are strictly contained with context-free languages. A regular language can be specified by productions in which the left-hand side has just one non-terminal, and the right-hand has just one terminal, or one terminal and one non-terminal. Alternatively, it can be specified by means of a (non-)deterministic finite automaton.

3 Decomposition of the GRAMMAR Constraint

We show here how to propagate the GRAMMAR constraint using a simple AND/OR decomposition based on the well known CYK parser. This parser uses dynamic programming bottom up to construct all possible parsings for all possible sub-strings. We backtrack over the table constructed by the parser to decompose the constraint into a Boolean formula. We introduce two types of Boolean variables: the variables $x(t, i, 1)$ which are *true* iff X_i, the ith CSP variable, has the terminal symbol t in its domain, and the variables $x(A, i, j)$ which are *true* iff the ith to $i + j - 1$th symbols can be parsed as the non-terminal A. The truth of $x(A, i, j)$ can be expressed in terms of the truth of other variables based on the CYK update rule: A is parsing for symbols i to $i + j - 1$ iff there is some production $A \rightarrow BC$ in the grammar, B is a parsing for symbols i to $i + k - 1$, and C is a parsing for symbols $i + k$ to $i + j - 1$. Algorithm 1 gives an $O(|G|n^3)$ time procedure for constructing the decomposition. This algorithm takes as input the grammar G and the constrained variables $X_1, \ldots, X_n$ and returns a set of Boolean formulae. The algorithm first creates a table V where each entry contains a set of non-terminals such that the non-terminal A belongs to $V[i,j]$ if A can parse the symbols i to $i+j-1$. In the second phase, the algorithm backtracks in the table V to create a variable $x(A,i,j)$ for each non-terminal $A \in V[i,j]$ that can contribute to the production of the non-terminal S at the top of the parsing tree.

```
input : A context-free grammar G in its Chomsky normal form
input : The constrained variables X_1, ..., X_n
output: A set of Boolean formulae equivalent to the GRAMMAR constraint or
        "Unsatisfiable" if the constraint is unsatisfiable
for i = 1 to n do
    V[i,1] ← {A | A → a ∈ G, a ∈ dom(X_i)} ∪ dom(X_i)
for j = 2 to n do
    for i = 1 to n − j + 1 do
        // Store in V[i,j] all the non-terminals that can generate the sequence
        // X_i ... X_{i+j−1}
        V[i,j] ← {A | A → BC ∈ G, k ∈ [1,j), B ∈ V[i,k], C ∈ V[i+k, j−k]}
if S ∉ V[1,n] then
    return "Unsatisfiable"
N ← {x(S,1,n)}                                              // Set of variables
Y ← ∅                                                       // Set of equivalences
for j = n downto 2 do
    for i = 1 to n − j + 1 do
        for x(A,i,j) ∈ N do
            // Store in D the pairs of variables on which the CYK rule applies
            D ← {⟨x(B,i,k), x(C,i+k,j−k)⟩ | k ∈ [1,j), A → BC ∈ G,
                    B ∈ V[i,k], C ∈ V[i+k, j−k]}
            for ⟨a,b⟩ ∈ D do
                N ← N ∪ {a,b} // Add nodes to the decomposition
            Y ← Y ∪ {x(A,i,j) ≡ ⋁_{⟨a,b⟩∈D} a ∧ b} // Add relation
for i = 1 to n do
    N ← N ∪ {x(a,i,1) | a ∈ dom(X_i), A → a ∈ G, x(A,i,1) ∈ N}
    Y ← Y ∪ {x(A,i,1) ≡ x(a,i,1) | A → a ∈ G, x(A,i,1) ∈ N, a ∈ dom(X_i)}
    dom(X_i) ← {a | x(a,i,1) ∈ N}
return The set of clauses Y
```

Algorithm 1. CYK-prop(G, $[X_1, \ldots, X_n]$)

Example 2. Consider again the context-free grammar, $\mathcal{G}$ from Example 1, again applied to a sequence of length 3.

$$A \to aA \mid a \qquad B \to bB \mid b \qquad S \to AB$$

Algorithm 1 constructs the following formulae:

$$x(A,1,1) \equiv x(a,1,1)$$
$$x(A,2,1) \equiv x(a,2,1)$$
$$x(B,3,1) \equiv x(b,3,1)$$
$$x(A,1,2) \equiv x(a,1,1) \wedge x(A,2,1)$$
$$x(B,2,2) \equiv x(b,2,1) \wedge x(B,3,1)$$
$$x(S,1,3) \equiv (x(A,1,1) \wedge x(B,2,2)) \vee \ (x(A,1,2) \wedge x(B,3,1))$$

The formulae created by Algorithm 1 can be represented by a rooted DAG. Every leaf is labelled with a variable $x(t,i,1)$ where t is a terminal symbol and i is an integer between 1 and n. Every inner-node is either a conjunction or a disjunction. Formulae of the form $x \equiv b$ are represented by a single leaf node with two labels: x and b. For formulae of the form $x \equiv (a_1 \wedge b_1) \vee \ldots \vee (a_k \wedge b_k)$, we create k and-nodes with two children each, a_i and b_i. We label each and-node with the expression $a_i \wedge b_i$. The k and-nodes have the or-node labelled with x as common parent.

Based on this DAG, we propose the following CNF decomposition. For every or-node x with children $c_1, \ldots, c_k$, we post the following constraint forcing at least one child to be *true* when the or-node x is *true*.

$$\neg x \vee c_i \vee \ldots \vee c_k \tag{1}$$

For every and-node x with children c_1 and c_2, we post the following constraints to enforce all children to be *true* whenever the and-node x is *true*.

$$\neg x \vee c_1 \tag{2}$$
$$\neg x \vee c_2 \tag{3}$$

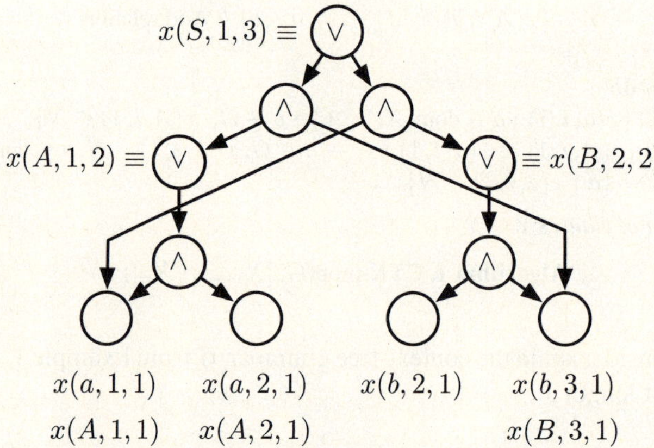

Fig. 1. DAG corresponding to the example grammar

For every node x, except the root $x(S, 1, n)$, we post the following constraint on its ancestors $a_1, \ldots, a_k$, to force the node x to be *true* only if one of its ancestors is *true*.

$$\neg x \vee a_1 \vee \ldots \vee a_k \tag{4}$$

We force the root node $x(S, 1, n)$ to be *true*. Finally, for every position $1 \leq i \leq n$, we force one and only one terminal to be *true*.

$$\bigvee_t x(t, i, 1)\ \forall\, 1 \leq i \leq n \tag{5}$$

$$\neg x(t, i, 1) \vee \neg x(u, i, 1)\ \forall\, i\ \forall\, t \neq u \tag{6}$$

Note that constraints (4) are redundant as they are logically implied by the others. However, they are added to the encoding to ensure that unit propagation on the decomposition prunes all possible values.

Example 3. Let w be the node $x(b, 2, 1) \wedge x(B, 3, 1)$, y be the node $x(A, 1, 2) \wedge x(B, 3, 1)$, and z be the node $x(A, 1, 1) \wedge x(B, 2, 2)$ in the DAG of Figure 1. We show the CNF clauses constraining the variable y.

Clause (1) applied to $x(S, 1, 3)$ becomes $\neg x(S, 1, 3) \vee y \vee z$. This ensures that if $x(S, 1, 3)$ is *true*, one of its children is also *true*. Clauses (2) and (3) applied to y become $\neg y \vee x(A, 1, 2)$ and $\neg y \vee x(B, 3, 1)$. If the and-node y is *true*, both of its children are also *true*. Clause (4) constrains the variable y in three different ways. When the clause is directly applied to y, it becomes $\neg y \vee x(S, 1, 3)$ forcing y to be *true* only if it produces $x(S, 1, 3)$. Similarly, the node $x(A, 1, 2)$ belongs to a parsing tree only if y is *true*. We therefore have $\neg x(A, 1, 2) \vee y$. Finally, the node $x(B, 3, 1)$ is *true* only if either of its parents y or w is *true*. We therefore have $\neg x(B, 3, 1) \vee w \vee y$. There are no other constraints on variable y.

4 Theoretical Properties

We first prove that this decomposition of the global GRAMMAR constraint is correct. The correctness follows quite quickly from the proof of the correctness of the CYK parser, and is similar to the correctness proofs for the previous propagators for the GRAMMAR constraint [3,2].

Theorem 1. *The* GRAMMAR *constraint is satisfiable iff* $x(S, 1, n)$ *can be* true.

Proof: Suppose the GRAMMAR constraint is satisfiable. There exists a parsing tree T proving that the sequence $X_1, \ldots, X_n$ belongs to the language. We first prove that for every node in the parsing tree, there is a corresponding variable created by Algorithm 1. We then show that all these variables can be set to *true*. The first phase of the algorithm (line 0 to line 7) stores in $V[i, j]$ every non-terminal that can produce the symbols for X_i to X_{i+j-1}. The second phase of the algorithm (line 9 to line 24) creates a node $x(A, i, j)$ for every terminal A that can produce the symbols for X_i to X_{i+j-1} and participates to the production of the non-terminal S at the root of the parsing tree. The correctness of this statement follows from [3,2]. Therefore, for every node in the parsing tree T, we have a corresponding variable $x(X, i, j)$.

We prove by induction on the depth of the parsing tree that every variable corresponding to a node in the parsing tree can be set to *true*. As a base case, the leaves of the parsing tree correspond to the nodes $x(X_i, i, 1)$ in the DAG that we set to *true*. The other leaves of the DAG are set to *false*. The clauses (5) and (6) are satisfied since there is one and only one leaf set to *true* at each position. Let A be a node in the parsing tree with children B and C where A generates a sequence of length j at position i and B generates a sequence of length k. Consequently, there exists a production $A \to BC \in G$, a variable $x(A, i, j)$, a variable $x(B, i, k)$, and a variable $x(C, i + k, j - k)$. On line 19, Algorithm 1 has made the node $x(A, i, j)$ the parent of the pair $x(B, i, k) \wedge x(C, i + k, j - k)$ since the production $A \to BC$ and both nodes $x(B, i, k)$ and $x(C, i + k, j - k)$ exist. By our induction hypothesis, we assume that the variables $x(B, i, k)$ and $x(C, i + k, j - k)$ are *true*. The and-node can be set to *true* while satisfying the clauses (2) and (3). Since the and-node is *true*, we can set the variable $x(A, i, j)$ to *true* and satisfy clause (1). Finally, the clause (4) is satisfied for the variables $x(B, i, k)$ and $x(C, i+k, j-k)$ and the and-node. When applying the induction step to all nodes in the parsing tree in post-order, we obtain that the root node $x(S, 1, n)$ can be set to *true*.

Suppose there exists a solution to the CNF clauses where $x(S, 1, n)$ is *true*. Clause 1 guarantees that at least one child is also *true*. This child is an and-node with two children that are also *true* thanks to the clauses (2) and (3). We continue this reasoning until reaching the leaf nodes. All the visited nodes form a parsing tree whose leaves, when listed from left to right, are a sequence satisfying the GRAMMAR constraint. ■

Notice that the constraint (4) was not used in the second part of proof of Theorem 1. This constraint is not necessary to detect the satisfiability of the constraint. Constraint (4) is in fact redundant. It is however essential to prove our next result.

We show that the decomposition of the GRAMMAR constraint does not hinder propagation. This is less immediate than the previous result. In particular, we find it surprising that unit propagation alone is enough to achieve GAC here. This does not follow directly from the completeness proofs for previous GAC propagators [3,2]. Indeed, we had to add redundant constraints to the decomposition to give this property.

Theorem 2. *Unit propagation on the CNF clauses achieves GAC on the* GRAMMAR *constraint.*

Proof: We assume that all CNF clauses are consistent. The constraint (4) guarantees that every node that can be *true* has an ancestor that can also be *true*. By successively applying the argument from a leaf node x, we obtain a path connecting the leaf x to the root node $x(S, 1, n)$ such that every variable on this path can be set to *true*. Let $x(A, i, j)$ be a variable on the path. Let $c_1, \ldots, c_n$ be the child variables of $x(A, i, j)$ in the DAG. From the constraint (1), we conclude that there exists at least one and-node among the children that can be *true*. Let c_i be one such child that has b_1 and b_2 as children. The constraints (2) and (3) guarantee that both children can be *true*. We repeat this argument until reaching the leaves. Every node thus explored form a parsing tree whose leaves are a support for the variable x. Therefore, one can build a support for every node in the DAG that can be set to *true*.

The constraint (5) ensures that if a character belongs to all supports, its corresponding leaf is fixed to *true*. Finally, the constraint (6) ensures that a character fixed to *true* removes all supports for the other characters at the same position. ■

Finally, we show that we can propagate this decomposition efficiently. The run-time complexity of Algorithm 1 is the same as that of the CYK parser, i.e. $\Theta(n^3|G|)$ where $|G|$ is the size of the grammar.

Theorem 3. *The running time complexity of Algorithm 1 is $O(|G|n^3)$ where n is the length of the sequence and $|G|$ is the number of productions in the grammar.*

Proof: Line 2 iterates n times over the $O(|G|)$ productions resulting in a time complexity of $O(|G|n)$. The set $V[i,j]$ created on line 7 tests all combinations of productions and integers between 1 and j for a total number of $O(|G|n)$ tests. Since there are $O(n^2)$ sets $V[i,j]$, the complexity sums up to $O(|G|n^3)$. The running time of the *for loop* on line 12 is dominated by the computation on line 15. Let Z be the set of non-terminals in the grammar. Let $f(A)$ be the number of productions in the grammar G whose left hand side is the non-terminal A. We have $\sum_{A\in Z} f(A) = |G|$. Line 15 takes $O(nf(A))$ time to execute as we test for each production that generates A and every integer k. The cumulative time spent on this line is therefore given by the following expression.

$$O(\sum_{j=2}^{n}\sum_{i=1}^{n-j+1}\sum_{A\in Z} nf(A)) = O(n\sum_{j=1}^{n}\sum_{i=1}^{n}\sum_{A\in Z} f(A)) \tag{7}$$

$$= O(|G|n^3) \tag{8}$$

The running time of Algorithm 1 is thus $O(|G|n)+O(|G|n^3)+O(|G|n^3)=O(|G|n^3)$. ■

The size of the graph and the number of CNF clauses are bounded by the number of and-nodes in the DAG which is $O(n^3|G|)$. Notice that whilst Algorithm 1 performs $\Theta(n^3|G|)$ tests on line 7, not all these tests add a non-terminal to the set $V[i,j]$. Moreover, not all the non-terminals in $V[i,j]$ lead to the creation of a node on lines 15 to 18.

We are now ready to analyse the running time complexity of maintaining GAC on the decomposition. We assume that the solver wakes up a constraint only when a variable in its scope is fixed to a specific value. For a CNF clause of arity k, this event occurs at most k times down the branch of the search tree. We have no assumptions regarding in which order the constraints are awaken. However, we assume that the propagator of a CNF clause of arity k maintains GAC in $O(k)$ time down a branch of the search tree. This assumption can be satisfied by encoding the k-ary CNF clause $\bigvee_{i=1}^{k} x_i$ using the following clauses: $x_1 \vee y_2$, $\neg y_i \vee x_i \vee y_{i+1}$ for $1 < i < k$, and $\neg y_k \vee x_k$. Since each of the k clauses is awaken at most three times down a branch of the search tree and each propagation takes constant time, propagating the original CNF clause requires $O(k)$ time down a branch of the search tree. Notice that other implementations of the CNF clause propagator might be more efficient in practice. See [13] for instance for an implementation using watched literals.

Theorem 4. *Amortised over a branch of the search tree of length k, we can enforce GAC k times on the* GRAMMAR *constraint using the decomposition in $O(n^3|G|)$ time.*

Proof: We assume that propagating a CNF clause of arity k takes $O(k)$ time down a branch of the search tree. We conclude that the propagation time, down a branch of the search tree, is proportional to the number of literals in the CNF clauses. Since the graph inducing the CNF clauses is of size $O(n^3|G|)$, the number of literals in the CNF clauses is also $O(n^3|G|)$. Consequently, we obtain a running time complexity of $O(n^3|G|)$ down a branch of the search tree. ■

This improves upon the $\Theta(n^3|G|)$ time complexity of the monolithic propagators for the GRAMMAR constraint given in [2,3]. We note that our decomposition is the first incremental propagator proposed in the literature.

5 Regular Languages

In some cases, we can specify problem constraints using a simple grammar. For instance, we often only need a regular language [1]. Regular languages are strictly contained within context-free languages. They can be specified with productions of the form of $A \to aB$ or $A \to a$. We show that for regular languages, Algorithm 1 creates a smaller DAG, resulting in faster propagation.

Theorem 5. *Unit propagation on the CNF decomposition enforces GAC on the* REGULAR *constraint in* $O(n|G|)$ *time.*

Proof: If all productions are of the form of $A \to aB$ or $A \to a$, a node $x(A, i, j)$ can belong to a parsing tree only if $i = n - j + 1$. The size of the graph is therefore bounded by $O(n|G|)$ and-nodes which limits the number of literals in the CNF clauses to $O(n|G|)$. Using the same assumption and argument as Theorem 4, we conclude that propagating the CNF-clauses down a branch of the search tree takes $O(n|G|)$ time. ■

The running time complexity for pruning regular languages using this decomposition matches the complexity of the propagator for the REGULAR constraint based on dynamic programming [1]. In fact, the clauses constructed by Algorithm 1 are essentially the hidden variable encoding of the ternary decomposition of the REGULAR constraint given in [2].

Example 4. The language $a^n b^m$ used in Example 1 can be recognized by the automaton of Figure 2. This automaton can be translated to a regular grammar as follows.

$$S \to aA \qquad A \to aA \mid bB \mid b \qquad B \to bB \mid b$$

Algorithm 1 constructs the graph depicted in Figure 3 over a sequence of three variables. From this graph, we construct clauses representing the Boolean formulae:

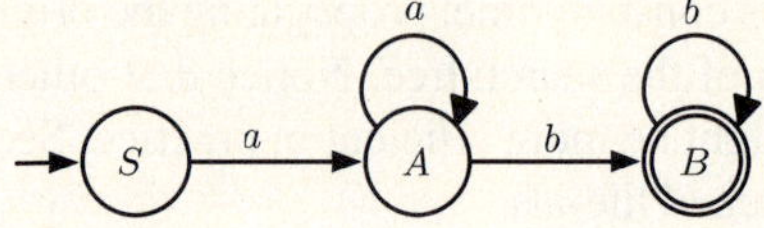

Fig. 2. Automaton recognizing the language $a^n b^m$ for $n, m \geq 1$

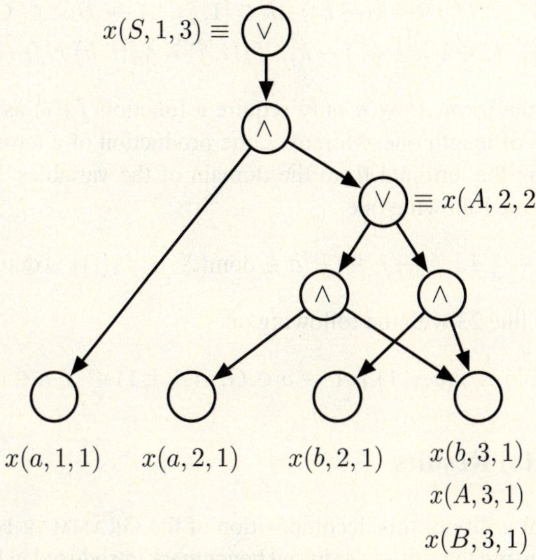

Fig. 3. DAG corresponding to the regular grammar of Example 4

$$x(a,1,1) \wedge (x(a,2,1) \wedge x(b,3,1)) \vee (x(b,2,1) \wedge x(b,3,1))$$

This gives constraints logically equivalent to:

$$X_1 = a, (X_2 = a \wedge X_3 = b) \vee (X_2 = b \wedge X_3 = b)$$

6 Conditional Productions

We have also found it useful in practice to go slightly outside context-free grammars. These extensions permit us to specify in a simple manner that, for instance, a work day must have a span of between 6 to 8 hours, or that a certain activity can only be executed after 2pm. To specify such conditions, we make productions in the grammar conditional on Boolean functions of the relevant indices. This can be quickly incorporated into our decomposition. We attach the Boolean functions $f_A(i,j)$, $f_B(i,j)$, and $f_C(i,j)$ to every production $A \rightarrow BC \in G$. These functions restrict where the production can be applied in a sequence. For instance, the non-terminal A can only be produced by the production $A \rightarrow BC$ if A generates a sub-string of length j starting at position i where $f_A(i,j)$ is *true*. Similarly, the production can be applied only if B generates a sub-string of length j starting at position i where $f_B(i,j)$ is *true*. To support these constrained productions, we change line 7 in Algorithm 1 with the following one.

$$V[i,j] \leftarrow \{A \mid A \rightarrow BC \in G,\ k \in [1,j),\ B \in V[i,k],\ C \in V[i+k, j-k],$$
$$f_A(i,j) \wedge f_B(i,k) \wedge f_C(i+k, j-k)\}$$

We also replace line 15 with the following one.

$$D \leftarrow \{\langle x(B,i,k),\ x(C,i+k,j-k)\rangle \mid k \in [1,j),\ A \rightarrow BC \in G,$$
$$B \in V[i,k],\ C \in V[i+k,j-k],\ f_A(i,j) \wedge f_B(i,k) \wedge f_C(i+k,j-k))\}$$

Productions of the form $A \rightarrow a$ only require a function $f_A(i)$ as they necessarily produce sequences of length one. Moreover, the production of a terminal can be controlled by removing the terminal from the domain of the variables X_i. We therefore replace line 2 with the following one.

$$V[i,1] \leftarrow \{A \mid A \rightarrow a \in G,\ a \in \text{dom}(X_i),\ f_A(i)\} \cup \text{dom}(X_i)$$

We also replace line 23 with the following one.

$$Y \leftarrow Y \cup \{x(A,i,1) \equiv x(a,i,1) \mid A \rightarrow a \in G, x(A,i,1) \in N, a \in \text{dom}(X_i), f_A(i)\}$$

7 Experimental Results

To test the practical utility of this decomposition of the GRAMMAR constraint, we ran some experiments using the shift-scheduling benchmark introduced in [4]. The schedule of an employee in a company is subject to the following rules. An employee either works on an activity a_i, has a break (b), has lunch (l), or rests (r). When working on an activity, the employee works on that activity for a minimum of one hour. An employee can change activities after a break or a lunch. A break is fifteen minutes long and a lunch is one hour long. Lunches and breaks are scheduled between periods of work. A part-time employee works at least three hours but less than six hours a day and has one break. A full-time employee works between six and eight hours a day and have a break, a lunch, and a break in that order. Employees rest at the beginning and the end of the day. At some time of the day, the business is closed and employees must either rest, break, or have lunch. We divide a day into 96 time slots of 15 minutes. During time slot t, at least $d(t,a_i)$ employees must be assigned to activity a_i. Our goal is to minimize first the number of employees and then the number of hours worked.

We model the schedule of an employee with a sequence of 96 characters (one per time slot) that must be accepted by the following grammar G.

$$R \rightarrow rR \mid r \qquad L \rightarrow lL \mid l \qquad A_i \rightarrow a_iA_i \mid a_i$$
$$W \rightarrow A_i \qquad P \rightarrow WbW \qquad F \rightarrow PLP$$
$$S \rightarrow RPR \mid RFR$$

We add some restrictions on some productions. For $W \rightarrow A_i$, we have $f_W(i,j) \equiv j \geq 4$ since an employee works on an activity for at least one continuous hour. In $F \rightarrow PLP$, we have $f_L(i,j) \equiv (j = 4)$ since a lunch is one hour long. In $S \rightarrow RPR$, we have $f_P(i,j) \equiv 13 \leq j \leq 24$ since a part-time employee works at least three hours and at most six hours plus a fifteen minute break. In $S \rightarrow RFR$, we have $f_F(i,j) \equiv 30 \leq j \leq 38$ which represents between six and eight hours of work plus an hour and a half of idle time for the lunch and the breaks. Finally, the productions $A_k \rightarrow a_kA_k \mid a_k$ are constrained with $f_{A_k}(i,j) \equiv \mathit{open}(i)$ where $\mathit{open}(t)$ returns *true* if t is within business hours. When solving the problem with m employees, the model consists of m sequences $S_1, \ldots, S_m$ subject to this GRAMMAR constraint. The 0/1 variable $x(j,t,c)$ is set to 1 if the tth character of sequence S_j is c. We post the constraint $\sum_j x(j,t,a_i) \geq d(t,a_i)$ in order to satisfy the demand for each activity a_i at time t. To break symmetry, we force the sequences to be in lexicographical order.

We implemented a program that takes as input a benchmark instance and the grammar G and prepares the input for the MiniSat+ solver [5]. MiniSat+ is a pseudo-Boolean solver that allows constraints of the form $x_1 + \ldots + x_n \geq k$ where x_i is a Boolean variable. Such inequality constraints are useful to make sure that the demand $d(t,a_i)$ is satisfied. CNF clauses are encoded with linear equations where the sum of the literals in a clause must be equal to or greater than one. The negation of a variable x is expressed with $1 - x$. We tested two CNF encodings of the GRAMMAR constraint: one encoding that includes the redundant clause (4) allowing unit propagation to achieve GAC as well as one encoding where the clauses (4) are omitted and GAC is not maintained.

We also implemented a CP model in ILog Solver 6.2 using either this decomposition of the GRAMMAR constraint or the previous monolithic propagator for the GRAMMAR constraint based on the CYK parser [2,3]. The model has a matrix of variables where each row corresponds to the schedule of an employee and is subject to a GRAMMAR constraint. Each column is subject to a global cardinality constraint (GCC) to ensure that the number of occurrences of an activity satisfies the demand. We added lexicographic constraints between the rows of the column to break symmetries. We used a static variable that was essential to the success of the experiment: we filled in the table from left to right, and assigned variables to the values r, b, l, a_1 and a_2 in that order.

Our experiments used MiniSat+ on a Intel Dual Core 2.0 GHz with 1 Gb of RAM using Mac OS X 10.4.8 and ILog Solver on a AMD Dual Core Opteron 2.2 GHz with 4 Gb of RAM. The reader should be careful when comparing the times as the clock speeds of the computers are slightly different. MiniSat+ is halted after finding the optimal solution or when the search is suspended by a lack of memory. ILog solver was halted after one hour of computation as it never proved the optimality of a solution. Table 1 presents the results for 17 satisfiable instances of the benchmark involving one or two activities. The CP model performed very well at finding a good solution. Many solutions were returned after a few hundreds of backtracks. However, no solutions were proved optimal after one hour of computation. Notice that the decomposition performs significantly better than the monolithic propagator as it explores many more backtracks within the same period of time. The decomposition therefore explores a larger portion of the search tree. For some instances, it finds some satisfiable solutions within one hour whereas the monolithic propagator does not.

The MiniSat+ solver returned a feasible solution for all instances regardless of the encoding. For 8 instances, the solver also proved optimality of the solutions. However, the two encodings we used did not prove optimality for the same instances. The main weakness of the MiniSat+ solver was its memory consumption as 9 times out of 17, the search was stopped by the lack of memory. Notice that the encoding that omits clauses of the form (4) is often faster than the encoding achieving GAC. We conjecture that, in this case, MiniSat is finding itself the redundant constraints using no-good learning.

Even though Algorithm 1 can produce a graph with up to $O(n^3|G|)$ nodes, we noticed that in practice many nodes are never created. The size of the resulting DAG

Table 1. Benchmark problems solved by MiniSat+. *GAC SAT*: results from MiniSat+ with all CNF clauses; *SAT*: results from MiniSat+ with all CNF clauses but clause (4); Mono: results from a CP solver using the monolithic propagator; Decomp: results from a CP solver using the decomposition; $|A|$: number of activities; #: problem number; m: number of employees; sol: number of worked hours (boldfonted if best solution found amongst the different methods); time (s): CPU time in seconds to find and prove the optimality of a solution. Times are omitted when the search is suspended by a lack of memory; bt: number of backtracks (boldfonted if least backtracks amongst methods that prove optimality); opt: solution was proved optimal. ILog solver did not prove any problems optimal within one hour of computation.

$\|A\|$	#	m	GAC SAT				SAT				Mono		Decomp	
			sol	time	bt	opt	sol	time	bt	opt	sol	bt	sol	bt
1	2	4	**26.0**	2666	507215	√	**26.0**	1998	**443546**	√	26.75	28072	26.25	625683
1	3	6	37.25		1128199		**36.75**		1953562		37.0	34788	37.0	4771577
1	4	6	**38.0**	256	**84999**	√	**38.0**	287	91151	√	-	15539	**38.0**	56488
1	5	5	**24.0**	153	67376	√	**24.0**	60	**40008**	√	**24.0**	40163	**24.0**	7914413
1	6	6	**33.0**	98	48638	√	**33.0**	70	**40361**	√	-	11537	**33.0**	33405
1	7	8	49.5		236066		49.5		682715		**49.0**	27635	**49.0**	2663721
1	8	3	**20.5**	80	36348	√	**20.5**	44	**25502**	√	21.0	24343	**20.5**	635589
1	10	9	**54.0**		202699		54.25		507749		-	9365	-	519446
2	1	5	**25.0**	453	146234		**25.0**	301	**103918**	√	**25.0**	1180	**25.0**	3828461
2	2	10	58.75		313644		59.0		151076		**58.0**	14887	**58.0**	2116602
2	3	6	**38.25**		236850		**38.25**		214203		41.0	1419	41.0	214201
2	4	11	71.25		230777		**69.75**		239519		-	9983	-	774942
2	5	4	**23.75**	2945	644496	√	**23.75**	1876	**522780**	√	26.5	25573	26.25	117105
2	6	5	**26.75**	4831	**777572**	√	27.25		2162816		**26.75**	10681	**26.75**	1054531
2	8	5	**31.5**		244837		31.75		391858		32.0	218	**31.5**	3771831
2	9	3	**19.0**	2283	701474	√	**19.0**	1227	**481395**	√	19.25	20473	**19.0**	45516
2	10	8	**55.0**		372870		**55.0**		333520		-	9968	-	909857

is much smaller in practice than the theoretical bound of $O(n^3|G|)$. For instance, the grammar G for problems with one activity can be written in Chomsky normal form in 15 productions. The upper bound on the number of and-nodes in the DAG is $15\frac{96^3}{2} =$ 6635520 nodes whilst there were 71796 nodes on average with these instances.

We also tried modelled the schedule of an employee using an automaton. Due to the constraints on the number of hours a full-time and a part-time employee must work, many states in the automaton needed to be duplicated resulting in an automaton with several thousands of states. Moreover, patterns such as those produced by the non-terminals P and W cannot be reused in an automaton without further duplicating states. The DAG based on the regular language ended up much larger than the one produced by the context-free grammar.

8 Related Work

Vempaty introduced the idea of representing the solutions of a CSP by a deterministic finite automaton [6]. Such automaton can be used to answer questions about satisfiability, validity and equivalence. Amilhastre generalized these ideas to non-deterministic automata, and proposed heuristics to minimize the size of the automata [7]. This approach was then applied to configuration problems [8]. Boigelot and Wolper developed decision procedures for arithmetic constraints based on automata [9].

Pesant introduced the REGULAR constraint and gave a complete propagation algorithm based on dynamic programming [1]. Coincidently Beldiceanu, Carlsson and Petit proposed specifying global constraints by means of finite automaton augmented with counters [10]. Propagators for such automaton are constructed automatically from the specification of the automaton by means of a decomposition into simpler constraints. Quimper and Walsh proposed a closely related decomposition of the REGULAR constraint and showed that it was effective and efficient in practice [2]. Demassay et al. [4] used a column generation technique to solve a shift scheduling problem. The columns are generated with a CP solver using the COST-REGULAR constraint, a variation of the REGULAR constraint while the optimization process is driven by the simplex method. Côté et al. [11] encoded the REGULAR constraint into a MIP and efficiently solved some instances of the shift scheduling problem using the same automaton as Demassay et al. This encoding takes the modelling of constraints using formal languages beyond the scope of constraint programming. One of our contributions is to continue this theme by taking constraints specified using formal languages into the domain of SAT solvers.

Quimper and Walsh proposed the GRAMMAR constraint and gave two different propagators, one based on the CYK and the other on the Earley parser [2]. Coincidently, Sellmann proposed the GRAMMAR constraint and gave a propagator based on the CYK parser [3]. Finally Golden and Pang proposed the use of string variables which are specified using regular expressions or finite automata and show how to propagate matching, containment, cardinality and other constraints on such string variables [12].

9 Conclusion

We have studied the global GRAMMAR constraint. This restricts a sequence of variables to belong to a context-free language. Such a constraint is useful for a wide range of problems in scheduling, rostering and related domains. Based on an AND/OR decomposition, we showed how the GRAMMAR constraint can be converted into clauses in conjunctive normal form. This decomposition does not hinder propagation since unit propagation on the decomposition achieves GAC on the original GRAMMAR constraint. Using this decomposition, we can enforce GAC on the GRAMMAR constraint in $O(n^3)$ time. By using the decomposition, we also improve upon existing propagators by being incremental. On specialized languages, running time can be even better. In particular, on regular languages we require just $O(n|\delta|)$ time where $|\delta|$ is the size of the transition table of the automaton recognizing the language. Experiments on a shift scheduling problem with a state of the art SAT solver demonstrated that we can solve problems this way that defeat existing constraint solvers. The decomposition of global constraints opens up a number of possibilities which we are only starting to explore. For example, it may make it easier to construct no-goods, as well as cost measures for over-constrained problems. Finally, a decomposition may make it easier to construct constraint based branching heuristics.

Acknowledgements

The second author is funded by DCITA and the ARC through Backing Australia's Ability and the ICT Centre of Excellence program. We would like to thank Louis-Martin Rousseau for useful comments and for providing the benchmark.

References

1. Pesant, G.: A regular language membership constraint for finite sequences of variables. In: Wallace, M. (ed.) CP 2004. LNCS, vol. 3258, pp. 295–482. Springer, Heidelberg (2004)
2. Quimper, C.-G., Walsh, T.: Global grammar constraints. In: Benhamou, F. (ed.) CP 2006. LNCS, vol. 4204. Springer, Heidelberg (2006)
3. Sellmann, M.: The theory of grammar constraints. In: Benhamou, F. (ed.) CP 2006. LNCS, vol. 4204, pp. 530–544. Springer, Heidelberg (2006)
4. Demassey, S., Pesant, G., Rousseau, L.: A cost-regular based hybrid column generation approach. Constraints 11, 315–333 (2006)
5. Eén, N., Sörensso, N.: Translating pseudo-Boolean constraints into SAT. Journal on Satisfiability, Boolean Modelling and Computation 2, 1–26 (2006)
6. Vempaty, N.R.: Solving constraint satisfaction problems using finite state automata. In: 10th National Conf. on AI, pp. 453–458. AAAI, Stanford, California, USA (1992)
7. Amilhastre, J.: Representation par automate d'ensemble de solutions de problèmes de satsifaction de contraintes. PhD thesis, Universite Montpellier II / CNRS, LIRMM (1999)
8. Amilhastre, J., Fargier, H., Marquis, P.: Consistency restoration and explanations in dynamic CSPs - application to configuration. Artificial Intelligence 135, 199–234 (2002)
9. Boigelot, B., Wolper, P.: Representing arithmetic constraints with finite automata: An overview. In: Van Hentenryck, P. (ed.) CP 2002. LNCS, vol. 2470, pp. 1–19. Springer, Heidelberg (2002)
10. Beldiceanu, N., Carlsson, M., Petit, T.: Deriving filtering algorithms from constraint checkers. In: Wallace, M. (ed.) CP 2004. LNCS, vol. 3258, pp. 107–122. Springer, Heidelberg (2004)
11. Côté, M.C., Gendron, B., Rousseau, L.M.: The regular constraint for integer programming modeling. In: 4th Int. Conf. on Integration of AI and OR Techniques in Constraint Programming (CPAIOR 07), pp. 29–43 (2007)
12. Golden, K., Pang, W.: Constraint reasoning over strings. In: Rossi, F. (ed.) CP 2003. LNCS, vol. 2833, pp. 377–391. Springer, Heidelberg (2003)
13. Moskewicz, M., Madigan, C., Zhao, Y., Zhang, L., Malik, S.: CHAFF: engineering an efficient SAT solver. In: Proc. of the 38th Design Automation Conf (DAC'01), pp. 530–535 (2001)

Structural Relaxations by Variable Renaming and Their Compilation for Solving MinCostSAT

Miquel Ramírez[1] and Hector Geffner[2]

[1] Universitat Pompeu Fabra
Passeig de Circumvalació 8
08003 Barcelona Spain
miquel.ramirez@upf.edu

[2] ICREA & Universitat Pompeu Fabra
Passeig de Circumvalació 8
08003 Barcelona Spain
hector.geffner@upf.edu

Abstract. Searching for optimal solutions to a problem using lower bounds obtained from a relaxation is a common idea in Heuristic Search and Planning. In SAT and CSPs, however, explicit relaxations are seldom used. In this work, we consider the use of explicit relaxations for solving MinCostSAT, the problem of finding a minimum cost satisfying assignment. We start with the observation that while a number of SAT and CSP tasks have a complexity that is exponential in the treewidth, such models can be relaxed into weaker models of bounded treewidth by a simple form of variable renaming. The relaxed models can then be compiled in polynomial time and space, so that their solutions can be used effectively for pruning the search in the original problem. We have implemented a MinCostSAT solver using this idea on top of two off-the-shelf tools, a d-DNNF compiler that deals with the relaxation, and a SAT solver that deals with the search. The results over the entire suite of 559 problems from the 2006 Weighted Max-SAT Competition are encouraging: SR(w), the new solver, solves 56% of the problems when the bound on the relaxation treewidth is set to $w = 8$, while Toolbar, the winner, solves 73% of the problems, Lazy, the runner up, 55%, and MinCostChaff, a recent MinCostSAT solver, 26%. The relation between the proposed relaxation method and existing structural solution methods such as cutset decomposition and derivatives such as mini-buckets is also discussed.

1 Introduction

The idea of searching for optimal solutions to a problem using lower bounds obtained from a relaxation has been common in both Heuristic Search and Planning. In Pattern Databases, for example, certain state variables are abstracted away from the problem, and the resulting weaker problem is solved exhaustively. A table stored in memory saves the distance to the goal from any state of the relaxation which provides then a lower bound in the original problem for any state

C. Bessiere (Ed.): CP 2007, LNCS 4741, pp. 605–619, 2007.

where the value of the variables that have not been abstracted away coincides [1]. The best results for the Rubik's Cube, for example, have been obtained in this way [2]. Likewise, some of the best domain-independent planners use distance estimators obtained from an explicit relaxation where 'deletes' are dropped out of the problem [3].

In SAT and CSPs, the general idea of solving a problem by first solving a relaxation is implicit in many methods, even if explicit relaxations are seldom used. For example, node-consistency can be thought as a relaxation where non-unary constraints are excluded, and similarly, arc-consistency can be thought as iterating over relaxed problems that contain a single constraint [4].

In this work, we consider the use of explicit relaxations and their use in MinCostSAT: the problem of obtaining a minimum cost satisfying assignment of a CNF formula, where the cost of an assignment adds up the cost of the literals that are true [5]. We start with the observation that while a number of tasks over graphical models such as SAT and CSPs have a complexity that is exponential in the treewidth of the underlying interaction graph [6], such models can be relaxed into weaker models of bounded treewidth by a suitable form of variable renaming, where a variable that appears in many factors (clauses, constraints, etc.) is replaced by many fresh new variables that appear in few. Provided that the relaxed model has a bounded treewidth, the relaxation can be compiled in polynomial time and space, so that its solutions, obtained from the compiled representation without search can be used to prune the search in the original problem, very much as it is done with Pattern Databases in Heuristic Search.

Using these ideas, we have implemented a MinCostSAT solver that we call SR(w), on top of two off-the-shelf tools: the d-DNNF compiler due to Darwiche [7] and the MiniSAT 2.0 solver due to Sörensson & Eén [8]. Given a MinCost-SAT problem over a CNF theory T, SR(w) maps T into the 'renamed' relaxation T^- which is compiled into d-DNNF [9], a form akin to OBDDs that supports a number of queries and transformations in polynomial time and in particular, MinCostSAT (called 'preferred models' in [10]). The compilation is exponential in the treewidth of the relaxation T^- that we control and call the *target treewidth* w. The optimal solution to the original theory T is obtained by performing a DPLL-style branch-and-bound search over T implemented on top of MiniSAT exploiting both the lower bounds obtained from the compilation of T^- and capabilities such Unit Propagation and Clause Learning. The resulting MinCostSAT solver, SR(w), is then evaluated empirically over the entire suite of problems from the 2006 Weighted Max-SAT competition [11].

2 MinCostSAT

MinCostSAT is the problem of obtaining a minimum cost satisfying truth assignment of a CNF propositional formula. If the formula is denoted by T, the cost $c(s)$ of a truth assignment s over T is defined as follows:

$$c(s) \stackrel{\text{def}}{=} \begin{cases} \sum_{l:s\models l} c(l) & \text{if } s \models T \\ \infty & \text{otherwise} \end{cases} \quad . \tag{1}$$

where l stands for literals and $c(l)$ stands for the cost of literal l. The optimal cost $c^*(T)$ of T is the cost of the best (minimum cost) assignment s. In some formulations, costs are defined only on *positive literals*, with the costs of *negative literals* assumed to be zero [12]. Non-negative costs on negative literals $\neg x$ can then be captured by introducing new positive literals x' set to $x' \equiv \neg x$. In this work we do not need this assumption and accommodate costs on both positive and negative literals. Without loss of generality, however, we assume that all costs are *non-negative*; indeed, a positive increment can always be added to the cost of any pair of complementary literals x and $\neg x$ without changing the solutions so that none has negative cost and at most one has a positive cost.

MinCostSAT is a (boolean) special case of the class of constraint optimization problems called *Valued CSPs* (VCSPs)[13]. Another special case of VCSPs closely related to MinCostSAT is Weighted MAX-SAT, where the cost of an assignment reflects the costs of the clauses that are violated by it [14]. The transformation of one into the other is simple and involves the addition of a linear number of variables or clauses, and they both subsume other variations like MAX-SAT, (Weighted) MIN-ONE, (Weighted) MAX-ONE, and (Weighted) Partial MAX-SAT [5,15].

3 Relaxing Graphical Models by Renaming Variables

Current state-of-the-art MinCostSAT and Weighted MAX-SAT perform a branch and bound search, pruning the space by various forms of constraint propagation that take into account both the constraints and their weights [16,17,18,19]. In this work, we approach the search in MinCostSAT from a slightly different perspective. *Rather than pruning values by local consistency methods, we compute explicit lower bounds by solving optimally a global relaxation.* This relaxation is defined structurally in terms of the *constraint* or *interaction* graph that represents the interactions among the variables in the problem [6].

Relaxations by Variable Renaming

We start with the observation that any graphical model can be relaxed into a weaker model of bounded treewidth by a simple form of variable renaming, where a variable that appears in many factors is replaced by many fresh new variables that appear in few. For example, a graphical model over variables $x_1, \ldots, x_n$ where there is a factor for each variable pair, has an interaction graph that is a full clique and a treewidth equal to $n-1$. Yet, if a variable x_i is replaced by a different 'alias' variable x_i^j in each of the factors where it appears, a relaxed model is obtained with treewidth $n-2$. Actually, if the same is done for all the variables $x_1, \ldots, x_n$, the treewidth of the relaxed model is reduced to 1.

If T is the propositional MinCostSAT theory, we will refer by T^- to the relaxed theory obtained by replacing some or all occurrences of some variables x_i in T by a set of new variables x_i^j that we call 'aliases'. There is a lot of freedom in the choice of the variables x_i in T to rename, in the number x_i^j of aliases to introduce for each renamed variable x_i, and in the scope of these aliases (i.e., the set of clauses in T where x_i is replaced by x_i^j). A *renaming scheme* defines these three aspects.

For simplicity, we consider only schemes where the scopes of the clauses including the aliases are disjoint (no occurrence of a renamed x_i is replaced by more than one alias), and span all the clauses where x_i appears (so that renamed variables x_i do not appear in the relaxation T^-). Such schemes can be described by defining the set of variables x_i in T to be renamed (relaxed) along with the alias x_i^j to be used in place of x_i in each of the clauses where x_i appears. For example, given a theory T with four clauses:

$$C_1 : x_1 \vee x_2 \ , \ C_2 : \neg x_1 \vee x_3 \ , \ C_3 : x_2 \vee \neg x_3 \ , \ C_4 : x_1 \vee x_4$$

an admissible renaming can be obtained by replacing x_2 by the alias x_2^1 in clause C_1 and by the alias x_2^2 in C_3, resulting in the relaxation T^-:

$$C_1' : x_1 \vee x_2^1 \ , \ C_2 : \neg x_1 \vee x_3 \ , \ C_3' : x_2^2 \vee \neg x_3 \ , \ C_4 : x_1 \vee x_4$$

The interaction graphs of both of these theories are displayed in Figure 1, from which it is possible to see that T has treewidth 2, while T^- has treewidth 1.

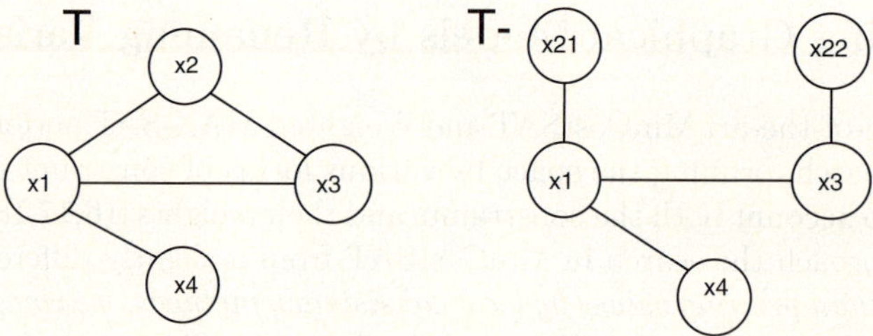

Fig. 1. The interactions graphs of T and T^- where variable x_2 in T is renamed into the aliases x_2^1 and x_2^2. The corresponding treewidths are 2 and 1.

We say that variable x_i is *fully renamed* when the different occurrences of x_i in T are replaced by different aliases x_i^j in T^-.[1] When the variables are renamed fully, the only aspect that a renaming scheme must define is the set of variables to rename. For this we make use of the notion of w-cutsets: these are sets of variables x_i in T whose instantiation ensures that the (induced) treewidth of the resulting theory is bounded by w. This notion, introduced in [20], has been proposed as an alternative way for combining structural and search methods: basically, one can choose an small target treewidth w, search then exhaustively over the possible instantiations v of the w-cutset C_w, solving the resulting theories T_v by structural methods with a complexity exponential only on w. For a bounded w, the complexity of this method is dominated by the exhaustive search over the possible instantiations over the w-cutset variables and hence is exponential in $|C_w|$.

[1] It is assumed that no variable in T appears twice in a given clause. If not, multiple occurrences can be collapsed into one when they all have the same sign, and else the clause is a tautology and can be deleted.

The method that we propose makes use of the w-cutset notion too but by *using renaming rather than instantiation for simplifying T into a tractable form*, does not require an exhaustive search over the w-cutset variables, except in the worst case.

The theory T^- obtained by *renaming fully* all the variables x_i in a w-cutset of T, can be processed indeed in time that is exponential in w, in the same way as the theory T_v that is obtained from T by *instantiating* such variables. Yet, while in the latter case the complexity bound follows from the (induced) treewidth of its interaction graph, in the former, it does not. This is because treewidth is a rough structural notion affected by the *size of the clauses,* a size that can be reduced by *instantiating* variables in a clause but not by *renaming* such variables. Finer structural measures like *hypertree width* [21] that take into account the size and scope of the constraints, can be used instead for characterizing the complexity bounds that follow from renaming. We will take however a simpler route and refer to the *simplified (induced) treewidth* of a theory T as the (induced) treewidth of its *simplified interaction graph*: this is the interaction graph of T *with the nodes representing the variables that occur in a single clause of T removed.*

Theorem 1. *Let T be a CNF formula and let S be a w-cutset for T. Then the relaxation T^- obtained by fully renaming each variable x_i in S has a* simplified treewidth *bounded by w.*

A simplified treewidth bounded by w ensures a complexity exponential in w over the typical queries in graphical models provided that variables that appear in a single factor can be eliminated in time that does not grow with the size of the factor. This is certainly true in our context for variables that appear in a single clause, as individual clauses can be compiled into d-DNNF (see below) in linear-time [9]. The alias variables x_i^j that result from fully renaming a variable x_i in T fall into this class. Note also that *simplified treewidth* of w implies *treewidth* of w when no factor has a size greater than w.

For simplicity, when no confusion arises, we will use the term treewidth to refer to simplified treewidth, and refer to the relaxation method that maps the theory T into T^- according to Theorem 1, as *w-cutset renaming.* This is a polynomial and fast operation. The theory T^- above, whose interaction graph is shown in Figure 1 is a w-cutset renaming relaxation of T, with $w = 1$ for the w-cutset $S = \{x_2\}$.

In order to compute a w-cutset, the *GWC* algorithm presented in [22] can be used. The *GWC* algorithm greedily and incrementally builds a minimal set of variables S that ensures $|C_i/S| \leq w$ over the maximal cliques C_i in the min-fill tree-decomposition of the model. In our solver, we just substitute the *min-fill* ordering by *minimum induced width* (MIW) [6] which scales up better for large theories at a small cost in size of the cutsets.

In the experiments, we consider also an alternative relaxation method that we call *w-mini-bucket renaming* as it is based on the mini-bucket approximation scheme [23]. The w-mini-bucket renaming scheme runs the mini-buckets procedure *symbolically.* That is, propagating only the scopes of the primitive and induced functions but not the functions themselves. Each scope keeps track also of the set of primitive functions (clauses) it was derived from. If $x_1, \cdots, x_i, \cdots, x_k, \cdots, x_n$ is the ordering in which the variables are processed, then when processing the bucket of variable x_i, if the number of variables $x_k \neq x_i, k \geq i$ appearing on that bucket is above the w bound, the scopes in the bucket are partitioned into sets $s_1, \ldots, s_m$ none of which has more than w variables $x_k, k > i$. The variable x_i is then renamed into x_i^j in all the clauses that are associated with the scopes in s_j.

Like w-cutset renaming, w-mini-bucket renaming yields relaxations T^- with treewidth bounded by w, but unlike the former it does not use full variable renaming, as an alias may end up appearing in different clauses. As we will see, the experimental results for the two methods tend to be similar, with an slight edge for w-cutset renaming.

4 Compiling the Relaxation into d-DNNF

If the relaxation T^- has bounded (simplified) treewidth, then all the MinCost-SAT sub-problems problems $T^- \cup s^-$ arising in the search where s^- is a set of T^- literals, can be solved from scratch in polynomial time and space by variable elimination [24]. A more efficient solution, which is more elegant too, can be obtained however by compiling the formula in a suitable way so that the solutions to these sub-problems can be efficiently 'retrieved' from a compiled representation. For formulas expressed in CNF, Darwiche's CNF to d-DNNF compiler [7] allows us to do exactly that in time and space exponential in the formula treewidth [9].

A formula T in d-DNNF is a rooted DAG (Directed Acyclic Graph) whose leaves are the positive and negative literals associated with the variables in T along with the constants **true** and **false**, and whose internal nodes stand for conjunctions or disjunctions (AND and OR nodes, respectively). A d-DNNF formula is thus in Negated Normal Form (NNF) as it contains only the connectives for conjunctions, disjunctions, and negations, and negation occurs only in literals [9]. The d-DNNF representation enforces two additional constraints, decomposability (no variable shared among sub-formulas represented by the children of an AND node) and determinism (no model shared among sub-formulas represented by the children of an OR node), that enable a large number of otherwise intractable queries and transformations to be done in time which is linear in the size of the DAG representation [25]. For example, the procedure for computing the cost of a formula T in d-DNNF can be expressed in term of the value of the function $c^*(n)$ computed bottom up over the nodes n of the DAG as follows [10]:

$$c^*(n) = \begin{cases} 0 & \text{if } n = \textbf{true} \\ \infty & \text{if } n = \textbf{false} \\ c(L) & \text{if } n = L \text{ where } L \text{ is a literal different than } \textbf{true} \text{ and } \textbf{false} \\ \sum_i c^*(n_i) & \text{if } n \text{ is an AND node with children } n_i \\ \min_i c^*(n_i) & \text{if } n \text{ is an OR node with children } n_i \end{cases} \tag{2}$$

If the DAG represents the compilation of T^- then the cost $c^*(T^-)$ is given by the value $c^*(n)$ of the root node, while the cost $c^*(T^- \cup s^-)$ of the theory T^-

extended with a set of literals s^- is obtained from the same bottom-up recursion but setting the costs $c(L)$ of the literals L whose negation is in s^- to ∞. Finally, while the costs $c^*(T^- \cup s^-)$ are obtained in a single bottom-up pass over the DAG, a minimum cost model M of T can be obtained by a subsequent top-down pass, collecting the literals in the leaves that can be reached from the root node, following all of the children of every reached AND node, and a single best child (min. cost) of every reached OR node [10].

In order to ensure that the relaxation T^- compiles in time and space exponential in the target (simplified) treewidth w set for the relaxation, we must instruct the d-DNNF compiler to use an elimination ordering over the variables in T^- (in the form of a decomposition tree [26]) related to the variable ordering used for obtaining T^- from T. For this, if T^- was obtained by w-cutset renaming, we just place the alias variables x_i^j first in the ordering, while if T^- was obtained by w-mini-bucket renaming, the aliases x_i^j are introduced in place of the renamed variables x_i in the order in which they were 'eliminated' (symbolically) during the relaxation. These elimination orders ensure that the compiler processes the relaxed theories T^- in time and space exponential in the target width w in the worst case.

5 The Cost of Renamed Variables

If there are costs $c(x_i) > 0$ or $c(\neg x_i) > 0$ associated to variables x_i in T that have been renamed in T^-, we need to decide how to allocate these costs to their aliases x_i^j. One possibility is to ignore such costs by setting the costs of all alias literals to zero. This ensures that the compilation of T^- yields lower bounds for T, but they are not as informed as they could be. Setting the costs of the all the alias literals x_i^j and $\neg x_i^j$ to the cost of the corresponding literals x_i and $\neg x_i$ can lead to overestimation and hence does not necessarily produce lower bounds. Actually, a simple option that uses the costs over renamed variables x_i and yields lower bounds is to transfer these costs to a particular, designated alias variable x_i^j, thus setting $c(x_i^j)$ and $c(\neg x_i^j)$ to $c(x_i)$ and $c(\neg x_i)$ respectively, leaving the cost of all other alias literals in zero. This is actually the choice that we have made in our solver where such designated alias variables are selected greedily using the idea of Maximal Independent Sets (MIS) [27,12]. We have also tried an scheme where the cost of a renamed literal is split uniformly over it alias literals, that also ensures admissibility (lower bounds), but found the results to be slightly inferior.

A MIS ω is a subset of clauses that is maximally independent in the sense that no two clauses in ω share a variable. We build a MIS greedily, starting from the set S of clauses in T^- that include some alias variable x_i^j. Then iteratively a clause C with maximum "average cost" defined in [12]:

$$\frac{\sum_{l_i \in C} c(l_i)}{|\{l_i \in C_j\}|} \tag{3}$$

is chosen and added to ω, while all clauses featuring an alias variable x_i^k coming from the same renamed variable x_i as an alias variable x_i^j in C are removed from S. This process continues until no more clauses are left in S. The alias literals x_i^j or $\neg x_i^j$ in a clause of ω get then all the weight from the renamed literals x_i and $\neg x_i$, ensuring that this cost allocation yields a lower bound over the relaxation and also that the alias literals that get these weights are more tightly constrained.

6 The Search

The search algorithm looks for the best model of T by looking for the best model of the relaxation T^- that satisfies the constraints $x_i^k = x_i^j$ for all the aliases x_i^k and x_i^j of the same renamed variables x_i in T. This is achieved by a branch-and-bound DPLL-style search over T whose state s is a set s of literals over the renamed variables x_i that represents the commitments made so far. Initially s is empty. Then in each step, the best model M of $T^- \cup s^-$ and its cost $c^*(T^- \cup s^-)$ are computed, where s^- is the set of alias literals that correspond to s: namely, all x_i^j (resp. $\neg x_i^j$) are in s^- if x_i (resp. $\neg x_i$) in s. The lower bound $LB(s)$ is set to $c^*(T^- \cup s^-)$. The search does not continue beneath s if either $LB(s)$ is not smaller than the current upper bound (a bound conflict), the boolean constraint propagation procedures derives an *empty clause* (a logical conflict), or if M has no discrepancies (a solution). Else, a variable x_i with a discrepancy in M is selected (an alias pair x_i^j and x_i^k such that $x_i^j \neq x_i^k$ in M) the state s is extended with either x_i or $\neg x_i$, and the process is iterated. By setting a small target width w, the relaxation procedure that yields T^- from T, ensures that the compilation of T^- can be done in polynomial time and space, and the compilation in turn ensures that the best model M of $T^- \cup s^-$ and its costs can be computed efficiently for any set of literals s^-.

This basic search procedure is implemented on top of MiniSAT 2.0 [8], thus relying on the efficient boolean constraint propagation provided by the *two-literal watching* rule [28] which is performed right after every commitment. We also use its (dynamic) VSIDS variable selection heuristic [28] but branch only on the variables x_i that have been renamed, choosing always first the value x_i or $\neg x_i$ with least cost $c(x_i)$ or $c(\neg x_i)$. For relaxations T^- obtained by w-cutset renaming this means that in the worst case, the size of the search space will be exponential in the size of the w-cutset used. Within this space, however, the lower bounds $LB(s)$ obtained from the compiled relaxation and the pruning that they produce, will normally keep the search away from this worst case scenario, as the experimental results below show.

7 Learning from Bound Conflicts

The implementation of the search on top of a SAT solver benefits from the ability of to learn new clauses during search after *logical failures*. It is well known that *clause learning* is a key technique in current solvers that can reduce the search space quite drastically [29,30]. The success of *learning from logical conflicts* in SAT, suggested to look at the problem of *learning from bound conflicts* as when the lower bound $LB(s)$ does not improve the current upper bound UB for a given state s; i.e., when $LB(s) \geq UB$. In the context of solvers whose inference is based on *unit propagation*, this problem has been approached in [31] and [12] where a set of literals that explains the bound conflict is obtained and negated. Our solver, however, does not use only unit resolution but also and mainly optimal inference over the compiled relaxation T^-. The trivial way to learn in such setting is by simply recording the clause $\neg s$ when $LB(s) \geq UB$. This, however, while enables us to preserve the conflict-directed implementation of MiniSAT, has not pruning effect. A much more effective alternative is to find the smallest possible subset s' in s that explains the bound conflict, i.e., a subset $s' \subseteq s$ such that $LB(s') \geq UB$. Interestingly, it is possible to use the compiled d-DNNF representation of T^- for computing such 'causes' for failure even if there is no guarantee that such causes are minimal. The idea is simple and requires only a single downward pass over the DAG representing the compilation of T^-.

Basically, starting from the root node of the DAG representing the compilation of T^- we perform a top-down scan, skipping some nodes, while collecting the literals l in the leaves that are reached, retaining from this set only the literals l in s. Of course, if no node is skipped in this scan, we will get back the set s itself. Yet as we will see there are three types of nodes n that can be skipped because the commitments beneath them in the graph, if any, are not relevant either to the cost of their parent node in the graph or the bound failure. For this, let $c^*(n)$ be the cost of node in n in the DAG when evaluated in the context of the commitments s^- and let $c_0^*(n)$ be the value of the same node when evaluated in the context with no commitments at all (i.e., with s^- assumed empty, as in the beginning of the search).

Clearly if $c^*(n) = c_0^*(n)$, it means that the commitments beneath n are not relevant to its cost given s^0. Likewise, if n is an OR-node, the commitments beneath the child n_1 are not relevant to the cost of n either if $c_0^*(n_1) > c^*(n)$. Last, if n is an AND-node, the commitments beneath the child n_1 can be ignored if $c_0^*(n_1) + c^*(n_2) \geq UB$ as the commitments beneath the other child n_2 suffice to explain the bound failure.

By performing and exhaustive scan of the DAG representing T^- after finding that $LB(s) \geq UB$, starting from the root node while skipping nodes as above, it is then possible to get a reduced set of alias literals $t^- \subseteq s^-$ such that $LB(t) \geq UB$ as well. The *conflict clause* $\neg t$ is then fed to the 1st Unique Implication Point [29] heuristic implemented by MiniSAT 2.0, that derives the *blocking clause* and the decision level to backtrack to.

8 Empirical Evaluation

The MinCostSAT solver SR(w) accepts a MinCostSAT problem in the form of a cost function c and a CNF theory T. Using w-cutset renaming, it then maps T into a relaxation T^- which is compiled in d-DNNF using Darwiche's c2d compiler, and sets the cost of the renamed literals according to the MIS procedure described above. It then carries a DPLL-style branch-and-bound search on top of

MiniSAT 2.0 that benefits from the lower bounds obtained from the relaxation, as well as from unit propagation and clause learning from both logical and bound conflicts.

The experiments below have all been run on a grid consisting of 76 nodes, each one being a dual-processor Xeon "Woodcrest" dual core computer, with a clock speed of 2.33 GHz and 8 Gb of RAM. Execution time was limited to 1,800 seconds.

Overall Performance

Table 1 compares SR(w) against three state-of-the-art Weighted-MAX SAT and MinCostSAT solvers over the 559 problems of the 2006 Weighted SAT Competition [11]: the winner of the competition, *toolbar* [17], the runner-up, *Lazy* [32], and the recent MinCostSAT solver, *MinCostChaff* [12] all ran on the same platform. The problems were converted into MinCostSAT by adding a *slack* variable x into each non-unary clause and setting $c(x)$ to the weight of the clause. Unary clauses over a literal x ($\neg x$) were removed and their weight was assigned to $\neg x$ (x) resp. Last, hard clauses, represented with a very large weight in Weighted MAX-SAT, were modeled as hard clauses (crisp constraints).

The competition problems fall into different categories: *MinCostSAT*, where all clauses are hard constraints and literals are weighted, *Weighted Max-SAT*, where all clauses are soft and weights are associated to constraints, and *Weighted Partial Max-SAT* which have a mix of both hard and soft constraints. This is explicitly indicated in Table 1.

The value of the target treewidth w used in the SR(w) solver is $w = 8$. The performance for other values of w is analyzed below. From the results shown, it is clear that SR(w) does well in relation to state-of-the-art MinCostSAT and Weighted-MAX solvers, trailing only Toolbar, while showing an slight edge over Lazy, which does a lot better in these instances than MinCostChaff. The best relative performance of SR(w) is on the Weighted Partial Max-SAT problems, where in two domains (WCSP; dense tight and sparse tight) manages to solve 10 and 17 instances where the other solvers solve none.

Impact of Target Width, Learning, and Renaming Schemes

Table 2 shows the number of problems solved by SR(w) for different bounds $w = 1, 2, 4, 8, 16, \ldots$ on the (simplified) treewidth of the relaxation. Interestingly, the best coverage is not obtained for the extreme values of w but for $w = 8$ and $w = 16$. The last column shows the results corresponding to the relaxation $T^- = T$. In such a case, the theories T, if they compile, are solved without search (no variables are renamed), so that column is testing the CNF to d-DNNF compiler, which does pretty well, solves by itself the same number of problems as MinCostChaff. Further details on some of the instances for various values of w are shown in Table 3 and Table 4, illustrating the typical trade-off between search and inference: for relaxations with larger w, the search visits less number of nodes, but the compilation is more expensive in terms of space and time, and the overhead per node in

Table 1. Overall performance over the 2006 Weighted SAT Competition instances. S is the number of solved instances in each domain and T the average time needed to solve them in seconds. Domains are split into native *MinCostSAT*, *Weighted Partial Max-SAT*, and *Weighted Max-SAT*. Times for SR(w) include the relaxation, compilation and search, for the target treewidth fixed at $w = 8$ which results in the best coverage over these instances.

		SR(w)		toolbar-3.1		Lazy		MinCostChaff	
Set Name	N	S	T	S	T	S	T	S	T
Auctions (paths)	30	20	136.28	28	244.49	21	123.69	0	0
Auctions (sched.)	30	18	131.97	30	82.93	28	0.65	6	317
Auctions (regions)	30	30	171.07	30	3.39	30	41.39	13	173
Max-Clique (brock)	12	0	–	4	59.14	4	66.57	0	0
Max-Clique (c-fat)	7	3	23.92	7	10.99	7	0.07	1	973
Max-Clique (ham.)	6	2	23.92	5	67.03	5	119.02	3	627
Max-Clique (John.)	4	2	1.40	3	34.96	3	25.98	2	782
Max-Clique (Kell.)	2	1	16.63	1	20.67	1	27.50	0	0
Max-Clique (Mann)	4	1	0.06	2	48.63	1	0.18	1	1,472
Max-Clique (p_hat)	12	1	1,813.73	7	385.63	7	367.21	3	1,591
Max-Clique (san)	11	0	–	4	649.00	1	6.03	0	0
Max-Clique (sanr)	4	0	–	3	463.08	2	466.25	0	0
Max-One	45	40	130.65	45	129.93	30	357.29	1	1,623
WCSP (SPOT5)	21	9	16.24	5	81.03	3	533.96	2	277
QCP	25	6	242.99	11	133.25	7	255.79	25	43
MinCostSAT	243	133	54.7%	185	76.1%	150	61.7%	57	23.5%
WCSP (S-L)	20	20	40.22	18	344.46	10	351.52	17	252
WCSP (D-L)	20	10	722.98	16	446.24	13	629.06	3	339
WCSP (D-T)	30	10	546.82	0	0.00	0	0.00	0	0
WCSP (S-T)	20	17	413.89	0	0.00	0	0.00	0	0
WCSP (SPOT5)	21	9	16.24	4	83.02	3	655.94	8	1,189
Wt. Partial Max-SAT	111	66	59.5%	38	34.2%	26	23.4%	28	25.2%
WCSP (S-L)	20	13	6.93	20	3.33	18	299.49	15	285
WCSP (D-L)	20	11	656.23	20	17.51	20	260.34	1	970
WCSP (D-T)	30	27	270.02	30	33.44	0	0.00	0	0
WCSP (S-T)	20	13	60.22	20	161.54	0	0.00	0	0
Wt. Max-Cut (spin.)	5	2	0.43	3	49.71	2	0.14	2	820
Wt. Max-Cut (brock)	12	2	0.10	12	9.20	12	11.62	0	0
Wt. Max-Cut (c-fat)	7	4	15.44	7	7.35	7	15.50	1	881
Wt. Max-Cut (hamm.)	6	0	–	4	67.97	5	285.10	3	638
Wt. Max-Cut (john.)	4	1	12.10	3	54.79	3	47.45	2	731
Wt. Max-Cut (keller)	2	0	–	2	10.33	2	11.20	0	0
Wt. Max-Cut (mann)	4	2	78.20	4	1,034.70	4	640.47	1	1,492
Wt. Max-Cut (p-hat)	12	6	193.53	12	1,138.46	12	7.03	2	1,415
Wt. Max-Cut (san)	11	1	541.14	11	54.73	11	36.53	0	0
Wt. Max-Cut (sanr)	4	1	1,575.30	4	39.59	4	16.86	0	0
Wt. Ramsey	48	33	124.83	35	3.27	29	42.72	34	17
Wt. Max-SAT	205	116	56.6%	187	91.2%	129	62.9%	61	29.8%
Total	559	315	56.4%	410	73.3%	305	54.6%	146	26.1%

Table 2. Impact of target treewidth parameter w in SR(w): Number of problems solved for each value of w. The last column with $w = tw$, means no relaxation at all so that $T^- = T$. In such a case, the problem is solved without search from the d-DNNF compilation of T, when the compilation is successful.

Domains	I	w=1	w=2	w=4	w=8	w=16	w=32	w=64	w=tw
Auction (paths)	30	5	10	12	20	25	24	7	29
Auction (sched.)	30	18	17	18	18	20	22	17	26
Auction (regions)	30	24	25	28	30	30	30	29	30
Max-Clique	62	10	10	11	10	10	6	4	11
Max-One	45	42	42	42	40	17	0	0	9
WCSP (SPOT5)	42	8	8	8	18	8	7	0	12
QCP	25	10	10	9	6	0	0	0	0
WCSP (S-L)	40	12	22	32	33	31	0	0	0
WCSP (D-L)	40	1	1	3	21	0	0	0	0
WCSP (D-T)	60	0	0	2	37	28	0	0	9
WCSP (S-T)	40	1	0	0	30	29	0	0	2
Wt. Max-Cut (spin.)	5	1	2	2	2	1	0	0	1
Wt. Max-Cut	62	2	7	7	17	10	0	0	7
Wt. Ramsey	48	25	25	26	33	15	0	0	10
Total Solved	559	159	179	200	315	224	89	57	146
% solved		28.4%	32.0%	35.8%	56.4%	40.1%	15.9%	10.2%	26.1%

Table 3. A closer look at some instances from the SPOT5 domain: tw is the instance upper bound treewidth as estimated by the MIW ordering, w is the treewidth bound that produced the best total time for SR(w) over each instance, and *Relax*, *Comp*, and *Search* are the relaxation, compilation and search times all in seconds.

Problem	# vars.	# Clauses	tw	w	# Nodes	Relax	Comp	Search	Total
8.wcsp.dir	20	21	6	4	2	0.001	0.010	0.000	0.011
1502.wcsp.dir	515	427	7	4	20	0.045	0.040	0.003	0.088
503.wcsp.dir	317	849	13	12	7	0.036	0.120	0.002	0.158
404.wcsp.dir	187	966	23	16	162	0.022	0.070	0.019	0.111
54.wcsp.dir	154	441	23	8	428	0.011	0.040	0.036	0.087
29.wcsp.dir	139	629	31	16	98	0.016	0.080	0.026	0.122
1504.wcsp.dir	1,577	6,312	43	32	339	0.853	16.380	38.971	56.204
505.wcsp.dir	552	3,296	46	45	3	0.182	19.230	0.132	19.544
408.wcsp.dir	392	3,013	55	32	1372	0.113	0.670	10.458	11.241
42.wcsp.dir	361	1,883	61	32	10,654	0.084	4.660	733.013	737.757

the search (which is linear in the size of the compilation) is greater. Indeed most of the failures for widths $w \leq 32$ are search timeouts.

Table 5 shows the combined impact of the treewidth bound w, the renaming scheme (w-cutset vs. w-mini-buckets), and learning (turned on and off) on two instances. As it can be seen, learning can help a lot, in particular, for small values of w, while the differences between the results obtained with w-cutset and w-mini-bucket renaming are not so clear cut.

Table 4. A closer look at the performance for various relaxation treewidths w over the *29.wcsp.dir* instance from Table 3. *d-DNNF size* denotes the number of nodes in the d-DNNF DAG while *# nodes* refers to the number of nodes during search.

w	d-DNNF size	# Nodes	Relax.	Comp.	Search	Total
1	5,581	453,758	0.03	0.04	131.14	131.21
2	5,130	76,231	0.02	0.03	7.65	7.7
4	4,922	4,737	0.02	0.03	0.41	0.46
8	11,240	482	0.02	0.05	0.07	0.13
16	25,721	98	0.02	0.08	0.03	0.12
30	35,822	3	0.01	0.32	0	0.34

Table 5. Number of nodes in the search and total run-time (in parenthesis) over a random Max-3-SAT instance. w denotes the treewidth bound on the relaxation. MIW estimate was 29.

	w-mini-buckets renaming		w-cutset renaming	
w	Learning	No learning	Learning	No learning
1	21,373 (21.99)	98,461 (102.6)	14,399 (15.88)	Timeout
2	25,162 (28.3)	129,859 (143.63)	9,302 (10.1)	556,181 (546.47)
4	64,716 (76.61)	146,377 (168.29)	11,218 (18.71)	75,511 (105.81)
8	11,627 (60.63)	18,473 (96.17)	4,889 (40.08)	9,669 (67.25)
16	474 (196.96)	695 (300.37)	238 (186.59)	737 (533.52)

9 Discussion

We have presented an structural relaxation scheme based on renaming variables that maps a CNF theory T into a relaxation T^- with a (simplified) treewidth bounded by a parameter w. We have then used this relaxation for developing a MinCostSAT solver that obtains its lower bounds from a suitable compilation of the relaxation into d-DNNF. The observed performance of this solver, implemented on top of a state-of-the-art SAT solver that benefits also from efficient unit propagation and clause learning, suggests that the idea of compiling structural relaxations for guiding the search, is an idea worth exploring in further depth that may be applicable in other contexts too. This approach is closely related to other methods that aim to combine structural and search-methods and in particular to Dechter's mini-buckets. Indeed, if the relaxation is done by the scheme that mimics mini-buckets which we call w-mini-bucket renaming, we would be obtaining the same sort of structural lower bounds. On the other hand, by appealing to *explicit relaxations*, our approach is more general as it is not tied to a particular renaming scheme, can benefit from existing tools such as SAT solvers and d-DNNF compilers, and deals in a natural way with dynamic variable ordering. Just in time for the last version of this paper, we have learned about an independent but closely related relaxation scheme in the context of Bayesian Networks to appear at UAI-07 [33].

Acknowledgements

We thank the anonymous reviewers for useful comments, R. Dechter for an informative exchange on treewidth, and N. Sörenssón, D. Le Berre, and Z. Fu for answering various questions about MiniSAT and MinCostChaff. We also thank the authors of the tools, the c2d compiler and MiniSAT, used in our solver, and R. Isla from UPF for help with the cluster. H. Geffner is partially supported by grant TIN2006-15387-C03-03 from MEC, Spain.

References

1. Culberson, J.C., Schaeffer, J.: Pattern Databases. Comp. Int. 14 (1998)
2. Korf, R.E.: Finding Optimal Solutions to Rubik's Cube Using Pattern Patabases. In: Proc. AAAI-98 (1998)
3. Bonet, B., Geffner, H.: Planning as Heuristic Search. Art. Int. 129 (2001)
4. Mackworth, A.K.: Consistency in Networks of Relations. Art. Int. 8 (1977)
5. Li, X.Y.: Optimization Algorithms for the Minimum–Cost Satisfiability Problem. PhD thesis, North Carolina State University (2004)
6. Dechter, R.: Constraint Processing. Morgan Kauffman, San Francisco (2003)
7. Darwiche, A.: New Advances in Compiling CNF to Decomposable Negational Normal Form. In: Proc. ECAI'04 (2004)
8. Eén, N., Söressón, N.: MiniSAT: an Extensible SAT Solver. Technical report, Chalmers University (2005)
9. Darwiche, A.: Decomposable Negation Normal Form. Journal of the ACM 48(4), 608–647 (2001)
10. Marquis, P., Darwiche, A.: Compiling Propositional Weighted Bases. Artificial Intelligence 157(1–2), 81–113 (2004)
11. Argelich, J., et al.: First Evaluation of Max-SAT solvers (2006), Available at `http://www.iiia.csic.es/maxsat06`
12. Fu, Z., Malik, S.: Solving the Minimum Cost Satisfiability Problem using SAT Based Branch-and-Bound Search. In: Proc. of ICCAD'06 (2006)
13. Bistarelli, S., Montanari, U., Rossi, F., Schiex, T., Verfaille, G., Fargier, H.: Semiring-Based CSPs and Valued CSPs: Frameworks, Properties and Comparison. Constraints 4(3), 199–240 (2004)
14. Papadimitrou, C.H.: Computational Complexity. Addison-Wesley, Reading (1994)
15. Giunchiglia, E., Maratea, M.: Solving Optimization Problems with DLL. In: Proc. of ECAI'06 (2006)
16. Larrosa, J., Heras, F.: Resolution in Max-SAT and its Relation to Local Consistency in Weighted CSPs. In: Proc. of IJCAI-05, pp. 193–199 (2005)
17. Larrosa, J., Heras, F.: New Inference Rules for Efficient Max-SAT Solving. In: Proc. AAAI'06 (2006)
18. Li, C.M., Manyá, F., Planes, J.: Detecting Disjoint Inconsistent Subformulas for Computing Lower Bounds for Max-SAT. In: Proc. AAAI'06 (2006)
19. de Givry, S., Larrosa, J., Messeguer, P., Schiex, T.: Solving Max-SAT as Weighted CSP. In: Rossi, F. (ed.) CP 2003. LNCS, vol. 2833, pp. 363–376. Springer, Heidelberg (2003)
20. Dechter, R.: Enhancement Schemes for Constraint Processing: Backjumping, Learning and Cutset Decomposition. Artificial Intelligence 43(3), 273–312 (1990)

21. Gottlob, G., Leone, N., Scarcello, F.: Hypertree decompositions and tractable queries. J. Comput. Syst. Sci. 64(3), 579–627 (2002)
22. Bidyuk, B., Dechter, R.: On Finding Minimal w-cutset. In: Proc. UAI-04 (2004)
23. Dechter, R.: Mini–Buckets: a General Scheme for Generating Approximations in Automated Reasoning. In: Proc. of IJCAI-97, pp. 1297–1303 (1997)
24. Dechter, R.: Bucket Elimination: a Unifying Framework for Reasoning. Artificial Intelligence 113(1–2), 41–85 (1999)
25. Darwiche, A., Marquis, P.: A Knowledge Compilation Map. Journal of AI Research 17, 229–264 (2002)
26. Darwiche, A.: Recursive Conditioning. Artificial Intelligence 126(1–2), 5–41 (2001)
27. Coudert, O., Madre, J.C.: New Ideas for Solving Covering Problems. In: Proc. of DAC'95, pp. 641–646 (1995)
28. Moskewicz, M.W., Madigan, C.F., et al.: Chaff: Engineeering an Efficient SAT Solver. In: Proc.of DAC-01 (2001)
29. Zhang, L., Madigan, C.F., et al.: Efficient Conflict Driven Learning in a Boolean Satisfiability Solver. In: Proc. of ICCAD'01 (2001)
30. Silva, J.P.M., Sakallah, K.A.: GRASP – A New Search Algorithm for Satisfiability. In: Proc. of ICCAD'96, pp. 220–227 (1996)
31. Manquinho, V., Marques-Silva, J.: Search Pruning Techniques in SAT-based Branch-and-Bound Algorithms for the Binate Covering Problem. IEEE Trans. on CAD and Integrated Circuit and Systems 21, 505–516 (2002)
32. Alsinet, T., Manyá, F., Planes, J.: Improved Exact Solvers for Weighted Max-SAT. In: Proc. of the 8th SAT conference (2005)
33. Choi, A., Chavira, M., Darwiche, A.: Node splitting: A scheme for generating upper bounds in bayesian networks. In: Proceedings UAI-07 (to appear, 2007)

Bound-Consistent Deviation Constraint

Pierre Schaus, Yves Deville, and Pierre Dupont

Department of Computing Sciences and Engineering
Université catholique de Louvain, Belgium
{pierre.schaus,yves.deville,pierre.dupont}@uclouvain.be

Abstract. Deviation is a recent constraint to balance a set of variables with respect to a given mean. We show that the propagators recently introduced are not bound-consistent when the mean is rational. We introduce bound-consistent propagators running in linear time with respect to the number of variables. We evaluate the improvement in terms of efficiency and pruning obtained with the new propagators on the Balanced Academic Curriculum Problem.

1 Introduction

Global constraints to obtain a balanced assignment on a set of variables has not received much attention up to now. Some possible applications for such constraints are the following: fairly distribute the night and weekend shifts in physician scheduling in emergency rooms [2], balance the tardiness of tasks in a scheduling problem, balance the violations among soft global constraints, balance the load of work between periods in a timetabling problem [1], and generate spatially balanced scientific experiments [3].

The constraint `deviation` has been recently introduced in [7]. This constraint guarantees an assignment on a set of variables to be balanced around a given mean. More precisely `deviation` constrains a set of variables to present a given mean and constrains the sum of deviations to this mean. A closely related constraint using a different measure of balance is `spread` [5,6]. The propagators for `spread` run in quadratic time with respect to the number of variables against linear time for `deviation` . The semantic of `deviation` is given in the following definition.

Definition 1. *Given n finite domain variables $\mathcal{X} = (X_1, X_2, ..., X_n)$, one integer value s and one finite domain variable Δ, $\mathtt{deviation}(\mathcal{X}, s, \Delta)$ holds if and only if*

$$\sum_{i=1}^{n} X_i = s \quad \text{and} \quad \Delta \geq \sum_{i=1}^{n} |n \cdot X_i - s|.$$

In other words, $\mathtt{deviation}(\mathcal{X}, s, \Delta)$ is the conjunction of two constraints. One sum constraint enforcing the sum of the variables to be equal to s and one deviation constraint enforcing the sum of absolute deviations of $n \cdot X_i$ to the sum s to be less than or equal to Δ [1]. Another formulation is that the mean

[1] Bound-consistency is $\mathcal{NP}$-Complete when it is constrained to be equal to Δ [7].

C. Bessiere (Ed.): CP 2007, LNCS 4741, pp. 620–634, 2007.

(or average) of variables X_i must be equal to s/n and the sum of deviations to this mean must be smaller than Δ/n. The definition of `deviation` might seem restrictive since the sum is fixed. However in many practical applications the sum is known: one often needs to distribute (weighted) items into categories (nurses, shifts,...) and balance the loads of the categories.

The domain of a variable A is denoted $Dom(A)$, the maximum and minimum values in $Dom(A)$ are denoted $A^{\min}$ and $A^{\max}$ respectively.

Two propagators can be imagined for the `deviation` constraint:

1. Increasing of $\Delta^{\min}$ given domains of variables in $\mathcal{X}$ and value s.
2. Narrowing of $Dom(X_i)$ given the values $\Delta^{\min}$, s and the domains $Dom(X_j)$ with $X_j \in \mathcal{X}$ and $i \neq j$.

This paper gives bound-consistent filtering algorithms for both propagators running in linear time $\Theta(n)$.

Section 2 motivates the need for new propagators by explaining the weaknesses of the bounds computed in [7]. The improved bound-consistent ones considered in this paper are introduced. Section 3 and 4 give linear time filtering algorithms for propagators 1 and 2 respectively. Finally, Section 5 experiments the improvement made by the new propagators on the Balanced Academic Curriculum Problem.

2 Weakness of Existing Propagators

This section starts with some notations useful for the rest of the paper. Then the weaknesses of the bounds computed in [7] are explained and the improved bound-consistent ones considered in this paper are introduced.

An integer interval between integer numbers a and b is denoted $[a..b] \subseteq \mathbb{Z}$ while the rational interval is denoted $[a,b] \subseteq \mathbb{Q}$. An assignment on the variables $\mathcal{X} = (X_1, X_2, ..., X_n)$ is denoted by the tuple x and the ith entry of this tuple by $x[i]$. We denote by $s^{\downarrow}$ the largest multiple of n from s not larger than s: $s^{\downarrow} = \lfloor s/n \rfloor \cdot n$ and by $s^{\uparrow}$ the value $s^{\downarrow} + n$. The rational interval domain of X_i is $I_i^{\mathbb{Q}} = [X_i^{\min}, X_i^{\max}]$ and its integer interval domain is $I_i^{\mathbb{Z}} = [X_i^{\min} .. X_i^{\max}]$.

Definition 2 (Bound Consistency). *A global constraint $C(X_1, ..., X_k)$ is bound-consistent if and only if the minimum value and maximum value of every variable X_i with $i \in [1..k]$ has a support in the constraint assuming the other variables $X_{j \neq i}$ take their value from $[X_j^{\min}..X_j^{\max}]$.*

Filtering algorithms from [7] are simple and efficient (run-time in $\Theta(n)$). However, for integer finite domains, these algorithms are bound-consistent only when $s \bmod n = 0$ that is when the mean s/n is an integer. The reason is the relaxing assumption that the domains are rational intervals instead of integer intervals when computing the bounds. Definition 3 gives the expressions of the computed bounds in [7] and the bound-consistent ones considered in this paper.

Definition 3. $\underline{\Delta}^{\mathbb{Q}}$ *denotes the minimal sum of deviations with rational interval domains:*

$$\underline{\Delta}^{\mathbb{Q}} = \min_x \{\sum_{i=1}^{n} |n \cdot x[i] - s| \mid \forall i: \; x[i] \in I_i^{\mathbb{Q}} \text{ and } \sum_{i=1}^{n} x[i] = s\}. \tag{1}$$

$\underline{\Delta}^{\mathbb{Z}}$ *denotes the minimal sum of deviations with integer interval domains obtained by substituting* $\mathbb{Q}$ *by* $\mathbb{Z}$ *in equation (1).*

$\overline{X}_i^{\mathbb{Q}}$ *denotes the maximal consistent value for* X_i *with rational interval domains:*

$$\overline{X}_i^{\mathbb{Q}} = \max_x \{ \, x[i] \mid \forall j: \; x[j] \in I_j^{\mathbb{Q}} \text{ and } \sum_{j=1}^{n} x[j] = s \text{ and} \sum_{j=1}^{n} |n \cdot x[j] - s| \leq \Delta^{\max}\}. \tag{2}$$

$\overline{X}_i^{\mathbb{Z}}$ *denotes the maximal consistent value for* X_i *with integer interval domains obtained by substituting* $\mathbb{Q}$ *by* $\mathbb{Z}$ *in equation (2).*

Corresponding definitions for $\underline{X}_i^{\mathbb{Q}}$ *and* $\underline{X}_i^{\mathbb{Z}}$ *are obtained by replacing maximization over* x *by minimization in equation (2).*

The two propagators described in [7] filtering Δ and $\mathcal{X}$ apply respectively the filtering rules

$$\Delta^{\min} \leftarrow \max(\Delta^{\min}, \underline{\Delta}^{\mathbb{Q}}) \quad \text{and} \tag{3}$$

$$Dom(X_i) \leftarrow Dom(X_i) \cap [\underline{X}_i^{\mathbb{Q}}, \overline{X}_i^{\mathbb{Q}}] \quad \forall i \in [1..n]. \tag{4}$$

These filtering rules are bound-consistent if the domains of the X_i's are rational intervals $[X_i^{\min}, X_i^{\max}]$. When the domains of the X_i's are integer intervals $[X_i^{\min}..X_i^{\max}]$, the corresponding bound-consistent filtering rules are obtained by substituting $\mathbb{Q}$ by $\mathbb{Z}$ in equations (3) and (4). Nevertheless, rules (3) and (4) can be used for integer domains as well since they are obtained by relaxing the domains to rational intervals. The relations between the bounds are $\underline{X}_i^{\mathbb{Z}} \geq \underline{X}_i^{\mathbb{Q}}$, $\overline{X}_i^{\mathbb{Z}} \leq \overline{X}_i^{\mathbb{Q}}$ and $\underline{\Delta}^{\mathbb{Z}} \geq \underline{\Delta}^{\mathbb{Q}}$. In the particular case of $s \bmod n = 0$, the bounds are completely equivalent. As illustrated in the two following examples, the relaxing assumption of rational interval domains can lead to miss some possible filtering with respect to a bound-consistent filtering.

Example 1 (Filtering of Δ). Assume two variables $\mathcal{X} = (X_1, X_2)$ with domains $[-5..5]$ and a sum constraint $s = 1$. Obviously $\underline{\Delta}^{\mathbb{Q}} = 0$ is obtained with the tuple $x = (0.5, 0.5)$ while $\underline{\Delta}^{\mathbb{Z}} = 2$ is obtained with the tuple $x = (1, 0)$ or $x = (0, 1)$.

Example 2 (Filtering of $\mathcal{X}$). Assume ten variables with domains $[-5..5]$, a sum constraint $s = 7$ and a maximum sum of deviations $\Delta^{\max} = 42$. One can see that $\overline{X}_i^{\mathbb{Q}} = \frac{7}{10} + \frac{21}{10} = 2.8$ and $\underline{X}_i^{\mathbb{Q}} = \frac{7}{10} - \frac{21}{10} = -1.4$. This solution is obtained if eight variables are assigned to the mean 7/10 and the other two are as far as possible from the mean that is one above the mean and the other below the mean at an equal distance $\frac{21}{10}$. For this configuration, the maximum deviation $\Delta^{\max} = 42$ is reached. When only integer assignments are permitted, the result is $\overline{X}_i^{\mathbb{Z}} = 1$ and $\underline{X}_i^{\mathbb{Z}} = 0$. Indeed, for an assignment composed of seven values 1 and three values 0, the maximal deviation is reached ($\Delta^{\max} = 42$). Clearly there is no other integer assignment with a lower deviation. Hence the filtering of [7] would achieve $Dom(X_i) = [-1..2]$ while a bound-consistent filtering would give $Dom(X_i) = [0..1]$.

3 A Bound-Consistent Lower Bound for the Deviation

The previous section shows in Example 1 that when every domain overlaps the mean, the lower bound for the deviation computed by propagators in [7] is equal to 0 since every variable can be assigned to the mean s/n. This lower bound is not bound-consistent when the mean is rational (when $s \bmod n \neq 0$). Next theorem gives a lower bound for Δ that can be computed in constant time and greater than 0 in this case.

Theorem 1. *A lower bound for the deviation* Δ *is:*

$$0 \leq 2 \cdot (n - s \bmod n) \cdot (s \bmod n) \leq \underline{\Delta}^{\mathbb{Z}}.$$

Proof. This lower bound is obtained by enlarging every domain $Dom(X_i)$ such that s/n gets inside: $\forall i \in [1..n] : s/n \in [X_i^{\min}, X_i^{\max}]$. Then in an assignment of minimum deviation, every variable are either assigned to $s^{\downarrow}$ or to $s^{\uparrow} = s^{\downarrow} + n$. If we denote by y the number of variables ($n \cdot X_i$) assigned to $s^{\downarrow}$, the sum constraint can be written: $y \cdot s^{\downarrow} + (n-y) \cdot (s^{\downarrow} + n) = s \cdot n$. Hence $y = n - (s - s^{\downarrow}) = n - s \bmod n$. Using this, a lower bound of $\underline{\Delta}^{\mathbb{Z}}$ is $(n - s \bmod n) \cdot (s \bmod n) + (s \bmod n) \cdot (n - s \bmod n) = 2 \cdot (n - s \bmod n) \cdot (s \bmod n)$. □

The lower bound introduced in Theorem 1 is bound-consistent only if every domain overlaps the mean s/n. The remaining of this section introduces a linear time algorithm to compute a valid assignment satisfying the sum constraint and minimizing the sum of deviations in the general case when the domains do not necessarily overlap the mean. More formally the algorithm computes a tuple x satisfying the relation [2]:

$$\underset{x}{\operatorname{argmin}}\{(\sum_{i=1}^{n} |n \cdot x[i] - s|) | \forall i : x[i] \in I_i^{\mathbb{Z}} \text{ and } \sum_{i=1}^{n} x[i] = s\}.$$

To alleviate notations, the tuple $n \cdot x$ is used instead of x. Note that $n \cdot x$ corresponds to an integer assignment only if it is composed of values which are multiple of n. The algorithm executes in two phases: a greedy part followed by a repair part.

- Greedy: The sum constraint is dropped. Each $n \cdot x[i]$ is set to the closest multiple of n from s in $Dom(n \cdot X_i)$.

[2] $\operatorname{argmin}_x f(X)$ is the set of x such that $f(x)$ is minimal.

– Repair: If the sum constraint is satisfied that is $\sum_{i=1}^{n} x[i] = s$, then $n \cdot x$ is a solution to the problem. Otherwise the sum is larger or smaller than s. We consider the larger case: $\sum_{i=1}^{n} x[i] > s$ (the other case is similar). Then some entries of $n \cdot x$ must be decreased until the sum constraint is satisfied. An entry $n \cdot x[i] = s^{\uparrow} > n \cdot X_i^{\min}$ is called an *overlapping* entry. The choice of the entries to decrease is important. Decreasing an entry which is smaller than s by n results in an augmentation by n of the sum of deviations. But decreasing an overlapping entry by n (that is from $n \cdot x[i] = s^{\uparrow}$ to $s^{\downarrow}$) only increases the sum of deviations by $(2 \cdot (s \bmod n) - n)$ (see Figure 1). This last quantity is smaller or equal to n. Consequently, all overlapping entries are first considered in any order to be decreased by n to satisfy the sum constraint. If the sum constraint is not yet satisfied after this operation, the following property holds:
$$\forall i : n \cdot x[i] \leq s \text{ or } n \cdot X_i^{\min} \geq s.$$
In other words, each entry $n \cdot x[i]$ lies either on the lower bound of the corresponding variable domain or lies below s and can if necessary be further decreased. Consequently every entry below s, not yet on its lower bound, can be decreased at most to its lower bound $(n \cdot X_i^{\min})$. This results in an augmentation of the sum of deviations equal to the amount of the decreasing. These entries are used to satisfy the sum constraint. They are decreased maximally in an arbitrary order until the sum constraint is satisfied.

The greedy part is achieved by iterating once over the variables. There are at most n overlapping variables candidates to a repair. Finally, there are at most n variables needed to be further decreased to satisfy the sum constraint. Hence the total complexity is $\Theta(n)$ to compute the bound-consistent lower bound $\underline{\Delta}^{\mathbb{Z}}$.

Lemma 1. *The greedy + repair algorithm computes an assignment x such that $\sum_{i=1}^{n} x[i] = s$ and $\sum_{i=1}^{n} |n \cdot x[i] - s| = \underline{\Delta}^{\mathbb{Z}}$.*

Proof. It can be verified that tuple x after the greedy part until the termination of the algorithm satisfies the following invariant:

$$x \in \min_{y}\{(\sum_{i=1}^{n} |n \cdot y[i] - s|) \mid \sum_{i=1}^{n} y[i] = \sum_{i=1}^{n} x[i] \text{ and } \forall j :\ y[j] \in I_j^{\mathbb{Q}}\}.$$

Since each modifiation of x make the sum over x strictly closer to s and since the algorithm terminates whenever the sum is equal to s, the correctness follows. □

Example 3 (Computing $\underline{\Delta}^{\mathbb{Z}}$). Assume six variables with domain bounds represented on Figure 2 and given in the following table:

i	1	2	3	4	5	6
$X_i^{\max}$	16	12	14	16	12	15
$X_i^{\min}$	11	10	12	15	10	12
$n \cdot X_i^{\max}$	96	72	84	96	72	90
$n \cdot X_i^{\min}$	66	60	72	90	60	72

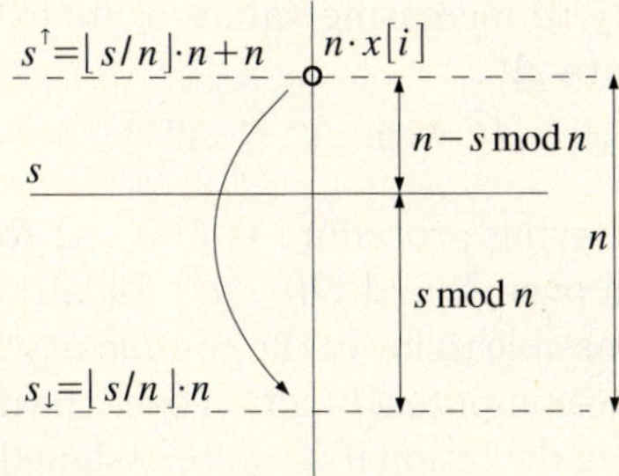

Fig. 1. Decreasing of an overlapping variable by n. The horizontal plain line represents the sum constraint s. The horizontal dashed lines are placed at $s^{\uparrow}$ and $s^{\downarrow}$.

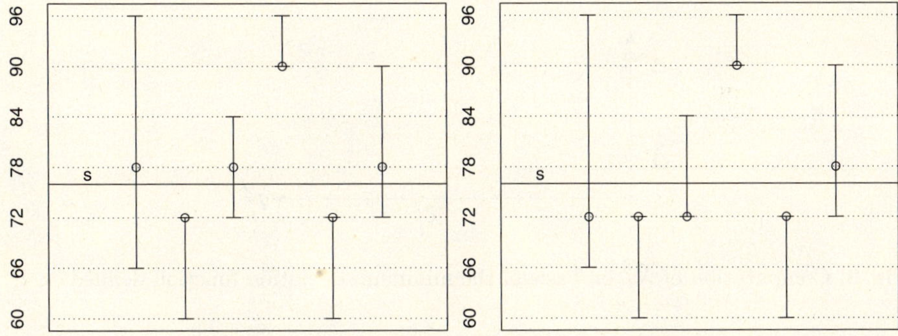

Fig. 2. Illustration of Example 3 to compute $\underline{\Delta}^{\mathbb{Z}}$. Horizontal lines represents the multiples of $n = 6$. On the left, the result of the greedy part and on the right the result of the repair part are represented with symbol $\circ$.

The sum constraint is $s = 76$. After completion of the greedy part, the tuple $n \cdot x$ is equal to $(78, 72, 78, 90, 72, 78)$. An illustration of $n \cdot x$ is given on the left of Figure 2 (symbols $\circ$). For this tuple $\sum_{j=1}^{n} n \cdot x[j] = 468 > 456$. Since the sum is too high, some entries of $n \cdot x$ must be decreased. First candidates are overlapping entries $n \cdot x[1]$, $n \cdot x[3]$ and $n \cdot x[6]$. The decrease by $n = 6$ of any two of them is sufficient to satisfy the sum constraint. The right of Figure 2 shows the final tuple $n \cdot x$. The value of $\underline{\Delta}^{\mathbb{Z}}$ is then $\sum_{j=1}^{n} |n \cdot x[j] - s| = 32$.

4 Bound-Consistent Lower and Upper Bounds for X_i

This section explains how to compute $\overline{X_i}^{\mathbb{Z}}$ the maximum value in $I_i^{\mathbb{Z}}$ consistent with `deviation`$(\mathcal{X}, s, \Delta)$. Note that computing $\underline{X_i}^{\mathbb{Z}}$ is a similar problem symmetric with respect to s. The previous section gives an algorithm to find the minimum deviation in linear time. A shaving process using this algorithm can be sketched:

– Assign X_i successively to increasing values of its extended domain $I_i^{\mathbb{Z}}$.
– For each value compute $\underline{\Delta}^{\mathbb{Z}}$.
– $\overline{X}_i^{\mathbb{Z}}$ is the largest value in $I_i^{\mathbb{Z}}$ with $\underline{\Delta}^{\mathbb{Z}} \leq \Delta^{\max}$.

The complexity of this shaving procedure is $\mathcal{O}(e \cdot n)$ for X_i where e is the the size of the largest domain over $\mathcal{X}$ and $\mathcal{O}(e \cdot n^2)$ for all variables in $\mathcal{X}$.

A better algorithm is possible to lower the complexity to $\Theta(n)$. Indeed, for each variable X_i, it is possible to compute a function over the domain interval $I_i^{\mathbb{Z}}$ giving for each value the minimum deviation if X_i were assigned to that value. As shown in Subsection 4.1, this function has a simple analytical form composed of two contiguous increasing linear functions. Given this function, $\overline{X}_i^{\mathbb{Z}}$ is found in constant time by intersecting it with the horizontal line at $\Delta^{\max}$ (see Figure 3). Subsection 4.2 gives an algorithm to compute the function for every variable in $\Theta(n)$.

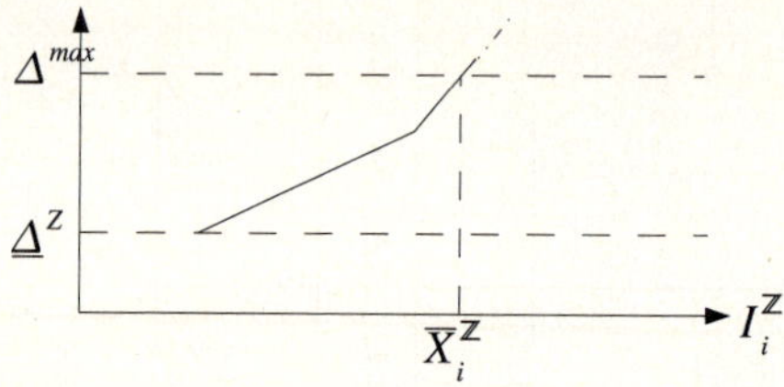

Fig. 3. Computation of $\overline{X}_i^{\mathbb{Z}}$ on basis of the minimum deviation function defined on $I_i^{\mathbb{Z}}$

4.1 Function of the Minimum Deviation on $I_i^{\mathbb{Z}}$

The computation of the function giving the minimum deviation on the domain of X_i is conceptually based on any assignment m_i on $\mathcal{X}$ which maximizes the ith entry among all the assignments of minimal sum of deviations $\underline{\Delta}^{\mathbb{Z}}$:

$$m_i \in \underset{n \cdot x}{\operatorname{argmax}}\{x[i] \big| \forall j \neq i : \; x[j] \in I_j^{\mathbb{Z}} \text{ and } \sum_{j=1}^{n} |n \cdot x[j] - s| = \underline{\Delta}^{\mathbb{Z}} \text{ and } \sum_{j=1}^{n} x[j] = s\}.$$

Any assignment with the ith entry larger than $m_i[i]$ has a deviation larger than the deviation of m_i. If $m_i[i] \geq n \cdot X_i^{\max}$, then $\overline{X}_i^{\mathbb{Z}} = X_i^{\max}$. We now assume $m_i[i] < n \cdot X_i^{\max}$.

The minimum deviation function on $[m_i[i], n \cdot X_i^{\max}]$ can take different forms following the value $m_i[i]$. Three cases are possible for $m_i[i]$ given in Property 1.

Property 1

– If $m_i[i] < s^{\downarrow}$ then $m_i[i] = n \cdot X_i^{\max}$.
– If $m_i[i] = s^{\downarrow}$ then $\forall j \neq i$: either $m_i[j] = n \cdot X_i^{\min}$ or $m_i[j] \leq s^{\downarrow}$.
– If $m_i[i] \geq s^{\uparrow}$ then $\forall j \neq i$: either $m_i[j] = n \cdot X_i^{\min}$ or $m_i[j] \leq s^{\uparrow}$.

Property 1 can be verified starting from an assignment obtained from the greedy+repair algorithm from Section 3 and then by increasing the ith entry as much as possible while keeping the sum constraint satisfied and the deviation unchanged. Each case from Property 1 is considered in turn in the next three paragraphs giving the evolution of the minimum deviation on $I_i^{\mathbb{Z}}$ for each case.

Case $m_i[i] < s^{\downarrow}$:

In this case, $n \cdot \overline{X}_i^{\mathbb{Z}} = m_i[i]$ because the entry $m_i[i]$ cannot be increased since it is already to its maximum possible value.

Case $m_i[i] = s^{\downarrow}$:

If $m_i[i]$ is increased by n, the only entries which can be decreased are below $s^{\downarrow}$ (Property 1). Consequently when $m_i[i]$ is increased by n the deviation increases by $n - (s - s^{\downarrow}) + (s^{\uparrow} - s)$. Term n represents the decrease of an entry below $s^{\downarrow}$ and the term $-(s - s^{\downarrow}) + (s^{\uparrow} - s)$ represents the increase by n of $m_i[i]$. If $m_i[i]$ is further increased by n, the deviation increases by $2 \cdot n$. Indeed, $m_i[i] \geq s^{\uparrow}$ and the other entries candidate to be decreased are below $s^{\downarrow}$.

Example 4. This example considers 4 variables with domains given in next table:

i	1	2	3	4
$X_i^{\max}$	7	5	6	7
$X_i^{\min}$	3	0	5	5
$n \cdot X_i^{\max}$	28	20	24	28
$n \cdot X_i^{\min}$	12	0	20	20

The sum constraint is $s = 17$. Hence $s^{\downarrow} = 16$ and $s^{\uparrow} = 20$. The assignment $m_1 = (16, 12, 20, 20)$ is represented on Figure 4 with symbols $\circ$. The deviation of this assignment is 12. If $m_1[1]$ is increased by 4 that is from 16 to 20, the deviation increases by $-(s - s^{\downarrow}) + (s^{\uparrow} - s) = -1 + 3$. For the sum constraint

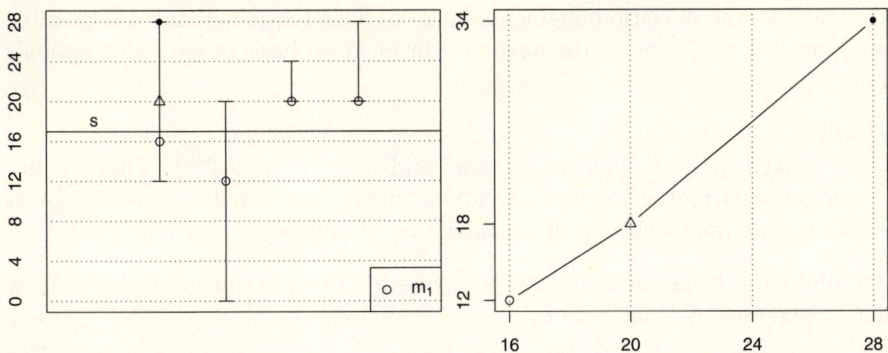

Fig. 4. Figure of Example 4. On the left is the representation of m_1 with symbols $\circ$ and the successive values of $m_1[1]$. On the right is the evolution of the deviation with the successive values of $m_1[1]$.

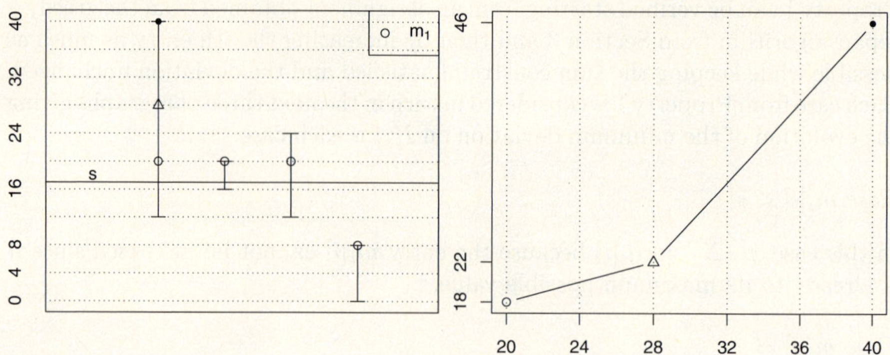

Fig. 5. Figure of Example 5. On the left is the representation of m_1 and the successive values of $m_1[1]$. On the right is the evolution of the deviation with the successive values of $m_1[1]$.

$s = 17$ to remain satisfied, another entry must be decreased by 4. The only possible entry is $m_1[2]$ making the deviation increase by 4. The deviation of m_1 is thus increased from 12 to 18 when $m_1[1]$ is set to 20 (represented by the symbols $\triangle$ on the Figure 4). If $m_1[1]$ is further increased, the deviation is increased by $2 \cdot 4 = 8$ at every step. Hence when $m_1[1]$ is increased to 28 the deviation is 34 (represented by the symbol $\bullet$)

Case $m_i[i] \geq s^{\uparrow}$*:*

If $m_i[i]$ is increased by n the deviation of m_i increases by n. For the sum constraint to remain satisfied, another entry must also be decreased by n. To keep the deviation of m_i minimal, priority must be given to entries $m_i[j] = s^{\uparrow} > n \cdot X_j^{\min}$. Indeed, the decrease of such an entry induces a smaller increase in the deviation than for an entry under s. The whole effect on the deviation is an augmentation of $n-(s^{\uparrow}-s)+(s-s^{\downarrow}) = 2.(s-s^{\downarrow})$. Note that if only entries $n \cdot X_j^{\min} < m_i[j] \leq s^{\downarrow}$ are available, the deviation augments by $2 \cdot n$. This reasoning makes it possible to predict the evolution of the deviation in $\Theta(1)$ on basis of two information's about m_i:

- $m_i[i]$.
- $o_i = \#\{m_i[j] | j \neq i \text{ and } m_i[j] = s^{\uparrow} \text{ and } m_i[j] > n \cdot X_j^{\min}\}$. This number corresponds to the number of entries in m_i that can be decreased by n causing an augmentation of the deviation of only $-(s^{\uparrow} - s) + (s - s^{\downarrow})$.

The minimum deviation increases by $2 \cdot (s - s^{\downarrow})$ every n during o_i steps. After that it increases by $2 \cdot n$ every n.

Example 5. This example cosiders 4 variables with domains given in next table:

i	1	2	3	4
$X_i^{\max}$	10	5	6	2
$X_i^{\min}$	3	4	3	0
$n \cdot X_i^{\max}$	40	20	24	8
$n \cdot X_i^{\min}$	12	16	12	0

The sum constraint is $s = 17$. Hence $s^{\downarrow} = 16$ and $s^{\uparrow} = 20$. Assignment $m_1 = (20, 20, 20, 8)$ is represented on Figure 5 with symbol $\circ$. The deviation of this assignment is 18 and $o_1 = 2$ because of the second and third entries. The evolution of the deviation is given on the Figure 5.

4.2 Computation of the Evolution of the Minimum Deviation for Every Variable

The previous subsection explains how the minimum deviation on $I_i^{\mathbb{Z}}$ evolves starting from a special assignment called m_i. We briefly summarize the possible cases of evolution of the deviation when $m_i[i]$ is incremented by n.

- $m_i[i] < s^{\downarrow}$: The deviation can not increase anymore.
- $m_i[i] = s^{\downarrow}$: The deviation increases first by $n - (s - s^{\downarrow}) + (s^{\uparrow} - s)$ the first time $m[i]$ is increased by n. Then it increases by $2 \cdot n$ every increase by n of $m_i[i]$.
- $m_i[i] \geq s^{\uparrow}$: The deviation increases by $2 \cdot (s - s^{\downarrow})$ every n during o_i steps. After that it increases by $2 \cdot n$ every increase by n of $m_i[i]$.

The only necessary information to predict the evolution of the deviation is the entry $m_i[i]$ and the counter o_i. To simplify the notations we denote by $m[i]$ the entry $m_i[i]$ and by $o[i]$ the counter o_i. Algorithm 1 computes $m[i]$ and $o[i]$ for $1 \leq i \leq n$ in $\Theta(n)$. The algorithm assumes that the `deviation` constraint is consistent.

- Lines 4-5 do a greedy assignment for each variable multiple of n closest from s inside its domain.
- Lines 9-13 consider the case when the sum constraint is (by chance) respected after the greedy assignment.
- Lines 15-21 try to make the sum constraint satisfied by moving assignment of variables which overlap the value s.
- Lines 22-23 update the sets *overlaps* and *overlaps*$(s^{\uparrow})$ after the possible modifications in lines 15-23.
- Lines 24-31 consider the case where the sum constraint could be satisfied after modifications of lines 15-23.
- Lines 32-35 and 36-41 holds respectively when the sum is too large or too low even after the modifications of lines 15-23. If the sum is too large, some entries must be decreased. It is implicitly assumed that entries $j \neq i$ can be potentially decreased. Hence $m[i] = nx[i]$ and $o[i]$ is 0 because, all other entries are already at their minimum or under s. If the sum it too small, $m[i]$ is obtained by increasing $nx[i]$ such that the sum is satisfied. If the ith entry was overlapping, $o[i]$ is the current number of overlapping entries minus one.

Algorithm 1. Compute m and o

Data: $\mathcal{X}$ and s such that $s \in [\sum_{i=1}^{n} X_i^{\min}, \sum_{i=1}^{n} X_i^{\max}]$
Result: m and o

```
nx, m, o integer arrays of size n
sum ← 0                                              /* Σ_{i=1}^{n} nx[i] */
s* ← (s − s↓) ≤ (s↑ − s) ? s↓ : s↑    /* the multiple of n closest to s */
for i ← 1 to n do
    Set nx[i] to the multiple of n closest to s in [n · X_i^min, n · X_i^max]
overlaps ← {i | nx[i] = s↑ > n · X_i^min or nx[i] = s↓ < n · X_i^max}
overlaps(s↑) ← {i ∈ overlaps | nx[i] = s↑}
sum ← Σ_{i=1}^{n} nx[i]
if sum = n · s then
    for i ← 1 to n do
        m[i] ← nx[i]
        if i ∈ overlaps(s↑) then o[i] ← #overlaps(s↑) − 1
        else o[i] ← #overlaps(s↑)
else
    if ( sum > n · s and s* = s↑ ) or ( sum < n · s and s* = s↓ and s* ≠ s )
    then
        δ ← sum > n · s ? −n : n
        for i ∈ overlaps do
            if sum = n · s then break
            else
                nx[i] ← nx[i] + δ
                sum ← sum + δ
        overlaps ← {i | nx[i] = s↑ > n · X_i^min or nx[i] = s↓ < n · X_i^max}
        overlaps(s↑) ← {i ∈ overlaps | nx[i] = s↑}
    if sum = n · s then
        for i ← 1 to n do
            if i ∈ overlaps and #overlaps(s↑) > 0 then
                m[i] = s↑
                o[i] = #overlaps(s↑) − 1
            else
                m[i] = nx[i]
                o[i] = #overlaps(s↑)
    else if sum > n · s then
        for i ← 1 to n do
            m[i] = nx[i]
            o[i] = 0
    else                                                  /* sum < n · s */
        for i ← 1 to n do
            m[i] = nx[i] + n · s − sum
            if n · X_i^min < s < n · X_i^max and #overlaps(s↑) > 0 then
                o[i] = #overlaps(s↑) − 1
            else o[i] = #overlaps(s↑)
```

It can be seen that Algorithm 1 has a time complexity of $\Theta(n)$. Indeed, in all cases a constant number of operations is performed for each variable.

Example 6. This example considers the following domains:

i	1	2	3	4	5	6
$X_i^{\max}$	16	11	14	14	12	15
$X_i^{\min}$	11	9	12	13	10	12
$n \cdot X_i^{\max}$	96	66	84	84	72	90
$n \cdot X_i^{\min}$	66	54	72	78	60	72

The sum constraint is $s = 74$, $n \cdot s = 444$ and $s^* = s^{\downarrow} = 72$.

- Lines 4-8: After the greedy assignment, $nx = (72, 66, 72, 78, 72, 72)$. The sum is 432 which is smaller than 444. Hence the condition to execute lines 9-13 is not satisfied. We have also $overlaps = \{1, 3, 6\}$ and $overlaps(s^{\uparrow}) = \phi$.
- Lines 15-23 will result in $nx = (78, 66, 78, 78, 72, 72)$. The sum is now 444, $overlaps = \{1, 3, 6\}$ and $overlaps(\text{sup}) = \{1, 3\}$.
- Since $sum = n.s$ is satisfied, lines 24-32 are executed next. Entries 1, 3 and 6 satisfy the if statement line 26 while entries 2, 4 and 5 does not. Hence results are $m = (78, 66, 78, 78, 72, 78)$ and $o = (1, 2, 1, 2, 2, 1)$

5 Experimental Results

This section compares the existing propagators from [7] with the presented bound-consistent propagators on the Balanced Academic Curriculum Problem (BACP). We also give an expression of the minimum difference between two deviation values and experiment the usage of this difference to speed up the Branch and Bound search. All experiments were performed on an Intel® Pentium® M 1.86GHz with 1GB of memory and with the Gecode 1.3.1 Solver.

The objective of the BACP is to assign courses to periods while balancing the workload of periods and respecting prerequisites relations between pair of courses. The CP model we consider to solve BACP is precisely the one introduced in [4]. The objective function in [4] is to minimize the maximum load over periods. In contrast, our objective function is to minimize the deviation of loads of periods from the mean load.

The search performed to solve BACP is a DFS Branch and Bound search. Hence, each time a solution is found, the next solution is constrained to have a smaller deviation. More information can be given on the next solution to be found. Indeed the smallest difference δ between two possible deviation values is

$\delta = \min\{2 \cdot s \bmod n\ ,\ 2 \cdot (n - s \bmod n)\}$ when $s \bmod n \neq 0$.
$\delta = 2 \cdot n$ when $s \bmod n = 0$.

The expression $\min\{2 \cdot s \bmod n\ ,\ 2 \cdot (n - s \bmod n)\}$ can be understood easily. The value $2 \cdot s \bmod n$ corresponds to the move represented by arrows labeled 1 on Figure 6 while the value $2 \cdot (n - s \bmod n)$ corresponds to the move represented

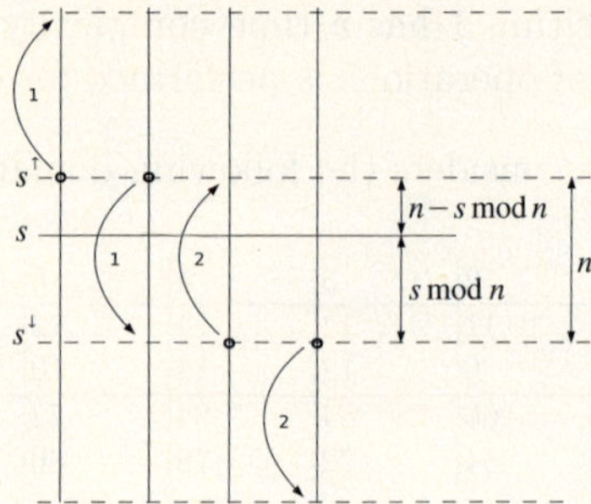

Fig. 6. Illustration of the smallest distance between two possible deviations

with arrows labeled 2. The value δ can be used to speed-up the Branch and Bound search. Indeed, if a solution is found with a deviation of Δ, the next solution can be constrained to present a deviation less than or equal to $\Delta - \delta$.

Three real instances are available on CSPLIB. These instances are summarized in the following table:

n (#periods)	#courses	#prerequisites	s (total load)	s mod n
8	46	38	133	5
10	42	34	134	4
12	66	65	204	0

We report here the instances of 8 and 10 periods because the instance with 12 periods presents an integer mean load ($s \bmod n = 0$). Hence proposed propagators, as checked experimentally, behave exactly as the ones from [7] on the instance with 12 periods.

The two instances were solved with 4 configurations:

- the propagators proposed in [7] (Deviation),
- the bound-consistent propagators (BC Deviation),
- the propagators proposed in [7] with the lower bound from Theorem 1 and the value δ during the Branch and Bound search (Deviation*) and
- the bound-consistent propagators and the value δ during the Branch and Bound search (BC Deviation*).

Table 1 gives statistics on the last 5 bounds found during the Branch and Bound search for each configuration. The reported statistics are the time and the number of leaf nodes explored so far (# L.N.). The last line gives the statistics to prove the optimality of the last bound found.

It appears from Table 1 that the new propagators become really useful when the upper bound $\Delta^{\max}$ becomes tight. Moreover, the new propagators permit to prove optimality of the last bound within less than one second for both instances while it not possible in a reasonable time (not finished after 20 minutes) with existing propagators from [7]. The usage of the lower bound and the δ value permits to prove the optimality of the last bound with propagators from [7]. We

Table 1. Instances of 8 and 10 periods. Statistics about the last 5 bounds during the B&Bound The time and the number of leaf nodes (# L.N.) are given for each bound

8 Periods					8 Periods				
	Deviation		BC Deviation			Deviation*		BC Deviation*	
Bound	Time(ms)	# L.N.	Time(ms)	# L.N.	Bound	Time(ms)	# L.N.	Time(ms)	# L.N.
50	20	447	40	**441**	62	20	365	20	**320**
46	30	454	40	**443**	56	20	370	20	**325**
40	30	456	40	**445**	50	20	375	20	**330**
36	40	559	40	**450**	40	20	378	20	**332**
30	40	561	40	**451**	30	30	483	20	**337**
proof	∞	∞	40	**1517**	proof	30	1644	20	**1172**
10 Periods					10 Periods				
84	50	857	60	857	84	40	855	50	**770**
76	50	862	60	862	76	40	860	60	**822**
64	50	864	60	864	64	40	862	60	**826**
56	70	1060	60	**891**	56	60	1058	60	**853**
48	18370	368486	60	**896**	48	24660	574539	60	**858**
proof	∞	∞	60	**3288**	proof	24660	2021299	60	**3191**

Table 2. Comparison of the propagators on 500 randomized versions of the 8 periods instance: number of unsolved instances

	$s \bmod n = 0$	$s \bmod n \neq 0$
Nb instances	55	445
Deviation	0	391
BC Deviation	0	0
Deviation*	0	229
BC Deviation*	0	0

can also see that even with the bound consistent propagators, the number of explored nodes is decreased: $1,172 < 1,517$ for 8 periods and $3,191 < 3,288$ for 10 periods.

The objective of the next experiments is to study on more instances the gain obtained with the new propagators. We generated 500 instances from the original 8 periods instance. For each instance, the weight given to each course is a random integer in [1..5] and 30 prerequisites relations are randomly chosen out the 38. Each instance was solved with the four configurations. The time limit given is of 5 seconds. Table 2 gives the number of unsolved instances.

It appears that all instances can be easily solved with the bound-consistent propagators. This is not the case with propagators from [7] since 301 instances remain unsolved. The use of the lower bound from Theorem 1 and the δ value permits to solve 162 additional instances with propagators from [7]. The value $s \bmod n$ has a strong influence on the old propagators but it does not influence the new propagators. All the 55 instances with $s \bmod n = 0$ could be solved with all configurations. This is not surprising since propagators proposed in [7] are also bound-consistent in this case.

6 Conclusion

The `deviation` constraint recently introduced in [7] guarantees an assignment on a set of variables to be balanced around a given mean. It constrains the set of variables to present a given mean and the deviation with respect to this mean. The main advantage of the propagators proposed in [7] is their simplicity. However, these propagators are bound-consistent only when the mean is an integer. We experiment on the Balanced Academic Curriculum Problem (BACP) that instances are very difficult to solve with propagators from [7] when this property does not hold. We give a simple lower bound on the deviation which can be found in constant time and help to solve some additional problems when the sum is not a multiple of n. Our main contributions are bound-consistent propagators for any rational mean value running in linear time. In contrast with propagators presented in [7], bound-consistent propagators solve efficiently any instance of the BACP from CSPLIB. Finally, we give a way to speedup the Branch and Bound search when the objective is to minimize the deviation.

Acknowledgment. The authors wish to thank Grégoire Dooms for various interesting discussions, especially for the Theorem 1 which was the starting point of this article. Tkanks to the reviewers for their helpful comments. This research is supported by the Walloon Region, project Transmaze (516207).

References

1. Castro, C., Manzano, S.: Variable and value ordering when solving balanced academic curriculum problem. In: Proc. of the ERCIM WG on constraints (2001)
2. Gendreau, M.l., Ferland, J., Gendron, B., Hail, N., Jaumard, B., Lapierre, S., Pesant, G., Soriano, P.: Physician scheduling in emergency rooms. In: Proc. of PATAT (2006)
3. Gomes, C., Sellmann, M., van Es, C., van Es, H.: The challenge of generating spatially balanced scientific experiment designs. In: Proc. of CP-AI-OR (2004)
4. Hnich, B., Kiziltan, Z., Walsh, T.: Modelling a balanced academic curriculum problem. In: Proceedings of CP-AI-OR (2002)
5. Pesant, G., Regin, J.-C.: Spread: A balancing constraint based on statistics. In: van Beek, P. (ed.) CP 2005. LNCS, vol. 3709, pp. 460–474. Springer, Heidelberg (2005)
6. Schaus, P., Deville, Y., Dupont, P., Régin, J.C.: Simplication and extension of spread. In: 3th Workshop on Constraint Propagation And Implementation (2006)
7. Schaus, P., Deville, Y., Dupont, P., Régin, J.C.: The deviation constraint. In: Proceedings of CP-AI-OR, vol. 4510, pp. 269–284 (2007)

Constructive Interval Disjunction

Gilles Trombettoni[1] and Gilles Chabert[2]

[1] University of Nice-Sophia and COPRIN Project, INRIA, 2004 route des lucioles, 06902 Sophia.Antipolis cedex, B.P. 93, France
[2] ENSIETA, 2 rue François Verny, 29806 Brest cedex 09, France
trombe@sophia.inria.fr, gilles.chabert@ensieta.com

Abstract. This paper presents two new filtering operators for numerical CSPs (systems with constraints over the reals) based on *constructive disjunction*, as well as a new splitting heuristic. The fist operator (CID) is a generic algorithm enforcing constructive disjunction with intervals. The second one (3BCID) is a hybrid algorithm mixing constructive disjunction and *shaving*, another technique already used with numerical CSPs through the algorithm 3B. Finally, the splitting strategy learns from the CID filtering step the next variable to be split, with no overhead.

Experiments have been conducted with 20 benchmarks. On several benchmarks, CID and 3BCID produce a gain in performance of orders of magnitude over a standard strategy. CID compares advantageously to the 3B operator while being simpler to implement. Experiments suggest to fix the CID-related parameter in 3BCID, offering thus to the user a promising variant of 3B.

1 Introduction

We propose in this paper new advances in the use of two refutation principles of constraint programming: shaving and constructive disjunction. We first introduce shaving and then proceed to constructive disjunction that will be considered an improvement of the former.

The shaving principle is used to compute the singleton arc-consistency (SAC) of finite-domain CSPs [3] and the 3B-consistency of numerical CSPs [7]. It is also in the core of the SATZ algorithm [9] proving the satisfiability of boolean formula. Shaving works as follows. A value is temporarily assigned to a variable (the other values are temporarily discarded) and a partial consistency is computed on the remaining subproblem. If an inconsistency is obtained then the value can be safely removed from the domain of the variable. Otherwise, the value is kept in the domain. This principle of refutation has two drawbacks. Contrarily to arc consistency, this consistency is not incremental [2]. Indeed, the work of the underlying refutation algorithm on the *whole* subproblem is the reason why a *single value* can be removed. Thus, obtaining the *singleton arc consistency* on finite-domain CSPs requires an expensive fixed-point propagation algorithm where all the variables must be handled again every time a single value is removed [3]. SAC2 [1] and SAC-optim [2] and other SAC variants obtain better average or worst time complexity by managing heavy data structures

C. Bessiere (Ed.): CP 2007, LNCS 4741, pp. 635–650, 2007.

for the supports of values (like with AC4) or by duplicating the CSP for every value. However, using these filtering operators inside a backtracking scheme is far from being competitive with the standard MAC algorithm in the current state of research. In its QuickShaving [8], Lhomme uses this shaving principle in a pragmatic way, i.e., with no overhead, by learning the promising variables (i.e., those that can possibly produce gains with shaving in the future) during the search. Researchers and practitioners have also used for a long time the shaving principle in scheduling problems. On numerical CSPs, the 2B-consistency is the refutation algorithm used by 3B-consistency [7]. This property limited to the bounds of intervals explains that 3B-consistency filtering often produces gains in performance.

Example. *Figure 1 (left) shows the first two steps of the 3B-consistency algorithm. Since domains are continuous, shaving does not instantiate a variable to a value but restricts its domain to a sub-interval of fixed size located at one of the endpoints. The subproblems are represented with slices in light gray. The 2B-consistency projects every constraint onto a variable and intersects the result of all projections. In the leftmost slice, 2B-consistency leads to an empty box since the projections of the first and the second constraint onto* x_2 *are two intervals* I_1 *and* I_2 *with empty intersection. On the contrary, the fixed-point of projections in the rightmost slice is a nonempty box (with thick border).*

The second drawback of shaving is that the pruning effort performed by the partial consistency operator to refute a given value is lost, which is not the case with constructive disjunction[1].

Constructive disjunction was proposed by Van Hentenryck et al. in the nineties to handle efficiently disjunctions of constraints, thus tackling a more general model than the standard CSP model [17]. The idea is to propagate independently every term of the disjunction and to perform the union of the different pruned search spaces. In other terms, a value removed by every propagation process (run with one term/constraint of the disjunct) can be safely removed from the ground CSP. This idea is fruitful in several fields such as scheduling, where a common constraint is that two given tasks cannot overlap, or 2D bin packing problems where two rectangles must not overlap.

Constructive disjunction can also be used to handle the classical CSP model (where the problem is viewed as a conjunction of constraints). Indeed, every variable domain can be viewed as a unary disjunctive constraint that imposes one value among the different possible ones ($x = v_1 \vee ... \vee x = v_n$, where x is a variable and $v_1, ..., v_n$ are the different values). In this specific case, similarly to shaving, the constructive disjunction principle can be applied as follows. Every value in the domain of a variable is assigned in turn to this variable (the other values are temporarily discarded), and a partial consistency on the corresponding subproblems is computed. The search space is then replaced by the union of the resulting search spaces. One advantage over shaving is that the

[1] Note that optimized implementations of SAC reuse the domains obtained by subfiltering in subsequent calls to the shaving of a same variable.

(sub)filtering steps performed during constructive disjunction are better reused. This constructive "domain" disjunction is not very much exploited right now while it can sometimes produce impressive gains in performance. In particular, in addition to *all-diff* constraints [14], incorporating constructive domain disjunctions into the famous Sudoku problem (launched, for instance, when the variables/cases have only two remaining possible values/digits) often leads to a backtrack-free solving. The same phenomenon is observed with shaving but at a higher cost [15].

This observation has precisely motivated the research described in this paper devoted to the application of constructive domain disjunction to numerical CSPs. The continuous nature of interval domains is particularly well-suited for constructive domain disjunction. By splitting an interval into several smaller intervals (called *slices*), constructive domain disjunction leads in a straightforward way to the *constructive interval disjunction* (`CID`) filtering operator introduced in this paper.

After useful notations and definitions introduced in Section 2, Sections 3 and 4 describe the *CID* partial consistency and the corresponding filtering operator. A hybrid algorithm mixing shaving and CID is described in Section 5. Section 6 presents a new CID-based splitting strategy. Finally, experiments are presented in Section 7.

2 Definitions

The algorithms presented in this paper aim at solving systems of equations or, more generally, numerical CSPs.

Definition 1. *A* **numerical CSP** *(NCSP)* $P = (X, C, B)$ *contains a set of constraints* C *and a set* X *of* n *variables. Every variable* $x_i \in X$ *can take a real value in the interval* $\mathbf{x_i}$ *and* $\mathbf{B}$ *is the cartesian product (called a* **box***)* $\mathbf{x_1} \times ... \times \mathbf{x_n}$*. A solution of* P *is an assignment of the variables in* X *satisfying all the constraints in* C*.*

Remark 1. Since real numbers cannot be represented in computer architectures, the bounds of an interval $\mathbf{x_i}$ should actually be defined as floating-point numbers.

CID filtering performs a union operation between two boxes.

Definition 2. *Let* B_l *and* B_r *be two boxes corresponding to a same set* V *of variables.*
We call **hull** *of* B_l *and* B_r*, denoted by* `Hull`(B_l, B_r)*, the minimal box including* B_l *and* B_r*.*

To compute a bisection point based on a new (splitting) strategy, we need to calculate the *size* of a box. In this paper, the size of a box is given by its perimeter.

Definition 3. *Let* $B = \mathbf{x_1} \times ... \times \mathbf{x_n}$ *be a box. The* **size** *of* B *is* $\sum_{i=1}^{n}(\overline{\mathbf{x_i}} - \underline{\mathbf{x_i}})$*, where* $\overline{\mathbf{x_i}}$ *and* $\underline{\mathbf{x_i}}$ *are respectively the upper and lower bounds of the interval* $\mathbf{x_i}$*.*

3 CID-consistency

The CID-consistency is a new partial consistency that can be obtained on numerical CSPs. Following the principle given in introduction (i.e., combining interval splitting and constructive disjunction), the CID(2)-consistency can be formally defined as follows (see Figure 1).

Definition 4. (CID(2)-consistency)
Let $P = (X, C, B)$ be an NCSP. Let F be a partial consistency.

Let B_i^l be the sub-box of B in which $\mathbf{x_i}$ is replaced by $[\underline{\mathbf{x_i}}, \check{\mathbf{x}}_\mathbf{i}]$ (where $\check{\mathbf{x}}_\mathbf{i}$ is the midpoint of $\mathbf{x_i}$). Let B_i^r be the sub-box of B in which $\mathbf{x_i}$ is replaced by $[\check{\mathbf{x}}_\mathbf{i}, \overline{\mathbf{x_i}}]$. A variable x_i in X is CID(2)-consistent w.r.t. P and F if $B = Hull(F(X, C, B_i^l), F(X, C, B_i^r))$. The NCSP P is CID(2)-consistent if all the variables in X are CID(2)-consistent.

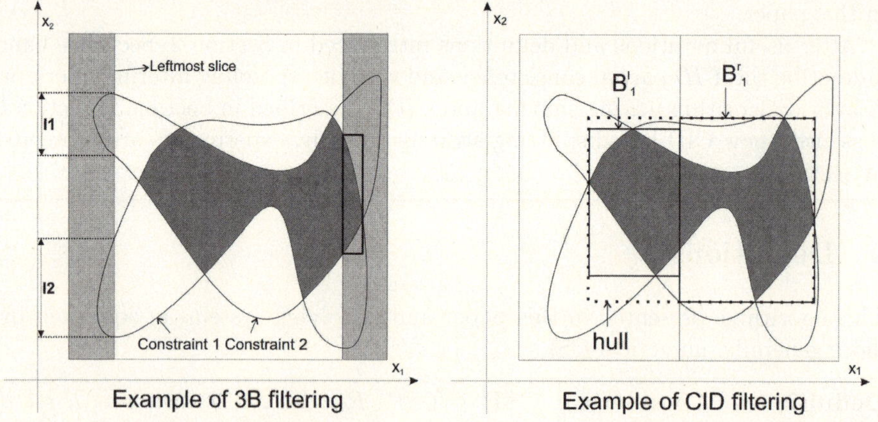

Fig. 1. Shaving and CID-consistency on a simple example with two constraints. The constraints are represented with their intersection in dark gray. **Left:** The first two steps of 3B. **Right:** the result of `VarCID` on variable x_1 (with 2 slices). The subboxes B_1^l and B_1^r are represented with thick borders; the resulting box appears in dotted lines.

For every dimension, the number of slices considered in the CID(2)-consistency is equal to 2. The definition can be generalized to the CID(s)-consistency in which every variable is split into s slices.

In practice, like 3B-w-consistency, the CID-consistency is obtained with a precision that avoids a slow convergence onto the fixed-point. We will consider that a variable is CID(2,w)-consistent if the hull of the corresponding left and right boxes resulting from subfiltering reduces no variable more than w.

Definition 5. (CID(2,w)-consistency)
With the notations of Definition 4, put $B' = Hull(F(X, C, B_i^l), F(X, C, B_i^r))$.

A variable x_i in X is CID(2,w)-consistent if $|\mathbf{x_i}| - |\mathbf{x'_i}| \leq w$, where $\mathbf{x_i}$ and $\mathbf{x'_i}$ are the domain of x_i in resp. B and B'.
The NCSP is CID(2,w)-consistent if all the variables in X are CID(2,w)-consistent.

Algorithm CID details the CID(s,w)-consistency filtering algorithm. Like the 3B-consistency algorithm, CID iterates on all the variables until a stop criterion, depending on w, is reached (see Definition 5): the Repeat loop is interrupted when no variable interval has been reduced more than w [2].

Every variable x_i is "*varcided*", i.e., handled by the procedure VarCID. The domain of x_i is split into s slices of size $\frac{|\mathbf{x_i}|}{s}$ each by the procedure SubBox. The partial consistency operator F (e.g., 2B or a variant of the latter called Box-consistency [16]) filters the corresponding sub-boxes, and the union of the resulting boxes is computed by the Hull operator. Note that if the subfiltering operator F applied to a given sub-box sliceBox detects an inconsistency, then the result sliceBox' is empty, so that there is no use of performing the union of sliceBox' with the current box in construction.

```
Algorithm CID (s: number of slices, w: precision, in-out P = (X,C,B): an NCSP,
F: subfiltering operator and its parameters)
    repeat
        P_old ← P
        LoopCID (X, s, P, F)
    until StopCriterion(w, P, P_old)
end.
Procedure LoopCID (X, s, in-out P, F)
    for every variable xi ∈ X do
        VarCID (xi, s, P, F)
    end
end.
Procedure VarCID (xi, s, (X, C, in-out B), F)
    B' ← empty box
    for j ← 1 to s do
        sliceBox ← SubBox (j, s, xi, B)  /* the j^th sub-box of B on xi */
        sliceBox' ← F(X, C, sliceBox) /* perform a partial consistency */
        B' ← Hull(B', sliceBox')        /* Union with previous sub-boxes */
    end
    B ← B'
end.
```

4 A CID-Based Solving Strategy

To find all the solutions of a numerical CSP, we propose a strategy including a bisection operation, CID filtering and an interval Newton [10]. Between two bisections, two operations are run in sequence:

1. a call to CID (how to fix the parameters is discussed just below),
2. a call to an interval Newton operator.

[2] From a theoretical point of view, in order that the stop criterion leads to a (non unique) fixed-point, it is necessary to return the box obtained just before the last filtering, i.e., the box in P_{old} in Algorithm CID.

The Right Set of Parameters for CID Filtering

First of all, the subfiltering operators we chose for `CID` are `2B` and `Box`. The classical user-defined parameter `w-hc4` (percentage of the interval width) is used by the subfiltering operator (`Box` or `2B`) inside CID to control the propagation loop. The parameter s is the number of slices used by the `VarCID` procedure.

Although useful to compute the CID-consistency property, the fixed-point repeat loop used by Algorithm `CID` does not pay off in practice (see below). In other words, running more than once `LoopCID` on all the variables is always counterproductive, even if the value of w is finely tuned. Thus, we have set the parameter w to ∞, that is, we have discarded w from the user-defined parameters.

Endowed with the parameters s and `w-hc4`, CID filtering appears to be an efficient general-purpose operator that has the potential to replace 2B/Box (alone) or 3B. For some (rare) benchmarks however, the use of only 2B/Box appears to be more efficient.

To offer a compromise between pure 2B/Box and `CID`, we introduce a third parameter n' defined as the number of variables that are varcided between two bisections in a round-robin strategy: given a predefined order between variables, a `VarCID` operation is called on n' variables (modulo n), starting at the lattest varcided variable plus one in the order. (This information is transmitted through the different nodes of the tree search.) Thus, if n' is set to 0, then only 2B/Box filtering is called between two bisections; if $n' = n$ (n is the number of variables in the system), then `CID` is called between two bisections.

We shall henceforth consider that `CID` has three parameters: the number of slices `s`, the propagation criterion `w-hc4` of `2B/Box` used for subfiltering and the number `n'` of varcided variables.

Default Values for CID Parameters

So far, we have proposed an efficient general-purpose combination of CID, interval Newton and bisection. However, such a strategy is meaningful only if default values for `CID` are available. In our solver, the default values provide the following CID operator: `CID(s=4, w-hc4=10%, n'=n)`.

Experiments have led us to select $s = 4$ (see Section 7.2):

- The optimal number of slices lies between 2 and 8.
- Selecting $s = 4$ generally leads to the best performance. In the other cases, the performance is not so far from the one obtained with a tuned number of slices.

Discarded Variants

Several variants of CID or combinations of operators have been discarded by our experiments. Mentioning these discarded algorithms may be useful.

First, different combinations of bisection, CID and interval Newton have been tried. The proposed combination is the best one, but adding an interval Newton to the 2B/Box subfiltering (i.e., inside CID filtering) produces interesting results as well.

Second, we recommend to forget the fixed-point parameter w in CID. Indeed, a lot of experiments confirmed that relaunching LoopCID several times in a row between two bisections is nearly *never* useful. The same phenomenon has been observed if the relaunch criterion concerns several dimensions, i.e., if the reduction of box size (perimeter or volume) is sufficiently large. A third experiment running LoopCID twice between two splits leads to the same conclusion. Finally, the same kind of experiments have been conducted with no more success to determine which specific variables should be varcided again in an adaptive way. All these experiments give us the strong belief that one LoopCID, i.e., varciding all the variables once, is rather a *maximal* power of filtering.

Third, in a previous workshop version of this paper, we had proposed a CID246 variant of CID, in which the number s of slices was modified between two splits: it was alternatively 2, 4 or 6 : $s = ((i\, modulo\, 3) + 1) \times 2)$, where i indicates the ith call to LoopCID. The comparison with the standard CID was not fair because the parameter s in CID was set to 2. It turns out that CID with $s = 4$ yields nearly the same results as CID246 while being simpler.

Finally, we also investigated the option of a reentrant algorithm, under the acronym k-CID. As k-B-consistency [7] generalizes the 3-B-consistency, it is possible to use $(k-1)$-CID as subfiltering operator inside a k-CID algorithm. Like 4-B-consistency, 2-CID-consistency remains a theoretical partial consistency that is not really useful in practice. Indeed, the pruning power is significant (hence a small number of required splits), but the computational time required to obtain the solutions with 2-CID plus bisection is often not competitive with the time required by 1-CID plus bisection.

5 3B, CID and a 3BCID Hybrid Version

As mentioned in the introduction, the CID partial consistency has several points in common with the well-known 3B-consistency partial consistency [7].

Definition 6. (3B(s)-consistency)
Let $P = (X, C, B)$ be an NCSP. Let B_i^l be the sub-box of B in which $\mathbf{x_i}$ is replaced by $[\underline{\mathbf{x_i}}, \underline{\mathbf{x_i}} + \frac{|\mathbf{x_i}|}{s}]$. Let B_i^r be the sub-box of B in which $\mathbf{x_i}$ is replaced by $[\overline{\mathbf{x_i}} - \frac{|\mathbf{x_i}|}{s}, \overline{\mathbf{x_i}}]$.

Variable x_i is 3B(s)-consistent w.r.t. P if $2B(X, C, B_i^l) \neq \emptyset$ and $2B(X, C, B_i^r) \neq \emptyset$. The NCSP P is 3B(s)-consistent if all the variables in X are 3B(s)-consistent.

For practical considerations, and contrarily to finite-domain CSPs, a partial consistency of an NCSP is generally obtained with a precision w [7]. This precision avoids a slow convergence to obtain the property. Hence, as in CID, a parameter w is also required in the outer loop of 3B.

When the subfiltering operator is performed by *Box consistency*, instead of 2B-consistency, we obtain the so-called *Bound consistency* property [16].

The 3B algorithm follows a principle similar to CID, in which VarCID is replaced by a shaving process, called VarShaving in this paper. In particular, both algorithms are not incremental, hence the outside repeat loop possibly reruns the treatment of all the variables, as shown in Algorithm 3B.

```
Algorithm 3B (w: stop criterion precision, s : shaving precision, in-out
P = (X,C,B): an NCSP, F: subfiltering operator and its parameters)
    repeat
        for every variable xi ∈ X do
        |   VarShaving (xi, s, P, F)
        end
    until StopCriterion(w, P)
end.
```

The procedure VarShaving reduces the left and right bounds of variable x_i by trying to refute intervals with a width at least equal to $\frac{|x_i|}{s}$. The following proposition highlights the difference between 3B filtering and CID filtering.

Proposition 1. *Let $P = (X, C, B)$ be an NCSP. Consider the box B' obtained by* CID(s,w) *w.r.t.* 2B *and the box B'' obtained by* 3B(s,w) [3]. *Then,* CID(s,w) *filtering is stronger than* 3B(s,w) *filtering, i.e., B' is included in or equal to B''.*

This theoretical property is based on the fact that, due to the hull operation in VarCID, the whole box B can be reduced on several, possibly all, dimensions. With VarShaving, the pruning effort can impact only x_i, losing all the temporary reductions obtained on the other variables by the different calls to F.

Proposition 1 states that the pruning capacity of CID is greater than the one of 3B. In the general case however, 3B-consistency and CID-consistency are not comparable because s is the exact number of calls to subfiltering F inside VarCID (i.e., the upper bound is reached), while s is an upper bound of the number of calls to 2B by VarShaving. Experiments will confirm that a rough work on a given variable with CID (e.g., setting $s = 4$) yields better results than a more costly work with 3B (e.g., setting $s = 10$).

The 3BCID Filtering Algorithm

As mentioned above, the 3B and CID filtering operators follow the same scheme, so that several hybrid algorithms have been imagined. The most promising version, called 3BCID, is presented in this paper.

3BCID manages two parameters: the numbers s_{CID} and s_{3B} of slices for the CID part and the shaving part. Every variable x_i is handled by a shaving and a VarCID process as follows.

The interval of x_i is first split into s_{3B} slices handled by shaving. Using a subfiltering operator F, a simple shaving procedure tries to refute these slices to

[3] An additional assumption related to floating-point numbers and to the fixed-point criterion is required in theory to allow a fair comparison between algorithms: the 2B/Box subfiltering operator must work with a subdivision of the slices managed by 3B and CID.

the left and to the right (no dichotomic process is performed). Let s_{left} (resp. s_{right}) be the leftmost (resp. rightmost) slice of x_i that has not been refuted by subfiltering, if any. Let $\mathbf{x_i'}$ be the remaining interval of x_i, i.e., $\overline{s_{left}} \leq \underline{\mathbf{x_i'}} \leq \overline{\mathbf{x_i'}} \leq \underline{s_{right}}$.

Then, if $\mathbf{x_i'}$ is not empty, it is split into s_{CID} slices and handled by CID. One performs the hull of the (at most) $s_{\text{CID}} + 2$ boxes handled by the subfiltering operator F: s_{left}, s_{right} and the s_{CID} slices between s_{left} and s_{right}.

It is straightforward to prove that the obtained partial consistency is stronger than 3B(s_{3B})-consistency.

The experiments will show that 3BCID with $s_{\text{CID}} = 1$ can be viewed as an improved version of 3B where constructive disjunction produces an additional pruning effect with a low overhead.

6 A New CID-Based Splitting Strategy

There are three main splitting strategies (i.e., variable choice heuristics) used for solving numerical CSPs. The simplest one follows a *round-robin* strategy and loops on all the variables. Another heuristic selects the variable with the largest interval. A third one, based on the *smear function* [10], selects a variable x_i implied in equations whose derivative w.r.t. x_i is large.

The round-robin strategy ensures that all the variables are split in a branch of the search tree. Indeed, as opposed to finite-domain CSPs, note that a variable interval is generally split (i.e., instantiated) several times before finding a solution (i.e., obtaining a small interval of width less than the precision). The largest interval strategy also leads the solving process to not always select a same variable as long as its domain size decreases. The strategy based on the smear function sometimes splits always the same variables so that an interleaved schema with round-robin, or a preconditionning phase, is sometimes necessary to make it effective in practice.

We introduce in this section a new CID-based splitting strategy. Let us first consider different box sizes related to (and learnt during) the VarCID procedure applied to a given variable x_i :

- Let $\texttt{OldBox}_i$ be the box B just before the call to VarCID on x_i. Let $\texttt{NewBox}_i$ be the box obtained after the call to VarCID on x_i.
- Let $B_i^{l'}$ and $B_i^{r'}$ be the left and right boxes computed in VarCID, after a reduction by the F filtering operator, and before the Hull operation.

The ratio ratioBis leads to an "intelligent" splitting strategy. The ratio ratioBis= $\frac{f(Size(B_i^{l'}),Size(B_i^{r'}))}{Size(NewBox)}$, where f is any function that aggregates the size of two boxes (e.g., sum), in a sense computes the size lost by the Hull operation of VarCID. In other words, $B_i^{l'}$ and $B_i^{r'}$ represent precisely the boxes one would obtain if one splits the variable x_i (instead of performing the hull operation) immediately after the call to VarCID; NewBox is the box obtained by the `Hull` operation used by `CID` to avoid a combinatorial explosion due to a choice point.

Thus, after a call to `LoopCID`, the CID principle allows us to learn about a good variable interval to be split: *one selects the variable having led to the lowest* `ratioBis`. Although not related to constructive disjunction, similar strategies have been applied to finite-domain CSPs [4,13].

Experiments, not reported here, have compared a large number of variants of `ratioBis` with different functions f. The best variant is `ratioBis` $= \frac{Size(B_i^{l'})+Size(B_i^{r'})}{Size(NewBox)}$.

7 Experiments

We have performed a lot of comparisons and tests on a sample of 20 instances. These tests have helped us to design efficient variants of CID filtering.

7.1 Benchmarks and Interval-Based Solver

Twenty benchmarks are briefly presented in this section. Five of them are sparse systems found in [11]: `Hourglass`, `Tetra`, `Tangent`, `Ponts`, `Mechanism`. They are challenging for general-purpose interval-based techniques, but the algorithm `IBB` can efficiently exploit a preliminary decomposition of the systems into small subsystems [11]. The other benchmarks have been found in the Web page of the COPRIN research team or in the COCONUT Web page where the reader can find more details about them [12]. The precision of the solutions. i.e., the size of interval under which a variable interval is not split, is $1e-08$ for all the benchmarks, and $5e-06$ for `Mechanism`. `2B` is used for all the benchmarks but one because it is the most efficient local consistency filtering when used alone inside `3B` or `CID`. `Box+2B` is more adequate for `Yamamura8`. All the selected instances can be solved in an acceptable amount of time by a standard algorithm in order to make possible comparisons between numerous variants. No selected benchmark has been discarded for any other reason!

All the tests have been performed on a `Pentium IV 2.66 Ghz` using the interval-based library in `C++` developed by the second author. This new solver provides the main standard interval operators such as `Box`, `2B`, interval Newton [10]. The solver provides round-robin, largest-interval and CID-based splitting strategies. Although recent and under developement, the library seems competitive with up-to-date solvers like `RealPaver` [5]. For all the presented solving techniques, including `3B` and `3BCID`, an interval Newton is called just before a splitting operation iff the width of the largest variable interval is less than $1e-2$.

7.2 Results Obtained by `CID`

Table 1 reports the results obtained by `CID`(s, `w-hc4`, n'), as defined in Section 4.

The drastic reduction in the number of required bisections (often several orders of magnitude) clearly underlines the filtering power of `CID`. In addition,

Table 1. Comparison between [CID + interval Newton + round-robin bisection strategy] and [a standard strategy]: 2B/Box + interval Newton + round-robin splitting. n is the number of variables. The column #s yields the number of solutions. The first column w-hc4 is the user-defined parameter w-hc4 used by 2B or Box. The last 3 columns s, w-hc4 and n' indicate the values of parameters that have been tuned for CID (first CID column). The second CID column reports the results of CID when $s = 4$ and w-hc4 $= 10\%$, i.e., when only n' is tuned. The third CID column reports the results of CID when $s = 4$ and $n' = n$, i.e., when only w-hc4 is tuned. The fourth CID column reports the results of CID with the default values for parameters, i.e., $s = 4$, w-hc4 $= 10\%$, $n' = n$. Every cell contains two values: the CPU time in seconds to compute all the solutions (top), and the number of required bisections (bottom). For every benchmark, the best CPU time is bold-faced.

Name	n	#s	w-hc4	2B/Box + Newton	CID $(s, \texttt{whc4}, n')$	CID $(4, 10\%, n')$	CID $(4, \texttt{whc4}, n)$	CID $(4, 10\%, n)$	s	w-hc4	n'
BroydenTri	32	2	15%	758 2e+07	**0.12** 46	0.28 44	0.19 65	0.45 50	4	80%	40
Hourglass	29	8	5%	24 1e+05	**0.44** 109	0.44 109	0.52 80	0.52 80	4	10%	17
Tetra	30	256	0.02%	401 1e+06	**10.1** 2116	11.6 1558	11.7 1690	14.5 1320	4	30%	20
Tangent	28	128	15%	32 1e+05	**3.7** 692	3.7 692	4.9 447	5.1 450	4	50%	28
Reactors	20	38	5%	156 1e+06	**15.6** 2588	16.4 2803	16.7 2381	17.7 2156	4	15%	18
Trigexp1	30	1	20%	371(3.4) 5025	**0.12** 1	0.15 3	0.14 2	0.14 3	8	2%	30
Discrete25	27	1	0.01%	5.2 1741	**0.62** 2	1.08 3	0.84 12	2.13 99	8	0.5%	35
I5	10	30	2%	692 3e+06	**126** 23105	147 60800	150 20874	157 32309	6	2%	5
Transistor	12	1	10%	179 1e+06	**66** 11008	79.4 31426	91.4 16333	91.4 16333	8	10%	6
Ponts	30	128	5%	10.8 34994	**2.7** 388	2.9 338	2.9 380	3.1 304	4	30%	25
Yamamura8	8	7	1%	13 1032	**7.5** 104	9.5 60	9.5 60	9.5 60	4	10%	4
Design	9	1	10%	395 3e+06	**275** 200272	278 256000	313 76633	313 76633	5	10%	2
D1	12	16	5%	4.1 35670	**1.7** 464	1.7 464	1.7 464	1.7 464	4	10%	12
Mechanism	98	448	0.5%	TO(111) 24538	**43.1** 3419	45.2 3300	46.6 2100	47.8 2420	4	2%	50
Hayes	8	1	0.01%	155 3e+05	**75.8** 1e+05	77 1e+05	111 81750	147 58234	4	80%	2
Kin1	6	16	10%	84 70368	**76.8** 6892	76.8 6892	83.5 4837	87.4 4100	4	10%	3
Eco9	8	16	10%	26 2e+05	**18** 55657	19.4 46902	26.6 10064	26.6 10064	3	10%	1
Bellido	9	8	10%	**80** 7e+05	94.4 1e+05	94.4 1e+05	106 45377	106 45377	4	10%	3
Trigexp2-9	9	0	20%	61.8 3e+05	**50.4** 4887	65.14 14528	62.4 11574	68.4 9541	6	10%	9
Trigexp2-5	5	0	20%	**3.0** 13614	3.8 10221	4.6 4631	6.2 2293	6.6 1887	2	20%	1
Caprasse	4	18	30%	**2.6** 37788	2.73 18176	3.0 12052	4.7 5308	5.1 5624	2	5%	1

impressive gains in running time are obtained by CID for the benchmarks on the top of the table, as compared to standard strategy using 2B or 2B+Box, an interval Newton and a round-robin splitting policy[4].

CID often obtains better running times than the standard strategy, except on Bellido, Trigexp2-5 and Caprasse, for which the loss in performance is small. However, it is not reasonable to propose to the user an operator for which three parameters must be tuned by hand. That is why we have also reported the last three CID columns where only 0 or 1 parameter has been tuned. The default values (fourth CID column with $s = 4$, w-hc4= 10%, $n' = n$) yield very good results: it outperforms the standard strategy in 15 of the 21 instances. In particular, setting $s = 4$ provides the best results in 12 of the 21 instances.

The second and third CID columns report very good results obtained by a filtering algorithm with only one parameter to be tuned (like with 2B or Box). Hence, since CID with only parameter n' to be tuned (second CID column) allows a continuum between pure 2B and CID ($n' = 0$ amounts to a call to 2B), a first recommendation is to propose this CID variant in interval-based solvers.

The second recommendation comes from a combinatorial consideration. In a sense, constructive interval disjunction can be viewed as a "polynomial-time splitting" since VarCID performs a polynomial-time hull after having handled the different slices. However, the exponential aspect of (classical) bisection becomes time-consuming only when the number of variables becomes high. This would explain why CID cannot pay off on Trigexp2-5 and Caprasse which have a very small number of variables and lead to no combinatorial explosion due to bisection. (The intuition is confirmed by the better behavior of CID on the (scalable) variant of Trigexp2 with 9 variables.) Thus, the second recommendation would be to use CID on systems having a minimal number of variables, e.g., 5 or 8.

7.3 Comparing CID, 3B and 3BCID

Table 2 reports the results obtained by CID, 3B and 3BCID (see Section 5). All the results have been obtained with a parameter w-hc4 set to 5%.

Several trials have been performed for every algorithm, and the best result is reported in the table. For 3B, seven values have been tried for the parameter s_{3B}: 4, 5, 7, 10, 20, 50, 100.

For CID, nine values of the parameters have been tried: five values for the number of slices s_{CID} (2, 3, 4, 6, 8; fixing $n' = n$), and four values for the parameter n' (1, $0.5n$, $0.75n$, $1.2n$; fixing $s_{CID} = 4$). For 3BCID, eight combinations of parameters have been tried: four values for s_{CID} (1,2,3,4) combined with two values for s_{3B} (10, 20).

The main conclusions drawn from Table 2 are the following:

- 3BCID and CID always outperform 3B. Even the standard strategy outperforms 3B for 9 benchmarks in the bottom of the table.

[4] Note that this strategy is inefficient for Trigexp1 (solved in 371 seconds) and for Mechanism (that is not solved after a timeout (TO) of several hours). However, a reasonable running time can be obtained with a variant of 2B that push *all* the constraints of the NCSP in the propagation queue after every bisection.

Table 2. Comparison between CID, 3B and 3BCID. The first three columns recall resp. the name of the benchmark, its number of variables and the CPU time in seconds required by the strategy 2B/Box + Newton + bisection with round-robin. The other columns report the CPU time required to solve the benchmarks with CID, 3B and 3BCID. The best CPU time result is bold-faced.

Name	n	2B/Box	CID	3B	3BCID($s_{CID}=1$)	3BCID($s_{CID}=2$)
BroydenTri	32	758	0.23	0.22	**0.18**	0.19
Hourglass	29	24	0.45	0.73	**0.43**	0.50
Tetra	30	401	**13.6**	20.7	17.1	18.8
Tangent	28	32	4.13	8.67	**3.18**	4.13
Reactors	20	156	18.2	24.2	**15.5**	16.9
Trigexp1	30	3.4	**0.10**	0.26	0.12	0.11
Discrete25	27	5.2	1.37	2.19	1.26	**1.13**
I5	10	692	139	144	**115**	123
Transistor	12	179	71.5	77.9	49.3	**46.9**
Ponts	30	10.8	**3.07**	5.75	4.19	4.43
Yamamura8	8	13	**9.0**	9.1	10.3	10.7
Design	9	395	300	403	**228**	256
D1	12	4.1	1.78	2.99	**1.64**	1.76
Mechanism	98	111	**79**	185	176	173
Hayes	8	155	**99**	188	102	110
Kinematics1	6	84	**76.1**	136	76.6	81.4
Eco9	8	26	**19.3**	40.1	27.0	30.3
Bellido	9	**80**	95	143	**93**	102
Trigexp2-9	9	61.8	52.2	74.5	**39.9**	45.1
Caprasse	4	**2.6**	**3.1**	9.38	4.84	5.35

– 3BCID is competitive with CID. 3BCID is better than CID concerning 11 benchmarks. CID remains even better for Mechanism. We wonder if it is related to its large number of variables.

The good news is that the best value for s_{CID} in 3BCID is often $s_{CID} = 1$. In only four cases, the best value is greater, but the value $s_{CID} = 1$ also provides very good results. This suggests to propose 3BCID with $s_{CID} = 1$ as an alternative of 3B. In other words, 3BCID with $s_{CID} = 1$ can be viewed as a promising implementation of 3B. This is transparent for a user who has to specify the same parameter s_{3B}, the management of constructive disjunction being hidden inside 3BCID (that performs a Hull operation of at most 3 boxes since $s_{CID} = 1$).

7.4 Comparing Splitting Strategies

Table 3 applies the three available splitting strategies to CID with $n' = n$ and $s = 4$. We underline some observations.

The new CID-based splitting strategy is better than the other strategies on 13 of the 20 instances, especially on Design. The largest interval strategy is the best on only one instance. The round-robin strategy is the best on 6 instances.

Table 3. Comparison on CID with three splitting strategies: Round-robin, Largest interval and the new CID-based strategy.

Filtering	CID	CID	CID
Splitting	Round-robin	Largest Int.	CID-based
BroydenTri	0.21	0.18	**0.17**
Hourglass	0.52	0.51	**0.37**
Tetra	**12.1**	28.2	16.4
Tangent	**3.7**	21.7	5.2
Reactors	17.0	13.2	**12.7**
Trigexp1	0.15	0.19	**0.14**
Discrete25	**0.84**	1.49	1.06
I5	**151**	421	179
Transistor	93	**36**	41
Ponts	2.92	5.51	**2.31**
Yamamura8	9.5	6.9	**5.1**
Design	318	334	**178**
D1	**1.72**	2.96	2.50
Mechanism	47	49	**46**
Hayes	**115**	564	318
Kinematics1	83	70	**63**
Eco9	26.7	31.4	**26.1**
Bellido	107	102	**99**
Trigexp2-9	62	55	**53**
Caprasse	5.16	5.43	**5.04**

On the 7 instances for which the CID-based strategy is not the best, the loss in performance is significant on Hayes.

The behavior of the CID-based strategy with $s = 6$ (not reported here) is even better, the round-robin strategy being the best on only 3 instances. This would suggest that the ratioCID learned during a VarCID operation is more accurate with a higher number of slices.

8 Conclusion

This paper has introduced two new filtering operators based on the constructive disjunction principle exploited in combinatorial problems. The first experimental results are very promising and we believe that CID and 3BCID have the potential to become standard operators in interval constraint solvers. The CID operator also opens the door to a new splitting strategy learning from the work of CID filtering.

The experiments lead to clear recommendations concerning the use of these new filtering operators. First, CID can be used with fixed values of parameters s and w-hc4, letting the user only tune the third parameter n' (i.e., the number of variables that are varcided between 2 bisections). This allows the user to select in a sense a rate of CID filtering, $n' = 0$ producing the pure 2B/Box. Used this way, CID could maybe subsume existing filtering operators. Second, 3BCID with $s = 1$ can be provided as a promising alternative of a 3B operator.

Several questions remain open. It seems that, due to combinatorial considerations, CID is not convenient for small problems while it seems more interesting for large-scale systems. A more complete experimental study should confirm or contradict this claim. Also, 3BCID should be compared to the weak-3B operator implemented in RealPaver [5][5]. A comparison with filtering algorithms based on linearization, like Quad [6], will be performed as well.

Moreover, the CID-based splitting strategy merits a deeper experimental study. In particular, a comparison with the *smear* function will be performed once the latter is implemented in our solver.

An interesting future work is to propose *adaptive* variants of CID that can choose which specific variable should be varcided or bisected next.

Acknowledgements

Special thanks to Olivier Lhomme for useful discussions about this research. Also thanks to Bertrand Neveu, Arnold Neumaier and the anonymous reviewers.

References

1. Barták, R., Erben, R.: A new Algorithm for Singleton Arc Consistency. In: Proc. FLAIRS (2004)
2. Bessière, C., Debruyne, R.: Optimal and Suboptimal Singleton Arc Consistency Algorithms. In: Proc. IJCAI, pp. 54–59 (2005)
3. Debruyne, R., Bessière, C.: Some Practicable Filtering Techniques for the Constraint Satisfaction Problem. In: Proc. IJCAI, pp. 412–417 (1997)
4. Geelen, P.A.: Dual Viewpoint Heuristics for Binary Constraint Satisfaction Problems. In: Proc. ECAI'92, pp. 31–35 (1992)
5. Granvilliers, L., Benhamou, F.: RealPaver: An Interval Solver using Constraint Satisfaction Techniques. ACM Trans. on Mathematical Software 32(1), 138–156 (2006)
6. Lebbah, Y., Michel, C., Rueher, M.: A Rigorous Global Filtering Algorithm for Quadratic Constraints. Constraints Journal 10(1), 47–65 (2005)
7. Lhomme, O.: Consistency Tech. for Numeric CSPs. In: IJCAI, pp. 232–238 (1993)
8. Lhomme, O.: Quick Shaving. In: Proc. AAAI, pp. 411–415 (2005)
9. Min Li, C., Anbulagan: Heuristics Based on Unit Propagation for Satisfiability Problems. In: Proc. IJCAI, pp. 366–371 (1997)
10. Neumaier, A.: Interval Methods for Systems of Equations. Cambridge University Press, Cambridge (1990)
11. Neveu, B., Chabert, G., Trombettoni, G.: When Interval Analysis helps Interblock Backtracking. In: Benhamou, F. (ed.) CP 2006. LNCS, vol. 4204, pp. 390–405. Springer, Heidelberg (2006)
12. Web page of COPRIN: www-sop.inria.fr/coprin/logiciels/ALIAS/Benches/benches.html
    COCONUT benchs:
    www.mat.univie.ac.at/~neum/glopt/coconut/Benchmark/Benchmark.html

[5] An implementation of both operators in a same solver would lead to a fair comparison.

13. Refalo, P.: Impact-Based Search Strategies for Constraint Programming. In: Wallace, M. (ed.) CP 2004. LNCS, vol. 3258, pp. 557–571. Springer, Heidelberg (2004)
14. Régin, J.C.: A Filtering Algorithm for Constraints of Difference in CSPs. In: Proc. AAAI, pp. 362–367 (1994)
15. Simonis, H.: Sudoku as a Constraint Problem. In: CP Workshop on Modeling and Reformulating Constraint Satisfaction Problems, pp. 13–27 (2005)
16. Van Hentenryck, P., Michel, L., Deville, Y.: Numerica: A Modeling Language for Global Optimization. MIT Press, Cambridge (1997)
17. Van Hentenryck, P., Saraswat, V., Deville, Y.: Design, Implementation, and Evaluation of the Constraint Language CC(FD). J. Logic Programming 37(1–3), 139–164 (1994)

An LP-Based Heuristic for Optimal Planning

Menkes van den Briel[1], J. Benton[2], Subbarao Kambhampati[2], and Thomas Vossen[3]

[1] Arizona State University, Department of Industrial Engineering,
[2] Department of Computer Science and Engineering,
Tempe AZ, 85287, USA
{menkes,j.benton,rao}@asu.edu
[3] University of Colorado, Leeds School of Business,
Boulder CO, 80309, USA
vossen@colorado.edu

Abstract. One of the most successful approaches in automated planning is to use heuristic state-space search. A popular heuristic that is used by a number of state-space planners is based on relaxing the planning task by ignoring the delete effects of the actions. In several planning domains, however, this relaxation produces rather weak estimates to guide search effectively. We present a relaxation using (integer) linear programming that respects delete effects but ignores action ordering, which in a number of problems provides better distance estimates. Moreover, our approach can be used as an admissible heuristic for optimal planning.

Keywords: Automated planning, improving admissible heuristics, optimal relaxed planning

1 Introduction

Many heuristics that are used to guide heuristic state-space search planners are based on constructing a relaxation of the original planning problem that is easier to solve. The idea is to use the solution to the relaxed problem to guide search for the solution to the original problem. A popular relaxation that has been implemented by several planning systems, including UNPOP [17,18], HSP [4,5], and FF [15], involves using *relaxed actions* in which the delete effects of the original actions are ignored.

For example, FF estimates the distance between an intermediate state and the goals by creating a planning graph [3] using relaxed actions. From this graph, FF extracts in polynomial time a relaxed plan whose corresponding plan length is used as an inadmissible, but effective, distance estimate. One can transform this approach into an admissible heuristic by finding the optimal relaxed plan, also referred to as h^+ [14], but computing such a plan is NP-Complete [8]. In order to extract the optimal relaxed plan one must extend the relaxed planning graph to level off [3] so that all reachable actions can be considered.

Although ignoring delete effects turns out to be quite effective for many planning domains, there are some obvious weaknesses with FF's relaxed plan heuristic. For example, in a relaxed plan no atom changes more than once, if an

C. Bessiere (Ed.): CP 2007, LNCS 4741, pp. 651–665, 2007.

atom becomes true it remains true as it is never deleted. However, in a plan corresponding to the original problem an atom may be added and deleted several times. In order to improve the quality of the relaxed plan we consider a relaxation based on *relaxed orderings*.

In particular, we view a planning problem as a set of interacting network flow problems. Given a planning domain where states are defined in terms of n boolean or multi-valued state variables (i.e. fluents), we view each fluent as a separate flow problem, where nodes correspond to the values of the fluent, and arcs correspond to the transitions between these values. While network flow problems are computationally easy, what makes this flow problem hard is that the flows are "coupled" as actions can cause transitions in multiple fluents.

We set up an IP formulation where the variables correspond to the number times each action is executed in the solution plan. The objective is to minimize the number of actions, and the constraints ensure that each pre-condition is supported. However, the constraints do not ensure that pre-conditions are supported in a correct ordering. Specifically, for pre-conditions that are deleted we setup balance of flow constraints. That is, if there are m action instances in the plan that cause a transition from value f of fluent c, then there must be m action instances in the plan that cause a transition to value f of c. Moreover, for pre-conditions that are not deleted we simply require that they must be supported.

The relaxation that we pursue in this paper is that we are not concerned about the specific positions of where the actions occur in the plan. This can, to some extent, be thought of as ignoring the ordering constraints that ensure that the actions can be linearized into a feasible plan. An attractive aspect of our formulation is that it is not dependent on the length of the plan. Previous integer programming-based formulations for planning, such as [7,9,21], use a step-based encoding. In a step-based encoding the idea is to set up a formulation for a given plan length and increment it if no solution can be found. The problem with such an encoding is that it may become impractically large, even for medium sized planning tasks. In a step-based encoding, if l steps are needed to solve a planning problem then l variables are introduced for each action, whereas in our formulation we require only a single variable for each action.

The estimate on the number of actions in the solution plan, as computed by our IP formulation, provides a lower bound on the optimal (minimum number of actions) plan. However, since solving an IP formulation is known to be computationally intractable, we use the linear programming (LP) relaxation which can be solved in polynomial time. We will see that this double relaxation is still competitive with other admissible heuristics after we add non-standard and strong valid inequalities to the formulation. In particular, We show that the value of our LP-relaxation with added inequalities, gives very good distance estimates and in some problem instances even provides the optimal distance estimate.

While the current paper focuses on admissible heuristics for optimal sequential planning, the flow-based formulation can be easily extended to deal with more general planning problems, including cost-based planning and over-subscription planning. In fact, a generalization of this heuristic leads to state-of-the-art performance in oversubscription planning with non-uniform actions costs, goal utilities as well as dependencies between goal utilities [2].

This paper is organized as follows. In Section 2 we describe our action selection formulation and describe a number of helpful constraints that exploit domain structure. Section 3 reports some experimental results and related work is described in Section 4. In Section 5 we summarize our main conclusions and describe some avenues for future work.

2 Action Selection Formulation

We find it useful to do the development of our relaxation in terms of multi-valued fluents (of which the boolean fluents are a special case). As such, we will use the SAS+ formalism [1] rather than the usual STRIPS/ADL one as the background for our development. SAS+ is a planning formalism that defines actions by their prevail-conditions and effects. Prevail-conditions describe which variables must propagate a certain value during the execution of the action and effects describe the pre- and post-conditions of the action.

To make the connection between planning and network flows more straightforward, we will restrict our attention to a subclass of SAS+ where each action that has an post-condition on a fluent also has a pre-condition on that fluent. We emphasize that this restriction is made for ease of exposition and can be easily removed; indeed our work in [2] avoids making this restriction.

2.1 Notation

We define a SAS+ planning task as a tuple $\Pi = \langle C, A, s_0, s_* \rangle$, where

- $C = \{c_1, ..., c_n\}$ is a finite set of state variables, where each state variable $c \in C$ has an associated domain V_c and an implicitly defined extended domain $V_c^+ = V_c \cup \{u\}$, where u denotes the *undefined value*. For each state variable $c \in C$, $s[c]$ denotes the value of c in state s. The value of c is said to be *defined* in state s if and only if $s[c] \neq u$. The total state space $S = V_{c_1} \times ... \times V_{c_n}$ and the partial state space $S^+ = V_{c_1}^+ \times ... \times V_{c_n}^+$ are implicitly defined.
- A is a finite set of actions of the form $\langle pre, post, prev \rangle$, where *pre* denotes the pre-conditions, *post* denotes the post-conditions, and *prev* denotes the prevail-conditions. For each action $a \in A$, $pre[c], post[c]$ and $prev[c]$ denotes the respective conditions on state variable c. The following two restrictions are imposed on all actions: (1) Once the value of a state variable is defined, it can never become undefined. Hence, for all $c \in C$, if $pre[c] \neq u$ then $pre[c] \neq post[c] \neq u$; (2) A prevail- and post-condition of an action can never define a value on the same state variable. Hence, for all $c \in C$, either $post[c] = u$ or $prev[c] = u$ or both.
- $s_0 \in S$ denotes the initial state and $s_* \in S^+$ denotes the goal state. We say that state s is *satisfied* by state t if and only if for all $c \in C$ we have $s[c] = u$ or $s[c] = t[c]$. This implies that if $s_*[c] = u$ for state variable c, then any defined value $f \in V_c$ satisfies the goal for c.

While SAS+ planning allows the initial state, the goal state and the pre-conditions of an action to be partial, we assume that s_0 is a total state and that all preconditions are defined for all state variables on which the action has post-conditions (i.e. $pre[c] = u$ if and only if $post[c] = u$). The assumption that s_0 is a total state is common practice in automated planning. However, the assumption that all preconditions are defined is quite strong, therefore, we will briefly discuss a way to relax this second assumption in Section 5.

An important construct that we use in our action selection formulation is the so-called *domain transition graph* [13]. A domain transition graph is a graph representation of a state variable and shows the possible ways in which values can change. Specifically, the domain transition graph DTG_c of state variable c is a labeled directed graph with nodes for each value $f \in V_c$. DTG_c contains a labeled arc (f_1, f_2) if and only if there exists an action a with $pre[c] = f_1$ and $post[c] = f_2$ or $pre[c] = u$ and $post[c] = f_2$. The arc is labeled by the set of actions with corresponding pre- and post-conditions. For each arc (f_1, f_2) with label a in DTG_c we say that there is a *transition* from f_1 to f_2 and that action a has an *effect* in c.

We use the following notation.

- $DTG_c = (V_c, E_c)$: is a directed domain transition graph for every $c \in C$
- V_c: is the set of possible values for each state variable $c \in C$
- E_c: is the set of possible transitions for each state variable $c \in C$
- $V_c^a \subseteq V_c$ represents the prevail condition of action a in c
- $E_c^a \subseteq E_c$ represents the effect of action a in c
- $A_c^E := \{a \in A : |E_c^a| > 0\}$ represents the actions that have an effect in c, and $A_c^E(e)$ represents the actions that have the effect e in c
- $A_c^V := \{a \in A : |V_c^a| > 0\}$ represents the actions that have a prevail condition in c, and $A_c^V(f)$ represents the actions that have the prevail condition f in c
- $V_c^+(f)$: to denote the in-arcs of node f in the domain transition graph G_c;
- $V_c^-(f)$: to denote the out-arcs of node f in the domain transition graph G_c;

Moreover, we define the *composition* of two state variables, which is related to the parallel composition of automata [10], as follows.

Definition 1. *(Composition) Given the domain transition graph of two state variables c_1, c_2, the composition of DTG_{c_1} and DTG_{c_2} is the domain transition graph $DTG_{c_1||c_2} = (V_{c_1||c_2}, E_{c_1||c_2})$ where*

- $V_{c_1||c_2} = V_{c_1} \times V_{c_2}$
- $((f_1, g_1), (f_2, g_2)) \in E_{c_1||c_2}$ *if* $f_1, f_2 \in V_{c_1}$, $g_1, g_2 \in V_{c_2}$ *and there exists an action* $a \in A$ *such that one of the following conditions hold.*
  - $pre[c_1] = f_1$, $post[c_1] = f_2$, *and* $pre[c_2] = g_1$, $post[c_2] = g_2$
  - $pre[c_1] = f_1$, $post[c_1] = f_2$, *and* $prev[c_2] = g_1$, $g_1 = g_2$
  - $pre[c_1] = f_1$, $post[c_1] = f_2$, *and* $g_1 = g_2$

We say that $DTG_{c_1||c_2}$ is the composed domain transition graph of DTG_{c_1} and DTG_{c_2}.

Example. Consider the set of actions $A = \{a, b, c, d\}$ and set of state variables $C = \{c_1, c_2\}$ whose domain transition graphs have $V_{c_1} = \{f_1, f_2, f_3\}$, $V_{c_2} = \{g_1, g_2\}$ as the possible values, and $E_{c_1} = \{(f_1, f_3), (f_3, f_2), (f_2, f_1)\}$, $E_{c_2} = \{(g_1, g_2), (g_2, g_1)\}$ as the possible transitions as shown in Figure 1. Moreover, $A^E_{c_1} = \{a, b, c\}$, $A^E_{c_2} = \{b, d\}$ are the actions that have an effect in c_1 and c_2 respectively, and $A^V_{c_1} = \emptyset$, $A^V_{c_2} = \{a\}$ are the actions that have a prevail condition in c_1 and c_2 respectively. The effect and prevail condition of action a are represented by $E^a_{c_1} = (f_1, f_3)$ and $V^a_{c_2} = g_1$ respectively and the set of in-arcs for node g_1 is given by $V^+_{c_2}(g_1) = \{(g_2, g_1)\}$. Note that, since prevail conditions do not change the value of a state variable, we do not consider them to be transitions. The common actions in the composed domain transition graph, that is, actions in $A^E_{c_1} \cap A^E_{c_2}$ can only be executed simultaneously in the two domain transition graphs. Hence, in the composition the two domain transition graphs are synchronized on the common actions. The other actions, those in $A^E_{c_1} \backslash A^E_{c_2} \cup A^E_{c_2} \backslash A^E_{c_1}$, are not subject to such a restriction and can be executed whenever possible.

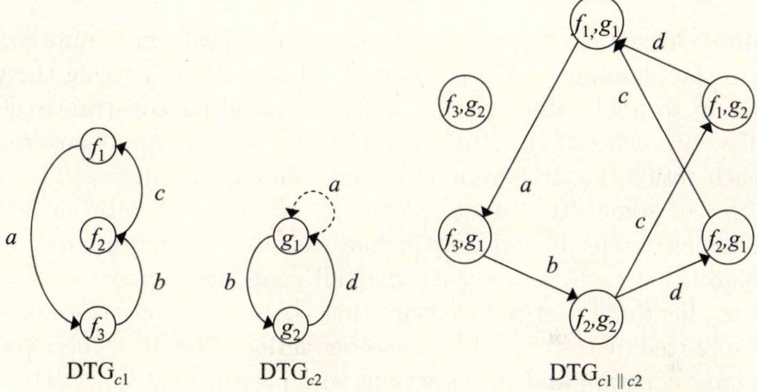

Fig. 1. Two domain transition graphs and their composition

2.2 Formulation

Our action selection formulation models each domain transition graph in the planning domain as an appropriately defined network flow problem. Interactions between the state variables, which are introduced by the pre-, post-, and prevail-conditions of the actions, are modeled as side constraints on the network flow problems. The variables in our formulation indicate how many times an action is executed, and the constraints ensure that all the action pre-, post-, and prevail-conditions must be respected. Because we ignore action ordering, we are solving a relaxation on the original planning problem. Our relaxation, however, is quite different from the more popular relaxation that ignores the delete effects of the actions.

Variables. We define two types of variables. We create one variable for each ground action and one for each state variable value. The action variables indicate how many times each action is executed and the variables representing state variable values indicate which values are achieved at the end of the solution plan. The variables are defined as follows.

- $x_a \in \mathbb{Z}^+$, for $a \in A$; $x_a \geq 0$ is equal to the number of times action a is executed.
- $y_{c,f} \in \{0, 1\}$, for $c \in C$, $f \in V_c$; $y_{c,f}$ is equal to 1 if the value f in state variable c is achieved at the end of the solution plan, and 0 otherwise.

Objective function. The objective function that we use minimizes the number of actions. Note, however, that we can deal with action costs by simply multiplying each action variable with a cost parameter c_a. Goal utilities can be dealt with by including the summation $\sum_{c \in C, f \in V_c : f = s_*[c]} u_{c,f} y_{c,f}$, where $u_{c,f}$ denotes the utility parameter for each goal.

$$\sum_{a \in A} x_a \tag{1}$$

Constraints. We define three types of constraints. Goal constraints ensure that the goals in the planning task are achieved. This is done by fixing the variables corresponding to goal values to one. Effect implication constraints define the network flow problems of the state variables. These constraints ensure that the effect of each action (i.e. transition in the domain transition graph) is supported by the effect of some other action. That is, one may execute an action that deletes a certain value if and only if one executes an action that adds that value. These constraints also ensure that all goals are supported. The prevail condition implication constraints ensure that the prevail conditions of an action must be supported by the effect of some other action. The M in these constraints denotes a large constant and allows actions with prevail conditions to be executed multiple times as long as their prevail condition is supported at least once. Note that, the initial state automatically adds the values that are present in the initial state.

- Goal constraints for all $c \in C$, $f \in V_c$: $f = s_*[c]$

$$y_{c,f} = 1 \tag{2}$$

- Effect implication constraints for all $c \in C$, $f \in V_c$

$$\sum_{e \in V_c^+(f) : b \in A_c^E(e)} x_b + 1\{\text{if } f = s_0[c]\} = \sum_{e \in V_c^-(f) : a \in A_c^E(e)} x_a + y_{c,f} \tag{3}$$

- Prevail condition implication constraints for all $c \in C$, $f \in V_c$: $a \in A_c^V(f)$

$$\sum_{e \in V_c^+(f) : b \in A_c^E(e)} x_b + 1\{\text{if } f = s_0[c]\} \geq x_a / M \tag{4}$$

One great advantage of this IP formulation over other step-based encodings is its size. The action selection formulation requires only one variable per action, whereas a step-based encoding requires one variable per action for each plan step. In a step-based encoding, if l steps are needed to solve a planning problem then l variables are introduced for each action.

Note that any feasible plan satisfies the above constraints. In a feasible plan all goals are satisfied, which is expressed by the constraints (2). In addition, in a feasible plan an action is executable if and only if its pre-conditions and prevail conditions are supported, which is expressed by constraints (3) and (4). Since any feasible will satisfy the constraints above, the formulation provides a relaxation to the original planning problem. Hence, an optimal solution to this formulation provides a bound (i.e. an admissible heuristic) on the optimal solution of the original planning problem.

2.3 Adding Constraints by Exploiting Domain Structure

We can substantially improve the quality of LP-relaxation of the action selection formulation by exploiting domain structure in the planning problem. In order to automatically detect domain structure in a planning problem we use the so-called *causal graph* [22]. The causal graph is defined as a directed graph with nodes for each state variable and directed arcs from source variables to sink variables if changes in the sink variable have conditions in the source variable. In other words, there is an arc in the causal graph if there exists an action that has an effect in the source variable and an effect or prevail condition in the source variable. We differentiate between two types of arcs by creating an effect causal graph and a prevail causal graph as follows ([16] use labeled arcs to make the same distinction).

Definition 2. *(Effect causal graph) Given a planning task* $\Pi = \langle C, A, s_0, s_* \rangle$, *the effect causal graph* $G_\Pi^{effect} = (V, E^{effect})$ *is an undirected graph whose vertices correspond to the state variables of the planning task.* G_Π^{effect} *contains an edge* (c_1, c_2) *if and only if there exists an action a that has an effect in* c_1 *and an effect in* c_2.

Definition 3. *(Prevail causal graph) Given a planning task* $\Pi = \langle C, A, s_0, s_* \rangle$, *the prevail causal graph* $G_\Pi^{prevail} = (V, E^{prevail})$ *is a directed graph whose nodes correspond to the state variables of the planning task.* $G_{prevail_\Pi}$ *contains a directed arc* (c_1, c_2) *if and only if there exists an action a that has a prevail condition in* c_1 *and an effect in* c_2.

By analyzing the effect causal graph, the prevail causal graph, and the domain transition graphs of the state variables, we are able to tighten the constraints of the integer programming formulation and improve the value of the corresponding LP relaxation. In particular, we add constraints to our formulation if certain (global) causal structure and (local) action substructures are present in the causal graphs and domain transition graphs respectively.

Example. The effect causal graph and prevail causal graph corresponding to the example shown in Figure 1 is given by Figure 2. Since action b has an effect in state variables c_1 and c_2 there is an edge (c_1, c_2) in G_{Π}^{effect}. Similarly, since action a has an effect in c_1 and a prevail condition in c_2 there is an arc (c_2, c_1) in $G_{\Pi}^{prevail}$.

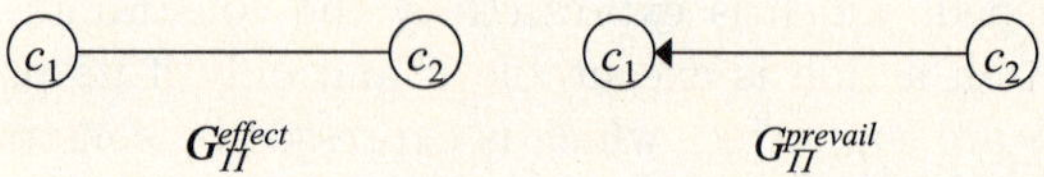

Fig. 2. The effect causal graph and prevail causal graph corresponding to Figure 1

Type 1 Domain Structure Constraints. The first set of domain structure constraints that we add to the action selection formulation deals with cycles in the causal graph. Causal cycles are undesirable as they describe a two-way dependency between state variables. That is, changes in a state variable c_1 will depend on conditions in a state variable c_2, and vice versa. It is possible that causal cycles involve more than two state variables, but we only consider 2-cycles (i.e. cycles of length two). A causal 2-cycle may appear in the effect causal graph and in the prevail causal graph. Note that, since the effect causal graph is undirected, any edge in the effect causal graph corresponds to a 2-cycle.

For every 2-cycle involving state variables c_1 and c_2 we create the composition $DTG_{c_1||c_2}$ if the following conditions hold.

- For all $a \in A_{c_1}^E$ we have $a \in (A_{c_2}^E \cup A_{c_2}^V)$
- For all $a \in A_{c_2}^E$ we have $a \in (A_{c_1}^E \cup A_{c_1}^V)$

In other words, for every action a that has an effect in state variable c_1 (c_2) we have that a has an effect or prevail condition in state variable c_2 (c_1). This condition will restrict the composition to provide a complete synchronization of the two domain transition graphs. Now, for each composed domain transition graph that is created we define an appropriately defined network flow problem. The corresponding constraints ensure that the two-way dependencies between state variables c_1 and c_2 are respected.

- Type 1 domain constraints for all $c_1, c_2 \in C$ such that $DTG_{c_1||c_2}$ is defined and $f \in V_{c_1}$, $g \in V_{c_2}$

$$\sum_{e \in V_{c_1||c_2}^+(f,g):b \in A_{c_1||c_2}^E(e)} x_b + 1\{\text{if } f = s_0[c_1] \wedge g = s_0[c_2]\} =$$

$$\sum_{e \in V_{c_1||c_2}^-(f,g):a \in A_{c_1||c_2}^E(e)} x_a \tag{5}$$

Example. In order to provide some intuition as to why these constraints are important and help improve the action selection formulation, consider the following scenario. Assume we are given the set of actions $A = \{a, b\}$ and the set of state variables $C = \{c_1, c_2\}$, such that $E^a_{c_1} = (f_1, f_2)$, $E^a_{c_2} = (g_2, g_3)$, $E^b_{c_1} = (f_2, f_3)$, and $E^b_{c_2} = (g_1, g_2)$. The effect implication constraint (3) allows the effect of action a support the effect of action b in c_1, and it allows the effect of action b support the effect of action a in c_2. However, in the composed domain transition graph, it is clear that neither action a or b can support each other. Hence, if actions a and b are selected in the solution plan, then the solution plan must include one or more other actions in order to satisfy the network flow constraints in the composed domain transition graph.

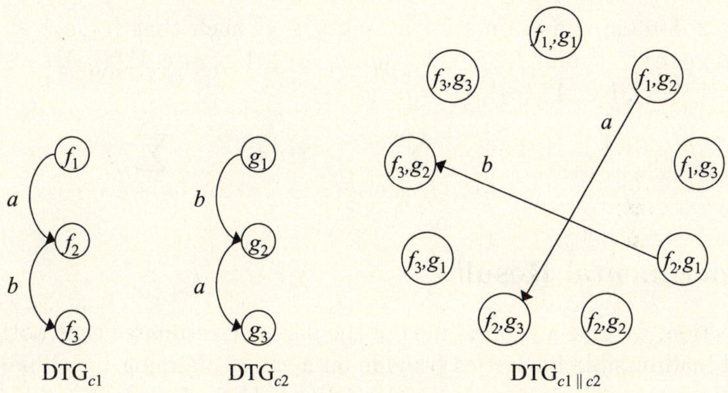

Fig. 3. Actions a and b can both support each other in either DTG_{c_1} and DTG_{c_2}, but not in $DTG_{c_1||c_2}$

Type 2 Domain Structure Constraints. The second set of domain structure constraints that we add to the action selection formulation deals with the structure given in Figure 4. That is, we have an arc (c_1, c_2) in the prevail causal graph that is not in a 2-cycle. In addition, we have a pair of actions a and b that have different prevail conditions in c_1 and different effects in c_2, such that a supports b in c_2.

Since actions a and b are mutex (action b deletes a post-condition of action a) they cannot be executed in parallel. Therefore, in a solution plan we must have that either a is executed before b, or that b is executed before a. If the solution plan executes a before b, then the network flow problem corresponding to state variable c_1 must have flow out of f_1. On the other hand, if b is executed before a, then the network flow problem corresponding to state variable c_2 must have flow out of g_3. These flow conditions may seem rather obvious, they are ignored by the action selection formulation. Therefore, we add the following constraints to our formulation to ensure that the flow conditions with respect to the domain structure given in Figure 4 are satisfied.

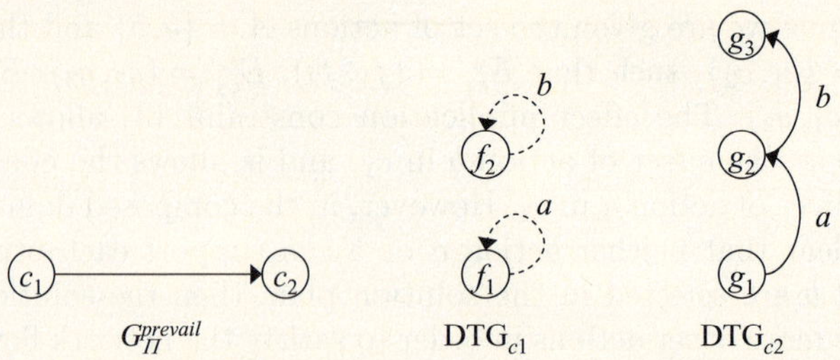

Fig. 4. Domain structure for type 2 domain structure constraints

– Type 2 domain constraints for all $c_1, c_2 \in C$ such that $(c_1, c_2) \in E^{prevail}$, $(c_2, c_1) \notin E^{prevail}$ and $f_1, f_2 \in V_{c_1}$, $g_1, g_2, g_3 \in V_{c_2}$, $e_1 \in V_{c_2}^{+}(g_2)$, $e_2 \in V_{c_2}^{-}(g_2)$: $a \in A_{c_2}^{E}(e_1)$, $b \in A_{c_2}^{V}(e_2)$, $g_3 = head(e_2)$

$$x_a + x_b - 1 \leq \sum_{e \in V_{c_1}^{-}(f_1) : a' \in A_c^E(e)} x_{a'} + \sum_{e \in V_{c_2}^{-}(g_3) : b' \in A_c^E(e)} x_{b'} \qquad (6)$$

3 Experimental Results

In this section, we give a general idea of the distance estimates that both admissible and inadmissible heuristics provide on a set of planning benchmarks from the international planning competitions (IPCs). In particular, we will compare the results of our action selection formulation (with and without the domain structure constraints) with four distance estimates: (1) the admissible distance estimate given by a step based formulation that is very similar to Lplan [9], (2) the admissible distance estimate h^+, which represents the length of the optimal relaxed plan in which the delete effects of the actions are ignored [14], (3) the inadmissible distance estimate h^{FF}, which represents the relaxed plan heuristic of the FF planner [15], and (4) the optimal distance estimate given by Satplanner [19] using the -opt flag.

We use Logistics and Freecell from IPC2, Driverlog and Zenotravel from IPC3, and TPP from IPC5. In addition, we included a few results on well known Blocksworld problems. We focus on these domains mainly because we assume that all pre-conditions are defined. There are several planning domains where this assumption does not hold which limits our experimentation. In Section 5, however, we briefly discuss how we can relax this assumption. All our tests were performed on a 2.67GHz Linux machine with 1GB of memory using a 15 minute timeout. The heuristics that use linear programming were solved using ILOG CPLEX 10.1 [11], a commercial LP/IP solver.

Table 1 summarizes the results. The results represent the distance estimate in terms of the number of actions from the initial state to the goals. LP and LP$^-$ shows the results of our action selection formulation with and without the domain structure constraints respectively. Lplan shows the results of a formulation that is very similar Lplan (the actual planner is not publicly available). They were

Table 1. Distance estimates from the initial state to the goal (values shown shown in bold equal the optimal distance). A dash '-' indicates a timeout of 15 minutes, and a star '*' indicates that the value was rounded to the nearest decimal.

Problem	LP	LP^-	Lplan	h^+	h^{FF}	Optimal
logistics4-0	**20**	16.0*	17	19	19	20
logistics4-1	**19**	14.0*	15	17	17	19
logistics4-2	**15**	10.0*	11	13	13	15
logistics5-1	**17**	12.0*	13	15	15	17
logistics5-2	**8**	6.0*	7	**8**	**8**	8
logistics6-1	**14**	10.0*	11	13	13	14
logistics6-9	**24**	18.0*	19	21	21	24
logistics12-0	42	32.0*	33	39	39	-
logistics15-1	67	54.0*	-	63	66	-
freecell2-1	**9**	**9**	**9**	**9**	**9**	9
freecell2-2	**8**	**8**	**8**	**8**	**8**	8
freecell2-3	**8**	**8**	**8**	**8**	9	8
freecell2-4	**8**	**8**	**8**	**8**	9	8
freecell2-5	**9**	**9**	**9**	**9**	**9**	9
freecell3-5	12	12	13	13	14	-
freecell13-3	55	55	-	-	95	-
freecell13-4	54	54	-	-	94	-
freecell13-5	52	52	-	-	94	-
driverlog1	**7**	3.0*	**7**	6	8	7
driverlog2	**19**	12.0*	13	14	15	19
driverlog3	11	8.0*	9	11	11	12
driverlog4	15.5*	11.0*	12	12	15	16
driverlog6	**11**	8.0*	9	10	10	11
driverlog7	**13**	11.0*	12	12	15	13
driverlog13	24	15.0*	16	21	26	-
driverlog19	96.6*	60.0*	-	89	93	-
driverlog20	89.5*	60.0*	-	84	106	-
zenotravel1	**1**	**1**	**1**	**1**	**1**	1
zenotravel2	**6**	3.0*	5	4	4	6
zenotravel3	**6**	4.0*	5	5	5	6
zenotravel4	**8**	5.0*	6	6	6	8
zenotravel5	**11**	8.0*	9	**11**	**11**	11
zenotravel6	**11**	8.0*	9	11	13	11
zenotravel13	24	18.0*	19	23	23	-
zenotravel19	66.2*	46.0*	-	62	63	-
zenotravel20	68.3*	50.0*	-	-	69	-
tpp01	**5**	3.0*	**5**	4	4	5
tpp02	**8**	6.0*	7	7	7	8
tpp03	**11**	9.0*	10	10	10	11
tpp04	**14**	12.0*	13	13	13	14
tpp05	**19**	15.0*	17	17	17	19
tpp06	25	21.0*	23	21	21	-
tpp28	-	150.0*	-	-	88	-
tpp29	-	-	-	-	104	-
tpp30	-	174.0*	-	-	101	-
bw-sussman	4	4	**6**	5	5	6
bw-12step	4	4	8	4	7	12
bw-large-a	**12**	**12**	**12**	**12**	**12**	12
bw-large-b	16	16	**18**	16	16	18

obtained by running a step-based encoding that finds minimum length plans. The values in this column represent the plan length at which the LP-relaxation returns a feasible solution. h^+ shows the length of the optimal relaxed plan and h^{FF} shows the length of FF's extracted relaxed plan. Finally, Optimal shows the results of Satplanner using the -opt flag, which returns the minimum length plan. Note that, Satplanner does not solve a relaxation, but the actual planning problem, so the values in this column represent the optimal distance estimate.

When comparing the results of LP with Lplan and h^+, we see that in many problem instances LP provides better distance estimates. However, there are a few instances in the Freecell and Blocksworld domains in which both Lplan and h^+ provide better estimates. The action selection formulation does clearly outperform both Lplan and h^+ in terms of scalability and time to solve the LP-relaxation. Lplan, generally takes the most time to solve each problem instance as it spends time finding a solution on a plan length for which no feasible solution exists. Both Lplan and h^+ fail to solve several of the large instances within the 15 minutes timeout. The LP-relaxation of the action selection formulation typically solves all small and some medium sized problem instances in less than one second, but the largest problem instances take several minutes to solve and on the largest TPP problem instances it times out at 15 minutes.

When we compare the results of LP with h^{FF} we are comparing the difference between an admissible and an inadmissible heuristic. The heuristic computation of FF's relaxed plan is very fast as it solves most problem instances in a fraction of a second. However, the distance estimate it provides is not admissible as it can overestimate the minimum distance between two states (see for example, driverlog7 and zenotravel6). The results that our action selection formulation provides are admissible and thus can be used in an optimal search algorithm. Moreover, in some problem instances the quality of our distance estimate is outstanding. For example, in the Logistics, Driverlog, and Zenotravel domains, the distance estimate given by LP equals the optimal distance in all problem instances for which Satplanner found the optimal solution.

Finally, when comparing the results of LP with LP$^-$ we see that the domain structure constraints help improve the value of the LP-relaxation in many problem instances except in instances in the Freecell and Blocksworld domains. Both these domains seem to have domain structure that we have not captured yet in our constraints. While this may seem like a problem, we rather take this as a challenge, as we believe that more domain structure can be exploited.

4 Related Work

Admissible heuristics for optimal planning (such as, minimize the number of actions in the solution plan or minimize the cost of the actions in the solution plan) are very scarce and often provide poor distance estimates. On the other hand, inadmissible heuristics are plentiful and have shown to be very effective in solving automated planning problems. HSPr* [12] is one of the few approaches that describes admissible heuristics for planning. HSPr* creates an appropriately defined shortest-path problem to estimate the distance between two states. Our work differs from HSPr* as we use linear programming to solve a relaxation of the original planning problem.

The use of linear programming as an admissible heuristic for optimal planning was introduced by the Lplan planning system [9]. However, the idea was never incorporated in other planning systems due to poor performance results. Lplan sets up an IP formulation for step-based planning. Thus, when the LP-relaxation of the IP has a solution for plan length l, but not for plan length $l-1$, then the minimum length plan must be at least l steps long. The drawbacks with the LP-relaxation to a step-based encoding is that goal achievement can be accumulated over different plan steps. In general, the quality of the LP-relaxation of an IP formulation depends on how the problem is formulated ([21] describe the importance of developing strong IP formulations in automated planning).

5 Conclusions

We described an integer programming formulation whose LP-relaxation can be used as an admissible heuristic for optimal planning, including planning problems that involve costs and utilities. In fact, in ongoing work we have successfully incorporated our LP-based heuristic in a search algorithm that solves oversubscription planning problems [2].

Our action selection formulation and the heuristic it provides differs in two ways from other formulations that have been used in planning: (1) we do not use a step based encoding, and so, do not have to deal with a bound on the plan length in the IP formulation, and (2) we ignore action ordering, which provides a rather different view on relaxed planning than the more popular approach that ignores the delete effects of the actions.

The experimental results show that the action selection formulation oftentimes provides better distance estimates than a step-based encoding that is similar to Lplan [9]. It outperforms this step-encoding with respect to scalability and solution time, making it a viable distance estimate for a heuristic state-space planner. Moreover, in most problem instances it outperforms h^+ [14], which provides the optimal relaxed plan length when delete effects are ignored. Hence, the relaxation based on ignoring action orderings seems to be stronger than the relaxation based on ignoring delete effects.

Unlike most admissible heuristics that have been described in the planning literature, we can use the action selection formulation to provide an admissible distance estimate for various optimization problems in planning, including but not limited to, minimizing the number of actions, minimizing the cost of actions, maximizing the number of goals, and maximizing the goal utilities. There are several interesting directions that we like to explore in future work.

First, we would like to relax the assumption that all preconditions are defined. This would allow us to create a general action selection formulation and tackle a much broader range of planning domains. We simply need to replace the current action variables with variables that represent the action effects the action prevail conditions. In case an action has one or more undefined pre-conditions we create one effect variable for each possible value that the pre-condition may take and introduce an extra prevail variable as well. We have a preliminary implementation of this general action selection formulation [2], but have not yet extended it with the domain structure constraints.

Second, it would be interesting to analyze planning domains more carefully and see if there are more domain structures that we can exploit. We already have encountered two domains, namely Freecell and Blocksworld, that may suggest that other domain structures could be discovered.

Acknowledgements. This research is supported in part by the NSF grant IIS308139, the ONR grant N000140610058, and by the Lockheed Martin subcontract TT0687680 to Arizona State University as part of the DARPA integrated learning program.

References

1. Bäckström, C., Nebel, B.: Complexity results for SAS+ planning. Computational Intelligence 11(4), 625–655 (1995)
2. Benton, J., van den Briel, M.H.L., Kambhampati, S.: A hybrid linear programming and relaxed plan heuristic for partial satisfaction planning problems. In: Proceedings of the 17th International Conference on Automated Planning and Scheduling (to appear 2007)
3. Blum, A., Furst, M.: Fast planning through planning graph analysis. In: Proceedings of the 14th International Joint Conference on Artificial Inteligence, pp. 1636–1642 (1995)
4. Bonet, B., Loerincs, G., Geffner, H.: A fast and robust action selection mechanism for planning. In: Proceedings of the 14th National Conference on Artificial Intelligence, pp. 714–719 (1997)
5. Bonet, B., Geffner, H.: Planning as heuristic search. Aritificial Intelligence 129(1), 5–33 (2001)
6. Botea, A., Müller, M., Schaeffer, J.: Fast planning with iterative macros. In: Proceedings of the 20th International Joint Conference on Artificial Intelligence, pp. 1828–1833 (2007)
7. van den Briel, M.H.L., Kambhampati, S., Vossen, T.: Reviving integer programming Approaches for AI planning: A branch-and-cut framework. In: Proceedings of the 15th International Conference on Automated Planning and Scheduling, pp. 310–319 (2005)
8. Bylander, T.: The computational complexity of propositional STRIPS planning. Artificial Intelligence 26(1-2), 165–204 (1995)
9. Bylander, T.: A linear programming heuristic for optimal planning. In: Proceedings of the 14th National Conference on Artificial Intelligence, pp. 694–699 (1997)
10. Cassandras, C.G., Lafortune, S.: Introduction to Discrete Event Systems. Kluwer Academic Publishers, Dordrecht (1999)
11. ILOG Inc.: ILOG CPLEX 8.0 user's manual. Mountain View, CA (2002)
12. Haslum, P., Geffner, H.: Admissible heuristics for optimal planning. In: Proceedings of the International Conference on Artificial Intelligence Planning and Scheduling (2000)

13. Helmert, M.: The Fast Downward planning system. Journal of Artificial Intelligence Research 26, 191–246 (2006)
14. Hoffmann, J.: Where "ignoring delete lists" works: Local search topology in planning benchmarks. Journal of Artificial Intelligence Research 24, 685–758 (2005)
15. Hoffmann, J., Nebel, B.: The FF planning system: Fast plan generation through heuristic search. Journal of Artificial Intelligence Research 14, 253–302 (2001)
16. Jonsson, P., Bäckström, C.: Tractable plan existence does not imply tractable plan generation. Annals of Mathematics and Artificial Intelligence 22(3), 281–296 (1998)
17. McDermott, D.: A heuristic estimator for means-ends analysis in planning. In: Proceedings of the 3rd International Conference on Artificial Intelligence Planning Systems, pp. 142–149 (1996)
18. McDermott, D.: Using regression-match graphs to control search in planning. Artificial Intelligence 109(1-2), 111–159 (1999)
19. Rintanen, J., Heljanko, K., Niemelä, I.: Planning as satisfiability: parallel plans and algorithms for plan search. Albert-Ludwigs-Universität Freiburg, Institut für Informatik, Technical report 216 (2005)
20. Vidal, V.: A lookahead strategy for heuristic search planning. In: Proceedings of the 14th International Conference on Automated Planning and Scheduling, pp. 150–159 (2004)
21. Vossen, T., Ball, B., Lotem, A., Nau, D.S.: On the use of integer programming models in AI planning. In: Proceedings of the 18th International Joint Conference on Artificial Intelligence, pp. 304–309 (1999)
22. Williams, B.C., Nayak, P.P.: A reactive planner for a model-based executive. In: Proceedings of the 15th International Joint Conference on Artificial Intelligence, pp. 1178–1195 (1997)

A Cost-Based Model and Algorithms for Interleaving Solving and Elicitation of CSPs*

Nic Wilson, Diarmuid Grimes, and Eugene C. Freuder

Cork Constraint Computation Centre
Department of Computer Science
University College Cork, Ireland
n.wilson@4c.ucc.ie, d.grimes@4c.ucc.ie, e.freuder@4c.ucc.ie

Abstract. We consider Constraint Satisfaction Problems in which constraints can be initially incomplete, where it is unknown whether certain tuples satisfy the constraint or not. We assume that we can determine such an unknown tuple, i.e., find out whether this tuple is in the constraint or not, but doing so incurs a known cost, which may vary between tuples. We also assume that we know the probability of an unknown tuple satisfying a constraint. We define algorithms for this problem, based on backtracking search. Specifically, we consider a simple iterative algorithm based on a cost limit on which unknowns may be determined, and a more complex algorithm that delays determining an unknown in order to estimate better whether doing so is worthwhile. We show experimentally that the more sophisticated algorithms can greatly reduce the average cost.

1 Introduction

In Constraint Satisfaction Problems it is usually assumed that the CSP is available before the solving process begins, that is, the elicitation of the problem is completed before we attempt to solve the problem. As discussed in the work on Open Constraints and Interactive CSPs [1,2,3,4,5], there are situations where it can be advantageous and natural to interleave the elicitation and the solving. We may not need all the complete constraints to be available in order for us to find a solution. Furthermore, it may be expensive, in terms of time or other costs, to elicit some constraints or parts of the constraints, for example, in a distributed setting. Performing a constraint check in certain situations can be computationally very expensive. We may need to pay for an option to be available, or for the possibility that it may be available. Some constraints may be related to choices of other agents, which they may be reluctant to divulge because of privacy issues or convenience, and so it could cost us something to find these out. Or they may involve an uncertain parameter, such as the capacity of a resource, and it could be expensive, computationally or otherwise, to determine more certain information about this.

* This material is based upon works supported by the Science Foundation Ireland under Grant No. 05/IN/I886.

C. Bessiere (Ed.): CP 2007, LNCS 4741, pp. 666–680, 2007.

In this paper we consider approaches for solving such partially-specified CSPs which take these costs into account. Constraints may be initially incomplete: it may be unknown whether certain tuples satisfy the constraint or not. It is assumed in our model that we can determine such an unknown tuple, i.e., find out whether this tuple is in the constraint or not, but doing so incurs a known cost, which may vary between tuples. We also assume that we know the probability of an unknown tuple satisfying a constraint. An optimal algorithm for this situation is defined to be one which incurs minimal expected cost in finding a solution.

Example

To illustrate, consider a problem with two variables X and Y, where X takes values 1, 2, 3 and 4, so $D(X) = \{1, 2, 3, 4\}$, and the domain, $D(Y)$, of Y is $\{5, 6\}$. There are two incomplete constraints, the first, c_1, is a unary constraint on X, and the second, c_2, is a binary constraint on the two variables. It is (currently) unknown if $X = 1$ satisfies constraint c_1. The probability p_1 that it does so is 0.9. We can determine (i.e., find out) if $X = 1$ satisfies constraint c_1, but this test incurs a cost of $K_1 = 50$. We write $c_1(X = 1) = v_1$, where v_1 represents an unknown boolean value. It is also unknown if values 2, 3 and 4 satisfy c_1. We have $c_1(X = 2) = v_2$, $c_1(X = 3) = v_3$ and $c_1(X = 4) = v_4$. The cost of determining unknowns v_2, v_3 and v_4 is each 70, and the probability of success of each is 0.8. Tuples $(2, 6)$, $(3, 5)$ and $(4, 6)$ all satisfy the binary constraint, whereas tuples $(2, 5)$, $(3, 6)$ and $(4, 5)$ do not. It is unknown whether tuples $(1, 5)$ and $(1, 6)$ satisfy the constraint. We have $c_2(X = 1, Y = 5) = v_5$, and $c_2(X = 1, Y = 6) = v_6$, and $c_2(X = 2, Y = 6) = c_2(X = 3, Y = 5) = c_2(X = 4, Y = 6) = 1$. The other tuples have value 0. Unknowns v_5 and v_6 each have cost 200 and probability of success 0.1.

Consider a standard backtracking search algorithm with variable ordering X, Y and value ordering $1, 2, 3, 4$ for X and $5, 6$ for Y. The algorithm will first incur a cost of 50 in determining v_1. This unknown will be determined successfully with 90% chance, and if so, then $X = 1$ satisfies c_1. After that, v_5 will be determined, costing 200, but with only 0.1 chance of success. If both v_1 and v_5 are successfully determined then $(X = 1, Y = 5)$ is a solution of the CSP. However, this has only chance $0.9 \times 0.1 = 0.09$ of happening, and cost $50 + 200 = 250$ is incurred.

It can be shown that the expected cost incurred by this algorithm is approximately 464 and can be written as $E_1 + qE_2$, where $q = 0.1 + 0.9^3 = 0.829$, $E_1 = 50 + 0.9(200 + 0.9 \times 200) = 392$ and $E_2 = 70 + 0.2(70 + 0.2 \times 70) = 86.8$. ($E_1$ is the expected cost in the $X = 1$ branch, E_2 is the expected cost conditional on having reached the $X = 2$ constraint check, and q is the chance that the algorithm fails to find a solution with $X = 1$.) This is far from optimal, mainly because determining unknowns v_5 and v_6 is very expensive, and they also have only small chance of success. An optimal algorithm for this problem (i.e., one with minimal expected cost) can be shown to have expected cost $E_2 + (0.2^3 \times 389.5) \approx 90$, which can be achieved with a backtracking search algorithm which determines unknowns in the $X = 2, 3, 4$ branches before determining unknowns in the $X = 1$ branch. ■

Algorithms with low expected cost will clearly need to consider the costs and the probabilities. A backtracking algorithm should ideally not always determine any unknown it meets, but allow the possibility of delaying determining an unknown, to check whether it seems worthwhile doing so.

We define algorithms for this problem, based on backtracking search. Such algorithms can be crudely divided into three classes:

- Type 0: determining all unknowns to begin with;
- Type 1: determining unknowns as we meet them in the search;
- Type 2: making decisions about whether it's worth determining an unknown, making use of cost and probabilistic information.

The normal solving approaches for CSPs fall into Type 0, where the full CSP is elicited first and we then solve it, based on backtracking search with propagation at each node of the search tree. Algorithms for open constraints, which don't assume any cost or probability information, can be considered as being Type 1. In this paper we construct Type 2 algorithms, which make use of the cost and probabilistic information.

We consider a simple iterative algorithm based on a limit on the costs of unknowns that may be determined; for each cost limit value, we perform a backtracking search; if this fails to find a solution we increment the cost limit, and search again. With this algorithm it can easily happen that we pay a cost of determining an unknown tuple, only to find that that particular branch fails to lead to a solution for other reasons, as in the example, with unknown υ_1. A natural idea is to delay determining an unknown, in order to find out if it is worth doing so. Our main algorithm, described in Section 4, usually will not immediately determine an unknown, but explore more deeply first. The experimental results in Section 5 strongly suggest that this can be worthwhile.

Related Work: The motivation for this work is related to part of that for Open Constraints [1,2,3,6], and Interactive CSPs [4,5], with a major difference being our assumption of there being cost and probabilistic information available ([2] considers costs in optimisation problems, but in a rather different way). Although these kinds of methods could be used for our problem, not taking costs and probabilities into account will, unsurprisingly, tend to generate solutions with poor expected cost, as illustrated by the example and our experimental results.

Another approach is to ignore the probabilistic information, and look for complete assignments that will incur minimal cost to check if they are solutions. Weighted constraints methods e.g., [7] can be used to search for such assignments. If all the probabilities were equal to 1 then this would solve the problem. However, it may well turn out that all the lowest cost assignments also have relatively low probability. Consider the example with K_5 (the cost of determining υ_5) changed to be 10 instead of 200. The assignment which then needs minimum cost to discover if it's a solution is $(X_1 = 1, X_2 = 5)$; this again leads to a suboptimal algorithm. Alternatively, one could search for complete assignments which have highest probability of being a solution, as in Probabilistic CSPs [8].

Although this may perform satisfactorily if all the costs are equal, with varying costs it seems that the costs should be taken into account. Consider the example, but where p_5, the probability that $v_5 = 1$, is changed from 0.1 to 0.9. The assignment with greatest chance of being a solution is $(X_1 = 1, X_2 = 5)$; however the cost of finding this solution is 250, so trying this solution first is far from optimal.

The next section describes the model and problem more formally. Section 3 analyses the related problem of determining if a particular complete assignment is a solution. This analysis is important for our main algorithm, which is described in Section 4. Section 5 describes the experimental testing and results, and Section 6 discusses extensions.

2 A Formal Model for Interleaving Solving and Elicitation

Standard CSPs: Let V be a set of variables, which are interpreted as decision variables, so that we have the ability to choose values of them. Each variable $X \in V$ has an associated domain $D(X)$. For any subset W of V, let $D(W)$ be the set of assignments to W, which can be written as $\prod_{X \in W} D(X)$. Associated with each (standard) constraint c over V, is a subset V_c of V, which is called its *scope*. Define a (standard) constraint c over V to be a function from $D(V_c)$ to $\{0, 1\}$. We will sometimes refer to a set of constraints C over V as a *Constraint Satisfaction Problem (CSP) over* V. Let S be an assignment to all the variables V. S is said to satisfy constraint c if $c(S') = 1$, where S' is S restricted to V_c. S is a solution of CSP C (or, S *satisfies* C) if it satisfies each constraint in C.

The Unknowns: As well as decision variables V, we consider a disjoint set of variables $\mathcal{U}$, which we call the set of *unknowns*. These are uncertain variables, and we have no control over them. They are all boolean variables. We assume that, for any unknown $v \in \mathcal{U}$, we can determine (i.e., discover) the value of v, that is, whether $v = 1$ or $v = 0$. So we assume we have some procedure $Det(\cdot)$ that takes an unknown v as input and returns 1 or 0. We also assume that there is a certain cost $K_v \in [0, \infty)$ for executing this procedure on v, and that we have probabilistic information about the success of this procedure. In particular we assume that we know the probability p_v of success, i.e., the probability that $Det(v) = 1$.

Incomplete Constraints: An *incomplete constraint* c over $(V, \mathcal{U})$ has an associated subset V_c of V called its *scope*. c is a function from $D(V_c)$ to $\{0, 1\} \cup \mathcal{U}$. Hence, to any tuple $t \in D(V_c)$, c assigns 1, 0 or some unknown. c is intended as a partial representation of some standard constraint c^* over V_c. $c(t) = 1$ is interpreted as t satisfies the constraint c^*. Also, $c(t) = 0$ is interpreted as t doesn't satisfies the constraint c^*; otherwise, if $c(t) \in \mathcal{U}$, then it is unknown if t satisfies the constraint. We will sometimes refer to a set of incomplete constraints over $(V, \mathcal{U})$ as an *incomplete CSP*. An Expected Cost-based Interactive CSP (ECI CSP) is formally defined to be a tuple $\langle V, D, \mathcal{U}, K, p, C\rangle$, for set of variables V, set of unknowns $\mathcal{U}$, functions $K : \mathcal{U} \to [0, \infty)$, $p : \mathcal{U} \to [0, 1]$, and where C is a set of incomplete constraints over $(V, \mathcal{U})$.

Associated with an incomplete constraint c are two standard constraints with the same scope. The *known constraint* $\underline{c}$ is given by $\underline{c}(t) = 1$ if and only if $c(t) = 1$ (otherwise, $\underline{c}(t) = 0$). A tuple satisfies $\underline{c}$ if and only if it is known to satisfy c^*. The *potential constraint* $\overline{c}$ is given by $\overline{c}(t) = 0$ if and only if $c(t) = 0$ (otherwise, $\overline{c}(t) = 1$). A tuple satisfies $\overline{c}$ if it could potentially satisfy c^*. For a given set of incomplete constraints C, the *Known CSP* is the set of associated known constraints: $\underline{C} = \{\underline{c} : c \in C\}$, and the *Potential CSP* $\overline{C}$ is the set of associated potential constraints: $\{\overline{c} : c \in C\}$.

Suppose that $c(t) = v$, and we determine v and find out that $v = 1$. Then we now know that t does satisfy the constraint, so we can replace $c(t) = v$ by $c(t) = 1$. Define $c[v := 1]$ to be the incomplete constraint generated from c by replacing every occurrence of v by 1. We define $c[v := 0]$ analogously. More generally, let ω be an assignment to a set $\mathcal{W} \subseteq \mathcal{U}$ of unknowns, and let c be an incomplete constraint. $c[\omega]$ is the incomplete constraint obtained by replacing each v in $\mathcal{W}$ by its value $\omega(v)$. We define $C[\omega]$ to be $\{c[\omega] : c \in C\}$. $C[\omega]$ is thus the incomplete CSP updated by the extra knowledge ω we have about unknowns.

Incomplete CSP C *is solved by assignment* S *(to variables* V*) in the context* ω if S is a solution of the associated known CSP $\underline{C[\omega]}$. In other words, if S is known to be a solution of C given ω. An incomplete CSP C is *insoluble in the context* ω if the associated potential CSP $\overline{C[\omega]}$ has no solution. In this case, even if all the other unknowns are found to be equal to 1, the CSP is still insoluble.

Policies for Solving ECI CSPs

An algorithm for solving an incomplete CSP involves sequentially determining unknowns until we can find a solution. Of course, the choice of which unknown to determine next may well depend on whether previous unknowns have been determined successfully or not. In the example in Section 1, if we determine v_1 and discover that $v_1 = 0$ then there is no point in determining unknown v_5.

What we call a *policy* is a decision making procedure that sequentially chooses unknowns to determine. The choice of unknown to determine at any stage can depend on information received from determining unknowns previously. The sequence of decisions ends either with a solution to the known part of the CSP, or with a situation in which there is no solution, even if all the undecided unknown tuples are in their respective constraints. In more abstract terms a policy can be considered as follows:-

Given an assignment ω to some (possibly empty) set $\mathcal{W}$ of unknowns, a policy does one of the following:

(a) returns a solution of the Known CSP (given ω);
(b) returns "Insoluble" (it can only do this if the Potential CSP (given ω) is insoluble);
(c) choose another undetermined unknown.

In cases (a) and (b) the policy terminates. In case (c), the chosen unknown v is determined, with value $b = 1$ or 0. ω is then extended with $v = b$, and another choice is made by the policy, given $\omega \cup [v = b]$. The sequence continues until the problem is solved or proved unsatisfiable.

Define a *scenario* to be a complete assignment to all the unknowns. Let $\Pr(\alpha)$ be the probability of scenario α occurring. In the case of the variables $\mathcal{U}$ being independent, we have $\Pr(\alpha) = \prod_{v\,:\,\alpha(v)=1} p_v \times \prod_{v\,:\,\alpha(v)=0}(1 - p_v)$. In a scenario α, a policy iteratively chooses unknowns to determine until it terminates; let $\mathcal{W}_\alpha$ be the set of unknowns determined; the policy incurs a particular cost, say, K_α, which equals $\sum_{v \in \mathcal{W}_\alpha} K_v$. The expected cost of a policy is then equal to $\sum_\alpha \Pr(\alpha) K_\alpha$, where the summation is over all scenarios α.

Evaluating Policies. We evaluate policies in terms of their expected cost. So, we aim to define algorithms that implement policies which have relatively low expected cost.

Using Dynamic Programming to Generate an Optimal Policy

Although the problem involves minimising expected cost over all policies, the structure of the decisions—dynamically choosing a sequence from a (large) set of objects—does not fit very naturally into such formalisms as Influence Diagrams [9], Markov Decision Processes [10] and Stochastic Constraint Programming [11]. We describe below a simple dynamic programming [12] algorithm for generating an optimal policy.

Consider ECI CSP $\langle V, D, \mathcal{U}, K, p, C \rangle$. Let ω be an assignment to some set of unknowns $\mathcal{W} \subseteq \mathcal{U}$. Define $A(\omega)$ to be the minimal expected cost over all policies for solving $\langle V, D, \mathcal{U} - \mathcal{W}, K, p, C[\omega] \rangle$, the ECI CSP updated with ω. Then $A(\omega) = 0$ if either the associated Known CSP $\underline{C[\omega]}$ is soluble or the associated Potential CSP $\overline{C[\omega]}$ is insoluble. Otherwise, any policy chooses some unknown $v \in \mathcal{U} - \mathcal{W}$ to determine, incurring cost K_v and with chance p_v of finding that $v = 1$. If $v = 1$ then we have incomplete CSP $C(\omega \cup [v := 1])$ to solve, which has minimal expected cost $A(\omega \cup [v := 1])$. Therefore, $A(\omega)$ can be written as

$$\min_{v \in \mathcal{U} - \mathcal{W}} \big(K_v + p_v A(\omega \cup [v := 1]) + (1 - p_v) A(\omega \cup [v := 0]) \big).$$

The minimal expected cost over all policies for solving the original ECI CSP is equal to $A[\top]$, where $\top$ is the assignment to the empty set of variables. We can thus find the minimal expected cost by using a simple dynamic programming algorithm, iteratively applying the above equation, starting with all scenarios (or from minimal assignments ω such that $\overline{C[\omega]}$ is insoluble); we can also find an optimal policy in this way, by recording, for each ω, a choice $v \in \mathcal{U} - \mathcal{W}$ which minimises the expression for $A(\omega)$. However, there are $3^{|\mathcal{U}|}$ different possible assignments ω, so this optimal algorithm will only be feasible for problems with very small $|\mathcal{U}|$, i.e., very few unknowns (whereas problem instances in our experiments in Section 5 involve more than 2,000 unknowns). More generally, it seems that we will need to use heuristic algorithms.

3 Evaluating a Complete Assignment

In this section we consider the problem of testing if a given complete assignment is a solution of an ECI CSP $\langle V, D, \mathcal{U}, K, p, C\rangle$; the key issue is the order in which we determine the associated unknowns. This analysis is relevant for our main algorithm described in Section 4.

Associated with each potential solution S (i.e., solution of the associated potential CSP $\overline{C}$) is a set of unknowns, which can be written as: $\{c(S) : c \in C\} \cap \mathcal{U}$. An unknown v is in this set if and only if there exists some constraint c such that $c(S) = v$. Label these unknowns as $U = \{v_1, \ldots, v_m\}$; we abbreviate p_{v_i} to p_i, and K_{v_i} to K_i. We also define $r_i = K_i/(1 - p_i)$, where we set $r_i = \infty$ if $p_i = 1$. Assignment S is a solution of the unknown CSP if and only if each of the unknown values in U is actually a 1. In this section we assume that the unknowns are independent variables, so that the probability that S is a solution of the CSP is $p_1 p_2 \cdots p_m$, which we write as $P(U)$.

To evaluate set of unknowns $\{v_1, \ldots, v_m\}$, we determine them in some order until either we find one which fails, i.e., until $Det(v_i) = 0$, or until we have determined them all. Associated with an unknown v_i is the cost K_i and success probability p_i. Suppose we evaluate the unknowns in the sequence $v_1, \ldots, v_m$. We start by determining v_1, incurring cost K_1. If v_1 is successfully determined (this event has chance p_1), we go on to determine v_2, incurring additional cost K_2, and so on. The expected cost in evaluating these unknowns in this order is therefore $K_1 + p_1 K_2 + p_1 p_2 K_3 + \cdots + p_1 p_2 \cdots p_{m-1} K_m$. Let R_π be the expected cost incurred in evaluating unknowns $\{v_1, \ldots, v_m\}$ in the order $\pi(1), \pi(2), \ldots, \pi(m)$, i.e., with $v_{\pi(1)}$ first, and then $v_{\pi(2)}$, etc. Expected cost R_π is therefore equal to $K_{\pi(1)} + p_{\pi(1)} K_{\pi(2)} + p_{\pi(1)} p_{\pi(2)} K_{\pi(3)} + \cdots + p_{\pi(1)} p_{\pi(2)} \cdots p_{\pi(m-1)} K_{\pi(m)}$.

Proposition 1. *For a given set of unknowns $\{v_1, \ldots, v_m\}$, R_π is minimised by choosing π to order unknowns with smallest r_i ($= K_i/(1 - p_i)$) first, i.e., setting ordering $\pi(1), \pi(2), \ldots, \pi(m)$ in any way such that $r_{\pi(1)} \leq r_{\pi(2)} \leq \cdots \leq r_{\pi(m)}$.*

For a set of unknowns $U = \{v_1, \ldots, v_m\}$ we define $R(U)$ to be R_π, where π is chosen so as the minimise the cost, by ordering the unknowns to have smallest r_i first (as shown by Proposition 1).

Imagine a situation where we are given an ECI CSP, and a complete assignment S which is a possible solution. We will consider an expected-utility-based analysis of whether it is worth determining these unknowns, to test if S is a solution, where cost is negative utility. Suppose the utility of finding that S is a solution is Q. The chance of finding that S is a solution is $P(U)$, so the expected reward is $P(U) \times Q$. If we determine all the unknowns U (based on the minimal cost order) then the expected cost is $R(U)$. Therefore the overall expected gain is $(P(U) \times Q) - R(U)$, so there is a positive expected gain if and only if $P(U) \times Q > R(U)$, i.e., if and only if $Q > R(U)/P(U)$.

A natural approach, therefore, for solving an Expected Cost-based Interactive CSP is to search for solutions whose associated set of unknowns U has relatively low value of $R(U)/P(U)$. In particular, we can perform iterative searches based on an upper bound on $R(U)/P(U)$, where this upper bound is increased with each search. This is the basis of our main algorithm, described in the next section.

The monotonicity property, shown by the following proposition, is important since it allows the possibility of subtrees being pruned: if a partial assignment S has associated set of unknowns U, and we find that $R(U)/P(U)$ is more than our cost bound Q, then we can backtrack, since the set of unknowns U' associated with any complete assignment extending S will also have $R(U')/P(U') > Q$. Since $\mathcal{U}$ is finite, it is sufficient to show the result for the case when U' contains a single extra unknown (as we can then repeatedly add extra unknowns one-by-one to prove the proposition). The result for this case follows quite easily by expanding $R(U)$.

Proposition 2. *Let U and U' be any sets of unknowns with $U \subseteq U' \subseteq \mathcal{U}$. Then $R(U)/P(U) \leq R(U')/P(U')$.*

4 Iterative Expected Cost-Bound Algorithm

In this section we define our main algorithm for solving a given Expected Cost-based CSP $\langle V, D, \mathcal{U}, K, p, C \rangle$. The key idea behind this algorithm is to allow the possibility of delaying determining an unknown associated with a constraint check, until it has explored further down the search tree; this is in order to see if it is worth paying the cost of determining that unknown. The algorithm performs a series of depth-first searches; each search is generated by the procedure *TreeSearch*. The structure of each search is very similar to that of a standard backtracking CSP algorithm.

The behaviour in each search (i.e., in each call of *TreeSearch*) depends on the value of a global variable Q, which is involved in a backtracking condition, and is increased with each tree search. For example, in the experiments described in Section 5, we set $Q_{initial} = 20$ and define $Next(Q)$ to be $Q \times 1.5$, so that the first search has Q set to 20, the second search has $Q = 30$, and then $Q = 45$, and so on. The value of Q can be roughly interpreted as the cost that the algorithm is currently prepared to incur to solve the problem.[1]

The procedure *TopLevel* first initialises the cost incurred (`GlobalCost`) to zero. It then performs repeated tree searches until a solution is found (see procedure *ProcessNode*$(\cdot)$ below) or until all unknowns have been determined; in the latter case, it then performs one further tree search (which is then an ordinary CSP backtracking algorithm).

---

[1] Our experimental results for the main algorithm (without the size limit modification) tally very well with this interpretation, with the average Q for the last iteration being close to the average overall cost incurred (within 25% of the average cost for each of the four distributions used).

PROCEDURE *TopLevel*

```
GlobalCost := 0;    Q := Q_initial
repeat
    TreeSearch
    Q := Next(Q)
    until all unknowns have been determined
TreeSearch
```

PROCEDURE *TreeSearch*

```
Unknowns_root := ∅;
Construct child N of root node
ProcessNode(N)
```

The core part of the algorithm is the procedure *ProcessNode*(N). Let N be the current node, and let $Pa(N)$ be its parent, i.e., the node above it in the search tree. Associated with node N is the set $\texttt{Unknowns}_N$ of *current unknowns*. At a node, if any of the current unknowns evaluates to 0 then there is no solution below this node. Conversely, if all of the current unknowns at a node evaluate to 1 then the current partial assignment is consistent with all constraints that have been checked so far. If all the current unknowns at a leaf node evaluate to 1 then the current assignment is a solution.

At a search node, we perform, as usual, a constraint check for each constraint c whose scope V_c has just been fully instantiated (i.e., such that (i) the last variable instantiated is in the scope, and (ii) the set of variables instantiated contains the scope). A constraint check returns either 1, 0 or some unknown. The algorithm first determines if any constraint check fails, i.e., if it returns 0. If so, we backtrack to the parent node, in the usual way, assigning an untried value of the associated variable, when possible, and otherwise backtracking to *its* parent node. Propagation can be used in the usual way to eliminate elements of a domain which cannot be part of any solution extending the current assignment.

The set $\texttt{DirectUnknowns}_N$, of unknowns directly associated with the node N, is defined to be the set of unknowns which are generated by the constraint checks at the node. The set of *current unknowns* at the node, $\texttt{Unknowns}_N$, is then initialised to be the union of $\texttt{DirectUnknowns}_N$ and the current unknowns of the parent node.

The algorithm then tests to see if it is worth continuing, or if it is expected to be too expensive to be worth determining the current set of unknowns. The backtracking condition is based on the analysis in Section 3. We view Q as representing (our current estimate of) the value of finding a solution. Then the expected gain, if we determine all the unknowns in $\texttt{Unknowns}_N$, is $P(\texttt{Unknowns}_N) \times Q$ where $P(\texttt{Unknowns}_N)$ is the chance that all the current unknowns evaluate to 1. The expected cost of determining these unknowns sequentially is $R(\texttt{Unknowns}_N)$, as defined in Section 3, since we evaluate unknowns with smallest r_i first. So, determining unknowns $\texttt{Unknowns}_N$ is not worthwhile if the expected gain is less than the expected cost: $P(\texttt{Unknowns}_N) \times Q < R(\texttt{Unknowns}_N)$. Therefore we backtrack if $R(\texttt{Unknowns}_N)/P(\texttt{Unknowns}_N) > Q$.

We then construct a child node in the usual way, by choosing the next variable Y to instantiate, choosing a value y of the variable, and extending the current assignment with $Y = y$. If Y is the last variable to be instantiated then we use the *ProcessLeafNode*$(\cdot)$ procedure on the new node; otherwise we use the *ProcessNode*$(\cdot)$ procedure on the new node.

The *ProcessLeafNode*$(\cdot)$ procedure is similar to *ProcessNode*$(\cdot)$, except that we can no longer delay determining unknowns, so we determine each current unknown until we fail, or until all have been determined successfully. We determine an unknown with smallest $r_i = K_i/(1 - p_i)$ first (based on Proposition 1). If an unknown v_i is determined unsuccessfully, then there is no solution beneath this node. In fact, if N' is the furthest ancestor node of N which v_i is directly associated with (i.e. such that $\texttt{DirectUnknowns}_{N'} \ni v_i$), then there is no solution beneath N'. Therefore, we jump back to N' and backtrack to its parent node $Pa(N')$. If all the unknowns $\texttt{Unknowns}_N$ have been successfully determined then the current assignment, which assigns a value to all the variables V, has been shown to be a solution of the CSP, so the algorithm has succeeded, and we terminate the algorithm.

PROCEDURE *ProcessNode*(N)

> **if** any constraint check returns 0 **then** backtrack
> $\texttt{Unknowns}_N := \texttt{Unknowns}_{Pa(N)} \cup \texttt{DirectUnknowns}_N$
> **if** $R(\texttt{Unknowns}_N)/P(\texttt{Unknowns}_N) > Q$
>   **then** backtrack to parent node
> Construct child node N' of N
> **if** N' is a leaf node (all variables are instantiated)
>   **then** *ProcessLeafNode*(N') **else** *ProcessNode*(N')

PROCEDURE *ProcessLeafNode*(N)

> **if** any constraint check returns 0 **then** backtrack
> $\texttt{Unknowns}_N := \texttt{Unknowns}_{Pa(N)} \cup \texttt{DirectUnknowns}_N$
> **if** $R(\texttt{Unknowns}_N)/P(\texttt{Unknowns}_N) > Q$ **then** backtrack to parent node
> **while** Unknowns non-empty **do**:
>   Let v_i be unknown in $\texttt{Unknowns}_N$ with minimal r_i
>   Determine v_i;
> $\texttt{GlobalCost} := \texttt{GlobalCost} + K_i$
>   **if** v_i determined unsuccessfully
>   **then** Jump Back to furthest ancestor node associated with v_i
>   and backtrack to its parent node
> $\texttt{Unknowns}_N := \texttt{Unknowns}_N - \{v_i\}$
>   **end** (**while**)
> Return current (complete) assignment as a solution and STOP

If we apply this algorithm to the example in Section 1 (again using variable ordering X, Y, and numerical value ordering), no unknown will be determined until we reach an iteration where Q is set to being at least 87.5. Then the first leaf node N that the algorithm will reach is that associated with the assignment $(X =$

1, $Y = 5$). $\texttt{Unknowns}_N$ is equal to $\{v_1, v_5\}$. $r_1 = K_1/(1-p_1) = 50/0.1 = 500 > r_5 = 200/0.9$, so $R(\{v_1, v_5\}) = K_5 + p_5 K_1 = 205$, and $R(\{v_1, v_5\})/P(\{v_1, v_5\}) = 205/(0.9 \times 0.1) \approx 2278$, so the algorithm will backtrack; similarly for the leaf node associated with assignment ($X = 1$, $Y = 6$). The leaf node corresponding to ($X = 2$, $Y = 6$) has current set of unknowns $\{v_2\}$. Since $R(\{v_2\})/P(\{v_2\}) = 70/0.8 = 87.5 \geq Q$, unknown v_2 will be determined. If it evaluates to 1 then ($X = 2$, $Y = 6$) is a solution, and the algorithm terminates. Otherwise, v_3 and v_4 will be next to be determined. In fact, for this example, the algorithm generates an optimal policy, with expected cost of around 90.

One approach to improving the search efficiency of the algorithm is to set a limit SizeLimit on the size of the current unknown set $\texttt{Unknowns}_N$ associated with a node. If $|\texttt{Unknowns}_N|$ becomes larger than SizeLimit then we repeatedly determine unknowns, in increasing order of r_i, and remove the unknown from the current set until $|\texttt{Unknowns}_N| = \texttt{SizeLimit}$. It is natural then to change the backtracking condition to take this into account. In particular, we can change the test to be $(\texttt{CostDetSucc}_N + R(\texttt{Unknowns}_N))/P(\texttt{Unknowns}_N) > Q$, where $\texttt{CostDetSucc}_N$ is the cost incurred in (successfully) determining unknowns in ancestors of the current node, which can be considered as the cost that has already been spent in consistency checking of the current assignment.

In the algorithm whenever we determine an unknown in $\texttt{Unknowns}_N$ we choose an unknown v_i with minimum r_i. This is in order to minimise the expected cost of determining the set of current unknowns, because of Proposition 1. Alternatively, one could bias the ordering towards determining more informative unknowns. For example, suppose $\texttt{Unknowns}_N$ includes two unknowns v_i and v_j, where v_i is associated with a unary constraint, and v_j is associated with a constraint of larger arity. Even if r_i is slightly more than r_j, it may sometimes be better to determine v_i before v_j since v_i may well be directly associated with many other nodes in the search tree.

5 Experimental Testing

The problem instances used in the experiments were generated as follows: A soluble random binary extensional CSP is generated with parameters $\langle n, d, m, t \rangle$, where n is the number of variables, d the uniform domain size, m the graph density and t the constraint tightness, with the parameters chosen so that each instance is likely to be fairly easily soluble. For each constraint in this CSP we randomly select a number of the allowed tuples and randomly select the same number of the disallowed tuples to be assigned unknown. Each such tuple is assigned a different unknown v_i, which is assigned a probability p_i chosen independently from a uniform distribution taking values between 0 and 1. Each v_i is allocated its true value (which the algorithms only have access to when they determine u_i): this is assigned 1 with probability p_i, otherwise it is assigned 0 (where $v_i = 1$ means that the associated tuple satisfies the constraint).

We use four different distributions for cost, where costs are integers in our experiments. Each distribution has minimum value 1 and has median around 50. For $k = 1, 2, 3, 4$ using the kth distribution, each cost K_v is an independent sample of the random variable: $50 \times (2 \times \mathbf{rand})^k$ rounded up to be an integer, where **rand** is a random number taking values between 0 and 1 with a uniform distribution. Therefore $k = 1$ has a linear distribution, $k = 2$ is a scaled (and truncated) square root distribution, and so on.

The parameters for $\langle n, d, m, t \rangle$ were $\langle 20, 10, 0.163, 0.4 \rangle$ and $\langle 20, 10, 0.474, 0.3 \rangle$. Each problem set contained 100 problems. No problem was soluble without determining at least one unknown. For $\langle 20, 10, 0.163, 0.4 \rangle$, the first problem parameters, we generated four problem sets by using four different cost distributions; for the other problem set we used the linear ($k = 1$) cost distribution.

The following five algorithms were tested (where, according to the terminology in Section 1, the first is Type 1, and the others are Type 2):

Basic Algorithm: The basic algorithm works like a normal CSP depth-first search algorithm (maintaining arc consistency, and with min domain variable ordering) except that it determines each unknown as soon as it is encountered. As usual, a constraint check is performed as soon as all the variables in the constraint's scope are instantiated. When a constraint check returns an unknown v_i, we immediately determine v_i, incurring cost K_i. If v_i is determined successfully, i.e., v_i is found to be 1, then the constraint check is successful.

Basic Iterative (Cost-Bound Algorithm): This algorithm performs iterative searches, parameterised by increasing cost bound q; each search is similar to the basic algorithm, except that all unknowns with cost greater than q are removed from search for the current iteration (that is, they are set to 0, which allows for improved pruning through propagation). If a solution is found, search terminates; otherwise, the search is complete, after which search restarts with q incremented by a constant, q_{inc}. The process continues until either a solution has been found or all unknowns have been determined and the algorithm has proven insolubility. For the experiments reported below, q starts off with value 0, and q_{inc} is 5.

Main Iterative (Expected Cost-Bound Algorithm): This is the main algorithm described in Section 4. For this and the next two algorithms, $Q_{initial}$ is set to 20, with a multiplicative increment of 1.5.

Main Algorithm with Size Limit: This is the adapted version of the last algorithm discussed at the end of Section 4, which incorporates a limit `SizeLimit` on the cardinality of the set `Unknowns` of current unknowns, so that if |`Unknowns`| > `SizeLimit` then elements of `Unknowns` are determined until either one is found to be 0 or |`Unknowns`| = `SizeLimit`. In the experiments reported below, we set `SizeLimit` to 5.

Mixed Algorithm: This algorithm modifies the main Expected Cost-Bound algorithm by having, for each iteration, a cost bound q on each unknown being considered, in order to improve the search efficiency (because of additional propagation), whilst maintaining cost effectiveness. It therefore is a kind of hybrid of the main algorithm and the basic iterative cost-bound algorithm described above. Let `maxK` be the maximum cost of any unknown in the current problem

instance. On the first search all unknowns with cost greater than 30%(`maxK`) are removed from search, so that q starts at 30%(`maxK`); on each iteration this bound q is incremented by $q_{inc} = 5\%(\mathtt{maxK})$.
We also implemented a cost-based value ordering heuristic. The heuristic chooses the value which has minimum total cost over the constraints between the variable and its instantiated neighbors. The improvements for the iterative algorithms were minimal so we only present the results for the basic algorithm with the value ordering ("Basic Value").

Table 1. Results For Different Cost Distributions. Costs are Averaged Over 100 Problems. Bottom row gives mean search nodes for linear problem set.

	Basic	Basic Value	Basic Iterative	Main Iterative	Size Limit	Mixed
Linear ($k = 1$)	3272	2625	1711	152	495	178
Square ($k = 2$)	4574	3414	900	105	346	113
Cube ($k = 3$)	6823	4997	566	79	231	77
Fourth ($k = 4$)	11123	8401	344	50	180	52
Linear Search Nodes	57	55	652	2.1×10^6	1.2×10^6	1.2×10^5

Notes: Problem parameters $\langle 20, 10, 0.163, 0.4 \rangle$.

Discussion: Table 1 gives the results for the average costs on four different problem sets. These all had the same parameters $\langle n, d, m, t \rangle$ but costs were generated for unknowns using the distributions described above. The "main iterative" algorithm performs best in terms of average cost: the basic iterative algorithm incurs between around 7 to 11 times more cost for these instances, and the basic algorithm has average cost one or two orders of magnitude worse than the main iterative algorithm. (Naturally, all the algorithms do much better than determining all the unknowns prior to search, at a cost of more than 100,000.)

Unsurprisingly, the main iterative algorithm is vastly slower than the basic algorithms, generating on average around two million total search tree nodes for each problem instance, whereas the basic iterative generates only a few hundred. The last two algorithms both aim to improve the efficiency somewhat. The "Size Limit" algorithm cuts search tree nodes by more than 50% compared to the main algorithm, but incurs roughly three or more times as much average cost. The mixed algorithm trades off cost and search efficiency much more effectively for these instances, with only slightly worse average costs, but generating only a fraction of the search tree nodes, less than 6% for the linear distribution, and less than 30% for the other distributions.

The other problem set showed similar behaviour, though even more extreme: in the $\langle 20, 10, 0.0823, 0.75 \rangle$ problem set with the linear distribution, the mixed algorithm average cost was 222, compared to 5022 for the basic iterative. The size limit algorithm average cost was 1320, and generated more than nine times as many nodes as the mixed algorithm.

6 Extensions and Summary

Extending the algorithms: Our main algorithm can be considered as searching for complete assignments with small values of $R(U)/P(U)$, where U is the set of unknowns associated with the assignment, $P(U)$ is the probability that all of U are successfully determined (and hence that the assignment is a solution), and $R(U)$ is the expected cost of checking this. There are other ways of searching for assignments with small values of $R(U)/P(U)$, in particular, one could use local search algorithms or branch-and-bound algorithms. Such algorithms can be used to generate promising assignments, which we can sequentially test to see if they are solutions or not. If not, then we move on to the next potential solution (possibly updating the problem to take into account determined unknowns).

The efficiency of our main algorithm and a branch-and-bound algorithm would probably be greatly increased if one could design an efficient propagation mechanism of an upper bound constraint on $R(U)/P(U)$. Failing that, one might use a propagation method for weighted constraints [7] to prune subtrees of assignments with total associated cost above a threshold, or with probabilities below a threshold (the latter using a separate propagation, making use of the log/exponential transformation between weighted constraints and probabilistic constraints).

Extensions of the model: Our model of interleaving solving and elicitation is a fairly simple one. There are a number of natural ways of extending it to cover a wider range of situations. In particular, the framework and algorithms can be easily adapted to situations where there is a cost incurred for determining a *set* of unknowns (rather than a single unknown); for example, there may be a single cost incurred for determining all the unknowns in a particular constraint. The paper has focused especially on the case of the probabilities being independent; however, the model and algorithms can be applied in non-independent cases as well. Our model and algorithms also apply to the case where determining an unknown may leave it still unknown; unsuccessfully determining an unknown then needs to be reinterpreted as meaning that we are unable to find out if the associated tuple satisfies the constraint or not. Our current model allows a single unknown to be assigned to several tuples; although this can allow some representation of intensional constraints, we may also wish to allow non-boolean unknowns, for example, for a constraint $X - Y \geq \lambda$ where λ is an unknown constant.

In many situations, it could be hard to reliably estimate the success probabilities and costs, in particular, if a cost represents the time needed to find the associated information. However, since the experimental results indicate that taking costs and probabilities into account can make a very big difference to the expected cost, it could be very worthwhile making use of even very crude estimates of costs and probabilities.

Summary

The paper defines a particular model for when solving and elicitation are interleaved, which takes costs and success probabilities into account. A formal representation of such a problem is defined. A dynamic programming algorithm can be used to solve the problem optimally, i.e., with minimum expected cost; however this is only computationally feasible for situations in which there are few unknowns, i.e., very little unknown information. We define and experimentally test a number of algorithms based on backtracking search, with the most successful (though computationally expensive) ones being based on delaying determining an unknown until more information has been received.

References

1. Faltings, B., Macho-Gonzalez, S.: Open constraint satisfaction. In: Van Hentenryck, P. (ed.) CP 2002. LNCS, vol. 2470, pp. 356–370. Springer, Heidelberg (2002)
2. Faltings, B., Macho-Gonzalez, S.: Open constraint optimization. In: Rossi, F. (ed.) CP 2003. LNCS, vol. 2833, pp. 303–317. Springer, Heidelberg (2003)
3. Faltings, B., Macho-Gonzalez, S.: Open constraint programming. Artificial Intelligence 161(1–2), 181–208 (2005)
4. Cucchiara, R., Lamma, E., Mello, P., Milano, M.: An interactive constraint-based system for selective attention in visual search. In: International Syposium on Methodologies for Intelligent Systems, pp. 431–440 (1997)
5. Lamma, E., Mello, P., Milano, M., Cucchiara, R., Gavanelli, M., Piccardi, M.: Constraint propagation and value acquisition: why we should do it interactively. In: Proceedings of the Sixteenth International Joint Conference on Artificial Intelligence (IJCAI-99), pp. 468–477 (1999)
6. Lallouet, A., Legtchenko, A.: Consistencies for partially defined constraints. In: Proc. International Conference on Tools with Artificial Intelligence (ICTAI'05) (2005)
7. Larrosa, J., Schiex, T.: Solving weighted CSP by maintaining arc consistency. Artificial Intelligence 159(1–2), 1–26 (2004)
8. Fargier, H., Lang, J.: Uncertainty in Constraint Satisfaction Problems: a probabilistic approach. In: Moral, S., Kruse, R., Clarke, E. (eds.) ECSQARU 1993. LNCS, vol. 747, pp. 97–104. Springer, Heidelberg (1993)
9. Howard, R., Matheson, J.: Influence diagrams. In: Readings on the Principles and Applications of Decision Analysis, pp. 721–762 (1984)
10. Puterman, M.: Markov Decision Processes, Discrete Stochastic Dynamic Programming. John Wiley & Sons, Chichester (1994)
11. Tarim, S.A., Manadhar, A., Walsh, T.: Stochastic constraint programming: A scenario-based approach. Constraints 11(1), 53–80 (2006)
12. Bellman, R.: Dynamic Programming. Princeton University Press (1957)

On Universal Restart Strategies for Backtracking Search

Huayue Wu and Peter van Beek

School of Computer Science, University of Waterloo
Waterloo, Ontario, Canada N2L 3G1
{hwu,vanbeek}@cs.uwaterloo.ca

Abstract. Constraint satisfaction and propositional satisfiability problems are often solved using backtracking search. Previous studies have shown that a technique called randomization and restarts can dramatically improve the performance of a backtracking algorithm on some instances. We consider the commonly occurring scenario where one is to solve an ensemble of instances using a backtracking algorithm and wish to learn a good restart strategy for the ensemble. In contrast to much previous work, our focus is on universal strategies. We contribute to the theoretical understanding of universal strategies and demonstrate both analytically and empirically the pitfalls of non-universal strategies. We also propose a simple approach for learning good universal restart strategies and demonstrate the effectiveness and robustness of our approach through an extensive empirical evaluation on a real-world testbed.

1 Introduction

Constraint satisfaction and propositional satisfiability problems are often solved using backtracking search. It has been widely observed that backtracking algorithms can be brittle on some instances. Seemingly small changes to a variable or value ordering heuristic, such as a change in the ordering of tie-breaking schemes, can lead to great differences in running time. An explanation for this phenomenon is that ordering heuristics make mistakes. Depending on the number of mistakes and how early in the search the mistakes are made (and therefore how costly they may be to correct), there can be a large variability in performance between different heuristics. A technique called randomization and restarts has been proposed for taking advantage of this variability [1,2,3,4].

A restart strategy $(t_1, t_2, t_3, ...)$ is an infinite sequence where each t_i is either a positive integer or infinity. The idea is that a randomized backtracking algorithm is run for t_1 steps. If no solution is found within that cutoff, the algorithm is run for t_2 steps, and so on. The usual method for randomizing a backtracking algorithm is to randomize the variable or value ordering heuristics (e.g., [2,4]).

Luby, Sinclair, and Zuckerman [1] examine restart strategies in the more general setting of Las Vegas algorithms. A Las Vegas algorithm is a randomized algorithm that always gives the correct answer when it terminates, however the running time of the algorithm varies from one run to another and can be modeled

C. Bessiere (Ed.): CP 2007, LNCS 4741, pp. 681–695, 2007.

as a random variable. Let $f(t)$ be the probability that a backtracking algorithm $\mathcal{A}$ applied to instance x stops after taking exactly t steps; $f(t)$ is referred to as the runtime distribution of algorithm $\mathcal{A}$ on instance x. Luby, Sinclair, and Zuckerman [1] show that, given full knowledge of the runtime distribution of an instance, the optimal strategy for that instance is given by $(t^*, t^*, t^*, \ldots)$, for some fixed cutoff t^*. Of course, the runtime distribution of an instance is not known in practice.

A fixed cutoff strategy is an example of a non-universal strategy: designed to work on a particular instance—or, more precisely, a particular runtime distribution. When applied to another instance for which it was not designed, non-universal strategies are open to catastrophic failure, where the strategy provably will fail on the instance no matter how much time is alloted to the backtracking search. The failure is due to all cutoffs being too small, before there is sufficient probability of solving the instance. To avoid failure, such restart strategies are sometimes set with cutoffs much too high with a serious consequent hit in performance (see, e.g., Huang [5] and references therein).

In contrast to non-universal strategies, universal strategies are designed to be used on any instance. Luby, Sinclair, and Zuckerman [1] were the first to propose a universal strategy (hereafter, the Luby strategy). The Luby strategy is given by $(1, 1, 2, 1, 1, 2, 4, 1, 1, 2, 1, 1, 2, 4, 8, 1, \ldots)$ and grows linearly (each t_i is bounded above by $(i+1)/2$). Walsh [6] proposes the universal strategy $(1, r, r^2, \ldots)$, where the restart values are geometrically increasing. In practice, it has been found that a geometric factor in the range $1 < r < 2$ often works well on both SAT and CSP instances [6,7].

We consider a setting where an ensemble or sequence of instances are to be solved over time. Such a setting often arises in practice. For example, a common scenario in scheduling and rostering is that at regular intervals on the calendar a similar scheduling problem must be solved. For a further example, in our evaluation testbed of instruction scheduling, thousands of instances arise each time a compiler is invoked on some software project. In such a setting, the question we address is whether we can learn a good restart strategy in an offline manner from a small sample of the instances. In contrast to previous work, our focus is on learning good universal strategies.

In this paper, we make the following three contributions. First, we demonstrate both analytically and empirically the pitfalls of non-universal strategies, as learned by previously proposed approaches.

Second, we examine the worst-case performance of the universal strategies. The Luby universal strategy is known to be within a log factor of optimal in the worst-case [1]. However, bounds on the worst-case performance of the Walsh universal strategy are not known. We show that the performance of the Walsh strategy is not bounded with respect to the optimal value in the worst-case. The proof of the theorem provides some intuition behind good choices for the geometric factor that have previously been determined empirically. We also prove that the Walsh strategy guarantees a performance improvement under certain conditions.

Finally, we examine the practical performance of the universal strategies. Previous empirical evaluations have reported that the Luby universal strategy can perform poorly in practice (e.g., [4,8,9,10]) and the Walsh strategy has not been thoroughly evaluated empirically. We show that the performance of the universal strategies can sometimes be considerably improved by parameterizing the strategies and estimating the optimal settings for these parameters from a small sample of instances. The two parameters that we consider are a scale parameter s and a geometric factor parameter r. The Walsh strategy already contains the geometric factor. Luby, Sinclair, and Zuckerman [1, p.179] note that a geometric factor can also be incorporated into their universal strategy. For example, the first few terms of the Luby strategy with a geometric factor of 3 are given by, 1, 1, 1, 3, 1, 1, 1, 3, 1, 1, 1, 3, 9, ... The scale parameter, as the name suggests, scales, or multiplies, each cutoff in a restart strategy. For example, the first few terms of a scaled Walsh strategy are given by $(s, sr, sr^2, \ldots)$, for some given scale s and geometric factor r. Parameterizing the strategies improves performance while retaining any optimality and worst-case guarantees. We demonstrate the effectiveness and robustness of our approach through an extensive empirical evaluation on a real-world testbed of instruction scheduling problems.

2 Related Work

In this section, we relate our work to previously proposed methodologies for learning good restart strategies for an ensemble of instances. In each methodology, one begins by choosing a sample of instances from the ensemble.

Restart strategies are often informally chosen using trial-and-error methods where one runs experiments on a sample of instances in order to find good strategies (e.g., [4,11]). Zhan [7] performs extensive experiments to evaluate which geometric factor r for the universal strategies works best across problem classes. In preliminary work, we suggested that the universal strategies could be further parameterized using a scale factor s and that the parameters could be tuned to improve performance [12]. Independently, Eén and Sörensson [13] incorporates a scaled ($s = 150$) Walsh strategy into their SAT solver, but they offer no justification for the choice of value. More recently, Huang [5] extensively compares fixed cutoff restart strategies with particular scaled Luby and Walsh strategies on SAT benchmarks in the context of conflict clause learning. Huang notes that none of the strategies evaluated was consistently best across all benchmark families, which suggests that adapting a strategy to a benchmark family is important.

More formal methods for choosing good restart strategies have also been proposed. Ó Nualláin, de Rijke, and van Benthem [14] consider the case where an ensemble consists of instances drawn from two known runtime distributions—a runtime distribution for satisfiable instances and one for unsatisfiable—but the runtime distribution for any given instance is unknown. They sketch how estimates of these runtime distributions can be used to derive good restart strategies. However, the work is preliminary and no experimental results are reported.

Kautz et al. [8,9] consider the case where an ensemble consists of instances drawn from n different runtime distributions. They show that with this additional information, one can use dynamic programming to derive good restart strategies and that these restart strategies can be further improved by incorporating observations from during the search process itself. However, their approach is developed and experimentally evaluated in a scenario where a *new* instance is chosen each time the backtracking algorithm is restarted. Unfortunately, this is not a realistic scenario. In practice, one is interested in solving each instance in the ensemble, not just any instance.

Ruan, Horvitz, and Kautz [10] determine a good restart strategy as follows. One first empirically constructs the runtime distributions for each of the instances in the sample. The instances are then clustered such that the runtime distributions of the instances in a cluster have low variability. Each cluster of runtime distributions yields a sub-ensemble runtime distribution which is the normalized sum of the runtime distributions of the instances it contains. These sub-ensemble runtime distributions are then used to construct a single, final strategy using dynamic programming. However, the resulting learned strategies are non-universal and thus are open to catastrophic failure.

Gagliolo and Schmidhuber [15] propose learning a good restart strategy online as instances of the ensemble are solved. The restart strategy learned is an interleaving of the Luby universal strategy and a fixed cutoff. In essence, the fixed cutoff is determined by constructing a single runtime distribution from the samples seen so far, and choosing a restart strategy that minimizes the expected runtime on that runtime distribution. Because of the interleaved Luby strategy, the learned strategy is not open to catastrophic failure. However, we argue (see subsequent sections) that the fixed cutoff learned in this approach may not be useful in many practical settings.

3 Theoretical Results

In this section we contribute to the theoretical understanding of the universal restart strategies. For universal strategies there are two worst-case bounds of interest: worst-case bounds on the expected runtime of a strategy and worst-case bounds on the tail probability of a strategy. The tail probability is the probability that the strategy runs for more than t steps, for some t.

3.1 Bounds on Expected Runtime

Luby, Sinclair, and Zuckerman [1] show that, for any runtime distribution, the Luby strategy is within a log factor of the optimal fixed cutoff strategy for that distribution. They also show that, given no knowledge of the runtime distribution, no universal strategy can have a better bound than being within a log factor of optimal. The question we address is, how far can the Walsh strategy be from the optimal fixed cutoff strategy for a runtime distribution? Does it attain the best-possible log factor bound and, if not, can it be bound by some other polynomial or exponential function? Unfortunately, the answer is no to all of these questions. The first notable property we establish is that the Walsh strategy, although it appears to work well in practice, unfortunately comes with no formal guarantee on its worst-case performance as it can be *unbounded* worse than the optimal fixed cutoff strategy.

Theorem 1. *The expected runtime of a Walsh strategy of the form,* $(1, r, r^2, \ldots)$*,* $r > 1$*, can be unbounded worse than that of the optimal fixed cutoff strategy.*

Proof. The proof is constructive; given a Walsh strategy, we give a method for constructing a runtime distribution such that the expected runtime of the Walsh strategy on the runtime distribution is unbounded. Let $\mathcal{A}$ be the algorithm being applied by the strategy. For any given Walsh strategy of the form $(1, r, r^2, \ldots)$, $r > 1$, define a runtime probability distribution for $\mathcal{A}$ as follows,[1]

$$f(t) = \begin{cases} \frac{1}{l} & t = 1 \\ 1 - \frac{1}{l} & t = \infty \\ 0 & \text{otherwise} \end{cases}$$

where $l = r/(r-1)$. Note that the optimal strategy for this runtime distribution is the fixed cutoff strategy $(1, 1, 1, \ldots)$ with expected runtime l. The expected runtime $E[T]$ of the Walsh strategy is given by,

$$\begin{aligned} E[T] &= \frac{1}{l} + (1 - \frac{1}{l})\frac{(1+1)}{l} + (1 - \frac{1}{l})^2\frac{(1+1+r)}{l} + \cdots \\ &= \left(\sum_{i=0}^{\infty}(1 - \frac{1}{l})^i\right)\left(\frac{1}{l} + \frac{1}{l}(1 - \frac{1}{l}) + \frac{r}{l}(1 - \frac{1}{l})^2 + \cdots\right) \\ &= l\left(\frac{1}{l}\right)\left(1 + (1 - \frac{1}{l}) + r(1 - \frac{1}{l})^2 + \cdots\right) \\ &= 1 + (1 - \frac{1}{l})\sum_{i=0}^{\infty}(r - \frac{r}{l})^i \\ &= 1 + (1 - \frac{1}{l})\sum_{i=0}^{\infty}1^i. \end{aligned}$$

Thus the expected runtime $E[T]$ is unbounded with respect to that of the optimal fixed cutoff strategy. □

The proof of the theorem provides some practical guidance for selecting a value for the geometric factor r. Values in the range $1 < r < 2$ are safer, and the smaller the probability of a short run, the closer the geometric factor r must be to 1, or the strategy may not converge.

[1] Note that the condition $t = \infty$ in the runtime probability distribution simplifies the proof. However, for real CSP and SAT instances there always exists a t for which $P(T \leq t) = 1$; i.e. the runtime distributions are finite as a backtracking algorithm will always (eventually) terminate. At the expense of complicating the proof, the condition $t = \infty$ can also be formulated as $t = r^k$ and it can be shown that the Walsh strategy can be exponentially worse than the optimal fixed cutoff strategy.

3.2 Bounds on Tail Probability

Recall that the tail probability of an algorithm $\mathcal{A}$ on some instance is the probability that the algorithm runs for more than t steps on that instance, for some t. Similarly, the tail probability of a restart strategy on some instance is the probability that the strategy runs for more than t steps. Luby, Sinclair, and Zuckerman [1] show that, no matter what the runtime distribution of the original algorithm $\mathcal{A}$, if we apply $\mathcal{A}$ using the Luby strategy, the tail probability of the restart strategy decays superpolynomially as a function of t (i.e., faster than polynomially). Here we establish a more restricted result for the Walsh strategy by focusing on heavy-tailed probability distributions of the Pareto-Lévy form. Gomes et al. [3,4] show that this family of distributions can be a good fit to the runtime distributions of backtracking algorithms with randomized heuristics in the cases where restarts improve performance the most. In Pareto distributions, the tail probability has the form,

$$P[T > t] \sim Ct^{-\alpha}, \quad \text{where } \alpha > 0, C > 0.$$

In contrast to the classic exponentially decaying tail, a heavy-tailed distribution is one where the tail probability decays polynomially. In terms of a backtracking algorithm, a heavy-tail model implies that there is a significant probability that the backtracking search will run for a long time, and the longer the backtracking search has been running, the longer additional time it can be expected to run.

Theorem 2. *If the runtime distribution of the original algorithm $\mathcal{A}$ is a heavy-tailed probability distribution of the Pareto-Lévy form and $\mathcal{A}$ is applied using a Walsh strategy of the form, $(1, r, r^2, \ldots)$, $r > 1$, the tail probability of the restart strategy decays superpolynomially.*

Proof. Let $F(t) = 1 - Ct^{-\alpha}$ be the cumulative distribution of the runtime of algorithm $\mathcal{A}$; i.e., the probability that $\mathcal{A}$ stops after taking t or fewer steps. The idea is to first bound the tail probability of the restart strategy from above by a piecewise linear function which is further bounded by a smooth function that decays faster than heavy tail. Let $i_t = \arg\max_i(r^i \le t) = \lfloor \log_r t \rfloor$.

$$\begin{aligned} P[T > t] &\le P[T > r^{i_t}] \\ &= \prod_{l=0}^{i_t} \left(1 - F\left(r^l\right)\right) \\ &= C^{\lfloor \log_r t \rfloor + 1} \, r^{-\alpha \sum_{l=0}^{\lfloor \log_r t \rfloor} l} \end{aligned}$$

Since $\sum_{l=0}^{\lfloor \log_r t \rfloor} l = \frac{1}{2}(1 + \lfloor \log_r t \rfloor)\lfloor \log_r t \rfloor \ge \frac{1}{2}(1 + (\log_r t - 1))(\log_r t - 1) = \frac{1}{2}(\log_r^2 t - \log_r t)$, together with the fact that $r > 1$, we have,

$$\begin{aligned} P[T > t] &\le C^{\lfloor \log_r t \rfloor + 1} \, r^{-\frac{\alpha}{2}(\log_r^2 t - \log_r t)} \\ &= C^{\lfloor \log_r t \rfloor + 1} \, t^{-\frac{\alpha}{2}(\log_r t - 1)} \end{aligned}$$

In the case where $C < 1$, we have,

$$\begin{aligned} P[T > t] &\leq C^{\log_r t}\, t^{-\frac{\alpha}{2}(\log_r t - 1)} \\ &= t^{-\frac{\alpha}{2}\log_r t + R} \end{aligned}$$

where $R = \frac{\alpha}{2} + \log_r C$. In the case where $C \geq 1$, we have,

$$\begin{aligned} P[T > t] &\leq C^{\log_r t + 1}\, t^{-\frac{\alpha}{2}(\log_r t - 1)} \\ &= Ct^{-\frac{\alpha}{2}\log_r t + R} \end{aligned}$$

The basic form of the tail probability is $e^{-\log^2 t}$. Although slower than exponential, it no longer decays polynomially and thus is not heavy tailed. □

A practical consequence of the theorem is that for instances for which a Pareto distribution is a sufficiently good fit, the Walsh strategy is guaranteed to reduce the probability of very long runs. Moreover, it is quick to check that both the mean and the variance are finite for the cumulative distribution $P[T \leq t] = 1 - e^{-\log^2 t}$, and thus the mean and variance of the Walsh strategy are also finite. In contrast, the mean of the Pareto distribution is unbounded if $\alpha \leq 1$ and the variance is unbounded if $\alpha \leq 2$. Thus, for certain settings of the parameter α in the Pareto distribution, the Walsh strategy is guaranteed to give an expected performance gain over not performing restarts.

4 Analytical Study

In this section we use a simple analytic example to illustrate the pitfalls of using fixed cutoff and other non-universal strategies on an ensemble of instances. For the purposes of this study, we assume that there is no limit on computational resources—i.e., we wish to run the strategy on each instance in the ensemble until a solution is found. In such a scenario, the appropriate performance measure is the expected cost of solving the ensemble.

Consider an ensemble of n instances where the (unknown) runtime distribution of the kth instance is given by $f_k(t)$, $k = 0, \ldots, n-1$,

$$f_k(t) = \begin{cases} p & t = 10^k \\ 1-p & t = 10^n \\ 0 & \text{otherwise.} \end{cases}$$

where $p \geq \frac{1}{8}$ (the lower bound on p is to ensure that restarts are helpful for all possible values of n and k).

Following Gagliolo and Schmidhuber [15], suppose that we learn a fixed cutoff by collecting a sample of the ensemble, constructing a single runtime distribution for the sample, and finally choosing the fixed cutoff that minimizes the expected runtime of the strategy given the runtime distribution. In the limiting case where the sample is the entire ensemble, the runtime distribution would be given by,

$$f(t) = \begin{cases} p/n & t = 10^k, k = 0, \ldots, n-1 \\ 1-p & t = 10^n \\ 0 & \text{otherwise.} \end{cases}$$

It can easily be shown that (1, 1, ...) is the optimal fixed cutoff strategy for the above runtime distribution. However, if we actually run the strategy on each instance of the ensemble, the expected runtime of solving the ensemble is *unbounded* (i.e., the process will not terminate). This is true for any fixed cutoff strategy (t, t, ...) where $t < 10^{n-1}$. Further, if we interleave the learned cutoff with the Luby strategy, the result would only degrade the performance of the Luby.

Following Ruan, Horvitz, and Kautz [10], suppose that we learn a cutoff strategy by constructing a runtime distribution for each instance in the sample, clustering the runtime distributions into a small number of classes, and learning a restart strategy from the clustered runtime distributions. It can be shown that, under reasonable assumptions about the method for clustering the runtime distributions, unless the sample consists of the entire ensemble and the number of clusters is equal to n, the expected runtime of the learned strategy on the ensemble of instances can be unbounded.

As a point of comparison, it is easy to show that for each instance k with runtime distribution $f_k(t)$, $k = 0, \ldots, n-1$, the optimal restart strategy for that instance is the fixed cutoff strategy (t_k^*, t_k^*, ...) with $t_k^* = 10^k$. For the ensemble of n instances, if we use the optimal restart strategy for each instance (i.e., the fixed cutoff strategy (t_k^*, t_k^*, ...) is used on instance k), the expected runtime of solving the ensemble is $(10^n - 1)/(9p)$. Similarly, the expected runtime of the strategy using the cutoff $t = \infty$ (i.e., running the backtracking algorithm to completion on each instance) can be derived and is obviously finite. Thus, the non-universal restart strategies learned by previous proposals can be unbounded worse than the gold standard strategy of using the fixed cutoff t_k^* and unbounded worse than performing no restarts at all.

The universal strategies, by design, avoid this pitfall. But the question now is, how well do they perform? For a given n and p, we can experimentally determine the expected runtime of the Luby and Walsh strategies on the ensemble of instances, for various parameter settings. Table 1 summarizes a representative example, the case where $n = 6$ and $p = 1/8$. Ratios less then one in the table represent a speed-up; greater than one represent a slowdown. The default value of the scale parameter s is 1 and the default value of the geometric parameter r is 2 for the Luby strategy and 1.1 for the Walsh strategy.

There are two aspects of this analytic example that are worth noting. First, the pitfall that a learned non-universal restart strategy can be arbitrarily worse than no restarting at all arose even when perfect information about the runtime

Table 1. Ratio of expected runtime of the Luby and Walsh restart strategies over (a) the expected runtime of the gold standard strategy t_k^*, and (b) the expected runtime when no restarts are performed

	restarts using t_k^*		no restarts	
Parameter settings	Luby	Walsh	Luby	Walsh
Optimal	2.51	3.26	0.42	0.55
Default	14.17	3.30	2.39	0.56

distributions was available (i.e., the sample consisted of the entire ensemble). The pitfall is exacerbated when only estimates are available. In particular, the pitfall would be likely to arise whenever there exist instances in the ensemble that are inherently harder to solve than others. We would argue that these conditions would often hold in practice, an assertion that our empirical study in the next section supports. Second, the universal strategies avoid the pitfall and offer speedups for various parameter settings. In the next section, we introduce more realistic runtime distributions and study how robustly and accurately good parameter settings can be estimated and just how much the parameterized universal strategies can lead to performance gains.

5 Empirical Study

In this section we present the results of an extensive empirical evaluation of our approach on real-world scheduling instances. We performed two sets of experiments. In the first set of experiments, we consider a scenario that often arises in practice where a solution must be found within some given amount of computational resources. In these experiments we used a limit on the amount of CPU time. In such a scenario, the appropriate performance measure is the number of problems in the ensemble which are not solved. In the second set of experiments, we consider a scenario where a backtracking search is run to completion. In such a scenario, the appropriate performance measure is the expected time to solve all of the problems in the ensemble. We begin by presenting the experimental setup that is in common to the two sets of experiments, followed by the results of the experiments themselves.

5.1 Experimental Setup

We used instruction scheduling problems for multiple-issue pipelined processors in our experiments. Instruction scheduling is one of the most important steps in improving the performance of object code produced by a compiler. The task is to find a minimal length schedule for a basic block—a straight-line sequence of code with a single entry point and a single exit point—subject to precedence, latency, and resource constraints. We formulated a constraint programming model and solved the instances using backtracking search. In the model, there is a variable for each instruction, the domains of the variables are the time cycles in which the instruction could be scheduled, and the constraints consist of linear inequalities, global cardinality constraints, and other specialized constraints. The scheduler was able to solve almost all of the basic blocks that we found in practice, including basic blocks with up to 2600 instructions. We refer the reader to [16] for further details on the problem, the model, and the backtracking algorithm. The point we wish to emphasize here is that, prior to our examination of restart strategies, considerable effort went into improving the constraint programming model, backtracking algorithm, and heuristics to reduce the number of unsolved problems.

To randomize the backtracking algorithm, the dynamic variable ordering heuristic randomly picked a variable from the top 5 variables (or fewer, if there were fewer variables left). The backtracking algorithm is capable of performing three levels of constraint propagation:

Level = 0	bounds consistency
Level = 1	singleton bounds consistency
Level = 2	singleton bounds consistency to a depth of two

We repeated the experiments for each level of constraint propagation. For our experiments, we used scheduling instances that arise from the SPEC 2000 and MediaBench benchmark suites, two standard real-world benchmarks in compiler research. These benchmark suites consist of source code for software packages that are chosen to be representative of a variety of programming languages and types of applications. We had available to us a total of 6,377 hard scheduling instances from 28 different software packages. For our sample of instances, or training set, we used all 927 of the hard scheduling instances from the galgel, gap, mpeg, and jpeg software packages. We chose these four software packages for two reasons. First, the instances give approximately fifteen percent of the scheduling instances and, second, these software packages provide a good cross section of the data as they include both integer and floating point instructions as well as a variety of programming languages and types of applications. For our test set, we used the remaining 5,450 hard scheduling instances.

For each instance in the training and test sets, we collected 1000 samples of its runtime distribution by each time running the randomized backtracking algorithm on the instance and recording the amount of time taken in seconds. The samples are censored in that we ran the backtracking algorithm with a timeout mechanism; if the instance was not solved within 10 minutes, the backtracking algorithm was terminated and the maximum amount of 10 minutes was recorded. (All times were recorded to 1/100 of a second, the resolution of the system clock.) These empirical runtime distributions were then used to learn and test the various restart strategies.

All of the runtime experiments were performed on a cluster which consists of 768 machines running Linux, each with 4 GB of RAM and four 2.2 GHz processors.

5.2 Experiment 1

In our first set of experiments, we set a time limit of 10 minutes per instance and determined whether learning good parameter settings from a training set can reduce the number of problems in the test set which are not solved.

To learn good parameter settings for the Luby and Walsh strategies, we discretized the scale s into orders of magnitude, $10^{-1}, \ldots, 10^{5}$, and the geometric r into 2, 3, ..., 10 (Luby) and 1.1, 1.2, ..., 2 (Walsh). The best parameter settings were then estimated by choosing the values that minimized the expected number of instances not solved for the training set. The strategies with the estimated parameter settings were then evaluated on the test set. Table 2 summarizes the

Table 2. Expected number of scheduling instances in the test set *not* solved within a deadline of 10 minutes, for various fixed cutoff strategies (see text); the Luby and Walsh strategies with default, estimated, and optimal parameter settings; and various levels of constraint propagation

	Fixed cutoff			Luby			Walsh		
Level	t_k^*	$\hat{t}_{single}$	$t = 10\text{m}$	def.	est.	opt.	def.	est.	opt.
0	118.6	233.0	193.2	124.1	125.2	123.0	141.2	140.1	140.0
1	25.7	637.0	33.9	37.6	28.4	28.4	34.5	27.9	27.8
2	84.3	2,056.0	85.0	187.0	85.0	85.0	166.1	85.0	85.0

Table 3. Percentage increase in the expected number of scheduling instances in the test set *not* solved relative to the gold standard t_k^*, for various restart strategies and levels of constraint propagation

	Fixed cutoff			Luby			Walsh		
Level	t_k^*	$\hat{t}_{single}$	$t = 10\text{m}$	def.	est.	opt.	def.	est.	opt.
0	0.0%	96.5%	62.9%	4.6%	5.6%	3.7%	19.0%	18.1%	18.0%
1	0.0%	2,378.6%	31.9%	46.3%	10.5%	10.5%	34.2%	8.6%	8.2%
2	0.0%	2,338.9%	0.8%	121.8%	0.8%	0.8%	97.0%	0.8%	0.8%
Max	0.0%	2,378.6%	62.9%	121.8%	10.5%	10.5%	97.0%	18.1%	18.0%

results. Table 3 presents the same information except now stated in terms of percentage change. For comparison purposes, we show the results for three fixed cutoff strategies: (i) the gold standard strategy t_k^* where, for each instance k in the *test* set, the optimal fixed cutoff strategy for that instance is used; (ii) the fixed cutoff strategy $\hat{t}_{single}$ that would be learned from the training set by the method of Gagliolo and Schmidhuber [15]; and (iii) the fixed cutoff strategy where the cutoff is set equal to the deadline of 10 minutes; i.e., there are no restarts.

It can be seen that on this testbed the fixed cutoff strategy $\hat{t}_{single}$ performs poorly. Parameterizing the universal strategies and estimating good parameter settings can give quite reasonable performance improvements over the default or unparameterized universal strategies in some cases. Further, the parameter settings estimated from the training set lead to performance that approaches that of the optimal parameter settings (the parameter settings that, among all possible parameter settings, lead to the best performance on the test set). As well, it is worth noting that in some cases the default parameter settings lead to worse performance than when there are no restarts.

We also measured the robustness of our approach for learning good universal restart strategies by performing a sensitivity analysis. To be broadly useful, our approach should not rely on extremely accurate estimates of the optimal settings of the parameters. Rather, there should be a wide range of values for the parameters that are effective and small changes in the accuracy of the estimates should give small changes in the overall performance of the strategy.

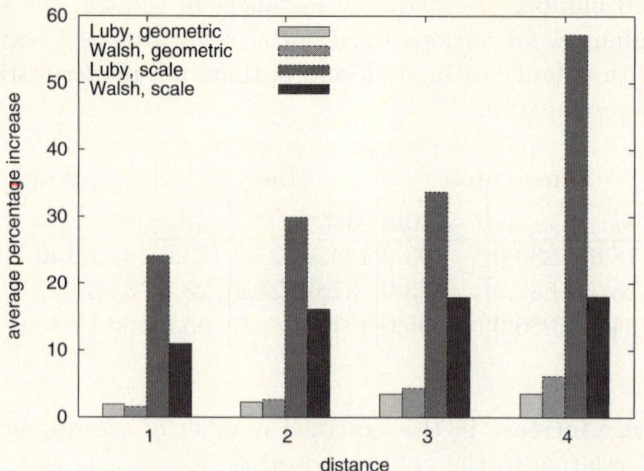

Fig. 1. Average (over all levels of constraint propagation) percentage increase in the expected number of instances *not* solved in the test set relative to the optimal parameter settings, for various distances

To measure the robustness, we began with the optimal parameter settings and systematically introduced inaccuracies in the parameters and observed the effect on performance. For each parameter setting that was a given distance from the optimal setting, we determined the percentage increase in the number of problems that could not be solved. For example, for a distance of 1, scale parameters that were one order of magnitude smaller and larger than the optimal setting were tested. The results are summarized in Figure 1. It can be seen that on this testbed: (i) the setting of the scale parameter is the most important for both the Luby and the Walsh strategies, (ii) estimates of the scale parameter that are off by one or two orders of magnitude are still effective, and (iii) the Walsh strategy is somewhat more robust than the Luby.

5.3 Experiment 2

In our second set of experiments, we removed the time limit and determined whether learning good parameter settings from a training set can reduce the time needed to solve all of the problems in the test set. Recall that in the runtime distributions that we gathered, the samples were censored in that the backtracking algorithm was terminated if an instance was not solved within 10 minutes. In this experiment we wished to run the backtracking algorithm to completion. It proved infeasible to actually do this on our benchmark instances—the instances that we let run without a timeout ran for days without terminating—and so we took a compromise approach as follows.

Gomes et al. [4] show that Pareto distributions of the form $F(t) = 1 - Ct^{-\alpha}$ are a good fit to runtime distributions that arise from backtracking algorithms with randomized heuristics when applied to a diverse set of problems. In our experimental runtime data, we replaced the timeouts by values sampled from the tail of a Pareto distribution with $C = 1$ and $\alpha = 0.5$. With these choices

Table 4. Expected time (days:hours:minutes) to solve *all* of the scheduling instances in the test set, for various fixed cutoff strategies (see text); the Luby and Walsh strategies with default, estimated, and optimal parameter settings; and various levels of constraint propagation

	Fixed cutoff			Luby			Walsh		
Level	t_k^*	$\hat{t}_{single}$	$t = \infty$	def.	est.	opt.	def.	est.	opt.
0	4:13:54	∞	295:07:03	62:13:07	7:14:29	7:14:29	17:17:19	7:03:53	7:03:53
1	1:00:22	∞	53:11:59	13:23:17	1:08:12	1:08:12	3:16:35	1:06:17	1:06:17
2	3:11:46	∞	122:23:52	49:18:45	3:23:00	3:23:00	13:22:30	3:17:04	3:17:04

Table 5. Percentage increase in the expected time to solve *all* of the scheduling instances in the test set relative to the gold standard t_k^*, for various restart strategies and levels of constraint propagation

	Fixed cutoff			Luby			Walsh		
Level	t_k^*	$\hat{t}_{single}$	$t = \infty$	def.	est.	opt.	def.	est.	opt.
0	0.0%	∞	6,348.4%	1265.8%	66.1%	66.1%	287.0%	56.4%	56.4%
1	0.0%	∞	5,169.1%	1275.9%	32.2%	32.2%	263.6%	24.3%	24.3%
2	0.0%	∞	3,423.8%	1326.3%	13.4%	13.4%	299.3%	6.3%	6.3%
Max	0.0%	∞	6,348.4%	1326.3%	66.1%	66.1%	299.3%	56.4%	56.4%

for C and α, of the instances that previously had timed out, approximately 59.2% of the instances are now "solved" within one hour, 91.9% are solved within one day, 98.9% are solved within one month, and all are solved within one year.

To learn good parameter settings for the Luby and Walsh strategies, we discretized the scale s into orders of magnitude, $10^{-1}, \ldots, 10^7$, and the geometric r into $2, 3, \ldots, 10$ (Luby) and $1.1, 1.2, \ldots, 2$ (Walsh). The best parameter settings were then estimated by choosing the values that minimized the time to solve all of the instances in the training set. The strategies with the estimated parameter settings were then evaluated on the test set. Table 4 summarizes the results. Table 5 presents the same information except now stated in terms of percentage change.

It can be seen that on this testbed parameterizing the universal strategies and estimating good parameter settings gives performance improvements over the default universal strategies in all cases (ranging from a minimum reduction of from 3 days down to 1 day to a maximum reduction of from 62 days down to 7 days). Further, the estimated parameter settings are accurate—in each case the estimated parameter settings turned out to be the optimal parameter settings. As well, we note that with just the default parameters, the Walsh strategy is much better than the Luby strategy. However, once we estimate and use good parameter settings, the Luby and Walsh strategies achieve quite comparable performance.

5.4 Discussion

We conclude this section with a discussion relating our experimental results with previous theoretical results, as at first glance it may appear that there is a conflict. Recall that Luby, Sinclair, and Zuckerman [1] show that, for any runtime distribution, the Luby strategy with default parameter settings is within a log factor of the optimal fixed cutoff strategy for that distribution. This may appear to contradict the experimental results that we report for the default Luby strategy. However, the theoretical result hides constant factors, which can be important in practice. The constant factors can in fact be large as one moves from the theoretician's time step to a more practical proxy such as clock time or number of backtracks. As well, we note that the optimality result does not hold in the case where limits are placed on computational resources, such as a deadline [17].

Recall also that Luby, Sinclair, and Zuckerman [1] show that, given no knowledge of the runtime distribution, no universal strategy can have a better bound than being within a log factor of optimal. This may appear to contradict the experimental results that we report for the universal strategies with estimated parameter settings. However, we note that the result does not hold in the case where we are allowed to sample from the ensemble—as we do here—and learn about the runtime distribution. As well, the theoretical result is a worst-case analysis and the proof relies on a pathological distribution which may not arise in practice.

6 Conclusions

We presented a theoretical worst-case analysis of the Walsh universal strategy. The analysis provides some insights into suitable ranges in practice for the geometric parameter of the strategy. We also presented an approach for learning good universal restart strategies in the commonly occurring scenario where an ensemble of instances is to be solved. We demonstrated the effectiveness and robustness of our approach through an extensive empirical evaluation on a real-world testbed. Together these results increase our theoretical understanding of universal restart strategies and increase their applicability in practice.

Acknowledgments. This work was made possible by the facilities of the Shared Hierarchical Academic Research Computing Network (SHARCNET).

References

1. Luby, M., Sinclair, A., Zuckerman, D.: Optimal speedup of Las Vegas algorithms. Information Processing Letters 47, 173–180 (1993)
2. Harvey, W.D.: Nonsystematic backtracking search. PhD thesis, Stanford University (1995)
3. Gomes, C., Selman, B., Crato, N.: Heavy-tailed distributions in combinatorial search. In: Proceedings of the Third International Conference on Principles and Practice of Constraint Programming, Linz, Austria, pp. 121–135 (1997)

4. Gomes, C., Selman, B., Crato, N., Kautz, H.: Heavy-tailed phenomena in satisfiability and constraint satisfaction problems. J. of Automated Reasoning 24, 67–100 (2000)
5. Huang, J.: The effect of restarts on the efficiency of clause learning. In: Proceedings of the 20th International Joint Conference on Artificial Intelligence, Hyderabad, India, pp. 2318–2323 (2007)
6. Walsh, T.: Search in a small world. In: Proceedings of the Sixteenth International Joint Conference on Artificial Intelligence, Stockholm, pp. 1172–1177 (1999)
7. Zhan, Y.: Randomisation and restarts. MSc thesis, University of York (2001)
8. Kautz, H., Horvitz, E., Ruan, Y., Gomes, C., Selman, B.: Dynamic restart policies. In: Proceedings of the Eighteenth National Conference on Artificial Intelligence, Edmonton, pp. 674–681 (2002)
9. Ruan, Y., Horvitz, E., Kautz, H.: Restart policies with dependence among runs: A dynamic programming approach. In: Proceedings of the Eighth International Conference on Principles and Practice of Constraint Programming, Ithaca, New York, pp. 573–586 (2002)
10. Ruan, Y., Horvitz, E., Kautz, H.: Hardness aware restart policies. In: IJCAI Workshop on Stochastic Search Algorithms (2003)
11. Bayardo Jr., R.J., Schrag, R.C.: Using CSP look-back techniques to solve real-world SAT instances. In: Proceedings of the Fourteenth National Conference on Artificial Intelligence, Providence, Rhode Island, pp. 203–208 (1997)
12. Wu, H., van Beek, P.: Restart strategies: Analysis and simulation (Doctoral Abstract). In: Proceedings of the Ninth International Conference on Principles and Practice of Constraint Programming, Kinsale, Ireland, p. 1001 (2003)
13. Eén, N., Sörensson, N.: An extensible SAT-solver. In: Giunchiglia, E., Tacchella, A. (eds.) SAT 2003. LNCS, vol. 2919, pp. 502–518. Springer, Heidelberg (2004)
14. Ó Nualláin, B., de Rijke, M., van Benthem, J.: Ensemble-based prediction of SAT search behaviour. Electronic Notes in Discrete Mathematics, vol. 9 (2001)
15. Gagliolo, M., Schmidhuber, J.: Learning restarts strategies. In: Proceedings of the 20th International Joint Conference on Artificial Intelligence, Hyderabad, India, pp. 792–797 (2007)
16. Malik, A.M., McInnes, J., van Beek, P.: Optimal basic block instruction scheduling for multiple-issue processors using constraint programming. In: Proceedings of the 18th IEEE International Conference on Tools with Artificial Intelligence, Washington, DC, pp. 279–287. IEEE Computer Society Press, Los Alamitos (2006)
17. van Moorsel, A.P.A., Wolter, K.: Analysis of restart mechanisms in software systems. IEEE Trans. on Software Engineering 32, 547–558 (2006)

Hierarchical Hardness Models for SAT

Lin Xu, Holger H. Hoos, and Kevin Leyton-Brown

University of British Columbia, 2366 Main Mall, Vancouver BC, V6T 1Z4, Canada
{xulin730,hoos,kevinlb}@cs.ubc.ca

Abstract. Empirical hardness models predict a solver's runtime for a given instance of an $\mathcal{NP}$-hard problem based on efficiently computable features. Previous research in the SAT domain has shown that better prediction accuracy and simpler models can be obtained when models are trained separately on satisfiable and unsatisfiable instances. We extend this work by training separate hardness models for each class, predicting the probability that a novel instance belongs to each class, and using these predictions to build a hierarchical hardness model using a mixture-of-experts approach. We describe and analyze classifiers and hardness models for four well-known distributions of SAT instances and nine high-performance solvers. We show that surprisingly accurate classifications can be achieved very efficiently. Our experiments show that hierarchical hardness models achieve higher prediction accuracy than the previous state of the art. Furthermore, the classifier's confidence correlates strongly with prediction error, giving a useful per-instance estimate of prediction error.

1 Introduction

For $\mathcal{NP}$-hard problems such as SAT, even the best known algorithms have worst-case running times that increase exponentially with instance size. In practice, however, many large instances of $\mathcal{NP}$-hard problems can still be solved within a reasonable amount of time. In order to understand this phenomenon, much effort has been invested in understanding the "empirical hardness" of such problems [15,18]. One recent approach uses linear basis-function regression to obtain models that can predict the time required for an algorithm to solve a given SAT instance [18]. These empirical hardness models can be used to gain insight into the factors responsible for an algorithm's performance, or to induce distributions of problem instances that are challenging for a given algorithm. They can also be leveraged to select among several different algorithms for solving a given problem instance [13,14,20] and can be applied in automated algorithm configuration and tuning [9]. Empirical hardness models have proven very useful for combinatorial auction winner determination [15], a prominent $\mathcal{NP}$-hard optimization problem. In Section 2, we introduce some background knowledge about empirical hardness models as well as our experimental setup.

Considering the SAT problem in particular, previous work has shown that if instances are restricted to be either only satisfiable or only unsatisfiable, very different models are needed to make accurate runtime predictions for uniform random SAT instances. Furthermore, models for each type of instance are simpler

C. Bessiere (Ed.): CP 2007, LNCS 4741, pp. 696–711, 2007.

and more accurate than models that must handle both types, which means that better empirical hardness models can be built if we know the satisfiability of instances. In this work we further investigate this idea by considering a variety of both structured and unstructured SAT instances and several state-of-the-art SAT solvers. The detailed experimental results are described in Section 3.

In Section 4, we study the feasibility of predicting the satisfiability of a novel SAT instance from a known distribution, using Sparse Multinomial Logistic Regression (SMLR) [11] as our classifier. Our experimental results are very promising. Even for uniform random 3-SAT instances generated at the phase transition, the prediction accuracy was greater than 86%. For the trickiest problems we encountered (SAT-encoded graph coloring problems on small-world graphs), the prediction accuracy was still greater than 73%.

Armed with a reasonably accurate (but imperfect) classifier, in Section 5 we consider the construction of hierarchical hardness models in order to make runtime predictions. We do so by using a mixture-of-experts approach with fixed ("clamped") experts—in other words, with conditional models trained on satisfiable instances and unsatisfiable instances separately. We evaluate both conditional models and then return a weighted sum of the two predictions, where these weights are given by a learned function that depends on both the instance features and the classifier's prediction. We found that using such hierarchical models improved overall prediction accuracy. Furthermore, the classifier's confidence correlated with prediction accuracy, giving useful per-instance evidence about the quality of the runtime prediction.

2 Background

For a given problem instance, empirical hardness models predict the runtime of an algorithm based on polytime-computable instance features. We have investigated a wide variety of different regression techniques in past work [15]. Here, we use the same linear basis-function ridge regression method that has previously proven to be very successful in predicting runtime on uniform random SAT and combinational auctions [18,15] and focus on combining models specialized to different types of instances.

2.1 Empirical Hardness Models

In order to predict the runtime of an algorithm $\mathcal{A}$ on a distribution $\mathcal{I}$ of problem instances, we run algorithm $\mathcal{A}$ on n instances drawn from $\mathcal{I}$ and compute for each instance $i \in \mathcal{I}$ a feature vector $\boldsymbol{x}_i = (x_{i,1}, \ldots, x_{i,k})$. We then fit a function $f(\boldsymbol{x})$ that, given the features $\boldsymbol{x}_i$ of an instance i, approximates $\mathcal{A}$'s runtime on i, y_i. To improve numerical stability by eliminating highly correlated features, we reduce the set of features through forward selection. Then we perform a basis function expansion of our feature set. Our basis functions can include arbitrarily complex functions of sets of features, or can simply be the raw features themselves; in this work, quadratic basis functions are used. Finally, we perform another pass of forward feature selection and select a subset of extended features $\boldsymbol{\phi}_i = \boldsymbol{\phi}(\boldsymbol{x}_i) = [\phi_1(\boldsymbol{x}_i), \ldots, \phi_d(\boldsymbol{x}_i)]$ for which our models achieve the best performance on a given validation data set.

We then use ridge regression to fit the free parameters $\boldsymbol{w}$ of the linear function $f_{\boldsymbol{w}}(\boldsymbol{x}_i) = \boldsymbol{w}^\top \phi(\boldsymbol{x}_i)$. We compute $\boldsymbol{w} = (\delta I + \boldsymbol{\Phi}^\top \boldsymbol{\Phi})^{-1} \boldsymbol{\Phi}^\top \tilde{\boldsymbol{y}}$, where $\tilde{y} = (\tilde{y}_1, \ldots, \tilde{y}_n)$, and $\tilde{y}_i$ is a transformation of the runtime y_i. In this work, we use $\tilde{y}_i = \log y_i$. The $n \times d$ matrix $\boldsymbol{\Phi}$ contains the feature values for all training instances, and δ is a small regularization constant that prevents arbitrarily large parameter values in $\boldsymbol{w}$ and increases numerical stability. Given a new, unseen instance j, a runtime prediction is made by computing its features $\boldsymbol{x}_j$ and evaluating $f_{\boldsymbol{w}}(\boldsymbol{x}_j) = \boldsymbol{w}^\top \phi(\boldsymbol{x}_j)$.

Empirical hardness models have a probabilistic interpretation. The features $\boldsymbol{x}$ and the empirical algorithm runtime y, when seen as random variables, are related as in the following graphical model:

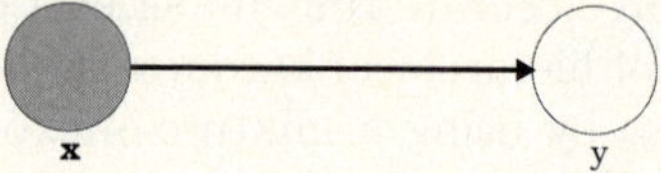

In this model, we observe the feature vector $\boldsymbol{x}$, and the probability distribution over runtime y is conditionally dependent on $\boldsymbol{x}$. Since we train a linear model using least squares fitting, we have implicitly chosen to represent $P(y|\boldsymbol{x})$ as a Gaussian with mean $\boldsymbol{w}^\top \phi(\boldsymbol{x})$ and some fixed variance β. What we call a prediction of an empirical hardness model is really $\mathbb{E}(y|\boldsymbol{x})$, the mean of this distribution conditioned on the observed feature vector.

2.2 Experimental Setup

For the experiments conducted throughout this study, we selected two distributions of unstructured SAT instances and two of structured instances:

- `rand3-fix`: uniform-random 3-SAT with 400 variables from the solubility phase transition (clauses-to-variables ratio 4.26) [2,19]; we generated 20,000 instances with a satisfiable/unsatisfiable ratio of 50.7/49.3.
- `rand3-var`: uniform-random 3-SAT with 400 variables and clauses-to-variables ratios randomly selected from 3.26 to 5.26; we generated 20,000 instances with a satisfiable/unsatisfiable ratio of 50/50.
- `QCP`: random quasi-group completion (the task of determining whether the missing entries of a partial Latin square can be filled in to obtain a complete Latin square [7]); using a range of parameter settings, we generated 30,620 SAT-encoded instances with a satisfiable/unsatisfiable ratio of 58.7/41.3.
- `SW-GCP`: graph-coloring on small-world graphs [6]; using a range of parameter settings, we generated 20,000 SAT-encoded instances with a satisfiable/unsatisfiable ratio of 55.9/44.1.

The latter two types of SAT distributions have been widely used as a model of hard SAT instances with interesting structure; we used the same instance generators and SAT encodings as the respective original studies. Each instance set was randomly split into training, validation and test sets, at a ratio of 70:15:15. All parameter tuning was performed with a validation set; test sets were used only to generate the final results reported in this paper. Note that since the test sets we used for our experiments are very big (at least 3000 instances each), we can expect similar performance for the whole distribution. For each instance, we computed the 84 features described by Nudelman et al. [18]; these features can be classified into nine categories: problem size, variable-clause graph, variable graph, clause graph, balance features, proximity to Horn formulae, LP-based, DPLL search space, and local search space. We used only raw features as basis functions for classification, because even a simple quadratic basis function expansion exceeded the 2GB of RAM available to us. For regression, we used raw features as well as quadratic basis functions for better runtime prediction accuracy. We evaluated the accuracy of logarithm runtime prediction using root mean squared error (RMSE). In order to reduce the number of redundant features, we used forward selection and kept the model with the smallest cross-validation error (this was done independently for each of the learned hardness models).

For uniform random 3-SAT instances, we ran four solvers that are known to perform well on these distributions: `kcnfs` [3], `oksolver` [12], `march_dl` [8], and `satz` [16]. For structured SAT instances, we ran six solvers that are known to perform well on these distributions: `oksolver`, `zchaff` [22], `sato` [21], `satelite` [4], `minisat` [5], and `satzoo` [5]. Note that in the 2005 SAT competition, `satelite` won gold medals for the Industrial and Handmade SAT+UNSAT categories; `minisat` and `zchaff` won silver and bronze, respectively, for Industrial SAT+UN SAT; and `kcnfs` and `march_dl` won gold and silver, respectively, in the Random SAT+UNSAT category.

All of our experiments were performed using a cluster consisting of 50 computers equipped with dual Intel Xeon 3.2GHz CPUs with 2MB cache and 2GB RAM, running Suse Linux 9.1. All runs of any solver that exceeded 1 CPU hour were terminated and recorded in our database of experimental results with a runtime of 1 CPU hour; this timeout occurred in fewer than 3% of all runs.

3 Conditional and Oracular Empirical Hardness Models

From previous research [18], we know that for uniform-random 3-SAT instances, much simpler and more accurate empirical hardness models can be learned when all instances are either satisfiable or unsatisfiable. In the following, we refer to these as *conditional* models, and to models trained on satisfiable and unsatisfiable instances as *unconditional* models. Let M_{sat} (M_{unsat}) denote a model trained only on satisfiable (unsatisfiable) instances. If we had an oracle that knew which conditional model performed better for a given instance, models equipped with such an oracle could achieve more accurate runtime predictions. We call such a (hypothetical) scheme an *oracular* model. (Note that our oracle chooses the *best* model for a particular instance, not the model trained on data with the same *satisfiability status* as the instance. This may seem counterintuitive; it will be discussed in detail below. For now, note simply that in most cases the two sorts of oracles would select the same model.) We can infer from the results of Nudelman et al. [18] that on uniform-random 3-SAT, oracular models could achieve much higher prediction accuracies than unconditional models. In fact, the performance of an oracular model bounds the performance of a conditional model from above.

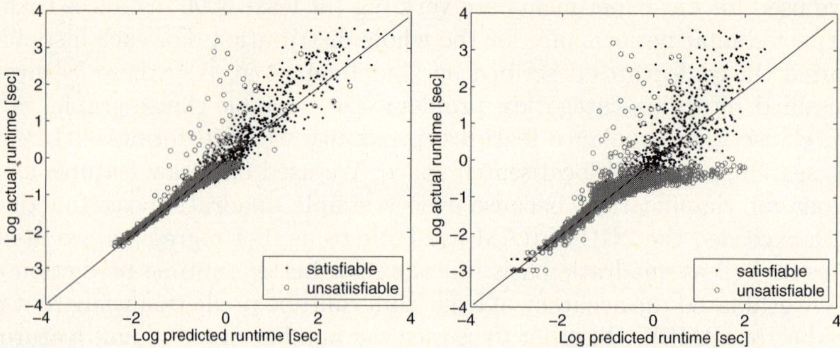

Fig. 1. Comparison of oracular model (left, RMSE=0.247) and unconditional model (right, RMSE=0.426). Distribution: `QCP`, solver: `satelite`.

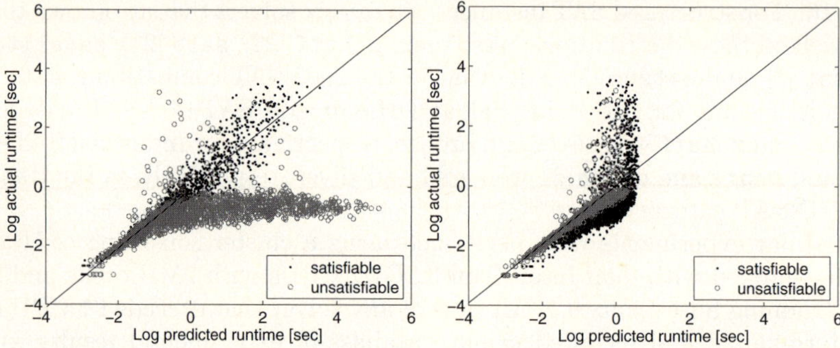

Fig. 2. Actual vs predicted runtime using only M_{sat} (left, RMSE=1.493) and only M_{unsat} (right, RMSE=0.683), respectively. Distribution: `QCP`, solver: `satelite`.

In the experiments conducted for this work, we found that the usefulness of oracular models extends to solvers and distributions not studied previously. Figure 1 shows the difference between using oracular models and unconditional models on structured SAT instances (distribution: `QCP`, solver: `satelite`). For oracular models, we observed almost perfect predictions of runtime for unsatisfiable instances and more noisy, but unbiased predictions for satisfiable instances (Figure 1, left). Figure 1 (right) shows that the runtime prediction for unsatisfiable instances made by unconditional models can exhibit both less accuracy and more bias.

Even though using the best conditional model can result in higher prediction accuracy, we found that there is a big penalty for using the wrong conditional model to predict the runtime of an instance. Figure 2 (left) shows that if we used M_{sat} for runtime prediction on an unsatisfiable instance, the prediction error was often very large. The large bias in the inaccurate predictions is due to the fact that models trained on different types of instances are very different. As shown in Figure 2 (right), similar phenomena occur when we use M_{unsat} to predict the runtime on a satisfiable instance.

Table 1. Accuracy of hardness models for different solvers and instance distributions

	RMSE for `rand3-var` models				RMSE for `rand3-fix` models			
Solvers	sat.	unsat.	unconditional	oracular	sat.	unsat.	unconditional	oracular
`satz`	5.481	3.703	0.385	0.329	0.459	0.835	0.420	0.343
`march_dl`	1.947	3.705	0.396	0.283	0.604	1.097	0.542	0.444
`kcnfs`	4.766	4.765	0.373	0.294	0.550	0.983	0.491	0.397
`oksolver`	8.169	4.141	0.443	0.356	0.689	1.161	0.596	0.497
	RMSE for `QCP` models				**RMSE for `SW-GCP` models**			
Solvers	sat.	unsat.	unconditional	oracular	sat.	unsat.	unconditional	oracular
`zchaff`	1.866	1.163	0.675	0.303	1.230	1.209	0.993	0.657
`minisat`	1.761	1.150	0.574	0.305	1.280	1.275	1.022	0.682
`satzoo`	1.293	0.876	0.397	0.240	0.709	0.796	0.581	0.384
`satelite`	1.493	0.683	0.426	0.247	1.232	1.226	0.970	0.618
`sato`	2.373	14.914	0.711	0.375	1.682	1.887	1.353	0.723
`oksolver`	1.213	1.062	0.548	0.427	1.807	2.064	1.227	0.601

Our results are consistent across data sets and solvers; as shown in Table 1, oracular models always achieved higher accuracy than unconditional models. The very large prediction errors in Table 1 for M_{sat} and M_{unsat} indicate that these models are very different. In particular, the RMSE for using models trained on unsatisfiable instances to predict runtimes on a mixture of instances was as high as 14.914 (distribution: `QCP`, solver: `sato`).

Unfortunately, oracular models rely on information that is unavailable in practice: the respective accuracies of our two models on a given (test) instance. Still, the prediction accuracies achieved by oracular models suggest that it may be promising to find some practical way of combining conditional models. For the rest of this paper, we will investigate the question of how this can be done. We will be guided both by the potential benefit of relying on conditional models (oracular models outperform unconditional models) and by the danger in doing so (if we make the wrong choices, prediction error can be much higher than when using an unconditional model).

4 Predicting the Satisfiability of SAT Instances

In this section, we will consider the most obvious candidate for a practical approximation of the oracle from the previous section: a classifier that predicts whether or not a given (test) instance is satisfiable. Even if this classifier were perfect—which it surely could not be in general, given the $\mathcal{NP}$-completeness of SAT—it would not choose the *better* of M_{sat} and M_{unsat} on a per-instance basis, as our oracular model does. However, on our datasets it would do nearly as well, making the same choices as the oracular model 98% of the time for `rand3-var`, 86% for `rand3sat-fixed`, 92% for `QCP`, and 77% for `SW-GCP`.

To build such models, we used Sparse Multinomial Logistic Regression (SMLR) [11], a recently developed, state-of-the-art sparse classification algorithm. Like relevance vector machines and sparse probit regression, SMLR learns classifiers

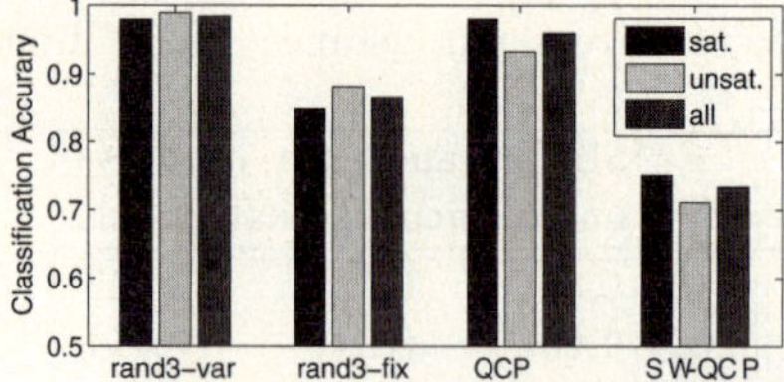

Dataset	Classification Accuracy on sat.	on unsat.	overall
rand3sat-var	0.9791	0.9891	0.9840
rand3sat-fix	0.8480	0.8814	0.8647
QCP	0.9801	0.9324	0.9597
SW-GCP	0.7516	0.7110	0.7340

Fig. 3. Classification accuracy for different data sets

that use sparsity-promoting priors to control the expressivity of the learned classifier, thereby tending to result in better generalization. SMLR encourages parameter weights either to be significantly large or exactly zero. It also learns a sparse multi-class classifier that scales favorably in both the number of training samples and the input dimensionality, which is important for our problems since we have tens of thousands of samples per data set. We also evaluated other classifiers, such as support vector machines [10], but we found that SMLR achieved the best classification accuracy.

We applied SMLR to build a classifier that would distinguish between satisfiable and unsatisfiable SAT instances, using the same set of raw features that were available to the regression model, although in this case we did not find it necessary to use a basis-function expansion of these features. The difference was in the response variable: here we defined it as the probability that an instance is satisfiable, rather than an algorithm's runtime on that instance. Of course, although the output of the classifier is real-valued, all the training data was labelled as satisfiable with probability 1 or with probability 0.

Since SAT is $\mathcal{NP}$-hard and our feature computation and model evaluation are polynomial-time, we cannot expect perfect classification results in general. However, $\mathcal{NP}$-hardness is a worst-case notion; there is no theoretical result that rules out *often* correctly guessing whether instances from known distributions are satisfiable. Complexity theory simply tells us that our classifier must sometimes make mistakes (unless $\mathcal{P} = \mathcal{NP}$); as we show below, it does. Indeed, $\mathcal{NP}$-hardness does not imply that all—or even most—instances of a problem are indeed intractable. This is precisely why these problems can be successfully tackled with heuristic algorithms, such as those studied here.

Considering the difficulty of the classification task, our experimental results are very good. Overall accuracy on test data (measured as the fraction of the time the classifier assigned more than 50% of probability mass to the correct class) was as high as 98%, and never lower than 73%. Furthermore, the classifier was usually very confident about the satisfiability of an instance (i.e., returned probabilities very close to 0 or 1), and the more confident the classifier was, the more accurate it tended to be. These results are summarized in Figures 3–5.

For the `rand3-var` data set (Figure 4, left), the overall classification error was only 1.6%. Using only the clauses-to-variables ratio (greater or less than 4.26) as the basis for predicting the satisfiability of an instance yields an error of 3.7%; therefore, by using SMLR rather than this simple classifier, the classification error is halved. On the `QCP` data set (Figure 4, right), classification accuracy was 96%, and the classifier was extremely confident in its predictions.

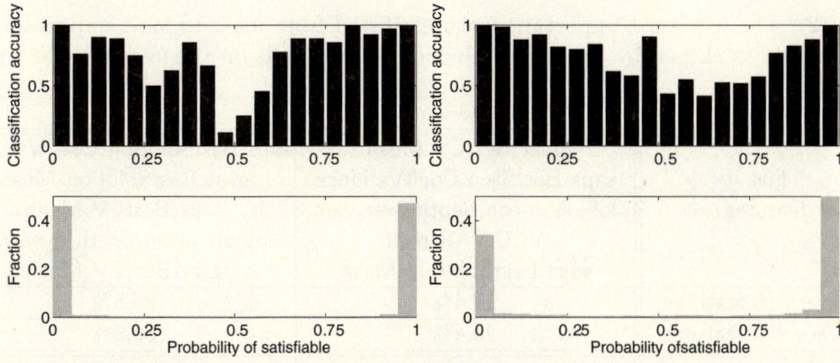

Fig. 4. Classification accuracy vs classifier output (top) and fraction of instances within the given set vs classifier output (bottom). Left: `rand3-var`, right: `QCP`.

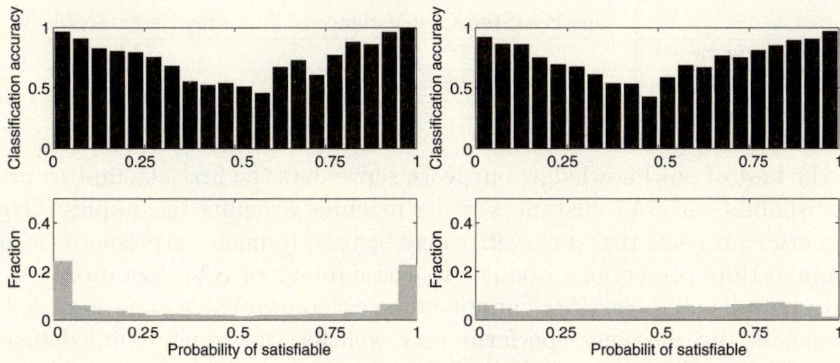

Fig. 5. Classification accuracy vs classifier output (top) and the fraction of instances within the given set vs classified output (bottom). Left: `rand3-fix`, right: `SW-GCP`.

Since all instances for `rand3sat-fix` (Figure 5, left) are generated at the phase transition, it is surprising to see a polynomial-time technique perform so well (accuracy of 86%). For `SW-GCP` (Figure 5, right) the classification accuracy is much lower (73%). We believe that this is primarily because our features are less predictive on this instance distribution, which is consistent with the results we obtained from unconditional hardness models for `SW-GCP`. Note that the fraction of instances for which the classifier was confident is smaller for the last two distributions than for `rand3-var` and `QCP`. However, even for `SW-GCP` we still see a strong correlation between the classifier's output and classification accuracy on test data.

One further interesting finding is that our classifiers can achieve very high accuracies even given very small sets of features. For example, on the `QCP` data, the SMLR classifier achieves an accuracy of 93% with only 5 features. The five most important features for classification on all four data sets are shown in Table 2. Interestingly, local-search based features turned out to be very important for classification in all four data sets.

Table 2. The five most important features (listed from most to least important) for classification as chosen by backward selection. (For details on the features, see [18].)

Data sets	rand3-var	rand3-fix
Five features	gsat_BestCV_Mean saps_BestStep_CoeffVariance lobjois_mean_depth_over_vars VCG_VAR_max saps_BestSolution_Mean	saps_BestSolution_CoeffVariance gsat_BestSolution_Mean saps_BestCV_Mean lobjois_mean_depth_over_vars gsat_BestCV_Mean
Accuracy (5 features)	98.4%	86.5%
Accuracy (all features)	98.4%	86.5%
Data sets	QCP	SW-GCP
Five features	lobjois_log_num_nodes_over_vars saps_BestSolution_Mean saps_BestCV_Mean vars_clauses_ratio saps_BestStep_CoeffVariance	vars_reduced_depth gsat_BestCV_Mean nvars VCG_VAR_min saps_BestStep_Mean
Accuracy (5 features)	93.0%	73.2%
Accuracy (all features)	96.0%	73.4%

To the best of our knowledge, our work represents the first attempt to predict the satisfiability of SAT instances using machine learning techniques. Overall, our experiments show that a classifier may be used to make surprisingly accurate polynomial-time predictions about the satisfiability of SAT instances. As discussed above, such a classifier cannot be completely reliable (unless $\mathcal{P} = \mathcal{NP}$). Nevertheless, our classifiers perform very well for the widely-studied instance distributions considered here. This finding may be useful in its own right. For example, researchers interested in evaluating incomplete SAT algorithms on large numbers of satisfiable instances drawn from a distribution that produces both satisfiable and unsatisfiable instances could use a complete search algorithm to label a relatively small training set, and then use the classifier to filter instances.

5 Hierarchical Hardness Models

Given our findings to far, it would be tempting to construct a hierarchical model that uses a classifier to pick the most likely conditional model and then simply returns that model's prediction. However, while this approach could sometimes be a good heuristic, it is not theoretically sound. Intuitively, the problem is that the classifier does not take into account the accuracies of the different conditional models. For example, recall Figure 2, which showed the prediction accuracy of M_{sat} and M_{unsat} for `satelite` on QCP. We saw that M_{sat} was much less accurate for unsatisfiable instances than M_{unsat} was for satisfiable instances. Thus if we encountered an instance that the classifier considered slightly more likely satisfiable than unsatisfiable, we would still expect to obtain a more accurate prediction from M_{unsat} than from M_{sat}.

A more principled way of combining conditional models can be derived based on the probabilistic interpretation of empirical hardness models introduced in

Section 2.1. As before (see Figure 6, left) we have a set of features that are always observed and a random variable representing runtime that is conditionally dependent on the features. Now we combine the features with our classifier's prediction s, yielding the feature vector $(\boldsymbol{x}, s)$. We also introduce a new random variable $z \in \{sat, unsat\}$, which represents the oracle's choice of which conditional model will perform best for a given instance. Instead of selecting one of the predictions from the two conditional models for runtime y, we use their weighted sum

$$P(y|(\boldsymbol{x}, s)) = \sum_{z \in \{sat, unsat\}} P(z|(\boldsymbol{x}, s)) \cdot P_{M_z}(y|(\boldsymbol{x}, s)), \quad (1)$$

where $P_{M_z}(y|(\boldsymbol{x}, s))$ is the probability of y evaluated according to model M_z. Since the models were fit using ridge regression, we can rewrite Eq. (1) as

$$P(y|(\boldsymbol{x}, s)) = \sum_{z \in \{sat, unsat\}} P(z|(\boldsymbol{x}, s)) \cdot \mathcal{N}(y|\boldsymbol{w}_z \boldsymbol{x}, \beta_z), \quad (2)$$

where $\boldsymbol{w}_z$ and β_z are the weights and standard deviation of model M_z. Thus, we will learn weighting functions $P(z|(\boldsymbol{x}, s))$ to maximize the likelihood of our training data according to $P(y|(\boldsymbol{x}, s))$. As a hypothesis space for these weighting functions we chose the commonly used softmax function

$$P(z = sat|(\boldsymbol{x}, s)) = \frac{e^{\boldsymbol{v}^\top (\boldsymbol{x}, s)}}{1 + e^{\boldsymbol{v}^\top (\boldsymbol{x}, s)}}, \quad (3)$$

where $\boldsymbol{v}$ is a vector of free parameters that must be learned [1]. Then we have the following loss function to minimize, where $\mathbb{E}(y_{i,z}|\boldsymbol{x})$ is the prediction of M_z and $\bar{y}_i$ is the real runtime:

$$\mathcal{L} = \sum_{i=1}^{N} \Bigg(\bar{y}_i - \Bigg(\sum_{k \in \{sat, unsat\}} P(z = k|(\boldsymbol{x}_i, s_i)) \cdot \mathbb{E}(y_{i,z}|\boldsymbol{x}_i) \Bigg) \Bigg)^2 . \quad (4)$$

This can be seen as a mixture-of-experts problem with the experts clamped to M_{sat} and M_{unsat} (see, e.g., [1]). For implementation convenience, we used an existing mixture of experts implementation, which is built around an EM algorithm and which performs iterative reweighted least squares in the M step [17]. We modified this code slightly to clamp the experts and to set the initial values of $P(z|(\boldsymbol{x}, s))$ to s (i.e., we initialized the choice of experts to the classifier's output). To evaluate the model and get a runtime prediction for test data, we simply compute the features $\boldsymbol{x}$ and the classifier's output s, and then evaluate

$$\mathbb{E}(y|(\boldsymbol{x}, s)) = \sum_{k \in \{sat, unsat\}} P(z|(\boldsymbol{x}, s)) \cdot \boldsymbol{w}_k^\top \phi(\boldsymbol{x}), \quad (5)$$

where $\boldsymbol{w}_k$ are the weights from M_k and $\phi(\boldsymbol{x})$ is the basis function expansion of $\boldsymbol{x}$. Thus, the classifier's output is not used directly to select a model, but rather as a feature upon which our weighting functions $P(z|(\boldsymbol{x}, s))$ depend, as well as for initializing the EM algorithm.

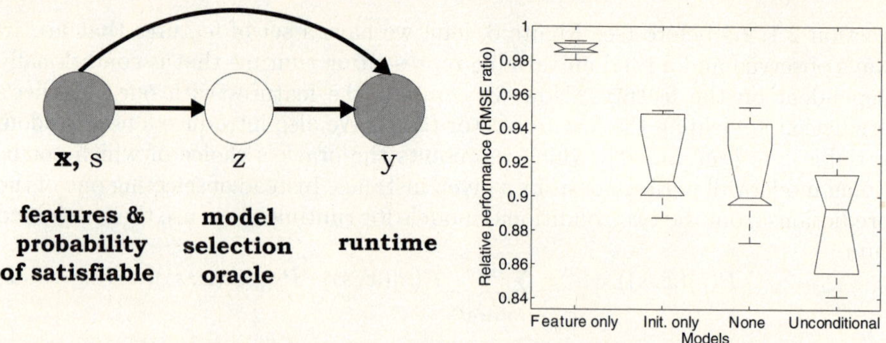

Fig. 6. Left: Graphical model for our mixture-of-experts approach. Right: Comparison of hierarchical hardness models' relative performance: RMSE of full hierarchical model ÷ RMSE of indicated model. Data set: QCP, Solvers: 6 solvers for QCP.

5.1 Experimental Results

Our first experiment used the QCP dataset to investigate the importance of the classifier's output to hierarchical models. Figure 6 (right) shows box plots comparing five scenarios. The first four are hierarchical models with classifier output used (1) both for EM initialization and as a feature to the weighting function; (2) only as a feature; (3) only for initialization; and (4) not at all. We also consider the case of an unconditional model. For each scenario except for the first we report the ratio between its RMSE and that of the first model. The best performance was achieved by full models (all ratios are less than 1). The ratio for keeping the feature only is nearly 1, indicating that the EM initialization is only slightly helpful. All of the hierarchical models outperform the unconditional model, indicating the power of leveraging conditional models; however, when we build a hierarchical model that disregards the classifier's output entirely we achieve only slightly better median RMSE than the unconditional model.

The broader performance of different unconditional, oracular and hierarchical models is shown in Table 3. For rand3-var, the accuracy of classification was very high (classification error was only 1.6%). Our experiments confirmed that hierarchical hardness models can achieve almost the same runtime prediction accuracy as oracular models for all four solvers considered in our study. Figure 7 shows that using the hierarchical hardness model to predict satz's runtime is much better than using the unconditional model.

On the rand3-fix dataset, results for all four solvers were qualitatively similar: hierarchical hardness models gave slightly but consistently better runtime predictions than unconditional models. On this distribution the gap in prediction accuracy between unconditional and oracular models is already quite small, which makes further significant improvements more difficult to achieve. Detailed analysis of actual vs predicted runtimes for satz (see Figure 8) showed that particularly for unsatisfiable instances, the hierarchical model tends to produce slightly more accurate predictions. Further investigation confirmed that those instances in Figure 8 (right) that are far away from the ideal prediction

Table 3. Comparison of oracular, unconditional and hierarchical hardness models. The second number of each entry is the ratio of the model's RMSE to the oracular model's RMSE. (*For SW-GCP, even the oracular model has large runtime prediction error.)

Solvers	RMSE (rand3-var models) oracular	uncond.	hier.	RMSE (rand3-fix models) oracular	uncond.	hier.
satz	0.329	0.385(85%)	0.344(96%)	0.343	0.420(82%)	0.413(83%)
march_dl	0.283	0.396(71%)	0.306(92%)	0.444	0.542(82%)	0.533(83%)
kcnfs	0.294	0.373(79%)	0.312(94%)	0.397	0.491(81%)	0.486(82%)
oksolver	0.356	0.443(80%)	0.378(94%)	0.497	0.596(83%)	0.587(85%)
Solvers	**RMSE (QCP models) oracular**	**uncond.**	**hier.**	**RMSE (SW-GCP models)* oracular**	**uncond.**	**hier.**
zchaff	0.303	0.675(45%)	0.577(53%)	0.657	0.993(66%)	0.983(67%)
minisat	0.305	0.574(53%)	0.500(61%)	0.682	1.022(67%)	1.024(67%)
satzoo	0.240	0.397(60%)	0.334(72%)	0.384	0.581(66%)	0.581(66%)
satelite	0.247	0.426(58%)	0.372(66%)	0.618	0.970(64%)	0.978(63%)
sato	0.375	0.711(53%)	0.635(59%)	0.723	1.352(53%)	1.345(54%)
oksolver	0.427	0.548(78%)	0.506(84%)	0.601	1.337(45%)	1.331(45%)

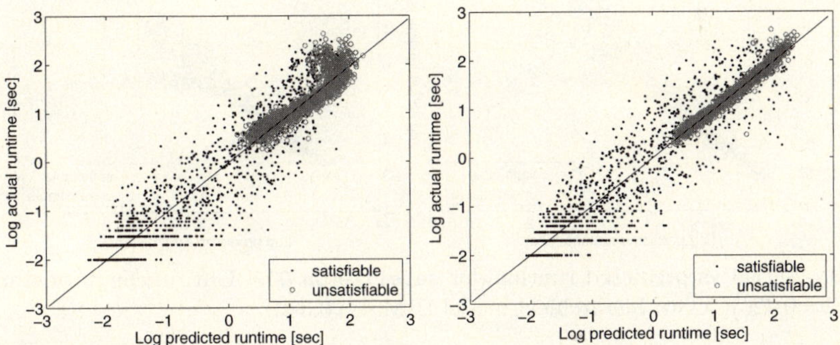

Fig. 7. Actual vs predicted runtime for satz on rand3-var. Left: unconditional model (RMSE=0.387); right: hierarchical model (RMSE=0.344).

line($y = x$) have low classification confidence. (We further discuss the relationship between classification confidence and runtime prediction accuracy at the end of this section.)

For the structured QCP instances, we observed similar runtime prediction accuracy improvements by using hierarchical models. Since the classification accuracy for QCP was higher than the classification accuracy for rand3-fix, we expected bigger improvements when using the hierarchical hardness model compared to the rand3-fix case. Our experimental results confirmed this hypothesis (Figure 9). For example, a hierarchical model for the satelite solver achieved a RMSE of 0.372, compared to 0.462 obtained from an unconditional model (whereas the oracular model yielded RMSE 0.247).

However, the runtime prediction accuracy obtained by hierarchical hardness models depends on the quality of the underlying conditional models (experts). In the case of data set SW-GCP (see Figure 10), we found that both unconditional and oracular models had fairly large prediction error (RMSE about 0.6; since

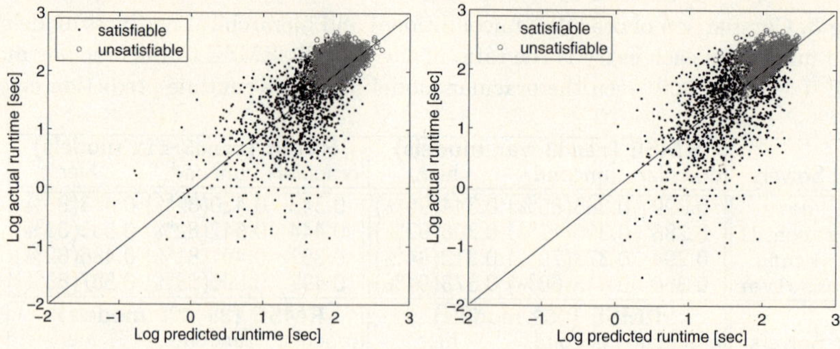

Fig. 8. Actual vs predicted runtime for `satz` on `rand3-fix`. Left: unconditional model (RMSE=0.420); right: hierarchical model (RMSE=0.413).

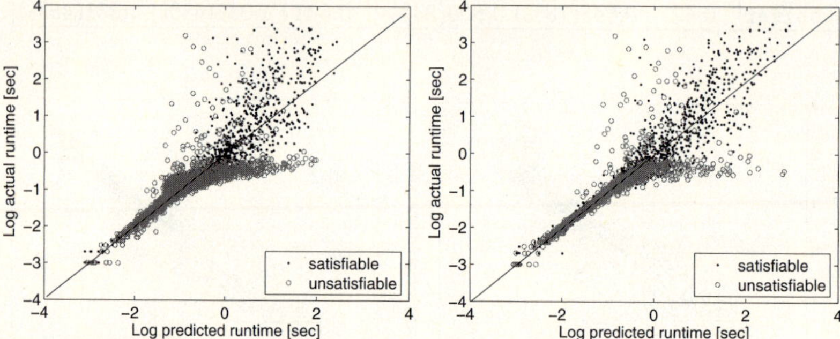

Fig. 9. Actual vs predicted runtime for `satelite` on `QCP`. Left: unconditional model (RMSE=0.426); right: hierarchical model (RMSE=0.372).

we used log runtime, this means that runtime predictions were off by about half an order of magnitude on average). As mentioned in Section 4, we believe that this is because our features are not as informative when applied to this data set as for the other three instance distributions. This is also consistent with the fact that the classification error on `SW-GCP` is much higher (26.6%, compared to 4.0% on `QCP` and 13.5% on `rand3sat-fix`).

When investigating the relationship between the classifier's confidence and regression runtime prediction accuracy, we found that higher classification confidence tends to be indicative of more accurate runtime predictions. This relationship is illustrated in Figure 11 for the `satelite` solver on the `QCP` data set: when the classifier is more confident about the satisfiability of an instance, both prediction error (Figure 11, left) and RMSE (Figure 11, right) are smaller.[1]

Though space constraints preclude a detailed discussion, we also observed that the features important for classification were similarly important for regression. For instance, only using the three features that were most important for

[1] Closer inspection of the raw data shown in Figure 11, left, revealed that a large number of the data points appear at $(0, 0)$ and $(1, 0)$. This is also reflected in the shape of the curve in the right pane of Figure 11.

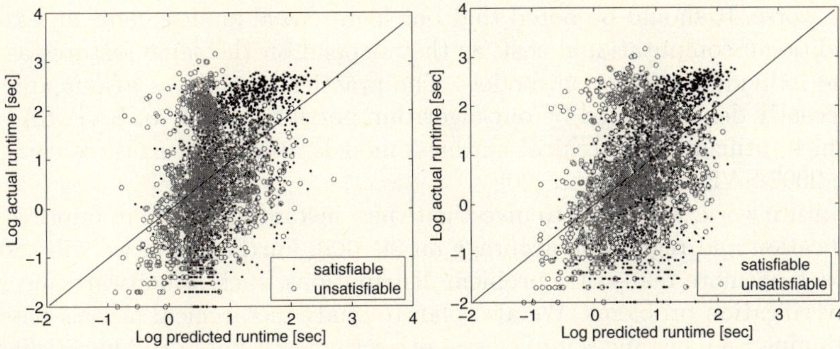

Fig. 10. Actual vs predicted runtime for `zchaff` on `SW-GCP`. Left: unconditional model (RMSE=0.993); right: hierarchical hardness model (RMSE=0.983).

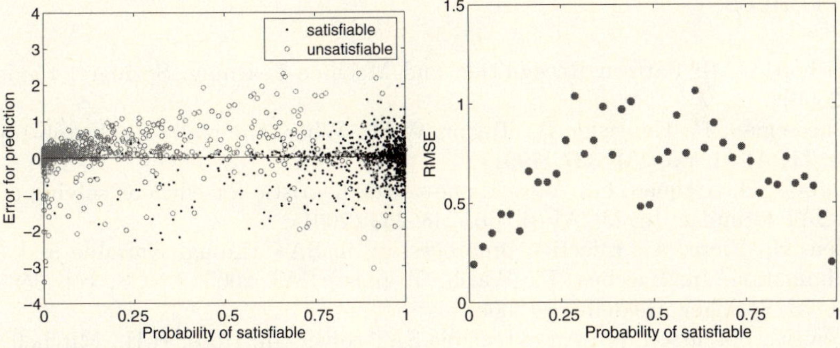

Fig. 11. Classifier output vs runtime prediction error (left); relationship between classifier output and RMSE (right). Data set: `QCP`, solver: `satelite`.

classification on `QCP` data, we achieved runtime prediction RMSE within 10% of the full model's accuracy for `satelite`.

6 Conclusions and Future Work

We have shown that there are big differences between models trained only on satisfiable and unsatisfiable instances, not only for uniform random 3-SAT (as was previously reported in [18]), but also for distributions of structured SAT instances, such as `QCP` and `SW-GCP`. Furthermore, these models have higher prediction accuracy than the respective unconditional models. A classifier can be used to distinguish between satisfiable and unsatisfiable instances with surprisingly high (though not perfect) accuracy. We have demonstrated how such a classifier can be combined with conditional hardness models into a hierarchical hardness model using a mixture-of-experts approach. In cases where we achieved high classification accuracy, the hierarchical models thus obtained always offered substantial improvements over an unconditional model. When the classifier was less accurate, our hierarchical models did not offer a substantial improvement over the unconditional model; however, hierarchical models were never significantly worse. It should be noted that our hierarchical models come at virtually no additional computational cost, as they depend on the same features as used for the individual regression models. The practical usefulness of our approach was recently demonstrated by our algorithm portfolio solver for SAT, SATzilla-07, which, utilizing hierarchical hardness models, placed 1st in three categories of the 2007 SAT competition [20].

In future work, we intend to investigate new instance features to improve both classification and regression accuracy on SW-GCP. Furthermore, we will test our approach on more real-world problem distributions, such as software and hardware verification problems. We also plan to study hierarchical models based on partitioning SAT instances into classes other than satisfiable and unsatisfiable—for example, such classes could be used to build different models for different underlying data distributions in heterogeneous data sets.

References

1. Bishop, C.M.: Pattern Recognition and Machine Learning. Springer, Heidelberg (2006)
2. Cheeseman, P., Kanefsky, B., Taylor, W.M.: Where the really hard problems are. In: IJCAI-91, pp. 331–337 (1991)
3. Dubois, O., Dequen, G.: A backbone-search heuristic for efficient solving of hard 3-SAT formulae. In: IJCAI-01, pp. 248–253 (2001)
4. Eén, N., Biere, A.: Effective preprocessing in SAT through variable and clause elimination. In: Bacchus, F., Walsh, T. (eds.) SAT 2005. LNCS, vol. 3569, pp. 61–75. Springer, Heidelberg (2005)
5. Eén, N., Sörensson, N.: An extensible SAT-solver. In: Hoos, H.H., Mitchell, D.G. (eds.) SAT 2004. LNCS, vol. 3542, pp. 502–518. Springer, Heidelberg (2005)
6. Gent, I.P., Hoos, H.H., Prosser, P., Walsh, T.: Morphing: Combining structure and randomness. In: AAAI-99, pp. 654–660 (1999)
7. Gomes, C., Selman, B., Crato, N., Kautz, H.: Heavy-tailed phenomena in satisfiability and constraint satisfaction problems. J. of Automated Reasoning 24(1), 67–100 (2000)
8. Heule, M., Maaren, H.V.: march_dl: Adding adaptive heuristics and a new branching strategy. J. on Satisfiability, Boolean Modeling and Computation 2, 47–59 (2006)
9. Hutter, F., Hamadi, Y., Hoos, H.H., Leyton-Brown, K.: Performance prediction and automated tuning of randomized and parametric algorithms. In: Benhamou, F. (ed.) CP 2006. LNCS, vol. 4204, pp. 213–228. Springer, Heidelberg (2006)
10. Joachims, T.: Making large-scale support vector machine learning practical. In: Advances in Kernel Methods: Support Vector Machines, pp. 169–184 (1998)
11. Krishnapuram, B., Carin, L., Figueiredo, M., Hartemink, A.: Sparse multinomial logistic regression: Fast algorithms and generalization bounds. IEEE Trans. on Pattern Analysis and Machine Intelligence, 957–968 (2005)
12. Kullmann, O.: Heuristics for SAT algorithms: Searching for some foundations. Technical report (September 1998)
13. Leyton-Brown, K., Nudelman, E., Andrew, G., McFadden, J., Shoham, Y.: Boosting as a metaphor for algorithm design. In: Rossi, F. (ed.) CP 2003. LNCS, vol. 2833, pp. 899–903. Springer, Heidelberg (2003)
14. Leyton-Brown, K., Nudelman, E., Andrew, G., McFadden, J., Shoham, Y.: A portfolio approach to algorithm selection. In: IJCAI-03, pp. 1542–1543 (2003)

15. Leyton-Brown, K., Nudelman, E., Shoham, Y.: Learning the empirical hardness of optimization problems: The case of combinatorial auctions. In: Van Hentenryck, P. (ed.) CP 2002. LNCS, vol. 2470, pp. 556–572. Springer, Heidelberg (2002)
16. Li, C.M., Anbulagan: Look-ahead versus look-back for satisfiability problems. In: Smolka, G. (ed.) Principles and Practice of Constraint Programming - CP97. LNCS, vol. 1330, pp. 341–355. Springer, Heidelberg (1997)
17. Murphy, K.: The Bayes Net Toolbox for Matlab. In: Computing Science and Statistics: Proc. of the Interface, vol. 33 (2001), `http://bnt.sourceforge.net/`
18. Nudelman, E., Leyton-Brown, K., Hoos, H.H., Devkar, A., Shoham, Y.: Understanding random SAT: Beyond the clauses-to-variables ratio. In: Wallace, M. (ed.) CP 2004. LNCS, vol. 3258, pp. 438–452. Springer, Heidelberg (2004)
19. Selman, B., Mitchell, D.G., Levesque, H.J.: Generating hard satisfiability problems. Artificial Intelligence 81, 17–29 (1996)
20. Xu, L., Hutter, F., Hoos, H.H., Leyton-Brown, K.: SATzilla-07: The design and analysis of an algorithm portfolio for SAT. In: CP-07 (2007)
21. Zhang, H.: SATO: an efficient propositional prover. In: Proc. of the Int'l. Conf. on Automated Deduction, pp. 272–275 (1997)
22. Zhang, L., Madigan, C.F., Moskewicz, M.W., Malik, S.: Efficient conflict driven learning in Boolean satisfiability solver. In: Proc. of the Int'l. Conf. on Computer Aided Design, pp. 279–285 (2001)

SATzilla-07: The Design and Analysis of an Algorithm Portfolio for SAT

Lin Xu, Frank Hutter, Holger H. Hoos, and Kevin Leyton-Brown

University of British Columbia, 2366 Main Mall, Vancouver BC, V6T 1Z4, Canada
{xulin730,hutter,hoos,kevinlb}@cs.ubc.ca

Abstract. It has been widely observed that there is no "dominant" SAT solver; instead, different solvers perform best on different instances. Rather than following the traditional approach of choosing the best solver for a given class of instances, we advocate making this decision online on a per-instance basis. Building on previous work, we describe a per-instance solver portfolio for SAT, SATzilla-07, which uses so-called empirical hardness models to choose among its constituent solvers. We leverage new model-building techniques such as censored sampling and hierarchical hardness models, and demonstrate the effectiveness of our techniques by building a portfolio of state-of-the-art SAT solvers and evaluating it on several widely-studied SAT data sets. Overall, we show that our portfolio significantly outperforms its constituent algorithms on every data set. Our approach has also proven itself to be effective in practice: in the 2007 SAT competition, SATzilla-07 won three gold medals, one silver, and one bronze; it is available online at http://www.cs.ubc.ca/labs/beta/Projects/SATzilla.

1 Introduction

The propositional satisfiability problem (SAT) is one of the most fundamental problems in computer science. SAT is interesting for its own sake, but also because instances of other $\mathcal{NP}$-complete problems can be encoded into SAT and solved by SAT solvers. This approach has proven effective for planning, scheduling, graph coloring and software/hardware verification problems. The conceptual simplicity of SAT facilitates algorithm development, and significant research and engineering efforts have led to sophisticated algorithms with highly-optimized implementations. By now, many such high-performance SAT solvers exist. Although there are some general patterns describing which solvers tend to be good at solving certain kinds of instances, it is still often the case that one solver is better than others at solving some problem instances from a given class, but dramatically worse on other instances. Indeed, we know that no solver can be guaranteed to dominate all others on unrestricted SAT instances [2]. Thus, practitioners with hard SAT problems to solve face a potentially difficult algorithm selection problem [26]: which algorithm(s) should be run in order to minimize some performance objective, such as expected runtime?

The most widely-adopted solution to such algorithm selection problems is to measure every candidate solver's runtime on a representative set of problem

C. Bessiere (Ed.): CP 2007, LNCS 4741, pp. 712–727, 2007.

instances, and then to use only the algorithm which offered the best (e.g., average or median) performance. We call this the "winner-take-all" approach. Its use has resulted in the neglect of many algorithms that are not competitive on average but that nevertheless offer very good performance on particular instances. The *ideal* solution to the algorithm selection problem, on the other hand, would be to consult an oracle that tells us the amount of time that each algorithm would take to solve a given problem instance, and then to select the algorithm with the best performance.

Unfortunately, computationally cheap, perfect oracles of this nature are not available for SAT or any other $\mathcal{NP}$-complete problem, and we cannot precisely determine an arbitrary algorithm's runtime on an arbitrary instance without actually running it. Nevertheless, our approach to algorithm selection in this paper is based on the idea of building approximate runtime predictors, which can be seen as heuristic approximations to perfect oracles. Specifically, we use machine learning techniques to build an *empirical hardness model*, a computationally inexpensive way of predicting an algorithm's runtime on a given problem instance based on features of the instance and the algorithm's past performance [24,19]. This approach has previously yielded effective algorithm portfolios for the winner determination problem (WDP) in combinatorial auctions [18,17]; however, there exist relatively few state-of-the-art solvers for WDP.

To show that algorithm portfolios based on empirical hardness models can also effectively combine larger sets of highly-optimized algorithms, we consider the satisfiability problem in this work. Specifically, we describe and analyze `SATzilla`, a portfolio-based SAT solver that utilizes empirical hardness models for per-instance algorithm selection. `SATzilla` goes back to 2003, when its original version was first submitted to the SAT competition. In that competition, `SATzilla` placed 2nd in the random instances category, 2nd in the handmade instances (satisfiable only) category, and 3rd in the handmade instances category. Here, we describe a substantially improved version of `SATzilla`, which uses new techniques, such as censored sampling and hierarchical hardness models, as well as an updated set of solvers. This new solver, dubbed `SATzilla-07`, was entered into the 2007 SAT competition and placed 1st in the handmade, handmade (unsatisfiable only) and random categories, 2nd in the handmade (satisfiable only) category, and 3rd in the random (unsatisfiable only) category. Here, we give a detailed description and performance analysis for `SATzilla-07`, something which was never published for the original of `SATzilla`.

There exists a fair amount of work related to ours. Lobjois et al. studied the problem of selecting between branch-and-bound algorithms [20] based on an estimate of search tree size due to Knuth. Gebruers et al. employed case-based reasoning to select a solution strategy for instances of a CP problem [8]. One problem with such classification approaches [12] is that they use a misleading error metric, penalizing misclassifications equally regardless of their cost. For the algorithm selection problem, however, using a sub-optimal algorithm is acceptable if the difference between its runtime and that of the best algorithm is small. (Our `SATzilla` approach can be considered to be a classifier with an error metric that depends on the difference in runtime between algorithms.)

Further related work includes "online" approaches that switch between algorithms during runtime. Gomes et al. built a portfolio of stochastic algorithms for quasi-group completion and logistics scheduling problems [10]; rather than choosing a single algorithm, their approach achieved performance improvements by running multiple algorithms. Lagoudakis & Littman employed reinforcement learning to solve an algorithm selection problem at each decision point of a DPLL solver for SAT in order to select a branching rule [16]. Low-knowledge algorithm control by Carchrae & Beck employed a portfolio of anytime algorithms, prioritizing each algorithm according to its performance so far [3]. Gagliolo & Schmidhuber learned dynamic algorithm portfolios that also support running several algorithms at once [7], where an algorithm's priority depends on its predicted runtime conditioned on the fact that it has not yet found a solution.

2 Building Portfolios with Empirical Hardness Models

The general methodology for building an algorithm portfolio we use in this work follows that of Leyton-Brown et al. [18] in its broad strokes, but we have made significant extensions here. Portfolio construction happens offline, as part of algorithm development, and comprises the following steps:

1. Identify a target distribution of problem instances.
2. Select a set of candidate solvers that have relatively uncorrelated runtimes on this distribution.
3. Use domain knowledge to identify features that characterize problem instances.
4. On a training set of problem instances, compute these features and run each algorithm to determine running times.
5. Optionally, identify one or more solvers to use for pre-solving instances, by examining the algorithms' runtimes. These pre-solvers will later be run for a short amount of time before features are computed (step 9 below), in order to ensure good performance on very easy instances.
6. Using a validation data set, determine which solver achieves the best average runtime (i.e., is the winner-take-all choice) on instances that would not have been solved by the pre-solvers.
7. Construct an empirical hardness model for each algorithm.
8. Choose the best subset of solvers to use in the final portfolio. We formalise and automatically solve this as a simple subset selection problem: from all given solvers, select a subset for which the respective portfolio (which uses the empirical hardness models learned in the previous step) achieves the lowest total runtime on the validation set.

Then, online, to solve a given instance, the following steps are performed:

9. Optionally, run each pre-solver for up to some fixed cutoff time.
10. Compute feature values. If feature computation cannot be finished for some reason (error, timeout), select the solver identified in step 6 above.

11. Otherwise, predict each algorithm's runtime using the empirical hardness models from step 7 above.
12. Run the algorithm predicted to be fastest. If one solver fails to finish its run (e.g., it crashes), run the algorithm predicted to be next-fastest.

In this work, we apply this general strategy to SAT and consider two different settings. In the first, discussed in Section 4, we investigate a problem distribution based on SAT-encoded quasi-group completion instances, which we obtained from an existing generator. On this fairly homogeneous distribution, we attempt to minimize average runtime. In our second setting, discussed in Section 5, we study several different distributions defined by sets of representative instances: the different categories of the SAT competition. These distributions are all highly heterogeneous. Our goal here is to maximize the SAT competition's scoring function: $Score(P, S_i) = 1000 \cdot SF(P, S_i)/\Sigma_j SF(P, S_j)$, where the speed factor $SF(P, S) = timeLimit(P)/(1 + timeUsed(P, S))$ reflects the fraction of the maximum time allowed for an instance S that was used by solver P.[1] Notice that when minimizing average runtime it does not much matter which solver is chosen for an easy instance on which all solvers are relatively fast, as the overall average will remain essentially unchanged. Given the competition's scoring function, however, we must *always* strive to choose the fastest algorithm.

3 Constructing Empirical Hardness Models

The success of an algorithm portfolio built using the methodology above depends on our ability to learn empirical hardness models that can accurately predict a solver's runtime for a given instance using efficiently computable features. In experiments presented in this paper, we use the same ridge regression method (linear in a set of quadratic basis functions) that has previously proven to be very successful in predicting runtime on uniform random k-SAT and on ombinatorial auction winner determination [24,19]. Other learning techniques (e.g., lasso regression, SVM regression, and Gaussian process regression) are also possible; it should be noted that our portfolio methodology is independent of the method used for estimating an algorithm's runtime.

Feature selection and ridge regression. To predict the runtime of an algorithm $\mathcal{A}$ on an instance distribution $\mathcal{D}$, we run algorithm $\mathcal{A}$ on n instances drawn from $\mathcal{D}$ and compute for each instance i a set of features $\boldsymbol{x}_i = [x_{i,1}, \ldots, x_{i,m}]$. We then fit a function $f(\boldsymbol{x})$ that, given the features $\boldsymbol{x}_i$ of instance i, yields a prediction, y_i, of $\mathcal{A}$'s runtime on i. Unfortunately, the performance of learning algorithms can suffer when some features are uninformative or highly correlated with other features, and in practice both of these problems tend to arise. Therefore, we first reduce the set of features by performing feature selection, in our case forward selection. Next, we perform a quadratic basis function expansion of our feature set to obtain additional pairwise product features $x_{i,j} \cdot x_{i,k}$ for $j = 1 \ldots m$ and $k = j + 1 \ldots m$. Finally, we perform another pass of forward selection on this

[1] Please see `http://www.satcompetition.org/2007/rules07.html` for details.

extended set to determine our final set of basis functions, such that for instance i we obtain an expanded feature vector $\boldsymbol{\phi}_i = \boldsymbol{\phi}(\boldsymbol{x}_i) = [\phi_1(\boldsymbol{x}_i), \ldots, \phi_d(\boldsymbol{x}_i)]$, where d is the number of basis functions. We then use ridge regression to fit the free parameters $\boldsymbol{w}$ of the function $f_{\boldsymbol{w}}(\boldsymbol{x})$ as follows. Let $\tilde{\boldsymbol{y}}$ be a vector with $\tilde{y}_i = \log y_i$. Let $\boldsymbol{\Phi}$ be an $n \times d$ matrix containing the vectors $\boldsymbol{\phi}_i$ for each instance in the training set, and let I be the identity matrix. Finally, let δ be a (small) regularization constant (to penalize large coefficients $\boldsymbol{w}$ and thereby increase numerical stability). Then, we compute $\boldsymbol{w} = (\delta I + \boldsymbol{\Phi}^\top \boldsymbol{\Phi})^{-1} \boldsymbol{\Phi}^\top \tilde{\boldsymbol{y}}$. Given a previously unseen instance j, a log runtime prediction is obtained by computing the instance features $\boldsymbol{x}_j$ and evaluating $f_{\boldsymbol{w}}(\boldsymbol{x}_j) = \boldsymbol{w}^\top \boldsymbol{\phi}(\boldsymbol{x}_j)$.

Accounting for Censored Data. As is common with heuristic algorithms for solving $\mathcal{NP}$-complete problems, SAT algorithms tend to solve some instances very quickly, while taking an extremely long amount of time to solve other instances. Indeed, this property of SAT solvers is precisely our motivation for building an algorithm portfolio. However, this property has a downside: runtime data can be very costly to gather, as individual runs can literally take weeks to complete, even when other runs on instances of the same size take only milliseconds. The common solution to this problem is to "censor" some runs by terminating them after a fixed cutoff time.

The bias introduced by this censorship can be dealt with in three ways. (We evaluate these three techniques experimentally in Section 4; here we discuss them conceptually.) First, censored data points can be discarded. Since the role of empirical hardness models in an algorithm portfolio can be seen as warning us away from instance-solver pairs that will be especially costly, this approach is highly unsatisfactory—the hardness models cannot warn us about parts of the instance space that they have never seen.

Second, we can pretend that all censored data points were solved at exactly the cutoff time. This approach is better, as it does record hard cases and recognizes them as being hard. (We have used this approach in past work.) However, it still introduces bias into hardness models by systematically underestimating the hardness of censored instances.

The third approach is to build models that do not disregard censored data points, but do not pretend that the respective runs terminated successfully at the cutoff time either. This approach has been extensively studied in the "survival analysis" literature in statistics, which originated in actuarial questions such as estimating a person's lifespan given mortality data and the ages and features of other people still alive. (Observe that this problem is the same as ours, except that for us data points are always censored at the same value. This subtlety turns out not to matter.) Gagliolo et al. showed that censored sampling can have substantial impact on the performance of restart strategies for solving SAT [21]. Different from their solution, we chose the simple, yet effective method by Schmee & Hahn [27] to deal with censored samples. In brief, this method consists of repeating the following steps until convergence:

1. Estimate the runtime of censored instances using the hardness model, conditioning on the fact that each runtime equals or exceeds the cutoff time.

2. Train a new hardness model using true runtimes for the uncensored instances and the predictions generated in the previous step for the censored instances.

Using Hierarchical Hardness Models. This section Summarizes Ideas from a Companion paper [29]. Previous research on empirical hardness models for SAT has shown that we can achieve better prediction accuracy and simpler models than with models trained on mixed instance sets ("unconditional models"; M_{uncond}) if we restrict ourselves to only satisfiable or unsatisfiable instances [24]. Of course, in practice we cannot divide instances in this way; otherwise we would not need to run a SAT solver in the first place. The idea of a hierarchical hardness model is to first predict an instance's satisfiability using a classification algorithm, and then to predict its hardness conditioned on the classifier's prediction. We use the Sparse Multinomial Logistic Regression (SMLR) classifier [14], but any classification algorithm that returns the probability of belonging to each class could be used. We train empirical hardness models (M_{sat}, M_{unsat}) using quadratic basis-function regression for both satisfiable and unsatisfiable training instances. Then we train a classifier to predict the probability that an instance is satisfiable. Finally, we build hierarchical hardness models using a mixture-of-experts approach with clamped experts: M_{sat} and M_{unsat}. We evaluate both models on test data, and weight each model's prediction by the predicted usefulness of that model. (Further details can be found in the companion paper [29].)

4 Evaluating SATzilla-07 on the QCP Data Set

In the following, we will describe the design and empirical analysis of an algorithm portfolio for solving relatively homogeneous QCP instances. The primary motivation for this part of our work was to demonstrate how our approach works in a relatively simple, yet meaningful, application scenario. At the same time, we did not want to make certain aspects of this application, such as solver selection, overly specific to the QCP instance distribution. The equally important goal of a full-scale performance assessment is addressed in Section 5, where we apply SATzilla-07 to a broad range of instances from past SAT competitions.

1. Selecting Instances. In the quasi-group completion problem (QCP), the objective is to determine whether the unspecified entries of a partial Latin square can be filled to obtain a complete Latin square. QCP instances are widely used in the SAT community to evaluate the performance of SAT solvers. We generated 23 000 QCP instances around the solubility phase transition, using the parameters given by Gomes & Selman [9]. Specifically, the order n was drawn uniformly from the interval $[26, 43]$, and the number of holes H (open entries in the Latin square) was drawn uniformly from $[1.75, 2.3] \times n^{1.55}$. We then converted the respective QCP instances to SAT CNF format. On average, the SAT instances in the resulting QCP data set have 3 784 variables and 37 755 clauses, but there is significant variability across the set. As expected, there were almost equal numbers of satisfiable and unsatisfiable instances (50.3% *vs* 49.7%).

2. Selecting Candidate Solvers. In order to build a strong algorithm portfolio, it is necessary to choose solvers whose runtimes are relatively uncorrelated. We have tended to find that solvers designed for different problem domains are less correlated than solvers designed for the same domain. On `QCP`, there is very little runtime correlation (Pearson's $r = -0.055$) between `Eureka` [23] (`INDUSTRIAL`) and `OKsolver` [15] (`RANDOM`), which makes these two solvers perfect candidates for `SATzilla-07`. On the other hand, the runtime correlation between `Eureka` (`INDUSTRIAL`) and `Zchaff_Rand` [22] (`INDUSTRIAL`) is much higher ($r = 0.81$), though still low enough to be useful.

These solvers were chosen because they are known to perform well on various types of SAT instances (as can be seen, e.g., from past SAT competition results). It should be noted, however, that on `QCP`, they are dominated by other solvers, such as `Satzoo` [5]; nevertheless, as previously explained, our goal in this evaluation was not to construct a highly `QCP`-specific portfolio, but to demonstrate and validate our general approach.

3. Choosing Features. Instance features are very important for building accurate hardness models. Good features should correlate well with (solver-specific) instance hardness, and they should be cheap to compute, since feature computation time counts as part of `SATzilla-07`'s runtime.

Nudelman et al. [24] described 84 features for SAT instances. These features can be classified into nine categories: problem size, variable-clause graph, variable graph, clause graph, balance features, proximity to Horn formulae, LP-based, DPLL probing, and local search probing. For the `QCP` data set, we ignored all LP-based features, because they were too expensive to compute. After eliminating features that were constant across our instance set, we ended up with 70 raw features. The computation time for the local search and DPLL probing features was limited to 4 CPU seconds each.

4. Computing Features and Runtimes. All our experiments were performed using a computer cluster consisting of 55 machines with dual Intel Xeon 3.2GHz CPUs, 2MB cache and 2GB RAM, running Suse Linux 9.1. All runs of any solver that exceeded 1 CPU hour were aborted (censored). The time for computing all features of a given instance was 13 CPU seconds on average and never exceeded 60 CPU seconds.

We randomly split our data set into training, validation and testing sets at a ratio of 70:15:15. All parameter tuning was performed on the validation set, and the test set was used only to generate the final results reported here. Although test and validation sets of 15% might seem small, we note that each of them contained 3 450 instances.

5. Identifying Pre-solvers. Since in this experiment, our goal was simply to minimize expected runtime, a pre-solving step was unnecessary.

6. Identifying the Winner-take-all Algorithm. We computed average runtimes for all solvers on the training data set, using the cutoff time of 3600 CPU seconds for unsuccesful runs and discarding those instances that were not solved

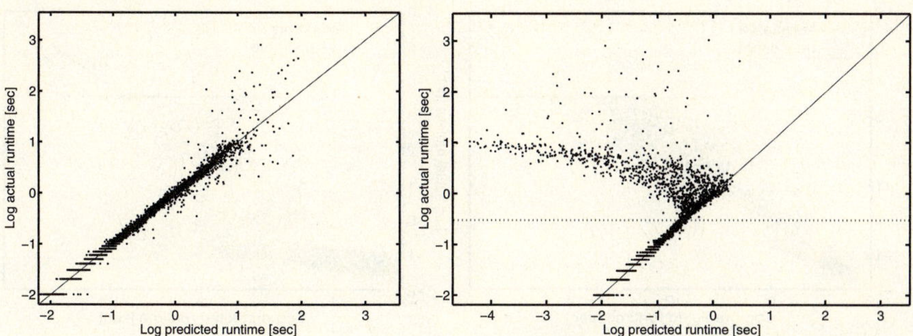

Fig. 1. Actual vs predicted runtime for OKsolver on selected (easy) instances from QCP with cutoff time $10^{-0.5}$. Left: trained with complete data; right: censored data points are discarded, RMSE for censored data: 1.713.

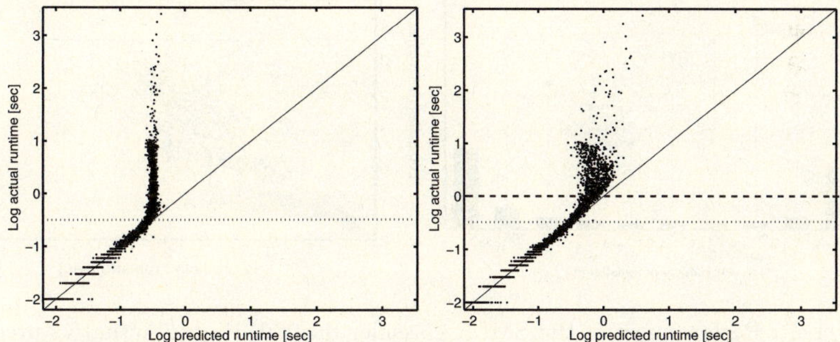

Fig. 2. Actual vs predicted runtime for OKsolver on selected (easy) instances from QCP with cutoff time $10^{-0.5}$. Left: set runtime for censored data points as cutoff time, RMSE for censored data: 0.883; right: using the method of Schmee & Hahn [27], RMSE for censored data: 0.608.

by any of the solvers (the latter applies to 5.2% of the instances from the QCP instance set). The average runtimes were 546 CPU seconds for OKsolver, 566 CPU seconds for Eureka, and 613 CPU seconds for Zchaff_Rand; thus, OKsolver was identified as the winner-take-all algorithm.

7. Learning Empirical Hardness Models. We learned empirical hardness models as described in Section 3. For each solver, we used forward selection to eliminate problematic features and kept the model with the smallest validation error. This lead to empirical hardness models with 30, 30 and 27 features for Eureka, OKsolver and Zchaff_Rand, respectively. When evaluating these models, we specifically investigated the effectiveness of our techniques for censored sampling and hierarchical models.

Censored Sampling. We gathered OKsolver runtimes on a set of all-satisfiable QCP instances of small order. The instances were chosen such that we could determine true runtimes in all cases; we then artificially censored our runtime

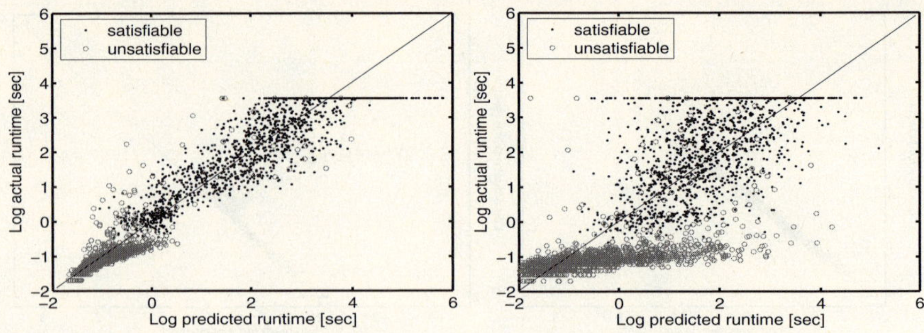

Fig. 3. Actual vs predicted runtime plots for `Eureka` on `QCP`. Left: model using a model selection oracle, RMSE=0.630; right: unconditional model, RMSE=1.111.

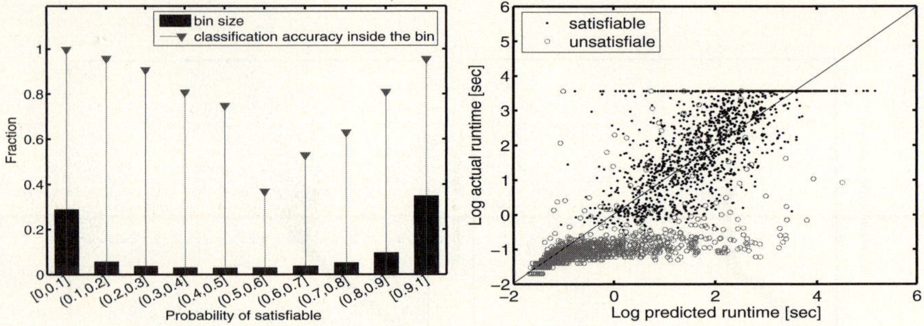

Fig. 4. Left: Performance of the SMLR classifier on `QCP`. Right: Actual vs predicted runtime for `Eureka` on `QCP` using a hierarchical hardness model, RMSE=0.938.

data, using a cutoff time of $10^{-0.5}$ CPU seconds, and compared the various methods for dealing with censored data surveyed in Section 3 on the resulting data. Fig. 1 (left) shows the runtime predictions achieved by the hardness model trained on ideal, uncensored data (RMSE=0.146). In contrast, Fig. 1 (right) shows that throwing away censored data points leads to very noisy runtime prediction for test instances whose true runtimes are higher than the cutoff time (RMSE for censored data: 1.713). Fig. 2 (left) shows the performance of a model trained on runtime data in which all censored points were labelled as having completed at exactly the cutoff time (RMSE for censored data: 0.883). Finally, Fig. 2 (right) shows that a hardness model trained using the method of Schmee & Hahn [27] yields the best prediction accuracy (RMSE for censored data: 0.608). Furthermore, we see good runtime predictions even for instances where the solver's runtime is up to half an order of magnitude (a factor of three) greater than the cutoff time. When runtimes get much bigger than this, the prediction becomes much noisier, albeit still better than we observed earlier. (We obtained similar results for the two other solvers, `Eureka` and `Zchaff_Rand`.

Hierarchical Hardness Models. Fig. 3 compares the runtime predictions made by a model with access to a model selection oracle ($M_{oracular}$), and an unconditional

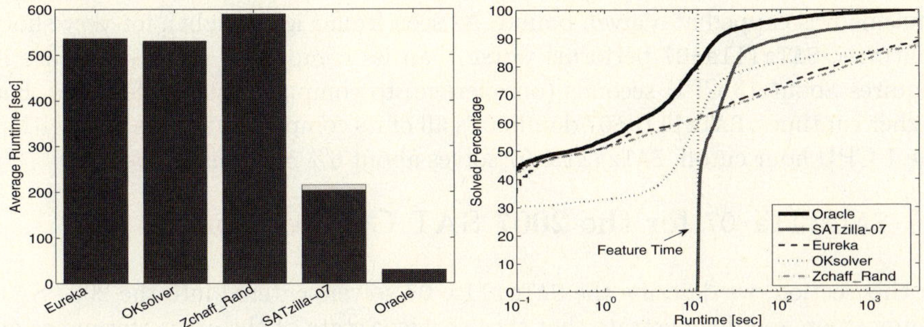

Fig. 5. Left: Average runtime for different solvers on QCP; the hollow box for SATzilla-07 represents the time used for computing instance features (13 CPU sec on average). Right: Empirical cumulative distribution functions (CDFs) for the same runtime data.

model (M_{uncond}) for the Eureka solver on the QCP instance set. $M_{oracular}$ defines an upper bound on performance with the conditional model. Overall, M_{uncond} tends to make considerably less accurate predictions (RMSE= 1.111) than $M_{oracular}$ (RMSE=0.630). We report the performance of the classifier and hierarchical hardness models in Fig. 4. The overall classification accuracy is 89%; as shown in Fig. 4 (left), the classifier is nearly certain, and usually correct, about the satisfiability of most instances. Although our hierarchical hardness model did not achieve the same runtime prediction accuracy as $M_{oracular}$, its performance is 36% closer to this ideal than M_{uncond} in terms of RMSE. (Note that hierarchical models are not guaranteed to achieve better performance than unconditional models, since the use of the wrong conditional model on certain instances can cause large prediction errors.) Similar results are obtained for the two other solvers, OKsolver and Zchaff_Rand.

8. Solver Subset Selection. Using our automated subset selection procedure, we determined that all three solvers performed strongly enough on QCP that dropping any of them would lead to reduced portfolio performance.

9. Performance Analysis. We compare the average runtime of SATzilla-07, an algorithm selection scheme based on a perfect oracle and all of SATzilla-07's component solvers in Fig. 5 (left). On the test data set, all component solvers have runtimes of around 600 CPU seconds on average; OKsolver, the "winner-take-all" choice, has an average runtime of 543 CPU seconds. SATzilla-07's average runtime, 205 CPU seconds, is much lower. Although SATzilla-07's performance is much better than any of its components, it still does significantly worse than the oracle. In particular, it chooses the same solver as the oracle only for 62% of the instances. However, in most of these cases, the runtimes of the solvers picked by SATzilla-07 and the oracle are very similar, and only for 12% of the QCP instances, the solver chosen by SATzilla-07 is more than 10 CPU seconds slower.

A more nuanced view of the algorithms' empirical performance is afforded by the cumulative distribution functions (CDFs) of their runtimes over the given instance set; these show the fraction of instances that would have been solved if runtime was capped at a given bound. As seen from Fig. 5 (right), for very short runtimes, SATzilla-07 performs worse than its component solvers, because it requires about 13 CPU seconds (on average) to compute instance features. For higher runtimes, SATzilla-07 dominates all of its component solvers, and within the 1 CPU hour cutoff, SATzilla-07 solves about 6% more instances.

5 SATzilla-07 for the 2007 SAT Competition

In this section, we describe the SATzilla-07 solvers entered into the 2007 SAT competition and demonstrate that these achieve state-of-the-art performance on a variety of real-world instance collections from past SAT competitions. The purpose of the SAT competitions is to track the state of the art in SAT solving, to assess and promote new solvers, and to identify new challenging benchmarks. In 2007, more than 30 solvers entered the SAT competition. Solvers were scored taking into account both speed and robustness. There were three main categories of instances, RANDOM, HANDMADE (or CRAFTED), and INDUSTRIAL.

We submitted three different versions of SATzilla-07 to the 2007 SAT competition. Two versions specifically targeted the RANDOM and HANDMADE categories.[2] In order to study an even more heterogeneous instance distribution, a third version of SATzilla-07 attempted to perform well in all three categories of the competition; we call this meta-category BIG-MIX.

Following our general procedure for portfolio construction (see Section 2), the three versions of SATzilla-07 were obtained as follows.

1. Selecting Instances. In order to train empirical hardness models for any of the above scenarios, we required instances that would be similar to those used in the real competition. For this purpose we used instances from the respective categories in all previous SAT competitions, as well as in the 2006 SAT Race (which only featured industrial instances). Instances that were repeated in previous competitions were also repeated in our data sets. Overall, there are 4 811 instances (all of them used in BIG-MIX), 2 300 instances in category RANDOM and 1 490 in category HANDMADE. About 75% of these instances can be solved by at least one solver within 1 800 CPU seconds on our reference machine.

2. Selecting Solvers. We considered a wide variety of solvers from previous SAT competitions and the 2006 SAT Race for inclusion in our portfolio. We manually analyzed the results of these competitions, selecting all algorithms that yielded the best performance on some subset of instances. Since our focus was on both satisfiable and unsatisfiable instances, we did not choose any incomplete algorithms (with the exception of SAPS as a pre-solver). In the end we selected seven high-performance solvers as candidates for SATzilla-07: Eureka [23], Zchaff_Rand [22], Kcnfs2006 [4], Minisat2.0 [6], March_dl2004 [11], Vallst [28], and Rsat [25]. Since preprocessing has proven to be an important element for some algorithms in previous SAT competitions, we considered seven additional solvers (labeled "+"

[2] We built a version of SATzilla-07 for the INDUSTRIAL category after the submission deadline and found its performance to be qualitatively similar to the results we present here: on average, it is twice as fast as the best single solver, Eureka.

in the following) that first run the Hyper preprocessor [1], followed by one of the above algorithms on the preprocessed instance. This doubled the number of our component solvers to 14.

3. Choosing features. In order to limit the additional cost for computing features, we limited the total feature computation time per instance to 60 CPU seconds. Again, we used the features of Nudelman et al. [24], but excluded a number of computationally expensive features, such as clause graph and LP-based features. The computation time for each of the local search and DPLL probing features was limited to 1 CPU second. The number of raw features used in SATzilla-07 is 48.

4. Computing features and runtimes. We collected feature and runtime data using the same environment and process as for the QCP data set, but because of time constraints and the large number of solvers, we reduced the cutoff time to 1 800 CPU seconds.

5. Identifying pre-solvers. Since the scoring function used in the 2007 SAT competition rewards quick algorithm runs, we cannot afford the feature computation for very easy instances (for which runtimes greater than one second are already too large). Thus, we have to solve easy instances before even computing any features. Good algorithms for pre-solving solve a large proportion of instances quickly; based on an examination of the training runtime data we chose March_dl2004 and the local search algorithm SAPS (UBCSAT implementation with the best fixed parameter configuration identified by Hutter et al. [13]) as pre-solvers. Within 5 CPU seconds on our reference machine, March_dl2004 solved 32%, 30.5%, and 29.9% of the instances in our RANDOM, HANDMADE and BIG-MIX data sets, respectively. For the remaining instances, we let SAPS run for 2 CPU seconds, because we found its runtime to be almost completely uncorrelated with March_dl2004 ($r = -0.014$ for the 398 remaining instances solved by both solvers). SAPS solved 12.0%, 6.9%, and 3.6% of the remaining RANDOM, HANDMADE and BIG-MIX instances, respectively.

6. Identifying winner-takes-all algorithm. Each solver's performance is reported in Table 1; as can be seen from this data, the winner-take-all solvers for BIG-MIX, RANDOM and HANDMADE happened always to be March_dl2004.

7. Learning empirical hardness models. We learned empirical hardness models as described in Section 3, using the Schmee & Hahn [27] procedure for dealing with censored data as well as hierarchical empirical hardness models [29].

8. Solver subset selection. Based on the results of automatic exhaustive subset search as outlined in Section 2, we obtained portfolios comprising the following solvers for our three data sets:

- BIG-MIX: Eureka, kcnfs2006, March_dl2004, Rsat;
- RANDOM: March_dl2004, kcnfs2006, Minisat2.0+;
- HANDMADE: March_dl2004, Vallst, March_dl2004+, Minisat2.0+, Zchaff_Rand+

Table 1. Percentage of instances solved by each algorithm and average runtime over these instances. "+" means with preprocessing; preprocessing is not carried out for industrial instances as it would often time out.

Solvers	BIG-MIX Avg. Time	BIG-MIX Solved [%]	RANDOM Avg. Time	RANDOM Solved [%]	HANDMADE Avg. Time	HANDMADE Solved [%]
Eureka	319	42	310	28	335	42
Kcnfs2006	287	37	257	56	428	26
March_dl2004	200	52	200	57	226	55
Minisat2.0	328	52	302	44	361	53
Rsat	318	52	318	45	333	52
Vallst	334	41	369	30	220	47
Zchaff_Rand	295	38	241	25	258	40
Eureka+	No preprocessing carried out for industrial instances		320	29	352	43
Kcnfs2006+			251	56	403	27
March_dl2004+			200	57	220	54
Minisat2.0+			313	44	355	53
Rsat+			310	44	365	52
Vallst+			366	30	191	48
Zchaff_Rand+			272	26	233	41

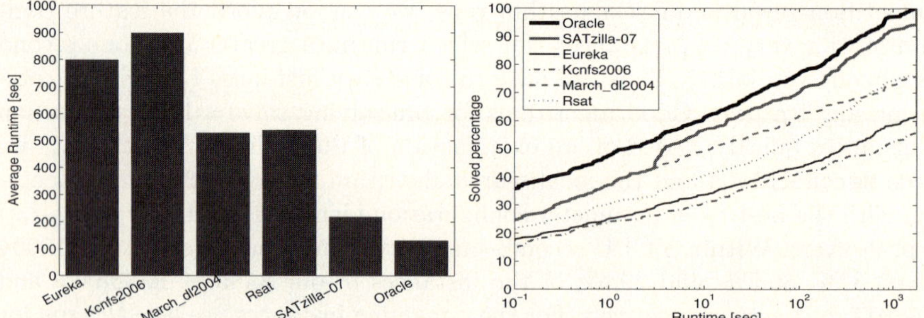

Fig. 6. Left: Average runtime, right: runtime CDF for different solvers on BIG-MIX; the average feature computation time was 6 CPU seconds

9. Performance analysis. For all three data sets we obtained excellent results: SATzilla-07 always outperformed all its constituent solvers in terms of average runtime and instances solved at any given time. The SAT/UNSAT classifierwas surprisingly effective in predicting satisfiability of RANDOM instances, where it reached a classification accuracy of 93%. For HANDMADE and BIG-MIX, the classification accuracy was still at a respectable 78% and 83% (i.e., substantially better than random guessing).

For BIG-MIX, the frequencies with which each solver was selected by a perfect oracle and SATzilla-07 were found to be similar. However, this does not mean that our hardness models made perfect predictions. Only for 27% of the instances, SATzilla-07 picked exactly the same solver as the oracle, but it selected a "good solver" (no more than 10 CPU seconds slower) for 66% of the instances. This indicates that many of the mistakes made by our models occur in situations where it does not matter much, because the selected and the best algorithms have very similar runtimes. Although the runtime predictions were not perfect, SATzilla-07 achieved very good performance (see Fig. 6). Its average runtime

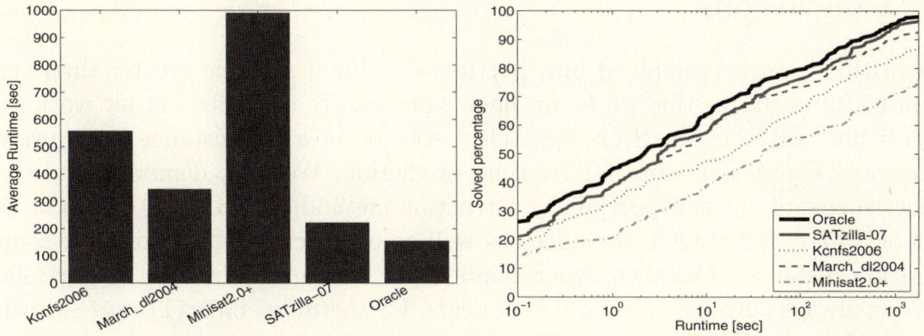

Fig. 7. Left: Average runtime, right: runtime CDF for different solvers on RANDOM; the average feature computation time was 3 CPU seconds

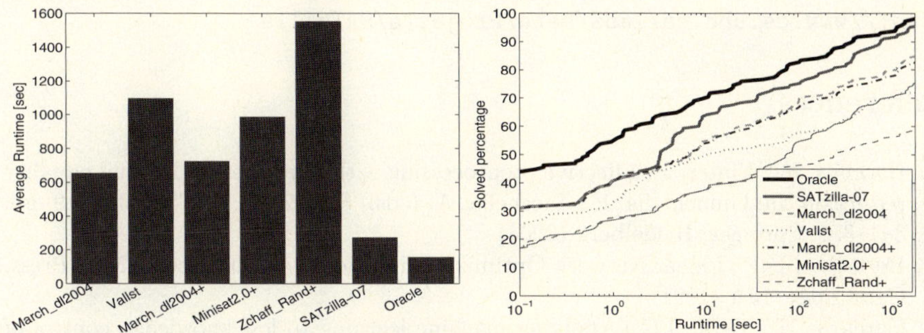

Fig. 8. Left: Average runtime, right: runtime CDF for different solvers on HANDMADE; the average feature computation time was 3 CPU seconds

(272 CPU seconds) was half that of the best single solver, March_dl2004 (530 CPU seconds), and it solved 17% more instances than any single solver within the given time limit.

For data set RANDOM, Fig. 7 (left) shows that SATzilla-07 performed better than the best solver, March_dl2004, with an average runtime that was 36% lower. However, this difference is not as large as for the QCP and BIG-MIX data sets, which is not surprising since even the oracle cannot improve much upon March_dl2004 in the RANDOM case. The runtime CDF plot (Fig. 7, right) shows that the performance of both, SATzilla-07 and March_dl2004, was close to that of the oracle, but SATzilla-07 dominated March_dl2004; in particular, for the same overall cutoff time, SATzilla-07 solved 5% more instances.

The performance results for HANDMADE were even better. Using five component solvers, SATzilla-07 was more than twice as fast on average than the best single solver (see Fig. 8, left). TThe CDF plot in Fig. 8 (right) shows that SATzilla-07 dominated all its components and solved 11% more instances than the best single solver; overall, its performance was found to be very close to that of the oracle.

6 Conclusions

Algorithms can be combined into portfolios to build a whole greater than the sum of its parts. In this work, we have significantly extended earlier work on algorithm portfolios for SAT that select solvers on a per-instance basis using empirical hardness models for runtime prediction. We have demonstrated the effectiveness of our new portfolio construction method, `SATzilla-07`, on a large set of SAT-encoded QCP instances as well as on three large sets of SAT competition instances. Our own experiments show that our `SATzilla-07` portfolio solvers always outperform their components. Furthermore, `SATzilla-07`'s excellent performance in the recent 2007 SAT competition demonstrates the practical effectiveness of our portfolio approach. `SATzilla` is an open project. We believe that with more solvers and training data added, `SATzilla`'s performance will continue to improve. `SATzilla-07` is available online at `http://www.cs.ubc.ca/labs/beta/Projects/SATzilla`.

References

1. Bacchus, F., Winter, J.: Effective preprocessing with hyper-resolution and equality reduction. In: Giunchiglia, E., Tacchella, A. (eds.) SAT 2003. LNCS, vol. 2919, pp. 341–355. Springer, Heidelberg (2004)
2. Bertsekas, D.P.: Linear Network Optimization, Algorithms and Codes. MIT Press, Cambridge, MA (1991)
3. Carchrae, T., Beck, J.C.: Applying machine learning to low-knowledge control of optimization algorithms. Computational Intelligence 21(4), 372–387 (2005)
4. Dubois, O., Dequen, G.: A backbone-search heuristic for efficient solving of hard 3-SAT formulae. In: IJCAI-01, pp. 248–253 (2001)
5. Eén, N., Sörensson, N.: An extensible SAT solver. In: Giunchiglia, E., Tacchella, A. (eds.) SAT 2003. LNCS, vol. 2919, pp. 502–518. Springer, Heidelberg (2004)
6. Eén, N., Sörensson, N.: Minisat v2.0 (beta). Solver description, SAT Race (2006)
7. Gagliolo, M., Schmidhuber, J.: Learning dynamic algorithm portfolios. Annals of Mathematics and Artificial Intelligence 47(3-4), 295–328 (2007)
8. Gebruers, C., Hnich, B., Bridge, D., Freuder, E.: Using CBR to select solution strategies in constraint programming. In: Muñoz-Ávila, H., Ricci, F. (eds.) ICCBR 2005. LNCS (LNAI), vol. 3620, pp. 222–236. Springer, Heidelberg (2005)
9. Gomes, C.P., Selman, B.: Problem structure in the presence of perturbations. In: AAAI-97, pp. 221–226 (1997)
10. Gomes, C.P., Selman, B.: Algorithm portfolios. Artificial Intelligence 126(1-2), 43–62 (2001)
11. Heule, M., Maaren, H.V.: march_dl: Adding adaptive heuristics and a new branching strategy. Journal on Satisfiability, Boolean Modeling and Computation 2, 47–59 (2006)
12. Horvitz, E., Ruan, Y., Gomes, C.P., Kautz, H., Selman, B., Chickering, D.M.: A Bayesian approach to tackling hard computational problems. In: Proc. of UAI-01, pp. 235–244 (2001)
13. Hutter, F., Hamadi, Y., Hoos, H.H., Leyton-Brown, K.: Performance prediction and automated tuning of randomized and parametric algorithms. In: Benhamou, F. (ed.) CP 2006. LNCS, vol. 4204, pp. 213–228. Springer, Heidelberg (2006)

14. Krishnapuram, B., Carin, L., Figueiredo, M., Hartemink, A.: Sparse multinomial logistic regression: Fast algorithms and generalization bounds. IEEE Transactions on Pattern Analysis and Machine Intelligence, 957–968 (2005)
15. Kullmann, O.: Investigating the behaviour of a SAT solver on random formulas (2002), `http://cs-svr1.swan.ac.uk/~csoliver/Artikel/OKsolverAnalyse.html`
16. Lagoudakis, M.G., Littman, M.L.: Learning to select branching rules in the DPLL procedure for satisfiability. In: LICS/SAT, vol. 9, pp. 344–359 (2001)
17. Leyton-Brown, K., Nudelman, E., Andrew, G., McFadden, J., Shoham, Y.: Boosting as a metaphor for algorithm design. In: Rossi, F. (ed.) CP 2003. LNCS, vol. 2833, pp. 899–903. Springer, Heidelberg (2003)
18. Leyton-Brown, K., Nudelman, E., Andrew, G., McFadden, J., Shoham, Y.: A portfolio approach to algorithm selection. In: IJCAI-03, pp. 1542–1543 (2003)
19. Leyton-Brown, K., Nudelman, E., Shoham, Y.: Learning the empirical hardness of optimization problems: The case of combinatorial auctions. In: Van Hentenryck, P. (ed.) CP 2002. LNCS, vol. 2470, pp. 556–572. Springer, Heidelberg (2002)
20. Lobjois, L., Lemaître, M.: Branch and bound algorithm selection by performance prediction. In: AAAI-98, pp. 353–358 (1998)
21. Schmidhuber, J., Gagliolo, M.: Impact of censored sampling on the performance of restart strategies. In: Benhamou, F. (ed.) CP 2006. LNCS, vol. 4204, pp. 167–181. Springer, Heidelberg (2006)
22. Mahajan, Y.S., Fu, Z., Malik, S.: Zchaff2004: an efficient SAT solver. In: Bacchus, F., Walsh, T. (eds.) SAT 2005. LNCS, vol. 3569, pp. 360–375. Springer, Heidelberg (2005)
23. Nadel, A., Gordon, M., Palti, A., Hanna, Z.: Eureka-2006 SAT solver. Solver description, SAT Race (2006)
24. Nudelman, E., Leyton-Brown, K., Hoos, H.H., Devkar, A., Shoham, Y.: Understanding random SAT: Beyond the clauses-to-variables ratio. In: Wallace, M. (ed.) CP 2004. LNCS, vol. 3258, pp. 438–452. Springer, Heidelberg (2004)
25. Pipatsrisawat, K., Darwiche, A.: Rsat 1.03: SAT solver description. Technical Report D-152, Automated Reasoning Group, UCLA (2006)
26. Rice, J.R.: The algorithm selection problem. Advances in Computers 15, 65–118 (1976)
27. Schmee, J., Hahn, G.J.: A simple method for regression analysis with censored data. Technometrics 21(4), 417–432 (1979)
28. Vallstrom, D.: Vallst documentation (2005), `http://vallst.satcompetition.org/index.html`
29. Xu, L., Hoos, H.H., Leyton-Brown, K.: Hierarchical hardness models for SAT. In: CP-07 (2007)

Filtering for Subgraph Isomorphism

Stéphane Zampelli[1], Yves Deville[1], Christine Solnon[2], Sébastien Sorlin[2], and Pierre Dupont[1]

[1] Université catholique de Louvain, Department of Computing Science and Engineering, Place Sainte-Barbe 2, 1348 Louvain-la-Neuve (Belgium)
{sz,yde,pdupont}@info.ucl.ac.be

[2] LIRIS, CNRS UMR 5205, University of Lyon I, 43 Bd du 11 Novembre, 69622 Villeurbanne Cedex (France)
{christine.solnon,sebastien.sorlin}@liris.cnrs.fr

Abstract. A subgraph isomorphism problem consists in deciding if there exists a copy of a pattern graph in a target graph. We introduce in this paper a filtering algorithm dedicated to this problem. The main idea is to label every node with respect to its relationships with other nodes of the graph, and to define a partial order on these labels in order to express compatibility of labels for subgraph isomorphism. This partial order over labels is used to filter domains. Labelings can also be strengthened by adding information from the labels of the neighbors. Such a strengthening can be applied iteratively until a fixpoint is reached. Practical experiments illustrate that our new filtering approach is more effective on difficult instances of scale free graphs than state-of-the-art algorithms and other CP approaches.

1 Introduction

Graphs are widely used in real-life applications to represent structured objects, e.g., molecules, images, or biological networks. In many of these applications, one looks for a copy of a pattern graph into a target graph [1]. This problem, known as subgraph isomorphism, is NP-complete [2] in the general case.

There exists dedicated algorithms for solving subgraph isomorphism problems, such as [3,4]. However, such dedicated algorithms can hardly be used to solve more general problems, with additional constraints, or approximate subgraph isomorphism problems, such as the one introduced in [5].

An attractive alternative to these dedicated algorithms is Constraint Programming (CP), which provides a generic framework for solving constraint satisfaction problems (CSP). Indeed, subgraph isomorphism problems may be formulated as CSP in a straightforward way [6,7]. To make CP competitive with dedicated approaches for these problems, [8] has introduced a global monomorphism constraint, and an associated filtering algorithm, together with redundant *Alldiff* constraints. [5] has extended this work to approximate subgraph isomorphism, and has shown that CP is competitive with dedicated approaches.

C. Bessiere (Ed.): CP 2007, LNCS 4741, pp. 728–742, 2007.

Contribution. In this paper, we introduce a new filtering algorithm for the subgraph isomorphism problem that exploits the global structure of the graph to achieve a stronger partial consistency. This work takes inspiration from the partition refinement procedure used in Nauty [9] and Saucy [10] for finding graph automorphisms: the idea is to label every node by some invariant property, such as node degrees, and to iteratively extend labels by considering labels of adjacent nodes. Similar labelings are used in [11,12] to define filtering algorithms for the graph isomorphism problem: the idea is to remove from the domain of a variable associated to a node v every node the label of which is different from the label of v. The extension of such a label-based filtering to subgraph isomorphism problems mainly requires to define a partial order on labels in order to express compatibility of labels for subgraph isomorphism: this partial order is used to remove from the domain of a variable associated to a node v every node the label of which is not compatible with the label of v. We show that this extension is more effective on difficult instances of scale free graphs than state-of-the-art subgraph isomorphism algorithms and other CP approaches.

Outline of the Paper. Section 2 presents the subgraph isomorphism problem and related CP models. Section 3 describes the theoretical framework of our filtering: it first introduces the concept of labeling, and shows how labelings can be used for filtering; it then shows that labelings can be iteratively strengthened by adding information from labels of neighbors. Section 4 introduces the practical framework and describes how to compute a label strengthening. An exact algorithm as well as an approximate version are provided. Experimental results are described in Section 5.

2 Subgraph Isomorphism

2.1 Definitions

An (undirected) *graph* $G = (N, E)$ consists of a *node set* N and an *edge set* $E \subseteq N \times N$, where an edge (u, v) is a couple of nodes.

A *subgraph isomorphism problem* between a pattern graph $G_p = (N_p, E_p)$ and a target graph $G_t = (N_t, E_t)$ consists in deciding whether G_p is isomorphic to some subgraph of G_t. More precisely, one should find an injective function $f : N_p \rightarrow N_t$ such that $\forall (u, v) \in N_p \times N_p, (u, v) \in E_p \Rightarrow (f(u), f(v)) \in E_t$. The problem is also called subgraph monomorphism problem or subgraph matching in the literature. The function f is called a *subgraph matching function.*

In the following, we assume $G_p = (N_p, E_p)$ and $G_t = (N_t, E_t)$ to be the underlying instance of subgraph isomorphism problem. We also define $Node = N_p \cup N_t$, $Edge = E_p \cup E_t$, $n_p = \#N_p$, $n_t = \#N_t$, $n = \#Node$, d_p and d_t the maximal degree of the graphs G_p and G_t, and $d = max(d_p, d_t)$.

2.2 CP Models for Subgraph Isomorphism

A subgraph isomorphism problem can be formulated as a CSP in a straightforward way [6,7,8]. A variable x_u is associated with every node u of the pattern graph and its domain is the set of target nodes. A global Alldiff constraint [13] ensures that the matching function is injective. Edge matching is ensured by a set of binary constraints:

$$\forall(u,v) \in N_p \times N_p,\ c2(x_u, x_v) \equiv ((u,v) \in E_p \Rightarrow (x_u, x_v) \in E_t)\ .$$

3 Theoretical Framework

This section introduces a new filtering algorithm for subgraph isomorphism. We will show in the next section how filtering can be achieved in practice from this theoretical work.

3.1 Subgraph Isomorphism Consistent Labelings

Definition 1. *A labeling l is defined by a triple $(\mathbb{L}, \preceq, \alpha)$ such that*

- *$\mathbb{L}$ is a set of labels that may be associated to nodes;*
- *$\preceq \subseteq \mathbb{L} \times \mathbb{L}$ is a partial order on $\mathbb{L}$;*
- *α : Node $\rightarrow \mathbb{L}$ is a total function assigning a label $\alpha(v)$ to every node v.*

A labeling induces a compatibility relation between nodes of the pattern graph and the target graph.

Definition 2. *The set of* compatible couples of nodes *induced by a labeling $l = (\mathbb{L}, \preceq, \alpha)$ is defined by $CC_l = \{(u,v) \in N_p \times N_t \mid \alpha(u) \preceq \alpha(v)\}$*

This compatibility relation can be used to filter the domain of a variable x_u associated with a node u of the pattern graph by removing from it every node v of the target graph such that $(u,v) \notin CC_l$.

The goal of this work is to find a labeling that filters domains as strongly as possible *without removing solutions* to the subgraph isomorphism problem, *i.e.*, if a node v of the pattern graph may be matched to a node u of the target graph by a subgraph matching function, then the label of v must be compatible with the label of u. This property is called subgraph isomorphism consistency.

Definition 3. *A labeling l is* subgraph isomorphism consistent *(SIC) iff for any subgraph matching function f, we have $\forall v \in N_p, (v, f(v)) \in CC_l$.*

In the context of graph isomorphism, such as in [9], as opposed to subgraph isomorphism studied here, an SIC labeling is often called an *invariant*. In this case, the partial ordering is replaced by an equality condition: two nodes are compatible if they have the same label.

Many graph properties, that are "invariant" to subgraph isomorphism, may be used to define SIC labelings such as, e.g., the three following SIC labelings:

- $l_{deg} = (\mathbb{N}, \leq, deg)$ where *deg* is the function that returns node degree;
- $l_{distance_k} = (\mathbb{N}, \leq, distance_k)$ where $distance_k$ is the function that returns the number of nodes that are reachable by a path of length smaller than k;
- $l_{clique_k} = (\mathbb{N}, \leq, clique_k)$ where $clique_k$ is the function that returns the number of cliques of size k that contains the node.

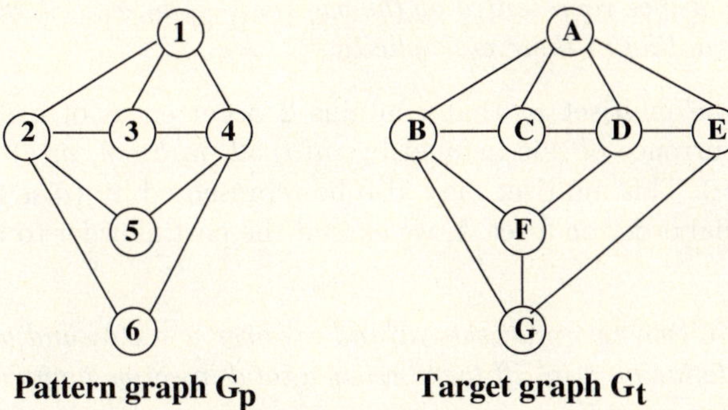

Fig. 1. Instance of subgraph isomorphism problem

Example. Let us consider for example the subgraph isomorphism problem displayed in Fig. 1. Note that this instance has no solution as G_p cannot be mapped into a subgraph of G_t. The labeling $l_{deg} = (\mathbb{N}, \leq, deg)$ assigns the following labels to nodes.

$$\begin{aligned} deg(A) = deg(B) = deg(D) = deg(2) = deg(4) = 4 \\ deg(C) = deg(E) = deg(F) = deg(G) = deg(1) = deg(3) = 3 \\ deg(5) = deg(6) = 2 \end{aligned}$$

Hence, the set of compatible couples induced by this labeling is

$$\begin{aligned} CC_{l_{deg}} &= \{(u,v) \mid u \in \{2,4\}, v \in \{A,B,D\}\} \\ &\cup \{(u,v) \mid u \in \{1,3,5,6\}, v \in \{A,B,C,D,E,F,G\}\} \end{aligned}$$

This set of compatible couples allows one to remove values C, E, F and G from the domains of the variables associated with nodes 2 and 4.

3.2 Strengthening a Labeling

We propose to start from an elementary SIC labeling that is easy to compute such as the l_{deg} labeling defined above, and to iteratively strengthen this labeling. The strength of labelings is defined with respect to the induced compatible couples as follows.

Definition 4. *Let l and l' be two labelings. l' is* strictly stronger than *l iff $CC_{l'} \subset CC_l$, and l'* is equivalent to *l iff $CC_{l'} = CC_l$.*

A stronger labeling yields a better filtering, as it contains less compatible couples.

To strengthen a labeling, the idea is to extend the label of a node by adding information from the labels of its neighbors. This information is a multiset (as several neighbors may have the same label). We shall use the following notations for multisets.

Definition 5. *Given an underlying set A, a* multiset *is a function $m : A \rightarrow \mathbb{N}$, such that $m(a)$ is the multiplicity (i.e., the number of occurrences) of a in m. The* *multiset m can also be represented by the bag* $\{a_0, \ldots, a_0, a_1, \ldots\}$ *where elements are repeated according to their multiplicity.*

For example, the multiset m that contains 2 occurrences of a, 3 occurrences of b, and 1 occurrence of c is defined by $m(a)$=2, $m(b)$=3, $m(c)$=1, and $\forall x \notin \{a, b, c\}, m(x)$=0. This multiset may also be represented by $\{a, a, b, b, b, c\}$.

Given a partial order on a set A, we extend the partial order to multisets over A as follows.

Definition 6. *Given two multisets* m *and* m' *over a set* A*, and a partial order* $\preceq \subseteq A \times A$*, we define* $m \preceq m'$ *iff there exists a total injective mapping* $t : m \rightarrow m'$ *such that* $\forall a_i \in m, a_i \preceq t(a_i)$*.*

In other words, $m \preceq m'$ iff for every element of m there exists a different element of m' which is greater or equal. For example, if we consider the classical ordering on $\mathbb{N}$, we have $\{3, 3, 4\} \preceq \{2, 3, 5, 5\}$, but $\{3, 3, 4\}$ is not comparable with $\{2, 5, 6\}$. Note that comparing two multisets is not trivial in the general case, especially if the order relation on the underlying set A is not total. This point will be handled in the next section.

We now define the labeling extension procedure.

Definition 7. *Given a labeling* $l = (\mathbb{L}, \preceq, \alpha)$*, the* neighborhood extension *of* l *is the labeling* $l' = (\mathbb{L}', \preceq', \alpha')$ *such that:*

- *every label of* $\mathbb{L}'$ *is composed of a label of* $\mathbb{L}$ *and a multiset of labels of* $\mathbb{L}$*, i.e.,* $\mathbb{L}' = \mathbb{L} \cdot (\mathbb{L} \rightarrow \mathbb{N})$*;*
- *the labeling function* α' *extends every label* $\alpha(v)$ *by the multiset of the labels of the neighbors of* v*, i.e.,* $\alpha'(v) = \alpha(v) \cdot m$ *where* $\forall l_i \in \mathbb{L}$*,* $m(l_i) = \#\{u \mid (u, v) \in Edge \wedge \alpha(u) = l_i\}$*;*
- *the partial order on the extended labels of* $\mathbb{L}'$ *is defined by* $l_1 \cdot m_1 \preceq' l_2 \cdot m_2$ *iff* $l_1 \preceq l_2$ *and* $m_1 \preceq m_2$*.*

The next theorem states that the neighborhood extension of a SIC labeling is a stronger (or equal) SIC labeling.

Theorem 1. *Let* $l = (\mathbb{L}, \preceq, \alpha)$ *be a labeling, and* $l' = (\mathbb{L}', \preceq', \alpha')$ *be its neighborhood extension. If* l *is an SIC labeling, then (i)* l' *is also SIC, and (ii)* l' *is stronger than or equal to* l*.*

Proof. (i): Let f be a subgraph matching function and $v \in N_p$. We show that $\alpha'(v) \preceq' \alpha'(f(v))$, that is $\alpha(v) \preceq \alpha(f(v))$ and $m \preceq m'$, with m (resp. m') the multiset of the labels of the neighbors of v in G_p (resp. of $f(v)$ in G_t):

- $\alpha(v) \preceq \alpha(f(v))$ because l is SIC;
- $m \preceq m'$ because m' contains, for each neighbor u of v, the label $\alpha(f(u))$ of the node matched to u by the subgraph matching function f; as l is SIC, $\alpha(u) \preceq \alpha(f(u))$, and thus $m \preceq m'$.

(ii) : This is a direct consequence of the partial order on the extended labels in $\mathbb{L}'$ (Definition 7) : $\alpha(u) \preceq \alpha(v)$ is one of the conditions to have $\alpha'(u) \preceq \alpha'(v)$. □

Example. Let us consider again the subgraph isomorphism problem displayed in Fig. 1, and the labeling $l_{deg} = (\mathbb{N}, \leq, deg)$ defined in 3.1. The neighborhood extension of l_{deg} is the labeling $l' = (\mathbb{L}', \preceq', \alpha')$ displayed below. Note that we only display compatibility relationships $l_i \preceq l_j$ such that l_i is the label of a node of the pattern graph and l_j is the label of a node of the target graph as other relations are useless for filtering purposes.

$$\begin{aligned}
\alpha'(A) &= 4 \cdot \{3,3,4,4\} \\
\alpha'(B) = \alpha'(D) &= 4 \cdot \{3,3,3,4\} \\
\alpha'(2) = \alpha'(4) &= 4 \cdot \{2,2,3,3\} \preceq' 4 \cdot \{3,3,4,4\} \text{ and } 4 \cdot \{3,3,3,4\} \\
\alpha'(C) &= 3 \cdot \{4,4,4\} \\
\alpha'(E) = \alpha'(F) &= 3 \cdot \{3,4,4\} \quad \preceq' 4 \cdot \{3,3,4,4\}, 3 \cdot \{4,4,4\} \text{ and } 3 \cdot \{3,4,4\} \\
\alpha'(1) = \alpha'(3) &= 3 \cdot \{3,4,4\} \quad \preceq' 4 \cdot \{3,3,4,4\}, 3 \cdot \{4,4,4\} \text{ and } 3 \cdot \{3,4,4\} \\
\alpha'(G) &= 3 \cdot \{3,3,4\} \\
\alpha'(5) = \alpha'(6) &= 2 \cdot \{4,4\} \qquad \preceq' 4 \cdot \{3,3,4,4\}, 3 \cdot \{4,4,4\} \text{ and } 3 \cdot \{3,4,4\}
\end{aligned}$$

Hence, the set of compatible couples induced by this extended labeling is

$$\begin{aligned}
CC_{l'} = &\{(u,v) \mid u \in \{2,4\}, v \in \{A,B,D\}\} \\
\cup &\{(u,v) \mid u \in \{1,3,5,6\}, v \in \{A,C,E,F\}\}
\end{aligned}$$

As compared to the initial labeling l_{deg}, this set of compatible couples allows one to further remove values B, D and G from the domains of the variables associated with nodes 1, 3, 5 and 6.

3.3 Iterative Labeling Strengthening

The strengthening of a labeling described in the previous section can be repeated by relabeling nodes iteratively, starting from a given SIC labeling l.

Definition 8. *Let $l = (\mathbb{L}, \preceq, \alpha)$ be an initial SIC labeling. We define the sequence of SIC labelings $l^i = (\mathbb{L}^i, \preceq^i, \alpha^i)$ such that $l^0 = l$ and l^{i+1} = neighborhood extension of l^i $(i \geq 0)$.*

A theoretical filter can be built on this sequence. Starting from an initial SIC labeling function $l = l^0$, we iteratively compute l^{i+1} from l^i and filter domains with respect to the set of compatible couples induced by l^i until either a domain becomes empty (thus indicating that the problem has no solution) or reaching some termination condition.

A termination condition is to stop iterating when the sequence reaches a fixpoint, *i.e.*, a step where any further relabeling cannot change the strength of the labeling. We show in [14] that such a fixpoint is reached in $O(n_p \cdot n_t)$ steps, when both the set of compatible couples and the number of different labels are not changed between two consecutive steps.

Example. Let us consider again the subgraph isomorphism problem displayed in Fig. 1, and let us suppose that the sequence of SIC labelings is started from

$l^0 = l_{deg} = (\mathbb{N}, \leq, deg)$ as defined in 3.1. After the first iteration, the neighborhood extension l^1 of l^0 is the labeling displayed in the example of section 3.2. To improve reading, we rename these labels as follows:

$$\begin{array}{rl}
\alpha^1(A) = 4 \cdot \{3,3,4,4\} & \text{renamed } m_1 \\
\alpha^1(B) = \alpha^1(D) = 4 \cdot \{3,3,3,4\} & \text{renamed } m_2 \\
\alpha^1(2) = \alpha^1(4) = 4 \cdot \{2,2,3,3\} & \text{renamed } m_3 \preceq^1 \{m_1, m_2\} \\
\alpha^1(C) = 3 \cdot \{4,4,4\} & \text{renamed } m_4 \\
\alpha^1(E) = \alpha^1(F) = \alpha^1(1) = \alpha^1(3) = 3 \cdot \{3,4,4\} & \text{renamed } m_5 \preceq^1 \{m_1, m_4\} \\
\alpha^1(G) = 3 \cdot \{3,3,4\} & \text{renamed } m_6 \\
\alpha^1(5) = \alpha^1(6) = 2 \cdot \{4,4\} & \text{renamed } m_7 \preceq^1 \{m_1, m_4, m_5\}
\end{array}$$

From labeling l^1, we compute the following extended labels and partial order:

$$\begin{array}{ll}
\alpha^2(A) = m_1 \cdot \{m_2, m_2, m_4, m_5\} & \text{renamed } n_1 \\
\alpha^2(B) = m_2 \cdot \{m_1, m_4, m_5, m_6\} & \text{renamed } n_2 \\
\alpha^2(C) = m_4 \cdot \{m_1, m_2, m_2\} & \text{renamed } n_3 \\
\alpha^2(D) = m_2 \cdot \{m_1, m_4, m_5, m_5\} & \text{renamed } n_4 \\
\alpha^2(E) = m_5 \cdot \{m_1, m_2, m_6\} & \text{renamed } n_5 \\
\alpha^2(F) = m_5 \cdot \{m_2, m_2, m_6\} & \text{renamed } n_6 \\
\alpha^2(G) = m_6 \cdot \{m_2, m_5, m_5\} & \text{renamed } n_7 \\
\alpha^2(1) = \alpha^2(3) = m_5 \cdot \{m_3, m_3, m_5\} & \text{renamed } n_8 \preceq^2 \{n_1, n_3\} \\
\alpha^2(2) = \alpha^2(4) = m_3 \cdot \{m_5, m_5, m_7, m_7\} & \text{renamed } n_9 \preceq^2 \{n_4\} \\
\alpha^2(5) = \alpha^2(6) = m_7 \cdot \{m_3, m_3\} & \text{renamed } n_{10} \preceq^2 \{n_1, n_3, n_5, n_6\}
\end{array}$$

The set of compatible couples induced by this labeling is

$$\begin{aligned}
CC_{l^2} = \{&(2, D), (4, D), (1, A), (1, C), (3, A), (3, C)\} \\
&\cup \{(u, v) \mid u \in \{5, 6\}, v \in \{A, C, E, F\}\}
\end{aligned}$$

This set of compatible couples allows one to remove values A and B from the domains of the variables associated with nodes 2 and 4. Hence, the domains of these two variables only contain one value (D), and thanks to the *alldiff* constraint on the variables, an inconsistency is detected.

4 Practical Framework

Algorithm 1 describes the overall filtering procedure. Starting from an initial SIC labeling, that may be, e.g., l_{deg}, this procedure first filters domains with respect to this initial labeling (line 1) and then iteratively extends this labeling (lines 4–8) and filters domains with respect to the new extended labeling (line 9) until some domain becomes empty, or a maximum number of iterations have been performed, or a fixpoint is reached.

Labeling extension (lines 4–8) is decomposed into three steps:

- lines 4–6: α^i is computed from α^{i-1}; this step is done in $\mathcal{O}(\#Edge)$;
- line 7: labels of $\mathbb{L}^i$ are renamed; this step is done in $\mathcal{O}(d \cdot \#Node)$;

Algorithm 1. Filtering procedure

Input: two graphs $G_p = (N_p, E_p)$ and $G_t = (N_t, E_t)$ such that $N_p \cap N_t = \emptyset$,
an initial SIC labeling $l^0 = (\mathbb{L}^0, \alpha^0, \preceq^0)$,
initial domains $D : N_p \rightarrow \mathcal{P}(N_t)$,
a limit k on the number of iterations

Output: filtered domains

1 **for** every node $u \in N_p$ **do**: $D(u) \leftarrow D(u) \cap \{v \in N_t | \alpha^0(u) \preceq^0 \alpha^0(v)\}$
2 $i \leftarrow 1$
3 **while** $\forall u \in N_p, D(u) \neq \emptyset$ **and** $i \leq k$ **and** *fixpoint not reached* **do**
4   **for** *every node* $u \in N_p \cup N_t$ **do**
5         $m^i_u \leftarrow$ multiset containing an occurrence of $\alpha^{i-1}(v), \forall (u, v) \in E_p \cup E_t$
6         $\alpha^i(u) \leftarrow \alpha^{i-1}(u) \cdot m^i_u$
7     $\mathbb{L}^i \leftarrow \{\alpha^i(u) | u \in N_p \cup N_t\}$; rename labels in $\mathbb{L}^i$ and α^i
8     $\preceq^i \leftarrow \{(\alpha^i(u), \alpha^i(v)) \mid u \in N_p \ \wedge \ v \in D(u) \ \wedge \ test(m^i_u, m^i_v, \preceq^{i-1})\}$
9   **for** every node $u \in N_p$ **do**: $D(u) \leftarrow D(u) \cap \{v \in N_t | \alpha^i(u) \preceq^i \alpha^i(v)\}$
10     $i \leftarrow i + 1$
11 **return** D

– line 8: the partial order $\preceq^i$ is computed, i.e., for every couple of nodes (u, v) such that u is a node of the pattern graph and v is a node of the target graph which was compatible with u at step $i - 1$, we test for the compatibility of the multisets m^i_u and m^i_v to determine if the labels of u and v are still compatible at step i. Testing the compatibility of two mulisets is not trivial. We show in 4.1 how to do this exactly in $\mathcal{O}(d^{5/2})$, so that line 8 has a time complexity of $\mathcal{O}(n_p \cdot n_t \cdot d^{5/2})$. We then show in 4.2 how to compute an order inducing a weaker filtering in $\mathcal{O}(n_t \cdot d \cdot (n_p + d_t \cdot \log n_t))$. These two variants are experimentally compared in Section 5.

The filtering step (line 9) is done in $\mathcal{O}(n_p \cdot n_t)$.

4.1 Exact Computation of the Partial Order

Given two multisets m_u and m_v, and a partial order $\preceq$, the function *test*$(m_u, m_v, \preceq)$ determines if $m_u \preceq m_v$, i.e., if there exists for each label occurrence in m_u a distinct label occurrence in m_v which is greater or equal according to $\preceq$.

Property 1. Let $G = (N = (N_u, N_v), E)$ be the bipartite graph such that N_u (resp. N_v) associates a different node with every label occurrence in the multiset m_u (resp. m_v), and E contains the set of edges (i, j) such that $i \preceq j$. We have $m_u \preceq m_v$ iff there exists a matching that covers N_u in G.

Hopcroft [15] proposes an algorithm for solving this problem in $\mathcal{O}(|N_u| \cdot |N_v| \cdot \sqrt{|N|})$. As the sizes of m_u and m_v are bounded by the maximal degree d, the test function can be done in $O(d^{5/2})$.

4.2 Computation of an Approximated Order

If $\preceq$ is a total order, the function $test(m_u, m_v, \preceq)$ can be implemented more efficiently, by sorting each multiset and matching every label of m_u with the smallest compatible label of m_v. In this case, the complexity of *test* is $\mathcal{O}(d \cdot \log d)$.

When $\preceq$ is not a total order, one may extend it into a total order $\leq$. This total order can then be used in the *test* function to determine if $m_u \leq m_v$. However, the total order introduces new label compatibilities so that $test(m_u, m_v, \leq)$ may return true while $test(m_u, m_v, \preceq)$ returns false. As a consequence, using this approximated order may induce a weaker filtering.

In this section, we first introduce the theoretical framework that defines a new neighborhood labeling extension based on a total order and proves its validity; then we show how it can be achieved in practice.

Neighborhood Labeling Extension Based on a Total Ord er. The next definition gives a simple condition on the total order to ensure its consistency with respect to the partial order, i.e., to ensure that $test(m_u, m_v, \preceq) = \text{True} \Rightarrow test(m_u, m_v, \leq) = \text{True}$.

Definition 9. *Let $l = (\mathbb{L}, \preceq, \alpha)$ be a labeling. A* consistent total order for l *is a total order $\leq$ on $\mathbb{L}$ such that $\forall u \in n_p, \forall v \in n_t, \alpha(u) \preceq \alpha(v) \Rightarrow \alpha(u) \leq \alpha(v)$*

We extend the order $\leq$ on multisets like for partial orders in Definition 6, i.e., $m \leq m'$ iff there exists an injective function $t : m \rightarrow m'$ such that $\forall a_i \in m, a_i \leq t(a_i)$. Hence, $m \preceq m' \Rightarrow m \leq m'$. Let us note however that this extension of $\leq$ to multisets only induces a partial order on multisets as some multisets may not be comparable.

We can then define a new neighborhood extension procedure, based on a consistent total order.

Definition 10. *Let $l = (\mathbb{L}, \preceq, \alpha)$ be a labeling, and $\leq$ be a consistent total order for l. The* neighborhood extension of l based on $\leq$ *is the labeling $l'_{\leq} = (\mathbb{L}', \preceq'_{\leq}, \alpha')$ where $\mathbb{L}'$ and α' are defined like in Definition 7, and the order relation $\preceq'_{\leq} \subseteq \mathbb{L}' \times \mathbb{L}'$ is defined by*

$$l_1 \cdot m_1 \preceq'_{\leq} l_2 \cdot m_2 \text{ iff } l_1 \preceq l_2 \wedge m_1 \leq m_2$$

The next theorem shows that the neighborhood extension $l'_{\leq}$ based on $\leq$ may be used in our iterative labeling process, and that it is stronger or equal to l. However, it may be weaker than the neighborhood extension based on the partial order $\preceq$. Indeed, the total order induces more compatible couples of labels than the partial order.

Theorem 2. *Let $l = (\mathbb{L}, \preceq, \alpha)$, $l' = (\mathbb{L}', \preceq', \alpha')$, and $l'_{\leq} = (\mathbb{L}', \preceq'_{\leq}, \alpha')$, be three labelings such that l' is the neighborhood extension of l and $l'_{\leq}$ is the neighborhood extension of l based on a consistent total order $\leq$.*

If l is an SIC labeling, then (i) $l'_{\leq}$ is SIC, (ii) $l'_{\leq}$ is stronger than (or equal to) l, and (iii) l' is stronger than (or equal to) $l'_{\leq}$.

Proof. (ii) and (iii): For labeling l', we have $l_1 \cdot m_1 \preceq' l_2 \cdot m_2$ iff $l_1 \preceq l_2 \wedge m_1 \preceq m_2$. As $\leq$ is consistent w.r.t. $\preceq$, we have $m \preceq m' \Rightarrow m \leq m'$. Hence, $CC_{l'} \subseteq CC_{l'_{\leq}} \subseteq CC_l$. (i) is a direct consequence of (iii), as l' is SIC (Theorem 1). □

Different consistent total orders may be derived from a given partial order, leading to prunings of different strength: the less new couples of compatible nodes are introduced by the total order, the better the filtering. However, we conjecture in [14] that finding the best consistent total order is NP-hard. Hence, we propose a heuristic algorithm that aims at computing a total order that introduces few new compatible couples without guarantee of optimality. Let us note L_p (resp. L_t) the set of labels associated with nodes of the pattern graph G_p (resp. target graph G_t). We shall suppose without loss of generality[1] that $L_p \cap L_t = \emptyset$. The idea is to sequence the labels of $L_p \cup L_t$, thus defining a total order on these labels, according to the following greedy principle: starting from an empty sequence, one iteratively adds some labels of $L_p \cup L_t$ at the end of the sequence, and removes these labels from L_p and L_t, until $L_p \cup L_t = \emptyset$.

To choose the labels added in the sequence at each iteration, our heuristic is based on the fact that the new couples of compatible nodes are introduced by new couples of compatible labels (e_p, e_t) such that $e_p \in L_p$ and $e_t \in L_t$. Hence, the goal is to sequence as late as possible the labels of L_p. To this aim, we first compute the set of labels $e_t \in L_t$ for which the number of labels $e_p \in L_p, e_p \preceq e_t$ is minimal. To break ties, we then choose a label e_t such that the average number of labels $e'_t \in L_t, e_p \preceq e'_t$, for every label $e_p \in L_p, e_p \preceq e_t$, is minimal. Then, we introduce in the sequence the selected label e_t, preceded by every label $e_p \in L_p$ such that $e_p \preceq e_t$.

The time complexity of this heuristic algorithm is in $\mathcal{O}(n_t \cdot \log n_t \cdot d_p \cdot d_t)$.

Practical Computation of an Approximate Partial Order. In practice, one has to compute a total order $\leq^{i-1}$ that approximates the partial order $\preceq^{i-1}$ at each iteration i of Algorithm 1. This must be done between lines 7 and 8. Then each call to the test function, line 8, is performed with the total order $\leq^{i-1}$ instead of the partial order $\preceq^{i-1}$.

In this case, the time complexity of the computation of $\preceq^i$ (line 8) is in $\mathcal{O}(n_t \cdot n_p \cdot d \cdot \log d)$. This complexity can be reduced to $\mathrm{O}(n_t \cdot n_p \cdot d)$ by first sorting all the multisets. When adding the time complexity of the computation of the total order by our heuristic algorithm, we obtain an overall complexity in $\mathcal{O}(n_t \cdot d \cdot (n_p + d_t \cdot \log n_t))$.

4.3 Filtering Within a Branch and Propagate Framework

In this section, we introduce two optimizations that may be done when filtering is integrated within a branch and propagate search, where a variable assignment is done at each step of the search.

[1] If a label e both belongs to L_p and L_t, it is always possible to rename e into e' in L_t (where e' is a new label), and to add a relation $e'' \preceq e'$ for every label $e'' \in L_p$ such that $e'' \preceq e$.

A first optimization provides an entailment condition for the filtering. If the initial labeling l^0 is such that the maximum label of the pattern graph is smaller or equal to the minimum label of the target graph, every label of nodes of the pattern graph is compatible with all the labels of nodes of the target graph so that no domain can be reduced by our filtering procedure.

A second optimization is done when, during the search, the variable associated with a pattern node is assigned to a target node. In this case, the neighborhood extension procedure is modified by forcing the two nodes to have a same new label which is not compatible with other labels as follows:

Definition 11. *Let $l = (\mathbb{L}, \preceq, \alpha)$ be an SIC labeling, and let $(u, v) \in N_p \times N_t$ such that $v \in x_u$. The propagation of $x_u = v$ on l is the new labeling $l' = (\mathbb{L}', \preceq'$ $, \alpha')$ such that*

- $\mathbb{L}' = \mathbb{L} \cup \{l_{uv}\}$ *where l_{uv} is a new label such that $l_{uv} \notin \mathbb{L}$;*
- $\preceq' = \preceq \cup \{(l_{uv}, l_{uv})\}$ *so that the new label l_{uv} is not comparable with any other label except itself;*
- $\alpha'(u) = \alpha'(v) = l_{uv}$ *and $\forall w \in Nodes \setminus \{u, v\}, \alpha'(w) = \alpha(w)$*

This labeling l' is used as a starting point of a new sequence of labeling extensions. Note that this propagation is done every time a domain is reduced to a singleton.

5 Experimental Results

Considered Instances. We evaluate our approach on graphs that are randomly generated using a power law distribution of degrees $P(d = k) = k^{-\lambda}$: this distribution corresponds to scale-free networks which model a wide range of real networks, such as social, Internet, or neural networks [16]. We have made experiments with different values of λ, ranging between 1 and 5, and obtained similar results. Hence, we only report experiments on graphs generated with the standard value $\lambda = 2.5$.

We have considered 6 classes of instances, each class containing 20 different instances. For each instance, we first generate a connected target graph which node degrees are bounded between d_{min} and d_{max}. Then, a connected pattern graph is extracted from the target graph by randomly selecting a percentage p_n (resp. p_e) of nodes (resp. edges).

All instances of classes A, B, and C are non directed feasible instances that have been generated with $d_{min} = 5$, $d_{max} = 8$, and $p_n = p_e = 90\%$. Target graphs in A (resp. B and C) have 200 (resp. 600 and 1000) nodes.

All instances of class D are directed feasible instances that have been generated with $d_{min} = 5$, $d_{max} = 8$, and $p_n = p_e = 90\%$. Target graphs have 600 nodes. Edges of target graphs have been randomly directed. To solve these directed instances, the filtering procedure is adapted by extending labelings with two multisets that respectively contain labels of successors and predecessors.

All instances of classes E and F are non directed instances that have been generated with $d_{min} = 20$, $d_{max} = 300$, and $p_n = 90\%$. Target graphs have

300 nodes. Instances of class E are feasible ones that have been generated with $p_e = 90\%$. Instances of class F are non feasible ones: for these instances, pattern graphs are extracted from target graphs by randomly selecting 90% of nodes and 90% of edges, but after this extraction, 10% of new edges have been randomly added.

For all experimentations reported below, each run searches for all solutions of an instance.

Comparison of Different Variants of Our Filtering Algorithm. Algorithm 1 has been implemented in Gecode (http://www.gecode.org), using CP (Graph) and CP(Map) [17,18] which provide graph and function domain variables. The global subgraph isomorphism constraint has been combined with $c2$ constraints (as defined in Section 2.2) and a global AllDiff constraint which are propagated by forward checking.

Table 1. Comparison of different variants of Algorithm 1: Exact (resp. Approx.) refers to the implementation of *test* described in 4.1 (resp. 4.2); k gives the maximum number of iterations. Each line successively reports the percentage of instances that have been solved within a CPU time limit of 600s on an Intel Xeon 3,06 Ghz with 2Go of RAM; the average run time for the solved instances; and the average number of failed nodes in the search tree for the solved instances.

	Solved instances (%)						Average time						Average failed nodes					
	Exact			Approx.			Exact			Approx.			Exact			Approx.		
	k=0	k=1	k=2	k=2	k=4	k=8	k=0	k=1	k=2	k=2	k=4	k=8	k=0	k=1	k=2	k=2	k=4	k=8
A	100	100	100	100	100	100	2.2	**0.6**	23.4	1.3	1.9	3.2	440	14	0	13	0	0
B	100	100	100	100	100	100	61.4	**5.6**	144.2	24.5	28.7	59.6	1314	8	0	3	0	0
C	45	100	45	100	100	100	439.2	**26.3**	495.8	101.8	110.4	227.8	1750	13	0	2	0	0
D	100	100	100	100	100	100	**0.7**	2.6	99.6	7.5	24.7	56.3	2	0	0	0	0	0
E	80	60	0	75	80	**85**	126.7	98.6	-	35.2	18.8	36.7	4438	159	-	39	13	7
F	23	20	0	38	63	**68**	186.4	109.9	-	45.0	10.5	3.9	18958	3304	-	2323	481	107

Table 1 compares different variants of Algorithm 1, obtained by either computing an exact partial order or an approximated one (as described in 4.1 and 4.2), and by considering different limits k on the number of iterations. In all variants, the initial labeling l^0 is the labeling l_{deg} defined in 3.1. Note that the order of l_{deg} is a total order so that in this case the exact and approximated variants are equivalent for $k = 1$.

Let us first compare the exact and approximated variants. The number of failed nodes with Approx./$k = 2$ is greater than Exact/$k = 2$, but it is smaller than with Exact/$k = 1$. This shows us that the total order computed by our heuristic algorithm is a quite good approximation of the partial order. When considering CPU-times, we note that Approx./$k = 2$ is significantly quicker than Exact/$k = 2$.

Table 1 also shows that the best performing variant differs when considering different classes of instances. Instances of class D are best solved when $k = 0$, i.e., with the simple l_{deg} labeling: these instances are easy ones, as adding a direction on edges greatly narrows the search space. Instances of classes A, B and C are more difficult ones, as they are not directed; these instances are best solved when $k = 1$, i.e., after one iteration of the exact labelling extension. Instances of classes E and F, which have significantly higher node degrees, are very difficult ones. For these instances, and more particularly for those of class F which are not feasible ones and which appear to be even more difficult, iterative labeling extensions actually improve the solution process and the best results are obtained when $k = 8$.

As a conclusion, these experimentations show us that (1) the approximated variant offers a good compromise between filtering's strength and time, and (2) the optimal limit k on the number of iterations depends on the difficulty of instances. The best average results are obtained with Approx./$k = 4$.

Comparison with State-of-the-Art Approaches. We now compare the variant Approx./k=4 of Algorithm 1 with a state-of-the-art algorithm coming from a C++ library called `vflib` [4], and with CP. We consider two different CP models:

- $c2$ is the model using $c2$ constraints described in Section 2.2;
- $c2 + c3$ is the model that additionnaly uses $c3$ constraints introduced in [8].

These two models are combined with a global Alldiff constraint. For $c2$ and Alldiff constraints, two levels of consistency are considered, i.e., Forward Checking (denoted by FC) and Arc Consistency (denoted by AC). Propagation of $c3$ follows [8]. All CP models have been implemented in Gecode using CP(Graph) and CP(Map).

Table 2. Comparison of state-of-the-art approaches. Each line successively reports the percentage of instances that have been solved within a CPU time limit of 600s on an Intel Xeon 3,06 Ghz with 2Go of RAM; the average run time for the solved instances; and the average number of failed nodes in the search tree for the solved instances.

	Solved instances (%)						Average time						Average failed nodes					
	vflib	c2		c2+c3		App.	vflib	c2		c2+c3		App.	vflib	c2		c2+c3		App.
		FC	AC	FC	AC	k=4		FC	AC	FC	AC	k=4		FC	AC	FC	AC	k=4
A	35	100	100	100	100	100	251.4	57.1	38.7	26.9	22.3	**1.9**	-	165239	19	67	0	0
B	0	0	0	0	0	**100**	-	-	-	-	-	**28.7**	-	-	-	-	-	0
C	0	0	0	0	0	**100**	-	-	-	-	-	**110.4**	-	-	-	-	-	0
D	100	100	100	5	0	100	**0.8**	7.9	81.7	542.7	-	24.7	-	2402	0	0	0	0
E	0	0	5	33	20	**80**	-	-	362.0	319.5	397.6	**18.8**	-	-	154	21	7	13
F	0	0	0	10	5	**63**	-	-	-	381.7	346.5	**10.5**	-	-	-	52	14	481

Table 2 compares all these approaches and shows us that, except for easy instances of class D which are best solved by `vflib`, all other classes of instances are best solved by Approx./k=4. When comparing the different CP models, we note that adding redundant $c3$ constraints significantly improves the solution process except for the easy instances of class D which are better solved with simpler models.

6 Conclusion

We introduced a new filtering algorithm for the subgraph isomorphism problem that exploits the global structure of the graph in order to achieve a stronger partial consistency. This work extends a filtering algorithm for graph isomorphism [12] where a total order defined on some graph property labelling is strengthened until a fixpoint. The extension to subgraph isomorphism has been theorically founded. The order is partial and can also be iterated until a fixpoint. However, using such a partial order is ineffective. Instead, one can map this partial order to a total order. Performing such a mapping is hard, and can be efficiently approximated throught a heuristic algorithm. Experimental results show that our propagators are efficient against state-of-the-art propagators and algorithms.

Future work includes the development of dynamic termination criteria for the iterative labeling, the experimental study of other degree distributions, the analysis of alternative initial labelings.

Acknowledgments

The authors want to thank the anonymous reviewers for the helpful comments. This research is supported by the Walloon Region, project Transmaze (WIST516207).

References

1. Conte, D., Foggia, P., Sansone, C., Vento, M.: Thirty years of graph matching in pattern recognition. IJPRAI 18(3), 265–298 (2004)
2. Garey, M., Johnson, D.: Computers and Intractability. Freeman and Co., New York (1979)
3. Ullmann, J.R.: An algorithm for subgraph isomorphism. J. ACM 23(1), 31–42 (1976)
4. Cordella, L., Foggia, P., Sansone, C., Vento, M.: An improved algorithm for matching large graphs. In: 3rd IAPR-TC15 Workshop on Graph-based Representations in Pattern Recognition, Cuen, pp. 149–159 (2001)
5. Zampelli, S., Deville, Y., Dupont, P.: Approximate constrained subgraph matching. In: van Beek, P. (ed.) CP 2005. LNCS, vol. 3709, pp. 832–836. Springer, Heidelberg (2005)
6. Régin, J.: Développement d'Outils Algorithmiques pour l'Intelligence Artificielle. Application à la Chimie Organique. PhD thesis (1995)
7. Rudolf, M.: Utilizing constraint satisfaction techniques for efficient graph pattern matching. In: Ehrig, H., Engels, G., Kreowski, H.-J., Rozenberg, G. (eds.) TAGT 1998. LNCS, vol. 1764, pp. 238–252. Springer, Heidelberg (2000)
8. Larrosa, J., Valiente, G.: Constraint satisfaction algorithms for graph pattern matching. Mathematical. Structures in Comp. Sci. 12(4), 403–422 (2002)

9. McKay, B.D.: Practical graph isomorphism. Congressus Numerantium 30, 45–87 (1981)
10. Darga, P.T., Liffiton, M.H., Sakallah, K.A., Markov, I.L.: Exploiting structure in symmetry detection for cnf. In: Proc. Design Automation Conference (DAC), pp. 530–534. IEEE/ACM (2004)
11. Sorlin, S., Solnon, C.: A global constraint for graph isomorphism problems. In: Régin, J.-C., Rueher, M. (eds.) CPAIOR 2004. LNCS, vol. 3011, pp. 287–301. Springer, Heidelberg (2004)
12. Sorlin, S., Solnon, C.: A new filtering algorithm for the graph isomorphism problem. In: Benhamou, F. (ed.) CP 2006. LNCS, vol. 4204. Springer, Heidelberg (2006)
13. Regin, J.C.: A filtering algorithm for constraints of difference in CSPs. In: Amer. Assoc. Artificial Intelligence. Proc. 12th Conf. American Assoc. Artificial Intelligence, vol. 1, pp. 362–367 (1994)
14. Zampelli, S., Deville, Y., Solnon, C., Sorlin, S., Dupont, P.: Filtering for subgraph matching. Technical Report INGIRR2007-03, Université Catholique de Louvain (2007)
15. Hopcroft, J.E., Karp, R.M.: An $n^{5/2}$ algorithm for maximum matchings in bipartite graphs. SIAM J. Comput. 2(4), 225–231 (1973)
16. Barabasi, A.L.: Linked: How Everything Is Connected to Everything Else and What It Means. Plume (2003)
17. Dooms, G., Deville, Y., Dupont, P.: Cp(graph): Introducing a graph computation domain in constraint programming. In: van Beek, P. (ed.) CP 2005. LNCS, vol. 3709, pp. 211–225. Springer, Heidelberg (2005)
18. Deville, Y., Dooms, G., Zampelli, S., Dupont, P.: Cp(graph+map) for approximate graph matching. In: van Beek, P. (ed.) CP 2005. LNCS, vol. 3709, pp. 33–48. Springer, Heidelberg (2005)

Solution Counting Algorithms for Constraint-Centered Search Heuristics

Alessandro Zanarini and Gilles Pesant

École Polytechnique de Montréal
Montreal, Canada
{azanarini,pesant}@crt.umontreal.ca

Abstract. Constraints have played a central role in CP because they capture key substructures of a problem and efficiently exploit them to boost inference. This paper intends to do the same thing for search, proposing constraint-centered heuristics which guide the exploration of the search space toward areas that are likely to contain a high number of solutions. We first propose new search heuristics based on solution counting information at the level of individual constraints. We then describe efficient algorithms to evaluate the number of solutions of two important families of constraints: occurrence counting constraints, such as `alldifferent`, and sequencing constraints, such as `regular`. In both cases we take advantage of existing filtering algorithms to speed up the evaluation. Experimental results on benchmark problems show the effectiveness of our approach.

1 Introduction

Constraint Programming (CP) is a powerful technique to solve combinatorial problems. It applies sophisticated inference to reduce the search space and a combination of variable and value selection heuristics to guide the exploration of that search space. Despite many research efforts to design generic and robust search heuristics and to analyze their behaviour, a successful CP application often requires customized, *problem-centered* search heuristics or at the very least some fine tuning of standard ones, particularly for value selection. In contrast, Mixed Integer Programming (MIP) and SAT solvers feature successful default search heuristics that basically reduce the problem at hand to a modeling issue.

Constraints have played a central role in CP because they capture key substructures of a problem and efficiently exploit them to boost inference. This paper intends to do the same thing for search, proposing *constraint-centered* heuristics. A constraint's consistency algorithm often maintains data structures in order to incrementally filter out values that are not supported by the constraint's set of valid tuples. These same data structures may be exploited to evaluate *how many* valid tuples there are. Up to now, the only visible effect of the consistency algorithms has been on the domains, projecting the set of tuples on each of the variables. Additional information about the number of solutions of a constraint can help a search heuristic to focus on critical parts of a problem

C. Bessiere (Ed.): CP 2007, LNCS 4741, pp. 743–757, 2007.

or promising solution fragments. Polytime approximate or exact algorithms to count the number of solutions of several common families of constraints were given in [12]. For some families, little work was required to provide close or even exact evaluations of the number of solutions for a constraint, given the existing consistency algorithm and its data structures.

There is a large body of scientific literature on search heuristics to solve CSPs. Most of the popular dynamic variable selection heuristics favour small domain size and large degree in the constraint graph (mindom, dom/deg, dom/ddeg, dom/wdeg, Brelaz). For value selection, minimizing the number of conflicts with neighbouring variables is popular. We mention below the closest related work on search. Kask et al. [9] approximate the total number of solutions extending a partial solution to a CSP and use it in a value selection heuristic, choosing the value whose assignment to the current variable gives the largest approximate solution count. An implementation optimized for binary constraints performs well compared to other popular strategies. Refalo [14] proposes a generic variable selection heuristic based on the impact the assignment of a variable has on the reduction of the remaining search space, computed as the Cartesian product of the domains of the variables. It reports promising results on benchmark problems. The main difference between our work and these is that we focus on individual constraints whereas they consider the problem as a whole. As an interesting connection for constraint-centered heuristics, Patel and Chinneck [10] investigate several variable selection heuristics guided by the constraints that are tight at the optimal solution of the relaxation, to find feasible solutions of MIPs.

Contributions. There are two main contributions in this work. First, we describe and experiment with new search heuristics based on solution counting information at the level of individual constraints. Second, we propose efficient algorithms to evaluate the number of solutions of two important families of constraints: occurrence counting constraints (`alldifferent`) and sequencing constraints (`regular`). With respect to [12], what is proposed for the former is a considerable improvement and for the latter it details what was only alluded to before.

Plan of the paper. Section 2 presents some key definitions and describes the search heuristics we propose. Section 3 gives an algorithm to compute the number of solutions of `regular` constraints. Section 4 summarizes the literature on counting solutions of `alldifferent` constraints and proposes a related algorithm more suited to our purpose. Section 5 presents comparative experimental results supporting our proposal. Finally Section 6 summarizes our work and mentions some of the arising research issues.

2 Generic Constraint-Centered Heuristic Search Framework

Whereas most generic dynamic search heuristics in constraint programming rely on information at the fine-grained level of the individual variable (e.g. its domain size and degree), we investigate dynamic search heuristics based on coarser, but more global, information. Global constraints are successful because they encapsulate powerful specialized filtering algorithms but firstly because they bring out the underlying structure of combinatorial problems. That exposed structure can also be exploited during search. The heuristics proposed here revolve around the knowledge of the number of solutions of individual constraints, the intuition being that a constraint with few solutions corresponds to a critical part of the problem with respect to satisfiability.

Definition 1 (solution count). *Given a constraint $\gamma(x_1, \ldots, x_k)$ and respective finite domains D_i $_{1 \le i \le k}$, let $\#\gamma(x_1, \ldots, x_k)$ denote the number of solutions of constraint γ.*

Search heuristics following the *fail-first principle* (detect failure as early as possible) and centered on constraints can be guided by a count of the number of solutions left for each constraint. We might focus the search on the constraint currently having the smallest number of solutions, recognizing that failure necessarily occurs through a constraint admitting no more solution.

max $= 0$;
for *each constraint* $\gamma(x_1, \ldots, x_k)$ **do**
    for *each unbound variable* $x_i \in \{x_1, \ldots, x_k\}$ **do**
        for *each value* $d \in D_i$ **do**
            if $\sigma(x_i, d, \gamma) >$ max **then**
                $(x^\star, d^\star) = (x_i, d)$;
                max $= \sigma(x_i, d, \gamma)$;
return branching decision "$x^\star = d^\star$";

Algorithm 1. The Maximum Solution Density (MaxSD) search heuristic

We can go one step further with solution count information and evaluate it for each variable-value pair in an individual constraint.

Definition 2 (solution density). *Given a constraint $\gamma(x_1, \ldots, x_k)$, respective finite domains D_i $_{1 \le i \le k}$, a variable x_i in the scope of γ, and a value $d \in D_i$, we will call*

$$\sigma(x_i, d, \gamma) = \frac{\#\gamma(x_1, \ldots, x_{i-1}, d, x_{i+1}, \ldots, x_k)}{\#\gamma(x_1, \ldots, x_k)}$$

the solution density[1] *of pair (x_i, d) in γ. It measures how often a certain assignment is part of a solution.*

We can favour the highest solution density available with the hope that such a choice generally brings us closer to satisfying the whole CSP. Our choice may combine information from every constraint in the model, be restricted to a single constraint, or even to a given subset of variables. Algorithms 1 to 3 define the search heuristics with which we will experiment in Section 5.

[1] Also referred to as *marginal* in some of the literature.

max $= 0$;
choose constraint $\gamma(x_1, \ldots, x_k)$ which minimizes $\#\gamma$;
for *each unbound variable* $x_i \in \{x_1, \ldots, x_k\}$ **do**
    for *each value* $d \in D_i$ **do**
        if $\sigma(x_i, d, \gamma) >$ max **then**
            $(x^\star, d^\star) = (x_i, d)$;
            max $= \sigma(x_i, d, \gamma)$;
return branching decision "$x^\star = d^\star$";

Algorithm 2. The Minimum Solution Count, Maximum Solution Density (MinSC;MaxSD) search heuristic

max $= 0$;
Let $S = \{x_i : |D_i| > 1 \text{ and minimum}\}$;
for *each variable* $x_i \in S$ **do**
    for *each constraint* γ *with* x_i *in its scope* **do**
        for *each value* $d \in D_i$ **do**
            if $\sigma(x_i, d, \gamma) >$ max **then**
                $(x^\star, d^\star) = (x_i, d)$;
                max $= \sigma(x_i, d, \gamma)$;
return branching decision "$x^\star = d^\star$";

Algorithm 3. The Smallest Domain, Maximum Solution Density (MinDom;MaxSD) search heuristic

3 Counting for Regular Constraints

The `regular`(X, Π) constraint [11] holds if the values taken by the sequence of finite domain variables $X = \langle x_1, x_2, \ldots, x_n \rangle$ spell out a word belonging to the regular language defined by the deterministic finite automaton $\Pi = (Q, \Sigma, \delta, q_0, F)$ where Q is a finite set of states, Σ is an alphabet, $\delta : Q \times \Sigma \to Q$ is a partial transition function, $q_0 \in Q$ is the initial state, and $F \subseteq Q$ is the set of final (or accepting) states. The filtering algorithm associated to this constraint is based on the computation of paths in a graph. The automaton is unfolded into a layered acyclic directed graph $G = (V, A)$ where vertices of a layer correspond to states of the automaton and arcs represent variable-value pairs. We denote by $v_{\ell,q}$ the vertex corresponding to state q in layer ℓ. The first layer only contains one vertex, v_{1,q_0}; the last layer only contains vertices corresponding to accepting states, $v_{n+1,q}$ with $q \in F$. This graph has the property that paths from the first layer to the last are in one-to-one correspondence with solutions of the constraint. The existence of a path through a given arc thus constitutes a support for the corresponding variable-value pair [11]. Figure 1 gives an example of a layered directed graph built for one such constraint on five variables.

The time complexity of the filtering algorithm is linear in the size of the graph (the number of variables times the number of transitions appearing in the automaton). Essentially, one forward and one backward sweep of the graph are sufficient. An incremental version of the algorithm, which updates the graph as the computation proceeds, has a time complexity that is linear in the size of the changes to the graph.

3.1 Counting Paths in the Associated Graph

Given the graph built by the filtering algorithm for `regular`, what is the additional computational cost of determining its number of solutions? As we already pointed out, every (complete) path in that graph corresponds to a solution. Therefore it is sufficient to count the number of such paths. We express this through a simple recurrence relation, which we can compute by dynamic programming. Let $\#op(\ell, q)$ denote the number of paths from $v_{\ell,q}$ to a vertex in the last layer. Then we have:

$$\#op(n+1, q) = 1$$
$$\#op(\ell, q) = \sum_{(v_{\ell,q}, v_{\ell+1,q'}) \in A} \#op(\ell+1, q'), \quad 1 \leq \ell \leq n$$

The total number of paths is given by

$$\#\texttt{regular}(X, \Pi) = \#op(1, q_0)$$

in time linear in the size of the graph even though there may be exponentially many of them. Therefore this is absorbed in the asymptotic complexity of the filtering algorithm.

The search heuristics we consider require not only *solution counts* of constraints but *solution densities* of variable-value pairs as well. In the graph of `regular`, such a pair (x_i, d) is represented by the arcs between layers i and $i+1$ corresponding to transitions on value d. The number of solutions in which $x_i = d$ is thus equal to the number of paths going through one of those arcs. Consider one such arc $(v_{i,q}, v_{i+1,q'})$: the number of paths through it is the product of the number of outgoing paths from $v_{i+1,q'}$ and the number of incoming paths to $v_{i,q}$. The former is $\#op(i+1, q')$ and the latter, $\#ip(i, q)$, is just as easily computed:

$$\#ip(1, q_0) = 1$$
$$\#ip(\ell+1, q') = \sum_{(v_{\ell,q}, v_{\ell+1,q'}) \in A} \#ip(\ell, q), \quad 1 \leq \ell \leq n$$

where $\#ip(\ell, q)$ denotes the number of paths from v_{1,q_0} to $v_{\ell,q}$.

In Figure 1, the left and right labels inside each vertex give the number of incoming and outgoing paths for that vertex, respectively. For example, the arc between the vertex labeled "2; 2" in layer L_3 and the vertex labeled "5; 2" in layer L_4 has $2 \times 2 = 4$ paths through it.

Let $A(i, d) \subset A$ denote the set of arcs representing variable-value pair (x_i, d). The solution density of pair (x_i, d) is thus given by:

$$\sigma(x_i, d, \texttt{regular}) = \frac{\sum_{(v_{i,q}, v_{i+1,q'}) \in A(i,d)} \#ip(i, q) \cdot \#op(i+1, q')}{\#op(1, q_0)}$$

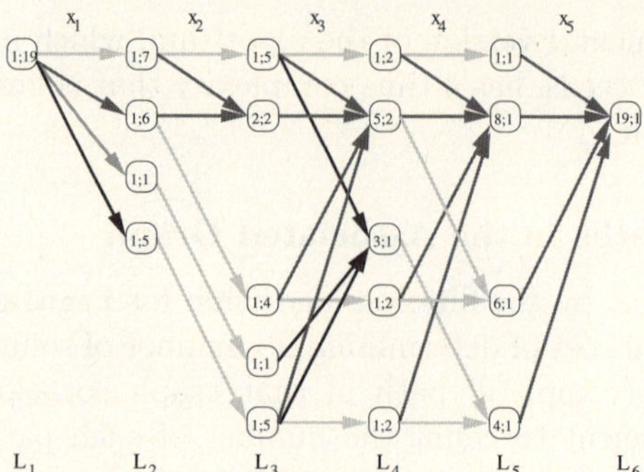

Fig. 1. The layered directed graph built for a `regular` constraint on five variables. Vertex labels represent the number of incoming and outgoing paths.

Once these quantities are tabulated, the cost of computing the solution density of a given pair is in the worst case linear in $|Q|$, the number of states of the automaton.

3.2 An Incremental Version

Because a constraint's filtering algorithm is called on frequently, the graph for `regular` is not created from scratch every time but updated at every call. Given that we already maintain data structures to perform incremental filtering for `regular`, should we do the same when determining its solution count and solution densities?

For the purposes of the filtering algorithm, as one or several arcs are removed between two given layers of the graph as a consequence of a value being deleted from the domain of a variable, other arcs are considered for removal in the previous (resp. following) layers only if the out-degree (resp. in-degree) of some vertices at the endpoints of the removed arcs becomes null. Otherwise no further updates need to be propagated. Consequently even though the total amount of work in the worst case is bounded above by the size of the graph, it is often much less in practice.

In the case of solution counting, the labels that we added at vertices contain finer-grained information requiring more extensive updates. Removing an arc will change the labels of its endpoints but also those of every vertex reachable downstream and of every vertex upstream which can reach that arc. Here the total amount of work in practice may be closer to the worst case. Therefore maintaining the additional data structures could prove to be too expensive.

3.3 A Lazy Evaluation Version

We may not be interested in the value of $\#op()$ and $\#ip()$ for every combination of arguments — for example in some search heuristics we may only want the solution densities for a particular variable. One way to avoid useless work is to lazily evaluate the $\#op()/\#ip()$ values as we require them. *Memory functions* combine the goal-oriented, top-down approach of recursive calls with the compute-once ability of dynamic programming. The request for a solution density triggers the computation of the required $\#op()/\#ip()$ values. If that value has been computed before, it is simply looked up in a table. Otherwise, it is computed recursively and tabulated before it is returned to avoid recomputing it. In some cases only a small fraction of the vertex labels are actually computed, especially if we do not require the solution count of the constraint: if we only compare variable-value pairs within a constraint, solution densities can be replaced by the number of solutions in which each pair participates, thus avoiding the computation of $\#op(1, q_0)$.

On the Nonogram problem introduced in Section 5, the lazy evaluation version was slightly faster than the version computing from scratch and up to five times faster than the version maintaining the data structures. Consequently we used the lazy evaluation version in our experiments.

4 Counting for Alldifferent Constraints

The `alldifferent` constraint restricts a set of variables to be pairwise different [15].

Definition 3 (Value Graph). *Given a set of variables $X = \{x_1, \ldots, x_n\}$ with respective domains $D_1, \ldots, D_n$, we define the* value graph *as a bipartite graph $G = (X \cup D_X, E)$ where $D_X = \bigcup_{i=1,\ldots,n} D_i$ and $E = \{\{x_i, d\} \mid d \in D_i\}$.*

There exists a bijection between a maximum matching of size $|X|$ on the value graph and a solution of the related `alldifferent` constraint. Finding the number of solutions is then equivalent to counting the number of maximum matchings on the value graph.
Maximum matching counting is also equivalent to the problem of computing the permanent of a (0-1) matrix. Given a bipartite graph $G = (V_1 \cup V_2, E)$, with $|V_1| = |V_2| = n$, the related $n \times n$ adjacency matrix A has element $a_{i,j}$ equal to 1 if and only if vertex i is connected to vertex j. The permanent of a $n \times n$ matrix A is formally defined as:

$$per(A) = \sum_{\sigma \in S_n} \prod_i a_{i,\sigma(i)} \tag{1}$$

where S_n denotes the symmetric group, i.e. the set of $n!$ permutations of $[n]$. Given a specific permutation, the product is equal to 1 if and only if all the elements are equal to 1 i.e. the permutation is a valid maximum matching in the related bipartite graph. Hence, the sum over all the permutations gives us the total number of maximum matchings. In the following, we will freely use both matrix and graph representations.

4.1 Computing the Permanent

Permanent computation has been studied for the last two centuries and it is still a challenging problem to address. Even though the analytic formulation of the permanent resembles that of the determinant, there has been few advances on its exact computation. In 1979, Valiant [16] proved that the problem is #P-complete, even for 0-1 matrices, that is, under reasonable assumptions, it cannot be computed in polynomial time. The focus then moved to approximating the permanent. We can identify at least four different approaches for approximating the permanent: elementary iterative algorithms, reductions to determinants, iterative balancing, and Markov Chain Monte Carlo methods.

Elementary Iterative Algorithms. Rasmussen proposed in [13] a very simple recursive estimator for the permanent. This method works quite well for dense matrices but it breaks down when applied to sparse matrices; its time complexity is $O(n^3\omega)$ recently improved to $O(n^2\omega)$ by Fürer [3] (here ω is a function satisfying $\omega \to \infty$ as $n \to \infty$). Further details about these approaches will be given in the next section.

Reduction to Determinant. The determinant reduction technique is based on the resemblance of the permanent and the determinant. This method randomly replaces some 1-entry elements of the matrix by uniform random elements $\{\pm 1\}$. It turns out that the determinant of the new matrix is an unbiased estimator of the permanent of the original matrix. The proposed algorithms either provide an arbitrarily close approximation in exponential time [2] or an approximation within an exponential factor in polytime [1].

Iterative Balancing. The work of Linial et al. [8] exploits a lower bound on the permanent of a doubly stochastic[2] $n \times n$ matrix B: $per(B) \geq n!/n^n$. The basic idea is to use the linearity of permanents w.r.t. multiplication with constants and transform the original matrix A to an approximated doubly stochastic matrix B and then exploit the lower bound. The algorithm that they proposed runs in $O(n^5 \log^2 n)$ and gives an approximation within a factor of e^n.

Markov Chain Monte Carlo Methods. Markov Chains can be a powerful tool to generate almost uniform samples. They have been used for the permanent in [6] but they impose strong restrictions on the minimum vertex degree. A notable breakthrough was achieved by Jerrum et al. [7]: they proposed the first polynomial approximation algorithm for general matrices with non-negative entries. Nonetheless this remarkable result has to face its impracticality due to a very high-computational complexity $\tilde{O}(n^{26})$ improved to $\Theta(n^{10} \log^2 n)$ later on.

Note that for our purposes we are not only interested in computing the total number of solutions but we also need that solution densities for each variable-value pair. Moreover, we need fast algorithms that work on the majority of the matrices; since the objective is to build a search heuristic based on counting information, we would prefer a fast algorithm with less precise approximation

[2] $\sum_i a_{i,j} = \sum_j a_{i,j} = 1$.

over a slower algorithm with better approximation guarantees. With that in mind, Markov Chain-based algorithms do not fit our needs (they are either too slow or they have a precondition on the minimum vertex degree). Determinant based algorithms are either exponential in time or give too loose approximations (within an exponential factor) as well as algorithms based on matrix scaling. The approach that seems to suit our needs better is elementary iterative algorithms. It combines a reasonable complexity with a good approximation. Although it gives poor results for sparse matrices, those cases are likely to appear close to the leaves of the search tree where an error by the heuristics has a limited negative impact.

4.2 Rasmussen's Estimator and Its Extensions

Suppose we want to estimate a function Q (in our case the permanent): a traditional approach is to design an estimator that outputs a random variable X whose expected value is equal to Q. The estimator is unbiased if $E(X)$ and $E(X^2)$ are finite. A straightforward application of Chebyshev's inequality shows that if we conduct $O(\frac{E(X^2)}{E(X)^2}\epsilon^{-2})$ independent and identically distributed trials and we take the mean of the outcomes then we have guarantee of ϵ-approximation. Hence the performance of a single run of the estimator and the ratio $\frac{E(X^2)}{E(X)^2}$ (*critical ratio*) determine the efficiency of the algorithm.

In the following, we denote by $A(n,p)$ the class of random (0-1) $n \times n$ matrices in which each element has independent probability p of being 1. We write X_A for the random variable that estimate the permanent of the matrix A; $A_{i,j}$ denotes the submatrix obtained from A by removing row i and column j. The pseudo-code of Rasmussen's estimator is shown in Algorithm 4; despite its simplicity compared to other techniques, the estimator is unbiased and shows good experimental behaviour. Rasmussen gave theoretical results for his algorithm applied to random matrices belonging to the class $A(n, p \geq 1/2)$. He proved that for "almost all" matrices of this class, the critical ratio is bounded by $O(n\omega)$ where ω is a function satisfying $\omega \to \infty$ as $n \to \infty$; the complexity of a single run of the estimator is $O(n^2)$, hence the total complexity is $O(n^3\omega)$. Here "almost all" means that the algorithm gives a correct approximation with probability that goes to 1 as $n \to \infty$. While this result holds for dense matrices, it breaks down for sparse matrices. Note however that there are still matrices belonging to $A(n, p = 1/2)$ for which the critical ratio is exponential. Consider for instance the upper triangular matrix:

$$\mathbf{U} = \begin{pmatrix} 1 & 1 & \dots & 1 \\ & 1 & \dots & 1 \\ & & \ddots & \vdots \\ & & & 1 \end{pmatrix}$$

For this particular matrix Rasmussen's estimator has expected value $E(X_U) = 1$ and $E(X_U^2) = n!$, hence the approximation is likely to be very poor.

```
if n = 0 then
    X_A = 1
else
    W = {j : a_{1,j} = 1};
    if W = ∅ then
        X_A = 0;
    else
        Choose j u.a.r. from W;
        Compute X_{A_{1,j}};
        X_A = |W| · X_{A_{1,j}};
```

Algorithm 4. Rasmussen's estimator

Fürer et al. [3] enhanced Rasmussen's algorithm with some branching strategies in order to pick up more samples in the critical parts of the matrix. It resembles very closely the exploration of a search tree. Instead of choosing u.a.r. a single column j from W, Fürer picks up a subset $J \subseteq W$ and it iterates on each element of J. The number of times it branches is logarithmic in the size of the matrix, and for a given branching factor he showed that a single run of the estimator still takes $O(n^2)$ time. The advantage of this approach resides in the theoretical convergence guarantee: the number of required samples is only $O(\omega)$ instead of Rasmussen's $O(n\omega)$, thus the overall complexity is $O(n^2\omega)$. Both Fürer and Rasmussen estimators allow to approximately compute the total number of solution of an `alldifferent` constraint. However if we need to compute the solution density $\sigma(x_i, d, \gamma)$ we are forced to recall the estimators on the submatrix $A_{i,d}$. Hence the approximated solution density is:

$$\sigma(x_i, d, \gamma) \approx \frac{E(X_{A_{i,d}})}{E(X_A)} \qquad (2)$$

Adding Propagation to the Estimator. A simple way to improve the quality of the approximation is to add propagation to Rasmussen's estimator. After randomly choosing a row i and a column j, we can propagate on the submatrix $A_{i,j}$ in order to remove all the 1-entries (edges) that do not belong to any maximum matching (the pseudo-code is shown in Algorithm 5). This broadens

```
if n = 0 then
    X_A = 1
else
    Choose i u.a.r. from {1...n};
    W = {j : a_{i,j} = 1};
    Choose j u.a.r. from W;
    Propagation on A_{i,j};
    Compute X_{A_{i,j}};
    X_A = |W| · X_{A_{i,j}};
```

Algorithm 5. Estimator with propagation

the applicability of the method; in matrices such as the upper triangular matrix, the propagation can easily lead to the identity matrix for which the estimator performs exactly. However, as a drawback, the propagation takes an initial precomputation of $O(\sqrt{n}m)$ plus an additional $O(n+m)$ each time it is called [15] (here m is the number of ones of the matrix i.e. edges of the graph). A single run of the estimator requires n propagation calls, hence the time complexity is $O(nm)$; the overall time complexity is then $O(n^2 m\omega)$.

A particularity of the new estimator is that it removes a priori all the 1-entries that do not lead to a solution. Hence it always samples feasible solutions whereas Rasmussen's ends up with infeasible solutions whenever it reaches a case in which $W = \emptyset$. This opens the door also to an alternative evaluation of the solution densities; given the set of solution samples S, we denote by $S_{x_i,d} \subseteq S$ the subset of samples in which $x_i = d$. The solution densities are approximated as:

$$\sigma(x_i, d, \gamma) \approx \frac{|S_{x_i,d}|}{|S|} \tag{3}$$

Experimental results showed a much better approximation quality for the computation of the solution densities using samples (3) instead of using submatrix counting (2). It is worth pointing out that Fürer's provides several samples in a single run but highly biased from the decisions taken close to the root of the search tree; thus it cannot be used to compute solution densities from samples. Due to the better results obtained using samples, we decide not to apply propagation methods to Fürer's.

Table 1. Estimators performance

% Removals	0.1	0.2	0.3	0.4	0.5	0.6	0.7
			Counting Error				
Rasmussen	1.32	1.76	3.66	5.78	7.19	13.80	22.65
Fürer	0.69	1.07	1.76	2.17	2.52	4.09	5.33
CountS	1.44	1.51	2.48	2.30	4.31	3.94	1.23
			Average Solution Density Error				
Rasmussen	1.13	1.83	3.12	5.12	7.85	13.10	23.10
Fürer	0.58	0.92	1.55	2.49	3.74	6.25	8.06
CountS	0.73	0.76	0.80	1.01	1.33	1.81	2.03
			Maximum Solution Density Error				
Rasmussen	3.91	6.57	11.60	19.86	30.32	42.53	40.51
Fürer	2.09	3.20	5.75	9.36	15.15	21.18	15.01
CountS	2.64	2.60	2.89	3.90	5.39	6.03	2.61

Estimator Benchmarks. We compared three estimators: Rasmussen's, Fürer's, and ours (the version based on samples, "CountS"). Due to the very high computational time required to compute the exact number of solutions, we performed systematic experiments on `alldifferent` of size 10, 11 and 12 with varying percentage of domain value removals. Table 1 shows the error on the total number of solutions, the average and the maximum error on the solution densities (all the errors are expressed in percentage). The number of samples used is 100 times the size of the instance. The time taken for counting is slightly higher than one tenth of a second for our methods compared to one tenth for Fürer's and a few hundredths for Rasmussen's. On the other side, exact counting can take up to thousands of seconds for very loose instances to a few hundredths of a second. Due to lack of room, we do not show the tests with a common time limit: the situation is pretty much the same, with our method showing the best approximations. Note that we also tested our method with instances of bigger size (up to 30) and even with few samples (10 times the instance size): the average error remains pretty low (again on the order of 2-4%) as well as the maximum error. The current implementation of our approach makes use of Ilog Solver 6.2; we believe that a custom implementation can gain in performance, avoiding the overhead due to model extraction and to backtrack information bookkeeping.

5 Experimental Results

We evaluate the proposed constraint-centered search heuristics on two benchmark problems modeled with the `alldifferent` and `regular` constraints.

Nonogram. A Nonogram (problem 12 of CSPLib) is built on a rectangular $n \times m$ grid and requires filling in some of the squares in the unique feasible way according to some clues given on each row and column. As a reward, one gets a pretty monochromatic picture. Each individual clue indicates how many sequences of consecutive filled-in squares there are in the row (column), with their respective size in order of appearance. Each sequence is separated from the others by at least one blank square but we know little about their actual position in the row (column). Such clues can be modeled with `regular` constraints (the actual automata $\mathcal{A}_i^r, \mathcal{A}_j^c$ are not difficult to derive but lie outside the scope of this paper):

$$\begin{array}{ll} \texttt{regular}((x_{ij})_{1\le j\le m}, \mathcal{A}_i^r) & 1 \le i \le n \\ \texttt{regular}((x_{ij})_{1\le i\le n}, \mathcal{A}_j^c) & 1 \le j \le m \\ x_{ij} \in \{0,1\} & 1 \le i \le n,\ 1 \le j \le m \end{array}$$

These puzzles typically require some amount of search, despite the fact that domain consistency is maintained on each clue. We experimented with 75 instances[3] of sizes ranging from 16×16 to 24×24.

We compared four search heuristics: random selection for both variable and value, dom/ddeg variable selection with min conflicts value selection, MaxSD, and MinSC;MaxSD. A variable selection heuristic based solely on domain size is not useful for this problem since every unbound variable has an identical domain of size 2. Note also that for the same reason the min conflicts value selection does not discriminate at all.

Table 2 reports the average and median number of backtracks and the total computation time for these heuristics. dom/ddeg is definitely ill-suited for

[3] Instances taken from http://www.blindchicken.com/~ali/games/puzzles.html

Table 2. Number of backtracks and computation time (in seconds) for 75 Nonogram instances

heuristic	avg btk	median btk	total time
random var/val	348.0	16	40.7
dom/ddeg ; min conflicts	33640.4	146	4405.2
MaxSD	236.0	2	57.0
MinSC;MaxSD	48.5	3	8.9

such a problem: the statistics reported should even be higher since ten instances where interrupted after five minutes of computation. A purely random heuristic performs fairly well here, which can be explained by the binary domains of the variables: even a random choice of value has a 50% chance of success. MaxSD performs better than the random heuristic in terms of backtracks but not enough to offset its higher computational cost, yielding a slightly higher computation time. MinSC;MaxSD is the best of the four, with a significantly lower average number of backtracks and the best computation time. The difference in performance between our two heuristics is actually strongly influenced by a few instances for which MaxSD behaved poorly: if we look at the median number of backtracks, the two are very close and markedly lower than for the random heuristic.

Quasigroup with Holes. A Latin Square of order n is defined on a $n \times n$ grid whose squares each contain an integer from 1 to n such that each integer appears exactly once per row and column. The Quasigroup with Holes (QWH) problem gives a partially-filled Latin Square instance and asks to complete it. It is easily modeled as:

$\texttt{alldifferent}((x_{ij})_{1 \leq j \leq n}) \quad 1 \leq i \leq n$
$\texttt{alldifferent}((x_{ij})_{1 \leq i \leq n}) \quad 1 \leq j \leq n$
$x_{ij} = d \quad (i, j, d) \in S$
$x_{ij} \in \{1, 2, \ldots, n\} \quad 1 \leq i, j \leq n$

We tested four search heuristics: dom/ddeg variable selection with min conflicts value selection (one of the most robust heuristics for QWH), MinDom;MaxSD, MaxSD, and a lazy version of MaxSD. For counting, we used an exact algorithm for 0.1 seconds and, in case of timeout, we ran CountS for another 0.1 seconds. Note that the counting is done only if a domain event occurs, that is, the counting algorithm is woken up in a way that is similar to constraint propagation. The lazy version of maximum solution density recounts at each event when the search is close to the tree root (whenever less than 20% of variables are assigned), every 2 events when the unbound variables are between 20% and 50% and every 3 events thereafter. The four heuristics were tested on 40 balanced QWH instances with about 41% of holes, randomly generated following [4]. We set the time limit to 1200 seconds. Table 3 shows the results. The heuristics based on maximum density were the ones performing better in term of backtracks (two orders of magnitude of difference), total time and number of instances solved. We also ran some tests on easier instances outside the phase transition: the dom/ddeg heuristic did better than our heuristics in terms of running time but not in

Table 3. Number of backtracks, computation time (in seconds) and the number of unsolved instances for 40 hard QWH instances of order 30

heuristic	avg btk	median btk	total time	unsolved
dom/ddeg ; min conflicts	788887.1	365230.5	19070.7	10
MinDom;MaxSD	17626.3	10001.5	25983.8	19
MaxSD	5634.0	2534.2	11371.3	1
LazyMaxSD	7479.6	2243.7	10258.0	2

terms of number of backtracks. It is worth mentioning that the number of backtracks by our heuristics only diminished slightly on these easier instances, so the heuristics appear fairly robust throughout the range. We also tried some simple combinations of the solution densities (i.e. for each variable-value pair the sum of the solution densities of the two `alldifferent` constraints) but we did not experience any significant improvement.

6 Conclusion and Open Issues

This paper advocated using constraints not only for inference but also for search. The key idea is to use solution counting information at the level of individual constraints. We showed that for some widely-used constraints such information could be computed efficiently, especially given the support already in place for domain filtering. We also proposed novel search heuristics based on solution counting and showed their effectiveness through experiments. From the point of view of CP systems, we are really introducing a new functionality for constraints alongside satisfiability testing, consistency and domain filtering, entailment, etc. As we argued, providing this support does not necessarily require a lot of extra work. It would, however, benefit from some thinking about how best to offer access to solution counts and solution densities, from a programming language design perspective.

We believe there are still several open issues regarding this work. Even though we have had some success with the search heuristics we proposed, little has been tried so far about combining the information originating from the different constraints, which should increase robustness in cases where the constraints give hugely conflicting information. We saw already that some compromises were attempted for the `alldifferent` constraint to cut down its computation time — a more in-depth investigation is required, including finding out a way to make it more incremental. Finally there are many more families of constraints for which efficient solution counting algorithms must be found.

Acknowledgements

The authors would like to thank the anonymous referees for helpful comments and Michael Mac-Vicar for conducting some experiments.

References

1. Barvinok, A.: Polynomial time algorithms to approximate permanents and mixed discriminants within a simply exponential factor. Random Structures and Algorithms 14, 29–61 (1999)
2. Chien, S., Rasmussen, L., Sinclair, A.: Clifford Algebras and Approximating the Permanent. In: Proc. 34th Annual ACM Symposium on Theory of Computing (STOC), pp. 222–231. ACM Press, New York (2002)
3. Fürer, M., Kasiviswanathan, S.P.: An Almost Linear Time Approximation Algorithm for the Permanent of a Random (0-1) Matrix. In: Wallace, M. (ed.) CP 2004. LNCS, vol. 3258, pp. 54–61. Springer, Heidelberg (2004)
4. Gomez, C.P., Shmoys, D.: Completing Quasigroups or Latin Squares: A Structured Graph Coloring Problem. In: Proc. Computational Symposium on Graph Coloring and Generalizations (2002)
5. Gomes, C.P., Sabharwal, A., Selman, B.: Model Counting: A New Strategy for Obtaining Good Bounds. In: Proc. AAAI'06, pp. 54–61 (2006)
6. Huber, M.: Exact Sampling from Perfect Matchings of Dense Regular Bipartite Graphs. Algorithmica 44, 183–193 (2006)
7. Jerrum, M., Sinclair, A., Vigoda, E.: A Polynomial-time Approximation Algorithm for the Permanent of a Matrix with Non-Negative entries. In: Proc. 33th Annual ACM Symposium on Theory of Computing (STOC), pp. 712–721. ACM Press, New York (2001)
8. Linial, N., Samorodnitsky, A., Wigderson, A.: A deterministic strongly polynomial algorithm for matrix scaling and approximate permanents. Combinatorica 20, 545–568 (2000)
9. Kask, K., Dechter, R., Gogate, V.: Counting-Based Look-Ahead Schemes for Constraint Satisfaction. In: Wallace, M. (ed.) CP 2004. LNCS, vol. 3258, pp. 317–331. Springer, Heidelberg (2004)
10. Patel, J., Chinneck, J.W.: Active-Constraint Variable Ordering for Faster Feasibility of Mixed Integer Linear Programs. Mathematical Programming (2006)
11. Pesant, G.: A regular language membership constraint for finite sequences of variables. In: Wallace, M. (ed.) CP 2004. LNCS, vol. 3258, pp. 482–495. Springer, Heidelberg (2004)
12. Pesant, G.: Counting Solutions of CSPs: A Structural Approach. In: Proc. IJCAI'05, pp. 260–265 (2005)
13. Rasmussen, L.E.: Approximating the permanent: a simple approach. Random Structures and Algorithms 5, 349–361 (1994)
14. Refalo, P.: Impact-Based Search Strategies for Constraint Programming. In: Wallace, M. (ed.) CP 2004. LNCS, vol. 3258, pp. 557–571. Springer, Heidelberg (2004)
15. Régin, J.-C.: A Filtering Algorithm for Constraints of Difference in CSPs. In: Proc. Twelfth National Conference on Artificial Intelligence (AAAI), vol. 1, pp. 362–367. AAAI Press, Stanford, California, USA (1994)
16. Valiant, L.G.: The complexity of computing the permanent. Theoretical Computer Science 8, 189–201 (1979)

Min-Domain Ordering for Asynchronous Backtracking*

Roie Zivan, Moshe Zazone, and Amnon Meisels

Department of Computer Science,
Ben-Gurion University of the Negev
Beer-Sheva, 84-105, Israel
{zivanr,moshezaz,am}@cs.bgu.ac.il

Abstract. Ordering heuristics are a powerful tool in CSP search algorithms. Among the most successful ordering heuristics are heuristics which enforce a *fail first* strategy by using the min-domain property [10,4,20,6]. Ordering heuristics have been introduced recently to *Asynchronous backtracking (ABT)*, for distributed constraints satisfaction (*DisCSP*) [27]. However, the pioneering study of dynamically ordered ABT, ABT_DO, has shown that a straightforward implementation of the min-domain heuristic does not produce the expected improvement over a static ordering. The best ordering heuristic for asynchronous backtracking was found to be the *Nogood-triggered* heuristic.

The present paper proposes an asynchronous dynamic ordering which does not follow the standard restrictions on the position of reordered agents in ABT_DO. Agents can be moved to a position that is higher than that of the target of the backtrack ($culprit$).

Combining the Nogood-triggered heuristic and the min-domain property in this new class of heuristics results in the best performing version of ABT_DO. The new version of retroactively ordered ABT is faster by a large factor than the best form of ABT.

1 Introduction

Distributed constraint satisfaction problems (*DisCSPs*) are composed of agents, each holding its local constraints network, that are connected by constraints among variables of different agents. Agents assign values to variables, attempting to generate a locally consistent assignment that is also consistent with all constraints between agents (cf. [24,21]). To achieve this goal, agents check the value assignments to their variables for local consistency and exchange messages with other agents, to check consistency of their proposed assignments against constraints with variables owned by different agents [24,2].

A search procedure for a consistent assignment of all agents in a distributed CSP ($DisCSP$), is a distributed algorithm. All agents cooperate in search for a globally consistent solution. The solution involves assignments of all agents to all their variables and exchange of information among all agents, to check the consistency of assignments with constraints among agents.

* Supported by the Lynn and William Frankel center for Computer Sciences and the Paul Ivanier Center for Robotics and Production Management.

C. Bessiere (Ed.): CP 2007, LNCS 4741, pp. 758–772, 2007.

Asynchronous Backtracking (*ABT*) is one of the most efficient and robust algorithms for solving distributed constraints satisfaction problems. Asynchronous Backtracking was first presented by Yokoo [25,24] and was developed further and studied in [9,3,17,2]. Agents in the *ABT* algorithms perform assignments asynchronously according to their current view of the system's state. The method performed by each agent is in general simple. Later versions of *ABT* use polynomial space memory and perform dynamic backtracking [3,2]. The versions of asynchronous backtracking in all of the above studies use a static priority order among all agents.

An asynchronous algorithm with dynamic ordering was proposed by [23], Asynchronous Weak Commitment (*AWC*). According to [24], *AWC* outperforms *ABT* on specific applications (N-queens, Graph-coloring). The heuristic used by *AWC* is very specific. Move any agent that sends back a *Nogood* to be first in the order of all agents [24]. However, in order to be complete, *AWC* uses exponential space for storing *Nogoods* [24]. This can be a problem when solving hard instances of *DisCSPs*.

An attempt to combine *ABT* with *AWC* was reported by [18]. In order to perform asynchronous finite reordering operations [18] propose that the reordering operation will be performed by abstract agents. In a later study the exact heuristic of *Dynamic Backtracking* [8] was proposed for *ABT* with dynamic ordering [16]. The results presented in both studies [18,16] show minor improvements to *ABT* with static ordering.

A general algorithm for dynamic ordering in asynchronous backtracking, *ABT_DO*, was presented in [27]. The *ABT_DO* algorithm uses polynomial space, similarly to standard *ABT*. In the *ABT_DO* algorithm the agents of the *DisCSP* choose orders dynamically and asynchronously. Agents in *ABT_DO* perform computation according to the current, most updated order they hold. There are three rules on the changes of orderings of agents in *ABT_DO*. Each agent can change the order of agents who have a lower priority than its own. An agent can propose an order change each time it replaces its assignment. Each order is time-stamped according to the assignments performed by agents [28].

Ordering heuristics are one of the most powerful tools for increasing the efficiency of standard *CSP* search algorithms [10,4,6,22]. Heuristics which are successful for sequential CSP algorithms were shown to fail to improve run-time when combined with asynchronous backtracking [28]. Thus, an investigation of ordering heuristics for asynchronous backtracking on *DisCSPs* is needed.

The results presented in [28] show that the performance of *ABT_DO* is highly dependent on the selected heuristic. The classic *Min-Domain* heuristic was implemented by including the current domain size of agents in the messages they send. Surprisingly, this heuristic which in centralized algorithms and in distributed algorithms using a sequential assignment protocol produces a large improvement over static order, was found not to be efficient for Asynchronous Backtracking. A heuristic which achieved a significant improvement was inspired by *Dynamic Backtracking* [8,1] in which the agent which sends a *Nogood* is advanced in the new order to be immediately after the agent to whom the *Nogood* was sent. The explanation for the success of this heuristic is that it does not cause the removal of relevant *Nogoods* as do other heuristics [28].

In the present paper we investigate the relation between the success of this heuristic and the *min-domain* heuristic which was found to be successful for sequential assignments (synchronous) algorithms on *DisCSPs* [5,14]. We demonstrate the effect of *Nogood* loss as a result of reordering on the failure of the *min domain* heuristic. Removal of *Nogoods* cause the return of values to the agent's domains. This harms the accuracy of the information that agents hold on the domain size of other agents. On the other hand, the *Nogood-triggered* heuristic of [27] does not lose valid information and moves agents with a potential of having a small domain to a higher position.

In order to maximize the *min-domain* property, a more flexible heuristic is proposed, which violates the restrictions on the ordering of agents in [27]. We study changes of order that move agents to a higher position, replacing agents that were ahead of them including the first agent. This new type of heuristics is termed *Retroactive ordering* and is based on a slightly modified version of ABT_DO.

The results presented in the present paper show that moving the $Nogood$ sender as high as possible in the priority order is successful only if the domain size of agents is taken into consideration. Our experiments show that the successful heuristics are those that support a *min-domain* scheme in which agents are moved to a higher position only if their current domain size is smaller than the current domain of agents they are moved in front of. Moving an agent before the agents which are included in the $Nogood$ actually *enlarges* its domain. The best heuristic in the present paper is that agents which generate a $Nogood$ are placed in the new order between the last and the second last agents in the generated $Nogood$. This heuristic is the asynchronous form of the Min-Domain heuristic. Agents are moved to a higher position only if their domain is smaller than the agents they pass on the way up. Our results on both random $DisCSPs$ and on structured $DisCSPs$ show that the proposed heuristic improves the best results to date [28] by a large factor.

Distributed $CSPs$ are presented in Section 2. A description of Asynchronous backtracking with dynamic ordering (ABT_DO) and its best heuristic is presented in Section 3. Section 4 presents an investigation of the existing heuristics and offers reasons for their performance in previous papers. Section 5 present the general scheme of retroactive heuristics for ABT_DO and a correctness proof. An extensive experimental evaluation, which compares standard and retroactive heuristics of ABT_DO is in Section 7. The experiments were conducted on randomly generated $DisCSPs$ and on Course Scheduling problems. Section 8 presents a discussion of the relation between the experimental results and the *min-domain* heuristic.

2 Distributed Constraint Satisfaction

A distributed constraint satisfaction problem - *DisCSP* is composed of a set of k agents $A_1, A_2, ..., A_k$. Each agent A_i contains a set of constrained variables $X_{i_1}, X_{i_2}, ..., X_{i_{n_i}}$. Constraints or **relations** R are subsets of the Cartesian product of the domains of the constrained variables. For a set of constrained variables $X_{i_k}, X_{j_l}, ..., X_{m_n}$, with domains of values for each variable $D_{i_k}, D_{j_l}, ..., D_{m_n}$, the constraint is defined as $R \subseteq D_{i_k} \times D_{j_l} \times ... \times D_{m_n}$. A **binary constraint** R_{ij} between any two variables X_j and X_i is a subset of the Cartesian product of their domains; $R_{ij} \subseteq D_j \times D_i$. In a distributed constraint satisfaction problem *DisCSP*, constrained variables can belong to different agents [25,21]. Each agent has a set of constrained variables, i.e. a *local constraint network*.

An assignment (or a label) is a pair $< var, val >$, where var is a variable of some agent and val is a value from var's domain that is assigned to it. A *compound label* (or a partial solution) is a set of assignments of values to a set of variables. A **solution** P to a *DisCSP* is a compound label that includes all variables of all agents, that satisfies all the constraints. Agents check assignments of values against non-local constraints by communicating with other agents through sending and receiving messages. Agents exchange messages with agents whose assignments may be in conflict [2]. Agents connected by constraints are therefore called *neighbors*. The ordering of agents is termed *priority*, so that agents that are later in the order are termed "lower priority agents" [24,2].

The following assumptions are routinely made in studies of $DisCSP$s and are assumed to hold in the present study [24,2].

1. All agents hold exactly one variable.
2. Messages arrive at their destination in finite time.
3. Messages sent by agent A_i to agent A_j are received by A_j in the order they were sent.

3 ABT with Dynamic Ordering

Each agent in ABT_DO holds a $Current\_order$ which is an ordered list of pairs. Every pair includes the ID of one of the agents and a counter. Each agent can propose a new order for agents that have lower priority (i.e. are in a lower position in the current order), each time it replaces its assignment. This way the sending of an ordering proposal message always coincides with an assignment message (an **ok?** message [26,27]). An agent A_i can propose an order according to the following rules:

1. Agents with higher priority than A_i and A_i itself, do not change priorities in the new order.
2. Agents with lower priority than A_i, in the current order, can change their priorities in the new order *but not to a higher priority than A_i itself* (This rule enables a more flexible order than in the centralized case).

The counters attached to each agent ID in the *order* list form a time-stamp. Initially, all time-stamp counters are set to zero and all agents start with the same $Current\_order$. Each agent A_i that proposes a new order, changes the order of the pairs in its own ordered list and updates the counters as follows:

1. The counters of agents with higher priority than A_i, according to the $Current\_order$, are not changed.
2. The counter of A_i is incremented by one.
3. The counters of agents with lower priority than A_i in the $Current\_order$ are set to zero.

In ABT, agents send **ok?** messages to their neighbors whenever they perform an assignment. In ABT_DO, an agent can choose to change its $Current\_order$ after changing its assignment. If that is the case, besides sending **ok?** messages an agent sends **order** messages to all lower priority agents. The **order** message includes the agent's new $Current\_order$.

An agent which receives an **order** message must determine if the received order is more updated than its own $Current\_order$. It decides by comparing the time-stamps lexicographically. Since orders are changed according to the above rules, every two orders must have a common prefix of agents' IDs. The agent that performs the change does not change its own position and the positions of higher priority agents.

When an agent A_i receives an order which is more up to date than its $Current\_order$, it replaces its $Current\_order$ by the received order. The new order might change the location of the receiving agent with respect to other agents (in the new $Current\_order$). In other words, one of the agents that had higher priority than A_i according to the old order, now has a lower priority than A_i or vice versa. Therefore, A_i rechecks the consistency of its current assignment and the validity of its stored $Nogoods$ (the explanations for removing values from its domain [26,27]) according to the new order. If the current assignment is inconsistent according to the new order, the agent makes a new attempt to assign its variable. In ABT_DO agents send **ok?** messages to all constraining agents (i.e. their neighbors in the constraints graph). Although agents might hold in their $Agent\_views$ assignments of agents with lower priorities, according to their $Current\_order$, they eliminate values from their domain *only if they violate constraints with higher priority agents.*

A $Nogood$ message (i.e. a message carrying a partial assignment which was found to be inconsistent [26,27]) is always checked according to the $Current\_order$ of the receiving agent. If the receiving agent is not the lowest priority agent in the $Nogood$ according to its $Current\_order$, it sends the $Nogood$ to the lowest priority agent and sends an **ok?** message to the sender of the $Nogood$. This is a similar operation to that performed in standard ABT for any unaccepted (inconsistent) $Nogood$ [2].

4 Investigation of Asynchronous Heuristics

In this section we offer explanations for the failure of the *min-domain* heuristic and the success of the *Nogood-triggered* heuristic when used in asynchronous backtracking [27,28]. Consider the example in Figure 1. The agents are ordered by their indices. Each agent has a single variable and three values, *a*, *b* and *c*, in its domain. The eliminated values are crossed and each points to its eliminating explanation (i.e. the assignment which caused its removal). The circled values represent the current assignments. In this example, agent A_5 has exhausted its domain and must create a $Nogood$. The $Nogood$ it generates includes the assignments of A_1 and A_2 therefore the $Nogood$ is sent to A_2. According to the rules of the ABT_DO algorithm agent A_2 can reorder agents A_3, A_4 and A_5. Now, if it will reorder them according to their current domain sizes then A_3 and A_4 will switch places. But, since both of the values eliminated from the domain of A_4 are in conflict with the assignment of A_3 then after they change places, these values will be returned to the domain of A_4 and its domain size will be larger than the domain of A_3.

In contrast, if A_2 reorders according to the *Nogood-triggered* heuristic then the only agent to change places is A_5 which is moved to be after A_2 and before A_3. Now, after A_2 replaces its assignment we get the situation in Figure 2. We can see that an agent with a small domain was moved forward while the others kept their domain sizes and places.

The example demonstrates why the *min-domain* heuristic fails when used in asynchronous backtracking. In asynchronous backtracking, all agents hold an assignment throughout the search. Conflicts with these assignments effect the size of domains of other agents. For each value which is removed from an agent's domain an explanation $Nogood$ is stored. When an agent is moved in front of an agent whose assignment is included in one of its $Nogoods$, this $Nogood$ must be eliminated and the corresponding value is returned to the domain. Thus, in contrast to sequential ordering algorithms, in asynchronous backtracking the resulting domain sizes after reordering cannot be anticipated by the ordering agent. The example demonstrates how this phenomena does not affect the *Nogood-triggered* heuristic.

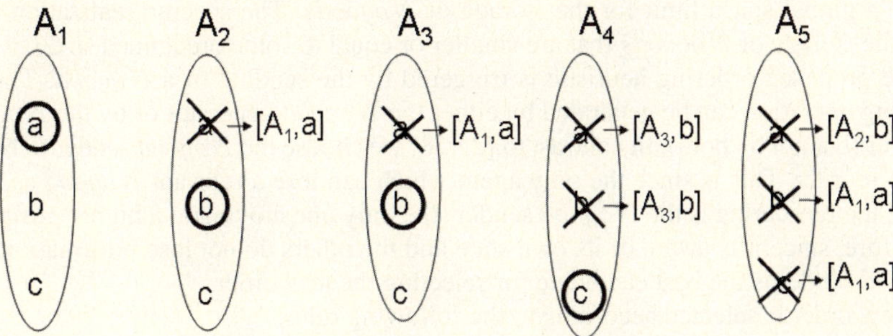

Fig. 1. Heuristics example before backtrack

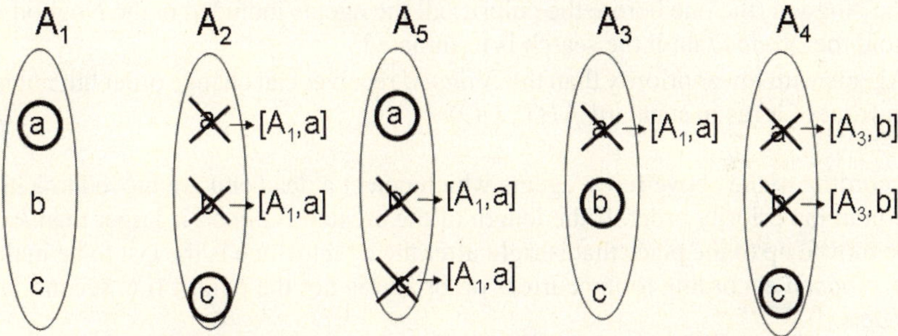

Fig. 2. After reordering using the NG-triggered heuristic

Following the example one can see that the *Nogood-triggered* heuristic is successful because in many cases it moves an agent with a small domain to a higher position. Only values whose *Nogood* explanation includes the assignment of the culprit agent are returned to the moving agent's domain. In fact, the agent can be moved up passed the culprit, and as long as it does not pass the second last assignment in the *Nogood* its domain size will stay the same. In Figure 2, Agent A_5 is moved right after agent A_2. Its domain size is one, since the *Nogoods* of its other two values are valid. If A_5 is moved before A_2 its domain size will stay the same as both eliminating *Nogoods* include only the assignment of A_1. However, if A_5 will be moved in front of A_1 then all its values will return to its domain. This possibility of moving an agent with a small domain beyond the culprit agent to a higher position is the basic motivation for retroactive ordering.

5 Retroactive Ordering Heuristics for ABT

In contrast to the rules of *ABT_DO* of the previous section, the present paper proposes a new type of ordering. The new type of ordering can change the order of agents with higher priority than the agent which replaces its assignment. A *retroactive* heuristic would enable moving the *Nogood* sender to a higher position than the *Nogood* receiver. In order to preserve the correctness of the algorithm, agents must be allowed to store *Nogoods*. In order to generate a general scheme for retroactive heuristics, one can define a global space limit for the storage of $Nogoods$. The specific realization is to limit the storage of $Nogoods$ that are smaller or equal to some predefined size k.

The proposed ordering heuristic is triggered by the sending of a $Nogood$. The re-ordering operation can be generated by either the $Nogood$ generator or by the $Nogood$ receiver (but not by both). In contrast to [27,28] we choose the $Nogood$ sender to be the one to reorder. This is since the only agent which can lose a relevant $Nogood$ as a result of the reordering is the $Nogood$ sender (the only one moving to a higher position). Therefore, since it is aware of its own state and the others do not lose information, the $Nogood$ sender is the best candidate for selecting the new order.
The new order is selected according to the following rules:

1. The $Nogood$ generator can be moved to any position in the new order.
2. If the Nogood generator is moved to a position which is before the second last in the Nogood (the one before the culprit) all the agents included in the Nogood must hold the $Nogood$ until the search is terminated.
3. Agents with lower priority than the $Nogood$ receiver can change order but not move in front of it (as in standard ABT_DO).

According to the above rules, agents which detect a dead end are moved to a higher position in the priority order. If the length of the created $Nogood$ is larger than k, they can be moved up to the place that is right after the agent which is the last to be included in the $Nogood$ according to the current order and is not the culprit (i.e. second last in the $Nogood$).

If the length of the created $Nogood$ is smaller or equal to k, the sending agent can be moved to a position before all the participants in the $Nogood$ and the $Nogood$ is sent and saved by all of them. In the extreme case where k is equal to the number of agents in the $DisCSP$ (i.e. $k = N$), the $Nogood$ sender can always move to be first in the priority order and the resulting algorithm is a generalization of AWC [24].

Figures 3 and 4 present the code of *Retroactive ABT_DO*. The difference from standard ABT_DO in the code performed when a $Nogood$ is received (Figures 3) derives from the different possible types of $Nogoods$. A $Nogood$ smaller or equal to k is actually a constraint that will be stored by the agent until the search is terminated. In the case of $Nogoods$ which are longer than k, the algorithm treats them as in standard ABT_DO i.e. accepts them only if the receiver is the lowest priority agent in the $Nogood$ and the $Nogood$ is consistent with the $Agent\_view$ and $current\_assignment$ of the receiver. In any case of acceptance of a $Nogood$, the agent searches for a new assignment only if it happens to be the lowest priority agent in the $Nogood$. As stated above, our choice is that only the $Nogood$ generator is allowed to change order.

Procedure **backtrack** (Figure 4) is largely changed in the retroactive heuristic version of ABT_DO. When an agent creates a $Nogood$ it determines whether it is larger than k or not. If it is larger then a single $Nogood$ is sent to the lowest priority agent in the $Nogood$ in the same way as in ABT_DO. Consequently, the agent selects a new order in which it puts itself not higher than the second lowest priority agent in the $Nogood$. When the $Nogood$ is smaller or equal to k, if it is the first time this $Nogood$ is generated, the $Nogood$ is sent to all the agents included in the $Nogood$ and the agent moves itself to an unlimited position in the new order (In this case the function **choose_new_order** is called with no limitations). In both cases, order messages are sent to all the lower priority agents in the new order. The assignment of the lowest priority agent in the $Nogood$

```
when received (ok?, (x_j, d_j) do:
  add (x_j, d_j) to agent_view;
  remove inconsistent nogoods;
  check_agent_view;

when received (order, received_order) do:
  if (received_order is more updated than Current_order)
     Current_order ← received_order;
     remove inconsistent nogoods;
     check_agent_view;

when received (nogood, x_j, nogood)
  old_value ← current_value
  if (nogood contains an agent x_k
        with lower priority than x_i and nogood.size > K)
     send (nogood, (x_i, nogood)) to x_k;
  else
     if (nogood consistent with {Agent_view ∪
           current_assignment} or nogood.size ≤ K)
        store nogood;
        if (nogood contains an agent x_k that is not its neighbor)
           request x_k to add x_i as a neighbor;
           add (x_k, d_k) to agent_view;
        if(x_i is with lowest priority in nogood)
           check_agent_view;
  if(old_value = current_value)
     send (ok?, (x_i, current_value)) to x_j;
```

Fig. 3. Retroactive ABT_DO algorithm (first part)

is removed from the *Agent_view*, the relevant *Nogoods* are removed and the agent attempts to re-assign its variable by calling **check_agent_view**.

Procedure **check_agent_view** (Figure 3)is slightly changed from that of *ABT_DO* [28] since the change of order in the new scheme is perfor med by the *Nogood* sender and not by its receiver.

6 Correctness of Retroactive *ABT_DO*

In order to prove the correctness of *Retroactive ABT_DO* we assume the correctness of the standard *ABT_DO* algorithm (see proof in [28]) and prove that the changes made for retroactive heuristics do not damage its correctness. We first prove the case for no *Nogood* storage ($k = 0$):

Theorem 1. Retroactive ABT_DO *is correct when* $k = 0$.

There are two differences between standard *ABT_DO* and *Retroactive ABT_DO* with $k = 0$. First, order is changed whenever a *Nogood* is sent and not when an assignment is replaced. This change does not make a difference in the correctness since when a *Nogood* is sent there are two possible outcomes. Either the *Nogood* receiver replaces its assignment, which makes it effectively the same as in standard *ABT_DO*, or the *Nogood* is rejected. A rejected *Nogood* can only be caused by a change of assignment

```
procedure backtrack
nogood ← resolve_inconsistent_subset;
if (nogood is empty)
   broadcast to other agents that there is no solution;
   stop;
select (x_j, d_j) where x_j has the lowest priority in nogood;
if(nogood.size > K)
   Current_order ← choose_new_order()
            where x_l has the second lowest priority in nogood;
   send (nogood, x_i, nogood) to x_j;
else if(is_new(nogood))
   new_position ← unlimited
   send (nogood, x_i, nogood) to all agents in nogood;
   store sent nogood;
Current_order ← choose_new_order(x_l)
send (order,Current_order) to lower priority agents;
remove (x_j, d_j) from agent_view;
remove all nogoods containing (x_j, d_j);
check_agent_view;

procedure check_agent_view
if(current_assignment is not consistent with all
      higher priority assignments in Agent_view)
   if(no value in D_i is consistent with all higher priority
         assignments in Agent_view)
      backtrack;
   else
      select d ∈ D_i where Agent_view and d are consistent;
      current_value ← d;
      send (ok?,(x_i, d)) to neighbors;
```

Fig. 4. The Retroactive ABT_DO algorithm (second part)

either of the receiving agent or of an agent with higher priority. In all of these cases, the most relevant order is determined lexicographically. Ties which could not have been generated in standard ABT_DO, are broken using the agents indexes.

The second change in the code for $k = 0$ is that in *Retroactive ABT_DO* a $Nogood$ sender can move to a position in front of the agent that receives the $Nogood$. Since the $Nogood$ sender is the only agent moving to a higher position, it is the only one that can lose a $Nogood$ as a result. However, the $Nogood$ sender removes all $Nogoods$ containing the assignment of the $Nogood$ receiver and it does not pass any other agent contained in the $Nogood$. Thus, no information is actually lost by this change. Moreover, the number of times two agents can move in front of one another without a higher priority agent changing its assignment is bounded by their domain sizes. □

Theorem 2. *$RetroactiveABT\_DO$ is correct when $n \geq k > 0$.*

In order to prove that $RetroactiveABT\_DO$ is correct for the case that $n \geq k > 0$ we need to show that infinite loops cannot occur. In the case of $Nogoods$ which are smaller or equal to k the case is very simple. All agents involved in the $Nogood$ continue to hold it, therefore the same assignment can never be produced again. The number of these Nogoods with a limited length is finite. In finite time the algorithm reaches a state in which no permanent $Nogoods$ are added. In this state, agents do not move in front of the second last in the $Nogoods$ generated and the previous proof holds. □

7 Experimental Evaluation

The common approach in evaluating the performance of distributed algorithms is to compare two independent measures of performance - time, in the form of steps of computation [12,24], and communication load, in the form of the total number of messages sent [12].

Non concurrent steps of computation, are counted by a method similar to the clock synchronization algorithm of [11]. Every agent holds a counter of computation steps. Every message carries the value of the sending agent's counter. When an agent receives a message it stores the data received together with the corresponding counter. When the agent first uses the received counter it updates its counter to the largest value between its own counter and the stored counter value which was carried by the message [29]. By reporting the cost of the search as the largest counter held by some agent at the end of the search, a measure of non-concurrent search effort that is close to Lamports logical time is achieved [11]. If instead of steps of computation, the number of non concurrent constraint checks is counted ($NCCC$s), then the local computational effort of agents in each step is measured [13,29].

The first set of experiments was conducted on random networks of constraints of n variables, k values in each domain, a constraints density of p_1 and tightness p_2 (which are commonly used in experimental evaluations of CSP algorithms [19,15]). The constraint networks were generated with 20 agents ($n = 20$) each holding exactly one variable, 10 values for each variable ($k = 10$) with two different constraints densities $p_1 = 0.4$ and $p_1 = 0.7$.. The tightness value p_2, is varied between 0.1 and 0.9, to cover all ranges of problem difficulty. For each pair of fixed density and tightness (p_1, p_2) 50 different random problems were solved by each algorithm and the results presented are an average of these 50 runs.

In order to confirm the dependency of the performance on the size of the current domain of the moved agents, we compared ABT_DO with ABT_DO with a retroactive heuristic in which agents are not allocated any additional $Nogood$ storage. Agents include in their messages the size of their current domains. This information is stored in the agent's $Agent\_views$ (as in [28]). A $Nogood$ generator moves itself to be in a higher position than the culprit agent but it moves in front of an agent *only if its current domain is smaller* than the domain of that agent. Otherwise, it places itself right after the culprit agent as in standard ABT_DO.

The Left Hand Side (LHS) of Figure 5 presents the results in $NCCCs$ for ABT_DO and Retroactive ABT_DO with the above heuristic. The retroactive version of ABT_DO (depicted in the figures as *min-domain*) improves the run-time performance of ABT_DO (depicted as ABT_DO_NG). In order to emphasize the relation to the *Min-Domain* property, a third line in Figures 5, 6 and 8 represents retroactive ABT_DO without checking the domain sizes (depicted in the figures as *After Second Last*). This version of retroactive ABT_DO was the slowest among the three. Similar results for the number of messages sent are presented on the Right Hand Side (RHS) of Figure 5. In the case of network load, both versions of *Retroactive* ABT_DO send less messages than standard ABT_DO. For high density problems the difference between the algorithms is similar but smaller (Figure 6).

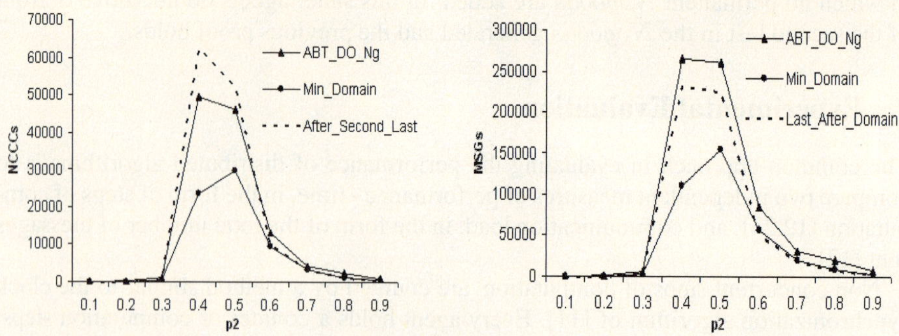

Fig. 5. Non concurrent constraint checks performed and messages sent by Retroactive ABT_DO and ABT_DO on low density DisCSPs ($p_1 = 0.4$)

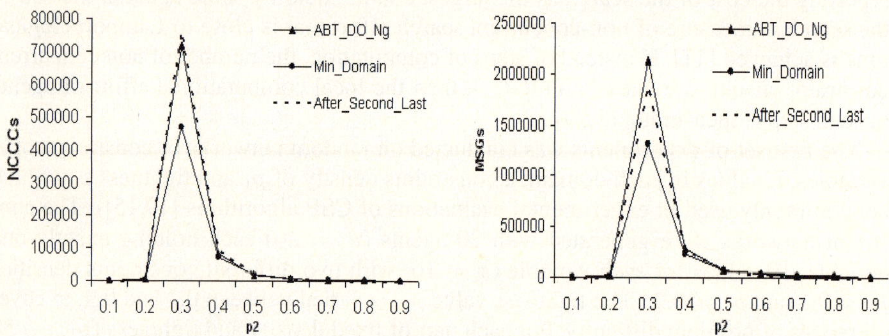

Fig. 6. Non concurrent constraint checks performed and messages sent by Retroactive ABT_DO and ABT_DO on high density DisCSPs ($p_1 = 0.7$)

In order to further demonstrate the dependency of the domain size of agents on the success of the selected heuristic we performed an additional experiment on random problems in which the size limit for keeping $Nogoods$ is varied[1]. A $Nogood$ generator which created a $Nogood$ of length larger than k places itself right after the $Nogood$ receiver as in standard ABT_DO. When the $Nogood$ generator creates a $Nogood$ smaller or equal to k, it places itself first in the priority order and sends the generated $Nogood$ to all the participating agents. In the case of $k = n$ the resulting algorithm is exactly AWC. In the case of $k = 0$ the resulting algorithm is standard ABT_DO. The LHS of Figure 7 presents the number of $NCCCs$ performed by the algorithm with k equal to 0, 1, 3 and n ($n = 15$). The results show similar performance when k is small. The performance of the algorithm deteriorates when $k = 3$ and the slowest performance is when $k = n$. Similar results in the number of messages are presented on the RHS of Figure 7.

The fact that a larger storage which enables more flexibility of the heuristic actually causes a deterioration of the performance might come as a surprise. However, one must

[1] In this experiment the problems were smaller ($n = 15$) since the algorithms run slower.

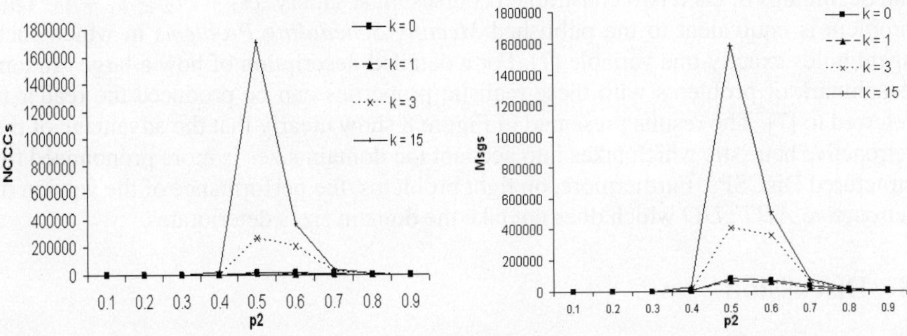

Fig. 7. Non concurrent constraint checks performed and messages sent by Retroactive ABT_DO with different limits on Nogood size ($p_1 = 0.4$)

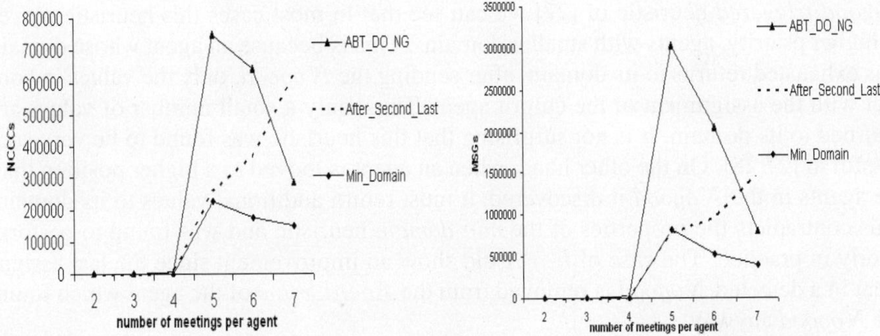

Fig. 8. Non concurrent constraint checks performed and messages sent by Retroactive ABT_DO and ABT_DO on Random Course Scheduling Problems

examine the effect of the specific heuristic used on the size of the domains of the agents which are moved up in the order of priorities. An agent creates a $Nogood$ when its domain empties. After sending the $Nogood$ it removes the assignment of the culprit agent from its $Agent\_view$ and returns to the domain only values whose eliminating $Nogood$ included the removed assignment. When the agent is moved in front of other agents whose assignments were included in the generated $Nogood$ it must return more values to its domain (the values whose explanation $Nogood$ included the assignment of the agent which was passed). This of course does not happen for the case of a $Nogood$ of size one and that is why for $k = 1$ we get better results. Thus, moving an agent as high as possible in the priority order actually results in moving upwards an agent with a larger domain.

In the next set of experiments, the successful versions of ABT with retroactive dynamic ordering were compared on realistic structured problems. The generated problems were course scheduling in which each variable assigned to an agent represents a single course which is taken by a number of students. Two variables are constrained if there is a student attending both courses. The constraints are arrival constraints, i.e. if the length of a course is t_1 and the time to get from one course to the other is t_2, then the beginnings of each two constrained courses must satisfy: $ct_1 - ct_2 \geq t_1 + t_2$. This problem is equivalent to the published *Meeting Scheduling Problems* in which each agent holds exactly one variable [7]. For a detailed description of how a large random benchmark of problems with these realistic properties can be produced the reader is referred to [7]. The results presented in Figure 8 show clearly that the advantage of the retroactive heuristic which takes into account the domain sizes is more pronounced for structured DisCSPs. Furthermore, on tight problems, the performance of the version of retroactive ABT_DO which does not take the domain sizes deteriorates.

8 Discussion

The results in the previous section show clearly the relation between the examined heuristics and the *Min-Domain* property of the generated search tree. A well known fact from centralized CSP algorithms [10,6] and from $DisCSP$ algorithms with a sequential assignment protocol [5] is that the *Min-Domain* heuristic is very powerful and improves the run of the same algorithms using a static order. If we investigate the *Nogood-triggered* heuristic of [27] we can see that in most cases this heuristic moves to higher priority, agents with smaller domains. This is because an agent whose domain was exhausted returns to its domain, after sending the $Nogood$, only the values in conflict with the assignment of the culprit agent. Thus, only a small number of values are returned to its domain. It is not surprising that this heuristic was found to be very successful in [27,28]. On the other hand, when an agent is moved to a higher position than the agents in the $Nogood$ it discovered, it must return additional values to its domain. This contradicts the properties of the *min-domain* heuristic and was found to perform poorly in practice. The case of $k = 1$ did show an improvement since the last assignment in a detected $Nogood$ is removed from the $Agent\_view$ of the agent which found the $Nogood$ anyway.

In our best performing heuristic, agents are moved higher in the priority order as long as their domain size is smaller than the domains of the agents before them and as long as they do not pass the second last in the $Nogood$ they have generated, which would result in returning more values to their domain. Since the agent moving to a higher position is not in conflict with the assignments of agents it has moved in front of, its move will not cause the loss of $Nogoods$ and therefore the information it holds on the size of the current domains of these agents remains valid. The retroactive ordering version has improved the results of [27,28] by a factor of 2. In the case of structured problems, this heuristic was found to improve the run of the standard ABT_DO by an even larger factor.

9 Conclusion

A general scheme for retroactive heuristics in Asynchronous Backtracking with dynamic agent ordering was presented. The flexibility of the heuristic is dependent upon the amount of memory that agents are allowed to use. However, moving agents to the highest position possible was found to deteriorate the performance of the algorithm. The best heuristic, moves to a higher priority only agents whose variable's domains are small but avoid the return of values to domains as a result of reordering. This brings to an extreme the exploitation of the *Min-Domain* property, and improves the run of the best heuristic reported so far [27,28] by a large factor.

References

1. Baker, A.B.: The hazards of fancy backtracking. In: Proceedings of the 12th National Conference on Artificial Intelligence (AAAI '94), Seattle, WA, USA, July 31 - August 4 1994, vol. 1, pp. 288–293. AAAI Press, Stanford, California, USA (1994)
2. Bessiere, C., Maestre, A., Brito, I., Meseguer, P.: Asynchronous backtracking without adding links: a new member in the abt family. Artificial Intelligence 161(1-2), 7–24 (2005)
3. Bessiere, C., Maestre, A., Messeguer, P.: Distributed dynamic backtracking. In: Proc. Workshop on Distributed Constraint of IJCAI01 (2001)
4. Bessiere, C., Regin, J.C.: Mac and combined heuristics: two reasons to forsake fc (and cbj?) on hard problems. In: Freuder, E.C. (ed.) CP 1996. LNCS, vol. 1118, pp. 61–75. Springer, Heidelberg (1996)
5. Brito, I., Meseguer, P.: Synchronous,asnchronous and hybrid algorithms for discsp. In: Wallace, M. (ed.) CP 2004. LNCS, vol. 3258. Springer, Heidelberg (2004)
6. Dechter, R.: Constraint Processing. Morgan Kaufman, San Francisco (2003)
7. Gent, I.P., Walsh, T.: Csplib: a benchmark library for constraints. In: Jaffar, J. (ed.) Principles and Practice of Constraint Programming – CP'99. LNCS, vol. 1713. Springer, Heidelberg (1999), `http://csplib.cs.strath.ac.uk/`
8. Ginsberg, M.L.: Dynamic Backtracking. J. of Artificial Intelligence Research 1, 25–46 (1993)
9. Hamadi, Y.: Distributed interleaved parallel and cooperative search in constraint satisfaction networks. In: Proc. Intelligent Agent Technology, 2001 (IAT-01), Singappore (2001)
10. Haralick, R.M., Elliott, G.L.: Increasing tree search efficiency for constraint satisfaction problems. Artificial Intelligence 14, 263–313 (1980)
11. Lamport, L.: Time, clocks, and the ordering of events in distributed system. Communication of the ACM 2, 95–114 (1978)
12. Lynch, N.A.: Distributed Algorithms. Morgan Kaufmann, San Francisco (1997)
13. Meisels, A., Razgon, I., Kaplansky, E., Zivan, R.: Comparing performance of distributed constraints processing algorithms. In: Alonso, E., Kudenko, D., Kazakov, D. (eds.) Adaptive Agents and Multi-Agent Systems. LNCS (LNAI), vol. 2636, pp. 86–93. Springer, Heidelberg (2003)
14. Meisels, A., Zivan, R.: Asynchronous forward-checking for distributed csps. Constraints 12(1) (2007)
15. Prosser, P.: An empirical study of phase transitions in binary constraint satisfaction problems. Artificial Intelligence 81, 81–109 (1996)
16. Silaghi, M.C.: Generalized dynamic ordering for asynchronous backtracking on discsps. In: AAMAS 2006, DCR workshop, Hakodate, Japan (2006)
17. Silaghi, M.C., Faltings, B.: Asynchronous aggregation and consistency in distributed constraint satisfaction. Artificial Intelligence 161(1-2), 25–54 (2005)
18. Silaghi, M.C., Sam-Haroud, D., Faltings, B.: Hybridizing abt and awc into a polynomial space, complete protocol with reordering. Technical Report 01/#364, EPFL (May 2001)
19. Smith, B.M.: Locating the phase transition in binary constraint satisfaction problems. Artificial Intelligence 81, 155–181 (1996)
20. Smith, B.M., Grant, S.A.: Trying harder to fail first. In: European Conference on Artificial Intelligence, pp. 249–253 (1998)
21. Solotorevsky, G., Gudes, E., Meisels, A.: Modeling and solving distributed constraint satisfaction problems (dcsps). In: Freuder, E.C. (ed.) CP 1996. LNCS, vol. 1118, pp. 561–562. Springer, Heidelberg (1996)
22. Wallace, R.J.: Factor analytic studies of csp heuristics. In: van Beek, P. (ed.) CP 2005. LNCS, vol. 3709, pp. 712–726. Springer, Heidelberg (2005)
23. Yokoo, M.: Asynchronous weak-commitment search for solving distributed constraint satisfaction problems. In: Proc. 1st Intrnat. Conf. on Const. Progr., Cassis, France, pp. 88–102 (1995)

24. Yokoo, M.: Algorithms for distributed constraint satisfaction problems: A review. Autonomous Agents & Multi-Agent Sys. 3, 198–212 (2000)
25. Yokoo, M., Durfee, E.H., Ishida, T., Kuwabara, K.: Distributed constraint satisfaction problem: Formalization and algorithms. IEEE Trans. on Data and Kn. Eng. 10, 673–685 (1998)
26. Yokoo, M., Hirayama, K.: Distributed Constraint Satisfaction Problems. Springer, Heidelberg (2000)
27. Zivan, R., Meisels, A.: Dynamic ordering for asynchronous backtracking on discsps. In: van Beek, P. (ed.) CP 2005. LNCS, vol. 3709, pp. 32–46. Springer, Heidelberg (2005)
28. Zivan, R., Meisels, A.: Dynamic ordering for asynchronous backtracking on discsps. Constraints 11(2,3), 179–197 (2006)
29. Zivan, R., Meisels, A.: Message delay and asynchronous discsp search. Archives of Control Sciences 16(2), 221–242 (2006)

Answer Set Optimization for and/or Composition of CP-Nets: A Security Scenario*

Stefano Bistarelli[1,2], Pamela Peretti[1], and Irina Trubitsyna[3]

[1] Dipartimento di Scienze, Università "G. d'Annunzio", Pescara, Italy
{bista,peretti}@sci.unich.it

[2] Istituto di Informatica e Telematica, CNR, Pisa, Italy
Stefano.Bistarelli@iit.cnr.it

[3] DEIS Università della Calabria, Rende, Italy
irina@deis.unical.it

Abstract. Defence trees are used to represent attack and defence strategies in security scenarios; the aim in such scenarios is to select the *best* set of countermeasures have to be applied to stop all the vulnerabilities. To represent the preference among the possible countermeasures of a given attack, defence trees are enriched with CP-networks (CP-net for short). However, for complex trees, composing CP-nets could be not always effective. In this paper we overcome these limitations by transforming each CP-net in an *Answer Set Optimization* (ASO) program. The ASO program, representing the overall scenario, is a special composition of the programs associated to each branch of the defence tree. The best set of countermeasure able to mitigate all the vulnerabilities is then obtained by computing the optimal answer set of the corresponding ASO program.

1 Introduction

Security has become today a fundamental part of the enterprise investment. In fact, more and more cases are reported showing the importance of assuring an adequate level of protection to the enterprise's assets. In order to focus the real and concrete threat, a risk management process is needed to identify, describe and analyze the possible vulnerabilities that have to be eliminated or reduced. The final goal of the process is to make security managers aware of the possible risks, and to guide them toward the adoption of a set of countermeasures which can bring the overall risk under an acceptable level.

Defence trees, DT [3], have been introduced as a methodology for the analysis of attack/defence security scenarios. A DT is an *and-or* tree, where leaves node represent the vulnerabilities and the set of countermeasures available for their mitigation, and nodes represent attacks composed by a set of actions that have to be performed as a whole, and or nodes represent attacks that can succeed also by completing only one of their child action. Notice that to defeat and attacks it is enough to patch one of the vulnerabilities (by selecting a single

* This paper is partially supported by the MIUR PRIN 2005-015491.

C. Bessiere (Ed.): CP 2007, LNCS 4741, pp. 773–781, 2007.

countermeasure), whilst to stop or attacks, one countermeasure for each of the actions composing the attack has to be selected.

The overall goal is to use the defence tree representation for the selection of the best set of countermeasures (w.r.t. specific preference criteria such as cost, efficiency, etc.), that can stop all the attacks to the system. To guide the selection, *CP-nets* [5] have been proposed to model preferences over attacks and countermeasures [4]. However, CP-nets are a graphical formalism that is good and elegant for representing small scenarios, but not so effective for big and complex scenarios. In particular, the methodology proposed in [4] aims at composing together the CP-nets associated to each branch of the tree. Each CP-net, in turn, represents the preferences among the countermeasure able to stop a specific attack.

In this paper the preference among countermeasures and the dependency between attacks and countermeasures, represented as a CP-net, are translated in *answer set optimization* (ASO) [8] programs. The and and or composition of the branch is then obtained by a syntactic composition of the ASO programs, whose semantics completely respects the intended meaning given in [4]. The semantics of the obtained ASO program provides a set of ordered answer sets representing the ordered sets of countermeasure to be adopted. To deal with ordered attacks (from the more to the less dangerous), the model is extended by introducing a corresponding rank among the preference rules of an ASO program. In this case, a preference cycle among countermeasure could be generated in the resulting CP-net. The use of ranked ASO program avoids this problem; in fact, the introduction of meta-preferences gives precedence to the adoption of countermeasures covering the more dangerous of the attacks (and removing in this way the possibility to obtain a cycle).

2 Defence Tree

Defence trees [3] are an extension of attack trees [12] and are used to represent attack strategies that can be used a mitigation factor.

The root of the tree is associated with an asset of the IT system under consideration and represents the attacker's goal. Leaf nodes in the attack tree represent simple subgoals which lead the attacker to damage the asset by exploiting a single vulnerability. Non-leaf nodes (including the tree root) can be of two different types: or-nodes and and-nodes. Subgoals associated with or-nodes are completed as soon as any of its child nodes is achieved, while and-nodes represent subgoals which require all of its child nodes to be completed (in the following we draw an horizontal line between the arcs connecting an and-node to its children to distinguish it from an or-node). The standard attack tree is then enriched by decorating every leaf node with a set of countermeasures. Each countermeasure associated with a leaf node represents a possible way of mitigating risk in an attack scenario where that specific vulnerability is used.

Notice that in order to mitigate the risks deriving from an or-attack, the system administrator has to introduce into the system *a countermeasure for*

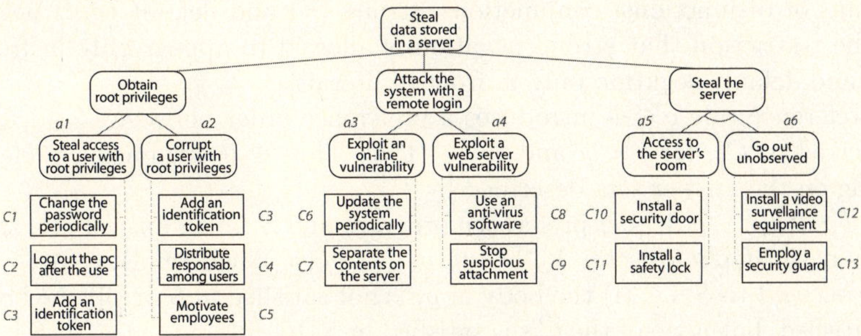

Fig. 1. An example of defence tree

each possible action of the branch. To mitigate the risks associated with an and-attack, instead, it *is enough to introduce a countermeasure for one of the attack actions* in the and-attack to stop the entire attack.

In the following example we use a defence tree to model an attack/defence scenario for an organization's IT system.

Example 1. An enterprise's server is used to store information about customers. Figure 1 shows the corresponding attack/defence scenario: rounded-box nodes denote the attack strategies and the different actions the attacker needs to perform, while square box denote the different countermeasures the system administrator can adopt. △

3 Answer Set Optimization Programs

Prioritized reasoning is an important extension of logic programming, that introduce preference on partial and complete solutions. A variety of approaches was proposed in the literature (see [10] for a survey of this topic). In this work we uses two approaches for representing and reasoning with preference statements: ASO and CR-prolog$_2$.

The ASO approach uses preference rules in order to express the preference relations among the combinations of atoms and introduces the preference order among these rules. Moreover a tool implementing the ASO semantics and its extensions, CHOPPER, has been recently proposed in [9].

An alternative way consists in the use of CR-prolog [1], a knowledge representation language based on the answer set semantic enriched with the introduction of consistency-restoring rules that allows a formalization of events or exceptions that are unlikely, unusual, or undesired. Its extension, CR-prolog$_2$ [2] admits the ordered disjunction in the head of rules and can be used to represent preferences intended as strict preferences (as in CR-prolog) or desires (LPOD [7]).

An answer set optimization program (ASO) is a pair $\langle \mathcal{P}, \Phi \rangle$, where $\mathcal{P}$ is an answer set program [11], called *Generating Program*, and Φ is called *Preference Program* and consists of a finite set of preference rules of the form $\varrho : \; C_1 > \cdots > C_k \leftarrow body$, where *body* is a conjunction of literals, i.e. atoms or negation of atoms, and C_is are *boolean combinations* of literals, i.e formulas built of atoms by means of disjunctions, conjunctions, strong ($\neg$) and default (*not*) negation with the restriction that strong negation is allowed to appear only in front of atoms and default negation only in front of literals.

A preference rule $\varrho \in \Phi$ introduces a preference order between $C_1, ..., C_k$: C_i is preferred to C_j, for $i < j$ and $i, j \in [1..k]$. Thus Φ determines a preference ordering on the answer sets described by $\mathcal{P}$.

Let $\Phi = \{\varrho_1, ..., \varrho_n\}$ be a preference program and S be an answer set, then S induces a *satisfaction vector* $V_S = (v_S(\varrho_1), ..., v_S(\varrho_n))$ where: a) $v_S(\varrho_j) = I$, if ϱ_j is *Irrelevant* to S, i.e. (i) the body of ϱ_j is not satisfied in S or (ii) the body of ϱ_j is satisfied, but none of the C_is is satisfied in S. b) $v_S(\varrho_j) = min\{i : S \models C_i\}$, otherwise. The satisfaction vectors are used to compare the answer sets.

Let S_1 and S_2 be two answer sets, then (i) $S_1 \geq S_2$ if $V_{S_1} \leq V_{S_2}$, i.e. if $v_{S_1}(\varrho_i) \leq v_{S_2}(\varrho_i)$ for every $i \in [1..n]$; (ii) $S_1 > S_2$ if $V_{S_1} < V_{S_2}$, i.e. if $V_{S_1} \leq V_{S_2}$ and for some $i \in [1..n]$ $v_{S_1}(\varrho_i) < v_{S_2}(\varrho_i)$.
A set of literals S is an *optimal answer set* of an ASO program $\langle \mathcal{P}, \Phi \rangle$ if S is an answer set of $\mathcal{P}$ and there is no answer set S' of $\mathcal{P}$ such then $S' > S$.

The ASO strategy is further extended by introducing *meta-preferences* among preference rules: a ranked ASO program is a sequence $\langle \mathcal{P}, \Phi_1, ..., \Phi_n \rangle$ consisting of a generating program $\mathcal{P}$ and a sequence of pairwise disjoint preference programs Φ_i. The rank of a rule $r \in \Phi_1 \cup \cdots \cup \Phi_n$, denoted $rank(r)$, is the unique integer i for which $r \in \Phi_i$.

Intuitively, the rank of the preference rule determines its importance: preference rules with lower rank are preferred over preference rules with higher rank. The optimal answer sets can be obtained in the following way: firstly, all answer sets optimal w.r.t. Φ_1 have to be selected; then, have to be selected the ones optimal w.r.t. Φ_2; and so on. More formally, $S_1 \geq_{rank} S_2$ if for every preference rule r' such that $v_{S_1}(r') \leq v_{S_2}(r')$ does not hold, there is a rule r'' such that $rank(r'') < rank(r')$ and $v_{S_1}(r'') < v_{S_2}(r'')$.

4 CP-Defence Trees

CP-networks [5] are a graphical formalism for representing and reasoning with preference statements which proposes a *ceteris paribus* (all else being equal) interpretation. The combination of defence trees and CP-nets has been recently proposed [4] as a methodology to help the system administrator to analyze a security scenario and to give him a model to represent preferences among countermeasure.

The resulting structure, called *CP-defence tree*, integrating the CP-net described in Figure 2 is presented in Figure 2(c). The CP-net graph G in Figure 2(a) highlights that the preference over countermeasures is conditioned by the corresponding attack. $CPT(A)$ describes the preference of protecting from each attack $a_i \in A$: the system administrator prefers to protect the action a_2 to the action a_1, a_1 to the action a_6 and so on. $CPT(C)$ collects the preferences among the countermeasures, that protect each action. For instance, for the action a_3 the countermeasure c_6 is preferable to c_7.

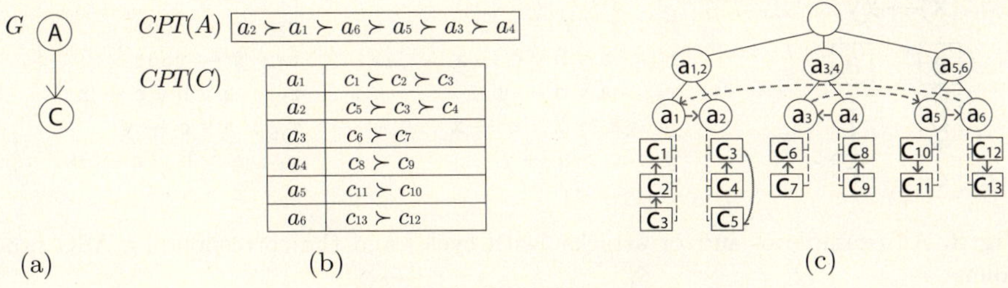

a_1	$c_1 \succ c_2 \succ c_3$
a_2	$c_5 \succ c_3 \succ c_4$
a_3	$c_6 \succ c_7$
a_4	$c_8 \succ c_9$
a_5	$c_{11} \succ c_{10}$
a_6	$c_{13} \succ c_{12}$

Fig. 2. A CP-defence tree

Considering Figure 2(c) the preference order over actions, described in $CPT(A)$, is represented with dotted arrows; while conditional preferences over countermeasures, described in $CPT(C)$, are represented by using solid arrows. The arrows are directed from the less preferred to the more preferred outcome.

Thus, given an IT system represented as the root of the tree, the corresponding CP-defence tree gives a graphical representation of the attack strategies that an attacker can pursue to damage the system, the different actions composing each attack and the countermeasures to be activated to stop them. Moreover, a preference order among attacks and countermeasures is highlighted.

4.1 *and/or* Composition of Attacks

In order to find the preferred defence strategy, the approach, consisting in the composition of preferences, was proposed in [4]. More in details, two different methods establishing the preference order among the countermeasures able to stop an and-attack and an or-attack were presented.

and-composition. To protect the system from an attack obtained by an and-composition of actions, the system administrator can stop any one of them. When an order among attacks is given the resulting strategy consist in the selection of the best countermeasure for the most dangerous of the actions.

Sometime not only the best countermeasure have to be activated but some of them (for instance because the countermeasure is only able to cover part of the attack). In this case the system administrator need to consider not only the best countermeasure, but the overall resulting countermeasure order.

More formally, given the and-attack, composed by two actions u and v, where $u \succ v$, and given the sets of countermeasures D_u and D_v, protecting from u and v respectively, and two partial order $(D_u, \succ_u)$ and $(D_v, \succ_v)$, the *and-composition* of preferences is a new partial order $(D_u \cup D_v, \succ_{v \wedge v})$, where a countermeasure c is preferred to a countermeasure c' if (i) it is preferred in at least one of the partial orders $(D_u, \succ_u)$, $(D_v, \succ_v)$, i.e. $c \succ_u c'$ or $c \succ_v c'$, otherwise (ii) c is the worst countermeasure in $(D_u, \succ_u)$, while c' is the best countermeasure in $(D_v, \succ_v)$, i.e $\forall x \in\ D_u,\ x \not\succ_u c$ and $\forall y \in\ D_v,\ c' \not\succ_v y$.

Thus, the and-composition, corresponding to the and-attack, preserves the partial orderings among the countermeasures, corresponding to each attack ac-

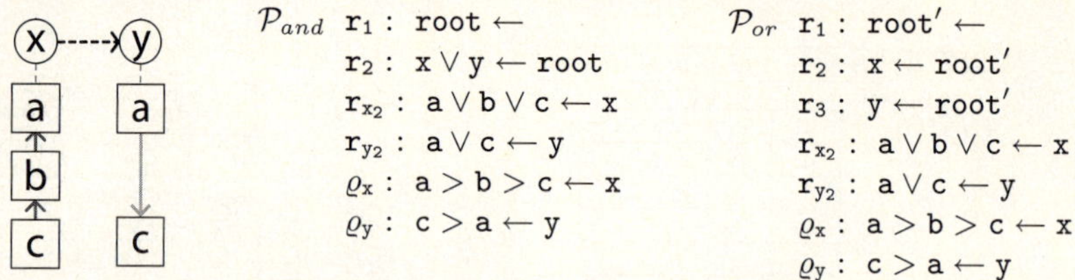

Fig. 3. An example of and/or attacks (with cycle) and the corresponding ASO programs

tion and introduces the *bridge preference rule*, connecting the corresponding orderings. As an example consider the defence tree in the left side of Figure 3, and consider an and-attack *root*, composed by two actions x and y, where $y \succ x$. The order obtained by and-composition is $c \succ a \succ b \succ c$. We can notice that in this case a cycle is obtained. Since the countermeasure of the worst attacks have to be considered as preferred, the cycle is broken by removing one of the preference among the countermeasure of the less dangerous attack x. More precisely, the preference relations, described in $(D_y, \succ_y)$ has to be considered as more important, and the relation $b \succ_x c$, generating (transitively) the conflict, has to be omitted.

As shown [6] not always is possible determine the most preferred outcome from a CP-net with an inconsistent preference order (i.e. cycle). In order to solve this problem we use the preference order over attacks in order to delete some edges from the induced preference graph and break the cycle. If we don't use this information we can obtain more that one outcome and we can't select the most preferred countermeasure to stop an and-attack.

Let us now to consider how to model this by using ASO programs.

Example 2. Consider the attack action depicted in left side of Figure 3, the attack action x and the preference order over the corresponding countermeasures a, b, and c generate the following ASO program $\langle \mathcal{P}_x, \Phi_x \rangle$:

$$\mathcal{P}_x \quad \mathtt{r_{x_1}} : \mathtt{x} \leftarrow, \ \ \mathtt{r_{x_2}} : \mathtt{a} \vee \mathtt{b} \vee \mathtt{c} \leftarrow \mathtt{x} \qquad \Phi_x \quad \varrho_{\mathtt{x}} : \mathtt{a} > \mathtt{b} > \mathtt{c} \leftarrow \mathtt{x}$$

where the rule r_{x_1} and r_{x_2} introduce the action and the possible countermeasures, while ϱ_x represents the preference order among them. The same result is obtained for the attack action y, the corresponding $\langle \mathcal{P}_y, \Phi_y \rangle$ program is:

$$\mathcal{P}_y \quad \mathtt{r_{y_1}} : \mathtt{y} \leftarrow, \ \ \mathtt{r_{y_2}} : \mathtt{a} \vee \mathtt{c} \leftarrow \mathtt{y} \qquad \Phi_y \quad \varrho_{\mathtt{y}} : \mathtt{c} > \mathtt{a} \leftarrow \mathtt{y}$$

In order to model the and-node *root*, a new program $\langle \mathcal{P}_{and}, \Phi_y, \Phi_x \rangle$ is generated combining the rules in $\langle \mathcal{P}_x, \Phi_x \rangle$ and $\langle \mathcal{P}_y, \Phi_y \rangle$ (see Figure 3). $\mathcal{P}_{and}$ introduces two new rules: r_1 represents the root action, while r_2 combines the action x and y in such way that only one of them must be stopped. The others rules are a added without any change. The answer sets of $\mathcal{P}_{and}$ are $M_1 = \{w, x, a\}$, $M_2 = \{w, x, b\}$, $M_3 = \{w, x, c\}$, $M_4 = \{w, y, c\}$ and $M_5 = \{w, y, a\}$. In order to establish the optimal answer set, the ASO semantics firstly constructs the satisfaction vectors $V_{M_1} = [\infty, 1]$[1], $V_{M_2} = [\infty, 2]$, $V_{M_3} = [\infty, 3]$, $V_{M_4} = [1, \infty]$ and $V_{M_5} = [2, \infty]$, reporting the satisfaction degree of

[1] In this application the irrelevance corresponds to the worst case.

each preference rule in the answer sets. Considering firstly ϱ_y and then ϱ_x the order among the answer set is $M_4 > M_5 > M_1 > M_2 > M_3$[2]. Concluding, the new order among the countermeasures is $c > a > b$. △

or-composition. The second method, called *or-composition*, was used to determine a preference order in the selection of the countermeasures able to stop an or-attack, i.e. an attack composed by a set of alternative actions one of which has to be successfully achieved to obtain the goal. The protection from this kind of attack consists in the protection from all the actions composing the or-attack. Intuitively, the most preferred strategy has to select the best countermeasure for each action or the countermeasure able to stop the bigger number of actions.

Again, in order to be able to select more than one countermeasure, a complete order among all of them need to be created. More formally, given the or-attack X, composed by k actions $u_1, \ldots, u_k$, the sets of countermeasures $D_{u_1}, \ldots, D_{u_k}$ protecting $u_1, \ldots, u_k$ respectively, and the orders among countermeasure $(D_{u_i}, \succ_{u_i})$ for $i = \{1, \ldots, k\}$, then the or-composition is a new order $(D_X, \succ_X)$. The order is defined over the set D_X, whose elements $C_1, ..., C_n$ are the sets of countermeasures covering all the attacks $u_1, ...u_k$, and $\succ_X$ is defined as follows: the set C is preferred to the set C' if there is a permutation π such that for all $i \in [1, \ldots, k]$, c_i is not worst than $c'_{\pi(i)}$, i.e. for $k = k'$, $\exists \pi$ s.t. $c_i \nprec c'_{\pi(i)}$. Notice also that when the same countermeasure is selected two times (to cover two different attacks), we consider its presence only one time.

Using the logic programming and the ASO semantics we can determine the preferred set of countermeasure faster than using the classical CP-net.

Example 3. As an example consider again the defence tree in the left side of Figure 3 and the or-attack *root'* composed by three action x and y. The corresponding ASO program $\langle \mathcal{P}_{or}, \Phi_y, \Phi_x \rangle$ is generated combing $\langle \mathcal{P}_x, \Phi_x \rangle$, $\langle \mathcal{P}_y, \Phi_y \rangle$ (see Figure 3). A new rule r_1, introduced in $\mathcal{P}_{or}$, represents *root'*, while the rules r_2, r_3 and r_4 model the or-attack, i.e. that all the three action must be stopped to stop the root.

The answer sets of $\mathcal{P}_{or}$ are $M_1 = \{root', x, y, a\}$ and $M_2 = \{root', x, y, c\}$[3] and describes the application of two alternative sets of countermeasures $\{a\}$ and $\{c\}$, protecting from the or-attack. In order to establish the optimal answer set, the ASO semantics firstly construct the satisfaction vectors $V_{M_1} = [1, 2]$ and $V_{M_2} = [2, 1]$. Then it compares these vectors, by firstly considering $\varrho_y \in \Phi_y$, obtaining that $V_{M_2} < V_{M_1}$. Concluding, M_2 is the optimal answer set and $\{c\}$ is the preferred set of countermeasures. △

Implementation. Given an IT system *root* and the corresponding CP-defence tree $\mathcal{T}$, the selection of the preferred defence strategy can be modelled by means of the corresponding logic program with preferences, then an ASO program

---

2. Notice that both the answer set M_1 and M_5 contain countermeasure a. However, we collect the countermeasure to be applied starting from the best model, so from M_4 we collect c from M_5 we collect a, and from M_2 we collect b.

3. We reminded that the ASO semantics [8] only collect minimal answer set, so among the set $M_1 = \{root', x, y, a\}$ and $M'_1 = \{root', x, y, b, a\}$ only M_1 is considered because M'_1 is not minimal.

solver can be used to automatically obtain the set of the best countermeasure. We used for our security scenario analysis CPDT-SOLVER. CPDT-SOLVER is an application-oriented version of CHOPPER [9], realizing ASO semantics over the ranked answer set optimization program, under the assumption that $I \equiv \infty$.

The same scenarios can be represented also by using the CR-Prolog$_2$ semantics, the only difference is that the preference among the countermeasures and the corresponding ordering can be written by using only one rule. An implementation is available for download from `http://www.krlab.cs.ttu.edu/Software/`.

5 Conclusion

In this paper we use the ASO semantics as an instrument to represent and solve the problem of countermeasure selection in a security scenario defined using a defence tree and a CP-net. The CP-net is used to describe the dependency among attacks and countermeasures, the preferences among the countermeasures, and (possibly) the order among attacks (depending from their seriousness or other parameters), whilst the defense tree represent the scenario associating each countermeasure to each attack action. The structure of the defence tree is built bottom-up by connecting with `and` nodes actions to be performed at a whole and with `or` node actions that by themselves can lead to a successful attack. In particular, the composition of CP-net needed to deal with `and`/`or` nodes is substituted by a composition of the corresponding ASO program. The composition of the ASO programs results extremely easy w.r.t. the composition of CP-net, and automatically remove cycles that can be obtained with `and`-composition.

References

1. Balduccini, M., Gelfond, M.: Logic programs with consistency-restoring rules. In: AAAI 2003. Int. Symp. on Logical Formalization of Commonsense Reasoning. Spring Symposium Series, pp. 9–18 (2003)
2. Balduccini, M., Mellarkod, V.S.: Cr-prolog2: Cr-prolog with ordered disjunction. In: ASP03 Answer Set Programming, vol. 78 (2003)
3. Bistarelli, S., Fioravanti, F., Peretti, P.: Defense tree for economic evaluations of security investment. In: 1st Int. Conf. on Availability, Reliability and Security (ARES'06), pp. 416–423 (2006)
4. Bistarelli, S., Fioravanti, F., Peretti, P.: Using cp-nets as a guide for countermeasure selection. In: ACM SAC2007. ACM Press, New York (2007)
5. Boutilier, C., Brafman, R.I., Domshlak, C., Hoos, H., Poole, D.: Cp-nets: A tool for representing and reasoning with conditional ceteris paribus preference statements. JAIR 21 (2004)
6. Brafman, R.I., Dimopolous, Y.: Extended semantics and optimization algorithms for cp-networks. Computational Intelligence 20(2), 218–245 (2004)
7. Brewka, G.: Logic programming with ordered disjunction. In: 18th Conf. on Artificial intelligence, pp. 100–105. American Association for AI (2002)
8. Brewka, G., Niemela, I., Truszczynski, M.: Answer set optimization. In: Proc. of the 18th Int. Joint Conf. on Artificial Intelligence, pp. 867–872 (2003)

9. Caroprese, L., Trubitsyna, I., Zumpano, E.: Implementing prioritized reasoning in logic programming. In: Proc. of the ICEIS (2007)
10. Delgrande, J.P., Schaub, T., Tompits, H., Wang, K.: A classification and survey of preference handling approaches in nonmonotonic reasoning. Computational Intelligence 20(2), 308–334 (2004)
11. Gelfond, M., Lifschitz, V.: Classical negation in logic programs and disjunctive databasesg. New Generation Computing 9, 365–385 (1991)
12. Schneier, B.: Attack trees: Modeling security threats. Dr. Dobb's Journal (1999)

Uncertainty in Bipolar Preference Problems

Stefano Bistarelli[1,2], Maria Silvia Pini[3], Francesca Rossi[3], and K. Brent Venable[3]

[1] Dipartimento di Scienze, Università "G. d'Annunzio", Pescara, Italy
[2] Istituto di Informatica e Telematica, CNR, Pisa, Italy
Stefano.Bistarelli@iit.cnr.it
[3] Dipartimento di Matematica Pura ed Applicata, Università di Padova, Italy
{mpini,frossi,kvenable}@math.unipd.it

Abstract. Preferences and uncertainty are common in many real-life problems. In this paper, we focus on bipolar preferences and on uncertainty modelled via uncontrollable variables. However, some information is provided for such variables, in the form of possibility distributions over their domains. To tackle such problems, we eliminate the uncertain part of the problem, making sure that some desirable properties hold about the robustness of the problem's solutions and its relationship with their preference. We also define semantics to order the solutions according to different attitudes with respect to the notions of preference and robustness.

1 Introduction

Bipolar preferences and uncertainty are present in many application fields, such as satellite scheduling, logistics, and production planning. For example, in multi-agent problems, agents may express their preferences in a bipolar way, and variables may be under the control of different agents. To give a specific example, just consider a conference reviewing system, where usually preferences are expressed in a bipolar scale. Uncertainty can arise for the number of available conference rooms at the time of the acceptance decision, and the goal could be to select the best papers while ensuring that they all can be presented. In general, in many real-life situations agents express what they like and what they dislike, thus often preferences are bipolar.

In this paper, bipolarity is handled via the formalism in [3]. Other formalisms can be found in [8,1,4,5]. We choose to generalize to bipolar preferences the soft constraints formalism [2] which is able to model problems with one kind of preferences (i.e., the negative preferences). Thus, each partial instantiation within a constraint will be associated to either a positive or a negative preference.

Another important feature, which arises in many real world problems, is uncertainty. We model uncertainty by the presence of *uncontrollable* variables. This means that the value of such variables will not be decided by us, but by Nature or by some other agent. Thus a solution will not be an assignment to all the variables but only to the controllable ones. A typical example of uncontrollable variable, in the context of satellite scheduling, is a variable representing the time when clouds will disappear. Although we cannot choose the value for such uncontrollable variables, we have some information on the plausibility of the values in their domains. In [7] this information, which is not bipolar,

C. Bessiere (Ed.): CP 2007, LNCS 4741, pp. 782–789, 2007.

is given by probability distributions. In this paper, we model this information by a possibility distribution over the values in the domains of such variables. Possibilities are useful when probability distributions are not available [11].

After defining formally bipolar preference problems with possibilistic uncertainty, we define the notion of preference and robustness for the solutions of such problems, as well as properties that they should respect, also in relation to the solution ordering. We then concentrate on problems with totally ordered preferences defined over real intervals, and we show how to eliminate the uncontrollable part of the problem by adding new constraints on the controllable part to recall part of the removed information. This approach is a generalization of the approach used in [9] to remove uncertainty from problems with negative preferences only. The additional constraints are then considered to define the robustness of the solutions. We define formally the preference and robustness of the solutions, and we define some desirable properties related to such notions that the solution ordering should have. Moreover, we introduce semantics that use such notions to order the solutions, and we show that they satisfy the desired properties on the solution ordering. In particular, they allow us to distinguish between highly preferred solutions which are not robust, and robust but not preferred solutions. Also, they guarantee that, if there are two solutions with the same robustness (resp., the same preference), then the ordering is given by their preference (resp., robustness).

2 Background: Bipolar Preference Problems

Bipolar preference problems [3] are based on a bipolar preference structure, which allows to handle both positive and negative preferences. This structure contains two substructures, one for each kind of preferences.

When dealing with negative preferences, two main properties should hold: combination should bring to worse preferences, and indifference should be better than all the other negative preferences. These properties can be found in a c-semiring [2], which is the structure used to represent soft constraints. A *c-semiring* is a tuple $(A, +, \times, \mathbf{0}, \mathbf{1})$ where: A is a set, $\mathbf{0}, \mathbf{1} \in A$, $+$ and $\times$ are the additive and the combination operators. Operator $+$ induces a partial order, written $\leq_S$, over A: $a \leq_S b$ iff $a + b = b$, $\mathbf{0}$ is its minimum and $\mathbf{1}$ its maximum. When $a \leq_S b$, we will say that *b is better than a*. Element $\mathbf{1}$ acts as indifference (in fact, $\forall a \in A, a \times \mathbf{1} = a$), and $\forall a, b \in A, a \times b \leq a, b$. This interpretation is natural when considering the weighted c-semiring $(R^+, min, +, +\infty, 0)$, where preferences are real positive numbers interpreted as costs, and thus as negative preferences. Such costs are combined via the sum $(+)$ and the best costs are the lower ones (min). From now on, a c-semiring will be denoted as: $(N, +_n, \times_n, \bot_n, \top_n)$.

When dealing with positive preferences, combination should bring to better preferences, and indifference should be lower than all the other positive preferences. These properties can be found in a *positive preference structure* [3], that is a tuple $(P, +_p, \times_p, \bot_p, \top_p)$, which is just like a negative one above, except that the combination operator $\times_p$ returns a better element rather than a worse one. An example of a positive preference structure is $(\Re^+, max, sum, 0, +\infty)$, where preferences are positive real numbers aggregated with sum and ordered by max (i.e., the best preferences are the highest ones).

When we deal with both positive and negative preferences, the same properties described above for a single kind of preferences should continue to hold. Moreover, all the positive preferences must be better than all the negative ones and there should exist an operator allowing for the compensation between positive and negative preferences. A bipolar preference structure links a negative and a positive structure by setting the highest negative preference to coincide with the lowest positive preference to model indifference. More precisely, a *bipolar preference structure* [3] is a tuple $(N, P, +, \times, \bot, \Box, \top)$ where, $(P, +_{|P}, \times_{|P}, \Box, \top)$ is a positive preference structure; $(N, +_{|N}, \times_{|N}, \bot, \Box)$ is a c-semiring; $+ : (N \cup P)^2 \longrightarrow (N \cup P)$ is an operator s.t. $a_n + a_p = a_p$, $\forall a_n \in N$ and $a_p \in P$; it induces a partial ordering on $N \cup P$: $\forall a, b \in P \cup N$, $a \leq b$ iff $a + b = b$; $\times : (N \cup P)^2 \longrightarrow (N \cup P)$ (called the *compensation operator*) is a commutative and monotonic operator. In the following, we will write $+_n$ instead of $+_{|N}$ and $+_p$ instead of $+_{|P}$. Similarly for $\times_n$ and $\times_p$. When $\times$ is applied to a pair in $(N \times P)$, we will sometimes write $\times_{np}$. An example of bipolar structure is the tuple (N=$[-1, 0]$, P=$[0, 1]$, $+$=max, $\times$, $\bot$=-1, $\Box$=0, $\top$=1), where $\times$ is s.t. $\times_p$= max, $\times_n$=min and $\times_{np}$=sum. Negative preferences are between -1 and 0, positive preferences between 0 and 1, compensation is sum, and the order is given by max.

A bipolar constraint is a constraint where each assignment of values to its variables is associated to one of the elements in a bipolar preference structure. A *bipolar CSP* (BCSP) $\langle S, V, C\rangle$ is a set of bipolar constraints C over a set of variables V defined on the bipolar structure S.

We will sometimes need to distinguish between two kinds of constraints in a BCSP. For this reason, we will use the notion of *RBCSP*, which is a tuple $\langle S, V, C_1, C_2\rangle$ such that $\langle S, V, C_1 \cup C_2\rangle$ is a BCSP.

Given a subset of variables $I \subseteq V$, and a bipolar constraint $c = \langle def, con\rangle$, the *projection of* c over I, written $c \Downarrow_I$, is a new bipolar constraint $\langle def', con'\rangle$, where $con' = con \cap I$ and $def(t') = \sum_{\{t | t\downarrow_{con'} = t'\}} def(t)$. In particular, the preference associated to each assignment to the variables in con', denoted with t', is the best one among the preferences associated by def to any completion of t', t, to an assignment to con. The notation $t \downarrow_{con'}$ indicates the subtuple of t on the variables of con'.

A *solution* of a bipolar CSP $\langle S, V, C\rangle$ is a complete assignment to all variables in V, say s. Its overall preference is $ovpref(s) = ovpref_p(s) \times ovpref_n(s) = (p_1 \times_p \ldots \times_p p_k) \times (n_1 \times_n \ldots \times_n n_l)$, where, for $i := 1, \ldots, k$, $p_i \in P$, for $j := 1, \ldots, l$, $n_j \in N$, and $\exists\langle def_i, con_i\rangle \in C$ s.t. $p_i = def_i(s \downarrow_{con_i})$ and $\exists\langle def_j, con_j\rangle \in C$ s.t. $n_j = def(s \downarrow_{con_j})$. This is obtained by combining all the positive preferences associated to its subtuples on one side, all the negative preferences associated to its subtuples on the other side, and then compensating the two preferences so obtained. This definition is in accordance with cumulative prospect theory [10] used in bipolar decision making. A solution s is *optimal* if there is no other solution s' with $ovpref(s') > ovpref(s)$. Given a bipolar constraint $c = \langle def, con\rangle$ and one of its tuple t, it is possible to define two functions pos and neg as follows: $pos(c)(t) = def(t)$ if $def(t) \in P$, otherwise $pos(c)(t) = \Box$, and $neg(c)(t) = def(t)$ if $def(t) \in N$, otherwise $neg(c)(t) = \Box$.

3 Uncertain Bipolar Problems

Uncertain bipolar problems (UBCSPs) are characterized by a set of variables, which can be controllable or uncontrollable, and by a set of bipolar constraints. Thus, a UBCSP is a BCSP where some of the variables are uncontrollable. Moreover, the domain of every uncontrollable variable is equipped with a possibility distribution, that specifies, for every value in the domain, the degree of plausibility that the variable takes that value. Formally, a possibility distribution π associated to a variable z with domain A_Z is a mapping from A_Z to a totally ordered scale L (usually $[0,1]$) s.t. $\forall a \in A_Z$, $\pi(a) \in L$ and $\exists\, a \in A_Z$ s.t. $\pi(a) = \mathbf{1}$, where $\mathbf{1}$ the top element of the scale L [11].

Definition 1 (UBCSP). *An uncertain bipolar CSP is a tuple $\langle S, V_c, V_u, C_c, C_{cu}\rangle$, where*

- *$S = (N, P, +, \times, \bot, \Box, \top)$ is a bipolar preference structure and $\leq_S$ is the ordering induced by operator $+$;*
- *$V_c = \{x_1, \ldots x_n\}$ is a set of controllable variables;*
- *$V_u = \{z_1, \ldots z_k\}$ is a set of uncontrollable variables, where every $z_i \in V_u$ has possibility distribution π_i with scale $[0,1]$;*
- *C_c is the set of bipolar constraints that involve only variables of V_c*
- *C_{cu} is a set of bipolar constraints that involve at least a variable in V_c and a variable in V_u and that may involve any other variable of $(V_c \cup V_u)$.*

In a BCSP, a solution is an assignment to all its variables. In a UBCSP, instead, a solution is an assignment to all its controllable variables.

An example of a UBCSP is presented in Figure 1 (a). It is defined by the tuple $\langle S, V_c = \{x, y\}, V_u = \{z_1, z_2\}, C_c, C_{cu}\}\rangle$, where S is the bipolar structure considered before, i.e., $\langle [-1, 0], [0, 1], max, \times, -1, 0, \mathbf{1}\rangle$, where $\times$ is s.t. $\times_p = max$, $\times_n = min$ and $\times_{np} = sum$. The set of controllable variables is composed by x and y, while the set of uncontrollable variables is composed by z_1 and z_2, which are characterized by the possibility distributions π_1 and π_2. The set of constraints C_c contains $\langle f, \{x, y\}\rangle$, while C_{cu} contains $\langle q, \{x, z_1\}\rangle$ and $\langle t, \{x, z_2\}\rangle$. Figure 1 (a) shows the positive and the negative preferences within such constraints and the possibility distributions π_1 and π_2 over the domains of z_1 and z_2. Other parts of Figure 1 will be described later.

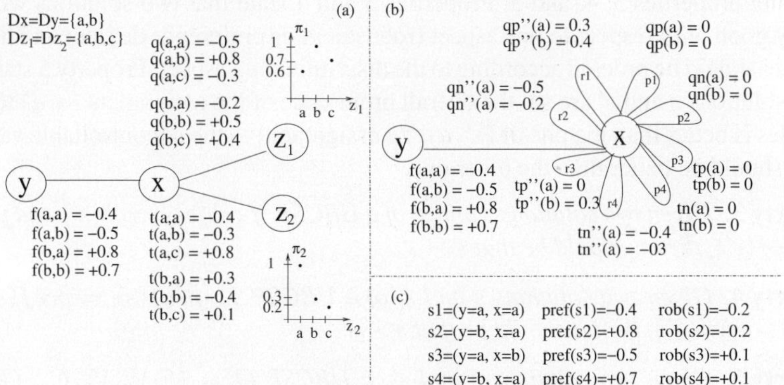

Fig. 1. How to handle a UBCSP

4 Preference, Robustness, and Desirable Properties

Given a solution s of a UBCSP, we will associate a preference degree to it, written $pref(s)$, which summarizes all the preferences in the controllable part and that can be obtained for some assignment to the uncontrollable variables decided by the Nature. It is reasonable to assume that $pref(s)$ belongs to the set of preferences in the considered bipolar preference structure.

When we deal with UBCSPs, we have to consider another interesting aspect that characterizes a solution, that is, its robustness with respect to the uncertainty, which measures what is the impact of Nature on the preference obtained by choosing that solution. The robustness of s will depend both on the preferences in the constraints connecting both controllable and uncontrollable variables to s and on such possibility distributions, and it is also reasonable that it will be an element of the bipolar preference structure. This will allow us to use the operators of such a structure over the robustness values. Before giving our definition of robustness of a solution s, that we will denote with $rob(s)$, we define two properties that such a definition should satisfy as in [6,9]. The first one states that, if we increase the preferences of any tuple involving uncontrollable variables, solution should have a higher value of robustness, the second one states that the same result should hold if we lower the possibility of any value of the uncontrollable variables.

Property 1. *Given solutions s and s' of a UBCSP, $\langle S, V_c, V_u, C_c, C_{cu}\rangle$, where every v_i in V_u is associated to a possibility distribution π_i, if $\forall \langle def, con\rangle \in C_{cu}$ and $\forall a$ assignment to the uncontrollable variables in con, $def((s,a)\downarrow_{con}) \leq_S def((s',a)\downarrow_{con})$, then it should be that $rob(s) \leq_S rob(s')$.*

Property 2. *Given a solution s of a UBCSP $Q_i = \langle S, V_c, V_u, C_c, C_{cu}\rangle$. Assume variables in V_u are described by a possibility distribution π_i, for $i = 1, 2$ s.t. $\forall a$ assignment to variables in V_u, $\pi_2(a) \leq \pi_1(a)$. Then it should be that $rob_{\pi_1}(s) \leq_S rob_{\pi_2}(s)$, where rob_{π_i} is the robustness computed in the problem with possibility distribution π_i.*

To understand which solutions are better than others in a UBCSP, it is reasonable to consider a solution ordering, which should be reflexive and transitive. The notions of robustness and preference should be related to this solution ordering, say $\succ$, by the following properties 3, 4, and 5. Properties 3 and 4 state that two solutions which are equally good with respect to one aspect (robustness or preference degree) and differ on the other should be ordered according to the discriminating aspect. Property 5 states that, if two solutions s and s' are s.t. the overall preference of the assignment (s, a) to all the variables is better than the one of (s', a), $\forall a$ assignment to the uncontrollable variables, then s should be better than the other one.

Property 3. *Given two solutions s and s' of a UBCSP, if $rob(s) = rob(s')$ and $pref(s) >_S pref(s')$, then it should be that $s \succ s'$.*

Property 4. *Given two solutions s and s' of a UBCSP s.t. $pref(s) = pref(s')$, and $rob(s) >_S rob(s')$, then it should be that $s \succ s'$.*

Property 5. *Given two solutions s and s', a UBCSP $Q = \langle S, V_c, V_u, C_c, C_{cu}\rangle$, s.t. $ovpref(s,a) >_S ovpref(s',a)$, $\forall a$ assignment to V_u, then it should be that $s \succ s'$.*

5 Removing Uncertainty: Preference, Robustness and Semantics

We now propose a procedure that extends to a bipolar context a common approach used to deal with uncertainty, that eliminates uncontrollable variables preserving as much information as possible [6,9]. Starting from this procedure, we define the robustness and preference degrees that satisfy the desirable properties mentioned above.

The procedure, that we call Algorithm *B-SP*, generalizes to the case of positive and negative totally ordered preferences defined over intervals of $\mathbb{Z}, \mathbb{Q}, \mathbb{R}$ (or structures isomorphic to them), Algorithm *SP* [9] for handling problems with fuzzy preferences and uncontrollable variables associated to possibility distributions. The algorithm takes as input a UBCSP $Q = \langle S, V_c, V_u, C_c, C_{cu}\rangle$, where every variable $z_i \in V_u$ has a possibility distribution π_i and where $S = \langle N, P, +, \times, \bot, \Box, \top\rangle$ is any bipolar preference structure with N and P totally ordered intervals of $\mathbb{Z}, \mathbb{Q}, \mathbb{R}$ (or structures isomorph to them). Then, the algorithm translates the UBCSP Q in the RBCSP $Q' = \langle S, V_c, C_c \cup C_{proj}, C_{rob}\rangle$ (that is, in the BCSP $\langle S, V, C \cup C_{rob}\rangle$). This problem Q' is obtained from Q by eliminating its uncontrollable variables and the bipolar constraints in C_{cu} relating controllable and uncontrollable variables, and by adding new bipolar constraints only among these controllable variables. These new constraints can be classified in two sets, that we call C_{rob} (robustness constraints) and C_{proj} (projection constraints), that we describe in the following. Starting from this problem Q', we then define the preference degree (resp., the robustness degree) of a solution considering the preference functions of the constraints in $C_c \cup C_{proj}$ (resp., in C_{rob}).

The set of *robustness constraints* C_{rob} is composed by the constraints obtained by reasoning on preference functions of the constraints in C_{cu} and on the possibilities associated to values in the domains of uncontrollable variables involved in such constraints. C_{rob} is built in three steps.

In the first step, that we denote *normalization*, every constraint $c = \langle def, con\rangle$ in C_{cu} s.t. $con \cap V_c = X$ and $con \cap V_u = Z$, is translated in two bipolar constraints $\langle defp, con\rangle$ and $\langle defn, con\rangle$, with preferences in $[0, 1]$, where, $\forall(t_X, t_Z)$ assignment to $X \times Z$, $defp(t_X, t_Z) = g_p(pos(c)(t_X, t_Z))$ and $defn(t_X, t_Z) = g_n(neg(c)(t_X, t_Z))$. If the positive (resp., negative) preferences are defined in the interval of $\mathbb{R}$ (or $\mathbb{Q}, \mathbb{Z}$), $P = [a_p, b_p]$ (resp., $N = [a_n, b_n]$) then g_p: $[a_p, b_p] \to [0, 1]$ (resp., g_n: $[a_n, b_n] \to [0, 1]$) is s.t. $x \mapsto \frac{x-a_p}{b_p-a_p}$ (resp., $x \mapsto \frac{x-a_n}{b_n-a_n}$) by using the classical division and subtraction operations of $\mathbb{R}$.

In the second step, denoted *uncontrollability elimination*, the constraint $\langle defp, con\rangle$ (resp., $\langle defn, con\rangle$) obtained before is translated in $\langle defp', X\rangle$ (resp., $\langle defn', X\rangle$), where, $\forall t_X$ assignment to X, $defp'(t_X) = \inf_{t_Z \in A_Z} \sup(defp(t_X, t_Z), c_S(\pi_Z(t_Z)))$, and $defn'(t_X) = \inf_{t_Z \in A_Z} \sup(defn(t_X, t_Z), c_S(\pi_Z(t_Z)))$, where c_S is an order reversing map w.r.t. $\leq_S$ in $[0, 1]$, s.t. $c_S(c_S(p)) = p$ and inf, which is the opposite of the sup operator (derived from operator $+$ of S), applied to a set of preferences, returns its worst preference w.r.t. the ordering $\leq_S$.

In the third step, denoted *denormalization*, the constraint $\langle defp', X\rangle$ (resp., $\langle defn', X\rangle$) is translated in $\langle defp'', X\rangle$ (resp., $\langle defn'', X\rangle$), where $\forall t_X$ assignment to X, $defp''(t_X) = g_p^{-1}(defp'(t_X))$, and $defn''(t_X) = g_n^{-1}(defn'(t_X))$. The map g_p^{-1}:$[0, 1] \to [a_p, b_p]$ is s.t. $y \mapsto [y(b_p - a_p) + a_p]$, and g_n^{-1}:$[0, 1] \to [a_n, b_n]$ is s.t. $y \mapsto [y(b_n - a_n) + a_n]$. Summarizing, given $c = \langle def, X \cup Z\rangle \in C_{cu}$, its corresponding robustness constraints in C_{rob} are the constraints $\langle defp'', X\rangle$ and $\langle defn'', X\rangle$ above.

Projection constraints are added to the problem in order to recall part of the information contained in the constraints in C_{cu} that will be removed later. They are useful to guarantee that the preference degree of a solution, say $pref(s)$, that we will define later, is a value that can be obtained in the given UBCSP. The set of projection constraints C_{proj} is defined as follows. Given a bipolar constraint $c = \langle def, con \rangle$ in C_{cu}, s.t. $con \cap V_c = X$ and $con \cap V_u = Z$, then the corresponding bipolar constraints in C_{proj} are $\langle defp, X \rangle$ and $\langle defn, X \rangle$, where $defp(t_X) = \inf_{\{t_Z \in A_Z\}} pos(c)\ (t_X, t_Z)$ and $defn(t_X) = \sup_{\{a \in A_Z\}} neg(c)\ (t_X, t_Z)$. In other words, $defn(t_X)$ (resp., $defp(t_X)$) is the best negative (resp., the worst positive) preference that can be reached for t_X in c for the various values t_Z in the domain of the uncontrollable variables in Z.

Let us show via an example how *B-SP* works. Consider the UBCSP $Q = \langle S, V_c = \{x, y\}, V_u = \{z_1, z_2\}, C_c, C_{cu} \rangle$ in Figure 1 (a). Figure 1 (b) shows the RBCSP $Q' = \langle S, V_c = \{x, y\}, C_c \cup C_{proj}, C_{rob} \rangle$, built by algorithm *B-SP*. C_c is composed by $\langle f, \{x, y\} \rangle$. C_{proj} is composed by $p1 = \langle qp, \{x\} \rangle$, $p2 = \langle qn, \{x\} \rangle$, $p3 = \langle tp, \{x\} \rangle$ and $p4 = \langle tn, \{x\} \rangle$, while C_{rob} by $r1 = \langle qp'', \{x\} \rangle$, $r2 = \langle qn'', \{x\} \rangle$, $r3 = \langle tp'', \{x\} \rangle$ and $r4 = \langle tn'', \{x\} \rangle$. Constraints in C_{rob} are obtained by assuming g_p the identity map, and $g_n : [-1, 0] \rightarrow [0, 1]$ s.t. $n \mapsto n + 1$.

Starting from the RBCSP $Q' = \langle S, V_c, C_c \cup C_{proj}, C_{rob} \rangle$, obtained applying algorithm *B-SP* to the BCSP Q, we associate to each solution of Q, a pair composed by a degree of preference and a degree of robustness. The preference of a solution is obtained by compensating a positive and a negative preference, where the positive (resp., the negative) preference is obtained by combining all positive (resp., negative) preferences of the appropriate subtuples of the solution over the constraints in $C_c \cup C_{proj}$, i.e., over initial constraints of Q linking only controllable variables and over new projection constraints. The robustness is obtained similarly, but considering only the constraints in C_{rob}, i.e., the robustness constraints. It is possible to prove that this definition of robustness satisfies Properties 1 and 2.

Definition 2 (preference and robustness). *Given a solution s of a UBCSP Q, let $Q' = \langle S, V_c, C_c \cup C_{proj}, C_{rob} \rangle$ the RBCSP obtained from Q by algorithm* B-SP. *The* preference *of s is $pref(s) = pref_p(s) \times pref_n(s)$, where $\times$ is the compensation operator of S, $pref_p(s) = \Pi_{\{\langle def, con \rangle \in C_c \cup C_{proj}\}}\ pos(c)(s \downarrow_{con})$, $pref_n(s) = \Pi_{\{\langle def, con \rangle \in C_c \cup C_{proj}\}}$ $neg(c)(s \downarrow_{con})$. The* robustness *of s is $rob(s) = rob_p(s) \times rob_n(s)$, where $rob_p(s) = \Pi_{\{\langle def, con \rangle \in C_{rob}\}}\ pos(c)(s \downarrow_{con})$, $rob_n(s) = \Pi_{\{\langle def, con \rangle \in C_{rob}\}}\ neg(c)(s \downarrow_{con})$.*

A solution of a BCSP is associated to a preference and a robustness degree. We here define *semantics* to order the solutions which depend on our attitude w.r.t. these two notions. Assume to have $A1 = (pref_1, rob_1)$ and $A2 = (pref_2, rob_2)$. The first semantics, which is called *Risky*, states that $A1 \succ_{Risky} A2$ iff $pref_1 >_S pref_2$ or ($pref_1 = pref_2$ and $rob_1 >_S rob_2$). The idea is to give more relevance to the preference degree. The second semantics, called *Safe*, states that $A1 \succ_{Safe} A2$ iff $rob_1 >_S rob_2$ or ($rob_1 =_S rob_2$ and $pref_1 >_S pref_2$). It represents the opposite attitude w.r.t. Risky semantics, since it considers the robustness degree as the most important feature. The last semantics, called *Diplomatic*, aims at giving the same importance to preference and robustness. $A1 \succ_{Dipl} A2$ iff ($pref_1 \geq_S pref_2$ and $rob_1 \geq_S rob_2$) and ($pref_1 >_S pref_2$ or $rob_1 >_S rob_2$). By definition, the Risky, Safe and Diplomatic semantics satisfy Properties 3 and 4. Additionally, Risky satisfies Property 5, if $\times$ in the bipolar structure is strictly monotonic. Property 3, 4 and 5 are desirable. However, there are semantics that don't satisfy them. For example, this happens with a semantics, that we denote *Mixed*, that generalizes the one adopted in [6]: $A1 \succ_{Mixed} A2$ iff $pref_1 \times rob_1 >_S pref_2 \times rob_2$, where $\times$ is the compensation operator in the bipolar structure.

6 Conclusions

We have studied problems with bipolar preferences and uncontrollable variables with a possibility distribution over such variables. Our technical development, although being an extension of two previous lines of work, which dealt with bipolarity only, or only uncertainty, was not strighforward, since it was not clear if it was possible to deal simultaneously with possibilistic uncertainty and bipolar preferences, making sure that desirable properties hold. In fact, such a task could have required a bipolarization of the possibility scale. Our results instead show that it is possible, without any added bipolarization, to extend the formalism in [9] to bipolar preferences and the one in [3] to uncertainty, preserving the desired properties.

Acknowledgements

This work has been supported by Italian MIUR PRIN project "Constraints and Preferences" (n. 2005015491).

References

1. Benferhat, S., Dubois, D., Kaci, S., Prade, H.: Bipolar possibility theory in preference modeling: representation, fusion and optimal solutions. Information Fusion 7(1) (2006)
2. Bistarelli, S., Montanari, U., Rossi, F.: Semiring-based constraint solving and optimization. Journal of the ACM 44(2), 201–236 (1997)
3. Bistarelli, S., Pini, M.S., Rossi, F., Venable, K.B.: Bipolar preference problems: framework, properties and solving techniques. In: Azevedo, F.; Barahona, P.; Fages, F.; Rossi, F. (eds.) CSCLP 2006. LNCS (LNAI), vol. 4651. Springer, Heidelberg (2001)
4. Dubois, D., Fargier, H.: On the qualitative comparison of sets of positive and negative affects. In: Godo, L. (ed.) ECSQARU 2005. LNCS (LNAI), vol. 3571, pp. 305–316. Springer, Heidelberg (2005)
5. Dubois, D., Fargier, H.: Qualitative decision making with bipolar information. In: KR'06, pp. 175–186 (2006)
6. Dubois, D., Fargier, H., Prade, H.: Possibility theory in constraint satisfaction problems: Handling priority, preference and uncertainty. Appl. Intell. 6(4), 287–309 (1996)
7. Fargier, H., Lang, J., Martin-Clouaire, R., Schiex, T.: A constraint satisfaction framework for decision under uncertainty. In: UAI-95, pp. 167–174. Morgan Kaufmann, San Francisco (1995)
8. Grabisch, M., Labreuche, Ch.: Bi-capacities - parts i and ii. Fuzzy Sets and Systems 151, 211–260 (2005)
9. Pini, M.S., Rossi, F., Venable, K.B.: Possibility theory for reasoning about uncertain soft constraints. In: Godo, L. (ed.) ECSQARU 2005. LNCS (LNAI), vol. 3571, pp. 800–811. Springer, Heidelberg (2005)
10. Tversky, A., Kahneman, D.: Advances in prospect theory: Cumulative representation of uncertainty. Journal of Risk and Uncertainty 5, 297–323 (1992)
11. Zadeh, L.A.: Fuzzy sets as a basis for the theory of possibility. Fuzzy sets and systems, 13–28 (1978)

An Analysis of Slow Convergence in Interval Propagation*

Lucas Bordeaux[1], Youssef Hamadi[1], and Moshe Y. Vardi[2,]**

[1]Microsoft Research Cambridge, UK
{lucasb,youssefh}@microsoft.com
[2]Rice University, USA
vardi@cs.rice.edu

Abstract. When performing interval propagation on integer variables with a large range, *slow-convergence* phenomena are often observed: it becomes difficult to reach the fixpoint of the propagation. This problem is practically important, as it hinders the use of propagation techniques for problems with large numerical ranges, and notably problems arising in program verification. A number of attempts to cope with this issue have been investigated, yet all of the proposed techniques only guarantee a fast convergence on specific instances. An important question is therefore whether slow convergence is *intrinsic* to propagation methods, or whether an improved propagation algorithm may exist that would avoid this problem. This paper proposes the first analysis of the slow convergence problem under the light of complexity results. It answers the question, by a negative result: if we allow propagators that are general enough, computing the fixpoint of constraint propagation is shown to be intractable. *Slow convergence is therefore unavoidable unless P=NP.* The result holds for the propagators of a basic class of constraints.

1 Motivation and Results of the Paper

Problems with Large Discrete Ranges. Constraint propagation is probably the most developed component of CP (Constraint Programming) solvers, and the propagation of many constraints has been intensely studied. In this paper we consider variables ranging over a discrete domain and focus on *interval* propagation techniques, which are often used when dealing with numerical constraints. (We assume that the reader is familiar with interval propagation, otherwise see [2,3,4,5].) The question we address, put quickly, is whether interval propagation is effective against variables with a large range. Note that a number of applications require variables with large ranges: the best example is perhaps software verification, an area that heavily relies on constraint solving, but in which CP

* An unabridged version of this paper including the missing proofs is available as a Microsoft Research Report.

** Part of this work was done while this author was visiting Microsoft Research, Cambridge, UK.

C. Bessiere (Ed.): CP 2007, LNCS 4741, pp. 790–797, 2007.

techniques have so far failed to have a significant impact. In verification problems, the ranges of numerical variables are typically extremely large, because the aim is typically one of the following:

- *To verify a property for all integers.* Typically, if the constraints are simple enough, so-called "small-domain" properties are used to bring the problem down to finite bounds. These properties guarantee that a solution can be found within some finite bounds, *iff* the problem is satisfiable. These bounds are however typically quite large: for instance for purely linear equality constraints, [13] proves that when we have m constraints over n variables, the variables can be restricted to the range $[0, n(ma)^{2m+1}]$, where a is the maximum of the absolute values of the coefficients of the linear constraints. If we have only 10 variables, 10 equalities and coefficients within $[-10, 10]$, this bound already goes as high as $10 \cdot 100^{21} = 10^{43}$. These bounds can be refined [15] but we cannot, in general, avoid the use of large numbers represented in infinite-precision.
- *To reflect machine encoding of numbers.* In this case we typically compute within bounds of about 2^{32} or 2^{64}. Extra care typically has to be taken, so that overflows are correctly handled (which requires "modular arithmetics"). Here the domains are smaller, but nonetheless large enough for the slow propagation problem to become a serious issue.

The Problem of Slow Convergence. When performing interval propagation on numerical variables with a large range, *slow-convergence* phenomena have been reported by many authors, *e.g.*, [8,11]: propagation tends to go on for a prohibitively long number of steps. The problem is easily understood by considering simple examples:

- Consider the problem $X_1 < X_2 \wedge X_2 < X_1$, with X_1 and X_2 ranging over $[0, 2^{30}]$. Bound propagation alone detects the inconsistency. On this example, standard propagation algorithms discover that $X_1 \in [1, 2^{30}]$ because $0 \leq X_2 < X_1$, then $X_2 \in [2, 2^{30}]$ because $1 \leq X_1 < X_2$, and propagation goes ahead narrowing a lower or upper bound by one unit at every step. We ultimately obtain empty intervals, but this requires about 2^{30} operations.
- As mentioned in [11], the problem sometimes even occurs when we have a single constraint. For instance if we take the constraint $2X_1 + 2X_2 = 1$ with X_1 and X_2 ranging over $[-2^{30}, 2^{30}]$, we have a similar problem as before: propagation slowly narrows the bounds of the intervals by a few units until reaching empty intervals.

To solve these two examples, propagation will typically take several seconds. The problem becomes much more severe whenever similar constraints are not stated by themselves, but together with other constraints. In this case the runtime can become arbitrarily high, as propagation may regularly reconsider many propagators between each reduction of the bounds of X_1 and X_2.

It would be a mistake to consider slow convergence as a mere curiosity arising only in annoying, yet artificial examples. Our experience is that the problem is unavoidable when solving problems in program verification, for instance problems from Satisfiability Modulo Theories[1]. In examples arising from our own experiments in software verification, reaching the fixpoint of one propagation step alone takes seconds or minutes on many instances, and up to 37 hours (in finite precision!) in some of the longer examples where we waited until completion. Note that propagation is supposed to be the fast part of constraint solving: it is done at every node of the branch & prune process, and we are supposed to be exploring many nodes per second.

Attempted Solutions. Several solutions to the slow convergence problem have been investigated in the literature. It was, for instance, suggested to:

- *Detect some cases of slow convergence and find ways to prevent them.* One way would be to use symbolic techniques to get rid of constraints of the form $X_1 < X_2 \wedge X_2 < X_1$ and similar "cycles of inequalities". A related approach was suggested (in the continuous of real-valued intervals) in [12]. Unfortunately, these methods only prevent particular cases of slow convergence.
- *Reinforce interval propagation by other reasoning techniques.* A noticeable recent work on the issue is [11], which use congruence computations in addition to interval propagation. Our experience, however, is that congruence reasoning hardly ever speeds-up propagation in practice, and that it is powerless against very simple cases of slow convergence, *e.g.*, $X_1 < X_2 \wedge X_2 < X_1$.
- *Find a new algorithm* that would avoid the pitfalls of the standard interval propagation algorithm, and that would provably converge quickly. So far no such algorithm has been proposed. (An interesting related work is [10] which uses extrapolation methods to "guess" the possible fixpoint; this is an exciting method but it offers, by definition, no proven guarantee.)
- *Interrupt propagation after a given number of steps*, for instance prevent the propagation of variables whose width have been reduced by less than 5%. This is a pragmatic solution that it easy to implement, its drawback is that it leaves a search space partially reduced, relying on more branching.
- *Do something else than interval propagation.* For instance in [8], the authors note the slow convergence phenomenon and introduce a method for dealing with certain linear constraints between 2 variables; another significant example is that state-of-the-art methods in satisfiability modulo theories use bound reasoning methods that are not based on interval propagation, but on linear relaxations [6].

Our Results. The approaches mentioned previously do not solve the slow convergence problem: no approach allows to compute the fixpoint of interval propagation while being guaranteed to avoid slow convergence. Can this problem be circumvented, or is there an unsuspected, *intrinsic* reason why slow convergence is unavoidable? We believe this is an important question for the field that, surprisingly, has not been studied in the literature on CP theory.

[1] www.smt-lib.org

The authors of [8] (introduction) are perfectly right in their analyzis of slow convergence: it is due to the fact that the number of steps is *proportional to the width of the intervals* (the width of an interval is here defined as the number of integer values in the interval). The question is whether we can reduce this to a number of steps that grows significantly less than linearly in the width. This can be stated precisely by saying that the complexity should be *polynomial in the number of bits of the integer values* encoded in the problem *i.e.*, poly-logarithmic in these integer values. In contrast, existing propagation algorithms are easily seen to be *polynomial in these integer values*, *i.e.*, exponential in the number of bits of their encodings. Following classical terminology we call an algorithm of the first type *strongly polynomial* and an algorithm of the second type *pseudo-polynomial* (formal definitions are to be found in Section 2). The question is therefore whether there exists a strongly polynomial algorithm for interval propagation. We answer this question by the negative, under the P $\neq$ NP assumption.

Our results make assumptions on the type of constraints that are propagated. We first state the result in the general case, where arbitrary user-defined "interval propagators" can be defined (Prop. 1 and 2). We next show in Prop. 3 that the result still holds even if we restrict ourselves to a simple class of propagators, namely linear constraints plus one simple non-linear operation (squaring). We leave open the question whether the intractability result still holds when we deal with purely linear constraints. However, it is clear that CP was never meant to deal solely with linear constraints and our results therefore show what we believe is an intrinsic problem of interval propagation methods.

The next section gives more formal definitions of interval propagation which, following a number of authors [1], we see as a form of fixpoint computation; Section 3 will then list our main results. The missing proofs, as well as a more detailed presentation, can be found in the unabridged version of this paper.

2 Interval Propagation and Fixpoint Computations

Closure Operators. Interval propagation is equivalent to the problem of computing certain fixpoints of functions on Cartesian products of intervals. A Cartesian product of intervals will be called *box*, for short:

Definition 1 (Box). *An n-dimensional* box *is a tuple* $B = \langle B_1 \cdots B_n \rangle$ *where each* B_i *is an interval. Inclusion over boxes is defined as follows:* $B \subseteq B'$ *iff* $B_1 \subseteq B'_1 \wedge \cdots \wedge B_n \subseteq B'_n$.

The functions we consider must have the following properties:

Definition 2 (Closure operator). *We call* closure operator *a function* f *which, given a box* B*, returns a box* $f(B)$*, with the following properties (for all* B, B'*):*

1. f *is "narrowing":* $f(B) \subseteq B$;
2. f *is monotonic: if* $B \subseteq B'$ *then we have* $f(B) \subseteq f(B')$;
3. f *is idempotent:* $f(f(B)) = B$.

Computational Problems related to Fixpoints. A fixpoint of a closure operator is a box that remains unchanged after application of the operator. We are interested in common fixpoints, defined as follows:

Definition 3 (Common Fixpoint of a set of closure operators). *Given a set of closure operators $\{f_1 \cdots f_m\}$, a common fixpoint of the operators is a box B satisfying $f_1(B) = B \wedge \cdots \wedge f_m(B) = B$.*

We are given an initial n-dimensional box B, and a set of closure operators $\{f_1 \cdots f_m\}$. We consider the following computational problems (the first two are "function problems" in which we aim at computing a result, the third is a "decision problem" in which we just aim at determining whether a certain result exists):

Problem 1 (Computation of Common Interval Fixpoint). *Compute a box B' such that (1) $B' \subseteq B$ and (2) B' is non-empty and (3) B' is a common fixpoint of $f_1, \ldots, f_m$. (a special return value is used to signal the case where no non-empty fixpoint exists.)*

Problem 2 (Computation of the Greatest Common Interval Fixpoint). *Compute a box B' such that (1) $B' \subseteq B$; (2) B' is a common fixpoint of $f_1, \ldots, f_m$ and (3) no box B'' such that $B' \subsetneq B'' \subseteq B$ is a common fixpoint of $f_1, \ldots, f_m$. (An empty box should be returned if no other such fixpoint exists.)*

Problem 3 (Existence of Common Interval Fixpoint). *Determine whether there exists a non-empty box $B' \subseteq B$ which is a common fixpoint of $f_1, \ldots, f_m$.*

Greatest Fixpoint Computation by "Chaotic Iteration". To compute a greatest fixpoint, the standard approach is to run what [1] refers to as a "chaotic iteration" algorithm which, in its simplest and least optimized form, can be presented as follows:

Algorithm 1. Standard Algorithm for Greatest Fixpoint Computation

---

while *there exists f_i such that $f_i(B) \neq B$* **do**
  Choose one such f_i
  $B \leftarrow f_i(B)$

The functions $f_1 \ldots f_m$ are applied to the box in turn, in any order that is computationally convenient, until we reach a state where nothing changes. A basic result, which directly follows from the Knaster-Tarski theorem [16], is that this algorithm, although non-deterministic, always converges to the greatest common fixpoint of $f_1 \ldots f_m$. (The uniqueness of this fixpoint shows in particular, that the box satisfying the requirements of Problem 2 is unique, and allows us to refer to it as *the* (unique) greatest common interval fixpoint.)

Strongly Polynomial *vs.* Pseudo-Polynomial Algorithms. Denoting by n the dimension of the considered box (*i.e.*, number of variables), m the number of operators whose fixpoint we compute, and w the maximum of the widths, we use the following definitions, which follow classical terminology:

- A *pseudo-polynomial* algorithm is an algorithm whose runtime is bounded in the worst case by $P(n, m, w)$, for some polynomial P;
- A *strongly polynomial* algorithm is an algorithm whose runtime is bounded in the worst case by $P(n, m, \log w)$, for some polynomial P.

It is straightforward to check that the classical "chaotic iteration" algorithm for interval propagation, as well as all the improved versions derived from it, are only pseudo-polynomial, and can therefore be subject to slow convergence.

3 Intractability of Interval Propagation

In this section we present our main results, which show that, under some well-defined assumptions concerning the operators, computing the fixpoint of these operators cannot be achieved in strongly polynomial time.

General Case. We first consider the "general case", in which the closure operators are defined as arbitrary functions. This captures, for instance, the ability of systems like Constraint Handling Rules (CHR) [7], in which the propagators can be user-defined.

We assume that the propagators $f_1 \ldots f_m$ are defined as programs (written in any appropriate language, like CHR), which have the additional guarantee to run in time polynomial in the length of the problem. This is because we want to show that the problem is intractable even when restricted to simple propagators (a hardness result would hardly be a surprise in the case where the execution of a propagator is itself intractable.) More precisely, the input of the fixpoint representation problem is as follows:

Input Representation 1. *The input is given as a box $B = \langle B_1 \ldots B_n \rangle$ together with a set of closure operators $\{f_1 \ldots f_m\}$ which are defined as programs whose runtime is guaranteed to be worst-case polynomial in the total input size.*

Proposition 1. *If the input is encoded using Representation 1, the problem of existence of a common interval fixpoint (Problem 3) is NP-complete.* [2]

[2] The hardness part of this result can alternatively be proven as a direct consequence of Prop. 3. We prove Prop. 1 separately for 3 reasons: it states the membership in NP under the more general assumptions (the closure operators need be polytime computable); it states the NP-hardness under the least restrictive assumptions (one-dimensional case, two operators); Prop. 2 is best presented by first presenting the proof of Prop. 1.

Note that the result even holds in dimension one and for only two operators. Indeed, if we consider non-idempotent narrowing operators instead of closure operators, it is easy to show that computing the fixpoint of one single operator in one dimension is NP-complete. One can show, by straightforward modifications of the proof, that the corresponding function problem, computing an arbitrary fixpoint (Problem 1), is FNP-complete[3]. Interestingly, propagation algorithms do not compute an arbitrary fixpoint, but the *largest* one (Problem 2). The problem is therefore an optimization problem and, in fact, its complexity is higher than FNP:

Proposition 2. *If the input is encoded using Representation 1, the computation of the greatest common fixpoint (Problem 2) is OptP-complete.*

OptP is a class introduced in [9] to characterize the complexity of optimization problems (many optimization problems are FNP-hard but not in FNP because the optimality of the result cannot be checked in polynomial time).

Basic Numerical constraints. We now refine our analysis to the case where we have "basic propagators": what if the user does not have the possibility to write her own propagators, but can only use a set of predefined propagators for basic constraints? For the sake of concreteness we now focus on a simple set of propagators, that we now define precisely.

Variables are numbered from 1 to n; the kth variable is denoted X_k and the interval that is associated with this variable is denoted $[l_k, r_k]$. The notation "$[l_k, r_k] \leftarrow rhs$" denotes an operator f which, given a box B, returns a box $f(B)$ in which the kth interval has been modified as specified by the right-hand side (*rhs*), and all other intervals are unchanged.

We consider the following operators for a constraint $X_i < X_j$:

$$\begin{aligned} [l_i, r_i] &\leftarrow [l_i, \min(r_i, r_j - 1)] \\ [l_j, r_j] &\leftarrow [\max(l_j, l_i + 1), r_j] \end{aligned} \tag{1}$$

(For readers who would have trouble with the notation: the upper bound of the ith interval, the one associated with X_i, is updated so that it is at most $r_j - 1$, and the lower bound of the jth interval is updated so that it is at least $l_j + 1$.)

We consider the following operators for a constraint $X_i = X_j^2$:

$$\begin{aligned} [l_i, r_i] &\leftarrow [\max(l_i, l_j^2), \min(r_i, r_j^2)] \\ [l_j, r_j] &\leftarrow [\max(l_j, \lceil\sqrt{l_i}\rceil), \min(r_j, \lfloor\sqrt{r_i}\rfloor)] \end{aligned} \tag{2}$$

We consider the following operators for a constraint $aX_i + bX_j = c$, where a, b and c are non-negative integer constants:

$$\begin{aligned} [l_i, r_i] &\leftarrow [\max(l_i, \lceil\tfrac{c - b \cdot r_j}{a}\rceil), \min(r_i, \lfloor\tfrac{c - b \cdot l_j}{a}\rfloor)] \\ [l_j, r_j] &\leftarrow [\max(l_j, \lceil\tfrac{c - a \cdot r_i}{b}\rceil), \min(r_j, \lfloor\tfrac{c - a \cdot l_i}{b}\rfloor)] \end{aligned} \tag{3}$$

[3] FNP, or "functional" NP, is closely related to NP, the difference being that instead of being asked whether a solution exists (say, to a SAT instance), we are asked to produce a solution [14].

Input Representation 2. *The problem is given as a box $B = \langle B_1 \ldots B_n \rangle$ together with a set of constraints $\{c_1 \ldots c_m\}$ which include the following 3 forms:*

1. $X_j < X_j$, *for some* $i, j \in 1..n$;
2. $X_i = X_j^2$, *for some* $i, j \in 1..n$; *or*
3. $aX_i + bX_j = c$, *for some* $i, j \in 1..n$ *and some constants* a, b *and* c.

Proposition 3. *If the input is encoded using Representation 2, the problem of existence of a common interval fixpoint (Section 2, Problem 3) is NP-complete.*

References

1. Apt, K.R.: The essence of constraint propagation. Theoretical Computer Science (TCS) 221(1-2), 179–210 (1999)
2. Apt, K.R., Zoeteweij, P.: An analysis of arithmetic constraints on integer intervals. Constraints (to appear)
3. Benhamou, F., Older, W.J.: Applying interval arithmetic to real, integer, and boolean constraints. J. of Logic Programming (JLP) 32(1), 1–24 (1997)
4. Cleary, J.G.: Logical arithmetic. Future Computing Systems 2(2), 125–149 (1987)
5. Davis, E.: Constraint propagation with interval labels. Artificial Intelligence 32(3), 281–331 (1987)
6. Dutertre, B., De Moura, L.M.: A fast linear arithmetic solver for DPLL(T). In: Ball, T., Jones, R.B. (eds.) CAV 2006. LNCS, vol. 4144, pp. 81–94. Springer, Heidelberg (2006)
7. Fruehwirth, T.W.: Theory and practice of constraint handling rules. J. of Logic Programming (JLP) 37(1-3), 95–138 (1998)
8. Jaffar, J., Maher, M.J., Stuckey, P.J., Yap, R.H.C.: Beyond finite domains. In: Borning, A. (ed.) PPCP 1994. LNCS, vol. 874, pp. 86–94. Springer, Heidelberg (1994)
9. Krentel, M.W.: The complexity of optimization problems. In: Proc. of ACM Symp. on Theory of Computing (STOC), pp. 69–76. ACM Press, New York (1986)
10. Lebbah, Y., Lhomme, O.: Accelerating filtering techniques for numeric CSPs. Artificial Intelligence 139(1), 109–132 (2002)
11. Leconte, M., Berstel, B.: Extending a CP solver with congruences as domains for program verification. In: Benhamou, F. (ed.) CP 2006. LNCS, vol. 4204, pp. 22–33. Springer, Heidelberg (2006)
12. Lhomme, O., Gottlieb, A., Rueher, M., Taillibert, P.: Boosting the interval narrowing algorithm. In: Proc.of Joint Int. Conf. and Symp. on Logic Programming (JICSLP), pp. 378–392. MIT Press, Cambridge (1996)
13. Papadimitiou, C.: On the complexity of integer programming. J. of the ACM 28(4), 765–768 (1981)
14. Papadimitriou, Ch.H.: Computational Complexity. Addison Wesley, Reading (1994)
15. Seshia, S.A., Bryant, R.A.: Deciding quantifier-free presburger formulas using parametrized solution bounds. Logical Methods in Computer Science, vol. 1(2) (2005)
16. Tarski, A.: A lattice-theoretic fixpoint theorem and its applications. Pacific J. of Mathematics 5, 285–309 (1955)

The Expressive Power of Valued Constraints: Hierarchies and Collapses

David A. Cohen[1], Peter G. Jeavons[2], and Stanislav Živný[2]

[1] Department of Computer Science, Royal Holloway, University of London, UK
d.cohen@rhul.ac.uk
[2] Computing Laboratory, University of Oxford, UK
{peter.jeavons,stanislav.zivny}@comlab.ox.ac.uk

Abstract. In this paper we investigate the ways in which a fixed collection of valued constraints can be combined to express other valued constraints. We show that in some cases a large class of valued constraints, of all possible arities, can be expressed by using valued constraints of a fixed finite arity. We also show that some simple classes of valued constraints, including the set of all monotonic valued constraints with finite cost values, cannot be expressed by a subset of any fixed finite arity, and hence form an infinite hierarchy.

1 Introduction

Building a computational model of a combinatorial problem means capturing the requirements and optimisation criteria of the problem using the resources available in some given computational system. Modelling such problems using *constraints* means expressing the requirements and optimisation criteria using some combination of basic constraints provided by the system. In this paper we investigate what kinds of relationships and functions can be expressed using a given set of allowed constraint types.

The classical constraint satisfaction problem (CSP) model considers only the feasibility of satisfying a collection of simultaneous requirements. Various extensions have been proposed to this model to allow it to deal with different kinds of optimisation criteria or preferences between different feasible solutions. Two very general extended frameworks that have been proposed are the semi-ring CSP framework and the valued CSP (VCSP) framework [2]. The semi-ring framework is slightly more general, but the VCSP framework is simpler, and sufficiently powerful to describe many important classes of problems [6,18].

In this paper we work with the VCSP framework. In this framework every constraint has an associated cost function which assigns a cost to every tuple of values for the variables in the scope of the constraint. The set of cost functions used in the description of the problem is called the *valued constraint language.*

As with all computing paradigms, it is desirable for many purposes to have a small language which can be used to describe a large collection of problems. Determining which problems can be expressed in a given language is therefore

C. Bessiere (Ed.): CP 2007, LNCS 4741, pp. 798–805, 2007.

a central issue in assessing the flexibility and usefulness of a constraint system, and it is this question that we investigate here.

We make use of a number of algebraic tools that have been developed for this question [15], and for the related question of determining the complexity of a constraint language [3,6]. By applying these tools to particular valued constraint languages, we show that some simple constraint classes provide infinite hierarchies of greater and greater expressive power, whereas other classes collapse to sets of cost functions of fixed arity which can express all the other cost functions in the class.

The paper is organised as follows. In Section 2, we define the standard valued constraint satisfaction problem and the notion of expressibility for valued constraints. In Section 3, we describe some algebraic techniques that have been developed for valued constraints in earlier papers and show how they can be used to investigate expressibility. In Section 4, we present our results. We show that some valued constraints of fixed arities can express constraints of all possible arities whereas some other sets of valued constraints cannot be expressed by any subset of fixed finite arity. Due to the page limit we only state our results, but all proofs are given in the full version of this paper [7]. Finally in Section 5, we summarise our results and suggest some important open questions.

2 Valued Constraints and Expressibility

In this section we define the valued constraint satisfaction problem and discuss how the cost functions used to define valued constraints can be combined to express other valued constraints. More detailed discussion of the valued constraint framework, and illustrative examples, can be found in [2,6].

Definition 1. *A* ***valuation structure****, Ω, is a totally ordered set, with a minimum and a maximum element (denoted 0 and ∞), together with a commutative, associative binary* ***aggregation operator****, $\oplus$, such that for all $\alpha, \beta, \gamma \in \Omega$, $\alpha \oplus 0 = \alpha$ and $\alpha \oplus \gamma \geq \beta \oplus \gamma$ whenever $\alpha \geq \beta$.*

Definition 2. *An instance of the* ***valued constraint satisfaction problem****,* VCSP*, is a tuple $\mathcal{P} = \langle V, D, C, \Omega \rangle$ where:*

- *V is a finite set of* ***variables****;*
- *D is a finite set of possible* ***values****;*
- *Ω is a valuation structure representing possible* ***costs****;*
- *C is a set of* ***valued constraints****. Each element of C is a pair $c = \langle \sigma, \phi \rangle$ where σ is a tuple of variables called the* ***scope*** *of c, and $\phi \in \Gamma$ is a mapping from $D^{|\sigma|}$ to Ω, called the* ***cost function*** *of c.*

Definition 3. *For any* VCSP *instance $\mathcal{P} = \langle V, D, C, \Omega \rangle$, an* ***assignment*** *for $\mathcal{P}$ is a mapping $s : V \rightarrow D$. The* ***cost*** *of an assignment s, denoted $Cost_{\mathcal{P}}(s)$, is given by the aggregation of the costs for the restrictions of s onto each constraint scope, that is,*

$$Cost_{\mathcal{P}}(s) \stackrel{\text{def}}{=} \bigoplus_{\langle\langle v_1, v_2, \ldots, v_m \rangle, \phi\rangle \in C} \phi(\langle s(v_1), s(v_2), \ldots, s(v_m) \rangle).$$

A ***solution*** *to $\mathcal{P}$ is an assignment with minimal cost.*

The complexity of finding an optimal solution to a valued constraint problem will obviously depend on the forms of valued constraints which are allowed in the problem [6]. In order to investigate different families of valued constraint problems with different sets of allowed constraint types, we use the notion of a **valued constraint language**, which is simply a set of possible cost functions mapping D^k to Ω, for some fixed set D and some fixed valuation structure Ω. The class of all VCSP instances where the cost functions of the valued constraints are all contained in a valued constraint language Γ will be denoted $\mathsf{VCSP}(\Gamma)$.

In any VCSP instance, the variables listed in the scope of each valued constraint are explicitly constrained, in the sense that each possible combination of values for those variables is associated with a given cost. Moreover, if we choose *any* subset of the variables, then their values are constrained implicitly in the same way, due to the combined effect of the valued constraints. This motivates the concept of **expressibility** for cost functions, which is defined as follows:

Definition 4. *For any* VCSP *instance $\mathcal{P} = \langle V, D, C, \Omega\rangle$, and any list $l = \langle v_1, \ldots, v_m\rangle$ of variables of $\mathcal{P}$, the* ***projection*** *of $\mathcal{P}$ onto l, denoted $\pi_l(\mathcal{P})$, is the m-ary cost function defined as follows:*

$$\pi_l(\mathcal{P})(x_1, \ldots, x_m) \stackrel{\text{def}}{=} \min_{\{s:V\to D \mid \langle s(v_1),\ldots,s(v_m)\rangle = \langle x_1,\ldots,x_m\rangle\}} Cost_{\mathcal{P}}(s).$$

We say that a cost function ϕ is ***expressible*** *over a valued constraint language Γ if there exists an instance $\mathcal{P} \in \mathsf{VCSP}(\Gamma)$ and a list l of variables of $\mathcal{P}$ such that $\pi_l(\mathcal{P}) = \phi$. We call the pair $\langle \mathcal{P}, l\rangle$ a* ***gadget*** *for expressing ϕ over Γ.*

Note that any cost function expressible over Γ can be added to Γ without changing the complexity of $\mathsf{VCSP}(\Gamma)$.

In this paper we shall examine the expressibility of cost functions over three particular valuation structures which can be used to model a wide variety of problems [6]:

Definition 5. *Let Ω be a valuation structure and let $\phi : D^m \to \Omega$ be a cost function.*

- *If $\Omega = \{0, \infty\}$, then we call ϕ a* ***crisp*** *cost function.*
- *If $\Omega = \mathbb{Q}_+$, the set of non-negative rational numbers with the standard addition operation, $+$, then we call ϕ a* ***finite-valued*** *cost function.*
- *If $\Omega = \overline{\mathbb{Q}}_+$, the set of non-negative rational numbers together with infinity, with the standard addition operation (extended so that $a + \infty = \infty$, for every $a \in \overline{\mathbb{Q}}_+$), then we call ϕ a* ***general*** *cost function.*

Note that with any *relation* R over D we can associate a crisp cost function ϕ_R on D which maps tuples in R to 0 and tuples not in R to ∞. On the other hand, with any m-ary cost function ϕ we can associate an m-ary crisp cost function defined by:

$$\mathsf{Feas}(\phi)(x_1, \ldots, x_m) \stackrel{\text{def}}{=} \begin{cases} \infty & \text{if } \phi(x_1, \ldots, x_m) = \infty \\ 0 & \text{if } \phi(x_1, \ldots, x_m) < \infty. \end{cases}$$

3 Expressive Power and Algebraic Properties

Adding a finite constant to any cost function does not alter the relative costs. Hence, for any valued constraint language Γ with costs in Ω, we define the **expressive power** of Γ, denoted $\langle\Gamma\rangle$, to be the set of all cost functions ϕ such that $\phi + c$ is expressible over Γ for some constant $c \in \Omega$ where $c < \infty$.

A number of algebraic techniques to determine the expressive power of a given valued constraint language have been developed in earlier papers. To make use of these techniques, we first need to define some key terms.

The i-th component of a tuple t will be denoted by $t[i]$. Note that any operation on a set D can be extended to tuples over D in the following way. For any function $f : D^k \to D$, and any collection of tuples $t_1, \ldots, t_k \in D^m$, define $f(t_1, \ldots, t_k) \in D^m$ to be the tuple $\langle f(t_1[1], \ldots, t_k[1]), \ldots, f(t_1[m], \ldots, t_k[m])\rangle$.

Definition 6 ([9]). *Let R be an m-ary relation over a finite set D and let f be a k-ary operation on D. Then f is a* ***polymorphism*** *of R if $f(t_1, \ldots, t_k) \in R$ for all choices of $t_1, \ldots, t_k \in R$.*

A valued constraint language, Γ, which contains only crisp cost functions (= relations) will be called a crisp constraint language. We will say that f is a polymorphism of a crisp constraint language Γ if f is a polymorphism of every relation in Γ. The set of all polymorphisms of Γ will be denoted $\mathsf{Pol}(\Gamma)$.

It follows from the results of [13] that the expressive power of a crisp constraint language is fully characterised by its polymorphisms:

Theorem 7 ([13]). *For any crisp constraint language Γ over a finite set*

$$R \in \langle\Gamma\rangle \Leftrightarrow \mathsf{Pol}(\Gamma) \subseteq \mathsf{Pol}(\{R\}).$$

Hence, a crisp cost function ϕ is expressible over a crisp constraint language Γ if and only if it has all the polymorphisms of Γ.

We can extend the idea of polymorphisms to arbitrary valued constraint languages by considering the corresponding feasibility relations:

Definition 8 ([3]). *The* ***feasibility polymorphisms*** *of a valued constraint language Γ are the polymorphisms of the corresponding crisp feasibility cost functions, that is,*

$$\mathsf{FPol}(\Gamma) \stackrel{\text{def}}{=} \mathsf{Pol}(\{\mathsf{Feas}(\phi) \mid \phi \in \Gamma\}).$$

However, to fully capture the expressive power of valued constraint languages it is necessary to consider more general algebraic properties, such as the following:

Definition 9 ([4]). *A list of functions, $\langle f_1, \ldots, f_k\rangle$, where each f_i is a function from D^k to D, is called a k-ary* ***multimorphism*** *of a cost function $\phi : D^m \to \Omega$ if, for all $t_1, \ldots, t_k \in D^m$, we have*

$$\sum_{i=1}^{k} \phi(t_i) \geq \sum_{i=1}^{k} \phi(f_i(t_1, \ldots, t_k)).$$

The next result shows that the multimorphisms of a valued constraint language are preserved by all the cost functions expressible over that language.

Theorem 10 ([6]). *If $\mathcal{F}$ is a multimorphism of a valued constraint language Γ, then $\mathcal{F}$ is a multimorphism of $\langle\Gamma\rangle$.*

Hence, to show that a cost function ϕ is *not* expressible over a valued constraint language Γ it is sufficient to identify some multimorphism of Γ which is not a multimorphism of ϕ.

It is currently an open question whether the set of multimorphisms of a valued constraint language completely characterizes the expressive power of that language. However, it was shown in [3] that the expressive power of a valued constraint language can be characterised by generalising the notion of multimorphism a little, to a property called a *fractional polymorphism*, which is essentially a multimorphism where each component function has an associated weight value.

Definition 11 ([3]). *A k-ary **weighted function** $\mathcal{F}$ on a set D is a set of the form $\{\langle r_1, f_1\rangle, \ldots, \langle r_n, f_n\rangle\}$ where each r_i is a non-negative rational number such that $\sum_{i=1}^{n} r_i = k$ and each f_i is a distinct function from D^k to D.*

*For any m-ary cost function ϕ, we say that a k-ary weighted function $\mathcal{F}$ is a k-ary **fractional polymorphism** of ϕ if, for all $t_1, \ldots, t_k \in D^m$,*

$$\sum_{i=1}^{k} \phi(t_i) \geq \sum_{i=1}^{n} r_i \phi(f_i(t_1, \ldots, t_k)).$$

For any valued constraint language Γ, we will say that $\mathcal{F}$ is a fractional polymorphism of Γ if $\mathcal{F}$ is a fractional polymorphism of every cost function in Γ. The set of all fractional polymorphisms of Γ will be denoted $\mathsf{fPol}(\Gamma)$.

It was shown in [3] that the feasibility polymorphisms and fractional polymorphisms of a valued constraint language effectively determine its expressive power.

Theorem 12 ([3]).

Let Γ be a valued constraint language with costs in $\overline{\mathbb{Q}}_+$ such that, for all $\phi \in \Gamma$, and all $c \in \mathbb{Q}_+$, $c\phi \in \Gamma$ and $\mathsf{Feas}(\phi) \in \Gamma$.

$$\phi \in \langle\Gamma\rangle \;\Leftrightarrow\; \mathsf{FPol}(\Gamma) \subseteq \mathsf{FPol}(\{\phi\}) \wedge \mathsf{fPol}(\Gamma) \subseteq \mathsf{fPol}(\{\phi\}).$$

4 Results

In this section we present our results. We consider the expressive power of crisp, finite-valued and general constraint languages. We consider the languages containing all cost functions up to some fixed arity over some fixed domain, and we also consider an important subset of these cost functions defined for totally ordered domains, the so-called *max-closed* relations, which are defined below.

The function Max denotes the standard binary function which returns the larger of its two arguments.

Definition 13. *A cost function ϕ is **max-closed** if $\langle \textsc{Max}, \textsc{Max} \rangle \in \mathsf{Mul}(\{\phi\})$.*

Definition 14. *For every $d \geq 2$ we define the following:*

- *$\mathbf{R}_{d,m}$ ($\mathbf{F}_{d,m}$, $\mathbf{G}_{d,m}$ respectively) denotes the set of all crisp (finite-valued, general respectively) cost functions over a domain of size d of arity at most m, and $\mathbf{R}_d = \cup_{m \geq 0} \mathbf{R}_{d,m}$, $\mathbf{F}_d = \cup_{m \geq 0} \mathbf{F}_{d,m}$, and $\mathbf{G}_d = \cup_{m \geq 0} \mathbf{G}_{d,m}$;*
- *$\mathbf{R}^{\max}_{d,m}$ ($\mathbf{F}^{\max}_{d,m}$, $\mathbf{G}^{\max}_{d,m}$ respectively) denotes the set of all crisp (finite-valued, general respectively) max-closed cost functions over an ordered domain of size d of arity at most m, and $\mathbf{R}^{\max}_d = \cup_{m \geq 0} \mathbf{R}^{\max}_{d,m}$, $\mathbf{F}^{\max}_d = \cup_{m \geq 0} \mathbf{F}^{\max}_{d,m}$, and $\mathbf{G}^{\max}_d = \cup_{m \geq 0} \mathbf{G}^{\max}_{d,m}$.*

Theorem 15. *For all $f \geq 2$ and $d \geq 3$,*

1. $\langle \mathbf{R}_{2,1} \rangle \subsetneq \langle \mathbf{R}_{2,2} \rangle \subsetneq \langle \mathbf{R}_{2,3} \rangle = \mathbf{R}_2$; $\langle \mathbf{R}_{d,1} \rangle \subsetneq \langle \mathbf{R}_{d,2} \rangle = \mathbf{R}_d$.
2. $\langle \mathbf{R}^{\max}_{2,1} \rangle \subsetneq \langle \mathbf{R}^{\max}_{2,2} \rangle \subsetneq \langle \mathbf{R}^{\max}_{2,3} \rangle = \mathbf{R}^{\max}_2$; $\langle \mathbf{R}^{\max}_{d,1} \rangle \subsetneq \langle \mathbf{R}^{\max}_{d,2} \rangle = \mathbf{R}^{\max}_d$.
3. $\langle \mathbf{F}^{\max}_{f,1} \rangle \subsetneq \langle \mathbf{F}^{\max}_{f,2} \rangle \subsetneq \langle \mathbf{F}^{\max}_{f,3} \rangle \subsetneq \langle \mathbf{F}^{\max}_{f,4} \rangle \cdots$
4. $\langle \mathbf{G}^{\max}_{2,1} \rangle \subsetneq \langle \mathbf{G}^{\max}_{2,2} \rangle \subsetneq \langle \mathbf{G}^{\max}_{2,3} \rangle = \mathbf{G}^{\max}_2$; $\langle \mathbf{G}^{\max}_{d,1} \rangle \subsetneq \langle \mathbf{G}^{\max}_{d,2} \rangle = \mathbf{G}^{\max}_d$.

The proof of Theorem 15 can be found in the full version of this paper [7], and we just give a brief sketch here. As any relation can be expressed as a propositional formula, the collapse described in Statement (1) follows from the standard SAT to 3-SAT reduction. The collapse of max-closed relations in Statement (2) is proved by adapting the SAT to 3-SAT reduction. However, this gives only a weaker result, $\mathbf{R}^{\max}_d = \langle \mathbf{R}^{\max}_{d,3} \rangle$. To show that any max-closed relation over a non-Boolean domain can be expressed by using only binary max-closed relations, we characterise the polymorphisms of $\mathbf{R}^{\max}_d$ and prove that $\mathbf{R}^{\max}_{d,2}$ does not have any extra polymorphisms. The separation result in Statement (3) is obtained by finding explicit multimorphisms for the finite-valued max-closed cost functions of each different arity. Finally, the collapse result in Statement (4) follows from a precise characterisation of the feasibility polymorphisms and fractional polymorphisms of $\mathbf{G}^{\max}_d$ obtained using the MIN-CUT MAX-FLOW theorem.

5 Conclusions and Open Problems

We have investigated the expressive power of valued constraints in general and max-closed valued constraints in particular.

In the case of relations, we built on previously known results about the expressibility of an arbitrary relation in terms of binary or ternary relations. We were able to prove in a similar way that an arbitrary max-closed relation can be expressed using binary or ternary max-closed relations. The results about the collapse of the set of all relations and all max-closed relations contrast sharply with the case of finite-valued max-closed cost functions, where we showed an infinite hierarchy. This shows that the VCSP is not just a minor generalisation of the CSP – finite-valued max-closed cost functions behave very differently from crisp max-closed cost functions with respect to expressive power. Finally, we showed the collapse of general max-closed cost functions by investigating their feasibility polymorphisms and fractional polymorphisms. This shows that allowing infinite costs in max-closed cost functions increases their expressive power substantially, and in fact allows them to express more finite-valued cost functions.

We remark that all of our results about max-closed cost functions obviously have equivalent versions for *min-closed* cost functions, that is, those which have the multimorphism ⟨Min, Min⟩. In the Boolean crisp case these are precisely the relations that can be expressed by a conjunction of **Horn** clauses.

One of the reasons why understanding the expressive power of valued constraints is important is for the investigation of **submodular functions**. A cost function ϕ is called submodular if it has the multimorphism ⟨Min, Max⟩. The standard problem of submodular function minimisation corresponds to solving a VCSP with submodular cost functions over the Boolean domain [5].

Submodular function minimisation (SFM) is a central problem in discrete optimisation, with links to many different areas [10,16]. Although it has been known for a long time that the ellipsoid algorithm can be used to solve SFM in polynomial time, this algorithm is not efficient in practice. Relatively recently, several new strongly polynomial combinatorial algorithms have been discovered for SFM [10,11,12]. Unfortunately, the time complexity of the fastest published algorithm for SFM is roughly of an order of $O(n^7)$ where n is the total number of variables [11].

However, for certain special cases of SFM, more efficient algorithms are known to exist. For example, the (weighted) Min-Cut problem is a special case of SFM that can be solved in cubic time [10]. Moreover, it is known that SFM over a Boolean domain can be solved in $O(n^3)$ time when the submodular function f satisfies various extra conditions [1,8,17]. In particular, in the case of non-Boolean domains, a cubic-time algorithm exists for SFM when f can be expressed as a sum of *binary* submodular functions [5].

These observations naturally raise the following question: What is the most general class of submodular functions that can be minimised in cubic time (or better)? One way to tackle this question is to investigate the expressive power of particular submodular functions which are known to be solvable in cubic time. Any fixed set of functions which can be *expressed* using such functions will have the same complexity [3].

One intriguing result is already known for submodular *relations*. In the case of relations, having ⟨Min, Max⟩ as a multimorphism implies having both Min and Max as polymorphisms. The ternary Median operation can be obtained by composing the operations Max and Min, so all submodular relations have the Median operation as a polymorphism. It follows that submodular relations are binary decomposable [14], and hence all submodular relations are expressible using binary submodular relations.

For finite-valued and general submodular cost functions it is an important open question whether they can be expressed using submodular cost functions of some fixed arity. If they can, then this raises the possibility of designing new, more efficient, algorithms for submodular function minimisation.

Acknowledgements. The authors would like to thank Martin Cooper, Martin Green, Chris Jefferson and András Salamon for many helpful discussions.

References

1. Billionet, A., Minoux, M.: Maximizing a supermodular pseudo-boolean function: a polynomial algorithm for cubic functions. Discrete Applied Mathematics 12, 1–11 (1985)
2. Bistarelli, S., Fargier, H., Montanari, U., Rossi, F., Schiex, T., Verfaillie, G.: Semiring-based CSPs and valued CSPs: Frameworks, properties, and comparison. Constraints 4, 199–240 (1999)
3. Cohen, D., Cooper, M., Jeavons, P.: An algebraic characterisation of complexity for valued constraints. In: Benhamou, F. (ed.) CP 2006. LNCS, vol. 4204, pp. 107–121. Springer, Heidelberg (2006)
4. Cohen, D., Cooper, M., Jeavons, P., Krokhin, A.: Soft constraints: Complexity and multimorphisms. In: Rossi, F. (ed.) CP 2003. LNCS, vol. 2833, pp. 244–258. Springer, Heidelberg (2003)
5. Cohen, D., Cooper, M., Jeavons, P., Krokhin, A.: A maximal tractable class of soft constraints. Journal of Artificial Intelligence Research (JAIR) 22, 1–22 (2004)
6. Cohen, D., Cooper, M., Jeavons, P., Krokhin, A.: The complexity of soft constraint satisfaction. Artificial Intelligence 170, 983–1016 (2006)
7. Cohen, D., Jeavons, P., Živný, S.: The expressive power of valued constraints: Hierarchies and Collapses. Technical Report CS-RR-07-02, Computing Laboratory, University of Oxford, Oxford, UK (April 2007)
8. Creignou, N., Khanna, S., Sudan, M.: Complexity Classification of Boolean Constraint Satisfaction Problems. In: SIAM Monographs on Discrete Mathematics and Applications. Society for Industrial and Applied Mathematics, Philadelphia, PA, vol. 7 (2001)
9. Denecke, K., Wismath, S.: Universal Algebra and Applications in Theoretical Computer Science. Chapman and Hall/CRC Press (2002)
10. Fujishige, S.: Submodular Functions and Optimization, 2nd edn. Annals of Discrete Mathematics, vol. 58. Elsevier, Amsterdam (2005)
11. Iwata, S.: A faster scaling algorithm for minimizing submodular functions. SIAM Journal on Computing 32, 833–840 (2003)
12. Iwata, S., Fleischer, L., Fujishige, S.: A combinatorial, strongly polynomial-time algorithm for minimizing submodular functions. Journal of the ACM 48, 761–777 (2001)
13. Jeavons, P.: On the algebraic structure of combinatorial problems. Theoretical Computer Science 200, 185–204 (1998)
14. Jeavons, P., Cohen, D., Cooper, M.: Constraints, consistency and closure. Artificial Intelligence 101(1–2), 251–265 (1998)
15. Jeavons, P., Cohen, D., Gyssens, M.: How to determine the expressive power of constraints. Constraints 4, 113–131 (1999)
16. Narayanan, H.: Submodular Functions and Electrical Networks, North-Holland, Amsterdam (1997)
17. Queyranne, M.: Minimising symmetric submodular functions. Mathematical Programming 82, 3–12 (1998)
18. Rossi, F., van Beek, P., Walsh, T. (eds.): The Handbook of Constraint Programming. Elsevier, Amsterdam (2006)

Eligible and Frozen Constraints for Solving Temporal Qualitative Constraint Networks*

Jean-François Condotta[1], Gérard Ligozat[2], and Mahmoud Saade[1]

[1] CRIL-CNRS, Université d'Artois, 62307 Lens Cedex, France
[2] LIMSI-CNRS, Université de Paris-Sud, 91403 Orsay, France
{condotta, saade}@cril.univ-artois.fr, ligozat@limsi.fr

Abstract. In this paper we consider the consistency problem for qualitative constraint networks representing temporal or spatial information. The most efficient method for solving this problem consists in a search algorithm using, on the one hand, the weak composition closure method as a local propagation method, and on the other hand, a decomposition of the constraints into subrelations of a tractable set. We extend this algorithm with the notion of eligibility and the notion of frozen constraints. The first concept allows to characterise constraints which will not be considered during the search. The second one allows to freeze constraints in order to avoid unnecessary updates.

1 Introduction

The temporal and spatial information concerning the situation of a particular set of entities can be represented using particular constraint networks [1, 2] called qualitative constraint networks (QCNs). Each constraint of a QCN represents a set of possible qualitative configurations between the temporal or spatial entities and is defined in terms of a set of basic relations. The consistency problem consists in deciding whether a given network has solutions which satisfy these constraints. A forceful method to check the consistency of a QCN consists in instantiating successively each constraint of the QCN by each one of the basic relations until a consistent scenario is found, or proved not to exist. This algorithm has been improved in efficiency by using tractable classes [3, 4, 5]. The general idea is to have a set *Split* of relations (containing all basic relations) for which the closure by weak composition method is complete. During search, the constraints are instantiated by relations in *Split* rather than by basic relations. We propose a refinement of this algorithm based on the notion of *eligibility*. The principle of the new algorithm is fairly simple: it consists in an early detection of constraints which do not need to be instantiated for deciding the consistency of the initial network.

In many applications, using qualitative constraints, two kinds of constraints are represented in a QCN. The first kind corresponds to constraints used to enforce complex structural requirements on the set of temporal or spatial objects present in the system. These constraints can be called *constraints of environment* or *structural constraints*. The second kind corresponds to critical constraints on the configurations on some objects. We refer to these constraints as to *critical constraints* or *constraints of position*.

* This work is supported in part by the CNRS and the ANR "Planevo" project nJC05_41940.

C. Bessiere (Ed.): CP 2007, LNCS 4741, pp. 806–814, 2007.

Even though these two categories of constraints are represented by relations of the same qualitative algebra, we can distinguish them on various points. In particular, considering only the constraints of environment can be assumed to yield a consistent set. It is the addition of constraints of position to this set which may result in an inconsistency. In that case, it is this last kind of constraints which may be *hard* to solve. The search of a solution must focus on them. Moreover, given a solution, only the partial solution concerning the critical constraints is of interest from the point of view of the user. In this paper, we introduce the concept of *frozen constraints* which allows to differentiate these two kinds of constraints. A frozen constraint is a constraint which cannot be modified during the search of a solution. Typically, structural constraints will be considered as frozen, whereas critical ones will not.

This paper is organized as follows: Section 2 gives a brief background on the temporal and spatial qualitative formalisms. Section 3 is devoted to study of the algorithm called $consistentE$ in which we introduce the concept of constraint eligibility. Section 4 describes experimental results for this algorithm. In Section 5, we introduce the concept of frozen constraints and we modify our algorithm in order to take this notion into account.

2 Background on Spatial and Temporal Qualitative Formalisms

We assume that we have a qualitative formalism defined on a finite set B of basic relations on a domain D. We assume that the arity of these relations is 2. We also assume that the basic relations constitute a partition of $\mathsf{D} \times \mathsf{D}$. A qualitative constraint network (QCN) is a pair composed of a set of variables and a set of constraints. The set of variables represents spatial or temporal entities of the system. A constraint consists of a set of basic relations (whose union is the set of possible instantiations of the two variables). Formally, a QCN is a pair (V, C), where V is a finite set of of n variables $v_0, \dots, v_{n-1}$ and C is a map which, to each pair (v_i, v_j) of V associates a subset $C(v_i, v_j)$ of basic relations $C(v_i, v_j) \subseteq \mathsf{B}$. $C(v_i, v_j)$ will be also denoted by C_{ij}. The set A is defined as the set of all subsets of the set of basic relations B ($A = 2^{\mathsf{B}}$). For $r \in \mathsf{A}$, and $x, y \in D$, we denote by $x\ r\ y$ the fact that there exists a basic relation $a \in r$ such that $(x, y) \in a$. Each element r of A may be considered as the union of all $a \in r$. We use the unqualified term "relation" to refer to such a union of basic relations. The set A is provided with the usual set-theoretic operations including intersection ($\cap$) and union ($\cup$). It is also provided with the operation of converse ($^{-1}$) and an operation of composition ($\circ$) called weak composition or qualitative composition. The weak composition $a \circ b$ of two basic relations of $a, b \in \mathsf{B}$ is the relation $r = \{c : \exists x, y, z \in \mathsf{D}, x\ a\ y, y\ b\ z \text{ and } x\ c\ z\}$. The weak composition of $r \circ s$ of $r, s \in \mathsf{A}$ is the relation $t = \bigcup_{a \in r, b \in s} \{a \circ b\}$. In the sequel, we shall use the following definitions:

Definition 1. *Let $\mathcal{N} = (V, C)$ a* QCN, *with $V = \{v_0, \dots, v_{n-1}\}$. A* partial solution *of $\mathcal{N}$ on $V' \subseteq V$ is a map σ from V' to* D *such that: $\sigma(v_i)\ \ C(v_i, v_j)\ \ \sigma(v_j)$, for each $v_i, v_j \in V'$. A* solution *of $\mathcal{N}$ is a partial solution of V. $\mathcal{N}$ is* consistent *iff it admits a solution. $\mathcal{N}$ is* $\circ$-closed *iff for each $v_k, v_i, v_j \in V$, $C(v_i, v_j) \subseteq C(v_i, v_k) \circ C(v_k, v_j)$. A* sub-QCN *$\mathcal{N}'$ of $\mathcal{N}$ is a* QCN *(V, C') where $C'(v_i, v_j) \subseteq C(v_i, v_j)$ for each $v_i, v_j \in V$.*

We note $\mathcal{N}' \subseteq \mathcal{N}$ *the fact that* $\mathcal{N}'$ *is a sub-*QCN *of* $\mathcal{N}$. *A* scenario *of* $\mathcal{N}$ *is a* sub-QCN (V, C') *of* $\mathcal{N}$ *such that* $C'(v_i, v_j) = \{a\}$ *with* $a \in \mathsf{B}$. *A* consistent scenario *of* $\mathcal{N}$ *is a scenario of* $\mathcal{N}$ *which admits a solution.* $\mathcal{N}' = (V', C')$ *is* equivalent *to* $\mathcal{N}$ *iff* $V = V'$ *and if the two* QCN*s have the same solutions.*

Given a QCN $\mathcal{N} = (V, C)$, there are several local constraint propagation algorithms which can be used to obtain in polynomial time ($O(|V|^3)$ for some of them) a sub-QCN which is $\circ$-closed and equivalent to $\mathcal{N}$. In brief, the principle of these algorithms is to iterate the operation $C(v_i, v_j) \leftarrow C(v_i, v_j) \cap (C(v_i, v_k) \circ C(v_k, v_j))$ for each 3-tuple of variables $v_i, v_j, v_k \in V$ until a fixed point is reached. In the following, the expression "method of closure by weak composition" will denote such an algorithm. The $\circ$-closed QCN obtained by application of the method of $\circ$-closure to a QCN $\mathcal{N}$ will be denoted by $wcc(\mathcal{N})$ and called the $\circ$-closure of $\mathcal{N}$. We have the following properties:

Proposition 1. *Let* $\mathcal{N}$ *and* $\mathcal{N}'$ *be two* QCN*s: (a)* $wcc(\mathcal{N}) \subseteq \mathcal{N}$, *(b)* $wcc(wcc(\mathcal{N})) = wcc(\mathcal{N})$, *(c) if* $\mathcal{N} \subseteq \mathcal{N}'$ *then* $wcc(\mathcal{N}) \subseteq wcc(\mathcal{N}')$.

3 The Search Algorithm with Eligibility

In this section we introduce a refinement of the algorithm proposed by Nebel [4] based on the notion of eligibility. The principle of this algorithm consists in an early detection of constraints which do not need to be instantiated for deciding consistency. In order to do so, at each step of the search, in particular during the closure by weak composition, we mark as non eligible each constraint defined by a relation belonging to the splitting set $Split$. Moreover, the selection of the next constraint to be instantiated is made among the constraints marked as eligible. The search terminates when all constraints are marked as non eligible. The main objective is to instantiate a minimal number of constraints. Algorithm 1 gives the definition of $consistentE$ (E stands for eligibility) which implements our approach. This function takes as a parameter a QCN $\mathcal{N}$ and returns a boolean value corresponding to the detection or not of the consistency of $\mathcal{N}$. $Split \subseteq \mathsf{A}$ is the set of relations used to split the constraints into tractable relations for the instantiations. $Split$ must contain all basic relations and be closed for the operation of converse. In the case of the Interval Algebra, $Split$ can be chosen as the set of convex relations or the set of ORD-Horn relations. The first step of the algorithm consists in marking as eligible each constraint of $\mathcal{N}$ defined by a relation not belonging to the set $Split$ and in marking as non eligible the other constraints. The algorithm returns the result of the recursive call of the function $consistentE'$. Each execution of this function begins with a call of the method of closure by weak composition. In addition to the usual component of triangulation, this method detects the new constraints which are defined by a relation of the set $Split$ at a given time. These constraints are marked as non eligible. The next step consists in selecting a constraint marked as eligible and processing it: first, the constraint is split into relations belonging to the set $Split$; then, each one of these relations is used to instantiate the chosen constraint. Search proceeds by calling again $consistentE'$. It terminates when all constraints are marked as non eligible or when all partial instantiations have failed.

Algorithm 1. Function $consistentE(\mathcal{N})$, with $\mathcal{N} = (V, C)$ and $n = |V|$.

```
for i, j ∈ 0 . . . n − 1
    if (C_ij ∈ Split) mark C_ij as non eligible else mark C_ij as eligible
endFor
return consistentE'(N)
```

Function $consistentE'(\mathcal{N})$, with $\mathcal{N} = (V, C)$.

```
if (wcc(N) == false) return false
Select a constraint C_ij such that C_ij is eligible
if such a constraint C_ij does not exist return true
Split C_ij into subrelations r_1, . . . , r_k such that r_l ∈ Split
for l ∈ 1 . . . k do
    C_ij ← r_l, C_ji ← C_ij^−1
    Mark C_ij and C_ji as non eligible
    if (consistentE'(N) == true) return true
endFor
return false
```

Function $wcc(\mathcal{N})$, with $\mathcal{N} = (V, C)$ and $n = |V|$.

```
do
    N' ← N
    for i, j, k ∈ 0 . . . n − 1
        C_ij ← C_ij ∩ (C_ik ∘ C_kj), C_ji ← C_ij^−1
        if (C_ij == ∅) return false
        if (C_ij ∈ Split) mark C_ij and C_ji as non eligible
    endFor
until (N' == N)
return true
```

The case where $consistentE$ returns **false** corresponds to the case where all possible partial solutions have been explored and have been detected as non consistent by the weak composition closure method. In the case where $consistentE$ terminates successfully, it is not guaranteed in general that the QCN $\mathcal{N}$ is a consistent network. Following the line of reasoning proposed by Nebel [4] we can prove that the QCN $\mathcal{N}$ we obtain is a $\circ$-closed QCN whose relations belong to $Split$. Hence, if the weak composition closure method is complete for $Split$, the obtained network is a consistent network.

Theorem 1. *If the method of closure by weak composition is complete for* $Split \subseteq 2^{\mathsf{B}}$, *then* $consistentE$ *is sound and complete for the consistency problem.*

4 Experimental Results About Eligibility

We have implemented a series of tests on a set of qualitative constraint networks on Allen's algebra. These QCNs have been randomly generated according to a model similar to those proposed in [6, 4]. This model has the following parameters: n is the number of variables of the network; $nonTrivialDensity$ (nTD) is a real number which corresponds to the probability of a constraint to be non trivial (*i.e.* different from B); $cardinalityDensity$ (cD) is a real number which corresponds to the probability of a basic relation to belong to a given non trivial constraint; $consistent$ indicates whether the generated network must be forced to be consistent by adding a consistent scenario. The experiments reported in this paper are concerned with QCNs on Allen's calculus generated with 50 variables, with $nonTrivialDensity \in \{0.25, 0.5, 0.75\}$. $cardinalityDensity$ varies from 0.05 until 0.95 by a step of 0.05. For lack of space, we only provide the results concerning consistent QCNs. For each data point, 100 QCNs have been generated and tested. All experiments have been implemented in JAVA using the QAT (Qualitative Algebra Toolkit) library [7]. We have compared the $consistentE$ algorithm and the algorithm proposed by Nebel [4]. The set of ORD-Horn relations [8, 9] is used for the set $Split$. During search the choice of constraints to be treated (line 2 of $consistentE'$) is dynamic. The first heuristics we use, called Dom consists in selecting a constraint having the lowest cardinality among all selectable constraints. The second heuristics is more original. We call it $DomTriangle$. As in the previous heuristics, this heuristics considers the constraints having the lowest cardinality. To each of these constraints C_{ij} the $DomTriangle$ heuristics associates the weight $\Sigma(|Cik| + |Ckj|$: C_{ik} and C_{kj} are not trivial) and chooses one constraint having a minimal weight.

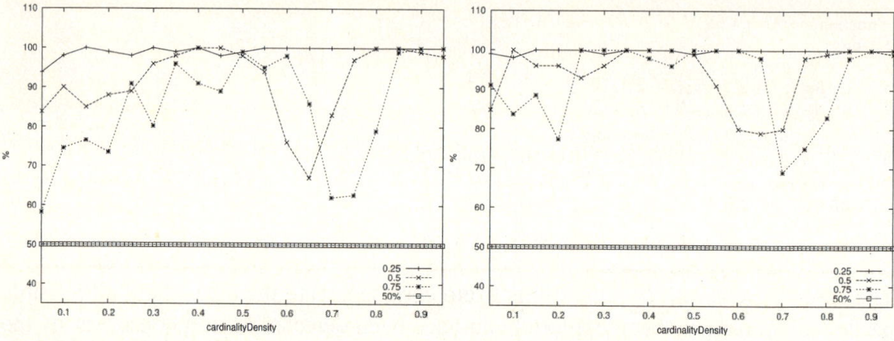

Fig. 1. Percentages of number of QCN solved faster by $consistentE$ for $nonTrivialDensity \in \{0.25, 0.5, 0.75\}$, with the Dom heuristics (left) and $DomTriangle$ heuristics (right)

By examining the graphs in Fig. 1 we note that for most of the QCNs generated, the algorithm $consistentE$ terminates earlier. The advantage is more pronounced when we use the $DomTriangle$ heuristics rather than Dom. Moreover, as a general rule, when the density $nonTrivialDensity$ is lower the advantage is higher. A plausible explanation of this phenomenon is that the lower this density is, the greater is the number of trivial relations, and then the greater the number of ORD-Horn relations, the earlier $consistentE$ terminates. Table **??** recapitulates the time and number of backtracks used during search. The average time is given in milliseconds. The first column indicates the time used by the first call of the method of closure by weak composition. The two following ones indicate the times of search used respectively by $consistentE$ and by Nebel's algorithm. In the last two columns, the numbers of backtracks are indicated. The resolution is particularly difficult for $cD \in \{0.6, 0.65\}$. In these phase the number of backtracks is very high. $consistentE$ is slower in some cases. These cases are always in the difficult phase. We have also made experiments for QCNs which are not forced to be consistent. The first results concerning these QCNs are similar.

Table 1. Comparison of $consistencyE$ and the Nebel's algo., Dom(left), DomTriangle(right)

nTD=0.5	T_{wcc}	T_E	T_N	BK_E	BK_N
cD=0.05	137	11	17	0	0
cD=0.1	138	9	14	0	0
cD=0.15	151	11	18	0	0
cD=0.2	162	14	24	0	0
cD=0.25	175	18	33	0	0
cD=0.3	198	24	45	0	0
cD=0.35	231	34	63	0	0
cD=0.4	268	55	98	0	0
cD=0.45	296	90	155	0	0
cD=0.5	290	296	387	0	0
cD=0.55	108	1289	1320	19	12
cD=0.6	72	**37566**	**34338**	1078	839
cD=0.65	59	**28751**	**27061**	785	640
cD=0.7	52	4964	10096	136	190
cD=0.75	47	717	987	0	2
cD=0.8	48	626	873	0	0
cD=0.85	42	520	752	0	0
cD=0.9	31	384	564	0	0
cD=0.95	17	179	281	0	0

nTD=0.5	T_{wcc}	T_E	T_N	BK_E	BK_N
cD=0.05	135	11	17	0	0
cD=0.1	132	6	13	0	0
cD=0.15	142	9	17	0	0
cD=0.2	154	13	24	0	0
cD=0.25	175	19	34	0	0
cD=0.3	198	26	47	0	0
cD=0.35	225	33	62	0	0
cD=0.4	262	56	98	0	0
cD=0.45	298	94	153	0	0
cD=0.5	281	290	380	0	0
cD=0.55	109	1642	1724	29	23
cD=0.6	68	6272	6325	162	139
cD=0.65	51	**14188**	**11260**	429	297
cD=0.7	45	1078	1283	7	7
cD=0.75	40	715	935	0	0
cD=0.8	38	625	879	0	0
cD=0.85	36	522	748	0	0
cD=0.9	24	368	570	0	0
cD=0.95	13	167	263	0	0

5 Frozen Constraints

In order to illustrate the concepts of constraints of environment and critical constraints, consider the q-queens problem. The problem consists in placing q queens (with q an integer number) on a chessboard of size $q \times q$ such that no queen can capture another queen. In order to represent this problem with qualitative constraints we can use a new qualitative algebra that we call $ACD25$ (Algebra of Cardinal Directions 25). It is based onto 25 basic relations defined on the discrete domain $\mathsf{D} = N \times N$. Roughly speaking, each one of these 25 relations (see Figure 2 (c)) corresponds to a particular cardinal direction (North, South, ...) and equally corresponds to a particular distance between the two points. The distance equals 0 (for the relation EQ), or 1 (for the relations $N, W, S, E, NW, SW, NE, SE$) or greater than 1 for the 16 remaining relations. Using the $ACD25$ algebra we can express the queens problem using a QCN $\mathcal{N} = (V, C)$ in the following way. A variable is introduced for each square of the chessboard and for each queen. Hence, we obtain $q \times (q+1)$ variables in V representing points of the plane of the integer number. A first set of constraints is necessary to define the structure of the object corresponding to the chessboard. These constraints are constraints of environment and give the relative position between a case and its adjacent cases, see Figure 2 (a). This set of constraints is always consistent. The critical constraints will correspond to the constraints on the positions of the queens. Firstly, we must constraint each queen to be on the chessboard, more precisely we can constraint each queen to be on exactly one line of the chessboard. For this, we force the ith queen to be to the east (resp. to the west) of the first square (resp. the last square) of the ith of the chessboard (see Figure 2 (b)). Finally, we define each constraint between two queens by the basic relations illustrated in Fig. 2 (c) to make sure that a queen cannot capture another queen. Note that given a solution of the QCN, we are only interested in the positions of the queens on the chessboard, *i.e.* the constraints equal to $\{EQ\}$ between a queen and a square. We now introduce the concept of frozen constraints. This concept is an elegant way of distinguishing and treating structural and critical constraints. A frozen constraint is just a constraint which cannot be modified during the search for a solution. Structural constraints will be considered as frozen, while critical constraints will not. The first one are used to constrain "the domain" of the problem.

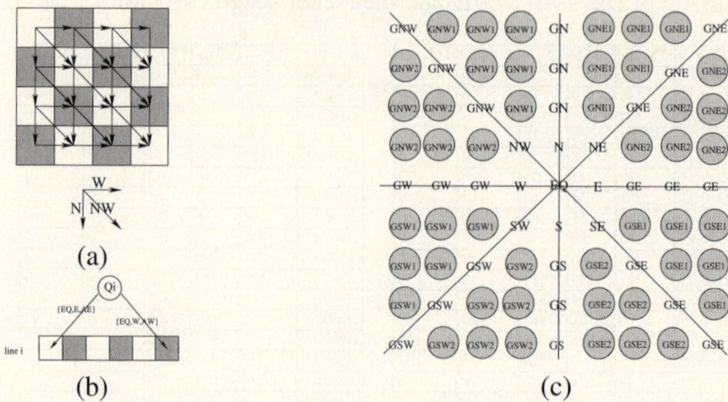

Fig. 2. (a) Constraints between the squares, (b) the constraint between a queen and its line, (c) the constraint between two queens

Algorithm 2. **Function** *consistentEF*$(\mathcal{N})$, *with* $\mathcal{N} = (V, C)$ *and* $n = |V|$.

1: **for** $i, j \in 0 \ldots n-1$
2:   **if** *(*$C_{ij} \in Split$*)* **or** *(*$(i,j) \in SFrozen$*)* *Mark* C_{ij} *as non eligible* **else** *Mark* C_{ij} *as eligible*
3: **endFor**
4: **return** $consistentEF'(\mathcal{N})$

Function $consistentEF'(\mathcal{N})$, *with* $\mathcal{N} = (V, C)$.
1: **if** $(wccF(\mathcal{N}) ==$ **false**) **return false**
2: *Select a constraint* C_{ij} *such that* C_{ij} *is eligible*
3: **if** *is such a constraint* C_{ij} *does not exist* **return true**
4: *Split* C_{ij} *in relations* $r_1, \ldots, r_k$ *such that* $r_l \in Split$
5: **for** $l \in 1 \ldots k$ **do**
6: $C_{ij} \leftarrow r_l$, $C_{ji} \leftarrow C_{ij}^{-1}$
7:   *Mark* C_{ij} *and* C_{ji} *as non eligible*
8:   **if** $(consistentEF'(\mathcal{N}) ==$ **true**) **return true**
9: **endFor**
10: **return false**

Function $wccF(\mathcal{N})$, *with* $\mathcal{N} = (V, C)$ *and* $n = |V|$.
1: **do**
2: $\mathcal{N}' \leftarrow \mathcal{N}$
3:   **for** $i, j \in 0 \ldots n-1$
4:   **if** *(*$(i,j) \notin SFrozen$*)*
5:   **for** $k \in 0 \ldots n-1$
6: $C_{ij} \leftarrow C_{ij} \cap (C_{ik} \circ C_{kj})$, $C_{ji} \leftarrow C_{ij}^{-1}$
7:   **if** $(C_{ij} == \emptyset)$ **return false**
8:   **if** *(*$C_{ij} \in Split$*)* *Mark* C_{ij} *and* C_{ji} *as non eligible*
9:   **endFor**
10:   **endFor**
11: **until** $(\mathcal{N}' == \mathcal{N})$
12: **return true**

We now extend the function $consistentE$ in order to take into account the concept of freezing. The freezing of a subset of the constraints will be made *a priori*. A frozen constraint cannot be selected or instantiated during the search, nor updated during the local propagation of constraints. This is translated into concrete terms in the definition of the function $consistentEF$ (E for eligibility and F for freezing) as defined in Algorithm 2. $SFrozen$ denotes the set of pairs of integer numbers representing the frozen constraints. The main modifications made w.r.t. the previous algorithm are the following ones. Firstly, we mark as non eligible each frozen constraint (line 2 of the function $consistentEF$). Secondly, the method of closure by weak composition is modified to consider only triangulation operations which can potentially modify a non frozen constraint. Applying this method is not guaranteed to yield an $\circ$-closed QCN but a weaker one that we denote by $\langle \circ, SFrozen \rangle$-closed. It is formally defined as follows:

Definition 2. *Let $\mathcal{N} = (V, C)$ be a* QCN. *Let $F \subseteq \{0, \ldots, n-1\} \times \{0, \ldots, n-1\}$ representing the set of frozen constraints. We say that $\mathcal{N}$ is $\circ$-closed w.r.t. F, denoted by $\langle \circ, F \rangle$-closed, iff $\forall i, j, k \in \{0, \ldots, n-1\}$, $(i, j) \notin F$ implies $C_{ij} \subseteq C_{ik} \circ C_{kj}$.*

Consider a set of QCNs defined on the same set of variables $V = \{v_0, \ldots, v_{n-1}\}$. Given a set $F \subseteq \{0, \ldots, n-1\} \times \{0, \ldots, n-1\}$ representing a set of frozen constraints on V and a set of relations $S \subseteq 2^{\mathsf{B}}$ representing a splitting set. We say that the method of $\langle \circ, F \rangle$-closure by weak composition is complete for S iff for any $\mathcal{N} = (V, C) \in \mathcal{Q}$, if $\mathcal{N}$ is $\langle \circ, F \rangle$-closed and for all $(i, j) \in (\{0, \ldots, n-1\} \times \{0, \ldots, n-1\}) \setminus F$ $C_{ij} \in S$ then $\mathcal{N}$ is a consistent QCN or contains the empty relation as a constraint. We have:

Theorem 2. *For any set of* QCN*s for which the closure by weak composition w.r.t. $SFrozen$ is complete for the set $Split$, $consistentEF$ is sound and complete.*

Consider the QCNs representing the q-queens problem. Take $SFrozen = \{(i, j) : C_{ij}$ is a constraint between two squares$\}$. Define $Split$ as the union of the set of basic relations of $ACD25$ and the universal relation. We can prove that the closure by weak composition w.r.t. $SFrozen$ is complete for the set $Split$.

6 Conclusion

We proposed and studied algorithms for solving QCNs based on concepts of eligible constraints and frozen constraints. We established the conditions under which these algorithms are sound and complete. Using experimental data, we showed the interest of our approach, in particular in terms of time of computation. Our experimental work is still in progress, especially for confronting $consistencyE$ and $consistencyEF$ to QCNs of greater sizes and to QCNs defined on other qualitative formalisms. It would be interesting to use other splitting sets than the set of ORD-Horn relations, such as the set of convex relations or the set of pointizable relations. Another future work consists in developing alternative methods of local propagation of constraints, similarly to the method of closure by weak composition. It would also be interesting to study the behavior of the algorithms under these new methods.

References

[1] Allen, a.J.F.: An interval-based representation of temporal knowledge. In: Proc. of the Seventh Int. Joint Conf. on Artificial Intelligence (IJCAI'81), pp. 221–226 (1981)

[2] Ligozat, G.: Reasoning about cardinal directions. Journal of Visual Languages and Computing 1(9), 23–44 (1998)

[3] Ladkin, P.B., Reinefeld, A.: Effective solution of qualitative interval constraint problems. Artificial Intelligence 57(1), 105–124 (1992)

[4] Nebel, B.: Solving hard qualitative temporal reasoning problems: Evaluating the efficienty of using the ORD-Horn class. In: Proceeding of the Twelfth Conference on Artificial Intelligence (ECAI'96) (1996)

[5] Renz, J., Nebel, B.: Efficient methods for qualitative spatial reasoning (1998)
[6] Beek, P.V., Manchak, D.W.: The design and experimental analysis of algorithms for temporal reasoning. Journal of Artificial Intelligence Research 4, 1–18 (1996)
[7] Condotta, J.F., Ligozat, G., Saade, M.: The QAT: A Qualitative Algebra Toolkit. In: Proceedings of the thirteenth international conference on Temporal Representation an Reasoning (TIME'2006), Hungary (2006)
[8] Nebel, B., Bürckert, H.J.: Reasoning About Temporal Relations: A Maximal Tractable Subclass of Allen's Interval Algebra. Journal of the ACM 42(1), 43–66 (1995)
[9] Ligozat, G.: A New Proof of Tractability for ORD-Horn Relations. In: Proc. of the Thirteenth Nat. Conference on Artificial Intelligence (AAAI'96), vol. 1, pp. 395–401 (1996)

The Log-Support Encoding of CSP into SAT

Marco Gavanelli

Dept. of Engineering, Ferrara University
http://www.ing.unife.it/docenti/MarcoGavanelli/

Abstract. Various encodings have been proposed to convert Constraint Satisfaction Problems (CSP) into Boolean Satisfiability problems (SAT). Some of them use a logical variable for each element in each domain: among these very successful are the *direct* and the *support* encodings.

Other methods, such as the *log*-encoding, use a logarithmic number of logical variables to encode domains. However, they lack the propagation power of the direct and support encodings, so many SAT solvers perform poorly on log-encoded CSPs.

In this paper, we propose a new encoding, called *log-support*, that combines the log and support encodings. It has a logarithmic number of variables, and uses support clauses to improve propagation. We also extend the encoding using a Gray code. We provide experimental results on Job-Shop scheduling and randomly-generated problems.

1 Introduction

One methodology for solving Constraint Satisfaction Problems (CSP) relies on the conversion into boolean satisfiability (SAT) problems. The advantage is the wide availability of free, efficient, SAT solvers, and the possibility to exploit advances in SAT solvers without reimplementing them in CP. SAT solvers have reached significant levels of efficiency, and new solvers are proposed, tested and compared every year in annual competitions [2,20]. There are both complete SAT solvers, based on systematic search (typically, variants of the DPLL procedure [6]), and incomplete solvers, often based on local search.

Very popular encodings [23,18] assign a SAT variable to each element of a CSP domain, i.e., for each CSP variable i and each value v in its domain, there is a logical variable $x_{i,v}$ that is true iff i takes value v. The reason for such a representation is that it lets the SAT solver achieve *pruning*: if the SAT solver infers that $x_{i,v}$ is $false$, then the corresponding CSP variable i cannot take value v. The most popular CSP-SAT encoding is the *direct* [23]; DPLL applied to a SAT encoded CSP mimics the Forward Checking on the original CSP [11,23]. The *support encoding* [12] has the same representation of domains, but a different representation of constraints. Unit propagation (used in DPLL solvers) applied to the support-encoded CSP achieves the same pruning of arc-consistency on the original CSP. Stronger types of consistency are proven in [3,7].

On the other hand, using a SAT variable for each value in a domain generates a huge search space. Indeed, it lets the SAT solver perform powerful propagation, but at a cost: the search space is exponential in the number of SAT variables.

In logarithmic encodings, each domain is represented by $\lceil \log_2 d \rceil$ SAT variables [15,14,9,23,18,1]. Such encodings can be tailored for specific constraints, such as

C. Bessiere (Ed.): CP 2007, LNCS 4741, pp. 815–822, 2007.

not equal [10]. In general, however, they lack the ability to remove single values from domains, which yields less powerful propagation when compared to CSP solvers. Constraints are usually represented as in the direct encoding.

In this paper, we propose a new encoding, called *Log-Support*, that uses support clauses in a logarithmic encoding. The codification of domains can be either the usual binary representation, or based on a Gray code, in order to maximise the propagation power of support clauses. We apply the new encodings on randomly generated problems and on benchmark job-shop scheduling problems, and compare the performances of the SAT solvers Chaff [17] and MiniSat [8] on the encoded problems.

2 Preliminaries and Notation

A *CSP* consists of a set of variables, ranging on domains, and subject to constraints. We focus on *binary CSPs*, where constraints involve at most two variables. We call n the number of variables, and d the maximum domain cardinality. The symbols i and j refer to variables, while v and w are domain values.

A *SAT problem* contains a formula built on a set of variables, which can take only values $true$ (or 1) and $false$ (or 0). We call them *logical variables* or *SAT variables* to distinguish them from CSP variables. The formula is often required to be in conjunctive normal form, i.e., a set of *clauses*, i.e., disjunctions of literals of the logical variables. A solution to a SAT problem is an assignment of values $true/false$ to the logical variables, such that all clauses are satisfied.

3 A Survey on Encodings

The Direct encoding. [23] uses a logical variable $x_{i,v}$ for each CSP variable i and domain value v. For each CSP variable i, a clause (called *at-least-one*) imposes that i takes at least one of the values in its domain: $x_{i,1} \vee x_{i,2} \vee \ldots \vee x_{i,d}$. *At-most-one* clauses forbid the variable i to take two values: $\forall j_1 \neq j_2$ we add $\neg x_{i,j_1} \vee \neg x_{i,j_2}$. Constraints are encoded with *conflict clauses*: for each pair of inconsistent assignments $i \leftarrow v$, $j \leftarrow w$ s.t. $(v,w) \notin c_{i,j}$, we have $\neg x_{i,v} \vee \neg x_{j,w}$.

For example, consider the CSP: $A \leq B$, with A and B ranging on $\{0,1,2\}$. The direct encoding produces the clauses:

at-least-one		$a_0 \vee a_1 \vee a_2$		$b_0 \vee b_1 \vee b_2$
at-most-one	$\neg a_0 \vee \neg a_1$	$\neg a_0 \vee \neg a_2$	$\neg b_0 \vee \neg b_1$	$\neg b_0 \vee \neg b_2$
		$\neg a_1 \vee \neg a_2$		$\neg b_1 \vee \neg b_2$
conflict	$\neg a_1 \vee \neg b_0$	$\neg a_2 \vee \neg b_0$	$\neg a_2 \vee \neg b_1$	

The Support Encoding. [16,12] represents domains as in the direct encoding, i.e., we have *at-least-one* and *at-most-one* clauses. Constraints are based on the notion of support. If an assignment $i \leftarrow v$ supports the assignments $j \leftarrow w_1$, $j \leftarrow w_2$, ..., $j \leftarrow w_k$, we impose that $x_{i,v} \rightarrow x_{j,w_1} \vee x_{j,w_2} \vee \ldots \vee x_{j,w_k}$ i.e., we impose a *support clause*: $\neg x_{i,v} \vee x_{j,w_1} \vee x_{j,w_2} \vee \ldots \vee x_{j,w_k}$.

The constraints of the previous example are represented as the support clauses: $\neg a_1 \vee b_1 \vee b_2$, $\neg b_0 \vee a_0$, $\neg a_2 \vee b_2$ and $\neg b_1 \vee a_0 \vee a_1$.

The Log Encoding. [15,23,10] uses $m = \lceil \log_2 d \rceil$ logical variables to represent domains: each of the 2^m combinations represents an assignment. For each CSP variable i we have logical variables x_i^b, where $x_i^b = 1$ iff bit b of the value assigned to i is 1. *At-least-one* and *at-most-one* clauses are not necessary; however, in case the cardinality of domains is not a power of two, we need to exclude the values in excess, with the so-called *prohibited-value clauses* [18] (although the number of these clauses can be reduced [10]). If v is not in the domain of i, and v is represented with the binary digits $\langle v_{m-1}, \dots, v_0 \rangle$, we impose $\neg \left(\bigwedge_{b=0}^{m-1} \neg(v_b \oplus x_i^b) \right)$ where $\oplus$ means exclusive-or. Intuitively, $\neg(s \oplus b)$ is the literal b if s is *true*, and $\neg b$ if s is false. We obtain the *prohibited-value* clause $\bigvee_{b=0}^{m-1} v_b \oplus x_i^b$.

Constraints can be encoded with conflict clauses. If two assignments $i \leftarrow v$, $j \leftarrow w$ are in conflict, and v_b and w_b are the binary representations of v and w, we impose a clause of length $2m$: $\left(\bigvee_{b=0}^{m-1} v_b \oplus x_i^b \right) \vee \left(\bigvee_{b=0}^{m-1} w_b \oplus x_j^b \right)$.

In the running example, we will have:

prohibited-value	$\neg a_1 \vee \neg a_0$	$\neg b_1 \vee \neg b_0$
conflict	$a_1 \vee \neg a_0 \vee b_1 \vee b_0$	$\neg a_1 \vee a_0 \vee b_1 \vee b_0$
	$\neg a_1 \vee a_0 \vee b_1 \vee \neg b_0$	

4 The Log-Support Encoding

In the log-encoding, conflict clauses consist of $2m$ literals; unluckily, the length of clauses typically influences negatively the performance of a SAT solver.

The DPLL applied to a support-encoded CSP performs a propagation equivalent to arc-consistency on the original CSP [12]. One could think of applying support clauses to log encodings; an intuitive formulation is the following. If an assignment $i \leftarrow v$ supports the assignments $j \leftarrow w_1, \dots, j \leftarrow w_k$, we could impose, as in the support encoding, that $v \rightarrow w_1 \vee \dots \vee w_k$, and then encode in binary form the values v and w_i. However, the binary form of a value is a conjunction, so the formula becomes $\left(\bigwedge_b \neg(v^b \oplus x_i^b)\right) \rightarrow \left(\bigwedge_b \neg(w_1^b \oplus x_j^b)\right) \vee \dots \vee \left(\bigwedge_b \neg(w_k^b \oplus x_j^b)\right)$ which, in conjunctive normal form, generates an exponential number of clauses[1].

We convert in clausal form only implications that have exactly one literal in the conclusion. Let us consider, as a first case, only the most significant bit. In our running example, the assignment $A \leftarrow 2$ supports only $B \leftarrow 2$. We can say that, whenever A takes value 2, the most significant bit of B must be 1: $a_1 \wedge \neg a_0 \rightarrow b_1$. We add the support clause $\neg a_1 \vee a_0 \vee b_1$, that is enough to rule out two conflicting assignments:

prohibited-values	$\neg a_1 \vee \neg a_0$	$\neg b_1 \vee \neg b_0$
support	$\neg a_1 \vee a_0 \vee b_1$	
conflict	$a_1 \vee \neg a_0 \vee b_1 \vee b_0$	

Note that this transformation is not always possible: we can substitute some of the conflict clauses with one support clause only if all the binary form of supported values agrees on the most significant bit.

[1] One could reduce the number of clauses by introducing new variables, as in [3].

Each support clause has length $m+1$ and removes $d/2$ conflict clauses (of length $2m$). This is a significant reduction of the number of conflict clauses when the assignments that satisfy the constraint are all grouped in the same half of the domain. This happens in many significant constraints (e.g, $>$, $\leq$, $=$).

To sum-up, this encoding has the same number ($n\lceil \log_2 d \rceil$) of logical variables required by the log-encoding, with a reduced number of conflict clauses (of length $2\lceil \log_2 d \rceil$), which are substituted by support clauses (of length $\lceil \log_2 d \rceil + 1$).

Improvements. The same scheme can be applied to the other direction (from B to A), and to other bits (not just to the most significant one). In the running example, we can add the support clauses $b_1 \vee b_0 \vee \neg a_0$, $b_1 \vee \neg b_0 \vee a_1$, $b_1 \vee \neg b_0 \vee \neg a_1$ and, in this case, remove all the conflict clauses.

Suppose that a value v in the domain of variable i conflicts with two consecutive values w and $w{+}1$ in the domain of j. Suppose that the binary representation of the numbers w and $w+1$ differs only for the least significant bit b_0. In this case, we can represent both the values w and $w+1$ using only the $m-1$ most significant bits, so we can impose one single conflict clause of length $2m-1$. This simple optimization can be considered as applying binary resolution [7] to the two conflict clauses, and can be extended to sets of consecutive conflicting values whose cardinality is a power of two.

4.1 Gray Code

The *Gray code* [13] uses a logarithmic number of bits, as the binary code; however, any two consecutive numbers differ only for one bit. So, by encoding the values in the CSP domains with a Gray code, all intervals of size 2 are representable, while in the classical binary code only half of them are representable. For instance, suppose that a CSP variable A has a domain represented in 4-bit binary code, and that during DPLL search its state is 001U, i.e., the first three bits have been assigned, while the last has not been assigned yet. We can interpret this situation as the current domain of A being $\{2, 3\}$. However, there is no combination that can represent the domain $\{3, 4\}$. In the 4-bit Gray code, $\{2, 3\}$ is represented by configuration 001U and $\{3, 4\}$ by 0U10.

With a Gray representation, the running example is encoded as follows:

prohibited-values	$\neg a_1 \vee a_0$	$\neg b_1 \vee b_0$
support	$\neg a_1 \vee a_0 \vee b_0$	$b_1 \vee b_0 \vee \neg a_0$
	$\neg a_1 \vee \neg a_0 \vee b_0$	$b_1 \vee b_0 \vee \neg a_1$
	$\neg a_1 \vee \neg a_0 \vee b_1$	$b_1 \vee \neg b_0 \vee \neg a_1$

By using a Gray code, the number of support clauses has increased from 4 to 6 (50%), while (in this case) no conflict clauses are necessary. The intuition is that a higher number of support clauses should allow for more powerful propagation, but in some cases it could also increase the size of the SAT problem. However, each support clause has one CSP value in the antecedent and one of the bits in the conclusion, so for each constraint there are at most $2d\lceil \log_2 d \rceil$ support clauses. The number of conflict clauses in the log-encoding cannot be higher than the number of pairs of elements in a domain, so d^2. Recall also that conflict clauses are longer than support clauses, so we can estimate the size of the (Gray) Log-Support encoding to be smaller than that of the log-encoding, when d is large.

5 Experimental Results

5.1 Randomly Generated Problems

The first set of experiments is based on randomly generated CSPs. A random CSP is often generated given four parameters [21]: the number n of variables, the size d of the domains, the probability p that there is a constraint on a given pair of variables, and the conditional probability q that a pair of assignments is consistent, given that there is a constraint linking the two variables.

In order to exploit the compact representation of log-encodings, we focussed on CSPs with a high number of domain values. In order to keep the running time within reasonable bounds, we had to keep small the number of CSP variables.

The Log-Support encoding was developed for constraints in which the set of satisfying assignments is connected, and we can easily foresee that a Gray code will have no impact on randomly generated constraint matrices. Thus, we used a different generation scheme, in which satisfying assignments have a high probability to be grouped in clusters. Note that also real-life constraints typically have their satisfying assignments grouped together, and not completely sparse.

For each constraint (selected with independent probability p) on variables A and B, we randomly selected a pair of values v and w respectively from the domains of A and B. The pair (v, w) works as an "attractor": the probability that a constraint is satisfied will be higher near (v, w) and smaller far from that point. Precisely, the probability that a pair of assignments (a, b) is satisfied is $q = 1-\alpha\sqrt{(a-v)^2+(b-w)^2}$, where α is a coefficient that normalises the value of q in the interval 0..1. A posteriori, we grouped the experiments with a same frequency of satisfied assignments, and plotted them in the graph of Figure 1.

These experiments were performed running zChaff 2004.5.13 [17] and MiniSat 1.14 [8] on a Pentium M715 processor 1.5GHz, with 512MB RAM. A memory limit was set at 150MB, and a timeout at 1000s. Each point is the geometric mean of at least 25 experiments, where the conditions of timeout or out of memory are represented by 1000s. Timing results include both the time spent for the encoding and for solving the problem; however, the encoding time was always negligible. Note that to perform the experiments we did not generate a DIMACS file, because the time for loading the DIMACS could have been large (see also the discussion in the next section).

From the graphs, we see that the log encoding is the slowest when the constraints are tight (q is small). This could be due to the fact that in the log-encoding we have limited propagation of constraints, which makes hard proving unsatisfiability. On the other hand, when the constraints are loose (q near 80-90%), the log encoding performs better than the direct and support encodings.

The support encoding is often the best option for MiniSat, while Gray was the best in the zChaff experiments. Moreover, the Log-Support/Gray encodings are

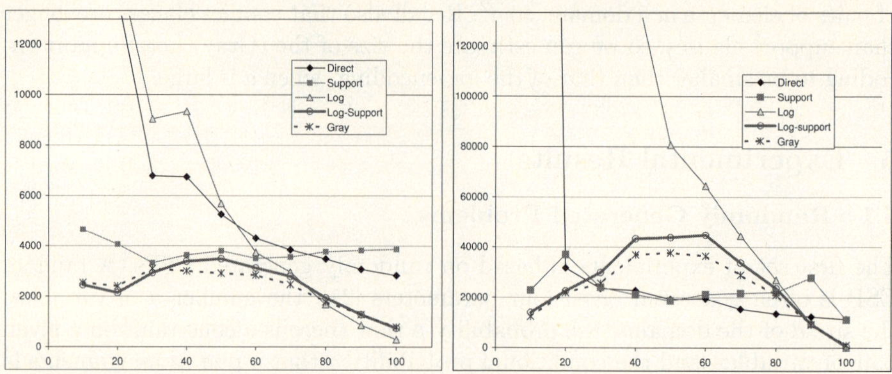

Fig. 1. Experiments on randomly-generated problems ($n = 7$, $d = 512$, $p = 30$ and q from 10 to 100). Times in ms. Left: Chaff, Right: MiniSat.

often competitive. For high values of q, the Log-Support/Gray encodings keep the same behaviour of the log-encoding. This is reasonable, because when q is high, few support clauses are inserted. On the other hand, when q is small, support clauses have a strong influence, and allow the SAT solver to detect infeasibility orders of magnitude faster than in the log-encoding. Both the Log-Support and the Gray encodings are typically faster than the direct encoding.

Finally, the Gray encoding is slightly faster than the Log-Support, probably due to the fact that more support clauses are present.

5.2 Job-Shop Scheduling Problems

We applied the encodings to the set of Job-Shop Scheduling Problems taken from the CSP competition 2006 [22] (and originally studied in [19]). These problems involve 50 CSP variables with variable domain sizes, from 114 to 159.

The results are in Figure 2: the plots show the number of problems that were solvable within a time limit given in abscissa (the higher the graph, the better).

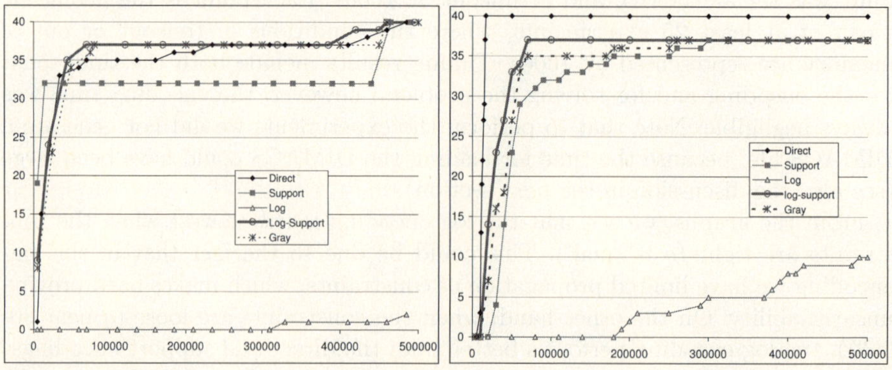

Fig. 2. Experiments on Job-Shop scheduling problems. Left: Chaff, right: MiniSAT.

The log encoding performed worst, and both Chaff and MiniSat were able to solve only a limited subset of the problems within 500s.

In the experiments performed with Chaff, the support encoding was able to solve some of the problems very quickly; however, given more time, the Log-Support was typically the best choice (it was able to solve more problems). In the experiments with MiniSat, the best encoding was the direct, possibly because of the special handling of binary clauses implemented in MiniSat. Notice that for both solvers the support encoding performed worse than the Log-Support and the Gray encodings. In these instances, the Gray encoding did not provide improvements with respect to the Log-Support.

Chaff required on average 65MB of RAM to solve a direct-encoded CSP, 56MB to solve a support-encoded CSP, and only 19MB to solve a problem encoded with Log-Support or Gray. The size of the generated SAT instance is also interesting. On average, a log-encoded CSP used 10^7 literals, from which we can estimate a DIMACS file of about 55MB. The Log-Support and Grey encodings needed on average $1.7 \cdot 10^6$ literals, with a DIMACS of about 9.5MB. The direct encoding used $2.3 \cdot 10^6$ literals (14MB), and the support $7 \cdot 10^6$ (45MB).

We can conclude that the Log-Support and Gray encodings are significant improvements with respect to the log encoding, both in terms of solution time and size of the generated SAT problem. The direct encoding is often faster than the Log-Support, but it requires more memory for Chaff to solve them, and the DIMACS file is much larger. Thus the Log-Support and Gray encodings could be interesting solution methods in cases with limited memory.

6 Conclusions and Future Work

We proposed two new encodings, called *Log-Support*, and *Gray*, for mapping CSPs into SAT. The Log-Support and Gray encodings use a logarithmic number of SAT variables for representing CSP domains, as in the well-known log-encoding. Experiments show that the new encodings outperform the traditional log-encoding, and is competitive with the direct and support encodings. Moreover, the size of the encoded SAT is typically a fraction of the size required by other encodings.

In future work, we plan to define a platform for defining CSPs, in the line of [5,4]. Such architecture could be populated with a variety of the many encodings proposed in recent years [1], and with the Log-Support/Gray encodings.

Other optimisations could be performed on the log encodings. We cite the *binary encoding* [9], that uses a logarithmic number of logical variables to encode domains, and it avoids imposing *prohibited value* clauses by encoding a domain value with a variable number of SAT variables. In future work, we plan to experiment with a variation of the Log-Support that exploits the same idea. Finally, we plan to experiment the various encodings with other solvers, in particular, local-search based.

Acknowledgements. This work has been partially supported by the MIUR PRIN 2005 project *Constraints and preferences as a unifying formalism for system analysis and solution of real-life problems.*

References

1. Ansótegui, C., Manyà, F.: Mapping problems with finite-domain variables to problems with boolean variables. In: Hoos, H.H., Mitchell, D.G. (eds.) SAT 2004. LNCS, vol. 3542. Springer, Heidelberg (2005)
2. Le Berre, D., Simon, L.: SAT competition (2005), www.satcompetition.org/2005/
3. Bessière, C., Herbrard, E., Walsh, T.: Local consistencies in SAT. In: Giunchiglia, E., Tacchella, A. (eds.) SAT 2003. LNCS, vol. 2919. Springer, Heidelberg (2004)
4. Cadoli, M., Mancini, T., Patrizi, F.: SAT as an effective solving technology for constraint problems. In: Esposito, F., Raś, Z.W., Malerba, D., Semeraro, G. (eds.) ISMIS 2006. LNCS (LNAI), vol. 4203, pp. 540–549. Springer, Heidelberg (2006)
5. Cadoli, M., Schaerf, A.: Compiling problem specifications into SAT. Artificial Intelligence 162(1-2), 89–120 (2005)
6. Davis, M., Logemann, G., Loveland, D.: A machine program for theorem-proving. Communications of the ACM 5, 394–397 (1962)
7. Dimopoulos, Y., Stergiou, K.: Propagation in CSP and SAT. In: Benhamou, F. (ed.) CP 2006. LNCS, vol. 4204, pp. 137–151. Springer, Heidelberg (2006)
8. Eén, N., Sörensson, N.: An extensible SAT-solver. In: Giunchiglia, E., Tacchella, A. (eds.) SAT 2003. LNCS, vol. 2919, pp. 502–518. Springer, Heidelberg (2004)
9. Frisch, A., Peugniez, T.: Solving non-boolean satisfiability problems with stochastic local search. In: Nebel, B. (ed.) IJCAI 2001, pp. 282–290 (2001)
10. Van Gelder, A.: Another look at graph coloring via propositional satisfiability. In: Computational Symposium on Graph Coloring and its Generalizations (2002)
11. Genisson, R., Jegou, P.: Davis and Putnam were already forward checking. In: Proc. of the 12th ECAI, pp. 180–184. Wiley, Chichester (1996)
12. Gent, I.P.: Arc consistency in SAT. In: van Harmelen, F. (ed.) ECAI'2002 (2002)
13. Gray, F.: Pulse code communication, U. S. Patent 2 632 058 (March 1953)
14. Hoos, H.: SAT-encodings, search space structure, and local search performance. In: Dean, T. (ed.) IJCAI 99, pp. 296–303. Morgan Kaufmann, San Francisco (1999)
15. Iwama, K., Miyazaki, S.: SAT-variable complexity of hard combinatorial problems. In: IFIP World Computer Congress, North-Holland, pp. 253–258 (1994)
16. Kasif, S.: On the parallel complexity of discrete relaxation in constraint satisfaction networks. Artificial Intelligence 45, 275–286 (1990)
17. Moskewicz, M.W., Madigan, C.F., Zhao, Y., Zhang, L., Malik, S.: Chaff: Engineering an efficient SAT solver. In: Proc. of DAC 2001, pp. 530–535. ACM Press, New York (2001)
18. Prestwich, S.: Local search on SAT-encoded colouring problems. In: Giunchiglia, E., Tacchella, A. (eds.) SAT 2003. LNCS, vol. 2919. Springer, Heidelberg (2004)
19. Sadeh, N.M., Fox, M.S.: Variable and value ordering heuristics for the job shop scheduling constraint satisfaction problem. Artificial Intelligence 86(1), 1–41 (1996)
20. Sinz, C.: The SAT race (2006), http://fmv.jku.at/sat-race-2006/
21. Smith, B.M., Dyer, M.E.: Locating the phase transition in binary constraint satisfaction problems. Artificial Intelligence 81(1-2), 155–181 (1996)
22. van Dongen, M., Lecoutre, C., Roussel, O.: Second international competition of CSP and Max-CSP solvers (2006), http://www.cril.univ-artois.fr/CPAI06/
23. Walsh, T.: SAT v CSP. In: Dechter, R. (ed.) CP 2000. LNCS, vol. 1894, pp. 441–456. Springer, Heidelberg (2000)

Groupoids and Conditional Symmetry

I.P. Gent[1], T. Kelsey[1], S.A. Linton[1], J. Pearson[2], and C.M. Roney-Dougal[3]

[1]School of Computer Science, University of St Andrews, St Andrews, UK
[2]Uppsala University, Department of Information Technology, Uppsala, Sweden
[3]School of Mathematics and Statistics, University of St Andrews, St Andrews, UK
{ipg,tom,sal}@cs.st-and.ac.uk, justin.pearson@it.uu.se,
colva@mcs.st-and.ac.uk

Abstract. We introduce groupoids – generalisations of groups in which not all pairs of elements may be multiplied, or, equivalently, categories in which all morphisms are invertible – as the appropriate algebraic structures for dealing with conditional symmetries in Constraint Satisfaction Problems (CSPs). We formally define the Full Conditional Symmetry Groupoid associated with any CSP, giving bounds for the number of elements that this groupoid can contain. We describe conditions under which a Conditional Symmetry sub-Groupoid forms a group, and, for this case, present an algorithm for breaking all conditional symmetries that arise at a search node. Our algorithm is polynomial-time when there is a corresponding algorithm for the type of group involved. We prove that our algorithm is both sound and complete – neither gaining nor losing solutions.

1 Introduction

Conditional symmetries in CSPs are parts of a problem that become interchangeable when some condition is satisfied. Typically the condition is that a subset of the variables have been given particular values. Definitions of conditional symmetry, together with initial approaches for identifying and breaking them, are given in [1,2,3,4]. A key problem is that the set of conditional symmetries of a CSP does not, in general, form a group. This motivates the research question: is there a suitable mathematical abstraction of conditional symmetry that can be used to identify, classify and break such symmeteries in an arbitrary CSP?

We describe groupoids as the class of mathematical objects that are the appropriate abstraction for conditional symmetries. Using groupoids we can describe, enumerate and analyse conditional symmetries for any CSP. Given a CSP, the Full Conditional Symmetry Groupoid, containing elements that capture both the symmetry and the condition under which it arises. This approach allows us to classify conditional symmetries in terms of the sub-groupoid(s) in which they are contained. Moreover, we can identify conditional symmetries that have properties that allow us to develop effective symmetry breaking techniques.

Groupoids are generalisations of groups, in which not all elements can be composed. A basic introduction to groupoids is given in [5]. The reason that we

C. Bessiere (Ed.): CP 2007, LNCS 4741, pp. 823–830, 2007.

have to leave groups behind when talking about conditional symmetries is that every element of a symmetry group can be applied to *all* partial assignments, and hence one cannot capture the concept of "condition".

2 Groupoids and Conditional Symmetries

We will use the following notation throughout: the set of variables will denoted with a V, individual variables $v_1, \ldots, v_n$ and sometimes w. For simplicity, we will assume that there is a single domain D for all variables (since constraints can be added to give different domains for chosen variables). A *literal* of a CSP is a pair (w, d) where $w \in V$ and $d \in D$.

Definition 1. *A* partial assignment *f is a set of literals that contains at most one literal for each variable. A partial assignment g is an* extension *of f, if $f \subseteq g$.*

We say that a partial assignment f is *complete* if $|f| = |V|$. That is, all variables are assigned values by f. A *solution* to a CSP is a complete partial assignment that violates no constraint.

Definition 2. *A* groupoid *is a set G, and a basis set B, together with a partial operation, composition, and two maps s and t from G to B that together satisfy the following:*

1. *composition, gh, of two elements, g and h in G is defined only when $t(g) = s(h)$ — this is what is meant by saying that the composition is partial;*
2. *if the products gh and hk are defined then $g(hk) = (gh)k$ is defined;*
3. *for every g in G there are left and right identity elements λ_g and ρ_g s.t. $\lambda_g g = g = g\rho_g$;*
4. *Each element has an inverse g^{-1} s.t. $gg^{-1} = \lambda_g$ and $g^{-1}g = \rho_g$.*

Often groupoids will be presented as collections of triples, $(s(g), g, t(g))$, with composition of two elements g and h can written as: $(s(g), g, t(g))(s(h), h, t(h)) = (s(g), gh, t(h))$, provided that $t(g) = s(h)$. convention of "acting from the right" so that gh means "do g then do h".

A *subgroupoid* of a group G is a subset of the elements of G that itself forms a groupoid under the same partial operation. The base set of a subgroupoid is the set of all sources and targets that occur for elements of the subgroupoid.

We now turn to formalising conditional symmetries as groupoid elements. The key problem in providing the definitions is that for composition to be defined, the target of one element has to be *equal* to the source of the next. This makes it impossible to represent sources and targets as the simple condition given by the constraint. Instead, we have a separate groupoid element for every partial assignment that satisfies a condition. We will develop the theory and show that this leads to well-defined groupoids and useful theoretical results.

We will denote the image of an object α under a map ϕ by α^ϕ. A *literal bijection* of a CSP is a bijection ϕ from the set of literals of the CSP to itself. The following definition begins the process of capturing the notion of a condition.

Definition 3. *A literal bijection is a* symmetry with respect to a, *where a is a subset of literals, if in its induced action on sets of literals, whenever f is a solution that contains a then f^ϕ is a solution and whenever f is a non-solution that contains a then f^ϕ is a non-solution.*

Before defining conditional symmetry groupoids, we need precise descriptions of conditions and symmetries arising from conditions. A *condition* is a predicate on literals. Any such predicate can be described by listing the sets of literals upon which it holds. If a symmetry in a CSP is present only when some condition holds, we will describe this situation by adding one generator to the conditional symmetry groupoid for each set of literals which satisfy the condition.

Definition 4. *We define the* full conditional symmetry groupoid G *of a CSP P to be the set of all triples as follows:*

$$G = \{(g, \pi, f) : g, f \text{ sets of literals}, \pi \text{ a symmetry with respect to } g, g^\pi = f\}.$$

The product (in this order) of two groupoid elements $(g, \pi, f), (h, \sigma, k)$ is defined only if $h = f$ in which case the product is $(g, \pi\sigma, k)$ and $g^{\pi\sigma}$ will equal k.

We work throughout with subgroupoids of the full conditional symmetry groupoid of the CSP. Note that if $(g, \pi, f) \in G$ and h is a set of literals that contains g, then $(h, \pi, h^\pi) \in G$, as π is a symmetry with respect to g only if it is a symmetry with respect to all extensions of g. We say that (h, π, h^π) is an *extension* of (g, π, f), and that the conditional symmetry groupoid is *closed under extensions.* We call the first entry of each triple its *precondition* and the last its *postcondition.*

Lemma 1. *With these definitions, the full conditional symmetry groupoid G of a CSP is a groupoid.*

Proof. The set of elements of G is clear, its base set is the power set of the set of literals. We must show that composition, where defined, is associative and that each element has left and right identities and inverses. Let $(g_1, \pi_1, f_1), (g_2, \pi_2, f_2)$ and $(g_3, \pi_3, f_3) \in G$, and suppose that $g_2 = f_1$ and $g_3 = f_2$. Then

$$((g_1, \pi_1, f_1)(g_2, \pi_2, f_2))(g_3, \pi_3, f_3) = (g_1, \pi_1\pi_2, g_1^{\pi_1\pi_2})(g_3, \pi_3, f_3).$$

Now, $g_2 = f_1 = g_1^{\pi_1}$, so $f_2 = g_2^{\pi_2} = g_1^{\pi_1\pi_2}$. Hence $g_3 = f_2 = g_1^{\pi_1\pi_2}$ and the product of the two groupoid elements in the previous displayed equation is defined, and is equal to $(g_1, \pi_1\pi_2\pi_3, g_1^{\pi_1\pi_2\pi_3})$. Conversely

$$\begin{aligned}(g_1, \pi_1, f_1)((g_2, \pi_2, f_2)(g_3, \pi_3, f_3)) &= (g_1, \pi_1, f_1)(g_2, \pi_2\pi_3, g_2^{\pi_2\pi_3}) \\ &= (g_1, \pi_1\pi_2\pi_3, g_1^{\pi_1\pi_2\pi_3}),\end{aligned}$$

as required. The right identity of (g, π, f) is $(f, 1, f)$, the left identity is $(g, 1, g)$, and the inverse is (f, π^{-1}, g), where by 1 we mean the identity mapping on the set of all literals.

Lemma 2. *The full conditional symmetry groupoid of a CSP has a well-defined partial action on the set of all sets of literals, which maps (non-)solutions to (non-)solutions.*

Proof. The action of an element (g, π, f) on a set h of literals is as follows. If $g \not\subseteq h$ then the condition of (g, π, f) is not satisfied, and so the action is undefined. If $g \subseteq h$ then $h^{(g,\pi,f)} := h^{\pi}$. To show that this is an action, we note that $h^{(g,\pi_1,f)(f,\pi_2,k)}$ is defined if and only if $g \subseteq h$ are sets of literals in which case we have

$$h^{(g,\pi_1,f)(f,\pi_2,k)} = h^{(g,\pi_1\pi_2,k)} = h^{\pi_1\pi_2} = (h^{(g,\pi_1,f)})^{(f,\pi_2,k)},$$

and that $h^{(g,1,f)} = h$ whenever $g \subseteq h$. Whenever h is a full assignment and $h^{(g,\pi,f)}$ is defined, then, since π is a symmetry with respect to g and $g \subseteq h$, h^{π} is a (non-)solution exactly when h is a (non-)solution.

Next we show that our notions of conditional symmetry strictly generalise the standard notions of unconditional symmetry.

Lemma 3. *The full conditional symmetry groupoid of a CSP P contains the group of all symmetries of P.*

Proof. Elements of the symmetry group of the CSP are of the form $(\emptyset, \pi, \emptyset)$.

In general, however, the full conditional symmetry groupoid of a CSP is far too large for practial computation, and we must restrict the situation somewhat.

Lemma 4. *The full conditional symmetry groupoid of a CSP P with $|V| = n$ and $|D| = d$ has order at least 2^{dn} and at most $2^{dn}(dn)!$.*

Proof. A precondition can be any subset of literals and the corresponding permutation can be any permutation of the full set of literals. The identity permutation is a symmetry with respect to any set of literals.

Of course, in practise we cannot identify *all* conditional symmetries of a CSP before solving it, so we identify as many non-identity conditional symmetries as possible, and then form the resulting groupoid.

Definition 5. *We say that a collection of conditional symmetry groupoid elements* $\{(g_i, \pi_i, f_i) \ : \ 1 \leq i \leq k\}$ generate *a conditional symmetry groupoid G if G is the smallest subgroupoid of the full conditional symmetry groupoid that contains all of the elements and is closed under extensions.*

The reason why any conditional symmetry groupoid is defined to be closed under extensions is that it must always be possible to consider conditions that are stronger than those initially given: if (v_1, α) implies some symmetry, then so does $\{(v_1, \alpha), (v_2, \beta)\}$. Later, when we discuss computing with conditional symmetry groupoids, we will describe a technique which avoids the creation of these additional elements.

Lemma 5. *The conditional symmetry groupoid G is generated by elements from $A := \{(g_i, \pi_i, f_i) \; : \; 1 \leq i \leq k\}$ if and only if each element of G is a product of elements that are extensions of elements of A and their inverses.*

Proof. We first show that the set of all elements of the conditional symmetry groupoid that are products of extensions of elements of A forms a groupoid and is closed under extensions. It is clear that it is closed under the partial product and the associativity follows from the associativity of the generalised conditional symmetry groupoid. If $(x_0, \sigma, x_k) = (x_0, \sigma_1, x_1)(x_1, \sigma_2, x_2) \cdots (x_k, \sigma_{k+1}, x_{k+1})$ is a product of extensions of elements of A, then we note that $(x, 1, x)$ is an extension of a left identity of an element of A, and similarly for $(y, 1, y)$, and that $(x_i, \sigma_i^{-1}, x_{i-1})$ and $(x_{i+1}, \sigma_{i+1}^{-1}, x_i)$ are extensions of right and left inverses of elements of A. Thus this set forms a groupoid. If (x, σ, y) is an extension of (x_0, σ, x_k) then it is clear that it is a product of elements of the form $(\overline{x_i}, \sigma_{i+1}, \overline{x_{i+1}})$, where $\overline{x_i}$ is a partial assignment that extends x_i.

Conversely, if (x, σ, y) is a product of extensions of elements of A then it must be contained in any groupoid that contains A, and so is an element of the groupoid generated by A. Thus the result follows.

3 Symmetry Breaking with Groupoids

Symmetry breaking by dominance detection for groups of symmetries uses the following principle: given the current search node g then for each previously found nogood f, and each symmetry π test the inclusion $f^\pi \subseteq g$. This can be done either by some supplied procedure, as in SBDD, or by adding new constraints that rule out all images under the symmetry group of extensions of f.

Lemma 6. *If $f \subseteq g$ are partial assignments, and (h, π, k) is an element of the full conditional symmetry groupoid, then $f^{(h,\pi,k)} \subseteq g^{(h,\pi,k)}$.*

Proof. If h is not a subset of f, then neither map is defined. Otherwise, $f^{(h,\pi,k)} = f^\pi = (f \setminus h)^\pi \cup k$ and $g^{(h,\pi,k)} = g^\pi = (g \setminus h)^\pi \cup k$. Since $(f \setminus h)^\pi \subseteq (g \setminus h)^\pi$, we have $f^\pi \subseteq g^\pi$ as required.

When implementing SBDD efficiently for groups or groupoids, the fact that groupoid actions are well-behaved with respect to extensions of partial assignments means that only failures at the top of subtrees need be stored during depth first search.

To check the dominance in SBDD in the group case we search for an element π of the symmetry group such that g is an extension of f^π. The situation with groupoids is a bit more complicated, as the action is only partial and so the following two cases have to be checked:

- Does there exist a groupoid element (h, γ, k) such that $f \subseteq h$ and $g \subseteq f^\gamma$?
- Otherwise we must search for some extension, f', of f and a groupoid element (h, γ, k) such that $f' \subseteq h$ and $g \subseteq f'^\gamma$.

Note that in case (ii) it is only worth considering extensions of f that assign values to no more variables than g, and one should only consider extensions that enable some new conditional symmetry to be used.

To avoid this two-case analysis, we *reverse* the normal process of SBDD and instead look for conditional symmetries that map the current partial assignment to a partial assignment that is an extension of the previous nogood.

Definition 6. *A partial assignment g is* dominated *by a nogood f with respect to a conditional symmetry groupoid G if there exists an element $(h, \gamma, k) \in G$ with $h \subseteq g$ and $f \subseteq g^\gamma$.*

This simplification is possible because groupoids *are* closed under inversion, and so if a map exists in one direction we can always consider its inverse.

Lemma 7. *Let G be a conditional symmetry groupoid of a CSP P and let a be a fixed partial assignment of P. The set of all elements of G of the form (a, π, a) form a group.*

Proof. Let $(a, \pi_1, a), (a, \pi_2, a) \in G$. The product $(a, \pi_1\pi_2, a)$ is defined and is of the correct form. Associativity holds because within this set of elements the product of two elements is always defined. The element $(a, 1, a) \in G$ and is the identity of this subgroup. The inverse $(a, \pi_1^{-1}, a) \in G$ is of the correct form.

Definition 7. *Let P be a CSP with conditional symmetry groupoid G generated by $X := \{(a_i, \pi_{ij}, b_i) : 1 \leq i \leq m, j \in \mathcal{J}_i\}$. Let A be a partial assignment, and let*

$$C := \bigcup_{a_i \subseteq A} a_i.$$

Then the local group at A with respect to X, *denoted $\mathcal{L}_X(A)$ is the group consisting of the permutations σ of all elements of G of the form (C, σ, C).*

It follows from Lemma 7 that the group at A is always a group, if nonempty. Since there is always the identity unconditional symmetry, the group at A is always nonempty, although it may be the trivial group $(C, 1, C)$.

Lemma 8. *Checking for dominance under the $\mathcal{L}_X(A)$ is sound.*

Proof. Since all elements of $\mathcal{L}_X(A)$ are symmetries with respect to a subset of A, they will all map (non-)solutions extending A to (non-)solutions.

We now consider a special case where checking for dominance under the group at A is also complete.

Theorem 1. *Let G be a conditional symmetry groupoid of a CSP P, generated by a set $X = \{(a_i, \pi_{ij}, a_i) : 1 \leq i \leq m, j \in \mathcal{J}_i\}$, where each a_i is a partial assignment. Assume that for $1 \leq i, k \leq m$ we have $a_i^{\pi_{kj}} = a_i$ for all $j \in \mathcal{J}_k$. Then checking for dominance under $\mathcal{L}_X(A)$ is complete as well as sound.*

Proof. Let $H := \mathcal{L}_X(A)$. We show that if $(g, \sigma, h) \in G$ and $g \subseteq A$ then $\sigma \in H$. It is clear that if σ is a product of π_{ij} for $a_i \subseteq A$ then $\sigma \in H$. We wish to show that if σ is a product including at least one π_{kj} for some $a_k \not\subseteq H$ then (g, σ, h) does not act on A. It is clear that no extension of (a_k, π_{kj}, a_k) can act on g as $a_k \not\subseteq A$, and hence that one cannot postmultiply any extension of (a_k, π_{kj}, a_k) to make it act on A. We show that one cannot premultiply any extension of (a_k, π_{kj}, a_k) by an element of G to make it act on A. Since $a_k^{\pi_{il}} = a_k$ for all l, if (x, σ, y) can premultiply an extension of (a_k, π_{kj}, a_k) then $a_k \subseteq y$ and so $a_k \subseteq x$ and hence $x \not\subseteq A$ and we are done.

Using this theorem, we can identify some special cases where testing dominance is possible in polynomial time.

Theorem 2. *Let G be a conditional symmetry groupoid of a CSP P, generated by a set $\{(a_i, \pi_{ij}, a_i) : 1 \leq i \leq m, j \in \mathcal{J}_i\}$ where each a_i is a partial assignment. Assume that for $1 \leq i, k \leq m$, whenever $a_i \cup a_k$ is a partial assignment then $a_i^{\pi_{kj}} = a_i$ for all $j \in \mathcal{J}_k$. If the actions of π_{ij} on the set of extensions of a_i all belong to a class of symmetries for which there exists a polynomial time algorithm to determine group dominance, then testing conditional symmetry dominance under the groupoid G can be done in polynomial-time at each node.*

Proof. By Theorem 1 it is both sound and complete to test each partial assignment A for dominance by previous nogoods using only the local group at A with respect to X. The local group at A with respect to X can be constructed in polynomial-time, by examining which conditions of which generators are subsets of A and then generating a group with the corresponding permutations. Hence

PREPROCESSING For each generator (a_i, π_{ij}, b_i) do

(i) If $a_i \neq b_i$ then return "inapplicable".
(ii) If π_{ij} is not a value symmetry on all literals in a_i, and on all literals involving variables not in a_i then return "inapplicable".
(ii) For each (a_k, π_{kl}, b_k) with $k \neq i$ such that $a_i \cup a_k$ is a partial assignment do
- If $a_i^{\pi_{kl}} \neq a_k$ then return "inapplicable".

AT NODE A

1. Make a set L of the generators of G such that $a_i \subseteq A$.
2. Construct the local group $\mathcal{L}_X(A)$, which is $\langle \sigma : (a, \sigma, a) \in L \rangle$.
3. For each nogood B do
   (a) If B contains any literals with different variables from those in A, consider the next nogood.
   (b) Otherwise, by repeatedly computing point stabilisers check whether there exists a $\sigma \in \mathcal{L}_X(A)$ such that for all $(w, \alpha) \in A$ with $(w, \beta) \in B$ for some β we have $(w, \alpha)^\sigma = (w, \beta)$.
   (c) If such a σ exists, return "dominated".
4. Return "not dominated".

Fig. 1. Algorithm for sound and complete conditional symmetry breaking

if there exists a polynomial-time algorithm for testing whether A is dominated by a nogood by an element of a group of symmetries then it can now be applied.

Corollary 1. *Let G be a conditional symmetry groupoid of a CSP P, generated by a set $\{(a_i, \pi_{ij}, a_i) : 1 \leq i \leq m, j \in \mathcal{J}_i\}$ where each a_i is a partial assignment. Assume that for $1 \leq i, k \leq m$, whenever $a_i \cup a_k$ is a partial assignment then $a_i^{\pi_{kj}} = a_i$ for all $j \in \mathcal{J}_k$. If the actions of π_{ij} on the set of extensions of a_i are value symmetries then testing conditional symmetry dominance is in P.*

Proof. This is immediate from Theorem 2 and [6].

Fig. 1 shows a polynomial-time algorithm which takes as input a set of conditional symmetry groupoid generators for a CSP and determines whether the conditions of Corollary 1 apply and if so tests for groupoid dominance.

As in SBDD, we can safely backtrack when dominated, and continue to the next search node otherwise. Our approach is not restricted to value symmetries. We can obtain polynomial-time algorithms whenever a polynomial-time algorithm exists for symmetry breaking in the unconditional case.

4 Conclusions and Further Work

We have shown that careful use of the theory of groupoids allows us fully to capture the notion of conditional symmetry in CSPs.

We have identified the algebraic structure of conditional symmetries. With this we can study the whole set of conditional symmetries of a problem, rather than just a small subset given to us by a programmer, and analyse sub- and super-groupoids. We have shown the enormous numbers of conditional symmetries and complicated structure that arises when we generate them all. We have provided definitions and algorithms for conditional symmetry breaking. We have defined a notion of dominance, allowing us to give an analogue of SBDD for conditional symmetries. We have also shown that it is possible to identify useful conditional symmetry sub-groupoids that are small enough to permit effective conditional symmetries breaking.

References

1. Gent, I.P., McDonald, I., Smith, B.M.: Conditional symmetry in the all-interval series problem. In: Symcon'03 (2003)
2. Gent, I.P., McDonald, I., Miguel, I., Smith, B.M.: Approaches to conditional symmetry breaking. In: SymCon'04 (2004)
3. Zhang, Y., Freuder, E.C.: Conditional interchangeability and substitutability. In: SymCon'04 (2004)
4. Walsh, T.: General symmetry breaking constraints. In: Benhamou, F. (ed.) CP 2006. LNCS, vol. 4204, pp. 650–664. Springer, Heidelberg (2006)
5. Brown, R.: From groups to groupoids: A brief survey. Bulletins of the London Mathematical Society 19, 113–134 (1987)
6. Roney-Dougal, C.M., Gent, I.P., Kelsey, T., Linton, S.A.: Tractable symmetry breaking using restricted search trees. In: ECAI'04, pp. 211–215 (2004)

Sampling Strategies and Variable Selection in Weighted Degree Heuristics*

Diarmuid Grimes and Richard J. Wallace

Cork Constraint Computation Centre and Department of Computer Science
University College Cork, Cork, Ireland
{d.grimes,r.wallace}@4c.ucc.ie

Abstract. An important class of CSP heuristics work by sampling information during search in order to inform subsequent decisions. An example is the use of failures, in the form of constraint weights, to guide variable selection in a weighted degree procedure. The present research analyses the characteristics of the sampling process in this procedure and the manner in which information is used, in order to better understand this type of strategy and to discover further enhancements.

1 Introduction

Recent years have seen the emergence of new and more powerful methods for choosing variables and variable assignments during CSP search. In the past most heuristics based their decisions on either the initial state of search or the current state of search. However newer heuristics use within-problem learning, basing their decisions on past states, in order to adapt to a given problem. Among these are Boussemart et al.'s "weighted-degree" heuristic (*wdeg*) [1] and a variation on the weighted degree strategy that we call "random probing" [2] [3]. The significance of these methods is that they can locate specific sources of failure, including at one extreme insoluble subproblems.

In this work, we study these techniques in order to characterise them more adequately, focusing on constraint weighting. (Although the following can be expanded to problems involving n-ary constraints, for simplicity we limit our discussion to binary CSPs.) We examine two aspects of these methods:

- the nature and quality of the information gained during sampling
- the manner in which this information is used during subsequent search

2 Characterising Algorithms Based on Constraint Weighting

2.1 Description of Heuristics Based on Constraint Weights

In the weighted degree procedure, a constraint's weight is incremented during consistency propagation whenever this constraint causes a domain wipeout. The *weighted degree* of a variable is the sum of the weights of the constraints in the current search state

* This work was supported by Science Foundation Ireland under Grants 00/PI.1/C075 and 05/IN/1886.

C. Bessiere (Ed.): CP 2007, LNCS 4741, pp. 831–838, 2007.

associated with the variable. The weighted degree heuristic (wdeg) chooses the variable with largest weighted degree. (So the heuristic acts identically to the forward-degree heuristic up until at least one failure has occurred.)

Domain information can also be incorporated by choosing the variable which minimises the ratio of domain-size to weighted degree (dom/wdeg). Given the general effectiveness of the dom/wdeg strategy, this is the method used in most experiments reported in this paper.

Random probing uses a more systematic method of sampling. It begins with a series of "random probes", in which variable selection is done randomly, and weights are incremented in the usual fashion but are not used to guide search. Probing is run to a fixed cutoff C, and for a fixed number of restarts R. On the last restart (final run), the cutoff is removed and the wdeg or dom/wdeg heuristic uses the accumulated weights for each variable. On the final run one can either use these weights as the final weights for the constraints or continue to update them, thereby combining global weights with weights that are local to the part of the search space one is in.

2.2 Characterisation of Constraint Weighting Procedures

The weighted degree procedures can be conceived in terms of an overall strategy that combines two heuristic principles: the Fail-First principle and an additional *Contention Principle*, which says that variables directly related to conflicts are more likely to *cause* failure if they are chosen instead of other variables. A somewhat more precise statement of this principle is:

Contention Principle. *If a constraint is identified as a source of contention, then variables associated with that constraint are more likely to cause failure after instantiation.*

This leads to the rule-of-thumb: *Choose the variable associated with the most contentious constraints,* which is the basis for the weighted degree heuristic.

The validity of the Contention Principle depends on the undirected character of constraints. Suppose the domain of variable x_k is wiped out after assigning values to variables x_1, x_2, ..., x_j. In this case, if x_k is assigned a value before these other variables, then at least one of the domains of the latter will be reduced. Moreover, the greater the number of partial assignments affecting x_k, the greater the likelihood that assigning x_k a value early in search will affect some other variable. (Note that a similar argument can be made even if the domain of x_k is only reduced.)

There are two aspects or phases in the weighted degree procedure (in any of its forms): a *sampling phase* and a *variable selection phase*. In the sampling phase, we are trying to sample likelihood of failure. This is done by tallying domain wipeouts. A "wipeout" is a complex event consisting of a set of domain deletions that comprise an entire domain. In addition, deletions are associated via episodes of constraint propagation with a set of assignments. A wipeout therefore has two aspects: the reduction itself and the 'context' of that reduction including both a set of assignments and the constraint C_{ik} associated with the final domain reduction. Constraint weights combine these events into event-classes involving all the assignment sets that can lead to a wipeout of D_k via constraint C_{ik} (note each of those assignment sets also leads to a wipeout of domain D_i via the same constraint).

In the weighted degree algorithm sampling is done in the context of systematic search. This means that the same basic event cannot be sampled more than once. At the same time, sampling is heavily *biased* in favour of assignment tuples related to the order of instantiation. Moreover, the bias changes during search because partial assignments are increasingly determined by the results of the sampling itself. This creates a negative feedback effect, since variables associated with high weights are selected earlier in search, after which their weights are less likely to increase since their constraints are removed from the current problem.

Random probing allows us to sample more systematically. In doing so, we may be able to uncover cases of "global contention", i.e. contention that holds across the entire search space. We also assume that variables associated with global contention are most likely to reduce overall search effort if they are instantiated at the top of the search tree.

In the variable selection phase, estimates of failure in the form of constraint weights are used to guide heuristic selection. As noted above, constraint weights give an estimate of overall contention associated with that variable. However, because of sampling biases as well as possible dependencies among failures, the relative values of these sums have an unknown relation to sizes of probabilities associated with the underlying compound events.

3 Experimental Methods and Reference Results

The bulk of the present analysis employs two sets of problems: 100 random binary and 100 random k-colouring problems. To facilitate data collection, problem parameters were chosen so that problems were fairly easy to solve, although in both cases, they are in the critical complexity region. The basic sets of problems had solutions. In most cases, results for more difficult problems of the same types corroborate the present ones. Unless otherwise noted, all results are for chronological backtracking using maintained arc consistency (MAC) with lexical value ordering. In experiments on search efficiency, search was for one solution. For all results using the random probing strategy, means given are means over 10 experiments, each experiment having a different random seed.

Table 1. Search Efficiency on Random and k-Colour. Problems with Selected Heuristics.

heuristic	random	colouring
lexical	253,607	4,547,058
max static deg	2000	22,460
Brelaz	3101	910
min dom/fwddeg	1621	1285
max fwddeg	2625	347,306
min dom/wdeg	1538	1029
max wdeg	2070	16,866

Notes. Random problems are <50,10,0.183,0.631>. k-colour problems are <50,6,0.27>, where 6 is number of colours and 0.27 is density. Measure is mean search nodes.

Since we are trying to assess quality of search given different kinds and amounts of information, measures of effort are confined to the search itself. So results for random probing are for the final run following the sampling phase. In the final run, weights were no longer incremented after failure ("frozen weights"). This allows us to assess quality of information provided by the probing without contamination by further updating during the final run.

Selected results for various heuristics are shown in Table 1. These include the foundation heuristics used by weighted degree and random probing, namely maximum forward-degree and minimum domain/forward-degree. To indicate problem difficulty, results for lexical variable ordering are also included.

4 Search Efficiency with Weighted Degree Strategies

Elsewhere we have collected results for a variety of problems using weighted degree and random probing; these included both soluble and insoluble and random and structured problems ([2], [3]). In these papers we have shown that, even with preprocessing work included, the random probing approach improves over dom/wdeg and in some cases by orders of magnitude. This work demonstrates the generality of the basic effects that we wish to study in more depth in this paper.

Results for weighted degree using either max wdeg or min dom/wdeg as the heuristic are shown at the bottom of Table 1. As expected, when the basic heuristics are elaborated by incorporating the constraint weights, there is consistent improvement in average search effort.

Probing results for random problems are shown in Table 2. The first thing that should be noted is that for random problems every combination of restarts and node cutoff gives an improvement over dom/wdeg. In the best cases there is about a 25% improvement. At the same time, some combinations of restarts and cutoffs give better overall performance than others. This means that different probing regimes yield information of varying quality, so this is a significant aspect of probing. (Partial results have been collected for random binary problems with the same parameters that had no solutions. Similar improvements were found as for those reported above.)

Corresponding data for colouring problems are shown in Table 3. Somewhat different parameter values were tested with the expectation that good estimates of failure would

Table 2. Search Efficiency with Random Probing with Different Restarts and Cutoff (random)

	Restarts				
Cutoff	10	20	40	80	160
25	1498	1369	1316	1263	1228
50	1346	1287	1237	1174	1205
100	1314	1228	1173	1223	1174
200	1237	1245	1196	1211	1177

Notes. <50,10,0.183,0.631> problems.
final run after probing, mean search nodes across ten experiments, dom/frowdeg.

Table 3. Search Efficiency with Random Probing with Different Restarts and Cutoff (colouring)

	Restarts			
Cutoff	10	40	100	200
50	6129	4526	3118	3710
100	5988	4123	3996	—
500	6463	4698	3837	—

Notes. <50,6,0.27> k-colouring problems.
Otherwise as in Table 2.

require more extensive search than with random problems because with inequality constraints propagation cannot occur until a domain is reduced to one value. In this case, search after random probing is consistently inferior to the interleaving strategy used by weighted degree, although these results are closer to those for the strong heuristics listed in Table 1 than for the weak ones.

Results obtained to date suggest that interleaving after probing does not improve search to a significant degree and may sometimes impair it. Thus, for the random problems, using 40 restarts and a 50-node cutoff gave a mean of 1285 search nodes (versus 1237 in Table 2). Comparable results were found for the colouring problems using 40 or 100 restarts with a 50-node cutoff. For much more difficult problems of this type, freezing weights sometimes yields marked improvements in performance [3].

Another issue is whether probing with a node cutoff can mask a varying number of failures and, therefore, differences in quality of sampling. In fact, there is a high degree of consistency in the relation between failures and nodes. Thus, for the random problems a failure-count cutoff of 50 was associated with a node-count of about 70, with a total range of 60-87 across 100 problems and 4000 runs. Similar results were found for the colouring problems. This means the basic results would not be altered if failures were used instead of nodes. Nonetheless, in some subsequent experiments we use failure-cutoffs in order to control this factor directly.

5 Empirical Analyses of Sampling and Variable Selection

Weighted-degree heuristics estimate the likelihood that failure will be induced by tallying actual failures. Previous work has not addressed the issue of the actual method of sampling or considered alternative sampling strategies. The key issues involve quality of sampling. In the first place, we can consider the specific type of event sampled. Because we are looking for indicators that predict the likelihood of inducing failure, it may be possible to sample events related to failure other than domain wipeout. In the second place, we can sample under different methods of search, that differ in the degree of consistency established or the manner in which conflict is detected.

5.1 Sampling Based on Different Specific Events Related to Failure

Here we look at sampling contention that is either an elaboration of failure counts or is based on domain reductions. We consider the following:

- wipeout-tallies in which in each case the relevant constraint weight is increased by the size of the domain reduction leading to the wipeout
- tallies of all deletions; i.e. whenever a domain is reduced in size during constraint propagation, the weight of the constraint involved is incremented by 1
- tallies of all deletions where constraint weights are increased by the size of the domain reduction
- tallies of all deletions *except* those leading to a wipeout

The last-mentioned 'strategy' was included to evaluate the hypothesis that sampling is related to contention rather than to failure in particular.

Table 4. Search Efficiency with Different Sampling Strategies (Mean search nodes per problem)

	dom/wdeg	random probe-dom/wdeg (40R50C)
wipeouts	1538	1265
wipe by #del	1592	1261
alldel	1523	1426
alldel by #del	1496	1461
dels/nowipe	1530	1499

Notes. <50,10,0.183,0.631> problems. "R" and "C" are restarts and node-cutoff on each run before the final one.

The results show that any of these events can indicate contention (Table 4). For the dom/wdeg heuristic, sampling either deletions and failures gives comparable results. With random probing, direct sampling of failure is reliably better than sampling deletions. This is further evidence that effectiveness of search after probing is affected by quality of sampling, since events directly associated with failure (i.e. with greater degrees of contention) are better predictors of fail-firstness than conflicts that do not necessarily imply failure. Nonethess, search is very efficient in all cases.

5.2 Sampling Based on Different Search Procedures

We compared three search methods for information gathering that weight constraints that either cause domain wipeouts in systematic search or cause conflict in local search. The first uses the breakout method for preprocessing weight generation (similar to [4]), these weights are then used during complete search with dom/wdeg. The second uses forward checking with random probing for information gathering, and the third is random probing using MAC as in earlier sections. All three methods were followed by complete search with MAC, using frozen weights. For both FC and MAC random probing, there were 100 restarts with a *failure* cutoff of 30. Breakout was run to a total weight cutoff of 3000. Thus, each method generated the same amount of information.

Table 5. Search Efficiency with Information. Gathered under Different Search Procedures.

	probe-dom/wdeg	probe-wdeg
Breakout	1863	3890
FC-probes	1492	3198
MAC-probes	1198	1595

Notes: <50,10,0.183,0.631> problems. Mean search nodes for the final run across ten experiments.

As seen in Table 5, the weights learnt by MAC were superior to those learnt by either FC or breakout for these problems. The magnitude of the improvement when using MAC is even clearer if the domain size factor is removed from the heuristic. (Note that if either breakout or FC produced weights of similar quality to MAC then, because of the speedup they offer over MAC, they would be more efficient for preprocessing).

5.3 Analysis of Variable Selection

To further analyse the quality of search with sampling, measures of *promise* and *fail-firstness* were collected. These are measures of the quality of search under two different conditions: (i) when search is on a solution path, i.e. the present partial assignment can be extended to a solution, (ii) when a mistake has been made and search is in an insoluble subtree [5]. Quality is assessed by measuring the degree of adherence to an optimal policy under each condition. It was expected that sampling would have its major effect on fail-firstness.

Table 6. Adherence-to-Policy Assessments and Selected. Descriptive Measures for Orderings Based on Sampling.

heuristic	policy measures		descriptive measures		
	promise	badtree	|dom|	fwd-deg	faildepth
dom/fwddeg	.00041	437	3.3	8.2	7.7
dom/wdeg	.00042	366	3.3	8.2	7.4
random probe (40R 50C)	.00046	282	3.4	8.7	7.1

Notes. <50,10,0.183,0.631> problems. Means of 100 problem-means. "badtree" is mean mistake-tree size. "|dom|" and "fwd-deg" are for variables chosen in search.

For fail-first assessments, search was for one solution; this gives somewhat less reliable results than with all-solutions search, but it is much less time-consuming. (Promise calculations necessarily involve an all-solutions search.) To cope with the fact that variable selection under interleaved sampling or random probing is not well-defined or easily replicated, the following strategy was used. After a run, the solution was saved in the order obtained. Quality assessment was based on this ordering, which was therefore fixed throughout search. Although search is less efficient here than it would be if the ordering were dynamic, it allows better assessment of information gained by the end of sampling both for interleaved and sample-first methods. For comparison, the same method was used with orderings produced by the min dom/fwddeg heuristic.

Results of this analysis show that the major difference is in the fail-firstness of these orderings, reflected in the magnitudes of mistake-tree sizes (Table 6). Measures of promise are highly similar. With colouring problems, in contrast, the mean mistake-tree size was appreciably greater for random probing-dom/wdeg than for dom/wdeg, 10,100 versus 318. Clearly, some features of these problems interfered with adequate sampling.

6 Conclusions

We developed a rationale for the weighted degree approach in terms of two principles of performance, one of which is the well-known Fail-First Principle. We were also able to show why another, the Contention Principle, is necessary in any complete explanation of the weighted degree approach. To demonstrate the actual operation of the Fail-First Principle, we showed that fail-firstness is indeed enhanced by strategies based on sampling and that differences in overall efficiency of search are related to this property. We have also been able to make some predictions on the basis of the Contention Principle regarding novel sources of contention that were verified experimentally.

In these procedures, sampling produces estimates of the probability of failure. This information is used in turn to predict differences in fail-firstness in order to inform variable selection. We have given a detailed account of the nature of this sampling and the use of this information in search.

In the course of this analysis, we were able to identify two potential shortcomings of the original weighted degree method: a feedback relation between sampling and variable selection that can hamper the discrimination of degrees of contention, and the inability to use estimates of failure for selections early in search. Random probing was designed to address these difficulties. However, the present work shows that there are marked differences in effectiveness of different sampling strategies with different problems and with different search strategies. The basis for these differences remains to be clarified. Now that we have a more adequate analytical framework, we should be able to pursue these and other issues in a more informed manner.

References

1. Boussemart, F., Hemery, F., Lecoutre, C., Sais, L.: Boosting systematic search by weighting constraints. In: Proc. Sixteenth European Conference on Artificial Intelligence-ECAI'04, pp. 146–150 (2004)
2. Grimes, D., Wallace, R.J.: Learning from failure in constraint satisfaction search. In: Ruml, W., Hutter, F. (eds.) Learning for Search: Papers from the 2006 AAAI Workshop, pp. 24–31. Tech. Rep. WS-06-11 (2006)
3. Grimes, D., Wallace, R.J.: Learning to identify global bottlenecks in constraint satisfaction search. In: 20th International FLAIRS Conference (2007)
4. Eisenberg, C., Faltings, B.: Using the breakout algorithm to identify hard and unsolvable subproblems. In: Rossi, F. (ed.) CP 2003. LNCS, vol. 2833, pp. 822–826. Springer, Heidelberg (2003)
5. Beck, J.C., Prosser, P., Wallace, R.J.: Trying again to fail-first. In: Faltings, B.V., Petcu, A., Fages, F., Rossi, F. (eds.) CSCLP 2004. LNCS (LNAI), vol. 3419, pp. 41–55. Springer, Heidelberg (2005)

A Case for Simple SAT Solvers*

Jinbo Huang

Logic and Computation Program
National ICT Australia
Canberra, ACT 0200 Australia
jinbo.huang@nicta.com.au

Abstract. As SAT becomes more popular due to its ability to handle large real-world problems, progress in efficiency appears to have slowed down over the past few years. On the other hand, we now have access to many sophisticated implementations of SAT solvers, sometimes boasting large amounts of code. Although low-level optimizations can help, we argue that the SAT algorithm itself offers opportunities for more significant improvements. Specifically, we start with a no-frills solver implemented in less than 550 lines of code, and show that by focusing on the central aspects of the solver, higher performance can be achieved over some best existing solvers on a large set of benchmarks. This provides motivation for further research into these more important aspects of SAT algorithms, which we hope will lead to future significant advances in SAT.

1 Introduction

Modern clause learning technology coupled with data structures for fast unit propagation has greatly enhanced the efficiency and scalability of SAT, making it practical to tackle real-world instances with millions of clauses. However, over the past few years progress appears to have slowed down considerably. For example, MiniSat 2.0, winner of SAT Race 2006 [13], solved no more instances in the race than SatELiteGTI from 2005, and Cadence MiniSat v1.14 actually solved three fewer instances than MiniSat v1.13 from 2005. Even more unfortunately, our benchmarking shows that MiniSat 2.0 solves 59 fewer instances than BerkMin, a solver written in 2002 based on the same clause learning framework [4], on a set of 251 instances distributed by Miroslav Velev[1] given a one-hour time limit.

In this paper we would like to investigate what contributes to such substantial differences in performance between solvers. To begin with, clearly, difference in the efficiency of implementation alone would not explain these differences in performance we are witnessing, as that would imply, for example, that BerkMin would outperform MiniSat 2.0 in general, which is not true. Given a set of 311 instances from IBM [14] also used in our benchmarking, MiniSat 2.0 solves 103 more instances than BerkMin.

* National ICT Australia is funded by the Australian Government's *Backing Australia's Ability* initiative, in part through the Australian Research Council.

[1] http://www.miroslav-velev.com/sat_benchmarks.html.

C. Bessiere (Ed.): CP 2007, LNCS 4741, pp. 839–846, 2007.

In fact, we venture to argue that the sophistication of implementation, although responsible for some of the solver efficiency, may not be as critical as the choices made in the central aspects of the solver. In support of this argument, we start with a simple clause learning SAT solver written in less than 550 lines of C++ (excluding comments and blank lines), called TINISAT [5], and show that by improving its decision heuristic, a consistently high performance across different benchmark families, including IBM and Velev, can be achieved.

While our experiments with TINISAT speak to the importance of the decision heuristic, there are other important aspects of clause learning, such as the backtracking scheme, restart policy, and clause deletion policy. To offer a more complete picture, and to illustrate how a simple and effective implementation is possible, we devote the following section to a story that attempts to unify the various aspects of clause learning around a central theme so that their importance can be better understood. We then describe the experiments done regarding the decision heuristic, and finally the experiments that demonstrate the performance of TINISAT on a large number of industrial benchmarks.

2 A Unifying View of Clause Learning

Clause learning originated in SAT as a means of pruning DPLL search trees. The early SAT solver GRASP [9], for example, used clause learning to achieve a form of *nonchronological backtracking* where branches known to contain no solutions were skipped over during backtracking. Although the learning method introduced by GRASP has been adopted by later SAT solvers, a subtle yet critical change has occurred in how backtracking is done after learning a clause, starting with Chaff [10]. In fact, the backtracking scheme used by Chaff, and most of its successors, is so different from GRASP's that the overall SAT algorithm is no longer a binary DPLL search.

Repeated Probing. To better understand this change, we have previously proposed an alternative formulation of clause learning as a simple 3-step cycle [5], which we now refer to as *repeated probing* and give as Algorithm 1.

This formulation makes it explicit that clause learning is no traditional binary search enhanced with pruning, but something very different and, in fact, simpler: It is a sequence of resolutions (line 2) and all components of the solvers serve a common purpose of guiding the resolution process. Using this formulation as the basis, we now embark on a unifying account of clause learning SAT algorithms. We start with a review of the learning process itself [9], now understood as a resolution process of which the learned clause is the final resolvent [2].

Algorithm 1. Repeated Probing

```
1: set variables till hitting a conflict; return SAT if all variables are set without conflict
2: derive a new clause by resolution; return UNSAT if empty clause is derived
3: unset some variables and go back to step 1.
```

Clause Learning as Resolution. The process of learning commences upon the generation of an empty clause under a particular assignment of truth values to a subset of the variables, and ends with the derivation of a new clause that is entailed by the set of existing clauses. Recall that there are two types of assignments: decision assignments and implications produced by unit propagation. As is customary, we label each (decision or implication) assignment with the decision level in which it is made. In this paper we assume that the decision level is initially 1, and is incremented before each decision is made—hence the very first decision is made in level 2. This will allow us to label the literals that are implied by the CNF formula with level 1, and use level 0 to signify a fatal conflict. Note that the last case arises when a conflict occurs in decision level 1, at which point the CNF formula is immediately declared unsatisfiable without the need to go through the usual learning process.

To give a precise description of the learning process, we enlist the notion of the *antecedent clause* [9] for an implication, which is defined to be the clause that became unit and produced the implication. For example, after the assignments $[A, \overline{B}]$, the clause $c_1 : \overline{A} \vee B \vee \overline{C}$ becomes unit, and $\overline{C}$ is implied; clause c_1 is then the antecedent clause for the implication $\overline{C}$. Note that given any clause *cl*, if a literal of *cl* has become false due to an implication, then clause *cl* can always be resolved against the antecedent clause for that implication.

The learning process maintains a clause *cl* that is initialized to be the clause in which a conflict has just occurred (that is, whose literals have all been assigned false). Clause *cl* is then repeatedly updated to be the resolvent of itself and the antecedent clause for some implication that has made one of its literals false. Learning methods generally agree on the order of the resolution steps, but differ on the condition for terminating the loop. One of the most polular methods is 1-UIP [15], which terminates the resolution loop when clause *cl* contains exactly one literal whose value is assigned in the current decision level.

A Common Purpose. Once one commits to a particular learning method, it becomes clear that the sequence of clauses learned is completely determined by the sequence of assignments made. Now, note that the latter is determined in turn by nothing other than the combination of the decision heuristic, backtracking scheme, restart policy, and (recursively) the learned clauses that have been added to the CNF formula (assuming a fixed implementation of unit propagation). For unsatisfiable instances, the sequence of learned clauses ends in the empty clause and determines the time and space efficiency of the algorithm. For satisfiable instances, the sequence of assignments made determines the exact point at which a solution is discovered.

Hence in all cases, the various components of the SAT solver can be understood as serving a single, common purpose—that of determining the sequence of assignments made and the sequence of clauses learned. Accordingly, the effectiveness of these components can be understood solely in terms of their contributions to the early termination of these sequences.

Backtracking Schemes. To understand the role of backtracking, let us now go back to the *repeated probing* process given in Algorithm 1. Observe that each probing is a flat sequence of (decision and implication) assignments leading to a conflict (line 1), and each pair of consecutive probings share a prefix by means of partially (or completely as a special case) erasing the assignments of the previous probing in reverse chronological order (line 3)—this erasing of assignment is exactly what is known as *backtracking.*

Backtracking in systematic depth-first search has traditionally been understood as a means of (recursively) exploring each branch of a search node until a solution is found in one. This is no longer the case in modern clause learning. In the formulation of Algorithm 1, backtracking amounts to a heuristic for deciding what prefix of the current sequence of assignments should carry over to the next. The only property required of the heuristic is, naturally, that there should not be an empty clause after backtracking.

The weakest condition that guarantees this requirement is to erase all assignments in levels $\geq \beta$, where β is the highest decision level among literals in the clause just learned. This is in fact the backtracking scheme used in GRASP.

Any decision level $< \beta$, therefore, is a perfectly legal level to backtrack to. Hence Algorithm 1 subsumes the framework of *unrestricted backtracking* described in [8]. Although unrestricted backtracking can potentially result in better performance, one has yet to come up with heuristics that compute good backtracking points. Most current clause learning SAT solvers backtrack to (i.e., erase assignments in levels down to but excluding) the *assertion level*, which is the *second highest* decision level among literals in the learned clause, resulting in a generally more aggressive jump[2] than GRASP's backtracking.

Restarts. A restart is a backtrack to decision level 1, where all assignments are erased except those implied by the CNF formula. In the context of Algorithm 1, the utility of a restart can be best understood as giving the solver an opportunity to make better decisions than it did in the last probing now that new information is available in the form of the newly learned clauses [5].

Practical restart policies, however, do not guarantee that new decisions made after a restart will be better than those made in the previous probing. One must therefore also take into account the overhead of too frequent restarts (e.g., a restart after each conflict), which arises from the erasing and redoing of assignments that may not have been necessary.

Completeness. Using 1-UIP learning and under the assumption that all clauses are kept, repeated probing as given in Algorithm 1 is complete in that it will always terminate with an answer given sufficient resources.[3] The key reason is that each clause learned by 1-UIP is guaranteed to be distinct from all existing clauses. In fact a stronger statement holds: Each of these learned clauses is guaranteed to be subsumed by no existing clause [16]. Since there is only a finite

[2] To our knowledge whether this type of backtracking can benefit solvers for the more general constraint satisfaction problems is an interesting open question.

[3] Zhang and Malik [17] proved the completeness of a restricted version of Algorithm 1 where the solver always backtracks to the assertion level, in which case learned clauses need not be kept to ensure completeness.

number of distinct clauses over a given number of variables, and each iteration of Algorithm 1 produces a distinct clause, the loop must eventually terminate, on both satisfiable and unsatisfiable instances.

Clause Deletion. When employed, clause deletion adds another dimension to what determines the sequences of assignments and conflicts, as it affects both the unit propagation and the learning process. As a direct result, different clauses will be learned and different decisions made. This means that clause deletion can be a double-edged knife: The reduced memory requirement and unit propagation cost must be balanced against the potentially larger number of probings required. In practice, solvers that employ clause deletion use heuristics to estimate the usefulness of clauses and decide which clauses should be deleted at what time.

The completeness of the algorithm can also be impacted by clause deletion. Some solvers intentionally ignore this issue as it does not seem to matter in most practical cases [4]. Other solvers provide for increasingly long periods between deletions, or delete clauses in such a way that the total number of clauses monotonically increases, thus ensuring completeness [10].

Concluding Remarks. In this section we have presented a comprehensive and unifying view of modern clause learning SAT algorithms based on formulating them as the process of repeated probing instead of DPLL search. This view exposes the true semantics of these SAT algorithms as pure resolution procedures, rather than DPLL searches enhanced with pruning. With this understanding, the various components of a clause learning SAT solver, including the decision heuristic, backtracking scheme, restart policy, and implementation of unit propagation, are all unified behind a single, common purpose—that of guiding the resolution process, which provides new insights into the roles played by and the effectiveness of the respective components.

3 A Simple SAT Solver

TINISAT is directly implemented in the framework of repeated probing (Algorithm 1). Pseudocode for its top-level procedure can be found in [5]. The final version (with the new decision heuristic described below) has about 550 lines of code, which breaks down as follows: CNF parsing (92 lines), clause pool maintenance (83 lines), unit propagation (53 lines), clause learning (55 lines), decision heuristic (67 lines), main loop (17 lines), miscellaneous (183 lines).

Restart Policy. Given the set of experiments reported in [5] where different restart policies are compared, we decided to use Luby's policy [7] (where a "unit run" is 512 conflicts; see [5] for details), and devote our first set of experiments to the discovery of a more robust decision heuristic.

Decision Heuristic. Our quest for a good decision heuristic was motivated by the comparative performance of MiniSat and Berkmin described in the beginning of the paper: MiniSat drastically outperforms BerkMin on the IBM benchmarks, but equally drastically underperforms it on the Velev benchmarks.

Upon studying the documentations of the two solvers, we found that one major difference between them was the decision heuristic: BerkMin favors variables from recent conflict clauses, while MiniSat selects variables based on their scores only. To verify if this was indeed a major reason for the drastic difference of solver performance between benchmark groups, we did the following experiment: We implemented a BerkMin-type heuristic in TINISAT, ran the solver on the same IBM and Velev benchmarks, and compared its performance with that of MiniSat. We used two versions of MiniSat for this purpose, MiniSat 2.0 and MiniSat 1.14, as the former employs preprocessing while the latter and TINISAT don't. This helps ensure that what we observe is not just due to whether preprocessing is used.

In the results, we saw a shift of advantage similar to the case of BerkMin vs. MiniSat: TINISAT with the BerkMin-type heuristic solved significantly fewer IBM instances, but significantly more Velev instances, than both versions of MiniSat. We then changed the decision heuristic of TINISAT to the MiniSat type, so that it simply selected a variable of the highest score, and started to repeat our experiment. It quickly became evident that TINISAT was now doing very poorly on the Velev benchmarks.

The conclusion we drew from these experiments was that a new decision heuristic was needed if the solver was to achieve a more robust performance across different types of problems. After an extensive set of further experiments, we found that the BerkMin type heuristic can be more robust if coupled with a type of phase selection heuristic suggested in [12,11].

The overall heuristic now used in TINISAT is as follows. For each literal a score is kept that is initially the number of its occurrences in the original clauses. On learning a clause, the score of every literal is incremented by 1 for each of its occurrences in clauses involved in resolution. The scores of all literals are halved once every 128 conflicts. When a decision is called for, we pick a free variable with the highest score (sum of two literal scores) from the most recently learned clause that has not been satisfied; if no such clause exists (at most 256 clauses are searched for this purpose) we pick any free variable with the highest score.

The variable is then set to a value as follows: Each variable has a field called *phase*, initially set to the value with the higher score. On backtracking, every variable whose assignment is erased has its *phase* set to that assignment, except for variables set in the latest decision level. When chosen for decision, a variable is set to its *phase*. However, this heuristic is bypassed if the two values differ in score by more than 32, in which case the value with the higher score is used. The intuition behind this phase selection heuristic is that the assignments made prior to the last decision level did not lead to any conflict and may have satisfied some subsets of the CNF, and hence repeating those same assignments may tend to avoid solving some subproblems multiple times [12,11].

4 Final Experiments

We present here an extensive set of experiments conducted to evaluate the performance of TINISAT against BerkMin, MiniSat 1.14, and MiniSat 2.0. An

Table 1. Performance of TINISAT

Velev benchmarks (251)					
Time	TINISAT	TINISATELite	BM	MS 1.14	MS 2.0
10min	124	131	99	95	92
15min	136	146	115	98	93
20min	153	152	121	98	93
30min	164	163	139	106	97
60min	183	182	161	116	102
IBM benchmarks (311)					
Time	TINISAT	TINISATELite	BM	MS 1.14	MS 2.0
10min	238	248	172	238	269
15min	244	257	179	253	278
20min	253	267	183	257	290
30min	262	276	192	268	296
60min	279	289	201	280	304
SAT Race Q1 mixed benchmarks (50)					
Time	TINISAT	TINISATELite	BM	MS 1.14	MS 2.0
10min	40	45	37	38	40
15min	44	47	41	39	43
20min	46	48	42	41	43
30min	48	49	43	42	44
60min	49	49	47	42	44
SAT Race Q2 mixed benchmarks (50)					
Time	TINISAT	TINISATELite	BM	MS 1.14	MS 2.0
10min	31	36	28	32	32
15min	33	38	31	34	34
20min	35	39	31	38	35
30min	40	45	34	40	36
60min	43	45	37	41	39
SAT Race final mixed benchmarks (100)					
Time	TINISAT	TINISATELite	BM	MS 1.14	MS 2.0
10min	49	59	38	53	59
15min	58	70	43	58	68
20min	61	74	46	66	71
30min	70	81	49	72	71
60min	77	87	63	76	74

additional solver called TINISATELite, created by coupling TINISAT with the SATELITE preprocessor [3], was also used. All experiments were run on a cluster of 16 AMD X2 Dual Core Processors running at 2GHz with 4GB of RAM under Linux, except those with BerkMin and MiniSat 1.14 on Velev, which were run on AMD Athlon 64 processors at 2GHz with 2GB of RAM (prior to a hardware upgrade). A one-hour time limit applied to all runs of all solvers.

Five benchmark groups have been used: 251 instances from Miroslav Velev, 311 instances from IBM Formal Verification [14], and the three groups of 50, 50, and 100 instances used in the first qualification round, second qualification round, and final round, respectively, of SAT Race 2006 [13]. The results are summarized in Table 1 (detailed results available at http://rsise.anu.edu.au/~jinbo/tinisat). For each benchmark group and each solver, we report the number of instances solved in 10, 15, 20, 30, and 60 minutes.

A high performance of TINISAT can be observed. For the 60-minute cut-off, for example, both TINISAT and TINISATELite outperform all other solvers in four of the groups. Most interestingly, the high degree of sensitivity to problem type exhibited by BerkMin and MiniSat on the Velev and IBM benchmarks appears to have been remedied in TINISAT, and a significant improvement in overall performance has been achieved: Out of the 762 instances, TINISAT and TINISATELite solves 68 and 89 more instances, respectively, than MiniSat 2.0.

5 Conclusion and Future Work

We have shown that by focusing on the central aspects of clause learning, a simple solver can significantly outperform the best existing solvers with more sophisticated implementations. Our successful quest for better decision heuristics also provides evidence that there is still considerable room for improvement even within the confines of the current clause learning framework. Some concrete opportunities for further improvement we see include more effective clause deletion policies, more flexible backtracking, dynamic restart policies, and hybridization of decision heuristics based on variable activity (as in typical clause learning solvers) and unit propagation lookahead (as in Satz [6] and its variants, which defeat clause learning solvers on many random and handmade problems).

References

1. Beame, P., Kautz, H., Sabharwal, A.: Understanding the power of clause learning. In: IJCAI, pp. 1194–1201 (2003)
2. Beame, P., Kautz, H.A., Sabharwal, A.: Towards understanding and harnessing the potential of clause learning. JAIR 22, 319–351 (2004)
3. Eén, N., Biere, A.: Effective preprocessing in SAT through variable and clause elimination. In: Bacchus, F., Walsh, T. (eds.) SAT 2005. LNCS, vol. 3569, pp. 61–75. Springer, Heidelberg (2005)
4. Goldberg, E., Novikov, Y.: BerkMin: A fast and robust SAT-solver. In: DATE, pp. 142–149 (2002)
5. Huang, J.: The effect of restarts on the efficiency of clause learning. In: IJCAI, pp. 2318–2323 (2007)
6. Li, C.M., Anbulagan: Heuristics based on unit propagation for satisfiability problems. In: IJCAI, pp. 366–371 (1997)
7. Luby, M., Sinclair, A., Zuckerman, D.: Optimal speedup of Las Vegas algorithms. Information Processing Letters 47(4), 173–180 (1993)
8. Lynce, I., Silva, J.P.M.: Complete unrestricted backtracking algorithms for satisfiability. In: SAT (2002)
9. Marques-Silva, J., Sakallah, K.: GRASP—A new search algorithm for satisfiability. In: ICCAD, pp. 220–227 (1996)
10. Moskewicz, M., Madigan, C., Zhao, Y., Zhang, L., Malik, S.: Chaff: Engineering an efficient SAT solver. In: DAC, pp. 530–535 (2001)
11. Pipatsrisawat, K., Darwiche, A.: A lightweight component caching scheme for satisfiability solvers. In: SAT, pp. 294–299 (2007)
12. Pipatsrisawat, T., Darwiche, A.: SAT solver description: Rsat. In: SAT-Race (2006)
13. Sinz, C.: SAT Race (2006), `http://fmv.jku.at/sat-race-2006`
14. Zarpas, E.: Benchmarking SAT solvers for bounded model checking. In: Bacchus, F., Walsh, T. (eds.) SAT 2005. LNCS, vol. 3569, pp. 340–354. Springer, Heidelberg (2005)
15. Zhang, L., Madigan, C., Moskewicz, M., Malik, S.: Efficient conflict driven learning in a Boolean satisfiability solver. In: ICCAD, pp. 279–285 (2001)
16. Zhang, L.: On subsumption removal and on-the-fly CNF simplification. In: Bacchus, F., Walsh, T. (eds.) SAT 2005. LNCS, vol. 3569, pp. 482–489. Springer, Heidelberg (2005)
17. Zhang, L., Malik, S.: Validating SAT solvers using an independent resolution-based checker: Practical implementations and other applications. In: DATE, pp. 10880–10885 (2003)

CP-Based Local Branching*

Zeynep Kiziltan[1], Andrea Lodi[2], Michela Milano[2], and Fabio Parisini[2]

[1] Computer Science Dep., University of Bologna, Italy
zeynep@cs.unibo.it
[2] D.E.I.S., University of Bologna, Italy
{alodi,mmilano}@deis.unibo.it

Abstract. Local branching is a general purpose heuristic search method successfully used in Mixed Integer Programming (MIP). We propose its integration and extension in Constraint Programming (CP).

1 Local Branching Search Strategy

Formal Background. A Constraint Satisfaction Problem (CSP) consists of a set of variables $X = [X_1, ..., X_n]$, each with a finite domain $\mathcal{D}(X_i)$ of values, and a set of constraints specifying allowed combinations of values for subsets of variables. A solution $\bar{X} = [\bar{X}_1, ..., \bar{X}_n]$ is an assignment of X satisfying the constraints. CP typically solves a CSP by exploring the space of partial assignments using a backtrack tree search, enforcing a local consistency property using either specialised or general purpose propagation algorithms. In constraint optimisation problems, even if a value in a domain can participate in a feasible solution, it can be pruned if it cannot be a part of a better solution (called cost-based filtering [4])). CP makes use of branch-and-bound search for finding the optimal solution. We can exploit the additive bounding procedure [3] for computing tight bounds for optimisation problems. This technique works using reduced-costs which are computed as a result of the solution of a linear program. A reduced-cost is associated to a variable and represents the additional cost to pay to the optimal solution when it becomes part of the optimal solution.

Local Branching in MIP. The basic idea of Local Branching [2] is that, given a reference solution to an optimisation problem, its neighbourhood can be defined through a linear constraint stating a maximum Hamming distance wrt such a solution. Thus, such a neighbourhood can be searched using tree search with the hope of improving the solution quality. After the optimal solution in the neighbourhood is found, the incumbent solution is updated to this new solution and the search continues from this better solution. Assume we have a tree search method for solving an optimisation problem P whose constrained variables are X. For a given integer parameter k, the neighbourhood $\mathcal{N}(\bar{X}, k)$ is the set of feasible solutions of P satisfying the additional local branching constraint $\Delta(X, \bar{X}) \leq k$ which ensures that the sought assignment of X has at

* Andrea Lodi and Michela Milano are partially supported by the University of Padova "Integrating Integer and Constraint Programming" (grant 2005 - CPDA051592).

C. Bessiere (Ed.): CP 2007, LNCS 4741, pp. 847–855, 2007.

most k values different than the reference solution $\bar{X}$. Given $\bar{X}$, the solution space associated with the current branching node is partitioned by means of the disjunction $\Delta(X, \bar{X}) \leq k \;\vee\; \Delta(X, \bar{X}) \geq k + 1$. Exploring each exhaustively guarantees completeness. The neighbourhood structure is general-purpose, that is, it is independent of the problem. The scheme can be made heuristic by imposing limits on the subtree exploration. In [2] several ideas are borrowed from the metaheuristic literature to enhance the heuristic behaviour. The method is particularly effective because the local branching constraints, stated as linear equations in the MIP model, contribute to the computation of the problem bound. We refer the reader to [2] for the full description of the algorithm.

CP-based Local Branching. The local branching framework is not specific to MIP. It can be integrated in any tree search. We therefore suggest the use of general-purpose neighbourhood structures within a tree search with constraint propagation. Like in MIP, neighbourhoods can be constructed via additional constraints in the original model and such constraints can be used both to tighten the problem bound and for filtering purposes. Since this is a new constraint problem, CP can directly be used to find the initial feasible solution and search the neighbourhood, exploiting the power of constraint propagation. Thus, complex constraints can be solved and infeasible solutions in the neighbourhoods can be detected effectively by constraint propagation, which are difficult tasks for a pure local search algorithm. Moreover, solution quality improves quickly by local search around the best found solution, which we miss in the classical CP framework. Furthermore, the use of tree search for performing local search guarantees completeness unlike classical local search algorithms. Consequently, we expect the following advantages over a pure CP-based or local search: (1) we obtain better solutions within a time limit; (2) we improve solution quality quicker; (3) we are able to prove optimality; (4) we prove optimality quicker. And finally, the technique is general and applicable to any optimisation problem modelled with constraints in contrast to many local search techniques designed only for specific problems. We stress that we do not propose a mere implementation of local branching in CP. We significantly change and extend the original framework so as to accommodate it in the CP machinery smoothly and successfully. Our contributions are:

Bound of the neighbourhood. Using a linear programming solver for computing the bound of each neighbourhood is not computationally affordable in CP. We have therefore studied a lighter way to compute the bound of the neighbourhood which is efficient, effective and incremental.

Cost-based filtering. Cost-based filtering can be applied when reduced-costs are available. Its use in CP is more aggressive than in MIP where it is mainly applied during preprocessing (variable fixing). We show how we can extract valid reduced-costs from the additive bounding procedure.

Restarting. In [2], diversification techniques are applied when for instance the subtree rooted at the left node is proved to contain no improving solutions, instead of simply reversing the last local branching constraint and exploring the rest of the tree using the same search method as of the subtrees. We propose a new diversification scheme which finds a new feasible solution by keeping all the reversed branching constraints and *restarts* local branching from the new incumbent solution using the regular local branching framework. This diversification and its variations are applied together with intensification mechanisms described next. Due to lack of space, we refer the reader to [6] for details.

Discrepancy. The parameter k is essential to the success of the method as it defines the size of the neighbourhood. We propose two uses of k: (1) the traditional one, with k being fixed for each neighbourhood; (2) the variable one, with k ranging between k_1 and k_2. In this way, the neighbourhood defined by k_1 is searched first. While no improving solution is found, the neighbourhood is enlarged up until k_2-discrepancy subtree is completely explored. In addition, the neighbourhoods are visited in slices. Instead of posting the constraint $\Delta(X, \bar{X}) \leq k$, we impose k constraints of the form $\Delta(X, \bar{X}) = j$ with $j = 1 \ldots k$. We show why this is important for the computation of the bound.

Heuristics. As search proceeds in local branching, we gather a set of incumbent solutions $\bar{X}_1, ..., \bar{X}_m$ which are feasible and which get closer to the optimal solution. We can exploit these incumbent solutions as a guide to search the subtrees. Being independent of the problem, such heuristics would provide us with a general method suitable for this search strategy. We have developed a number of useful heuristics, however we will not discus them here for reasons of space.

2 Additive Bounding for Local Branching

To integrate local branching in CP, we need a local branching constraint $\Delta(X, \bar{X}) \leq k$, where $\bar{X}$ is an assignment of X representing the current reference solution and k is an integer value. The constraint holds iff the sought assignment of X has at most k different values than $\bar{X}$. This constraint enforces that the Hamming distance between X and $\bar{X}$ is at most k. The CP model we consider is:

$$\min \sum_{i \in N} C_{iX_i} \tag{1}$$

$$\text{subject to } \mathit{AnySide\_cst}(X) \tag{2}$$

$$\Delta(X, \bar{X}) \leq k \tag{3}$$

$$X_i \in \mathcal{D}(X_i) \quad \forall i \in N \tag{4}$$

where C_{iX_i} is the cost of assigning variable X_i, $\mathit{AnySide\_cst}(X)$ is any set of constraints on domain variables X. The purpose of this section is to exploit the delta constraint (3), that implicitly represents the structure of the explored tree, to tighten the problem bound and to perform cost based filtering [4]. To this purpose, we have developed a local branching constraint $\mathit{lb\_cst}(X, \bar{X}, k, C)$ which combines together the Δ constraint and the cost function $C = \min \sum_{i \in N} C_{iX_i}$. Using this constraint alone provides very poor problem bounds, and thus poor filtering. If instead we recognize in the problem a combinatorial relaxation *Rel* which can be solved in polynomial time and provide a bound LB_{Rel} and a set of reduced-costs $\bar{c}$, we can feed the local branching constraint with $\bar{c}$ and obtain an improved bound in an additive bounding fashion. Additive bounding is an effective procedure for computing bounds for optimisation problems [3]. It consists in solving a sequence of relaxations of P, each producing an improved bound. Assume, we have a set of bounding procedures $B_1, ..., B_m$. We write $B_i(c)$ for the ith bounding procedure when applied to an instance of P with cost matrix c. Each B_i returns a lower bound LB_i and a reduced-cost matrix $\bar{c}$. This cost matrix is used by the next bounding procedure $B_{i+1}(\bar{c})$. The sum of the bounds $\sum_{i\in\{1,...,m\}} LB_i$ is a valid lower bound for P. An example of the relaxation *Rel* is the Assignment Problem if the side constraints contain an *alldifferent*. Another example is a Network Flow Problem if the side constraints contain a global cardinality constraint. Clearly, a tighter bound can always be found feeding an LP solver with the linear relaxation of the whole problem, including the local branching constraints, as done in [2]. We have experimentally noticed that this relaxation is too expensive in computational time to be used in a CP setting.

To explain how additive bounding can improve the bound obtained by the local branching constraints, we use the usual mapping between CP and 0-1 Integer Programming (IP) models. Note that this model is useful to understand the structure of the problems we are considering, but it is not solved by an IP solver. We devise a special purpose linear time algorithm as we explain next. We define a directed graph $G = (N, A)$ where arc $(i, j) \in A$ iff $j \in \mathcal{D}(X_i)$ where $\mathcal{D}(X_i) \subseteq N$ and $N = \{1, \ldots, n\}$. The corresponding IP model contains x_{ij} variables and $\bar{x}$ as the IP equivalent variables and $\bar{X}$. The additive bounding procedure uses two relaxations which correspond to *Rel* and *Loc_Branch* that considers the *lb_cst*$(X, \bar{X}, k, C)$. The solution of *Rel* produces the optimal solution X^*, with value LB_{Rel} and a reduced-cost matrix $\bar{c}$. We can feed the second relaxation *Loc_Branch* with the reduced-cost matrix $\bar{c}$ from *Rel* and we obtain:

$$LB_{Loc\_Branch} = \min \sum_{i\in N} \sum_{j\in N} \bar{c}_{ij}\, x_{ij} \tag{5}$$

$$\text{s.t.} \sum_{(i,j)\in S} (1 - x_{ij}) \leq k \quad S = \{(i, j) | \bar{x}_{ij} = 1\} \tag{6}$$

$$x_{ij} \in \{0, 1\}, \qquad \forall (i, j) \in A \tag{7}$$

To have a tighter bound, we divide this problem into k problems corresponding to each discrepancy from 1 to k and transforming the constraint (6) into $\sum_{(i,j)\in S}(1 - x_{ij}) = d$ with $d = 1$ *to* k. The optimal solution of each of these subproblems can be computed as follows. We start from $\bar{X} = [\bar{X}_1, ..., \bar{X}_n]$ and then extract and sort in non-decreasing order the corresponding reduced-costs $\bar{c}_{sorted} = sort(\bar{c}_{1\bar{X}_1}, ..., \bar{c}_{n\bar{X}_n})$. The new bound LB_{Loc_Branch} is the sum of the first $n - d$ smallest reduced-costs from $\bar{c}_{sorted}$. Overall, a valid bound for the problem is $LB = LB_{Loc\_Branch} + LB_{Rel}$. The use of the additive bounding here is different from its use in [7], since we are starting from a reference solution $\bar{X}$ which is not the optimal solution X^* computed by the first relaxation.

2.1 Cost-Based Filtering

After computing the lower bound in an additive fashion, we need an associated reduced-cost matrix so as to apply cost-based filtering [4]. To do this, we have to compute the reduced-cost matrix of the following problem:

$$LB_{Loc\_Branch} = \min \sum_{(i,j)\in S} \bar{c}_{ij}\, x_{ij} \tag{8}$$

$$\sum_{(i,j)\in S} x_{ij} = n - d \tag{9}$$

$$x_{ij} \in [0,1], \qquad \forall (i,j) \in S \tag{10}$$

This problem is the d-th subproblem (5)-(7) obtained by: (i) removing variables $x_{ij}, \forall (i,j) \notin S$, (ii) writing constraint (6) in equality form with $k = d$ and (iii) relaxing the integrality requirement on the remaining variables. It is easy to see that the two problems are indeed equivalent. First, the integrality conditions are redundant as shown by the counting algorithm used in the previous section to solve the problem. Second, since the variables $x_{ij}, (i,j) \notin S$ do not contribute to satisfy constraint (9) they can be dropped to 0 because their reduced-costs are non-negative. The dual of such a linear program is as follows:

$$LB_{Loc\_Branch} = \max (n-d)\pi_0 + \sum_{(i,j)\in S} \pi_{ij} \tag{11}$$

$$\pi_0 + \pi_{ij} \leq \bar{c}_{ij}, \qquad \forall (i,j) \in S \tag{12}$$

$$\pi_{ij} \leq 0, \qquad \forall (i,j) \in S \tag{13}$$

Let us partition set S into $S_{\min}$ containing the $n-d$ pairs (i,j) having the smallest reduced-costs and $S_{\max}$ containing the remaining d pairs. We also define $\bar{c}_{\max} = \max_{(i,j)\in S_{\min}} \bar{c}_{ij}$. Then, it is not difficult to prove the following result.

Theorem 1. *The dual solution (i) $\pi_0 = \bar{c}_{\max}$, (ii) $\pi_{ij} = 0, \forall (i,j) \in S_{\max}$ and (iii) $\pi_{ij} = \bar{c}_{ij} - \pi_0, \forall (i,j) \in S_{\min}$ is optimal for system (11)-(13).*

We can now construct the reduced-cost matrix $\hat{c}$ associated with the optimal solution of system (8)-(10) as $\hat{c}_{ij} = 0, \forall (i,j) \in S_{\min}$ and $\hat{c}_{ij} = \bar{c}_{ij} - \bar{c}_{\max}, \forall (i,j) \in S_{\max}$. Finally, the reduced-costs of the variables $x_{ij}, (i,j) \notin S$ do not change.

2.2 Incremental Computation of the Bound

While exploring the subtrees, decisions are taken on variable instantiation and as a consequence constraints are propagated and some domains are pruned. We can therefore update the problem lower bound by taking into account the most recent situation of the domains. The challenge is to do this in an incremental way, not incurring much extra overhead. The first bound LB_{Rel} can be recomputed, possibly incrementally. Using the new solution, we can update the second bound LB_{Loc_Branch} in a simple way by using some special data structures. Consider the sets $S_{\min}$ and $S_{\max}$ defined previously. More precisely, we consider a list $S_{\max}$ initially containing d ordered pairs (i, j) corresponding to the variable-value assignment of the d greatest reduced-costs from $\bar{c}_{sorted}$ and $S_{\min}$ containing the $n-d$ ordered pairs (i, j) corresponding to the $n-d$ smallest reduced-costs from $\bar{c}_{sorted}$. Whilst $S_{\min}$ contains the assignments (variable index - value) that should remain the same w.r.t. $\bar{X}$ since they have the smallest reduced-costs, $S_{\max}$ contains the assignments that should change w.r.t. $\bar{X}$ and that conceptually assume a value corresponding to a 0 reduced-cost. Note that initially there are n pairs whose first index goes from 1 to n in $S_{\min} \cup S_{\max}$.

Assignment of j to X_i We distinguish four cases:

- $(i, j) \in S_{\max}$: A variable that was supposed to change w.r.t. $\bar{X}$ is instead assigned the value in $\bar{X}$. We should update $S_{\min}$ and $S_{\max}$ by maintaining them ordered, as well as LB_{Loc_Branch}: 1) remove (i, j) from $S_{\max}$; 2) remove $(h, k) = max_{(m,n) \in S_{\min}} \bar{c}_{mn}$ from $S_{\min}$ and add it ordered in $S_{\max}$; 3) $LB_{Loc\_Branch} = LB_{Loc\_Branch} + \bar{c}_{ij} - \bar{c}_{hk}$.
- $(i, k) \in S_{\max}$ with $k \neq j$: A variable that was supposed to change w.r.t. $\bar{X}$, indeed changes. In the bound, this variable was assuming a value corresponding to a 0 reduced-cost, while now it assumes the value j whose reduced-cost $\bar{c}_{ij}$ may or may not be 0. We should update LB_{Loc_Branch}: $LB_{Loc\_Branch} = LB_{Loc\_Branch} + \bar{c}_{ij}$.
- $(i, j) \in S_{\min}$: No changes are necessary because a variable that was supposed to remain the same w.r.t. $\bar{X}$ remains the same.
- $(i, k) \in S_{\min}$ with $k \neq j$:A variable that was supposed to remain the same w.r.t. $\bar{X}$ instead changes. We should update $S_{\min}$ and $S_{\max}$ as well as LB_{Loc_Branch}: 1) remove $(h, k) = min_{(m,n) \in S_{\max}} \bar{c}_{mn}$ from $S_{\max}$ and insert it in the last position of $S_{\min}$; 2) remove (i, k) from $S_{\min}$; 3) $LB_{Loc\_Branch} = LB_{Loc\_Branch} - \bar{c}_{ij} + \bar{c}_{hk}$.

Removal of j from $\mathcal{D}(X_i)$. The only important case is when $(i, j) \in S_{\min}$, where a variable that was supposed to remain the same w.r.t. $\bar{X}$ and that contributed to the computation of the bound changes. We assume X_i changes to a value corresponding to the smallest reduced-cost (possibly 0) whose index is k, and then update $S_{\min}$ and $S_{\max}$ as well as LB_{Loc_Branch}: 1) remove $(h, k) = min_{(m,n) \in S_{\max}} \bar{c}_{mn}$ from $S_{\max}$ and insert it in the last position of $S_{\min}$; 2) remove (i, j) from $S_{\min}$; 3) $LB_{Loc\_Branch} = LB_{Loc\_Branch} + \bar{c}_{hk} - \bar{c}_{ij}$. That is, the number of variables which must change is decreased from from d to $d-1$.

3 Experimental Results

We have conducted experiments to support the expected benefits of local branching in CP as stated in Section 1. Experiments are done using ILOG Solver 6.0 and ILOG Scheduler 6.0 on a 2Ghz pentium IV processor running Windows XP with 512 MB RAM. Due to lack of space, we here report a summary of the experimental set up and the results. Details can be found in [6]. ATSPTW is a time constrained variant of the Asymmetric Travelling Salesman Problem in which each city has an associated visiting time and must be visited within a specific time window. It is a difficult problem with applications in routing and scheduling. The difficulty stems from its co-existing optimisation and scheduling parts. Solving an ATSPTW thus requires strong optimisation and feasibility reasoning. Since the motivation of our work is to combine the power of constraint propagation for solving feasibility problems with a local search method successful in tackling optimisation problems, ATSPTW is our choice of problem domain to test the benefits of local branching in CP. In the experiments, we adopt the model in [5]. We test different variations of local branching in CP with a pure CP-based search (called *CP*) which exploits backtracking in depth-first search with constraint propagation along with suitable problem-specific search heuristics. The *alldifferent* constraints and the cost function C in the model allow us to exploit the cost-based filtering of [4] in *CP*. Moreover, they allow us to use the Assignment Problem as *Rel* and apply the cost-based filtering described in Section 2 in local branching. As we want local branching to improve solution quality and to prove optimality fast, we consider setting k to 3 or 5 (called LB_3 and LB_5 resp.) and apply a variation of restarting if the subtree rooted at the left node does not have any improving solution. We also adopt a hybrid method (called LB_H) which starts as LB_3 but may end up as LB_5 (if no improving solution is found), exploiting different discrepancy values. In all local branching methods, the initial feasible solution is found using *CP* and each subtree is searched in increasing value of discrepancy with a general heuristic specifically developed for local branching. The experiments are performed on 242 heterogeneous instances taken from `http://elib.zib.de`. The results appear in tables in which the participating number of instances are indicated in paranthesis.

Table 1. Instances where the methods provide different solution cost

(a) 5 minutes cut off.

Method (86)	# times providing best solution	Average % gap from the best solution CP	LB_3	LB_5
The best				
CP	15	0	5.51	7.24
LB_3	13	12.77	0	22.99
LB_5	28	25.65	4.72	0
Best				
CP	3	0	0	0.73
LB_3	30	15.97	0	0.07
LB_5	27	17.75	0	0

(b) 30 minutes cut off.

Method (54)	# times providing best solution	Average % gap from the best solution CP	LB_3	LB_5	LB_H
The best					
CP	8	0	5.42	6.07	5.46
LB_3	2	11.67	0	0.52	0.52
LB_5	8	20.69	3.82	0	2.70
LB_H	7	26.28	3.77	30.01	0
Best					
CP	0	N/A	N/A	N/A	N/A
LB_3	20	9.98	0	4.41	0
LB_5	23	11.81	0.65	0	0
LB_H	29	11.21	0.51	3.04	0

In Table 1(a), we report statistics on the instances for which the methods provide solutions with different cost by the cut off time. We show in the second column how many times a method provides the best solution and in the third the average gap of the provided solution w.r.t. the best one obtained from the other methods. The first group of rows are about the instances for which only 1 method gives the best solution, whilst in the second multiple methods provide the best solution. Note that we here are not interested in any run-time. All methods are allowed to run until the cut off time and thus we are interested in the best solution possible. The aim is to support our thesis that we can obtain better solutions within a time limit. We observe that LB_5 and LB_3 are the winners in the groups, respectively. Moreover, for the instances where CP is the preferred method (the CP rows in both groups), the average gap of the solutions provided by LB_3 and LB_5 are much smaller than the gap of the CP solutions when LB_3 or LB_5 is preferred. In Table 2(a), we report statistics on the instances for which the methods provide equally good solutions by the cut off time. We give statistics by dividing the instances into three disjoint groups. In the first, none of the methods can prove optimality by the cut off time, so we compare the average time to find the best solution. In the second, all methods prove optimality, so we check the average total run-time required to prove optimality. The third group contains the instances which are a mix w.r.t. completeness of the search. Since we cannot compare run-times in this case, we look at the number of times each method proves optimality. Such statistics help us support our theses that we can improve solution quality quicker and we can prove optimality (quicker). We observe that LB_3 is the winner in all groups, with LB_5 being preferrable over CP in two. Local branching thus provides clear benefits over CP when solving ATSPTW. The results in the tables support our theses. It is however difficult to decide between LB_3 and LB_5. In Tables 1(b) and 2(b), similar results are reported when we impose a 30 minute cutoff time instead. In addition, we compare with the previous methods also the hybrid method LB_H. Even if more time is given to all methods, the benefits of local branching, in particular of LB_H, are apparent. The results indicate that LB_H is the most robust method, combining the advantages of LB_3 and LB_5.

Table 2. Instances where the methods provide the same solution cost

(a) 5 minutes cut off.

Method	Average comparison
All are cut off (7)	Best solution time
CP	179.02
LB_3	98.63
LB_5	103.16
None is cut off (132)	Total run-time
CP	38.04
LB_3	35.43
LB_5	60.50
Min. one & max. two are cut off (13)	# times proving optimality
CP	5
LB_3	11
LB_5	7

(b) 30 minutes cut off.

Methods	Average comparison
All are cut off (2)	Best solution time
CP	1184. 25
LB_3	611. 68
LB_5	490.02
LB_H	450. 88
None is cut off (175)	Total run-time
CP	185.52
LB_3	113.39
LB_5	142.69
LB_H	114. 05
Min. one & max. three are cut off (6)	# times proving optimality
CP	1
LB_3	5
LB_5	5
LB_H	4

References

1. Harvey, W., Ginsberg, M.L.: Limited discrepancy search. In: IJCAI-95, pp. 607–615. Morgan Kaufmann, San Francisco (1995)
2. Fischetti, M., Lodi, A.: Local branching. Math. Prog. 98, 23–47 (2003)

3. Fischetti, M., Toth, P.: An additive bounding procedure for combinatorial optimization problems. Oper. Res. 37, 319–328 (1989)
4. Focacci, F., Lodi, A., Milano, M.: Optimization-oriented global constraints. Constraints 7, 351–365 (2002)
5. Focacci, F., Lodi, A., Milano, M.: A hybrid exact algorithm for the TSPTW. INFORMS J. on Comp. 14(4), 403–417 (2002)
6. Kiziltan, Z., Lodi, A., Milano, M., Parisini, F.: CP-based Local Branching. Technical Report OR/07/8, University of Bologna (2007)
7. Lodi, A., Milano, M., Rousseau, L.M.: Discrepancy based additive bounding for the alldifferent constraint. In: Rossi, F. (ed.) CP 2003. LNCS, vol. 2833, pp. 510–524. Springer, Heidelberg (2003)

Strong Controllability of Disjunctive Temporal Problems with Uncertainty

Bart Peintner[1], Kristen Brent Venable[2], and Neil Yorke-Smith[1]

[1] Artificial Intelligence Center, SRI International
{peintner,nysmith}@ai.sri.com
[2] University of Padova, Italy
kvenable@math.unipd.it

Abstract. The Disjunctive Temporal Problem with Uncertainty (DTPU) is an extension of the Disjunctive Temporal Problem (DTP) that accounts for events not under the control of the executing agent. We investigate the semantics of DTPU constraints, refining the existing notion that they are simply disjunctions of STPU constraints. We then develop the first sound and complete algorithm to determine whether Strong Controllability holds for a DTPU. We analyze the complexity of our algorithm with respect to the number of constraints in different classes, showing that, for several common subclasses of DTPUs, determining Strong Controllability has the same complexity as solving DTPs.

1 Introduction

The Simple Temporal Problem (STP) [1] is a temporal constraint formalism widely used for modeling and solving real-world planning and scheduling problems. Several extensions of this framework have been proposed in the literature. The Disjunctive Temporal Problem (DTP) [2] allows for non-convex and non-binary constraints by introducing disjunctions of STP constraints. The *Simple Temporal Problem with Uncertainty* (STPU) [3] extends the STP by allowing two classes of events, *controllable* and *uncontrollable*. Uncontrollable events are controlled by exogenous factors, often referred to as 'Nature'. The concept of *consistency* of an STP is replaced by varying notions of *controllability* of an STPU. The level of controllability for a problem describes the conditions under which an executor can guarantee all constraints will be satisfied, w.r.t. Nature's behavior. In problems that exhibit Strong Controllability (SC), there exists a time assignment to all events that ensures all constraints will be satisfied whatever Nature's realisation of the uncontrollable events.

The recently introduced *Disjunctive Temporal Problem with Uncertainty* (DTPU) [4] allows for both disjunctive constraints and contingent events. Such a coexistence is intrinsic to many real-world planning and scheduling problems (e.g., [5]). In this paper we focus on Strong Controllability of DTPUs, which provides an appropriate notion of solution for application domains such as production planning, and in situations where the entire schedule of actions must be known in advance. We present a sound and complete algorithm to determine whether Strong Controllability of a DTPU holds. We then analyze the complexity of the algorithm with respect to the quantity of different constraint types and we show that for several common subclasses of DTPUs, determining SC has the same complexity as solving a classical DTP without uncertainty.

C. Bessiere (Ed.): CP 2007, LNCS 4741, pp. 856–863, 2007.

2 Background

Temporal Problems. A *Simple Temporal Problem* [1] is defined by a set of time-point variables X, which represent instantaneous events, and a set of quantitative constraints $\mathcal{C}$, which restrict the temporal distance between events. STP constraints are binary and convex, taking the form $X_j - X_i \in [a_{ij}, b_{ij}]$. A distinguished event, denoted *TR*, marks the start of time. Unary domain constraints thus can be modeled as binary relations to *TR*. Solving an STP equates to deciding consistency and deriving its minimal network. An STP is consistent iff it has a *solution*: an assignment to all variables such that all constraints are satisfied. Consistency can be tested with an All-Pairs Shortest Path algorithm, requiring $\mathcal{O}(n^3)$ time for n variables [1]. The *minimal network* is the tightest representation of the constraints that includes all solutions to the problem.

The *Disjunctive Temporal Problem* [2] generalizes the STP by admitting non-binary temporal relations. DTP constraints consist of disjunctions of STP constraints: $X_{j1} - X_{i1} \in [a_{i1j1}, b_{i1j1}] \vee X_{j2} - X_{i2} \in [a_{i2j2}, b_{i2j2}] \vee \cdots \vee X_{j\ell} - X_{i\ell} \in [a_{i\ell j\ell}, b_{i\ell j\ell}]$. Note that a variable may appear in more than one disjunct. While the worst-case complexity of solving a DTP is **NP**-hard [2], in practice efficient solving techniques have been developed (e.g., [6]), and tractability results are known for some classes of DTPs (e.g., [7]). A simple way to solve a DTP is to consider the *component STPs* obtained by selecting one disjunct from each constraint. A DTP is consistent iff it contains a consistent component STP. A search through the meta space of component STPs is the heart of most constraint-based DTP solvers (e.g., [6]); these solvers have been shown to be very efficient. The time complexity of the search depends on the number of component STPs. In the worst case, for m constraints with a maximum of k disjuncts each, there are $\mathcal{O}(k^m)$ component STPs, and the complexity is $\mathcal{O}(n^2 m k^m)$ [6].

Temporal Problem with Uncertainty. The STP and DTP formalisms assume that all events are under the complete control of the execution agent. Recognizing that this assumption is often not valid, the *Simple Temporal Problem with Uncertainty* (STPU) [3] distinguishes two classes of variables, *controllable* V_c and *uncontrollable* V_u. The values of controllable variables are chosen by the execution agent and correspond to events in standard STPs. The values of uncontrollable variables, by contrast, are determined by exogenous factors ('Nature'); such a *realisation* is observed but cannot be controlled by the execution agent. The only information known prior to observation of an uncontrollable variable λ is that Nature will ensure that its value respects a single *contingent constraint* $\lambda - \mathbf{X} \in [\mathbf{a}, \mathbf{b}]$, with $a \geq 0$. Contingent constraints are assumed independent, and Nature is assumed to be consistent. Besides contingent constraints, which we distinguish by using a bold typeface, all other constraints in an STPU are *executable*.

The semantics of STPU constraints can be summarized as follows:

1. ***Contingent STPU constraints*** (S) model a priori information the agent is given about when an event controlled by Nature can occur (e.g., "An experiment will end (uncontrollable) between 5 and 10 minutes after it begins (controllable)").
2. ***Executable STPU constraints*** (S_e) model requirements the agent has between variables it controls and those controlled by Nature (e.g., "Data cannot be sent (controllable) until 3 minutes after the experiment ends (uncontrollable)").

3. ***(Executable) STP constraints*** (S_c) model temporal constraints between events under the control of the agent (e.g., "The experiment cannot start until after 2 p.m.").

Controllability of an STPU is the analogue of consistency of an STP. Three forms have been defined [3]: strong, weak and dynamic. In this paper we extend the notion of *Strong Controllability* (SC), a guarantee that a single assignment to all controllable variables in the STPU will satisfy all constraints, regardless of the realisation. The time complexity of determining strong controllability of an STPU is in class **P** [3].

3 Extending the DTP with Contingent Events

In the sequel, we will indicate with *constraint* a disjunctive temporal constraint and with *disjunct* a single simple temporal constraint. Representationally, the extension of an STPU to a DTPU is straightforward: we relax the restriction that each constraint be binary and convex, and allow disjunctive constraints [4]. Like the STPU, we divide the variables into two classes, controllable and uncontrollable, and retain the restriction that each process of uncertain duration is represented by a single contingent constraint between the process's start and end time-points.

Definition 1 (DTPU). *A* Disjunctive Temporal Problem with Uncertainty *is a tuple* $\langle V_c, V_u, C, C_u \rangle$*, where* V_c*,* V_u *are the sets of executable and uncontrollable variables, respectively,* C *is a finite set of disjunctive temporal constraints over* $V_c \cup V_u$*, and* $C_u \subseteq C$ *is the set of binary contingent constraints, one for each element of* V_u*.*

Notice that w.r.t. the original definition in [4], the set of contingent constraints now appears explicitly. A solution to a DTPU, $s = s_c \cup s_u$ is a complete assignment to all variables $V = V_c \cup V_u$ that satisfies all constraints in C. The controllable part of the assignment, s_c, is the *decision*, and the uncontrollable part, s_u, is the *realisation*.

Example 1. Consider the example of a Mars rover (Figure 1) tasked with drilling into a rock (D denotes the start of the drilling action, D' its end), taking an image (I, I'), and sending data collected during each action back to Earth (S, S'). The drilling task consists of a preparation phase followed by two minutes of drilling. The preparation phase has variable duration, depending in part on whether the type of rock requires a different drill bit than is currently installed. The image task must occur at time 15, which is when the object to photograph will be visible. Drilling causes significant vibration, so the image cannot be taken during the last two minutes or during the minute after drilling ends. Only in the small window $[25, 30]$ can the rover begin data transmission.

The problem can be formalized as a DTPU as follows. The constraints describe the durations and temporal ordering between the activities. In this example, $V_c = \{TR, D, S, I, I'\}$, $V_u = \{D', S'\}$, and C contains nine constraints, two of which are disjunctive. The filled arrows represent contingent constraints: C_u contains two constraints, $\mathbf{S' - S \in [4, 5]}$ and $\mathbf{D' - D \in [5, 10] \vee [15, 20]}$.

We define a *component STPU* P' of a DTPU P to be an STPU obtained by selecting one disjunct from each constraint. Note that P' may include only a subset of the uncontrollable variables of P. The DTPU in Figure 1 has four component STPUs, one for each combination of disjuncts in the two disjunctive constraints.

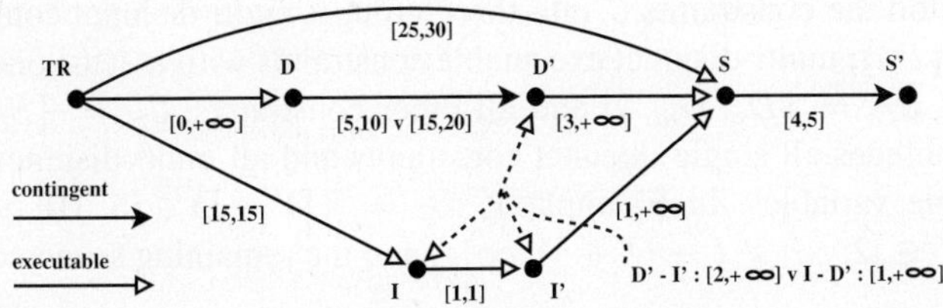

Fig. 1. Dashed arrows depict disjunctive constraints that involve more than two variables

In addition to constraints of type S, S_c and S_e, a DTPU features the types:

1. ***DTP*** (D)**:** A disjunction of two or more STP constraints (e.g., "The image action must be ended 2 minutes before drilling begins (controllable) or the image action must be started after drilling begins (controllable)").
2. ***Executable DTPU*** (D_e)**:** A disjunction of two or more executable STPU disjuncts (e.g., "The image action must end 2 minutes before drilling ends (uncontrollable) or the image action must start at least 1 minute after drilling ends (uncontrollable)").
3. ***Mixed executable DTPU*** (D_{me})**:** A disjunction of STP and executable STPU constraints (e.g., "The image action must end before drilling starts (controllable) or the image action must start at least 1 minute after drilling ends (uncontrollable)").
4. ***Contingent DTPU*** (D_c)**:** A disjunction of two or more contingent STPU constraints. *Nature chooses which disjunct will be satisfied.* (e.g., "Drilling can take 5–10 minutes or 15–20, depending on whether the correct bit is installed").

It is important to recognize that by choosing a duration for uncertain processes (i.e., choosing a time for an uncontrollable variable), Nature is in effect 'choosing' a disjunct from the contingent constraint modeling that process.

An eighth constraint type would be *mixed DTPU constraints* that contain both contingent and executable disjuncts. Such constraints are outside our definition of a DTPU, which specifies exactly one contingent constraint to model each uncontrollable variable. Contingent constraints model the behavior of Nature: what the modeler declares *will* happen, not what should happen. Thus, by definition, one of contingent disjuncts of a mixed DTPU constraint will always be satisfied, making the executable disjuncts superfluous. If there were a realisation not satisfying one of the contingent disjuncts, then the model of Nature would be incomplete.

4 Strong Controllability of a DTPU

We now address the problem of testing the Strong Controllability of a DTPU. Motivating examples for SC include production planning, where schedules must be known in advance because of possible dependencies among activities performed by other agents, and safety-critical domains where advanced approval is mandated of the schedule. Additionally, when the executing agent lacks resources to reason about dynamic controllability, as may be the case for a Mars rover, it can operate with SC.

Let us partition the constraints $\mathcal{C}$ into three groups: multi-disjunct contingent constraints, $\mathcal{C}_C = \{D_c\}$; multi-disjunct executable constraints with at least one executable STPU disjunct, $\mathcal{C}_E = \{D_e, D_{me}\}$; and all other constraints, $\mathcal{C}_S = \{S, S_e, S_c, D\}$. Note that $\mathcal{C}_S$ includes all single disjunct constraints and all multi-disjunct constraints over controllable variables. In Example 1, $\mathcal{C}_C = \{\mathbf{D' - D} \in [\mathbf{5, 10}] \vee [\mathbf{15, 20}]\}$, $\mathcal{C}_E = \{D' - I' \in [2, \infty) \vee I - D' \in [1, \infty)\}$, and the remaining seven constraints in $\mathcal{C}_S$.

In general, it is not true that a DTPU is SC if it contains an SC component STPU, since Nature can in effect choose a disjunct, and thus a decision strongly controlling only one disjunct of a contingent DTPU constraint is not sufficient. However, this relationship does hold if $\mathcal{C}_C = \emptyset$, which we say is a *Simple-Natured* DTPU. The converse is false unless $\mathcal{C}_E = \emptyset$, since an SC solution may satisfy different disjuncts in different realisations. When $\mathcal{C}_E = \emptyset$, we say that the DTPU is *Simple-Nature-Dependent*, since all executable constraints that depend on uncontrollables are simple (single-disjunct).

We combine the idea of using the SC test for STPUs [8] with the now-standard meta-CSP search of a DTP solver [6]. In our algorithm DTPU-SC, the DTPU constraints are treated as CSP variables whose values correspond to the disjuncts of the DTPU constraint. Hence, for each DTPU constraint $C_i \in \mathcal{C}$ with disjuncts $D(C_i)$, a meta-CSP variable C_i is created with a domain consisting of the disjuncts $c_{ij} \in D(C_i)$.

Pseudocode of DTPU-SC is given in Algorithm 1. The three methods correspond to the three classes of constraints, $\mathcal{C}_S$, $\mathcal{C}_C$, and $\mathcal{C}_E$, defined above. Initially, DTPU-SC is called with partial component STPs A and A_C empty, i.e., DTPU-SC$(\emptyset, \emptyset, \mathcal{C}_S, \mathcal{C}_C, \mathcal{C}_E)$. DTPU-SC either returns the empty set, indicating that DTPU P is not SC, or it returns a set of decisions S such that any $s_c \in S$ strongly controls P.

Since finding a single SC component STPU is not sufficient for determining SC of DTPUs, DTPU-SC must efficiently keep track of which component STPUs each assignment controls during search. To help explain the operation of the algorithm, we will first look at three special cases. Then we will address the general case.

Case 1: STPU First, consider the trivial case in which all constraints are single-disjunct. Since only $\mathcal{C}_S$ contains constraints, and all these constraints are simple, the DTPU P is an STPU; thus SC can be determined with the existing STPU algorithm [8].

Case 2: Totally Simple Second, consider the case in which multi-disjunct constraints are present, but the sets $\mathcal{C}_C$ and $\mathcal{C}_E$ are empty. In this common case, all constraints involving uncontrollable variables have only a single disjunct. The DTPU is Simple-Natured, and moreover is also Simple-Nature-Dependent; altogether, we describe the DTPU as *Totally Simple*. An example of a Totally Simple DTPU is $V_d = \{TR, X\}$, $V_u = \{Z\}$, $\mathcal{C} = \{X - TR \in [1, 2] \vee [5, 8], \mathbf{Z - TR} \in [\mathbf{8, 10}], Z - X \in [1, 5]\}$.

By the above, we can check SC by checking each component STPU for SC. If a decision controls any component STPU, it controls the DTPU as well. It is straightforward to adapt existing meta-CSP DTP solvers to implement this algorithm. The first method in Algorithm 1 does exactly this; the call to the second method, ALL-PATHS-SC, in line 4 simply returns the minimal network of A in the case of a Totally Simple DTPU. Before the incremental consistency check for a disjunct over an uncontrollable variable (line 10), we convert the disjunct into a set of STP constraints using a call to

Algorithm 1. Determine SC, return controlling minimal network

```
DTPU-SC(A, A_C, C_S, C_C, C_E)
1: S ← ∅
2: if C_S = ∅ then                                  {A is a disjunct combination of C_S}
3:    G ← minimal-network(A)
4:    S ← ALL-PATHS-SC(A, A_C, C_C, C_E, G)
5: else
6:    C_i ← select-variable(C_S), C'_S ← C_S − {C_i}
7:    for each disjunct c_ij of D(C_i) do
8:       A'_C ← A_C ∪ c_ij                          {A'_C is an STP that ignores uncontrollable variables}
9:       A' ← A' ∪ sc-transform(A'_C, c_ij)         {Transform c_ij into disjuncts over controllable variables}
10:      if consistent(A') then
11:         S ← DTPU-SC(A', A'_C, C'_S, C_C, C_E)
12:         if S ≠ ∅ then return S
13: return S                                        {Set of SC decisions or nil}
ALL-PATHS-SC(A, A_C, C_C, C_E, G)
1: if C_C = ∅ then G ← G ∩ SATISFY-C_E(A, A_C, C_E)
2: else
3:    C_i ← select-variable(C_C), C'_C ← C_C − {C_i}
4:    for each disjunct c_ij of D(C_i) do
5:       A'_C ← A_C ∪ c_ij
6:       A' ← A ∪ sc-transform(A'_C, c_ij)
7:       if consistent(A') then
8:          G ← ALL-PATHS-SC(A', A'_C, C'_C, C_E, G)
9:          if G = ∅ then return ∅                  {Fail if ANY disjunct fails}
10:      else return ∅
11: return G
SATISFY-C_E (A, A_C, C_E)
1: H ← ∅                                            {H will hold all assignments that satisfy any combination of C_E}
2: if C_E = ∅ then H ← minimal-network(A)           {A represents a complete component STPU}
3: else
4:    C_i ← select-variable(C_E), C'_E ← C_E − {C_i}
5:    for each disjunct c_ij of D(C_i) do
6:       A' ← A ∪ sc-transform(A_C, c_ij)           {Returns at most 1 constr.}
7:       if consistent(A') then H ← H ∪ SATISFY-C_E(A', A_C, C'_E)
8: return H
```

sc-transform, which is a transformation adapted from STPUs [8]. sc-transform converts a single disjunct (i.e., STPU constraint) over uncontrollable variables into an equivalent set of disjuncts over controllable variables. If the input disjunct is contingent, this set can be as large as the number of constraints over uncontrollable variables; if it is executable, only a single disjunct will be produced.

The complexity of DTPU-SC for the case of a Totally Simple DTPU is the same as solving a DTP: $\mathcal{O}(n^2 S k^S)$, where $S = |\mathcal{C}_S|$. The only additions to the DTP algorithm are lines 8 and 9, both of which amortize to $\mathcal{O}(1)$ time.

Case 3: Simple-Nature-Dependent When $\mathcal{C}_C$ is non-empty, i.e., if the DTPU contains multi-disjunct contingent constraints, Nature chooses the disjunct that must be satisfied for each contingent constraint, and an SC decision must control *any* combination of disjuncts from C_C. Contrary to intuition, we cannot simply break the disjunctive constraints apart. Consider the constraint $\mathbf{D}' - \mathbf{D} \in [\mathbf{5}, \mathbf{10}] \vee [\mathbf{15}, \mathbf{20}]$: if we break the constraint into two STPU constraints, they will simply be inconsistent with one another.

The second method, ALL-PATHS-SC, extends the partial component STP A (generated by the first method, i.e., by search through the C_S constraints) using every feasible disjunct combination of the constraints in C_C. For each combination, it intersects the set of decisions that control it with the set of decisions that control the previously checked combinations. Thus, ALL-PATHS-SC returns the set G of all decisions that control each combination. The call to the third method, SATISFY-C_E, in line 1 simply returns the minimal network of A if C_E is empty.

For the Simple-Nature-Dependent DTPU, where C_E is empty and C_C non-empty, the time complexity is $\mathcal{O}(n^2 Sk^S + n^2(S)k^C k^S)$, where $C = |C_C|$. The S element describes the maximum number of consistency checks in ALL-PATHS-SC in line 7.

Case 4: General DTPU In the general case, both C_C and C_E are non-empty. The constraints in C_E contain uncontrollable variables, but (since they are executable constraints) only one disjunct must be satisfied for any realisation, and the agent may choose which disjunct. With C_E constraints, however, it is possible that a single SC decision satisfies different disjuncts for different realisations. Hence, for each decision under consideration, we must determine for each feasible disjunct combination in C_C whether there is a feasible disjunct combination in C_E as well. While this is not difficult for a single decision, DTPU-SC is searching in the meta-CSP space, and therefore is effectively reasoning about sets of decisions at once (recall that a minimal network represents a set of decisions). Hence, method ALL-PATHS-SC must maintain a potentially *non-convex* list of decisions G: the union of decisions that satisfy at least one disjunct combination of C_E for each disjunct combination of C_C considered so far.

The third method in Algorithm 1, SATISFY-C_E, searches through all disjunct combinations of C_E for those consistent with the SC decisions given as input (in the partial STP A). Upon finding consistent disjunct combinations, it adds the resulting minimal network to a union H. H therefore represents a non-convex set of decisions that control the assignment to C_C. Upon return, in line 1 of ALL-PATHS-SC, H is intersected with G, assuring that G contains only assignments that control all combinations of C_C considered so far. We note that efficient data structures and simplification methods for G and H are key to reducing the complexity in practice of the repeated intersections.

In the general case, DTPU-SC considers $k^S k^C k^E$ disjunct combinations, where $E = |C_E|$. Therefore, SATISFY-C_E requires $\mathcal{O}(n^2 E k^E k^C k^S)$. Analyzing the intersection performed in line 1 of ALL-PATHS-SC yields $\mathcal{O}(n^2 k^S S k^{S^{k^C}})$. Since testing consistency of a DTP is **NP**-hard, it is no surprise that deciding SC with DTPU-SC is thus in the complexity class **EXPSPACE**.

Case 5: Simple-Nature Finally, we specialize the general case to the Simple-Natured DTPU, where C_E is non-empty but C_C is empty, i.e., all contingent constraints are simple. Using the above analysis, now $C = 0$, reducing the complexity to $\mathcal{O}(n^2 k^S (S + E k^S k^E))$. We suspect that Simple-Nature DTPUs occur frequently in practice because the need to model processes with uncertain, non-convex durations is relatively rare.

5 Related and Future Work

Uncertainty in planning and scheduling tasks has been addressed in the literature in different ways. For example in the *Conditional Temporal Problem* [9] it is the presence in the problem of the variables (all of which are controllable) that is unknown. A similar type of decision-point based uncertainty is captured in the *Temporal Plan Network* [10], where decision nodes are used to explicitly introduce choices in activity execution that the planner must make. Outside of the literature descended from the STP, there is a large body of work on fuzziness and uncertainty in temporal reasoning (e.g., [11]). Another interesting relation is that between DTPUs and Quantified CSPs [12]. Informally, Strong Controllability corresponds to a forall-then-exists quantification over uncontrollable and controllable variables, respectively.

For the future, we aim to analyze dynamic and weak controllability of DTPUs and derive algorithms for testing them. We would also like to explore the potential of mixed DTPU constraints with suitable semantics to capture decision-point based uncertainty.

Acknowledgments. This material is based in part upon work supported by the Defense Advanced Research Projects Agency (DARPA) under Contract No. NBCHD030010. Any opinions, findings and conclusions or recommendations expressed in this material are those of the authors and do not necessarily reflect the views of DARPA or the DOI-NBC.

References

1. Dechter, R., Meiri, I., Pearl, J.: Temporal constraint networks. Artificial Intelligence 49, 61–95 (1991)
2. Stergiou, K., Koubarakis, M.: Backtracking algorithms for disjunctions of temporal constraints. Artificial Intelligence 120, 81–117 (2000)
3. Vidal, T., Fargier, H.: Handling contingency in temporal constraint networks: From consistency to controllabilities. JETAI 11, 23–45 (1999)
4. Venable, K.B., Yorke-Smith, N.: Disjunctive temporal planning with uncertainty. In: Proc. of IJCAI'05, pp. 1721–1722 (2005)
5. Muscettola, N., Nayak, P.P., Pell, B., Williams, B.C.: Remote Agent: To boldly go where no AI system has gone before. Artificial Intelligence 103, 5–47 (1998)
6. Tsamardinos, I., Pollack, M.E.: Efficient solution techniques for disjunctive temporal reasoning problems. Artificial Intelligence 151, 43–89 (2003)
7. Satish Kumar, T.K.: On the tractability of restricted disjunctive temporal problems. In: Proc. of ICAPS'05., pp. 110–119 (2005)
8. Vidal, T., Ghallab, M.: Dealing with uncertain durations in temporal constraint networks dedicated to planning. In: Proc. of ECAI-96, pp. 48–52 (1996)
9. Tsamardinos, I., Vidal, T., Pollack, M.E.: CTP: A new constraint-based formalism for conditional, temporal planning. Constraints 8, 365–388 (2003)
10. Kim, P., Williams, B.C., Abramson, M.: Executing reactive, model-based programs through graph-based temporal planning. In: Proc. of IJCAI'01, pp. 487–493 (2001)
11. Dubois, D., Fargier, H., Prade, H.: Fuzzy scheduling. European J. of Operational Research 147, 231–252 (2003)
12. Bordeaux, L., Monfroy, E.: Beyond NP: Arc-consistency for quantified constraints. In: Van Hentenryck, P. (ed.) CP 2002. LNCS, vol. 2470, pp. 371–386. Springer, Heidelberg (2002)

Exploiting Single-Cycle Symmetries in Branch-and-Prune algorithms

Vicente Ruiz de Angulo and Carme Torras

Institut de Robòtica i Informàtica Industrial (CSIC-UPC)
Llorens i Artigas 4-6, 08028-Barcelona, Spain
{ruiz,torras}@iri.upc.edu

Abstract. As a first attempt to exploit symmetries in continuous constraint problems, we focus on permutations of the variables consisting of one single cycle. We propose a procedure that takes advantage of these symmetries by interacting with a Branch-and-Prune algorithm without interfering with it. A key concept in this procedure are the classes of symmetric boxes formed by bisecting a n-dimensional cube at the same point in all dimensions at the same time. We quantify these classes as a function of n. Moreover, we propose a simple algorithm to generate the representatives of all these classes for any number of variables at very high rates. A problem example from the chemical field and a kinematics solver are used to show the performance of the approach in practice.

1 Symmetry in Continuous Constraints Problems

Symmetry exploitation in discrete constraint problems has received a great deal of attention lately [6,4,5,11]. On the contrary, symmetries have been largely disregarded in continuous constraint solving, despite the important growth in both theory and applications that this field has recently experienced [12,1,9].

Continuous (or numerical) constraint solving is often tackled using Branch-and-Prune algorithms [13], which iteratively locate solutions inside an initial domain box, by alternating box subdivision (branching) and box reduction (pruning) steps. Motivated by a molecular conformation problem, in this paper we deal with the most simple type of box symmetry, namely that in which domain variables (i.e., box dimensions) undergo a single-cycle permutation leaving the constraints invariant. This can be seen, thus, as a form of constraint symmetry in the terminology introduced in [3].

We are interested in solving the following general Continuous Constraint Satisfaction Problem (CCSP): Find all points $\mathbf{x} = (x_1, \ldots, x_n)$ lying in an initial box of $\mathbb{R}^n$ satisfying the constraints $f_1(\mathbf{x}) \in C_1, \ldots, f_m(\mathbf{x}) \in C_m$, where f_i is a function $f_i : \mathbb{R}^n \to \mathbb{R}$, and C_i is an interval in $\mathbb{R}$.

We assume the problem is tackled using a Branch-and-Prune (B&P) algorithm. The only particular feature that we require of this algorithm is that it has to work with boxes in $\mathbb{R}^n$.

We say that a function $s : \mathbb{R}^n \to \mathbb{R}^n$ is a point symmetry of the problem if there exists an associated permutation $\sigma \in \Sigma_m$ such that $f_i(\mathbf{x}) = f_{\sigma(i)}(s(\mathbf{x}))$

C. Bessiere (Ed.): CP 2007, LNCS 4741, pp. 864–871, 2007.

and $C_i = C_{\sigma(i)}$, $\forall i = 1, \ldots, m$. We consider symmetry as a property that relates points that are equivalent as regards to a CCSP. Concretely, from the above definition one can conclude that $\mathbf{x}$ is a solution to the problem iff $s(\mathbf{x})$ is a solution to the problem. Let s and t be two symmetries of a CCSP with associated permutations σ_s and σ_t. It is easy to see that the composition of symmetries $s(t(\cdot))$ is also a symmetry with associated permutation $\sigma_s(\sigma_t(\cdot))$.

An interesting type of symmetries are permutations of the components of $\mathbf{x}$. Let D be a finite set. A cycle of length k is a permutation ψ such that there exist distinct elements $a_1, \ldots a_k \in D$ such that $\psi(a_i) = \psi(a_{(i+1) mod\ k})$ and $\psi(z) = z$ for any other element $z \in D$. Such a cycle is represented as $(a_1, \ldots a_k)$. Every permutation can be expressed as a composition of disjoint cycles. In this paper we focus on a particular type of permutations, namely those constituted by a single cycle. In its simplest form, this is $s(x_1, x_2, \ldots x_n) = (x_{\theta(1)}, x_{\theta(2)}, \cdots x_{\theta(n)}) = (x_2, x_3 \ldots x_n, x_1)$, where $\theta(i) = (i+1)\ mod\ n$.

Example: $n = 3, m = 4, \mathbf{x} = (x_1, x_2, x_3) \in [-1,1] \times [-1,1] \times [-1,1]$,

$$\begin{aligned}
f_1(\mathbf{x}) &: & x_1^2 + x_2^2 + x_3^2 \in [5,5] &\equiv\ x_1^2 + x_2^2 + x_3^2 = 5 \\
f_2(\mathbf{x}) &: & 2x_1 - x_2 \in [0,\infty] &\equiv\ 2x_1 - x_2 \geqslant 0 \\
f_3(\mathbf{x}) &: & 2x_2 - x_3 \in [0,\infty] &\equiv\ 2x_2 - x_3 \geqslant 0 \\
f_4(\mathbf{x}) &: & 2x_3 - x_1 \in [0,\infty] &\equiv\ 2x_3 - x_1 \geqslant 0
\end{aligned}$$

There exists a symmetry $s(x_1, x_2, x_3) = (x_2, x_3, x_1)$. The constraint permutation associated to s is $\sigma(1) = 1$, $\sigma(2) = 3$, $\sigma(3) = 4$, and $\sigma(4) = 2$.

For $n \geqslant 3$ there is never a unique symmetry for a given problem. If there exists a symmetry s, then for example $s^2(\mathbf{x}) = s(s(\mathbf{x}))$ is another symmetry. In general, using the convention of denoting $s^0(\mathbf{x})$ the identity mapping, $\{s^i(\mathbf{x}), i = 0 \ldots n-1\}$ is the set of different symmetries that can be obtained by composing $s(\mathbf{x})$ with itself, while for $i \geqslant n$ we have that $s^i(\mathbf{x}) = s^{i\ mod\ n}(\mathbf{x})$. Thus, a single-cycle symmetry generates by composition $n-1$ symmetries, excluding the trivial identity mapping. Some of them may have different numbers of cycles. The algorithm presented in this paper deals with all the compositions of a single-cycle symmetry, even if some of them are not single-cycle symmetries. The gain obtained with the proposed algorithm will be shown to be generally proportional to the number of different compositions of the selected symmetry. Therefore, when several single-cycle symmetries exist in a CCSP problem, the algorithm should be used with that generating the most symmetries by composition, i.e., with that having the longest cycle.

2 Box Symmetry

Since B&P algorithms work with boxes, we turn our attention now to the set of points symmetric to those belonging to a box $\mathcal{B} \subseteq \mathbb{R}^n$.

Let s be a single-cycle symmetry corresponding to the circular variable shifting θ introduced in the preceding section, and $\mathcal{B} = [\underline{x}_1, \overline{x}_1] \times \ldots \times [\underline{x}_n, \overline{x}_n]$ a box in $\mathbb{R}^n$. The *box symmetry* function S is defined as $S(\mathcal{B}) = \{s(\mathbf{x})\ \ s.t.\ \ \mathbf{x} \in \mathcal{B}\} =$

$[\underline{x}_{\theta(1)}, \overline{x}_{\theta(1)}] \times \ldots \times [\underline{x}_{\theta(n)}, \overline{x}_{\theta(n)}] = [\underline{x}_2, \overline{x}_2] \times \ldots \times [\underline{x}_n, \overline{x}_n] \times [\underline{x}_1, \overline{x}_1]$. The box symmetry function has also an associated constraint permutation σ, which is the same associated to s. S^i will denote S composed i times. We say, then, that $S^i(\mathcal{B})$ and $S^j(\mathcal{B})$ are symmetric boxes, $0 \leqslant i, j < n$, $i \neq j$.

As in the case of point symmetry, box symmetry has implications for the CCSP. If there is no solution inside a box $\mathcal{B}$, there is no solution inside any of its symmetric boxes either. A box $\mathcal{B}_f \subseteq \mathcal{B}$ is a solution iff $S^i(\mathcal{B}_f) \subseteq S^i(\mathcal{B})$ is a solution box for any $i \in \{1 \ldots n-1\}$.

Box symmetry is an equivalence relation defining symmetry equivalence classes. Let $R(\mathcal{B})$ be the set of *different* boxes in the symmetry class of $\mathcal{B}$, $R(\mathcal{B}) = \{S^i(\mathcal{B}), i \in \{0, \ldots, n-1\}\}$. We define the *period* $P(\mathcal{B})$ of a box $\mathcal{B}$ as $P(\mathcal{B}) = |R(\mathcal{B})|$. Therefore $R(\mathcal{B}) = \{S^i(\mathcal{B}), i \in \{0, \ldots, P(\mathcal{B}) - 1\}\}$. For example, for box $\mathcal{B}' = [0,4] \times [2,5] \times [2,5] \times [0,4] \times [2,5] \times [2,5]$, $P(\mathcal{B}') = 3$.

In the following sections we will show that the implications of box symmetry for a CCSP can be exploited to save much computing time in a meta-algorithm that uses the B&P algorithm as a tool without interfering with it.

3 Algorithm to Exploit Box Symmetry Classes

The algorithm we will propose to exploit box symmetry makes much use of the symmetry classes formed by bisecting a n-dimensional cube I^n (i.e., of period 1) in all dimensions at the same time and at the same point, resulting in 2^n boxes. We will denote L and H the two subintervals into which the original range I is divided. For example, for $n = 2$, we have the following set of boxes $\{L \times L, L \times H, H \times L, H \times H\}$ whose periods are 1, 2, 2 and 1, respectively. And their symmetry classes are: $\{L \times L\}$, $\{L \times H, H \times L\}$, and $\{H \times H\}$. Representing the two intervals L and H as 0 and 1, respectively, and dropping the $\times$ symbol, the sub-boxes can be coded as binary numbers. Let $\mathbb{SR}_n$ be the set of representatives, formed by choosing the smallest box in binary order from each class. For example, $\mathbb{SR}_2 = \{00, 01, 11\}$. Note that the cube I^n to be partitioned can be thought of as the the set of binary numbers of length n, and that $\mathbb{SR}_n$ is nothing more than a subset whose elements are different under circular shift.

Section 4 will show how many components $\mathbb{SR}_n$ has, how they are distributed and, more importantly, how can they be generated. The symmetry exploitation algorithm we propose below uses the B&P algorithm as an external routine. Thus, the internals of the B&P algorithm do not need to be modified.

The idea is to first divide the initial box into a number of symmetry classes. Next, one needs to process only a representative of each class with the B&P algorithm. At the end, by applying box symmetries to the solution boxes obtained in this way, one would get all the solutions lying in the space covered by the whole classes, i.e., the initial box. The advantage of this procedure is that the B&P algorithm would have to process only a fraction of the initial box. Assuming that the initial box is a n-cube covering the same interval $[x_l, x_h]$ in all dimensions, we can directly apply the classes associated to $\mathbb{SR}_n$. A procedure to exploit single-cycle symmetries in this way is presented in Algorithm 1.

Algorithm 1. CSYM algorithm

Input: A n-cube, $[x_l, x_h] \times \cdots \times [x_l, x_h]$; S: a single-cycle box symmetry; $B\&P$: a B&P algorithm.
Output: A set of boxes covering all solutions.

1 $SolutionBoxSet \leftarrow EmptySet$
2 $x^* \leftarrow$ SELECTBISECTIONPOINT(x_l, x_h)
3 **foreach** $\mathbf{b} \in \mathbb{SR}_n$ **do**
4 $\quad \mathcal{B} \leftarrow$ GENERATESUBBOX$(\mathbf{b}, x_l, x_h, x^*)$
5 $\quad SolutionBoxSet \leftarrow SolutionBoxSet \cup$ PROCESSREPRESENTATIVE$(\mathcal{B})$
6 **return** $SolutionBoxSet$

Algorithm 2. The PROCESSREPRESENTATIVE function

Input: A box $\mathcal{B}$; S: a single-cycle box symmetry; $B\&P$: a B&P algorithm.
Output: The set of solution boxes contained in $\mathcal{B}$ and its symmetric boxes.

1 $SolSet \leftarrow B\&P(\mathcal{B})$
2 $SymSolSet \leftarrow SolSet$
3 **for** $i{=}1{:}\ P(\mathcal{B}) - 1$ **do**
4 $\quad SymSolSet \leftarrow SymSolSet \cup$ APPLYSYMMETRY$(SolSet, S^i)$
5 **return** $SymSolSet$

The operator GENERATESUBBOX$(\mathbf{b}, x_l, x_h, x^*)$ returns the box corresponding to binary code $\mathbf{b}$ when $[x_l, x_h]$ is the range of the initial box in all dimensions and x^* is the point in which this interval is bisected. The iterations over line 4 of Algorithm 1 generate a set of representative boxes such that, together with their symmetries, cover the initial n-cube.

PROCESSREPRESENTATIVE$(\mathcal{B})$ returns all the solution boxes associated to $\mathcal{B}$, that is, the solutions inside $\mathcal{B}$ and inside its symmetric boxes. Since the number of symmetries of $\mathcal{B}$ is $P(\mathcal{B})$, the benefits of exploiting the symmetries of a class representative is proportional to its period.

4 An Illustrative Example

Molecules can be modeled as mechanical chains by making some reasonable approximations, such as constant bond length and constant angle between consecutive bonds. Finding all valid conformations of a molecule can be formulated as a distance-geometry [2] problem in which some distances between points (atoms) are fixed and known, and one must find the set of values of unknown (variable) distances by solving a set of constraints consisting of equalities or inequalities of determinants formed with subsets of the fixed and variable distances [2].

The problem can be solved using a B&P algorithm [9,8]. Figure 1(a) displays the known and unknown distances of the cycloheptane, a molecule composed of a ring of seven carbon atoms. The distance between two consecutive atoms of the ring is constant and equal everywhere. The distance between two atoms

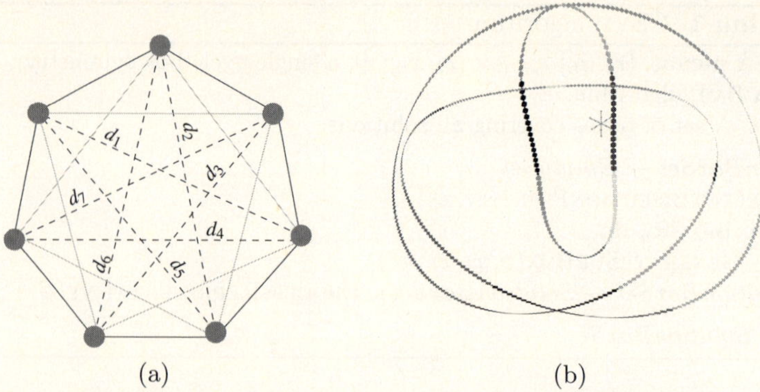

Fig. 1. (a) Cycloheptane. Disks represent carbon atoms. Constant and variable distances between atoms are represented with continuous and dashed lines, respectively. (b) Three-dimensional projection of the cycloheptane solutions. The lightest (yellow) boxes are the solutions found inside the representatives using the B&P algorithm (line 1 in Algorithm 2). The other colored boxes are the solutions obtained by applying symmetries to the yellow boxes (line 4 in Algorithm 2).

connected to a same atom is also known and constant no matter the atoms. The problem has several symmetries. One is $s(d_1, \ldots, d_7) = (d_{\theta(1)}, d_{\theta(2)}, \ldots, d_{\theta(7)}) = (d_2, d_3 \ldots, d_7, d_1)$. When this symmetry is exploited with the CSYM algorithm the problem is solved in 4.64 minutes, which compares very favorably with the 31.6 minutes spent when using the algorithm in [8] alone. Thus, a reduction by a factor close to $n = 7$ (i.e., the length of the symmetry cycle) in computing time is obtained, which suggests that the handling of box symmetries doesn't introduce a significant overhead. Figure 1(b) shows a projection into d_1 d_2 and d_3 of the solutions obtained using CSYM.

5 Counting and Generating Box Symmetry Classes

Let us define some quantities of interest:

-$\mathcal{N}_n$: Number of elements of $\mathbb{SR}_n$.

-$\mathcal{FP}_n$: Number of elements of $\mathbb{SR}_n$ that correspond to full-period boxes , i.e., boxes of period n.

-$\mathcal{N}_n^p$: Number of elements of $\mathbb{SR}_n$ having period p.

Polya's theorem [7] could be used to determine some of these quantities for a given n by building a possibly huge polynomial and elucidating some of its coefficients. We present a simpler way of calculating them by means of the formulae below. A demonstration of their validity as well as expressions for similar quantities distinguishing the number of 1's can be found in [10]. We begin with $\mathcal{FP}_n$:

$$\mathcal{FP}_n = \frac{2^n}{n} - \sum_{p \in div(n),\ p<n} \frac{p}{n}\, \mathcal{FP}_p. \tag{1}$$

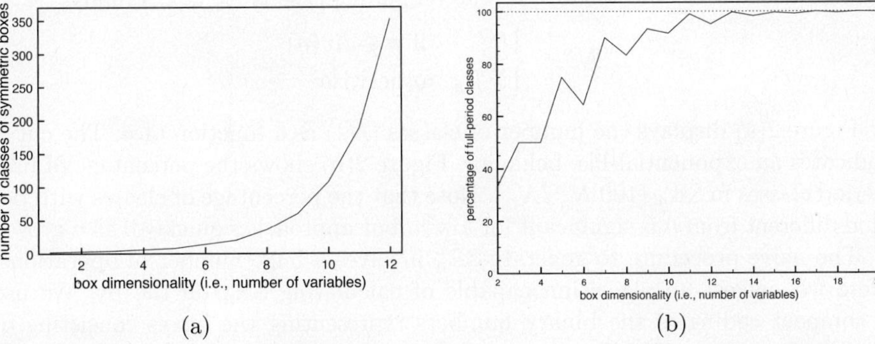

(a) (b)

Fig. 2. (a) Number of elements of $\mathbb{SR}_n$ as a function of n. (b) Percentage of full-period elements in $\mathbb{SR}_n$ as a function of n.

This recurrence has a simple baseline condition: $\mathcal{FP}_1 = 2$. $\mathcal{N}_n$ is calculated with

$$\mathcal{N}_n = \frac{2^n}{n} + \sum_{p \in div(n),\ p<n} \frac{n-p}{n}\, \mathcal{FP}_p. \tag{2}$$

Algorithm 3. ClassGen algorithm

Input: *sum* is the sum of the digits that remain to be written on the right (from position *pos* to *m*); *pos*: the index of the next position to be written; *ctrol*: the index of the current control element, whose value cannot be surpassed in the next position; *m*: the length of the code; *A*: array where class codes are being generated.

Output: A set of codes representing classes, $\mathbb{SR}$.

```
SR ← EmptySet
if pos = m then
    if sum < A[ctrol] then        /* otherwise, SR will remain EmptySet */
        A[m] ← sum
        SR ← {A};
else
    if pos ≠ 1 then
        LowerLimit = 0
        UpperLimit ← MINIMUM(A[ctrol], sum)
    else
        LowerLimit = ⌈sum/m⌉
        UpperLimit ← sum
    for i = UpperLimit to LowerLimit do
        A[pos] ← i
        if i = A[ctrol] then                   /* i = A[ctrol] = UpperLimit */
            SR ← SR ∪ CLASSGEN(sum − i, pos + 1, ctrol + 1, m, A)
        else SR ← SR ∪ CLASSGEN(sum − i, pos + 1, 1, m, A); /* i < A[ctrol] */
return SR
```

This formula is valid for $n > 1$. The remaining case is $\mathcal{N}_1 = 2$. Finally,

$$\mathcal{N}_n^p = \begin{cases} 0 & \text{if } p \notin div(n) \\ \mathcal{FP}_p & \text{otherwise} \end{cases} \tag{3}$$

Figure 2(a) displays the number of classes ($\mathcal{N}_n$) as a function of n. The curve indicates an exponential-like behavior. Figure 2(b) shows the percentage of full-period classes in $\mathbb{SR}_n$ ($100\,\mathcal{N}_n^n/\mathcal{N}_n$). Note that the percentage of classes with period different from n is significant for low n, but approaches quickly 0 as n grows.

The naive procedure to generate $\mathbb{SR}_n$ involves a huge number of operations. Here we suggest an algorithm capable of calculating $\mathbb{SR}_n$ on the fly. We use a compact coding of the binary numbers representing the boxes consisting of chains of numbers. The first number in the code is the number of 0's appearing before the first 1. The i-th number in the code for $i > 1$ is the number of 0's between the $(i-1)$-th and the i-th 1's. For example, the number 0100010111 is codified as 13100. The length of this numerical codification is the number of 1's of the codified binary number, which has been denoted by m.

Algorithm 3, explained in [10], generates $\mathbb{SR}_{nm}^n$, the subset of the elements of $\mathbb{SR}_n$ having m 1's and period n, from which the whole $\mathbb{SR}_n$ can be obtained, as showed also in [10]. The algorithm outputs a list of codes in decreasing numerical order. For instance, the output obtained when requesting $\mathbb{SR}_{93}^9$ with $\text{ClassGen}(6, 1, 1, 3, A)$ is: $\{600, 510, 501, 420, 411, 402, 330, 321, 312\}$.

6 Conclusions

We have approached the problem of exploiting symmetries in continuous constraint satisfaction problems using B&P algorithms. Our approach is general and could be used also with other box-oriented algorithms, such as Branch-and-Bound for nonlinear optimization. The particular symmetries we have tackled are single-cycle permutations of the problem variables.

The suggested strategy is to bisect the domain, the initial n-cube, simultaneously in all dimensions at the same point. This forms a set of boxes that can be grouped in box symmetry classes. A representative of each class is selected to be processed by the B&P algorithm and all the symmetries of the representative are applied to the resulting solutions. In this way, the solutions within the whole initial domain are found, while having processed only a fraction of it –the set of representatives– with the B&P algorithm. The time savings tend to be proportional to the number of symmetric boxes of the representative. Therefore, symmetry exploitation is complete for full-period representatives.

We have also developed a method for generating the classes resulting from bisecting a n-cube. The numerical analysis of the classes revealed that the average number of symmetries of the class representatives tends quickly to n as the number of variables, n, grows. These are good news, since n is the maximum number of symmetries attainable with single-cycle symmetries of n variables. However, for small n there is still a significant fraction of the representatives not having the maximum number of symmetries. Another weakness of the proposed strategy is the exponential growth in the number of classes as a function of n.

The problems with small and large n should be tackled with a more refined subdivision of the initial domain in box symmetry classes, which is left for near future work. We are also currently approaching the extension of this work to deal with permutations of the problem variables composed of several cycles.

Acknowledgments

This work has been partially supported by the Spanish Ministry of Education and Science through the contract DPI2004-07358 and by the "Comunitat de Treball dels Pirineus" under contract 2006ITT-10004.

References

1. Benhamou, F., Goulard, F.: Universally Quantified Interval Constraints. In: Dechter, R. (ed.) CP 2000. LNCS, vol. 1894, pp. 67–82. Springer, Heidelberg (2000)
2. Blumenthal, L.: Theory and aplications of distance geometry. Oxford University Press, Oxford (1953)
3. Cohen, D., Jeavons, P., Jefferson, Ch., Petrie, K.E., Smith, B.M.: Symmetry Definitions for Constraint Satisfaction Problems. Constraints 11(2-3), 115–137 (2006)
4. Flener, P., Frisch, A.M., Hnich, B., Kiziltan, Z., Miguel, I., Pearson, J., Walsh, T.: Breaking Row and Column Symmetries in Matrix Models. In: Van Hentenryck, P. (ed.) CP 2002. LNCS, vol. 2470, pp. 462–476. Springer, Heidelberg (2002)
5. Gent, I.P., Harvey, W., Kelsey, T.: Groups and Constraints: Symmetry Breaking During Search. In: Van Hentenryck, P. (ed.) CP 2002. LNCS, vol. 2470, pp. 415–430. Springer, Heidelberg (2002)
6. Meseguer, P., Torras, C.: Exploiting symmetries within constraint satisfaction search. Artificial Intelligence 129, 133–163 (2001)
7. Polya, G., Read, R.C.: Combinatorial enumeration of groups, graphs and chemical compounds. Springer, New York (1987)
8. Porta, J.M., Ros, L.l., Thomas, F., Corcho, F., Canto, J., Perez, J.J.: Complete maps of molecular loop conformational spaces. Journal of Computational Chemistry (to appear)
9. Porta, J.M., Ros, L.l., Thomas, F., Torras, C.: A Branch-and Prune Solver for Distance Constraints. IEEE Trans. on Robotics 21(2), 176–187 (2005)
10. de Angulo, R.V., Torras, C.: Exploiting single-cycle symmetries in continuous constraint satisfaction problems. IRI_DT 2007/02 (June 2007), `http://www.iri.upc.edu/people/ruiz/articulos/symmetriesreport1.pdf`
11. Puget, J.-F.: Symmetry Breaking Revisited. Constraints 10(1), 23–46 (2005)
12. Sam-Haroud, D., Faltings, B.: Consistency Techniques for Continuous Constraints. Constraints 1(1-2), 85–118 (1996)
13. Vu, X.-H., Silaghi, M., Sam-Haroud, D., Faltings, B.: Branch-and-Prune Search Strategies for Numerical Constraint Solving. Swiss Federal Institute of Technology (EPFL) LIA-REPORT, vol. 7 (2006)

Constraint Symmetry for the Soft CSP

Barbara M. Smith[1], Stefano Bistarelli[2,3], and Barry O'Sullivan[4]

[1] School of Computing, University of Leeds, U.K.
bms@comp.leeds.ac.uk
[2] Istituto di Informatica e Telematica, CNR, Pisa, Italy
stefano.bistarelli@iit.cnr.it
[3] Dipartimento di Scienze, Universitá degli Studi "G. d'Annunzio", Pescara, Italy
bista@sci.unich.it
[4] Cork Constraint Computation Centre, University College Cork, Ireland
b.osullivan@4c.ucc.ie

Abstract. We introduce a definition of constraint symmetry for soft CSPs, based on the definition of constraint symmetry for classical CSPs. We show that the constraint symmetry group of a soft CSP is a subgroup of that of an associated classical CSP instance. Where it is smaller, we can successfully exploit the additional symmetries using conditional symmetry breaking. We demonstrate, in a case-study of graph colouring, that eliminating the symmetry of the soft CSP combined with conditional symmetry breaking can lead to huge reductions in the search effort to find an optimal solution to the soft CSP.

1 Introduction

The importance of exploiting symmetry in combinatorial search problems is well known. In this paper we focus on symmetries in soft constraint satisfaction problems (CSPs). We follow previous work [2,4], but introduce a definition of constraint symmetry for soft CSPs based on constraint symmetry for classical CSPs [5]. We show that the constraint symmetry group of a soft CSP is a subgroup of the constraint symmetry group of the associated classical CSP instance in which the soft constraints are treated as hard constraints. Symmetries of the classical CSP that are not symmetries of the soft CSP can be expressed as conditional symmetries [6]. Conditional symmetry breaking can reduce search effort if the optimal solution is also a solution to the classical CSP, or the proof of optimality requires proving that there is no such solution. The additional symmetries can sometimes be expressed as conditional symmetries that become active earlier in the search. We demonstrate the usefulness of these ideas in a case-study of graph colouring.

We first outline the semiring framework for soft constraints, which is defined and discussed in more detail in [3,1,8].

A classical CSP instance P is a triple $\langle V, D, C\rangle$ where V is a set of variables, D is a universal domain, specifying the possible values for those variables, and C is a set of constraints. Each constraint $c_i \in C$ consists of a *scope*, a list of variables from V, and a *relation* over D. A *solution* to P is a mapping from V into D whose restriction to each constraint scope is in the corresponding relation, i.e. is allowed by the constraint.

Soft constraints associate a qualitative or quantitative value either to the entire constraint or to each assignment of its variables [3]. In this paper, we use the framework

C. Bessiere (Ed.): CP 2007, LNCS 4741, pp. 872–879, 2007.

of semiring-based constraints [1]. A semiring structure S is a 5-tuple $\langle A, +, \times, \mathbf{0}, \mathbf{1} \rangle$; as with a classical CSP, we also have a set of variables V with domain D. A is a set of values, representing the levels of preference (or importance or cost) associated with constraints or assignments; $\mathbf{0}$ and $\mathbf{1}$ are elements of A corresponding to complete unacceptability and complete satisfaction respectively. A classical CSP fits into this framework: the assignments allowed by a constraint have value $\mathbf{1}$ and those it forbids have value $\mathbf{0}$. In general, in the semiring framework, a constraint c_i is a *function*: given an assignment to the variables in its scope, it returns a value in A.

The operator $\times$ is used to combine preference levels, for instance to compute the preference level of a complete assignment from the preference levels of the individual constraints. Combining a completely violated constraint, with semiring value $\mathbf{0}$, with any other preference level, gives $\mathbf{0}$; combining any preference $a \in A$ with $\mathbf{1}$ gives a.

The operator $+$ is used to compare the levels of preference in A. A partial order $\leq_S$ is defined over A such that $a \leq_S b$ (b is preferred to a) iff $a+b = b$. Within the ordering, $\mathbf{1}$ is the best element of A and $\mathbf{0}$ is the worst. An optimal solution to a semiring-based soft CSP $\langle V, D, C, S \rangle$ is a complete assignment whose preference level is at least as great as, or incomparable with, any other complete assignment.

2 Constraint Symmetry

In [5], a constraint symmetry of a classical CSP instance is defined as an automorphism of a graph that represents the constraints, the microstructure complement; an automorphism of a graph or hypergraph is a bijective mapping of the vertices that preserves the edges. We can adapt the definitions of microstructure complement and constraint symmetry to semiring-based soft CSPs.

Definition 1 (Microstructure Complement of a Semiring-based CSP Instance). *For any semiring-based CSP instance $P = \langle V, D, C, S \rangle$, the* microstructure complement *of P is a hyperedge-labelled hypergraph with the set of vertices $V \times D$. For every assignment whose semiring value $\neq \mathbf{1}$, there is a hyperedge joining the vertices of the associated tuple, labelled with the semiring value. There is also an edge, with label $\mathbf{0}$, joining any pair of nodes representing different values for the same variable.*

Definition 2 (Soft Constraint Symmetry). *A* constraint symmetry *of a soft CSP instance is an automorphism of its microstructure complement that preserves the hyperedge labels.*

This is a more restrictive definition of symmetry in soft CSPs than the definitions given in [2,4], which are analogous to solution symmetry as defined in [5]. As in classical CSPs, the difficulty of identifying solution symmetries without solving the instance makes constraint symmetry a more practically useful idea.

The semiring operators $\times$ and $+$ do not affect the microstructure complement. Moreover, the automorphisms of the microstructure complement depend only on which hyperedges have the same label, rather than on the value of the label. Hence, the symmetries of a soft CSP do not depend on how complete assignments are valued, but only on which sets of assignments are given the same preference values by the constraints.

Given a soft CSP instance P_s, there is an associated classical CSP instance P_h, in which the soft constraints of P_s become hard constraints. Let G_h, G_s be the microstructure complement of P_h and P_s respectively. Since they have the same vertex set, an automorphism of G_s corresponds to a bijective mapping on the vertices of G_h. Every hyperedge in G_s is a hyperedge in G_h, and any mapping of G_s that maps hyperedges to hyperedges with the same label must translate into a mapping of hyperedges to hyperedges in G_h. Hence, any automorphism of G_s that preserves the hyperedge labels must be an automorphism of G_h and the constraint symmetry group of P_s is a subgroup of that of P_h.

3 The Symmetries of the Soft n-Queens Problem

As an example of constraint symmetry in soft CSPs, we consider a soft version of the n-queens problem, that allows solutions that do not satisfy all the constraints. As usual, n queens are to be placed on squares of an $n \times n$ chessboard so that no two queens are in the same row, column or diagonal. In the CSP model of the problem the variables $v_1, \ldots, v_n$ represent the rows of the chessboard, and the values represent the columns. The nodes of the microstructure complement correspond to the squares of the board. The automorphisms of the graph, and so the constraint symmetries of this problem, are the eight symmetries of the chessboard: reflections in the horizontal and vertical axes; rotations through 90°, 180° and 270°; reflections in the two main diagonals; and the identity symmetry, denoted by $x, y, r90, r180, r270, d1, d2, i$ respectively.

Suppose that in the soft CSP, the value of the constraint $v_i = v_j$ is $|i - j|/n$, so that $|i - j|/n$ is the label on the edge joining the vertices $\langle v_i, k\rangle$ and $\langle v_j, k\rangle$, for $k = 1, 2, ..., n$. Similarly, the value of $|v_i - v_j| = |i - j|$ is $|i - j|/n$. If the constraint is satisfied, the value is $\mathbf{1}$. Hence the set of values A, when $n = 4$, say, is $\{\mathbf{0}, \frac{1}{4}, \frac{1}{2}, \frac{3}{4}, \mathbf{1}\}$. In the microstructure complement, any edge joining two nodes corresponding to squares in different rows has a value different from $\mathbf{0}$, whereas edges joining nodes corresponding to squares in the same row represent assigning two values to the same variable and so have semiring value $\mathbf{0}$. Because the rows are now distinguished from the columns, the chessboard symmetries are not all symmetries of the soft CSP. For example, $r90$ applied to a solution with two queens in the first column gives a layout with two queens in the first row, which is not a solution. In the microstructure complement of the 4-queens instance, $r90$ maps edges with labels $\frac{1}{4}$, $\frac{1}{2}$ and $\frac{3}{4}$ to edges with label $\mathbf{0}$. However, $x, y, r180$ and i map rows into rows and do preserve the edge labels; this is the symmetry group of the soft CSP.

4 Conditional Symmetries

In solving a CSP, it is important to eliminate as much of the symmetry as possible; any remaining symmetry in the problem may cause wasted effort in exploring subtrees that are symmetrically equivalent to subtrees already explored. As in classical CSPs, several methods are available to eliminate symmetry in soft CSPs; we can add further constraints (with semiring value $\mathbf{0}$) to the CSP that ideally can be satisfied by exactly one solution in each symmetry equivalence class, or we can use a dynamic symmetry breaking method, as explored in [2,4].

The example of soft n-queens shows that a soft CSP instance P_s may have fewer symmetries than its classical counterpart P_h in which the soft constraints become hard constraints. If so, eliminating the symmetries of P_h in solving P_s would risk losing solutions. However, in solving the soft CSP, the search may explore subproblems in which any solution must also be a solution to P_h. The symmetries of P_h are then applicable, and eliminating only the symmetries of P_s may lead to unnecessary search.

As an example, we consider a graph colouring problem. Colouring the nodes of a graph so that no adjacent nodes have the same colour can be represented as a classical CSP, with variables $v_1, v_2, ..., v_n$ representing the nodes in the graph. The domain of each variable is $\{0, 1, ..., k-1\}$ where k is the number of colours allowed, For each edge (i, j) in the graph there is a constraint in the CSP that $v_i \neq v_j$. If k colours are not sufficient to colour the graph, we might want to find the 'best' colouring with the colours available, by attaching a cost to any assignment that does not satisfy the constraints. Suppose that the value of the assignment $\{v_i = l, v_j = l\}$, where nodes i and j are adjacent, is $\max(2, l)$. We might view this as a simplification of a timetabling problem, where the cost of a clash for two events that should be at different times depends on when the clash occurs. We combine the costs of violating constraints using arithmetic addition, and we seek a solution with minimum overall cost. As each successive solution is found, future solutions are constrained to have a smaller total cost, by adding a constraint on c, a variable representing the value of the solution. When it can be proved that no better solution exists, the incumbent solution has been proved optimal.

In the classical CSP, the colours are interchangeable; hence, the size of the symmetry group is $k!$, ignoring any symmetry in the graph. In the soft CSP, with the valuation given, only the colours 0, 1, 2 are interchangeable. In a solution with overall cost 2, there is one edge whose vertices have the same colour. Any better solution has *no* edge whose vertices have the same colour. If the search finds a solution with $c = 2$, a constraint will be added that in future $c < 2$. Given the costs of constraint violations, the search will look for solutions with $c = 0$, corresponding to semiring value $\mathbf{1}$, i.e. it will look for a solution to the classical CSP, P_h. At this point, the symmetries of the classical CSP become valid, and it would be legitimate to eliminate them.

Ideally, the search should use the symmetries of P_h where possible, and the symmetries of the soft CSP, P_s, otherwise. The symmetries of P_h that are not also symmetries of P_s can be viewed as *conditional* symmetries [6]. Conditional symmetries exist only within a subproblem; in this case, within the subproblem where the semiring value is constrained to be $\mathbf{1}$.

The conditional symmetries just described will only be useful in practice if the search looks for solutions with semiring value $\mathbf{1}$; if the optimal solution to the soft CSP has many violated constraints, the conditional symmetries will never become relevant. However, some of these symmetries can be active even when the optimal solution is not close to a solution to P_h. Consider the edges of the graph where the constraints of P_h are violated, i.e. the edges whose nodes have the same colour. If the largest colour assigned to the nodes of any of these edges is i, with $i \geq 2$, then the colours $i+1, ..., k-1$ are interchangeable. These are symmetries that are conditional on the value of $maxCol$, a variable representing the largest colour used in a solution. Since $maxCol \leq c$, whenever a new solution is found and the constraint on c is tightened, this translates into a tighter constraint on $maxCol$. There is a hierarchy of symmetries conditional on $maxCol$: some will become active at an early stage of the search, while as the search progresses and better solutions are found, more colours can be treated as interchangeable. Experimental results showing the effect of eliminating both types of conditional symmetry are given in the next section.

5 Experimental Evaluation

Experiments with symmetry breaking, including conditional symmetry breaking, are presented in this section. More details can be found in a longer version of the paper [9].

We consider the soft graph colouring problem described in the last section, where the aim is to find the best colouring with k colours. Recall that the symmetries of the soft CSP are that the colours 0, 1, 2 are interchangeable. In addition, there are conditional symmetries; in a subproblem where the value of the solution is constrained to be 0 (semiring value $\mathbf{1}$), all the colours are interchangeable, and if the largest colour assigned to adjacent vertices cannot be more than i, the colours $i+1$, ..., $k-1$ are interchangeable.

In the CSP, the domain values represent the colours. Symmetries due to interchangeable values can easily be eliminated using SBDS (Symmetry Breaking During Search) [7], a dynamic symmetry breaking method that adds constraints on backtracking to a choice point, say between $v_i = j$ and $v_i \neq j$. It uses a function for each symmetry to construct the symmetric equivalent of $v_i \neq j$ and adds this constraint on the $v_i \neq j$ branch, if the symmetry is not yet broken on the path to this point. For instance, for the symmetry σ_{jl} that transposes the values j and l, it posts $v_i \neq l$. If σ_{jl} is conditional on $c = 0$, SBDS constructs the constraint $c \neq 0 \vee v_i \neq l$; the constraints for other conditional symmetries are analogous.

For our experiments we randomly generated connected graphs with 20 nodes, with the probability of an edge between a pair of nodes set as 0.7. For these graphs, the chromatic number, γ, i.e. the minimum number of colours required to give a perfect colouring, is between 7 and 9. The problems were solved using ILOG Solver 6.0, using its default optimization search to minimize the value of the solution.

We first solved 20 instances with $k = \gamma$, i.e. there is a perfect colouring. Symmetry breaking makes little or no difference for 19 of the instances. However, the 20th instance takes 1,530 backtracks to solve with conditional symmetry breaking, around 750,000 if just the soft symmetries (that the colours 0, 1, 2 are interchangeable) are eliminated, and nearly 1.5 million with no symmetry breaking. A solution with value 2 is found easily, both with and without symmetry breaking; both types of conditional symmetry then become unconditional, and all colours are interchangeable. Symmetry breaking, especially conditional symmetry breaking, is clearly worthwhile here, even though it makes no difference for most individual instances.

Table 1 shows the results for a second set of 20 instances, which have optimal value 2 when $k = \gamma - 1$. We solved these using no symmetry breaking and three different symmetry-breaking strategies. First, only the symmetries of the soft CSP are broken. Secondly, we used the remaining symmetries of the classical CSP, conditional on $c = 0$.

Table 1. Comparison of symmetry-breaking using SBDS for soft graph colouring instances whose optimal value is 2

No symmetry breaking			Soft symmetries		Cond. symmetries: $c = 0$		Cond. symmetries: *maxCol*$\leq l$		
F	P	time	P	time	P	time	F	P	time
55,993.8	267,615.4	48.19	92,774.5	12.99	56,051.45	6.38	20,107.4	20,165.05	2.51

Table 2. Comparison of symmetry-breaking using SBDS for soft graph colouring instances whose optimal value is 4

Soft symmetries			Cond. symmetries: *maxCol* $\leq l$		
F	P	time	F	P	time
69,510.1	587,828.9	82.40	58,924.5	383,446.45	61.52

Since the optimal value is 2, the proof of optimality requires proving that there is no solution with value 0, and the conditional symmetries come into play at the proof stage. Finally, we made the symmetries that transpose j, l where $2 < j < l$, conditional on *maxCol* $< j$ rather than on $c = 0$. This allows the symmetry to be eliminated at an earlier stage in the search. In Table 1, the columns headed 'F' show the average number of backtracks to find a solution with value 2; the columns headed 'P' show the average total number of backtracks, including the proof of optimality. The average time is in seconds on a 1.7GHz Pentium PC running Windows 2000. For the first three strategies, finding the optimal solution takes the same number of backtracks for every instance, and the 'F' column is not repeated. With no symmetry breaking, the total search effort is dominated by the proof of optimality. On the other hand, with symmetries conditional on *maxCol*, the proof of optimality takes little additional effort once the optimal solution is found; furthermore, it takes less than half as much effort to find the optimal solution than with no symmetry breaking.

Finally, Table 2 shows the results for 20 instances whose optimal value is 4 when $k = \gamma - 1$; the optimal solutions have exactly two edges whose vertices are assigned the same colour. These instances cannot be solved in a reasonable time without symmetry breaking, and we do not show the results of using the symmetries conditional on $c = 0$, because they never become active. For each instance, the search was terminated after 2 million backtracks. The limit was never reached with the conditional symmetries, but with just the soft symmetries, the proof of optimality was not completed in 5 of the 20 instances, although the optimal solution was found. The averages for 'P' and run time for the soft symmetries are based on the remaining 15 instances only, and so are underestimates. If 2 million backtracks for each of the cutoff instances were included in the average number of backtracks, it would increase to over 900,000. The symmetries conditional on the value of *maxCol* are clearly very useful. For most instances, the conditional symmetries have little or no effect on the search effort to find the optimal solution, but they speed up the proof of optimality considerably.

The results presented in this section demonstrate that if the symmetry group of the classical CSP is larger than that of the soft CSP, eliminating the resulting conditional symmetries can lead to huge reductions in search effort. Making these symmetries conditional on the value of the solution being the semiring value **1** is most useful when the search has to prove that there is no such solution, as in Table 1. If the optimal solution is worse, so that subproblems in which the value of the solution is constrained to be **1** never arise, these conditional symmetries never become active, and offer no benefit. However, some of the additional symmetries may still be relevant during the search, conditional on some other aspect of the solution. Table 2 shows that eliminating the symmetries as early in the search as possible can give large reductions in search effort, both in finding the optimal solution and in proving optimality.

6 Discussion and Conclusions

We have enriched the notions of *symmetry for satisfiability* and *symmetry for all solutions* for soft CSPs [2,4] with the notion of *constraint symmetry*, defined analogously to constraint symmetry for classical CSPs [5]. It was previously noted that symmetries in soft CSPs are rarer than in classical CSPs [2,4]; we have shown that the constraint symmetry group of a soft CSP instance P_s is a subgroup of that of the classical CSP instance P_h in which the soft constraints become hard constraints, and in practice may be smaller. The additional symmetries can be successfully exploited by using *conditional* symmetry breaking. They can be eliminated in any subproblem in which the solution to P_s is constrained to be a solution to P_h, i.e. to have semiring value **1**; this happens either if the optimal solution to P_s is also a solution to P_h, or if the proof of optimality requires proving that there is no such solution.

The graph colouring example shows that the additional symmetries may become applicable at an earlier stage in the search, conditional on some property of the solution, not necessarily its value. Although the graph colouring example is an artificial one constructed for illustration purposes, conditional soft symmetries that do not depend on the value of the solution can occur in more realistic problems. For example, a simplified version of a university timetabling problem was constructed for a competition in connection with the PATAT conference in 2002-3[1], to test metaheuristic algorithms. The problem has classes to be scheduled over 5 days with 9 hours in each day. In a feasible timetable, every class is assigned a timeslot and a room; the hard constraints affecting the assignment of classes to timeslots are that no student attends more than one class at the same time. In the CSP defined by these hard constraints, the timeslots are interchangeable. There are also soft constraints that no student should have a class in the last slot of the day, more than two classes consecutively, or a single class on any day. The soft constraints destroy much of the symmetry, although the days as a whole are still interchangeable. However, in any subproblem in which the "no class at the end of the day" soft constraint is satisfied in day i, there is a reversal symmetry: we can reverse the timetable for the first 8 timeslots of that day. Hence this is a conditional symmetry, whose condition is that there is no class assigned to the last timeslot of day i.

Soft CSPs provide a context in which conditional symmetries come into their own; whenever a soft CSP instance P_s has fewer symmetries than its classical CSP counterpart P_h, the additional symmetries will hold in the subproblem in which the solution

[1] See http://www.idsia.ch/Files/ttcomp2002/.

value is $\mathbf{1}$, if not sooner. In general, identifying conditional symmetries in a classical CSP instance is difficult; there is no practicable way to identify the symmetries of all the subproblems that could arise during search. Conditional symmetry breaking has hitherto relied on insight to identify useful conditional symmetries, as in [6]. However, the conditional symmetries that arise in soft CSPs are well-defined: they are the constraint symmetries of P_h that are not constraint symmetries of P_s.

Our empirical results on graph colouring problems demonstrate that eliminating both the symmetry of the soft CSP and the conditional symmetry can lead to huge reductions in the search effort to find an optimal solution. Where the soft CSP has less symmetry than its classical counterpart, the additional symmetries will apply whenever the solution is constrained to have semiring value $\mathbf{1}$; however, some of these symmetries may apply even when the search is considering much worse solutions. It is important to use the conditional symmetries: the more symmetry is eliminated, and the earlier in search, the better the results.

Acknowledgments

This work was completed while the first author was employed at the Cork Constraint Computation Centre and was supported by Science Foundation Ireland under Grant No. 05/IN/I886. The second author is partially supported by the MIUR project PRIN 2005-015491.

References

1. Bistarelli, S.: Semirings for Soft Constraint Solving and Programming. LNCS, vol. 2962. Springer, Heidelberg (2004)
2. Bistarelli, S., Kelleher, J., O'Sullivan, B.: Symmetry Breaking in Soft CSPs. In: Proceedings of AI-2003, BCS Conference Series, pp. 199–212. Springer, Heidelberg (2004)
3. Bistarelli, S., Montanari, U., Rossi, F.: Semiring-based constraint solving and optimization. Journal of ACM 44(2), 201–236 (1997)
4. Bistarelli, S., O'Sullivan, B.: Combining branch & bound and SBDD to solve soft CSPs. In: Proceedings of SymCon Workshop (2004)
5. Cohen, D., Jeavons, P., Jefferson, C., Petrie, K.E., Smith, B.M.: Symmetry Definitions for Constraint Programming. Constraints 11, 115–137 (2006)
6. Gent, I.P., Kelsey, T., Linton, S.A., McDonald, I., Miguel, I., Smith, B.M.: Conditional Symmetry Breaking. In: van Beek, P. (ed.) CP 2005. LNCS, vol. 3709, pp. 256–270. Springer, Heidelberg (2005)
7. Gent, I.P., Smith, B.M.: Symmetry Breaking During Search in Constraint Programming. In: Horn, W. (ed.) Proceedings ECAI'2000, pp. 599–603 (2000)
8. Meseguer, P., Rossi, F., Schiex, T.: Soft constraints. In: Rossi, F., van Beek, P., Walsh, T. (eds.) Handbook of Constraint Programming, vol. 9, pp. 281–328. Elsevier, Amsterdam (2006)
9. Smith, B.M., Bistarelli, S., O'Sullivan, B.: Constraint Symmetry for the Soft CSP. Technical Report CPPod-22-2007, CPPod Research Group (2007) Available from `http://www.dcs.st-and.ac.uk/~cppod/publications/reports/cppod-22-2007.pdf`

Breaking Value Symmetry*

Toby Walsh

NICTA and UNSW
Sydney, Australia
tw@cse.unsw.edu.au

1 Introduction

One common type of symmetry is when values are symmetric. For example, if we are assigning colours (values) to nodes (variables) in a graph colouring problem then we can uniformly interchange the colours throughout a colouring. For a problem with value symmetries, all symmetric solutions can be eliminated in polynomial time [1,2]. However, as we show here, both static and dynamic methods to deal with symmetry have computational limitations. With static methods, pruning all symmetric values is NP-hard in general. With dynamic methods, we can take exponential time on problems which static methods solve without search.

2 Background

A constraint satisfaction problem consists of a set of variables, each with a domain of values, and a set of constraints specifying allowed combinations of values for given subsets of variables. A solution is an assignment of values to variables satisfying the constraints. Variables take one value from a given finite set. Symmetry occurs in many constraint satisfaction problems. A *value symmetry* is a permutation of the values that preserves solutions. More formally, a value symmetry is a bijective mapping σ on the values such that if $X_1 = d_1, \ldots, X_n = d_n$ is a solution then $X_1 = \sigma(d_1), \ldots, X_n = \sigma(d_n)$ is also. A *variable symmetry*, on the other hand, is a permutation of the variables that preserves solutions. More formally, a variable symmetry is a bijective mapping σ on the indices of variables such that if $X_1 = d_1, \ldots, X_n = d_n$ is a solution then $X_{\sigma(1)} = d_1, \ldots, X_{\sigma(n)} = d_n$ is also. Symmetries are problematic as they increase the size of the search space. For instance, if we have m interchangeable values, symmetry increases the size of the search space by a factor of $m!$.

Many constraint solvers explore the space of partial assignments enforcing some local consistency. We consider four local consistencies for finite domain variables Given a constraint C, a *support* is assignment to each variable of a value in its domain which satisfies C. A constraint is *generalized arc consistent* (*GAC*) iff for each variable, every value in its domain belongs to a support. A set of constraints is GAC iff each constraint is

* NICTA is funded by the Australian Government's Department of Communications, Information Technology and the Arts and the Australian Research Council through Backing Australia's Ability and the ICT Centre of Excellence program. Thanks to Chris Jefferson and Jean-Francois Puget for useful comments.

C. Bessiere (Ed.): CP 2007, LNCS 4741, pp. 880–887, 2007.

GAC. On binary constraints, GAC is simply called arc consistency (AC). A set of binary constraints is *singleton arc consistent* (*SAC*) iff we can assign every variable with each value in its domain and make the resulting problem arc consistent (AC). Finally, a set of binary constraint is k*-consistent* iff each $k-1$ assignment can be consistently extended to a kth variable, and is *strongly* k*-consistent* iff it is j-consistency for all $j \leq k$. We will compare local consistency properties applied to sets of constraints, c_1 and c_2 which are logically equivalent. As in [4], a local consistency property Φ on c_1 is as strong as Ψ on c_2 iff, given any domains, if Φ holds on c_1 then Ψ holds on c_2; Φ on c_1 is stronger than Ψ on c_2 iff Φ on c_1 is as strong as Ψ on c_2 but not vice versa; Φ on c_1 is equivalent to Ψ on c_2 iff Φ on c_1 is as strong as Ψ on c_2 and vice versa.

3 Static Methods

One simple and common mechanism to deal with symmetry is to add constraints which eliminate symmetric solutions [5]. Suppose we have a set Σ of value symmetries. Based on [6], we can eliminate all symmetric solutions by posting a global constraint which ensures that the solution is ordered lexicographically before any of its symmetries. More precisely, we post the global constraint $\text{ValSymBreak}(\Sigma, [X_1, \ldots, X_n])$ which ensures $[X_1, \ldots, X_n] \leq_{\text{lex}} [\sigma(X_1), \ldots, \sigma(X_n)]$ for all $\sigma \in \Sigma$ where X_1 to X_n is a fixed ordering on the variables. Unfortunately, pruning *all* values from such a symmetry breaking constraint is NP-hard.

Theorem 1. *Deciding if* $\text{ValSymBreak}(\Sigma, [X_1, \ldots, X_n])$ *is GAC is NP-complete, even when* $|\Sigma|$ *is linearly bounded.*

Proof: Membership in NP follows by giving a support for every possible assignment. To prove it is NP-hard, we give a reduction from a 3-SAT problem in N Boolean variables and M clauses. We construct a CSP with $N+M+1$ variables over $4N+2$ possible values. The first $4N$ values partition into $2N$ interchangeable pairs. The values $4i-3$ and $4i-2$ are interchangeable, as are $4i-1$ and $4i$ for $1 \leq i \leq N$. The values $4i-3$ and $4i-2$ represent x_i being true, whilst the values $4i-1$ and $4i$ represent x_i being false. The final two values, $4N+1$ and $4N+2$ are not interchangeable. The first N CSP variables represent a "truth assignment". We have $X_i \in \{4i-3, 4i-2, 4i-1, 4i\}$ for $1 \leq i \leq N$. The next M CSP variables ensure at least one literal in each clause is true. For example, if the ith clause is $x_j \vee \neg x_k \vee x_l$, then the domain of X_{N+i} is $\{4j-3, 4j-2, 4k-1, 4k, 4l-3, 4l-2\}$. The final variable X_{N+M+1} is a "switch" and has the domain $\{4N+1, 4N+2\}$. Note that all variables have symmetric domains.

We have two sets of constraints. First, we have the constraints $odd(X_{N+M+1}) \rightarrow odd(X_i)$ for $1 \leq i \leq N$ and $odd(X_{N+M+1}) \rightarrow even(X_{N+j})$ for $1 \leq j \leq M$. Second, we have the constraints $odd(X_{N+M+1}) \rightarrow PHP(N, N+1)$ and $even(X_{N+M+1}) \rightarrow PHP(N, N)$ where $PHP(i, j)$ is a pigeonhole constraint which holds iff the variables X_1 to X_i take j distinct values. Note that $PHP(N, N+1)$ is unsatisfiable and that $PHP(N, N)$ is satisfiable. Thus, the constructed CSP is unsatisfiable if $X_{N+M+1} = 4N+1$ and satisfiable if $X_{N+M+1} = 4N+2$. Note that if we take any solution of the CSP and permute any of the interchangeable values, we still have a solution. Thus, if

Σ is the set of symmetries induced by these interchangeable values, it is permissible to add VALSYMBREAK($\Sigma, [X_1, \ldots, X_n]$) to this CSP.

Suppose our branching heuristic sets the switch variable X_{N+M+1} to $4N + 1$. Enforcing AC on the binary constraints prunes the domains of X_i to $\{4i - 3, 4i - 1\}$ for $1 \leq i \leq N$. Similarly, the domain of X_{N+i} is reduced to $\{4j - 2, 4k, 4l - 2\}$. Consider now finding a support for VALSYMBREAK given this particular subproblem. X_{N+i} can only take the value $4j - 2$ if X_j had previously been assigned $4j - 3$. In other words, X_{N+i} can only take the value $4j - 2$ if x_j is set to true in the "truth assignment". Similarly, X_{N+i} can only take the value $4k$ if X_k had previously been assigned $4k - 1$. In other words, X_{N+i} can only take the value $4k$ if x_k is set to false in the "truth assignment". Finally, X_{N+i} can only take the value $4l - 2$ if X_j had previously been assigned $4l - 3$. In other words, X_{N+i} can only take the value $4l - 2$ if x_l is set to true in the "truth assignment". Thus, at least one of the literals in the ith clause must have been set to true in the "truth assignment". Hence, there is a support for VALSYMBREAK iff the original 3-SAT problem is satisfiable. By Theorem 3, $|\Sigma|$ can be linearly bound. □

This is a somewhat surprising result. Whilst it is polynomial to eliminate all symmetric solutions either statically [2] or dynamically [1], it is NP-hard to lookahead and prune all symmetric values. Equivalently, whilst we can avoid visiting symmetric leaves of the search tree in polynomial time, avoiding symmetric subtrees is NP-hard.

4 Dynamic Methods

An alternative to static methods which add constraints to eliminate symmetric solutions are dynamic methods which modify the search procedure to ignore symmetric branches. For example, with value symmetries, the GE-tree method can dynamically eliminate all symmetric leaves in a backtracking search procedure in $O(n^4 \log(n))$ time [1]. However, as we show now, such dynamic methods may not prune *all* symmetric subtrees which static methods can do. Suppose we are at a particular node in the search tree explored by the GE-tree method. Consider the current and all past variables seen so far. The GE-tree method can be seen as performing forward checking on a static symmetry breaking constraint over this set of variables. This prunes symmetric assignments from the domain of the *next* branching variable. Unlike static methods, the GE-tree method does not prune *deeper* variables. By comparison, static symmetry breaking constraints can prune deeper variables, resulting in interactions with the problem constraints and additional domain prunings. For this reason, static symmetry breaking methods can solve certain problems exponentially quicker than dynamic methods.

Theorem 2. *There exists a model of the pigeonhole problem with n variables and $n+1$ interchangeable values such that, given any variable and value ordering, the GE-tree method explores $O(2^n)$ branches, but which static symmetry breaking methods can solve in just $O(n^2)$ time.*

Proof: The $n + 1$ constraints in the CSP are $\bigvee_{i=1}^{n} X_i = j$ for $1 \leq j \leq n + 1$, and the domains are $X_i \in \{1, \ldots, n + 1\}$ for $1 \leq i \leq n$. The problem is unsatisfiable by a simple pigeonhole argument. Any of the static methods for breaking value symmetry presented later in this paper will prune $n+1$ from every domain in $O(n^2)$ time. Enforcing

GAC on the constraint $\bigvee_{i=1}^{n} X_i = n+1$ then proves unsatisfiability. On the other hand, the GE-tree method irrespective of the variable and value ordering, will only terminate each branch when $n-1$ variables have been assigned (and the last variable is forced). A simple calculation shows that the size of the GE-tree more than doubles as we increase n by 1. Hence we will visit $O(2^n)$ branches before declaring the problem is unsatisfiable. □

This theoretical result supports the experimental results in [2] showing that static methods for breaking value symmetry can outperform dynamic methods. Given the intractability of pruning all symmetric values in general, we focus in the rest of the paper on a common and useful type of value symmetry where symmetry breaking methods have been proposed that take polynomial time: we will suppose that values are ordered into partitions, and values within each partition are uniformly interchangeable.

5 Generator Symmetries

One way to propagate VALSYMBREAK is to decompose it into individual lexicographical ordering constraints, $[X_1, \ldots, X_n] \leq_{\text{lex}} [\sigma(X_1), \ldots, \sigma(X_n)]$ and use one of the propagators proposed in [7] or [8]. Even if we ignore the fact that such a decomposition may hinder propagation (see Theorem 2 in [8]), we have to cope with Σ, the set of symmetries being exponentially large in general. For instance, if we have m interchangeable values, then Σ contains $m!$ symmetries. To deal with large number of symmetries, Aloul *et al.* suggest breaking only those symmetries corresponding to generators of the group [9]. Consider the generators which interchange adjacent values within each partition. If the m values partition into k classes of interchangeable values, there are just $m-k$ such generators. Breaking *just* these symmetries eliminates *all* symmetric solutions.

Theorem 3. *If Σ is a set of symmetries induced by interchangeable values, and Σ_g is the set of generators corresponding to interchanging adjacent values then posting* VALSYMBREAK$(\Sigma_g, [X_1, \ldots, X_n])$ *eliminates all symmetric solutions.*

Proof: Assume VALSYMBREAK$(\Sigma_g, [X_1, \ldots, X_n])$. Consider any two interchangeable values, j and k where $j < k$, Let $\sigma_j \in \Sigma_g$ be the symmetry which swaps just j with $j+1$. To ensure $[X_1, \ldots, X_n] \leq_{\text{lex}} [\sigma_j(X_1), \ldots, \sigma_j(X_n)]$, j must occur before $j+1$ in X_1 to X_n. By transitivity, j therefore occurs before k. Thus, for the symmetry σ' which swaps just j with k, $[X_1, \ldots, X_n] \leq_{\text{lex}} [\sigma'(X_1), \ldots, \sigma'(X_n)]$. Consider now any symmetry $\sigma \in \Sigma$. The proof proceeds by contradiction. Suppose $[X_1, \ldots, X_n] >_{\text{lex}} [\sigma(X_1), \ldots, \sigma(X_n)]$. Then there exists some j with $X_j > \sigma(X_j)$ and $X_i = \sigma(X_i)$ for all $i < j$. Consider the symmetry σ' which swaps just X_j with $\sigma(X_j)$. As argued before, $[X_1, \ldots, X_n] \leq_{\text{lex}} [\sigma'(X_1), \ldots, \sigma'(X_n)]$. But this contradicts $[X_1, \ldots, X_n] >_{\text{lex}} [\sigma(X_1), \ldots, \sigma(X_n)]$ as σ and σ' act identically on the first j variables in X_1 to X_n. Hence, $[X_1, \ldots, X_n] \leq_{\text{lex}} [\sigma(X_1), \ldots, \sigma(X_n)]$. □

Not surprisingly, reducing the number of symmetry breaking constraints to linear comes at a cost. We may not prune all symmetric values.

Theorem 4. *If Σ is a set of symmetries induced by interchangeable values, and Σ_g is the set of generators corresponding to interchanging adjacent values then GAC on* VALSYMBREAK$(\Sigma, [X_1, \ldots, X_n])$ *is stronger than GAC on* $[X_1, \ldots, X_n] \leq_{\text{lex}} [\sigma(X_1), \ldots, \sigma(X_n)]$ *for all* $\sigma \in \Sigma_g$.

Proof: Clearly it is at least as strong. To show it is stronger, suppose all values are interchangeable with each other. Consider $X_1 = 1$, $X_2 \in \{1, 2\}$, $X_3 \in \{1, 3\}$, $X_4 \in \{1, 4\}$ and $X_5 = 5$. Then enforcing GAC on VALSYMBREAK$(\Sigma, [X_1, \ldots, X_5])$ prunes 1 from X_2, X_3 and X_4. However, $[X_1, \ldots, X_5] \leq_{\text{lex}} [\sigma(X_1), \ldots, \sigma(X_5)]$ is GAC for all $\sigma \in \Sigma_g$.. □

Finally, it is not hard to see that there are other sets of generators for the symmetries induced by interchangeable values which do not necessarily eliminate all symmetric solutions (e.g. with the generators which interchange the value 1 with any i, we do not eliminate either the assignment $X_1 = 1$, $X_2 = 2$ or the symmetric assignment $X_1 = 1$, $X_2 = 3$).

6 Puget's Decomposition

With value symmetries, a second method that eliminates all symmetric solutions is a decomposition due to [2]. Consider a surjection problem (where each value is used at least once) with interchangeable values. We can channel into dual variables, Z_j which record the first index using the value j by posting the binary constraints: $X_i = j \rightarrow Z_j \leq i$ and $Z_j = i \rightarrow X_i = j$ for all $1 \leq i \leq n$, $1 \leq j \leq m$. We can then eliminate all symmetric solutions by insisting that interchangeable values *first* occur in some given order. That is, we place strict ordering constraints on the Z_k within each class of interchangeable values. Puget notes that any problem can be made into a surjection by introducing m additional new variables, X_{n+1} to X_{n+m} where $X_{n+i} = i$. These variables ensure that each value is used at least once. In fact, we don't need additional variables. It is enough to ensure that each Z_j has a dummy value, which means that j is not assigned, and to order (dummy) values appropriately. Unfortunately, Puget's decomposition into binary constraints hinders propagation.

Theorem 5. *If Σ is a set of symmetries induced by interchangeable values, then GAC on* VALSYMBREAK$(\Sigma, [X_1, \ldots, X_n])$ *is stronger than AC on Puget's decomposition into binary constraints.*

Proof: It is clearly at least as strong. To show it is stronger, suppose all values are interchangeable with each other. Consider $X_1 = 1$, $X_2 \in \{1, 2\}$, $X_3 \in \{1, 3\}$, $X_4 \in \{3, 4\}$, $X_5 = 2$, $X_6 = 3$, $X_7 = 4$, $Z_1 = 1$, $Z_2 \in \{2, 5\}$, $Z_3 \in \{3, 4, 6\}$, and $Z_4 \in \{4, 7\}$. Then all Puget's symmetry breaking constraints are AC. However, enforcing GAC on VALSYMBREAK$(\Sigma, [X_1, \ldots, X_5])$ will prune 1 from X_2. □

If *all* values are interchangeable with each other, we only need to enforce a slightly stronger level of local consistency to prune all symmetric values. More precisely, enforcing singleton arc consistency on Puget's binary decomposition will prune all symmetric values.

Theorem 6. *If all values are interchangeable and Σ is the set of symmetries induced by this then GAC on* VALSYMBREAK$(\Sigma, [X_1, \ldots, X_n])$ *is equivalent to SAC on Puget's decomposition into binary constraints.*

Proof: Suppose Puget's encoding is AC. We will show that there is at least one support for VALSYMBREAK. We assign Z_1 to Z_m in turn, giving each the smallest remaining value in their domain, and enforcing AC on the encoding after each assignment. This will construct a support without the need for backtracking. At each choice point, we ensure that a new value is used as soon as possible, thus giving us the most freedom to use values in the future. Suppose now that Puget's encoding is SAC. Then, by the definition of SAC, we can assign any variable with any value in its domains and be sure that the problem can be made AC without a domain wipeout. But if the problem can be made AC, it has support. Thus every value in every domain has support. Hence enforcing SAC on Puget's decomposition ensures that VALSYMBREAK is GAC. □

We might wonder if singleton arc-consistency is enough for arbitrary value symmetries. That is, does enforcing SAC on Puget's encoding prune all symmetric values? We can prove that no fixed level of local consistency is sufficient. Given the intractability of pruning all symmetric values in general, this result is not surprising.

Theorem 7. *For any given k, there exists a value symmetry and domains for which Puget's encoding is strongly k-consistent but is not $k+1$-consistent.*

Proof: We construct a CSP problem with $2k+1$ variables over $2(k+1)$ possible values. The $2(k+1)$ values partition into $k+1$ pairs which are interchangeable. More precisely, the values i and $k+1+i$ are interchangeable for $1 \leq i \leq k+1$. The first k variables of the CSP have $k+1$ values between them (hence, one value is not taken). More precisely, $X_i \in \{i, i+1\}$ for $1 \leq i \leq k$. The remaining $k+1$ variables then take the other $k+1$ values. More precisely, $X_{k+i} = k+1+i$ for $1 \leq i \leq k+1$. The values 1 to $k+1$ need to be used by the first k variables, X_1 to X_k so that the last $k+1$ variables, X_{k+1} to $X_{2(k+1)}$ can use the values $k+2$ to $2(k+1)$. But this is impossible by a pigeonhole argument. Puget's encoding of this is strongly k-consistent. since any assignment of $k-1$ or less variables can be extended to an additional variable. On the other hand, enforcing $k+1$-consistency will discover that the CSP has no solution. □

Finally, we compare this method with the previous method based on breaking the symmetries corresponding to the generators which interchange adjacent values.

Theorem 8. *If Σ is a set of symmetries induced by interchangeable values, and Σ_g is the set of generators interchanging adjacent values then AC on Puget's decomposition for Σ is stronger than GAC on $[X_1, \ldots, X_n] \leq_{\text{lex}} [\sigma(X_1), \ldots, \sigma(X_n)]$ for all $\sigma \in \Sigma_g$.*

Proof: Suppose Puget's decomposition is AC. Consider the symmetry σ which interchanges j with $j+1$. Consider any variable and any value in its domain. We show how to construct a support for this assignment. We assign every other variable with j if it is in its domain, otherwise any value other than $j+1$ and failing this, $j+1$. Suppose this is not a support for $[X_1, \ldots, X_n] \leq_{\text{lex}} [\sigma(X_1), \ldots, \sigma(X_n)]$. This means that in the sequence from X_1 to X_n, we had to use the value $j+1$ before the value j. However, as

Puget's decomposition is AC, there is a value in the domain of Z_j smaller than Z_{j+1}. This contradicts $j+1$ having to be used before j. Hence, this must be a support. Thus $[X_1, \ldots, X_n] \leq_{\text{lex}} [\sigma(X_1), \ldots, \sigma(X_n)]$ is GAC for all $\sigma \in \Sigma_g$. To show that AC on Puget's decomposition is stronger consider again the example used in the proof of Theorem 4. The lexicographical ordering constraint for each generator $\sigma \in \Sigma_g$ is GAC without any domain pruning. However, enforcing AC on Puget's decomposition prunes 1 from X_2, X_3 and X_4. □

7 Value Precedence

A third method to break symmetry due to interchangeable values uses the global *precedence* constraint [3]. PRECEDENCE($[X_1, \ldots, X_n]$) holds iff $\min\{i \mid X_i = j \vee i = n+1\} < \min\{i \mid X_i = k \vee i = n+2\}$ for all $j < k$. That is, the first time we use j is before the first time we use k for all $j < k$. Posting such a constraint eliminates all symmetric solutions due to interchangeable values. In [10], a GAC propagator for such a precedence constraint is given which takes $O(nm)$ time. It is not hard to show that PRECEDENCE($[X_1, \ldots, X_n]$) is equivalent to VALSYMBREAK($\Sigma, [X_1, \ldots, X_n]$) where Σ is the set of symmetries induced by interchangeable values. Hence, enforcing GAC on such a precedence constraint prunes all symmetric values in polynomial time. Precedence constraints can also be defined when values partition into several interchangeable classes; we just insist that values within each class first occur in a fixed order. In [10], a propagator for such a precedence constraint is proposed which takes $O(n \prod_i m_i)$ time where m_i is the size of the ith class of interchangeable values. This is only polynomial if we can bound the number of classes of interchangeable values. This complexity is now not so surprising. We have shown that pruning all symmetric values is NP-hard when the number of classes of interchangeable values is unbounded.

8 Related Work

Puget proved that symmetric solutions can be eliminated by the addition of suitable constraints [5]. Crawford *et al.* presented the first general method for constructing variable symmetry breaking constraints [6]. Petrie and Smith adapted this method to value symmetries by posting a suitable lexicographical ordering constraint for each value symmetry [13]. Puget and Walsh independently proposed propagators for such symmetry breaking constraints [7,8]. To deal with the exponential number of such constraints, Puget proposed a global propagator which does forward checking in polynomial time [7]. To eliminate symmetric solutions due to interchangeable values, Law and Lee formally defined value precedence and proposed a specialized propagator for a pair of interchangeable values [3]. Walsh extended this to a propagator for any number of interchangeable values [10]. An alternative way to break value symmetry statically is to convert it into a variable symmetry by channelling into a dual viewpoint and using lexicographical ordering constraints on this dual view [14,12]. A number of dynamic methods have been proposed to deal with value symmetry. Van Hentenryck *et al.* gave a labelling schema for eliminating all symmetric solutions due to interchangeable values [15]. Inspired by this method, Roney-Dougal *et al.* gave a polynomial method to construct a GE-tree, a search tree without value symmetry [1]. Finally, Sellmann and van

Hentenryck gave a $O(nd^{3.5} + n^2d^2)$ dominance detection algorithm for eliminating all symmetric solutions when both variables and values are interchangeable [16].

9 Conclusion

Value symmetries can be broken either statically (by adding constraints to prune symmetric solutions) or dynamically (by modifying the search procedure to avoid symmetric branches). We have shown that both approaches have computational limitations. With static methods, we can eliminate all symmetric solutions in polynomial time but pruning all symmetric values is NP-hard in general (or equivalently, we can avoid visiting symmetric leaves of the search tree in polynomial time but avoiding symmetric subtrees is NP-hard). With dynamic methods, we typically only perform forward checking and can take exponential time on problems which static methods solve without search.

References

1. Roney-Dougal, C., Gent, I., Kelsey, T., Linton, S.: Tractable symmetry breaking using restricted search trees. In: Proc. of ECAI-2004 (2004)
2. Puget, J.F.: Breaking all value symmetries in surjection problems. In: van Beek, P. (ed.) CP 2005. LNCS, vol. 3709. Springer, Heidelberg (2005)
3. Law, Y., Lee, J.: Global constraints for integer and set value precedence. In: Wallace, M. (ed.) CP 2004. LNCS, vol. 3258. Springer, Heidelberg (2004)
4. Debruyne, R., Bessière, C.: Some practicable filtering techniques for the constraint satisfaction problem. In: Proc. of the 15th IJCAI (1997)
5. Puget, J.F.: On the satisfiability of symmetrical constrained satisfaction problems. In: Komorowski, J., Raś, Z.W. (eds.) ISMIS 1993. LNCS, vol. 689. Springer, Heidelberg (1993)
6. Crawford, J., Luks, G., Ginsberg, M., Roy, A.: Symmetry breaking predicates for search problems. In: Proc. of the 5th Int. Conf. on Knowledge Representation and Reasoning (KR '96) (1996)
7. Puget, J.F.: An efficient way of breaking value symmetries. In: Proc. of the 21st National Conf., AAAI, Stanford, California, USA (2006)
8. Walsh, T.: General symmetry breaking constraints. In: Benhamou, F. (ed.) CP 2006. LNCS, vol. 4204.Springer, Heidelberg (2006)
9. Aloul, F., Ramani, A., Markov, I., Sakallah, K.: Solving difficult SAT instances in the presence of symmetries. In: Proc. of the Design Automation Conf. (2002)
10. Walsh, T.: Symmetry breaking using value precedence. In: Proc. of the 17th ECAI (2006)
11. Bessiere, C., Hebrard, E., Hnich, B., Walsh, T.: The complexity of global constraints. In: Proc. of the 19th National Conf. on AI. AAAI, Stanford, California, USA (2004)
12. Law, Y., Lee, J.: Symmetry Breaking Constraints for Value Symmetries in Constraint Satisfaction. Constraints 11(2-3), 221–267 (2006)
13. Petrie, K.E., Smith, B.M.: Symmetry Breaking in Graceful Graphs. Technical Report APES-56a-2003, APES Research Group (2003)
14. Flener, P., Frisch, A., Hnich, B., Kiziltan, Z., Miguel, I., Pearson, J., Walsh, T.: Breaking row and column symmetry in matrix models. In: Van Hentenryck, P. (ed.) CP 2002. LNCS, vol. 2470. Springer, Heidelberg (2002)
15. Hentenryck, P.V., Agren, M., Flener, P., Pearson, J.: Tractable symmetry breaking for CSPs with interchangeable values. In: Proc. of the 18th IJCAI (2003)
16. Sellmann, M., Hentenryck, P.V.: Structural symmetry breaking. In: Proc. of 19th IJCAI (2005)

Author Index

Printing: Mercedes-Druck, Berlin
Binding: Stein + Lehmann, Berlin

Lecture Notes in Computer Science

Sublibrary 2: Programming and Software Engineering

For information about Vols. 1–4039
please contact your bookseller or Springer

Vol. 4749: B.J. Krämer, K.-J. Lin, P. Narasimhan (Eds.), Service-Oriented Computing – ICSOC 2007. XIX, 629 pages. 2007.

Vol. 4741: C. Bessiere (Ed.), Principles and Practice of Constraint Programming – CP 2007. XV, 890 pages. 2007.

Vol. 4670: V. Dahl, I. Niemelä (Eds.), Logic Programming. XII, 470 pages. 2007.

Vol. 4634: H.R. Nielson, G. Filé (Eds.), Static Analysis. XI, 469 pages. 2007.

Vol. 4615: R. de Lemos, C. Gacek, A. Romanovsky (Eds.), Architecting Dependable Systems IV. XIV, 435 pages. 2007.

Vol. 4610: B. Xiao, L.T. Yang, J. Ma, C. Muller-Schloer, Y. Hua (Eds.), Autonomic and Trusted Computing. XVIII, 571 pages. 2007.

Vol. 4609: E. Ernst (Ed.), ECOOP 2007 – Object-Oriented Programming. XIII, 625 pages. 2007.

Vol. 4608: H.W. Schmidt, I. Crnkovic, G.T. Heineman, J.A. Stafford (Eds.), Component-Based Software Engineering. XII, 283 pages. 2007.

Vol. 4591: J. Davies, J. Gibbons (Eds.), Integrated Formal Methods. IX, 660 pages. 2007.

Vol. 4589: J. Münch, P. Abrahamsson (Eds.), Product-Focused Software Process Improvement. XII, 414 pages. 2007.

Vol. 4574: J. Derrick, J. Vain (Eds.), Formal Techniques for Networked and Distributed Systems – FORTE 2007. XI, 375 pages. 2007.

Vol. 4556: C. Stephanidis (Ed.), Universal Access in Human-Computer Interaction, Part III. XXII, 1020 pages. 2007.

Vol. 4555: C. Stephanidis (Ed.), Universal Access in Human-Computer Interaction, Part II. XXII, 1066 pages. 2007.

Vol. 4554: C. Stephanidis (Ed.), Universal Acess in Human Computer Interaction, Part I. XXII, 1054 pages. 2007.

Vol. 4553: J.A. Jacko (Ed.), Human-Computer Interaction, Part IV. XXIV, 1225 pages. 2007.

Vol. 4552: J.A. Jacko (Ed.), Human-Computer Interaction, Part III. XXI, 1038 pages. 2007.

Vol. 4551: J.A. Jacko (Ed.), Human-Computer Interaction, Part II. XXIII, 1253 pages. 2007.

Vol. 4550: J.A. Jacko (Ed.), Human-Computer Interaction, Part I. XXIII, 1240 pages. 2007.

Vol. 4542: P. Sawyer, B. Paech, P. Heymans (Eds.), Requirements Engineering: Foundation for Software Quality. IX, 384 pages. 2007.

Vol. 4536: G. Concas, E. Damiani, M. Scotto, G. Succi (Eds.), Agile Processes in Software Engineering and Extreme Programming. XV, 276 pages. 2007.

Vol. 4530: D.H. Akehurst, R. Vogel, R.F. Paige (Eds.), Model Driven Architecture - Foundations and Applications. X, 219 pages. 2007.

Vol. 4523: Y.-H. Lee, H.-N. Kim, J. Kim, Y.W. Park, L.T. Yang, S.W. Kim (Eds.), Embedded Software and Systems. XIX, 829 pages. 2007.

Vol. 4498: N. Abdennahder, F. Kordon (Eds.), Reliable Software Technologies - Ada-Europe 2007. XII, 247 pages. 2007.

Vol. 4486: M. Bernardo, J. Hillston (Eds.), Formal Methods for Performance Evaluation. VII, 469 pages. 2007.

Vol. 4470: Q. Wang, D. Pfahl, D.M. Raffo (Eds.), Software Process Dynamics and Agility. XI, 346 pages. 2007.

Vol. 4468: M.M. Bonsangue, E.B. Johnsen (Eds.), Formal Methods for Open Object-Based Distributed Systems. X, 317 pages. 2007.

Vol. 4467: A.L. Murphy, J. Vitek (Eds.), Coordination Models and Languages. X, 325 pages. 2007.

Vol. 4454: Y. Gurevich, B. Meyer (Eds.), Tests and Proofs. IX, 217 pages. 2007.

Vol. 4444: T. Reps, M. Sagiv, J. Bauer (Eds.), Program Analysis and Compilation, Theory and Practice. X, 361 pages. 2007.

Vol. 4440: B. Liblit, Cooperative Bug Isolation. XV, 101 pages. 2007.

Vol. 4408: R. Choren, A. Garcia, H. Giese, H.-f. Leung, C. Lucena, A. Romanovsky (Eds.), Software Engineering for Multi-Agent Systems V. XII, 233 pages. 2007.

Vol. 4406: W. De Meuter (Ed.), Advances in Smalltalk. VII, 157 pages. 2007.

Vol. 4405: L. Padgham, F. Zambonelli (Eds.), Agent-Oriented Software Engineering VII. XII, 225 pages. 2007.

Vol. 4401: N. Guelfi, D. Buchs (Eds.), Rapid Integration of Software Engineering Techniques. IX, 177 pages. 2007.

Vol. 4385: K. Coninx, K. Luyten, K.A. Schneider (Eds.), Task Models and Diagrams for Users Interface Design. XI, 355 pages. 2007.

Vol. 4383: E. Bin, A. Ziv, S. Ur (Eds.), Hardware and Software, Verification and Testing. XII, 235 pages. 2007.

Vol. 4379: M. Südholt, C. Consel (Eds.), Object-Oriented Technology. VIII, 157 pages. 2007.

Vol. 4364: T. Kühne (Ed.), Models in Software Engineering. XI, 332 pages. 2007.

Vol. 4355: J. Julliand, O. Kouchnarenko (Eds.), B 2007: Formal Specification and Development in B. XIII, 293 pages. 2006.

Vol. 4354: M. Hanus (Ed.), Practical Aspects of Declarative Languages. X, 335 pages. 2006.

Vol. 4350: M. Clavel, F. Durán, S. Eker, P. Lincoln, N. Martí-Oliet, J. Meseguer, C. Talcott, All About Maude - A High-Performance Logical Framework. XXII, 797 pages. 2007.

Vol. 4348: S.T. Taft, R.A. Duff, R.L. Brukardt, E. Ploedereder, P. Leroy, Ada 2005 Reference Manual. XXII, 765 pages. 2006.

Vol. 4346: L. Brim, B. Haverkort, M. Leucker, J. van de Pol (Eds.), Formal Methods: Applications and Technology. X, 363 pages. 2007.

Vol. 4344: V. Gruhn, F. Oquendo (Eds.), Software Architecture. X, 245 pages. 2006.

Vol. 4340: R. Prodan, T. Fahringer, Grid Computing. XXIII, 317 pages. 2007.

Vol. 4336: V.R. Basili, D. Rombach, K. Schneider, B. Kitchenham, D. Pfahl, R.W. Selby (Eds.), Empirical Software Engineering Issues. XVII, 193 pages. 2007.

Vol. 4326: S. Göbel, R. Malkewitz, I. Iurgel (Eds.), Technologies for Interactive Digital Storytelling and Entertainment. X, 384 pages. 2006.

Vol. 4323: G. Doherty, A. Blandford (Eds.), Interactive Systems. XI, 269 pages. 2007.

Vol. 4322: F. Kordon, J. Sztipanovits (Eds.), Reliable Systems on Unreliable Networked Platforms. XIV, 317 pages. 2007.

Vol. 4309: P. Inverardi, M. Jazayeri (Eds.), Software Engineering Education in the Modern Age. VIII, 207 pages. 2006.

Vol. 4294: A. Dan, W. Lamersdorf (Eds.), Service-Oriented Computing – ICSOC 2006. XIX, 653 pages. 2006.

Vol. 4290: M. van Steen, M. Henning (Eds.), Middleware 2006. XIII, 425 pages. 2006.

Vol. 4279: N. Kobayashi (Ed.), Programming Languages and Systems. XI, 423 pages. 2006.

Vol. 4262: K. Havelund, M. Núñez, G. Roşu, B. Wolff (Eds.), Formal Approaches to Software Testing and Runtime Verification. VIII, 255 pages. 2006.

Vol. 4260: Z. Liu, J. He (Eds.), Formal Methods and Software Engineering. XII, 778 pages. 2006.

Vol. 4257: I. Richardson, P. Runeson, R. Messnarz (Eds.), Software Process Improvement. XI, 219 pages. 2006.

Vol. 4242: A. Rashid, M. Aksit (Eds.), Transactions on Aspect-Oriented Software Development II. IX, 289 pages. 2006.

Vol. 4229: E. Najm, J.F. Pradat-Peyre, V.V. Donzeau-Gouge (Eds.), Formal Techniques for Networked and Distributed Systems - FORTE 2006. X, 486 pages. 2006.

Vol. 4227: W. Nejdl, K. Tochtermann (Eds.), Innovative Approaches for Learning and Knowledge Sharing. XVII, 721 pages. 2006.

Vol. 4218: S. Graf, W. Zhang (Eds.), Automated Technology for Verification and Analysis. XIV, 540 pages. 2006.

Vol. 4214: C. Hofmeister, I. Crnkovic, R. Reussner (Eds.), Quality of Software Architectures. X, 215 pages. 2006.

Vol. 4204: F. Benhamou (Ed.), Principles and Practice of Constraint Programming - CP 2006. XVIII, 774 pages. 2006.

Vol. 4199: O. Nierstrasz, J. Whittle, D. Harel, G. Reggio (Eds.), Model Driven Engineering Languages and Systems. XVI, 798 pages. 2006.

Vol. 4192: B. Mohr, J.L. Träff, J. Worringen, J. Dongarra (Eds.), Recent Advances in Parallel Virtual Machine and Message Passing Interface. XVI, 414 pages. 2006.

Vol. 4184: M. Bravetti, M. Núñez, G. Zavattaro (Eds.), Web Services and Formal Methods. X, 289 pages. 2006.

Vol. 4166: J. Górski (Ed.), Computer Safety, Reliability, and Security. XIV, 440 pages. 2006.

Vol. 4158: L.T. Yang, H. Jin, J. Ma, T. Ungerer (Eds.), Autonomic and Trusted Computing. XIV, 613 pages. 2006.

Vol. 4157: M. Butler, C. Jones, A. Romanovsky, E. Troubitsyna (Eds.), Rigorous Development of Complex Fault-Tolerant Systems. X, 403 pages. 2006.

Vol. 4143: R. Lämmel, J. Saraiva, J. Visser (Eds.), Generative and Transformational Techniques in Software Engineering. X, 471 pages. 2006.

Vol. 4134: K. Yi (Ed.), Static Analysis. XIII, 443 pages. 2006.

Vol. 4119: C. Dony, J.L. Knudsen, A. Romanovsky, A. Tripathi (Eds.), Advanced Topics in Exception Handling Techniques. X, 302 pages. 2006.

Vol. 4111: F.S. de Boer, M.M. Bonsangue, S. Graf, W.-P. de Roever (Eds.), Formal Methods for Components and Objects. VIII, 447 pages. 2006.

Vol. 4089: W. Löwe, M. Südholt (Eds.), Software Composition. X, 339 pages. 2006.

Vol. 4085: J. Misra, T. Nipkow, E. Sekerinski (Eds.), FM 2006: Formal Methods. XV, 620 pages. 2006.

Vol. 4079: S. Etalle, M. Truszczyński (Eds.), Logic Programming. XIV, 474 pages. 2006.

Vol. 4067: D. Thomas (Ed.), ECOOP 2006 – Object-Oriented Programming. XIV, 527 pages. 2006.

Vol. 4066: A. Rensink, J. Warmer (Eds.), Model Driven Architecture – Foundations and Applications. XII, 392 pages. 2006.

Vol. 4063: I. Gorton, G.T. Heineman, I. Crnkovic, H.W. Schmidt, J.A. Stafford, C.A. Szyperski, K. Wallnau (Eds.), Component-Based Software Engineering. XI, 394 pages. 2006.

Vol. 4054: A. Horváth, M. Telek (Eds.), Formal Methods and Stochastic Models for Performance Evaluation. VIII, 239 pages. 2006.

Vol. 4053: M. Ikeda, K.D. Ashley, T.-W. Chan (Eds.), Intelligent Tutoring Systems. XXVI, 821 pages. 2006.

Vol. 4044: P. Abrahamsson, M. Marchesi, G. Succi (Eds.), Extreme Programming and Agile Processes in Software Engineering. XII, 230 pages. 2006.